For more resources, visit the Web site for

Crossroads and Cultures

A HISTORY OF THE WORLD'S PEOPLES

bedfordstmartins.com/smith

FREE ONLINE STUDY GUIDE
Get instant feedback on your progress with

- Chapter self-tests
- Key terms review
- Map quizzes
- Timeline activities
- Note-taking outlines

FREE HISTORY RESEARCH AND WRITING HELP
Refine your research skills and find plenty of good sources with

- A database of useful images, maps, documents, and more at *Make History*
- A guide to online sources for history
- Help with writing history papers
- A tool for building a bibliography
- Tips on avoiding plagiarism

160°W　140°W　120°W　100°W　80°W　60°W　40°W　20°W

Arctic Circle

**NORTH
AMERICA**

R O C K Y   M T S.

APPALACHIAN MTS.

Mississippi R.

Gulf of
Mexico

Tropic of Cancer

PACIFIC   OCEAN

ATLANTIC
OCEAN

Caribbean Sea

Equator

Amazon R.

A N D E S   M T S.

**SOUTH
AMERICA**

Tropic of Capricorn

ATLANTIC
OCEAN

| 0 | | 1000 | | 2000 | | 3000 miles |
| 0 | 1000 | 2000 | 3000 kilometers | | | |

Antarctic Circle

N
W　E
S

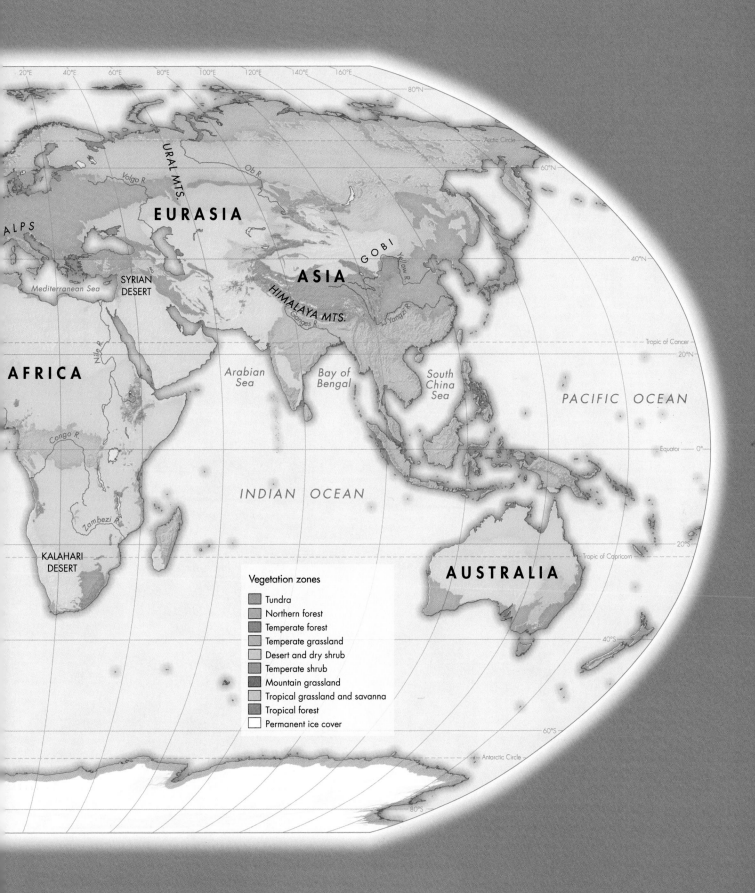

80°N

60°N

ALPS

EURASIA

URAL MTS.

Volga R.

Ob R.

Arctic Circle

ASIA

GOBI

Yellow R.

40°N

SYRIAN
DESERT

Mediterranean Sea

HIMALAYA MTS.

Ganges R.

Yangzi R.

Nile R.

AFRICA

Arabian
Sea

Bay of
Bengal

South
China
Sea

Tropic of Cancer

20°N

PACIFIC OCEAN

Congo R.

INDIAN OCEAN

Equator   0°

Zambezi R.

KALAHARI
DESERT

Tropic of Capricorn   20°S

AUSTRALIA

40°S

Vegetation zones

Tundra
Northern forest
Temperate forest
Temperate grassland
Desert and dry shrub
Temperate shrub
Mountain grassland
Tropical grassland and savanna
Tropical forest
Permanent ice cover

60°S

Antarctic Circle

80°S

Crossroads and Cultures

A History of the World's Peoples

Bonnie G. Smith
Rutgers University

Marc Van De Mieroop
Columbia University

Richard von Glahn
University of California, Los Angeles

Kris Lane
Tulane University

Bedford/St. Martin's
Boston ■ New York

FOR BEDFORD/ST. MARTIN'S

Publisher for History: Mary Dougherty
Executive Editor for History: Elizabeth M. Welch
Director of Development for History: Jane Knetzger
Senior Developmental Editor: Heidi Hood
Senior Production Editor: Anne Noonan
Senior Production Supervisor: Andrew Ensor
Executive Marketing Manager: Jenna Bookin Barry
Associate Editor: Jennifer Jovin
Assistant Production Editor: Laura Deily
Editorial Assistant: Emily DiPietro
Production Assistant: Elise Keller
Copy Editor: Dan Otis
Map Editor: Charlotte Miller
Indexer: Leoni Z. McVey
Cartography: Mapping Specialists, Ltd.
Photo Researcher: Rose Corbett Gordon
Permissions Manager: Kalina K. Ingham
Senior Art Director: Anna Palchik
Text Designer: Jerilyn Bockorick
Cover Designer: Billy Boardman
Cover Art: Registan Square Illuminated at Night
K.M. Westermann/CORBIS
Composition: Cenveo Publisher Services
Printing and Binding: RR Donnelley and Sons

President: Joan E. Feinberg
Editorial Director: Denise B. Wydra
Director of Marketing: Karen R. Soeltz
Director of Production: Susan W. Brown
Associate Director, Editorial Production: Elise S. Kaiser
Managing Editor: Elizabeth M. Schaaf

Library of Congress Control Number: 2011943843

Manufactured in the United States of America.

7 6 5 4 3 2
f e d c b a

For information, write: Bedford/St. Martin's, 75 Arlington Street, Boston, MA 02116   (617-399-4000)

ISBN: 978-0-312-41017-9 (Combined edition)
ISBN: 978-0-312-57158-0 (Loose leaf)
ISBN: 978-0-312-44213-2 (Volume 1)
ISBN: 978-0-312-57159-7 (Loose leaf)
ISBN: 978-0-312-44214-9 (Volume 2)
ISBN: 978-0-312-57160-3 (Loose leaf)
ISBN: 978-0-312-57161-0 (Volume A)
ISBN: 978-0-312-57167-2 (Volume B)
ISBN: 978-0-312-57168-9 (Volume C)

A CONVERSATION WITH THE AUTHORS

The Story Behind *Crossroads and Cultures*

Bonnie G. Smith
Rutgers University

Marc Van De Mieroop
Columbia University

Richard von Glahn
University of California,
Los Angeles

Kris Lane
Tulane University

Bedford/St. Martin's is proud to publish *Crossroads and Cultures: A History of the World's Peoples,* which incorporates the best current cultural history into a fresh and original narrative that connects global patterns of development with life on the ground. This new synthesis highlights the places and times where people interacted and exchanged goods and ideas and in doing so joined their lives to the broad sweep of global history. Below the authors discuss their goals and approach.

Q. How does the title *Crossroads and Cultures: A History of the World's Peoples* tell the story of your book?

Crossroads

Bonnie: From the beginning we knew that we would be stressing interactions and engagements among the world's peoples. We looked for the places where they would meet—the **crossroads**—whether those were actual places or the intersections reflected in the practices of everyday life. We

want students to see how crossroads, interactions, and connections among the world's peoples have changed over time and continue to shape their own lives.

Richard: This focus is a result of our recognition that world history is not simply a matter of covering more areas of the world; it requires rethinking what matters in world history. World history must center on cross-cultural interactions and the ways in which peoples and cultures are influenced and are sometimes transformed by political engagement, cultural contact, economic exchange, and social encounters with other societies.

Cultures

Bonnie: The second half of our title reflects our heartfelt judgment that the past is shaped by **cultures**. Beliefs, ways of living, artistic forms, technology, and intellectual accomplishments are fundamental to historical development and are a part of the foundation of politics and economies. Cultures also produce structures such as caste, class, ethnicity, race, religion, gender, and sexuality—all of which are important themes in our book.

> **"We looked for the places where the world's peoples would meet—the crossroads—whether those were actual places or the intersections reflected in the practices of everyday life."**

A History of the World's Peoples

Marc: The book's subtitle, ***A History of the World's Peoples***, is crucial. History often focuses on kings and states, but in the end the peoples of the past are the most interesting to study, however difficult that may be considering the nature of the sources for world history. People interact with their immediate and more distant neighbors, and these interactions are, indeed, often a cause of historical change.

Bonnie: *Crossroads and Cultures* focuses on people—individual and collective historical actors—who have lived the history of the world and produced global events. We want to capture their thoughts and deeds, their everyday experiences, their work lives, and their courageous actions—all of which have helped to create the crossroads we travel today.

Q. To follow up on the idea of "crossroads," what are some of the places and interactions that you emphasize in the book, and why?

Marc: In the ancient world, the period that I cover in the book (Part 1, from human origins to 500 C.E.), two regions figured prominently by virtue of their location—the Middle East and Central Asia. From earliest times, the Middle East formed a nexus of interactions among the African, European, and Asian continents, which I try to convey when I discuss the first human migrations out of Africa and when I show how the Roman and Persian empires met—and yes, battled! But I emphasize as well that vast open areas also served as crossroads in antiquity. Indeed, Central Asia, an enormous region, acted as a highway for contacts between the cultures at its fringes: China, South Asia, the Middle East, and Europe. Seas also can play this role, and I include the gigantic Pacific Ocean, which, although a formidable barrier, functioned as a road for migration for centuries.

Richard: Since I also deal with a period remote from the present (Part 2, 500–1450 C.E.), I try to balance my coverage between familiar and recognizable places that remain crossroads today—Rome and Jerusalem, Baghdad and Istanbul, Beijing and Delhi, the Nile Delta and the Valley of Mexico—and places that have faded from view, such as the trading cities of the West African savanna; Melaka, the greatest port of Asia in the fifteenth century; Samarkand, which had a long history as the linchpin of the Central Asian Silk Road; and the Champagne fairs in France, which operated as a "free trade" zone and became the incubator of new business practices that enabled Europeans to surpass the older economic centers of the Mediterranean world.

Kris: Since my section of the book (Part 3, 1450–1750) treats the early modern period, when the entire globe was interconnected for the first time in recorded history, I have almost too many crossroads to choose from. In this period, Seville and Lisbon emerged as hugely rich and important ports and sites of redistribution, but so also did Manila, Nagasaki, and Macao. Most of the obvious crossroads of this seafaring era were ports, but great mining centers like Potosí, deep in the highlands of present-day Bolivia, also became world-class cosmopolitan centers. In other books many of these sites have been treated simply as nodes in an expanding European world, but I try to show how local people and other non-European residents made Manila and Potosí quite different from what the king of Spain might have had in mind. Indeed, I emphasize crossroads as places of personal opportunity rather than imperial hegemony.

Bonnie: The crossroads that we describe are often the obvious ones of war, empire building, and old and new forms of trade, but we also enthusiastically feature the more ordinary paths that people traveled. For example, in my own section of the book (Part 4, 1750 to the present), I trace the route of the young Simon Bolivar, whose travels in Spain, France, and the new United States helped to inspire his own liberation struggles. I also follow the rough road from factory to factory along which a seven-year-old English orphan, Robert Blincoe, traveled. His life occurred at the crossroads of industrial development, where he suffered deliberate torture as the world began industrializing. For me, these personal journeys—filled with interactions—are at the heart of our endeavor to make history vivid and meaningful for students.

> "The crossroads that we describe are often the obvious ones of war, empire building, and old and new forms of trade, but we also enthusiastically feature the more ordinary paths that people traveled."

Q. Author teams of world history textbooks typically divide the work based on geographic specialty. Why did you decide to take responsibility for eras instead of regions?

Bonnie: Our goal is to show the interactions of the world's peoples over time and space. Had we divided history by region, our purpose would have been confounded from the start. Many books still take a "civilizational" approach, shifting from one region or nation to another and dividing each author's coverage according to national specialization. We aimed for a more interconnected result by each taking responsibility for narrating developments across the globe during a particular period of time.

Marc: When we look at any period globally, we can see certain parallels between the various parts of the world. There is a huge benefit to weighing what happened in different places at the same time.

Richard: Right. World history fundamentally is about making comparisons and connections. Defining our subject matter by time period rather than by geographic region enabled us to see the connections or parallel developments that make societies part of world history—as well as the distinctive features that make them unique. Our format has the virtue of bringing a coherent perspective to the many stories that each part of the book tells.

Kris: In my chapters, certain themes, such as slavery and the spread of silver money, took on new meaning as I traced them across cultures in ways that regional specialists had not considered. Writing the book this way entailed a huge amount of reading, writing, and reconsideration, but I feel it was a great decision. It allowed each of us to explore a bit before coming back together to hash out differences.

Q. The table of contents for *Crossroads and Cultures* blends both thematic and regional chapters. Why did you organize the book this way?

Bonnie: There is no orthodoxy in today's teaching of world history. Although textbooks often follow either a regional or a thematic structure, we felt that neither of these told the story that a blended approach could tell.

Richard: I particularly relished the opportunity to develop thematic chapters—for example, on cross-cultural trade and business practices, or on educational institutions and the transmission of knowledge—that illustrate both convergence and diversity in history. The thematic chapters were especially suitable for introducing individuals from diverse levels of society, to help students appreciate personal experiences as well as overarching historical trends.

Kris: In my period, the rapid integration of the world due to expanding maritime networks had to be balanced against the persistence of land-based cultures that both borrowed from new technologies and ideas and maintained a regional coherence. The Aztecs, the Incas, the Mughals, and the Ming were all land-based, tributary empires headed by divine kings, but whereas the first two collapsed as a result of European invasion, the latter two were reinforced by contact with Europeans, who introduced powerful new weapons. I felt it was necessary to treat these empires in macroregional terms before grappling with more sweeping themes. I found that in the classroom my students made better connections themselves after having time to get a firm handle on some of these broad regional developments.

> "Defining our subject matter by time period rather than by geographic region enabled us to see the connections or parallel developments that make societies part of world history—as well as the distinctive features that make them unique."

Q. Each chapter includes a Counterpoint section as substantial as the main sections of the narrative itself. What purposes do the Counterpoints serve?

Kris: The **Counterpoint** feature helps students and teachers remember that alternative histories—or paths—are not only possible but that they exist alongside "master narratives." In each chapter we have selected a people, a place, or a movement that functions as a Counterpoint to the major global development traced in that chapter. Some Counterpoints highlight different responses to similar circumstances—the successful resistance of the Mapuche of Chile against the European conquistadors, for example, in a chapter that tells the story of the collapse of the Aztec and Incan empires. Other Counterpoints show cultures adapting to a particular environment that either enables persistence or requires adaptation—such as the Aborigines of Australia, gatherer-hunters by choice, in a chapter that treats the rise of agriculture and spread of settled farming. Counterpoint is about human difference and ingenuity.

Richard: The Counterpoint feature is fundamental to our approach. It reminds us that there is much diversity in world history and helps us to think about the causes underlying divergence as well as convergence.

Marc: Right. It helps counter the idea that everyone goes through the same stages of evolution and makes the same choices. There is no uniform history of the world, as nineteenth-century scholars used to think.

Bonnie: One of my favorite Counterpoints centers on the importance of nonindustrialized African women farmers to the world economy during the Industrial Revolution. From a pedagogical standpoint, Counterpoints not only expose basic questions that historians grapple with but also offer material within a single chapter for compare-and-contrast exercises.

Q. Each chapter also offers a special feature devoted to the way that people made their living at different times and at different crossroads in the past. Would you explain how this Lives and Livelihoods feature works?

Richard: The **Lives and Livelihoods** feature helps us provide more in-depth study of one of our key themes, namely how people's lives intersect with larger cross-cultural interactions and global change.

Bonnie: We often spotlight new means of making a living that arose as the result of cross-cultural exchange or that contributed to major global developments. For example, the Lives and Livelihoods feature in Chapter 6 shows students how papermaking originated as a carefully guarded invention in classical China and became a worldwide technology that spawned numerous livelihoods. Similarly, the feature in Chapter 24 on workers on the trans-Siberian railroad exemplifies influence in both directions: the workers built a transportation network that advanced interconnections and fostered global change—change that they and their families experienced in turn.

> **"The Lives and Livelihoods feature supports one of our key themes: how people's lives intersect with larger cross-cultural interactions and global change."**

Q. *Crossroads and Cultures* has a rich art and map program, and it also includes plentiful primary-source excerpts and clear reading aids. Can you talk about how you had students in mind as you developed these features of the book?

Kris: Throughout the book we chose **images** to match as closely as we could the themes we wanted to stress. We did not conceive of the images as mere illustrations but rather as documents worthy of close historical analysis in their own right, products of the same places and times we try to evoke in the text.

Richard: And our carefully developed **map program** provides sure-footed guidance to where our historical journey is taking us—a crucial necessity, since we travel to so many places not on the usual Grand Tour! Our **Seeing the Past** and **Reading the Past** features, which provide excerpts from visual and written primary sources, give students direct exposure to the ideas and voices of the people we are studying. These features also help students build their analytical skills by modeling how historians interpret visual and written evidence.

Bonnie: Among the many reading aids, one of my favorites is the chapter-opening **Backstory**, which provides a concise overview of previously presented material to situate the current chapter for the student. It is at once a review and an immediate preparation for the chapter to come.

Richard: And we use every opportunity—at the start of chapters and sections, in the features, and at the end of each chapter—to pose **study questions** to help students think about what they are reading and make connections across time and space.

Kris: We wanted to hit as many bases as possible in order to make our book accessible for different kinds of learners. I imagine I'm like most teachers in that I never teach a course in exactly the same way each year. I like to use or emphasize different aspects of a textbook each time I assign it, sometimes hammering on chronology or working through study questions and sometimes paying closer attention to maps, works of art, or material culture. It all needs to be there; I like a complete toolbox.

Q. You have written many well-received and influential works. What response to *Crossroads and Cultures: A History of the World's Peoples* would please you most?

Bonnie: Our hope is that our approach to world history will engage students and help them master material that can otherwise seem so remote, wide-ranging, and seemingly disconnected from people's lives.

Richard: I would like from students who read this book what I want from my own students: a recognition and appreciation of the diversity of human experience that fosters understanding not only of the past and where we have come from but also of our fellow world citizens and the future that we are making together.

Kris: The practical side of me wants simply to hear, "At last, a world history textbook that works." The idealistic side wants to hear, "Wow, a world history textbook that makes both me and my students think differently about the world and about history."

Marc: And I hope that students start to realize not only that the pursuit of answers to such questions is absorbing and satisfying but also that the study of history is fun!

Crossroads and Cultures: A History of the World's Peoples **makes its new synthesis accessible and memorable for students through a strong pedagogical design, abundant maps and images, and special features that heighten the narrative's attention to the lives and voices of the world's peoples. To learn more about how the book's features keep the essentials of world history in focus for students, see the "How to Use This Book" introduction on the following pages.**

HOW TO USE THIS BOOK

STEP 1

Use the part opener's features to understand the place, time, and topic of the era.

PLACE
Ask yourself what regions are covered.

TIME
Ask yourself what era is under investigation.

TOPIC
Ask yourself what topics or themes are emphasized.

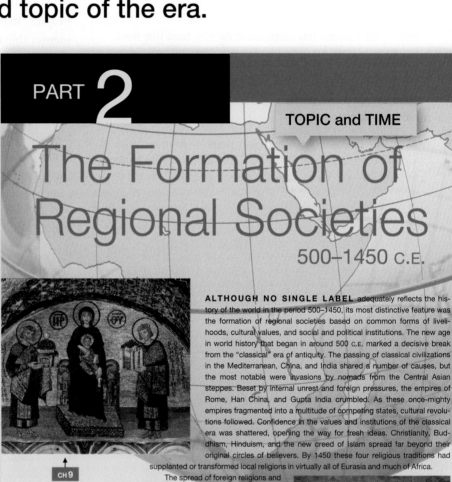

PART 2

TOPIC and TIME

The Formation of Regional Societies

500–1450 C.E.

ALTHOUGH NO SINGLE LABEL adequately reflects the history of the world in the period 500–1450, its most distinctive feature was the formation of regional societies based on common forms of livelihoods, cultural values, and social and political institutions. The new age in world history that began in around 500 C.E. marked a decisive break from the "classical" era of antiquity. The passing of classical civilizations in the Mediterranean, China, and India shared a number of causes, but the most notable were invasions by nomads from the Central Asian steppes. Beset by internal unrest and foreign pressures, the empires of Rome, Han China, and Gupta India crumbled. As these once-mighty empires fragmented into a multitude of competing states, cultural revolutions followed. Confidence in the values and institutions of the classical era was shattered, opening the way for fresh ideas. Christianity, Buddhism, Hinduism, and the new creed of Islam spread far beyond their original circles of believers. By 1450 these four religious traditions had supplanted or transformed local religions in virtually all of Eurasia and much of Africa.

CH 9

The spread of foreign religions and the lifestyles and livelihoods they promoted produced distinctive regional societies. By 1000, Europe had taken shape as a coherent society and culture even as it came to be divided between the Roman and Byzantine Christian churches. The shared cultural values of modern East Asia—rooted in the literary and philosophical traditions of China but also assuming distinctive national forms—also emerged during the first millennium C.E. During this era, too, Indian civilization expanded into Southeast Asia and acquired a new unity expressed through the common language of Sanskrit. The rapid expansion of Islam across Asia, Africa, and

CH 10 ➡

266

TOPIC
Read the part overview to learn how the chapters that follow fit into the larger story.

CHAPTERS IN THIS PART ▼

9   The Worlds of Christianity and Islam, 400–1000
10 Religion and Cross-Cultural Exchange in Asia, 400–1000
11 Societies and Networks in the Americas and the Pacific, 300–1200
12 The Rise of Commerce in Afro-Eurasia, 900–1300
13 Centers of Learning and the Transmission of Culture, 900–1300
14 Crusaders, Mongols, and Eurasian Integration, 1050–1350
15 Collapse and Revival in Afro-Eurasia, 1300–1450

CH 11

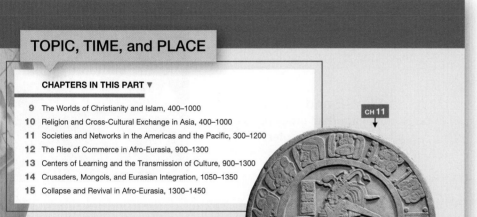

even parts of Europe demonstrated the power of a shared reli-

500–1450 C.E.

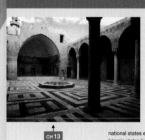

CH 13

faiths grew ever wider. The rise of steppe empires—above all, the explosive expansion of the Mongol empires—likewise transformed the political and cultural landscape of Asia. Historians today recognize the ways in which the Mongol conquests facilitated the movement of people, goods, and ideas across Eurasia. But contemporaries could see no farther than the ruin sowed by the Mongols wherever they went, toppling cities and laying waste to once-fertile farmlands.

After 1300 the momentum of world history changed. Economic growth slowed, strained by the pressure of rising populations on productive resources and the effects of a cooling climate, and then it stopped altogether. In the late 1340s the Black Death pandemic devastated the central Islamic lands and Europe. It would take centuries before the populations in these parts of the world returned to their pre-1340 levels.

By 1400, however, other signs of recovery were evident. Powerful national states emerged in Europe and China, restoring some measure of stability. Strong Islamic states held sway in Egypt, Anatolia (modern Turkey), Iran, and India. The European Renaissance—the intense outburst of intellectual and artistic creativity envisioned as a "rebirth" of the classical civilization of Greece and Rome—flickered to life, sparked by the economic vigor of the Italian city-states. Similarly, Neo-Confucianism—a "renaissance" of China's classical learning—whetted the intellectual and cultural aspirations of ed...

Eurasia's major land-based economies struggled to regain their earlier prosperity.

In 1453 Muslim Ottoman armies seized Constantinople and deposed the Byzantine Christian emperor, cutting the last thread of connection to the ancient world. The fall of Constantinople symbolized the end of the era discussed in Part 2. Denied direct access to the rich trade with Asia, European monarchs and merchants began to shift their attention to the Atlantic world. Yet just as Columbus's discovery of the "New World" (in fact, a very ancient one) came as a surprise, the idea of a new world order centered on Europe—the modern world order—was still unimaginable.

CH 15

TIME and PLACE
Scan the timeline to see how events and developments in different regions of the world fit together.

	500	750	1000	1250	1500
Americas	• 500 First permanent settlements in Chaco Canyon 500–1000 Andean state of Tiwanaku 550–650 Collapse of Teotihuacán	800–900 Collapse of the Maya city-states Rise of Chimu state 900 700–900 Heyday of Andean state of Wari	950–1150 Height of Toltec culture • 1050 Consolidation of Cahokia's dominance	• 1200 Incas move into Cuzco region • 1150 Abandonment of pueblos in Chaco Canyon • 1325 Aztecs found Tenochtitlán 1250–1300 Collapse of Cahokia	Columbus reaches the Americas 1492 • 1430–1532 Inca Empire
Europe	• 507 Clovis defeats Visigoths and converts to Christianity 590–604 Papacy of Gregory I	Charles Martel halts Muslim advance into Europe 732 • • 793 Earliest record of Viking raids on Britain Charlemagne crowned emperor 800 •	• 988 Rus prince Vladimir converts to Christianity • 1066 Norman conquest of England	• 1150 Founding of first university at Paris 1347–1350 Outbreak of Black Death 1400–1550 Italian Renaissance 1150–1300 Heyday of the Champagne fairs 1337–1453 Hundred Years' War Reconquista Mongol conquest of Kiev 1240 • 1270–1300 Introduction of overseas navigational aids completed 1492	
Middle East	• 527–565 Reign of Byzantine emperor Justinian I 570–632 Life of Muhammad	• 680 Permanent split between Shi'a and Sunni Islam 750–850 Abbasid caliphate at its height 661–743 Umayyad caliphate	First Crusade ends with Christian capture of Jerusalem 1099 • Saladin recaptures Jerusalem 1187	• 1120 Founding of order of Knights of the Temple • 1291 Mamluks recapture Acre, last Christian stronghold in Palestine • 1258 Mongols sack Baghdad 1347–1360 Outbreak of Black Death	• 1453 Fall of Constantinople to the Ottomans
Africa	• 500 Spread of camel use; emergence of trans-Saharan trade routes	• 750 Islam starts to spread via trans-Saharan trade routes	969 Fatimids capture Egypt Fall of kingdom of Ghana 1076 •	Reign of Sunjata, founder of 1250–1517 Mamluk dynasty Mali Empire 1230–1255 • 1250 Kingdom of Benin founded 1100–1500 Extended dry period in West Africa prompts migrations	
Asia and Oceania	581–618 Sui Empire • 668 Unification of Korea under Silla rule 618–907 Tang Empire 755–763 An Lushan rebellion 600–1000 Polynesian settlement of Pacific Islands		850–1267 Chola kingdom 939 Vietnam achieves independence from China 960–1279 Song Empire	1100–1500 Easter Island's stone monuments 1336–1573 Ashikaga Shogunate Formation of first Hawaiian 1206–1526 Delhi Sultanate 1368–1644 Ming Empire chiefdoms 1200–1400 1271–1368 Yuan Empire 1392–1910 Korean Yi dynasty	

STEP 2

Use the chapter's introductory features to understand the place, time, and topic of this chapter.

15

AT A CROSSROADS ▶

The fall of Constantinople to the Ottoman Turks in 1453 marked the end of the Byzantine Empire and heralded the coming age of gunpowder weapons. The Ottoman forces under Sultan Mehmed II breached the massive walls of Constantinople using massive cannons known as *bombards*. The Turkish cannons appear in the center of this book illustration of the siege of Constantinople, published in France in 1455. (The Art Archive/Bibliothèque Nationale Paris.)

PLACE and TOPIC
An important crossroads opens every chapter.

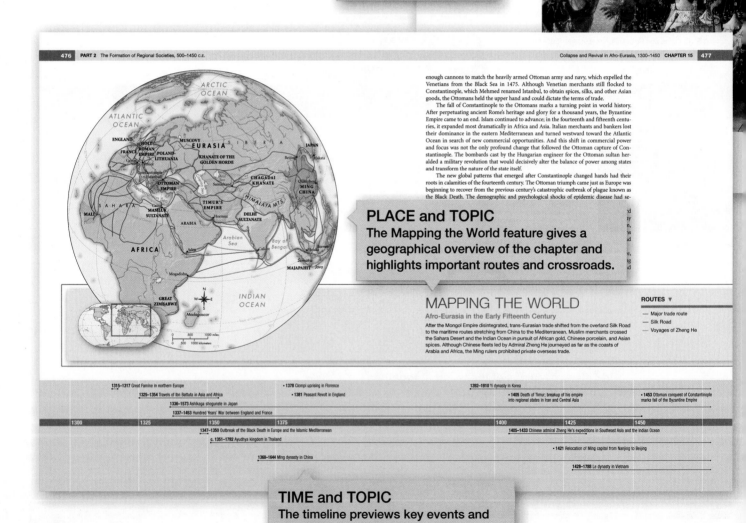

enough cannons to match the heavily armed Ottoman army and navy, which expelled the Venetians from the Black Sea in 1475. Although Venetian merchants still flocked to Constantinople, which Mehmed renamed Istanbul, to obtain spices, silks, and other Asian goods, the Ottomans held the upper hand and could dictate the terms of trade.

The fall of Constantinople to the Ottomans marks a turning point in world history. After perpetuating ancient Rome's heritage and glory for a thousand years, the Byzantine Empire came to an end. Islam continued to advance; in the fourteenth and fifteenth centuries, it expanded most dramatically in Africa and Asia. Italian merchants and bankers lost their dominance in the eastern Mediterranean and turned westward toward the Atlantic Ocean in search of new commercial opportunities. And this shift in commercial power and focus was not the only profound change that followed the Ottoman capture of Constantinople. The bombards cast by the Hungarian engineer for the Ottoman sultan heralded a military revolution that would decisively alter the balance of power among states and transform the nature of the state itself.

The new global patterns that emerged after Constantinople changed hands had their roots in calamities of the fourteenth century. The Ottoman triumph came just as Europe was beginning to recover from the previous century's catastrophic outbreak of plague known as the Black Death. The demographic and psychological shocks of epidemic disease had se-

PLACE and TOPIC
The Mapping the World feature gives a geographical overview of the chapter and highlights important routes and crossroads.

MAPPING THE WORLD
Afro-Eurasia in the Early Fifteenth Century

After the Mongol Empire disintegrated, trans-Eurasian trade shifted from the overland Silk Road to the maritime routes stretching from China to the Mediterranean. Muslim merchants crossed the Sahara Desert and the Indian Ocean in pursuit of African gold, Chinese porcelain, and Asian spices. Although Chinese fleets led by Admiral Zheng He journeyed as far as the coasts of Arabia and Africa, the Ming rulers prohibited private overseas trade.

ROUTES ▼
— Major trade route
— Silk Road
— Voyages of Zheng He

1315–1317 Great Famine in northern Europe
• 1370 Ciompi uprising in Florence
1392–1910 Yi dynasty in Korea
1325–1354 Travels of Ibn Battuta in Asia and Africa
• 1381 Peasant Revolt in England
• 1405 Death of Timur; breakup of his empire into regional states in Iran and Central Asia
• 1453 Ottoman conquest of Constantinople marks fall of the Byzantine Empire
1336–1573 Ashikaga shogunate in Japan
1337–1453 Hundred Years' War between England and France
1300   1325   1350   1375   1400   1425   1450
1347–1350 Outbreak of the Black Death in Europe and the Islamic Mediterranean
1405–1433 Chinese admiral Zheng He's expeditions in Southeast Asia and the Indian Ocean
c. 1351–1782 Ayudhya kingdom in Thailand
• 1421 Relocation of Ming capital from Nanjing to Beijing
1368–1644 Ming dynasty in China
1428–1788 Le dynasty in Vietnam

TIME and TOPIC
The timeline previews key events and developments discussed in the chapter.

Collapse and Revival in Afro-Eurasia

1300–1450

armies of the Ottoman sultan Mehmed II encircled Constantinople, the Byzantine emperor Constantine XI received a visit from a fellow Christian, a Hungarian engineer named Urban. Urban had applied metallurgical skills acquired in Hungary's rich iron and copper mines to the manufacture of large cannons known as *bombards*. He came to the Byzantine capital to offer his services to repel the Ottoman assault. But although Urban was a Christian, he was a businessman, too. When Constantine could not meet his price, Urban quickly left for the sultan's camp. Facing the famed triple walls of Constantinople, Mehmed promised to quadruple the salary Urban requested and to provide any materials and manpower the engineer needed.

Seven months later, in April 1453, Ottoman soldiers moved Urban's huge bronze bombards—with barrels twenty-six feet long, capable of throwing eight-hundred-pound shot—into place beneath the walls of Constantinople. Although these cumbersome cannons could fire only seven rounds a day, they battered the walls of Constantinople, which had long been considered impenetrable. After six weeks of siege the Turks breached the walls and swarmed into the city. The vastly outnumbered defenders, Emperor Constantine among them, fought to the death.

Urban's willingness to put business before religious loyalty helped tip the balance of power in the Mediterranean. During the siege, the Genoese merchant community at Constantinople—along with their archrivals, the Venetians—maintained strict neutrality. Although the Italian merchants, like Urban, were prepared to do business with Mehmed II, within a decade the Venetians and Ottomans were at war. Venice could not produce

BACKSTORY

In the fourteenth century, a number of developments threatened the connections among the societies of the Afro-Eurasian world. The collapse of the Mongol empires in China and Iran in the mid-1300s disrupted caravan traffic across Central Asia, diverting the flow of trade and travel to maritime routes across the Indian Ocean. Although the two centuries of religious wars known as the Crusades ended in 1291, they had hardened hostility between Christians and Muslims. As the power of the Christian Byzantine Empire contracted, Muslim Turkish sultanates—the Mamluk regime in Egypt and the rising Ottoman dynasty in Anatolia (modern Turkey)—gained control of the eastern Mediterranean region. Yet the Crusades and direct contact with the Mongols had also whetted European appetites for luxury and exotic goods from the Islamic world and Asia. Thus, despite challenges and obstacles, the Mediterranean remained a lively crossroads of commerce and cross-cultural exchange.

Fourteenth-Century Crisis and Renewal in Eurasia

FOCUS How did the Black Death affect society, the economy, and culture in Latin Christendom and the Islamic world?

Islam's New Frontiers

FOCUS Why did Islam expand dramatically in the fourteenth and fifteenth centuries, and how did new Islamic societies differ from established ones?

The Global Bazaar

FOCUS How did the pattern of international trade change during the fourteenth and fifteenth centuries, and how did these changes affect consumption and fashion tastes?

COUNTERPOINT Age of the Samurai in Japan, 1185–1450

FOCUS How and why did the historical development of Japan in the fourteenth and fifteenth centuries differ from that of mainland Eurasia?

bazaar, and this isolation contributed to the birth of Japan's distinctive national culture. For most Afro-Eurasian societies, however, the maritime world increasingly became the principal crossroads of economic and cultural exchange.

OVERVIEW QUESTIONS

The major global development in this chapter: Crisis and recovery in fourteenth- and fifteenth-century Afro-Eurasia.

As you read, consider:

1. In the century after the devastating outbreak of plague known as the Black Death, how and why did Europe's economic growth begin to surpass that of the Islamic world?

2. Did the economic revival across Eurasia after 1350 benefit the peasant populations of Europe, the Islamic world, and East Asia?

3. How did the process of conversion to Islam differ in Iran, the Ottoman Empire, West Africa, and Southeast Asia during this period?

4. What political and economic changes contributed to the rise of maritime commerce in Asia during the fourteenth and fifteenth centuries?

STEP 3

Use the chapter tools to understand what is important.

Focus questions, which also appear at the start and end of the chapter, tell you what you need to learn from each major section.

Topical headings in the margin focus on important topics and are useful for reviewing the chapter.

Marginal glossary definitions provide further explanation of key terms boldfaced in the narrative.

Islam's New Frontiers

FOCUS
Why did Islam expand dramatically in the fourteenth and fifteenth centuries, and how did new Islamic societies differ from established ones?

In the fourteenth and fifteenth centuries, Islam continued to spread to new areas, including central and maritime Asia, sub-Saharan Africa, and southeastern Europe. In the past, Muslim rule had often preceded the popular adoption of Islamic religion and culture. Yet the advance of Islam in Africa and Asia came about not through conquest, but through slow diffusion via merchants and missionaries. The universalism and egalitarianism of Islam appealed to rising merchant classes in both West Africa and maritime Asia.

During this period, Islam expanded by adapting to older ruling cultures rather than seeking to eradicate them. Timur, the last of the great nomad conquerors, and his descendants ruled not as Mongol khans but as Islamic sultans. The culture of the Central Asian states, however, remained an eclectic mix of Mongol, Turkish, and Persian traditions, in contrast to the strict adherence to Muslim law and doctrine practiced under the Arab regimes of the Middle East and North Africa. This pattern of cultural adaptation and assimilation was even more evident in West Africa and Southeast Asia.

Islamic Spiritual Ferment in Central Asia 1350–1500

The spread of Sufism in Central Asia between 1350 and 1500 played a significant role in the process of cultural assimilation. **Sufism**—a mystical tradition that stressed self-mastery, practical virtues, and spiritual growth through personal experience of the divine—had already emerged by 1200 as a major expression of Islamic values and social identity. Sufism appeared in many variations and readily assimilated local cultures to its beliefs and practices. Sufi mystics acquired institutional strength through the communal solidarity of their brotherhoods spread across the whole realm of Islam. In contrast to the orthodox scholars and teachers known as *ulama*, who made little effort to convert nonbelievers, Sufi preachers were inspired by missionary zeal and welcomed non-Muslims to their lodges and sermons. This made them ideal instruments for the spread of Islam to new territories.

Timur

One of Sufism's most important royal patrons was Timur (1336–1405), the last of the Mongol emperors. Born near the city of Samarkand (SAM-ar-kand) when the Mongol Ilkhanate in Iran was on the verge of collapse, Timur—himself a Turk—grew up among Mongols who practiced Islam. He rose to power in the 1370s by reuniting quarreling Mongol tribes in common pursuit of conquest. Although Timur lacked the dynastic pedigree enjoyed by Chinggis Khan's descendants, like Chinggis he held his empire together by the force of his personal charisma.

From the early 1380s, Timur's armies relentlessly pursued campaigns of conquest, sweeping westward across Iran into Mesopotamia and Russia and eastward into India. In 1400–1401 Timur seized and razed Aleppo and Damascus, the principal Mamluk cities in Syria. In 1402 he captured the Ottoman sultan in battle. Rather than trying to consolidate his rule in Syria and Anatolia (modern Turkey), however, Timur turned his attention eastward. He was preparing to march on China when he fell ill and died early in 1405. Although Timur's empire quickly fragmented, his triumphs would serve as an inspiration to later empire builders, such as the Mughals in India and the Manchus in China. Moreover, his support of Sufism would have a lasting impact, helping lay the foundation for a number of important Islamic religious movements in Central Asia.

The institutions of Timur's empire were largely modeled on the Ilkhan synthesis of Persian civil administration and Turkish-Mongol military organization. Like the Ilkhans and the Ottomans, Timur's policies favored settled farmers and urban populations over pastoral nomads, who were often displaced from their homelands. While Timur allowed local princes a degree of autonomy, he was determined to make Samarkand a grand imperial capital.

Sufism A tradition within Islam that emphasizes mystical knowledge and personal experience of the divine.

Again, as with Islam in West Africa, the intellectual ferment of the Renaissance was nurtured in an urban environment. Humanist scholars shunned the warrior culture of the old nobility while celebrating the civic roles and duties of townsmen, merchants, and clerics. Despite their admiration of classical civilization, the humanists did not reject Christianity. Rather, they sought to reconcile Christian faith and doctrines with classical learning. By making knowledge of Latin and Greek, history, poetry, and philosophy the mark of an educated person, the humanists transformed education and established models of schooling that would endure down to modern times.

Nowhere was the revolutionary impact of the Renaissance felt more deeply than in visual arts such as painting, sculpture, and architecture. Artists of the Renaissance exuded supreme confidence in the ability of human ingenuity to equal or even surpass the works of nature. The new outlook was exemplified by the development of the techniques of perspective, which artists used to convey a realistic, three-dimensional quality to physical forms, most notably the human body. Human invention also was capable of improving on nature by creating order and harmony through architecture and urban planning. Alberti advocated replacing the winding narrow streets and haphazard construction of medieval towns with planned cities organized around straight boulevards, open squares, and monumental buildings whose balanced proportions corresponded to a geometrically unified design.

Above all, the Renaissance transformed the idea of the artist. No longer mere manual tradesmen, artists now were seen as possessing a special kind of genius that enabled them to express a higher understanding of beauty. In the eyes of contemporaries, no one exemplified this quality of genius more than Leonardo da Vinci (1452–1519), who won renown as a painter, architect, sculptor, engineer, mathematician, and inventor. Leonardo's father, a Florentine lawyer, apprenticed him to a local painter at age eighteen. Leonardo spent much of his career as a civil and military engineer in the employ of the Duke of Milan, and developed ideas for flying machines, tanks, robots, and solar power that far exceeded the engineering capabilities of his time. Leonardo sought to apply his knowledge of natural science to painting, which he regarded as the most sublime art (see Seeing the Past: Leonardo da Vinci's *Virgin of the Rocks*).

The final Counterpoint section offers an important exception to the Major Global Development discussed in the chapter.

ce was rooted in the rich soil of Italy's
comm[...] from the Islamic world and Asia. In-
tern[...] roduction across maritime Asia and
gave[...] d consumption. In Japan, however,
grow[...] fostered the emergence of a national
cult[...] ted the rest of East Asia.

Cultural Innovations

COUNTERPOINT
Age of the Samurai in Japan 1185–1450

In Japan as in Europe, the term *Middle Ages* brings to mind an age of warriors, a stratified society governed by bonds of loyalty between lords and vassals. In Japan, however, the militarization of the ruling class intensified during the fourteenth and fifteenth centuries, a time when the warrior nobility of Europe was crumbling. Paradoxically, the rise of the **samurai** (sah-moo-rye) ("those who serve") warriors as masters of their own estates was accompanied by the increasing independence of peasant communities.

Phonetic spellings follow many potentially unfamiliar terms.

from[...] apter, Japan became more isolated
a pe[...] ural exchanges with China reached
cont[...] invasion of Japan in 1281, ties with
[...] panese see this era as the period in
which Japan's unique national identity—expressed most distinctly in the ethic of *bushidō* (boo-shee-doe), the "Way of the Warrior"—took its definitive form. Samurai warriors became the

> **FOCUS**
>
> How and why did the historical development of Japan in the fourteenth and fifteenth centuries differ from that of mainland Eurasia?

samurai Literally, "those who serve"; the hereditary warriors who dominated Japanese society and culture from the twelfth to the nineteenth centuries.

LIVES AND LIVELIHOODS

> Lives and Livelihoods features underscore the connections between daily life and global developments.

Urban Weavers in India

Industry and commerce in India, especially in textiles, grew rapidly beginning in the fourteenth century. Specialized craftsmen in towns and regional groups of merchants formed guilds that became the nuclei of new occupational castes, *jati* (JAH-tee). Ultimately these new occupational castes would join with other forces in Indian society to challenge the social inequality rooted in orthodox Hindu religion.

It was growth in market demand and technological innovations such as block printing that drove the rapid expansion of India's textile industries. Luxury fabrics such as fine silks and velvet remained largely the province of royal workshops or private patronage. Mass production of textiles, on the other hand, was oriented toward the manufacture of cheaper cotton fabrics, especially colorful chintz garments. A weaver could make a woman's cotton *sari* in six or seven days, whereas a luxury garment took a month or more. Domestic demand for ordinary cloth grew steadily, and production for export accelerated even more briskly. At the beginning of the sixteenth century, the Portuguese traveler Tomé Pires, impressed by the craftsmanship of Indian muslins and calicoes (named after the port of Calicut), observed that "they make enough of these to furnish the world."[1]

Weaving became an urban industry. It was village women who cleaned most of the cotton and spun it into yarn; they could easily combine this simple if laborious work with other domestic chores. But peasants did not weave the yarn into cloth, except for their own use. Instead, weaving, bleaching, a...
professional...
living in sep...

Like oth...
pation that c...
Families of w...
guilds with b...
within their g...
not have excl...
could include...
could becom...

Indian Block-Printed Textile, c. 1500
Block-printed textiles with elaborate designs were in great demand both in India and throughout Southeast Asia, Africa, and the Islamic world. Craftsmen carved intricate designs on wooden blocks (a separate block for each color), which were then dipped in dye and repeatedly stamped on bleached fabric until the entire cloth was covered. This cotton fabric with geese, lotus flower, and rosette designs was manufactured in Gujarat in western India. (Ashmolean Museum, University of Oxford/...

...tions for social recognition. Amid the whirl and congestion of city life, it was far more difficult than in villages to enforce the laws governing caste purity and segregation. As a fourteenth-century poet wrote about the crowded streets of his hometown of Jaunpur in the Ganges Valley, in the city "one person's caste-mark gets stamped on another's forehead, and a brahman's holy thread will be found hanging around an untouchable's neck."[2] Brahmans objected to this erosion of caste boundaries, to little avail. Weaver guilds became influential patrons of temples and often served as trustees and accountants in charge of managing temple endowments and revenues.

In a few cases the growing economic independence of weavers and like-minded artisans prompted complete rejection of the caste hierarchy. Sufi preachers and *bhakti* (BAHK-tee)—devotional movements devoted to patron gods and goddesses—encouraged the disregard of caste distinctions in favor of a universal brotherhood of devout believers. The fifteenth-century bhakti preacher Kabir, who was strongly influenced by Sufi teachings, epitomized the new social radicalism coursing through the urban artisan classes. A weaver himself, Kabir joined the dignity of manual labor to the purity of spiritual devotion, spurning the social pretension and superficial piety of the brahmans ("pandits") and Muslim clerics ("mullahs"):

a trinity of labor, charity, and spiritual devotion. The Sikhs, who gained a following principally among traders and artisans in the northwestern Punjab region, drew an even more explicit connection between commerce and piety. In the words of a hymn included in a sixteenth-century anthology of Sikh sacred writings:

> The true Guru [teacher] is the merchant;
> The devotees are his peddlers.
> The capital stock is the Lord's Name, and
> To enshrine the truth is to keep His account.[4]

Sikh communities spurned the distinction between pure and impure occupations. In their eyes, holiness was to be found in honest toil and personal piety, not ascetic practices, book learning, or religious rituals.

1. Tomé Pires, *The Suma Oriental of Tomé Pires*, ed. and trans. Armando Cortes (London: Hakluyt Society, 1944), 1:53.
2. Vidyapati Thakur, *Kirtilata*, quoted in Eugenia Vanina, *Urban Crafts and Craftsmen in Medieval India (Thirteenth–Eighteenth Centuries)* (New Delhi: Munshiram Manoharlal, 2004), 443.
3. Quoted in Vanina, *Urban Crafts and Craftsmen*, 149.
4. *Sri Guru Granth Sahib*, trans. Gophal Singh (Delhi: Gur Das Kapur & Sons, 1960), 2:427.

QUESTIONS TO CONSIDER

1. In what ways did the organization of textile production reinforce or challenge the prevailing social norms of Hindu society?
2. In what ways did religious ideas and movements reflect the new sense of dignity among prosperous Indian merchants and craftsmen?

...at ease...
...mullahs...
...ome
...toil,
...sure.
...elesced
...red on

...h India. Delhi: Oxford University Press, 1985.
...India (Thirteenth–Eighteenth Centuries). New Delhi: Munshiram Manoharlal, 2004.

SEEING THE PAST

> Reading the Past and Seeing the Past features provide direct exposure to important voices and ideas of the past through written and visual primary sources.

Leonardo da Vinci's *Virgin of the Rocks*

Leonardo's Botanical Studies with Star-of-Bethlehem, Grasses, Crowfoot, Wood Anemone, and Another Genus,
c. 1500–1506 (The Royal Collection © 2011 Her Majesty Queen Elizabeth II/Bridgeman Art Library.)

Virgin of the Rocks, c. 1483–1486
(Erich Lessing/Art Resource.)

While living in Milan in the early 1480s, Leonardo accepted a commission to paint an altarpiece for the chapel of Milan's Confraternity of the Immaculate Conception, a branch of the Franciscan order. Leonardo's relationship with the friars proved to be stormy. His first version of the painting (now in the Louvre), reproduced here, apparently displeased his patrons and was sold to another party. Only after a fifteen-year-long dispute over the price did Leonardo finally deliver a modified version in 1508.

In portraying the legendary encounter between the child Jesus and the equally young John the Baptist during the flight to Egypt, Leonardo replaced the traditional desert setting with a landscape filled with rocks, plants, and water. Leonardo's dark grotto creates an aura of mystery and foreboding, from which the figures of Mary, Jesus, John, and the angel Uriel emerge as if in a vision. A few years before, Leonardo had written about "coming to the entrance of a great cavern, in front of which I stood for some time, stupefied and uncomprehending. . . . Suddenly two things arose in me, fear and desire: fear of

the menacing...
the cavern; de...
there was any...
thing within."[1]

Fantastic as the scen...
might seem, Leonardo's
meticulous rendering of
rocks and pl...
based on cl...
of nature. Th...
lehem flowe...
left of the pa...
izing purity a...
also appear...
contempora...
cal drawing...
Geologists h...
Leonardo's f...
sandstone n...
and his prec...
of plants wh...
most likely t...

Master...
the *Virgin* o...
display Leonardo's careful study of human an...
landscapes, and botany. Although he admire...
tion of nature, Leonardo also celebrated the h...
rational and aesthetic capacities, declaring th...
arts may be called the grandsons of God."[2]

1. Arundel ms. (British Library), p. 115 recto, cited i...
Leonardo da Vinci: The Marvelous Works of Nat...
(Oxford: Oxford University Press, 2006), 78.
2. John Paul Richter, ed., *The Notebooks of Leonar...*
of 1883 ed.; New York: Dover, 1970), Book IX, 3...

EXAMINING THE EVIDENCE

1. How does Leonardo express the conne... between John (at left) and Jesus throug... gesture, and their relationships with th... Mary and the angel Uriel?
2. The friars who commissioned the painting sought to celebrate the sanctity and purity of their patron, the Virgin Mary. Does this painting achieve that effect?

Thus, China influenced patterns of international trade not only as a producer, as with

READING THE PAST

A Spanish Ambassador's Description of Samarkand

In September 1403, an embassy dispatched by King Henry III of Castile arrived at Samarkand in hopes of enlisting the support of Timur for a combined military campaign against the Ottomans. Seventy years old and in failing health, Timur lavishly entertained his visitors, but made no response to Henry's overtures. The leader of the Spanish delegation, Ruy Gonzalez de Clavijo, left Samarkand disappointed, but his report preserves our fullest account of Timur's capital in its heyday.

The city is rather larger than Seville, but lying outside Samarkand are great numbers of houses that form extensive suburbs. These lay spread on all hands, for indeed the township is surrounded by orchards and vineyards. . . . In between these orchards pass streets with open squares; these are all densely populated, and here all kinds of goods are on sale with breadstuffs and meat. . . .

Samarkand is rich not only in foodstuffs but also in manufactures, such as factories of silk. . . . Thus trade has always been fostered by Timur with the view of making his capital the noblest of cities; and during all his conquests . . . he carried off the best men to people Samarkand, bringing thither the master-craftsmen of all nations. Thus from Damascus he carried away with him all the weavers of that city, those who worked at the silk looms; further the bow-makers who produce those cross-bows which are so famous; likewise armorers; also the craftsmen in glass and porcelain, who are known to be the best in all the world. From Turkey he

had brought their gunsmiths who make the arquebus. . . . So great therefore was the population now of all nationalities gathered together in Samarkand that of men with their families the number they said must amount to 150,000 souls . . . [including] Turks, Arabs, and Moors of diverse sects, with Greek, Armenian, Roman, Jacobite [Syrian], and Nestorian Christians, besides those folk who baptize with fire in the forehead [i.e., Hindus]. . . .

The markets of Samarkand further are amply stored with merchandise imported from distant and foreign countries. . . . The goods that are imported to Samarkand from Cathay indeed are of the richest and most precious of all those brought thither from foreign parts, for the craftsmen of Cathay are reputed to be the most skillful by far beyond those of any other nation.

Source: Ruy Gonzalez de Clavijo, *Embassy to Tamerlane, 1403–1406*, trans. Guy Le Strange (London: Routledge, 1928), 285–289.

EXAMINING THE EVIDENCE

1. What features of Timur's capital most impressed Gonzalez de Clavijo?
2. How does this account of Samarkand at its height compare with the chapter's description of Renaissance Florence?

South...
and Rai...

496

502

STEP 5

Review what you have learned.

Remember to visit the Online Study Guide for more review help.

REVIEW

Online Study Guide
bedfordstmartins.com/smith

Review the Major Global Development discussed in the chapter.

The major global development in this chapter ▶ Crisis and recovery in fourteenth- and fifteenth-century Afro-Eurasia.

Review the Important Events from the chapter.

IMPORTANT EVENTS

1315–1317	Great Famine in northern Europe
1325–1354	Travels of Ibn Battuta in Asia and Africa
1336–1573	Ashikaga shogunate in Japan
1337–1453	Hundred Years' War between England and France
1347–1350	Outbreak of the Black Death in Europe and the Islamic Mediterranean
c. 1351–1782	Ayudhya kingdom in Thailand
1368–1644	Ming dynasty in China
1378	Ciompi uprising in Florence
1381	Peasant Revolt in England
1392–1910	Yi dynasty in Korea
1405	Death of Timur; breakup of his empire into regional states in Iran and Central Asia
1405–1433	Chinese admiral Zheng He's expeditions in Southeast Asia and the Indian Ocean
1421	Relocation of Ming capital from Nanjing to Beijing
1428–1788	Le dynasty in Vietnam
1453	Ottoman conquest of Constantinople marks fall of the Byzantine Empire

Review the Key Terms.

KEY TERMS

Black Death (p. 478)
humanism (p. 498)
janissary corps (p. 489)
Little Ice Age (p. 479)
Neo-Confucianism (p. 486)
oligarchy (p. 483)

pandemic (p. 478)
Renaissance (p. 498)
samurai (p. 501)
shogun (p. 503)
Sufism (p. 488)
theocracy (p. 489)
trade diaspora (p. 492)

CHAPTER OVERVIEW QUESTIONS

1. How and why did Europe's economic growth begin to surpass that of the Islamic world in the [...] after the Black Death?

2. Did the economic revival across Eurasia a[...] benefit the peasant populations of Europe[...] Islamic world, and East Asia?

3. How did the process of conversion to Islam differ in Iran, the Ottoman Empire, West Africa, and Southeast Asia during this period?

4. What political and economic changes contributed to the rise of maritime commerce in Asia during the fourteenth and fifteenth centuries?

Answer these big-picture questions posed at the start of the chapter.

SECTION FOCUS QUESTIONS

1. How did the Black Death affect society, the [...] omy, and culture in Latin Christendom and [...] Islamic world?

2. Why did Islam expand dramatically in the fourteenth and fifteenth centuries, and how did new Islamic societies differ from established ones?

3. What were the principal sources of growth in international trade during the fourteenth and fifteenth centuries, and how did this trade affect patterns of consumption and fashion tastes?

4. How and why did the historical development of Japan in the fourteenth and fifteenth centuries differ from that of mainland Eurasia?

Explain the main point of each major section of the chapter.

MAKING CONNECTIONS

1. What social, economic, and technological c[...] strengthened the power of European mona[...] during the century after the Black Death?

2. How and why did the major routes and con[...] ties of trans-Eurasian trade change after the collapse of the Mongol empires in Central Asia?

3. In what ways did the motives for conversion to Islam differ in Central Asia, sub-Saharan Africa, and the Indian Ocean during this era?

4. In this period, why did the power and status of the samurai warriors in Japan rise while those of the warrior nobility in Europe declined?

Connect ideas and practice your skills of comparison and analysis.

507

VERSIONS AND SUPPLEMENTS

Adopters of *Crossroads and Cultures: A History of the World's Peoples* and their students have access to abundant extra resources, including documents, presentation and testing materials, the acclaimed Bedford Series in History and Culture volumes, and much, much more. See below for more information, visit the book's catalog site at bedfordstmartins .com/smith/catalog, or contact your local Bedford/St. Martin's sales representative.

Get the Right Version for Your Class

To accommodate different course lengths and course budgets, *Crossroads and Cultures: A History of the World's Peoples* is available in several different formats, including three-hole punched loose-leaf Budget Books versions and e-books, which are available at a substantial discount.

- Combined edition (Chapters 1–31)—available in hardcover, loose-leaf, and e-book formats
- Volume 1: To 1450 (Chapters 1–16)—available in paperback, loose-leaf, and e-book formats
- Volume 2: Since 1300 (Chapters 15–31)—available in paperback, loose-leaf, and e-book formats
- Volume A: To 1300 (Chapters 1–14)—available in paperback
- Volume B: 500–1750 (Chapters 9–22)—available in paperback
- Volume C: Since 1750 (Chapters 23–31)—available in paperback

Your students can purchase *Crossroads and Cultures: A History of the World's Peoples* in popular e-book formats for computers, tablets, and e-readers by visiting bedfordstmartins .com/ebooks. The e-book is available at a discount.

Online Extras for Students

The book's companion site at bedfordstmartins.com/smith gives students a way to read, write, and study by providing plentiful quizzes and activities, study aids, and history research and writing help.

FREE **Online Study Guide.** Available at the companion site, this popular resource provides students with quizzes and activities for each chapter, including multiple-choice self-tests that focus on important concepts; flashcards that test students' knowledge of key terms; timeline activities that emphasize causal relationships; and map quizzes intended to strengthen students' geography skills. Instructors can monitor students' progress through an online Quiz Gradebook or receive e-mail updates.

FREE **Research, Writing, and Anti-plagiarism Advice.** Available at the companion site, Bedford's **History Research and Writing Help** includes **History Research and Reference Sources**, with links to history-related databases, indexes, and journals; **More Sources and How to Format a History Paper**, with clear advice on how to integrate primary and secondary sources into research papers and how to cite and format sources correctly; **Build a Bibliography**, a simple Web-based tool known as the Bedford Bibliographer that generates bibliographies in four commonly used documentation styles; and **Tips on Avoiding Plagiarism**, an online tutorial that reviews the consequences of plagiarism and features exercises to help students practice integrating sources and recognize acceptable summaries.

Resources for Instructors

Bedford/St. Martin's has developed a rich array of teaching resources for this book and for this course. They range from lecture and presentation materials and assessment tools to course management options. Most can be downloaded or ordered at bedfordstmartins.com/smith/catalog.

HistoryClass for Crossroads and Cultures. *HistoryClass*, a Bedford/St. Martin's Online Course Space, puts the online resources available with this textbook in one convenient and completely customizable course space. There you and your students can access an interactive e-book and primary source reader; maps, images, documents, and links; chapter review quizzes; interactive multimedia exercises; and research and writing help. In *HistoryClass* you can get all our premium content and tools and assign, rearrange, and mix them with your own resources. For more information, visit yourhistoryclass.com.

Bedford Coursepack for Blackboard, WebCT, Desire2Learn, Angel, Sakai, or Moodle. We have free content to help you integrate our rich materials into your course management system. Registered instructors can download coursepacks easily and with no strings attached. The coursepack for *Crossroads and Cultures: A History of the World's Peoples* includes book-specific content as well as our most popular free resources. Visit bedfordstmartins.com/ coursepacks to see a demo, find your version, or download your coursepack.

Instructor's Resource Manual. Written by Rick Warner, an experienced teacher of the world-history survey course, the instructor's manual offers both experienced and first-time instructors tools for preparing lectures and running discussions. It includes chapter review material, teaching strategies, and a guide to chapter-specific supplements available for the text.

Computerized Test Bank. The test bank includes a mix of fresh, carefully crafted multiple-choice, matching, short-answer, and essay questions for each chapter. It also contains the Overview, Focus, Making Connections, Lives and Livelihoods, Reading the Past, and Seeing the Past questions from the textbook and model answers for each. The questions appear in Microsoft Word format and in easy-to-use test bank software that allows instructors to easily add, edit, resequence, and print questions and answers. Instructors can also export questions into a variety of formats, including WebCT and Blackboard.

The Bedford Lecture Kit: Maps, Images, Lecture Outlines, and i>clicker Content. Look good and save time with *The Bedford Lecture Kit*. These presentation materials are downloadable individually from the Instructor Resources tab at bedfordstmartins.com/smith/catalog and are available on *The Bedford Lecture Kit* Instructor's Resource CD-ROM. They provide ready-made and fully customizable PowerPoint multimedia presentations that include lecture outlines with embedded maps, figures, and selected images from the textbook and extra background for instructors. Also available are maps and selected images in JPEG and PowerPoint formats; content for i>clicker, a classroom response system, in Microsoft Word and PowerPoint formats; the Instructor's Resource Manual in Microsoft Word format; and outline maps in PDF format for quizzing or handing out. All files are suitable for copying onto transparency acetates.

Make History—Free Documents, Maps, Images, and Web Sites. *Make History* combines the best Web resources with hundreds of maps and images, to make it simple to find the source material you need. Browse the collection of thousands of resources by course or by topic, date, and type. Each item has been carefully chosen and helpfully annotated to make it easy to find exactly what you need. Available at bedfordstmartins.com/makehistory.

Videos and Multimedia. A wide assortment of videos and multimedia CD-ROMs on various topics in world history is available to qualified adopters through your Bedford/ St. Martin's sales representative.

Package and Save Your Students Money

For information on free packages and discounts up to 50%, visit bedfordstmartins.com/smith/catalog, or contact your local Bedford/St. Martin's sales representative.

Sources of Crossroads and Cultures. The authors of *Crossroads and Cultures* have carefully developed this two-volume primary source reader themselves to reflect the textbook's geographic and thematic breadth and the key social, cultural, and political developments discussed in each chapter. *Sources of Crossroads and Cultures* extends the textbook's emphasis on the human dimension of global history through the voices of both notable figures and everyday individuals. With a blend of major works and fresh perspectives, each chapter contains approximately six sources, an introduction, document headnotes, and questions for discussion. Available free when packaged with the print text.

Sources of Crossroads and Cultures e-Book. The reader is also available as an e-book for purchase at a discount.

The Bedford Series in History and Culture. More than one hundred titles in this highly praised series combine first-rate scholarship, historical narrative, and important primary documents for undergraduate courses. Each book is brief, inexpensive, and focused on a specific topic or period. For a complete list of titles, visit bedfordstmartins.com/ history/series. Package discounts are available.

Rand McNally Historical Atlas of the World. This collection of almost seventy full-color maps illustrates the eras and civilizations in world history from the emergence of human societies to the present. Available for $3.00 when packaged with the print text.

The Bedford Glossary for World History. This handy supplement for the survey course gives students historically contextualized definitions for hundreds of terms—from *abolitionism* to *Zoroastrianism*—that they will encounter in lectures, reading, and exams. Available free when packaged with the print text.

World History Matters: A Student Guide to World History Online. Based on the popular "World History Matters" Web site produced by the Center for History and New Media, this unique resource, edited by Kristin Lehner (The Johns Hopkins University), Kelly Schrum (George Mason University), and T. Mills Kelly (George Mason University), combines reviews of 150 of the most useful and reliable world history Web sites with an introduction that guides students in locating, evaluating, and correctly citing online sources. Available free when packaged with the print text.

Trade Books. Titles published by sister companies Hill and Wang; Farrar, Straus and Giroux; Henry Holt and Company; St. Martin's Press; Picador; and Palgrave Macmillan are available at a 50% discount when packaged with

Bedford/St. Martin's textbooks. For more information, visit bedfordstmartins.com/tradeup.

A Pocket Guide to Writing in History.   This portable and affordable reference tool by Mary Lynn Rampolla provides reading, writing, and research advice useful to students in all history courses. Concise yet comprehensive advice on approaching typical history assignments, developing critical reading skills, writing effective history papers, conducting research, using and documenting sources, and avoiding plagiarism—enhanced with practical tips and examples throughout—have made this slim reference a best-seller. Package discounts are available.

A Student's Guide to History.   This complete guide to success in any history course provides the practical help students need to be effective. In addition to introducing students to the nature of the discipline, author Jules Benjamin teaches a wide range of skills from preparing for exams to approaching common writing assignments, and he explains the research and documentation process with plentiful examples. Package discounts are available.

Worlds of History: A Comparative Reader.   Compiled by Kevin Reilly, a widely respected world historian and community college teacher, *Worlds of History* fosters historical thinking through thematic comparisons of primary and secondary sources from around the world. Each chapter takes up a major theme—such as patriarchy, love and marriage, or globalization—as experienced by two or more cultures. "Thinking Historically" exercises build students' capacity to analyze and interpret sources one skill at a time. This flexible framework accommodates a variety of approaches to teaching world history. Package discounts are available.

NOTE ON DATES AND USAGE

Where necessary for clarity, we qualify dates as B.C.E. ("Before the Common Era") or C.E. ("Common Era"). The abbreviation B.C.E. refers to the same era as B.C. ("Before Christ"), just as C.E is equivalent to A.D. (*anno Domini,* Latin for "in the year of the Lord"). In keeping with our aim to approach world history from a global, multicultural perspective, we chose these neutral abbreviations as appropriate to our enterprise. Because most readers will be more familiar with English than with metric measures, however, units of measure are given in the English system in the narrative, with metric and English measures provided on the maps.

We translate Chinese names and terms into English according to the *pinyin* system, while noting in parentheses proper names well established in English (e.g., Canton, Chiang Kai-shek). Transliteration of names and terms from the many other languages traced in our book follow the same contemporary scholarly conventions.

BRIEF CONTENTS

15 Collapse and Revival in Afro-Eurasia, 1300–1450 *474*

PART 3   The Early Modern World, 1450–1750

16 Empires and Alternatives in the Americas, 1430–1530 *512*
17 The Fall of Native American Empires and the Rise of an Atlantic World, 1450–1600 *546*
18 Western Africa in the Era of the Atlantic Slave Trade, 1450–1800 *580*
19 Trade and Empire in the Indian Ocean and South Asia, 1450–1750 *612*
20 Consolidation and Conflict in Europe and the Greater Mediterranean, 1450–1750 *646*
21 Expansion and Isolation in Asia, 1450–1750 *682*
22 Transforming New Worlds: The American Colonies Mature, 1600–1750 *718*

PART 4   The World from 1750 to the Present

23 Atlantic Revolutions and the World, 1750–1830 *758*
24 Industry and Everyday Life, 1750–1900 *790*
25 The Rise of Modern Nation-States, 1850–1900 *824*
26 Imperial Order and Disorder, 1850–1914 *856*
27 Wars, Revolutions, and the Birth of Mass Society, 1910–1929 *890*
28 Global Catastrophe: the Great Depression and World War II, 1929–1945 *924*
29 The Emergence of New Nations in a Cold War World, 1945–1970 *958*
30 Technological Transformation and the End of Cold War, 1960–1992 *988*
31 A New Global Age, 1989 to the Present *1022*

CONTENTS

A Conversation with the Authors: The Story Behind
  Crossroads and *Cultures*   vii
How to Use This Book   xii
Versions and Supplements   xxi

Note on Dates and Usage   xxiii
Maps   xxxv
Special Features   xxxvii
Acknowledgments   xxxviii

PART 3 — The Early Modern World, 1450–1750

15 Collapse and Revival in Afro-Eurasia, 1300–1450   474

Major Global Development ▶ Crisis and recovery in fourteenth- and fifteenth-century Afro-Eurasia.

Backstory   475

Fourteenth-Century Crisis and Renewal in Eurasia   478
  The "Great Mortality": The Black Death of 1347–1350   479
  Rebuilding Societies in Western Europe, 1350–1492   482
  Ming China and the New Order in East Asia, 1368–1500   485

Islam's New Frontiers   488
  Islamic Spiritual Ferment in Central Asia, 1350–1500   488
  Ottoman Expansion and the Fall of Constantinople, 1354–1453   489
  Commerce and Culture in Islamic West Africa   491
  Advance of Islam in Maritime Southeast Asia   492

The Global Bazaar   493
  Economic Prosperity and Maritime Trade in Asia, 1350–1450   494
  China's Overseas Overture: The Voyages of Zheng He, 1405–1433   498
  Commerce and Culture in the Renaissance   499

COUNTERPOINT Age of the Samurai in Japan, 1185–1450   501
  "The Low Overturning the High"   503
  The New Warrior Order   503

Conclusion   505 | *Notes*   505
Resources for Research   506 | *Review*   507

▶ READING THE PAST A French Theologian's View of the Black Death   482
▶ READING THE PAST A Spanish Ambassador's Description of Samarkand   490
▶ LIVES AND LIVELIHOODS Urban Weavers in India   496
▶ SEEING THE PAST Leonardo da Vinci's *Virgin of the Rocks*   502

16 Empires and Alternatives in the Americas, 1430–1530   512

Major Global Development ▶ The diversity of societies and states in the Americas prior to European invasion.

Backstory   513

Many Native Americas   516

Tributes of Blood: The Aztec Empire, 1325–1521   519
  Humble Origins, Imperial Ambitions   520
  Enlarging and Supplying the Capital   523
  Holy Terror: Aztec Rule, Religion, and Warfare   523
  Daily Life Under the Aztecs   526
  The Limits of Holy Terror   529

Tributes of Sweat: The Inca Empire, 1430–1532   529
  From Potato Farmers to Empire Builders   530
  The Great Apparatus: Inca Expansion and Religion   530
  Daily Life Under the Incas   534
  The Great Apparatus Breaks Down   537

COUNTERPOINT The Peoples of North America's Eastern Woodlands, 1450–1530   538

Conclusion   542 | *Notes*   542
Resources for Research   542 | *Review*   544

▶ SEEING THE PAST An Aztec Map of Tenochtitlán   521
▶ SEEING THE PAST The Coyolxauhqui Stone   524
▶ LIVES AND LIVELIHOODS The Aztec Midwife   528
▶ READING THE PAST An Andean Creation Story   533

17

The Fall of Native American Empires and the Rise of an Atlantic World, 1450–1600 *546*

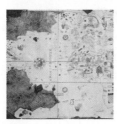

Major Global Development ▶ European expansion across the Atlantic and its profound consequences for societies and cultures worldwide.

Backstory *547*

Guns, Sails, and Compasses: Europeans Venture Abroad *551*
　Motives for Exploration *551*
　Technologies of Exploration *552*
　Portugal Takes the Lead *553*

New Crossroads, First Encounters: The European Voyages of Discovery, 1492–1521 *555*
　Christopher Columbus in a New World *555*
　From Independence to Servitude: The Encomienda System *559*
　Columbus's Successors *560*
　The Columbian Exchange *561*

Spanish Conquests in the Americas, 1519–1600 *562*
　The Fall of Aztec Mexico *562*
　The Fall of Inca Peru *564*
　The Conquest: Myths and Realities *565*

A New Empire in the Americas: New Spain and Peru, 1535–1600 *567*
　American Silver and the Global Economy *567*
　American Silver and Everyday Life *569*

Brazil by Accident: The Portuguese in the Americas, 1500–1600 *570*
　Native Encounters and Foreign Competitors *570*
　Bitter Sugar: Slavery and the Plantation Complex in the Early Atlantic World, 1530–1600 *572*

COUNTERPOINT The Mapuche of Chile: Native America's Indomitable State *573*
　A Culture of Warfare *573*
　Uprisings Against the Spanish *574*

Conclusion *576* | *Notes* *577*
Resources for Research *577* | *Review* *579*

▶ READING THE PAST Tlatelolcan Elders Recall the Conquest of Mexico *564*
▶ SEEING THE PAST Malintzin and the Meeting Between Moctezuma and Cortés *566*
▶ READING THE PAST First Encounter in Brazil: Cabral's Report to King Manoel of Portugal *571*
▶ LIVES AND LIVELIHOODS Atlantic Sugar Producers *574*

18

Western Africa in the Era of the Atlantic Slave Trade, 1450–1800 *580*

Major Global Development ▶ The rise of the Atlantic slave trade and its impact on early modern African peoples and cultures.

Backstory *581*

Many Western Africas *585*

Landlords and Strangers: Peoples and States in West Africa *588*
　Empire Builders and Traders *589*
　Sculptors and Priest-Kings *590*

Land of the Blacksmith Kings: West Central Africa *593*
　Farmers and Traders *593*
　Smiths and Kings *594*

Strangers in Ships: Gold, Slavery, and the Portuguese *595*
　From Voyages of Reconnaissance to Trading Forts, 1415–1650 *595*
　Portuguese Strategy in the Kingdom of Kongo *598*
　Portuguese Strategy in Angola *599*

Northern Europeans and the Expansion of the Atlantic Slave Trade, 1600–1800 *600*
　The Rise and Fall of Monopoly Trading Companies *601*
　How the Mature Slave Trade Functioned *604*
　The Middle Passage *605*
　Volume of the Slave Trade *606*

COUNTERPOINT The Pygmies of Central Africa *607*
　Life in the Congo Rain Forest *607*
　Pygmy-Bantu Relations *608*

Conclusion *609* | *Notes* *609*
Resources for Research *610* | *Review* *611*

▶ LIVES AND LIVELIHOODS West Africa's Gold Miners *588*
▶ READING THE PAST Al-Sa'di on Jenne and Its History *591*
▶ SEEING THE PAST Art of the Slave Trade: A Benin Bronze Plaque *592*
▶ READING THE PAST Alonso de Sandoval, "General Points Relating to Slavery" *596*

19

Trade and Empire in the Indian Ocean and South Asia, 1450–1750 *612*

Major Global Development ▶ The Indian Ocean trading network and the impact of European intrusion on maritime and mainland South Asia.

Backstory *613*

Trading Cities and Inland Networks: East Africa *617*
Port Towns and Beginnings *617*
Indian Ocean Connections *619*
Links to the Interior *620*

Trade and Empire in South Asia *620*
Vijayanagara's Rise and Fall, 1336–1565 *621*
The Power of the Mughals *623*
Gunpowder Weapons and Imperial Consolidation, 1500–1763 *625*
Everyday Life in the Mughal Empire *630*

European Interlopers *632*
Portuguese Conquistadors, 1500–1600 *632*
The Dutch and English East India Companies, 1600–1750 *635*

COUNTERPOINT Aceh: Fighting Back in Southeast Asia *640*
The Differing Fortunes of Aceh and Melaka *640*
Aceh, "the Veranda of Mecca" *640*

Conclusion *642* | *Notes* *643*
Resources for Research *643* | *Review* *645*

▶ READING THE PAST Portuguese Report of a Vijayanagara Festival *624*
▶ SEEING THE PAST Reflections of the Divine in a Mughal Emerald *629*
▶ LIVES AND LIVELIHOODS Cinnamon Harvesters in Ceylon *636*
▶ READING THE PAST Dutch Merchants Learn How to Act in Aceh *641*

20

Consolidation and Conflict in Europe and the Greater Mediterranean, 1450–1750 *646*

Major Global Development ▶ Early modern Europe's increasing competition and division in the face of Ottoman expansion.

Backstory *647*

The Power of the Ottoman Empire, 1453–1750 *650*
Tools of Empire *651*
Expansion and Consolidation *651*
Daily Life in the Ottoman Empire *655*

Europe Divided, 1500–1650 *658*
Everyday Life in Early Modern Europe *659*
Protestant and Catholic Reformations *661*
Imperial Spain and Its Challenges *665*
The Seventeenth-Century Crisis *667*

European Innovations in Science and Government, 1550–1750 *670*
The Scientific Revolution *670*
The Emergence of Capitalism *672*
New Political Models: Absolutism and Constitutionalism *673*

COUNTERPOINT The Barbary Pirates *677*
Reign of the Sea Bandits *677*
The Barbary Wars *678*

Conclusion *679* | *Notes* *679*
Resources for Research *680* | *Review* *681*

▶ READING THE PAST Weapons of Mass Destruction: Ottomans vs. Persians in Baghdad *655*
▶ LIVES AND LIVELIHOODS Ottoman Coffeehouse Owners and Patrons *658*
▶ SEEING THE PAST Gift Clocks for the Emperors of China *664*
▶ READING THE PAST An Exiled European Muslim Visits the Netherlands *669*

21

Expansion and
Isolation in Asia,
1450–1750   *682*

Major Global Development ▶ The general trend toward political and cultural consolidation in early modern Asia.

Backstory   683

Straddling Eurasia: Rise of the Russian Empire,
1462–1725   686
   Consolidation in Muscovite Russia   687
   The Romanovs' New Frontiers   689

China from Ming to Qing Rule, 1500–1800   690
   Late Ming Imperial Demands and Private Trade   691
   Manchu Expansion and the Rise of the Qing
     Empire   693
   Everyday Life in Ming and Qing China   695
   The Flourishing of Art and Culture   696

Japan in Transition, 1540–1750   697
   Rise of the Tokugawa Shogunate and the Unification
     of Japan   698
   Everyday Life and Culture in Tokugawa Japan   700
   Emergence of a National Culture   702

Korea, a Land in Between, 1392–1750   705
   Capital and Countryside   705
   Everyday Life in Choson Korea   706

Consolidation in Mainland Southeast Asia,
1500–1750   708
   Political Consolidation   708
   Commercial Trends   710

COUNTERPOINT "Spiritual Conquest"
in the Philippines   711
   Arrival of the Spanish   712
   The Limits of "Spiritual Conquest"   714

Conclusion   714 | *Notes*   715
Resources for Research   715 | *Review*   717

▶ SEEING THE PAST   Blue-on-White: Ming Export
   Porcelain   692
▶ LIVES AND LIVELIHOODS   Silk Weavers in China   696
▶ READING THE PAST   Selections from the Hidden
   Christians' Sacred Book   700
▶ READING THE PAST   Scenes from the Daily Life
   of a Korean Queen   707

22

Transforming New
Worlds: The American
Colonies Mature,
1600–1750   *718*

Major Global Development ▶ The profound social, cultural, and environmental changes in the Americas under colonial rule.

Backstory   719

The World that Silver Made: Spanish America,
1570–1750   723
   Governing and Profiting from the Colonies   724
   Everyday Life in Spanish America   729

Gold, Diamonds, and the Transformation of Brazil,
1695–1800   732
   Boom Times for Colonial Brazil   733
   Everyday Life in Golden-Age Brazil   735

Bitter Sugar, Part Two: Slavery and Colonialism in the
Caribbean, 1625–1750   737
   Pirates and Planters   738
   The Rise of Caribbean Slave Societies   740

Growth and Change in British and French North
America, 1607–1750   741
   Experiments in Commercial Colonialism   741
   Everyday Life in the Northern Colonies   745

COUNTERPOINT   The Maroons of Suriname   748
   From Persecution to Freedom   748
   Suriname's Distinctive Maroon Culture   749

Conclusion   750 | *Notes*   750
Resources for Research   750 | *Review*   752

▶ READING THE PAST   An Iraqi Traveler's Impressions
   of Potosí   727
▶ SEEING THE PAST   *Gentlemen of Esmeraldas*   730
▶ LIVES AND LIVELIHOODS   Caribbean
   Buccaneers   738
▶ READING THE PAST   A Swedish Traveler's Description
   of Quebec   747

23

Atlantic Revolutions and the World, 1750–1830 *758*

Major Global Development ▶ The Atlantic revolutions and their short- and long-term significance.

Backstory *759*

The Promise of Enlightenment *762*
A New World of Ideas *762*
Enlightenment and the Old Order *765*
Popular Revolts in an Age of Enlightenment *767*

Revolution in North America *767*
The British Empire and the Colonial Crisis, 1764–1775 *768*
The Birth of the United States, 1775–1789 *768*

The French Revolution and the Napoleonic Empire *771*
From Monarchy to Republic, 1789–1792 *771*
War, Terror, and Resistance, 1792–1799 *773*
Napoleon's Reign, 1799–1815 *774*
Muhammad Ali and the Revolutionary Spirit in Egypt *774*

Revolution Continued in the Western Hemisphere *777*
Revolution in Haiti, 1791–1804 *777*
Revolutions in Latin America, 1810–1830 *778*
New Ideologies and Revolutionary Legacies *783*

COUNTERPOINT Religious Revival in a Secular Age *784*
Christianity's Great Awakening *785*
Government and Religion Allied *785*

Conclusion *786* | *Notes* *787*
Resources for Research *788* | *Review* *789*

▶ SEEING THE PAST Portrait of Catherine the Great *766*
▶ LIVES AND LIVELIHOODS The Cowboy Way of Life *782*
▶ READING THE PAST Simon Bolivar on Latin American Independence *784*
▶ READING THE PAST Phillis Wheatley, "On Being Brought from Africa to America" *786*

24

Industry and Everyday Life, 1750–1900 *790*

Major Global Development ▶ The Industrial Revolution and its impact on societies and cultures throughout the world.

Backstory *791*

The Industrial Revolution Begins, 1750–1830 *794*
The Global Roots of Industrialization *794*
Great Britain: A Culture of Experimentation *795*
World Trade and the Rise of Industry *796*
The Technology of Industry *798*

Industrialization After 1830 *798*
Industrial Innovation Gathers Speed *799*
Challenge to British Dominance *802*
Industrialization in Japan *802*
Economic Crises and Solutions *804*

The Industrial Revolution and the World *806*
The Slow Disintegration of Qing China *807*
Competition in West and South Asia *809*
A New Course for Africa *810*

Industry and Society *812*
The Changing Middle Class *812*
The New Working Class *813*
The Sexual Division of Labor *815*

The Culture of Industry *815*
Industry and the Arts *817*

COUNTERPOINT African Women and Slave Agriculture *818*
Women and Farming in Africa *818*
Women Slaves in the North American South *819*

Conclusion *820* | *Notes* *820*
Resources for Research *821* | *Review* *823*

▶ READING THE PAST Industry Comes to the British Countryside *797*
▶ LIVES AND LIVELIHOODS Builders of the Trans-Siberian Railroad *800*
▶ SEEING THE PAST Japan's Industrious Society *803*
▶ READING THE PAST Mexican Women on Strike *816*

25

The Rise of Modern Nation-States,
1850–1900 *824*

Major Global Development ►The causes and consequences of nation building in the nineteenth century.

Backstory *825*

Modernizing Nations *828*
 "What Is a Nation?" *829*
 Latin American Nation Building *829*
 The Russian Empire's New Course *832*
 A Unified Italy and a United Germany *836*

Emerging Powers: The United States and Japan *838*
 Expansion and Consolidation of the United States *838*
 Dramatic Change in Japan *841*

The Culture of Nations *843*
 The Culture of Tradition *843*
 Westernization *845*
 National Institutions *846*

COUNTERPOINT Outsiders Inside the Nation-State *849*
 People of Color *849*
 Women *850*
 The Struggle for Citizens' Rights *851*

Conclusion *852* | *Notes* *853*
Resources for Research *853* | *Review* *855*

► READING THE PAST The Russian People Under Serfdom *835*
► SEEING THE PAST The Korean Flag *844*
► LIVES AND LIVELIHOODS Historians of the Nation-State *846*
► READING THE PAST "Good Wives, Wise Mothers" Build Japan *848*

26

Imperial Order and Disorder,
1850–1914 *856*

Major Global Development ►The accelerated competition among nineteenth-century nation-states for empire.

Backstory *857*

Building Empires *860*
 Imperialism: What Is It? *860*
 Takeover in Asia *861*
 Europeans Scramble for Africa *864*
 Japan's Imperial Agenda *868*
 Technology, Environment, and the Imperial Advantage *868*

Imperial Society *869*
 Changing Conditions of Everyday Life *869*
 Medicine, Science, and Well-Being in the Colonies *872*
 Migrants and Diasporas *874*

Culture in an Imperial Age *878*
 The Culture of Everyday Life *878*
 Art and Empire *879*

Imperial Contests at the Dawn of the Twentieth Century *880*
 Clashes for Imperial Control *881*
 Growing Resistance to Foreign Domination *883*

COUNTERPOINT The West Copies from the World *885*
 Changes in the Arts *885*
 Expansion of Ideas *886*
 Lifestyles Transformed *886*

Conclusion *887* | *Notes* *887*
Resources for Research *888* | *Review* *889*

► READING THE PAST Rubber Workers in Congo *871*
► SEEING THE PAST Imperial Architecture in Saigon *872*
► LIVES AND LIVELIHOODS Indentured Laborers *876*
► READING THE PAST The United States Overthrows the Hawaiian Queen *882*

27

Wars, Revolutions, and the Birth of Mass Society, 1910–1929 *890*

Major Global Development ▶ The wars of the decade 1910 to 1920 and their role in the creation of mass culture and society.

Backstory 891

Revolutions, Local Wars, and World War 894
  Revolutionaries and Warriors: Mexico, China, and the Balkans 894
  Fighting World War I 896
  Civilians at War: The Home Front 900

Revolution in Russia and the End of World War I 902
  Revolution in Russia 902
  Ending the War: 1918 904

Postwar Global Politics 905
  The Paris Peace Conference, 1919–1920 905
  Struggles for Reform and Independence 908
  Postwar Imperial Expansion 912

An Age of the Masses 913
  Mass Society 913
  Culture for the Masses 914
  Mobilizing the Masses 916

COUNTERPOINT A Golden Age for Argentineans 919
  A Flourishing Economy and Society 919
  Argentina's Cultural Riches 920

Conclusion 920 | *Notes* 921
Resources for Research 922 | *Review* 923

▶ SEEING THE PAST Wartime Propaganda 901
▶ READING THE PAST Communism Spreads in China 911
▶ READING THE PAST Léopold Sédar Senghor, "To the Senegalese Soldiers Who Died for France" 912
▶ LIVES AND LIVELIHOODS The Film Industry 916

28

Global Catastrophe: The Great Depression and World War II, 1929–1945 *924*

Major Global Development ▶ The causes and outcomes of the Great Depression and World War II.

Backstory 925

1929: The Great Depression Begins 928
  Economic Disaster Strikes 928
  Social Effects of the Great Depression 930
  Protesting Poverty 931

Militarizing the Masses in the 1930s 932
  The Rise of Stalinism 933
  Japanese Expansionism 935
  Hitler's Rise to Power 936
  Democracies Mobilize 938

Global War, 1937–1945 939
  Europe's Road to War 940
  The Early Years of the War, 1937–1943 940
  War and the World's Civilians 945

From Allied Victory to the Cold War, 1943–1945 950
  The Axis Defeated 950
  Postwar Plans and Uncertainties 951

COUNTERPOINT Nonviolence and Pacifism in an Age of War 953
  Traditional Tactics: The Example of Nigerian Women 953
  Gandhi and Civil Disobedience 953

Conclusion 954 | *Notes* 955
Resources for Research 955 | *Review* 957

▶ READING THE PAST Promoting Business in the Great Depression 930
▶ READING THE PAST "Comfort Women" in World War II 942
▶ LIVES AND LIVELIHOODS Soldiers and Soldiering 946
▶ SEEING THE PAST Technological Warfare: Civilization or Barbarism? 952

29

The Emergence of New Nations in a Cold War World, 1945–1970 *958*

Major Global Development ▶ The political transformations of the postwar world and their social and cultural consequences.

Backstory *959*

World Politics and the Cold War *962*
  The New Superpowers *962*
  The Cold War Unfolds, 1945–1962 *963*
  The People's Republic of China, 1949 *965*
  Proxy Wars and Cold War Alliances *965*

Decolonization and the Birth of Nations *969*
  The End of Empire in Asia *970*
  The Struggle for Independence in the Middle East *972*
  New Nations in Africa *973*

World Recovery in the 1950s and 1960s *975*
  Expanding Economic Prosperity *976*
  Building and Rebuilding Communism *978*

Cultural Dynamism amid Cold War *980*
  Confronting the Heritage of World War *980*
  Liberation Culture *981*
  The Culture of Cold War *982*

COUNTERPOINT The Bandung Conference, 1955 *983*
  Shared Goals *984*
  Divisive Issues *985*

Conclusion *985* | *Notes* *985*
Resources for Research *986* | *Review* *987*

▶ LIVES AND LIVELIHOODS Cosmonauts and Astronauts *966*
▶ SEEING THE PAST African Liberation on Cloth *975*
▶ READING THE PAST The Great Leap Forward in China *978*

30

Technological Transformation and the End of Cold War, 1960–1992 *988*

Major Global Development ▶ The technological revolution of the late twentieth century and its impact on societies and political developments around the world.

Backstory *989*

Advances in Technology and Science *992*
  The Information Revolution *992*
  The Space Age *994*
  A New Scientific Revolution *995*

Changes in the World Economy *996*
  The Rising Pacific Economy *996*
  Multinational Corporations *998*
  Global Changes in Work *998*
  The Knowledge Economy *1000*
  Postindustrial Family Life *1002*

Politics and Protest in an Age of Cold War *1003*
  Democracy and Dictatorship in Latin America *1003*
  Domestic Revolution and a Changing International Order *1006*
  Activists Challenge the Superpowers *1009*

The End of the Cold War Order *1012*
  A Shifting Balance of Global Power *1012*
  A Change of Course in the West *1014*
  The Collapse of Communism in the Soviet Bloc *1014*

COUNTERPOINT Agrarian Peoples in a Technological Age *1017*
  Local Farmers Against Multinational Corporations *1018*
  Government Measures to Protect Farmers *1018*

Conclusion *1019* | *Notes* *1019*
Resources for Research *1020* | *Review* *1021*

▶ READING THE PAST Japan Transforms Business Practices *999*
▶ LIVES AND LIVELIHOODS Global Tourism *1000*
▶ READING THE PAST Terror and Resistance in El Salvador *1006*
▶ SEEING THE PAST The Iranian Revolution as Visual News *1010*

31

A New Global Age, 1989 to the Present *1022*

Major Global Development ▶ The causes and consequences of intensified globalization.

Backstory *1023*

The Impact of Global Events on Regions and Nations *1026*
   North Versus South *1026*
   Advancing Nations in the Global Age *1027*

Global Livelihoods and Institutions *1031*
   Global Networks and Changing Jobs *1032*
   Neoliberalism and the Global Economy *1033*
   Beyond the Nation-State *1033*
   Global Cities *1036*

The Promises and Perils of Globalization *1037*
   Environmental Challenges *1038*
   Population Pressures and Public Health *1040*
   Worldwide Migration *1044*
   Terrorism Confronts the World *1045*
   Global Economic Crisis *1047*

Cultures Without Borders *1048*
   The Quest for Human Rights *1048*
   Religion Worldwide *1048*
   Global Literature and Music *1049*

COUNTERPOINT Who Am I? Local Identity in a Globalizing World *1052*
   Ethnic Strife and New Nations *1052*
   Movements to Protect Tradition *1052*

Conclusion *1053* | *Notes* *1054*
Resources for Research *1054* | *Review* *1056*

▶ **READING THE PAST** Testimony to South Africa's Truth and Reconciliation Commission *1030*
▶ **READING THE PAST** Assessing Livelihoods for Women in a Global Economy *1035*
▶ **SEEING THE PAST** The Globalization of Urban Space *1037*
▶ **LIVES AND LIVELIHOODS** Readers of the Qur'an *1050*

   Index *I-1*

MAPS

Chapter 15

Mapping the World Afro-Eurasia in the Early Fifteenth Century *476*
Map 15.1 Spread of the Black Death, 1347–1451 *480*
Map 15.2 Europe and the Greater Mediterranean, 1453 *485*
Map 15.3 The Ming Empire, 1449 *486*
Spot Map Ottoman Expansion, c. 1200–1453 *490*
Map 15.4 The Indian Ocean and Southeast Asia, c. 1450 *495*
Spot Map Japan, 1185–1392 *503*

Chapter 16

Mapping the World The Western Hemisphere, c. 1500 *514*
Map 16.1 Main Settlement Areas in the Americas, c. 1492 *517*
Spot Map Kwakiutl Culture Area, c. 1500 *519*
Map 16.2 The Aztec Empire, 1325–1521 *520*
Spot Map Lake Texcoco and Tenochtitlán, c. 1500 *522*
Spot Map Cuzco, c. 1500 *530*
Map 16.3 The Inca Empire, 1325–1521 *531*
Map 16.4 Native Peoples of North America, c. 1500 *539*

Chapter 17

Mapping the World European Exploration and Conquest, c. 1450–1600 *548*
Map 17.1 The East Atlantic, c. 1500 *554*
Map 17.2 European Voyages of Discovery, c. 1420–1600 *556–557*
Spot Map Cortés's Invasion of the Aztec Empire, 1519–1521 *563*
Spot Map Pizarro's Invasion of the Inca Empire, 1531–1533 *564*
Map 17.3 European Claims in the Americas, c. 1600 *568*
Spot Map The Mapuche of Chile, c. 1550 *573*

Chapter 18

Mapping the World Africa and the Atlantic, c. 1450–1800 *582*
Map 18.1 Western Africa, c. 1500 *586*
Spot Map Kongo Territory, c. 1500 *594*
Map 18.2 The Early Atlantic Slave Trade, c. 1450–1650 *597*
Map 18.3 West Central Africa, c. 1500–1635 *600*
Map 18.4 The Atlantic Slave Trade at Its Height, c. 1650–1800 *602*
Spot Map Pygmies of the Congo Rain Forest *607*

Chapter 19

Mapping the World The Indian Ocean and South Asia, 1450–1750 *614*
Spot Map East African Port Cities *617*
Map 19.1 Indian Ocean Trade, c. 1500 *618*
Map 19.2 The Mughal Empire, c. 1700 *625*

Spot Map Sikh Rebellion, 1710–1715 *632*
Map 19.3 Portugal's Seaborne Empire, c. 1600 *634*
Map 19.4 Dutch and English Colonies in South and Southeast Asia, to 1750 *638*
Spot Map Aceh *640*

Chapter 20

Mapping the World Europe and the Greater Mediterranean, c. 1600 *648*
Map 20.1 The Ottoman Empire, 1453–1683 *652*
Map 20.2 World Trade, c. 1720 *660–661*
Map 20.3 Protestant and Catholic Reformations in Europe *663*
Spot Map Route of the Spanish Armada, 1588 *666*
Map 20.4 War of the Spanish Succession, 1701–1714 *676*
Spot Map The Barbary Coast, c. 1560 *677*

Chapter 21

Mapping the World Eurasian Trade and Empires, c. 1700 *684*
Map 21.1 Rise of Russia, 1462–1725 *687*
Spot Map St. Petersburg, c. 1750 *689*
Map 21.2 The Qing Dynasty, 1644–1799 *694*
Spot Map Tokugawa Japan *698*
Spot Map Choson Korea *705*
Map 21.3 Southeast Asian Trade, c. 1500–1700 *709*
Map 21.4 Maritime Trade Between the Americas and Asia, 1571–1800 *712*

Chapter 22

Mapping the World New World Colonies, c. 1750 *720*
Map 22.1 Spanish America, 1580–1750 *724*
Map 22.2 Colonial Brazil, 1695–1750 *733*
Map 22.3 The Caribbean in the Great Age of Piracy, c. 1650–1730 *737*
Map 22.4 British and French North America, c. 1650–1750 *742*
Spot Map Chesapeake Bay, c. 1650–1700 *743*
Spot Map The Maroons of Suriname *748*

Chapter 23

Mapping the World Wars and Revolutions in the Atlantic World, 1750–1830 *760*
Spot Map Pugachev Uprising in Russia, 1773 *767*
Map 23.1 Colonial Crisis and Revolution in North America, 1754–1789 *769*
Map 23.2 Napoleonic Europe, 1796–1815 *775*
Map 23.3 Haitian Rebellion and Independence, 1791–1804 *778*
Map 23.4 Revolutions in Latin America, 1810–1830 *780*
Spot Map Arabia, 1802–1807 *786*

Chapter 24

Mapping the World The Spread of Industrialization *792*
Map 24.1 Industrialization in Europe, c. 1900 *795*
Map 24.2 The Spread of Railroads, c. 1900 *799*
Spot Map Industrializing Japan, c. 1870–1900 *804*
Map 24.3 Qing China, 1830–1911 *808*
Spot Map Industrializing India, c. 1857–1900 *810*
Map 24.4 Africa, 1750–1880 *811*

Chapter 25

Mapping the World Nation-States, c. 1880 *826*
Map 25.1 Latin America, c. 1900 *830*
Map 25.2 The Crimean War and Postwar Settlement, 1853–1856 *833*
Spot Map Unification of Italy, 1859–1870 *837*
Spot Map Unification of Germany, 1866–1871 *838*
Map 25.3 U.S. Civil War and Westward Expansion *839*
Map 25.4 Japan, c. 1860–1889 *842*

Chapter 26

Mapping the World The Spread of Imperialism, 1850–1914 *858*
Map 26.1 Imperial Division of Asia, c. 1850–1900 *862*
Spot Map Modernization Projects in Egypt *864*
Map 26.2 Imperial Division of Africa, c. 1880–1914 *866*
Spot Map The Sino-Japanese War, 1894 *868*
Map 26.3 Global Migration, c. 1800–1910 *874–875*
Spot Map The Spanish-American War, 1898 *881*
Map 26.4 Imperialism in the Pacific, c. 1840–1914 *883*

Chapter 27

Mapping the World Wars and Revolutions, 1910–1929 *892*
Spot Map The Mexican Revolution, 1910–1911 *895*
Map 27.1 World War I in Europe and the Middle East, 1914–1918 *898*
Map 27.2 The Peace of Paris in Central and Eastern Europe, 1920 *906*
Map 27.3 The Mandate System in Africa and the Middle East, 1924 *907*
Map 27.4 Turkey Under Mustafa Kemal, 1923 *909*
Spot Map Japanese-occupied Territories in China, 1918–1922 *910*
Spot Map Ireland, 1921 *910*
Spot Map Argentina, c. 1920 *919*

Chapter 28

Mapping the World World War II, 1937–1945 *926*
Map 28.1 Japanese Expansion, 1931–1942 *935*

Spot Map Italian Invasion of Ethiopia, 1935–1936 *940*
Map 28.2 Nazi Expansion, 1933–1939 *941*
Map 28.3 World War II in Europe, North Africa, and the Soviet Union, 1939–1945 *943*
Map 28.4 World War II in the Pacific, 1937–1945 *944*
Spot Map Major Concentration Camps and Extermination Sites in Europe *945*

Chapter 29

Mapping the World Independence Movements and New Nations *960*
Map 29.1 Divided Germany *965*
Map 29.2 Regional Alliances, 1948–1955 *968*
Map 29.3 Partition of India, 1947 *970*
Map 29.4 New States of Southeast Asia, 1945–1999 *971*
Spot Map The Arab-Israeli War of 1948–1949 *972*
Map 29.5 New States in Africa and the Middle East, 1945–2011 *974*

Chapter 30

Mapping the World OPEC, Pacific Tigers, and World Migration *990*
Map 30.1 The Pacific Tigers, c. 1960–1995 *997*
Map 30.2 South and Central America, 1960–1992 *1004*
Spot Map The United States and the Vietnam War, c. 1968–1975 *1008*
Spot Map The Soviet War in Afghanistan, 1979–1989 *1009*
Map 30.3 The Middle East, 1967–1990 *1013*
Spot Map Solidarity Protests in Poland, 1981–1983 *1015*
Map 30.4 Post–Cold War Eastern Europe and Central Asia, c. 1990 *1017*

Chapter 31

Mapping the World A New Global Age *1024*
Spot Map Conflict and Genocide in Sub-Saharan Africa *1027*
Map 31.1 South Africa After Apartheid *1031*
Spot Map Mercosur, 2011 *1036*
Map 31.2 The Global Environment of the Early Twenty-First Century *1039*
Map 31.3 The World's Peoples, c. 2010 *1042–1043*
Map 31.4 Wars in Afghanistan and Iraq, 2001–2011 *1046*
Spot Map Arab Spring, 2010–2011 *1047*

SPECIAL FEATURES

Lives and Livelihoods

Urban Weavers in India   *496*
The Aztec Midwife   *528*
Atlantic Sugar Producers   *574*
West Africa's Gold Miners   *588*
Cinnamon Harvesters in Ceylon   *636*
Ottoman Coffeehouse Owners and Patrons   *658*
Silk Weavers in China   *696*
Caribbean Buccaneers   *738*
The Cowboy Way of Life   *782*
Builders of the Trans-Siberian Railroad   *800*
Historians of the Nation-State   *846*
Indentured Laborers   *876*
The Film Industry   *916*
Soldiers and Soldiering   *946*
Cosmonauts and Astronauts   *966*
Global Tourism   *1000*
Readers of the Qur'an   *1050*

Reading the Past

A French Theologian's View of the Black Death   *482*
A Spanish Ambassador's Description of Samarkand   *490*
An Andean Creation Story   *533*
Tlatelolcan Elders Recall the Conquest of Mexico   *564*
First Encounter in Brazil: Cabral's Report to King Manoel of Portugal   *571*
Al-Sa'di on Jenne and Its History   *591*
Alonso de Sandoval, "General Points Relating to Slavery"   *596*
Portuguese Report of a Vijayanagara Festival   *624*
Dutch Merchants Learn How to Act in Aceh   *641*
Weapons of Mass Destruction: Ottomans vs. Persians in Baghdad   *655*
An Exiled European Muslim Visits the Netherlands   *669*
Selections from the Hidden Christians' Sacred Book   *700*
Scenes from the Daily Life of a Korean Queen   *707*
An Iraqi Traveler's Impressions of Potosí   *727*
A Swedish Traveler's Description of Quebec   *747*
Simon Bolivar on Latin American Independence   *784*
Phillis Wheatley, "On Being Brought from Africa to America"   *786*

Industry Comes to the British Countryside   *797*
Mexican Women on Strike   *816*
The Russian People Under Serfdom   *835*
"Good Wives, Wise Mothers" Build Japan   *848*
Rubber Workers in Congo   *871*
The United States Overthrows the Hawaiian Queen   *882*
Communism Spreads in China   *911*
Léopold Sédar Senghor, "To the Senegalese Soldiers Who Died for France"   *912*
Promoting Business in the Great Depression   *930*
"Comfort Women" in World War II   *942*
The Great Leap Forward in China   *978*
Japan Transforms Business Practices   *999*
Terror and Resistance in El Salvador   *1006*
Testimony to South Africa's Truth and Reconciliation Commission   *1030*
Assessing Livelihoods for Women in a Global Economy   *1035*

Seeing the Past

Leonardo da Vinci's *Virgin of the Rocks*   *502*
An Aztec Map of Tenochtitlán   *521*
The Coyolxauhqui Stone   *524*
Malintzin and the Meeting Between Moctezuma and Cortés   *566*
Art of the Slave Trade: A Benin Bronze Plaque   *592*
Reflections of the Divine in a Mughal Emerald   *629*
Gift Clocks for the Emperors of China   *664*
Blue-on-White: Ming Export Porcelain   *692*
Gentlemen of Esmeraldas   *730*
Portrait of Catherine the Great   *766*
Japan's Industrious Society   *803*
The Korean Flag   *844*
Imperial Architecture in Saigon   *872*
Wartime Propaganda   *901*
Technological Warfare: Civilization or Barbarism?   *952*
African Liberation on Cloth   *975*
The Iranian Revolution as Visual News   *1010*
The Globalization of Urban Space   *1037*

ACKNOWLEDGMENTS

Writing *Crossroads and Cultures* has made real to us the theme of this book, which is connections among many far-flung people of diverse livelihoods and talents. From the first draft to the last, the authors have benefited from repeated critical readings by many talented scholars and teachers who represent an array of schools and historical interests. Our sincere thanks go to the following instructors, who helped us keep true to our vision of showing connections among the world's people and whose comments often challenged us to rethink or justify our interpretations. Crucial to the integrity of the book, they always provided a check on accuracy down to the smallest detail.

Alemseged Abbay, *Frostburg State University*

Heather J. Abdelnur, *Augusta State University*

Wayne Ackerson, *Salisbury University*

Kathleen Addison, *California State University, Northridge*

Jeffrey W. Alexander, *University of Wisconsin–Parkside*

Omar H. Ali, *The University of North Carolina at Greensboro*

Monty Armstrong, *Cerritos High School*

Pierre Asselin, *Hawai'i Pacific University*

Eva Baham, *Southern University at Baton Rouge*

William Bakken, *Rochester Community and Technical College*

Thomas William Barker, *The University of Kansas*

Thomas William Barton, *University of San Diego*

Robert Blackey, *California State University, San Bernardino*

Chuck Bolton, *The University of North Carolina at Greensboro*

Robert Bond, *San Diego Mesa College*

James W. Brodman, *University of Central Arkansas*

Gayle K. Brunelle, *California State University, Fullerton*

Samuel Brunk, *The University of Texas at El Paso*

Jurgen Buchenau, *The University of North Carolina at Charlotte*

Clea Bunch, *University of Arkansas at Little Rock*

Kathy Callahan, *Murray State University*

John M. Carroll, *The University of Hong Kong*

Giancarlo Casale, *University of Minnesota*

Mark Chavalas, *University of Wisconsin–La Crosse*

Yinghong Cheng, *Delaware State University*

Mark Choate, *Brigham Young University*

Sharon Cohen, *Springbrook High School*

Christine Colin, *Mercyhurst College*

Eleanor Congdon, *Youngstown State University*

Dale Crandall-Bear, *Solano Community College*

John Curry, *University of Nevada, Las Vegas*

Michelle Danberg-Marshman, *Green River Community College*

Francis Danquah, *Southern University at Baton Rouge*

Sherrie Dux-Ideus, *Central Community College*

Peter Dykema, *Arkansas Tech University*

Tom Ewing, *Virginia Polytechnic Institute and State University*

Angela Feres, *Grossmont College*

Michael Fischbach, *Randolph-Macon College*

Nancy Fitch, *California State University, Fullerton*

Terence Anthony Fleming, *Northern Kentucky University*

Richard Fogarty, *University at Albany, The State University of New York*

Nicola Foote, *Florida Gulf Coast University*

Deanna Forsman, *North Hennepin Community College*

John D. Garrigus, *The University of Texas at Arlington*

Trevor Getz, *San Francisco State University*

David Goldfrank, *Georgetown University*

Charles Didier Gondola, *Indiana University–Purdue University Indianapolis*

Sue Gronewold, *Kean University*

Christopher Guthrie, *Tarleton State University*

Anne Hardgrove, *The University of Texas at San Antonio*

Donald J. Harreld, *Brigham Young University*

Todd Hartch, *Eastern Kentucky University*

Janine Hartman, *University of Cincinnati*

Daniel Heimmermann, *The University of Texas at Brownsville*

Cecily M. Heisser, *University of San Diego*

Timothy Henderson, *Auburn University at Montgomery*

Ted Henken, *Baruch College, The State University of New York*

Marilynn J. Hitchens, *University of Colorado Denver*

Roy W. Hopper, *University of Memphis*

Timothy Howe, *St. Olaf College*

Delridge Hunter, *Medgar Evers College, The City University of New York*

Bruce Ingram, *Itawamba Community College*

Erik N. Jensen, *Miami University*

Steven Sandor John, *Hunter College, The City University of New York*

Deborah Johnston, *Lakeside School*

David M. Kalivas, *Middlesex Community College*

Carol Keller, *San Antonio College*

Ian Stuart Kelly, *Palomar College*

Linda Kerr, *University of Alberta*

Charles King, *University of Nebraska at Omaha*

Melinda Cole Klein, *Saddleback College*

Ane Lintvedt-Dulac, *McDonogh School*

Ann Livschiz, *Indiana University–Purdue University Fort Wayne*

George E. Longenecker, *Vermont Technical College*

Edward Lykens, *Middle Tennessee State University*

Susan Maneck, *Jackson State University*

Chandra Manning, *Georgetown University*

Michael Marino, *The College of New Jersey*

Thomas Massey, *Cape Fear Community College*

Mary Jane Maxwell, *Green Mountain College*

Christine McCann, *Norwich University*

Patrick McDevitt, *University at Buffalo, The State University of New York*

Ian F. McNeely, *University of Oregon*

M. E. Menninger, *Texas State University–San Marcos*

Kathryn E. Meyer, *Washington State University*

Elizabeth Mizrahi, *Santa Barbara City College*

Max Okenfuss, *Washington University in St. Louis*

Kenneth Orosz, *Buffalo State College, The State University of New York*

Annette Palmer, *Morgan State University*

David Perry, *Dominican University*

Jared Poley, *Georgia State University*

Elizabeth Ann Pollard, *San Diego State University*

Dana Rabin, *University of Illinois at Urbana-Champaign*

Norman G. Raiford, *Greenville Technical College*

Stephen Rapp, *Universität Bern*

Michele Reid, *Georgia State University*

Chad Ross, *East Carolina University*

Morris Rossabi, *Queens College, The City University of New York*

Steven C. Rubert, *Oregon State University*

Eli Rubin, *Western Michigan University*

Anthony Santoro, *Christopher Newport University*

Linda B. Scherr, *Mercer County Community College*

Hollie Schillig, *California State University, Long Beach*

Michael Seth, *James Madison University*

Jessica Sheetz-Nguyen, *University of Central Oklahoma*

Rose Mary Sheldon, *Virginia Military Institute*

David R. Smith, *California State Polytechnic University, Pomona*

Ramya Sreenivasan, *University at Buffalo, The State University of New York*

John Stavens, *Bristol Eastern High School*

Catherine Howey Stearn, *Eastern Kentucky University*

Richard Steigmann-Gall, *Kent State University*

Anthony J. Steinhoff, *The University of Tennessee at Chattanooga*

Stephen J. Stillwell, *The University of Arizona*

Heather Streets, *Washington State University*

Jean Stuntz, *West Texas A&M University*

Guy Thompson, *University of Alberta*

Hunt Tooley, *Austin College*

Wendy Turner, *Augusta State University*

Rick Warner, *Wabash College*

Michael Weber, *Gettysburg College*

Theodore Weeks, *Southern Illinois University*

Guy Wells, *Lorain County Community College*

Sherri West, *Brookdale Community College*

Kenneth Wilburn, *East Carolina University*

Pingchao Zhu, *University of Idaho*

Alexander Zukas, *National University*

Many colleagues, friends, and family members have helped us develop this work as well. Bonnie Smith wishes to thank in particular Michal Shapira and Molly Giblin for their research assistance and Patrick Smith, who gave helpful information on contemporary world religions. Her colleagues at Rutgers, many of them pioneers in world history, were especially helpful. Among these, expert historian Donald R. Kelley shaped certain features of the last section of the book and always cheered the author on. Marc Van De Mieroop thanks the friends and colleagues who often unknowingly provided insights and information used in this book, especially Irene Bloom, William Harris, Feng Li, Indira Peterson, Michael Sommer, and Romila Thapar. Richard von Glahn thanks his many colleagues at UCLA who have shaped his thinking about world history, especially Ghislaine Lydon, Jose Moya, Ron Mellor, Sanjay Subrahmanyam, and Bin Wong. He is also grateful for the exposure to pathbreaking scholarship on world history afforded by the University of California's Multi-Campus Research Unit in World History. Kris Lane thanks the many wonderful William & Mary students of History 192, "The World Since 1450," as well as colleagues Abdul-Karim Rafeq, Scott Nelson, Chitralekha Zutshi, Hiroshi Kitamura, Philip Daileader, Chandos Brown, and Ron Schechter. All offered valuable advice on framing the early modern period. He also owes a huge debt to the University of Minnesota for graduate training and teaching assistant experience in this field.

We also wish to acknowledge and thank the publishing team at Bedford/St. Martin's, who are among the most talented people in publishing that we as a group have ever worked with and who did so much to bring this book into being. Among them, our special thanks go to former publisher for history Patricia A. Rossi, who inspired the conceptual design of the book and helped bring us together. The current publisher for history, Mary Dougherty, then picked up the reins from Tisha and advanced the project, using her special combination of professional expertise and personal warmth. It is hard to convey sufficiently our heartfelt appreciation to president Joan E. Feinberg and editorial director Denise Wydra. They always kept us alert to Bedford's special legacy of high-quality textbooks, a legacy based on the benefits a book must have for students and teachers alike. We aimed to be part of that legacy while writing *Crossroads and Cultures*.

President emeritus and founder Charles Christensen was also present at the beginning of this project, and he always cheerfully lent his extraordinary knowledge of publishing to the making and actual production of this book. We know that it would have been less than it is without his wisdom. Alongside all these others, director of development for history Jane Knetzger patiently and skillfully guided the development process, during which each chapter (and sentence) was poked and prodded. We thank Jane for being such a quiet force behind the progress of *Crossroads and*

Cultures. Special thanks go to senior editor and expert facilitator Heidi Hood and the editorial assistants who joined Heidi in providing invaluable help on many essential tasks: Lynn Sternberger, Jennifer Jovin, and Emily DiPietro. All of them moved the project along in myriad ways that we hardly know. We also appreciate the countless schedules, tasks, and layouts juggled so efficiently and well by senior production editor Anne Noonan. On the editorial team were John Reisbord and Daniel Otis, who helped edit and polish our final draft. All along the way Rose Corbett Gordon and Charlotte Miller, our superb photo researcher and talented map editor, respectively, provided us with striking and thought-provoking images and up-to-date, richly informative, and gorgeous maps. No author team could ask for more than to have the book's content laid out in such a clear and attractive design as that provided by Jerilyn Bockorick, with assistance from senior art director Anna Palchik. Jerilyn's special attention to the overall look of our work makes us feel that we and our readers are especially lucky. Senior designer Billy Boardman created our six beautiful covers with help from senior art director Donna Dennison. We are grateful for their craft in building the book's appeal.

Crossroads and Cultures has a wealth of materials for students and teachers to help support the text. Editor Annette Fantasia has guided our creation of the sourcebook that accompanies the main book, and we could hardly have achieved this task without her help; she also edited the instructor's resource manual. The work of associate editor Jack Cashman, who supervised the development of the other elements in our impressive array of supplements, will be appreciated by all teachers and students who use these materials. Jenna Bookin Barry, senior executive marketing manager; Sally Constable, senior market development manager; and Katherine Bates, market development manager, have worked tirelessly at our side to ensure that the book is in the best shape to meet the needs of students and teachers. We are deeply grateful for all the work they have done in the past and all that they will do in so sincerely advocating for the success of *Crossroads and Cultures* in today's classrooms.

Among the authors' greatest *Crossroads* experiences has been our relationship with brilliant executive editor Elizabeth M. Welch and her support team of ace development editors Sylvia Mallory, Margaret Manos, and Jim Strandberg. Beth has guided many a successful book from inception to completion—all to the benefit of tens of thousands of students and their instructors. We thank her for bringing us her historical, conceptual, visual, and publishing talent, all of which she has offered with such generosity of spirit, good humor, and grace. It has been a privilege for all of us to work with Beth and to have spent these *Crossroads* years with the entire Bedford team.

Finally, our students' questions and concerns have shaped much of this work, and we welcome all our readers' suggestions, queries, and criticisms. We know that readers, like our own students, excel in spotting unintended glitches and also in providing much excellent food for thought. Please contact us with your comments at our respective institutions.

Bonnie G. Smith
Marc Van De Mieroop
Richard von Glahn
Kris Lane

AT A CROSSROADS ▶

The fall of Constantinople to the Ottoman Turks in 1453 marked the end of the Byzantine Empire and heralded the coming age of gunpowder weapons. The Ottoman forces under Sultan Mehmed II breached the massive walls of Constantinople using massive cannons known as *bombards*. The Turkish cannons appear in the center of this book illustration of the siege of Constantinople, published in France in 1455. (The Art Archive/Bibliothèque Nationale Paris.)

Collapse and Revival in Afro-Eurasia

1300–1450

I n August 1452, as the armies of the Ottoman sultan Mehmed II encircled Constantinople, the Byzantine emperor Constantine XI received a visit from a fellow Christian, a Hungarian engineer named Urban. Urban had applied metallurgical skills acquired at Hungary's rich iron and copper mines to the manufacture of large cannons known as *bombards*. He came to the Byzantine capital to offer his services to repel the Ottoman assault. But although Urban was a Christian, he was a businessman, too. When Constantine could not meet his price, Urban quickly left for the sultan's camp. Facing the famed triple walls of Constantinople, Mehmed promised to quadruple the salary Urban requested and to provide any materials and manpower the engineer needed.

Seven months later, in April 1453, Ottoman soldiers moved Urban's huge bronze bombards—with barrels twenty-six feet long, capable of throwing eight-hundred-pound shot—into place beneath the walls of Constantinople. Although these cumbersome cannons could fire only seven rounds a day, they battered the walls of Constantinople, which had long been considered impenetrable. After six weeks of siege the Turks breached the walls and swarmed into the city. The vastly outnumbered defenders, Emperor Constantine among them, fought to the death.

Urban's willingness to put business before religious loyalty helped tip the balance of power in the Mediterranean. During the siege, the Genoese merchant community at Constantinople—along with their archrivals, the Venetians—maintained strict neutrality. Although the Italian merchants, like Urban, were prepared to do business with Mehmed II, within a decade the Venetians and Ottomans were at war. Venice could not produce

Fourteenth-Century Crisis and Renewal in Eurasia

FOCUS How did the Black Death affect society, the economy, and culture in Latin Christendom and the Islamic world?

Islam's New Frontiers

FOCUS Why did Islam expand dramatically in the fourteenth and fifteenth centuries, and how did new Islamic societies differ from established ones?

The Global Bazaar

FOCUS How did the pattern of international trade change during the fourteenth and fifteenth centuries, and how did these changes affect consumption and fashion tastes?

COUNTERPOINT Age of the Samurai in Japan, 1185–1450

FOCUS How and why did the historical development of Japan in the fourteenth and fifteenth centuries differ from that of mainland Eurasia?

BACKSTORY

In the fourteenth century, a number of developments threatened the connections among the societies of the Afro-Eurasian world. The collapse of the Mongol empires in China and Iran in the mid-1300s disrupted caravan traffic across Central Asia, diverting the flow of trade and travel to maritime routes across the Indian Ocean. Although the two centuries of religious wars known as the Crusades ended in 1291, they had hardened hostility between Christians and Muslims. As the power of the Christian Byzantine Empire contracted, Muslim Turkish sultanates—the Mamluk regime in Egypt and the rising Ottoman dynasty in Anatolia (modern Turkey)—gained control of the eastern Mediterranean region. Yet the Crusades and direct contact with the Mongols had also whetted European appetites for luxury and exotic goods from the Islamic world and Asia. Thus, despite challenges and obstacles, the Mediterranean remained a lively crossroads of commerce and cross-cultural exchange.

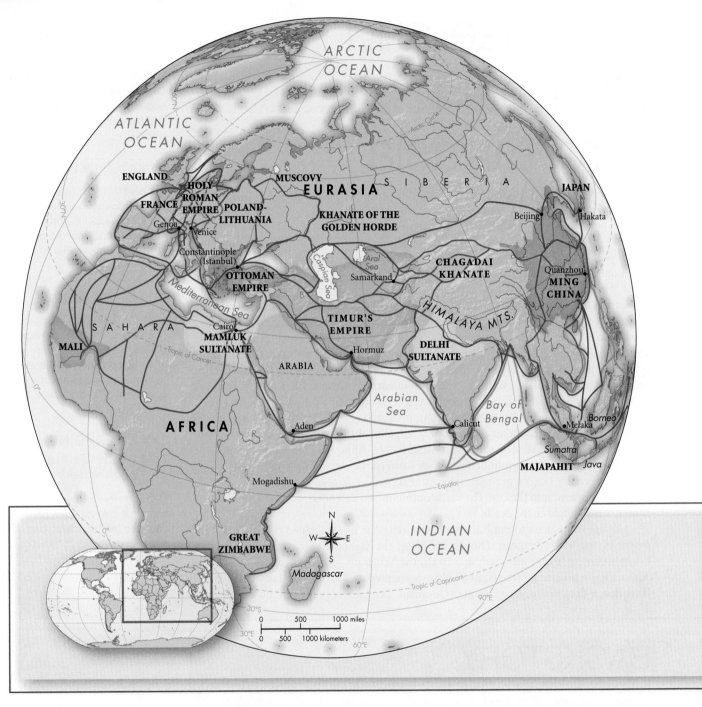

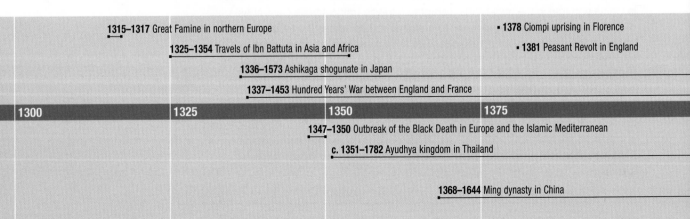

1315–1317 Great Famine in northern Europe

1325–1354 Travels of Ibn Battuta in Asia and Africa

1336–1573 Ashikaga shogunate in Japan

1337–1453 Hundred Years' War between England and France

• **1378** Ciompi uprising in Florence

• **1381** Peasant Revolt in England

| 1300 | 1325 | 1350 | 1375 |

1347–1350 Outbreak of the Black Death in Europe and the Islamic Mediterranean

c. 1351–1782 Ayudhya kingdom in Thailand

1368–1644 Ming dynasty in China

enough cannons to match the heavily armed Ottoman army and navy, which expelled the Venetians from the Black Sea in 1475. Although Venetian merchants still flocked to Constantinople, which Mehmed renamed Istanbul, to obtain spices, silks, and other Asian goods, the Ottomans held the upper hand and could dictate the terms of trade.

The fall of Constantinople to the Ottomans marks a turning point in world history. After perpetuating ancient Rome's heritage and glory for a thousand years, the Byzantine Empire came to an end. Islam continued to advance; in the fourteenth and fifteenth centuries, it expanded most dramatically in Africa and Asia. Italian merchants and bankers lost their dominance in the eastern Mediterranean and turned westward toward the Atlantic Ocean in search of new commercial opportunities. And this shift in commercial power and focus was not the only profound change that followed the Ottoman capture of Constantinople. The bombards cast by the Hungarian engineer for the Ottoman sultan heralded a military revolution that would decisively alter the balance of power among states and transform the nature of the state itself.

The new global patterns that emerged after Constantinople changed hands had their roots in calamities of the fourteenth century. The Ottoman triumph came just as Europe was beginning to recover from the previous century's catastrophic outbreak of plague known as the Black Death. The demographic and psychological shocks of epidemic disease had severely tested Europe's political and economic institutions—indeed, even its Christian faith.

The Black Death also devastated the Islamic world. Economic depression struck hard in Egypt, Syria, and Mesopotamia, the heartland of Islam. However, Europe's economy recovered more quickly. One consequence of the plague was the slow demise of serfdom, which contributed to the growing political and economic power of European monarchs and the urban merchant classes. By 1500 European merchants, bankers, and artisans had surpassed their Muslim counterparts in innovation and efficiency.

In Asia, the fourteenth century witnessed the rise and fall of the last Mongol empire, that of Timur (also known as Tamerlane). The end of the Mongol era marked the passing of nomadic rule, the resurgence of agrarian bureaucratic states such as Ming China and

MAPPING THE WORLD
Afro-Eurasia in the Early Fifteenth Century

After the Mongol Empire disintegrated, trans-Eurasian trade shifted from the overland Silk Road to the maritime routes stretching from China to the Mediterranean. Muslim merchants crossed the Sahara Desert and the Indian Ocean in pursuit of African gold, Chinese porcelain, and Asian spices. Although Chinese fleets led by Admiral Zheng He journeyed as far as the coasts of Arabia and Africa, the Ming rulers prohibited private overseas trade.

ROUTES ▼

— Major trade route
— Silk Road
— Voyages of Zheng He

1392–1910 Yi dynasty in Korea

• **1405** Death of Timur; breakup of his empire into regional states in Iran and Central Asia

• **1453** Ottoman conquest of Constantinople marks fall of the Byzantine Empire

1400 | 1425 | 1450

1405–1433 Chinese admiral Zheng He's expeditions in Southeast Asia and the Indian Ocean

• **1421** Relocation of Ming capital from Nanjing to Beijing

1428–1788 Le dynasty in Vietnam

the Ottoman Empire, and the shift of trade from the overland Silk Road to maritime routes across the Indian Ocean. Commerce attained unprecedented importance in many Asian societies. The flow of goods across Eurasia and Africa created new concentrations of wealth, fostered new patterns of consumption, and reshaped culture. The European Renaissance, for example, although primarily understood as a rebirth of the classical culture of Greece and Rome, also drew inspiration from the wealth of goods that poured into Italy from the Islamic world and Asia. By contrast, Japan remained isolated from this global bazaar, and this isolation contributed to the birth of Japan's distinctive national culture. For most Afro-Eurasian societies, however, the maritime world increasingly became the principal crossroads of economic and cultural exchange.

OVERVIEW
QUESTIONS

The major global development in this chapter: Crisis and recovery in fourteenth- and fifteenth-century Afro-Eurasia.

As you read, consider:

1. In the century after the devastating outbreak of plague known as the Black Death, how and why did Europe's economic growth begin to surpass that of the Islamic world?

2. Did the economic revival across Eurasia after 1350 benefit the peasant populations of Europe, the Islamic world, and East Asia?

3. How did the process of conversion to Islam differ in Iran, the Ottoman Empire, West Africa, and Southeast Asia during this period?

4. What political and economic changes contributed to the rise of maritime commerce in Asia during the fourteenth and fifteenth centuries?

Fourteenth-Century Crisis and Renewal in Eurasia

FOCUS

How did the Black Death affect society, the economy, and culture in Latin Christendom and the Islamic world?

No event in the fourteenth century had such profound consequences as the **Black Death** of 1347–1350. The unprecedented loss of life that resulted from this **pandemic** abruptly halted the economic expansion that had spread throughout Europe and the Islamic heartland in the preceding three centuries. Although the population losses were as great in the Islamic world as in Latin Christendom, the effects on society, the economy, and ideas diverged in important ways.

Largely spared the ravages of the Black Death, following the collapse of the Mongol empires in the fourteenth century Asian societies and economies faced different challenges. Expanding maritime trade and the spread of gunpowder weapons gave settled empires a decisive edge over nomadic societies, an edge that they never again relinquished. The founder of the Ming dynasty (1368–1644) in China rejected the Mongol model of "universal empire" and strove to restore a purely Chinese culture and social order. The prestige, stability, and ruling ideology of the Ming state powerfully influenced neighbors such as Korea and Vietnam—but had far less effect on Japan.

Black Death The catastrophic outbreak of plague that spread from the Black Sea to Europe, the Middle East, and North Africa in 1347–1350, killing a third or more of the population in afflicted areas.

pandemic An outbreak of epidemic disease that spreads across an entire region.

The "Great Mortality": The Black Death of 1347–1350

On the eve of the Black Death, Europe's agrarian economy already was struggling under the strain of climatic change. Around 1300 the earth experienced a shift in climate. The warm temperatures that had prevailed over most of the globe for the previous thousand years gave way to a **Little Ice Age** of colder temperatures and shorter growing seasons; it would last for much of the fourteenth century. The expansion of agriculture that had occurred in the Northern Hemisphere during the preceding three centuries came to a halt. The Great Famine of 1315–1317, when severe winters and overly wet summers brought on successive years of crop failure, killed 10 percent of the population in northern Europe and the British Isles. Unlike famine, though, the Black Death pandemic struck the ruling classes as hard as the poor. Scholars estimate that the Black Death and subsequent recurrences of the pandemic killed approximately one-third of the population of Europe.

Although the catastrophic mortality (death rates) of the Black Death is beyond dispute, the causes of the pandemic remain mysterious. The Florentine poet Giovanni Boccaccio (1313–1375), an eyewitness to the "great mortality," described the appearance of apple-sized swellings, first in the groin and armpits, after which these "death-bearing plague boils" spread to "every part of the body, wherefrom the fashion of the contagion began to change into black or livid blotches . . . in some places large and sparse, and in others small and thick-sown." The spread of these swellings, Boccaccio warned, was "a very certain token of coming death."[1]

The prominence of these glandular swellings, or buboes, in eyewitness accounts has led modern scholars to attribute the Black Death to bubonic plague, which is transmitted by fleas to rats and by rats to humans. Yet the scale of mortality during the Black Death far exceeds levels expected in plague outbreaks. Moreover, in Egypt the Black Death struck in winter, when bubonic plague is usually dormant, and the chief symptom was spitting blood rather than developing buboes, suggesting an airborne form of the plague. The pandemic killed as many livestock, especially cattle, as it did humans. Although it is difficult to identify the Black Death with any single modern disease, there is no doubt that the populations of western Eurasia had no previous experience of the disease, and hence no immunity to it. Outbreaks of plague continued to recur every decade or two for the next century, and intermittently thereafter.

Boccaccio and other eyewitnesses claimed that the Black Death had originated in Central Asia and traveled along overland trade routes to the Black Sea. The first outbreak among Europeans occurred in 1347 at the Genoese port of Caffa, on the Crimean peninsula. At that time Caffa was under siege by Mongols of the Golden Horde. Legend relates that the Mongols used catapults to lob corpses of plague victims over the city walls. Whether or not the Mongols really used this innovative type of germ warfare, the Genoese fled, only to spread the plague to the seaports they visited throughout the Mediterranean. By the summer of 1350 the Black Death had devastated nearly all of Europe (see Map 15.1).

The historian William McNeill has suggested that the Black Death was a byproduct of the Mongol conquests. He hypothesized that Mongol horsemen carried the plague bacillus from the remote highland forests of Southeast Asia into Central Asia, and then west to the Black Sea and east to China. The impact of the plague on China remains uncertain, however. The Mongol dynasty of Kubilai (Qubilai) (KOO-bih-lie) Khan already was losing its hold on China in the 1330s, and by the late 1340s China was afflicted by widespread famine, banditry, and civil war. By the time the Ming dynasty took control in 1368, China's population had fallen substantially. Yet Chinese sources make no mention of the specific symptoms of the Black Death, and there is no evidence of pandemic in the densely populated areas of South and Southeast Asia.

The demographic collapse resulting from the Black Death was concentrated in Europe and the Islamic lands ringing the Mediterranean. In these regions population growth halted for over a century. England's population did not return to pre-plague levels for four hundred years.

Causes and Spread of the Black Death

Demographic Consequences

Little Ice Age Name applied by environmental historians to periods of prolonged cool weather in the temperate zones of the earth.

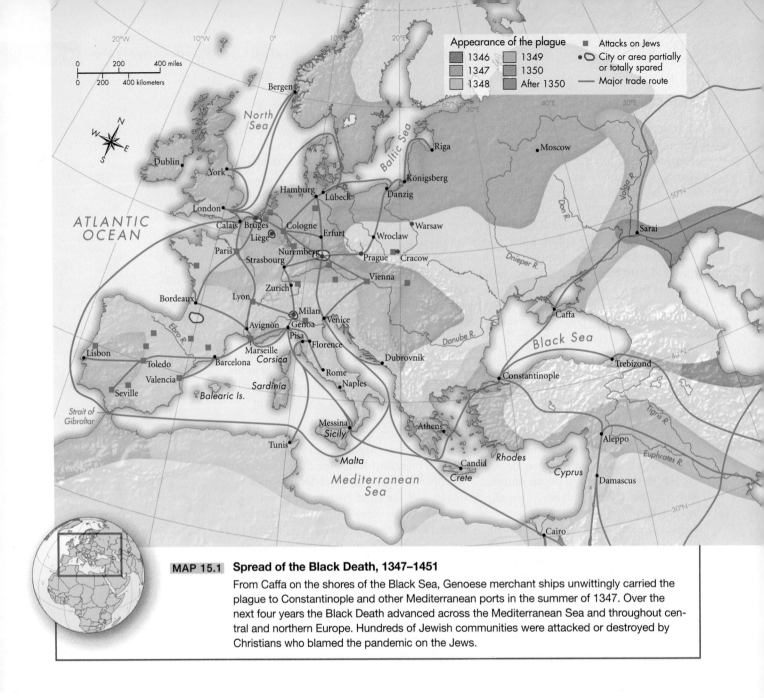

MAP 15.1 **Spread of the Black Death, 1347–1451**

From Caffa on the shores of the Black Sea, Genoese merchant ships unwittingly carried the plague to Constantinople and other Mediterranean ports in the summer of 1347. Over the next four years the Black Death advanced across the Mediterranean Sea and throughout central and northern Europe. Hundreds of Jewish communities were attacked or destroyed by Christians who blamed the pandemic on the Jews.

Population losses from the Black Death were equally devastating in the Islamic parts of the Mediterranean. Italian ships brought the plague to Alexandria in the autumn of 1347. The Egyptian historian al-Maqrizi (al-mak-REE-zee) recorded that twenty thousand people died each day in Cairo, then the most populous city in the world. Although this estimate surely is exaggerated, the plague probably did cause more than one hundred thousand deaths in Cairo alone. In the Islamic world, as in Europe, the loss of human lives and livestock seriously disrupted agriculture. While rural inhabitants flocked to the towns in search of food and work, urban residents sought refuge in the countryside from the contagion that festered in crowded cities.

Decline of the Mamluk Sultanate

The devastation of the plague dealt a serious blow to the agricultural economy of the Mamluk (MAM-luke) Sultanate, which ruled over Egypt and Syria. The scarcity of labor following the pandemic prompted a return to pastoral nomadism in many rural areas, and the urban working classes who survived benefited from rising wages. "The wages of skilled artisans, wage workers, porters, servants, stablemen, weavers, masons, construction workers, and the like have increased manyfold," wrote al-Maqrizi, who served as Cairo's market inspector from 1399 to 1405. But, he added, "of this class only a few remain, since most have died."[2]

The Mamluk Sultanate depended on agricultural wealth for its support, so population losses and declining agricultural production following the Black Death undermined the Mamluk government. A struggle for power broke out among rival factions. Bureaucratic mismanagement compounded the economic distress. Faced with decreasing revenues, the sultanate tried to squeeze more taxes from urban commerce and industry. But the creation of state monopolies in the spice trade and the sugar industry throttled private enterprise and undermined the commercial vitality of Cairo and Damascus. The impoverishment of the urban artisan and merchant classes further weakened the Mamluk regime, leading to its ultimate downfall at the hands of Ottoman conquerors in 1517. In the fall of the Mamluk Sultanate, we can see how the plague produced a chain of interconnected consequences. Population decline led to agricultural decline, which in turn produced economic problems, undermined political authority, and created the conditions for significant social, political, and military upheaval.

Although the horrific mortality caused by the Black Death afflicted Latin Christendom and the Islamic world in equal measure, their responses to the epidemic diverged in significant ways. Christians interpreted the plague as divine punishment for humanity's sins (see Reading the Past: A French Theologian's View of the Black Death). Acts of piety and atonement proliferated, most strikingly in the form of processions of flagellants (from *flagella*, a whip used by worshipers as a form of penance), whose self-mutilation was meant to imitate the sufferings of Christ. In many places Christians blamed vulnerable minorities—such as beggars, lepers, and especially Jews—for corrupting Christian society. Although the Roman Church, kings, and local leaders condemned attacks against Jews, their appeals often went unheeded. For example, the citizens of Strasbourg threw the municipal council out of office for trying to protect the city's Jewish population and then burned nine hundred Jews on the grounds of the Jewish cemetery. The macabre images of death and the corruption of the flesh in European painting and sculpture in the late fourteenth and fifteenth centuries vividly convey the anguish caused by the Black Death.

Christian Responses to the Black Death

Dance of Death

The scourge of the Black Death pandemic dramatically influenced attitudes toward death in Latin Christendom. Literary and artistic works such as this woodcut of skeletons dancing on an open grave vividly portrayed the fragility of life and the dangers of untimely death. For those unprepared to face divine judgment, the ravages of disease and death were only a prelude to the everlasting torments of hell. (akg-images/ Imagno.)

A French Theologian's View of the Black Death

This account of the Black Death comes from Jean de Venette (d. c. 1368), a monk and master of theology at the University of Paris who compiled, probably in the late 1350s, a chronicle of his own lifetime.

Some said that this pestilence was caused by infection of the air and waters. . . . As a result of this theory. . . . the Jews were suddenly and violently charged with infecting wells and water and corrupting the air. . . . In Germany and other parts of the world where Jews lived, they were massacred and slaughtered by Christians, and many thousands were burned everywhere, indiscriminately. . . . But in truth, such poisonings, granted that they actually were perpetrated, could not have caused so great a plague nor have infected so many people. There were other causes; for example, the will of God and the corrupt humors and evil inherent in air and earth. . . .

After the cessation of the epidemic, or plague, the men and women who survived married each other. There was . . . fertility beyond the ordinary. Pregnant women were seen on every side. . . . But woe is me! The world was not changed for the better but for the worse by this renewal of the population. For men were more avaricious and grasping than before, even though they had far greater possessions. They were more covetous and disturbed each other more frequently with suits, brawls, disputes, and pleas. Nor by the mortality resulting from this terrible plague inflicted by God was peace between kings and lords established. On the contrary, the enemies of the king of France and of the Church were stronger and wickeder than before and stirred up wars on sea and on land. Greater evils than before pullulated everywhere in the world. And this factor was very remarkable. Although there was an abundance of all goods, yet everything was twice as dear, whether it were utensils, victuals, or merchandise, hired helpers or peasants and serfs, except for some hereditary domains which remained abundantly stocked with everything. Charity began to cool, and iniquity with ignorance and sin to abound, for few could be found in the good towns and castles who knew how or were willing to instruct children in the rudiments of grammar.

Source: Richard A. Newhall, ed., *The Chronicle of Jean de Venette* (New York: Columbia University Press, 1953), 50–51.

EXAMINING THE EVIDENCE

1. How did Venette's interpretation of the causes of the epidemic differ from those of his European contemporaries?

2. In Venette's view, what were the social and moral consequences of the Black Death?

Muslim Responses to the Black Death

Muslims did not share the Christian belief in "original sin," which deemed human beings inherently sinful, and so they did not see the plague as a divine punishment. Instead, they accepted it as an expression of God's will, and even a blessing for the faithful. The Muslim cleric Ibn al-Wardi (IB-unh al-wahr-dee), who succumbed to the disease in 1349, wrote that "this plague is for Muslims a martyrdom and a reward, and for the disbelievers a punishment and rebuke."[3] Most Muslim scholars and physicians rejected the theory that the pandemic was spread through contagion, counseling against abandoning stricken family members. The flagellants' focus on atonement for sin and the scapegoating of Jews seen in Christian Europe were wholly absent in the Islamic world.

Rebuilding Societies in Western Europe 1350–1492

Just as existing religious beliefs and practices shaped Muslim and Christian responses to the plague, underlying conditions influenced political and economic recovery in the two regions. Latin Christendom recovered more quickly than Islamic lands. In Europe, the death toll caused an acute labor shortage. Desperate to find tenants to cultivate their lands, the nobility had to offer generous concessions, such as release from labor services, that liberated the peasantry from the conditions of serfdom. The incomes of the nobility and the Church declined by half or more, and many castles and monasteries fell into ruin. The shortage of labor enabled both urban artisans and rural laborers to bargain for wage increases. Rising wages improved living standards for ordinary people, who began to consume more meat, cheese, and beer. At the same time, a smaller population reduced the demand for grain and manufactured goods such as woolen cloth. Many nobles, unable to find tenants, converted their agricultural land into pasture. Hundreds of villages were abandoned. In much of central Europe, cultivated land reverted back to forest. Thus, the plague redrew the economic map of Europe, shifting the economic balance of power.

Economic change brought with it economic conflict, and tensions between rich and poor triggered insurrections by rural peasants and the urban lower classes throughout western Europe. In the Italian city-states, the working classes of Florence, led by unemployed wool workers, revolted against the patricians (the wealthy families who controlled the city's government) in 1378. Their demand for a greater share of wealth and political rights alarmed the city's artisan guilds, which allied with the patricians to suppress what became known as the Ciompi revolt ("uprising by the little people"). While the revolt failed, it clearly demonstrated the awareness of Florence's working classes that the plague had undermined the status quo, creating an opportunity for economic and political change.

The efforts of elites to respond to the new economic environment could also lead to conflict. In England, King Richard II's attempt to shift the basis of taxation from landed wealth to a head tax on each subject incited the Peasant Revolt of 1381. Led by a radical preacher named John Ball, the rebels presented a petition to the king that went beyond repeal of the head tax to demand freedom from the tyranny of noble lords and the Christian Church:

> Henceforward, that no lord should have lordship but that there should be proportion between all people, saving only the lordship of the king; that the goods of the holy church ought not to be in the hands of men of religion, or parsons or vicars, or others of holy church, but these should have their sustenance easily and the rest of the goods be divided between the parishioners, . . . and that there should be no villeins [peasants subject to a lord's justice] in England or any serfdom or villeinage, but all are to be free and of one condition.[4]

In the end the English nobles mustered militias to suppress the uprising. This success could not, however, reverse the developments that had produced the uprising in the first place. High wages, falling rents, and the flight of tenants brought many estates to the brink of bankruptcy. Declining aristocratic families intermarried with successful entrepreneurs, who coveted the privileges of the titled nobility and sought to emulate their lifestyle. A new social order began to form, one based on private property and entrepreneurship rather than nobility and serfdom, but equally extreme in its imbalance of wealth and poverty.

Perhaps nowhere in Europe was this new social order more apparent than in Italy. In the Italian city-states, the widening gap between rich and poor was reflected in their governments, which increasingly benefited the wealthy. Over the course of the fifteenth century, the ideals and institutions of republican (representative) government on which the Italian city-states were founded steadily lost ground. A military despot wrested control of Milan in 1450. Venice's **oligarchy**—rule by an exclusive elite—strengthened its grip over the city's government and commerce. In Florence, beset by constant civil strife after the Ciompi uprising, the Medici family of bankers dominated the city's political affairs. Everywhere, financial power was increasingly aligned with political power.

In the wake of the Black Death, kings and princes suffered a drop in revenues as agricultural production fell. Yet in the long run, royal power grew at the expense of the nobility and the Church. In England and France, royal governments gained new sources of income and established bureaucracies of tax collectors and administrators to manage them. The rulers of these states transformed their growing financial power into military and political strength by raising standing armies of professional soldiers and investing in new military technology. The French monarchy, for instance, capitalized on rapid innovations in gunpowder weapons

Social Unrest and Rebellion

Rise of National States

oligarchy Rule by a small group of individuals or families.

to create a formidable army and to establish itself as the supreme power in continental Europe. Originally developed by the Mongols, these weapons had been introduced to Europe via the Islamic world by the middle of the fourteenth century.

Hundred Years' War

The progress of the Hundred Years' War (1337–1453) between England and France reflected the changing political landscape. On the eve of the Black Death pandemic, the war broke out over claims to territories in southwestern France and a dispute over succession to the French throne. In the early years of the conflict, the English side prevailed, thanks to the skill of its bowmen against mounted French knights. As the war dragged on, the English kings increasingly relied on mercenary armies, paid in plunder from the towns and castles they seized. By 1400, combat between knights conducted according to elaborate rules of chivalry had yielded to new forms of warfare. Cannons, siege weapons, and, later, firearms undermined both the nobility's preeminence in war and its sense of identity and purpose. An arms race between France and its rivals led to rapid improvements in weaponry, especially the development of lighter and more mobile cannons. Ultimately the French defeated the English, but the war transformed both sides. The length of the conflict, the propaganda from both sides, and the unified effort needed to prosecute the increasingly costly war all contributed to the evolution of royal governments and the emergence of a sense of national identity.

Consolidating State Power

To strengthen their control, the monarchs of states such as France, England, and Spain relied on new forms of direct taxation, as well as financing from bankers. The French monarchy levied new taxes on salt, land, and commercial transactions, wresting income from local lords and town governments. The kings of England and France promoted domestic industries such as textiles and metallurgy to enhance their national power. The marriage of Isabella of Castile and Ferdinand of Aragon in 1469 created a unified monarchy in Spain. This expansion of royal power in Spain depended heavily on loans from Genoese bankers, who also financed the maritime ventures of the Portuguese and Spanish monarchs into the Atlantic Ocean. Thus, in all three of these states, new economic conditions contributed to the growth of monarchical power (see Map 15.2).

Ultimately, consolidation of monarchical power in western Europe would create new global connections. In their efforts to consolidate power, Ferdinand and Isabella, like so many rulers in world history, demanded religious conformity. In 1492 they conquered Granada, the last Muslim foothold in Spain, and ordered all Jews and Muslims to convert to Christianity or face banishment. With the *Reconquista* (Spanish for "reconquest") of Spain complete, Ferdinand and Isabella turned their crusading energies toward exploration. That same year, they sponsored the first of Christopher Columbus's momentous transatlantic voyages in pursuit of the fabled riches of China.

Wheeled Cannon

The Hundred Years' War between England and France touched off an arms race that spurred major advances in the technology of warfare. Initially, gunsmiths concentrated on making massive siege cannons capable of firing shot weighing hundreds of pounds. By 1500, however, military commanders favored more mobile weapons, such as this wheeled cannon manufactured for the Holy Roman Emperor Maximilian I. (Erich Lessing/Art Resource.)

MAP 15.2

Europe and the Greater Mediterranean, 1453

The century following the Black Death witnessed the growth of royal power and territorial consolidation across Europe, most notably in England and France. But central Europe and Italy remained politically fragmented. The Ottoman conquest of Constantinople in 1453 extinguished the Byzantine Empire and sharpened the conflict between Christendom and the Islamic world in southeastern Europe.

Ming China and the New Order in East Asia 1368–1500

State building in East Asia, too, fostered the development of national states. The Yuan dynasty established in China by the Mongol khan Kubilai had foundered after his death in 1294. Kubilai's successors wrung as much tribute as they could from the Chinese population, but they neglected the infrastructure of roads, canals, and irrigation and flood-control dikes that the Chinese economy depended on. By the time the Mongol court at Dadu (modern Beijing) began to enlist the services of the Confucian-educated elite in the late 1330s, economic distress and social unrest already had taken a heavy toll. When peasant insurrections and civil wars broke out in the 1350s, the Mongol leaders abandoned China and retreated to their steppe homeland. After a protracted period of war and devastation, a Chinese general of peasant origin restored native rule, founding the Ming dynasty in 1368 (see Map 15.3).

MAP 15.3

The Ming Empire, 1449

After expelling the Mongols, the rulers of the Ming dynasty rebuilt the Great Wall to defend China from nomad invasions. Emperor Yongle moved the Ming capital from Nanjing to Beijing and launched expeditions commanded by his trusted aide Zheng He that voyaged throughout Southeast Asia and the Indian Ocean.

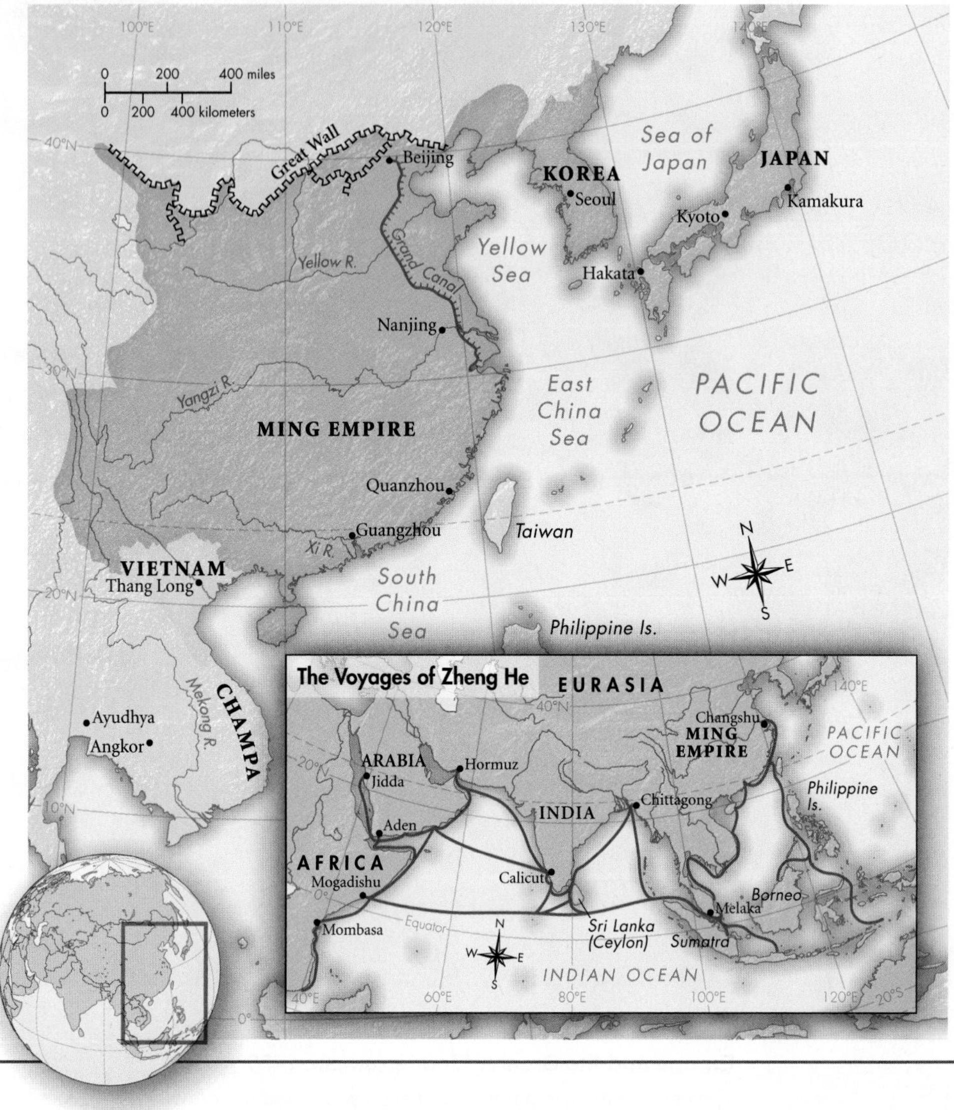

Ming Autocracy

The Ming founder, Zhu Yuanzhang (JOO yuwen-JAHNG) (r. 1368–1398)—better known by his imperial title, Hongwu (hoong-woo)—resurrected the basic Chinese institutions of civil government. But throughout his life Hongwu viewed the scholar-official class with suspicion. Born a peasant, Hongwu saw himself as a populist crusading against the snobbery and luxurious lifestyle of the rich and powerful. Once in command, he repeatedly purged high officials and exercised despotic control over his government. Hongwu reinstituted the civil service examinations system to select government officials, but he used the examinations and the state-run school system as tools of political indoctrination, establishing the teachings of twelfth-century Neo-Confucian philosopher Zhu Xi (JOO shee) as the standard for the civil service exams. Zhu shared the Neo-Confucian antipathy toward Buddhism as a foreign religion and sought to reassert the Confucian commitment to moral perfection and the betterment of society. **Neo-Confucianism** advocated a strict moral code and a patriarchal social hierarchy, and the Ming government supported it with the full force of imperial law. Thus, Hongwu drew on tradition and a belief in China's cultural superiority as he created a new state.

This strong sense of Chinese superiority can be seen in many of Hongwu's policies. Determined to eradicate any taint of Mongol customs, Hongwu rejected the Mongol model of a multiethnic empire and turned his back on the world of the steppe nomads. He located his

Neo-Confucianism The reformulation of Confucian doctrines to reassert a commitment to moral perfection and the betterment of society; dominated Chinese intellectual life and social thought from the twelfth to the twentieth centuries.

capital at Nanjing, on the south bank of the Yangzi River, far from the Mongol frontier. Foreign embassies were welcome at the Ming court, which offered trading privileges in return for tribute and allegiance to the Chinese emperor. But Hongwu distrusted merchants as much as he did intellectuals. In 1371 he forbade Chinese merchants from engaging in overseas commerce and placed foreign traders under close government scrutiny.

Hongwu's son, the Emperor Yongle (r. 1402–1424), reversed his father's efforts to sever China from the outside world. Instead, Yongle embraced the Mongol vision of world empire and rebuilt the former Mongol capital of Dadu, creating the modern city of Beijing. Throughout his reign Yongle campaigned to subdue the Mongol tribes along the northern frontier, but with little success. He also wanted to expand southward. In 1405 he launched a series of naval expeditions under Admiral Zheng He (JUNG-huh) that, as we will see, projected Chinese power deep into the Indian Ocean, and in 1407 he invaded and conquered Vietnam (see again Map 15.3). Nonetheless, Yongle's reign did not represent a complete break with that of Hongwu. Like his father, Yongle was an autocrat who promoted Neo-Confucian policies, even as he sought to reestablish some of the global connections Hongwu had tried to sever.

The impact of Hongwu's policies went far beyond the realms of court politics and international diplomacy. He envisioned his empire as a universe of self-sufficient and self-governing villages, where men worked in the fields and women remained at home. The Neo-Confucian ideology of Hongwu emphasized the patriarchal authority of the lineage, and his policies deprived women of many rights, including a share in inheritance. It outlawed the remarriage of widows. By the fourteenth century, many elite families practiced foot binding, which probably originated among courtesans and entertainers. From around age six the feet of young girls were tightly bound with bandages, deforming the bones and crippling them. The feet of adult women ideally were no more than three to four inches long; they were considered a mark of feminine beauty and a symbol of freedom from labor. Foot binding accompanied seclusion in the home as a sign of respectable womanhood.

Ming Patriarchal Society

Despite the strictures of patriarchal society, in the households of nonelite groups, women played an essential economic role. Women worked alongside men in rice cultivation and performed most tasks involved in textile manufacture. As national and international markets for Chinese silk expanded beginning in the twelfth century, male artisans in urban workshops took over skilled occupations such as silk weaving. But the spread of cotton, introduced from India in the thirteenth century, gave peasant women new economic opportunities. Most cotton was grown, ginned (removing the seeds), spun into yarn, and woven into cloth within a single household, principally by women. Confucian moralists esteemed spinning, weaving, and embroidery as "womanly work" that would promote industriousness and thrift; they became dismayed, however, when women displayed entrepreneurial skill in marketing their wares. Nevertheless, women did engage in commercial activities, suggesting that there were limits to the moralists' control of women's lives.

The Ming dynasty abandoned its designs for conquest and expansion after the death of Yongle in 1424. Yet the prestige, power, and philosophy of the Ming state continued to influence its neighbors, with the significant exception of Japan (see Counterpoint: Age of the Samurai in Japan, 1185–1450). Vietnam regained its independence from China in 1427, but under the long-lived Le dynasty (1428–1788), Vietnam retained Chinese-style bureaucratic government. The Le rulers oversaw the growth of an official class schooled in Neo-Confucianism and committed to forcing its cultural norms, kinship practices, and hostility to Buddhism on Vietnamese society as a whole. In Korea, the rulers of the new Yi dynasty (1392–1910) also embraced Neo-Confucian ideals of government. Under Yi rule the Confucian-educated elite acquired hereditary status with exclusive rights to political office. In both Vietnam and Korea, aristocratic rule and Buddhism's dominance over daily life yielded to a "Neo-Confucian revolution" modeled after Chinese political institutions and values.

Neo-Confucianism in Vietnam and Korea

Islam's New Frontiers

FOCUS

Why did Islam expand dramatically in the fourteenth and fifteenth centuries, and how did new Islamic societies differ from established ones?

In the fourteenth and fifteenth centuries, Islam continued to spread to new areas, including central and maritime Asia, sub-Saharan Africa, and southeastern Europe. In the past, Muslim rule had often preceded the popular adoption of Islamic religion and culture. Yet the advance of Islam in Africa and Asia came about not through conquest, but through slow diffusion via merchants and missionaries. The universalism and egalitarianism of Islam appealed to rising merchant classes in both West Africa and maritime Asia.

During this period, Islam expanded by adapting to older ruling cultures rather than seeking to eradicate them. Timur, the last of the great nomad conquerors, and his descendants ruled not as Mongol khans but as Islamic sultans. The culture of the Central Asian states, however, remained an eclectic mix of Mongol, Turkish, and Persian traditions, in contrast to the strict adherence to Muslim law and doctrine practiced under the Arab regimes of the Middle East and North Africa. This pattern of cultural adaptation and assimilation was even more evident in West Africa and Southeast Asia.

Islamic Spiritual Ferment in Central Asia 1350–1500

The spread of Sufism in Central Asia between 1350 and 1500 played a significant role in the process of cultural assimilation. **Sufism**—a mystical tradition that stressed self-mastery, practical virtues, and spiritual growth through personal experience of the divine—had already emerged by 1200 as a major expression of Islamic values and social identity. Sufism appeared in many variations and readily assimilated local cultures to its beliefs and practices. Sufi mystics acquired institutional strength through the communal solidarity of their brotherhoods spread across the whole realm of Islam. In contrast to the orthodox scholars and teachers known as *ulama*, who made little effort to convert nonbelievers, Sufi preachers were inspired by missionary zeal and welcomed non-Muslims to their lodges and sermons. This made them ideal instruments for the spread of Islam to new territories.

Timur   One of Sufism's most important royal patrons was Timur (1336–1405), the last of the Mongol emperors. Born near the city of Samarkand (SAM-ar-kand) when the Mongol Ilkhanate in Iran was on the verge of collapse, Timur—himself a Turk—grew up among Mongols who practiced Islam. He rose to power in the 1370s by reuniting quarreling Mongol tribes in common pursuit of conquest. Although Timur lacked the dynastic pedigree enjoyed by Chinggis Khan's descendants, like Chinggis he held his empire together by the force of his personal charisma.

From the early 1380s, Timur's armies relentlessly pursued campaigns of conquest, sweeping westward across Iran into Mesopotamia and Russia and eastward into India. In 1400–1401 Timur seized and razed Aleppo and Damascus, the principal Mamluk cities in Syria. In 1402 he captured the Ottoman sultan in battle. Rather than trying to consolidate his rule in Syria and Anatolia (modern Turkey), however, Timur turned his attention eastward. He was preparing to march on China when he fell ill and died early in 1405. Although Timur's empire quickly fragmented, his triumphs would serve as an inspiration to later empire builders, such as the Mughals in India and the Manchus in China. Moreover, his support of Sufism would have a lasting impact, helping lay the foundation for a number of important Islamic religious movements in Central Asia.

The institutions of Timur's empire were largely modeled on the Ilkhan synthesis of Persian civil administration and Turkish-Mongol military organization. Like the Ilkhans and the Ottomans, Timur's policies favored settled farmers and urban populations over pastoral nomads, who were often displaced from their homelands. While Timur allowed local princes a degree of autonomy, he was determined to make Samarkand a grand imperial capital.

Sufism A tradition within Islam that emphasizes mystical knowledge and personal experience of the divine.

He forcibly relocated artists, craftsmen, scholars, and clerics from many regions and put them into service in Samarkand (see Reading the Past: A Spanish Ambassador's Description of Samarkand). The citadel and enormous bazaar built by Timur have long since perished, but surviving mosques, shrines, and tombs illuminate Timur's vision of Islamic kingship: all-powerful, urbane and cosmopolitan, and ostentatious in its display of public piety.

After Timur's death in 1405, his sons carved the empire into independent regional kingdoms. Like Timur, his successors sought to control religious life in royal capitals such as Herat and Samarkand by appointing elders (*shayks*) and judges (*qadis*) to administer justice, supervise schools and mosques, and police public morality. Yet Sufi brotherhoods and the veneration of Sufi saints exerted an especially strong influence over social life and religious practice in Central Asia. Timur had lavished special favor on Sufi teachers and had strategically placed the shrines of his family members next to the tombs of important Sufi leaders. The relics of Timur in Samarkand, along with the tombs of Sufi saints, attracted pilgrims from near and far.

Elsewhere in the Islamic world, a number of religious movements combined the veneration of Sufi saints and belief in miracles with unorthodox ideas derived from Shi'ism, the branch of Islam that maintains that only descendants of Muhammad's son-in-law Ali have a legitimate right to serve as caliph. Outside the major cities, Islamic leadership passed to Sufis and popular preachers. One of the most militant and influential of these radical Islamic sects was the Safavid (SAH-fah-vid) movement founded by a Sufi preacher, Safi al-Din (SAH-fee al-dean) (1252–1334). Like other visionary teachers, Safi preached the need for a purified Islam cleansed of worldly wealth, urban luxury, and moral laxity. His missionary movement struck a responsive chord among the pastoral Turk and Mongol tribes of Anatolia and Iran. The Safavids roused their followers to attack Christians in the Caucasus region, but they also challenged Muslim rulers such as the Ottomans and Timur's successors. At the end of the fifteenth century, a charismatic leader, Shah Isma'il (shah IS-mah-eel), combined Safavid religious fervor with Shi'a doctrines to found a **theocracy**—a state subject to religious authority. It would rule Iran for more than two centuries and shape modern Iran's distinctive Shi'a religious culture.

Timur Enthroned
We can glean some sense of Timur's self-image from the *Book of Victories*, a chronicle of Timur's campaigns commissioned by one of his descendants in the 1480s. This scene portrays the moment in 1370 when Timur declared himself successor to the Chagadai khans. (Rare Books and Manuscripts Department, The Sheridan Libraries, The Johns Hopkins University.)

Ottoman Expansion and the Fall of Constantinople 1354–1453

The spread of Islam in Central Asia would have profound consequences for the region. In the eyes of Europeans, however, the most significant—and alarming—advance was the Ottoman expansion into the Balkan territories of southeastern Europe. The Byzantine state was severely shaken by the Black Death, and in 1354 the Ottomans took advantage of this weakness to invade the Balkans. After a decisive victory in 1389, the Ottoman Empire annexed most of the Balkans except the region around Constantinople itself, reducing it to an isolated enclave.

The growing might of the Ottoman Empire stemmed from two military innovations: (1) the formation of the **janissary corps**, elite army units composed of slave soldiers, and (2) the use of massed musket fire and cannons, such as the bombards of Urban, the Hungarian engineer whom we met at the start of this chapter. In the late fourteenth century the Ottomans adopted the Mamluk practice of organizing slave armies that would be more reliably loyal to the sultan than the unruly *ghazi* ("holy warrior") bands that Osman

theocracy A state ruled by religious authorities.

janissary corps Slave soldiers who served as the principal armed forces of the Ottoman Empire beginning in the fifteenth century; also staffed much of the Ottoman state bureaucracy.

A Spanish Ambassador's Description of Samarkand

In September 1403, an embassy dispatched by King Henry III of Castile arrived at Samarkand in hopes of enlisting the support of Timur for a combined military campaign against the Ottomans. Seventy years old and in failing health, Timur lavishly entertained his visitors, but made no response to Henry's overtures. The leader of the Spanish delegation, Ruy Gonzalez de Clavijo, left Samarkand disappointed, but his report preserves our fullest account of Timur's capital in its heyday.

The city is rather larger than Seville, but lying outside Samarkand are great numbers of houses that form extensive suburbs. These lay spread on all hands, for indeed the township is surrounded by orchards and vineyards. . . . In between these orchards pass streets with open squares; these are all densely populated, and here all kinds of goods are on sale with breadstuffs and meat. . . .

Samarkand is rich not only in foodstuffs but also in manufactures, such as factories of silk. . . . Thus trade has always been fostered by Timur with the view of making his capital the noblest of cities; and during all his conquests . . . he carried off the best men to people Samarkand, bringing thither the master-craftsmen of all nations. Thus from Damascus he carried away with him all the weavers of that city, those who worked at the silk looms; further the bow-makers who produce those cross-bows which are so famous; likewise armorers; also the craftsmen in glass and porcelain, who are known to be the best in all the world. From Turkey he had brought their gunsmiths who make the arquebus. . . . So great therefore was the population now of all nationalities gathered together in Samarkand that of men with their families the number they said must amount to 150,000 souls . . . [including] Turks, Arabs, and Moors of diverse sects, with Greek, Armenian, Roman, Jacobite [Syrian], and Nestorian Christians, besides those folk who baptize with fire in the forehead [i.e., Hindus]. . . .

The markets of Samarkand further are amply stored with merchandise imported from distant and foreign countries. . . . The goods that are imported to Samarkand from Cathay indeed are of the richest and most precious of all those brought thither from foreign parts, for the craftsmen of Cathay are reputed to be the most skillful by far beyond those of any other nation.

Source: Ruy Gonzalez de Clavijo, *Embassy to Tamerlane, 1403–1406*, trans. Guy Le Strange (London: Routledge, 1928), 285–289.

EXAMINING THE EVIDENCE

1. What features of Timur's capital most impressed Gonzalez de Clavijo?

2. How does this account of Samarkand at its height compare with the chapter's description of Renaissance Florence?

(r. 1280–1324), the founder of the Ottoman state, had gathered as the core of his army. At first, prisoners and volunteers made up the janissary corps. Starting in 1395, however, the Ottomans imposed a form of conscription known as *devshirme* (dev-SHEER-may) on the Christian peoples of the Balkans to supplement Turkish recruits. Adolescent boys conscripted through the devshirme were taken from their families, raised as Muslims, and educated at palace schools for service in the sultan's civil administration as well as the army. The Mamluks purchased slaves from Central Asia, but the Ottomans obtained a cheaper and more abundant supply from within their empire. At the same time, they created a government and military wholly beholden to the sultan. Janissaries were forbidden to marry and forfeited their property to the sultan upon their death.

Practical concerns dictated Ottoman policies toward Christian communities. Where Christians were the majority of the population, the Ottomans could be quite tolerant. Apart from the notorious devshirme slave

Ottoman Expansion, c. 1200–1453

Ottoman territory
- By c. 1300
- By c. 1360
- By c. 1453
- Tributary state
- Major battle

WALLACHIA
Danube R.
Kosovo 1389
BALKANS
Black Sea
Constantinople (Istanbul) 1453
ANATOLIA

levy, the Ottoman impositions were less burdensome than the dues the Balkan peoples had owed the Byzantine emperor. The Ottomans allowed Balkan Christians freedom to practice their religion, and they protected the Greek Orthodox Church, which they considered indispensable to maintaining social order. In Anatolia and other places where Christians were a minority, however, the Ottomans took a much harder line, seeing such minorities as a potential threat to the Ottoman order. Muslim governors stripped Christian bishops of their authority, seized church properties and revenues, and curbed public worship. By 1500 Christian society in Anatolia had nearly vanished; most Christians had converted to Islam.

Like the Ming emperors of China, Ottoman rulers favored the creation of a stable peasant society that would serve as a reliable source of revenue. A married peasant with a plot of land that could be worked by two oxen became the basic unit of Ottoman society. The state controlled nearly all cultivated land, but peasant families enjoyed permanent rights to farm the land they occupied. The government sold the rights to collect land taxes (a practice known as tax farming) to merchants and other wealthy individuals, including non-Muslims such as Greeks and Jews. The practice of tax farming guaranteed revenues for the state, but it distanced Ottoman officials from their subjects.

Despite their own nomadic origins, the Ottomans regarded nomadic tribes, like religious minorities, as a threat to stability. Many nomads were forcibly deported and settled in the Balkans and western Anatolia, where they combined farming with stock raising. Due to heavy taxes imposed on animal herds, nomads had to earn additional income through transport, lumbering, and felt and carpet manufacture. The push toward such activities created by harsh Ottoman policies was matched by the pull of global trade connections. Strong demand from European customers and the imperial capital of Istanbul (the name Mehmed II gave to Constantinople) stimulated carpet weaving by both peasants and herders.

The patriarchal family, in which the wife is subject to her husband's control, was a pillar of Ottoman law, just as it was in Ming China. Although the Ottoman state barred women from owning cultivated land, it did not infringe on women's rights to a share of family inheritance, as prescribed in the Qur'an. Thus, although men usually controlled property in the form of land and houses, women acquired wealth in the form of money, furnishings, clothes, and jewelry. Women invested in commercial ventures, tax farming, and moneylending. Because women were secluded in the home and veiled in public— long-established requirements to maintain family honor and status in the central Islamic lands—women used servants and trusted clients to help them conduct their business activities.

The final defeat of the Byzantine Empire by Ottoman armies in 1453 shocked the Christian world. Mehmed II's capture of Constantinople also completed a radical transformation of the Ottoman enterprise. The Ottoman sultans no longer saw themselves as roving ghazi warriors, but as monarchs with absolute authority over a multinational empire at the crossroads of Europe and Asia: "ruler of the two seas and the two continents," as the inscription over Mehmed's palace gate proclaimed. A proudly Islamic regime, the Ottoman sultanate aspired to become the centerpiece of a broad cosmopolitan civilization spanning Europe, Asia, and Africa.

Commerce and Culture in Islamic West Africa

West African trading empires and the merchants they supported had long served as the vanguard of Islam in sub-Saharan Africa. The Mali Empire's adoption of Islam as its official religion in the late thirteenth century encouraged conversion to Islam throughout the West African savanna. Under Mali's protection, Muslim merchant clans expanded their activities throughout the towns of the savanna and the oasis trading posts of the Sahara. Islam continued to prosper despite the collapse of Mali's political dominion in the mid-fourteenth century.

Timbuktu Manuscript
Timbuktu became the hub of Islamic culture and intellectual life in the western Sahara. Scholars and students at Timbuktu assembled impressive libraries of Arabic texts, such as this twelfth-century Qur'an. Written mostly on paper imported from Europe, Timbuktu's manuscripts were preserved in family collections after the city's leading scholars were deported to North Africa by Moroccan invaders in 1591. (Candace Feit.)

Muslim Merchants and Scholars

The towns of Jenne and Timbuktu, founded along the Niger River by Muslim merchants in the thirteenth century, emerged as the new crossroads of trans-Saharan trade. Jenne benefited from its access to the gold mines and rain forest products of coastal West Africa. Timbuktu's commercial prosperity rose as trade grew between West Africa and Mamluk Egypt. Islamic intellectual culture thrived among the merchant families of Timbuktu, Jenne, and other towns.

As elsewhere in the Islamic world, West African trader families readily combined religious scholarship with mercantile pursuits. Thus, in West Africa, trade and Islamic culture went hand in hand. In fact, West Africa saw the development of a profitable trade *in* Islamic culture. Since the eleventh century, disciples of renowned scholars had migrated across the Sahara and founded schools and libraries. The Moroccan Muslim scholar and traveler Ibn Battuta (IB-uhn ba-TOO-tuh), who visited Mali in 1352–1353, voiced approval of the people's "eagerness to memorize the great Qur'an: they place fetters on their children if they fail to memorize it and they are not released until they do so."[5] Books on Islamic law, theology, Sufi mysticism, medicine, and Arabic grammar and literature were staple commodities of trans-Saharan trade. The Muslim diplomat Hasan al-Wazzan (hah-SAHN al-wah-zan), whose *Description of Africa* (published in Italian in 1550) became a best-seller in Europe, wrote that in Timbuktu "the learned are greatly revered. Also, many book manuscripts coming from the Berber [North African] lands are sold. More profits are realized from sales of books than any other merchandise."[6]

Muslim Clerics and Native Religious Leaders

Muslim clerics wielded considerable influence in the towns. Clerics presided over worship and festival life and governed social behavior by applying Muslim law and cultural traditions. Yet away from the towns the majority of the population remained attached to ancestral beliefs in nature spirits, especially the spirits of rivers and thunder. Healer priests, clan chiefs, and other ritual experts shared responsibility for making offerings to the spirits, providing protection from evil demons and sorcerers, and honoring the dead. Much to the chagrin of purists such as Ibn Battuta, West African rulers maintained their authority in rural areas by combining Muslim practices with indigenous rituals and traditions. Islam in West Africa was largely urban, and West African rulers knew that their control of the countryside depended on religious accommodation.

trade diaspora A network of merchants from the same city or country who live permanently in foreign lands and cooperate with one another to pursue trading opportunities.

Advance of Islam in Maritime Southeast Asia

Muslim Arab merchants had dominated maritime commerce in the Indian Ocean and Southeast Asia since the seventh century. Not until the thirteenth century, however, did Islam begin to gain converts in Malaysia and the Indonesian archipelago. By 1400 Arab and Gujarati traders and Sufi teachers had spread Islam throughout maritime Asia. The dispersion of Muslim merchants took the form of a **trade diaspora**, a network of merchant settlements dispersed across foreign lands but united by common origins, religion, and language, as well as by business dealings.

Political and economic motives strongly influenced official adoption of Islam. In the first half of the fourteenth century, the Majapahit (mah-jah-PAH-hit) kingdom (1292–1528), a bastion of Hindu religion, conquered most of Java and the neighboring islands of Bali and Madura and forced many local rulers in the Indonesian archipelago to submit tribute. In response, many of these rulers adopted Islam as an act of resistance to dominance by the Majapahit kings. By 1428 the Muslim city-states of Java's north coast, buoyed by the profits of trade with China, secured their independence from Majapahit. Majapahit's dominion over the agricultural hinterland of Java lasted until 1528, when a coalition of Muslim princes forced the royal family to flee to Bali, which remains today the sole preserve of Hinduism in Southeast Asia.

Cosmopolitan port cities, with their diverse merchant communities, were natural sites for religious innovation. The spread of Islam beyond Southeast Asia's port cities, however, was slow and uneven. Javanese tradition attributes the Islamization of the island to a series of preachers, beginning with Malik Ibrahim (mah-leek EE-bra-heem) (d. 1419), a Gujarati spice trader of Persian ancestry. Because merchants and Sufi teachers played a far greater role than orthodox ulama in the spread of Islam in Southeast Asia, relatively open forms of Islam flourished. The Arab shipmaster Ibn Majid (IB-uhn maj-jid), writing in 1462, bemoaned the corruption of Islamic marriage and dietary laws among the Muslims of Melaka (mah-LAK-eh): "They have no culture at all. The infidel marries Muslim women while the Muslim takes pagans to wife. . . . The Muslim eats dogs for meat, for there are no food laws. They drink wine in the markets and do not treat divorce as a religious act.[7] Enforcement of Islamic law often was suspended where it conflicted with local custom. Southeast Asia never adopted some features of Middle Eastern culture often associated with Islam, such as the veiling of women.

Local pre-Islamic religious traditions persisted in Sumatra and Java long after the people accepted Islam. The most visible signs of conversion to Islam were giving up the worship of idols and the consumption of pork and adopting the practice of male circumcision. In addition, the elaborate feasting and grave goods, slave sacrifice, and widow sacrifice (*sati*) that normally accompanied the burials of chiefs and kings largely disappeared. Yet Southeast Asian Muslims continued to honor the dead with prayers and offerings adapted to the forms of Islamic rituals. Malays and Javanese readily adopted veneration of Sufi saints and habitually prayed for assistance from the spirits of deceased holy men. Muslim restrictions on women's secular and religious activities met with spirited resistance from Southeast Asian women, who were accustomed to active participation in public life. Even more than in West Africa, Islam in Southeast Asia prospered not by destroying existing traditions, but by assimilating them.

In regions such as West Africa and Southeast Asia, then, Islam diffused through the activities of merchants, teachers, and settlers rather than through conquest. The spread of Islam in Africa and Asia also followed the rhythms of international trade. While Europe recovered slowly from the Black Death, thriving commerce across the Indian Ocean forged new economic links among Asia, Africa, and the Mediterranean world.

Politics of Conversion

Religious Diversity

The Global Bazaar

Dynastic changes, war, and the Black Death roiled the international economy in the fourteenth century. Yet even before the end of the century, trade and economic growth were reviving in many areas. The maritime world of the Indian Ocean, largely spared both pandemic and war, displayed unprecedented commercial dynamism. Pepper and cotton textiles from India, porcelain and silk from China, spices and

FOCUS

How did the pattern of international trade change during the fourteenth and fifteenth centuries, and how did these changes affect consumption and fashion tastes?

other exotic goods from Southeast Asia, and gold, ivory, and copper from southern Africa circulated through a network of trading ports that spanned the Indian Ocean, Southeast Asia, and China. These trading centers attracted merchants and artisans from many lands, and the colorful variety of languages, dress, foods, and music that filled their streets gave them the air of a global bazaar.

The crises of the fourteenth century severely disrupted the European economy, but by 1450 Italy regained its place as the center within Latin Christendom of finance, industry, and trade. Previously, European craftsmen had produced only crude imitations of Islamic luxury wares. By the early fifteenth century, however, mimicry had blossomed into innovation, and Italian production of luxury goods surpassed Islamic competitors' in both quantity and quality. Wealth poured into Italy, where it found new outlets in a culture of conspicuous consumption. In contrast, the Islamic heartlands of the Middle East never recaptured their former momentum. In sum, the crises of the fourteenth century did not destroy the shared economy and commerce of the Afro-Eurasian world, but they did reshape them in profound and long-lasting ways (see Map 15.4).

Economic Prosperity and Maritime Trade in Asia 1350–1450

In Kubilai Khan's day, hostility among the Mongol khanates disrupted Central Asian caravan trade. Thus when the Venetian traveler Marco Polo returned home in 1292, he traveled by ship rather than retracing the overland route, known as the Silk Road, that had brought him to China two decades before. Polo's experience was a sign of things to come. After 1300 maritime commerce largely replaced inland trade over the ancient Silk Road. Asian merchants from India to China would seize the opportunities presented by the new emphasis on maritime commerce.

India: Cotton and Pepper

In India, improvements in spinning wheels and looms, and above all the invention of block printing of fabrics in the fourteenth century, led to a revolution in cotton textile manufacture. Using block printing (carved wooden blocks covered with dye), Indian weavers produced colorful and intricately designed fabrics—later known in Europe as chintz, from the Hindi *chint* ("many-colored")—that were far cheaper than luxury textiles such as silk or velvet. Gujarat in the northwest and the Tamil lands in southeastern India became centers of cotton manufacture and trade. Although cotton cultivation and weaving spread to Burma, Thailand, and China, Indian fabrics dominated Eurasian markets (see Lives and Livelihoods: Urban Weavers in India).

Along with textiles, India was famous for its pepper, for which Europeans had acquired a taste during the age of the Crusades. Muslim merchants from Gujarat controlled both cotton and pepper exports from the cities of Calicut and Quilon (KEE-lon). By 1500 Gujarati merchants had created a far-flung trade network across the Indian Ocean from Zanzibar to Java. Gujarati *sharafs* (from the Persian word for "moneylender") and Tamil *chettis* ("traders") acted as bankers for merchants and rulers alike in nearly every Indian Ocean port.

China: Silk and Porcelain

China's ocean-going commerce also flourished in the fourteenth century. The thriving trade between India and China deeply impressed Ibn Battuta, who found thirteen large Chinese vessels, or *junks*, anchored at Calicut when he arrived there in 1341. These junks, Battuta tells us, carried a complement of a thousand men and contained "four decks with rooms, cabins, and saloons for merchants; a cabin has chambers and a lavatory, and can be locked by its occupant, who takes along with him slave girls and wives."[8]

Silk had long dominated China's export trade, but by the eleventh century domestic silk-weaving was flourishing in Iran, the Byzantine Empire, and India. Because Iranian and Byzantine silk manufacturers were better positioned to respond to changing fashions in the Islamic world and Europe, China primarily exported raw silk rather than finished fabrics. At the same time, China retained its preeminent place in world trade by exporting porcelain, which became known as "chinaware."

Much admired for their whiteness and translucency, Chinese ceramics already had become an important item of Asian maritime trade in the tenth century. Bulky and fragile,

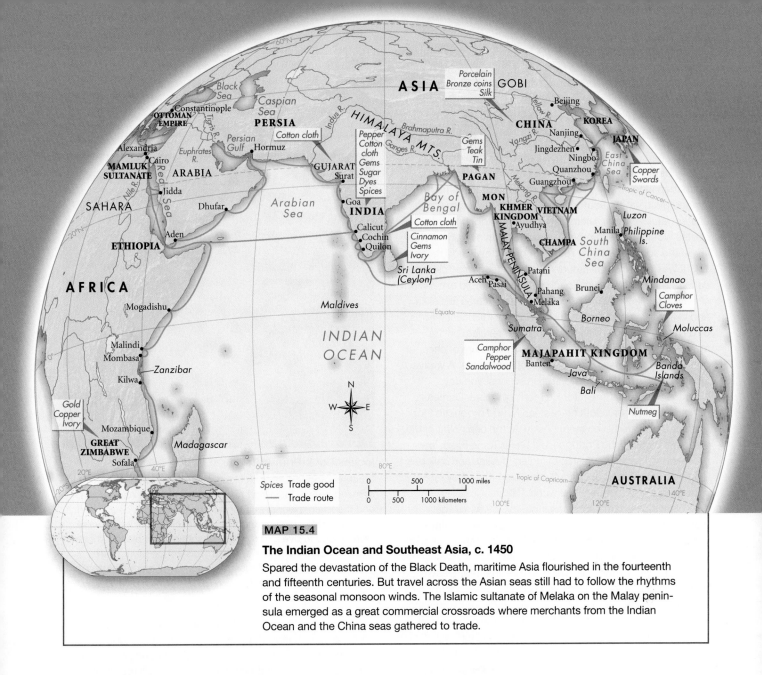

MAP 15.4

The Indian Ocean and Southeast Asia, c. 1450

Spared the devastation of the Black Death, maritime Asia flourished in the fourteenth and fifteenth centuries. But travel across the Asian seas still had to follow the rhythms of the seasonal monsoon winds. The Islamic sultanate of Melaka on the Malay peninsula emerged as a great commercial crossroads where merchants from the Indian Ocean and the China seas gathered to trade.

ceramic wares were better suited to transport by ship than overland by camel or cart. In the thirteenth century, artisans at Jingdezhen (JING-deh-JUHN) in southern China perfected the techniques for making true porcelains, which transform into glass the glaze and pigments, as well as the body of the piece. Porcelain wares, which were harder and whiter than previous types of ceramics, could be made into thin yet strong vessels. Although the Chinese preferred monochromatic (single-colored) porcelains that imitated the colors and texture of jade, consumers in the Islamic world prized intricate designs executed with the metallic pigments used by glassmakers. Muslim merchants introduced the cobalt blue pigment (which Chinese potters called "Mohammedan blue") used to create blue-and-white decorated porcelains. By 1400, Jingdezhen had become the largest manufacturing city in the world, housing more than one thousand kilns with some seventy thousand craftsmen engaged in several dozen specialized tasks. Thus, technological innovation and the demands of the international marketplace shaped both the production and decoration of Chinese ceramics.

The most avid consumers of Chinese porcelains were in the Islamic world, reflecting the global nature of the Chinese ceramics industry. Muslims used Chinese porcelains both as eating and drinking vessels and to decorate mosques, tombs, and other holy places. Imports of Chinese porcelain devastated local ceramic manufacturing in many parts of maritime Asia,

Urban Weavers in India

Industry and commerce in India, especially in textiles, grew rapidly beginning in the fourteenth century. Specialized craftsmen in towns and regional groups of merchants formed guilds that became the nuclei of new occupational castes, *jati* (JAH-tee). Ultimately these new occupational castes would join with other forces in Indian society to challenge the social inequality rooted in orthodox Hindu religion.

It was growth in market demand and technological innovations such as block printing that drove the rapid expansion of India's textile industries. Luxury fabrics such as fine silks and velvet remained largely the province of royal workshops or private patronage. Mass production of textiles, on the other hand, was oriented toward the manufacture of cheaper cotton fabrics, especially colorful chintz garments. A weaver could make a woman's cotton *sari* in six or seven days, whereas a luxury garment took a month or more. Domestic demand for ordinary cloth grew steadily, and production for export accelerated even more briskly. At the beginning of the sixteenth century, the Portuguese traveler Tomé Pires, impressed by the craftsmanship of Indian muslins and calicoes (named after the port of Calicut), observed that "they make enough of these to furnish the world."[1]

Weaving became an urban industry. It was village women who cleaned most of the cotton and spun it into yarn; they could easily combine this simple if laborious work with other domestic chores. But peasants did not weave the yarn into cloth, except for their own use. Instead, weaving, bleaching, and dyeing cloth were skilled tasks performed by professional urban craftsmen, or in some cases by artisans living in separate weavers' settlements in the countryside.

Like other trades in India, weaving was a hereditary occupation that conferred a distinct *jati* caste status and identity. Families of weavers belonged to one of a number of regional guilds with branches in different towns, and members married within their guilds. Unlike European guilds, Indian guilds did not have exclusive monopolies over their trades. A single town could include a number of different weaving guilds, which could become fierce economic and social rivals.

Indian Block-Printed Textile, c. 1500

Block-printed textiles with elaborate designs were in great demand both in India and throughout Southeast Asia, Africa, and the Islamic world. Craftsmen carved intricate designs on wooden blocks (a separate block for each color), which were then dipped in dye and repeatedly stamped on bleached fabric until the entire cloth was covered. This cotton fabric with geese, lotus flower, and rosette designs was manufactured in Gujarat in western India. (Ashmolean Museum, University of Oxford/ Bridgeman Art Library.)

Increased affluence brought further social and economic differentiation to the ranks of weavers. Although guild leaders negotiated orders from merchants and princes, artisans could freely sell their own wares through urban shops and country fairs. The most successful weavers became merchants and brokers, buying more looms and hiring others to work under their supervision. By the fourteenth century some weavers had begun to add the honorific title *chetti* (merchant) to their names.

Southeast Asia: Spices and Rain Forest Products

from the Philippines to East Africa. Chinese porcelains became potent prestige goods among the tribal societies of the Philippines and Indonesia, who attributed magical powers to them.

In mainland Southeast Asia, the shift in political power from the inland rice-growing regions toward coastal port cities reflected the new prominence of maritime trade in the region's economic life. Burma exported cotton to China as early as 1400 and became an important source of metals, gems, and teak for shipbuilding. The profits of maritime commerce fueled the emergence of Ayudhya (a-YOOD-he-ya) in Thailand as the dominant power in mainland Southeast Asia in the late fourteenth century. By 1400 Ayudhya was challenging Majapahit for control of the Southeast Asian trade routes between India and China.

The rising prosperity of weavers whetted their aspirations for social recognition. Amid the whirl and congestion of city life, it was far more difficult than in villages to enforce the laws governing caste purity and segregation. As a fourteenth-century poet wrote about the crowded streets of his hometown of Jaunpur in the Ganges Valley, in the city "one person's caste-mark gets stamped on another's forehead, and a brahman's holy thread will be found hanging around an untouchable's neck."[2] Brahmans objected to this erosion of caste boundaries, to little avail. Weaver guilds became influential patrons of temples and often served as trustees and accountants in charge of managing temple endowments and revenues.

In a few cases the growing economic independence of weavers and like-minded artisans prompted complete rejection of the caste hierarchy. Sufi preachers and *bhakti* (BAHK-tee)—devotional movements devoted to patron gods and goddesses—encouraged the disregard of caste distinctions in favor of a universal brotherhood of devout believers. The fifteenth-century bhakti preacher Kabir, who was strongly influenced by Sufi teachings, epitomized the new social radicalism coursing through the urban artisan classes. A weaver himself, Kabir joined the dignity of manual labor to the purity of spiritual devotion, spurning the social pretension and superficial piety of the brahmans ("pandits") and Muslim clerics ("mullahs"):

> I abandoned kin and caste, I weave my threads at ease
>
> I quarrel with no one, I abandoned the pandits and mullahs,
>
> I wear what I have woven; forgetful of myself, I come close to God.[3]

In Kabir's mind, genuine piety was rooted in honest toil, devotion to family, and abstinence from sensual pleasure.

By the seventeenth century, such ideas had coalesced into a separatist religious movement, Sikhism, centered on a trinity of labor, charity, and spiritual devotion. The Sikhs, who gained a following principally among traders and artisans in the northwestern Punjab region, drew an even more explicit connection between commerce and piety. In the words of a hymn included in a sixteenth-century anthology of Sikh sacred writings:

> The true Guru [teacher] is the merchant;
>
> The devotees are his peddlers.
>
> The capital stock is the Lord's Name, and
>
> To enshrine the truth is to keep His account.[4]

Sikh communities spurned the distinction between pure and impure occupations. In their eyes, holiness was to be found in honest toil and personal piety, not ascetic practices, book learning, or religious rituals.

---

1. Tomé Pires, *The Suma Oriental of Tomé Pires*, ed. and trans. Armando Cortes (London: Hakluyt Society, 1944), 1:53.
2. Vidyapati Thakur, *Kirtilata*, quoted in Eugenia Vanina, *Urban Crafts and Craftsmen in Medieval India (Thirteenth–Eighteenth Centuries)* (New Delhi: Munshiram Manoharlal, 2004), 443.
3. Quoted in Vanina, *Urban Crafts and Craftsmen*, 149.
4. *Sri Guru Granth Sahib*, trans. Gophal Singh (Delhi: Gur Das Kapur & Sons, 1960), 2:427.

QUESTIONS TO CONSIDER

1. In what ways did the organization of textile production reinforce or challenge the prevailing social norms of Hindu society?

2. In what ways did religious ideas and movements reflect the new sense of dignity among prosperous Indian merchants and craftsmen?

For Further Information:

Ramaswamy, Vijaya. *Textiles and Weavers in Medieval South India*. Delhi: Oxford University Press, 1985.

Vanina, Eugenia. *Urban Crafts and Craftsmen in Medieval India (Thirteenth–Eighteenth Centuries)*. New Delhi: Munshiram Manoharlal, 2004.

Thus, China influenced patterns of international trade not only as a producer, as with ceramics, but as a market for exported goods large enough to shape production elsewhere in the world. China was the principal market for the international trade in pepper, and it was Chinese demand that drove the rapid expansion of pepper cultivation in Southeast Asia, in particular Sumatra, during the fifteenth century. In return for exports of pepper, sandalwood, tin and other metals, fine spices, and exotic products of the tropical rain forests, Southeast Asia imported cotton cloth from India and silks, porcelain, and bronze coins from China. In the wake of this trade boom, Indian and Chinese merchant communities sprouted across maritime Southeast Asia. The trade diasporas of Gujarati Muslims and Chinese from Guangzhou

Wedding Present of Chinese Porcelains

Avid demand in the Muslim world stimulated development of China's renowned blue-and-white porcelains. This Persian miniature from around 1480 illustrates the story of a Chinese princess who in a gesture of diplomacy is sent to marry a Turkish nomad chieftain. The dowry that accompanies the reluctant bride includes blue-and-white porcelains and brass wares of Turkestan design. (The Art Archive/Topkapi Museum Istanbul/ Gianni Dagli Orti.)

(Canton) and Quanzhou (CHYWAN-joe) created networks of cultural as well as economic influence, ultimately altering the balance of political power as well (see again Map 15.4).

China's Overseas Overture: The Voyages of Zheng He 1405–1433

The growth of South Asian maritime trade attracted the attention of the Chinese government, and in the early fifteenth century, the Ming dynasty in China took a more active role in maritime Southeast Asia, becoming a rival for political and economic supremacy. From the 1390s Malay princes in Sumatra appealed to the Ming court for protection against the demands of the Majapahit kings. In 1405 the Ming emperor Yongle decided to intervene by sending a naval expedition to halt the expansionist aggression of Majapahit and Ayudhya and to assert Chinese authority over the maritime realm.

Zheng He's Mission

Yongle entrusted the fleet to the command of a young military officer named Zheng He (1371–1433). Zheng was born into a Muslim family who had served the Mongol rulers of the Yuan dynasty. In 1383, Zheng He, then age twelve, was conscripted into the eunuch corps (castrated males employed as guardians of the imperial household) and placed in the retinue of the prince who would become Emperor Yongle. Zheng assisted the prince in the overthrow of his nephew that brought Yongle to the throne in 1402, and became his most trusted confidant.

For his mission to Southeast Asia, Yongle equipped Zheng He with a vast armada, a fleet of sixty-three ships manned by nearly twenty-eight thousand sailors, soldiers, and officials. Zheng's seven-masted flagship, more than four hundred feet long, was a marvel of Chinese nautical engineering. His fleet later became known as the "treasure ships" because of the cargoes of exotic goods and tribute they brought back from Southeast Asia, India, Arabia, and Africa. But Zheng's primary mission was political, not economic. Yongle, as we have seen, had a vision of world empire, in part borrowed from the Mongols, in which a multitude of princes would pay homage to Ming sovereignty. The constant flow of foreign embassies, the display of exotic tribute, and the emperor's pivotal role as arbitrator of disputes among lesser rulers were crucial to his sense of imperial dignity.

Departing in November of 1405, Zheng's fleet sailed first to Java in a show of force designed to intimidate Majapahit. He then traveled to Sumatra and Melaka and across the Indian Ocean to Ceylon and Calicut. No sooner had Zheng He returned to China in the

Renaissance A period of intense intellectual and artistic creativity in Europe, beginning in Italy in the fourteenth century as a revival of the classical civilization of ancient Greece and Rome.

humanism The study of the humanities (rhetoric, poetry, history, and moral philosophy), based on the works of ancient Greek and Roman writers, that provided the intellectual foundations for the Renaissance.

autumn of 1407 than Yongle dispatched him on another voyage. Yongle had recently launched his invasion of Vietnam, and the purpose of the second voyage was to curtail Ayudhya's aggression and establish a Chinese presence at strategic ports such as Melaka along the Straits of Sumatra. Altogether Yongle commissioned six expeditions under Zheng He's command. During the fourth and subsequent voyages, Zheng He sailed beyond India to Arabia and down the east coast of Africa.

The projection of Chinese power over the sea-lanes of maritime Asia led to far-reaching economic and political changes. The close relations Zheng He forged with rulers of port cities strengthened their political independence and promoted their commercial growth. Under the umbrella of Chinese protection, Melaka flourished as the great cross-roads of Asian maritime trade.

The high cost of building and equipping the treasure ships depleted the Ming treasury, however, and after Yongle's death in 1424, Confucian ministers at the Ming court prevailed on his young successor to halt the naval expeditions. In 1430, Yongle's successor nonetheless overcame bureaucratic opposition and dispatched Zheng He on yet another voyage, his seventh. After traveling once again to Africa, Zheng died during his return home. With the passing of the renowned admiral, enthusiasm for the expeditions evaporated. Moreover, the Ming court faced a new threat: a resurgent Mongol confederation in the north. In 1449 a foolish young Ming emperor led a military campaign against the Mongols, only to be taken captive. The Ming court obtained the emperor's release by paying a huge ransom, but its strategic priorities had been completely transformed. Turning its back on the sea, the Ming state devoted its energies and revenues to rebuilding the Great Wall, much of which had crumbled to dust, as a defense against further Mongol attacks. The Great Wall that survives today was largely constructed by the Ming dynasty.

The Last of the Treasure Fleets

The shift in Chinese policy did not mean the end of Chinese involvement in maritime trade. Chinese merchants continued to pursue trading opportunities in defiance of the imperial ban on private overseas commerce. Even though Muslim merchants dominated Asian maritime commerce, Chinese merchant colonies dotted the coasts of Southeast Asia. Melaka's rulers converted to Islam but welcomed merchants from every corner of Asia. The population probably reached one hundred thousand before Melaka was sacked by the Portuguese in 1511. The Portuguese, like the Chinese before them, were drawn to Southeast Asian waters by the tremendous wealth created by maritime trade. Spurred by the growing European appetite for Asian spices, the violent intrusion of the Portuguese would transform the dynamics of maritime trade throughout Asia.

Commerce and Culture in the Renaissance

European expansion in the late fourteenth and early fifteenth centuries was preceded and influenced by a period of dramatic cultural change. The century after the outbreak of the Black Death marked the beginning of a sweeping transformation in European culture known as the **Renaissance**. In its narrow sense *Renaissance* (French for "rebirth") refers to the revival of ancient Greek and Roman philosophy, art, and literature that originated in fourteenth-century Italy. Scholars rediscovered classical learning and began to emulate the language and ideas of Greek and Roman philosophers and poets; these individuals became known as humanists, students of the liberal arts or humanities. The new intellectual movement of **humanism** combined classical learning with Christian piety and dedication to civic responsibilities.

At the same time the Renaissance inaugurated dramatic changes in the self-image and lifestyle of the wealthy. The new habits of luxurious living and magnificent display diverged sharply from the Christian ethic of frugality. Innovations in material culture and aesthetic values reflected crucial changes in the Italian economy and its relationship to the international trading world of the Mediterranean and beyond. These transformations in turn led to a reorientation of Europe away from Asia and toward the Atlantic world.

The Black Death had hit the Italian city-states especially hard. Some contemporary observers claimed that the pandemic had radically reshaped the social order. Although

Italy's Economic Transformation

artisan guilds became a powerful force in urban government for a time in Florence, Siena, and other cities, over the long term the patrician elite of wealthy merchants and landowners reasserted their oligarchic control. The rich became richer, and status and power were increasingly measured in visible signs of wealth.

Still, the economies of the Italian city-states underwent fundamental transformation. Diminishing profits from trade with the Islamic world prompted many Italian merchants to abandon commerce in favor of banking. Squeezed out of the eastern Mediterranean by the Turks and Venetians, Genoa turned its attention westward. Genoese bankers became financiers to the kings of Spain and Portugal and supplied the funds for their initial forays into the Atlantic in search of new routes to African gold and Asian spices. European monarchs' growing reliance on professional armies, naval fleets, and gunpowder weapons also stimulated demand for banking services, forcing them to borrow money to meet the rising costs of war.

Italy became the primary producer of luxury goods for Europe, displacing the Islamic world and Asia. Before 1400, Islamic craftsmanship had far surpassed that of Latin Christendom. The upper classes of Europe paid handsome sums to obtain silk and linen fabrics, ceramics, rugs, glass, metalwork, and jewelry imported from the Mamluk Empire. "The most beautiful things in the world are found in Damascus," wrote Simone Sigoli, a Florentine who visited the city in 1386. "Such rich and noble and delicate works of every kind that if you had money in the bone of your leg, without fail you would break it to buy these things. . . . Really, all Christendom could be supplied for a year with the merchandise of Damascus."[9] But the Black Death, Timur's invasions, and Mamluk mismanagement devastated industry and commerce in Egypt and Syria. According to a census of workshops in Alexandria recorded in 1434, the number of looms operating in the city had fallen to eight hundred, compared with fourteen thousand in 1395.

Seizing the opportunity these developments created, Italian entrepreneurs first imitated and then improved on Islamic techniques and designs for making silk, tin-glazed ceramics known as *maiolica* (my-OH-lee-kah), glass, and brassware. By 1450 these Italian products had become competitive with or eclipsed imports from Egypt and Syria. Italian firms captured the major share of the international market for luxury textiles and other finished goods, and the Islamic lands were reduced to being suppliers of raw materials such as silk, cotton, and dyestuffs.

A Culture of Consumption   Along with Italy's ascent in finance and manufacturing came a decisive shift in attitudes toward money and its use. The older Christian ethics of frugality and disdain for worldly gain gave way to prodigal spending and consumption. This new inclination for acquisition and display cannot be attributed simply to the spread of secular humanism. Indeed, much of this torrent of spending was lavished on religious art and artifacts, and the Roman papacy stood out as perhaps the most spendthrift of all. Displaying personal wealth and possessions affirmed social status and power. Civic pride and political rivalry fueled public spending to build and decorate churches and cathedrals. Rich townsmen transformed private homes into palaces, and artisans fashioned ordinary articles of everyday life—from rugs and furniture to dishes, books, and candlesticks—into works of art. Public piety blurred together with personal vanity. Spending money on religious monuments, wrote the fifteenth-century Florentine merchant Giovanni Rucellai (ROO-chel-lie) in his diary, gave him "the greatest satisfaction and the greatest pleasure, because it serves the glory of God, the honor of Florence, and my own memory."[10]

"Magnificence" became the watchword of the Renaissance. Wealthy merchants and members of the clergy portrayed themselves as patrons of culture and learning. Their private townhouses became new settings for refined social intercourse and conspicuous display. Magnificence implied the liberal spending and accumulation of possessions that advertised a person's virtue, taste, and place in society. "The magnificence of a building," the architect Leon Battista Alberti (1404–1472) declared, "should be adapted to the dignity of its owner."[11] Worldly goods gave tangible expression to spiritual refinement. The paintings of Madonnas and saints that graced Renaissance mansions were much more than objects of devotion: they were statements of cultural and social values. Thus, as with Islam in West Africa, changes in commerce and culture were closely linked. New commercial wealth created an expanded market for art, which was in turn shaped by the values associated with commerce.

Again, as with Islam in West Africa, the intellectual ferment of the Renaissance was nurtured in an urban environment. Humanist scholars shunned the warrior culture of the old nobility while celebrating the civic roles and duties of townsmen, merchants, and clerics. Despite their admiration of classical civilization, the humanists did not reject Christianity. Rather, they sought to reconcile Christian faith and doctrines with classical learning. By making knowledge of Latin and Greek, history, poetry, and philosophy the mark of an educated person, the humanists transformed education and established models of schooling that would endure down to modern times.

Nowhere was the revolutionary impact of the Renaissance felt more deeply than in visual arts such as painting, sculpture, and architecture. Artists of the Renaissance exuded supreme confidence in the ability of human ingenuity to equal or even surpass the works of nature. The new outlook was exemplified by the development of the techniques of perspective, which artists used to convey a realistic, three-dimensional quality to physical forms, most notably the human body. Human invention also was capable of improving on nature by creating order and harmony through architecture and urban planning. Alberti advocated replacing the winding narrow streets and haphazard construction of medieval towns with planned cities organized around straight boulevards, open squares, and monumental buildings whose balanced proportions corresponded to a geometrically unified design.

Above all, the Renaissance transformed the idea of the artist. No longer mere manual tradesmen, artists now were seen as possessing a special kind of genius that enabled them to express a higher understanding of beauty. In the eyes of contemporaries, no one exemplified this quality of genius more than Leonardo da Vinci (1452–1519), who won renown as a painter, architect, sculptor, engineer, mathematician, and inventor. Leonardo's father, a Florentine lawyer, apprenticed him to a local painter at age eighteen. Leonardo spent much of his career as a civil and military engineer in the employ of the Duke of Milan, and developed ideas for flying machines, tanks, robots, and solar power that far exceeded the engineering capabilities of his time. Leonardo sought to apply his knowledge of natural science to painting, which he regarded as the most sublime art (see Seeing the Past: Leonardo da Vinci's *Virgin of the Rocks*).

The flowering of artistic creativity in the Renaissance was rooted in the rich soil of Italy's commercial wealth and nourished by the flow of goods from the Islamic world and Asia. International trade also invigorated industrial and craft production across maritime Asia and gave birth there to new patterns of material culture and consumption. In Japan, however, growing isolation from these cross-cultural interactions fostered the emergence of a national culture distinct from the Chinese traditions that dominated the rest of East Asia.

Cultural Innovations

COUNTERPOINT
Age of the Samurai in Japan 1185–1450

In Japan as in Europe, the term *Middle Ages* brings to mind an age of warriors, a stratified society governed by bonds of loyalty between lords and vassals. In Japan, however, the militarization of the ruling class intensified during the fourteenth and fifteenth centuries, a time when the warrior nobility of Europe was crumbling. Paradoxically, the rise of the **samurai** (sah-moo-rye) ("those who serve") warriors as masters of their own estates was accompanied by the increasing independence of peasant communities.

In contrast to the regions explored earlier in this chapter, Japan became more isolated from the wider world during this era. Commercial and cultural exchanges with China reached a peak in the thirteenth century, but after the failed Mongol invasion of Japan in 1281, ties with continental Asia became increasingly frayed. Thus, many Japanese see this era as the period in which Japan's unique national identity—expressed most distinctly in the ethic of *bushidō* (boo-shee-doe), the "Way of the Warrior"—took its definitive form. Samurai warriors became the

FOCUS

How and why did the historical development of Japan in the fourteenth and fifteenth centuries differ from that of mainland Eurasia?

samurai Literally, "those who serve"; the hereditary warriors who dominated Japanese society and culture from the twelfth to the nineteenth centuries.

Leonardo da Vinci's *Virgin of the Rocks*

Virgin of the Rocks, c. 1483–1486
(Erich Lessing/Art Resource.)

Leonardo's Botanical Studies with Star-of-Bethlehem, Grasses, Crowfoot, Wood Anemone, and Another Genus,
c. 1500–1506 (The Royal Collection © 2011 Her Majesty Queen Elizabeth II/Bridgeman Art Library.)

the menacing darkness of the cavern; desire to see if there was any marvelous thing within."[1]

Fantastic as the scene might seem, Leonardo's meticulous renderings of rocks and plants were based on close observation of nature. The Star of Bethlehem flowers at the lower left of the painting, symbolizing purity and atonement, also appear in the nearly contemporaneous botanical drawing shown here. Geologists have praised Leonardo's highly realistic sandstone rock formations and his precise placement of plants where they would most likely take root.

Masterpieces such as the *Virgin of the Rocks* display Leonardo's careful study of human anatomy, natural landscapes, and botany. Although he admired the perfection of nature, Leonardo also celebrated the human mind's rational and aesthetic capacities, declaring that "we by our arts may be called the grandsons of God."[2]

While living in Milan in the early 1480s, Leonardo accepted a commission to paint an altarpiece for the chapel of Milan's Confraternity of the Immaculate Conception, a branch of the Franciscan order. Leonardo's relationship with the friars proved to be stormy. His first version of the painting (now in the Louvre), reproduced here, apparently displeased his patrons and was sold to another party. Only after a fifteen-year-long dispute over the price did Leonardo finally deliver a modified version in 1508.

In portraying the legendary encounter between the child Jesus and the equally young John the Baptist during the flight to Egypt, Leonardo replaced the traditional desert setting with a landscape filled with rocks, plants, and water. Leonardo's dark grotto creates an aura of mystery and foreboding, from which the figures of Mary, Jesus, John, and the angel Uriel emerge as if in a vision. A few years before, Leonardo had written about "coming to the entrance of a great cavern, in front of which I stood for some time, stupefied and uncomprehending. . . . Suddenly two things arose in me, fear and desire: fear of

1. Arundel ms. (British Library), p. 115 recto, cited in Martin Kemp, *Leonardo da Vinci: The Marvelous Works of Nature and Man* (Oxford: Oxford University Press, 2006), 78.
2. John Paul Richter, ed., *The Notebooks of Leonardo da Vinci* (rpt. of 1883 ed.; New York: Dover, 1970), Book IX, 328 (para. 654).

EXAMINING THE EVIDENCE

1. How does Leonardo express the connection between John (at left) and Jesus through position, gesture, and their relationships with the figures of Mary and the angel Uriel?

2. The friars who commissioned the painting sought to celebrate the sanctity and purity of their patron, the Virgin Mary. Does this painting achieve that effect?

patrons of new forms of cultural expression whose character differed markedly from the Chinese traditions cherished by the old Japanese nobility. A culture based on warriors, rather than Confucian scholars, created a different path for the development of Japanese society.

"The Low Overturning the High"

During the Kamakura period (1185–1333), the power of the **shogun**, or military ruler, of eastern Japan was roughly in balance with that of the imperial court and nobility at Kyoto in the west. Warriors dominated both the shogun's capital at Kamakura (near modern Tokyo) and provincial governorships, but most of the land remained in the possession of the imperial family, the nobility, and religious institutions based in Kyoto. The shoguns appointed low-ranking samurai among their retainers to serve as military stewards on local estates, with responsibility for keeping the peace.

After the collapse of the Kamakura government in 1333, Japan was wracked by civil wars. In 1336 a new dynasty of shoguns, the Ashikaga (ah-shee-KAH-gah), came to power in Kyoto. Unlike the Kamakura shoguns, the Ashikaga aspired to become national rulers. Yet not until 1392 did the Ashikaga shogunate gain uncontested political supremacy, and even then it exercised only limited control over the provinces and local samurai.

Rise of the Samurai

In the Kamakura period, the samurai had been vassals subordinated to warrior clans to whom they owed allegiance and service. But wartime disorder and Ashikaga rule eroded the privileges and power of the noble and monastic landowners. Most of their estates fell into the hands of local samurai families, who formed alliances known as *ikki* ("single resolve") to preserve order. The *ikki* brotherhoods signed pacts pledging common arbitration of disputes, joint management of local shrines and festivals, and mutual aid against outside aggressors.

Just as samurai were turning themselves into landowners, peasants banded together in village associations to resist demands for rents and labor service from their new samurai overlords. These village associations began to assert a right to self-government, claiming legal powers formerly held by the noble estate owners.

Like the *ikki* leagues, villages and districts created their own autonomous governments. Their charters expressed resistance to outside control while requiring strict conformity to the collective will of the community. As one village council declared, "Treachery, malicious gossip, or criminal acts against the village association will be punished by excommunication from the estate."[12] Outraged lords bewailed this reversal of the social hierarchy, "the low overturning the high," but found themselves powerless to check the growing independence of peasant communities.

The political strength of the peasants reflected their rising economic fortunes. Japan's agrarian economy improved substantially with the expansion of irrigated rice farming. The village displaced the manorial estate as the basic institution of rural society. Rural traders, mostly drawn from the affluent peasantry, formed merchant guilds and obtained commercial privileges from local authorities. Japan in

Japan, 1185–1392

the fifteenth century had little involvement in foreign trade, and there were few cities apart from the metropolis of Kyoto, which had swelled to 150,000 inhabitants by mid-century. Yet the prosperity of the agrarian economy generated considerable growth in artisan crafts and trade in local goods.

The New Warrior Order

After the founding of the Ashikaga shogunate, provincial samurai swarmed the streets of Kyoto seeking the new rulers' patronage. Their reckless conduct prompted the shoguns to issue regulations forbidding samurai to possess silver swords, wear fine silk clothing, gamble, stage tea-drinking competitions, and consort with loose women—to little effect. In this world of "the low overturning the high," warriors enjoyed newfound wealth while much of the old nobility was reduced to abject poverty.

shogun The military commander who effectively exercised supreme political and military authority over Japan during the Kamakura (1185–1333), Ashikaga (1338–1573), and Tokugawa (1603–1868) shogunates.

Night Attack on the Sanjo Palace

The Heiji Revolt of 1159 marked a key turning point in the shift from aristocratic to warrior rule in Japan. This scene from a thirteenth-century scroll painting depicts the samurai rebels storming the imperial palace and taking the emperor hostage. Although the leaders of the insurrection were captured and executed, the revolt plunged Japan into civil wars that ended only when the Kamakura shogun seized power in 1185. (Werner Forman/Art Resource.)

Cultural and Social Life of the Samurai

While derided by courtiers as uneducated and boorish, the shoguns and samurai became patrons of artists and cultural life. The breakdown of the traditional social hierarchy allowed greater intermingling among people from diverse backgrounds. By the early fifteenth century the outlandish antics of the capital's samurai had been tempered by a new sense of elegance and refinement. The social and cultural worlds of the warriors and courtiers merged, producing new forms of social behavior and artistic expression.

In the early years of the Ashikaga shogunate, the capital remained infatuated with Chinese culture. As the fourteenth century wore on, however, this fascination with China was eclipsed by new fashions drawn from both the court nobility and Kyoto's lively world of popular entertainments. Accomplishment in poetry and graceful language and manners, hallmarks of the courtier class, became part of samurai self-identity as well. A new mood of simplicity and restraint took hold, infused with the ascetic ethics of Zen Buddhism, which stressed introspective meditation as the path to enlightenment.

The sensibility of the Ashikaga age was visible in new kinds of artistic display and performance, including poetry recitation, flower arrangement, and the complex rituals of the tea ceremony. A new style of theater known as *nō* reflected this fusion of courtly refinement, Zen religious sentiments, and samurai cultural tastes. The lyrical language and stylized dances of *nō* performances portrayed samurai as men of feeling rather than ferocious warriors. Thus, the rise of warrior culture in Japan did not mean an end to sophistication and refinement. It did, however, involve a strong focus on cultural elements that were seen as distinctly Japanese.

In at least one area, developments in Japan mirrored those in other parts of the world. The warriors' dominance over Ashikaga society and culture led to a decisive shift toward patriarchal authority. Women lost rights of inheritance as warrior houses consolidated landholdings in the hands of one son who would continue the family line. Marriage and sexual conduct were subject to stricter regulation. The libertine sexual mores of the Japanese aristocracy depicted in Lady Murasaki's *Tale of Genji* (c. 1010) gave way to a new emphasis on female chastity as an index of social order. The profuse output of novels, memoirs, and diaries written by court women also came to an end by 1350. Aristocratic women continued to hold positions of responsibility at court, but their literary talents were devoted to keeping official records rather than expressing their personal thoughts.

By 1400, then, the samurai had achieved political mastery in both the capital and the countryside and had eclipsed the old nobility as arbiters of cultural values. This warrior culture, which combined martial prowess with austere aesthetic tastes, stood in sharp contrast to the veneration of Confucian learning by the Chinese literati and the classical ideals and ostentatious consumption prized by the urban elite of Renaissance Italy.

Conclusion

The fourteenth century was an age of crisis across Eurasia and Africa. The population losses resulting from the Black Death devastated Christian and Muslim societies and economies. In the long run Latin Christendom fared well: the institution of serfdom largely disappeared from western Europe; new entrepreneurial energies were released; and the Italian city-states recovered their commercial vigor and stimulated economic revival in northern Europe. However, the once-great Byzantine Empire succumbed to the expanding Ottoman Empire and, under fire by Urban's cannon, came to an end in 1453. Although the Ottoman conquest of the Balkan peninsula threatened Latin Christendom, the central Islamic lands, from Egypt to Mesopotamia, never regained their former economic vitality. Still, the Muslim faith continued to spread, winning new converts in Africa, Central Asia, and Southeast Asia.

The fourteenth century also witnessed the collapse of the Mongol empires in China and Iran, followed by the rise and fall of the last of the Mongol empires, that of Timur. In China, the Ming dynasty spurned the Mongol vision of a multinational empire, instead returning to an imperial order based on an agrarian economy, bureaucratic rule, and Neo-Confucian values. New dynastic leaders in Korea and Vietnam imitated the Ming model, but in Japan the rising samurai warrior class forged a radically different set of social institutions and cultural values.

The Black Death redirected the course of European state-making. Monarchs strengthened their authority, aided by advances in military technology, mercenary armies, and fresh sources of revenue. The intensifying competition among national states would become one of the main motives for overseas exploration and expansion in the Atlantic world. At the same time, the great transformation in culture, lifestyles, and values known as the Renaissance sprang from the ruin of the Black Death. But the Renaissance was not purely an intellectual and artistic phenomenon. Its cultural innovations were linked to crucial changes in the Italian economy and the international trading world of the Mediterranean and beyond.

Asia was largely spared the ravages of the Black Death pandemic. Maritime Asia, from China to the east coast of Africa, enjoyed a robust boom in trade during the fifteenth century, in contrast to the sluggish economic recovery in much of Europe and the Islamic world. The intrusion of the Portuguese into the Indian Ocean in 1498 would upset the balance of political and economic power throughout Asian waters and dramatically alter Asia's place in what became the first truly global economy. But the arrival of the Europeans would have far more catastrophic effects on the societies of the Americas, which were unprepared for the political and economic challenges—and especially the onslaught of epidemic disease—that followed Columbus's landing in the Caribbean islands in 1492.

NOTES

1. Giovanni Boccaccio, *The Decameron* (New York: Modern Library, 1931), 8–9.
2. Quoted in Adel Allouche, *Mamluk Economics: A Study and Translation of Al-Maqrizi's* Ighathah (Salt Lake City: University of Utah Press, 1994), 75–76 (translation slightly modified).
3. Quoted in Michael W. Dols, "Ibn al-Wardi's *Risalah al-naba' 'an al'waba'*: A Translation of a Major Source for the History of the Black Death in the Middle East," in *Near Eastern Numismatics, Iconography, Epigraphy and History: Studies in Honor of George C. Miles*, ed. Dickran K. Kouymjian (Beirut, Lebanon: American University of Beirut, 1974), 454.
4. *Anonimalle Chronicle*, in *The Peasants' Revolt of 1381*, ed. R. B. Dobson (London: Macmillan, 1970), 164–165.
5. Ibn Battuta, "The Sultan of Mali," in *Corpus of Early Arabic Sources for West African History*, trans. J. F. P. Hopkins, ed. N. Levtzion and J. F. P. Hopkins (Cambridge, U.K.: Cambridge University Press, 1981), 296.
6. Leo Africanus, *History and Description of Africa*, trans. John Poy (London: Hakluyt Society, 1896), 3:825.
7. Shihab al-Din Ahmad ibn Majid, "Al'Mal'aqiya," in *A Study of the Arabic Texts Containing Material of South-East Asia*, ed. and trans. G. R. Tibbetts (Leiden, Netherlands: Brill, 1979), 206.

8. Ibn Battuta, *Travels in Asia and Africa, 1325–1354*, trans. H. A. R. Gibb (London: Routledge & Kegan Paul, 1929), 235.

9. Simone Sigoli, "Pilgrimage of Simone Sigoli to the Holy Land," in *Visit to the Holy Places of Egypt, Sinai, Palestine and Syria in 1384 by Frescobaldi, Gucci, and Sigoli*, trans. Theophilus Bellorini and Eugene Hoade (Jerusalem: Franciscan Press, 1948), 182.

10. Quoted in Lisa Jardine, *Worldly Goods: A New History of the Renaissance* (New York: Doubleday, 1996), 126.

11. Quoted in Richard A. Goldthwaite, *Wealth and the Demand for Art in Italy, 1300–1600* (Baltimore: Johns Hopkins University Press, 1993), 220.

12. Declaration of Oshima and Okitsushima shrine association, dated 1298, quoted in Pierre François Souyri, *The World Turned Upside Down: Medieval Japanese Society* (New York: Columbia University Press, 2001), 136.

RESOURCES FOR RESEARCH

Fourteenth-Century Crisis and Renewal in Eurasia

William McNeill's landmark work drew attention to the profound impact of epidemic diseases on world history. The exact cause of the Black Death remains a subject of debate, as the works of Cantor and Herlihy show, but few dispute that the pandemic had lasting consequences for European history. The influence of the Black Death in the Islamic world is less well studied, but Borsch's recent study seeks to explain why the economic depression it caused lasted longer in Egypt than in Europe.

Borsch, Stuart J. *The Black Death in Egypt and England: A Comparative Study.* 2005.

British History in Depth: The Black Death. http://www.bbc.co.uk/history/british/middle_ages/black_01.shtml

Brook, Timothy. *The Confusions of Pleasure: Commerce and Culture in Ming China.* 1998.

Cantor, Norman. *In the Wake of the Plague: The Black Death and the World It Made.* 2001.

Herlihy, David. *The Black Death and the Transformation of the West.* 1997.

McNeill, William H. *Plagues and Peoples.* 1976.

Islam's New Frontiers

The study of Islam in Africa has advanced rapidly in recent years. Robinson serves as a good overview; the essays in Levtzion and Pouwells provide comprehensive regional coverage. Imber provides the best introduction to the early history of the Ottoman Empire.

Dunn, Ross E. *The Adventures of Ibn Battuta: A Muslim Traveler of the 14th Century.* 1989.

Imber, Colin. *The Ottoman Empire, 1300–1650: The Structure of Power,* 2d ed. 2009.

Levtzion, Nehemia, and Randall L. Pouwells, eds. *The History of Islam in Africa.* 2000.

Manz, Beatrice Forbes. *The Rise and Rule of Tamerlane.* 1989.

Robinson, David. *Muslim Societies in African History.* 2004.

The Global Bazaar

New scholarship has erased the older image of this period as "the Dark Ages." The original understanding of the Renaissance as an intellectual and artistic movement centered in Italy has been broadened to include transformative changes in trade, industry, material culture, and lifestyles. Similarly, accounts of voyages of Zheng He—lucidly described by Levathes—have opened a window on the vigorous cultural and economic interchange across Asia; Reid examines this topic in greater detail.

Burke, Peter. *The European Renaissance: Centres and Peripheries.* 1998.

Finlay, Robert. *The Pilgrim Art: Cultures of Porcelain in World History.* 2010.

Goldthwaite, Richard A. *Wealth and the Demand for Art in Italy, 1300–1600.* 1993.

Jardine, Lisa. *Worldly Goods: A New History of the Renaissance.* 1996.

Levathes, Louise. *When China Ruled the Seas: The Treasure Fleet of the Dragon Throne, 1405–1433.* 1994.

Reid, Anthony. *Southeast Asia in the Age of Commerce, 1350–1750.* Vol. 1, *The Land Below the Winds;* Vol. 2, *Expansion and Crisis.* 1989, 1993.

COUNTERPOINT: Age of the Samurai in Japan, 1185–1450

Recent years have seen a wave of revisionist scholarship on medieval Japan. Souyri's work stands out for its finely detailed depiction of social diversity. *Tale of the Heike,* an account of the struggle between warlords that led to the founding of the Kamakura shogunate, provides a sharp contrast to earlier courtly literature such as Lady Murasaki's *Tale of Genji.*

Adolphson, Mikael S. *The Gates of Power: Monks, Courtiers, and Warriors in Premodern Japan.* 2000.

Mass, Jeffrey P., ed. *The Origins of Japan's Medieval World: Courtiers, Clerics, Warriors, and Peasants in the Fourteenth Century.* 1997.

McCullough, Helen Craig, trans. *Tale of the Heike.* 1988.

Souyri, Pierre-François. *The World Turned Upside Down: Medieval Japanese Society.* 2001.

Wakita, Haruko. *Women in Medieval Japan: Motherhood, Household Economy, and Sexuality.* 2006.

▶ **For additional primary sources from this period**, see *Sources of Crossroads and Cultures.*

▶ **For Web sites, images, and documents related to topics in this chapter**, see Make History at bedfordstmartins.com/smith.

REVIEW

The major global development in this chapter ▶ Crisis and recovery
in fourteenth- and fifteenth-century Afro-Eurasia.

IMPORTANT EVENTS

1315–1317	Great Famine in northern Europe
1325–1354	Travels of Ibn Battuta in Asia and Africa
1336–1573	Ashikaga shogunate in Japan
1337–1453	Hundred Years' War between England and France
1347–1350	Outbreak of the Black Death in Europe and the Islamic Mediterranean
c. 1351–1782	Ayudhya kingdom in Thailand
1368–1644	Ming dynasty in China
1378	Ciompi uprising in Florence
1381	Peasant Revolt in England
1392–1910	Yi dynasty in Korea
1405	Death of Timur; breakup of his empire into regional states in Iran and Central Asia
1405–1433	Chinese admiral Zheng He's expeditions in Southeast Asia and the Indian Ocean
1421	Relocation of Ming capital from Nanjing to Beijing
1428–1788	Le dynasty in Vietnam
1453	Ottoman conquest of Constantinople marks fall of the Byzantine Empire

KEY TERMS

Black Death (p. 478)	**pandemic** (p. 478)
humanism (p. 498)	**Renaissance** (p. 498)
janissary corps (p. 489)	**samurai** (p. 501)
Little Ice Age (p. 479)	**shogun** (p. 503)
Neo-Confucianism (p. 486)	**Sufism** (p. 488)
	theocracy (p. 489)
oligarchy (p. 483)	**trade diaspora** (p. 492)

CHAPTER OVERVIEW QUESTIONS

1. How and why did Europe's economic growth begin to surpass that of the Islamic world in the century after the Black Death?

2. Did the economic revival across Eurasia after 1350 benefit the peasant populations of Europe, the Islamic world, and East Asia?

3. How did the process of conversion to Islam differ in Iran, the Ottoman Empire, West Africa, and Southeast Asia during this period?

4. What political and economic changes contributed to the rise of maritime commerce in Asia during the fourteenth and fifteenth centuries?

SECTION FOCUS QUESTIONS

1. How did the Black Death affect society, the economy, and culture in Latin Christendom and the Islamic world?

2. Why did Islam expand dramatically in the fourteenth and fifteenth centuries, and how did new Islamic societies differ from established ones?

3. What were the principal sources of growth in international trade during the fourteenth and fifteenth centuries, and how did this trade affect patterns of consumption and fashion tastes?

4. How and why did the historical development of Japan in the fourteenth and fifteenth centuries differ from that of mainland Eurasia?

MAKING CONNECTIONS

1. What social, economic, and technological changes strengthened the power of European monarchs during the century after the Black Death?

2. How and why did the major routes and commodities of trans-Eurasian trade change after the collapse of the Mongol empires in Central Asia?

3. In what ways did the motives for conversion to Islam differ in Central Asia, sub-Saharan Africa, and the Indian Ocean during this era?

4. In this period, why did the power and status of the samurai warriors in Japan rise while those of the warrior nobility in Europe declined?

PART 3

The Early Modern World
1450–1750

MAJOR GLOBAL CHANGES occurred between 1450 and 1750, as regional societies gave way to multiethnic empires, and horse-borne raiders gave way to cannon and long-distance sailing craft. Historians call this era "early modern" because it was marked by a general shift toward centralized, bureaucratic, monetized, and technologically sophisticated states. Yet nearly all of these "modern" states also clung to divine kingship and other remnants of the previous age, and most sought to revive and propagate older religious or philosophical traditions. Some states embraced mutual tolerance, but many others fought bitterly over matters of faith.

One of the most striking breaks with the past was the creation of new linkages between distant regions, most notably the Americas and the rest of the world. Early globalization accelerated changes in everything from demography to commerce to technology, allowing populations to grow and many individuals to get rich. Yet globalization also enabled the spread of disease, and some technical innovations increased the scale and deadliness of warfare; early modernity did not promise longer and better lives for everyone. The shift to modernity was not a uniquely Western phenomenon either, although western Europeans were key players in its spread, usually as traders, missionaries, or conquerors.

Beginning in around 1450, Iberians—the people of Spain and Portugal—used new ships and guns to venture into the Atlantic, where they competed in overseas colonization, trade, and conquest. They set out to claim new territories for their monarchs and to spread their Roman Catholic faith. They did both at the expense of many millions of native peoples, first in Africa and the East Atlantic and then throughout the Americas and beyond. Wherever they went, Iberians moved quickly from plunder to the creation of settled colonies, creating a new trading sphere that historians call the "Atlantic world." Other Europeans soon followed in the Iberians' wake, but the silver of Spanish America became the world's money.

Modernity affected Africa most deeply via the slave trade. The older flow of captive workers to the Muslim Middle East and Indian Ocean basin continued well into early modern times, but it was soon overshadowed by a more urgent European demand in the Atlantic. This desire for slaves to staff distant plantations and mines fueled

CHAPTERS IN THIS PART ▼

16 Empires and Alternatives in the Americas, 1430–1530

17 The Fall of Native American Empires and the Rise of an Atlantic World, 1450–1600

18 Western Africa in the Era of the Atlantic Slave Trade, c. 1450–1800

19 Trade and Empire in the Indian Ocean and South Asia, 1450–1750

20 Consolidation and Conflict in Europe and the Greater Mediterranean, 1450–1750

21 Expansion and Isolation in Asia, 1450–1750

22 Transforming New Worlds: The American Colonies Mature, 1600–1750

CH 18

existing antagonisms within Africa even as it spawned new ones, each generating captives and refugees to be traded abroad for select commodities, including firearms, textiles, and metal ware. Europeans did not penetrate, much less conquer, sub-Saharan Africa at this time, however, in part due to their general lack of resistance to tropical disease.

In the vast Indian Ocean basin a freer model of interaction and integration developed. Islamic merchants had come to dominate these seas by 1450, not through imperial means but rather by establishing trading networks from East Africa to Southeast Asia. Luxury products from the African interior were traded abroad for spices, cloth, porcelain, and other compact valuables. Ships also carried bulk commodities and religious pilgrims. After 1500, European interlopers discovered that in such a thriving, diverse, and politically decentralized region, they would have to compete fiercely for space. This they did, first by establishing coastal trading forts, then by moving inland.

On the Eurasian mainland, with the aid of modern firearms, powerful Ottoman, Russian, Safavid, and Mughal leaders turned from regional consolidation to massive imperial expansion by the sixteenth century. Each combined religious fervor with considerable political ambitions, but several of these states, notably the Ottomans and Mughals, embraced religious diversity. Collecting tributes in cash and establishing the appropriate bureaucracies to collect them were shared objectives. Unlike the Safavids and Mughals, the Ottomans sought to extend their empire overseas, taking on Venice and the Habsburgs in the Mediterranean and the Portuguese in the Indian Ocean. Russia would venture abroad under Peter the Great.

Europe remained mostly embroiled in religious and political conflict. The religious schism known as the Protestant Reformation touched off over a century of bloody war after 1500, and doctrinal disputes would carry on well into modern times. Warfare itself was transformed from knightly contests and town sieges to mass infantry mobilization and bombardment of strategic fortresses. These models would be exported, along with armed sailing ships. Europe's political fractures enabled the rise of market economies as well, with more states sponsoring overseas colonizing ventures

CH 19

CH 20

over time to augment their share of business. New forms of government emerged, and also a marked tendency to question ancient authorities. From this came a revolution in science, emphasizing physical observation and secular reasoning, and at the end of the early modern period, a new intellectual movement known as the Enlightenment.

In East Asia, by contrast, introversion rather than foreign engagement was the rule in early modern times. Although both China and Japan had strong seafaring traditions by 1450, state policies from the fifteenth to sixteenth centuries gradually discouraged external affairs. Despite official isolation, both regions proved to be extraordinarily dynamic. Political consolidation and population growth were matched with a general shift from tributary to money economies. In the Chinese Ming and Qing empires this led to a massive rise in demand for silver, stimulating global circulation of this mostly American-produced metal. Porcelain and silk, much of it produced by poor women working in the household, were sent abroad in exchange. With the patronage of newly wealthy merchants and bureaucrats, the arts flourished on a scale not seen before.

By 1700, the American colonies were not the neo-Europes their first colonizers had envisioned. Centuries of ethnic and cultural mixture, forced labor regimes, frontier expansion, and export-oriented economies all led to the formation of distinct societies. Native populations were recovering in some areas, and African and African-descended populations had grown to dominate whole regions. Europeans continued to migrate to the colonies in search of new livelihoods, but most soon adopted the nativist attitudes of earlier colonizers. In much of the Americas, the different outlooks of European colonizers and colonists would prove irreconcilable by the end of the early modern era.

CH 21 →

	1400		1500	
Americas	1325–1521 Aztec Empire	1430–1532 Inca Empire · Columbus reaches the Americas 1492 · · Portuguese reach Brazil 1500	Spanish conquest of Aztecs 1519–1521 · Spanish conquest of Inca 1532–1536	Discovery of silver at Potosí 1545 ·
Europe		1462–1505 Ivan III unites Russia · Christian reconquest of Spain completed 1492 · 1473–1543 Copernicus	· 1517 Luther confronts Catholic Church, sparking the Protestant Reformation	
Middle East		· 1453 Ottoman conquest of Constantinople	Ottoman conquest of Egypt 1517 · 1520–1566 Reign of Suleiman the Magnificent	Battle of Lepanto 1571
Africa	First sub-Saharan Africans captured and taken to Portugal 1441 ·	· 1450 Height of kingdom of Benin · 1464–1492 Reign of Songhai emperor Sunni Ali	1506–1543 Reign of Afonso I of Kongo	
Asia and Oceania	1405–1433 Voyages of Ming admiral Zheng He · 1421 Relocation of Ming capital to Beijing 1428–1788 Vietnamese Le dynasty		· 1498 Vasco da Gama reaches India Portuguese establish fort in Ceylon 1517 ·	

Despite these profound transformations, many people remained largely unaffected by the currents of early modernity. Though not densely populated, most of North and South America, Polynesia, Oceania, central and southern Africa, and highland Asia remained beyond the zone of sustained contact with foreigners. New commodities and biological transfers were only beginning to be felt in many of these places at the end of the early modern period. As a result of their long isolation, inhabitants of these regions would be among the most drastically affected by modernity's next wave.

CH 22

1600	1700	1800

- **1625** Dutch settle New Amsterdam; English establish colony on Barbados
- **1763** Rio de Janeiro becomes capital of Brazil
- **1607** English establish colony at Jamestown, Virginia
- **1695–1800** Brazil's "gold rush"
- **1608** French establish colony at Quebec City

- **1588** English defeat Spanish Armada
- **1618–1648** Thirty Years' War
- **1712–1714** War of the Spanish Succession
- **1643–1715** Reign of Louis XIV
- **1712** Peter the Great founds St. Petersburg
- **1600** English East India Company founded
- **1642–1727** Newton
- **1688** England's Glorious Revolution
- **1700–1800** The Enlightenment

- Last Ottoman siege at Vienna defeated **1683**
- **1736–1747** Nadir Shah reunites Iran
- **1600–1629** Peak of Safavid Empire
- **1722** Fall of Safavid Empire

- **1591** Moroccan raiders conquer Songhai Empire
- **1680s** Rise of kingdom of Asante
- **1750–1800** Height of Atlantic slave trade
- **1624–1663** Reign of Queen Nzinga in Ndongo
- **1638–1641** Dutch seize São Jorge da Mina and Luanda
- **1720s** Rise of kingdom of Dahomey

- **1602–1867** Tokugawa Shogunate
- **1736–1799** Reign of Qing emperor Qianlong
- **1644** Manchu invasion of Beijing; Ming Empire replaced by Qing
- **1751** Qing annexation of Tibet
- **1500–1763** Mughal Empire

AT A CROSSROADS ▲

Perched on a granite ridge high above Peru's Urubamba River, the Inca site of Machu Picchu continues to draw thousands of visitors each year. First thought to be the lost city of Vilcabamba, then a convent for Inca nuns, Machu Picchu is now believed to have been a mid-fifteenth-century palace built for the Inca emperor and his mummy cult. It was probably more a religious site than a place of rest and recreation. (The Art Archive/Gianni Dagli Orti.)

Empires and Alternatives in the Americas

1430–1530

Many Native Americas

FOCUS What factors account for the diversity of native American cultures?

Tributes of Blood: The Aztec Empire, 1325–1521

FOCUS What core features characterized Aztec life and rule?

Tributes of Sweat: The Inca Empire, 1430–1532

FOCUS What core features characterized Inca life and rule?

COUNTERPOINT: The Peoples of North America's Eastern Woodlands, 1450–1530

FOCUS How did the Eastern Woodlanders' experience differ from life under the Aztecs and Incas?

In 1995, American archaeologist Johan Reinhard and his assistants discovered a tomb atop Mount Ampato, a peak overlooking the Peruvian city of Arequipa. Inside were the naturally mummified remains of a fourteen-year-old girl placed there some five hundred years earlier. Material and written evidence suggests she was an *aclla* (AHK-yah), or "chosen woman," selected by Inca priests from among hundreds of regional headmen's daughters. Most aclla girls became priestesses in temples and palaces dedicated to the Inca emperor or the imperial sun cult. Others became the emperor's concubines or wives. Only the most select, like the girl discovered on Mount Ampato, were chosen for the "debt-payment" sacrifice, or *capacocha* (kah-pah-KOH-chah), said to be the greatest honor of all.

According to testimonies collected soon after the Spanish conquest of the Incas in 1532 (discussed in the next chapter), the capacocha sacrifice was a rare and deeply significant event preceded by numerous rituals. First, the victim, chosen for her (and rarely, his) physical perfection, trekked to Cuzco, the Inca capital, to be feasted and blessed. The child's father brought gifts and sacred objects from his province and in turn received fine textiles from the emperor. Following an ancient Andean tradition, reciprocal ties between ruler and ruled were reinforced through such acts of ritualized gift exchange, feasting, and finally, sacrifice. The girl, too, received fine alpaca and cotton skirts and shawls, along with tiny gold and silver votive objects, a necklace of shell beads, and tufts of tropical bird feathers. These items adorned her in her tomb, reached after a long journey on foot from Cuzco.

As suggested by later discoveries in Chile and Argentina, at tomb-side the aclla girl was probably given a beaker filled with beer brewed from maize. In a pouch she carried coca leaves. The sacred coca, chewed throughout the Andes, helped fend off the headaches

BACKSTORY

By the fifteenth century, the Americas had witnessed the rise and fall of numerous empires and kingdoms, including the classic Maya of Mesoamerica, the wealthy Sicán kingdom of Peru's desert coast, and the Cahokia mound builders of the Mississippi Basin. Just as these cultures faded, there emerged two new imperial states that borrowed heavily from their predecessors. The empires treated in this chapter, the Aztec and Inca, were the largest states ever to develop in the Americas, yet they were not all-powerful. About half of all native Americans, among them the diverse peoples of North America's eastern woodlands, lived outside their realms.

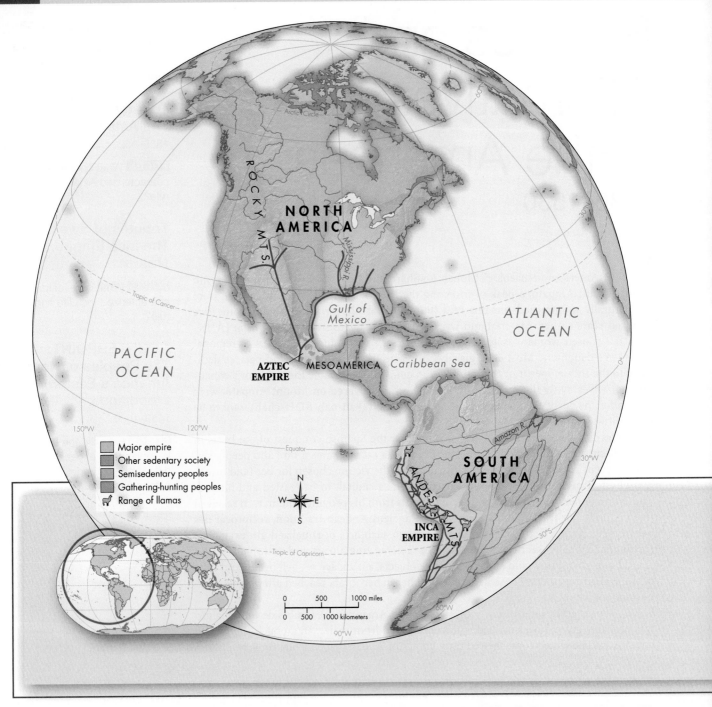

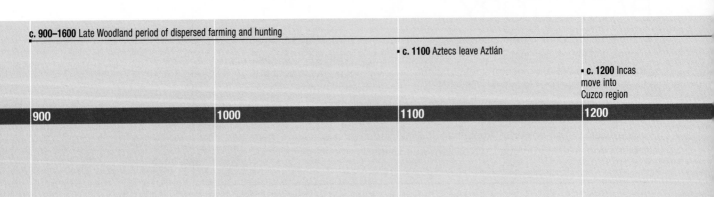

c. 900–1600 Late Woodland period of dispersed farming and hunting

▪ **c. 1100** Aztecs leave Aztlán

▪ **c. 1200** Incas move into Cuzco region

900   **1000**   **1100**   **1200**

and nausea brought on by oxygen starvation at high altitude, whereas the maize beer induced sleepiness. Barely conscious of her surroundings, the girl was lowered into her grass-lined grave, and, according to the forensic anthropologists who examined her skull, struck dead with a club. Other Inca sacrificial victims appear to have been buried alive and left to freeze to death, as described in postconquest accounts.

Why did the Incas sacrifice children, and why in these ways? By combining material, written, and oral evidence, scholars are beginning to solve the riddle of the Inca mountain mummies. From what is now known, it appears that death, fertility, reciprocity, and imperial links to sacred landscapes were all features of the capacocha sacrifice. Although macabre practices such as this may challenge our ability to empathize with the leaders, if not the common folk, of this distant culture, with each new fact we learn about the child mummies, the closer we get to understanding the Inca Empire and its ruling cosmology.

The Incas and their subjects shared the belief that death occurred as a process rather than in an instant, and that proper death led to an elevated state of consciousness. In this altered state a person could communicate with deities directly, and in a sense join them. If the remains of such a person were carefully preserved and honored, they could act as an oracle, a conduit to the sacred realms above and below the earth. Mountains, as sources of springs and rivers, and sometimes fertilizing volcanic ash, held particular spiritual significance.

In part, it was this complex of beliefs about landscape, death, and the afterlife that led the Incas to mummify and otherwise preserve respected ancestors, including their emperors, and to bury chosen young people atop mountains that marked the edges, or heights, of empire. Physically perfect noble children such as the girl found on Mount Ampato were thus selected for the role of communicants with the spirit world. Their sacrifice unified the dead, the living, and the sacred mountains, and also bound together a far-flung empire that was in many ways as fragile as life itself.[1]

MAPPING THE WORLD

The Western Hemisphere, c. 1500

Native Americans inhabited the entire Western Hemisphere from the Arctic Circle to the tip of South America. Their societies varied tremendously in density and political sophistication, largely as a result of adaptation to different natural environments. Empires were found only in the tropical highlands of Mesoamerica and the Andes, but large chiefdoms based on farming could be found in eastern Canada, the bigger Caribbean islands, and the lower Amazon Basin. Gatherer-hunters were the most widespread of all native American cultures, and despite their relatively small numbers they proved most resistant to conquest by settled neighbors.

ROUTES ▼

— Inca road
— Other trade route

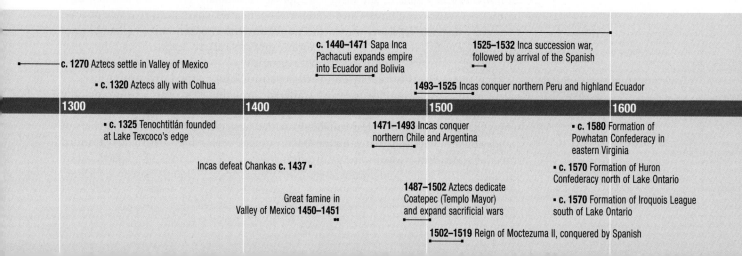

c. **1270** Aztecs settle in Valley of Mexico

• c. **1320** Aztecs ally with Colhua

c. **1440–1471** Sapa Inca Pachacuti expands empire into Ecuador and Bolivia

1525–1532 Inca succession war, followed by arrival of the Spanish

1493–1525 Incas conquer northern Peru and highland Ecuador

1300   1400   1500   1600

• c. **1325** Tenochtitlán founded at Lake Texcoco's edge

1471–1493 Incas conquer northern Chile and Argentina

• c. **1580** Formation of Powhatan Confederacy in eastern Virginia

Incas defeat Chankas c. **1437** •

• c. **1570** Formation of Huron Confederacy north of Lake Ontario

Great famine in Valley of Mexico **1450–1451**

1487–1502 Aztecs dedicate Coatepec (Templo Mayor) and expand sacrificial wars

• c. **1570** Formation of Iroquois League south of Lake Ontario

1502–1519 Reign of Moctezuma II, conquered by Spanish

But this fragility was not evident to the people gathered at the capacocha sacrifice. By about 1480, more than half of all native Americans were subjects of two great empires, the Aztec in Mexico and Central America and the Inca in South America. In part by drawing on ancient religious and political traditions, both empires excelled at subduing neighboring chiefdoms through a mix of violence, forced relocation, religious indoctrination, and marriage alliances. Both empires demanded allegiance in the form of tribute. Both the Aztecs and Incas were greatly feared by their many millions of subjects. Perhaps surprisingly, these last great native American states would prove far more vulnerable to European invaders than their nonimperial neighbors, most of whom were gatherer-hunters and semisedentary villagers. Those who relied least on farming had the best chance of getting away.

OVERVIEW
QUESTIONS

The major global development in this chapter: The diversity of societies and states in the Americas prior to European invasion.

As you read, consider:

1. In what ways was cultural diversity in the Americas related to environmental diversity?

2. Why was it in Mesoamerica and the Andes that large empires emerged in around 1450?

3. What key ideas or practices extended beyond the limits of the great empires?

Many Native Americas

FOCUS

What factors account for the diversity of native American cultures?

Population Density

Environmental and Cultural Diversity

Scholars once claimed that the Western Hemisphere was sparsely settled prior to the arrival of Europeans in 1492, but we now know that by the end of the fifteenth century the overall population of the Americas had reached some 60 million or more. Vast open spaces remained, but in places the landscape was more intensively cultivated and thickly populated than western Europe (see Map 16.1). Fewer records for nonimperial groups survive than for empire builders such as the Incas and Aztecs, but by combining archaeological, artistic, anthropological, linguistic, and historical approaches, scholars have shed much new light on these less-studied cultures. Outside imperial boundaries, coastal and riverside populations were densest. This was true in the Caribbean, the Amazon and Mississippi river basins, the Pacific Northwest, parts of North America's eastern seaboard, and the upper Río de la Plata district of southeastern South America.

Ecological diversity gave rise in part to political and cultural diversity. America's native peoples, or Amerindians, lived scattered throughout two vast and ecologically diverse continents. They also inhabited a variety of tropical, temperate, and icy environments that proved more or less suitable to settled agriculture. Some were members of wandering, egalitarian gatherer-hunter bands; others were subjects of rigidly stratified imperial states. In between were many alternatives: traveling bands of pilgrims led by prophets, as in Brazil and southeastern North America; chiefdoms based on fishing,

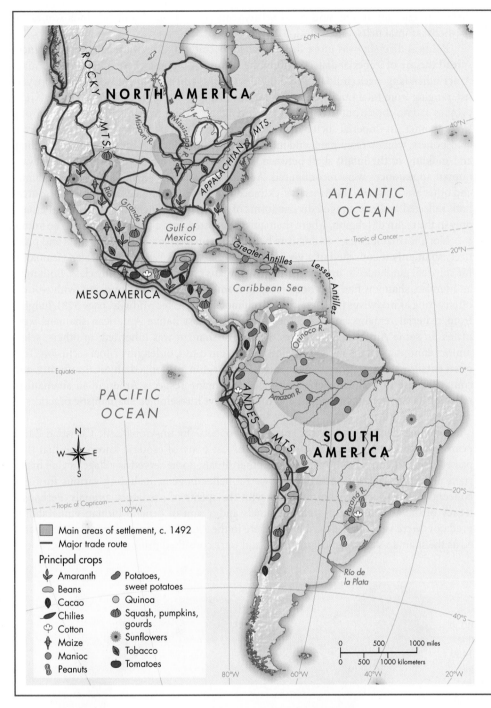

MAP 16.1

**Main Settlement Areas
in the Americas, c. 1492**

Most native Americans settled in regions that supported intensive agriculture. In Mesoamerica and greater North America, maize, beans, and squash were key crops. Andean peoples also grew these crops, but they relied more on potatoes and related tubers, supplemented by quinoa. People throughout the tropical Americas grew cotton, and tobacco was even more widespread. The trade routes shown here linked peoples from very different cultures, mostly to exchange rare items such as shells, precious stones, gold dust, and bird feathers, but seeds for new crops also followed these paths.

whaling, or farming, as in the Pacific Northwest and Greater Antilles; large confederacies of chiefdoms as in highland Colombia and northeastern North America; commercially vibrant and independent city-states as in the Maya heartland of Central America. Others, such as the peoples of coastal Ecuador and the Lesser Antilles, had mastered the sea, routinely ferrying goods and ideas from one continent to the other, and throughout the Caribbean islands. Gold working and maize farming were among the many technologies that traversed American waters. Long-distance overland traders were equally important, carrying copper and tropical feathers from Central America to North America's desert Southwest in exchange for turquoise or, in South America, trekking between distant jungle, mountain, and coast settlements to trade gold and precious stones for seashells, animal pelts, and salt.

Political diversity was more than matched by cultural diversity. The Aztecs and Incas spread the use of imperial dialects within their empires, but elsewhere hundreds of distinct Amerindian languages could be heard. Modes of dress and adornment were even more varied, ranging from total nudity and a few tattoos to highly elaborate ceremonial dress. Arctic peoples had no choice but to bundle up, yet even their style choices distinguished one group from another. In imperial societies strict rules of dress and decorum separated elites from commoners, women from men, and juniors from seniors. Lip and ear piercing, tooth filing, and molding of the infant skull between slats of wood were but a few of the many ways human appearances were reconfigured. Architecture was just as varied, as were ceramics and other arts. In short, the Americas' extraordinary range of climates and natural resources both reflected and encouraged diverse forms of material and linguistic expression. Perhaps only in the realm of religion, where shamanism persisted, was a unifying thread to be found.

Shamanism

Not a formal ideology or doctrine but rather a broadly similar set of beliefs and practices, **shamanism** consisted of a given tribe's or chiefdom's reliance on healer-visionaries for spiritual guidance. In imperial societies shamans constituted a priestly class. Both male and female, shamans had functions ranging from fortuneteller to physician, with women often acting as midwives (see Lives and Livelihoods: The Aztec Midwife, page 528). Judging from material remains and eyewitness accounts, most native American shamans were males. In some Amerindian cultures the role of shaman was inherited; in others, select juniors announced their vocation following a vision quest, or lengthy ritual seclusion. This often entailed a solo journey to a forest or desert region, prolonged physical suffering, and controlled use of hallucinogenic substances. In many respects Amerindian shamanism reflected its Central Asian origins, and in other ways it resembled shamanistic practices in sub-Saharan Africa.

Often labeled "witch-doctors" or "false prophets" by unsympathetic Christian Europeans, shamans maintained and developed a vast body of esoteric knowledge that they passed along to juniors in initiations and other rituals. Some served as village or clan historians and myth-keepers. Most used powerful hallucinogens, including various forms of concentrated tobacco, to communicate with the spirits of predatory animals. Perhaps a legacy of the ancient era of great mammals and a sign of general human vulnerability, predators were venerated almost everywhere in the Americas. Animal spirits were regarded as the shaman's alter ego or protector, and were consulted prior to important occasions

Canadian War Club

This stone war club with a fish motif was excavated from a native American tomb in coastal British Columbia, Canada, and is thought to date from around 1200 to 1400 C.E. Such items at first suggest a people at war, but this club was probably intended only for ceremonial use. Other clubs from the same tomb share its overt sexual symbolism. Modern Tsimshian inhabitants of the region, who still rely on salmon, describe the exchange of stone clubs in their foundation myths. (National Museum of the American Indian, Smithsonian Institution. Catalog number: 5/5059. Photo by Katherine Fogden.)

shamanism Widespread system of religious belief and healing originating in Central Asia.

such as royal marriages, births, and declarations of war. Shamans also mastered herbal remedies for virtually all forms of illness, including emotional disorders. These rubs, washes, and infusions were sometimes highly effective, as shown by modern pharmacological studies. Shamans nearly always administered them along with complex chants and rituals aimed at expelling evil spirits. Shamans, therefore, combined the roles of physician and religious leader, using their knowledge and power to heal both body and spirit.

The many varieties of social organization and cultural practice found in the early modern Americas reflect both creative interactions with specific environments and the visions of individual political and religious leaders. Some Amerindian gatherer-hunters lived in swamplands and desert areas where subsistence agriculture was impossible using available technologies. Often such gathering-hunting peoples traded with—or plundered—their farming neighbors. Yet even farming peoples, as their ceramic and textile decorations attest, did not forget their past as hunters. As in other parts of the world, big-game hunting in the early modern Americas was an esteemed, even sacred activity among urban elites, marked by elaborate taboos and rituals.

Just as hunting remained important to farmers, agriculture could be found among some of the Americas' least politically complex societies, again characterized by elaborate rituals and taboos. According to many early modern observers, women controlled most agricultural tasks and spaces, periodically making offerings and singing to spirits associated with human fertility. Staple foods included maize, potatoes, and manioc, a lowland tropical tuber that could be ground into flour and preserved. Agricultural rituals were central in most cultures, and at the heart of every imperial state. With the ebb and flow of empires, many groups shifted from one mode of subsistence to another, from planting to gathering-hunting and back again. Some, such as the Kwakiutl (KWAH-kyu-til) of the Pacific Northwest, were surrounded by such abundant marine and forest resources that they never turned to farming. Natural abundance combined with sophisticated fishing and storage systems allowed the Kwakiutl to build a settled culture of the type normally associated with agricultural peoples. Thus, the ecological diversity of the Americas helped give rise to an equally diverse array of native American cultures, many of which blurred the line between settled and nomadic lifestyles.

Range of Livelihoods

Kwakiutl Culture Area, c. 1500

Tributes of Blood: The Aztec Empire 1325–1521

Mesoamerica, comprised of modern southern Mexico, Guatemala, Belize, El Salvador, and western Honduras, was a land of city-states after about 800 C.E. Following the decline of ancient cultural forebears such as Teotihuacán (tay-oh-tee-wah-KAHN) in the Mexican highlands and the classic Maya in the greater Guatemalan lowlands, few urban powers, with the possible exception of the Toltecs, managed to dominate more than a few neighbors at a time.

FOCUS

What core features characterized Aztec life and rule?

This would change with the arrival in the Valley of Mexico of a band of former gatherer-hunters from a mysterious northwestern desert region they called Aztlán (ost-LAWN), or "place of cranes." As newcomers these "Aztecs," who later called themselves Mexica (meh-SHE-cah, hence "Mexico"), would suffer a number of humiliations at the hands of powerful city-dwellers centered on Lake Texcoco, now overlain by Mexico City. The Aztecs were at first regarded as coarse barbarians, but as with many conquering outsiders, in time they would have their revenge (see Map 16.2).

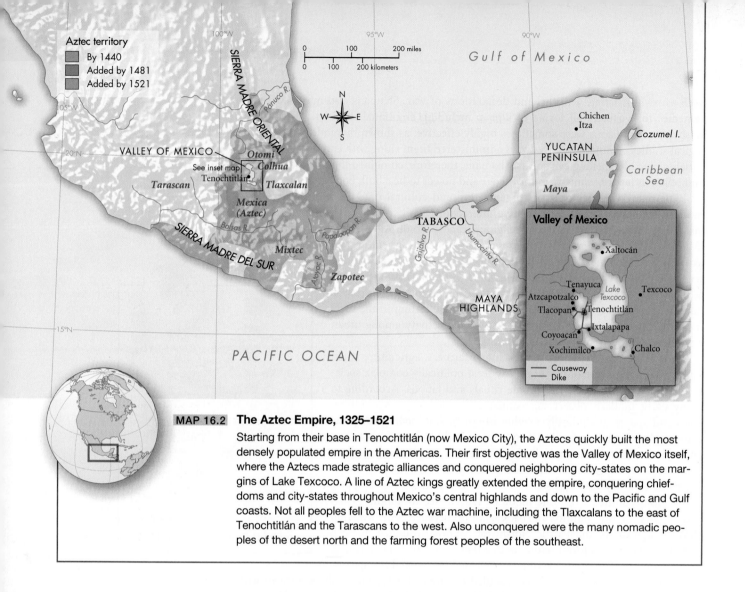

MAP 16.2 **The Aztec Empire, 1325–1521**

Starting from their base in Tenochtitlán (now Mexico City), the Aztecs quickly built the most densely populated empire in the Americas. Their first objective was the Valley of Mexico itself, where the Aztecs made strategic alliances and conquered neighboring city-states on the margins of Lake Texcoco. A line of Aztec kings greatly extended the empire, conquering chiefdoms and city-states throughout Mexico's central highlands and down to the Pacific and Gulf coasts. Not all peoples fell to the Aztec war machine, including the Tlaxcalans to the east of Tenochtitlán and the Tarascans to the west. Also unconquered were the many nomadic peoples of the desert north and the farming forest peoples of the southeast.

Humble Origins, Imperial Ambitions

Unlike the classic Maya of preceding centuries, the Aztecs did not develop a phonetic writing system. They did, however, preserve key aspects of their history in a mix of oral and symbolic, usually painted or carved, forms. Aztec elders developed and maintained a series of chronicles of the kind historians call master narratives, or state-sponsored versions of the past meant to glorify certain individuals or policies. These narratives related foundation myths, genealogies, tales of conquest, and other important remembrances. Though biased, fragmentary, and otherwise imperfect, many Aztec oral narratives were preserved by dozens of young native scribes writing in Nahuatl (NAH-watt), the Aztec language, soon after the Spanish Conquest of 1519–1521 (discussed in the next chapter).

Historical Documentation
Why is it that the Spanish victors promoted rather than suppressed these narratives of Aztec glory? In one of history's many ironic twists, Spanish priests arriving in Mexico in the 1520s taught a number of noble Aztec and other Mesoamerican youths to adapt the Latin alphabet and Spanish phonetics to various local languages, most importantly Nahuatl. The Spanish hoped that stories of Aztec rule and religion, once collected and examined, would be swiftly discredited and replaced with Western, Christian versions. Not only did this quick conversion not happen as planned, but an unintended consequence of the information-gathering campaign was to create a vast and diverse body of Mesoamerican literature written in native languages.

Despite the agony of the immediate postconquest years, the Aztecs were a quick study in the production of written historical documents. Indeed, most of what we know of Aztec history relies heavily on these hybrid and often enigmatic sixteenth-century sources (see Seeing the Past: An Aztec Map of Tenochtitlán). Aside from interviews with the elders,

An Aztec Map of Tenochtitlán

Tenochtitlán, from the *Codex Mendoza* (The Granger Collection, New York.)

contains an illustrated history of Aztec conquests, crimes and punishments, and even a map of Tenochtitlán, the Aztec capital. This symbol-filled map is reproduced here.

According to legend, the Aztec capital came into existence when an eagle landed on a cactus in the middle of Lake Texcoco. This image, now part of the Mexican national flag, is at the center of the map. Beneath the cactus is a picture of a stone carving of a cactus fruit, a common Aztec symbol for the human heart, emblem of sacrifice. Beneath this is a third symbol labeled afterwards by a Spanish scribe "Tenochtitlán."

The city, or rather its symbol, marks the meeting of four horizontal, spatial quarters as well as a vertical axis linking the sky, earth, and watery underworld. In each quarter are various Aztec nobles, only one of whom, Tenochtli (labeled "Tenuch" on the map), is seated on a reed mat, the Aztec symbol of supreme authority. He was the Aztecs' first emperor; the name "Tenochtli" means "stone cactus fruit."

The lower panel depicts the Aztec conquests of their neighbors in Colhuacan and Tenayuca. Framing the entire map are symbols for dates, part of an ancient Mesoamerican system of time keeping and prophesying retained by the Aztecs. Finally, barely legible in the upper left-hand corner is the somewhat jarring signature of André Thevet, a French priest and royal cosmographer who briefly possessed the *Codex Mendoza* in the late sixteenth century.

Named for Mexico's first Spanish viceroy, the *Codex Mendoza* was painted by Aztec artists about a dozen years after the Spanish Conquest of 1519–1521. It was commissioned by the viceroy as a gift for the Holy Roman emperor and king of Spain, Charles V. After circulating among the courts of Europe, the *Codex Mendoza* landed in the Bodleian Library in Oxford, England, where it remains. Much of the document consists of tribute lists, but it also

EXAMINING THE EVIDENCE

1. What does this map reveal about the Aztec worldview?

2. How might this document have been read by a common Aztec subject?

several painted books, or codices, marked with precise dates, names, and other symbols, survive, along with much archaeological and artistic evidence. In combining these sources with Spanish eyewitness accounts of the conquest era, historians have assembled a substantial record of Aztec life and rule.

Aztec Origins   According to most accounts, the Aztecs arrived in the Valley of Mexico sometime in the thirteenth century, but it was not until the early fourteenth that they established a permanent home. The most fertile sites in the valley were already occupied by farmers who had no interest in making room for newcomers, but the Aztecs were not dissuaded; they had a reputation for being tough and resourceful. Heeding an omen in the form of an eagle perched on a cactus growing on a tiny island near the southwest edge of Lake Texcoco, the refugees settled there in 1325. Reclaiming land from the shallow lakebed, they founded a city called Tenochtitlán (teh-noach-teet-LAWN), or "cactus fruit place." Linked to shore by three large causeways, the city soon boasted imposing stone palaces and temple-pyramids.

The Aztecs quickly transformed Tenochtitlán into a formidable capital. By 1500 it was home to some two hundred thousand people, ranking alongside Nanjing and Paris among the world's five or six most populous cities at the time. At first the Aztecs developed their city by trading military services and lake products such as reeds and fish for building materials, including stone, lime, and timber from the surrounding hillsides. They then formed marriage alliances with regional ethnic groups such as the Colhua, and by 1430 initiated the process of imperial expansion.

Intermarriage with the Colhua, who traced their ancestry to the mighty Toltec warriors, lent the lowly Aztecs a new, elite cachet. At some point the Aztecs tied their religious cult, focused on the war god Huitzilopochtli (weetsy-low-POACH-tlee), or "hummingbird-on-the-left" to cults dedicated to more widely known deities, such as Tlaloc, a powerful water god. Also known to the distant Maya, the fearsome Tlaloc resembled a goggle-wearing crocodile, and was usually surrounded by shells and other marine symbols. A huge, multilayered pyramid faced with carved stone and filled with rubble, now referred to by archaeologists as the Templo Mayor, or "Great Temple," but called by the Aztecs Coatepec, or "Serpent Mountain," became the centerpiece of Tenochtitlán. At its top, some twenty stories above the valley floor, sat twin temple enclosures, one dedicated to Huitzilopochtli, the other to Tlaloc. Like many imperial structures, Coatepec was built to awe and intimidate. In the words of one native poet:

Lake Texcoco and Tenochtitlán, c. 1500

Map legend:
— Causeway
— Major road
— Major canal
— Aqueduct

A Great Temple
B Ritual center
C Palace
D Assembly hall

0   0.5   1 mi.
0   0.5   1 km

> Proud of itself
> Is the City of Mexico-Tenochtitlán
> Here no one fears to die in war
> This is our glory
>
> This is Your Command
> Oh Giver of Life
> Have this in mind, oh princes
> Who could conquer Tenochtitlán?
> Who could shake the foundation of heaven?[2] *

As these words suggest, the Aztecs saw themselves as both stagehands and actors in a grand-scale cosmic drama centered on their great capital city.

---

* Miguel Leon-Portilla. *Pre-Columbian Literatures of Mexico*, by and Leon-Portilla, translated from the Spanish by Grace Lobanov. Copyright © 1969 by The University of Oklahoma Press. Used by permission of the publisher.

Enlarging and Supplying the Capital

With Tenochtitlán surrounded by water, subsistence and living space became serious concerns amid imperial expansion. Fortunately for the Aztecs, Lake Texcoco was shallow enough to allow an ingenious form of land reclamation called *chinampa* (chee-NAHM-pah). Still visible in a few Mexico City neighborhoods today, **chinampas** were long, narrow terraces built by hand from dredged mud, reeds, and rocks, bordered by interwoven sticks and live trees. Chinampa construction also created rows of deep canals, which served as waterways, or suburban "canoe roads." Because the Aztecs lacked iron or bronze metallurgy, wheeled vehicles, and draft animals, construction of large-scale agricultural works such as chinampas and massive temple-pyramids such as Coatepec absorbed the labors of many thousands of workers. Their construction, therefore, is a testimony to the Aztecs' ability to command and organize large amounts of labor.

Over time, Tenochtitlán's canals accumulated algae, water lilies, and silt. Workers periodically dredged and composted this organic material to fertilize maize, bean, and tomato plantings on the newly formed island-terraces. Established chinampa lands encompassing several square miles were eventually used for building residences, in part to help ease urban crowding. Always hoping not to anger Tlaloc, the fickle water god, by the mid-fifteenth century the Aztecs countered problems such as chronic flooding and high salt content at their end of the lake with dikes and other complex, labor-intensive public works.

Earlier, in the fourteenth century, an adjacent "twin" city called Tlatelolco (tlah-teh-LOLE-coe) had emerged alongside Tenochtitlán. Tlatelolco served as the Aztec marketplace. Foods, textiles, and goods from throughout Mesoamerica and beyond were exchanged here. Highly prized cocoa beans from the hot lowlands served as currency in some exchanges, and more exotic products, such as turquoise and the iridescent tail feathers of the quetzal bird, arrived from as far away as northern New Mexico and southern Guatemala, respectively. Though linked by trade, these distant regions fell well outside the Aztec domain. No matter how far they traveled, all products were transported along well-trod footpaths on the backs of human carriers. Only when they arrived on the shores of Lake Texcoco could trade goods be shuttled from place to place in canoes. Tlatelolco served as crossroads for all regional trade, with long-distance merchants, or *pochteca* (poach-TEH-cah), occupying an entire precinct. For the Aztecs, Tenochtitlán was the center of the political and spiritual universe. Tlatelolco was the center of Aztec commerce, connecting the peoples of the Valley of Mexico to diverse societies scattered across the Americas.

Genuine Aztec imperial expansion began only in around 1430, less than a century before the arrival of Europeans. An auspicious alliance between Tenochtitlán and the neighboring city-states of Texcoco and Tlacopan led to victory against a third, Atzcapotzalco (otts-cah-poat-SAUL-coh). Tensions with Atzcapotzalco extended back over a century to the Aztecs' first arrival in the region, and these early slights were not forgotten. Whether motivated by revenge or something else, the Aztecs used the momentum of this victory to overtake their allies and lay the foundations of a regional, tributary empire. Within a generation they controlled the entire Valley of Mexico, exacting tribute from several million people representing many distinct cultures. The Nahuatl language helped link state to subjects, although many newly conquered and allied groups continued to speak local languages. These persistent forms of ethnic identification, coupled with staggering tribute demands, would eventually help bring about the end of Aztec rule.

Holy Terror: Aztec Rule, Religion, and Warfare

A series of six male rulers, or *tlatoque* (tlah-TOE-kay, singular *tlatoani*), presided over Aztec expansion. When a ruler died, his successor was chosen by a secret council of elders from among a handful of eligible candidates. Aztec kingship was sacred in that each tlatoani traced his lineage back to the legendary Toltec warrior-sages. For this, the incorporation of the Colhua lineage had been essential. In keeping with this Toltec legacy, the Aztec

chinampa A terrace for farming and house building constructed in the shallows of Mexico's Lake Texcoco by the Aztecs and their neighbors.

The Coyolxauhqui Stone

Coyolxauhqui Stone (The Art Archive/Museo del Templo Mayor Mexico/Gianni Dagli Orti.)

Like many imperial peoples, the Aztecs sought to memorialize their deities in stone. The Aztec war god Huitzilopochtli was central, but as in other traditions, so were his mother and other female relatives. Huitzilopochtli's mother was Coatlicue (kwat-lih-KWAY), "Serpent Skirt," a fearsome and not obviously maternal figure. Huitzilopochtli's birth was said to be miraculous; Coatlicue had been inseminated by downy feathers while sweeping a temple, a ruse of the trickster-creator god Tezcatlipoca (tess-caught-lee-POH-cah), "Smoking Mirror."

A daughter, Coyolxauhqui (coe-yole-SHAU-key), "She Who is Adorned with Copper Bells," was so outraged at her mother's suspicious pregnancy that she incited her four hundred siblings to attempt matricide. Coatlicue was frightened at the prospect, but her unborn child, Huitzilopochtli, spoke from the womb to calm her. Upon the arrival of the angry children, dressed for war and led by Coyolxauhqui, Huitzilopochtli burst out of his mother's womb fully grown. He quickly prepared for battle and confronted his sister, whom he dismembered with a fire serpent. Huitzilopochtli went on to rout his other siblings, running them down like a proper Aztec warrior, stripping and sacrificing each without mercy.

The circular stone shown here, discovered by electrical workers near Mexico City's cathedral in 1979, depicts Coyolxauhqui dismembered on the ground. Some ten feet across, this stone apparently sat at the base of the Aztec Templo Mayor. Sacrificed warriors from all over the Aztec Empire probably got a good look at it before climbing the temple stairs to their deaths. Although shown in defeat, Coyolxauhqui is the ideal woman warrior, her serpent belt buckled with a human skull. Earth Monster knee- and elbow-pads, as well as heel-cups, add to her fearsome appearance, as do serpent ties on her severed arms and legs. An elaborate headdress and huge, Toltec-style ear-spools top off the battlefield ensemble.

EXAMINING THE EVIDENCE

1. How does the Coyolxauhqui stone reflect women's roles in Aztec society?

2. What does the stone suggest about death in Aztec thought?

Empire was characterized by three core features: human sacrifice, warfare, and tribute. All were linked to Aztec and broader Mesoamerican notions of cosmic order, specifically the fundamental human duty to feed the gods.

Sacrifice   Like most Mesoamerican peoples, the Aztecs traced not only their own but all human origins to sacrifices made by a wide range of deities. In most origin stories male and female gods threw themselves into fires, drew their own blood, and killed and dismembered one another, all for the good of humankind. These forms of sacrifice were considered essential to the process of releasing and renewing the generative powers that drove the cosmos (see Seeing the Past: The Coyolxauhqui Stone).

According to Aztec belief, humans were expected to show gratitude by following the example of their creators in an almost daily ritual cycle. Much of the sacred calendar had been inherited from older Mesoamerican cultures, but the Aztecs added many new holidays to celebrate their own special role in cosmic history. The Aztecs' focus on sacrifice also appears to have derived from their acute sense that secular and spiritual forces were

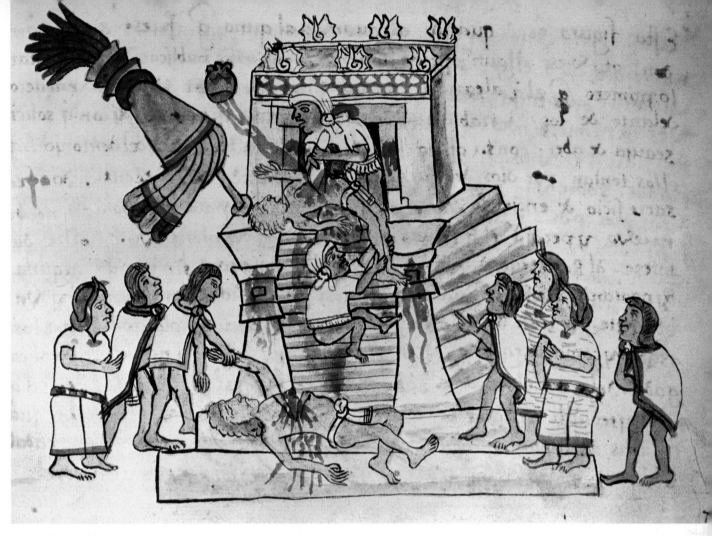

Aztec Human Sacrifice

This image dates from just after the Spanish Conquest of Mexico, but it was part of a codex about Aztec religious practices and symbols. Here a priest is removing the beating heart of a captive with a flint knife as an assistant holds his feet. The captive's bloody heart, in the form of a cactus fruit, ascends, presumably to the gods (see the same icon in Seeing the Past: An Aztec Map of Tenochtitlán, page 521). At the base of the sacrificial pyramid lies an earlier victim, apparently being taken away by noble Aztec men and women responsible for the handling of the corpse. (Scala/Art Resource, NY.)

inseparable and interdependent. Affairs of state were affairs of heaven, and vice versa. Tenochtitlán was thought to be the foundation of heaven, its enormous temple-pyramids the center of human-divine affairs. Aztec priests and astrologers believed that the universe, already in its fifth incarnation after only three thousand years, was inherently unstable, always on the verge of chaos and collapse. Only human intervention in the form of sustained sacrificial ritual could stave off apocalypse.

As an antidote, or at least a brake against impending doom, the gods had given humans the "gift" of warfare. Human captives, preferably able-bodied, energetic young men, were to be hunted and killed so that the release of their blood and spirits might satisfy the gods. Warrior sacrifice was so important to the Aztecs that they believed it kept the sun in motion. Thus the act of human sacrifice, which involved removing the hearts of live victims using a flint knife, was in part a reenactment of several creator gods' own acts of self-sacrifice.

Devout Aztec subjects, rather like the classic Maya before them, also took part in non-lethal cosmic regeneration rituals in the form of personal bloodletting, or **autosacrifice**. According to a number of eyewitness sources, extremities and genitals were bled using thorns and stone blades, with public exhibition of suffering as important as blood loss. Blood offerings were absorbed by thin sheets of reed paper, which were burnt before an

autosacrifice The Mesoamerican practice of personal blood-letting as a means of paying debts to the gods.

altar. These bloodlettings, like captive sacrifices, emphasized the frailty of the individual, the pain of life, and most of all indebtedness to the gods. Autosacrifice was, in short, a physical expression of the empathy and subordination humans were to feel before their creators. Human blood fueled not only the Aztec realm, but the cosmos.

Warfare   Given these sacrificial obligations, Aztec warfare was aimed not at the annihilation, but rather at live capture of enemies. This is not to say that "stone age" weapons technology was an impediment to determined killers: two-handed broadswords with razor-sharp obsidian blades could slice feather-clad warriors to ribbons, and ceramic projectiles could be hurled from slings with deadly accuracy. Spears, lances, clubs, and other weapons were equally menacing. Still, according to most sources, Aztec combat was ideally a stylized and theatrical affair similar to royal jousts in contemporary Eurasia, with specific individuals paired for contest.

In the field, Aztec warriors were noted for their fury, a trait borrowed from their patron deity, Huitzilopochtli. Chronic enemies such as the Tlaxcalans of east-central Mexico, and the Tarascans to the west, apparently learned to match the ferocious Aztec style. Despite their proximity to Tenochtitlán, they remained unconquered when Europeans arrived. Some enemies, such as the nearby Otomí, were eventually overwhelmed, then incorporated into Aztec warrior ranks.

All Mesoamerican warriors considered death on the battlefield the highest honor. But live capture was the Aztecs' main goal, and most victims were marched naked and bound to the capital to be sacrificed. Although charged with religious meaning, Aztec warrior sacrifices were also intended to horrify enemies; visiting diplomats were made to watch them, according to sources. Aztec imperial expansion depended in part on religious terror, or the ability to appear chosen by the gods for victory.

Tribute   In addition to sacrificial victims, the Aztecs demanded **tribute** of conquered peoples, a common imperial practice worldwide. In addition to periodic labor drafts for temple building and other public works, tribute lists included useful things such as food, textiles, and craft goods, crucial subsidies for the empire's large priestly and warrior classes. Redistribution of certain tribute items to favored subjects of lower status, a tactic also practiced by the Incas, further helped cement loyalties. Other tribute items were purely symbolic. Some new subjects were made to collect filth and inedible insects, for example, just to prove their unworthiness before the Aztec sovereign. As an empire that favored humiliation over co-optation and promotion of new subjects, the Aztecs faced an ever-deepening reservoir of resentment.

Daily Life Under the Aztecs

Class Hierarchy   Aztec society was highly stratified, and class divisions firm. As in most imperial societies, Mexica nobles regarded commoners, particularly farming folk, as uncouth and generally beneath contempt. In between were imperial bureaucrats, priests, district chiefs, scribes, merchants, and artisans. Although elites at several levels showed off the fruits of their subordinates' labors in lavish displays, most Aztec art seems to have been destined not for wealthy people's homes but rather for temples, tombs, and religious shrines. Despite heavy emphasis on religious ceremonies, the Aztecs also maintained a multitiered civil justice system. In many instances, and quite unlike most of the world's imperial cultures, including the Incas, Aztec nobles received harsher punishments than commoners for similar misdeeds.

Class hierarchy was further reinforced by a host of detailed dress and speech codes, along with many other social rules and rituals. The tlatoani, for example, could not be touched or even looked in the face by any but his closest relatives, consorts, and servants. Even ranking nobles were supposed to lie face down on the ground and put dirt in their mouths before him. Nobles guarded their own rank with vigilance, going so far as to develop a restricted form of speech. Chances for social advancement were severely limited, but some men, all of whom were expected to serve in the military for a period, gained status on the battlefield.

At the base of the social pyramid were peasants and slaves. Some peasants were ethnic Aztecs, but the vast majority belonged to city-states and clans that had been conquered after 1430. In either case, peasants' lives mostly revolved around producing food for subsistence

tribute Taxes paid to a state or empire, usually in the form of farm produce or artisan manufactures but sometimes also human labor or even human bodies.

and providing overlords with tribute goods and occasional labor. Slavery usually took the form of crisis-driven self-indenture; it was not an inherited social status. Chattel slavery existed, in which slaves were treated as property and traded in the marketplace, but slavery remained unimportant to the overall Aztec economy.

Merchants, particularly the mobile pochteca, responsible for long-distance trade, occupied an unusual position. Although the pochteca sometimes accumulated great wealth, they remained resident aliens much like other ethnic merchant communities operating in the contemporary Mediterranean and Indian Ocean basins. They had no homeland, but made a good living supplying elites with exotic goods, including slaves. Yet even among merchants there seems to have been little interest in capital accumulation in the form of money, land, or saleable goods. There is no evidence of complex credit instruments, industrial-style production, or real estate exchange of the sort associated with early merchant capitalism in other parts of the world at this time. The Aztec state remained at root tributary, the movement of goods mostly a reflection of power relations underpinned by force. Merchants, far from influencing politics, remained ethnic outsiders. Thus, both the Aztec economy and social structure reinforced the insularity of Aztec elites. The inflexible Aztec society could not incorporate outsiders, and economic exchange, even long-distance trade, did little to add new ideas and beliefs to Aztec culture.

Women's Roles

The life of an Aztec woman was difficult even by early modern standards. Along with water transport and other heavy household chores, maize grinding and tortilla making became the core responsibilities of most women in the Valley of Mexico, and indeed throughout Mesoamerica. Without animal- or water-driven grain mills, food preparation was an arduous, time-consuming task, particularly for the poor. Only noblewomen enjoyed broad exemption from this and other forms of manual work.

Sources suggest that some women achieved shaman status, performing minor priestly roles and working as surgeons and herbalists. Midwifery was also a fairly high-status, female occupation (see Lives and Livelihoods: The Aztec Midwife). These were exceptions; women's lives were mostly hard under Aztec rule. Scholars disagree, however, as to whether male political and religious leaders viewed women's substantial duties and contributions as complementary or subordinate. Surviving texts do emphasize feminine mastery of the domestic sphere and its social value. However, this emphasis may simply reflect male desire to limit the sphere of women's actions, since female reproductive capacity was also highly valued as an aid to the empire's perpetual war effort.

Indeed, Aztec society was so militarized that giving birth was referred to as "taking a captive." This comparison reflects the generalized Aztec preoccupation with pleasing their gods: women were as much soldiers as men in the ongoing war to sustain human life. Women's roles in society were mostly domestic rather than public, but the home was a deeply sacred space. Caring for it was equivalent to caring for a temple. Sweeping was a genuine ritual, for example, albeit one with hygienic benefits. Hearth tending, maize grinding, spinning, and weaving were also highly ritualized tasks, each accompanied by chants and offerings. Insufficient attention to any of these daily rituals put families and entire lineages at risk.

Children's Lives

Aztec children, too, lived a scripted existence, their futures predicted at birth by astrologers. Names were derived from birthdates, and in a way amounted to a public badge of fate. According to a variety of testimonies taken just after the Spanish Conquest, Aztec society at all levels emphasized duty and good comportment rather than rights and individual freedom. Parents were admonished to police their children's behavior and to help mold all youths into useful citizens. Girls and boys at every social level were assigned tasks considered appropriate for their sex well before adolescence. By age fourteen, children of both sexes were fully engaged in adult work. One break from the constant chores was instruction between ages twelve and fifteen in singing and playing instruments, such as drums and flutes, for cyclical religious festivals. Girls married at about age fifteen, and boys nearer twenty, a pattern roughly in accordance with most parts of the world at the time. Elder Aztec women usually served as matchmakers, and wedding ceremonies tended to be elaborate, multiday affairs. Some noblemen expanded their prestige by retaining numerous wives and siring dozens of children.

The Aztec Midwife

Aztec Midwife

Women were expected to be tough in Aztec culture, which described giving birth as "taking a captive." But as in war, medical attention was often required, so a trained class of professional midwives stood by to administer aid. This image accompanies a description in Nahuatl, the Aztec language, of the midwife's duties written soon after the Spanish Conquest. (Firenze, Biblioteca Medicea Laurenziana, Ms. Med. Palat. 219, c. 132v.)

In Aztec culture, childbirth was a sacred and ritualized affair. Always life-threatening for mother and child, giving birth and being born were both explicitly compared to the battlefield experience. Aside from potential medical complications, the Aztecs considered the timing of a child's birth critical in determining his or her future. This tricky blend of physical and spiritual concerns gave rise to the respected and highly skilled livelihood of midwife. It is not entirely clear how midwives were chosen, but their work and sayings are well described in early postconquest records, particularly the illustrated books of Aztec lore and history collectively known as the *Florentine Codex*. The following passage, translated directly from sixteenth-century Nahuatl, is one such description. Note how the midwife blends physical tasks, such as supplying herbs and swaddling clothes, with shamanistic cries and speeches.

And the midwife inquired about the fate of the baby who was born.

When the pregnant one already became aware of [pains in] her womb, when it was said that her time of death had arrived, when she wanted to give birth already, they quickly bathed her, washed her hair with soap, washed her, adorned her well. And then they arranged, they swept the house where the little woman was to suffer, where she was to perform her duty, to do her work, to give birth.

If she were a noblewoman or wealthy, she had two or three midwives. They remained by her side, awaiting her word. And when the woman became really disturbed internally, they quickly put her in a sweat bath [a kind of sauna]. And to hasten the birth of the baby, they gave the pregnant woman cooked *ciuapatli* [literally, "woman medicine"] herb to drink.

And if she suffered much, they gave her ground opossum tail to drink, and then the baby was quickly born. [The midwife] already had all that was needed for the baby, the little rags with which the baby was received.

And when the baby had arrived on earth, the midwife shouted; she gave war cries, which meant the woman had fought a good battle, had become a brave warrior, had taken a captive, had captured a baby.

Then the midwife spoke to it. If it was a boy, she said to it: "You have come out on earth, my youngest one, my boy, my young man." If it was a girl, she said to it: "My young woman, my youngest one, noblewoman, you have suffered, you are exhausted.". . . [and to either:] "You have come to arrive on earth, where your relatives, your kin suffer fatigue and exhaustion; where it is hot, where it is cold, and where the wind blows; where there is thirst, hunger, sadness, despair, exhaustion, fatigue, pain. . . ."

And then the midwife cut the umbilical cord. . . .

Source: Selection from the *Florentine Codex* in Matthew Restall, Lisa Sousa, and Kevin Terraciano, eds., *Mesoamerican Voices: Native-Language Writings from Colonial Mexico, Oaxaca, Yucatan, and Guatemala* (New York: Cambridge University Press, 2005), 216–217.

QUESTIONS TO CONSIDER

1. Why was midwifery so crucial to the Aztecs?
2. How were boys and girls addressed by the midwife, and why?

For Further Information:
Carrasco, Davíd, and Scott Sessions. *Daily Life of the Aztecs, People of the Sun and Earth*, 2d ed. Indianapolis, IN: Hackett Publishing, 2008.
Clendinnen, Inga. *Aztecs: An Interpretation*. New York: Cambridge University Press, 1994.

Food and Scarcity

At around harvest time in September, Aztec subjects of all classes ate maize, beans, and squash lightly seasoned with salt and ground chili peppers. During other times of the year, and outside the chinampa zone, food could be scarce, forcing the poor to consume roasted insects, grubs, and lake scum. Certain items, such as frothed cocoa, were reserved for elites. Stored maize was used to make tortillas year-round, but two poor harvests in a row, a frequent occurrence in densely populated highland Mexico, could reduce rations considerably.

In addition to periodic droughts, Aztec subjects coped with frosts, plagues of locusts, volcanic eruptions, earthquakes, and floods. Given such ecological uncertainty, warfare was reserved for the agricultural off-season, when hands were not needed for planting, weeding, or harvesting. In the absence of large domesticated animals and advanced metallurgy, agricultural tasks throughout Mesoamerica demanded virtual armies of field laborers equipped only with fire-hardened digging sticks and obsidian or flint knives.

Animal protein was scarce in highland Mexico, especially in urban areas where hunting opportunities were limited and few domestic animals were kept. Still, the people of Tenochtitlán raised significant numbers of turkeys and plump, hairless dogs (the prized Xolo breed of today). Even humble beans, when combined with maize, could constitute a complete protein, and indigenous grains such as amaranth were also highly nutritious. Famines still occurred, however, and one in the early 1450s led to mass migration out of the Valley of Mexico. Thousands sold themselves into slavery to avoid starvation.

The Limits of Holy Terror

As the Aztec Empire expanded in the later fifteenth century, sacrificial debts grew to be a consuming passion among pious elites. Calendars filled with sacrificial rites, and warfare was ever more geared toward satisfying what must have seemed a ballooning cosmic budget.

Underlying Weaknesses

By 1500 the Aztec state had reached its height, and some scholars have argued that it had even begun to decline. Incessant captive wars and related tribute demands had reached their limits, and old enemies such as the Tlaxcalans and Tarascans remained belligerent. New conquests were blocked by difficult terrain, declining tributes, and resistant locals. With available technologies, there was no place else for this inherently expansive empire to grow, and even with complex water works in place, agricultural productivity barely kept the people fed. Under the harsh leadership of Moctezuma II ("Angry Lord the Younger") (r. 1502–1520), the future did not look promising. Although there is no evidence to suggest the Aztec Empire was on the verge of collapse when several hundred bearded, sunburnt strangers of Spanish descent appeared on Mexico's Gulf Coast shores in 1519, points of vulnerability abounded.

Tributes of Sweat: The Inca Empire 1430–1532

At about the same time as the Aztec expansion in southernmost North America, another great empire emerged in the central Andean highlands of South America. There appears to have been no significant contact between them. Like the Aztecs, the Incas burst out of their highland homeland in the 1430s to conquer numerous neighboring cultures and huge swaths of territory. They demanded tribute in goods and labor, along with allegiance to an imperial religion. Also like the Aztecs, the Incas based their expansion on a centuries-long inheritance of technological, religious, and political traditions.

FOCUS

What core features characterized Inca life and rule?

Despite enormous geographical, technological, and cultural barriers, by 1500 the Incas ruled one of the world's most extensive, ecologically varied, and rugged land empires, stretching nearly three thousand miles along both sides of the towering Andean mountain range from just north of the equator to central Chile. Like most empires ancient and modern, extensive holdings proved to be a mixed blessing (see Map 16.3, page 531).

From Potato Farmers to Empire Builders

Inca Origins

Thanks to abundant archaeological evidence and early postconquest interviews and narratives, much is known about the rise and fall of the Inca state. Still, like the early Ottoman, Russian, and other contemporary empires, numerous mysteries remain. As in those cases, legends and sagas of the formative period in particular require careful and skeptical analysis. The Inca case is somewhat complicated by the fact that their complex knotted-string records, or *khipus* (also *quipus*, KEY-poohs), have yet to be deciphered.

Scholars agree that the Incas emerged from among a dozen or so regional ethnic groups or allied clans living in the highlands of south-central Peru between 1000 and 1400 C.E. Living as scattered and more-or-less egalitarian potato and maize farmers, the Incas started out as one of many similar groups of Andean mountaineers. Throughout the Andes, clan groupings settled in and around fertile valleys and alongside lakes between eighty-five hundred and thirteen thousand feet above sea level. Though often graced with clear mountain springs and fertile soils, these highland areas were subject to periodic frosts and droughts, despite their location within the tropics. Even more than in the Aztec realm, altitude (elevation above sea level), not latitude (distance north or south of the equator), was key.

Environment and Exchange

Anthropologist John Murra once described Inca land use as a "**vertical archipelago**," a stair-step system of interdependent environmental "islands." Kin groups occupying the altitudes best suited to potato and maize farming established outlying settlements in cold uplands, where thousands of llamas and alpacas—the Americas' only large domestic animals—were herded, and also in hot lowlands, where cotton, peanuts, chilis, and the stimulant coca were grown. People, animals, and goods traveled constantly between highland and lowland ecological zones using well-maintained and often stone-paved trails and hanging bridges, yet the incredibly rugged nature of the terrain (plus the stubborn nature of llamas) made use of wheeled vehicles impractical.

vertical archipelago Andean system of planting crops and grazing animals at different altitudes.

Clans with highland ties and even some states of considerable size inhabited Peru's long desert coast. Here, urban civilization was nearly as old as that of ancient Egypt. Andean coast dwellers engaged in large-scale irrigated agriculture, deep-sea fishing, and long-distance trade. Trading families outfitted large balsawood rafts with cotton sails and plied the Pacific as far as Guatemala. Inland trade links stretched over the Andes and deep into the Amazon rain forest. Stopping at pilgrimage sites along the way, coast-dwelling traders exchanged salt, seashells, beads, and copper hatchets for exotic feathers, gold dust, and pelts. The Incas would move rapidly to exploit all of these diverse Andean regions and their interconnections, replacing old exchange systems and religious shrines with their own. Around 1200 C.E. they established a base near Cuzco (KOOS-coh), deep in the highlands of Peru not far from the headwaters of the Amazon, and soon after 1400 they began their remarkable drive toward empire.

The Great Apparatus: Inca Expansion and Religion

Cuzco, located in a narrow valley at a breathtaking altitude of over two miles above sea level, served as the Incas' political base and religious center. Like the Aztecs, the Incas saw their capital as the hub of the universe, calling it the "navel of the world." An array of dirt paths and stone-paved roads radiated out in all directions and tied hundreds of subsidiary shrines to the cosmically-ordained center. Much like the Aztecs' Tenochtitlán, Cuzco served as both the preeminent religious pilgrimage site and the empire's administrative capital. Compared with the Aztec capital, however, the city was modest in size, perhaps home to at most fifty thousand. Still, Cuzco had the advantage of being stoutly built

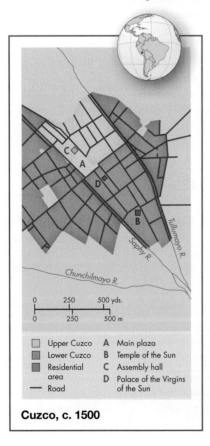

☐ Upper Cuzco	**A** Main plaza
▨ Lower Cuzco	**B** Temple of the Sun
▦ Residential area	**C** Assembly hall
— Road	**D** Palace of the Virgins of the Sun

Cuzco, c. 1500

of hewn stone. Whereas most of Tenochtitlán's temples and palaces were dismantled in the centuries following the Spanish Conquest, Cuzco's colossal stone foundations still stand.

For obscure reasons, the Incas in the early fifteenth century began conquering their neighbors. In time each emperor, or Sapa ("Unique") Inca, would seek to add more territory to the realm, called Tawantinsuyu (tuh-wahn-tin-SUE-you), or, "The Four Quarters Together." The Sapa Inca was thought to be descended from the sun and was thus regarded as the natural lord and sustainer of all humanity. To worship the sun was to worship the Inca, and vice versa. Devotion to lesser mountain and ancestor deities persisted, however, absorbed over time by the Incas in a way reminiscent of the Roman Empire's assimilation of regional deities and shrines. This religious inclusiveness helped the empire spread quickly even as the royal cult of the sun was inserted into everyday life. In a similar way, *runasimi*, later mislabeled "Quechua" (KETCH-wah) by the Spanish, became the Incas' official language even as local languages continued to be spoken.

Inca expansion was so rapid that the empire reached its greatest extent within a mere four generations of its founding. In semilegendary times, Wiracocha Inca (r. 1400–1438) was said to have led an army of followers to defeat an invading ethnic group called the Chankas near Cuzco. According to several royal sagas, this victory spurred Wiracocha to improve the defensive position of his people further by annexing the fertile territories of other neighbors. Defense turned to offense, and thus was primed the engine of Inca expansion.

Wiracocha's successor, Pachacuti Inca Yupanki (r. 1438–1471), was far more ambitious, so much so that he is widely regarded as the true founder of the Inca Empire. Substantial archaeological evidence backs this claim. Pachacuti (literally "Cataclysm") took over much of what is today Peru, including many coastal oases and the powerful Chimú kingdom. Along the way, Pachacuti perfected the core strategy of Inca warfare: amassing and mobilizing such overwhelming numbers of troops and backup forces that actual fighting was usually unnecessary.

Thousands of peasants were conscripted to bear arms, build roads, and carry grain. Others herded llamas, strung bridges, and cut building stone. With each new advance, huge masonry forts and temples were constructed in the imperial style, leaving an indelible Inca stamp on the landscape still visible today from Ecuador to Argentina. Even opponents such as the desert-dwelling Chimú, who had their aqueducts cut off to boot, simply capitulated in the face of the Inca juggernaut. Just after the Spanish Conquest, Pachacuti was remembered by female descendants:

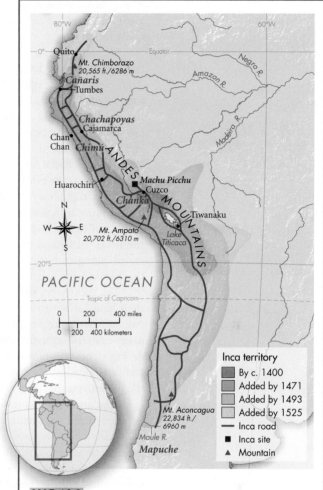

MAP 16.3

The Inca Empire, 1325–1521

Starting from their base in Cuzco, high in the Andes, the Incas built the most extensive empire in the Americas, and the second most populous after that of the Aztecs. They linked it by a road system that rivaled that of the ancient Romans. Inca expansion was extremely rapid as each ruler competed with his predecessor to extend tributary control. Some groups, such as the Cañaris and Chachapoyas, resisted Inca domination for many years, and the Mapuche of Chile were never conquered.

Imperial Expansion

> As [Pachacuti] Inca Yupanki remained in his city and town of Cuzco, seeing that he was lord and that he had subjugated the towns and provinces, he was very pleased. He had subjugated more and obtained much more importance than any of his ancestors. He saw the great apparatus that he had so that whenever he wanted to he could subjugate and put under his control anything else he wanted.[3]

These early colonial remembrances underscore the Sapa Inca's tremendous power. Pachacuti could at any time deploy the "great apparatus" of empire as his personal conquest machine.

Pachacuti's successors continued in the same vein, extending conquests southward deep into what are today Chile and Argentina, and also eastward down the slope of the Andes and into the upper Amazon Basin. It is from this last region, the quarter the Incas called Antisuyu (auntie-SUE-you), that we derive the word *Andes*. On the northern frontier, the Incas fought a series of bitter wars with Ecuadorian ethnic groups to extend Inca rule into the southernmost part of present-day Colombia (see again Map 16.3). Here the imperial Inca conquest machine met its match: instead of capitulating, awestruck by the Inca, many Ecuadorian and Colombian highlanders fought to the death.

According to most sources, Inca advances into new territory were couched in the rhetoric of diplomacy. Local headmen were told they had two options: (1) to retain power by accepting Inca sovereignty and all the tributary obligations that went with it, or (2) to defy the Inca and face annihilation. Most headmen went along, particularly once word of the Incas' battlefield prowess spread. Those who did not were either killed in battle or exiled, along with their subject populations, to remote corners of the empire. Several of these exile colonies are still identifiable today in southern Ecuador and northern Bolivia.

The Incas seem to have been most interested in dominating productive peoples and their lands, although they also succeeded to some extent in spreading their imperial solar cult. Whatever their motives, like the Aztecs they defined political domination in simple, easily understood terms: tribute payment. Conquered subjects showed submission by rendering significant portions of their surplus production—and also labor—to the emperor and his subordinates. Tribute payment was a grudgingly accepted humiliation throughout the Andes, one that many hoped to shake off at the first opportunity.

Inca Religion

Scholars argue that to understand Inca religion one must set aside familiar distinctions between sacred and secular and between life and death. As the chapter-opening description of child sacrifice suggests, a continuum of life was assumed throughout the Andes, despite permanent loss of consciousness, and spirit and body were deemed inseparable. Likewise, features in the landscape, ranging from mountain springs and peaks to ordinary boulders, were almost always thought to house or emit spiritual energy (see Reading the Past: An Andean Creation Story). Even practical human-made landforms, such as irrigation canals, walls, and terraces, were commonly described as "alive." These sacred places, **wakas** (or *huacas*), received sacrifices of food, drink, and textiles from their human caretakers in exchange for good harvests, herd growth, and other bounties. In addition, most Andeans venerated images and amulets carved from wood, shell, stone, metal, and bone.

Andeans also venerated the human corpse. As long as something tangible remained of one's deceased relatives or ancestors, they were not regarded as entirely dead. It was generally thought wise to keep them around. Of course it helped that the central Andes' dry highland and coastal climates were ideal for mummification: preservation often required little more than removal of internal organs. In wetter areas, the dead were sometimes smoked over a slow fire, a process that led some outsiders to suspect cannibalism. In fact, it would have been fairly common in Inca times to encounter a neighbor's "freeze-dried" or smoked grandparents hanging from the rafters, still regarded as very much involved in household affairs. Andeans sometimes carried ancestor mummies to feasts and pilgrimages as well. Thus, Inca society included both past and present generations.

The Incas harnessed these and other core features of Andean society at its most ancient, yet like the Aztecs they put a unique stamp on the vast and diverse region they came to dominate. Though warlike, the Incas rarely sacrificed captive warriors, a ritual archaeologists now know was practiced among ancient coastal Peruvians. As for cannibalism, it was something the Incas associated with barbaric forest dwellers. Inca stone architecture, though clearly borrowing from older forms such as those of Tiwanaku, a temple complex in modern Bolivia, is still identifiable thanks to the frequent use of trapezoidal (flared) doors, windows, and niches (see the illustration of Machu Picchu in At a

waka A sacred place or thing in Andean culture.

An Andean Creation Story

The small Peruvian town of Huarochirí (wahr-oh-chee-REE), located in the high Andes east of Lima, was the target of a Spanish anti-idolatry campaign at the end of the sixteenth century. The Spanish conquest of the Incas, which began in 1532 (see Chapter 17), had little effect on the everyday life of Andean peasants, and many clung tenaciously to their religious beliefs. In Huarochirí, Spanish attempts to root out these beliefs and replace them with Western, Christian ones produced written testimonies from village elders in phonetically rendered Quechua, the most commonly spoken language in the Inca Empire. Like the Aztec codices, the resulting documents—aimed at eradicating the beliefs they describe—have unwittingly provided modern researchers with a rare window on a lost mental world. The passage here, translated directly from Quechua to English, relates an Andean myth that newly arrived or converted Christians considered a variation on the biblical story of Noah and the Great Flood. In the Christian story, God, angered by the wickedness of man, resolves to send a flood to destroy the earth. He spares only Noah, whom he instructs to build an ark in which Noah, his family, and a pair of every animal were saved from the Great Flood.

> In ancient times, this world wanted to come to an end. A llama buck, aware that the ocean was about to overflow, was behaving like somebody who's deep in sadness. Even though its owner let it rest in a patch of excellent pasture, it cried and said, "In, in," and wouldn't eat. The llama's owner got really angry, and he threw a cob from some maize he had just eaten at the llama. "Eat, dog! This is some fine grass I'm letting you rest in!" he said. Then that llama began speaking like a human being. "You simpleton, whatever could you be thinking about? Soon, in five days, the ocean will overflow. It's a certainty. And the whole world will come to an end," it said. The man got good and scared. "What's going to happen to us? Where can we go to save ourselves?" he said. The llama replied, "Let's go to Villca Coto mountain. There we'll be saved. Take along five days' food for yourself." So the man went out from there in a great hurry, and himself carried both the llama buck and its load. When they arrived at Villca Coto mountain, all sorts of animals had already filled it up: pumas, foxes, guanacos [wild relatives of the llama], condors, all kinds of animals in great numbers. And as soon as that man had arrived there, the ocean overflowed. They stayed there huddling tightly together. The waters covered all those mountains and it was only Villca Coto mountain, or rather its very peak, that was not covered by the water. Water soaked the fox's tail. That's how it turned black. Five days later, the waters descended and began to dry up. The drying waters caused the ocean to retreat all the way down again and exterminate all the people. Afterward, that man began to multiply once more. That's the reason there are people until today.

[The scribe who recorded this tale, an Andean converted by Spanish missionaries, then adds this comment:] "Regarding this story, we Christians believe it refers to the time of the Flood. But they [i.e., non-Christian Andeans] believe it was Villca Coto mountain that saved them."

Source: Excerpt from *The Huarochirí Manuscript: A Testament of Ancient and Colonial Andean Religion*, trans. and ed. Frank Salomon and George L. Urioste (Austin: University of Texas Press, 1991), 51–52.

EXAMINING THE EVIDENCE

1. What do the similarities and differences between the Andean and Judeo-Christian flood stories suggest?

2. What do the differences between them reveal?

For Further Information:
Spalding, Karen. *Huarochirí: An Andean Society Under Inca and Spanish Rule*. Stanford: Stanford University Press, 1988.
Urton, Gary. *Inca Myths*. Austin: University of Texas Press, 1999.

Crossroads, page 512). It is worth noting, however, that the cult of the sun, which the Incas transformed and elevated to something new and imperial, proved far less durable than local religious traditions once the empire fell. Despite the Incas' rhetoric of diplomacy, most Andeans appear to have associated their rule with tyranny. Like the Aztecs, they failed to inspire loyalty in their subjects, who saw Inca government as a set of institutions designed to exploit, rather than protect, the peoples of the empire.

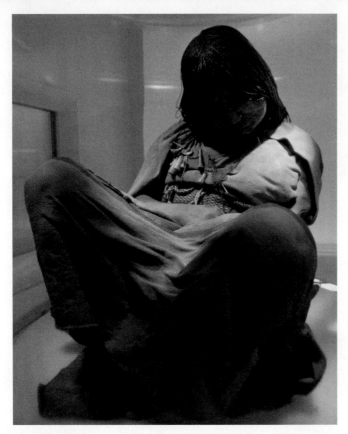

Inca Mummy

The Incas did not sacrifice humans as often as the Aztecs did, but headmen in newly conquered regions were sometimes required to give up young sons or daughters for live burial on high mountains. The victims, including this adolescent girl found in a shallow tomb atop 20,000-foot Mount Lullaillaco in the Argentine Andes, died of exposure after the long climb, but the Incas believed them to remain semiconscious and in communication with the spirit world. The girl seen here wears fine camelid-fiber garments bound by a *chumbi* (traditional Andean belt) and silver *topos* (shawl pins). She is also adorned with a shell necklace and other amulets, and her hair is pleated as described in early postconquest accounts. Such sacrifices were known as *capacocha*, or "debt payment." (AP Photo/Natacha Pisarenko.)

Daily Life Under the Incas

Inca society, like Aztec society, was highly stratified, with few means of upward mobility. Along with class gradations tied to occupation, the Incas maintained a variety of divisions and ranks according to sex, age, and ethnic or regional origin. Everyday life thus varied tremendously among the Inca's millions of subjects, although the vast peasant majority probably had much in common with farming folk the world over. Seasonal work stints for the empire were a burden for men, whereas women labored constantly to maintain households, raise children, and care for elderly kin. Unlike that of the Aztec, the Inca legal system, in common with most such systems in early modern times, appears to have been more harshly punitive against commoners than nobles. Exemplary elite behavior was expected, but not so rigidly enforced.

At the pinnacle of society was the Sapa Inca himself, the "son of the Sun." As in most imperial cultures, the emperor's alleged divinity extended to matters of war; he was believed to be the greatest warrior in the world. As a sign of unworthiness, everyone who came before him was obliged to bear a symbolic burden, such as a load of cloth or large water vessel. Only the Inca's female companions had intimate, daily contact with him. Although the ideal royal couple according to Inca mythology was a sibling pair, it was in fact dozens of wives and concubines who assured that there would be numerous potential heirs. Unlike monarchs in Europe and parts of Africa, the imperial household did not practice primogeniture, or the automatic inheritance of an estate or title by the eldest son. Neither did they leave succession to a group of elders, the method preferred by the Aztecs. Violent succession struggles predictably ensued. Though barred from the role of Inca themselves, ambitious noblewomen came to exercise considerable behind-the-scenes power over imperial succession.

Just beneath the Inca imperial line was an assortment of Cuzco-based nobles, readily identifiable by their huge ear-spools and finely woven tunics. Rather like their Aztec counterparts, they spoke a dialect of the royal language forbidden among commoners. Among this elite class were

Class Hierarchy   decorated generals and hereditary lords of prominent and ancient clans. Often drawn from these and slightly lower noble ranks was a substantial class of priests and astrologers, charged with maintaining a vast array of temples and shrines.

Many noble women and girls deemed physically perfect, like the sacrificial victim described at the start of this chapter, were also selected for religious seclusion, somewhat like nuns in contemporary Western societies. Seclusion was not always permanent, because some of these women were groomed for marriage to the Inca. Still more noblewomen, mostly wives and widows, were charged with maintaining the urban households and country estates of the Incas, dead and alive.

Next came a class of bureaucrats, regional military leaders, and provincial headmen. Bureaucrats kept track of tribute obligations, communal work schedules, and land appropriations. Following conquest, up to two-thirds of productive land was set aside in the name of the ruling Inca and the cult of the sun. Bureaucrats negotiated with headmen as to which lands these would be, and how and when their subjects would be put to work on behalf of their new rulers. If negotiations failed, the military was called in for a show of force. Lower-ranking Inca military men, like bureaucrats, often faced service at the most hostile fringes of empire. They had little beyond the weak hold of local power to look forward to. As a result, in sharp distinction with the Aztecs, death in battle was not regarded as a glorious sacrifice among the Incas, but rather as yet another humiliation. Furthermore, many officers were themselves provincial in origin and thus had little hope of promotion to friendlier districts closer to the imperial core.

The Inca and his substantial retinue employed and received tribute from numerous artisans, mostly conquered provincials. Such specialists included architects, khipu-keepers, civil engineers, metalworkers, stonecutters, weavers, potters, wood-carvers, and many others. Unlike the Aztecs, the Incas did not tolerate free traders, instead choosing to manage the distribution of goods and services as a means of exercising state power. Partly as a result, chattel, or market-oriented, slavery appears not to have existed under the Incas, although some conquered young men and women spared from death or exile were absorbed into the labor force as personal servants. Most Inca subjects and tribute payers were peasants belonging to kin groups whose lives revolved around agriculture and rotational labor obligations. For them, the rigors of everyday life far outweighed the extra demands of Inca rule. Only in the case of recently conquered groups, or those caught in the midst of a regional rebellion or succession conflict, was this not true. Even then, subsistence remained the average Andean's most pressing concern; battlefields were abandoned at planting and harvest times.

Andean artisans living under Inca rule produced remarkable textiles, metalwork, and pottery, but the empire's most visible achievements were in the fields of architecture and civil engineering. The Incas' extensive road systems, irrigation works, and monumental temples were unmatched by any ancient American society. No one

Inca Road
Stretching nearly 10,000 miles across mountains, plains, deserts, and rain forests, the Inca Royal Road held one of the world's most rugged and extensive empires together. Using braided fiber bridges to span chasms and establishing inns and forts along the road, the Incas handily moved troops, supplies, and information—in the form of khipu records and messages—across vast distances. The Royal Road had the unintentional consequence of aiding penetration of the empire by Spanish conquistadors on horseback. (akg-images/ Aurélia Frey.)

Material Achievements

else moved or carved such large stones or ruled such a vast stretch of terrain. Linking coast, highlands, and jungle, the Incas' roads covered nearly ten thousand miles. Draft workers and soldiers paved them with stones whenever possible, and many sections were hewn into near-vertical mountainsides by hand. Grass weavers spanned breathtaking gorges with hanging bridges strong enough to sustain trains of pack llamas for years at a time. These engineering marvels enabled the Incas to communicate and move troops and supplies across great distances with amazing speed, yet they also served the important religious function of facilitating pilgrimages and royal processions. Massive irrigation works and stone foundations, though highly practical, were similarly charged with religious power. Thus, the Inca infrastructure not only played an important practical role in imperial government, but it also expressed the Incas' belief in the connection between their own rule and the cosmic order.

The Incas appropriated and spread ancient Andean metalworking techniques, which were much older and thus far more developed than those of Mesoamerica. On the brink of a genuine Bronze Age by 1500, Inca metallurgy ranged from fine decorative work in specially prepared alloys to toolmaking for the masses. As in many parts of the early modern world, the forging of metals was as much a religious as an artistic exercise in the Andes, and metals themselves were regarded as semidivine. Gold was associated with the sun in Inca cosmology, and by extension with the Sapa Inca and his solar cult. Silver was associated with the moon and with several mother goddesses and Inca queens and princesses. Copper and bronze, considered less divine than gold and silver, were put to more practical uses.

Another ancient Andean tradition inherited by the Incas was weaving. Weaving in fact predates even ceramics in the Andes. Inca textiles, made mostly from native Peruvian cotton and alpaca fibers, were of extraordinary quality, and cloth became in essence the coin of the realm. Cooperative regional lords were rewarded by the Incas with substantial gifts of blankets and ponchos, which they could then redistribute among their subjects. Unlike some earlier coastal traditions, Inca design features favored geometric forms over representations of humans, animals, or deities. Fiber from the vicuña, a wild relative of the llama, was reserved for tunics and other garments worn only by the Sapa Inca. Softer than cashmere, it was the gold standard of Andean textile components. Some women became master weavers, but throughout most of the Inca Empire men wove fibers spun into thread by women, a gendered task division later reinforced by the Spanish.

With such an emphasis on textiles, it may come as no surprise that the Incas maintained a record-keeping system using knotted strings. Something like the Chinese abacus, or accounting device, in its most basic form, the **khipu** enabled bureaucrats and others to keep track of tributes, troop movements, ritual cycles, and other important matters. Like bronze metallurgy, the khipu predates the Inca Empire, but was most developed by Inca specialists. Although the extent of its capabilities as a means of data management remains a subject of intense debate, the khipu was sufficiently effective to remain in use for several centuries under Spanish rule, long after alphabetic writing was introduced.

Social Relations

Other ancient Andean traditions appropriated and spread by the Incas include reciprocity, the expectation of equal exchange and returned favors, complementary gender roles, and a tendency to view all social relations through the lens of kinship. Villagers, for example, depended on one another for aid in constructing homes, maintaining irrigation works, and tilling and harvesting fields. Whereas they chafed at service to the Inca ruler, they regarded rotational group work and communal care for disadvantaged neighbors not as burdens, but rather—after the work was done—as excuses for drinking parties and other festivities. Even in such a reciprocal environment, stresses and strains accumulated. In some villages, aggression was periodically vented during ritual fights between clan divisions.

Throughout the Andes, women occupied a distinct sphere from that of men, but not a subordinate one. For example, sources suggest that although the majority of Andeans living under Inca rule were patrilineal, or male-centered, in their succession preferences, power frequently landed in the hands of sisters and daughters of headmen. Literate Inca descendants described a world in which both sexes participated equally in complementary agricultural tasks, and also in contests against neighboring clans. Women exempted from rotational labor duties handled local exchanges of food and craft goods. Whether or not they were allowed to accumulate property as a result of these exchanges remains unknown.

Women's fertility was respected, but never equated with warfare, as in Aztec society. Interestingly, Andean childbirth was almost regarded as a nonevent, and rarely involved midwives. The Andean creator god, Wiracocha (weer-ah-COACH-ah), somewhat similar to the Aztecs' Tlaloc, had both male and female aspects. As in many traditional societies, Andean social hierarchy was described in terms of age and proximity of kin relation. "Mother" and "father," for example, were terms used to describe both gods and the most prominent earthly individuals (including one's parents). Next in line were numerous aunts, uncles, cousins, and so on down the family tree. Almost any respected elder was referred to as "uncle" or "aunt."

As in most early modern societies, parents treated Inca children much like miniature adults, and dressed them accordingly. Parents educated children by defining roles and duties early, using routine chores deemed appropriate to one's sex and status as the primary means of education. Girls and boys also participated in community and even state-level

khipu Knotted cotton or alpaca fiber strings used by the Incas and other Andeans to record tributes, troop numbers, and possibly narratives of events.

work projects. The expectation of all children was not to change society but to reproduce and maintain it through balanced relations with deities and neighbors. Contact with the Inca himself was an extremely remote possibility for most children living in the empire. A rare exception was capacocha sacrificial victims, such as the headman's daughter described at the opening of this chapter.

Just as maize was native to highland Mesoamerica and served as the base for urban development, the potato was the indigenous staple of the central Andes. A hearty, high-yield tuber with many varieties, the potato could be roasted, stewed, or naturally freeze-dried and stored for long periods. Control of preserved food surpluses was a hallmark of enduring imperial states, in large part because marching armies needed to eat. Maize could also be dried or toasted for storage and snacking, but among Andeans it was generally reserved for beer making. Along with maize, many lowland dwellers subsisted on manioc, peanuts, beans, and chili peppers.

Unique in the Americas, though common in much of Eurasia and Africa, Andean pastoralism played a critical role in Inca expansion. Andean domesticated animals included the llama, alpaca, and guinea pig. Llamas, in addition to carrying light loads, were sometimes eaten, and alpacas provided warm cloth fiber, much appreciated in the cold highlands. Slaughter of domestic animals, including fertilizer-producing guinea pigs, usually accompanied ritual occasions such as weddings or harvest festivals. Although like most early modern elites, the Inca and other nobles preferred to dine on freshly hunted deer, wild pig, and other meats. The average Andean diet was overwhelmingly vegetarian. Nevertheless, a common component of Inca trail food was *charqui* (hence "jerky"), bits of dried and salted llama flesh. Apparently for cultural rather than practical reasons, llamas and alpacas were never milked. Like many other peoples, Andeans restricted consumption of and even contact with certain animal fluids and body parts.

Khipu

The Incas did not invent the knotted-string record-keeping method known as khipu, but they used it extensively as they rapidly built their vast empire. Khipu masters braided and knotted cords of different colors and thicknesses in many combinations. Some khipus were kept as stored records and others sent as messages carried across the Andes by relay runners. (The Art Archive/Archaeological Museum Lima/Gianni Dagli Orti.)

Food and Subsistence

The high Inca heartland, though fertile, was prone to periodic droughts and frosts. The warmer coast was susceptible to catastrophic floods related to the so-called El Niño phenomenon, or periodic fluctuation in the eastern Pacific Ocean's surface temperature and resulting onshore moisture flow. Only by developing food storage techniques and exploiting numerous microenvironments were the Incas and their subjects able to weather such events. Added to these cyclical catastrophes were volcanic eruptions, earthquakes, mudslides, tsunamis, and plagues of locusts. Still, the overall record suggests that subsistence under the Incas, thanks to the "vertical archipelago," was much less precarious than under the Aztecs.

The Great Apparatus Breaks Down

In its simplest form Inca expansion derived from a blend of religious and secular impulses. As in Aztec Mexico, religious demands seem to have grown more and more urgent, possibly even destabilizing the empire by the time of the last Sapa Inca. As emperors died, their mummy cults required permanent and extravagant maintenance. In a context where the dead were not separate from the living, such obligations could not be shirked. The most eminent of mummies in effect tied up huge tracts of land. Logically, if vainly, successive emperors strove to make sure their mummy cults would be provided for in equal or better fashion. Each hoped his legacy might outshine that of his predecessor. Given the extraordinary precedent set by Pachacuti Inca, some scholars have argued that excessive mummy veneration effectively undermined the Inca Empire.

Despite this potentially unsustainable drive to conquer new territories, it was the Incas' notable organizational and diplomatic skills that held their enormous, geographically fractured empire together until the arrival of the Spanish in 1532. The Incas' ability to control the distribution of numerous commodities over great distances, to maintain communications and transport despite the absence of written texts and wheeled vehicles, to erect temples and centralize religious observation, and finally, to monopolize violence, all marked them as an imperial people.

As with the Aztecs, however, rapid growth by means of competitive violence sowed seeds of discontent. On the eve of the Spanish arrival both empires appear to have been on the verge of contraction rather than expansion, with rebellion at court and in the provinces the order of the day. The Incas had never done well against Amazonian and other lowland forest peoples, and some such enemies kept up chronic raiding activities. Highlanders such as the Cañaris of Ecuador and the Chachapoyas of northern Peru had cost the Incas dearly in their conquest, only just completed in 1525 after more than thirty years. Like the Tlaxcalans of Mexico, both of these recently conquered groups would ally with Spanish invaders in hopes of establishing their independence once and for all.

The Inca state was highly demanding of its subjects, and enemy frontiers abounded. Yet it seems the Incas' worst enemies were ultimately themselves. A nonviolent means of royal succession had never been established. This was good for the empire in that capable rather than simply hereditary rulers could emerge one after another, but bad in that the position of Sapa Inca was always up for grabs. In calmer times, defense against outside challengers would not have been much trouble, but the Spanish had the good fortune to arrive in the midst of a civil war between two rivals to the throne, Huascar and Atawallpa (also "Atahualpa"). By 1532 Atawallpa defeated his half-brother in a series of epic battles, only to fall prey to a small number of foreign interlopers.

COUNTERPOINT
The Peoples of North America's Eastern Woodlands 1450–1530

FOCUS
How did the Eastern Woodlanders' experience differ from life under the Aztecs and Incas?

By 1450 a great variety of native peoples, several million in all, inhabited North America's eastern woodlands. East of the Great Plains, dense forests provided raw materials for shelter, cooking, and transportation, as well as habitat for game. Trees also yielded nuts and other edible byproducts, and served as fertilizer for crops when burned. The great mound-building cultures of the Mississippi Basin had mostly faded by this time, their inhabitants having returned to less urban, more egalitarian ways of life. Villages headed by elected chiefs, not empires headed by divine kings, were the most common form of political organization (see Map 16.4).

Most of what we know about the diverse native inhabitants of eastern North America in early modern times derives from European documents from the contact period (1492–1750), plus archaeological studies. Although far less is known about them than about the Aztecs or Incas, the evidence suggests that Eastern Woodlands peoples faced significant changes in both their politics and everyday lives at the dawn of the early modern period, just before Europeans arrived to transform the region in other ways. Climate change may have been one important factor spurring conflict and consolidation.

Eastern Woodlands peoples were like the Aztecs in at least one sense. Most were maize farmers who engaged in seasonal warfare followed by captive sacrifice. According to archaeological evidence, both maize planting and warrior sacrifice spread into the region from Mesoamerica around the time of the Toltecs (800–1100 C.E.). The century prior to European contact appears to have been marked by rapid population growth, increased warfare, and political reorganization. Multisettlement ethnic alliances or leagues, such as the Iroquois Five Nations of upstate New York and the Powhatan Confederacy of Tidewater, Virginia, were relatively new to the landscape. Some confederacies were formed for

Population Growth and Political Organization

MAP 16.4

Native Peoples of North America, c. 1500

To the north of Mesoamerica, hundreds of native American groups, most of them organized as chiefdoms, flourished in a wide array of climate zones, from the coldest Arctic wilderness to the hottest subtropical deserts. Populations were highest where maize and other crops could be grown, as in the Mississippi Valley, Great Lakes, and eastern woodlands regions. Dense, sedentary populations also developed in the Pacific Northwest, where peoples such as the Kwakiutl lived almost entirely from gathering, hunting, and fishing. Nomadic hunters lived throughout the Great Plains, the Rocky Mountains, the Sierra Nevada, and the desert Southwest. Conflict between sedentary farmers and nomadic hunters was common, and some groups formed alliances to defend themselves against these and other attackers.

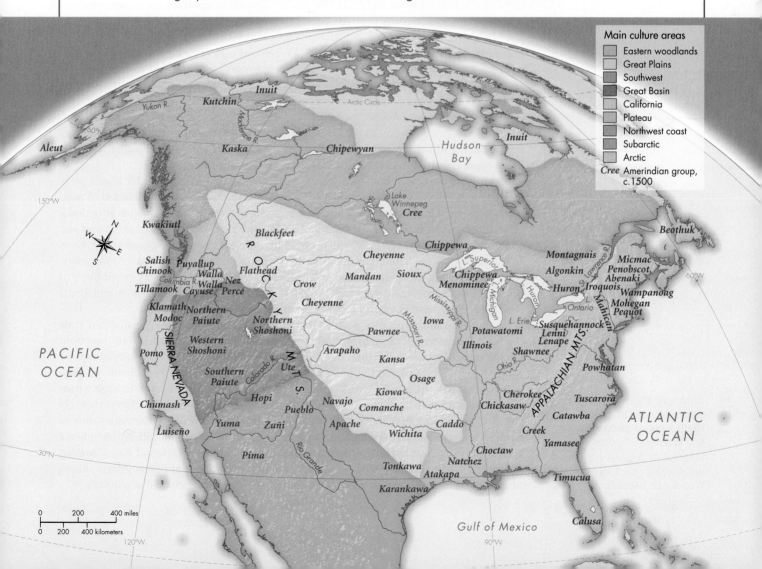

Huron Wampum Belt

For many Eastern Woodlands peoples such as the Huron, seashells like the New England quahog (a variety of clam) were sacred trade goods. Shell beads, generically called *wampum* after the arrival of Europeans, were woven into ceremonial belts whose geometrical designs and color schemes represented clans and sometimes treaties between larger groups. The linked-hands motif in this belt suggests a treaty or covenant. (National Museum of the American Indian, Smithsonian Institution. Catalog number: 1/2132. Photo by Katherine Fogden.)

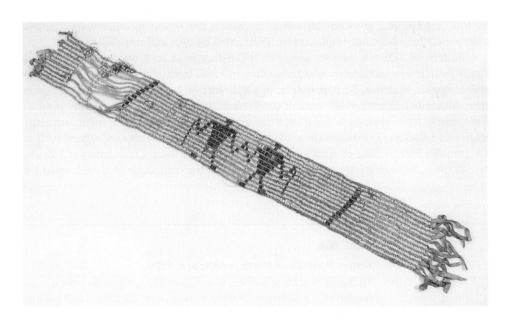

temporary defensive or offensive purposes, and others were primarily religious. Village populations sometimes exceeded two thousand inhabitants, and confederacies counted up to twenty thousand or more. As in the Andes, clan divisions were fairly common, but overall population densities were considerably lower.

Gathering-hunting groups, which made up a minority of the total Eastern Woodlands population, tended to occupy large but rocky, cold, or otherwise challenging landscapes. Notably, thanks to their varied diet, these nonsedentary peoples seem to have suffered fewer vitamin and mineral deficiencies than settled maize eaters. Even maize farmers, however, were generally taller than their European (or Mesoamerican) contemporaries. Throughout the eastern forests, including the vast Great Lakes region, metallurgy was limited to simple manipulation of native copper. Raw copper, found in abundance in northern Michigan, was regarded as a sacred substance and was associated with chiefly power. Beads made from polished seashells, or **wampum**, were similarly prized.

Nearly all Eastern Woodlands groups, including small gatherer-hunter bands, were headed by chiefs. These men were usually exceptional warriors or shamans elected by popular agreement. Chiefs retained power, however, only by redistributing goods at periodic ceremonies; generosity was the hallmark of leadership. Since surplus food, game, and war booty were far from predictable, chiefs could be unceremoniously deposed at any time. Few chiefdoms were hereditary. As in many societies, individual Eastern Woodlanders, particularly young men, yearned for independence even as circumstances forced them to cooperate and subordinate their wills to others. If the chief's generosity was a centripetal force, egalitarian desires formed a powerful centrifugal one.

Matrilineal Society

Some agricultural peoples, such as the Huron of central Ontario, Canada, had male chiefs or headmen but were organized matrilineally. This meant that society was built around clans of mothers, daughters, and sisters. Matrilineal clans occupied **longhouses**, or wooden multifamily residential buildings, typical of most Eastern Woodlands peoples. Elder women consulted with chiefs regularly, and all women played a part in urging men to war. Agriculture was regarded as a strictly female preserve among the Huron, closely linked to human fertility. Huron men were relegated to risky, perennial activities such as hunting, warfare, and tree felling. Their sphere of influence lay almost entirely outside the village. Men's exploits abroad, including adolescent vision quests, conferred status. Among all Eastern Woodlanders, public speech making, or rhetoric, was as highly prized among adult men as martial expertise. Only the most esteemed men participated in councils.

wampum Beads made of seashells; used in eastern North America as currency and to secure alliances.

longhouse A wooden communal dwelling typical of Eastern Woodlands peoples.

Children's lives were generally unenviable among North America's Eastern Woodlanders (keeping in mind that this was true of childhood throughout the early modern world). Thanks to a multitude of vermin and pathogens, generally poor nutrition, smoky residences, and manifold hazards of war and accident, relatively few children survived to adulthood. Partly for these reasons, Eastern Woodlands cultures discouraged severe discipline for children, instead allowing them much freedom.

Playtime ended early for surviving girls and boys, however, as each was schooled before puberty in the arts and responsibilities deemed appropriate for their sex. Girls learned to farm and cook, boys to hunt and make war. Soon after puberty young people began to "try out" mates until a suitable match was found. This preference for trial marriage over forced arrangements was found in the Andes and other parts of the Americas as well. Though this and the seemingly casual practice of divorce among Eastern Woodlanders were considered scandalous by early modern European standards, stable monogamy prevailed.

Warfare was endemic throughout the Eastern Woodlands in the summer season, when subsistence itself was less of a battle. In form, these wars resembled blood feuds, or vengeance cycles. According to European witnesses, wars among the Iroquois, Mahicans, and others were spawned by some long-forgotten crime, such as the rape or murder of a clan member. As such, they did not constitute struggles over land or other natural resources, which were relatively abundant, but rather male contests intended to prove courage and preserve honor.

Warfare closely resembled hunting in that successful warriors gained status for their ability to ambush and capture their equivalents from the opposite camp. These unlucky individuals were then brought to the captor's longhouse for what can only be described as an excruciating ordeal, nearly always followed by slaughter and ritual consumption. (Female and child captives, by contrast, were "adopted" as replacements for lost kin.) The religious significance of captive sacrifice among Eastern Woodlands peoples has been less clearly explained than that of the Aztecs and other Mesoamericans, but it seems to have been tied to subsistence anxieties.

Religious thought among Eastern Woodlands peoples varied, but there were commonalities. Beyond the realm of everyday life was a complex spirit world. Matrilineal societies such as the Huron traced their origins to a somewhat malevolent female spirit whose grandsons were responsible for various technical innovations and practices considered essential to civilized human life. The sky itself was often more important than the sun or moon in Eastern Woodlands mythologies, and climatic events were associated with enormous bird spirits, such as the thunderbird.

Like Andean peoples, many Eastern Woodlanders believed that material things such as boulders, islands, and personal charms contained life essences, or "souls." Traders and warriors, in particular, took time to please spirits and "recharge" protective amulets with offerings and incantations. Periodic feasts were also imbued with spiritual energy, but were unlike those of the Aztecs or Incas in that none was held on a specified date. As in many nonurban societies, religious life was an everyday affair, not an institutionalized one. Instead of priesthoods, liturgies, and temples, most Eastern Woodlands peoples relied on elders and shamans to maintain traditions and remind juniors of core beliefs.

Dreams and visions were carefully analyzed for clues to personal and group destinies. Dreams were also analyzed for evidence of witchcraft, or malevolent spell casting, within the group. Stingy or secretive individuals were sometimes suspected of this practice, often associated with jealousy, greed, and other socially unacceptable impulses. As in many semisedentary cultures worldwide, malicious witchcraft was blamed for virtually all sickness and death.

Unlike many other native American groups, most Eastern Woodlanders did not regard death as a positive transition. They believed that souls lived on indefinitely and migrated to a new home, usually a recognizable ethnic village located in the western distance. Even dogs' souls migrated, as did those of wild animals. The problem with this later

Children's Lives

Warfare

Religion

existence was that it was unsatisfying. Dead souls were said to haunt the living, complaining of hunger and other insatiable desires. The Huron sought to keep their dead ancestors together and send them off well through elaborate burial rituals, but it was understood that ultimately little could be done for them.

Conclusion

By the time Europeans entered the Caribbean Sea in 1492, the two continents and many islands that make up the Americas were home to over 60 million people. Throughout the Western Hemisphere, native American life was vibrant and complex, divided by language, customs, and sometimes geographical barriers, but also linked by religion, trade, and war. Cities, pilgrimage sites, mountain passes, and waterways served as crossroads for the exchange of goods and ideas, often between widely dispersed peoples. Another uniting factor was the underlying religious tradition of shamanism.

The many resources available in the highland tropics of Mesoamerica and the Andes Mountains promoted settled agriculture, urbanization, and eventually empire building. Drawing on the traditions of ancestors, imperial peoples such as the Aztecs and Incas built formidable capitals, road systems, and irrigation works. As the Inca capacocha and Aztec warrior sacrifices suggest, these empires were driven to expand at least as much by religious beliefs as by material desires. In part as a result of religious demands, both empires were in crisis by the first decades of the sixteenth century, when Europeans possessing steel-edged weapons, firearms, and other technological advantages first encountered them. Other native peoples, such as the Huron, Iroquois, and Powhatan of North America's eastern woodlands, built chiefdoms and confederacies rather than empires, and to some degree these looser structures would prove more resilient in the face of European invasion.

NOTES

1. For the archaeologist's own account of these discoveries, see Johan Reinhard, *The Ice Maiden: Inca Mummies, Mountain Gods, and Sacred Sites in the Andes* (Washington, DC: National Geographic, 2005).
2. Miguel León-Portilla, *Pre-Columbian Literatures of Mexico* (Norman: University of Oklahoma Press, 1969), 87.
3. Juan de Betanzos, *Narrative of the Incas*, c. 1557, trans. Roland Hamilton and Dana Buchanan (Austin: University of Texas Press, 1996), 92.

RESOURCES FOR RESEARCH

Many Native Americas

Native American history has long been interdisciplinary, combining archaeology, anthropology, history, linguistics, geography, and other disciplines. Here is a small sample of works on the last centuries before European arrival plus several venerable encyclopedias.

Conrad, Geoffrey, and Arthur Demarest. *Religion and Empire.* 1984.

Denevan, William, ed. *The Native Population of the Americas in 1492*, 2d ed. 1992.

National Museum of the American Indian, Washington, DC: http://www.nmai.si.edu/.

Steward, Julian, ed. *The Handbook of South American Indians*, 7 vols. 1946–1959.

Sturtevant, William E., ed. *The Handbook of North American Indians*, 20 vols. 1978–2008.

Trigger, Bruce, ed. *The Cambridge History of the Native Peoples of the Americas*, 3 vols. 1999.

Tributes of Blood: The Aztec Empire, 1325–1521

Scholarship on the Aztecs has exploded in recent years. The following small sample includes new works that synthesize the perspectives of history, anthropology, and comparative religions.

Carrasco, Davíd. *City of Sacrifice: The Aztec Empire and the Role of Violence in Civilization*. 1999.

Carrasco, Davíd, and Scott Sessions. *Daily Life of the Aztecs, People of the Sun and Earth*, 2d ed. 2008.

Clendinnen, Inga. *Aztecs, an Interpretation*. 1994.

For more on Mexico City's Templo Mayor, see: http://archaeology.asu.edu/tm/index2.htm.

Hassig, Ross. *Aztec Warfare: Imperial Expansion and Political Control*, 2d ed. 2006.

Townsend, Richard F. *The Aztecs*, rev. ed. 2000.

Tributes of Sweat: The Inca Empire, 1430–1532

As with the Aztecs, studies of the Incas have proliferated in recent years. Exciting work has taken place in many fields, including archaeology, linguistics, history, and anthropology.

D'Altroy, Terrence. *The Incas*. 2002.

McEwan, Gordon F. *The Incas: New Perspectives*. 2006.

On khipus, see also Prof. Urton's Web site: http://khipukamayuq.fas.harvard.edu.

Urton, Gary. *Signs of the Inka Khipu: Binary Coding in the Andean Knotted-String Records*. 2004.

Von Hagen, Adriana, and Craig Morris. *The Cities of the Ancient Andes*. 1998.

COUNTERPOINT: The Peoples of North America's Eastern Woodlands, 1450–1530

The history of North America's Eastern Woodlands peoples was pioneered by Canadian and U.S.-based anthropologists and historians. It has continued to grow and broaden in scope. Indigenous voices are best heard in James Axtell's documentary history.

The American Indian Studies Research Institute, University of Indiana, Bloomington. http://www.indiana.edu/%7Eaisri/index.shtml.

Axtell, James. *Natives and Newcomers: The Cultural Origins of North America*. 2001.

Axtell, James, ed. *The Indian Peoples of Eastern North America: A Documentary History of the Sexes*. 1981.

Richter, Daniel. *The Ordeal of the Longhouse: The Peoples of the Iroquois League in the Era of European Colonization*. 1992.

Trigger, Bruce. *The Children of Aataentsic: A History of the Huron People to 1660*, 2d ed. 1987.

▶ **For additional primary sources from this period**, see *Sources of Crossroads and Cultures*.

▶ **For Web sites, images, and documents related to topics in this chapter**, see Make History at bedfordstmartins.com/smith.

REVIEW

The major global development in this chapter ▶ The diversity of societies
and states in the Americas prior to European invasion.

IMPORTANT
EVENTS

c. 900–1600	Late Woodland period of dispersed farming and hunting
c. 1100	Aztecs leave Aztlán
c. 1200	Incas move into Cuzco region
c. 1270	Aztecs settle in Valley of Mexico
c. 1320	Aztecs ally with Colhua
c. 1325	Tenochtitlán founded at Lake Texcoco's edge
c. 1437	Incas defeat Chankas
c. 1440–1471	Sapa Inca Pachacuti expands empire into Ecuador and Bolivia
1450–1451	Great famine in Valley of Mexico
1471–1493	Incas conquer northern Chile and Argentina
1487–1502	Aztecs dedicate Coatepec (Templo Mayor) and expand sacrificial wars
1493–1525	Incas conquer northern Peru and highland Ecuador
1502–1519	Reign of Moctezuma II, conquered by Spanish
1525–1532	Inca succession war, followed by arrival of the Spanish
c. 1570	Formation of Huron Confederacy north of Lake Ontario and of Iroquois League south of Lake Ontario
c. 1580	Formation of Powhatan Confederacy in eastern Virginia

KEY
TERMS

autosacrifice (p. 525)   **tribute** (p. 526)
chinampa (p. 523)   **vertical archipelago**
khipu (p. 536)   (p. 530)
longhouse (p. 540)   **waka** (p. 532)
shamanism (p. 518)   **wampum** (p. 540)

CHAPTER OVERVIEW
QUESTIONS

1. In what ways was cultural diversity in the Americas related to environmental diversity?

2. Why was it in Mesoamerica and the Andes that large empires emerged in around 1450?

3. What key ideas or practices extended beyond the limits of the great empires?

SECTION FOCUS
QUESTIONS

1. What factors account for the diversity of native American cultures?

2. What core features characterized Aztec life and rule?

3. What core features characterized Inca life and rule?

4. How did the Eastern Woodlanders' experience differ from life under the Aztecs and Incas?

MAKING
CONNECTIONS

1. Compare the Aztec and Inca empires with the Ming (see Chapter 15). What features did they share? What features set them apart?

2. How did Aztec and Inca sacrificial rituals differ, and why?

3. What were the main causes of warfare among native American peoples prior to the arrival of Europeans?

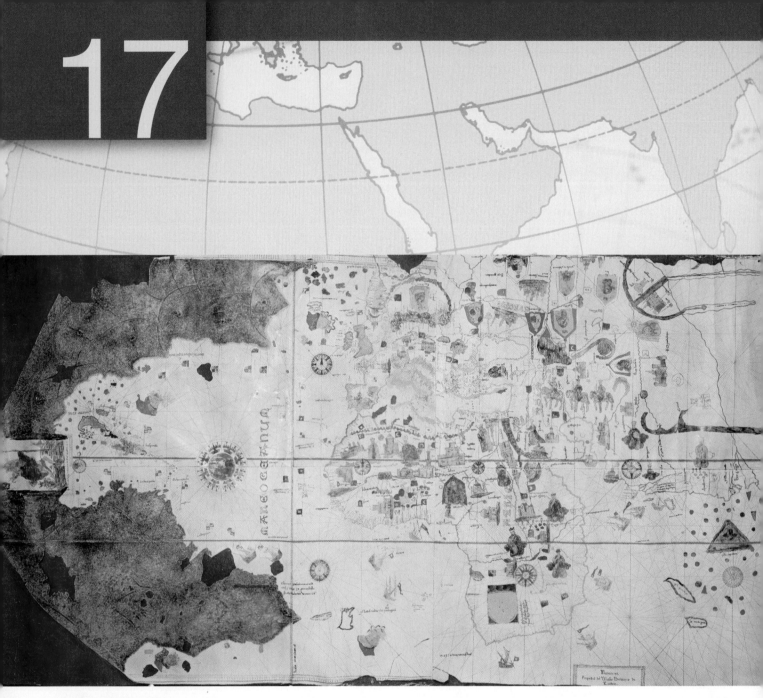

AT A CROSSROADS ▲

Painted on calfskins, portolan ("port finder") charts were used by mariners in the Mediterranean and North Atlantic beginning in the late fourteenth century. In addition to ports, the charts showed coasts and islands and corresponded, at least theoretically, to compass bearings. Like medieval manuscript illuminators, chart-makers occasionally filled blank or unknown spaces with renditions of ships, sea monsters, and freakish foreigners. After Christopher Columbus's momentous transatlantic voyage in 1492, portolan charts began to depict new European discoveries in the Americas with great accuracy. This 1500 map by Juan de la Cosa, who sailed with Columbus, is the earliest such chart. (Museo Naval, Madrid/Bridgeman Art Library.)

The Fall of Native American Empires and the Rise of an Atlantic World

1450–1600

The woman the Aztecs called Malintzin (mah-LEEN-tseen) was only a young girl when she was traded away by her parents around 1510. Malintzin was sent to serve a noble family living in what is today the state of Tabasco, on the Gulf coast of Mexico. She herself was of noble birth, a native speaker of the Aztec language, Nahuatl (NAH-watt). Malintzin's new masters were Chontal Maya speakers, and soon she learned this language, quite different from her own.

Throughout Malintzin's servitude in Tabasco, stories circulated there and in the neighboring Yucatan peninsula of bearded strangers. One day in the year 1519 eleven large vessels filled with these strangers arrived in Tabasco. The Tabascans assembled an attack when one party came ashore in a rowboat, but they were quickly defeated. In exchange for

BACKSTORY

By the mid-1400s, some 60 million people inhabited the Americas, about half of them subjects of the Aztec and Inca empires (see Chapter 16). These empires relied on far-flung tribute networks and drew from diverse cultural traditions even as they spread their own religious practices and imperial languages. Outside the Aztec and Inca realms, smaller states and chiefdoms occupied much of the hemisphere. Conflict between groups, whether in Peru, Brazil, Mexico, or eastern North America, was frequent.

The inhabitants of western Eurasia and North Africa were slowly recovering from the Black Death of 1347–1350 (see Chapter 15). Weakened nobilities and rebounding populations stimulated trade, political consolidation, and the adoption of new technologies for war and transport. The long-distance trade in luxury goods such as silk and spices also recovered, but by the early 1400s the rise of the Ottoman Empire in the eastern Mediterranean intensified competition and limited western European access to overland routes such as the Silk Road. The Asian luxury trade drained Europe of precious metals, prompting enterprising Italians and the seafaring Portuguese and Spanish of the Iberian peninsula to seek gold in Africa, to plant slave-staffed sugar colonies in the islands of the Mediterranean and eastern Atlantic, and to search for sea routes to Asia. In so doing they would link distant continents and initiate the development of a new Atlantic world.

Guns, Sails, and Compasses: Europeans Venture Abroad

FOCUS Why and how did Europeans begin to cross unknown seas in the fifteenth century?

New Crossroads, First Encounters: The European Voyages of Discovery, 1492–1521

FOCUS What were the main sources of conflict between Europeans and native Americans in the first decades after contact?

Spanish Conquests in the Americas, 1519–1600

FOCUS What factors enabled the Spanish to conquer the Aztec and Inca empires?

A New Empire in the Americas: New Spain and Peru, 1535–1600

FOCUS Why was the discovery of silver in Spanish America so important in the course of world history?

Brazil by Accident: The Portuguese in the Americas, 1500–1600

FOCUS How and why did early Portuguese Brazil develop differently from Spanish America?

COUNTERPOINT: The Mapuche of Chile: Native America's Indomitable State

FOCUS How did the Mapuche of Chile manage to resist European conquest?

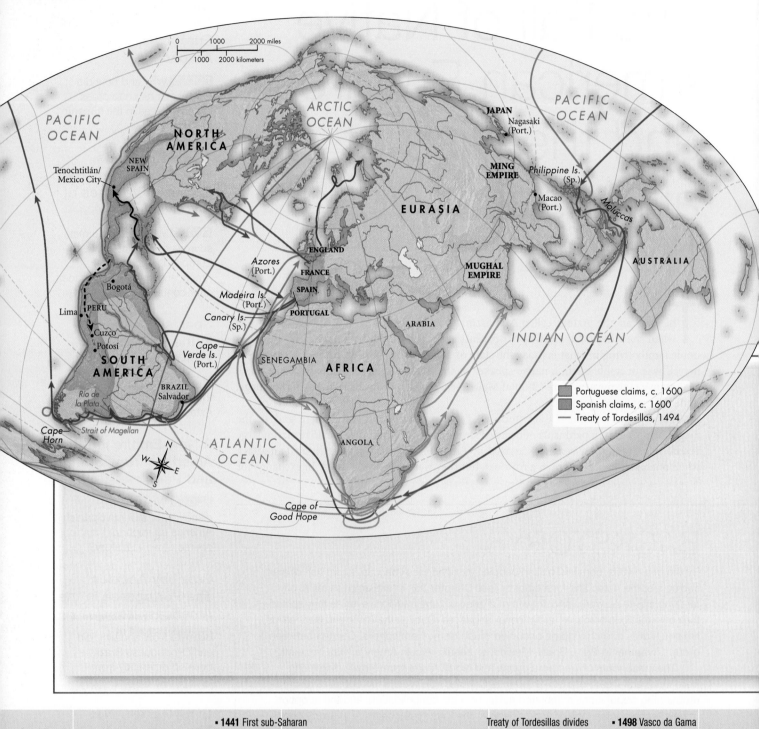

Portuguese claims, c. 1600
Spanish claims, c. 1600
Treaty of Tordesillas, 1494

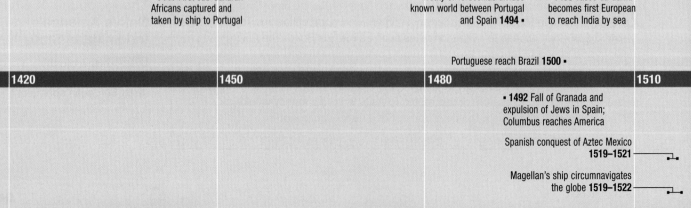

• **1441** First sub-Saharan
Africans captured and
taken by ship to Portugal

Treaty of Tordesillas divides
known world between Portugal
and Spain **1494** •

• **1498** Vasco da Gama
becomes first European
to reach India by sea

Portuguese reach Brazil **1500** •

1420	1450	1480	1510

• **1492** Fall of Granada and
expulsion of Jews in Spain;
Columbus reaches America

Spanish conquest of Aztec Mexico
1519–1521

Magellan's ship circumnavigates
the globe **1519–1522**

peace, they offered the strangers gold and feather work, and also several servant girls, among them Malintzin. When asked through an interpreter where the gold had come from, the Tabascans said "Mexico."

The strangers' interpreter was a bearded Spanish castaway called Jerónimo de Aguilar. He had lived several years in the Yucatan, but had now been ransomed by his countrymen. Aguilar soon discovered that Malintzin knew the language of Aztec Mexico. Their strangers' leader, Hernando Cortés, took a special interest in her for this reason, but as several of the strangers would later write, he also considered her the most beautiful and intelligent of the group of young female captives.

Twice given away now, and less certain than ever of her future, Malintzin joined the bearded foreigners in their cramped, floating homes. Heading west in the direction of the Aztec heartland, they reached a tiny island within sight of the mainland. Here Cortés ordered a party ashore to make contact with local villagers and, through them, to initiate a conversation with a group of traveling Aztec representatives. Only Nahuatl was spoken.

Suddenly the bilingual Malintzin was thrust into a mediating role of global significance. She passed along in Nahuatl the words the Spanish castaway gave her in Chontal Mayan. Then she did the reverse when the Aztec ambassadors replied. Aguilar made sense of the Mayan replies in the strangers' language for Cortés, who was already planning a risky march to take over the Aztec capital. Malintzin soon learned Castilian Spanish,

MAPPING THE WORLD
European Exploration and Conquest, c. 1450–1600

Combining a variety of shipbuilding and navigating technologies in innovative ways, and arming themselves with powerful new guns, western Europeans set out in search of spices, gold, and slaves. Some also sought Christian allies and converts. Merchants shared knowledge and pooled capital in Portugal's capital of Lisbon, the first seat of truly global maritime exploration. Soon after the Portuguese came the Spanish, among them settlers, traders, missionaries, and—most famously—conquistadors. These toppled the great American empires of the Aztecs and Incas within a generation of Columbus's landing in the Caribbean. The French, Dutch, and English followed the Iberian lead, but had little to show for their efforts before 1600.

ROUTES ▼

European exploration

→ Portuguese, 1487–1500

→ Spanish, 1492–1522

→ English, 1497–1580

→ French, 1534–1536

→ Dutch, 1596

Spanish conquistadors

→ Hernando Cortés, 1519–1521

--→ Francisco Pizarro, 1531–1533

1532–1536 Spanish conquest of Inca Peru

1549 Portuguese establish royal capital of Salvador; first Jesuits arrive in Brazil

1572 Mita labor draft and mercury amalgamation formalized in Potosí

1555 French establish colony in Brazil's Guanabara Bay

1540

1570

1600

1545 Discovery of silver deposits at Potosí

1570–1571 Inquisition established in Lima and Mexico City

1592 Potosí reaches peak production

1564 Discovery of mercury mines in Huancavelica, Peru

1567 Portuguese drive French from Brazil

1599 Great Mapuche uprising in Chile

rendering Aguilar unnecessary. From here until the end of the conquest campaigns in 1521, Malintzin served as Cortés's key to Aztec Mexico.

In the midst of conquest Malintzin bore Cortés a son, but she ultimately married another Spaniard and lived with the respect given to European ladies in the first years of colonial rule. Malintzin joined a host of other former Aztec subjects who helped the foreigners build Mexico City from the rubble of the former Aztec capital of Tenochtitlán, and eventually a vast Christian kingdom called New Spain.

In modern Mexican mythology Malintzin, or Malinche (mah-LEEN-cheh), as she is commonly known, is regarded as a traitor, a collaborator, even a harlot. Recent scholars have shown these characterizations to be both anachronistic and unfair. Malintzin was not seen as a traitor in her own day, even by the Aztecs. In their paintings of the conquest, Nahuatl-speaking artists working shortly after the arrival of the Spanish often placed Malintzin at the center, poised and confident, speech scrolls emanating from her mouth. For a culture that called its kings *tlatoque*, or "speakers," this was significant.

But why was it mostly southern Europeans who were sailing across the Atlantic in Malintzin's and Cortés's time? In part it was because residents of the old European crossroads of Iberia (the peninsula occupied by Spain and Portugal), including colonies of Italian merchants, had begun charting the eastern Atlantic at least a century before. Also, in finishing what they called the *Reconquista* (Reconquest) of their homeland, Christian Iberians were driven to outflank the growing Ottoman Empire in North Africa and to revive the global crusade against Islam. Over time, a mix of commercial, political, and religious motives inspired the merchants and monarchs of Portugal and Spain, Europe's southwestern-most kingdoms, to develop the technologies needed to navigate open seas, exploring first the west coast of Africa and then crossing the vast Atlantic itself. Flush with capital, Italian bankers helped fund these enterprises (as we saw in Chapter 15).

The Iberian encounter with the Americas that resulted from all of these factors was an accident of monumental significance. In quest of legendary Asian riches, Columbus and his successors landed instead in the vast and populous but previously isolated regions they called the New World. It was new to them, of course, but hardly so to its roughly 60 million native American inhabitants. Cultural misunderstandings, political divisions among indigenous peoples, and European firearms aided conquest and settlement, but germs made the difference in a way not seen anywhere in Africa or Asia. Only certain Pacific Islanders proved as vulnerable.

Among the manifold effects of European expansion across the Atlantic was a biological exchange of profound importance for all humanity. Dubbed by historian Alfred Crosby "the Columbian Exchange," this was the first major biological relinking of the earth since the continents had drifted apart in prehuman times. Although the Columbian Exchange brought many deadly diseases to the Americas, it also brought new animals for transport, plowing, and consumption. Among the many effects of this global exchange was rapid population growth in parts of the world where American crops such as potatoes and maize took root. As a result of European expansion to the west, the Atlantic became a global crossroads, the center of a new pattern of exchange that would have consequences for the entire world.

Finally, we should not make the mistake of assuming that Europeans met little or no significant resistance in the Americas. As we shall see in the Counterpoint that concludes this chapter, one group of native Americans who successfully fought off European conquest, in part by adopting the horse and turning it against their oppressors, were the Mapuche of Chile.

OVERVIEW
QUESTIONS

The major global development in this chapter: European expansion across the Atlantic and its profound consequences for societies and cultures worldwide.

As you read, consider:

1. What were the main biological and environmental consequences of European expansion into the Atlantic after 1492?

2. What roles did misunderstanding and chance play in the conquests of the Aztecs and Incas?

3. How did Eurasian demand for silver and sugar help bring about the creation of a linked Atlantic world?

Guns, Sails, and Compasses: Europeans Venture Abroad

Since late medieval times, Nordic and southern European mariners had been venturing farther and farther out to sea, testing seasonal winds and following currents as they founded new colonies and connected markets to regions of supply. Sailors and navigators shared information, but as in the Mediterranean, colonizing distant lands was a competitive, religiously charged, and violent process, one that also entailed fusing technologies from around the world. In the fifteenth century tiny Portugal emerged as the world's first truly global maritime empire. Neighboring Spain followed, spurred on by Christopher Columbus and a crusading spirit.

FOCUS

Why and how did Europeans begin to cross unknown seas in the fifteenth century?

Motives for Exploration

Early modern Europeans had many reasons for engaging in overseas ventures, but most shared a common interest in accumulating wealth, gaining power against their rivals, and spreading Christianity. Commerce was a core motive for expansion, as European merchants found themselves starved for gold and silver, which they needed to purchase Asian spices, silks, gems, and other luxuries. With the exception of Mediterranean coral and, increasingly, guns, Europe produced little to offer in exchange for eastern luxuries. In part because of Europe's relative poverty, ambitious monarchs and princes adopted violent means to extend their dominions overseas and to increase their tax and tribute incomes. Finally, Europe's many Christian missionaries hoped to spread their religion throughout the globe. These motives would shape the early encounters between Europeans and the peoples of the Americas, as well as the subsequent hybrid societies that would emerge in the conquered lands.

"Gold is most excellent," wrote Christopher Columbus in a letter to the king and queen of Spain. "Gold constitutes treasure, and anyone who has it can do whatever he likes in the world."[1] Columbus, a native of the Italian city-state of Genoa, knew what he was talking about. Genoese merchants had long traded for gold in North Africa, where Muslim traders who crossed the Sahara from West Africa brought it to exchange for a variety of goods. African gold lubricated Mediterranean and European trade, but population growth, commercial expansion, and intensifying competition among Christian and Islamic states

Gold and Spices

strained supplies. It was thus the well-placed Portuguese, who established a North African foothold in Morocco in 1415, who first sought direct access to African gold.

Italian merchants made some of their greatest profits on spices, which were used as both medicines and flavoring agents. Since most spices came from the farthest tropical margins of Asia, they rose considerably in value as they passed through the hands of mostly Islamic middlemen in the Indian Ocean and eastern Mediterranean. Indian pepper and Indonesian nutmeg were but a few of the many desired drugs and condiments that Portuguese and other European merchants hoped to purchase more cheaply by sailing directly to the source. This entailed either circumnavigating Africa or finding a western passage to the Pacific.

Slaves and Sugar

Throughout the Mediterranean basin, slaves were prized as field laborers and household servants, and demand for them grew with the expansion of commercial agriculture and the rise of wealthy merchant families. Prices also rose as source regions near the Black Sea were cut off after 1453 by the Ottomans. As the word *slave* suggests, most captives came initially from the Slavic regions of eastern Europe. Others were prisoners of war taken in battles and pirate raids. In part to meet growing Christian European demand, increasing numbers of sub-Saharan Africans were transported to North African ports by caravan. As with gold, southern European merchants engaged in this trade were quick to seek captives by sailing directly to West Africa.

Sugar, yet another exotic commodity in high and growing demand in Europe, required large investments in land, labor, and machinery. Produced mostly by enslaved workers on eastern Atlantic islands such as Portuguese Madeira by the mid-fifteenth century, cane sugar, in medieval times considered a spice or drug, increasingly became a common commodity in Europe as both a sweetener and preservative. As sugar took the place of honey in Old World cuisines, few consumers pondered its growing connection to overseas enslavement. In time, European demand for sugar would lead to the establishment of the Atlantic slave trade and the forced migration of millions of Africans to the Americas.

Technologies of Exploration

Firearms Manufacture

As they set sail for new horizons, Europeans employed innovations in three technological spheres: gun making, shipbuilding, and navigation. First was firearms manufacture. Gunpowder, a Chinese invention, had been known since at least the ninth century C.E. Chinese artisans experimented with rockets and bombs, but it was late medieval and early modern Europeans who developed gunpowder and gun making to their greatest destructive effect.

Europeans had also borrowed and improved on ancient Chinese papermaking and movable type technologies, and by 1500 they published treatises detailing the casting and operation of bronze and iron cannon. Soon, crude handguns and later muskets transformed field warfare, first in Europe, then worldwide. As gun and powder technologies improved and fighters acquired shooting and reloading skills, contingents of musketeers replaced archers, crossbowmen, and other foot soldiers.

Shipbuilding and Navigation

The second key technological leap was in ship construction. Although numerous small, swift-sailing vessels traversed the Mediterranean in late medieval times, long-distance carriers were cumbersome and even dangerous when overloaded. The Roman-style galley, used mostly in the Mediterranean, was a long and narrow fighting vessel propelled by captive oarsmen with occasional help from sails. Galleys functioned effectively where seas were calm, distances short, and prisoners plentiful. Galleys also worked well to defend against pirates and for massive showdowns, but they were almost useless for carrying cargo.

The galley proved unreliable for the rougher waters and longer voyages common in the North Atlantic. Here, in the old trading ports and fishing villages of Portugal, Spain, western France, the Netherlands, and England, shipwrights combined more rigid North Sea hull designs and square sail rigs with some of the defensive features of the galley, such as the high aft-castle, or fortified cabin built on the rear deck. They also borrowed and incorporated the galley's triangular or lateen sails, which in turn had been adapted from the Arabian *dhows* of the Indian Ocean.

The resulting hybrid vessel combinations, which included the caravel form used by ocean-crossing mariners such as Columbus, proved greater than the sum of their parts. Although slow and unwieldy by modern standards, these late-fifteenth-century European ships were the world's most durable, swift-sailing, and maneuverable means of heavy transport to date. Later modified into galleons, frigates, and clippers, they would serve as the basic models for virtually all European carriers and warships until the advent of steam technology in the early nineteenth century.

European innovations in navigational technology also propelled overseas expansion. Learned cosmographers believed the world to be more or less spherical by Columbus's time, but finding one's way from port to port beyond sight of land was still a source of worry. One aid in this dilemma was the magnetic compass, like gunpowder and printing a fairly ancient Chinese invention developed in a novel way by Europeans. We know from travelers' accounts that sailors in the Indian Ocean also used compasses in medieval and early modern times, but rarely in combination with sea charts, which contained detailed compass bearings and harbor descriptions. The combination of charts and compasses soon changed European navigators' perceptions of what had formerly been trackless seas.

Another borrowed instrument, apparently Arabic in origin, was the astrolabe. A calculator of latitude (one's location north or south of the equator), it proved even more critical for long-distance maritime travel than the compass. Precise knowledge of latitude was essential for early modern sailors in particular since longitude, a more complicated east-west calculation, was little known until the invention of seaworthy clocks in the mid-eighteenth century.

Thus armed with an impressive ensemble of borrowed and modified tools, weapons, and sailing vessels, Europeans were well poised to venture out into unknown or unfamiliar worlds. Add the recent development of the printing press, and they were also able to publicize their journeys in new if not altogether honest ways.

Portuguese Ship

The Portuguese were the first Europeans to develop ocean-going ships for extended, return voyages. Initially they combined rigid hull designs from the Atlantic with maneuverable triangular sails of Arabic origin to build caravels, but these small vessels had limited cargo space and were vulnerable to attack. This evocative image from a contemporary manuscript shows Vasco da Gama's flagship, the *St. Gabriel*, on its way to India in 1497–1498 with every stitch of canvas out. For such long trips the Portuguese chose to sacrifice the maneuverability of the caravel in favor of maximizing sail surface and relying on trade winds. The resulting ships, which could carry up to 1200 tons of cargo and were built like floating fortresses, are known as "carracks." Portugal's national symbol until recent times, the red cross of the Order of Christ identified such ships as Portuguese. (The Art Archive/Science Academy Lisbon/Gianni Dagli Orti.)

Portugal Takes the Lead

Historians have long wondered why tiny Portugal, one of Europe's least populated and developed kingdoms, led the way in overseas expansion. A closer look at key factors helps solve this puzzle. First, the kingdom of Portugal was an ancient maritime crossroads straddling two vibrant commercial spheres, the Mediterranean and northeast Atlantic. Coastal shipping had grown efficient in late medieval times while overland transport between northern and southern Europe remained slow, costly, and prone to banditry. Well before 1400, long-distance merchants from as far away as Venice and Stockholm put in at Lisbon,

Overseas Incentives

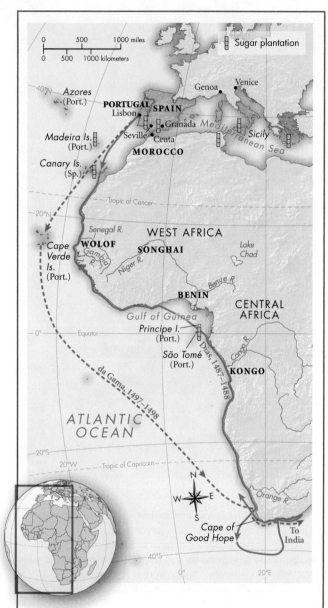

MAP 17.1

The East Atlantic, c. 1500

The Portuguese were the first Europeans to seek a sea route to Asia, and they did so by making their way south along the Atlantic coast of Africa. The diseases of tropical Africa limited Portuguese colonization to a few fortified enclaves, but they established lucrative settlement colonies in the eastern Atlantic island chains of the Azores, Madeiras, and Cape Verdes, along with the wet tropical island of São Tomé in the Gulf of Guinea. By 1500 the Portuguese had discovered that the fastest way to round the tip of Africa was to follow the prevailing winds and currents that swept to the west of the African coast before turning southeast.

the Portuguese capital, to break up their long journeys. Commercial competition was fostered by Portugal's kings, and along with money and exotic goods, important shipbuilding and sailing knowledge was exchanged. Capital, in the form of money, ships, and goods, also accumulated in the hands of powerful merchant clans, many of them foreign.

Other factors besides accumulating capital and foreign merchants pushed the Portuguese abroad. By the 1430s, fishermen regularly ventured far out into the Atlantic in pursuit of better catches. Moreover, arable land in Portugal grew scarce as populations grew and large estates expanded, rendering overseas colonization ever more attractive. Also, religious and strategic concerns drove Portuguese nobles to capture the Islamic port city of Ceuta (SYOO-tah), on Morocco's Mediterranean coast, in 1415. Crusade-like ventures such as this continued to overlap with commercial ones throughout early modern times. Thus, the push of limited resources at home and the pull of opportunities abroad stimulated Portuguese expansion.

With support from ambitious nobles such as Prince Henry "the Navigator" (1394–1460), Portuguese and foreign investors pooled capital accumulated in shipping and moneylending and invested it in a variety of new technologies to create a far-flung network of settlement colonies and *feitorias* (fay-toe-REE-ahs), or fortified trading posts. Some invested in overseas plantations in the eastern Atlantic and Mediterranean, others in the gold and slave trades of West Africa (see Map 17.1).

Gaining confidence with each new experience, Portuguese merchants and sailors learned to navigate the complex currents and prevailing winds of the West African coast. By 1430 they had come upon the Azores and Madeiras, uninhabited island chains in the eastern Atlantic. With incentives from the Crown and some Italian merchant investment, Portuguese settlers immediately colonized and farmed these islands. The Canaries, farther south, were somewhat different. Inhabited by dozens of bands and chiefdoms descended from pre-Islamic Moroccan immigrants, these rugged volcanic islands posed distinct political and moral challenges. "They go about naked without any clothes," wrote one Portuguese chronicler, "and have little shame at it; for they make a mockery of clothes, saying they are but sacks in which men put themselves."[2]

What was to be done? Should the inhabitants of the Canary Islands be conquered and their lands taken over by Europeans, and if so, by what right, and by whom? The presence of indigenous Canarians in fact spurred competition among a variety of European adventurers. Among them were Spanish missionaries and militant French and Portuguese nobles, but Spanish nobles under Isabella and Ferdinand, Columbus's future sponsors, ultimately won title to the islands. The Guanches (HWAN-chehs), as the Europeans called the largest group of native inhabitants, lost to the point of annihilation. A few survivors were enslaved and made to work on sugar plantations. In many ways, the Canarian experience foretold Iberian, and more generally European, actions in the Americas. When they stood in the way of European ambitions, the interests of indigenous peoples counted for little or nothing.

Always in search of gold, which the eastern Atlantic islands lacked, and spurred on by Prince Henry, the Portuguese in 1444 reached the mouth of the Senegal River. On the Senegal, the Portuguese traded Arabian warhorses for gold dust with representatives of the Muslim Wolof kingdoms. They also traded, and on a few occasions raided, for slaves. The victims of these 1440s raids and exchanges were the first Africans to be shipped en masse across Atlantic waters. Most ended up in the households and artisan workshops of Lisbon.

Portuguese reconnaissance in the eastern Gulf of Guinea in the 1480s led to contacts with the kingdom of Benin and also to settlement of the offshore islands of Príncipe and São Tomé. Some captives from Benin were forced to plant and refine sugar on São Tomé. The slave-staffed tropical sugar plantation, which would define the economy and culture of colonial Brazil and much of the Caribbean basin from the fifteenth to nineteenth centuries, found a prototype here off the coast of central Africa in the years just before Columbus's famous voyages. Iberians developed similar plantations in the Canaries and Madeira.

By 1488, Bartolomeu Dias rounded Africa's Cape of Good Hope, and ten years later, Vasco da Gama became the first European to reach India by sea. Given the momentum, cumulative knowledge, and overall success of the Portuguese enterprise, it is understandable that when in the early 1480s Christopher Columbus proposed to open a westward route to "the Indies," the Portuguese king, on the advice of his cosmographers, declined. Columbus's calculations were in doubt, as was the need for an alternative of any kind. Once in the Indian Ocean, the Portuguese used their sturdy ships and superior firepower to terrifying effect, taking more than a dozen key ports from their mostly Muslim inhabitants by 1510. The emphasis on capturing ports reflected Portuguese ambitions. They sought to dominate the existing maritime Asian trade, not to establish a colonial land empire. Thus, as we shall see, Portuguese and Spanish expansion would take very different forms.

Origins of the Atlantic Slave Trade

Push to Asia

New Crossroads, First Encounters: The European Voyages of Discovery 1492–1521

Portugal's Spanish neighbors had long been interested in overseas expansion as well, although by Columbus's time they lagged far behind. Spanish sailors and shipbuilders were as competent as those of Portugal, and some nobles and merchant families were tied to the early African trade. What would quickly distinguish Spain's overseas enterprises from Portugal's, however, was a stronger tendency to acquire large landmasses by force, colonize them with large numbers of settlers, and force Catholicism on all inhabitants. To some extent this pattern of expansion derived from the centuries-long Christian Reconquest of the Iberian peninsula that ended with the defeat of the Muslim caliphate of Granada in January 1492. As if fated, it was at Ferdinand and Isabella's royal military encampment, Santa Fe de Granada, that Columbus received his license to sail across the Ocean Sea, the name then given to the Atlantic.

> **FOCUS**
> What were the main sources of conflict between Europeans and native Americans in the first decades after contact?

Christopher Columbus in a New World

Christopher Columbus, born in the Italian city of Genoa in 1451, was just one of many ambitious merchants who came of age in the dynamic, profit-seeking East Atlantic world centered on Lisbon. Columbus married Felipa de Perestrelo, a Portuguese noblewoman, but did not settle down. Instead, he spent most of his time sailing on Portuguese merchant vessels bound for West Africa, England, and even Iceland. He soon became obsessed with a scheme to sail west to China and Japan, which he had read about in the already two-hundred-year-old account of the Venetian merchant Marco Polo. In around 1485 Columbus left for Spain,

feitoria A Portuguese overseas trading post, usually fortified.

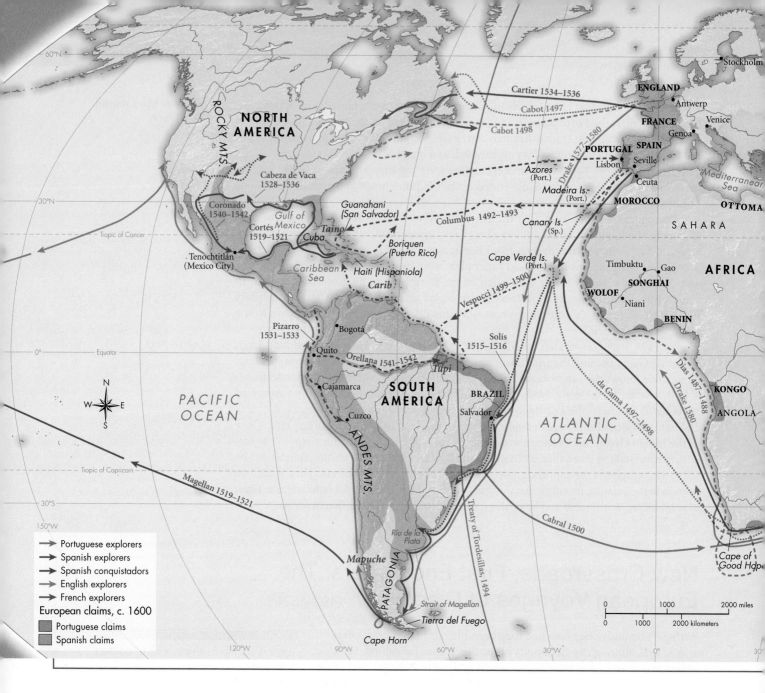

where he eventually won the sponsorship of Isabella and Ferdinand. By 1492 he was off to cross the Atlantic in search of the successors of Qubilai Khan, China's famed thirteenth-century Mongol ruler. "I set out for Your Highnesses' Canary Islands," he wrote to Ferdinand and Isabella in his ship's log, "in order to begin my journey from there and sail until I should arrive in the Indies, there to deliver Your Highnesses' embassy to those princes."[3]

On October 12, 1492, barely a month after leaving his last stopover point in the Canary Islands, Christopher Columbus and his mostly Spanish crew made contact with the native Taino (tah-EE-no) inhabitants of Guanahani, one of the smaller Bahama Islands. Unable to communicate with them, Columbus imagined himself somewhere near Japan, or at least "east of India." He christened the island San Salvador, or "Holy Savior," as a religious gesture of thanks, and called the native Bahamians and all other indigenous peoples he subsequently encountered "Indians" (see Map 17.2).

Remarking in his journal that the "Indians" he met in the Bahamas were tall, well built, scantily clad, and ignorant of iron weapons, Columbus proposed that they would make excellent slaves. The Indians reminded him of the native Canary Islanders whom the

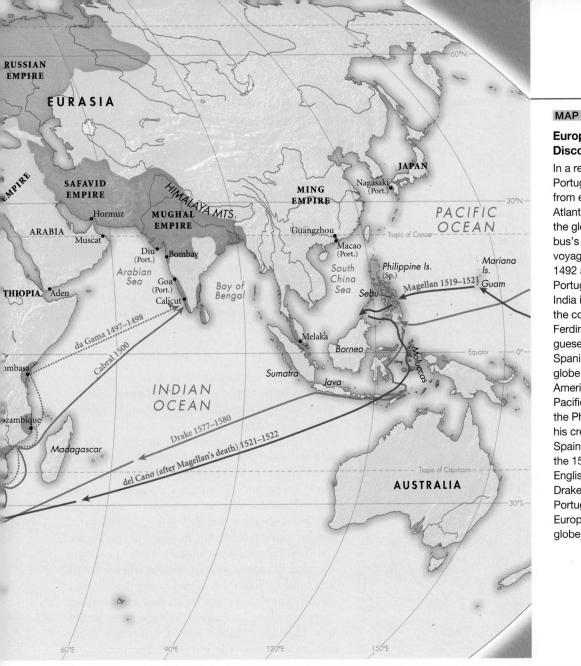

MAP 17.2

European Voyages of Discovery, c. 1420–1600

In a remarkably short time, the Portuguese and Spanish went from exploring the eastern Atlantic to circumnavigating the globe. Christopher Columbus's first Spanish-sponsored voyage across the Atlantic in 1492 and Vasco da Gama's Portuguese-sponsored trip to India in 1497–1498 heightened the competition, and by 1519 Ferdinand Magellan, a Portuguese navigator sailing for the Spanish, set out to circle the globe by rounding South America and crossing the Pacific. Magellan was killed in the Philippines, but some of his crew survived to return to Spain in 1522. It was not until the 1577–1580 voyage of the English privateer Francis Drake, led by a kidnapped Portuguese pilot, that another European circumnavigated the globe.

Spanish and Portuguese had conquered and enslaved. True to his word, Columbus eventually shipped some five hundred Caribbean natives to the markets of Seville.

After the first landfall in the Bahamas, Columbus sailed southwest to Cuba, then east to the large island known locally as Haiti. He renamed it "Española" ("Hispaniola," "Little Spain" in English) and began looking for a town site to settle in the name of his queen. In the course of this and three subsequent voyages, Christopher Columbus claimed and named everything and everyone that came into his view for his royal Spanish sponsors. In his logbook, Columbus constantly reiterated his hopes of finding gold, spices, and news of "the Great Khan." He died in 1506, still believing he was near China.

For the diverse American peoples who met Columbus and his crewmembers, the heavily clothed and armed foreigners provoked mixed feelings. They brought some useful goods, including hatchets and sewing needles, but when their incessant demands for food, gold, and sexual companionship were not met, they turned violent, torturing, raping, and murdering native islanders at will. No one, least of all Columbus, seemed willing to punish the newcomers or rein them in. Before long, some frustrated Taino hosts returned the violence in kind,

Exploring the Caribbean

Early Native American–Spanish Relations

Columbus Meets Native Americans

On October 12, 1492, the Italian navigator Christopher Columbus reached the Bahama Islands, and soon afterward Haiti, which he renamed "Española," partly pictured here. The native Taino welcomed Columbus, hoping to recruit him as an ally against fierce neighbors the admiral dubbed "Caribs," and later, "cannibals." News of these meetings soon spread throughout Europe, and very early images such as this one accompanying a portion of one of Columbus's published letters show how difficult it was for European artists to imagine what was to them a truly "New World." Even the ship is drawn from medieval tradition, since we know that Columbus sailed in what were then the most sleek and modern caravels. (Corbis.)

but this only led to massive vengeance raids organized by better-armed colonists. In the most extreme cases, native women killed their children, then themselves, to avoid violation.

Columbus, meanwhile, kept looking for China, and for gold. The "Indians" seemed not to have much interest in the yellow metal, preferring instead a gold-copper alloy. From this, Columbus concluded that the Indians were not only "natural slaves," but they knew no commerce; they were ignorant of price. Finally, seeing no churches, mosques, or synagogues, the only religious structures he knew, Columbus assumed all Indians were ignorant of religion as well and came to regard his arrival in the "Indies" as a divinely sanctioned event. He claimed in his writings that the Indians, particularly his Taino allies, needed him for religious indoctrination, instruction in the ways of work and trade, and physical protection.

Caribs Protection was essential due to the presence of "evil" Indians, as Columbus described them, chronic enemies of the Taino. The word *Caribbean* derives from Carib, or *caribe*, apparently an ethnic term. Groups of so-called Caribs did in fact inhabit the smaller islands to the east and south of Borinquen, the large island renamed Puerto Rico, or "Rich Port," by the Spanish. Although culturally similar to the Taino, these Caribs were said to have a particularly bad habit: they ate human flesh.

"Man-eating" natives were in some ways a predictable New World wonder, the sort of marvel medieval travelers had often described for sensation-hungry readers. Columbus happily played along. It appears he blended the Latin *canis* (dog) and local ethnic name *caribe* to produce a new word: *canibal*, or "cannibal." *Carib* and *cannibal* soon became interchangeable terms in the lexicon of Spanish conquest, and the image of the cannibal stuck fast in the European imagination. Indeed, almost as quickly as news of the Indies reached Europe, printers rushed to illustrate the alleged atrocities of the Caribbean "dog-people."

Given the circumstantial nature of the evidence, historians and anthropologists remain divided as to whether the so-called Caribs practiced cannibalism. What mattered for Columbus and his followers was that their allies, the "good Indians," said they did. With such a legal pretext (the eating of human flesh being regarded as a clear violation of natural law in the Western tradition), the newcomers could claim to be serving a necessary

Dog-Faced Cannibals

European readers of chivalry tales and travel accounts expected the American "New World" to yield fantastic and horrible creatures. Early news from the Caribbean and Brazil suggested the existence of humans with doglike, omnivorous appetites, seeming to confirm the alleged observations of Marco Polo and other medieval travelers. In this 1527 woodcut, a German artist fused Weimaraner-like dogs' heads with naked German butchers, one with a raised steel cleaver, to represent native Americans. Since this image predates the Spanish conquest of the Incas by five years, the horned llama-like animal at lower left is of special interest. (Courtesy of the John Carter Brown Library at Brown University.)

police role. By this argument, the Spanish alone could adequately "protect" and "punish"—that is, take over Western-style functions of government in the "New World." Thus, drawing on a variety of assumptions and preconceptions, Europeans imposed their own interpretations on the social and cultural patterns of New World peoples, interpretations that justified European domination.

Spanish sovereignty in the Americas was soon defined against the backdrop of Portugal's older overseas claims. With the pope's backing, in 1494 the Spanish and Portuguese split the world into two zones of influence. According to the terms of the Treaty of Tordesillas, the Spanish were to rule everyone living 370 leagues (roughly 1110 miles) or more west of the Canaries; all inhabitants beyond this line were now subjects of the crown of Spain according to European law. Africa, Asia, and eventually Brazil, which was not known to Europeans until 1500, fell to the Portuguese.

Why was the Roman Catholic pope involved in an agreement of this kind? First, fifteenth-century Europeans regarded his authority as above that of secular rulers. More important, however, was the matter of spreading the Christian gospel, a job Columbus himself embraced. Iberian monarchs, all pious Catholics at this time, promised to sponsor the conversion of everyone their subjects encountered abroad and also to continue the medieval fight against "infidels." Commerce may have supplied the initial and most powerful motive for overseas expansion, but a drive for religious and cultural hegemony soon came to play an important part in European colonization.

Treaty of Tordesillas

From Independence to Servitude: The Encomienda System

Although missionaries were present in the Caribbean from the 1490s, early Spanish colonization of this vast island region amounted mostly to a mad dash for gold and slaves. Early Spanish settlers had little interest in working the land themselves, preferring instead to live from the rents and labor provided by native American slaves and tribute payers. As news of massive abuse and alarming death rates among the Taino and captive Caribs reached Spain, Queen Isabella demanded an end to Amerindian slavery. After 1503 only violent rebels and alleged cannibals were to be enslaved.

Compromise on Native American Slavery

Would the Taino then be free in exchange for accepting Catholicism and Spanish protection against the Caribs? No, in large part because their labor was thought necessary to mine gold, which Spain's monarchs desperately wanted. Compromise came in the form of the *encomienda* system. Native villages headed by chieftains were entrusted to leading Spanish citizens in a manner resembling medieval European feudalism: village farming folk were to offer labor and surplus produce to their "lord" in exchange for military protection. Chiefs served as middlemen, exempted from tribute and manual work. The Spanish *encomenderos* who received these fiefdoms were self-styled men-at-arms, and from their ranks would come the conquerors of the mainland.

Indians deemed good and faithful subjects of Crown and Church paid tributes to their encomendero, or "trustee," as he was called, in farm products, textiles, and other local goods, twice a year. Adult men were also required to lend their labor to the encomendero from time to time, helping him clear farmland, round up livestock, and construct buildings. For his part, the encomendero was to protect his tributaries from outside attack and ensure their conversion to Christianity. However reciprocal in theory, the encomienda system was in fact used mostly to round up workers for the gold mines. It looked like slavery to the few Spanish critics who denounced it, and even more so to the many thousands of native peoples who suffered under it.

Bartolomé de Las Casas's Defense of Native American Rights

"And on the Day of Judgment it shall all be more clear," thundered Bartolomé de Las Casas in a sermon-like tract, "when God has His vengeance for such heinous and abominable insults as are done in the Indies by those who bear the name of Christians."[4] Las Casas was a Hispaniola encomendero's son turned Dominican priest who emerged as the leading defender of native American rights in early modern times. Some historians have argued that he represented another, more humanitarian side of the Spanish character in the otherwise violently acquisitive era of Columbus and his successors. Through constant pleading at court, and in widely publicized university debates and publications, Las Casas helped to suppress the indigenous slave trade and sharply restrict the encomienda system by the early 1540s. For the Tainos who first met Columbus, the reforms came too late. By 1510 there were only a few hundred encomienda subjects where a decade before there had been hundreds of thousands. By almost any measure, the Columbian era in the Caribbean was a disaster.

Columbus's Successors

Columbus's accomplishments as a navigator spawned dozens of like-minded expeditions (see again Map 17.2). These included the four voyages of Amerigo Vespucci (1497–1504), a Florentine merchant for whom the continents of the Western Hemisphere would later be named. Vespucci gained most fame as an early publicist of the new lands and peoples that southern Europeans were rapidly encountering throughout the American tropics. Vespucci came to realize that the Americas were not part of Asia. This did not, however, prevent him from embracing other European preconceptions. In relating his voyages to Brazil to Medici rulers in Florence, Vespucci calmly described the roasting and eating of human flesh among the local inhabitants. His reports only added to the European fixation on native American cannibalism.

Early Global Reconnaissance

Other voyages of reconnaissance included those of Juan de Solís and Ferdinand Magellan. Both were seasoned Portuguese explorers sailing in the service of Spain, and both, like Columbus, sought a westward route to Asia. Solís sailed up the Río de la Plata estuary near modern Buenos Aires in 1516, but was captured and killed in a skirmish with local inhabitants. Magellan learned details of the Argentine coast and its currents and winds from survivors of the Solís expedition, then organized a much more ambitious voyage to the Moluccas, or Maluku, in what is today Indonesia. The epic journey that followed, arguably one of the boldest ever undertaken, was recorded by yet another Italian, the Venetian Antonio de Pigafetta.

encomienda A feudal-style grant of a native American village to a conquistador or other Spaniard.

Columbian Exchange Historian Alfred Crosby's term for the movement of American plants, animals, and germs to the rest of the world and vice versa.

Of the five ships that left Spain in 1519, two were wrecked before Magellan reached the treacherous straits at the southern tip of South America that still bear his name. When food ran short, crewmembers shot, salted, and ate penguins and sea lions. Encounters with the native inhabitants of Tierra del Fuego and the neighboring mainland were mostly brief and hostile, reminiscent of Columbus's early encounters. Always the good publicist,

Pigafetta described exchanges and conflicts with primitive giants, giving rise to the legend of Patagonia, or "the land of Big Foot."

Once in the Pacific, Magellan set a northwesterly course that eventually led to Guam, in the Mariana Islands east of the Philippines. The four-month ocean crossing had left much of the crew suffering from malnutrition, and many others died from the effects of scurvy, a debilitating disease caused by lack of vitamin C. Magellan then sailed to the Philippine island of Sebu, where he became embroiled in a dispute between local chieftains. Alarmed to find Muslim merchants active in the region, Magellan sought to create an alliance with new converts to Christianity through a show of force. Instead, he and forty crewmembers were killed. Only one vessel managed to escape and return to Spain in 1522 by following the new Portuguese sailing route through the Indian and Atlantic oceans. For the first time in recorded history, the world had been circumnavigated (see again Map 17.2).

Meanwhile, in the Caribbean, Spanish colonists became rapidly disillusioned with the fabled "West Indies" of Columbus. Unhappiest of all were newly arrived immigrants from the Iberian peninsula, desperate young men with dreams of gold and a more promising future in a new world. Such men, and most immigrants were men in the early years, fanned out across the Caribbean in search of new sources of wealth, both human and metallic. Most failed, and many died, but some eventually found what they sought: fabled continental empires rich beyond belief.

The Columbian Exchange

In a landmark 1972 book, historian Alfred Crosby argued that the most significant consequences of 1492 were not political or even commercial, but biological.[5] What Crosby called the **Columbian Exchange** referred to the massive interoceanic transfer of animals (including humans), plants, and diseases that followed in Columbus's wake. Many of these transfers, such as the introduction of rats and smallpox to the Americas, were unintentional. Yet all had profound consequences.

TVRCICVM
FRVMENTVM.
Türckisch korn.

Maize

Perhaps the most globally transformative native American crop (vying with the potato), maize was first domesticated in highland Mexico some 7000 years ago. This 1542 German depiction is the most accurate to survive from the first decades after maize was introduced to Europe. Similar varieties soon transformed global dietary patterns, particularly in sub-Saharan Africa. Some cultures adopted maize only as livestock feed. (*De Historia Stirpium*, 1542, Leonhard Fuchs, Typ 565.42.409(B), Houghton Library, Harvard University.)

Since European explorers circled the globe shortly after Columbus's time, this process of biological exchange was almost from the start a worldwide phenomenon. Indigenous cuisines, farming practices, and transportation modes were changed, sometimes for the better. Northern European populations, for example, grew rapidly following the introduction of Andean potatoes, which thrived in cool, wet climates. South and Southeast Asian cuisines were forever changed after the introduction of American capsicum peppers and peanuts, which flourished in the Old World tropics.

But European cattle, sheep, pigs, goats, horses, and other large domestic mammals also rapidly altered landscapes, sometimes with catastrophic consequences. In the worst case, the highlands of central Mexico were quickly denuded and reduced to deserts following the introduction of sheep in the sixteenth century. Lacking predators, and having access to vast new pastures, their populations exploded. Similar processes of environmental transformation were later repeated in Australia, New Zealand, Argentina, and the western United States.

Biological and Environmental Transformations

Epidemic Diseases and Population Loss

As in the case of ship borne rats, many unwanted exchanges took place in the first phases of global interaction. Worst among these were diseases, mostly caused by viruses, bacteria, and blood parasites, introduced to previously unexposed hosts. Since Africa and Eurasia had long been linked by waves of trade, warfare, migration, and pilgrimage, the repeated spread of diseases such as smallpox, measles, and mumps had allowed people over time to develop immunity against these and other pathogens. As seen in Chapter 15, pandemics of plague could be devastating in Africa and Eurasia, but never to the extent that they would be in long-isolated regions overseas. The peoples of the Americas, Australia, and Polynesia proved tragically vulnerable in this regard; they suffered what was probably the worst demographic collapse in history.

In the early modern Americas poor hygiene and medical care, chronic warfare, forced labor, and malnutrition all accompanied European conquest, rendering new disease agents more destructive. Documentary evidence suggests that throughout the Americas and Pacific Islands, indigenous populations declined by almost 90 percent within a century. Recovery and acquired immunity came slowly. With the introduction of malaria, yellow fever, and other mosquito-borne blood parasites—as deadly for Europeans as anyone else—America's lowland tropics did not recover their precontact populations until the introduction of insect-killing pesticides following World War II. On the plus side, world food exchanges spurred rapid population growth in Europe, Africa, and Asia, and contributed to the rebound of the Americas. Overall, the spread of American food crops boosted world population significantly before the end of early modern times. The peoples of the Americas, however, paid a steep price for these new and more productive connections between the world's societies.

Spanish Conquests in the Americas 1519–1600

FOCUS

What factors enabled the Spanish to conquer the Aztec and Inca empires?

Two men disappointed by their prospects in the Caribbean islands were Hernando Cortés and Francisco Pizarro. Cortés gained fame by the 1520s as conqueror of the Aztecs, and Pizarro after 1532 as conqueror of the Incas. Their extraordinary actions on the American mainland gave rise to the almost mythical Spanish-American livelihood of **conquistador**, or conqueror. Like Columbus, neither man acted alone, but both altered the course of global history. Also like Columbus, these two famous conquistadors, though made hugely rich by their exploits, both ended their lives unappreciated and disgraced. The sword of conquest was double-edged.

The Fall of Aztec Mexico

As we saw in Chapter 16, the people known as Aztecs called themselves Mexica (meh-SHEE-cah). By the time Spaniards arrived on Central America's Atlantic shores in the late 1510s, the Mexica ruled much of Mesoamerica, often by terror. The empire centered on the fertile highlands surrounding modern Mexico City, but extended south to the Pacific coast and east into Guatemala. Cortés would soon discover, however, that the Aztec Empire was vulnerable.

The Road to Tenochtitlán

A brash and ambitious leader, Hernando Cortés left his base in southern Cuba after a dispute with his sponsor, the governor. In Yucatan, as we have seen, he found an extraordinarily valuable translator in the person of Malintzin. By September of 1519 Cortés set out for the interior from the new town of Veracruz on Mexico's Gulf coast. With him were Malintzin and several hundred horses and well-armed men. The Spanish also brought with them fierce mastiffs, huge dogs bred for war. After a series of attacks on both Aztec allies and enemies, the Spanish and several thousand new allies entered Tenochtitlán in November 1519 as guests of the emperor, Moteuczoma, or "Moctezuma," II.

conquistador Spanish for "conqueror," a new livelihood in the Americas after Columbus.

Shortly after being welcomed and treated to a feast by the curious and gracious Moctezuma, Cortés and his followers managed to capture and imprison the unsuspecting emperor. Fearful for their ruler's life, the Aztec people, now leaderless, faced great uncertainty. Not afraid to use terror in his own way, Cortés ordered that anyone who opposed the Spanish and their allies would be publicly cut to pieces and fed to the dogs. Treachery, terror, and seizure of indigenous leaders were in fact stock tactics developed by Spanish conquistadors in the course of their decades of Caribbean slave raiding. These tactics proved even more effective against mainland imperial peoples who depended on divine kings. Attached to their subsistence plots, settled farmers had nowhere to run.

There followed almost eight months of looting and destruction, accompanied by a mix of open battles and informal skirmishes. Some former Aztec subjects supported the Spanish, most significantly the Tlaxcalans, but others resisted violently. Soon unfamiliar diseases such as smallpox and influenza swept through Tenochtitlán and the entire Valley of Mexico, decimating a vast and densely populated region already facing food shortages. Ironically, the people who would give the world maize, tomatoes, chocolate, vanilla, and a thousand other life-sustaining and pleasurable foods were now receiving only the most deadly ingredients of the Columbian Exchange: viruses and bacteria. Cortés ordered that images of the Virgin Mary be placed atop Aztec temples to assert the power of the invaders' Christian deities.

Cortés's Invasion of the Aztec Empire, 1519–1521

Aztec Empire, 1519
Cortés's original route, 1519
Cortés's retreat, 1520
Cortés's return route, 1520–1521

Spanish Setbacks

While Cortés went to negotiate with soldiers sent by Cuba's governor to arrest him in early 1520, the Spaniards left behind in Tenochtitlán provoked a siege by massacring Aztec nobles. Rushing to the city with Cuban recruits whom he had just won over, Cortés reached his comrades only to be trapped by the Aztec warriors. The desperate Spaniards brought out the captive emperor, Moctezuma, in hopes of calming tempers, but he was killed in a hail of stones. The besieged Spanish tried to flee Tenochtitlán, but there was no sneaking out of a city linked to the mainland by only three narrow causeways. Cortés and a handful of conquistadors escaped at the head of the pack, but many other Spaniards, about half the total number, fell into Aztec hands. One Spanish soldier recalled: "As we marched along we were followed by the Mexicans who hurled arrows and darts at us and stones from their slings, and the way in which they surrounded us and continually attacked us was terrifying."[6] According to Aztec accounts, when the city's male warriors fell dead or exhausted, women warriors took over, attacking the foreign enemy with equal vigor (see Reading the Past: Tlatelolcan Elders Recall the Conquest of Mexico). Despite the ravages of disease and the loss of their emperor, the Aztecs were still capable of dishing out terror in kind.

Final Victory

Cortés and his bedraggled Spanish forces eventually regrouped with aid from the Tlaxcalans, their staunchest allies, but it was over a year before Tenochtitlán and its twin city of Tlatelolco fell. Cut off from the mainland, the Aztecs faced starvation, then attack by land and water. Cortés ordered thirteen small, European-style sailing vessels built on the shores of Lake Texcoco, and armed with cannon these helped pound remaining Aztec warrior contingents in canoes. By August 1521 Cortés and his men and allies had forced the Aztecs to retreat to Tlatelolco. Soon, both cities were occupied and pillaged. Yet the Aztec capital proved hard to hold. Angry at the lack of valuable plunder, the Spanish responded to persistent urban rebels by razing virtually all residential buildings.

Soon after, a successor emperor to Moctezuma was captured and killed, after having been tortured for allegedly hiding booty. Dissatisfied conquistadors then fanned out across Mesoamerica in search of riches and empires. The self-promoting Cortés traveled to Spain in hopes of consolidating his gains, but found little support from the emperor Charles V. The material and political conquest of the Aztec center had not

Tlatelolcan Elders Recall the Conquest of Mexico

In what would become New Spain, or colonial Mexico, Spanish missionaries quickly introduced European-style writing systems. Indigenous scribes picked them up within a few decades of the conquest, rendering Nahuatl, Maya, and other local languages in a Latinate script with Spanish phonetics. Formal documents, including histories and sermons, were produced in this manner, but also interviews, myths, genealogies, criminal testimonies, and a host of everyday transactions. The following excerpt is a direct English translation of a Nahuatl document from about 1540 relating the conquest of both Tenochtitlán and its "twin city," Tlatelolco. The Tlatelolcan elders relating the story to junior scribes apparently witnessed and participated in the events in question.

> And when they reached Yacocolco here, Spaniards were captured on the Tlilhuacan [tleel-WALK-on] road, as well as all the people from the various altepetl [allied city-states]. Two thousand died there, and the Tlatelolcans were exclusively responsible for it. At this time we Tlatelolcans set up skull racks; skull racks were in three places. One was in the temple courtyard at Tlillan, where the heads of our [present] lords [the Spaniards] were strung; the second was in Yacocolco, where the heads of our lords [the Spaniards] were strung, along with the heads of two horses; the third place was in Çacatla, facing the Cihuateocalli (see-wah-tayoh-CAH-yee) [Woman-Temple]. It was the exclusive accomplishment of the Tlatelolcans. After this they drove us from there and reached the marketplace. That was when the great Tlatelolcan warriors were entirely vanquished. With that the fighting stopped once and for all. That was when the Tlatelolcan women all let loose, fighting, striking people, taking captives. They put on warriors' devices, all raising their skirts so that they could give pursuit.

Source: James Lockhart, ed. and trans. *We People Here: Nahuatl Accounts of the Conquest of Mexico* (Berkeley: University of California Press, 1993), 265–267.

EXAMINING THE EVIDENCE

1. What does this document tell us about Aztec political identity during the conquest?

2. What does it tell us about military culture and gender roles?

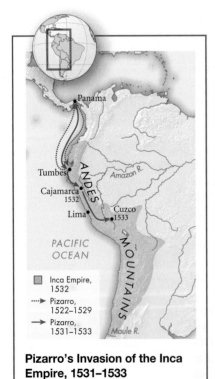

Pizarro's Invasion of the Inca Empire, 1531–1533

been easy, and at the fringes conquest was far from over. Far more difficult would be the winning of the hearts and minds of millions of former Aztec subjects now anxious to assert their own agendas. This would be the long story of colonial Mexico, a "New Spain" so unlike its Iberian namesake.

The Fall of Inca Peru

When Francisco Pizarro left the small Spanish settlement of Panama City in 1522 in search of "Pirú," a mythical chieftain, he had no idea that events high in the Andes Mountains to the south would conspire to favor his dream of repeating the success of Cortés. But as with Cortés and his many companions and aides, an empire—even with guns, germs, and steel on one's side—could not be toppled overnight.

In fact it took a decade of coastal reconnaissance and humiliating failure before Pizarro at last marched into what is today the Republic of Peru. In the meantime he had acquired Quechua translators immersed for several years in Castilian Spanish; a small army of men with horses, armor, and state-of-the-art weapons; and a license from Charles V. By late 1532, when Pizarro's forces began their inland march across a coastal desert reminiscent of southern Spain, Peru at last seemed ripe for the taking.

Tawantinsuyu (tuah-wahn-tin-SUE-you), as the Incas called their empire, was in deep crisis in 1532. A five-year battle over succession had recently ended with Atawallpa (also Atahualpa) emerging the winner. According to several eyewitness accounts, when

Pizarro Meets Atawallpa

Throughout colonial times native and European artists depicted the day in 1532 when Inca emperor Atawallpa met Francisco Pizarro. This is the first known image of the Peruvian encounter, a woodcut accompanying an eyewitness account published in Seville, Spain, in 1534. It depicts Atawallpa on a litter holding up what is probably the prayer book given him by the priest Vicente de Valverde, also pictured. Pizarro stands back with his fellow Spaniards, armed but not poised to attack. In the distance is a European-style castle presumably meant to stand for an Inca city. Notably absent is the native Andean interpreter whom we know only by his Christian name, "Little Philip." (Courtesy of the John Carter Brown Library at Brown University.)

Pizarro and his 168 men climbed into the Andes to meet Atawallpa in the sacred city of Cajamarca, the new Sapa Inca was flush with victory. Atawallpa did not feel vulnerable, and in fact intended, rather like Moctezuma in Mexico, to draft the strangely bearded and well-armed foreigners into his service. Though their horses, firearms, and steel swords were cause for wonder, the Inca did not mistake the Spanish for gods.

According to survivor testimonies, in November 1532 Pizarro and his men captured Atawallpa in a surprise attack reminiscent of Cortés's seizure of Moctezuma. Humiliated, Atawallpa was held hostage for nearly a year as his subjects scrambled to gather up gold and silver to free him. The Incas possessed far more gold and silver than the Aztecs, and the hoard of metals offered to free their leader, whom most Andeans regarded as a divine being, was staggering. Suddenly Pizarro and his followers were rich beyond their wildest dreams.

Thus "Peru" became instantly synonymous with great wealth among Europeans, an association that would soon be reinforced by the discovery of immensely rich silver mines. Despite the ransom, however, Atawallpa was killed on Pizarro's orders in 1533. The treachery was complete, and by 1534 Tawantinsuyu was in Spanish hands.

The Conquest: Myths and Realities

How did a small number of Spanish men manage to topple two of the world's most populous and extensive empires in a relatively short time? Some biologists and anthropologists have claimed that these great, isolated indigenous empires faced inevitable defeat because they lacked iron, sufficient protein, draft animals, wheeled vehicles, writing, acquired immunity to numerous pathogens, and other advantages. Historians have long puzzled over this riddle, too, but more with an eye on human actors and the timing of events.

For their part, the conquistadors and their Spanish contemporaries regarded these victories as the will of their Christian God. Spain's enemies—and internal critics such as Las Casas—emphasized the conquistadors' "sins" of treachery, cruelty, lust, and greed. By the nineteenth century, historians less interested in judging the Spanish focused on the leadership abilities of individuals. They emphasized the intelligence and tenacity of Cortés and Pizarro, and the apparent weakness and indecisiveness of their adversaries, Moctezuma and Atawallpa. This emphasis on "great men" was aided by the conquistadors' own insistence that they were mistaken for gods everywhere they went.

Malintzin and the Meeting Between Moctezuma and Cortés

This image, taken from the early postconquest document known as the *Florentine Codex*, was drawn and colored by an indigenous Mexican artist who had been exposed to European prints and paintings while being schooled by Spanish friars. In it, Malintzin translates the words between Aztec emperor Moctezuma and Hernando Cortés at their momentous first meeting.

Malintzin Interprets for Cortés and Moctezuma
(The Granger Collection, New York.)

EXAMINING THE EVIDENCE

1. How does this drawing reflect the indigenous artist's instruction by Spanish friars?

2. To what extent is it a reflection of Malintzin's perceived importance in the conquest of Mexico?

Factors of Conquest

Recently, historians have focused on other causal factors. These include the importance of indigenous allies and interpreters; the conquistadors' accumulated experience as "Indian fighters" in the Caribbean; internal imperial politics and the timing of Spanish arrival; indigenous adaptation to Spanish fighting methods; contrasting goals of warfare; and of course, the introduction of novel weapons, animals, and diseases. Most historians agree that the conquests resulted from the convergence of these many variables—a number of them, such as the appearance of Malintzin the able translator, completely unpredictable (see Seeing the Past: Malintzin and the Meeting Between Moctezuma and Cortés).

A final point worth emphasizing is that indigenous peoples were not overawed by Spanish horses and technology, nor did they view the newcomers as gods. As this quote from a Spanish soldier who participated in the conquest of Mexico suggests, Aztec warriors adapted rapidly to the threat of cannon and armored opponents on horseback:

> One day an Indian I saw in combat with a mounted horseman struck the horse in the chest, cutting through to the inside and killing the horse on the spot. On the same day I saw another Indian give a horse a sword thrust in the neck that laid the horse dead at his feet. . . . Among them are extraordinary brave men who face death with absolute determination.[7]

The evidence from Inca Peru barely differs. After the capture of Atawallpa in 1532, Andean warriors quickly learned to avoid open field engagements where they might be run down by mounted Spaniards, preferring instead to ambush their enemies as they crossed rivers and traveled through narrow canyons. Simple stones and slingshots proved a surprising match for guns and steel-edged weapons in these conditions. Rebellions and raids continued for decades in the Mexican and Peruvian backcountry, but the rapid Spanish conquest of the Aztec and Inca imperial cores was sealed by those empires' own former subjects; although they did not know what was in store for them, most were anxious for something different.

A New Empire in the Americas: New Spain and Peru 1535–1600

Within a few generations of conquest, Spanish settlers penetrated deep into the Americas, transforming the world's largest overseas land empire into the world's greatest source of precious metals. Spain's monarchs in turn used this mineral bounty to pursue their religious and territorial ambitions in Europe and beyond. Merchants used it to link the world economy in unprecedented ways. But for the millions of native Americans subjected to Spanish rule, life would revolve around negotiating a measure of freedom within an imperial system at least as taxing as those of the Aztecs and Incas.

FOCUS

Why was the discovery of silver in Spanish America so important in the course of world history?

American Silver and the Global Economy

In 1545 an indigenous prospector came across silver outcrops on a high, red mountain in what is today south-central Bolivia. The Cerro Rico, or "Rich Hill," of Potosí (poh-toe-SEE), as it was soon known, turned out to be the most concentrated silver deposit ever discovered (see Map 17.3). Indeed, no other silver strike approached the extraordinary wealth of Potosí until modern times. This and related silver discoveries in early Spanish America radically transformed not only life in the colonies, but the global economy. As we will see in subsequent chapters, in regions as distant as China and South Asia, American silver affected people's livelihoods in profound and unexpected ways. Even before Potosí, silver mines had been discovered in highland Mexico in around 1530, and many new finds followed. Mexican districts such as Zacatecas (zah-cah-TAY-cus) and Guanajuato (hwan-uh-WAH-toe) were expanding rapidly by the 1550s and would continue to drive Mexico's economy well into the modern period.

Although the Spanish quickly adopted efficient Old World techniques of tunneling and refining, the silver boom also spurred important technical innovations. Chief among these was the use of mercury to separate silver from crushed ore. Amalgamation, as this process is known, was practiced in antiquity, but it was Bartolomé de Medina, a merchant working in the Mexican mines of Pachuca in the mid-1550s, who developed and patented a low-energy, large-scale refining process suitable for New World environments. Medina's invention revolutionized Spanish-American silver mining even as it spread one of the world's most persistent toxins, mercury.

Refining Innovations

Amalgamation was implemented in Potosí on a large scale after 1572 as part of a crown initiative to stimulate production. Although Spain itself produced substantial mercury, New World sources had been avidly sought since Potosí's discovery. Before long, the mine owners' dreams came true; in the Peruvian highlands southeast of Lima, the mercury mines of Huancavelica (wan-kah-bell-EE-cah) were discovered in 1564. Thus the Spanish paired Andean mercury with Andean silver, touching off an enormous boom in production. Potosí yielded tens of millions of ounces of silver annually by the 1580s. It was enough to pave the main streets of the town with silver bricks during religious processions.

Even with abundant mercury, silver production remained costly. Unlike gold panning, underground mining required massive capital inputs, especially in labor and technology. Water-powered silver-processing mills, first developed in Germany, were among the most complex machines in use in early modern times. Mercury remained expensive despite a crown monopoly meant to assure availability. Less often calculated, although well known even in the sixteenth century, were the environmental and health costs of mercury pollution. Soils, rivers, and refinery workers' clothing were saturated with mercury, leading to a range of neurological disorders and birth defects. "Trembling like someone with mercury poisoning" became a common colonial metaphor for fright, akin to "shaking like a leaf."

Environmental Hazards

More costly than mercury and machines combined was labor. Mining was hard and deadly work, attracting few volunteers. African and African-descended slaves supplemented

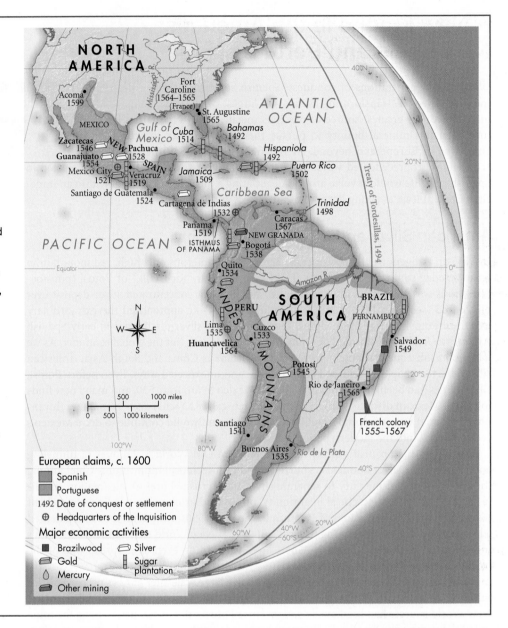

MAP 17.3

European Claims in the Americas, c. 1600

Beginning in the 1510s, the Spanish used bases in Cuba and on the Isthmus of Panama to launch the conquests of the Aztec and Inca empires. In search of similar empires, Spanish explorers drove deep into the interiors of North and South America; by the 1540s they had penetrated the U.S. Southwest and South America's Río de la Plata basin, and made their way down the Amazon. Other conquests in Central America, northwest Mexico, and New Granada led to the creation of a vast Spanish-American Empire, under the twin capitals of Mexico City and Lima. Portuguese Brazil, by contrast, consisted only of a few small settlements along the Atlantic coast, but by 1600 it was the world leader in sugar production, increasingly dependent on the labor of enslaved Africans.

The Mine Draft

mita A Spanish revival of the Inca draft labor system.

repartimiento An allotment of indigenous laborers in colonial Mexico, similar to the Andean mita.

the workforce from an early date in boomtowns such as Zacatecas and Potosí, but Spanish-American silver mines came to rely mostly on native American draft and wageworkers. The draft, or *mita* (MEE-tah) as it was called in the Andes, entailed a year of service in Potosí, Huancavelica, or some other mining center, followed by six years of work in one's own home region, usually in subsistence farming or herding. In Mexico the Spanish implemented a similar system called *repartimiento* (reh-par-tee-MYEN-toe).

Drafted indigenous laborers received a small wage and rations during their work stints, but given the danger of these jobs and the high cost of living in mining towns, the mita and repartimiento proved hugely disruptive of indigenous lifeways. Many considered draft work a death sentence. The miners of Huancavelica, in particular, faced lifelong degenerative illnesses caused by mercury poisoning. Others were killed by cave-ins and falls. Furthermore, indigenous women and children forced to occupy Spanish-American mining towns suffered from contaminated food, air, and water supplies. Exposure to heavy metals, a hazard usually associated with modern industrialization, was probably worst for native American draftees and African slaves engaged in refining tasks. Here in

The Rich Mountain of Potosí
This c. 1603 image of Potosí's famous Cerro Rico shows not only the legendary red mountain with its silver veins but also workers, most of them native Andeans, refining silver by mercury amalgamation, and antlike llamas carrying ore down the mountain. The ore-crushing mill in the foreground is powered by a stream of water supplied by canals coming down from artificial reservoirs built high in a neighboring mountain range. (The Hispanic Society of America Museum and Library, New York.)

the mills mercury was routinely vaporized, and large quantities of lead, arsenic, and other heavy metals were smelted along with silver. Such was the human cost of making money.

Potosí boomed in the first years of the mita, reaching peak production in 1592, but heightened demand for mine laborers in this remote and unhealthy site only worsened an already dramatic indigenous demographic collapse. Most eligible workers who remained in the region quickly learned to avoid the most dangerous tasks, and many sold whatever they could to pay a cash fee for exemption. Mine owners were increasingly forced to pay wages to stay in business.

American Silver and Everyday Life

The silver bonanza of the sixteenth century altered livelihoods worldwide. In the Spanish colonies, everything from ranch work to church building was connected in one way or another to the flow of silver. The armies of dependent miners living in towns such as Potosí and Zacatecas spurred merchants and landowners to expand their inventories, crops, and livestock herds. Mule-drivers, weavers, tanners, and countless other specialists came to rely on the continued productivity of the mines for their sustenance. In town centers, indigenous and mixed-heritage market women took advantage of crown-mandated tax exemptions to carve out a lucrative space as well. But along with this new orientation of the colonial economy toward silver production came an intensification of conversion efforts on the part of Spanish missionaries. Worldwide, Spanish-American silver funded a massive expansion of the Catholic Church.

Whereas most indigenous peoples adapted quickly to Spanish legal and civic traditions and even tolerated the oppressive obligations of mine work, most resisted total conversion to Catholicism. Confident in the universality of their religion, European missionaries expected indigenous populations to accept Christianity as the one true faith. When they did not, the process of cultural exchange shifted from conversion to coercion. After a brief period of optimism, in which a small number of newly arrived European priests met and mingled with tens of thousands of indigenous subjects, violence erupted. Within a few decades of military conquest, the Catholic Church was commonly using prosecution, public humiliation, and even torture and execution throughout Spanish America.

Challenges of Religious Conversion

Native Americans were not the only victims of religious intolerance. Offices of the **Inquisition**, a branch of the Catholic Church dedicated to enforcing orthodox beliefs and practices, were established in Mexico City and Lima in 1570 and Cartagena in 1610. Their purpose was to punish alleged deviants and heretics among the Spanish settlers, including a number of secretly practicing Jews and a few Muslims. In the indigenous majority (soon exempted from prosecution by the Inquisition due to their newness to the faith), complete conversion was limited by long-held, core religious beliefs. Most native American converts rejected monotheism, belief in a single, supreme god. Instead, they adopted the Christian God, his holy intermediaries, and saints on their own terms, as new additions to an already crowded pantheon. There were other misunderstandings. Thousands of native converts were baptized, only to return the next day to request that this new and pleasant ceremony be performed again. Catholic missionary priests became pessimistic and often angry with their seemingly stubborn parishioners. Conversion, unlike military conquest, was a slow process that depended on more than missionary zeal. It also required missionaries to achieve a better understanding of would-be converts.

It was only after some priests learned to speak indigenous languages fluently that Europeans began to fathom, and in some cases transform, native cosmologies. One way around the obstacle of conflicting core beliefs was to ignore elders and focus conversion efforts on native youths, particularly boys. Upon maturity, they would presumably serve as exemplary believers, leaders in the new faith. Many such boys were removed from their parents' custody, taught to read and write, and ordered to collect and collate essential myths and sagas. These stories were then rewritten by European priests to match Christian history and beliefs.

Yet even as the missionaries succeeded with some native men, they failed miserably with women. Indigenous women, despite repeated sexual assaults by conquistadors, merchants, overseers, and even priests, carried on with their lives, teaching their children the old ways and also pressing for social recognition and advancement within the new social order. Some, like Malintzin, refashioned themselves as something in between Spanish and indigenous, often bearing **mestizo** (meh-STEE-soh) or mixed-heritage children. But the extraordinary persistence of indigenous American languages, religious practices, food ways, and dress through modern times is due mostly to humble indigenous women, unsung keepers of the hearth. Despite the determination of Spanish priests and conquistadors to remake the Americas to serve European interests and ambitions, indigenous culture would continue to play a powerful role in colonial society.

Brazil by Accident: The Portuguese in the Americas 1500–1600

FOCUS

How and why did early Portuguese Brazil develop differently from Spanish America?

Despite some notable similarities with their Spanish neighbors north and south, the Portuguese followed a distinct path in colonizing Brazil. The general trend in the century after contact in 1500 was from benign neglect and small-scale trade with indigenous coast-dwellers toward a more formal royal presence and settled plantation agriculture, mostly concentrated along the northeast coast. By 1600, Brazil was the world's largest sugar producer. It also became the prime destination for sub-Saharan African slaves. A key stimulus for this tectonic shift in colonial policy and economy was French encroachment between 1503 and 1567. The arrival of French traders and religious refugees in Brazil forced the Portuguese to briefly take their eyes off India.

Native Encounters and Foreign Competitors

It was on the way to India in early 1500 that the Portuguese captain Pedro Alvares Cabral and his large fleet were blown westward from Cape Verde, in West Africa. Toward the end of April the fleet unexpectedly sighted land, which the captain dubbed the "Island of the True Cross." The landmass was later found not to be an island, but rather a mountainous stretch of the continent of South America. Columbus and the Spanish were at this time only

Inquisition A branch of the Catholic Church established to enforce orthodoxy.

mestizo A person of mixed European and native American ancestry.

First Encounter in Brazil: Cabral's Report to King Manoel of Portugal

On May 1, 1500, Pedro Alvares Cabral's scribe, Pero Vaz de Caminha, recorded the first known meeting between Europeans and Tupi-speaking tribespeople in a letter to the king. Unlike the Tainos who met Columbus, the indigenous peoples who met Cabral and his crew had no gold—perhaps luckily. Unimpressed, the foreigners dispatched a small vessel home to Lisbon to report on their "discovery," and the great fleet sailed on to India.

In appearance they are dark, somewhat reddish, with good faces and good noses, well shaped. They go naked, without any covering; neither do they pay more attention to concealing or exposing their shame than they do to showing their faces, and in this respect they are very innocent. Both [captives taken from a canoe to see Cabral] had their lower lips bored and in them were placed pieces of white bone, the length of a handbreadth, and the thickness of a cotton spindle and as sharp as an awl [pointed tool] at the end. . . . Their hair is smooth, and they were shorn, with the hair cut higher than above a comb of good size, and shaved to above the ears. And one of them was wearing below the opening, from temple to temple towards the back, a sort of wig of yellow birds' feathers . . . very thick and very tight, and it covered the back of the head and the ears. This was glued to his hair, feather by feather, with a material as soft as wax, but it was not wax. Thus the headdress was very round and very close and very equal, so that it was not necessary to remove it when they washed. . . .

One of them saw . . . some white rosary beads; he made a motion that they should give them to him, and he played much with them, and put them around his neck; and then he took them off and wrapped them around his arm. He made a sign towards the land and then to the beads and to the collar of the captain, as if to say that they would give gold for that. We interpreted this so, because we wished to, but if he meant that he would take the beads and also the collar, we did not wish to understand because we did not intend to give it to him. And afterwards he returned the beads to the one who gave them to him. . . .

There were also among them four or five young women just as naked, who were not displeasing to the eye, among whom was one with her thigh from the knee to the hip and buttock all painted with black paint and all the rest in her own color; another had both knees and calves and ankles so painted, and her privy parts so nude and exposed with such innocence that there was not there any shame.

Source: William Brooks Greenlee, trans., *The Voyage of Pedro Alvares Cabral to Brazil and India* (Nendeln/Lichtenstein: Kraus Reprint Limited, 1967, reproduced by permission of the Hakluyt Society, 1938), 10–21.

EXAMINING THE EVIDENCE

1. Why might Cabral's scribe have been so keen to describe the physical features, piercings, and personal adornments of Tupi men and women in such detail in a letter to the king of Portugal?

2. What does the passage concerning the captain's collar reveal about European and indigenous attitudes and communication?

---

beginning to touch upon its northern shores, and had no sense of its size. The huge portion of the continent claimed by Portugal would later be called Brazil (see again Map 17.3).

Brazil was of little interest to Portugal for some time despite the fact that it fell within the domain delineated by the 1494 Treaty of Tordesillas, signed with Spain and sanctioned by the pope (see Reading the Past: First Encounter in Brazil: Cabral's Report to King Manoel of Portugal). Without gold or some other lucrative export, there seemed to be little point in colonizing this distant land. Brazil's one obvious resource, and what earned it its name, was brazilwood, a tree with a deep-red, pithy heart. Portuguese traders, soon followed by French competitors, set up posts all along Brazil's vast coast to barter with indigenous Tupi speakers for precut, red-hearted logs.

Cut and carried to shore by indigenous men, brazilwood was then shipped to Europe, where dye was extracted and sold at profit. Native Brazilians willingly participated in this trade because it brought them tangible benefits: metal hatchets, knives, sewing needles, and other utilitarian items, along with beads, mirrors, bells, and other personal and ritual adornments. For some, it also brought military alliances against traditional enemies. In several places Portuguese *degredados*, or criminal castaways, survived their tropical exile and married into eminent indigenous families, becoming translators and commercial middlemen.

Early Dyewood Trade

This use of criminal exiles to spearhead colonization was quite different from Spanish practices in the Americas.

**Portuguese Response
to French Competition**

French competition for control of Brazil and its dyewood pressed the Portuguese to assert their claims more forcefully. A fleet of warships was sent from Lisbon in 1532 to protect Portuguese traders and to punish French interlopers. Land claims were to be organized differently, too. After 1534 Brazil was carved into fifteen proprietary colonies, granted by King Manoel to courtiers ranging from noble warriors to scholars. Brazil's proprietary governors were told to encourage permanent settlement by farmers and artisans from their home districts. This was similar to Spanish plans in the early Caribbean, but the models the king had in mind were Madeira and the Azores, Portugal's earlier experiments with overseas settlement colonies. Brazil's new proprietors were also expected to organize the defense of their holdings against French and indigenous enemies. The closest the Spanish ever came to such private colonization schemes was Charles V's grant of parts of Venezuela to German banking families in the 1530s and 1540s, all of which failed.

With few exceptions, the Brazilian proprietary colonies also failed; the French were still a menace, and native Brazilians, not Portuguese colonists, had the run of the land. In 1549 the Crown tried another strategy: Salvador, a defensible hamlet located at the tip of the wide Bay of All Saints in northeastern Brazil, was made the royal capital and seat of a governor general. Jesuit missionaries, only a half dozen of them at first, also arrived. They soon fanned out across Brazil to convert tens of thousands of native, Tupi-speaking allies to Roman Catholicism. From here forward, enemies of the Crown or faith, indigenous and otherwise, would be given no quarter.

French Retreat from Brazil

The French did not easily give up on their Brazilian enterprise, and in fact redoubled their efforts at midcentury. In 1555 they established a new colony in Guanabara Bay, near modern Rio de Janeiro (see again Map 17.3). The colony's leader proved incapable of sorting out disputes between Catholics like himself and numerous Protestant refugees, or Huguenots. Divided by religion, like France itself at the time (as we will see in Chapter 20), the French colony was doomed. The Portuguese drove out Catholics and Protestants alike by 1567. As for indigenous enemies, including the allies of the French, Portuguese wars and slaving expeditions would continue throughout colonial times.

Bitter Sugar: Slavery and the Plantation Complex in the Early Atlantic World 1530–1600

A search for precious metals and gems came up short soon after the royal capital of Salvador was established in 1549, but the Portuguese found other ways beyond brazilwood to profit from a tropical colony. On Brazil's northeast coast, sugar cane was planted along the banks of several rivers as early as the 1530s. By 1570, Brazil was the world's number-one sugar producer, a position it still holds. Cane sugar was Brazil's answer to Spanish-American silver. It was an exotic cash crop with a growing market abroad. Europeans, in particular, could not get enough of it. First indigenous, then African, slaves were made to do the bulk of the burdensome work required to produce sugar (see Lives and Livelihoods: Atlantic Sugar Producers).

**Dependence on Enslaved
Africans**

Sugar growers in the region surrounding Salvador competed vigorously with their counterparts in Pernambuco, one of the few surviving proprietary colonies to the north. Each region vied for the greater share of total output, with Pernambuco usually ahead. Native Brazilian slaves were exploited in large numbers in both regions, but well before 1600 Portuguese planters turned to Africa for still more enslaved laborers. Indigenous workers died in large numbers from disease and abuse, as happened in the early Spanish Caribbean, and were also prone to run away to the interior. As will be seen in greater detail in the next chapter, the Portuguese had the advantage of established market ties with dozens of western African chiefdoms and states from Senegambia to Angola. More even than the Spanish, they sought to replace indigenous cane cutters with enslaved Africans.

Though more resistant to Old World diseases than their native American co-workers, Africans died in alarming numbers in the early cane fields of Brazil. Many were literally worked to death. Instead of moderating workloads, improving nutrition and medical care, and encouraging family formation, Portuguese masters opted to exhaust the labor power of their slaves, the vast majority of them young men. The reason was as logical as it was cold-hearted: having direct access to more and more captives at relatively low cost in western Africa, sugar planters "used up" laborers much like mine owners did mita workers in Peru. Even when female slaves were introduced and families formed, high child mortality rates discouraged reproduction. Brazil would subsequently become so dependent on Africa for labor that by the time the slave trade ended in the nineteenth century over 40 percent of all slaves transported across the Atlantic had landed in this single destination.

COUNTERPOINT
The Mapuche of Chile: Native America's Indomitable State

The climate of southern Chile, a land of rugged coasts and dense forests, is wet and cool. Gently rolling hills are interspersed with picturesque lakes, rivers, and volcanoes. Near the coast is a temperate rain forest comparable to parts of the Pacific Northwest of the United States and Canada. Fish and wildlife are abundant and varied. Towering araucaria pines yield nuts rich in fat and protein, and vitamin-packed wild berries abound in the thickets. This is the homeland of the Mapuche (mah-POOH-cheh), or Araucanians (a term derived from the Bay of Arauca), one of the Americas' most resilient native cultures. Across nearly five centuries, they successfully resisted attempted conquests by the Incas, the Spanish, and the Chilean nation-state.

> **FOCUS**
>
> How did the Mapuche of Chile manage to resist European conquest?

Today, more than five hundred years after Columbus, the Mapuche, half a million strong, are still proclaiming their independence. It was only in the 1880s that Chilean armed forces managed to partially subdue the Mapuche using modern weapons and threats of annihilation, a process similar to that used against native peoples of western North America and the Argentine *pampas*, or plains, in the same era. But what of colonial times, the era of the conquistadors? There was substantial gold in the Mapuche heartland, yet the Spanish failed to conquer them despite knowing this since the time of Pizarro. Why?

A Culture of Warfare

The historical record suggests that successful Mapuche resistance owed much to entrenched cultural patterns. As poets, ex-captives, and Mapuche commentators themselves have noted since the sixteenth century, this was a fiercely independent people raised to fight. The Mapuche reared boys for a life of warfare, apparently before as well as after Spanish arrival in the region. Girls were raised to produce and store the food surpluses needed for the war effort. Despite their access to horses, iron and steel-edged weapons, and firearms, the Spanish fared little better than the Incas against the native Chileans.

There were early successes, however. The first conquistadors in Chile, headed by Pedro de Valdivia, in fact managed to reduce a large number of Mapuche to encomienda servitude by 1550. Rich gold deposits were subsequently discovered, and Mapuche men were forced to

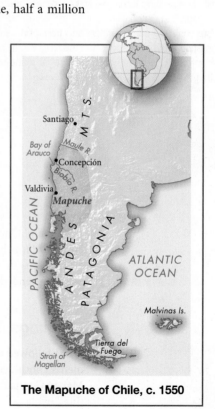

The Mapuche of Chile, c. 1550

Atlantic Sugar Producers

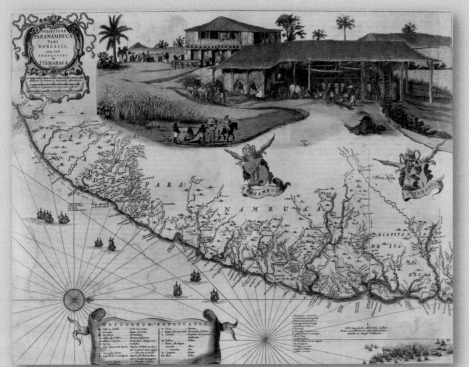

Found in countless foods and beverages, and now a major global source of biofuels, cane sugar was once a rare commodity. Introduced to the Mediterranean by Muslim traders and colonists in the eighth or ninth century C.E., sugar was at first a medicine and high-status condiment. Its source, sugar cane, a tall, thick grass, was eventually planted in Egypt, Sicily, Cyprus, and southern Iberia, and by at least the fourteenth century was processed not only by Muslims but also by Christian landowners in southern Spain and Portugal. Though later associated exclusively with slavery, sugar making in this era was done by a mixed free and enslaved labor force. Before long, women joined men in both cane fields and processing plants.

Sugar cane is so tough that considerable energy is required to extract maximum juice. Efficient presses were thus a technical hurdle for commercial producers. Like silver refining, sugar making required technical expertise and a complex sequence of chemical processes that allowed for few errors. In the Mediterranean basin, cane millers borrowed from long-established techniques of wine grape and olive pressing. Specialists were required to design and build ever larger and more powerful machines, which were among the most complex mechanical apparatus known at the time.

Animals such as oxen were often used for power, but waterwheels were preferred for their greater efficiency. In the

Sugar Plantations

Enslaved sugar-makers worked not only in fields but also in powerful mills and refining furnaces. Men, women, and children were all involved. This Dutch 1662 image of Pernambuco, Brazil, depicts enslaved sugar refinery and transport workers during the intense harvest period when the mills ran all night. The Dutch controlled Pernambuco and its sugar plantations from 1630 to 1654. (Courtesy of the John Carter Brown Library at Brown University.)

work them. Once it became clear that the Spanish were only after gold and captive laborers, the Mapuche resisted violently. To drive their point home, they captured, killed, and ate portions of Valdivia's corpse in a great public ceremony. Mapuche cannibalism was plainly intended to terrorize the enemy.

Uprisings Against the Spanish

What followed was a general uprising lasting from 1553 to 1557. Raids on Spanish settlements continued until 1598, when the Mapuche captured and ate yet another governor, Martín García de Loyola, a close relative of the founder of the Catholic Jesuit order, Ignatius Loyola (see Chapter 20). This incident was followed by a mass uprising in 1599, in

generally dry and sometimes frost-prone Mediterranean basin, access to warm, well-watered plains and consistently flowing millstreams was severely limited. Bounded by ecological and capital constraints, mill ownership remained a dream of most sugar producers. This soon proved equally true in the Atlantic islands and Brazil. For their part, mill workers, particularly the women and sometimes children who fed canes through the rollers, faced loss of limbs and sometimes death. "And in these Mills (during the season of making Sugar) they work both day and night," wrote English visitor Richard Flecknoe in 1654, "the work of immediately applying the canes to the Mill being so perilous [that] if through drowsiness or heedlessness a finger's end be but engaged between the posts, their whole body inevitably follows."[1] Rendering the precious juice into white crystal sugar was also difficult and labor intensive. Workers had to boil the juice in huge copper vats, then reduce it in a series of smaller vats into a concentrated syrup they poured into molds to crystallize. Women were usually in charge of whitening the resulting brown sugar loaves with wet clay and removing them from the molds and packing them for shipment. European consumers considered white sugar purer than brown, "purged" of imperfections. Each phase of the process required skill and close monitoring, and fires had to be stoked throughout the night. Sugar making thus produced a number of task-specific livelihoods, such as purger (purifier), mold-maker, and crating supervisor. Given its complexity, high capital investment, and careful attention to timing, sugar making has been described as an early modern precursor of industrial, or factory, production. However labeled, sugar work was monotonous and occasionally deadly.

On the consumer end of sugar making, first Muslim and then Jewish and Christian chefs made the most of the new sweetener, inventing a wide variety of candies, pastries, and preserves. Thus was born the livelihood of confectioner, or candy-maker. When American cacao took Europe by storm in the 1600s, the specialty of chocolatier emerged.

Europeans' taste for sugar grew slowly at first, but by 1600, sugar was an ordinary ingredient in many foods. Sugar's association with slavery also gradually increased. Numerous slaves labored in the early cane fields and mills of the eastern Atlantic islands of Madeira and the Canaries, but the pattern replicated in the Americas—predominantly African slaves manning large plantations—appeared first on the Portuguese island of São Tomé, off equatorial West Africa. By 1550, the so-called plantation complex was established in the Spanish Caribbean and Brazil. In the Americas, as in the Canaries, with the decimation of local cultures indigenous slavery gave way to African slavery.

---

1. E. Bradford Burns, ed., *A Documentary History of Brazil* (New York: Alfred A. Knopf, 1966), 82.

QUESTIONS TO CONSIDER

1. How did the rise of Atlantic sugar affect the global economy?
2. How did it transform livelihoods?

For Further Information:

Mintz, Sidney W. *Sweetness and Power*. New York: Viking, 1985.
Schwartz, Stuart B., ed. *Tropical Babylons: Sugar and the Making of the Atlantic World, 1450–1680*. Chapel Hill: University of North Carolina Press, 2004.

which established rebels united with Mapuches who had been subjected to Spanish rule. It was a resounding success. No Spanish town remained south of the Biobío River after 1600, and Spanish attempts to reconquer the Mapuche and occupy their lands failed throughout the colonial period.

What factors besides a culture of warfare allowed the Mapuche to succeed when so many other native American cultures fell to European invaders? As in North America's Great Plains, the inadvertent introduction of horses by the Spanish greatly enhanced Mapuche warrior mobility. Steel and iron guns, knives, and swords were also captured and quickly adopted. Further, the Mapuche "Columbian Exchange" included Old World foods and animals such as wheat, apples, chickens, and pigs, markedly increasing their subsistence base.

Mapuche Man and Woman

The Mapuche peoples of Chile proved as resistant to the Spanish as they had been to the Incas. Hostilities began in 1549, and by 1599 Mapuche warriors had destroyed all inland Spanish settlements south of the Biobío River. This image, painted by a Spanish priest who fled the Mapuche in 1600, depicts a Mapuche woman with her spinning equipment and trademark horned hairstyle. To the left is the great Mapuche leader Lautaro, who led the first uprisings. As is evident, the Mapuche adopted Spanish-style helmets and body armor, which they fashioned from the raw hides of introduced cattle. Like the Plains peoples of North America, the Mapuche also adopted the horse to great effect. (Courtesy of the University of Oviedo Library, Spain.)

Despite their new mounts and access to new weapons, Chile's native warriors did not alter their overall style of warfare. Rather than face the better-armed Spanish on the open field, as these European-trained fighters would have liked, the Mapuche preferred night attacks, long-distance raiding, captive-taking, and other tactics later termed *guerrilla*, or "little war," by the Spanish. Very long native-style bamboo lances remained the weapon of choice, not to be replaced by cumbersome and inaccurate handguns or dueling rapiers, and Mapuche men continued to fight barefoot. Alliances were another key to success. The great uprising of 1599 linked culturally related neighbors in a confederacy that the Spanish termed "the Indomitable State."

As a result of sustained Mapuche resistance, southern Chile became a permanent frontier of Spanish South America, a region of defensive rather than offensive operations. The Mapuche, though still frequently at war with their European neighbors, had proved the fact of their independence. Throughout the Spanish world, they became legendary. Only in the late nineteenth century was a tenuous peace established with the Chilean government and reservations created. Like many treaties between nation-states and indigenous peoples, this peace brought not integration but marginalization and poverty. As a result, the Mapuche are still fighting.

Conclusion

The first wave of European overseas expansion in the Atlantic was transformative in many ways, and would not be repeated in Africa, Asia, or Oceania for several centuries. Hundreds of isolated cultures were brought into contact with one another, often for the first time. Agents of the Columbian Exchange, European farmers and ranchers migrated to new landscapes, which they and their plants, livestock, and germs quickly transformed. Millions of sub-Saharan Africans, most of them captive laborers, joined a fast-emerging Atlantic, and soon globally integrated, world.

Spearheading this transformation were the uniquely positioned and highly motivated Portuguese, armed and outfitted to undertake risky voyages of reconnaissance and chart new routes to commercial gain abroad. By the 1440s they were trading for gold and slaves in sub-Saharan Africa, and by the 1540s they had reached Japan. Although most interested in commerce, the Portuguese also carried with them a militant Christianity that they promoted with some success alongside their expanding global network of trading posts. In Brazil they took another tack, establishing hundreds of slave-staffed sugar plantations.

Early modern Spaniards sought the same gold, spices, sugar, and slaves that motivated their Portuguese neighbors, but after encountering the Americas, they turned away from trading posts in favor of territorial conquest. Those they defeated were forced to extract wealth and accept conversion to the Catholic faith. Ironic as it may seem, it was imperial peoples such as the Aztecs and Incas who proved most vulnerable to the Spanish onslaught, and more especially to foreign disease. Mobile, scattered cultures such as the Mapuche of Chile proved far more resistant. Even at the margins, however, violent conquest and the beginnings of the Atlantic slave trade transformed livelihoods for millions. Some individuals swept up in the early phases of colonial encounter and the Columbian Exchange, such as young Malintzin, found advantages and even a means to social gain. Countless others found themselves reduced to servitude in an emerging social order defined by race as much as by wealth or ancestry. This new order forged in the Americas would soon affect much of western Africa.

NOTES

1. Christopher Columbus, *The Four Voyages*, trans. J. M. Cohen (New York: Penguin, 1969), 300.
2. Gomes Eannes de Azurara, quoted in John H. Parry and Robert G. Keith, *New Iberian World: A Documentary History of the Discovery of Latin America to the Seventeenth Century* (New York: Times Books, 1984), 1:256.
3. Geoffrey Symcox and Blair Sullivan, *Christopher Columbus and the Enterprise of the Indies: A Brief History with Documents* (Boston: Bedford/St. Martin's, 2004).
4. Bartolomé de las Casas, *An Account, Much Abbreviated, of the Destruction of the Indies*, ed. Franklin Knight, trans. Andrew Hurley (Indianapolis: Hackett, 2003), 61.
5. Alfred Crosby, *The Columbian Exchange: Biological and Cultural Consequences of 1492*, 2d ed. (Westport, CT: Praeger, 2003).
6. Bernal Díaz del Castillo, *The History of the Conquest of New Spain*, ed. Davíd Carrasco, trans. A. P. Maudslay (Albuquerque: University of New Mexico Press, 2008), 230.
7. Quoted in Ross Hassig, *Aztec Warfare: Imperial Expansion and Political Control* (Norman: University of Oklahoma Press, 1992), 124.

RESOURCES FOR RESEARCH

General Works

There are several fine general surveys of early Latin America, but the following are exceptional for their helpful models and explanations of key colonial institutions such as the encomienda and early plantation complex, plus the tricky business of analyzing writings and images from the early postconquest era.

Brown University, John Carter Brown Library Archive of Early American Images. http://www.brown.edu/Facilities/John_Carter_Brown_Library/pages/ea_hmpg.html.

Library of Congress, Exploring the Early Americas. http://www.loc.gov/exhibits/earlyamericas/.

Lockhart, James, and Stuart B. Schwartz. *Early Latin America*. 1983.

Schwartz, Stuart B., ed. *Implicit Understandings: Observing, Reporting, and Reflecting on the Encounters Between Europeans and Other Peoples in the Early Modern Era*. 1994.

University of Texas, Latin American Network Information Center. http://www.info.lanic.utexas.edu/la/region/history.

Guns, Sails, and Compasses: Europeans Venture Abroad

The topic of early Iberian overseas expansion has drawn scholarly attention for many years, and several of the following works, though relatively old, are still considered classics.

Fernández Armesto, Felipe. *Before Columbus: Exploration and Colonization from the Mediterranean to the Atlantic, 1229–1492*. 1987.

Newitt, Malyn. *A History of Portuguese Overseas Expansion, 1400–1668*. 2005.

Parry, J. H. *The Age of Reconnaissance*. 1963.

Phillips, William D., and Carla Rahn Phillips. *The Worlds of Christopher Columbus*. 1992.

Symcox, Geoffrey, and Blair Sullivan. *Christopher Columbus and the Enterprise of the Indies: A Brief History with Documents*. 2004.

New Crossroads, First Encounters: The European Voyages of Discovery, 1492–1521

The literature on the Columbian Exchange and environmental transformations has grown in recent years, with special emphasis on the role of disease as a major factor distinguishing European success in the Americas from their less penetrating early experiences in Africa and Asia.

Alchon, Suzanne Austin. *A Pest in the Land: New World Epidemics in a Global Perspective*. 2003.

Cook, Noble David. *Born to Die: Disease and New World Conquest, 1492–1650*. 1998.

Crosby, Alfred. *The Columbian Exchange: Biological and Cultural Consequences of 1492*, 2d ed. 2003.

Emmer, Pieter C., ed. *General History of the Caribbean*. Vol. 2. *New Societies: The Caribbean in the Long Sixteenth Century*. 1997.

Melville, Elinor. *A Plague of Sheep: Environmental Consequences of the Conquest of Mexico*. 1994.

Spanish Conquests in the Americas, 1519–1600

Recent scholarship on the Spanish conquests has evolved to emphasize the many factors, such as the help of thousands of indigenous allies, that enabled relatively small numbers of Europeans to bring down two of the world's most populous empires.

Powers, Karen V. *Women in the Crucible of Conquest: The Gendered Genesis of Spanish American Society, 1500–1600*. 2005.

Restall, Matthew. *Seven Myths of the Spanish Conquest*. 2003.

Schwartz, Stuart B., ed. *Victors and Vanquished: Spanish and Nahua Views of the Conquest of Mexico*. 2000.

Townsend, Camilla. *Malintzin's Choice: An Indian Woman in the Conquest of Mexico*. 2006.

Wood, Stephanie. *Transcending Conquest: Nahua Views of Spanish Colonial Mexico*. 2003.

A New Empire in the Americas: New Spain and Peru, 1535–1600

Good regional and topical studies of colonial Spanish America abound. The following have been selected to highlight the themes of this chapter. Bakewell's treatment of early mining, trade, and administration is superlative.

Bakewell, Peter. *A History of Latin America to 1825*, 3d ed. 2009.

Clendinnen, Inga. *Ambivalent Conquests: Maya and Spaniard in Yucatan, 1517–1570*, 2d ed. 2003.

Gibson, Charles. *The Aztecs Under Spanish Rule*. 1964.

Mangan, Jane E. *Trading Roles: Gender, Ethnicity, and the Urban Economy in Colonial Potosí*. 2005.

Brazil by Accident: The Portuguese in the Americas, 1500–1600

The early history of Brazil is becoming a more popular topic, mostly focusing on European-indigenous relations.

Bethell, Leslie, ed. *Colonial Brazil*. 1986.

Hemming, John. *Red Gold: The Conquest of the Brazilian Indians, 1500–1760*. 1978.

Léry, Jean de. *History of a Voyage to the Land of Brazil*. Translated by Janet Whatley. 1990.

Metcalf, Alida. *Go-Betweens in the History of Brazil, 1500–1600*. 2005.

Schwartz, Stuart B. *Sugar Plantations and the Formation of Brazilian Society*. 1985.

COUNTERPOINT: The Mapuche of Chile: Native America's Indomitable State

Few studies of the colonial Mapuche have been published in English. The following are three important exceptions.

Dillehay, Tom. *Monuments, Empires, and Resistance: The Araucanian Polity and Ritual Narratives*. 2007.

Jones, Kristine. "Warfare, Reorganization and Redaptation at the Margins of Spanish Rule: The Southern Margin (1573–1882)." In *The Cambridge History of the Native Peoples of the Americas*, vol. 3, pt. 2, 138–187. Edited by Stuart B. Schwartz and Frank Salomon. 1999.

Padden, Robert C. "Cultural Adaptation and Militant Autonomy Among the Araucanians of Chile." In *The Indian in Latin American History: Resistance, Resilience, and Acculturation*, rev. ed. 71–91. Edited by John Kicza. 2000.

▶ **For additional primary sources from this period,** see *Sources of Crossroads and Cultures.*

▶ **For Web sites, images, and documents related to topics in this chapter,** see Make History at bedfordstmartins.com/smith.

The major global development in this chapter ▶ European expansion across the Atlantic and its profound consequences for societies and cultures worldwide.

IMPORTANT EVENTS

1441	First sub-Saharan Africans captured and taken by ship to Portugal
1492	Fall of Granada and expulsion of Jews in Spain; Columbus reaches America
1494	Treaty of Tordesillas divides known world between Portugal and Spain
1498	Vasco da Gama becomes first European to reach India by sea
1500	Portuguese reach Brazil
1519–1521	Spanish conquest of Aztec Mexico
1519–1522	Magellan's ship circumnavigates the globe
1532–1536	Spanish conquest of Inca Peru
1545	Discovery of silver deposits at Potosí
1549	Portuguese establish royal capital of Salvador; first Jesuits arrive in Brazil
1555	French establish colony in Brazil's Guanabara Bay
1564	Discovery of mercury mines in Huancavelica, Peru
1567	Portuguese drive French from Brazil
1570–1571	Inquisition established in Lima and Mexico City
1572	Mita labor draft and mercury amalgamation formalized in Potosí
1592	Potosí reaches peak production
1599	Great Mapuche uprising in Chile

KEY TERMS

Columbian Exchange (p. 560)

conquistador (p. 562)

encomienda (p. 560)

feitoria (p. 555)

Inquisition (p. 570)

mestizo (p. 570)

mita (p. 568)

repartimiento (p. 568)

CHAPTER OVERVIEW QUESTIONS

1. What were the main biological and environmental consequences of European expansion into the Atlantic after 1492?

2. What roles did misunderstanding and chance play in the conquests of the Aztecs and Incas?

3. How did Eurasian demand for silver and sugar help bring about the creation of a linked Atlantic world?

SECTION FOCUS QUESTIONS

1. Why and how did Europeans begin to cross unknown seas in the fifteenth century?

2. What were the main sources of conflict between Europeans and native Americans in the first decades after contact?

3. What factors enabled the Spanish to conquer the Aztec and Inca empires?

4. Why was the discovery of silver in Spanish America so important in the course of world history?

5. How and why did early Portuguese Brazil develop differently from Spanish America?

6. How did the Mapuche of Chile manage to resist European conquest?

MAKING CONNECTIONS

1. How did Spanish and Portuguese imperial aims differ from those of the Incas and Aztecs (see Chapter 16)?

2. How would you compare the Spanish conquest of Mexico with the Ottoman conquest of Constantinople discussed in Chapter 15?

3. What role did European consumers play in the rise of the American plantation complex?

4. How did global demand for silver affect the lives of ordinary people in the Spanish colonies?

AT A CROSSROADS ▶

This dramatic brass plaque depicts the oba, or king, of Benin in a royal procession, probably in the sixteenth century. He is seated sidesaddle on a seemingly overburdened horse, probably imported and sold to him by Portuguese traders. The larger attendants to each side shade the monarch while the smaller ones hold his staff and other regal paraphernalia. Above, as if walking behind, are two armed guards. (Image copyright © The Metropolitan Museum of Art/Art Resource, NY.)

Western Africa in the Era of the Atlantic Slave Trade

1450–1800

I n 1594 a youth of about seventeen was captured in a village raid in the interior of western Africa. The Portuguese, who controlled the Atlantic port of Luanda, where the young captive was taken, called this vast region Angola, a corruption of the Kimbundu term for "blacksmith." The young man was now a nameless body to be branded, examined like a beast, and sold; he was also, in the words of his captors, "a black." In Luanda, the captive was housed in a stifling barracks with many others, perhaps including some who spoke his language and probably even a few who came from his village. Most, however, were strangers whose words, looks, hairstyles, and "country marks," or ritual scars, were unfamiliar.

Eventually, men dressed in black robes appeared among the captives. These odd-looking men were Roman Catholic priests, members of the Jesuit order. They had only recently established a missionary base in Luanda. In grave tones and mostly unintelligible

BACKSTORY

Prior to 1450, the lives of most western Africans focused on hoe agriculture, supplementary herding and hunting, and in some places mining and metallurgy. Chiefdoms were the dominant political form throughout the region, from the southern fringes of Morocco to the interior of Angola, although several expansive kingdoms rose and fell along the Niger and Volta rivers, notably Old Ghana, which thrived from about 300 to 1000, and most recently, as the early modern period dawned, Mali, which flourished from about 1200 to 1400.

Trade in many commodities extended over vast distances, often monopolized by extended families or ethnic groups. Muslim traders were dominant along the southern margins of the Sahara Desert after about 1000 C.E. Some western African merchants traded slaves across the Sahara to the Mediterranean basin, and others raided vulnerable villages for captives, some of whom were sent as far away as the Red Sea and Indian Ocean. Islam predominated by 1450 along many trade routes into the savanna, or grasslands, but most western Africans retained local religious beliefs, usually combining ancestor veneration with healing and divination practices similar to native American shamanism (see Chapter 16).

Many Western Africas

FOCUS What range of livelihoods, cultural practices, and political arrangements typified western Africa in early modern times?

Landlords and Strangers: Peoples and States in West Africa

FOCUS What economic, social, and political patterns characterized early modern West Africa?

Land of the Blacksmith Kings: West Central Africa

FOCUS What economic, social, and political patterns characterized early modern West Central Africa?

Strangers in Ships: Gold, Slavery, and the Portuguese

FOCUS How did the early Portuguese slave trade in western Africa function?

Northern Europeans and the Expansion of the Atlantic Slave Trade, 1600–1800

FOCUS What were the major changes in the Atlantic slave trade after 1600?

COUNTERPOINT: The Pygmies of Central Africa

FOCUS How did the Pygmies' rain forest world differ from the better-known environment of savannas and farms?

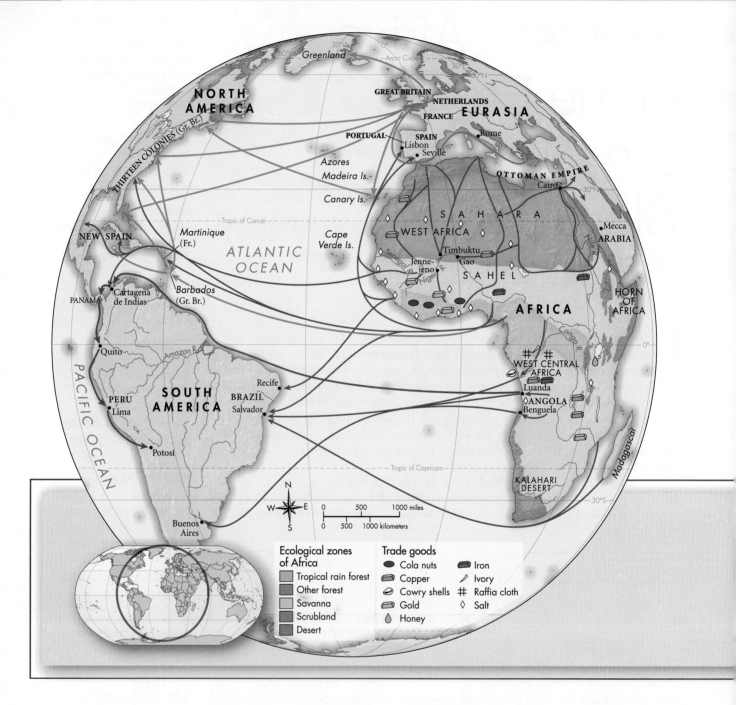

Ecological zones of Africa
- Tropical rain forest
- Other forest
- Savanna
- Scrubland
- Desert

Trade goods
- Cola nuts
- Copper
- Cowry shells
- Gold
- Honey
- Iron
- Ivory
- Raffia cloth
- Salt

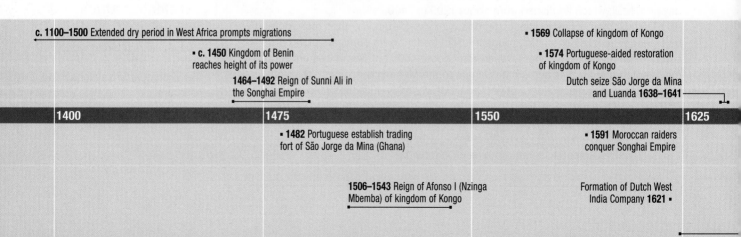

c. 1100–1500 Extended dry period in West Africa prompts migrations

c. 1450 Kingdom of Benin reaches height of its power

1464–1492 Reign of Sunni Ali in the Songhai Empire

1482 Portuguese establish trading fort of São Jorge da Mina (Ghana)

1506–1543 Reign of Afonso I (Nzinga Mbemba) of kingdom of Kongo

1569 Collapse of kingdom of Kongo

1574 Portuguese-aided restoration of kingdom of Kongo

Dutch seize São Jorge da Mina and Luanda **1638–1641**

1591 Moroccan raiders conquer Songhai Empire

Formation of Dutch West India Company **1621**

1400   1475   1550   1625

words, they spoke to the captives. The young man must have listened with puzzlement. At last, after several weeks, each captive was sprinkled with water and made to accept a lump of salt on the tongue. After this conversion ritual, names were assigned. The young man was now called "Domingo," "Sunday" in Portuguese. Once in the Americas, Spanish scribes recorded his name as "Domingo Angola, black slave." His sale records are the only evidence we have of his existence.

Domingo was one of the lucky ones. He survived barracks life in Luanda and then the grueling two-month voyage, or "middle passage," from Luanda to Cartagena de Indias, a bustling port on the Caribbean coast of present-day Colombia. More than one in five died during these ordeals. After stumbling out of the sickening hold of the slave ship and into the bright Caribbean sun, Domingo Angola would have been washed, oiled, examined for signs of contagious illness, and fed a simple meal of maize gruel and tough, salted beef. Both foods were new to him, and they would form the core of his diet for the rest of his enslaved life in Spanish South America.

After being transported by ship to Panama, Domingo was sold to a merchant on his way to Quito, the former northern Inca capital high in the Andes Mountains of Ecuador. There, according to notary records for the year 1595, he was sold yet again, this time to two merchants planning a multiyear sales trip to the distant silver-mining town of Potosí, several thousand miles to the south. In all, Domingo spent almost another year of hard and dangerous tropical travel. Documents listing travel costs say he fell ill while waiting for a ship on the Pacific coast and had to be treated. In Potosí, Domingo was sold yet again, and probably not for the last time. He had not yet turned nineteen.[1]

Meanwhile, back in Angola, a terrifying story arose about men and women such as Domingo who had been captured and taken away across the sea. People began to imagine that they were being captured to feed a distant race of cannibals. These "people eaters," red in color, lived somewhere beyond the sunset, it was said, on the far side of an

MAPPING THE WORLD

Africa and the Atlantic, c. 1450–1800

The vast and ecologically diverse continent of Africa had long been linked together by trade in salt, copper, iron, cola nuts, and other commodities. It had also been connected since ancient times to the Mediterranean and the Indian Ocean maritime worlds. Goods traded beyond Africa consisted mostly of gold and ivory, but there was also substantial traffic in human captives. After 1450 the Portuguese extended this pattern into the growing Atlantic world, establishing fortified trading posts all along Africa's west coast.

ROUTES ▼

→ Slave and trade route, c. 1450–1800

→ Voyage of Domingo Angola, c. 1594–1597

→ Voyages of Olaudah Equiano, c. 1755–1797

▪ **1672** Formation of English Royal African Company

1750–1800 Atlantic slave trade reaches highest volume

| 1700 | 1775 | 1850 |

▪ **1807** British declare Atlantic slave trade illegal

1624–1663 Reign of Queen Nzinga in the Ndongo kingdom of Angola

enormous lake, and there they butchered ordinary Angolans. Human blood was their wine, brains their cheese, and roasted and ground long-bones their gunpowder. The red people—the sunburnt Portuguese—were slavish devotees of Mwene Puto, God of the Dead. How else to explain the massive, ceaseless traffic in souls, what Angolans called the "way of death"?[2]

Domingo's long journey from western Africa to highland South America was not unusual, and in fact he would have met many other Angolans arriving in Potosí via Brazil and Buenos Aires. Victims of the Atlantic slave trade in this period were constantly on the move, some sailing from Africa as far as India, the Molucca Islands in the East Indies, and even Japan. This trend of slave mobility diminished somewhat with the rise of plantation agriculture in the seventeenth and eighteenth centuries, but Africans continued to work on sailing ships and in port cities all over the world. On land or at sea, massive disruption and shuffling of ethnic groups was typical of the Atlantic slave trade and what historians call the **African diaspora**, or "great scattering" of sub-Saharan African peoples. As we will see in the next chapter, millions of slaves were sent across the Indian Ocean from East Africa as well, a phenomenon predating the Atlantic trade but in the end not as voluminous. This chapter focuses on western or "Atlantic" Africa, a vast portion of the continent that geographers normally split into two parts: West and West Central Africa (see Mapping the World, page 583).

Although slavery and slave trading were established practices in western Africa prior to the arrival of Europeans, both institutions and their effects changed dramatically as a result of the surge in European demand for African slaves that coincided with European colonization of the Americas. Beginning in the late sixteenth century, new patterns of behavior emerged. African warriors and mercenaries focused more and more on attacking and kidnapping their neighbors in order to trade them to foreign slavers for weapons, stimulants, and luxury goods; coastal farmers abandoned arable lands vulnerable to raiders; formerly protective traditions and customs were called into question; and Islam and Christianity made new inroads. We now know that even cultures inhabiting zones far inland from the Atlantic coast, such as the Batwa, or Pygmies, of the Congo rain forest, were affected by reverberations of the slave trade. They were driven deeper into the forest as other internal migrants, forced to move under pressure from slavers, expanded their farms and pasturelands. There, as we will see in the Counterpoint to this chapter, the Pygmies forged a lifestyle far different from that of their settled neighbors.

African diaspora The global dispersal, mostly through the Atlantic slave trade, of African peoples.

OVERVIEW
QUESTIONS

The major global development in this chapter: The rise of the Atlantic slave trade and its impact on early modern African peoples and cultures.

As you read, consider:

1. How did ecological diversity in western Africa relate to cultural developments?

2. What tied western Africa to other parts of the world prior to the arrival of Europeans along Atlantic shores?

3. How did the Atlantic slave trade arise, and how was it sustained?

Many Western Africas

It has been estimated that the African continent, comprising a little over 20 percent of the earth's landmass, was home to 100 million people at the time of Columbus's famous 1492 transatlantic voyage. About 50 million people inhabited West and West Central Africa, what we refer to here as "western Africa." Western Africa thus had a population comparable to that of all the Americas at that time. It contained several dozen aspiring tributary states in various stages of expansion and contraction, along with a vast number of permanent agricultural and mobile, warrior-headed chiefdoms. There were also wide-ranging pastoral or herding groups, trading peoples, fishing folk, and scattered bands of desert and rain forest gatherer-hunters. The array of livelihoods was wide, yet the vast majority of western Africans lived as hoe agriculturalists, primarily cultivators of rice, sorghum, millet, and cotton (see Map 18.1).

Cultural Diversity

Religious ideas and practices varied as much as livelihoods, but most Africans south of the Sahara, like many peoples the world over, placed great emphasis on fertility. Fertility rituals were an integral aspect of everyday life; some entailed animal sacrifice, and others, rarely, human sacrifice. Also as in many other early modern societies, discord, illness, and material hardship were often thought to be the products of witchcraft. The capacity to identify and punish witches helped define power in many societies.

Islam, introduced by long-distance traders and warriors after the seventh century C.E., became dominant in the dry *sahel* (from the Arabic for "shore") and savanna, or grassland, regions just south of the Sahara, and along the rim of the Indian Ocean. Christian and Jewish communities were limited to tiny pockets in the northeastern Horn and along the Maghreb, or Mediterranean coast. Over two thousand languages were spoken on the continent, most of them derived from four major roots. All told, Africa's cultural and linguistic diversity easily exceeded that of Europe in the era of Columbus.

Even where Islam predominated, local notions of the spirit world survived. Most western Africans believed in a distant creator deity, sometimes equated with Allah, and everyday ritual tended to emphasize communication with ancestor spirits, who helped placate a host of other, potentially malevolent forces. As in many ancient cosmologies, animal and plant spirits were considered especially potent.

Places were also sacred. Rather like Andean *wakas*, western African **génies** (JEHN-ees) could be features in the landscape: boulders, springs, rivers, lakes, and groves. Trees were especially revered among peoples living along the southern margins of the savanna, and villagers built alongside patches of old-growth forest. Through periodic animal sacrifice, western Africans sought the patronage of local tree spirits, since they were literally most rooted in the land.

Environmental Challenges

Western Africa fell entirely within the lowland tropics and was thus subject to a number of endemic diseases and pests. The deadly falciparum variety of malaria and other serious mosquito-borne fevers attacked humans in the hot lowlands, and the wide range of the tsetse fly, carrier of the fatal trypanosomiasis virus, limited livestock grazing and horse breeding. As in modern times, droughts could be severe and prolonged in some densely populated regions, spurring mass migration and warfare. Western Africans nevertheless adapted to these and other environmental challenges, in the case of malaria developing at least some immunity against the disease.

Animal Husbandry and Metalsmithing

In the arid north where Islam predominated, beasts of burden included camels, donkeys, and horses. Cattle were also kept in the interior highlands and far south, where they were safe from tsetse flies. Arabian warhorses were greatly prized, and were widely traded among kingdoms and chiefdoms along the southern margins of the Sahara. They were most valued where fly-borne disease made breeding impossible. Other domestic animals included goats, swine, guinea fowl, sheep, and dogs. In general, animal **husbandry**, as in greater Eurasia, was far more developed in western Africa than in the Americas. There were also more large wild mammals in sub-Saharan Africa than in any other part of the world, and these featured prominently in regional cosmologies.

génie A sacred site or feature in the West African landscape.

husbandry Human intervention in the breeding of animals.

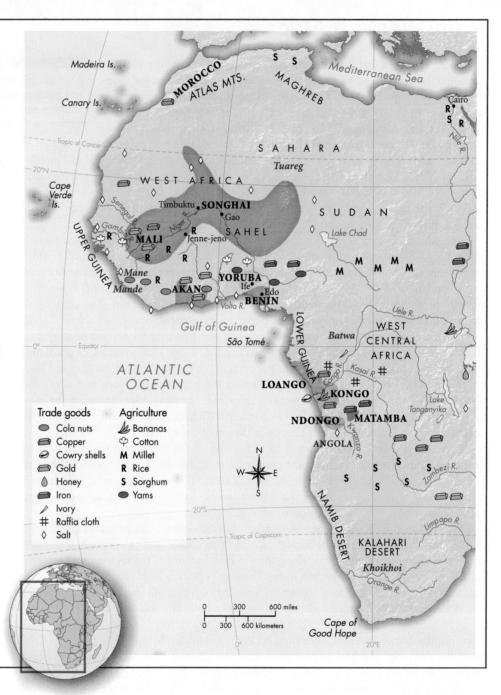

MAP 18.1

Western Africa, c. 1500

The huge regions of West and West Central Africa were of key importance to early modern global history as sources of both luxury commodities and enslaved immigrants. But western Africa was also marked by substantial internal dynamism. The Songhai Empire on the middle Niger rose to prominence about the time of Columbus. Large kingdoms and city-states also flourished on the Volta and lower Niger rivers and near the mouth of the Congo (Zaire). Rain forests and deserts were home to gatherer-hunters such as the Batwa (Pygmies) and Khoikhoi. Since tropical diseases severely limited the raising of large livestock, most western Africans used iron hand tools to plant and harvest millet, sorghum, rice, bananas, and, after trade with the Americas, maize and manioc.

Mining and metalsmithing technologies were also highly developed and widely dispersed. Throughout West and West Central Africa, copper and copper-alloy metallurgical techniques had grown complex by 1500. Goldsmithing was also advanced, though less widespread. This was in part because African gold was being increasingly drawn away into commercial trade networks extending to the Mediterranean Sea and Indian Ocean. To a large extent, western Eurasia's "bullion famine" spurred early European expansion into Africa.

Since ancient times, Africans had been great producers and consumers of iron. Whether in Mali or Angola, African ironmongers were not simply artisans but also shamanlike figures and even **paramount chiefs**—heads of numerous village clans. In fact, throughout sub-Saharan Africa, metalwork was a closely guarded and mystical pro-

paramount chief A chief who presided over several headmen and controlled a large area.

cess similar to alchemy (the transmutation of base metals into gold) in contemporary Europe, the Middle East, and China. African metalsmiths produced great quantities of tools, ornaments, and lasting works of art. They made the iron hoes most people tended crops with, and sometimes they traded in bulk over vast distances.

Africa's internal trade was linked to craft specialization, but mostly it served to redistribute basic commodities. Those who mined or collected salt, for example, usually bartered it for other necessities such as cloth. Highly prized in the vast West African interior, where springs and deposits were extremely scarce, Saharan salt was an essential dietary supplement. Similarly, manufactured goods such as agricultural tools were widely traded for food, textiles, and livestock, but bits of gold, copper, and iron also served as currency. Among the most important trade goods were cola nuts, the sharing of which cemented social relations in much of West Africa, particularly among elites.

Copper and bronze bracelets were prized by some of western Africa's coastal peoples, and eventually they were standardized into currency that the Portuguese called *manillas* (mah-KNEE-lahs). In some areas seashells such as the cowry, brought all the way from the Maldive Islands off the west coast of India, functioned in the same way. The desire for brightly colored cotton textiles from India fueled Africa's west coast demand for shell and copper-bronze currency, which in time would also contribute to the expansion of the Atlantic slave trade. Africa's east coast, meanwhile, remained integrated into the vast and mostly separate Indian Ocean trade circuit through the monsoon-seasonal export of ivory, gold, and to a lesser extent, human captives, as we will see in Chapter 19.

African societies linked by trade were sometimes also bound by political ties. A shared desire to both expand household units and improve security led many Africans to form short- and long-term confederations and conglomerates. Like the Iroquois and Powhatan confederacies of eastern North America (discussed in Chapter 16), some of these alliances had a religious core, but just as often such collaborative actions were spurred by ecological stresses such as droughts. In this politically fluid context, ethnic and other forms of identity often blended and blurred as groups merged and partially or wholly adopted each other's languages, cosmologies, farming techniques, and modes of dress and adornment.

Nevertheless, as in the Americas, intergroup conflict was hardly unusual in western Africa prior to the arrival of Europeans. Expansionist, tributary empires such as Mali and Songhai grew independently of outside forces, and both managed to make lifelong regional and internal enemies. The motives of African warfare varied, but they frequently had to do with the control of resources, and especially people, sometimes as slaves put to work on agricultural estates. As in other parts of the early modern world, European trading and political meddling on Africa's Atlantic coast would spawn or exacerbate major new conflicts that would reverberate deep within the continent. Full-blown imperialism would come much later, with the development of new technologies and antimalarial drugs, but it would benefit in part from this earlier political disruption.

A Young Woman from West Africa

Since at least medieval times, West African women surprised outside visitors with their independence, visibility, and political influence, in both Islamic and non-Islamic societies. This drawing by an English artist during a slave-trading voyage to West Africa in around 1775 depicts a young woman with elaborately braided hair, pearl earrings, and a choker strung with coral or large stones. It is possible that she is a member of an elite family given these proudly displayed ornaments, but we do not know. The portrait reveals neither her identity nor her destiny, though it is clear that she made a strong impression on the foreign artist. (National Maritime Museum, London/The Image Works.)

Trade, Politics, and Warfare

West Africa's Gold Miners

Implements of the Gold Trade
West Africa was long legendary for its gold, which was first traded across the Sahara and later to Europeans arriving along the Atlantic coast. In the Akan region of present-day Ghana, gold dust circulated as currency, with portions measured by merchants in a hanging balance against tiny, fancifully designed brass weights. Gold dust was stored in brass boxes and dished out with decorated brass spoons. Smaller exchanges employed cowry shells, brought to Atlantic Africa from the Maldive Islands in the Indian Ocean. (Aldo Tutino/Art Resource, NY.)

Until 1650, gold was a more valuable West African export than slaves, and it remained highly significant for many years afterward. The mines and their workers, some of whom were enslaved, were controlled by local kings, whose agents traded the gold to long-distance merchants with ties to Europeans on the coast. Gold diggings were concentrated along the upper reaches of the Senegal, Niger, and Volta rivers, mostly in and around streams flowing down from eroded mountain ranges. Sources describing West African gold mining in early modern times are rare, but anecdotal descriptions combined with somewhat later eyewitness accounts suggest that women did many

of the most strenuous tasks. The Scottish traveler Mungo Park described nonenslaved West African women miners among the Mande of the upper Niger in the 1790s as follows:

> About the beginning of December, when the harvest is over, and the streams and torrents have greatly subsided, the Mansa, or chief of the town, appoints a day to begin *sanoo koo*, "gold washing"; and the women are sure to have themselves in readiness by the time appointed. . . . On the morning of their departure, a bullock is killed for the first day's

Landlords and Strangers: Peoples and States in West Africa

FOCUS

What economic, social, and political patterns characterized early modern West Africa?

According to mostly archaeological and some textual references, West Africans in the period following 700 C.E. faced several radical new developments. Two major catalysts for change were the introduction and spread of Islam after the eighth century and a long dry period lasting from roughly 1100 to 1500 C.E. At least one historian has characterized human relations in this era in terms of "landlords" and "strangers," a reference to the tendency toward small and scattered agricultural communities offering safe passage and hospitality to a variety of travelers and craft specialists.[3] In return, these "strangers"—traders, blacksmiths, tanners, bards, and clerics—offered goods and services. The model "landlord" was an esteemed personage or even group of elders capable of ensuring the security and prosperity of a wide range of dependents and affiliates, usually conceived of as members of an extended family.

entertainment, and a number of prayers and charms are used to ensure success; for a failure on that day is thought a bad omen. . . . The washing of the sands of the streams is by far the easiest way of obtaining the gold dust, but in most places the sands have been so narrowly searched before that unless the stream takes some new course, the gold is found but in small quantities. While some of the party are busied in washing the sands, others employ themselves farther up the torrent, where the rapidity of the stream has carried away all the clay, sand, etc., and left nothing but small pebbles. The search among these is a very troublesome task. I have seen women who have had the skin worn off the tops of their fingers in this employment. Sometimes, however, they are rewarded by finding pieces [nuggets] of gold, which they call *sanoo birro*, "gold stones," that amply repay them for their trouble. A woman and her daughter, inhabitants of Kamalia, found in one day two pieces of this kind.

Mande men, according to Park, participated in excavating deep pits in gold-bearing hills "in the height of the dry season," producing clay and other sediments "for the women to wash; for though the pit is dug by the men, the gold is always washed by the women, who are accustomed from their infancy to a similar

operation, in separating the husks of corn from the meal." To be efficient, panning required intense concentration and careful eye-hand coordination, and use of several pans to collect concentrates. This skill was appreciated, as Park explains: "Some women, by long practice, become so well acquainted with the nature of the sand, and the mode of washing it, that they will collect gold where others cannot find a single particle." Gold dust was then stored in quills (the hollow shafts of bird feathers) plugged with cotton, says Park, "and the washers are fond of displaying a number of these quills in their hair."

Source: Mungo Park, *Travels in the Interior Districts of Africa*, ed. and introduced by Kate Ferguson Masters (Durham, NC: Duke University Press, 2000), 264–267.

QUESTIONS TO CONSIDER

1. Why was West African gold mining seasonal?

2. How were tasks divided between men and women, and why?

3. Was gold washing demeaning labor, or could it be a source of pride?

For Further Information:
Philip D. Curtin. *Economic Change in Precolonial Africa: Senegambia in the Era of the Slave Trade*. Madison: University of Wisconsin Press, 1975.

Empire Builders and Traders

The late medieval dry period also witnessed the rise of mounted warriors: the stranger as conqueror and captive-taker. On the banks of the middle and upper Niger River rose the expansionist kingdoms of Mali and Songhai, both linked to the Mediterranean world via the caravan terminus of Timbuktu (see again Map 18.1). Both empires were headed by devout, locally born Muslim rulers. One, Mansa Musa (*mansa* meaning "conqueror") of Mali, made the pilgrimage to Mecca in 1325. Musa spent so much gold during a stop in Cairo that his visit became legend.

It was gold, concentrated near the headwaters of the Senegal, Niger, and Volta rivers, that put sub-Saharan Africa on the minds—and maps—of European and Middle Eastern traders and monarchs. Most West African mines were worked by farming peoples forced to pay tribute in gold dust unearthed in the fallow (inactive) season (see Lives and Livelihoods: West Africa's Gold Miners). As in North America, India, and many other parts of the world at this time, warfare was also limited by the seasonal demands of subsistence agriculture. Yet land was a less-prized commodity than labor in West Africa. Prestige derived not from own-

Politics of the Gold Trade

ership of farmland or mines but from control over productive people, some of whom—and in places like Songhai, many of whom—were enslaved. Captive-taking was thus integral to warfare at all political levels, from the smallest chiefdom to the largest empire. Like the seasonal production of gold, the seasonal production of slaves, who for centuries had been sent north across the Sahara to Mediterranean markets and east to those of the Red Sea and Indian Ocean, would vastly expand once Europeans arrived on Atlantic shores.

With the exception, as we will see, of the Songhai Empire, West African politics in this period was mostly confederated. Dozens of paramount chiefs or regional kings relied on a host of more-or-less-loyal tributaries and enslaved laborers for their power, wealth, and sustenance. In general, as in much of Southeast Asia (see Chapter 19), early modern West Africa witnessed the periodic rise of charismatic and aggressive rulers, with few bureaucrats and judges. Rulers typically extended their authority by offering to protect vulnerable agricultural groups from raiders. Some coastal rice growers in Upper Guinea drifted in and out of these kinds of regional alliances, depending on political and environmental conditions. Alliances did not always spare them from disaster. Still, as actors in the Columbian Exchange, enslaved rice farmers from this region transferred techniques and perhaps grains to the plantations of North and South America.

From Western Sudan to Lower Guinea, town-sized units predominated, many of them walled or otherwise fortified. Archaeologists are still discovering traces of these extensive enclosures, some of which housed thousands of inhabitants. As in medieval Europe, even when they shared a language, walled cities in neighboring territories could be fiercely competitive. These were not tribal units but rather highly stratified and populous urban enclaves.

Songhai Empire   Dating to the first centuries C.E., West Africa was also home to sizable kingdoms. Old Ghana flourished from about 300 to 1000 C.E., followed by Mali, which thrived from about 1200 to 1400. From about the time of Columbus, the Songhai Empire, centered at Gao, rose to prominence under Sunni Ali (r. 1464–1492). Similar to the mansas of Mali, Sunni Ali was a conqueror, employing mounted lancers and huge squads of boatmen to great and terrifying effect. Sunni Ali's successor, Muhammad Touré, extended Songhai's rule even farther. At his zenith Touré, who took the title *askiya* (AH-skee-yah), or hereditary lord, and later *caliph*, or supreme lord, controlled a huge portion of West Africa (see again Map 18.1). Ultimately, like many Eurasian contemporaries, he was limited more by sheer logistics and distance than armed resistance.

The wealth and power of Songhai derived from the merchant crossroads cities of the middle Niger: Jenne, Gao, and Timbuktu (see Reading the Past: Al-Sa'di on Jenne and Its History). Here gold from the western mines of the upper Niger and Senegal, salt from the Sahara, and forest products from the south such as cola nuts and raffia palm fiber were exchanged, along with a host of other commodities. Slaves, many of them taken in Songhai's wars of expansion, were also traded to distant buyers in North and East Africa. Stately Timbuktu, meanwhile, retained its reputation as a major market for books and a center of Islamic teachings.

Touré's successors were less aggressive than he, and as Songhai's power waned in the later sixteenth century, the empire fell victim to mounted raiders from distant Morocco. With alarming audacity, and greatly aided by their state-of-the-art firearms and swift mounts, the Moroccans (among them hundreds of exiled Spanish Muslims, or Moriscos) captured the cities of Gao and Timbuktu in 1591. As their victory texts attest, these foreign conquistadors took home stunning quantities of gold and a number of slaves. Yet unlike their Spanish and Portuguese contemporaries in the Americas, they failed to hold on to their new conquest. The mighty Sahara proved a more formidable barrier to colonial governance than the Atlantic Ocean. After the fall of Songhai there emerged a fractured dynasty of Moroccan princes, the Sa'dis, who were in turn crushed by new, local waves of warfare in the late seventeenth and early eighteenth centuries. Most fell victim to the Sahara's best-known nomads, the Tuareg (TWAH-regh).

Sculptors and Priest-Kings

Farther south, near the mouth of the Niger River, was the rain forest kingdom of Benin, with its capital at Edo. Under King Ewuare (EH-woo-AH-reh) (r. c. 1450–1480), Benin

Al-Sa'di on Jenne and Its History

The historian known as Al-Sa'di (1594–c. 1656) was an imam, or religious scholar, descended from the Moroccan Sa'dis who invaded and toppled the Songhai Empire on the middle Niger River in 1591. He lived in the cities of Timbuktu and Jenne, and he appears to have learned most of what he knew about the region's past from a mix of written Arabic sources and local oral historians who spoke the Songhai language. The following passage, from about 1655, is translated from Al-Sa'di's Arabic history of the middle Niger region from medieval times to his own.

> Jenne is a large, well-favored and blessed city, characterized by prosperity, good fortune, and compassion. God bestowed these things upon that land as innate characteristics. It is the nature of Jenne's inhabitants to be kind, charitable, and solicitous for one another. However, when it comes to matters of daily life, competitiveness is very much a part of their character, to such an extent that if anyone attains a higher status, the rest uniformly hate him, though without making this apparent or letting it show. Only if there occurs some change of fortune—from which God protect us—will each of them display his hatred in word and deed.
>
> Jenne is one of the great markets of the Muslims. Those who deal in salt from the mine of Taghaza meet there with those who deal in gold from the mine of Bitu. These two blessed mines have no equal in the entire world. People discovered their great blessing through going to them for business, amassing such wealth as only God—Sublime is He—could assess. This blessed city of Jenne is why caravans come to Timbuktu from all quarters—north, south, east, and west. Jenne is situated to the south and west of Timbuktu beyond the two rivers [the Niger and Bani]. When the [Bani] river is in flood, Jenne becomes an island, but when the flood abates, the water is far from it. It begins to be surrounded by water in August, and in February the water recedes again. . . .
>
> With the exception of Sunni Ali [of Songhai], no ruler had ever defeated the people of Jenne since the town was founded. According to what its people tell, Sunni Ali besieged them for seven years, seven months, and seven days, finally subduing them and ruling over them. His army was encamped at Joboro [original site of Jenne, south of the city] and they would attack the people of Jenne daily until the flood encircled the city. Then he would retire with his army to a place called Nibkat Sunni ("the hillock of Sunni"), so named because he stayed there. His army would remain there and keep watch until the waters receded and then would return to Joboro to fight. I was told by Sultan Abd Allah son of Sultan Abu Bakr that this went on for seven years. Then famine struck and the people of Jenne grew weak. Despite that, they contrived to appear still strong, so that Sunni Ali had no idea what condition they were really in. Weary of the siege at last, he decided to return to Songhai. Then one of the Sultan of Jenne's senior army commanders, said to be the grandfather of Unsa Mani Surya Muhammad, sent word to Sunni Ali and revealed the secret, and told him not to return home until he saw how things would turn out. So Sunni Ali exercised patience and became even more eager [to take Jenne].
>
> Then the sultan took counsel with his commanders and the senior men of his army. He proposed that they should surrender to Sunni Ali, and they agreed. . . . So the Sultan of Jenne and his senior army commanders rode forth to meet Sunni Ali, and when he got close to him he dismounted and walked towards him on foot. Sunni Ali welcomed him and received him with honor. When he saw that the sultan was only a young man, he took hold of him and seated him beside him on his rug and said, "Have we been fighting with a boy all this time?" Then his courtiers told him that the young man's father had died during the siege, and that he had succeeded him as sultan. This is what lies behind the custom of the Sultan of Songhai sitting together with the Sultan of Jenne on a single rug until this day.

Source: John O. Hunwick, ed. and trans., *Timbuktu and the Songhay Empire: Al-Sadi's Tarikh al-sudan Down to 1613 and Other Contemporary Documents* (Leiden, the Netherlands: Brill, 1999), 13–21.

EXAMINING THE EVIDENCE

1. How does Al-Sa'di characterize the city and people of Jenne?

2. Why is the city's location on the Niger River important?

3. How does Al-Sa'di characterize the Songhai Empire founder Sunni Ali's conquest of Jenne?

Art of the Slave Trade: A Benin Bronze Plaque

Copper and bronze metallurgy were advanced arts in western Africa long before the arrival of Europeans. Metal sculpture, in the form of lifelike busts, historical plaques, and complex representations of deities, was most developed in western Nigeria and the kingdom of Benin. Realistic representations of elite men and women appear to have served a commemorative function, as did relief-sculpted plaques depicting kings, chiefs, and warlords in full regalia. Beginning in the 1500s, sculptors in Benin and neighboring lands began to depict Portuguese slave traders and missionaries, bearded men with helmets, heavy robes, and trade goods, including primitive muskets. This plaque depicts Portuguese slavers with a cargo of manillas, the bronze bracelets that served as currency in the slave trade until the mid-nineteenth century.

EXAMINING THE EVIDENCE

1. How were Portuguese newcomers incorporated into this traditional Benin art form?

2. How might this bronze representation of foreigners and their trade goods have been a commentary on the slave trade?

Plaque of Portuguese Traders with Manillas
(Gift of Mr. and Mrs. Klaus G. Perls, 1991 (1991.17.13). The Metropolitan Museum of Art, New York, NY/Art Resource, NY.)

reached the height of its power in the mid-fifteenth century, subjecting dozens of neighboring towns and chiefdoms to tributary status. Benin grew wealthy in part by exporting cloth made by women working on domestic looms in tributary villages. This trade expanded substantially with the arrival of Portuguese coastal traders around 1500, revitalizing Benin's power. Some of the most accomplished sculptors in African history worked under King Ewuare and his successors, producing a stunning array of cast brass portraits of Benin royalty, prominent warriors, and even newly arrived Europeans. This was but one of the many specialized livelihoods afforded by urban living (see Seeing the Past: Art of the Slave Trade: A Benin Bronze Plaque).

Yoruba City-States

Just west of Benin were a number of city-states ruled by ethnic Yoruba clans. At their core was the city of Ife (EE-feh), founded in around 1000 C.E. Ife metalsmiths and sculptors were as accomplished as those of Benin, and their large cast works, especially in copper, have been hailed as inimitable. As in the precontact Americas, Yoruba political leaders, called **obas**, performed a mix of political and religious duties. Most of these priest-kings were men, but a significant number were women. One of the obas' main functions was to negotiate with an array of ancestor deities thought to govern key aspects of everyday life. Some slaves later taken from this region to the Americas appear to have adapted these ideas to Christian monotheism, masking multiple ancestor worship behind the Roman Catholic cult of saints.

Akan City-States

oba A priest-king or queen of the Yoruba culture (modern southern Nigeria).

Urban life also matured along the banks of the lower Volta River, in what is today Ghana, at the beginning of early modern times. Here Akan peoples had formed city-states, mostly by controlling regional gold mines and trading networks. The Akan initially focused on transporting gold and cola nuts to the drier north, where these commodities found a ready market among the imperial societies of the middle Niger. With the arrival of Europeans on the Atlantic coast in the late fifteenth century, however, many Akan traders turned their attention toward the south. Throughout early modern times, women held great power in Akan polities, and matrilineal inheritance was the recognized standard. Matrilineal societies were relatively rare in West Africa, but other exceptions included the nomadic Tuareg. Even in patrilineal empires such as Mali and Songhai, women could wield considerable power, especially in matters of succession.

Land of the Blacksmith Kings: West Central Africa

Human interaction in West Central Africa, called by some historians "land of the blacksmith kings," was in part defined by long-term control of copper and iron deposits. As in West Africa, however, the vast majority of people were engaged in subsistence agriculture, limited to hoe tilling because the tsetse fly eliminated livestock capable of pulling plows. For this reason, few people other than gatherer-hunters such as the Pygmies inhabited the most prominent geographical feature of the region, Africa's great equatorial forest (see again Mapping the World, page 583). Most preferred to farm the surrounding savanna and fish along the Atlantic coast and major riverbanks.

> **FOCUS**
>
> What economic, social, and political patterns characterized early modern West Central Africa?

The Congo (Zaire) River basin and estuary, second only to the Amazon in terms of forest cover and volume of freshwater catchment, were of central importance to human history in West Central Africa. Although patterns of belief and material culture varied, most people spoke derivations of Western Bantu, an ancestral root language. Islam was known in some areas but remained marginal in influence. Most inhabitants of West Central Africa lived in matrilineal or patrilineal kin-based villages, a small minority of them subordinate to paramount chiefs or small kings. In all, the region was marked by a cultural coherence similar to that of Mesoamerica (discussed in Chapter 16).

Farmers and Traders

The hoe-agriculturalists who formed the vast majority of West Central Africans grew mostly millet and sorghum, complemented by yams and bananas in certain areas. Bananas, a crop introduced to the region some time before 1000 C.E., enabled farmers to exploit the forest's edge more effectively and devote more energy to textile making and other activities. Some forested areas were too wet for staple crops but still offered game, medicinal plants, and other products. Pygmy forest dwellers, for example, traded honey, ivory, and wild animal skins to their farming neighbors for iron points and food items. Tsetse flies and other pests limited the development of animal husbandry in West Central Africa, except in the drier south. In the vast plains of southern Angola, livestock survived, but rains were highly uncertain.

Farmers

Wherever they lived, West Central Africans, like Europeans and Asians, embraced a host of native American crops in the centuries following Columbus's voyages. Maize became a staple throughout Central Africa, along with cassava (manioc), peanuts, chili peppers, beans, squash, and tobacco. Peanuts, probably introduced by the Portuguese from Brazil soon after 1500, were locally called *nguba* (NGOO-bah), from which the American term "goober peas" derives.

As the introduction of American crops demonstrates, West Central Africa may have had less direct ties to global trade than coastal West Africa, but it was still part of the system. Likewise, the internal African trade networks were of great importance to West Central African life. As in West Africa, salt was traded over great distances, along with food products, textiles, metal goods, and other items. Raffia palm fiber was used to manufacture a supple and durable cloth, and coastal lagoons were exploited for cowry shells for trade.

Traders

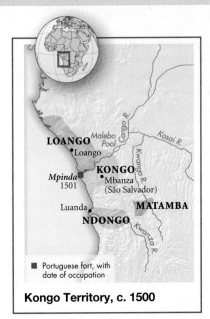

Kongo Territory, c. 1500

Throughout the region political power came to be associated with control of these sorts of trade goods and also of routes of access to the interior. For example, in around 1300 two kingdoms arose above and below the Malebo Pool alongside the Congo River. This was the first major cataract, and hence portage site, for all traders moving between the coast and interior. The kings of Loango, living above the falls but also controlling access to the Atlantic coast, taxed trade and also drew legitimacy from their role as caretakers of an ancient religious shrine. Below the falls and to the south, in Kongo—a kingdom misnamed by the Portuguese after the title of its warlords, the **manikongos** (mah-nee-CONE-goes)—leaders came to power in part by monopolizing copper deposits. The kings of Kongo also controlled access to cowry shells, the region's main currency.

Smiths and Kings

As in West Africa, power also derived from the mystique surrounding metallurgy. The introduction of ironworking to the region sometime early in the Common Era had made the majority of farmers dependent on smiths for hoes, blades, and other implements. Making the most of this reliance, some blacksmiths became kings. By 1500, Kongo commanded an area stretching inland from the right bank of the Congo River south and east some 185 miles, absorbing numerous villages, slaves, and tributaries along the way. A few small kingdoms existed to the north and east, often with copper deposits serving as their lifeblood. These kingdoms eventually challenged Kongo directly, in part because they were subjected to Kongo slave-raiding. In what is today Angola, just north of the Kwanza River, there emerged in the sixteenth century the Ndongo (NDOAN-go) kingdom. Just northeast of Ndongo lay the Matamba kingdom. Initially tributaries of Kongo, the people of Matamba shifted their relations in favor of Ndongo as Portuguese influence there grew in the sixteenth century. By 1600, the Portuguese held forts deep in Ndongo country, using them to procure slaves from farther inland.

Less is known about the peoples of the more isolated and forested middle Congo basin, but archaeologists have recently shown that large chiefdoms were being consolidated there as early as the thirteenth century, and they lasted into early modern times. Here, innovations in sword manufacture seem to have enabled some paramount chiefs to monopolize trade along Congo River tributaries. Like elites everywhere, these chiefs considered themselves the spiritual kin of various predatory lords of the animal kingdom, in this case the leopard and eagle.

We know less about women's livelihoods than men's, but it appears that in early modern West Central Africa, as in many preindustrial societies, women tended to work mostly at domestic tasks such as child rearing, food preparation, and other aspects of household management. Men were frequently engaged in hunting, herding, trade, and warfare, so women's responsibilities often extended to agriculture. In many places, women planted yams in hard soils by slicing through the crust with machetes made by village men. Almost everywhere, women tended the food crops and men cleared forest.

Women formed the foundation of West Central African society in terms of both subsistence and reproduction. Yet

Mbundu Blacksmiths
This late-seventeenth-century watercolor depicts a Mbundu blacksmith and assistant at work. As the assistant operates the typical African bellows with rods attached to airbags, the master smith hammers a crescent-shaped iron blade on an anvil. Other blades, including what may be a sickle or hoe, lie on the ground to the left of the anvil. In the background a curious audience looks on. (Illumination by Padre Giovanni Antonio Cavazzi da Montecuccolo (died 1692) from the Manoscritti Araldi; reproduction courtesy of Michele Araldi.)

women did still more. Evidence for the early modern period is slim, but it appears that while men controlled metal smelting and smithing, women both managed and worked in mining crews. Some were probably enslaved, but others were likely associated with ethnic groups famed for their expertise in these tasks. Even children were employed in mines, particularly salt and copper mines. Experienced West and West Central African miners, including women and children, were probably among the first slaves sent by the Portuguese to work the gold mines of the Spanish Caribbean. Many later found their skills in demand in Colombia, Mexico, Peru, and Brazil.

Strangers in Ships: Gold, Slavery, and the Portuguese

As we saw in Chapter 17, the Portuguese arrived in western Africa soon after 1400 in search of gold and a sea route to India. For well over a century they were the only significant European presence in the region. During that time, a number of Portuguese explorers, merchants, missionaries, and even criminal castaways established a string of *feitorias*, or fortified trading posts, and offshore island settlements. There were no great marches to the interior, no conquests of existing empires. Instead, the Portuguese focused their efforts on extracting Africa's famed wealth in gold, ivory, and slaves through intermediaries. In a pattern that would be continued in Asia, the Portuguese sought to dominate maritime trade.

FOCUS

How did the early Portuguese slave trade in western Africa function?

From Voyages of Reconnaissance to Trading Forts 1415–1650

On the wide Gambia River the Portuguese sailed far inland, seeking the famed gold of Mali, at this time an empire in decline but still powerful in the interior (see again Map 18.1). The warring states of the region were happy to trade gold for horses, which were far more valuable than the crude European guns available at this time. Chronic conflicts yielded a surplus of captives. With explicit backing from the pope, Portuguese merchants did not hesitate to accept African slaves as payment. Once in Portuguese hands, each healthy young male was reduced to an accounting unit, or *peça* (PEH-sah) literally "piece." Women, children, the disabled, and the elderly were discounted in terms of fractions of a peça.

African enslavement of fellow Africans was widespread long before the arrival of Europeans, and the daily experience of slavery in most African households, farms, or mines was no doubt unpleasant. What differed with the arrival of the Portuguese in the fifteenth century was a new insistence on innate African inferiority—in a word, racism—and with it a closing of traditional avenues of reentry into free society, if not for oneself, then for one's children, such as faithful service, or in Islamic societies, religious conversion. The Portuguese followed the pope's decree that enslaved sub-Saharan Africans be converted to Catholicism, but they also adopted an unstated policy that regarded black Africans as "slaves by nature." To sidestep the paradox of African spiritual equality and alleged "beastly" inferiority, the Portuguese claimed that they sold only captives taken in "just war." Many such slaves were sold, like young Domingo Angola, to the Spanish, who took the Portuguese sellers at their word (see Reading the Past: Alonso de Sandoval, "General Points Relating to Slavery").

Iberian demand for African slaves remained limited prior to American colonization. Word of goldfields in the African interior encouraged the Portuguese to continue their dogged search for the yellow metal. By 1471 caravels reached West Africa's so-called Gold Coast, and in 1482 the Portuguese established a feitoria in present-day Ghana. Built by

Racism as Justification for Slavery

manikongo A "blacksmith" king of Kongo.

peça Portuguese for "piece," used to describe enslaved Africans as units of labor.

Alonso de Sandoval, "General Points Relating to Slavery"

Alonso de Sandoval (1577–c. 1650) was a Jesuit priest born in Seville, Spain, and raised in Lima, Peru. He spent most of his adult life administering sacraments to enslaved Africans arriving at the Caribbean port city of Cartagena de Indias, in present-day Colombia. In 1627 he published a book entitled *On Restoring Ethiopian Salvation*. In it, he focused on cultural aspects of sub-Saharan African societies as he understood them, with the aim of preaching to Africans more effectively, but he also discussed the Atlantic slave trade and its justifications.

The debate among scholars on how to justify the arduous and difficult business of slavery has perplexed me for a long time. I could have given up on explaining it and just ignored it in this book. However, I am determined to discuss it, although I will leave the final justification of slavery to legal and ecclesiastical authorities. . . . I will only mention here what I have learned after many years of working in this ministry. The readers can formulate their own ideas on the justice of this issue. . . .

A short story helps me explain how to morally justify black slavery. I was once consulted by a captain who owned slave ships that had made many voyages to these places. He had enriched himself through the slave trade, and his conscience was burdened with concern over how these slaves had fallen into his hands. His concern is not surprising, because he also told me that one of their kings imprisoned anyone who angered him in order to sell them as slaves to the Spaniards. So in this region, people are enslaved if they anger the king. . . .

There is a more standard way in which slaves are traded and later shipped in fleets of ships to the Indies. Near Luanda are some black merchants called pombeiros worth a thousand pesos. They travel inland eighty leagues [c. 250 miles], bringing porters with them to carry trade goods. They meet in great markets where merchants gather together to sell slaves. These merchants travel 200 or 300 leagues [c. 650–1000 miles] to sell blacks from many different kingdoms to various merchants or pombeiros. The pombeiros buy the slaves and transport them to the coast. They must report to their masters how many died on the road. They do this by bringing back the hands of the dead, a stinking, horrific sight. . . .

I have spent a great deal of time discussing this subject because slaves are captured in many different ways, and this disturbs the slave traders' consciences. One slave trader freely told me that he felt guilty about how the slaves he had bought in Guinea had come to be enslaved. Another slave trader, who had bought 300 slaves on foot, expressed the same concerns, adding that half the wars fought between blacks would not take place if the Spanish [or more likely, Portuguese] did not go there to buy slaves. . . . The evidence, along with the moral justifications argued by scholars, is the best we can do to carefully address this irredeemable situation and the very difficult business of the slave trade.

Source: Alonso de Sandoval, *Treatise on Slavery*, ed. and trans. Nicole Von Germeten (Indianapolis, IN: Hackett Publishers, 2008), 50–55.

EXAMINING THE EVIDENCE

1. Who was Alonso de Sandoval, and why did he write this passage?

2. How does Sandoval try to justify African enslavement?

3. Are Africans themselves involved in this discussion?

Early Portuguese Slave Trade

enslaved Africans, São Jorge da Mina, or "St. George of the mine," served for over a century as Portugal's major West African gold and slaving fort.

After 1500, as slave markets in Spanish America and Brazil emerged, new trading posts were established in choice spots all along the West African coast. It so happened that invasions of Mande and Mane (MAH-nay) peoples into modern Guinea, Liberia, Sierra Leone, and Ivory Coast in the fifteenth and sixteenth centuries produced yet more streams of captives through the seventeenth century (see Map 18.2). As in the first years after their arrival, the Portuguese continued to trade copper, iron, textiles, horses, and guns (now much more advanced) for gold, ivory, and a local spice called malaguetta pepper, but by the early 1500s the shift toward slave trading was evident. The coexistence of rising

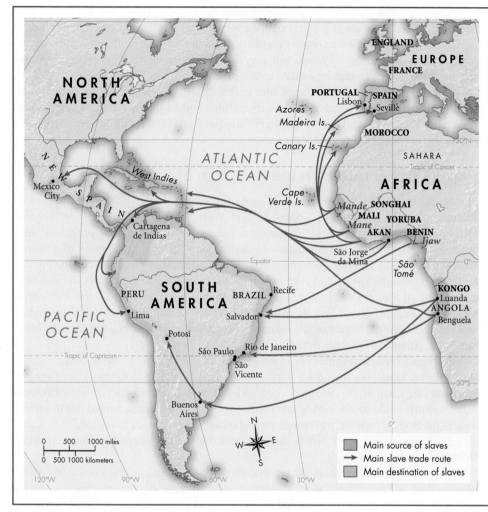

MAP 18.2

The Early Atlantic Slave Trade, c. 1450–1650

The first enslaved Africans transported by ship in Atlantic waters arrived in Portugal in 1441. The Portuguese won a monopoly on African coastal trade from the pope, and until 1500, they shipped most enslaved African captives to the eastern Atlantic islands, where plantations were booming by the 1450s. Soon after 1500, Portuguese slave traders took captives first to the Spanish Caribbean (West Indies), then to the mainland colonies of New Spain and Peru. Claimed by the Portuguese in 1500, Brazil was initially a minor destination for enslaved Africans, but this changed by about 1570, when the colony's sugar production ballooned. Another early Atlantic route took slaves south to Buenos Aires, where they were marched overland to the rich city of Potosí. Death rates on the ships and on overland marches were always high in this traffic in human lives.

Main source of slaves
→ Main slave trade route
Main destination of slaves

demand for slaves in the Americas and increased supply in Africa as the result of warfare made the dramatic growth of the Atlantic slave trade all but inevitable.

Throughout western Africa the Portuguese both extracted and transported wealth. They frequently ferried luxury goods such as cola nuts and textiles, as well as slaves, between existing African trade zones. As we will see, a similar pattern would emerge when the Portuguese reached India, and later China, Japan, and the Spice Islands. Virtually everywhere the Portuguese docked their lumbering but well-armed ships, Africans found that they benefited as much from access to the foreigners' shipping, which was relatively secure and efficient, as from their goods. As a result, many competing coastal lords made the most of these new trade ties, often to the detriment of more isolated and vulnerable neighbors.

At times commerce with the Portuguese, which increasingly turned to the import of bronze and copper bracelets, or manillas, as currency, would upend a region's balance of power, touching off a series of interior conflicts. Some such conflicts were ignited by Portuguese convicts, who survived abandonment along the coast to establish marriage alliances with local chiefdoms. As seen in Chapter 17 in the case of Brazil, this was in fact the Portuguese plan, to drop expendable subjects like seeds along the world's coasts. Some took root, learned local languages, and built trading posts. In several West African coastal enclaves, mulatto or "Eurafrican" communities developed. These mixed communities were nominally Catholic, but much cultural blending occurred. Some scholars now refer to these new intermediaries of global exchange as "Atlantic creoles."

New Markets in the Niger Delta

After 1510, the Portuguese moved eastward. Here among the Niger delta's vast tidal flats and mangroves, Ijaw (EE-jaw) boatmen were initially willing to trade an adult male captive for fewer than a dozen copper manillas. Rates of exchange moderated with competition and a steadier flow of goods, but overall, Portuguese demand for slaves remained relatively low and was met by other captive-producing zones. What historians call the "Nigerian diaspora" mostly developed later in this densely populated region, in the seventeenth and eighteenth centuries. By then rival Dutch and English slavers had begun operating posts to the west and east of the Niger delta (see Map 18.4, page 602). After 1650 this region was known simply as the Slave Coast.

Portuguese Strategy in the Kingdom of Kongo

Portuguese interest in Atlantic Africa shifted southeastward after 1500, based in part on alliances with the kingdom of Kongo. Within West Central Africa generally, ongoing cycles of trade, war, and drought profoundly influenced relationships with outsiders. Once again, local nobles forced the Portuguese to operate according to local systems of influence and local rules. Still, whereas Portuguese slavers were to be largely displaced by the French, English, and Dutch in West and even northern West Central Africa by 1650, in the southern portion of the continent they held on for much longer. As a result, the fortunes of Kongo and Angola became ever more intimately entwined with those of Brazil, Portugal's vast colony on the other side of the Atlantic. Historians now speak of a functionally separate South Atlantic slave trade circuit.

Missionary Efforts

Portuguese Soldier

Here a Benin artist depicts a Portuguese soldier in what appears to be light armor and a crested metal helmet typical of the later sixteenth century. Portuguese soldiers like this one aided several African allies, including the Christian kings of Kongo, as they fought for regional supremacy and engaged in the growing slave trade. (Snark/Art Resource, NY.)

Portuguese religious initiatives in Africa had long been split between armed conflict with Muslim kingdoms in the far north, epitomized by the 1415 conquest of Ceuta in Morocco (see Chapter 17), and more peaceful, although scattered and inconsistent, missionary efforts in the south. Portuguese missionaries, like merchants, tended not to survive long in the tropical interior, where malaria and other diseases took a heavy toll. Thus scores of Franciscans, Jesuits, and others died denouncing the persistent **fetishism** (roughly, "idolatry") of their local hosts.

Quite unlike their Spanish contemporaries in the Americas, the Portuguese made barely a dent in African religious traditions, despite centuries of contact. This was not for lack of trying—the Portuguese worked much harder at conversion than did later-arriving northern Europeans—but rather due to a mix of hardening Portuguese racism and sub-Saharan Africa's punishing disease regime. Falciparum malaria, in particular, severely restricted the movements of European missionaries, who also faced language barriers and other cultural obstacles. The obvious solution was to train African priests, and for a time this option was pursued and even sponsored by the Portuguese royal family.

In the early sixteenth century, African priests were trained in Lisbon, in the university city of Coimbra, and even in Rome. African seminaries also were established, notably in the Cape Verde Islands and the island of São Tomé, located off the western coast in the Gulf of Guinea. Despite promising beginnings, however, these endeavors met with sharp opposition from an increasingly racist and self-righteous Portuguese clergy. A similar process had taken place in Spanish America, where ambitious plans for training and ordaining a native American clergy were scrapped within a few generations of contact. Emerging colonial racial hierarchies, indelibly linked to status, trumped the universal ideal of spiritual equality. An African clergy could also prove subversive of the slave trade and other such commercial projects. Already in decline before 1600, most of the local African seminaries languished in the seventeenth and early eighteenth centuries. Only with the Enlightenment-inspired reforms of the later eighteenth century (discussed in Chapter 23) were African novices again encouraged to become priests beyond the secular, or parish, level, and only after the abolition of slavery did their numbers become significant. Thus, although the Atlantic slave trade would result in the forced migration of millions of Africans and the creation of new hybrid cultural communities in the Americas, in Africa itself the racial basis of the trade inhibited cultural merger and exchange.

This did not mean that Christianity had no impact on early modern Atlantic Africa. Rather, it meant that its presence was less deeply felt than might otherwise have been the case. Aside from the offshore islands, only in Kongo and Angola did Christianity play a critical historical role. Beginning in the 1480s, the Portuguese applied their usual blend of trade, military alliances, and religious proselytizing to carve out a niche in West Central Africa. By 1491 they had managed to convert much of the Kongo aristocracy to Roman Catholicism. Key among the converts was the paramount chief's son, Nzinga Mbemba, who later ruled as Afonso I (r. 1506–1543).

Afonso's conversion was apparently genuine. He learned to read, studied theology tirelessly, and renamed Mbanza, the capital city, São Salvador ("Holy Savior"). One of his sons became a priest in Lisbon and returned to Kongo following consecration in Rome. He was one of the earliest exemplars of western African indigenous clergy.

Ultimately, however, Christianity, like copper, tended to be monopolized by Kongo's elites; the peasant and craft worker majority was virtually ignored. Most Kongolese commoners recognized deities called **kitomi** (key-TOE-mee), each looked after by a local (non-Catholic) priest. Meanwhile, Portuguese military aid buttressed Kongo politically while fueling the slave trade.

Here, as elsewhere in Africa, the slave trade, though it offered considerable gains, also exacerbated existing dangers and conflicts and almost always created new ones. King Afonso wrote to the king of Portugal in 1526, complaining that "every day the merchants carry away our people, sons of our soil and sons of our nobles and vassals, and our relatives, whom thieves and people of bad conscience kidnap and sell to obtain the coveted things and trade goods of that [Portuguese] Kingdom."[4] Even in its earliest days, the slave trade in West Central Africa was taking on a life of its own.

Kongo-Portuguese Slaving Alliance

As a result of Kongo's slaving-based alliance with the Portuguese, King Afonso's successors faced growing opposition from every direction. The kingdom of Kongo finally collapsed in 1569. São Salvador was sacked, and its Christian nobles were humiliated and sold into slavery in the interior. Lisbon responded to the fall of its staunchest African ally with troops, in this case six hundred Portuguese harquebusiers (the precursor of musketeers). With this violent intervention, the monarchy was effectively restored in 1574. In exchange, Kongo traders called *pombeiros* (pohm-BEH-rohs) supplied their Portuguese saviors with a steady stream of slaves. The process of propping up regimes in exchange for captives was to continue throughout the long history of the slave trade.

Portuguese Strategy in Angola

A second pillar of Portuguese strategy in West Central Africa entailed establishing a permanent military colony in Angola, home of the young man named Domingo whose story began this chapter. Beginning with the port city of Luanda, this new colony was to become one of the largest and longest-lived clearinghouses for the Atlantic slave trade (see Map 18.3). It was perhaps here more than anywhere else in Africa that the Portuguese, aided again by droughts and other factors, managed to radically alter local livelihoods.

According to Portuguese documents and climatological evidence, the major stimulus to the early Angolan slave trade was a severe and prolonged drought affecting the interior in the 1590s. The drought uprooted numerous groups of villagers already weakened by slave-raiding, and these luckless refugees in turn were preyed upon by still more parasitic and aggressive warrior-bandits calling themselves Imbangala. The Imbangala, organized around secret military societies, soon became slaving allies of the Portuguese. These were probably Domingo Angola's captors.

Employing terrifying tactics, including human sacrifice and—allegedly—cannibalism, Imbangala raiders eventually threatened to snuff out the Ndongo kingdom. That Ndongo survived at all, in fact, depended on the creativity and wile of a powerful woman, Queen Nzinga (r. 1624–1663). Following the maxim "if you can't beat 'em, join 'em," Queen Nzinga sought to thwart the Imbangala by allying with their sometime business partners, the Portuguese. In Luanda she was baptized "Dona Ana," or "Queen Ann."

fetishism The derogatory term used by Europeans to describe western African use of religious objects.

kitomi Deities attended by Kongo priests prior to the arrival of Christian Europeans.

pombeiro A slave-trade middleman in the West Central African interior.

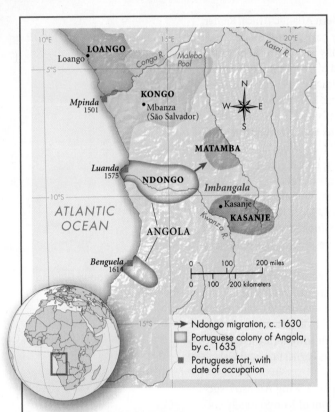

MAP 18.3 **West Central Africa, c. 1500–1635**

No African region was more affected by European interlopers in early modern times than West Central Africa, the Atlantic world's main source of enslaved captives, nearly all of them shipped abroad by the Portuguese. At first, Portuguese missionaries and diplomats vied for the favor of the kings of Kongo. Before long, however, the Portuguese shifted their interest south to Luanda, a base built almost exclusively for slave trading. Peoples of the interior suffered periodic slave raids as the Portuguese extended their networks south to Benguela. Some refugees migrated eastward, only to encounter new enemies— most of them allies of the Portuguese.

Adopting the example of the kings of Kongo, Queen Nzinga promised to supply slaves to her new friends. She soon discovered that the Portuguese had little authority over the Imbangala, however. Their warriors continued to attack the Ndongo, who were forced to move to a new homeland, in deserted Matamba. From this newer, more secure base Queen Nzinga built her own aggressive slaving and trading state. When the Dutch occupied Luanda in the 1640s, the queen adapted, trading slaves to them in exchange for political immunity for her followers. Before her death at the age of eighty-one, Queen Nzinga reestablished ties with the Portuguese, who again controlled the coast in the 1650s.

To the south and west, meanwhile, Imbangala warriors began to intermingle with various peoples, eventually establishing the kingdom of Kasanje (see again Map 18.3). After 1630, Kasanje merchant-warriors operated alternately as slavers and middlemen, taking or trading for captives from the east. Farther south, other warriors began to interact with Portuguese settlers around the Atlantic port of Benguela. By the later seventeenth century Benguela rivaled Luanda as the key conduit for the South Atlantic slave trade.

By this time, Portuguese trade in Africa focused almost entirely on slaves. Overall, West Central Africa, mostly Kongo and Angola, supplied over 5 million, or nearly half of the about 12 million recorded slaves sent to the Americas between 1519 and 1867. The victims were overwhelmingly peasants, poor millet and sorghum farmers struggling to eke out a living in a largely drought-prone and war-torn region. Very occasionally, as in the case of Kongo, the enslaved included nobles and prominent warriors. At least two-thirds of all African captives sent across the Atlantic were men, a significant number of them boys. Some historians have argued that growing demand for young men abroad and the African desire to be rid of these potentially vengeful captives proved mutually reinforcing. Into the vortex were thrust young men such as Domingo Angola, who was sent all the way to the Andean boomtown of Potosí.

Due to Portuguese entrenchment on the West Central African coast and a fairly formalized system of enslavement, a majority of Angolan and Kongolese slaves reached the Americas as baptized Catholics more or less fluent in Kimbundu or Kikongo, the common languages of the coast, and sometimes even Portuguese. Ethnic differences existed, but on the whole slaves given the monikers "Kongo" and "Angola," like Domingo, had more in common than any comparable group of Africans taken to the Americas.

Northern Europeans and the Expansion of the Atlantic Slave Trade 1600–1800

FOCUS

What were the major changes in the Atlantic slave trade after 1600?

Other Europeans had vied for a share of the Portuguese Atlantic slave trade since the mid-sixteenth century, among them famous figures such as the English corsair Francis Drake, but it was only after 1600 that competition grew significantly. First the French, then the English, Dutch, Danish,

Queen Nzinga's Baptism
Here the same late-seventeenth-century artist who painted the Mbundu blacksmiths (see page 594) portrays the baptism of the central African Queen Nzinga. Queen Nzinga's Catholic baptism did not prevent her from making alliances with non-Catholics, both African and European, in long and violent struggles with neighbors and the Portuguese in her district of Matamba, Angola. Some witnesses say she was attended by dozens of male servants dressed as concubines. (Illumination by Padre Giovanni Antonio Cavazzi da Montecuccolo (died 1692) from the Manoscritti Araldi; reproduction courtesy of Michele Araldi.)

and other northern Europeans forcibly displaced Portuguese traders all along the western shores of Africa. Others set up competing posts nearby. By 1650, the Portuguese were struggling to maintain a significant presence even in West Central Africa. They began to supplement western African slaves with captives transshipped from their outposts in the Indian Ocean, primarily Mozambique and Madagascar. As a result, slaves arriving in Brazil in the seventeenth century were of increasingly diverse ethnic origins (see Map 18.4).

Since it was both profitable and logistically complex, the slave trade was among the most thoroughly documented commercial activities of early modern times. Beginning after 1650, we can cross-check multiple documents for numbers of slaves boarded, origin place-names, and age or sex groupings. These sources, a bland accounting of mass death and suffering, suggest that the volume of the trade grew slowly, expanding gradually after 1650 and very rapidly only after 1750. The British, despite profiting greatly from the slave trade in western Africa through the 1790s, when volume peaked, suddenly reversed policy under pressure from abolitionists in 1807. After 1808, the British Navy actively suppressed the Atlantic slave trade until it was formally abolished by international treaty in 1850. Despite these measures, contraband slaving continued, mostly between Angola and Brazil. In terms of numbers of lives, families, and communities destroyed, the Atlantic slave trade was primarily a modern phenomenon with deep early modern roots.

The Rise and Fall of Monopoly Trading Companies

Following the example of the Spanish and Portuguese, northern European participation in the Atlantic slave trade grew in tandem with colonization efforts in the Americas. Tobacco-producing Caribbean islands such as Barbados and Martinique and mainland North American regions such as Virginia and the Carolinas were initially staffed with indentured, or contracted, European servants and only a small number of African slaves. As sugar cultivation increased in the Caribbean after 1650 and tobacco took off in Virginia,

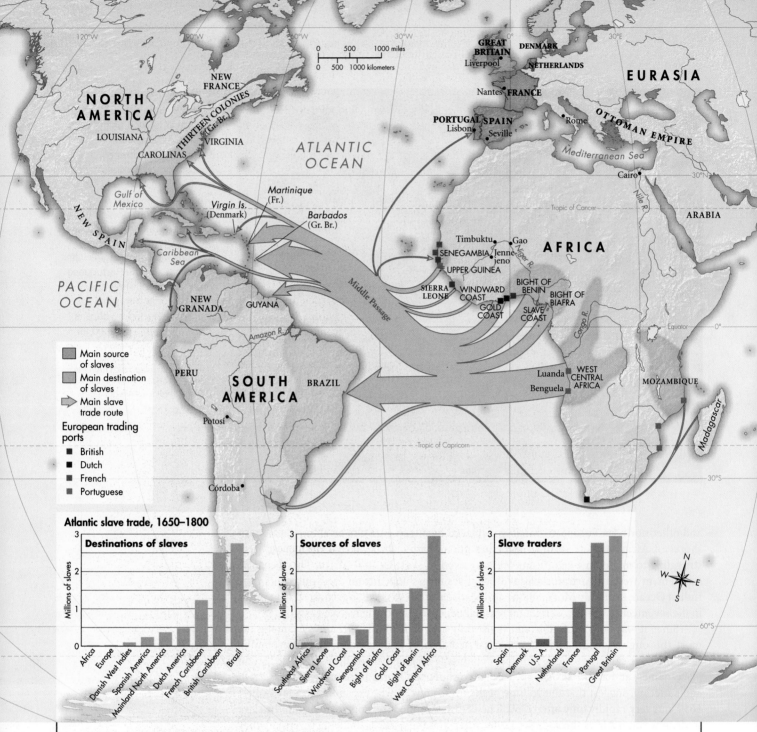

MAP 18.4 The Atlantic Slave Trade at Its Height, c. 1650–1800

Though always terrible and deadly, the Atlantic slave trade grew dramatically after 1650. The Portuguese were no longer the only slave traders, and demand was no longer limited to Spanish America and Brazil. New slaving nations included the Netherlands, England, France, and Denmark, all of which had colonies in the Caribbean and on the North American mainland that relied on plantation agriculture. The regions from which enslaved Africans came also shifted during this long period. West Central Africa remained a major source region, but the Upper Guinea Coast was increasingly overshadowed by the so-called Slave Coast located between the Bight of Benin and the Bight of Biafra.

however, planters shifted overwhelmingly to African slavery. This had been their wish, as their documents attest, and a declining supply of poor European contract laborers, particularly after 1700, accelerated the trend.

Origins of American Racism

For historians of the North Atlantic, this transition from indentured servitude to African slavery has raised a host of questions about the origins of American racism. In sum, can modern notions of racial difference be traced to early modern American slavery and the Atlantic slave trade? Some prominent scholars of English and French colonialism have argued that racist ideologies grew mostly *after* this shift from European to African labor. Before that, they argue, "white" and "black" workers were treated by masters and overseers with equal cruelty. In Virginia and Barbados during the early to mid-1600s, for instance, black and white indentured servants labored alongside each other, experiencing equal exploitation and limited legal protection in the brief years before racial slavery was codified by law. Scholars working in a broader historical context, however—one that takes into account Spanish, Portuguese, Dutch, and Italian experiences in the Atlantic, Mediterranean, and beyond—have been less convinced by this assertion. They argue that while racist notions hardened with the expansion of slavery in the Caribbean and North America after 1650—and grew harder still following the Scientific Revolution with its emphasis on biological classification—European views of sub-Saharan Africans had virtually never been positive. Put another way, racism was more a cause of slavery than a result.

Although numerous challengers were gathering force by 1600, Portuguese slavers remained the most significant suppliers to early English and French planters in the Americas. As we have seen, the Portuguese had a distinct advantage in that over several centuries they had established the financial instruments and supply networks necessary to run such a complex and risky business. To compete, northern Europeans were forced to establish state-subsidized monopoly trading companies. The highly belligerent Dutch West India Company was founded in 1621 to attack Spanish and Portuguese colonial outposts and take over Iberian commercial interests in the Atlantic. Several slaving forts in western Africa were eventually seized. São Jorge da Mina fell in 1638, and Luanda, Angola, in 1641. Although these colonial outposts were returned in subsequent decades, the era of Portuguese dominance was over.

The French, whose early overseas activities had been stunted by the religious wars described in Chapter 20, finally organized a monopoly trading company in 1664 to supply their growing Caribbean market. The English, fresh from their own civil conflicts, followed suit by forming the Royal African Company in 1672. By 1700, the French and English were fighting bitterly to supply not only their own colonial holdings but also the highly lucrative Spanish-American market. Dutch slavers also competed, supplying nearly one hundred thousand slaves to the Spanish up to the 1730s. After 1650, Spanish-Americans were not

Formation of Northern European Trading Companies

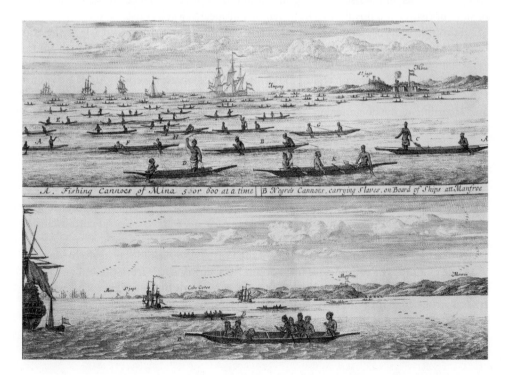

Filling the Slave Ships
The upper half of this 1732 engraving by Dutch artist Johannes Kip shows West African fishermen in canoes off the coast of present-day Ghana, with the old Portuguese fortress of São Jorge da Mina in the distance. The lower half shows slaves being ferried to a Dutch ship in a somewhat longer canoe, with a string of other European slave-trading forts in the distance. Slave ships often cruised African coasts for several months, acquiring a diverse range of captives before crossing the Atlantic. (Beinecke Rare Book and Manuscript Library, Yale University.)

buying as many slaves as in the first century after conquest, but unlike other colonists they paid for them with gold and silver. Danish slavers also entered the competition by the 1670s, when they established several Caribbean sugar plantations in the Virgin Islands.

The company model did not last. By 1725, if not before, most of the northern European monopoly companies had been dismantled. Stuck with costly forts, salaried officers, and state-mandated contract obligations, they proved to be too inflexible and inefficient to survive in a world of limited information and shifting supply and demand. Thus the French, English, and Dutch resorted to a system more like that long practiced by the Portuguese, in which small numbers of private merchants, often related to one another by marriage if not blood, pooled capital to finance individual voyages. Like their Mediterranean predecessors in Venice, Genoa, and elsewhere, the trade in slaves was but one of many overlapping ventures for most of these investors. Their profits, usually averaging 10 percent or so, were reinvested in land, light industry, and numerous other endeavors. In time, investors inhabiting bustling slave ports such as Liverpool, England, and Nantes, France, had little to do with the actual organization of slaving voyages. Nonetheless, the profits slavery produced would flow through these ports into Europe, fueling the continent's economic growth and development.

How the Mature Slave Trade Functioned

The slave trade proved most lucrative when European investors cut every possible corner. Profit margins consistently trumped humanitarian concerns. By the late seventeenth century, ships were packed tightly, food and water rationed sparingly, and crews kept as small as possible. Unlike other shipping ventures at this time, the value of the captives held as cargo far exceeded the costs of ship and crew on typical slaving voyages. In part this was a reflection of the considerable risks involved.

European Risk and Profit

Risks and uncertainties abounded in the slave trade. Despite a growing number of more or less friendly European forts scattered along Africa's vast Atlantic coast, slavers were mostly on their own when it came to collecting captives. In short, the system was much more open and African-dominated than has generally been acknowledged. Ships spent an average of three months cruising coastal towns and estuaries in search of African middlemen willing to trade captives for commodities. By the late seventeenth century, competition was on the rise, affecting supply and thus price. Violence, mostly in the form of slave uprisings and hostile attacks by fellow Europeans, was a constant concern.

European ship captains in charge of this dangerous and drawn-out leg of the trip hoped to receive at the other end a bounty of 2 to 5 percent on all surviving slaves. Somewhat like modern human traffickers, they were in fact betting their lives on a relatively small fortune. As we saw with regard to Portuguese missionaries, western Africa was notoriously unhealthy for "unseasoned" Europeans, due mostly to endemic falciparum malaria, and according to the documentary record, as many as one in ten ship captains died before leaving the African coast for the Americas. Few who survived repeated the trip. Ships' doctors had scant remedies on hand even for common ailments such as dysentery, which also afflicted slaves and crewmembers to a great extent. When not ill themselves, doctors inspected slaves before embarkation, hoping to head off premature death or the spread of disease aboard ship and thereby to protect the investment.

African Gains and Losses

On the African consumer side, few northern European products were attractive enough to stimulate trade. More than anything, Africans wanted colorful cotton fabrics from India to supplement their own usually indigo-dyed or plain products. Thus the Dutch, French, English, and others followed the Portuguese example yet again by importing huge quantities of cotton cloth from South Asia, cowry shells from the Indian Ocean, and iron, brass, and copper from parts of Europe, particularly Spain and Sweden. European traders struggled to meet the particular and often shifting demands of each slaving region's inhabitants. Cloth was the most sought-after trade item throughout the period of the slave trade, constituting at least two-thirds of imports carried by British slavers between the 1690s and 1808. Other tastes were introduced by Europeans. By 1700, American plantation commodities such as rum and tobacco were being exchanged for slaves in significant quantities. Thus, the Atlantic slave trade was a global concern, drawing in people and goods from around the world.

It is clear from many contemporary sources that chiefs and kings throughout western Africa greatly augmented their prestige by accumulating and redistributing the commodities they procured through the slave trade. The captives they sent abroad were not their kin, and western Africans appear to have had no sense of the overall magnitude of this commerce in human bodies. There were few internal brakes on captive-taking besides the diminishing pool of victims and shifting political ambitions; the African desire to hold dependents to boost prestige and provide domestic labor meshed with European demands. Along these lines, whereas female war captives might be absorbed into elite households, men and boys were generally considered dangerous elements and happily gotten rid of. It so happened that European planters and mine owners in the colonies valued men over women by a significant margin. Thus, however immoral and disruptive of African life it appears in retrospect, the slave trade probably seemed at the time to be mutually beneficial for European buyers and African sellers. Only the slaves themselves felt otherwise.

The Middle Passage

It is difficult to imagine the suffering endured by the more than 12 million African captives forced to cross the Atlantic Ocean in early modern times. The ordeal itself has come to be known as the **Middle Passage** (see again Map 18.4). As noted at the opening of this chapter, some West Central Africans imagined the slavers' ships to be floating slaughterhouses crossing a great lake or river to satisfy white cannibals inhabiting a distant, sterile land. Portuguese sailors unambiguously dubbed them "death ships" or "floating tombs." Perhaps troubled by this sense of damnation, Portuguese priests in Luanda, Benguela, and elsewhere baptized as many slaves as they could before departure. Portuguese ships were virtually all named for Catholic saints.

Slave Conditions and Mortality

Northern Europeans, increasingly in charge of the slave trade after 1650, took a more dispassionate approach. Slaves, as far as they were concerned, were a sort of highly valued livestock requiring efficient but impersonal handling. Put another way, the care and feeding of slaves were treated as pragmatic matters of health, not faith. Rations were the subsistence minimum of maize, rice, or millet gruel, with a bit of fish or dried meat added from time to time. Men, women, and children were assigned separate quarters. Women were given a cotton cloth for a wrap, whereas men were often kept naked, both to save money and to discourage rebellion by adding to their already abject humiliation. Exercise was required on deck in the form of dancing to drums during daylight hours. Like cattle, slaves were showered with seawater before the nighttime lockdown. The hold, ventilated on most ships after initial experiences with mass suffocation and heatstroke, was periodically splashed with vinegar.

Despite these measures, slave mortality on the one- to three-month voyage across the Atlantic was high. On average, between 10 and 20 percent of slaves did not survive the cramped conditions, physical abuse, and generally unsanitary environment aboard ship. This high mortality rate is all the more alarming in that these slaves had been selected for their relative good health in the first place, leaving countless other captives behind to perish in makeshift barracks, dungeons, and coastal agricultural plots. Many more died soon after landing in the Americas, often from dysentery and other intestinal ailments. Some who were emotionally overwhelmed committed suicide along the way by hurling themselves into the ocean or strangling themselves in their chains. A few enraged men managed to kill a crewmember or even a captain before being summarily executed. Slaves from different regions had trouble communicating. Thus successful slave mutinies, in which women as well as men participated, were rare but not unknown.

The general conditions of the Middle Passage worsened over time. In the name of increased efficiency, the situation belowdecks went from crowded to crammed between the seventeenth and eighteenth centuries. On average, crews of 30 to 40 common

Middle Passage The Atlantic crossing made by slaves taken from Africa to the Americas.

sailors oversaw 200 to 300 slaves in around 1700, whereas the same number oversaw 300 to 400 slaves after 1750. These are only averages; even in the 1620s, some ships carried 600 or more slaves.

Although some Iberian clergymen protested the horrors of this crossing as early as the sixteenth century, it took the extraordinary eighteenth-century deterioration of conditions aboard slave ships to awaken the conscience of participating nations. In England, most importantly, African survivors of the Middle Passage such as Olaudah Equiano (c. 1745–1797) were called to testify before Parliament by the late eighteenth century. "Permit me, with the greatest deference and respect," Equiano began his 1789 autobiography, "to lay at your feet the following genuine Narrative, the chief design of which is to excite in your august assemblies a sense of compassion for the miseries which the Slave-Trade has entailed on my unfortunate countrymen."[5] Such testimonies, backed by the impassioned pleas of prominent Quakers and other religious figures, were finally heard. Abolition of the Atlantic slave trade, first enforced by the British in 1808, would come much more easily than abolition of slavery itself.

Volume of the Slave Trade

It is important to note that the trans-Saharan and East African slave trades preceded the Atlantic one discussed here, and that these trades continued apace throughout early modern times. In fact, the volume of the Atlantic trade appears only to have eclipsed these other avenues to foreign captivity after 1600. That said, the Atlantic slave trade ultimately constituted the greatest forced migration in early modern world history. Compared with the roughly 2 million mostly free European migrants who made their way to all parts of the Americas between the voyage of Columbus in 1492 and the British abolition of the slave trade in 1808, the number of enslaved Africans to cross the Atlantic and survive is astounding—between 10 and 12 million.

Olaudah Equiano

Olaudah Equiano, whose slave name was Gustavus Vassa, became a celebrity critic of the Atlantic slave trade in the late eighteenth century after writing a memoir of his experiences as a slave and free man of color in Africa, North America, the Caribbean, and Europe. The book, published in 1789, offered a rare victim's perspective on the Atlantic slave trade and the daily humiliations and punishments suffered by slaves in the Americas. (British Library, London/© British Library Board. All Rights Reserved/Bridgeman Art Library.)

Also astounding is the fact that the vast majority of these Africans arrived in the last half century of the slave trade, that is, after 1750. Up until 1650 a total of approximately 710,000 slaves had been taken to American markets, most of them to Spanish America (262,700). Brazil was the next largest destination, absorbing about a quarter of a million slaves to that date. São Tomé, the sugar island in the Gulf of Guinea, and Europe (mostly Iberia) absorbed about 95,000 and 112,000 slaves, respectively. Madeira and the Canaries imported about 25,000 African slaves, and the English and French West Indies, 21,000 and 2500, respectively. The average annual volume for the period up to 1650 was approximately 7500 slaves per year.

Eighteenth-Century Explosion

The second (1650–1750) and third (1750–1850) stages of the Atlantic slave trade witnessed enormous, historically transformative growth. By 1675, nearly 15,000 slaves were being carried to the colonies annually, and by 1700 nearly 30,000. The total volume of the trade between 1700 and 1750 was double that of the previous fifty years, bringing some 2.5 million slaves to the Americas. The trade nearly doubled yet again between 1750 and 1800, when some 4 million Africans were transported. By this time the effect of the Atlantic slave trade on western African societies was considerable. The trade was increasingly restricted by British naval interdiction after 1808, but slavers still managed to move some 3 million slaves, mostly to Brazil, and to a lesser extent Cuba and the United States, by 1850. Northern U.S. shipbuilders were key suppliers to Brazilian slavers to the very end.

It appears that in the first three centuries of the Atlantic slave trade most African captives came from the coastal hinterland. This changed only after about 1750, when colonial demand began to outstrip local sources of supply. Thereafter, slaves were brought to the coast from increasingly distant interior regions. In West Africa this amounted to something of an inversion of the caravan trading routes fanning out from the Niger River basin, but in West Central Africa entirely new trails and trade circuits were formed. Also, whereas war captives and drought refugees had been the main victims in the past, now random kidnapping and slave-raiding became widespread.

COUNTERPOINT
The Pygmies of Central Africa

As in the Americas, certain forest, desert, and other margin-dwelling peoples of Africa appear to have remained largely immune to the effects of European conquest, colonization, and trade throughout early modern times. But such seeming immunity is difficult to gauge, especially since we now know some margin-dwelling groups once thought to be naturally isolated were in fact refugees from conquest and slaving wars. Many were driven from the more accessible regions where they had once hunted or otherwise exploited nature to survive. Distinct cultures such as the Batwa (BAH-twah), a major Pygmy group of the great Congo rain forest, and the Khoikhoi (COY-coy) and other tribespeople of southern Africa's Kalahari Desert, were until only recently thought to have been unaffected by outsiders before the nineteenth century. Recent scholarship, and most surviving gatherer-hunters themselves, suggest otherwise.

> **FOCUS**
> How did the Pygmies' rain forest world differ from the better-known environment of savannas and farms?

Life in the Congo Rain Forest

Still, for the Pygmies, as for many of the world's tropical forest peoples, life has long been distinct from that of settled agriculturalists. Even now, Pygmies live by exploiting the natural forest around them, unaided by manufactured goods. These forests, marked by rugged terrain and washed by superabundant rains, make agriculture and herding impossible. Short of cutting down huge swaths of trees, which in this region often leads to massive soil erosion, neither can be practiced. This is not to say space is limited. Indeed, the Congo River basin is home to the world's second-largest rain forest, after that of the Amazon in South America; it is vast. As in the Amazon, most forest animals are modest in size, with the important exception of the African elephant, which early modern Pygmies occasionally hunted for food and tusks.

Until recent times, most Pygmies were gatherer-hunters. Their superior tracking abilities, limited material possessions, and knowledge of useful forest products such as leaves for dwellings and natural toxins for bow hunting allowed them to retreat in times of external threats such as war. Herding and farming Bantu-speaking and Sudanic neighbors were at a disadvantage in Pygmy country, which

Pygmies of the Congo Rain Forest

Modern-day Pygmies
Here Baka Pygmies of Cameroon and the Central African Republic hunt in the Congo rain forest using nets, sticks, and vines. The woman also carries a machete for butchering the catch and a basket for the meat. Pygmy hunters arrange nets fashioned from vines in forest enclosures to catch small antelope and other game lured or scared into the trap by chants and songs. (Martin Harvey/Peter Arnold/Photolibrary.)

seems to have prevented Pygmy militarization or formation of defensive confederacies. The Congo rain forest is also attractive in that it is much less affected by malarial mosquitoes than the surrounding farmland. In recent times only a few Pygmy groups, such as the much-studied Mbuti (M-BOOH-tee), have remained separate enough from neighboring farmers and herders to retain their famously short stature and other distinct characteristics. The Pygmies' highly distinctive singing style and instrumentation, most of it Mbuti, has become renowned with the rise of world music recording and distribution.

Everyday Pygmy life has been examined in most detail by anthropologists, many of whom have emphasized differences between Pygmy and neighboring Bantu rituals. Whereas Bantu speakers have venerated dead ancestors in a way that has deeply affected their long-term settlement patterns, warfare, and kin groupings, the Pygmies have long preferred to "let go" of their dead—to move on, as it were. Similarly, whereas Bantu coming-of-age rituals such as circumcision have tended to be elaborate and essential to social reproduction, Pygmies have traditionally marked few distinct phases in life. Most important, the Pygmies have venerated the forest itself as a life-giving spirit, whereas outsiders have treated it as a threatening space and potential source of evil. Has it always been so?

Legendary since ancient Egyptian times for their small, reedlike bodies, simple lifestyles, good-natured humor, and melodious music, the Pygmies have long been held up as the perfect counterpoint to urban civilization and its discontents. It is only recently that the Pygmies and other nonsedentary peoples like them have been treated historically, as makers rather than "nonactors" or victims of history. The absence of written records produced by the Pygmies themselves has made this task difficult, but anthropologists, historians, linguists, and archaeologists working together have made considerable headway.

Pygmy-Bantu Relations

It seems that some time after 1500, the introduction of iron tools and banana cultivation to the central African interior began to alter settlement patterns and overall demography. This change placed Pygmies and Bantu neighbors in closer proximity, as more and more forest was cut for planting and Bantu moved into Pygmy territory. Bantu speakers, some of them refugees from areas attacked by slavers or afflicted by drought, appear to have displaced some Pygmy groups and to have intermarried with others. They seem to have adopted a variety of Pygmy religious beliefs, although Bantu languages mostly displaced original Pygmy ones. Also after 1500, American crops such as peanuts and manioc began to alter sedentary life at the forest's edge, leading to still more interaction, not all of it peaceful, between the Pygmies and their neighbors. Pygmies adopted American capsicum peppers as an everyday spice.

Were the Pygmies driven from the rain forest's edge into its heart as a result of the slave trade? Perhaps in some places, yes, but the evidence is clearer for increased interaction with Bantu migrants. Early effects of globalization on Pygmy life are more easily tracked in terms of foods adopted as a result of the Columbian Exchange. Despite these exchanges and conflicts, the Pygmies have managed to retain a distinct identity that is as intertwined with the rhythms of the forest as it is with the rhythms of settled agriculture.

Although the story of the Pygmies' survival is not as dramatic as that of the Mapuche of Chile (see Chapter 17), their culture's richness and resilience serve as testaments to their peoples' imagination, will, and ingenuity. Their extraordinary adaptation to the rain forest—probably in part a result of early modern historical stresses, which pushed them farther into the forest—reminds us of a shared human tendency to make the most of a given ecological setting, but also that the distinction between civilized and "primitive" life-styles is a false one, or at least socially constructed.

Conclusion

Western African societies grew and changed according to the rhythms of planting, harvest, trade, and war, and these rhythms continued to define everyday life in early modern times. Droughts, diseases, and pests made subsistence more challenging in sub-Saharan Africa than in most parts of the world, yet people adapted and formed chiefdoms, kingdoms, and empires, often underpinned, at least symbolically, by the control of iron and other metals. Iron tools helped farmers clear forest and till hard soils.

Islam influenced African society and politics across a broad belt south of the Sahara and along the shores of the Indian Ocean, but even this powerful religious tradition was to a degree absorbed by local cultures. Most African states and chiefdoms were not influenced by outside religious influences—or by the conquistadors who wished to impose them—until the late nineteenth century. It was malaria, a disease against which many sub-Saharan Africans had at least some acquired immunity, that proved to be the continent's best defense.

But Africa possessed commodities demanded by outsiders, and despite their failure to penetrate the interior in early modern times, it was these outsiders, first among them the seaborne Portuguese, who set the early modern phase of African history in motion. The Portuguese came looking for gold in the mid-fifteenth century, and once they discovered the dangers of malaria, they stuck to the coast and offshore islands to trade through intermediaries, including coastal chiefs and kings. First they traded for gold, but very soon for war captives. In return, the Portuguese brought horses, cloth, wine, metal goods, and guns. Local chiefs became powerful by allying with the newcomers, and they expanded their trading and raiding ventures deep into the continental interior. Thus began a symbiotic relationship, copied and expanded by the English, Dutch, French, and other northern Europeans, that swelled over four centuries to supply the Americas with some 12 million enslaved African laborers, the largest forced migration in world history. Among these millions of captives, most of whose names we shall never know, was young Domingo Angola, a West Central African teenager caught up in a widening global web of trade, conquest, and religious conversion.

NOTES

1. The story of Domingo Angola is reconstructed from notary documents found in the Ecuadorian National Archive in Quito (Archivo Nacional del Ecuador, Protocolos notariales 1:19 FGD, 1-x-1601, ff. 647–746, and 1:6 DLM, 5-x-1595, f. 287v.) and various studies of the early slave trade, especially Linda Heywood and John Thornton, *Central Africans, Atlantic Creoles, and the Foundation of the Americas, 1585–1660* (New York: Cambridge University Press, 2007). On the Jesuits in Luanda and their involvement in the slave trade at this time, see Dauril Alden, *The Making of an Enterprise: The Society of Jesus in Portugal, Its Empire, and Beyond, 1540–1750* (Stanford, CA: Stanford University Press, 1996), 544–546.
2. Joseph Miller, *Way of Death: Merchant Capitalism and the Angolan Slave Trade, 1730–1830* (Madison: University of Wisconsin Press, 1988), 4–5.
3. George E. Brooks, *Landlords and Strangers: Ecology, Society, and Trade in Western Africa, 1000–1630* (Boulder, CO: Westview Press, 1994).
4. This and other letters are published in António Brásio, ed., *Monumenta Missionaria Africana*, vol. 1, *África Ocidental (1471–1531)* (Lisbon: Agência Geral do Ultramar, 1952), 470–471. (Special thanks to José Curto of York University, Canada, for pointing out this reference.)
5. Olaudah Equiano, *The Interesting Narrative of the Life of Olaudah Equiano, Written by Himself*, 2d ed., introduction by Robert J. Allison (Boston: Bedford/St. Martin's, 2007), 7.

RESOURCES FOR RESEARCH

Many Western Africas

General surveys of precolonial Africa have proliferated in recent years, many incorporating a new range of findings from archaeology, climate studies, and linguistics. The Collins and Burns text is exceptional.

Bisson, Michael, S. Terry Childs, Philip de Barros, and Augustin Holl. *Ancient African Metallurgy: The Socio-cultural Context.* 2000.

Collins, Robert O., and James M. Burns. *A History of Sub-Saharan Africa.* 2007.

Connah, Graham. *African Civilizations: An Archeological Perspective*, 2d ed. 2001.

Ehret, Christopher. *The Civilizations of Africa: A History to 1800.* 2002.

McCann, James C. *Maize and Grace: Africa's Encounter with a New World Crop, 1500–2000.* 2005.

Northrup, David. *Africa's Discovery of Europe, 1450–1850.* 2002.

Webb, James L. A., Jr. *Humanity's Burden: A Global History of Malaria.* 2009.

Landlords and Strangers: Peoples and States in West Africa

Works on West Africa in the early modern period have begun to link internal developments to external factors such as the slave trade and the rise of global markets in a variety of innovative ways, including a focus on metals such as gold, copper, and bronze and crops such as rice, peanuts, and oil palm.

Brooks, George E. *Eurafricans in Western Africa: Commerce, Social Status, Gender, and Religious Observance from the Sixteenth to the Eighteenth Century.* 2003.

Brooks, George E. *Landlords and Strangers: Ecology, Society, and Trade in Western Africa, 1000–1630.* 1994.

Charney, Judith A. *Black Rice: The African Origins of Rice Cultivation in the Americas.* 2001.

Herbert, Eugenia. *Iron, Gender, and Power: Rituals of Transformation in African Societies.* 1993.

Herbert, Eugenia. *Red Gold of Africa: Copper in Precolonial History and Culture.* 1984.

Wright, Donald R. *The World and a Very Small Place in Africa: A History of Globalization in Niumi, The Gambia*, 2d ed. 2004.

Land of the Blacksmith Kings: West Central Africa

Works on early modern West Central Africa have become more detailed and transatlantic in nature in recent years, thanks in part to a host of newly discovered (or newly appreciated) sources in Portuguese, Spanish, and Italian.

Heywood, Linda M., and John Thornton. *Central Africans, Atlantic Creoles, and the Foundation of the Americas, 1585–1660.* 2007.

Hilton, Anne. *The Kingdom of Kongo.* 1985.

Sweet, James H. *Recreating Africa: Culture, Kinship, and Religion in the African-Portuguese World, 1441–1770.* 2003.

Vansina, Jan. *Paths in the Rainforest.* 1990.

Strangers in Ships: Gold, Slavery, and the Portuguese

Literature about the Atlantic slave trade is vast and fast growing. The following is only a small selection of helpful introductory works on the Portuguese era of the slave trade.

Barry, Boubacar. *Senegambia and the Atlantic Slave Trade.* 1998.

Blackburn, Robin. *The Making of New World Slavery from the Baroque to the Modern, 1492–1800.* 1997.

Hawthorne, Walter. *From Africa to Brazil: Culture, Identity, and an Atlantic Slave Trade, 1600–1830.* 2010.

Miller, Joseph. *Way of Death: Merchant Capitalism and the Atlantic Slave Trade, 1780–1830.* 1988.

Thomas, Hugh. *The Slave Trade: The Story of the Atlantic Slave Trade, 1440–1870.* 1997.

Northern Europeans and the Expansion of the Atlantic Slave Trade, 1600–1800

Among the burgeoning literature on the later stages of the Atlantic slave trade are these helpful works. Eltis and Klein offer clear overviews that draw in part from recently constructed databases.

Eltis, David. *The Rise of African Slavery in the Americas.* 2001.

Equiano, Olaudah. *The Interesting Narrative of the Life of Olaudah Equiano, Written by Himself*, 2d ed. Introduction by Robert J. Allison. 2007.

Handler, Jerome S., and Michael L. Tuite Jr. *The Atlantic Slave Trade and Slave Life in the Americas: A Visual Record* (University of Virginia/Virginia Foundation for the Humanities). http://hitchcock.itc.virginia.edu/Slavery/index.php.

Klein, Herbert. *The Atlantic Slave Trade.* 1999.

Law, Robin C. *The Slave Coast of West Africa, 1550–1750: The Impact of the Atlantic Slave Trade on an African Society.* 1990.

COUNTERPOINT: The Pygmies of Central Africa

The Mbuti Pygmy culture has been described in most detail by the anthropologist Colin Turnbull, and his works remain essential. Klieman offers a more historical look at Pygmy relations with Bantu neighbors over the long term.

Klieman, Kairn. *"The Pygmies Were Our Compass": Bantu and Batwa in the History of West Central Africa, Early Times to c. 1900 C.E.* 2003.

Turnbull, Colin. *The Forest People.* 1968.

Turnbull, Colin. *The Mbuti Pygmies: Change and Adaptation.* 1983.

Turnbull, Colin, Francis Chapman, and Michelle Kisliuk. *Mbuti Pygmies of the Ituri Rainforest.* Sound recording. 1992.

▶ **For additional primary sources from this period,** see *Sources of Crossroads and Cultures.*

▶ **For Web sites, images, and documents related to topics in this chapter,** see Make History at bedfordstmartins.com/smith.

The major global development in this chapter ▶ The rise of the Atlantic slave trade and its impact on early modern African peoples and cultures.

IMPORTANT EVENTS

c. 1100–1500	Extended dry period in West Africa prompts migrations
c. 1450	Kingdom of Benin reaches height of its power
1464–1492	Reign of Sunni Ali in the Songhai Empire
1482	Portuguese establish trading fort of São Jorge da Mina (Ghana)
1506–1543	Reign of Afonso I (Nzinga Mbemba) of kingdom of Kongo
1569	Collapse of kingdom of Kongo
1574	Portuguese-aided restoration of kingdom of Kongo
1591	Moroccan raiders conquer Songhai Empire
1621	Formation of Dutch West India Company
1624–1663	Reign of Queen Nzinga in the Ndongo kingdom of Angola
1638–1641	Dutch seize São Jorge da Mina and Luanda
1672	Formation of English Royal African Company
1750–1800	Atlantic slave trade reaches highest volume
1807	British declare Atlantic slave trade illegal

KEY TERMS

African diaspora (p. 584)
fetishism (p. 599)
génie (p. 585)
husbandry (p. 585)
kitomi (p. 599)
manikongo (p. 595)

Middle Passage (p. 605)
oba (p. 592)
paramount chief (p. 586)
peça (p. 595)
pombeiro (p. 599)

CHAPTER OVERVIEW QUESTIONS

1. How did ecological diversity in western Africa relate to cultural developments?
2. What tied western Africa to other parts of the world prior to the arrival of Europeans along Atlantic shores?
3. How did the Atlantic slave trade arise, and how was it sustained?

SECTION FOCUS QUESTIONS

1. What range of livelihoods, cultural practices, and political arrangements typified western Africa in early modern times?
2. What economic, social, and political patterns characterized early modern West Africa?
3. What economic, social, and political patterns characterized early modern West Central Africa?
4. How did the early Portuguese slave trade in western Africa function?
5. What were the major changes in the Atlantic slave trade after 1600?
6. How did the Pygmies' rain forest world differ from the better-known environment of savannas and farms?

MAKING CONNECTIONS

1. How does the Moroccan conquest of Songhai compare with the Spanish conquest of the Aztecs (see Chapter 17)?
2. How did gender roles differ between the kingdoms of West Africa and those of North America's Eastern Woodlands (see Chapter 16)?
3. How did the Portuguese experience in Africa differ from events in Brazil (see Chapter 17)?
4. How did growing European competition for enslaved Africans alter the nature of enslavement and trade in Africa itself?

AT A CROSSROADS ▶

In this exquisite miniature painting from the 1590s, the Mughal emperor Akbar receives the Persian ambassador Sayyid Beg in 1562. The painting is an illustration commissioned for Akbar's official court history, the *Akbarnama*, and thus would have been seen and approved by the emperor himself. The meeting is emblematic of the generally amiable relationship between the Mughals and their Safavid neighbors in Iran. (Victoria & Albert Museum, London/Art Resource, NY.)

Trade and Empire in the Indian Ocean and South Asia

1450–1750

Trading Cities and Inland Networks: East Africa

FOCUS How did Swahili Coast traders link the East African interior to the Indian Ocean basin?

Trade and Empire in South Asia

FOCUS What factors account for the fall of Vijayanagara and the rise of the Mughals?

European Interlopers

FOCUS What factors enabled Europeans to take over key Indian Ocean trade networks?

COUNTERPOINT: Aceh: Fighting Back in Southeast Asia

FOCUS Why was the tiny sultanate of Aceh able to hold out against European interlopers in early modern times?

Born to Persian immigrants in the Afghan city of Kandahar, Princess Mihr un-nisa (meer oon-NEE-sah), known to history as Nur Jahan, or "Light of the World," married the Mughal emperor Jahangir (jah-hahn-GEER) in 1611, at the age of thirty-four. As the emperor increasingly turned his attention to science and the arts, as well as to his addictions to wine and opium, Nur Jahan increasingly assumed the ruler's duties throughout the last decade of her husband's life, which ended in 1627. She had coins struck in her name, and most importantly, she made certain that a daughter from an earlier marriage and her brother's daughter both wed likely heirs to the Mughal throne.

As her husband withdrew from worldly affairs, Nur Jahan actively engaged them. After a visit from the English ambassador in 1613, she developed a keen interest in European manufactures, especially quality textiles. She established domestic industries in cloth manufacture and jewelry making and developed an export trade in indigo dye. Indigo from her farms was shipped to Portuguese and English trading forts along India's west coast, then sent to Lisbon, London, Antwerp, and beyond.

In 1614, Nur Jahan arranged for her niece, Arjumand Banu Begum (AHR-joo-mond bah-noo BEH-goom), to marry Jahangir's favorite son, Prince Khurram, known after he became emperor as Shah Jahan. Arjumand Banu Begum, who took the title Mumtaz Mahal,

BACKSTORY

For centuries before the rise of the Atlantic system (see Chapter 17), the vast Indian Ocean basin thrived as a religious and commercial crossroads. Powered by the annual monsoon wind cycle, traders, mainly Muslim, developed a flourishing commerce over thousands of miles in such luxury goods as spices, gems, and precious metals. The network included the trading enclaves of East Africa and Arabia and the many ports of South and Southeast Asia. Ideas, religious traditions— notably Islam—and pilgrimages moved along the same routes. Throughout the Indian Ocean basin, there was also a trade in enslaved laborers, mostly war captives, including many non-Africans, but this trade grew mostly after the rise of plantation agriculture in the later eighteenth century. The vast majority of the region's many millions of inhabitants were peasant farmers, many of them dependent on wet-rice agriculture.

At the dawn of the early modern period, Hindu kingdoms still flourished in southern India and parts of island Southeast Asia, but these were on the wane. By contrast, some Muslim kingdoms began an expansive phase. After 1500, a key factor in changes throughout the Indian Ocean basin was the introduction of gunpowder weapons from Europe.

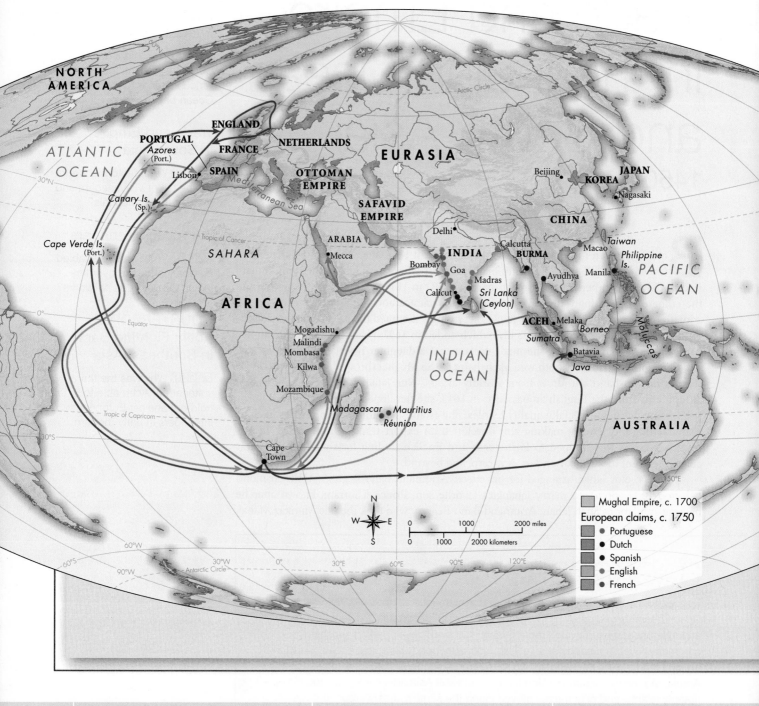

Legend:
- Mughal Empire, c. 1700
- European claims, c. 1750
  - Portuguese
  - Dutch
  - Spanish
  - English
  - French

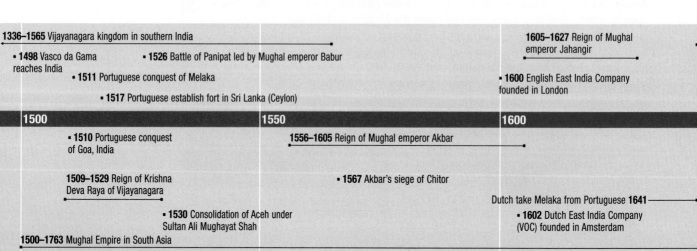

1336–1565 Vijayanagara kingdom in southern India

▪ **1498** Vasco da Gama reaches India

▪ **1526** Battle of Panipat led by Mughal emperor Babur

1605–1627 Reign of Mughal emperor Jahangir

▪ **1511** Portuguese conquest of Melaka

▪ **1600** English East India Company founded in London

▪ **1517** Portuguese establish fort in Sri Lanka (Ceylon)

1500   **1550**   **1600**

▪ **1510** Portuguese conquest of Goa, India

1556–1605 Reign of Mughal emperor Akbar

1509–1529 Reign of Krishna Deva Raya of Vijayanagara

▪ **1567** Akbar's siege of Chitor

Dutch take Melaka from Portuguese **1641**

▪ **1530** Consolidation of Aceh under Sultan Ali Mughayat Shah

▪ **1602** Dutch East India Company (VOC) founded in Amsterdam

1500–1763 Mughal Empire in South Asia

died in 1631 while bearing her fourteenth child for her emperor husband. Heartbroken, Shah Jahan went into mourning for two full years. He commissioned the construction of an extraordinary mausoleum for his beloved Mumtaz in the sacred city of Agra. This graceful structure of white marble, among the architectural wonders of the world, is known as the Taj Mahal.

Nur Jahan attended court with her head and breasts covered only by wisps of gauze. She rode horses proudly in public without her husband. Such conduct was not considered inappropriate for a woman of her status in her time. Like other South Asian noblewomen, Nur Jahan expressed her rank through public piety, commissioning a number of religious buildings, including her father's and her husband's mausoleums, as well as many elaborate gardens, several of which survive. She continued to play an active and sometimes controversial role in politics until her death in 1644, occasionally supporting rivals of Shah Jahan.

For most of the early modern period the lands surrounding the Indian Ocean remained in the hands of powerful local rulers, as exemplified by Nur Jahan. As in western Africa, but in stark contrast to much of the Americas, it took European interlopers several centuries to gain the lasting footholds that enabled the widespread imperial takeover after 1800 (discussed in Chapter 26). Again like western Africans and unlike the native peoples of the Americas, the inhabitants of the greater Indian Ocean basin had acquired over time at least some immunity to European microbes, so their resistance was not hobbled by waves of deadly disease.

Trade on the Indian Ocean during the age of sail followed the **monsoons**, semiannual alternating dry and humid winds generated by the seasonal heating and cooling of air masses above the vast Asian continent. To exploit these reliable winds, Arab sailors developed swift, triangular-rigged vessels. Southeast Asians introduced much larger square-riggers influenced by Chinese shipbuilding techniques, and by 1500 the Portuguese arrived from the North Atlantic in well-armed, sturdy vessels rigged with both square and triangular sails and capable of years-long voyages through heavy seas. It was the wide array of luxury trade goods, along with religious pilgrimage sites such as Mecca and Benares, that made this area a vibrant saltwater crossroads.

monsoon A wind system that influences large climatic regions such as the Indian Ocean basin and reverses direction seasonally.

MAPPING THE WORLD
The Indian Ocean and South Asia, 1450–1750

Harnessing the power of monsoon winds, Arab and Asian sailors traversed the Indian Ocean and Arabian Sea for centuries before the Portuguese arrived in the 1490s, in search of pepper and other commodities. In subsequent years, competing Eurasian interlopers, including the Ottomans, conquered key ports from East Africa to Southeast Asia in an attempt to control both exports to Europe and interregional trade. The Ottomans retreated after the mid-sixteenth century, but many Muslims continued to sail to the Arabian peninsula to make the pilgrimage to Mecca and to engage in trade.

ROUTES ▼

→ Portuguese *Carreira da India* (Voyage to India)
→ Dutch trade route
→ Major pilgrimage route

1641–1699 Sultanate of Women in Aceh

1764 British East India Company controls Bengal

1700 — 1750 — 1800

1658 Dutch drive Portuguese from Ceylon

1701 William Kidd hanged in London for piracy

1739 Persian raiders under Nadir Shah sack Delhi

The Indian Ocean basin, which some historians and linguists have termed the Afrasian Sea, was defined by interlinked maritime and overland networks. Despite repeated attempts, no state ever totally controlled the great basin's exchange of goods, people, and ideas. Religious diversity and relative political independence were the rule. Even Islam, the most widespread religion, was not practiced in exactly the same way in any two places. Muslims from East Africa, Arabia, Persia, and South, Southeast, and East Asia all maintained distinct identities despite a shared religion, distant mercantile connections, and even long-term residence and intermarriage in foreign ports.

India, with its huge, mostly Hindu population, lay at the center of the Afrasian Sea trading system. The black pepper of Malabar, on the southwest coast, was world-famous, as were the diamonds of Golconda, in the southern interior. But it was India's cotton fabrics, linking countless farmers, artisans, and brokers, that brought in most foreign exchange. As in the Mediterranean and Atlantic trading systems, gold from sub-Saharan Africa and later silver from the Americas were the essential lubricants of trade. Nur Jahan minted rupees in American silver and African gold.

The Portuguese reached India in 1498. They had three key goals: to monopolize the spice trade to Europe, to tax or take over key shipping lanes, and to fight the expansion of Islam and spread Christianity instead. With the brief exception of the Ottomans in the first half of the sixteenth century, no land-based empire in the region attempted to stop them. Persia's Safavids and South Asia's Mughals might have done so, but they preferred to play off the later-arriving English, French, and Dutch against the Portuguese—and against one another. Given these empires' overwhelming strength on land, this strategy made sense, but as in Africa, leaving sea power to the Europeans proved a fateful decision.

The arrival of the Portuguese coincided with the rise of the Islamic Mughal Empire in India beginning about 1500. Though a land empire much like China under the Ming (see Chapter 15), the Mughal state was thoroughly connected to the outside world. Wealthy and well armed, the Mughals seemed invincible to many neighbors and outsiders. Certainly European conquest was unthinkable in the seventeenth century, the era of Nur Jahan. Her life exemplifies both the colorful court life typical of Eurasia's so-called gunpowder empires, as well as the outward gaze and self-consciousness these states' rulers exhibited.

The term "gunpowder empire" was coined by historian Marshall Hodgson to help explain the rise of the Mughal, Safavid, Ottoman, and other states whose rapid expansion after 1500 was enabled by Western-style cannons, muskets, and other firearms.[1] Historians also apply the term to the Safavid and Ottoman states and the Spanish, Portuguese, and other European kingdoms that took their new and powerful weaponry abroad in the name of commerce and Christianity. Unlike their ocean-going European adversaries, however, the great land empires of Central and South Asia were motivated by neither trade nor religion; their goal in expanding was to extract tributes from neighboring populations.

Despite the rise and fall of gunpowder empires on land and at sea, historical records suggest that most inhabitants of the greater Indian Ocean carried on much as they had before. There were certain changes, however. Especially in cash-crop-producing regions, such as Ceylon (Sri Lanka) off India's south coast and Aceh in Indonesia, demands on ordinary laborers and on productive lands sharply increased. Religious change took place, too. Although Islamic land empires such as that of the Mughals advanced, Islam grew most notably in politically fractured Southeast Asia. As in western Africa and unlike in the Americas, very few people in this vast region adopted Christianity.

For a time, South Asia held competing Europeans at bay in spite of their advanced gun-making and shipbuilding technologies. Starting in the seventeenth century, however, the European powers began to exploit the region's open seas and political divisions to advance land-based conquest and colonization. As they had done in the Americas, Europeans divided the Indian Ocean's shores, waterways, and islands into rigidly controlled colonial plantations and monopoly trading zones. Local lords were co-opted or, if resistant, deposed. In the end, the relative peace, prosperity, and cultural diversity that had once blocked foreign control helped facilitate it.

OVERVIEW
QUESTIONS

The major global development in this chapter: The Indian Ocean trading network and the impact of European intrusion on maritime and mainland South Asia.

As you read, consider:

1. What environmental, religious, and political factors enabled trading enclaves to flourish in the Indian Ocean basin?

2. How did the rise and fall of India's land empires reflect larger regional trends?

3. How did Europeans insert themselves into the Indian Ocean trading network, and what changes did they bring about?

Trading Cities and Inland Networks: East Africa

The history of early modern East Africa is best understood in terms of linkages among the numerous Indian Ocean traders from as far away as China and the cities and peoples of the African interior. Brokering Africa's ties to Asia were merchant families and local princes clustered along a string of port towns and cities stretching from Ethiopia in the northeast to Mozambique in the southeast.

FOCUS

How did Swahili Coast traders link the East African interior to the Indian Ocean basin?

By 1500, it was mainly Muslims who lived in these thriving East African trading ports. Some were descendants of early Persian, Arabian, and South Asian overseas traders and missionaries, but the vast majority were native Africans, mostly Bantu speakers. Swahili, still commonly spoken in much of this region, is a Bantu language laced with Arabic terms. In early modern times, scribes recorded transactions in Swahili using Arabic script. Thus, the society and culture of East African trading ports blended African and Asian elements, reflecting the economic connections between the two regions.

Portuguese and Ottoman traders arrived in these ports around 1500, but neither managed to control more than a few of them at a time. Dutch, French, and English merchants arrived in the seventeenth century, but they, too, failed to monopolize East African trade. Offshore, the French established a minor presence on the huge island of Madagascar and then on much smaller Réunion, a future plantation colony, but neither island had been vital to the ancient monsoon trading circuit. As free from each other as they were from outsiders, the hundred-odd ports of East Africa's Swahili Coast remained largely independent until the imperial scramble of the late nineteenth century (discussed in Chapter 26).

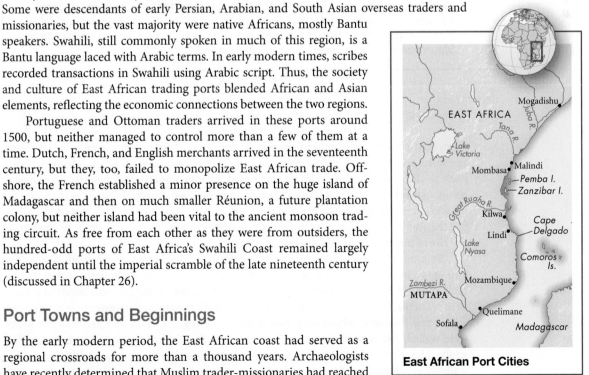

East African Port Cities

Port Towns and Beginnings

By the early modern period, the East African coast had served as a regional crossroads for more than a thousand years. Archaeologists have recently determined that Muslim trader-missionaries had reached

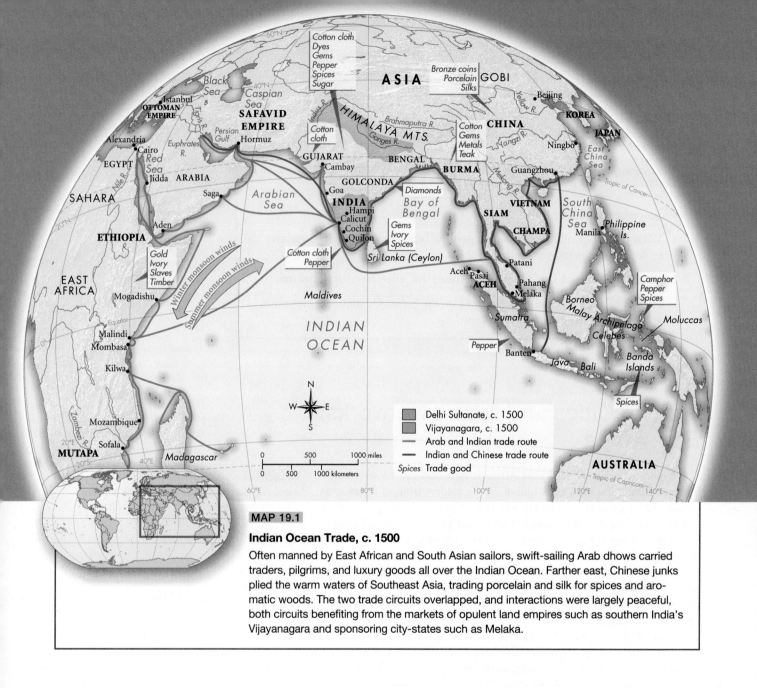

MAP 19.1

Indian Ocean Trade, c. 1500

Often manned by East African and South Asian sailors, swift-sailing Arab dhows carried traders, pilgrims, and luxury goods all over the Indian Ocean. Farther east, Chinese junks plied the warm waters of Southeast Asia, trading porcelain and silk for spices and aromatic woods. The two trade circuits overlapped, and interactions were largely peaceful, both circuits benefiting from the markets of opulent land empires such as southern India's Vijayanagara and sponsoring city-states such as Melaka.

many East African port towns by the eighth century C.E., soon after the founding of Islam. Seaborne trade in ivory, gold, ceramics, and other items was even older, however, dating back to classical antiquity. Early modern East African traders continued this commerce, bringing luxury goods from Central, South, and even East Asia to the coast in exchange for Africa's treasured raw materials. Traders also exchanged slaves for luxuries on occasion, but the scale of the Indian Ocean slave trade seems to have remained relatively small until the rise of plantations in the nineteenth century.

By modern urban standards, most East African trading ports were small towns. The largest, such as Kilwa, Sofala, Malindi, and Mombasa, had no more than 10,000 inhabitants at their height. Most towns were much smaller, home to only several hundred permanent residents. Quelimane (keh-lee-MAH-neh) and Mogadishu fell somewhere in between, with a few thousand inhabitants. Nearly all of the region's cities and many of the towns were walled, but only the most opulent had mosques of stone or coral block rather than adobe. Merchants, resident and foreign, occupied house blocks clustered within each city's walls. In exchange for tributes, local princes protected merchant families, negotiating with sometimes hostile inland chiefdoms for trade goods and subsistence items.

Indian Ocean Connections

East African traders exported elephant tusks and gold in exchange for South Asian cloth, much of it from Cambay in the Gujarat region of northwest India (see Map 19.1). They also imported Persian and even Chinese ceramics, along with spices, tobacco (after 1500), and a host of other items. African ivory was especially prized throughout Asia for its soft texture, and African gold, mostly from the southern interior, was always in high demand as currency. In much of India, women brought dowries of gold when they married, displaying it in the form of fine jewelry. As we have seen in previous chapters, African gold was an essential world currency prior to European expansion into the Americas.

Most goods were carried in **dhows** (dowz), swift, single-decked ships with triangular sails and about two hundred tons' capacity. Traders used smaller vessels and dugout canoes to navigate rivers such as the great Zambezi and to ferry goods through the treacherous coral reefs that lay between East Africa's towns.

Despite the extraordinary value of most Indian Ocean trade goods, shippers traveled only lightly armed. Although piracy had long been known, and was even expected in waters such as India's Malabar Coast, violent theft at sea seems to have become a serious threat to Indian Ocean commerce only after the arrival of the Portuguese, who sought to establish and defend their trading monopolies through brute force. Their actions in turn encouraged contraband trade and the fencing of stolen goods.

Chinese maritime visits to East Africa, though memorable, were few and far between. As we saw in Chapter 15, the famous Ming admiral Zheng He arrived first in Malindi in the late 1410s, and then at Mogadishu in the early 1430s. Zheng He's vessels were enormous, more than double the size of the largest Portuguese ships to arrive about a century later. In addition to the standard gold and ivory, the Ming admiral filled his ample holds with local items, including a veritable zoo for the Chinese emperor. There is no evidence of attempts to conquer or to establish trading posts or colonies, and afterward Chinese goods came to East Africa

Swahili Coast Traders

China's Retreat from the Indian Ocean

dhow A small sailing vessel with triangular rigs used in monsoon trade to East Africa.

Exchanger of Cambay

In this early-sixteenth-century watercolor, apparently by a self-taught Portuguese artist, a merchant in Cambay, on India's northwest coast, collects and changes gold, silver, and other coins of many mint marks and denominations. A tiny balance hangs behind him on one side, and a strongbox seems to float in midair on the other. To the right, people of many faiths, clothing styles, and colors come to seek his services. At least two are women bearing gold coins. (Ms 1889 at the Biblioteca Casanatense, Rome.)

again only through Southeast Asian intermediaries, often Muslim Malays. The Chinese retreat from the Indian Ocean left a void that early modern European interlopers were happy to fill.

Links to the Interior

Less often described than East Africa's ties to overseas merchants were its links to the African interior. The extent of each port's productive hinterlands or subsistence grounds was generally small, but coastal towns and cities did not simply face outward, as once believed. Almost all Swahili town-dwellers relied on nearby agricultural plots for their day-to-day survival, and many engaged in regular exchanges with independent cattle herders. Many Swahili elites owned slaves purchased from the interior, who produced food for both their masters and themselves. The African products in greatest demand overseas, however, came from the more densely populated southern interior.

Products from the Interior

This was most true of gold dust, traded northward from the mouth of the Zambezi River (see again Map 19.1). Its main sources were the many goldfields of the Mutapa kingdom (formerly Great Zimbabwe), located on the Zimbabwe Plateau. Here, as in parts of contemporary West Africa, men and women panned for gold in the agricultural off-season. A few mines went underground. The historical record is spotty, but it appears that an annual average of at least a ton of gold entered the Indian Ocean trade circuit during the sixteenth century.

Ivory was a different sort of product; collecting it required the hunting and slaughter of wild animals. Although modern demand for ivory has led to the extinction of elephants in parts of Africa, it appears that most of the tusks fed into the early modern Indian Ocean circuit were a byproduct of subsistence hunting. Hunters only went out seasonally, and without firearms. Bringing down an adult elephant with spears and longbows was an extremely dangerous business, and the compensation was not attractive enough to make it a livelihood. Aside from the dangers of ivory procurement, interior peoples such as the Shona speakers of the Mutapa kingdom were not easily pressured into market exchanges of any kind. With no particular need for Asian products, they carried ivory and gold to the seaports at their leisure.

An important export from the north Swahili Coast was lumber, specifically mangrove hardwoods for residential construction in desert regions of Arabia and the Red Sea. The exact ecological consequences of this enterprise have yet to be determined, but like the trade in tusks and gold, it appears not to have exhausted the resource. Extractive industries in the early modern period usually damaged the environment only in relation to their scale.

Arrival of the Portuguese

By 1500 trade was thriving throughout East Africa and its partners in the Indian Ocean basin. The arrival of the Portuguese at about that time would disrupt that valuable balance. With nothing to offer the well-off merchants of East Africa, India, and the Arabian Sea region, the Portuguese turned to force. Using their guns, stout vessels, and Mediterranean fort-building techniques, they sought to profit from the Indian Ocean trade by impeding it—that is, by enforcing monopolies on certain items and taking over vital ports. Ultimately this worked better in India than elsewhere, but the Portuguese tried desperately to gain control of East African trade, and even to penetrate the continent's southeast interior in search of Mutapa's fabled gold. Although they failed to conquer the Mutapa state, the Portuguese traded with its rulers and gained control of gold exports. As they had done in western Africa, in East Africa the Portuguese concentrated most of their energies on capturing and fortifying posts, or *feitorias*, which they established at Mozambique, Sofala, and Mombasa. The Dutch and English would soon follow.

Trade and Empire in South Asia

FOCUS
What factors account for the fall of Vijayanagara and the rise of the Mughals?

As in East Africa, despite competition and occasional violence, dozens of independent trading enclaves in South Asia prospered in early modern times. Many coastal cities and their surrounding hinterlands were subject to Muslim sultans or Hindu princes, most of whom drew their sustenance from the merchants they protected. Trading populations were larger than those of East

Africa and more diverse. Religious minorities included Jains, Jews, Parsis (Zoroastrians), and Christians. Among the region's most densely packed commercial crossroads, India's port cities maintained close ties to the subcontinent's rich and well-interconnected interior, at this time home to two major empires. One was in ascendance, the Muslim Mughal Empire in the north, and the other in decline, the Hindu kingdom of Vijayanagara (vizh-ah-ya-na-GAR-ah) in the south (see again Map 19.1).

Vijayanagara's Rise and Fall 1336–1565

Vijayanagara grew into an empire around 1500, only to disintegrate due to internal factionalism and external, mostly northern Muslim (although not Mughal) attacks. Because of its swift demise and the near-total loss of its written records, Vijayanagara remains one of the most enigmatic empires of the early modern period. With Muslim kingdoms dominating much of the subcontinent by the time the Portuguese arrived offshore around 1500, Hindu Vijayanagara appears to have been something of an anachronism. Like the contemporary Aztec and Inca empires of the Americas, Vijayanagara was neither a gunpowder empire nor an early modern, bureaucratic state. Its material record constitutes a major but still limited source for historians. Massive stone temple structures and lively artistic works hint at great opulence and power, but the nature of daily life for commoners remains obscure, although it has been reconstructed in part by archaeological work and from the observations of early European visitors.

Literally, "city of triumph," the kingdom of Vijayanagara was said to have been founded by two brothers in 1336. They chose the town site of Hampi, deep in the southern interior, to revive a purist version of the Hindu state. According to legend, the brothers had been captured in northern frontier wars and forced to convert to Islam in Delhi, but once back in their homeland they renounced that faith and sought the advice of Hindu Brahmans.

Hampi

This is an aerial view of part of Hampi, ancient capital of the Hindu kingdom of Vijayanagara in south-central India. The main temple rises in the smoky distance, marking the end of a long ceremonial promenade fronted by stone structures. The Tungabhadra River winds alongside, and all around are hills strewn with granite boulders, giving the city a primeval, almost timeless feel. Hampi fell to northern invaders in 1565. (Colin McPherson/Corbis.)

Hundreds of temples were quickly built along the Tungabadhra River gorge to venerate the state's patron deity, Virupaksha (vee-rooh-PAHK-shah), among others. Thus, the kingdom's identity was explicitly Hindu. By 1370, the empire covered most of southern India, with the exception of Malabar in the far southwest.

Divine Kingship

Whereas Muslim and Christian rulers were generally regarded as pragmatic "warriors of the faith," Hindu rulers were often seen as divine kings. Their most important duties involved performing the sacred rituals believed to sustain their kingdoms. Whether in Vijayanagara or in distant Bali in Southeast Asia, Hindu kingship relied on theatricality and symbolism quite removed from the everyday concerns of imperial administration. Early modern Hindu kings did participate in warfare and other serious matters, but their lives were mostly scripted by traditional sacred texts. Their societies believed that they would ensure prosperity in peacetime and victory in war by properly enacting their roles, which bordered on the priestly.

Life in Vijayanagara cycled between a peaceful period, when the king resided in the capital and carried out rituals, and a campaign season, when the king and his retinue traveled the empire battling with neighboring states and principalities. Like so much under Hindu rule, even victory on the field was scripted, and the warring season itself served as a reenactment of legendary battles. Each campaign started with a great festival reaffirming the king's divinity. Although he was renowned for his piety, it was his martial prowess that most set him apart from mere mortals. He was the exemplar of the **Kshatriya** (K-SHAH-tree-yah) or warrior **caste**, not the technically higher-ranking **Brahman** or priestly caste.

Krishna Deva Raya

Celebratory temple inscriptions record the names and deeds of many monarchs, but thanks to the records of foreign visitors the Vijayanagara king we know most about was Krishna Deva Raya (r. 1509–1529). Portuguese merchants and ambassadors traveled to his capital and court on several occasions, and all were stunned by the monarch's wealth and pomp. At his height, Krishna Deva Raya controlled most of India south of the Krishna River. Most of India's famed diamonds were mined nearby, providing a significant source of state revenue. But it was the constant flow of tribute from the *rajas*, the subject princes, that built his "city of triumph." Imperial demand drove the rajas to trade their products for Indian Ocean luxuries such as African gold and ivory. The king sat upon a diamond-studded throne, and two hundred subject princes attended him constantly at court. Each wore a gold ankle bracelet to indicate his willingness to die on the king's behalf.

Krishna Deva Raya welcomed the Portuguese following their 1510 conquest of Muslim-held Goa (GO-ah), a port on India's west coast that would become the keystone of Portugal's overseas empire. His armies required warhorses in the tens of thousands, and an arrangement with the Portuguese would give him easier access to horses from Arabia and Iraq. As they had done in western Africa, the Portuguese happily served as horse-traders to conquering non-Christian kings in exchange for access to key trade goods. Krishna Deva Raya used the imported mounts to extend Vijayanagara's borders north and south, and the Portuguese sent home some of the largest diamonds yet seen in Europe.

Imperial Organization

Vijayanagara shared some features with the roughly contemporaneous Aztec and Inca states—it was a tributary empire built on a combination of military force and religious charisma. Subject princes were required to maintain substantial armies and give surpluses to their king at periodic festivals; material display reaffirmed the king's divinity. Proper subordination of the rajas was equally important. Krishna Deva Raya was said to require so much gold from certain rajas that they were forced to sponsor pirates to generate revenue. Most tribute, however, came from the sale of farm products, cloth, and diamonds.

Above the rajas, Krishna Deva Raya appointed district administrators called *nayaks*. These were usually trusted relatives, and each oversaw a number of lesser kingdoms. The whole system was intended to both replicate and feed the center, with each raja and nayak sponsoring temple construction and revenue-generating projects of various sorts. Large-scale irrigation works improved agricultural yields, and at bridge crossings and city gates, officials taxed goods transported by ox-cart, donkey, and other means. The demands of the city and empire inevitably placed great pressure on southern India's forests and wetlands, and increased diamond mining sped deforestation and erosion of riverbanks. As in most

Kshatriya A member of the warrior caste in Hindu societies.

caste A hereditary social class separated from others in Hindu societies.

Brahman A member of the priestly caste in Hindu societies.

instances of imperial expansion, environmental consequences quickly became evident but were not, as far as we know, a major cause of decline.

Dependent as it was on trade, the expansion of Vijayanagara required a policy of religious tolerance similar to that later practiced by the Mughals. Jain merchants and minor princes were particularly important subjects since they helped link Vijayanagara to the world beyond India. Brahmanic or priestly law largely restricted Hindu trade to the land, whereas Jains could freely go abroad. Muslim coastal merchants were also allowed into the imperial fold, especially because they had far greater access than the Jains to luxury imports and warhorses. They had their own residential quarter in the city of Hampi. The early Portuguese policy in India was to exploit niches in this pre-existing trade system—not to conquer Vijayanagara, but simply to drive out competing Muslim merchants.

Though connected to the outside world mainly through the luxury goods trade, the empire's economy was based on large-scale rice cultivation. While kings and Brahmans reenacted the lives of the gods, the vast majority of Vijayanagara's subjects toiled their lives away as rice farmers. Around 1522 the Portuguese visitor Domingos Paes (see Reading the Past: Portuguese Report of a Vijayanagara Festival) described work on a huge, stone-reinforced reservoir: "In the tank I saw so many people at work that there must have been fifteen or twenty thousand men, looking like ants, so that you could not see the ground on which they walked."[2]

Rice Cultivation and Export

Vijayanagara's irrigated rice fed its people, but it was also a key export product. Special varieties were shipped as far abroad as Hormuz, on the Persian Gulf, and Aden, at the mouth of the Red Sea. More common rice varieties, along with sugar and some spices, provisioned the merchants of many Indian Ocean ports, including those of East Africa and Gujarat. It was through the sale of rice abroad that many subject princes obtained African gold for their king, with annual payments said to be in the thousands of pounds each by the time of Krishna Deva Raya. Hence, like luxury goods, rice was not only a key component in the trade relationships connecting the kingdom to the outside world; it also connected Vijayanagara's elites to each other, helping to define their political and social relationships.

Following Krishna Deva Raya's death in 1529, Vijayanagara fell victim first to internal succession rivalries, and then to Muslim aggressors. In 1565, under King Ramaraja, a coalition of formerly subject sultans defeated the royal army. Hampi, the capital city, was sacked, plundered, and abandoned; it was an overgrown ruin by 1568. Remnant Hindu principalities survived for a time in the southeast but eventually fell to the expansionist Mughals. By the seventeenth century only a few Hindu states remained around the fringes of South Asia, including remote Nepal. The Hindu principalities of Malabar, meanwhile, fell increasingly into the hands of Europeans and Muslim Gujarati merchants. Still, the memory of Vijayanagara's greatness and wealth lived on, to be revived much later by Hindu nationalists.

The Power of the Mughals

Another empire was expanding rapidly in India's north as Vijayanagara crumbled in the south. Beginning around 1500, under a Timurid (from Timur, the famed fourteenth-century Central Asian ruler discussed in Chapter 15) Muslim warlord named Babur (the "Tiger," r. 1500–1530), the Mughal Empire emerged as the most powerful, wealthy, and populous state yet seen in South Asia. By the time of Nur Jahan in the early 1600s, the Mughals (literally "Mongols," the great fourteenth-century emperors from whom the Mughals descended) had over 120 million subjects, a population comparable only to that of Ming China. Accumulating wealth from plunder and tribute and employing newly introduced gunpowder weapons and swift warhorses to terrifying effect, the Mughals subdued dozens of Hindu and Muslim principalities as they pushed relentlessly southward (see Map 19.2). Like many early modern empire builders, the Mughals were outsiders who adapted to local cultural traditions to establish and maintain legitimacy. In terms of Indian Ocean commerce, their rapid rise drove up demand for luxury imports, and, as in the case

Portuguese Report of a Vijayanagara Festival

The Portuguese merchant Domingos Paes (PAH-ish) visited Vijayanagara in 1520 with a larger diplomatic and commercial mission sent from Goa, the Portuguese trading post on India's southwest coast. Paes's report of the capital of Hampi and King Krishna Deva Raya's court, apparently written for the Portuguese court's official chronicler back in Lisbon, is among the richest to survive. Below, Paes describes part of a multiday festival that served to glorify the king and reaffirm the hierarchy of the state, and also to reenact cosmic battles.

At three o'clock in the afternoon everyone comes to the palace. They do not admit everyone at once . . . but there go inside only the wrestlers and dancing-women, and the elephants, which go with their trappings and decorations, those that sit on them being armed with shields and javelins, and wearing quilted tunics. As soon as these are inside they range themselves around the arena, each one in his or her place. . . . Many other people are then at the entrance gate opposite to the building, namely Brahmins, and the sons of the king's favorites, and their relations; all these noble youths who serve before the king. The officers of the household go about keeping order amongst all the people, and keep each one in his or her own place. . . .

The king sits dressed in white clothes all covered with [embroidery of] golden roses and wearing his jewels—he wears a quantity of these white garments, and I always saw him so dressed—and around him stand his pages with his betel [to chew], and his sword, and the other things which are his insignia of state. . . . As soon as the king is seated, the captains who waited outside make their entrance, each one by himself, attended by his chief people. . . . As soon as the nobles have finished entering, the captains of the troops approach with shields and spears, and afterwards the captains of archers. . . . As soon as these soldiers have all taken their places the women begin to dance. . . . Who can fitly describe to you the great riches these women carry on their persons?—collars of gold with so many diamonds and rubies and pearls, bracelets also on their arms and upper arms, girdles below, and of necessity anklets on their feet. . . .

Then the wrestlers begin their play. Their wrestling does not seem like ours, but there are blows [given], so severe as to break teeth, and put out eyes, and disfigure faces, so much so that here and there men are carried off speechless by their friends; they give one another fine falls, too. They have their captains and judges who are there to put each one on equal footing in the field, and also to award the honors to him who wins.

Source: Robert Sewell, *A Forgotten Empire (Vijayanagara): A Contribution to the History of India* (London: Sonnenschein, 1900), 268–271.

EXAMINING THE EVIDENCE

1. What does the selection suggest regarding social hierarchy and prescribed gender roles in Vijayanagara?

2. How does the divine kingship described here compare with that of the Incas (see Chapter 16)?

---

of Nur Jahan, some high-ranking Mughal nobles invested directly in exports of items such as indigo and gems.

Religious Toleration

Despite rule by Muslim overlords, most South Asians remained Hindus in early modern times, but those who converted to Islam enjoyed some benefits. Initially, conversion to Islam brought exemption from certain taxes, but these exemptions were suspended in the late sixteenth century under Emperor Akbar. As we will see, during and after his reign, lasting fusions between Hinduism and Islam emerged in various parts of the subcontinent.

Expanded Trade

Like its religion, South Asia's dynamic and highly productive economy was little changed after conquest. Under Mughal rule, South Asia's legendary textiles, grains, spices, gems, and many other products continued to find buyers worldwide. Truly new markets for Indian goods emerged in the Americas and parts of sub-Saharan Africa, supplied by Portuguese and other European shippers. Lacking commodities Indians wanted, European traders paid for South Asia's goods in hard cash. As a result India, like China, enjoyed a consistently favorable balance of trade throughout early modern times. Along with funding armies, this wealth from abroad fueled construction, especially of religious buildings. With royal sponsorship like that of Nur Jahan, many of India's most famous architectural gems, such as the Taj Mahal and Red Fort, were built along the Ganges River plain.

True to the Timurid heritage it shared with its Safavid Persian and Ottoman Turkish neighbors (discussed in the next chapter), Mughal rule in India was marked by both extraordinary court opulence and near-constant power struggles and rebellions. As in many other empires not constrained by rules of primogeniture, factionalism and succession crises eventually led to Mughal decline. Soon after 1700, this decline in central authority left Mughal India vulnerable to European as well as Persian imperial designs. Persian raiders sacked the capital of Delhi in 1739, and by 1763 the English East India Company won rights to tax former Mughal subjects in the vast province of Bengal, effectively exercising sovereignty in the Indian interior. Despite these top-level reversals of fortune, life for the bulk of South Asia's millions of poor farmers and artisans scarcely changed.

Gunpowder Weapons and Imperial Consolidation 1500–1763

The emperor, or "Mughal," Babur spent most of his life defeating Afghan warlords. Horses and archers were still critical in these early victories, as was Babur's charismatic leadership, but by the 1510s some of the emperor's most important forces were using matchlock guns in battle. By the 1526 Battle of Panipat, outside Delhi, Babur's armies had perfected the use of cannons (see again Map 19.2). As Babur recalled nonchalantly in his memoir, the *Baburnama*: "Mustafa the artilleryman fired some good shots from the mortars mounted on carts to the left of the center [flank]." Some 16,000 men were said to have died in this battle, and Babur celebrated by plundering the great city of Agra. In 1527, although hugely outnumbered by a Hindu Rajput alliance of some 80,000 cavalry and 500 armored war elephants, Babur and his army won handily. "From the center [flank of troops commanded by] our dear eldest son, Muhammad Humayun, Mustafa Rumi brought forward the caissons, and with matchlocks and mortars broke not only the ranks of the infidel but their hearts as well."[3] Gunpowder weapons continued to prove decisive as Babur and his successors drove south.

Humayun, as Babur's son was known, took over the

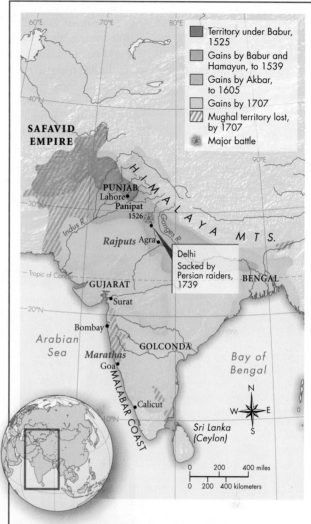

MAP 19.2   The Mughal Empire, c. 1700

Descendants of mounted Central Asian raiders, the Mughals expanded their control over the Indian subcontinent from the northwest after 1500. They did so with devastating, gunpowder-backed force followed by ethnic and religious accommodation. The majority of Mughal subjects did not practice the conquerors' Islamic faith, and some historians have even argued that India conquered the Mughals rather than the other way around. By 1700, the empire was approaching its greatest extent, after which rebellions and invasions began to force it to contract.

emerging Mughal Empire at his father's death in 1530, but he suffered setbacks. In 1535, he employed Ottoman military engineers and Portuguese gunners to attack the kingdom of Gujarat, a major textile exporter facing the Arabian Sea, but sources say his crippling addiction to opium cost valuable time and led to a forced withdrawal of troops. In the course of this ill-fated adventure, an Afghan warlord rose from the ashes to reconquer almost everything Babur had won in the north. Humayun went into exile in Safavid

Persia, but he returned to India aided by gun-toting Safavid forces. By 1555, Humayun had used this expanded firepower to regain his father's conquests, only to die in 1556 after hitting his head on the stairs of his library. Councilors decided the next Mughal would be Humayun's twelve-year-old son, Akbar.

Akbar the Great

India's historic role as an interfaith and intercultural crossroads was only heightened during the long reign of Akbar (literally "the Great," r. 1556–1605). Though founded by Timurid horsemen who regarded themselves as warriors of the Islamic faith in the Sunni tradition, by the time of Akbar a quick succession of marriages had linked Shi'ite Safavid and Hindu royalty to the central Mughal line. For over a century Persian remained the language of the court, and relations with the Safavids were friendly. Most notable, however, was the steady "Indianization" of the Mughal emperors themselves. The wealth and diversity of the subcontinent, not to mention the beauty and charm of Hindu Rajput princesses, absorbed them. Akbar was no exception; his son Jahangir, the next emperor, was born to a Hindu princess.

Taj Mahal

The Mughal emperor Shah Jahan (r. 1627–1658) commissioned this spectacular mausoleum, the Taj Mahal, in memory of his wife, Mumtaz Mahal. The structure includes Persian elements, in part because many Persian artisans worked in the Mughal court. But its quality of near-ethereal lightness, rising from the delicately carved white marble and long reflecting pool, marks it as Indian and Mughal. (Marco Pavan/Grand Tour/Corbis.)

This process of absorption was greatly accelerated by Akbar's eclectic personality. Fascinated with everything from yogic asceticism to the fire worship of India's Parsi, or Zoroastrian, minority, by the 1570s Akbar began formulating his own hybrid religion. It was a variety of emperor worship forced mostly upon high-ranking subjects. Somewhat like the early modern Inca and Japanese royal cults that tied the ruling house to the sun, Akbar's cult emphasized his own divine solar radiance. Staunch Muslim advisers rebelled against this seeming heresy in 1579, but Akbar successfully repressed them. In the end, Akbar's faith won few lasting converts—and left visiting Jesuit missionaries scratching their heads—yet its mere existence demonstrated an enduring Mughal tendency toward accommodation of religious difference.

Despite his eclecticism and toleration, Akbar clung to core Timurid cultural traditions, such as moving his court and all its attendant wealth and servants from one grand campsite to another. He was said to travel with no fewer than 100,000 attendants. He also never gave up his attachment to gunpowder warfare. Recalcitrant regional lords such as the Rajput Hindu prince Udai Singh defied Akbar's authority in the 1560s, only to suffer the young emperor's wrath. A protracted 1567 siege of the fortified city of Chitor ended with the deaths of some 25,000 defenders and their families. Akbar himself shot the commander of the city's defenses dead with a musket, and his massive siege cannons, plus the planting of explosive mines, brought down its formidable stone walls. A similar siege in 1569 employed even larger guns, hauled into position by elephants and teams of oxen. Few princes challenged Akbar's authority after these devastating demonstrations of Mughal firepower.

By the end of Akbar's reign, the Mughal Empire stretched from Afghanistan in the northwest to Bengal in the east, and south to about the latitude of Bombay (today Mumbai; see again Map 19.2). Emperor Jahangir (r. 1605–1627) was far less ambitious than his father Akbar, and as we saw in the opening paragraphs to this chapter, his addictions and interests led him to hand power to his favored wife, Nur Jahan, an effective administrator and business woman but not a conqueror. Jahangir's reign was nevertheless culturally significant. A devoted patron of the arts and an amateur poet, Jahangir took Mughal court splendor to new heights (see Seeing the Past: Reflections of the Divine in a Mughal Emerald). His illustrated memoir, the *Jahangirnama*, is a remarkably candid description of life at the top of one of the early modern world's most populous and wealthy empires.

Akbar's Successors

New conquests under Shah Jahan (r. 1628–1658) and Aurangzeb (aw-WRONG-zeb) (r. 1658–1707) carried the empire south almost to the tip of the subcontinent. These rulers had made few innovations in gunpowder warfare; as in the days of Babur, religion was as important a factor in imperial expansion as technology. Shah Jahan was an observant but tolerant Muslim, whereas Aurangzeb was a true holy warrior who called for a return to orthodoxy and elimination of unauthorized practices. Aurangzeb's religious fervor was a major force in the last phase of Mughal expansion.

The emperor's main foe was Prince Shivaji (c. 1640–1680), leader of the Hindu Marathas of India's far southwest. Aurangzeb employed European gunners, whose state-of-the-art weapons and high-quality gunpowder helped him capture several of Shivaji's forts, but he mostly relied on muskets, cannons, and other weapons designed and cast in India. Many large swivel guns were mounted on camels, a useful adaptation. For his part, Shivaji was never able to field more than a few hundred musketeers, relying instead on swift mounts and guerrilla raids. Despite a major offensive sent by Aurangzeb after Shivaji's death, the Marathas bounced back within a few decades and won recognition of their homeland.

Only with the accession of Aurangzeb's successor, Muhammad (r. 1720–1739), did Mughal stagnation and contraction set in. Rebellions by overtaxed peasants and nobles alike sapped the empire's overstretched bureaucratic and defensive resources, and Muhammad's guns proved increasingly outmoded. Europeans were by this time shifting to lighter and more mobile artillery, but the Mughals were casting larger and ever-more-unwieldy cannons. A cannon said to be capable of shooting 100-pound balls, dubbed "Fort Opener," was so heavy it had to be pulled by four elephants and thousands of oxen. Most of the time, it remained stuck in the mud between siege targets. Muhammad Shah

Jahangir Being Helped to Bed

This Mughal miniature from about 1635 shows the emperor Jahangir being put to bed by the ladies of his court after celebrating a Hindu new year's eve festival called Holi. As one of the illustrations in Jahangir's own memoir, the *Jahangirnama*, this image matches well with the emperor's self-description as a regular user of alcohol and other intoxicating substances. Though his interests were not as eclectic as those of his father, Akbar, Jahangir was tolerant of religious diversity. (© The Trustees of the Chester Beatty Library, Dublin.)

finally lost Delhi and the great Mughal treasury to Iran's Nadir Shah, successor to the Safavids, in 1739. The empire fell into disarray until the reign of Shah Alam II, who took the throne in 1759, only to fall under British influence in 1763. He ruled as a puppet of English East India Company until 1806.

Typical of early modern empire builders, the Mughals shifted between peaceful pragmatism and deadly force. They made a variety of alliances with subject peoples, offering them a share of power and the right to carry on established livelihoods. When not engaged in wars of expansion, emperors such as Akbar and Shah Jahan spent considerable time

Reflections of the Divine in a Mughal Emerald

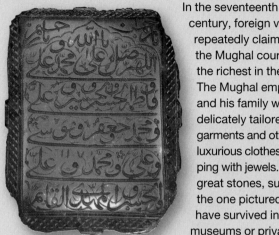

Mughal Emerald (Van Pelt Photography.)

In the seventeenth century, foreign visitors repeatedly claimed that the Mughal court was the richest in the world. The Mughal emperor and his family wore delicately tailored silk garments and other luxurious clothes, dripping with jewels. Many great stones, such as the one pictured here, have survived in museums or private collections. Fabulous gemstones weighing hundreds of carats were routinely exchanged and given as gifts to important visitors, loyal subjects, and favored heirs.

India's early modern rulers had direct access to precious metals, diamonds, rubies, and pearls, but emeralds—especially prized because green was the color of Islam—were hard to come by. Old mines in Egypt had long since played out, and sources in Afghanistan and Pakistan remained unknown, or at least untapped.

Emeralds were found, however, in faraway New Granada, the Spanish-American colony now roughly comprised by the Republic of Colombia. Beginning in the late sixteenth century, Spanish mine owners traded emeralds dug from the high Andes to Spanish and Portuguese merchants with ties to Goa, Portugal's most important trading post in India. From there, merchants traded the stones inland to intermediaries and even to the Mughal emperor himself. Once in the hands of the renowned artisans of the world's most opulent court, raw Colombian emeralds were faceted, tumbled, and carved for incorporation into a wide variety of royal jewels. Some were carefully inscribed with Arabic verses from the Qur'an or special prayers. The one pictured here contains a Shi'a prayer praising the Twelve Imams. It was meant to be sewn into a ritual garment, prayer-side in, as a protective amulet.

EXAMINING THE EVIDENCE

1. How does this precious object reflect patterns of early modern globalization?

2. Why would the royal owner commission a religious object of such magnificence?

---

mediating disputes, expanding palace structures, and organizing tribute collection. Elite tax-collectors and administrators called *zamindars* (SAW-mean-dars) lived off their shares of peasant and artisan tribute, ruling like chiefs over zones called *parganas*, similar to the Ottoman *timars* (discussed in the next chapter). Somewhat medieval in structure, this sort of decentralized rule bred corruption, which in turn led to waves of modernizing reform.

As in the similarly populous and cash-hungry empire of Ming China, Mughal tax reform moved in the direction of a centralized money economy (India's rulers had long enjoyed the privilege of minting gold, silver, and copper coins), stimulating both rural and urban markets. By Akbar's time, most taxes were paid in cash. Meanwhile, European merchants, ever anxious for Indian commodities such as pepper, diamonds, and cotton textiles, reluctantly supplied their South Asian counterparts with precious metals. As in China, this boost to the Mughal money supply was critical, since India had few precious metals mines of its own. The influx of cash, mostly Spanish-American silver pesos, continued even after the 1739 Persian sack of Delhi, but it was arguably a mixed blessing. As in contemporary China, and indeed in Spain itself, the heightened commercial activity and massive influx of bullion did not beget modern industrialization in India. Instead, it bred increased state belligerence and court grandeur. In a sense, the old "Mongolian" notions of governance were simply magnified, financed in a new, more efficient way. Even gunpowder weapons became little more than objects of show.

Tax Reform and Its Effects

Everyday Life in the Mughal Empire

Continuance of the Caste System

Despite its Islamic core and general policy of religious toleration, Mughal India remained sharply divided by status, or caste, as well as other types of social distinctions. India's caste divisions, like the so-called estates of Europe (nobility, clergy, and commoners), were thought to be derived from a divine order, or hierarchy, and could scarcely be challenged. Women's lives were circumscribed, if not oppressed, in virtually all but regal and wealthy merchant circles. The Hindu practice of **sati**, in which widows committed suicide by throwing themselves onto their husbands' funeral pyres, continued under Islamic rule,

sati The ancient Indian practice of ritual suicide by widows.

Building a Palace

This Mughal miniature from the 1590s is quite unusual in depicting ordinary working folk, along with a pair of animal helpers. Men of several colors, ages, and states of dress engage in heavy labor, transporting and lifting stones, beams, and mortar; splitting planks; setting stones; and plastering domes. Several women are sifting sand or preparing mortar, and at center-right are two well-dressed men who appear to be architects or inspectors. Two similar inspectors appear in the upper right, and only in the upper left corner do we glimpse the elite palace inhabitants, seemingly oblivious to the goings-on below. (Victoria & Albert Museum, London/Art Resource, NY.)

although there is much debate about its frequency. Akbar opposed the practice, but he did not ban it. Polygamy, sanctioned by Islam and embraced by Akbar and other rulers, was practiced by any man who could afford to support what amounted to multiple households.

Lower-caste folk, meanwhile, suffered regardless of gender. Men, women, and children were equally banished to a humiliated, slavelike existence in many areas, urban and rural. Worst off were the so-called Untouchables, who were relegated to disposing of human waste, animal carcasses, and other jobs requiring the handling of filth. Like those in many other parts of the early modern world, Mughal elites defined their own dignity most clearly by denying it to those around them—all the while displaying their innate goodness and superiority through ritualized, ostentatious acts of charity. After Akbar, the Mughal emperors had themselves publicly and lavishly weighed on their solar and lunar birthdays against piles of gold and silver coins, which they then distributed to the poor. Similar charitable practices were copied down to the lowest levels of society.

Farmers

As in much of the early modern world, the vast majority of Mughal subjects were subsistence farmers, many of them tied to large landlords through tributary and other customary obligations. The Mughal state thrived mostly by inserting itself into existing tributary structures, not by reordering local economies. Problems arose when Mughal rulers raised tax quotas sharply, or when droughts, floods, and other natural disasters upset the cycle of agricultural production. Unlike the Ming and Qing Chinese, or even the Spanish in Mexico, the Mughals devoted very little of their tremendous wealth to dams, aqueducts, and other massive public works projects. What was new, or modern, was that paper-pushing bureaucrats recorded farmers' tax assessments.

Even in good times, most South Asians lived on only a small daily ration of rice or millet, seasoned with ginger or cumin and—lightly—salt, an expensive state-monopoly item. Some fruits, such as mangoes, were seasonally available, but protein sources were limited. Even in times of bounty, religious dietary restrictions kept most people thin. After centuries of deforestation, people used animal dung as cooking fuel. Intensive agriculture using animal-drawn plows and irrigation works was widespread, but mass famines occurred with notable frequency. The Columbian Exchange was marginally helpful. After about 1600, American maize and tobacco were commonly planted, along with the capsicum peppers that came to spice up many South Asian dishes. Maize spurred population growth in some parts of India, whereas tobacco probably shortened some people's lives. Most tobacco was produced as a cash crop for elite consumption.

Urban Artisans

India's cities grew rapidly in Mughal times, in part due to stress-induced migration. Nine urban centers—among them Agra, Delhi, and Lahore—exceeded 200,000 inhabitants before 1700. After Akbar's rule, the shift to tax collection in cash was a major stimulus to urban growth and dynamism. Even smaller towns bustled with commercial activity as the economy became more thoroughly monetized, and all urban centers formed nuclei of artisan production.

A number of South Asian coastal and riverside cities and nearby hinterlands produced cotton and silk textiles in massive quantities. They usually followed the putting-out, or piecework, system, in which merchants "put out" raw materials to artisans working from home. As in China and northern Europe, women formed the backbone of this industry, not so much in weaving but rather in the physically harder tasks of fiber cleaning and spinning. Other, mostly male artisans specialized in woodworking, leather making, blacksmithing, and gem cutting. Perhaps the most visible artisanal legacy from Mughal times was in architecture. Highly skilled stonemasons produced Akbar's majestic Red Fort and Shah Jahan's inimitable Taj Mahal, both in the early Mughal capital of Agra.

Some men found employment in the shipyards of Surat, Calicut, and the Bay of Bengal, and others set sail with their seasonal cargoes of export goods and pilgrims. Gujarati Muslim merchants were dominant in the Arabian Sea even after the arrival of Europeans, but Hindus, Jains, and members of other faiths also participated. Unlike the Ottomans, the Mughals never developed a navy, despite their control of maritime

Gujarat since Akbar's conquest of the region in 1572 (see again Map 19.2). On land, by contrast, the empire's vast military apparatus absorbed many thousands of men. Frontier wars with fellow Muslims and southern Hindus were nearly constant. Christian Europeans were mostly seen as tangential commercial allies, technical advisers, and arms suppliers.

The Sikh Challenge

In the northwestern Punjab region an internal challenge of lasting significance emerged, this time mounted by leaders of a relatively new religious sect, Sikhism. Sikhism was something of a hybrid between Islam and Hinduism, but it tended more toward the latter and thus found deeper support among Hindu princes than among Islamic ones. Merchants and artisans were particularly attracted to the faith's recognition of hard work and abstinence (as we saw in Chapter 15). Peasant and artisan followers of Guru Gobind Singh (1666–1708) rebelled in 1710, and their plundering raids reached Delhi. The rebellion was violently quashed by Shah Farrukhsiyar (far-ROOK-see-yar) (r. 1713–1720) in 1715, but sporadic raids and uprisings continued until the end of the eighteenth century, when the Sikhs at last established a separate state.

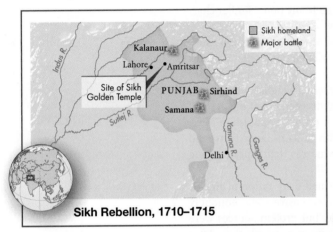

Sikh Rebellion, 1710–1715

In sum, the mighty Mughals ruled over the richest and most populous of Eurasia's early modern Islamic empires, and theirs remained by far the most culturally diverse. Mounted warriors used guns to crush or intimidate neighbors in new and terrifying ways, quickly absorbing huge swaths of terrain and millions of subject peoples. Yet generally, the resulting rule was neither intolerant nor authoritarian. As long as they paid cash tributes, regions could preserve their religious diversity and a degree of local autonomy. Problems arose with imperial overstretch, succession crises, and excessive taxation. Rebels, particularly non-Muslim ones, increasingly shook imperial foundations. More subtle but ultimately more serious were the inroads made by European commercial agents, in particular those of Britain's East India Company. These men, from Connecticut-born clerk Elihu Yale to Governor-general Robert Clive, formed the spearhead of a new imperialism.

European Interlopers

FOCUS

What factors enabled Europeans to take over key Indian Ocean trade networks?

Direct trade for Indian luxuries had been a dream of Europeans since the days of Marco Polo. Unfortunately, as the Portuguese explorer Vasco da Gama and his followers quickly discovered, Europeans had little that appealed to South Asians. With the exception of certain types of guns and clocks, the Portuguese had no products that could not be had in some form already, often more cheaply, and guns would soon be copied. Like Portugal, India was an ancient crossroads, but it was far larger and richer, and vastly more productive. Complex trade circuits had long linked India's rich interior and bustling ports to the wider world. In such a crowded marketplace, only silver and gold found universal acceptance because they functioned as money. Frustrated, the Portuguese turned to piracy, financing their first voyages by plunder rather than trade.

Portuguese Conquistadors 1500–1600

As would prove true in China, only precious metals opened India's doors of trade to newcomers. Even with powerful guns and swift ships on their side, the vastly outnumbered Portuguese had no choice but to part with their hard-won African gold and Spanish-American silver. Taking a somewhat different track than in western Africa, the Portuguese inserted themselves into Indian Ocean trade circuits with an uncompromising mix of belligerence and silver money. They were fortunate in that silver soon arrived in quantity through Portugal's growing Atlantic trade with the Spanish, particularly after 1550. Profits made in the slave trade were routinely reinvested in spices and other goods from India. Meanwhile, the security of all exchanges was guaranteed with brute force, and in some places, such as Goa in India and Melaka in Malaysia, outright conquest.

Portuguese Advances

Genuine Portuguese conquests in Asia were few but significant. Crown-sponsored conquistadors focused on strategic sites for their fortified trading posts, mostly traditional mercantile crossroads and shipping straits not effectively monopolized or defended by local princes. These *feitorías* resembled those already established along the western coast of Africa, but most proved far more expensive and difficult to maintain. The Indian Ocean's sea traffic was already huge, by comparison, and competition was fierce.

The Portuguese grand plan, one that was never realized, was to monopolize all trade in the Indian Ocean by extracting tolls and tariffs from local traders of various ethnicities and political allegiances. For a time they sold shipping licenses to Gujarati Muslim and other long-distance shippers. If traders failed to produce such licenses when passing through Portuguese-controlled ports, their goods were confiscated. On top of this, they had to pay duties.

Within a half-century of da Gama's 1498 voyage to India the Portuguese controlled access to the Persian Gulf, Red Sea, South China Sea, and Atlantic Ocean, along with many major coastal trading enclaves, from Mombasa on the coast of Kenya to Macao on China's Pearl River delta (see Map 19.3). Being so few in a region of millions, the Portuguese strategy was pragmatic. By tapping existing trade networks and setting up feitorías, they could efficiently collect spices and textiles, along with what were essentially extortion payments. Friends would be given silver, enemies lead. The method worked as long as the Portuguese faced no competition from other belligerent sea powers and remained unified and consistent in their use of violence.

Despite some early Ottoman attacks, seaborne trade competitors would not arrive until about 1600, but given the distance to Lisbon, it immediately proved impossible to enforce Portuguese unity and consistency in dealing with Indian Ocean merchants and princes. Ironically, it was "friendly" local merchants, rajas, and sultans—Arab, Hindu, and otherwise—who benefited most from Portuguese sponsorship and protection. As in western Africa, for several centuries the Portuguese unwittingly did as much to facilitate local aspirations as to realize their own. What they grandly called the "State of India," *Estado da Índia*, gradually proved more "Indian" than Portuguese, though for a short time it was highly profitable to the Crown.

Failed Efforts at Religious Conversion

Portugal's grand religious project was similarly absorbed. In 1498 Vasco da Gama expressed confidence in the spread of Roman Catholicism to East Africa: "On Easter day the Moors [Muslims] we had taken captive told us that in the town of Malindi [a Swahili port on the coast of Kenya] there were four vessels belonging to Christians from India, and if we should like to convey them there they would give us Christian pilots, and everything else we might need, including meats, water, wood, and other things."[4] Da Gama wrongly took this to mean that there was a pre-existing Christian base or network in the region upon which the Catholic Portuguese could build. Ultimately, Portuguese efforts to convert the many peoples of the Indian Ocean basin failed even more miserably than in Atlantic Africa, though not for lack of trying. Francis Xavier, an early Jesuit missionary (see Chapter 20), worked tirelessly and died an optimist. Whereas he focused on converting the region's countless slaves and lower-caste people, others sought to bend the will of monarchs such as Akbar, hoping they would set an example. Small Christian communities formed at Goa and other strongholds, but everywhere they went, Portuguese missionaries faced literally millions of hostile Muslims and perhaps equal or greater numbers of uninterested Hindus, Buddhists, Confucianists, Jains, Parsis, Sikhs, Jews, and others. In short, Christianity, at least in the form presented by the Portuguese, did not appeal to the vast majority of people inhabiting the Indian Ocean basin. As we will see in Chapter 21, only in

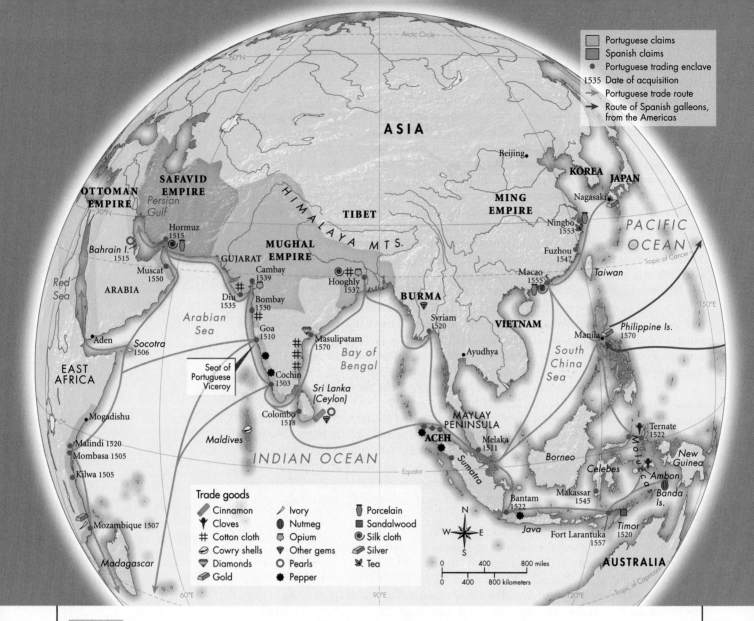

MAP 19.3

Portugal's Seaborne Empire, c. 1600

With their castle-like sailing vessels and potent gunpowder weapons, the Portuguese inserted themselves violently into the greater Indian Ocean basin beginning in 1498. From their stronghold in Goa, they monopolized regional and export trade in luxury goods, either by shipping these items themselves or by forcing others to purchase licenses. After 1580, the Portuguese were under Spanish rule, which linked the lucrative East and South Asia trade routes to New World silver arriving in the Philippines.

Japan, the Philippines, East Timor, and other select areas, mostly in the western Pacific, did early modern Catholic missionaries appear to strike a chord.

The "India Voyage"

Despite the failure of Christian missionary efforts, trade was brisk, at least for a time. The so-called *carreira da India* (cah-HEY-rah dah EENDJ-yah), or India voyage, became legendary in Portuguese culture, and for good reason. Even on successful trips, death rates on this annual sail between Lisbon and Goa were high due to poor onboard sanitation, prolonged vitamin C deprivation, questionable medical therapies such as bloodletting, and other health challenges typical of the era. Also, although early modern navigators were arguably more adept than medieval ones, shipwrecks were not uncommon on the India voyage. Unlike local dhows, sixteenth- and seventeenth-century Portuguese vessels were huge, round-hulled, and built for cargo rather than speed or maneuverability, and foundered due to overloading. The coral reefs of southeast Africa became a notorious graveyard of the carreira.

By the later sixteenth century, Portuguese monopolies on East Indian spices and sea-lanes had weakened considerably. With so much wealth at stake and so few enforcers on hand, corruption and contraband flourished. Spices were, after all, the drugs of their day, more valuable by weight than gold. Shipwrecks and piracy became more frequent throughout Portugal's ocean empire, as did competition from new, better-armed Europeans—Protestants, to boot. As Luiz Vaz de Camões (cah-MOYSH), veteran of many adventures in the East Indies, composed the triumphant poem that would become Portugal's national epic, *The Lusíads*, Portugal was actually on the eve of losing not only its heirless king but also its hard-won trading monopolies in the Indian Ocean. It was the Spanish under Philip II who would offer the first humiliation. Shortly after, Spain's sworn enemies, the Dutch, would deal the Portuguese a series of crushing blows.

Weakening of Portuguese Power

The Dutch and English East India Companies 1600–1750

As Portuguese fortunes declined and Mughal expansion continued toward the turn of the seventeenth century, South Asia's overseas trade underwent notable reorganization. This shift involved many players, including the familiar Gujarati merchants, the increasingly powerful Ottomans, Persia's expanding Safavids, and others. But ultimately it was Dutch and English newcomers, and to a lesser extent the French, who would have the greatest long-term impact. All formed powerful **trading companies** in the seventeenth and eighteenth centuries, each backed by state-of-the-art cannons and first-rate sailing ships.

Despite these important changes, it would be highly misleading to project the later imperial holdings of these foreigners back onto the seventeenth and early eighteenth centuries. Only the Dutch came close to establishing a genuine "Indian Ocean Empire" during early modern times. Meanwhile, East Africans, South and Southeast Asians, and other native peoples of the Indian Ocean continued to act independently, in their own interests. It was the sudden, unexpected collapse of the Mughals and other gunpowder-fueled Asian states in the later eighteenth century that allowed Europeans to conquer large landmasses and to plant colonies of the sort long since established in the Americas.

The Dutch East India Company, known by its Dutch acronym VOC, was founded in 1602. The company's aim was to use ships, arms, and Spanish-American silver to displace the Portuguese as Europe's principal suppliers of spices and other exotic Asian goods. Though not officially a state enterprise, the Dutch East India Company counted many ranking statesmen among its principal investors, and its actions abroad were as belligerent as those of any imperial army or navy. In the course of almost two centuries, the VOC extended Dutch influence from South Africa to Japan. Its most lasting achievement was the conquest of Java, base for the vast and diverse Dutch colony of Indonesia.

Dutch VOC

Although they never drove the Portuguese from their overseas capital at Goa, the mostly Protestant Dutch displaced their Catholic rivals nearly everywhere else. Their greatest early successes were in southern India and Java, followed by Sri Lanka (Ceylon), Bengal, Melaka, and Japan (see Map 19.4). In Southeast Asia their standard procedure was to follow conquest with enslavement and eventually plantation agriculture of the sort established by the Spanish and Portuguese in the Americas. They also imposed this sequence on Ceylon (see Lives and Livelihoods: Cinnamon Harvesters in Ceylon).

The monopolistic mentality of contemporary Europe is what drove Dutch aggression: profits were ensured not by open competition but by absolute control over the flow of commodities and the money to pay for them. Faced with competition from both regional authorities such as the Mughals and fellow foreign interlopers such as the English and Portuguese, the VOC concentrated on monopolizing spices. After seizing the pepper-growing region of southern Sumatra, the VOC turned to the riskier business of establishing plantations to grow coffee and other tropical cash crops. Like the Portuguese before them, the Dutch devoted at least as much cargo space to interregional trade as to exports. Thus clever local traders and many thousands of Chinese merchants benefited from the Dutch determination to monopolize trade.

trading companies Private corporations licensed by early modern European states to monopolize Asian and other overseas trades.

Cinnamon Harvesters in Ceylon

Harvesting Cinnamon

This engraving, based on a simpler one from 1672, depicts cinnamon harvesters in Ceylon (Sri Lanka). The Portuguese were the first Europeans to attempt to monopolize the global export of this spice, but local kings were difficult to conquer and control. Only in the later seventeenth century did the Dutch manage to establish plantation-type production, with the final product, the now familiar cinnamon sticks, monopolized by the Dutch East India Company. (The Granger Collection, New York.)

Long before the arrival of Europeans in 1506, the island of Sri Lanka, or Ceylon (its colonial name), was world-renowned for its cinnamon exports. As far away as Persia this wet tropical island off India's southeast tip, largely under control of competing Buddhist kings, was famous for its sapphires, rubies, pearls, and domesticated elephants (see again Map 19.3). Like India's pepper and Southeast Asia's cloves, mace, and nutmeg, Ceylonese cinnamon fetched extraordinary prices throughout Eurasia

and parts of Africa, where it was used as a condiment, preservative, and even medicine. As late as 1685 a Portuguese observer noted: "Every year a great number of vessels arrive from Persia, Arabia, the Red Sea, the Malabar Coast [of India], China, Bengal, and Europe to fetch cinnamon." Attempts to transplant the spice elsewhere, including Brazil, consistently failed, and early conquistador claims of finding cinnamon in Ecuador's eastern jungles proved false. As part of the Columbian Exchange,

Ceylonese cinnamon became a necessary ingredient in hot chocolate, a beverage developed in colonial Mexico that soon took Europe by storm.

The spice grew wild in forests belonging to the kingdom of Kandy, in Ceylon's southwest highlands. In 1517, the Portuguese struck a deal with the king of Kandy that allowed them to use and fortify the port of Colombo to monopolize cinnamon exports in exchange for cloth, metalware, and military assistance against rivals. The Portuguese did not engage directly in cinnamon production, but rather traded for it with the king and certain nobles. The king and his nobles in turn collected cinnamon as a tribute item produced on feudal-type estates called *para-wenia*. A special caste of male workers known as *chalias* was specifically responsible for planting, harvesting, slicing, drying, and packaging Ceylon's most prized crop. The chalias were not enslaved, but rather served as dependents of the king and various noblemen and military officers in exchange for the right to use land for subsistence farming in the off-season, plus rations of rice and occasionally a cash wage.

Cinnamon is derived from the shaved and dried inner bark of the small *Cinamomum verum* tree, a variety of laurel. Although the spice can be harvested wild, Ceylon's chalias pruned, transplanted, and even grew the trees from seed to maximize output and improve quality. With southwest Ceylon's white sand soils and reliable monsoon rains, the crop flourished year after year. Cinnamon is best when taken from young saplings three to five years old, no more than ten feet high, and about the thickness of a walking stick. Due to Ceylon's latitude, two harvests were possible, one concentrated in May-June and another in November-December. At harvest time the chalias cut ripe cinnamon trees with hatchets and then removed the bark. Daily collection quotas were set by the king and other holders of parawenia estates.

Next came peeling, the key process and the one for which the chalias were best known. As a seventeenth-century Portuguese writer described them: "These cinnamon peelers carry in their girdle a small hooked knife as a mark of their occupation." Working in pairs, one chalia made two lengthwise incisions on the ripe sticks using his hooked knife and carefully removed the resulting half-cylindrical strips of bark. His companion then used other tools to separate a gray outer bark from the thin, cream-colored inner bark. Leaving even a tiny amount of the outer bark on the inner bark made the cinnamon inedibly bitter. The inner bark was then left to dry, curling, thickening, and turning brown as it oxidized. The chalias then packaged the resulting "cinnamon sticks" in cloth-covered bundles weighing about 100 lbs. These were given to overlords; the king of Kandy alone was said to demand over 500 tons each year. Cinnamon was often bundled with black pepper for long sea voyages to help draw out moisture.

We have no documents written by the chalias to give us a sense of their views, but we do know that a leader of a 1609 rebellion against the Portuguese was a member of this caste and the son of a cinnamon cutter. Tapping into local discontent, the Dutch East India Company (VOC) displaced the Portuguese in 1658 after making an alliance with the king of Kandy. Once established on the island, the Dutch shifted to direct planting and harvesting, using enslaved laborers and totally monopolizing trade in cinnamon to maximize profits. The king was reduced to the status of client. Work on cinnamon plantations was not as difficult a livelihood as gem mining or pearl diving, but Dutch work demands were rigorous and punishments harsh for even light offenses. Dissatisfaction with the VOC administrators ran deep. The British took over Ceylon in 1796 following the collapse of the VOC, but their management of the cinnamon economy was not as careful or exacting, and both price and quality fell. Ceylon's export sector would be revived after 1800 with the introduction of American tropical crops adapted by British botanists: cinchona (quinine), cacao, and rubber.

QUESTIONS TO CONSIDER

1. How was cinnamon grown, harvested, and prepared for export?

2. How did cinnamon harvesting fit into traditional, pre-colonial landholding and labor systems?

3. How did Dutch rule change the lives and livelihoods of cinnamon harvesters? Of Sri Lanka (Ceylon) in general?

For Further Information:
Valentijn, François. *Description of Ceylon,* ed. Sinnappah Arasaratnam. London: Hakluyt Society, 1978 [orig. publ. 1720].
Winius, George D. *The Fatal History of Portuguese Ceylon: Transition to Dutch Rule.* New York: Cambridge University Press, 1971.

MAP 19.4

Dutch and English Colonies in South and Southeast Asia, to 1750

Although the Portuguese remained active in the Indian Ocean basin and South China Sea until the twentieth century, after 1600 the Dutch and English had largely displaced them. The East India Companies of these two countries sought to conquer and defend key trading enclaves, both against each other and against the later-arriving French. Outside the Spanish Philippines, only the Dutch managed to establish a significant land empire before 1750. In the hands of the company, or VOC, Dutch holdings grew to encompass most of Indonesia. The English and French would follow suit in South and Southeast Asia in subsequent decades.

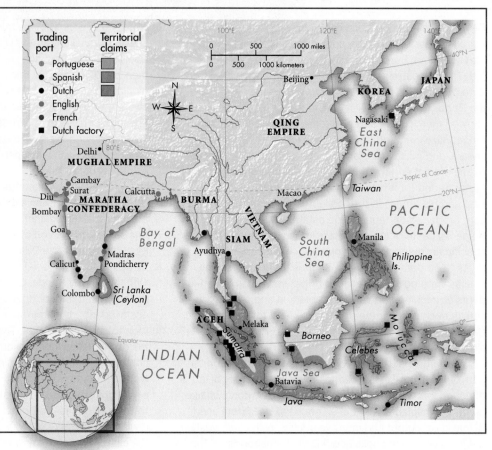

The VOC, like other Indian Ocean traders, relied on a steady supply of Spanish-American silver to lubricate commerce. Between 1600 and 1648, when these rival empires were at war, some silver was plundered from the Spanish in the Caribbean by Dutch pirates, but most was extracted through trade, both official and contraband. Recent research has revealed the importance of illegal Dutch slave traders in Buenos Aires after a major peace agreement was signed with Spain in 1648. The silver of Potosí in this case bypassed Europe entirely to go to Dutch trading posts in India, Southeast Asia, and China. Mexican silver, meanwhile, flowed out of Dutch Caribbean ports such as Curaçao, through Amsterdam, and into the holds of outbound company ships. Trade in Manila extracted still more Spanish silver. Though ever more divided in its political loyalties, the world was becoming ever more unified in its monetary system.

English East India Company

Compared with the VOC, the English East India Company (EIC), founded two years earlier in 1600, had more modest aims and much less capital. Nevertheless, it used brute force and a royal charter to displace the Portuguese in several strategic ports, especially around the Arabian peninsula and on the coasts of India. Given England's civil wars and other internal problems in the seventeenth century (discussed in the next chapter), progress was slow and uneven. Only in the late seventeenth century did English traders in India begin to amass considerable fortunes, mostly by exporting spices, gems, and cloth from their modest fortresses at Surat, Bombay, Madras, and Calcutta (see again Map 19.4). Like the VOC, however, the EIC grew increasingly powerful over time, eventually taking on a blatantly imperial role.

Two very different individuals from the turn of the eighteenth century illustrate the slow but steady ascent of the English East India Company. Elihu Yale, a native New Englander whose book collection was used to establish a college in Connecticut in his name, rose from the position of Company clerk to serve for over a dozen years as the

Dutch Headquarters in Bengal

This painting from 1665 depicts the Dutch East India Company (VOC) trading fort at Hugly, on the banks of the Ganges River branch of the same name in the Indian province of Bengal. As they did elsewhere along the rim of the rich and populous Indian Ocean basin, the Dutch sought to establish exclusive control over specific commodities, usually after driving out the Portuguese. In Bengal, the main export items were fine cotton print fabrics, which, along with a variety of products already circulating in the region, they traded mostly for Spanish-American silver. The VOC would eventually be displaced by the English East India Company. (Courtesy of Rijksmuseum, Amsterdam, The Netherlands.)

governor of the East India Company's fort at Madras. He quickly learned to exploit his post to export cloth, pepper, saltpeter, opium, and diamonds. Upon his return to England in 1699, Yale was the contemporary equivalent of a multimillionaire. Although he never visited New Haven, his philanthropic capital, skimmed from East India Company profits, was piously invested in colonial higher education.

At about the same time, England's Admiralty, under pressure from EIC investors, commissioned a Scottish-born but New York City–based privateer named William Kidd to search for English pirates interfering with Company-protected trade in the Indian Ocean, especially in the Red Sea. Instead, Kidd foolishly attacked and plundered a Mughal-sponsored merchantman off the southwest coast of India. Now a pirate himself, Kidd fled to Madagascar in the stolen vessel, then across the Atlantic to the Caribbean. Eventually, Kidd tried to contact his wife in New York, but he was captured and sent in chains to Boston, then London. At the urging of East India Company officials, whose friendship with Emperor Aurangzeb had been severely strained by the renegade pirate hunter's actions, Kidd was hanged in 1701. The company's interests in distant seas were, it seems, increasingly the government's.

COUNTERPOINT
Aceh: Fighting Back in Southeast Asia

FOCUS

Why was the tiny sultanate of Aceh able to hold out against European interlopers in early modern times?

The province and city of Aceh (AH-cheh), at the northwest tip of the island of Sumatra in Indonesia, was transformed but not conquered in early modern times. Like many trading enclaves linked by the Indian Ocean's predictable monsoon winds, Aceh was a Muslim sultanate that lived by exchanging the produce of its interior, in this case black pepper, for the many commodities supplied by other, distant kingdoms. Aceh's rulers participated directly in trade, dictating its terms and enjoying many of its benefits. Yet unlike most such enclaves, which fell like dominoes to European interlopers, Aceh held out. For a variety of reasons, but perhaps most importantly a newfound religious fervor, the Acehnese defeated a long string of would-be conquistadors.

The Differing Fortunes of Aceh and Melaka

Aceh's rulers were probably related to those of the less fortunate Malay trading city of Melaka. Melaka was a former fishing village with a fine natural harbor and highly strategic location on the east end of the narrow Melaka Strait. It was said to have been founded by a Hindu prince who converted to Islam in around 1420. Melaka's rulers forged deft, profitable alliances to regions as far away as China, but ties to the interior were weak, drawing predators. Melaka was attacked repeatedly by Javanese sultans, and in the end it fell to Portuguese cannons in 1511. Although Melakan forces had guns of their own and fought valiantly against the Europeans, when the tide turned they found themselves without a backcountry into which guerrilla warriors might flee and reorganize. The Dutch followed in 1641, displacing the Portuguese.

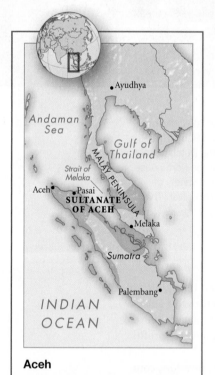

Aceh

Unlike Melaka, Aceh's influence reached deep into the interior and across hundreds of miles of coast. After defeating Portuguese invaders in 1518, Aceh emerged as one of the most assertive seaborne Islamic states in the entire Indian Ocean, tapping military aid from the distant Ottomans and shipping considerable quantities of pepper to the Mediterranean via the Red Sea. But Aceh's repeated efforts to conquer Portuguese-controlled Melaka failed, and by the late seventeenth century the kingdom declined as both a political and commercial force. Still, it was not until the late nineteenth century that the Dutch reduced Aceh to colonial status.

Aceh, "the Veranda of Mecca"

Aceh's early modern history has been gleaned from a variety of outside sources, and also local, sometimes official, chronicles, including epic poems written in Malay and Acehnese in the sixteenth and seventeenth centuries to celebrate the deeds of its sultans. Although poets tended to exaggerate the greatness of their patrons and to conflate or compress events, the epics express Acehnese Islamic pride, mostly as the region's bulwark against the militant Christian Portuguese. Ottoman, Portuguese, Dutch, and English sources note that Aceh was a great meeting place for Southeast Asian pilgrims on their way to Mecca, and it came to be known as *Serambi Mekkah*, the Veranda of Mecca.

Islamic Identity

Despite its intensely Islamic identity, Acehnese culture respected female independence. Women controlled and inherited nearly all property, from houses to rice fields, and at marriage men moved to their wives' households. Men in fact spent much of their time

Dutch Merchants Learn How to Act in Aceh

In this passage, originally composed in the Malay language just after 1600, a Dutch merchant in Aceh created a dialogue between an imaginary European visitor, "Daud," and a local informant, "Ibrahim." The sample exchange was meant to instruct future Dutch visitors. Should they come to Aceh for business, they would know something of the cultural intricacies of local exchange, and also how to ask about them. This passage describes the formal reception of a Gujarati merchant from western India by the local raja. Every detail of court etiquette was critical. To make mistakes in the course of observing and participating in these rituals, particularly when one had little knowledge of local languages, was to risk permanent expulsion, and in some cases death.

Daud: Who is it coming on this great elephant, who has such a crowd of people behind him?

Ibrahim: It is the Shahbandar with the Penghulu kerkun [secretary].

Daud: I also see some foreign traders sitting up there. Who are they?

Ibrahim: That is a Gujarati *nakhoda* [merchant], who has just come with his ship, and whom they are going to take to salute the raja.

Daud: What does it mean, that elephant caparisoned in red cloth, with those people in front of it playing on tambourines, trumpets, and flutes?

Ibrahim: The elephant you see and the man sitting in a palanquin [curtained couch] upon it, means that a letter is being brought from their raja to our lord. . . .

Daud: Who is seated up there?

Ibrahim: It is one of the sultan's *orangkaya* [courtier], that he has chosen for that.

Daud: And what is all that for?

Ibrahim: To honor the raja whose letter it is.

Daud: And what is that I see, so many men and slaves, each bringing a painted cloth in his hands?

Ibrahim: These are the presents which the nakhoda will offer to the king.

Daud: Is that the tariff he must pay for his goods, or must he pay another tariff?

Ibrahim: No, the tariff is extra, seven percent.

Daud: What honor will the raja give them in return?

Ibrahim: Indeed, when they enter the raja's palace, they will be given great honor.

Daud: What happens there?

Ibrahim: There they eat and drink, all sorts of food and fruits are brought, they play, dance, with all sorts of entertainments, they play on the trumpet, flute, clarinet, and *rebab,* and then the king asks for a garment of our local style to be brought, which he gives to the nakhoda.

Source: Frederick de Houtman, 1603, quoted in of Anthony Reid, *Southeast Asia in the Age of Commerce* (New Haven: Yale University Press, 1993), 2: 237–238. Credit: Anthony Reid. *Southeast Asia in the Age of Commerce*, Volume 2. Yale University Press, 1993. Copyright © Yale University Press, 1993. Used by permission of the publisher.

EXAMINING THE EVIDENCE

1. What does this dialogue suggest about the balance of power in Aceh?

2. What does it reveal about the interplay of rulership and trade?

away on business or engaged in religious study, leaving women in charge of most aspects of everyday life. Pre-Islamic kin structures governed daily affairs, while *ulama,* or religious scholars, oversaw matters of business and state. Criminal cases reveal that local custom could override Islamic prescriptions, especially when it came to capital punishment. The result was a somewhat mild, woman-friendly Southeast Asian blend of secular and religious life reminiscent of West Africa.

Aceh was immediately recognized as a powerful state by northern European visitors in the early seventeenth century. The first Dutch envoys were jailed from 1599 to 1601 for

Trade and Diplomacy

mishandling court etiquette (see Reading the Past: Dutch Merchants Learn How to Act in Aceh), but soon after, English visitors representing Queen Elizabeth I and the newly chartered East India Company made a better impression. Of particular interest to the Acehnese shah was Dutch and English hostility to Portugal, which also sent ambassadors. Playing competing Europeans off one another soon became an absorbing and sometimes profitable game. And the Europeans were by no means alone—sizable trading and diplomatic missions arrived in Aceh from eastern and western India, Burma, and Siam. Sultan Iskandar Muda used English and Dutch traders to drive the Gujaratis out of the pepper trade in the 1610s, only to force the Europeans out of it in the 1620s. He continued to ship pepper to Red Sea intermediaries, but steadily lost market share to both English and Dutch merchants, who turned to other Southeast Asian sources.

Sultanate of Women   Aceh's decline has been traditionally associated with the rise of female sultans in the seventeenth century, much as occurred in the Ottoman Empire at about the same time (as we will see in Chapter 20). Sultana Taj al-Alam Safiyat al-Din Shah ruled from 1641 to 1675. She was the daughter of the renowned conqueror and deft handler of foreign envoys, Iskandar Muda Shah (r. 1607–1636), but her politics focused mostly on domestic affairs, in part because Aceh was in a period of restructuring after her father's failed 1629 attack on Portuguese Melaka. Like her counterparts in Istanbul and Agra, Safiyat al-Din was a great patron of artists and scholars. Under her sponsorship, Acehnese displaced Malay as the language of state and the arts.

Safiyat al-Din was succeeded by three more sultanas, the last of whom, Kamalat Shah, was deposed following a 1699 decree, or **fatwa**, from Mecca declaring women unfit to serve as sultans. Careful reading of sources suggests that female sultans were not the cause of Aceh's declining power in the region, but rather a symptom of a general shift toward the Malay style of divine kingship. Even in decline, Aceh held out throughout early modern times and beyond against European attempts to subject it to colonial rule.

Conclusion

Thanks to reliable monsoon winds, the vast Indian Ocean basin had long been interconnected by ties of trade and religion, and this general pattern continued throughout early modern times. The region's countless farmers depended as they had for millennia on the monsoon rains.

Change came, however, with the rise of gunpowder-fueled empires both on land and at sea. Beginning about 1500, seaborne Europeans forcibly took over key ports and began taxing the trade of others, while Islamic warriors on horseback blasted resistant sultans and rajas into tribute-paying submission in South and Southwest Asia. Smaller sultanates and kingdoms also adopted gunpowder weapons after 1500, both to defend themselves against invaders and to attack weaker neighbors. Although such armed conflict could be deadly or at least disrupt everyday life, for most ordinary people in the long run it meant a rise in tribute demands, and in some places a turn to forced cultivation of export products such as cinnamon or pepper.

Despite the advances of increasingly belligerent Islamic and Christian empires throughout the Indian Ocean, most inhabitants, including India's 100 million-plus Mughal subjects, did not convert. Religious tolerance had long been the rule in this culturally complex region, and although the Portuguese were driven by an almost crusading fervor to spread Catholicism, in the end they were forced to deal with Hindus, Buddhists, Jews, and Muslims to make a profit. Later Europeans, most of them Protestants, scarcely bothered to proselytize prior to modern times, choosing instead to offer themselves as religiously neutral intermediaries, unlike the intolerant Portuguese.

fatwa A decree issued by Islamic religious officials.

The Mughals, like the kings of Vijayanagara before them, followed a tradition of divinely aloof religious tolerance, although conversion to the state faith had its benefits, particularly in trade. Emperor Akbar went so far as to create his own hybrid cult, although it never took root, and in the provinces Sikhism emerged as an alternative to Hinduism or Islam. As with Christianity, Islamic practices varied greatly throughout this vast region, and these differences were visible in customs of female mobility, dress, and access to positions of power. Nur Jahan represented a temporary period of Mughal openness to feminine power and public expression, and Aceh's Sultanate of the Women represented another in Southeast Asia.

Europeans sought to adapt to local cultures of trade when using force was impractical. For most of the early modern period, they had no choice, at least outside their tiny, fortressed towns. Only with the decline of great land empires such as that of the Mughals in the eighteenth century did this begin to change. Though it happened much more slowly than in contemporary Latin America or western Africa, by the end of the early modern period European imperial designs had begun to alter established lifeways throughout the Indian Ocean region. Expansion into the interior, first by overseas trading companies such as the English East India Company and the Dutch VOC, would grow in the nineteenth century into full-blown imperialism. Only a few outliers, such as the Muslim revivalist sultanate of Aceh, managed to hold out, and even their time would come.

NOTES

1. Marshall Hodgson, *The Venture of Islam,* 2 vols. (Chicago: University of Chicago Press, 1974), 2: 34.
2. Robert Sewell, *A Forgotten Empire (Vijayanagar): A Contribution to the History of India* (London: Sonnenschein, 1900), 245.
3. Thackston Wheeler, ed. and trans., *The Baburnama: Memoirs of Babur, Prince and Emperor* (Washington, D.C.: Smithsonian Institution, 1996), 326, 384.
4. Vasco da Gama, *The Diary of His Travels Through African Waters, 1497–1499,* ed. and trans. Eric Axelson (Somerset, U.K.: Stephan Phillips, 1998), 45.

RESOURCES FOR RESEARCH

General Works

The Indian Ocean has recently become a unit of study on par with the Atlantic and Mediterranean, but synthetic interpretations are still few. For the early modern period, Barendse's synthesis is essential.

Barendse, R. J. *The Arabian Seas: The Indian Ocean World of the Seventeenth Century.* 2002.

Risso, Patricia. *Merchants and Faith: Muslim Commerce and Culture in the Indian Ocean.* 1995.

The Sultan Qaboos Cultural Center at Washington D.C.'s Middle East Cultural Center maintains a superb site on the Indian Ocean in world history at http://www.indianoceanhistory .org/.

The University of Wisconsin's Center for South Asia maintains a Web site with links to texts, timelines, maps, and other materials relevant to the study of South Asia and the Indian Ocean. http://www.southasia.wisc.edu/resources.html.

Trading Cities and Inland Networks: East Africa

The following authors are among the leading specialists writing on early modern East Africa, including in their work both African and Portuguese perspectives.

Newitt, Malyn. *A History of Portuguese Overseas Expansion, 1400–1668.* 2005.

Pearson, Michael N. *Port Cities and Intruders: The Swahili Coast, India, and Portugal in the Early Modern Era.* 1998.

Trade and Empire in South Asia

The literature on maritime India is vast and growing, but the following works offer a good sense of both the questions being pursued and the types of sources available. Whereas works on Vijayanagara are few, and based mostly on art and archaeology, document-based studies on Mughal India have multiplied more rapidly than for any of the other gunpowder empires.

Dale, Stephen. *Indian Merchants and Eurasian Trade, 1600–1750.* 1994.

Mukhia, Harbans. *The Mughals of India.* 2004.

Pearson, Michael N. *The Portuguese in India* (The New Cambridge History of India, Part 1, vol. 1). 1987.

Schimmel, Annemarie. *The Empire of the Mughals: History, Art, and Culture.* Translated by Corinne Attwood. 2004.

Stein, Burton. *Vijayanagara.* 2005.

European Interlopers

The literature on Europe's "East India Companies" and related enterprises is voluminous, but recent work has attempted to go beyond a focus on business and bureaucracy to fathom cross-cultural meanings.

Boyajian, James C. *Portuguese Trade in Asia Under the Habsburgs, 1580–1640.* 1993.

Chaudhury, Sushil, and Michel Morineau, eds. *Merchants, Companies, and Trade: Europe and Asia in the Early Modern Era.* 1999.

Gaastra, Femme S. *The Dutch East India Company: Expansion and Decline.* 2003.

Keay, John. *The Honourable Company: A History of the East India Company.* 1993.

Ritchie, Robert C. *Captain Kidd and the War Against the Pirates.* 1986.

COUNTERPOINT: Aceh: Fighting Back in Southeast Asia

Work on the early modern history of island Southeast Asia has ballooned in recent years. The following authors treat Aceh in this wider context.

Lockard, Craig. *Southeast Asia in World History.* 2009.

Reid, Anthony. *Southeast Asia in the Age of Commerce.* 2 vols. 1988.

Reid, Anthony, ed. *Southeast Asia in the Early Modern Era: Trade, Power, and Belief.* 1993.

Reid, Anthony, ed. *Verandah of Violence: The Background to the Aceh Problem.* 2006.

▶ **For additional primary sources from this period,** see *Sources of Crossroads and Cultures*.

▶ **For Web sites, images, and documents related to topics in this chapter,** see Make History at bedfordstmartins.com/smith.

The major global development in this chapter ▶ The Indian Ocean trading network and the impact of European intrusion on maritime and mainland South Asia.

IMPORTANT EVENTS

1336–1565	Vijayanagara kingdom in southern India
1498	Vasco da Gama reaches India
1500–1763	Mughal Empire in South Asia
1509–1529	Reign of Krishna Deva Raya of Vijayanagara
1510	Portuguese conquest of Goa, India
1511	Portuguese conquest of Melaka
1517	Portuguese establish fort in Sri Lanka (Ceylon)
1526	Battle of Panipat led by Mughal emperor Babur
1530	Consolidation of Aceh under Sultan Ali Mughayat Shah
1556–1605	Reign of Mughal emperor Akbar
1567	Akbar's siege of Chitor
1600	English East India Company founded in London
1602	Dutch East India Company (VOC) founded in Amsterdam
1605–1627	Reign of Mughal emperor Jahangir
1641	Dutch take Melaka from Portuguese
1641–1699	Sultanate of Women in Aceh
1658	Dutch drive Portuguese from Ceylon
1701	William Kidd hanged in London for piracy
1739	Persian raiders under Nadir Shah sack Delhi
1764	English East India Company controls Bengal

KEY TERMS

Brahman (p. 622)
caste (p. 622)
dhow (p. 619)
fatwa (p. 642)
Kshatriya (p. 622)

monsoon (p. 615)
sati (p. 630)
trading companies (p. 635)

CHAPTER OVERVIEW QUESTIONS

1. What environmental, religious, and political factors enabled trading enclaves to flourish in the Indian Ocean basin?

2. How did the rise and fall of India's land empires reflect larger regional trends?

3. How did Europeans insert themselves into the Indian Ocean trading network, and what changes did they bring about?

SECTION FOCUS QUESTIONS

1. How did Swahili Coast traders link the East African interior to the Indian Ocean basin?

2. What factors account for the fall of Vijayanagara and the rise of the Mughals?

3. What factors enabled Europeans to take over key Indian Ocean trade networks?

4. Why was the tiny sultanate of Aceh able to hold out against European interlopers in early modern times?

MAKING CONNECTIONS

1. In what ways did Indian Ocean trade differ from the contemporary Atlantic slave trade (see Chapter 18)? What role did Africa play in each?

2. How did traditional kingdoms such as Vijayanagara differ from those of the Americas prior to the Spanish conquest (see Chapter 16)?

AT A CROSSROADS ▶

Court artists painted this 1588 Ottoman miniature to illustrate Suleiman the Magnificent's 1526 victory over Christian forces at the Battle of Mohacs, which left Hungary without a monarch and divided between the Habsburg and Ottoman empires. Traditional cavalry forces face off in the left foreground, but most prominent is the sultan himself in the upper right, on a white horse just behind a line of large Ottoman cannon. (Topkapi Palace Museum, Istanbul/ Giraudon/Bridgeman Art Library.)

Consolidation and Conflict in Europe and the Greater Mediterranean

1450–1750

The Power of the Ottoman Empire, 1453–1750

FOCUS What factors explain the rise of the vast Ottoman Empire and its centuries-long endurance?

Europe Divided, 1500–1650

FOCUS What sparked division in Europe after 1500, and why did this trend persist?

European Innovations in Science and Government, 1550–1750

FOCUS What factors enabled European scientific and political innovations in the early modern period?

COUNTERPOINT: The Barbary Pirates

FOCUS Why were the Barbary pirates of North Africa able to thrive from 1500 to 1800 despite Ottoman and European overseas expansion?

In 1590, forty-three-year-old Miguel de Cervantes Saavedra, an office clerk working in the Spanish city of Seville, applied for a colonial service job in South America. Such assignments usually went to applicants with nobler connections than Cervantes enjoyed, but perhaps he hoped his military service would count in his favor. Cervantes had been wounded in a major naval conflict, the Battle of Lepanto, in 1571, fighting against the mighty Ottomans. He also suffered five years of captivity in Algiers as the prisoner of North Africa's Barbary pirates. Despite all of this, he was turned down.

Before taking up his desk job in Seville, Cervantes had tried his hand at writing, publishing a modestly successful novel in 1585. Spain at this time was a literary leader in Europe. The novels, plays, and poems of Spain's "Golden Century" drew on medieval models, but they were both enriched and transformed by the changes resulting from overseas colonization and religious upheavals. Playwrights and poets rewrote the conquests of the Aztecs and Incas as tragedies, and one writer, "El Inca" Garcilaso de la Vega, son of a Spanish conquistador and an Inca princess, thrilled his Spanish readers with tales of a

BACKSTORY

Europe and the greater Mediterranean basin gradually recovered from the devastating Black Death of 1347–1350 (see Chapter 15), but the inhabitants of this geographically divided region faced many challenges at the start of the early modern period. Christian Europeans grew increasingly intolerant of religious diversity. In the most extreme case, Iberian Muslims and Jews were forced to convert to Catholicism or leave the peninsula after 1492, prompting a great diaspora, or scattering, largely into Morocco and Ottoman lands, but also into Italy, France, and northern Europe. Resource-poor and avid for Asian trade goods and precious metals, western Europeans raced to develop new technologies of war and long-distance transport to compete with one another as well as with non-Europeans abroad. In contrast, the Muslim Ottomans of the eastern Mediterranean had been expanding their tributary land empire since the fourteenth century. By the later fifteenth century they would take to the sea to extend their conquests into the Mediterranean and the Indian Ocean.

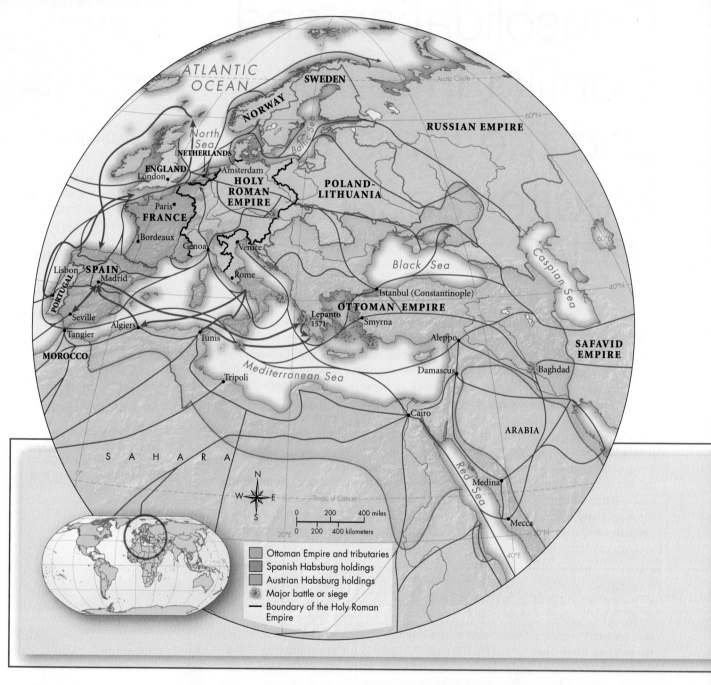

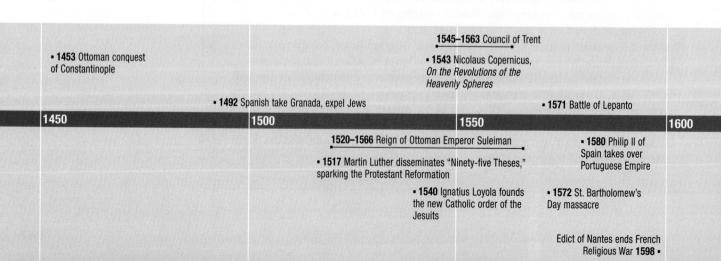

- **1453** Ottoman conquest of Constantinople

- **1492** Spanish take Granada, expel Jews

1545–1563 Council of Trent

- **1543** Nicolaus Copernicus, *On the Revolutions of the Heavenly Spheres*

- **1571** Battle of Lepanto

| 1450 | 1500 | 1550 | 1600 |

1520–1566 Reign of Ottoman Emperor Suleiman

- **1517** Martin Luther disseminates "Ninety-five Theses," sparking the Protestant Reformation

- **1540** Ignatius Loyola founds the new Catholic order of the Jesuits

- **1580** Philip II of Spain takes over Portuguese Empire

- **1572** St. Bartholomew's Day massacre

Edict of Nantes ends French Religious War **1598** -

vanished Inca paradise. He based his best-selling *Royal Commentaries of the Incas*, composed in the Spanish countryside, on stories told by his mother in Cuzco.

Cervantes never crossed the Atlantic, but he found plenty to inspire him in the vibrant crossroads city of Seville, Spain's largest city with over one hundred thousand inhabitants. Yet as Cervantes' 1605 masterpiece, *Don Quixote*, revealed, it was the author's experiences as a prisoner in Algiers that most prepared him to bridge cultures and upend literary conventions. Although regarded as the quintessential Spanish novel—set in the Spanish countryside, with poor Catholic villagers as its central characters—*Don Quixote* includes long passages describing the many peoples, especially forced converts to Christianity from Islam and renegade Christians living in North Africa, who routinely crossed borders and seas, risking their lives to find love or maintain family fortunes. Cervantes died in 1616, in the midst of a brief truce between Spain and its greatest rival of the day, the emerging Dutch Republic. "El Inca" Garcilaso died the same year.

Europe and the greater Mediterranean in the age of Cervantes was, like the Indian Ocean basin, home to diverse peoples who had long been linked by deep and multifaceted connections. Yet it was increasingly divided by political, religious, and ethnic conflict. Christians fought Jews and Muslims, and, in the movements known as the Protestant and Catholic reformations, one another. Emerging national identities based on language and shared religion began to harden, even as local and regional trade increased. Christian Europe viewed Ottoman expansion with alarm, and fear of growing Muslim power contributed to rising tension and conflict between Christians and Muslims. Piracy flourished from the Atlantic to the Indian Ocean, and war raged from the Low Countries to the Balkans, eventually engulfing nearly all of Europe by 1618. In the course of the Thirty Years' War that followed, Catholics and Protestants, led by ambitious princes, slaughtered each other by the tens of thousands. Economic woes compounded the chaos, exacerbated by a sudden drop in silver revenues from

MAPPING THE WORLD

Europe and the Greater Mediterranean, c. 1600

The Mediterranean was an ancient global crossroads, and its role in connecting Africa, Asia, and Europe only intensified during early modern times. After 1450, African gold and Spanish-American silver lubricated trade, but they also financed warfare, notably an increasingly bitter rivalry between the Ottoman and Habsburg empires. The period also witnessed the rise of the so-called Barbary pirates, based mostly in Algiers, Tunis, and Tripoli, who offered only a tenuous allegiance to the Ottomans against their Christian foes. Mediterranean trade, sea routes to the Indian Ocean, and overland routes to East Asia were all increasingly tied to Europe's North Atlantic trade. As trade grew, conflict became ever more intense.

ROUTES ▼

— Major trade route

→ Voyages of Miguel de Cervantes Saavedra, c. 1571–1609

→ Route of the Spanish Armada, 1588

1618–1648 Thirty Years' War

1642–1646 English Civil War

▪ **1687** Isaac Newton, *Principia Mathematica*

▪ **1688** Glorious Revolution in England

1650   **1700**   **1750**

1643–1715 Reign of Louis XIV of France

▪ **1640** Portugal wins independence from Spain

▪ **1683** Ottomans defeated in Vienna by Polish-Austrian alliance

1701–1714 War of the Spanish Succession

the mines of Spanish America. Prolonged cold weather led to a cycle of failed harvests. Amid growing anxiety, large-scale rebellions broke out from Scotland to the Persian frontier.

Out of this prolonged period of religious, political, and economic instability, which some historians have labeled the "seventeenth-century crisis," came profound and eventually world-changing innovations in science, government, and the economy. The combination of growing religious skepticism, deep interest in the physical world sparked by overseas discoveries, and new optical technologies led a small cluster of European intellectuals to turn to scientific inquiry, initiating what later would be hailed as a "scientific revolution." Political innovations included absolutism and constitutionalism, two novel approaches to monarchy. Whatever their political form, nearly all of Europe's competing states engaged in overseas expansion, using the Atlantic as a gateway to the wider world. With the support of their governments, merchants and investors in western Europe launched new efforts to challenge the long-established global claims of the Spanish and Portuguese.

Christian Europe's overseas expansion was driven in part by the rise of its powerful Sunni Muslim neighbor, the Ottoman Empire. The Ottoman state, which by 1550 straddled Europe, the Middle East, North Africa, Arabia, and parts of Central Asia, was strategically located between three vast and ancient maritime trade zones. To the west lay the Mediterranean, Atlantic, and all of Europe; to the east and north, the Silk Road and Black Sea region; and to the south, East Africa, Arabia, and the vast Indian Ocean basin. Along with such major commercial crossroads as Istanbul (formerly Constantinople), Aleppo, and Cairo, the Ottomans controlled key religious pilgrimage sites, including Mecca and Jerusalem. No early modern European state approached the Ottomans' size, military might, or cultural and religious diversity, and no contemporary Islamic empire, not even the mighty Mughals, did as much to offset rising Christian European sea power. The Ottomans were arguably the most versatile of the early modern "gunpowder empires."

OVERVIEW QUESTIONS

The major global development in this chapter: Early modern Europe's increasing competition and division in the face of Ottoman expansion.

As you read, consider:

1. To what degree was religious diversity embraced or rejected in early modern Europe and the greater Mediterranean, and why?

2. How did Christian Europe's gunpowder-fueled empires compare with that of the Ottomans?

3. What accounts for the rise of science and capitalism in early modern western Europe?

The Power of the Ottoman Empire 1453–1750

FOCUS

What factors explain the rise of the vast Ottoman Empire and its centuries-long endurance?

Founded by mounted Turkic warriors in the early fourteenth century, the Ottoman Empire grew rapidly after its stunning 1453 capture of the Byzantine capital, Constantinople (see Chapter 15). As in Mughal India, gunpowder weapons introduced by Christian Europeans sped the Ottomans' rise and helped them spread their dominions deep into Europe as well as the Middle East and North Africa. The Ottomans also took to the sea, challenging the Venetians, Habsburgs, and other contenders in the Mediterranean, as well as the Portuguese in the Indian Ocean. But it was arguably clever governance, minimal trade restrictions, and religious tolerance, not gunpowder weapons or naval proficiency, that permitted this most durable of Islamic empires to survive until the early twentieth century.

Tools of Empire

As we saw in Chapter 15, Mehmed II's conquest in 1453 of Constantinople not only shocked the Christian world but also marked a dramatic shift in the Ottoman enterprise. The sultans no longer viewed themselves as the roving holy warriors of Osman's day. Instead, they took on the identity of Islamic rulers with supreme authority over a multinational empire at the crossroads of Europe and Asia.

Devshirme System

Like other expansive realms, the Ottoman state faced the challenge of governing its frontier regions. To maintain control over the provinces, the Ottomans drew on the janissary corps, elite infantry and bureaucrats who owed direct allegiance to the sultan. Within a century of the capture of Constantinople, the janissaries were recruited nearly exclusively through the **devshirme** (dev-SHEER-may), the conscription of Christian youths from eastern Europe. Chosen for their good looks and fine physiques, these boys were converted to Islam and sent to farms to learn Turkish and to build up their bodies. The most promising were sent to Istanbul to learn Ottoman military, religious, and administrative techniques. Trained in Ottoman ways, educated in the use of advanced weaponry, and shorn of all family connections, the young men recruited through the devshirme were thus prepared to serve as janissaries wholly beholden to the sultan and dedicated to his service. In later years the janissaries would directly challenge the sultan's power, but for much of the early modern era, these crack soldiers and able administrators extended and supported Ottoman rule. A few rose to the rank of Grand Vizier (roughly, "Prime Minister").

Timar System

The **timar** system of land grants given in compensation for military service was another key means through which the Ottomans managed the provinces while ensuring that armed forces remained powerful. It was similar to Mughal India's *parganas* and Spanish America's *encomiendas* in that all three imperial systems were put in place to reward frontier warriors while preventing them from becoming independent aristocrats. Sultans snatched timars and gave them to others when their holders failed to serve in ongoing wars, an incentive to keep fighting. Even in times of stability, the timars were referred to as "the fruits of war." Timar-holders slowly turned new territories into provinces. Able administrators were rewarded with governorships. Although the timar and devshirme systems changed over time, it was these early innovations in frontier governance and military recruitment that stabilized and buttressed Ottoman rule in the face of succession crises, regional rebellions, natural disasters, and other shocks.

Expansion and Consolidation

Mehmed II's 1453 capture of Constantinople earned him the nickname "Conqueror." By 1464, Mehmed had added Athens, Serbia, and Bosnia to the Ottoman domain, and by 1475, the Golden Horde khanate of the Crimean peninsula was paying tribute to the Ottomans (see Map 20.1). In the Mediterranean, powerful Venice was put on notice that its days of dominance were coming to an end, and the Genoese were driven from their trading posts in the Black Sea. In 1480 the Ottomans attacked Otranto, in southern Italy, and in 1488 they struck Malta, a key Mediterranean island between Sicily and North Africa. At the imperial center, Constantinople, now named Istanbul, became a reflection of Mehmed's power, and also his piety. The city's horizon was soon dotted with hundreds of domes and minarets. With over one hundred thousand

devshirme The Ottomans' conscription of Christian male youths from eastern Europe to serve in the military or administration.

timar A land grant given in compensation for military service by the Ottoman sultan to a soldier.

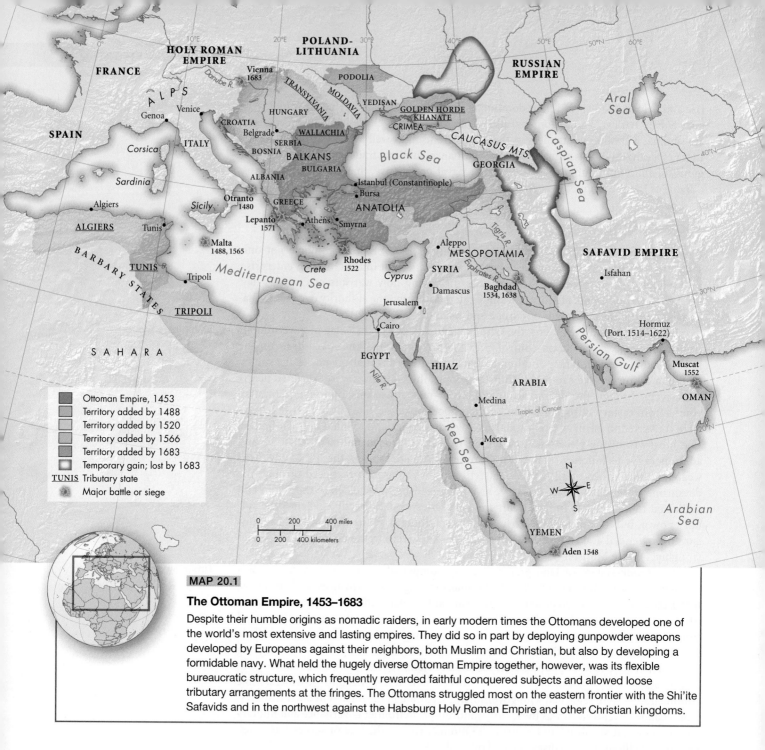

MAP 20.1

The Ottoman Empire, 1453–1683

Despite their humble origins as nomadic raiders, in early modern times the Ottomans developed one of the world's most extensive and lasting empires. They did so in part by deploying gunpowder weapons developed by Europeans against their neighbors, both Muslim and Christian, but also by developing a formidable navy. What held the hugely diverse Ottoman Empire together, however, was its flexible bureaucratic structure, which frequently rewarded faithful conquered subjects and allowed loose tributary arrangements at the fringes. The Ottomans struggled most on the eastern frontier with the Shi'ite Safavids and in the northwest against the Habsburg Holy Roman Empire and other Christian kingdoms.

inhabitants by the time of the sultan's death in 1481, Istanbul was one of the largest capitals in Eurasia.

The Ottomans turned newly obtained European artillery and highly trained janissary fighters on Islamic neighbors such as the Safavids and Mamluks in Syria and Egypt. Under Selim I (r. 1512–1520), called "the Grim," both were overwhelmed, although the Safavids would continue to challenge Ottoman power. Ottoman influence now touched the shores of the Indian Ocean, where Selim and the Ottomans challenged Portuguese expansion. The Muslim holy cities of Medina and Mecca became Ottoman protectorates, a boon for the state's religious reputation. Ottoman control of the Arabian peninsula would not be challenged until the end of the eighteenth century by the Wahhabi Saudis (discussed in Chapter 23).

Reign of Suleiman the Magnificent

Christian Europe again felt the sting of Ottoman artillery under Selim's successor, Suleiman (soo-lay-MAHN) (r. 1520–1566), called "the Magnificent." Suleiman ended

Istanbul's Skyline

When the former Constantinople became the capital of the Ottoman Empire, its rulers and court patrons soon transformed its architecture and overall skyline. The domes in the foreground make up part of the formerly Christian basilica Hagia Sophia, which was transformed into a mosque after 1453. In the distance rises Istanbul's imposing Blue Mosque, built between 1609 and 1616 for Sultan Ahmed I. (Photo by Ketan Gajria.)

the first year of his reign with the capture of two more symbolic prizes, Belgrade and Rhodes. The former feat gave Suleiman near-total control of eastern Europe, and the latter gave him effective rule over the eastern Mediterranean. In the western Mediterranean, the sultan supported Muslim pirates such as the Barbarossa brothers of Algiers, who targeted Europeans and held thousands of Christian captives for ransom (see Counterpoint: The Barbary Pirates). In 1565 the Ottomans laid siege to Malta. Though ultimately unsuccessful, this huge expedition provided yet another display of "the Great Turk's" naval capacity.

As the siege of Malta and other gunpowder-fueled seaborne offensives attested, Suleiman was determined to challenge the Habsburg Holy Roman Empire, as was his successor, Selim II (r. 1566–1574). But the Ottomans were dealt a terrible blow in 1571 when Habsburg forces sponsored by Spain's Catholic king Philip II (r. 1556–1598) overpowered Selim's navy at the Battle of Lepanto off the Greek coast (see again Map 20.1). Some six thousand janissaries armed with matchlock handguns faced off against over twenty thousand similarly armed European recruits and missionaries, among them the future author of *Don Quixote*. The Christians prevailed and commemorated their victory against the "infidels" in artwork ranging from painting to tapestry.

Although the Battle of Lepanto marked the beginning of a general decline in Ottoman sea supremacy, Selim II's will was far from broken. His forces managed to capture Tunis and Cyprus, and the navy was quickly rebuilt. A poet praised the sultan's vision:

Conflict with the Catholic Habsburgs

> If it were not for the body of Sultan Selim,
> This generous king, this source of happiness
> The enemy would have occupied
> The country from one end to the other
> God would not have helped us.
> Neither would he have granted us conquest.[1]

Battle with the Habsburgs reached a crescendo with the 1683 siege of Vienna. Ottoman gun technology had kept pace with that of western Europe, and some observers claimed that Ottoman muskets in fact had better range and accuracy than those used by Vienna's defenders. Heavy siege artillery was not employed here on the scale regularly practiced in Persia and Mesopotamia, however, and this may have proved a fatal mistake. Ottoman attempts to mine and blow up Vienna's walls failed just as tens of thousands of allies led by the Polish king arrived to save the day for the Habsburgs. At least fifteen thousand Ottoman troops were killed. Never again would the Ottomans pose a serious threat to Christian Europe.

Conflict with the Shi'ite Safavids

To the east, war with Persia occupied the sultans' attention throughout the sixteenth century. Since 1500, Safavid shahs had incited rebellions against Ottoman rule in outlying provinces, denouncing its Sunni leadership as corrupt and illegitimate. The Ottomans responded by violently persecuting both rebels and many innocents caught in between. Under Suleiman, campaigns against the Safavids in the 1530s and 1540s were mostly successful thanks to new guns, but territorial advances proved difficult to sustain. As one Ottoman eyewitness put it in the 1550s, "The territories called Persia are much less fertile than our country; and further, it is the custom of the inhabitants, when their land is invaded, to lay waste and burn everything, and so force the enemy to retire through lack of food."[2] The Safavids were just far enough away to prove unconquerable, leaving intermediate cities such as Baghdad as the key battlegrounds (see Reading the Past: Weapons of Mass Destruction: Ottomans vs. Persians in Baghdad).

Beginning in the late 1570s, Murad III took advantage of Safavid political instability to expand Ottoman influence beyond the frontier established by Suleiman. By the time a peace was arranged in 1590, the Ottomans controlled Mesopotamia and had established a firm presence in the Caucasus region. Still, the empire was rocked in the decades around 1600 by price inflation caused by a massive influx of Spanish-American silver, which flowed into the empire from Europe in exchange for Ottoman silks and spices. Ottoman attempts to fix prices of basic commodities and reduce the silver content of their coins only worsened the problem, and troops facing food shortages and poor pay rioted.

Some historians have argued that the Ottoman Empire was in decline following the reign of Suleiman the Magnificent, even though expansion continued into the seventeenth century, beginning with a long struggle for Hungary (1593–1606). Like Habsburg Spain, also said to be in decline in this era despite its vast size and wealth, Ottoman efforts to conquer new lands increasingly ended in stalemate, with military expenses far exceeding the value of the territory gained. The crushing weight of rising costs forced sultans and viziers to make humiliating concessions. Among the worst of these were losses to the Safavids that amounted to a total reversal of Murad III's gains. Frontier setbacks were not always evident from the center. Istanbul, with some four hundred thousand inhabitants by this time, was by far Eurasia's largest and most opulent city.

Sultanate of the Women

Murad IV (r. 1623–1640) managed to recapture Baghdad and several other eastern losses, but a crippling succession crisis ensued. Only after 1648 was the matter settled, with seven-year-old Mehmed IV (r. 1648–1687) on the throne. A child emperor required interim rule by regency, and in this case Mehmed's mother, Turhan, took control after fighting off challenges from other powerful women at court whose sons claimed a right to the throne. As a result of this direct feminine management of the Ottoman Empire, analogous to that of much tinier Aceh in these years (see Chapter 19), the period of Turhan's regency has been called "the Sultanate of the Women."

Indeed, as the Ottoman realm consolidated, court women became a powerful political force, despite their strict seclusion from society. First, the politics of succession dictated close control over the sultan's sexual life. Women came to dominate this key arena as early as the mid-sixteenth century. It was not seductive young wives and concubines who counted most, but rather elder women, particularly the Queen Mother. Second, much like

READING THE PAST

Weapons of Mass Destruction: Ottomans vs. Persians in Baghdad

In 1722 an Afghan army invaded the Safavid Empire from the east, seized the capital of Isfahan, and repulsed an Ottoman invasion from the west. The ambitious Afghan warlord Nadir Shah took over. Until his murder in 1747 Nadir attacked virtually all of Persia's neighbors, including the Mughals, but spent most of his energies fighting the Ottomans. Below is an excerpt from a chronicle of Nadir's campaigns written in around 1733 by an Armenian participant, Abraham of Erevan.

> After laying siege to the city [Baghdad] for forty-eight days, Nadir received the twenty-five cannons that he had left behind in Zohab. They began to place the cannons and to fire on the city. Both sides exchanged cannon fire. Since the Ottoman cannons were larger than Nadir's, they were capable of hurtling larger cannon balls. One particular cannon, the largest, could hurl a cannon ball filled with approximately forty *okhas* [about one hundred pounds] of gunpowder. Although Nadir's forces were not concentrated in one area, such a cannon ball was fired from the fort. It exploded in the middle of the camp and killed one hundred troops. Seeing such casualties, Nadir moved the front further back. After that, the Ottoman cannon balls could not harm his troops, but neither could his cannon balls reach Baghdad. Thus they faced each other for fifty-five days without firing their artillery. The Ottomans then fired the large cannon once again, but the explosion damaged a wall of the fortifications and destroyed many houses, after which the Turks did not use it again. After fifty-five days of siege, the Ottomans, fully armed, made a sudden sortie with the intention of attacking the Persians. . . . The Pasha, however, remained in the city and did not permit the citizens to leave either, for half of them were Persians and he suspected that they would join the troops of Nadir.

> The minute Nadir saw that the Ottomans had attacked him, he moved his troops forward without his cannons. The Ottomans, who had brought ten loaded cannons with them, began to fire on the Persian forces. Nadir then divided his troops into four groups so that he would not subject his entire army to the cannon fire. Having used their guns, the Ottomans could not reload their cannons fast enough, and while they were busy reloading, the Persians fell upon them from four sides and stopped the enemy from using its firepower. The two armies clashed and began to slaughter each other with swords and muskets for some seven hours. Eight thousand Ottomans and six thousand Persians perished. The Ottoman army suffered a defeat and fled back into the fortress and did not venture out again.

Source: Abraham of Erevan, *History of the Wars (1721–1738)*, ed. and trans. George A. Bournoutian (Costa Mesa, CA: Mazda Publishers, 1999), 77–78.

EXAMINING THE EVIDENCE

1. What role did cities such as Baghdad play in the battles between the Ottomans and Persians?

2. How do battles such as this one reveal the advantages and drawbacks of heavy guns?

Nur Jahan in Mughal India, powerful Ottoman women were important patrons of the arts and of pious works, and they figured prominently in royal rituals and mosque and hospital construction. The sultan was the ultimate patriarch, but it was his larger family that constituted the model of Ottoman society. Documents reveal that the royal harem, source of much lurid speculation by Europeans, was in fact a kind of sacred, familial space, more haven than prison.

Daily Life in the Ottoman Empire

As in most early modern states, the vast majority of Ottoman subjects lived in the countryside and were peasants and herders. Urban society, by contrast, was hierarchical, divided by occupation. Beneath the Osman royal family was the *askeri* (AS-keh-ree),

Social Structure

Istanbul Street Scene

This rare sixteenth-century Ottoman street scene depicts men and women exchanging a variety of goods near the famous bazaar of Istanbul, formerly Constantinople. A proud merchant holds up a bouquet of flowers, and another weighs what may be almonds. Two women with different head coverings bring what appear to be ducks and bread for sale, while a woman in the left foreground seems to be making a cash purchase from a merchant balancing a basket of fruit or flowers on his head. The exchanges take place right next to the Column of Constantine, a relic of Roman rule under the city's namesake emperor. (The Art Archive/Museo Correr Venice/Alfredo Dagli Orti.)

Women's Experience

caravanserai A roadside inn for merchants on the Silk Road and other overland trade routes.

or "military" class, which was exempt from taxes and dependent on the sultan for their well-being. In addition to military leaders, the askeri included bureaucrats and *ulama*, religious scholars versed in Arabic and canon law. Whereas the Safavids considered religious authorities superior to the shahs, the Ottoman sultans only took the advice of their chief ulama—a distinction that persists today in Shi'ite and Sunni states. Beneath the askeri was a much broader class of taxpayers called *reaya* (RAH-ya), or "the flock." The reaya included everyone from common laborers and artisans to traders and merchants. Thanks to a long-established Ottoman tradition of meritocracy and inclusion, provincial members of the lower classes could make considerable gains in status through education or military service.

In the countryside, peasant farmers' and pastoralists' lives revolved around cycles of planting and harvest, seasonal movement of animal herds, and the rhythms of commerce and religious observance. Some men were drafted into military service, leaving women to manage households, herds, and farms. Women in both rural and urban contexts also engaged in export crafts such as silk weaving, carpet making, and ceramic manufacture. Thus, although few country folk of either gender experienced urban life for more than a few days in a lifetime, rural life in the Ottoman Empire was shaped by the larger forces of international trade and the demands of the Ottoman military.

More mobile by far were merchants, whose livelihood was considered highly respectable. The merchants of trading crossroads such as Aleppo, Damascus, Smyrna, and Cairo profited handsomely from their access to Asian and African luxuries. Ottoman taxes on trade were relatively low, and the empire rarely resorted to the burdensome wartime demands made by European states on their often less-well-regarded merchant communities. On the flip side, the Ottoman state invested little in trading infrastructure beyond maintenance of **caravanserais**, or travelers' lodges located along otherwise desolate trade routes. Like the Inca roadside inns taken over by the Spanish after conquest in 1532, these structures also served a military purpose.

Recent research has revealed that ordinary women under Ottoman rule, much like court women, enjoyed more power than previously thought. Women had rights to their own property and investments, fully protected by shari'a, or Islamic law, before, during, and after marriage. This was, however, a rigidly patriarchal society. Women were expected to marry, and when they did they had few legal rights in relation to their husbands, who were permitted multiple wives and could divorce them at any time. Although women were treated as inferiors under Ottoman rule, it is worth noting that they had greater access to divorce than women in most early modern European societies.

The religious diversity of their subjects led the Ottomans to compromise in matters of gender. Islamic judges, or *qadis*, occasionally intervened in Christian married life, for example. Some Christian women won divorce by converting to Islam, as happened in the following case from Cyprus, decided in 1609: "Husna, daughter of Murad, Armenian wife, says before her husband Mergeri, son of Kuluk, Armenian: 'He always treats me cruelly. I do not want him.' He denies that. But now Husna becomes honored with Islam. After she takes the name Ayisha, her husband is invited to Islam, but he does not accept, so Ayisha's separation is ordered."[3] Although such conversions could be insincere, it is certain that religious diversity and legal oversight under Ottoman rule increased the range of options for female victims of domestic oppression.

Although devoutly Muslim at its core, the Ottoman state, with some 40 million subjects by the mid-seventeenth century, was at least as tolerant of religious diversity as the Islamic Mughal Empire, with policies similarly dictated by a practical desire to gain the cooperation of its diverse subjects. Religious tolerance and coexistence were most tested in frontier districts such as Cyprus and the Balkans. A description of Belgrade from 1660 illustrates just how diverse a frontier city could be: "On the banks of the river Sava there are three Gypsy neighborhoods, and on the banks of the Danube there are three neighborhoods of Greek unbelievers [i.e., Christians], as well as Serbs and Bulgarians also living in three neighborhoods. Right by the fortress is a neighborhood of Jews, those belonging to the seven communities known as the Karaim Jews. There is also a neighborhood of Armenian unbelievers. . . . All the rest are Muslim neighborhoods, so that families of the followers of Muhammad possess all the best, the most spacious and the airiest parts, located on the high or middle ground of the city."[4] Converts to Islam gained tax benefits (plus residential preferences, apparently), but punitive measures to force subjects to convert to the state religion were never used.

Religious Tolerance

Many Jews in the Ottoman Empire maintained their religious independence permanently. Some Jewish communities were centuries old and had local roots, but many more came as *Sephardim*, refugees from Iberian expulsions in the late fifteenth and early sixteenth centuries. Sephardic physicians, merchants, and tax collectors were a common sight in the capital city of Istanbul, and by the later sixteenth century many Ottoman towns had full-fledged Jewish communities. Members of the prominent Jewish Mendes family served as merchants, bankers, and advisers to the sultan in the sixteenth and seventeenth centuries.

In large part because of its incorporative nature and flexible structures, the Ottoman state proved one of the most durable in world history. Gunpowder weapons, though always important, were most critical in the early phases of expansion. Individual rulers varied widely in terms of aptitude and ambition, but the state itself remained quite stable. Fierce allegiance to Sunni Islam and control of its key shrines lent the Ottomans religious clout, yet their system of governance did not persecute Jews, Christians, or others who followed the state's rules regarding non-Muslims. Shi'ite Muslims faced more difficulties, by contrast, and this religious schism fueled a lasting rivalry with neighboring Persia.

Ottoman Rule: A Summing Up

Finally, in the realm of commerce, powerful merchants and trade guilds could be found in several Ottoman cities, notably Aleppo, but overseas ventures and entrepreneurial activities remained limited, at most sizable family businesses (see Lives and Livelihoods: Ottoman Coffeehouse Owners and Patrons). The state placed minimal restrictions on trade and provided some infrastructure in the form of caravanserais, but there was no policy equivalent to Iberian support of overseas commerce in the form of trading forts and convoys. In this regard the Ottoman Empire was profoundly different from the rising "merchant empires" of western Europe, where an increasingly global and highly competitive mercantile capitalism hitched state interests directly to those of bankers and merchants.

Ottoman Coffeehouse Owners and Patrons

Ottoman Coffeehouse

This late-sixteenth-century miniature depicts a packed Ottoman coffeehouse. The patrons and serving staff all appear to be male, but they represent many classes and age groups, and possibly several religious traditions. In the upper middle, elite men with large turbans are conversing; a worker prepares a tray of cups in a small room to their right. In the lower middle, one man appears to be speaking as others turn their attention to a backgammon game under way near his feet. When rebellions or other political troubles brewed, coffeehouses were a source of concern for Ottoman authorities. (The Trustees of the Chester Beatty Library, Dublin.)

An institution of modern life in much of the world today, the coffeehouse, or café, originated on the southern fringes of the Ottoman Empire in around 1450. The coffee bean, harvested from a small tree that scientists would later call *Coffea arabica*, had long been roasted, ground, and brewed in the Ethiopian and Somalian highlands of East Africa. At some point, coffee was transplanted to the highlands of Yemen, at the southern tip of the Arabian peninsula (see again Map 20.1). Here members of Sufi Muslim brotherhoods adopted coffee drinking to aid them in their all-night meditations and chants. Merchants sailing north on the Red Sea carried the new habit-forming beverage to Cairo and Constantinople. From there it spread quickly throughout the entire Mediterranean commercial world. By the late seventeenth century, there were coffeehouses in all the major cities of western Europe. By the early eighteenth century, coffee itself was planted in the tropical Americas.

Despite coffee's sobering effects, many *imams*, or religious scholars, were initially skeptical of its propriety. The

Europe Divided 1500–1650

Europe in the age of Ottoman ascendancy was diverse, fractured, and dynamic. By 1500, commerce and literacy were on the rise, populations were growing, and armies of craftsmen were perfecting technologies of warfare, manufacture, and navigation. Savvy publishers capitalized on demand for fiction long before Cervantes, but they also made available new thoughts on religion and science as well as new translations of classical works. Thus, the growth of literacy helped unsettle old notions of time, space, and human potential. A less visible transformation was taking place in the countryside, where traditional, reciprocal relationships tying peasants to feudal lords were increasingly replaced with commercial ones. Most notable in western Europe, especially in England, this shift entailed a rise in renting, sharecropping, and wage work, a proliferation of market-oriented farms owned by urban elites, and the privatization of lands formerly enjoyed as common community resources. Peasants displaced by this early capitalist restructuring of the countryside increasingly filled Europe's cities. Some went overseas to try their luck in the colonies.

word coffee apparently derives from *qahwa*, one of several Arabic terms for wine. Imams used this word since the beverage altered consciousness in a noticeable, if not necessarily debilitating, way. Eventually, coffee was decreed an acceptable drink in accordance with scripture, and was widely consumed during fasts such as Ramadan. Both men and women were allowed to drink coffee, but several *fatwas*, or religious prohibitions, were issued against female coffee vendors in the early sixteenth century. As a result, both the public sale and public consumption of coffee became male preserves in the Ottoman Empire.

Coffee's troubles were far from over. If coffee itself was declared wholesome, the places where it was commonly consumed were not. Coffeehouses, sometimes run by non-Muslims, proliferated in major market cities such as Cairo by the early 1500s, drawing hoards of lower-class traders, artisans, and even slaves. Unable to suppress the café even at the core of their empire, Ottoman religious leaders simply denounced them as places of iniquity, dens of sinners. Female musicians played and danced scandalously in some, conservative clerics argued, while other cafés promoted homosexual prostitution. Some coffeehouses served as well-known hangouts for opium and hashish addicts, further tainting their reputation. Then came the vice of tobacco smoking, introduced from the Americas by European merchants in the early seventeenth century.

As later proved true in Europe, there were other reasons to fear the coffeehouse. Ottoman officials suspected the cafés as hotbeds of insurrection and treason. Still, they proved impossible to suppress, and coffee vendors quickly sprang back into action when the authorities closed them down. The Ottomans finally relented, deciding that the coffeehouse was an ideal place to gauge popular reactions to state policy and planting spies. In an era before restaurants, and in a religious climate hostile to alcohol and hence taverns, the coffeehouse met a variety of social needs. It was first a place where traveling merchants far from the comforts of home could exchange information, buy their associates a few rounds of satisfying coffee, and perhaps relax with a game of backgammon and a water-cooled smoke. For men of the working class, the coffeehouse became a place of rest and collegiality, and occasionally of political ferment.

QUESTIONS TO CONSIDER

1. How did Islamic clerics' attitude toward coffee change? What factors might account for this shift?

2. How and why did the Ottoman state come to accept the coffeehouse as a social institution?

For Further Information:

Hattox, Ralph. *Coffee and Coffee Houses: The Origins of a Social Beverage in the Medieval Near East.* Seattle: University of Washington Press, 1985.

Schivelbusch, Wolfgang. *Tastes of Paradise: A Social History of Spices, Stimulants, and Intoxicants.* Translated by David Jacobson. New York: Vintage, 1993.

Everyday Life in Early Modern Europe

Historians estimate that Europe in 1492 had a population of about 70 million, or slightly more than the population of the Americas just prior to Columbus's arrival. By 1550, Europe counted some 85 million inhabitants, and it was still growing rapidly. This population increase was mostly due to reduced mortality rather than increased births. Unlike larger Ming China and Mughal India, Europe's high growth rate was not sustained. A series of epidemics and climatic events beginning in around 1600, coupled with the effects of the Thirty Years' War (1618–1648) and numerous other conflicts, led to population stagnancy and even decline. Europe's population in 1630 was below 80 million, and would not reach 100 million until just before 1700.

The Columbian Exchange was largely responsible for the sixteenth-century population increase. In both city and countryside, American crops radically altered European diets after 1500. Maize, potatoes, tomatoes, capsicum peppers, and many other foods reordered both peasant and elite tastes and needs. In some cases this sped population growth, and in others it simply spiced up an otherwise bland diet. Potatoes came to be associated with Ireland and

Changing Patterns of Consumption

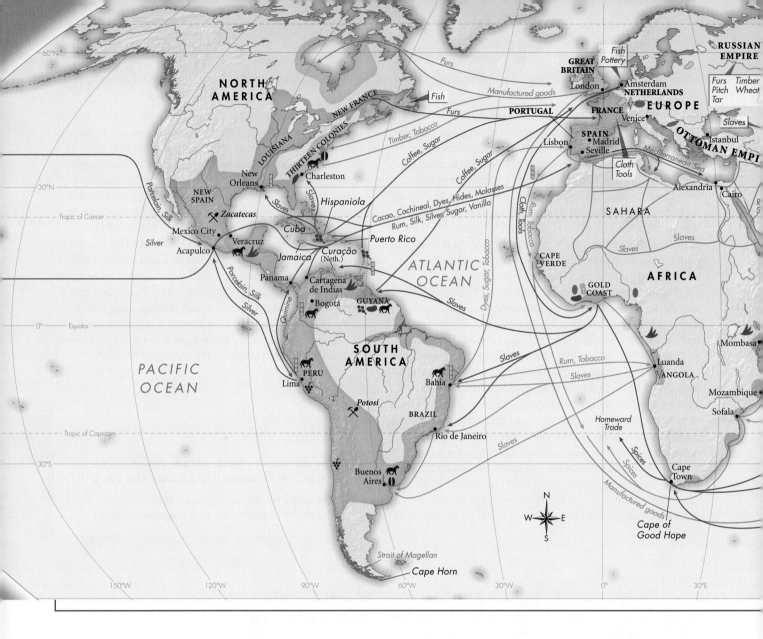

paprika with Hungary and Spain, but these and other American foods were widely embraced and helped spur an increasingly sophisticated consumer culture. American-grown sugar, tobacco, and later chocolate, vanilla, and coffee also figured prominently in Europe's taste revolution, as did Asian-grown tea and a host of exotic spices. European consumers also demanded new drugs such as opium and quinine bark, and merchants who trafficked in these and other tropical goods often made enormous profits. Thus, Europe's new connection with the Americas had a profound impact on its population, culture, and economy (see Map 20.2).

Environmental Transformations

The rise of commercial farming and peasant displacement, as well as overseas expansion, transformed ecosystems. Throughout Europe, more and more forest was cleared. Some princes passed decrees to limit deforestation, usually to preserve hunting grounds rather than for the good of the forest itself, but peasants still entered reserves in search of fuel and timber. Laws against such common use did little to relieve the stress, turning environmental problems into social ones. Shipbuilders, metalsmiths, and construction workers consumed forest as well, and wars and fires destroyed still more. By 1500, many Mediterranean cities, and even some northern European ones, relied on imported wood, sometimes looking as far afield as the Americas for new supplies. Not all environmental transformations were negative, however. The Dutch improved transportation by building canals and reclaimed land for agriculture from the sea by erecting dikes and filling wetlands.

Life Expectancy and Marriage Patterns

More people than ever crowded into European cities. Naples, London, and Paris were each home to more than two hundred thousand inhabitants by 1600. Nearly a dozen other

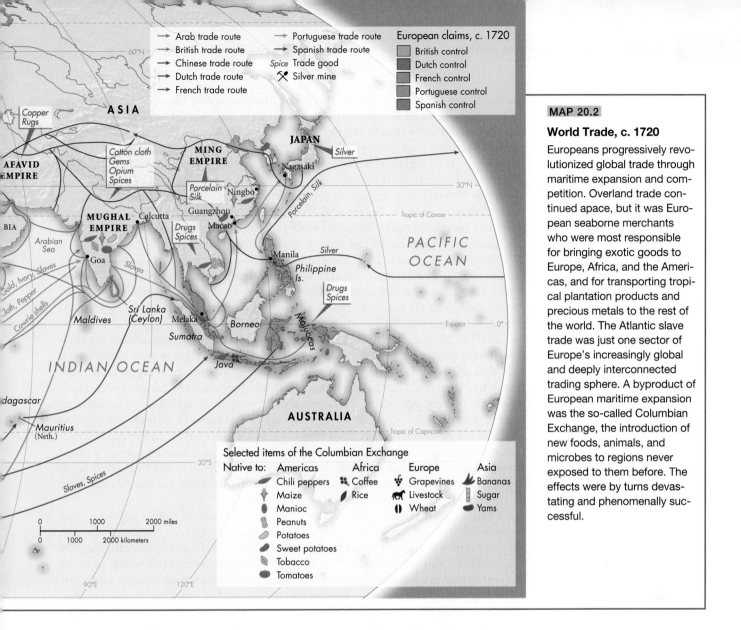

Legend (map):

- → Arab trade route
- → British trade route
- → Chinese trade route
- → Dutch trade route
- → French trade route
- → Portuguese trade route
- → Spanish trade route
- *Spice* Trade good
- ✕ Silver mine

European claims, c. 1720
- British control
- Dutch control
- French control
- Portuguese control
- Spanish control

ASIA

Copper Rugs

AFAVID EMPIRE

Cotton cloth, Gems, Opium, Spices

MING EMPIRE

JAPAN

Silver

Nagasaki

Porcelain, Silk

Ningbo

Guangzhou

Macao

Porcelain, Silk

PACIFIC OCEAN

30°N

Tropic of Cancer

MUGHAL EMPIRE

Calcutta

Arabian Sea

Drugs, Spices

Goa

Slaves

Silver

Manila

Philippine Is.

Gold, Ivory, Slaves

Cloth, Pepper

Cowrie shells

Maldives

Sri Lanka (Ceylon)

Melaka

Sumatra

Borneo

Moluccas

Java

Drugs, Spices

Equator   0°

INDIAN OCEAN

Madagascar

Mauritius (Neth.)

Slaves, Spices

AUSTRALIA

Tropic of Capricorn

30°S

90°E   120°E

0   1000   2000 miles
0   1000   2000 kilometers

Selected items of the Columbian Exchange

Native to:

Americas	Africa	Europe	Asia
Chili peppers	Coffee	Grapevines	Bananas
Maize	Rice	Livestock	Sugar
Manioc		Wheat	Yams
Peanuts			
Potatoes			
Sweet potatoes			
Tobacco			
Tomatoes			

MAP 20.2

World Trade, c. 1720

Europeans progressively revolutionized global trade through maritime expansion and competition. Overland trade continued apace, but it was European seaborne merchants who were most responsible for bringing exotic goods to Europe, Africa, and the Americas, and for transporting tropical plantation products and precious metals to the rest of the world. The Atlantic slave trade was just one sector of Europe's increasingly global and deeply interconnected trading sphere. A byproduct of European maritime expansion was the so-called Columbian Exchange, the introduction of new foods, animals, and microbes to regions never exposed to them before. The effects were by turns devastating and phenomenally successful.

cities in Iberia, the Netherlands, and Italy were close behind, with populations over one hundred thousand. Still, the vast majority of Europeans remained in the countryside. Life for most, including the nobility, was short. A lucky few survived into their eighties and even nineties in both urban and rural settings, but high infant mortality yielded overall life expectancies of only eighteen to thirty-six years.

Most early modern Europeans did not rush to marry, nor were they compelled to enter arranged marriages, as in some Asian societies. Women were between twenty and twenty-five, on average, when they married. Men married slightly later, between twenty-three and twenty-seven, in part due to itinerant work and military obligations. Relatively few children were born out of wedlock, at least according to surviving church records, but many were conceived before marriage. Most partners could expect to be widowed within twenty years, in which time half a couple's offspring would probably also have died. Moreover, one in ten women died in childbirth. In Europe, as in much of the world at this time, the prospect of death was never far away.

Protestant and Catholic Reformations

Like Islam, Christianity had long been subject to disagreements and schisms. Yet the critiques of Roman Catholicism presented by several sixteenth-century northern European theologians marked the deepest split thus far. Catholic reformers beginning with the German monk Martin Luther argued that the church had so deviated from early Christian

661

teachings that only radical reform could save the institution. For such reformers, the evident corruption and worldliness of the church were symptoms of a much deeper problem. In their view, the church had drifted into profound doctrinal and theological error. Inspired by a newfound faith in the individual that had its roots in Renaissance humanism (see Chapter 15), Luther and his followers emphasized the individual's ability to interpret scripture and communicate directly with God, without the intercession of priestly intermediaries. Although their opposition to Church teachings was theological, its implications were profoundly political. Outraged Catholic officials branded Luther and his followers Protestant (or protesting) heretics, and much of Europe fell into a century of bloody conflict fueled by religious hatred (see Map 20.3).

The Protestant Challenge

The challenge mounted by Luther amplified old complaints. Many ordinary people had grown dissatisfied with the Roman Catholic Church, particularly in northern Europe. Widespread abuse of benefices, or parish territories, reached a breaking point in the years around 1500, with far too many church officeholders concerned only with the financial rewards associated with their positions.

In 1517 Luther circulated "Ninety-five Theses"—propositions for academic debate— in which he charged that church policy encouraged priests to ignore their parishioners, keep concubines, and concentrate on money-grubbing. Worse, according to Luther, the church had corrupted Christian teachings on sin and forgiveness by inventing Purgatory, a spiritual holding pen where the deceased were purged of their sins before entering Heaven. Luther denounced the widespread sale of **indulgences**, written receipts that promised the payer early release from Purgatory, as a fraud. Heaven, Luther claimed, was the destination of the faithful, not the wealthy or gullible. Such teachings struck a chord among oppressed German peasants, many of whom took up arms in a 1525 rebellion. A social conservative, Luther withheld support from the uprising, but the revolutionary potential of Protestant Christianity was now revealed.

Church fathers balked at the notion of reform and ordered Luther defrocked and excommunicated. He responded by breaking away to form his own "Lutheran" church. Critiques similar to Luther's issued from the pens of the Swiss Protestant Ulrich Zwingli in 1523 and France's John Calvin in 1537. By the 1550s, Protestantism in a variety of forms was widespread in northern Europe, and its democratic and antiauthoritarian undercurrents soon yielded radical and unexpected political results. Still, most Europeans remained Catholic, revealing a deep, conservative countercurrent. That countercurrent soon resurfaced with a vengeance, although Catholicism, too, would be transformed.

Anglican Protestant Church

Another major schism occurred in 1534 when England's King Henry VIII declared his nation Protestant. Although Henry broke with the church for personal and political reasons rather than theological ones (the king wanted a divorce that the pope refused to grant), Anglican Protestantism was quickly embraced as the new state religion. Critics were silenced by Henry's execution of England's most prominent Catholic intellectual, Sir Thomas More, author of *Utopia* (1517). As in central and northern Europe, however, this early, mostly peaceful break hardly marked the end of Catholicism in England.

Founding of the Jesuit Order

The Catholic Church's leaders responded to Protestantism first with stunned disbelief, then vengeful anger. Some among the outraged Catholic majority launched strong but peaceful assaults. In Spain, for example, a Basque soldier calling himself Ignatius of Loyola became a priest and in 1534 founded a new religious order. Approved by the pope in 1540, the Society of Jesus, or Jesuits, soon became the Catholic Church's greatest educators and wealthiest property managers. More importantly for global history, they set out as missionaries to head off Protestant initiatives overseas. Within a few decades of Loyola's founding of the order there were Jesuit preachers in places as far-flung as Brazil, West Africa, Ceylon, and Japan (see Seeing the Past: Gift Clocks for the Emperors of China). Others stuck closer to home and won back converts in central Europe on the eve of the Thirty Years' War.

In the face of the Protestant challenge, some high officials within the church called for self-examination, and even the pope ultimately agreed that it was time for the church to

indulgence In early modern Europe, a note sold by the Catholic Church to speed a soul's exit from Purgatory.

MAP 20.3 **Protestant and Catholic Reformations in Europe**

In the midst of early overseas expansion, a great schism among Christians emerged in Europe. What Protestants called the Reformation was a fundamental questioning of Roman Catholic doctrine and practice. The dispute quickly produced violence and led some kingdoms, such as England, to break entirely from papal authority. France dissolved into civil war pitting Catholics against Protestants, and Spain and Portugal used their Inquisitions to persecute Protestants as heretics. A Catholic Reformation sought to reform and strengthen the church, but conflict continued to bubble up, leading soon after 1600 to the disastrous Thirty Years' War, the most deadly for civilians yet experienced in world history.

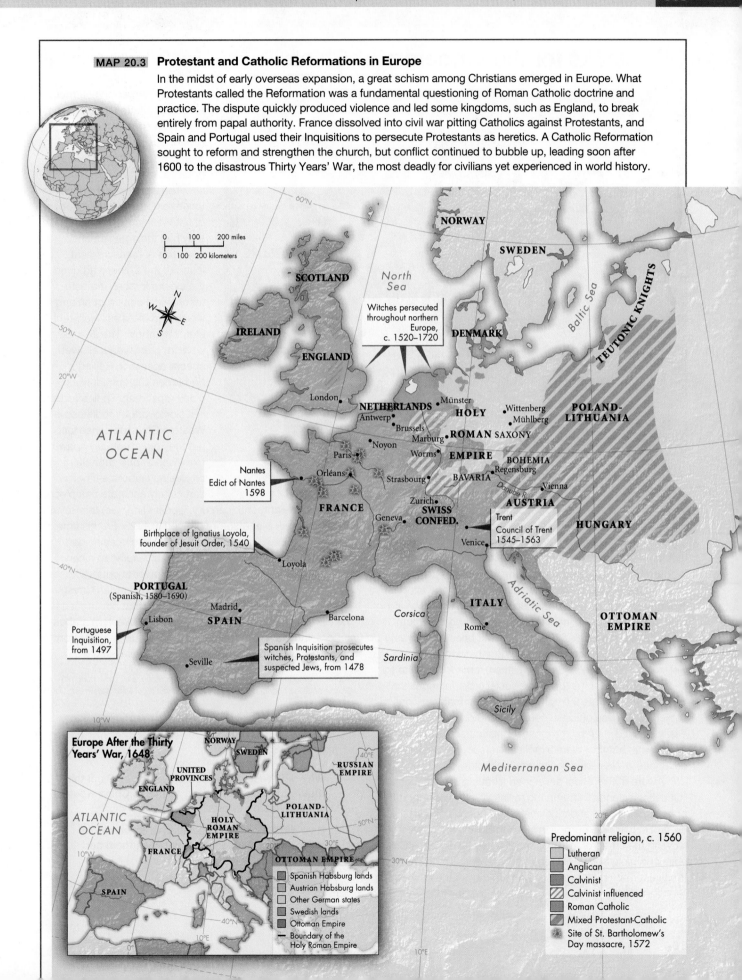

Witches persecuted throughout northern Europe, c. 1520–1720

Nantes
Edict of Nantes
1598

Birthplace of Ignatius Loyola, founder of Jesuit Order, 1540

Trent
Council of Trent
1545–1563

Portuguese Inquisition, from 1497

Spanish Inquisition prosecutes witches, Protestants, and suspected Jews, from 1478

PORTUGAL
(Spanish, 1580–1690)

Europe After the Thirty Years' War, 1648

Spanish Habsburg lands
Austrian Habsburg lands
Other German states
Swedish lands
Ottoman Empire
— Boundary of the Holy Roman Empire

Predominant religion, c. 1560

Lutheran
Anglican
Calvinist
Calvinist influenced
Roman Catholic
Mixed Protestant-Catholic
Site of St. Bartholomew's Day massacre, 1572

Gift Clocks for the Emperors of China

Courting the Qing: European Gift Clocks in the Forbidden City (The Palace Museum, Beijing/ChinaStock.)

With the exception of raw silver, China had little need of products introduced by Europeans hoping to trade for silk, porcelain, and eventually, tea. This presented a great problem for merchants short of silver, but it also challenged early modern European missionaries. The first Jesuits arrived in China in the 1550s, barely a decade after the pope's formal recognition of their order. They spent their first years trying to win poor converts inhabiting the cities along the South China Sea, but by the 1580s some Jesuit priests, such as the Italian Matteo Ricci, began working their way toward Beijing. Given China's huge population, it made sense to try to convert those at the top of the social order in hopes that they would mandate the conversion of their many millions of subjects. Chinese officials, courtiers, and princes were not easily swayed even by the most sophisticated philosophical arguments, but they were almost universally fascinated by advances in Western science and technology.

Aware of this, Ricci developed a special program of "Christian science," attempting to link Western cartography, optics, metallurgy, and clockmaking to notions of divine order. He carried a European clock to Beijing in hopes of wowing the emperor in 1601, and it proved a big hit. A Chinese chronicle from 1603 records the event as follows: "In the twenty-eighth year of the reign of Wanli of the Ming dynasty, the great Westerner Li Madou [Matteo Ricci] presented a self-sounding bell, a mysterious and unknown art. The great bell sounds the hours, at midday, one sound."

The Chinese were relatively uninterested in Western notions of timekeeping in itself because they had their own means and units of measurement. Instead, the Chinese admired the clocks for their intricate mechanical construction and welcomed them as "high-tech" status symbols. The Jesuits were for many years allowed special access to Beijing's Forbidden City primarily as clock repairmen. Their efforts to link clockwork to godliness in a Western Christian sense failed, but they did eventually spawn royal workshops capable of producing elaborate if not particularly accurate timepieces by the early eighteenth century. Under Qing rule, the Royal Office of Clock Manufacture opened in 1723. By this time, advances in English clock- and watchmaking coincided with increased British interest in China, leading to a new wave of gift timepieces meant to win favor at court. Those shown here are on display today in the Forbidden City, the Ming and Qing imperial palace in Beijing that now houses the Palace Museum. Gifts from a range of Western ambassadors, they reveal European states' centuries-long effort to curry favor with the powerful Chinese Empire.

Source: Catherine Pagani, *Eastern Magnificence and Western Ingenuity: Clocks of Late Imperial China* (Ann Arbor: University of Michigan Press, 2001).

EXAMINING THE EVIDENCE

1. Why did Western missionaries such as Ricci think that introducing European clocks to China would aid conversion efforts?

2. How did Chinese appreciation of these clocks reflect cultural differences between them and Europeans?

clarify its mission. The Council of Trent (1545–1563) yielded a new charter for the Roman Catholic Church. Far from offering compromises, however, Trent reaffirmed the Catholic Church's conservatism. Purgatory and indulgences were not eliminated, nor was priestly celibacy. Sacraments such as marriage were reinforced and sexual behavior more circumscribed than ever before. The church also policed ideas and banned books. Cervantes was fortunate to have only one sentence of *Don Quixote* removed. In some places, such as the staunchly Catholic Iberian world, the Holy Office of the Inquisition acted as enforcer of the new precepts, rooting out and punishing alleged deviance. Historians have shown that ordinary Catholics could be skeptical of the church's dogmatic claims, but much of what we know about these freethinkers comes from their Inquisition trial records.

Council of Trent

In the wake of Trent, France's Catholics began persecuting Huguenots, as Calvinist Protestants were known in France, in earnest. This culminated in the Saint Bartholomew's Day massacre of 1572, in which tens of thousands of Huguenots were slaughtered and their bodies mutilated (see again Map 20.3). Just back from America, horrified Huguenot Jean de Léry wrote how "civilized" French Christians had proved themselves far more barbaric than Brazil's Tupinamba cannibals, who at least killed one another according to rigid honor codes. Hostilities ended only in 1598 when the French king Henry IV signed the Edict of Nantes granting Protestants freedom to practice their religion. It helped that Henry IV was a former Protestant, but the Huguenots' troubles were not over.

French Wars of Religion

Imperial Spain and Its Challenges

With religiously and politically fractured kingdoms and duchies the rule in early modern Europe, unified Spain proved to be the exception. Largely financed by the wealth of their numerous overseas colonies, Spain's Catholic Habsburg monarchs sought to consolidate their gains in Europe, and more importantly, to challenge the much larger and more powerful Ottoman Empire to the east. As we have seen, the fight against the "Great Turk," to use the language of the day, forever altered the lives of veterans such as Miguel de Cervantes.

Philip II came to the throne of Spain in 1556, when his father, Holy Roman Emperor Charles V (r. 1516–1556), abdicated. The title of "Emperor" passed to Ferdinand, Charles's brother, but Philip inherited extensive holdings of his own. Taken together, his kingdoms were much larger and richer than his uncle's. Indeed, by 1598, the year of his death, Philip II ruled the world's first empire "upon which the sun never set." The distant Philippines were claimed and named for him in 1565. Still, governing a far-flung and culturally diverse empire brought more burden than pleasure. A forceful but pious monarch, Spain's so-called Prudent King would die doubting his own salvation.

Reign of Philip II

One of Philip's first concerns, inherited from his father, was centralization in the core kingdoms. Castile and Aragon had been nominally united with the marriage of Isabella and Ferdinand in 1469, but local nobles and semiautonomous cities such as Barcelona continued to challenge royal authority. Charles's attempts to assert his will had sparked rebellions in the 1520s, and regional resentments in Iberia itself continued to fester throughout the period of overseas expansion. Philip responded in part by turning Madrid, formerly a dusty medieval crossroads in central Castile, into a world-class capital and Spain's unequivocal center. The capital's building boom was funded in large part by American treasure. Palaces, churches, monasteries, and residential structures proliferated, often blending traditional Castilian and northern European architectural styles. Envious neighbors joked that the Spanish had discovered a magic formula for turning silver into stone.

Thanks to New World treasure, Spain had become Europe's most formidable state by the second half of the sixteenth century. Among other successes, Philip's forces had beaten, as we have seen, the Ottoman navy at Lepanto in 1571. Philip's biggest setback was the revolt of the Netherlands, a politically and religiously divided region inherited from his father. The so-called Dutch Revolt, which began in 1566, taxed Iberian resources severely before its end in 1648. This was a war the Spanish lost, despite enormous effort.

Annexation of Portugal

Two other key events in Philip II's reign were the assumption of the Portuguese throne in 1580 and the 1588 attempt to invade England by sea. Both events had global significance. Portugal's King Sebastian died without an heir in 1578, and the subsequent succession crisis ended only when Philip, whose mother was Isabella of Portugal, stepped in to take the crown. Legitimate or not, Philip's move required an armed invasion, and the Portuguese always regarded Spanish rule, which lasted from 1580 until 1640, as unlawful and oppressive. In global terms, Spanish-Portuguese union meant that one monarch now ruled a substantial portion of Europe, much of the Americas, and dozens of far-flung Asian and African ports, islands, and sea routes. No European challenger was even close.

Philip knew this, and he assumed his good fortune was a reflection of divine will. Like many powerful individuals at their peak, Philip overstretched his mandate. Irritated by English harassment of the Spanish in the Americas and by English aid to the Dutch rebels, and motivated first and foremost by a determination to bring England back into the Catholic fold, Philip decided to launch a full-scale invasion of the British Isles. Such an undertaking would require the concentration of an enormous amount of military resources, and as at Lepanto, the stakes were correspondingly huge.

The Spanish Armada

The Spanish **Armada** of 1588, the largest and most expensive naval force assembled up to that time, appears in retrospect to have been an ill-considered enterprise. Means of communication were few and slow, and most Spanish sailors were poorly equipped for foul weather. Neither side regarded the invasion as foolish at the time, however, and ultimately it was defeated due to a host of factors, only some of them within Spanish control. The Spanish stockpiled supplies for years, and even Cervantes took part, as a clerk charged with cataloguing stores of olive oil and other foods. When it came time to fight, English defenders such as the famous pirate Francis Drake, aided by numerous Dutch allies, were critical; they knew the English Channel and understood Spanish tactics and technology. English guns were also powerful, carefully placed, and well manned. Aiding this defense were harsh weather, contrary winds, poorly mounted cannon, and numerous other complications. Spanish luck went from bad to worse.

Ships not sunk by English and Dutch artillery were battered by waves and drawn off course by fierce gusts. The great Spanish fleet scattered, and the remaining vessels were forced to sail north around Scotland to avoid capture. Here in the cold North Atlantic, Spanish sailors died by the hundreds of hunger and exposure. Some survivors were captured off the coast of Ireland. The English, hardly the sea power they would later become, were jubilant. Subjects of the fiercely Protestant Elizabeth I had proved that mighty Philip and his great armada were not invincible after all.

Spain's misfortunes only compounded in the wake of the armada disaster, and although the world's most extensive empire was hardly crumbling, Philip II's successors faced a potent new competitor in the form of the breakaway Dutch Republic. The Dutch projected their power overseas beginning in the 1590s, and by 1640 the Dutch East and West India companies took over many of the key trading posts held by the joint Spanish-Portuguese Empire from the Caribbean islands to Japan. Beginning in 1630, the West India Company occupied northeastern Brazil, calling this vast territory New Holland. What the Dutch did not know was that at precisely this time the main sources of Spanish wealth, the great silver mines of Potosí in present-day Bolivia, were petering out. Much of the world was deeply affected. Declining silver revenues combined with other chance factors sparked what has become known as "the seventeenth-century crisis" (see Figure 20.1).

Route of the Spanish Armada, 1588

⟶ Advance of the Armada
⇢ Retreat of the Armada
✻ Major battle
▼ Shipwreck

armada A fleet of warships; usually used in reference to the Spanish naval fleet defeated by England in 1588.

Defeat of the Spanish Armada

Gunpowder weapons are very much on display in this dramatic 1601 painting by Dutch marine artist Hendrik Cornelisz Vroom of the 1588 Anglo-Dutch defeat of the Spanish Armada in the English Channel. High winds, shown by the stretched sail canvas, helped English and Dutch forces to outmaneuver and trap Spanish ships, which they blasted with their superior cannon. Several large vessels went down, and all on board drowned. Surviving Spanish ships sailed north around Scotland, where many crewmembers died of exposure. Others were captured in Ireland. It was one of the greatest naval defeats of early modern times. (Scala/White Images/Art Resource, NY.)

The Seventeenth-Century Crisis

Few topics have generated as much debate among historians as the seventeenth-century crisis, a complex series of events and trends that affected much of Europe and the Mediterranean basin from about 1600 to 1660. Some scholars have even claimed that no general crisis occurred, only a cluster of unrelated catastrophes. In any case, Europe's post-1660 rebound and push toward global maritime dominance seems remarkable. How did one of the world's most politically divided, religiously intolerant, and economically fractured regions give rise, in a relatively short time, to secular models of government, rational scientific inquiry, and financial capitalism, all hallmarks of modernity?

Historians focus on different causes, depending on their interpretive bent. Political and military historians focus on the "modern" horrors and early nationalism of the Thirty Years' War and related conflicts. Here, unlike in Asia and North Africa, gunpowder led to the dissolution rather than consolidation of empires. Economic historians focus on the shifting influx of American silver and its effects on food and other commodity prices. Some argue that inflated prices and economic depression had both negative and positive effects, sparking riots while prompting technical and financial innovations. Still other historians, informed by modern scientific techniques, focus on climate, analyzing ice cores and tree rings, along with traditional historical sources, to document the extent of the so-called Little Ice Age, which, as we will see, enveloped Europe from about 1550 to 1700. In the end it is hard to say which of these factors was most responsible for either the widespread turmoil or the swift turnaround that followed, but most historians agree that something transformative had occurred.

In the midst of a twelve-year truce between the Spanish and Dutch, the Thirty Years' War (1618–1648) broke out in

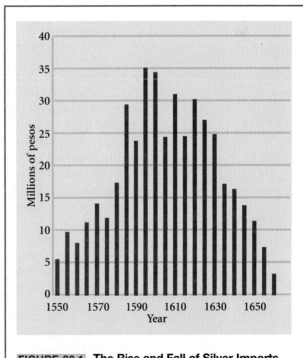

FIGURE 20.1   **The Rise and Fall of Silver Imports to Spain, 1550–1660**

The Thirty Years' War

Dutch artist Jan Maertszen de Jonghe graphically depicts the horrors of the battlefield in this 1634 rendering of the 1627 Battle of Dirschau, near Gdansk, Poland. The battle pitted Swedish king Gustav II, whose slain body appears in the foreground, against Polish-Lithuanian forces led by General Stanislaw Koniecpolski, shown here astride a chestnut horse. Soldiers and horses lie dead or wounded in this picture, but later in the Thirty Years' War, it was civilian casualties that reached levels not seen before in Europe. The Battle of Dirschau was one of several bloody encounters leading to stalemate in 1629, and this painting emphasizes the war's chaos and destruction more than its heroism. (akg-images.)

The Thirty Years' War

central Europe. This complex conflict pitted Christian factions against one another in a civil and international war that radically reshaped Europe's borders. The Thirty Years' War was devastating for civilians. Caught in the crossfire, they were forced to support occupying troops, only to be massacred for doing so when the tide turned and the other side's troops moved in.

In essence, the Thirty Years' War was over the internal politics of the Holy Roman Empire in central Europe (see again Map 20.3). This was really only a loose confederacy—since the days of Emperor Charles V, substantial autonomy had been ceded to an increasing number of Lutheran and Calvinist principalities and duchies. Inhabitants of these Protestant enclaves rightly feared a more assertive Catholic emperor. Emperor Ferdinand II was such a person, an ambitious, Jesuit-educated militant. When it became clear that Ferdinand might re-Catholicize central Europe, the various enemies of the Habsburgs sent aid, then joined the fray.

Before the war ground to a close, a variety of German and Bohemian princes, the kings of Denmark, Poland, and Sweden, plus the English, French, Dutch, and finally the Spanish had all been drawn into the conflict. Contemporary engravings and paintings from its last phase depict the full range of human cruelty, a blatant reminder, like the Saint Bartholomew's Day massacre, that Europeans were as capable of savagery as America's famous warrior cultures. At war's end at least a third of the population of Germany had died, and the region's infrastructure lay in ruins. From population decline to decreased agricultural production, the war was a manifestation of the seventeenth-century crisis.

Silver and Depression

It was also enormously costly in terms of money, the supply of which was shifting. Economic historians have found that throughout Europe prices rose even as demand fell. In one interpretation, an overabundance of silver in the late sixteenth century drove prices up, after which a sequence of plagues, droughts, wars, and other disasters killed off both consumers and suppliers of basic goods throughout Europe, leading to depression. A sustained drop in silver income beginning in around 1600 made hard money scarce when it was already overvalued, forcing many people to resort to barter. Thus, the fabulous wealth of the Americas proved both a blessing and a curse, shifting the global balance of power in Europe's favor at the same time that it led to dangerous and destructive economic volatility.

The Dutch Exception

Hard times for the masses could be good for some, and it appears that the Dutch fared rather well, particularly in comparison with the Spanish and Portuguese. The Netherlands' unique mix of financial capitalism, religious toleration, and overseas conquest seemed to

An Exiled European Muslim Visits the Netherlands

After an Ottoman-supported rebellion in Andalusia from 1569 to 1571, Spain's remaining forced converts to Christianity from Islam, or Moriscos, faced increasing persecution. Many fled to Morocco, Algeria, and other Muslim havens in North Africa, especially during a last wave of expulsions ordered by Philip III from 1609 to 1614. Among the refugees was Ahmad Ibn Qasim al-Hajari, born with the Spanish surname Bejarano in around 1569 in a village in Extremadura, not far from the birthplaces of Francisco Pizarro and Hernando Cortés. Al-Hajari went on to become a major spokesman for the Morisco community in exile, and he wrote and traveled widely. His best-known work, composed and circulated in both Arabic and Spanish, is called *The Supporter of Religion Against the Infidel* (c. 1637). In this passage, al-Hajari describes his visit to the Netherlands.

> About the Netherlands: You should know that I set out for that country deliberately, although it lies farther from our own country than France. But a man should seek protection from others or from himself, and after I had experienced the way French sailors were treating Muslims, I said: I will not return to my country in one of those ships, but I will go to the country of the Netherlanders, because they do not harm Muslims but treat them well. . . .
>
> After I reached the City of Amsterdam, I marveled at the beauty of its architecture and the style of its buildings, its cleanness and the great number of its inhabitants. Its population was almost like that of the City of Paris in France. There is no city in the world with so many ships as it has! One says that the total number of its ships, including the smaller and the bigger ones, is six thousand. As for the houses, each of these is painted and decorated with marvelous colors from top to bottom. Not one resembles another in the art of its painting. All the streets are made of paved stones. . . .
>
> One should know that the Netherlands consists of seventeen islands, all of which used to belong to the Sultan of al-Andalus [the king of Spain]. At a certain time, a man appeared in those lands who was held as a great scholar by them, called Luther, as well as another scholar called Calvin. Each of them wrote his view of the corruption and deviation from the religion of our lord Jesus and the Gospel that had come about in the religion of the Christians. They said the popes in Rome misled the people by worshiping idols and by the additions they introduced into the faith by forbidding priests and monks to marry, and many other things. All the people of the Netherlands . . . embraced this doctrine and they rose up against their sultan until today. The people of the Sultanate of the English also follow this doctrine. There are also many of them in France. Their scholars warn them against the popes and the worshiping of idols. They tell them they should not hate Muslims because they are the Sword of God on His earth against the worshipers of idols.

Source: Ahmad Ibn Qasim al-Hajari, *The Supporter of Religion Against the Infidel*, ed. and trans. P. S. Van Koningsveld, Q. al-Samarrai, and G. A. Wiegers (Madrid: Consejo Superior de Investigaciones Científicas, 1997), 194–195.

EXAMINING THE EVIDENCE

1. What aspects of the Netherlands most impress al-Hajari?

2. How clear is al-Hajari's understanding of the Protestant Reformation?

---

offset many of the difficulties faced by other states (see Reading the Past: An Exiled European Muslim Visits the Netherlands). The Dutch East India Company's spice-island takeovers in Southeast Asia were critical, as seen in Chapter 19, but Dutch pirates, many sponsored by the West India Company, were also busy capturing Spanish silver fleets in the Caribbean.

Historians have long suggested that the climatic change known as the Little Ice Age may have spurred rebellion and even war during the seventeenth century, but only recently have enough data been assembled to generate a fairly clear picture of the century's weather cycles. It now appears that four of the five coldest summers ever recorded in the Northern Hemisphere occurred in the seventeenth century, and that global volcanic activity was probably a major contributing factor to the cooldown. Global cooling shortened growing seasons just as Europeans were pushing into more marginal and thus vulnerable agricultural lands. In alpine valleys, for example, peasants and herders were driven from their highland homes by advancing glaciers. Unprecedented droughts ravaged traditionally wet regions such as Scotland in the 1630s and 1640s, sparking violent uprisings in the midst of an already unstable political climate.

Little Ice Age

The Little Ice Age affected regions far beyond European borders. The worst drought in five hundred years was recorded on the Yangzi River between 1641 and 1644, probably contributing to the 1644 fall of the Ming dynasty in China (discussed in Chapter 21). Ottoman territories were also hit: Egypt's Nile River fell to its lowest recorded levels between 1640 and 1643. Troops on the Persian frontier rebelled when their pay in silver coin proved insufficient to buy food.

Increased Persecutions

Within Europe, the seventeenth-century crisis took on more sinister social dimensions with the rise of witchcraft trials and Inquisition prosecutions. In Protestant Europe, thousands of women were executed for alleged acts of sorcery, and in Catholic Spain and its colonies an unprecedented number of Jews were killed by order of the Inquisition between 1637 and 1649. It is difficult to know why these repressive outbursts occurred in the midst of war, famine, and other problems, but the tendency to scapegoat vulnerable persons in uncertain times has been documented elsewhere. More positive outcomes of the seventeenth-century crisis included scientific discoveries and novel political ideas that eventually took on global importance.

European Innovations in Science and Government 1550–1750

FOCUS

What factors enabled European scientific and political innovations in the early modern period?

In the aftermath of the religious wars of the sixteenth and early seventeenth centuries, a new wave of political consolidation took place in northern and central Europe in the form of absolutist and constitutionalist monarchies. Many of these states, like their Spanish, Portuguese, and Dutch predecessors, took their expansionist energies overseas. Global expansion, as these earlier players had learned, entailed great risks and huge defense costs. In addition to building professional navies, states created licensing agencies and sponsored monopoly trading companies. Financial innovations included stock markets and double-entry accounting, essential ingredients of modern capitalism. Also emerging from the divided world of Europe was a new development aided by the printing press and other technologies: the "scientific revolution." Although restricted for many years to a small number of theorists and experimenters who shared their work in Latin treatises, Europe's embrace of science was to prove globally significant.

The Scientific Revolution

The rise of modern Western science is often described, rather like the Protestant Reformation, as a heroic struggle against a hidebound Catholic tradition. Certainly church patriarchs clung to traditional ideas when challenged by the new science. Still, it was very often Catholic-educated priests and seminarians, along with the odd basement alchemist, who broke the mold in early modern times. Even the Protestants' access to scientific books owed everything to the labors of countless Catholic monks who over centuries had transcribed, translated, and sometimes composed key treatises. They were in turn indebted to numerous medieval Islamic scholars based in cities such as Baghdad and Córdoba. Finally, in early modern times, the printing press and a general interest in technical improvements helped give thousands access to knowledge.

As with the "seventeenth-century crisis," historians have long debated whether or not Europe experienced a genuine "scientific revolution" in the early modern era. Skeptics argue that the key innovations of the period were too restricted to educated elites and court patrons to justify the term *revolution*. In contrast, proponents describe an unprecedented shift in worldview that resonated beyond the small circle of known "scientific rebels."

Call it what we may, European intellectuals after about 1550 increasingly expressed skepticism about received wisdom and began to employ mathematical formulas and empirical (observable) data in an effort to discover the rules by which nature operated. Inductive and deductive reasoning were guiding principles in their efforts. Inductive reasoning—deriving general principles from particular facts and empirical evidence—was most clearly articulated by the English statesman and writer Sir Francis Bacon. Its complement, deductive reasoning—the process of reasoning from a self-evident general principle to a specific fact—was the contri-

geocentrism The ancient belief that the earth is the center of the universe.

The Copernican Universe
The earth still appears quite large in relation to other planets in this 1660 rendering of a heliocentric, or sun-centered, cosmos, but the breakthrough initiated by Nicolaus Copernicus in 1543 is fully evident. Copernicus did not know that planets such as earth traced elliptical rather than perfectly circular orbits, but this was a minor error compared to the older view of a geocentric universe claimed since the days of the great ancient Greek philosopher Aristotle. (akg-images/historic-maps.)

bution of French thinker and mathematician René Descartes. One result of this new search for universal rules was a developing understanding of the way things worked, including the cosmos. Since this was akin to describing "Heaven" in a secular way, many churchmen bristled.

Early Breakthroughs

The first breakthroughs were made by a Polish monk, Nicolaus Copernicus. Copernicus was the first to systematically question the ancient Ptolemaic model of the cosmos, which was geocentric, or earth-centered. Copernicus's collected observations of solar, lunar, and planetary movements did not support **geocentrism**, suggesting instead that the stars and planets, including the earth, revolved around a fixed sun. Fearing ridicule, Copernicus did not publish his *On the Revolutions of the Heavenly Spheres* until 1543, the year of his death. Following Copernicus, the Danish astronomer Tycho Brahe compiled a wealth of "eyeball" data relating to planetary and stellar movements. This data was precise enough to help the German Johannes Kepler work out an elegant if not yet persuasive heliocentric, or sun-centered, model in which the planets circled the sun in elliptical orbits.

Many of Europe's most probing minds were open to the truth of **heliocentrism**, and some went on to risk not only reputations but lives to advance the project of wedding mathematics to observed phenomena. In works such as *The Advancement of Learning* (1605), Sir Francis Bacon attacked reliance on ancient writers and ardently supported the scientific method based on inductive reasoning and empirical experimentation. Bacon had his critics, but he was shielded from persecution by the Protestant English state, which he served as lord chancellor. By contrast, the Italian scientist Galileo Galilei is best remembered for his insistence, against an unforgiving Catholic Church, that nature was governed by mathematical laws. Although the Inquisition placed Galileo under house arrest, his use of new, high-grade telescopes to observe the moons of Jupiter furthered the cause of heliocentrism and challenged reliance on received wisdom.

Newton's Synthesis

Ultimately, minor deviations between Kepler's model and careful empirical observation were worked out in large part by the English scientist Isaac Newton. The elliptical planetary orbits discovered by Kepler, Newton argued through word and formula in *Principia Mathematica* (*Mathematical Principles*, 1687), resulted from the laws of motion, including the principle of gravity, which explained the forces that controlled the movement not only of

heliocentrism The early modern discovery that the sun is the center of our solar system.

planets but of objects on earth. The whole universe was brought together in one majestic system. Whereas Copernicus had feared publishing his findings in his lifetime, Newton faced a much more receptive audience. His synthesis would prevail until the twentieth century.

Advance of the New Science Beyond Europe

Other educated Europeans were testing boundaries in distant corners of the world. In the last years of the sixteenth century the Italian Jesuit Matteo Ricci stunned the Ming court with his vast knowledge of mechanics and mathematics. The Spanish-American metallurgist and parish priest Alvaro Alonso Barba went further, challenging received wisdom through experimentation in his 1627 treatise, *The Art of Metals*. Here in the remote silver mines of Potosí, high in the mountains of what is today Bolivia, Barba was sufficiently informed to comment on Galileo's observations of the moons of Jupiter as outlined in his 1610 publication, *Sidereus Nuncius* (*The Starry Messenger*).

The Emergence of Capitalism

Another great puzzle of early modern Europe regards the emergence of **capitalism**—an economic system in which private individuals or groups make their goods and services available on a free market and seek to take advantage of market conditions to profit from their activities. In developing a capitalist economic system, Europe diverged from the rest of the world, especially after 1650. To be sure, the desire to accumulate wealth and realize profits was by no means new. Ever since the introduction of agriculture and the production of surplus crops, some individuals and groups had accumulated great wealth. As we saw in Chapter 15, merchants in the fifteenth-century "global bazaar" avidly pursued profits from overseas trade. During early modern times, however, European merchants and entrepreneurs transformed their society in a way that none of their predecessors had.

Role of Trading Companies

Historians and economists remain divided as to how capitalism came about, as well as where it started. Most agree, however, that there were two overlapping stages: first commercial, and later industrial. Large trading companies such as the English East India Company and its Dutch competitor, the VOC, were especially important institutions in the commercial stage of capitalism. They spread the risks attached to expensive business enterprises and also took advantage of extensive communications and transportation networks. The trading companies organized commercial ventures on a larger scale than ever before in world history. They were supported by an array of businesses and services. Banks, for example, appeared in all the major commercial cities of Europe to safeguard funds and to grant loans to launch new ventures. Insurance companies mitigated financial losses from risky undertakings. Stock exchanges provided markets where investors could buy and sell shares in the trading companies, and they dealt in other commodities as well. Thus, innovative financial institutions and services created new connections among Europeans that facilitated expansion into global markets.

Rise of Wageworkers and the Bourgeoisie

In the countryside, meanwhile, innovations in mechanization and transport led to gains in productivity that exceeded population growth, especially in northwestern Europe. The arrival of potatoes and other New World crops boosted yields and filled peasant bellies. American sugar was increasingly used to preserve fruits through the long winter. Better food security enabled some peasants to sell their surplus labor for cash wages. Wages made peasants small-scale consumers, a new kind of market participant.

More dependable food supplies came with a social cost, however, most immediately felt by English peasants. Only landowners with secure titles to their property could take advantage of the new crops to practice commercial farming. Rich landowners therefore "enclosed" the land—that is, consolidated their holdings—and got Parliament to give them title to the common lands that in the past had been open to all. Land enclosure turned tenant farmers and sharecroppers into landless farm laborers. Many moved to the cities to seek work.

Cities became increasingly home to merchants, or burghers, as well as to wageworkers. The burghers, or **bourgeoisie**, grew to compete with the old nobility, particularly in England, the Netherlands, and parts of France, Germany, and Italy, as consumers of luxury goods. Especially after 1660 their economic power was boosting their political power.

capitalism In early modern Europe, a new way of conducting business by pooling money, goods, and labor to make a profit.

bourgeoisie In early modern Europe, a new class of burghers, or urban-dwelling merchants.

Europe's manufacturing sector was also deeply transformed. Beginning in the late Middle Ages, rising demand for textiles led to expanded production of woolen and linen fabrics. The major growth of the cloth industries took place in northern Europe beginning in the sixteenth century, when Spanish-American silver flowed through Spain to France, England, and Holland, despite ongoing conflicts. Asians did not much care for Europe's products, but colonists did. Millions of bolts of Dutch and French linens, as well as English woolens, were sent across the Atlantic, and even the Pacific, to Spanish and Portuguese colonies. Global interdependence grew ever tighter through the circulation of fabrics and silver. Europe's textile manufacturers begged Amsterdam and London merchants for Spanish-American dyes, along with Brazilian and Central American dyewood. Profits from growing international trade in textiles were then reinvested in more land for flax growing, larger weaving shops, and wages for increasing numbers of specialized workers. With the application of scientific principles and ever more innovative mechanical apparatus by the early eighteenth century, the stage was set for the emergence of industrial capitalism in England (discussed in Chapter 24).

England's commercial leadership in the eighteenth century had its origins in the mercantilism of the seventeenth century. European **mercantilism** was a system of economic regulations aimed at increasing the power of the state. It rested on the general premise that a nation's power and wealth were determined by its supply of precious metals, which were to be acquired by increasing exports (paid for with gold) and reducing imports to achieve domestic self-sufficiency. What distinguished English mercantilism was the notion that government economic regulations could and should serve the private interests of individuals and groups as well as the public needs of the state. For example, the Navigation Acts of the seventeenth century required that English goods be transported in English ships and restricted colonial exports to raw materials, enriching English merchants and manufacturers as well as the Crown.

Cornering the Atlantic slave trade and Indian Ocean cloth trade were England's two key overseas commercial objectives in the eighteenth century, and profits from both fueled industrial growth at home. As we will see in Chapter 22, English settlers amassed huge plantations in the Caribbean and North American mainland, based primarily on the labor of enslaved Africans, the profits from which they mostly sent home. English inroads in the Indian Ocean trade circuit, meanwhile, grew to eclipse all other European competitors. Capital that had been accumulated in the slave trade, Atlantic plantation complex, and East India monopolies was soon invested in industrial production in several English cities. Goods thus manufactured were subsequently forced on buyers in captive overseas markets, such as the North American colonies, enabling still greater capital accumulation in the imperial center. State power was exercised at every step, from the seizure of native American lands to the sale of African bodies, harsh reminders that the rise of industrial capitalism in England was not a magical or even a natural process, but rather the result of concerted applications of force in many parts of the world.

New Political Models: Absolutism and Constitutionalism

Europe in the wake of the Thirty Years' War witnessed the rise of two new state forms: absolutism and constitutionalism. Worn out by the costs of conflict, the Habsburg Empire fell into decline. A number of challengers sought to fill the void, including the commercially savvy Dutch, but it was the French under the Bourbon king Louis XIV who emerged pre-eminent. Not far behind, however, were the English, who despite a midcentury civil war moved to consolidate control over the British Isles and many overseas possessions by the early eighteenth century. As the great imperial rivals of the time, Britain and France developed distinct systems of governance later copied and modified by others. The monarchs of England found themselves sharply restricted by elected parliaments, whereas those of France sought absolute authority and claimed quasi-divinity. Despite their differing models of rule, the British and French managed to create the largest, most heavily armed, and widest-ranging navies yet seen in world history.

Although Spain's Philip II and other Habsburgs had acted in autocratic and grandiose ways since the mid-sixteenth century, no European monarch matched the heady blend of

Role of Textile Manufacture

Capitalism and Politics

mercantilism A system of economic regulations aimed at increasing the power of the state.

Absolutism in France

state drama and personal charisma of France's Louis XIV (r. 1643–1715). The "Sun-King," as he came to be known, personified the absolutist ruler who shared power with no one. Louis XIV spent much of his long reign centralizing state authority in order to make France a global contender. Though successful in the short run, Louis's form of **absolutism**—propped up in large part by rising taxes and a general contempt for the common masses—sowed the seeds of its own destruction.

Louis XIV came to the throne as a five-year-old, and his mother, Anne of Austria, and her Italian-born adviser and rumored lover, Cardinal Mazarin, ruled in his name. Under the regency, resistance quickly emerged in the form of the *Fronde*, a five-year period of instability from 1648 to 1653 that grew from a regional tax revolt into a potential civil war. Critics coined the term *Fronde*, French for a child's slingshot, to signify that the revolts were mere child's play. In fact, they posed an unprecedented threat to the Crown. Historians of the seventeenth-century crisis have often linked the uprisings to climate change, agricultural stresses, and price fluctuations. Whatever the Fronde's causes, nobles and district courts, or *parlements* (PARLE-mohn), asserted their power against the regency. In the end, the revolt was put down, and when Mazarin died in 1661, Louis XIV assumed total control. He would not forget the Fronde, drawing from it the lesson that the independent power of the French aristocracy must be eliminated and that all power and authority in France must derive from the king.

Like many other monarchs faced with entrenched power structures, Louis XIV spent the next several decades co-opting nobles and potential religious opponents through a mix of patronage and punishment. His rule was authoritarian, and like that of his Spanish Habsburg precursor, Philip II, intolerant of religious difference. After persecuting non-conformist Catholics in the 1660s, Louis exiled the country's remaining Huguenots, French Protestants whose protection had been guaranteed by Henry IV in the Edict of Nantes of 1598. Absolutism was extended to the press as well, with pro-state propaganda and harsh censorship of criticism the order of the day.

The French absolutist state also relied on loyal crown officers, called *intendants* (ON-tohn-don), whose authority superseded that of local parlements and nobles. These officials governed districts, or departments, in the king's name, administering justice, collecting taxes, and organizing defense. Loyal bureaucrats also included high-ranking commoners such as Jean-Baptiste Colbert, Louis's minister of finance. As a trusted favorite, Colbert also oversaw naval and overseas trade affairs, taking a close interest in French expansion in the Caribbean and North America. As the Ottomans had already shown, rewarding merit-worthy commoners with high office was as much a part of early modern government as containing the aspirations of high nobles. Building an overseas empire greatly expanded the scope of patronage politics.

Court Culture and State Power

More than any other early European monarch, Louis XIV arranged court life to serve as a sort of state theater. As in Inca Peru or Ming China, the ruler was allegedly divine, and physical proximity to him was regarded as both desirable and dangerous. A constant stream of propaganda in the form of poems, processions, statues, and medals celebrated the greatness of the monarch. "The state?" Louis asked rhetorically. "It is I."

To house his bulging court, which included growing numbers of fawning and reluctantly drafted nobles, Louis XIV ordered thousands of artisans and laborers to construct a palace befitting his magnificence. Built between 1662 and 1685, Versailles, just outside Paris, was to exceed the ambitious dimensions of Philip II's Escorial. Though hardly the pleasure dome outsiders and common folk imagined it to be, and far less opulent than the palace of Louis's near contemporary, Mughal emperor Shah Jahan, Versailles set a new model for European court grandeur. It was also a physical embodiment of Louis's political ideology. Versailles was a central point from which, at least in theory, all political power and authority flowed.

Tax increases helped to cover the costs of building and maintaining Versailles. The point of raising taxes during Louis XIV's rule was not simply to underwrite court opulence, however. More costly by far were the armed forces. Naval construction grew tremendously under Colbert's direction, but the professionalization and reorganization of land forces was even more extensive. By 1700 France, a country of some 20 million people, could field three hundred thousand soldiers. This was more than ten times the number of soldiers in England, a country with about half of France's total population.

absolutism A political theory holding that all power should be vested in one ruler; also such a system of government.

constitutionalism An early modern system of government based on a written charter defining a power-sharing arrangement between a monarch and representative bodies, or parliaments.

Palace of Versailles
In this 1668 aerial view of Versailles, painter Pierre Patel seeks to encompass the full grandeur and orderliness of French king Louis XIV's famous palace and retreat. Begun in 1661, Versailles instantly became a symbol of absolutist power, a virtual city unto itself. Many early modern rulers ordered the construction or expansion of similarly opulent structures, such as the Ottomans' Topkapi Palace in Istanbul and the Mughals' Red Fort complex in Delhi. (akg-images.)

Louis used his army and navy primarily to confront his powerful Habsburg neighbors to the east and south, although his aggression upset many others, including the English, Swedes, and Dutch. First were incursions into the Spanish Netherlands in the 1660s and 1670s, then into Germany in the 1680s and 1690s. Both conflicts ended with only minor gains for France, but Louis was feared enough to be dubbed the "Christian Turk." Meanwhile, the Crown sponsored French trading companies that vied with their Dutch and English counterparts to penetrate the markets of Africa, the Middle East, India, and Southeast Asia.

Most important in global terms was the War of the Spanish Succession (1701–1714). This long, bloody, and complex conflict proved disastrous for the French because most of Europe allied against them, fearing the consequences of French control over Spanish territories. It ended with England the ultimate victor and France forced to cede exclusive trading privileges with Spanish America (see Map 20.4). Military service, meanwhile, became a standard feature of life for French commoners, along with high taxes and periodic food shortages. Absolutism was good for centralizing authority, but not, as it would turn out, for keeping the peace.

The turmoil of seventeenth-century Europe resulted in both absolute monarchy and a lasting alternative form of government. **Constitutionalism** requires rulers to share power with representative bodies, or parliaments. In England, birthplace of constitutionalism, taxation was always at issue, but so were other matters such as religious freedom and class representation.

Constitutions were charters guaranteeing subjects certain rights, but which subjects and what rights? For a time, it was mostly elites whose economic and religious interests won out. Indeed, far from being democratically elected representatives of the popular classes, members of the constitutionalist parliament—whether in England, Holland, or Poland—were generally landlords and merchants. Some were prominent clergymen. None were artisans or peasants.

English constitutionalism did not emerge peacefully. Instead, when in 1641 King Charles I (r. 1625–1649) attempted to play absolutist monarch before England's centuries-old Parliament of wealthy property owners, he met a resistance so violent it cost him his life. Charles's timing, as historians of the seventeenth-century crisis have pointed out, could not have been worse: thousands were starving after a sequence of failed harvests. In what was surely among the most startling if not revolutionary acts of the early modern period, subjects decided that if the king was judged to be acting out-of-bounds, he should go.

England's showdown with the king had a long backstory. Charles had distrusted Parliament from the start of his rule and refused to call it into session throughout the 1630s.

Wars of Expansion

Constitutionalism in England

English Civil War

MAP 20.4

War of the Spanish Succession, 1701–1714

Unlike the Thirty Years' War of the previous century, the War of the Spanish Succession was openly understood to be a global power contest rather than a conflict over religious faith. With the Ottomans, Iberians, and even the Dutch in decline, the main contestants were Great Britain and France. Great Britain and its allies won the war, but in the Treaty of Utrecht they allowed the French prince to take the throne as Philip V in exchange for a monopoly on the slave trade to Spanish America and other concessions, such as the strategic Mediterranean post of Gibraltar and the island of Minorca.

The Cromwell Dictatorship and Restoration

The Glorious Revolution

Unconventional taxes and religious edicts eroded the king's support in England and provoked a rebellion in Scotland. Parliament was called in 1640 to meet this last crisis, but representatives surprised the monarch by demanding sweeping reforms. Many Protestants felt that the king supported Catholicism, the religion of his French wife, and the most radical among them, the Puritans, pushed hardest for checks on royal power. Charles reacted with force, touching off the English Civil War of 1642 to 1646.

After intense fighting, the Puritan faction under Oliver Cromwell emerged victorious. Cromwell and his Puritan supporters took over Parliament and brought Charles to trial. The king was convicted of tyranny and executed by beheading in 1649.

Cromwell, who styled himself "Lord Protector," proved instead to be a military dictator. Dissenters were killed or oppressed, and Cromwellian forces subjugated Scotland and Ireland with terror and mass displacement. Overseas conflicts with the Dutch and French resulted in few victories and expanded taxes. When Cromwell died in 1658, few English subjects mourned his passing. Instead, the reaction was a sweeping revival of Anglicanism and restoration of the monarchy in 1660.

King and Parliament, however, soon resumed their conflicts. After coming to power in 1685, James II ran afoul of Parliament with his absolutist tendencies and apparent desire to impose his and his wife's Catholicism on English subjects. In 1688 Parliament deposed James, an act that proved far less bloody than the removal of Charles I, and invited James's Protestant daughter Mary (r. 1689–1694) and her Dutch husband, William of Orange (r. 1689–1702), to assume the throne. The event was called the Glorious Revolution since it entailed the monarchs' signing an agreement to share power with Parliament. A genuine constitutional system, much copied worldwide in later years, was now in place.

COUNTERPOINT
The Barbary Pirates

To the vast land empire of the Ottomans and the fractured states of Europe, Africa's north coast, or Maghreb, offers a dual counterpoint. The early modern Maghreb consisted of sea-hugging city-states and tribal enclaves stretching from Morocco to present-day Libya. Although fiercely Islamic and sympathetic to the Ottoman cause against the Habsburgs and

> **FOCUS**
>
> Why were the Barbary pirates of North Africa able to thrive from 1500 to 1800 despite Ottoman and European overseas expansion?

their allies, no Maghribi city ever fell completely under the sway of the Ottoman Empire. Instead, the greatest threats to this centerless region's autonomy came from Christian Europe, whose merchants had long traveled to Africa in pursuit of slaves and gold. Energized by its gunpowder-fueled 1492 conquest of Granada, Spain invaded North Africa with fury, but struggled mightily and at great cost to hold onto a few rocky outposts. Subsequent European interlopers fared little better.

Reign of the Sea Bandits

After 1500, sea banditry flourished along what Europeans called the Berber, or Barbary, Coast. Early pirate leaders of great renown included Oruç and Hayreddin Barbarossa, Greek brothers from the island of Lesbos who settled in Algiers and ruled it from 1516 to 1546. The Barbarossa (Italian for "red beard") brothers were already famous for their bold raids on the coast of Italy. They briefly combined forces with neighboring Tunis to launch large-scale attacks and share out booty, but regional jealousies prevailed and the cities again competed. The raiders focused on capturing merchant vessels at sea, but what made the Barbarossas household names were their increasingly audacious land attacks and kidnappings. Hayreddin later strengthened ties to the Ottomans, but he remained independent of the sultan's orders.

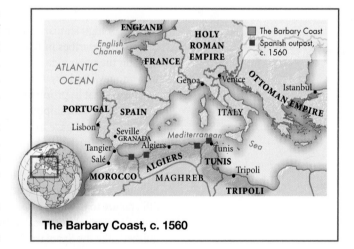

The Barbary Coast, c. 1560

As Ottoman sea power declined after 1580 and Atlantic shipping ballooned, other pirate bases sprang up along the west coast of Morocco. Key after 1600 was the tiny city of Salé (sah-LAY), whose pirate attacks on Spanish and Portuguese shipping were financed and sometimes manned by exiled Iberian Jews and Muslims. Some such foreign-born pirates were deeply involved in European court intrigues, acting as double agents and seeking support for pretenders to the Spanish-held Portuguese throne. Others were simply outlaws hoping to get rich at the expense of their former tormentors. Aside from these vengeful European "renegades," as they were called, a number of Morocco's own seafaring Berber tribes engaged in piracy and extortion as an extension of their culture. Countless young men came of age beneath the pirate flag.

By the time Miguel de Cervantes was held captive in Algiers in the late 1570s, Maghribi hostage trafficking and extortion rackets formed the core of a sophisticated business. The pirates used swift sailing vessels and state-of-the-art European guns to steal money and merchandise, but mostly they kidnapped Christian Europeans, preferably men and

Ransoming Christians

Piracy in the early modern Mediterranean entailed many daring captures at sea, along with several audacious ones on land. Unlike in the Americas, where piracy also thrived at this time, the Barbary pirates of Africa's north coast specialized in kidnapping and extortion. The ransom of Christian captives held in cities such as Algiers and Tunis was organized by Catholic religious orders, who collected sums from as far away as Spanish America to free men and women whose relatives in Spain, Italy, France, and elsewhere could produce no ransom. This seventeenth-century European engraving depicts Catholic priests heroically carrying ransom money, while Christian prisoners appear as cruelly mistreated victims cowering behind their Muslim captors. (The Art Archive.)

women of high status. Some hostages were mistreated and forced to do hard labor, but as Cervantes describes in *Don Quixote*, most were allowed to send letters to friends and relatives on the other side of the Mediterranean in hopes that they would raise sufficient ransom money. Barbary Coast extortion also consisted of selling safe passage to European shippers—that is, promising *not* to kidnap them or steal their merchandise in exchange for money, arms, and shipbuilding materials.

Unable to engage in the expensive conquest enterprises tried by the Spanish and Portuguese, northern European merchants, who were more answerable to shareholders than to kings after about 1600, struck deals with various sultans and tribal leaders in the Maghreb in exchange for safe passage. Maghribi leaders mostly welcomed these Protestant newcomers, because they had access to advanced weapons and shared their hatred of Catholic Iberians. Still, failure to pay for protection led to harsh reprisals. Some pirates raided as far away as the English Channel in the early 1600s, and before long thousands of northern Europeans languished, like the Spaniard Cervantes before them, in the jails of Algiers, Tunis, and Tripoli. In time, England, France, and the Netherlands funded permanent embassies in these and other competing city-states, but their primary purpose was to gather information and keep allied Muslim princes happy, not to seek the release of unlucky Christian subjects. After 1660, the English became a permanent presence in the Moroccan city of Tangier, a strategic base won from the Portuguese through royal marriage.

The Barbary Wars

Although internal divisions and poor leadership among Maghribi sovereigns became more evident over time, it was sustained rivalry among the Europeans that prevented any coordinated attack on the Barbary pirates until the early nineteenth century. Only then, when merchants from the fledgling United States reacted angrily to demands for protection money, did the Barbary pirates see a reversal in fortune. Outraged by what the merchants considered hypocrisy in an era of loudly proclaimed free trade, they proposed a new approach to the Mediterranean's piracy problem. In a pet project of President Thomas Jefferson, the United States won the support of traditional European powers, most significantly the French, to bomb the Barbary pirates into submission. The so-called Barbary Wars' unexpected result was near-total French takeover of North Africa, which ended only in the 1960s.

Conclusion

Fueled by gunpowder, silver, and religious fervor, Europe and the Mediterranean basin exploded after 1500 as the world's most belligerent region, but it was also the most commercially dynamic. Relative resource poverty had long compelled Europeans to trade with one another, but regional identities, exacerbated by religious differences, had led them to fight as often as they cooperated. This trend only continued in the late sixteenth century, when nationalist loyalties were hardened by the Protestant Reformation and its aftermath.

By contrast, in these years the Sunni Muslim Ottomans built a vast land empire encompassing eastern Europe, Southwest Asia, Egypt, and much of Arabia. They did so with force, but also by cleverly integrating new subjects into the ranks of government and the armed forces. Ottoman pragmatism also included a policy of religious tolerance. The Ottoman world became a haven for many of Europe's persecuted Jews, and conquered Christians were not forced to convert to Islam. Chronic wars with the Habsburgs and Safavids provided many opportunities for social advancement, but they also absorbed a huge portion of state resources, eventually bogging the empire down.

A battered Europe emerged from its seventeenth-century crisis to begin a new phase of national division. The century between 1650 and 1750 was no less bloody than the one before, but it marked the beginnings of three globally significant trends: a new science based on direct observation and experimentation, an increasingly capitalist economy, and increasingly centralized, national government. All of this sounds quite modern, but western Europe's competing kingdoms still saw the quest for wealth and power as a zero-sum game, in which gain by one side meant loss by the others, driving them to seek monopolies over resources and lay claim to ever more distant lands and peoples. To a degree, Europeans saw the world through the same mercantilist lens as the Portuguese of previous centuries, but the languages of science and rational economics, rather than religion, were increasingly used to justify conquest of traditional societies. Soon after, in the first years of the nineteenth century, it was a new language, that of free trade, rather than religious animosity that drove the fledgling United States and its European allies to attack the Barbary Coast pirates. Former Barbary captive Miguel de Cervantes of Spain could hardly have known what lay ahead for Europe and the greater Mediterranean, but his vision of a newly interconnected world continued to inspire his imagination. In the opening to the second part of *Don Quixote*, published in 1615, Cervantes jokingly claimed that he had received a letter from the Chinese emperor inviting him to establish a Spanish school at court for which his "world-famous" novel would be the main text. Cervantes claimed that he had declined the offer only because he was ill and could not afford the trip.

NOTES

1. Celalzade, Mustafa, *Selim-name* [In praise of Selim] (eds. Ahmet Uğur, Mustafa Huhadar), Ankara 1990; as it appears in Halil Berktay and Bogdan Murgescu, *The Ottoman Empire* (Thessaloniki: CDRSEE, 2005), 53.
2. Habsburg ambassador Ghiselin de Busbecq, quoted in Gérard Chaliand, ed., *The Art of War in World History from Antiquity to the Nuclear Age* (Berkeley: University of California Press, 1994), 457.
3. Jennings, Ronald C., *Christians and Muslims in Ottoman Cyprus and the Mediterranean World, 1571-1640*, New York – London 1993; as it appears in Halil Berktay and Bogdan Murgescu, *The Ottoman Empire* (Thessaloniki: CDRSEE, 2005), 116.
4. Evlija Celebi, Putopis. *Odlomci o jugoslovenskim zemljama* [Travel-records. Fragments about Yugoslav Countries], Sarajevo 1996; as it appears in Halil Berktay and Bogdan Murgescu, *The Ottoman Empire* (Thessaloniki: CDRSEE, 2005), 82.

RESOURCES FOR RESEARCH

General Works

Few historians have attempted to treat early modern Europe and the wider Mediterranean in a global context, but the following books are some of the best general syntheses in the field. Braudel remains the grand inspiration. Crosby challenges us to see what was special about growing European interest in numbers and calculation, which owed much to Islamic precedent.

Braudel, Fernand. *The Mediterranean and the Mediterranean World in the Age of Philip II.* 2 vols. Translated by Sian Reynolds. 1996.

Crosby, Alfred W. *The Measure of Reality: Quantification and Western Society, 1250–1600.* 1997.

Elliott, John H. *Spain, Europe, and the Wider World, 1500–1800.* 2009.

Elliott, John H. *Europe Divided, 1556–1598,* 2d ed. 2000.

Kamen, Henry. *Early Modern European Society.* 2000.

The Power of the Ottoman Empire, 1453–1750

Ottoman history is a vibrant field, and new work continues to link the empire to both West and East. A recent wave of regional studies of Ottoman Egypt and Syria joins better-known work on Ottoman eastern Europe and Anatolia. Giancarlo Casale's book takes the Ottomans overseas.

Casale, Giancarlo. *The Ottoman Age of Exploration.* 2010.

Goffman, Daniel. *The Ottomans and Early Modern Europe.* 2002.

Kafadar, Cemal. *Between Two Worlds: The Construction of the Ottoman State.* 1995.

Mansel, Philip. *Constantinople: City of the World's Desire, 1453–1924.* 1996.

Pierce, Leslie. *The Imperial Harem: Women and Sovereignty in the Ottoman Empire.* 1993.

Europe Divided, 1500–1650

Histories of the "seventeenth-century crisis" have come back into vogue in recent years, and now stress global linkages in trade, climate, and other spheres. Other authors, such as Davis and Schwartz, have expanded the study of women's self-fashioning and the popular religious toleration that existed despite harsh decrees from above.

Cunningham, Andrew, and Ole Peter Grell. *The Four Horsemen of the Apocalypse: Religion, War, Famine and Death in Reformation Europe.* 2000.

Davis, Natalie Zemon. *Women on the Margins: Three Seventeenth-Century Lives.* 1995.

"Introduction." AHR Forum: The General Crisis of the Seventeenth Century Revisited. *The American Historical Review* 113, no. 4 (October 2008): 1029–1030. http://www.jstor.org/stable/10.1086/ahr.113.4.1029.

Parker, Geoffrey. *Europe in Crisis, 1598–1648,* 2d ed. 2001.

Schwartz, Stuart B. *All Can Be Saved: Religious Tolerance and Salvation in the Iberian Atlantic World.* 2008.

Sturdy, David J. *Fractured Europe, 1600–1721.* 2002.

European Innovations in Science and Government, 1550–1750

Historians of science continue to debate the meaning and timing of the so-called Scientific Revolution, but when seen in a global context, the changes initiated in sixteenth-century Europe appear starkly important. Economic historians are even less in agreement with regard to the origins of modern capitalism, but the topic remains huge, and as treated by Chaudury, Pomeranz, and others, it has become more globally integrated.

Beik, William. *Louis XIV and Absolutism: A Brief Study with Documents.* 2000.

Chaudury, Sushil, and Michel Morineau, eds. *Merchants, Companies, and Trade: Europe and Asia in the Early Modern Era.* 1999.

Edwards, Philip. *The Making of the Modern English State, 1460–1660.* 2001.

Henry, John. *The Scientific Revolution and the Origins of Modern Science,* 2d ed. New York: Palgrave, 2002.

Pomeranz, Kenneth. *The Great Divergence: China, Europe, and the Making of the Modern World Economy.* 2000.

Smith, Pamela H., and Paula Findlen, eds. *Merchants and Marvels: Commerce, Science, and Art in Early Modern Europe.* 2002.

Smyth, Jim. *The Making of the United Kingdom, 1660–1800.* 2001.

COUNTERPOINT: The Barbary Pirates

The Barbary pirates have been a source of many legends, but serious historical research has also been undertaken. Braudel's classic study of the Mediterranean, cited above under General Works, includes considerable information on the sixteenth-century pirates, whereas Heers and Wolf provide more scope and detail.

Heers, Jacques. *The Barbary Corsairs.* 2003.

Pennell, C. R. *Bandits at Sea: A Pirates Reader.* 2001.

Vitkus, Daniel J., and Nabil Matar, eds. *Piracy, Slavery, and Redemption: Barbary Captivity Narratives from Early Modern England.* 2001.

Wolf, John B. *The Barbary Coast: Algeria Under the Turks.* 1979.

▶ **For additional primary sources from this period,** see *Sources of Crossroads and Cultures.*

▶ **For Web sites, images, and documents related to topics in this chapter,** see Make History at bedfordstmartins.com/smith.

The major global development in this chapter ▶ Early modern Europe's increasing competition and division in the face of Ottoman expansion.

IMPORTANT EVENTS

1453	Ottoman conquest of Constantinople
1492	Spanish take Granada, expel Jews
1517	Martin Luther disseminates "Ninety-five Theses," sparking the Protestant Reformation
1520–1566	Reign of Ottoman emperor Suleiman
1540	Ignatius Loyola founds the new Catholic order of the Jesuits
1543	Nicolaus Copernicus, *On the Revolutions of the Heavenly Spheres*
1545–1563	Council of Trent
1571	Battle of Lepanto
1572	St. Bartholomew's Day massacre
1580	Philip II of Spain takes over Portuguese Empire
1598	Edict of Nantes ends French Religious War
1618–1648	Thirty Years' War
1640	Portugal wins independence from Spain
1642–1646	English Civil War
1643–1715	Reign of Louis XIV of France
1683	Ottomans defeated in Vienna by Polish-Austrian alliance
1687	Isaac Newton, *Principia Mathematica*
1688	Glorious Revolution in England
1701–1714	War of the Spanish Succession

CHAPTER OVERVIEW QUESTIONS

1. To what degree was religious diversity embraced or rejected in early modern Europe and the greater Mediterranean, and why?

2. How did Christian Europe's gunpowder-fueled empires compare with that of the Ottomans?

3. What accounts for the rise of science and capitalism in early modern western Europe?

SECTION FOCUS QUESTIONS

1. What factors explain the rise of the vast Ottoman Empire and its centuries-long endurance?

2. What sparked division in Europe after 1500, and why did this trend persist?

3. What factors enabled European scientific and political innovations in the early modern period?

4. Why were the Barbary pirates of North Africa able to thrive from 1500 to 1800 despite Ottoman and European overseas expansion?

MAKING CONNECTIONS

1. How did battles for control of the Mediterranean compare with those for control of Indian Ocean trade (see Chapter 19)?

2. How globally important was the Protestant Reformation?

3. In what ways were the Barbary pirates similar to the Atlantic slave traders (see Chapter 18)? How were they different?

KEY TERMS

absolutism (p. 674)
armada (p. 666)
bourgeoisie (p. 672)
capitalism (p. 672)
caravanserai (p. 656)
constitutionalism (p. 674)
devshirme (p. 651)
geocentrism (p. 670)
heliocentrism (p. 671)
indulgence (p. 662)
mercantilism (p. 673)
timar (p. 651)

21

AT A CROSSROADS ▶

This life-size portrait from Beijing's Palace Museum depicts China's Emperor Qianlong (1711–1799) at a grand old age. The use of perspective—the illusion of three-dimensional space—reflects the influence of European Jesuit artists who resided at court after the early seventeenth century, but the emperor's pose reflects a Chinese taste for a more statuelike representation of imperial power. His elaborate silk garments and pearl-encrusted headgear and necklace suggest the wealth of the Qing treasury, which despite massive expenditures and waste, boasted a huge surplus in silver for much of the emperor's reign. (The Palace Museum, Beijing/©Hu Weibiao/ChinaStock.)

Expansion and Isolation in Asia

1450–1750

Wang Yangming (1472–1529) had trouble on his hands. As governor of the south western Chinese province of Jiangxi, he was expected to collect taxes and keep the peace for his Ming overlords. Wang had risen through the ranks of the civil service through a mix of intelligence, connections, and raw ambition. Now he was faced with a rebellious prince, Zhu Chen-hao, and his loyal followers. Acting as general, Wang successfully attacked the rebels with every weapon at hand, including novel bronze cannon probably copied from the Portuguese. More important than the suppression of the rebellion was the aftermath. Wang chose not to terrorize the populace and destroy the land as his predecessors might have, but instead moved quickly to rebuild, pardoning many rebels and winning their loyalty to the Ming emperor.

Wang Yangming's effective governorship won praise, but he was far better known as a philosopher. Wang was among the most renowned **Neo-Confucianists** of early modern China. As described in Chapter 15, the broad philosophical movement known as Neo-Confucianism was a revival of an ancient tradition. The fifth-century B.C.E. Chinese philosopher Kongzi (Latinized as "Confucius") envisioned the ideal earthly society as a mirror of divine harmony. Although he prescribed ritual ancestor worship, Confucius

BACKSTORY

By the fifteenth century, Russia, a largely agrarian society straddling Eurasia, had shaken off Mongol rule and was beginning to expand from its base in Moscow. Russian expansion would eventually lead to conflict with China, which by the fifteenth century was by far the world's most populous state. Self-sufficient, widely literate, and technically sophisticated, China vied with Europe for supremacy in both practical and theoretical sciences. As we saw in Chapter 15, the Ming dynasty had also become a global power capable of mounting long-distance sea voyages, yet by the 1430s its rulers had chosen to withdraw and focus on consolidating internal affairs. By contrast, Japan was deeply fractured in the fifteenth century, its many districts and several islands subject to feuding warlords. Korea, though less densely populated than either of its neighbors east or west, was relatively unified under the Yi dynasty, which came to power in the late fourteenth century. In mainland Southeast Asia, several Buddhist kingdoms were by this time undergoing a major reconfiguration. Neo-Confucianism was on the rise in Vietnam. The Philippine Islands, meanwhile, remained politically and ethnically diverse, in part due to their complex geography.

Straddling Eurasia: Rise of the Russian Empire, 1462–1725

FOCUS What prompted Russian territorial expansion?

China from Ming to Qing Rule, 1500–1800

FOCUS How did the shift to a silver cash economy transform Chinese government and society?

Japan in Transition, 1540–1750

FOCUS How did self-isolation affect Japan?

Korea, a Land in Between, 1392–1750

FOCUS How did life for common folk in early modern Korea differ from life in China or Japan?

Consolidation in Mainland Southeast Asia, 1500–1750

FOCUS What trends did mainland Southeast Asia share with China, Korea, Japan, and Russia?

COUNTERPOINT: "Spiritual Conquest" in the Philippines

FOCUS In contrast to the general trend of political consolidation in early modern Asia, why did the Philippines fall to a European colonizing power?

Neo-Confucianism The revival of Confucius's ancient philosophy stressing agrarian life, harmony between ruler and ruled, and respect for elders and ancestors.

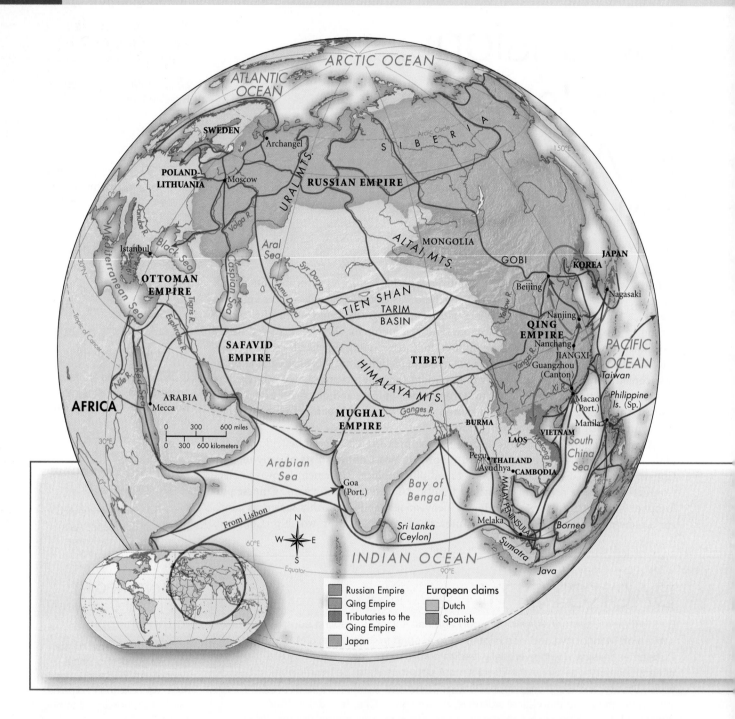

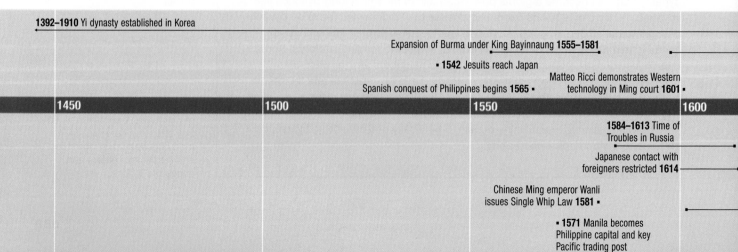

1392–1910 Yi dynasty established in Korea

Expansion of Burma under King Bayinnaung 1555–1581

• 1542 Jesuits reach Japan

Spanish conquest of Philippines begins 1565 •

Matteo Ricci demonstrates Western technology in Ming court 1601 •

1450 1500 1550 1600

1584–1613 Time of Troubles in Russia

Japanese contact with foreigners restricted 1614

Chinese Ming emperor Wanli issues Single Whip Law 1581 •

• 1571 Manila becomes Philippine capital and key Pacific trading post

developed a system of ethics rather than a formal religion. Education and scientific experimentation were highly valued, but so was submission to elders and other social superiors. Ideal Chinese citizens had duties rather than rights. Some of Confucius's core ideas were further developed by his fourth-century B.C.E. successor, Mengzi, or Mencius, whose commentaries inspired Wang Yangming.

As his response to the rebels in Jiangxi suggested, Wang was as much a man of action as he was a scholar. In fact, Wang saw no clear distinction between his military and intellectual lives, arguing that only by doing could one learn, and that action was in fact inseparable from learning. In addition to challenging older notions that privileged scholarly reflection in matters of policy, Wang argued that individuals possessed an innate sense of right and wrong, something akin to the Western notion of conscience. Some scholars have argued that at least one result of the wide diffusion of Wang's teachings was a heightened sense among Chinese elites of the worthiness of the individual as a historical actor.

Neo-Confucianists sought to restore order to societies they felt had descended into chaos and decadence. For Wang, putting Ming society back on track required forceful action. Other Neo-Confucianists argued in favor of more passive reflection, but Wang's ideas seemed to strike the right chord in early sixteenth-century China, and were widely promoted by educators, first in China and later in Korea and Vietnam. Japan borrowed more selectively from Neo-Confucianism. When blended with the underlying Buddhist beliefs already deeply rooted in all these regions, Neo-Confucianism emerged as a largely uncontroversial religion of state. A foundation for many legal as well as moral principles, it helped hold together millions of ethnically diverse and socially divided people. In other parts of Asia, however, religion fueled division and conflict. The Philippines were a battleground between recent converts to Islam and Roman Catholicism. Russia, meanwhile, was defining itself as a revived Byzantium, expanding frontiers across Asia in the name of Orthodox Christianity. Muslims and other non-Christians were treated as enemies of faith and state.

MAPPING THE WORLD

Eurasian Trade and Empires, c. 1700

With the decline of the Mongols, Central Asia returned to its former role as a trading crossroads, mostly for silk, gems, furs, and other high-value commodities, yet it also became a meeting ground for two new, expansive empires: Russia under the Romanovs and China under the Qing, or Manchu, dynasty. Despite their focus on land expansion, both empires sought trade ties with the outside world by sea, mostly to win foreign exchange in the form of silver. More isolated areas in the region included Korea and Japan, both of which experienced political consolidation influenced by the spread of Chinese Neo-Confucianist principles. Similar processes appeared in Vietnam, whereas most of mainland Southeast Asia remained under expansionist Buddhist kings.

ROUTES ▼

— Fur trade route

— Other trade route

➤ Spread of Neo-Confucianism

➤ Travels of Matteo Ricci, 1582–1598

1597–1630s Persecution of Japanese Christians

1644 Manchu invasion of Beijing; Ming dynasty replaced by Qing

1650　　　　**1700**　　　　**1750**

1627, 1636 Manchu invasions of Korea

1661–1722 Qing expansion under Emperor Kangxi

1751 Qing annexation of Tibet

1602–1867 Tokugawa Shogunate in Japan

1689–1725 Russian imperial expansion under Tsar Peter the Great

Over the course of early modern times, Asian monarchs varied between absolutist-style rulers, as in Ming and Qing China and in Russia, and more symbolic figureheads, as in Tokugawa Japan. Korea's Yi (yee) dynasty kings fell somewhere in between, as did some of the kings of mainland Southeast Asia. Ordinary people, as in most of the Middle East and Europe, had little chance to contact or communicate with their rulers, dealing only with royal intermediaries or provincial authorities. The vast majority of Asians worked at subsistence farming and paid tribute in cash or foodstuffs to landlords or royal administrators. Men were usually more mobile than women in that they were more likely to be caught up in public works or military drafts. Childhood—everywhere difficult to survive—was mostly an apprenticeship to adult labor.

Despite this continuity in everyday life, the early modern period was a time of sweeping change across Asia, sometimes sparked by the provocations of foreigners, but mostly resulting from long-range, internal developments. The overall trend was toward political consolidation under powerful dynasties. These centralizing governments sought to suppress internal dissent, encourage religious unity, and expand territorial holdings at the expense of weaker neighbors, often using new military technologies to achieve this end. Dependence on outsiders was for the most part limited to strategic items such as guns and hard currency. Whole new classes of bureaucrats and merchants flourished, and with them came wider literacy in vernacular languages, support of the arts, and conspicuous consumption. Despite some punishing episodes of war, rebellion, and natural disaster, the early modern period in East Asia was arguably more peaceful than in most of Europe, the Middle East, or Africa. It was an era of steady population growth, commercial expansion, political consolidation, and cultural florescence.

OVERVIEW
QUESTIONS

The major global development in this chapter: The general trend toward political and cultural consolidation in early modern Asia.

As you read, consider:

1. What factors led to imperial consolidation in Russia and China? Who were the new rulers, and what were the sources of their legitimacy?

2. Why was isolation more common in these empires than overseas engagement, and what were some of the benefits and drawbacks of isolation?

3. In what ways did early modern Asians transform their environments, and why?

Straddling Eurasia: Rise of the Russian Empire 1462–1725

FOCUS

What prompted Russian territorial expansion?

Whereas the emerging nation-states of western Europe expanded largely through overseas conquests, early modern Russia followed a land-based path of expansion and consolidation more like that of the Ottomans and other so-called gunpowder empires to the south and east. Beginning in 1462, Moscow-based princes combined new weapons technology with bureaucratic innovations to expand their holdings. By the time Tsar Peter the Great died in 1725, the Russian Empire encompassed a huge swath of northern Asia, stretching from the Baltic to the Pacific (see Map 21.1).

Russian imperialism was basically conservative, with Russian Orthodoxy, the state religion, serving as a kind of nationalist "glue" throughout early modern times. Religious and cultural unity, plus a tendency toward isolation, inhibited efforts at social and agricultural reform. Although Peter the Great would end his reign by copying elements of western European governance and science, Russia remained an essentially tributary, agricultural regime until the nineteenth century. Military reforms such as those embraced by the Ottomans were Peter's most modern legacy. Although a modest merchant class had long existed in cities such as Moscow and Novgorod, the majority of Russians remained **serfs**, bound peasants with little more freedom than slaves.

Consolidation in Muscovite Russia

After the fall of Constantinople in 1453, some Russian Christians prophesied that the principality of Muscovy was to be the new Byzantium, and Moscow the "third Rome." The

serf A dependent agricultural laborer attached to a property and treated much like a slave.

MAP 21.1 **Rise of Russia, 1462–1725**

Beginning with the consolidation of Muscovy in the mid-fifteenth century, Russia grew steadily to become one of the world's largest—albeit least densely populated—land empires. By the time of Peter the Great's death in 1725, the Russian Empire encompassed much of northern Eurasia and included key ports in the Atlantic, Arctic, and Pacific oceans, with links to the Mediterranean via the Black Sea and to Persia via the Caspian Sea. Alongside military and commercial endeavors, the Russians spread their Orthodox Christian faith as far as northwest North America.

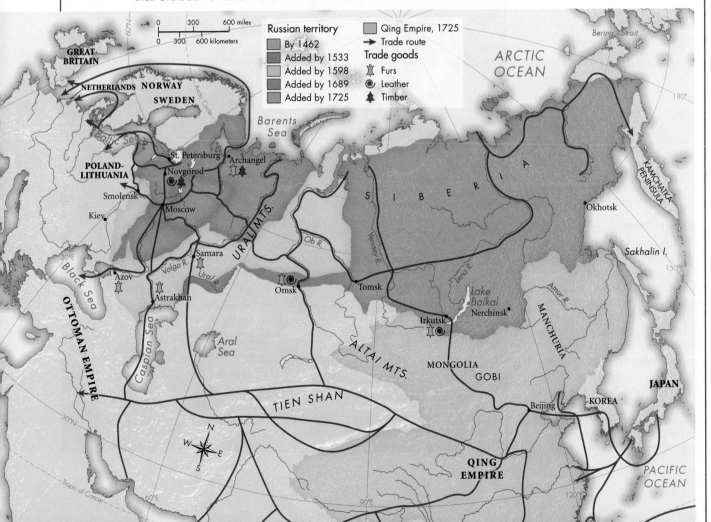

Rise and Expansion of Muscovy

Russian Orthodox Church was fiercely anti-Catholic and frequently energized by apocalyptic visionaries. These visionaries inspired a succession of grand princes who ruled Moscow following the Black Death, and each seemed more determined than the last to expand both Muscovy and the Orthodox Church's domain. As the early modern period progressed, the Ottomans and their allies came to pose the greatest threat to Russia in the south, and the Poles, Lithuanians, and Swedes periodically threatened in the west. The eastern Tatars, though in decline after Timur (see Chapter 15), were also a chronic menace.

Russia took shape under Moscow's grand prince, Ivan III (r. 1462–1505), nicknamed "the Great." Under Ivan the Great, the Muscovites expanded northward, tying landlocked Muscovy to the commercially vibrant Baltic Sea region. By the later sixteenth century, Russian monarchs began to allow English, Dutch, and other non-Catholic northwest European merchants to settle and trade in the capital. Like other Europeans, these merchants sought to circumvent the Ottomans and Middle Eastern intermediaries in the quest for East and South Asian fabrics and spices. As a result of alliances with foreign merchants, Muscovite rulers gained access to artillery, muskets, and other Western gunpowder technologies in exchange for furs and Asian textiles. These new weapons in turn fueled Russian imperial expansion, mostly across the steppes to the east and south (see again Map 21.1).

Peter the Great

Truly a giant of Russian history, the Romanov tsar Peter the Great spent much of his adult life trying to modernize and expand his vast realm, which spanned the Eurasian continent. He is shown here, tall in the saddle and supremely confident, at the 1709 Battle of Poltava (in present-day Ukraine), where he and his modernized army defeated Sweden's King Charles XII. The artist depicts Peter as blessed by an angel, whereas King Charles was forced to seek refuge with the Ottomans. (Tretyakov Gallery, Moscow/Bridgeman Art Library.)

Russia's next great ruler, and first tsar (literally, "Caesar"), was Ivan IV (r. 1533–1584), "the Terrible." Although remembered mostly for bizarre and violent behavior in his later years, Ivan IV was for the most part an effective monarch. In addition to conquering cities in the distant territories of the Golden Horde in the 1550s and acquiring lucrative fur-producing territories in Siberia, Ivan IV also reformed the Muscovite bureaucracy, judiciary, and treasury in a manner befitting a growing empire. The church, always at the heart of Russian politics, was also reorganized and partly subordinated to the state.

Ivan earned his nickname beginning in the 1560s when he established a personal fiefdom called the *oprichnina* (oh-preech-NEE-nah), which, like the Ottoman *timar* and *devshirme* systems, was in part intended to break the power of nobles and replace them with dependent state servants. This abrupt political shuffling crippled vital commercial cities such as Novgorod, however, and generally threw the empire into disarray. Meanwhile, wars begun in 1558 with Poland and Sweden went badly for Ivan's outgunned and undertrained forces. Things went no better on the southern front, and in 1571 Moscow fell to the eastern Tatars. Increasingly psychologically unstable during the last decade of his life, Ivan died of a stroke in 1584. Thanks in part to Ivan's personal disintegration, which included his killing of the heir apparent, Russia descended into chaos after Ivan's death. Historians have designated the subsequent three decades Russia's "Time of Troubles."

The Time of Troubles (1584–1613) was punctuated by succession crises, but it was also an era of famine, disease, military defeat, and social unrest, akin to Europe's "seventeenth-century crisis." Taking advantage of the dynastic chaos, the king of Poland and Lithuania tried to place his son on the Russian throne. The prospect of a Catholic ruler sparked Russia's first massive peasant rebellion, which ended with the humiliating occupation of Moscow by Polish forces. In 1613 an army of nobles, townspeople, and peasants drove out the intruders and put on the throne a nobleman, Michael Romanov (r. 1613–1645), founder of Russia's last royal line.

Time of Troubles

The Romanovs' New Frontiers

Under Romanov leadership, the seventeenth century saw the rebuilding and expansion of Muscovy and the slow but steady return to empire. Starting at 7 million in 1600, Russia's population roughly doubled by 1700. Impressive as this growth was, all of Russia's inhabitants could have fit into a small corner of China. Further, they looked more to leadership from the church, which had regained the authority it lost under Ivan the Terrible, than from the crown.

By the time of Peter the Great (r. 1689–1725), the Russian tsar faced a powerful and insubordinate church. Peter responded by prosecuting wandering preachers as enemies of the state. But what made Peter "great" was not his harsh dealings with the church but his relentless push to make Russia a competitor on par with France and other emerging western European nation-states. To this end, he kept stoking the fires of expansion-driven war, importing arms and military experts, building a navy, and professionalizing the armed forces. The Imperial Russian Army soon became not only a major force against the strongest of European and Central Asian challengers, but also a gargantuan consumer of state revenue.

Peter, a man of formidable size and boundless energy, is often remembered for his attempts to Westernize Russia, to purge it of what he regarded as backward, mostly Asian characteristics. Boyars, or nobles, were ordered to shave their beards and change their dress, and all courtiers were required to learn French. A new capital, St. Petersburg, was built on the Baltic shore in the French style, complete with a summer palace inspired by Louis XIV's Versailles. Not

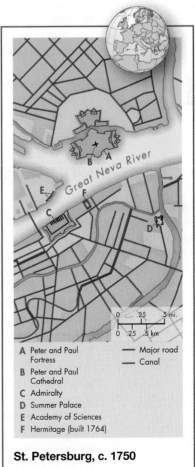

A Peter and Paul Fortress
B Peter and Paul Cathedral
C Admiralty
D Summer Palace
E Academy of Sciences
F Hermitage (built 1764)

—— Major road
—— Canal

St. Petersburg, c. 1750

everything Asian was bad, however. On southern expansion, Peter had this to say: "Approach as close to Constantinople and India as possible. He who rules there will be the real ruler of the world."[1]

Russian expansion across Asia was not only a military process. The growth of the fur trade reverberated ever more deeply through the many complex ecosystems of Siberia, and settling the great steppes of the south and east entailed wrenching social change and a wholesale transformation of the landscape. As frontier forts and agricultural colonization advanced, indigenous nomads were massacred, driven out, incorporated into trade or tributary networks, or forced to convert to Christianity. Well-watered riverbanks were tilled and planted in traditional fashion, and prairie grasslands became pasturage for large herds of domestic livestock. The steppe frontier was to some extent a haven for fugitives, too, including a number of runaway serfs, and it also proved to be a source of rebel leaders. The government was always playing catch-up, trying to bring order to the unruly fringe.

Foreign merchants, meanwhile, came to Russia not only from the west, but from the south and east. In addition to small colonies of northern Europeans, Moscow was home to thriving communities of Middle Eastern, Central Asian, South Asian, and Armenian merchants by the seventeenth century. As in most other mercantilist systems, however, the government granted foreign merchants only limited access to Russian urban markets and even less to interior supply regions. Thus Russian merchants continued to dominate both internal and long-distance trade, despite limited access to credit and precious metals. Mostly based in Moscow, they used distant ports such as Archangel, on the White Sea, to trade leather and other goods with the English and Dutch (see again Mapping the World, page 685). Furs were traded westward to eastern and central Europe, and also southward to the Ottoman and Persian empires. By the time of Peter the Great, England had become dependent on Russian timber, which it paid for with gold (coming mostly from Brazil by this time, as we will see in the next chapter).

The early modern Russian Empire, in sum, drew from a blend of religious self-confidence, demographic growth, commercial links, and the personal ambitions of its Moscow-based tsars. More gunpowder empire than modern state in many regards, Russia nevertheless grew to encompass more terrain than any other Eurasian state in its time, despite its relatively sparse population. The continued subjugation of the serf majority, however, would spark a new wave of rebellions before the end of the eighteenth century.

China from Ming to Qing Rule 1500–1800

FOCUS

How did the shift to a silver cash economy transform Chinese government and society?

By 1500, thanks to several millennia of intensive agriculture and a tradition of vast and innovative public works projects, China was home to at least 110 million people, almost twice as many as Europe. Moreover, China under the Ming dynasty (1368–1644) was virtually self-sufficient. Rice and other foodstuffs, along with livestock and manufactured goods, were transported and redistributed throughout the empire by way of a complex system of canals, roads, and fortified posts that had been constructed by drafted peasant laborers over the centuries.

Only silver was in short supply as Ming rulers shifted China's economy from copper or bronze currency and simple barter to silver money exchanges, especially after 1550. This shift to commercialization and a "hard money" economy necessitated links to the outside world. China's surplus of silk, a versatile fiber in demand abroad since antiquity, made exports not only possible, but highly profitable. Fine porcelain and lacquer wares also brought in considerable foreign exchange, and tea would later be added to the list. Western ideas and technologies arrived with Christian missionaries in the mid-sixteenth century, but they barely influenced Chinese culture. China, a technologically advanced and highly literate society, wanted only silver from the West, and, for a time, it managed to define its terms of connection and exchange with the outside world.

The final century of Ming rule, from about 1540 to 1644, witnessed a commercial revival and overall improvement in standards of living. It also saw the return of mounted enemies in the north, the Manchu. And, despite the general prosperity, there were no perfect guarantees against the famine and disease that plagued previous centuries due to the density of China's population and the primitive state of its medical care. Bureaucratic structures, though efficient by contemporary world standards, were inadequate to the task of mass relief. Peasant families could at best hope for community cooperation in hard times.

Late Ming Imperial Demands and Private Trade

The most important emperor of late Ming times was Wanli (r. 1573–1620). Wanli was a creature of the imperial palace and notoriously out of touch with his subjects, yet one of his policies had global implications. Previous emperors had enacted similar decrees on a small scale, but it was Wanli who ordered many of China's taxes collected in silver rather than in the form of labor service, rice, or other trade goods. The shift to hard currency eased price standardization across the empire. This was the "Single Whip Law" of 1581, so named since it bundled various taxes into one stinging payment.

Single Whip Law and the Shift to Hard Currency

Given China's immense population, approaching 200 million by this time, demand for silver soared. Portuguese merchants moved quickly to import Japanese silver acquired in exchange for guns, silk, and other items, but soon Chinese merchants all but eclipsed them. These merchants moored their ships in Nagasaki Bay alongside the Portuguese and later Dutch, but many more set up shop in Manila, the Philippine capital, where they exchanged silk, porcelain, and other goods for Spanish-American silver that had arrived from Mexico (see Map 21.3, page 709). Thanks to Wanli, a vibrant Chinese commercial colony emerged in Manila virtually overnight. Large numbers of Chinese merchants also settled in Thailand, Malaysia, and Java, where they offset the growing commercial power of Europeans.

Demand for Silver and the Manila Trade

Despite the great distances and risks involved, the Manila trade was particularly profitable for both Spanish and Chinese merchants. The annual transpacific voyages of the *naos de la China*, or "Manila galleons," that left Acapulco, Mexico, each year loaded with the silver of Potosí (Bolivia), Zacatecas (Mexico), and other American mining centers, continued unabated through the early nineteenth century. Like the arrival of the Atlantic silver fleet in Spain each fall, the safe arrival of the galleons in Manila was a longed-for and celebrated event in all quarters. Still more Spanish-American silver reached China from the West, traveling through Europe, the Middle East, and the Indian Ocean basin to ports such as Macao and Guangzhou (Canton). Since China, compared with contemporary Europe or India, valued silver at a relatively higher rate than gold, substantial profit could be made in almost any exchange. Put another way, the historically close relationship between favorable exchange rates and export profitability was quickly exploited by merchants on both sides of the exchange divide.

How China's economy managed to absorb millions of ounces of silver annually over the course of decades without dramatic price inflation or some other notable effect remains a matter of much scholarly debate. One outlet was government spending, for by the early seventeenth century Ming rulers became more like their western European contemporaries in outfitting costly armies. Defense against Manchu and other northern raiders as well as disgruntled peasants grew increasingly expensive, but in the end proved ineffectual. Were fluctuations in silver income to blame for Ming decline?

Echoing historians of the seventeenth-century crisis in Europe, scholars long claimed that a dip in silver revenues after about 1630 rendered the state unable to defend itself. More recent research, however, suggests no such dip occurred; silver kept pouring in through the 1640s. Other factors must have trumped the Ming state's budget issues. Meanwhile, private merchants who supplied the military with food, weapons, and other necessities clearly benefited from China's new, silver-based economy, as did those who exported silk to Manila and other overseas bazaars. Only in the nineteenth century would China's vast silver holdings begin to flow outward in exchange for opium and other imports brought by European traders.

Demand for Chinese Exports

China's new commercial links to the outside world stimulated the economy in several ways, especially in the coastal regions around Nanjing and Canton. Men continued to work in intensive rice agriculture since taxes in the form of raw commodities were still required despite rapid monetization of the overall economy. Women, however, were increasingly drawn into the production of silk thread and finished textiles for export. After silk, China's most admired product was its porcelain, known as "chinaware" in the West (see Seeing the Past: Blue-on-White: Ming Export Porcelain).

As in parts of northwest Europe described in the last chapter, Chinese textile making grew more efficient in response to export demands, but without the mechanization, standardization, and wage labor usually associated with modern industry. By the early sixteenth century not only finished fabrics were traded widely in China, but also their components, raw fiber and thread. Even mulberry leaves, which were fed to silkworms to produce thread, were traded on the open market. Only labor was not yet commodified in

SEEING THE PAST

Blue-on-White: Ming Export Porcelain

Ming Blue-on-White Export Porcelain (Paul Freeman/Bridgeman Art Library.)

Before industrialization, China's artisans produced a vast range of consumer goods, from ordinary metal nails to fine silk textiles. After silk, China was most renowned for its porcelain, a special variety of clay pottery fired to the point that it was transformed into glass. The center of this artisanal industry was (and remains) Jingdezhen (JING-deh-juhn) in southern China. The combination of properly mixed clay and high heat made it possible for artisans, mostly men, to fashion durable vessels, plates, and other items

of extraordinary thinness. Over many centuries, Chinese painters and calligraphers developed a range of styles and techniques for decorating porcelain, including the application of cobalt blue pigments that emerged from the kiln in stark contrast to the white base. The Ming developed this "blue-on-white" porcelain specifically for export, first, as we saw in Chapter 15, to the Muslim world and later to regions throughout the globe. The example shown here from about 1600 features Li Tieguai, a legendary Chinese religious figure, but many blue-on-white porcelain products were decorated with Western and other foreign images, including monograms and pictures of the Virgin Mary.

Porcelain making continued throughout the Qing period, as well, but with a shift toward individual artistic virtuosity rather than mass, anonymous production.

EXAMINING THE EVIDENCE

1. How did Ming craftsmen adapt their blue-on-white porcelain to match the tastes of foreign buyers?

2. Compare this Ming plate of around 1600 with the example on page 796 of "Wedgwood blue" china created in industrializing Britain around two centuries later. What aesthetic and physical qualities were the British manufacturers seeking to duplicate, and why?

the modern "hourly" or salaried sense. Unlike in neighboring Korea, chattel slavery, or full ownership of workers' bodies, was extremely rare in China, although penal labor—forced work by prisoners—was exploited in many public projects.

The explosive demand for export textiles that resulted from overseas expansion and American conquest had profound consequences for Chinese women. Women did most spinning and weaving in their own households in the form of piecework. This yielded essential income for the household but also added significantly to an already burdensome workload. Although being paid by the piece or task kept female workers at the mercy of male merchants, this new demand brought Chinese women, much like their Dutch and Irish contemporaries in the linen industry, fully into the global commercial economy. The products of their labors were consumed at the far edges of the world (see Lives and Livelihoods: Silk Weavers in China, page 696).

Manchu Expansion and the Rise of the Qing Empire

Some of the same environmental shocks that exacerbated the seventeenth-century crisis in Europe struck China in the last years of Ming rule. Droughts were particularly severe in the north from 1641 to 1644, but other factors also contributed to Ming decline. Court intrigues, often prompted by increasingly powerful eunuchs (castrated court officials), weakened Ming rulership just as China's economy grew in size and complexity. Manchu raids, meanwhile, became a severe threat and, consequently, a drain on resources as early as the 1620s. The Manchu were also on the march in Korea, which they reduced to tributary status in 1637. By 1642 the raiders reached Shandong province, but it was a local rebel, Li Zicheng, who ushered in the Manchu capture of Beijing in 1644. As the capital fell to Li, both the Ming emperor and his wife committed suicide rather than face the humiliation of captivity. To rid the capital of the rebels, a Ming official sought Manchu aid. The Manchus took advantage of the moment and occupied the capital. Calling themselves the Qing, or "Pure," dynasty, the Manchus quickly adapted to the role of ruling minority (see Map 21.2).

The transition to Qing rule after 1644 proved surprisingly smooth, and most Chinese subjects' lives were barely changed. Although the new Qing emperors maintained a distinct ethnic identity and often dealt harshly with dissenters, they tended to improve on rather than revolutionize established patterns of Chinese governance. As a result, the empire rebounded with remarkable speed. Under Qing rule, Western gunpowder technology was so fully embraced that it enabled the rapid conquest of much of Mongolia, Tibet, and the Amur River basin (claimed by Russia) by the 1750s. Tributaries from these distant provinces trekked to Beijing to pay homage to the "pure" emperor.

Qing Governance

The ascendancy of the Qing dynasty (1644–1911) was cemented with the accession of Emperor Kangxi (kang-shee) in 1661. By the end of his rule in 1722, China was for the first time in centuries an expansionist empire, with westward expansion by land China's principal aim. Mongolia, annexed in 1697, was a critical base for this project, and a buffer against Peter the Great's Russia. Even the traditionally defiant south began to give in, and by 1700 much of mainland Southeast Asia, including Burma, Thailand, Cambodia, and Vietnam, paid tribute to the Qing emperor in exchange for political autonomy. Kangxi's successors sought to follow his example. By 1751 Tibet and Nepal fell to the Qing. Chinese colonists, some of them hungry and homeless after floods and other disasters, were encouraged to move west with tax breaks, homesteads, and other incentives.

Qing Expansion

Most outlying regions were ruled indirectly, and some, like Korea, remained virtually autonomous, but by the 1750s, under the long-lived emperor Qianlong (chee-YEN-loong), China seemed to be reaching the limits of its bureaucratic and military capabilities. Victory in massive wars against southern Siberian peoples demonstrated Qing military might, but trouble was brewing, and not just at the fringes. Rebellions were now common throughout the realm. Subjects in the core districts grew increasingly restless, and guerrilla warfare and massacres of ethnic Chinese colonists became constant features of frontier life. Qianlong clung to power until 1796, and despite ballooning war costs, the emperor's reign

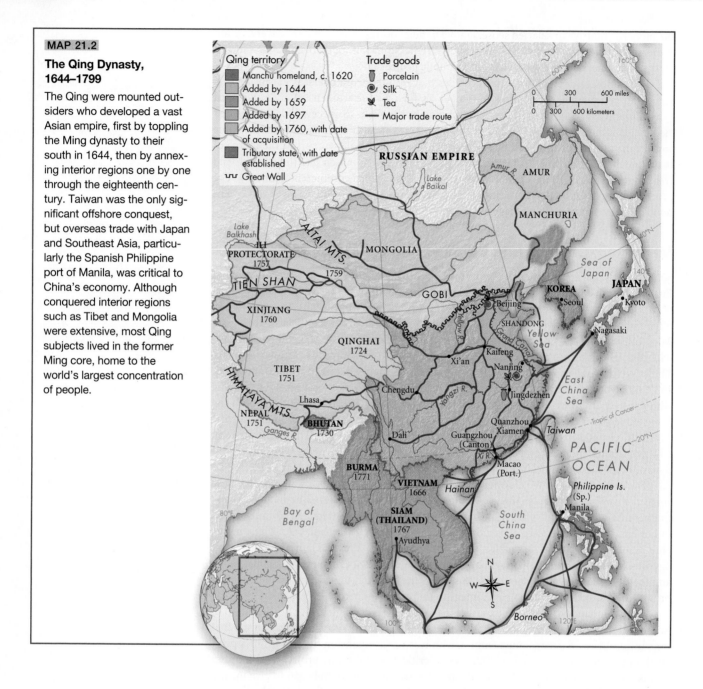

MAP 21.2

The Qing Dynasty, 1644–1799

The Qing were mounted outsiders who developed a vast Asian empire, first by toppling the Ming dynasty to their south in 1644, then by annexing interior regions one by one through the eighteenth century. Taiwan was the only significant offshore conquest, but overseas trade with Japan and Southeast Asia, particularly the Spanish Philippine port of Manila, was critical to China's economy. Although conquered interior regions such as Tibet and Mongolia were extensive, most Qing subjects lived in the former Ming core, home to the world's largest concentration of people.

had boasted some of the biggest treasury surpluses in early modern history. The silver of the Americas had funded Qing expansion.

Environmental Transformations

Historians have only recently begun to examine how China's environment was changed by the general expansion of trade and population in the Ming and Qing eras. The disasters most remarked upon by contemporaries were floods, but their relationship to human rather than divine action was rarely explored except by a few alert public works officials. Deforestation, though not in itself a cause of floods, often exacerbated them. As peasants cleared more and more land for planting and cut forests for firewood and building materials, effective rainfall catchment areas were greatly diminished. Monsoon rains thus swept away more and more exposed soil, creating massive erosion upstream and devastating river sedimentation downstream. The problem became so widespread that Chinese territorial expansion and colonization in Qing times were in part aimed at resettling peasants displaced by environmental catastrophes in the heartland. In early modern times China was arguably the most human-molded landscape in the world in proportion to its population, and subsistence requirements absorbed an extraordinary amount of energy even before the rise of the Ming.

Everyday Life in Ming and Qing China

Ming intellectuals made note of China's broad shift to commercialism as early as the sixteenth century, and most found it annoying. As in many traditional societies (except Islamic ones), merchants and traders were something of a suspect class, esteemed only slightly above actors and musicians. Chinese society as defined by Confucius emphasized production over exchange, the countryside over the city, and continuity over change or mobility. The ideal was a linked grouping of agriculturally self-sufficient provincial units overseen by patriarchal figures. These units were to be connected not by trade, but by a merit-based governing hierarchy headed by a divine monarch.

Struggles of the Common Folk

Within this model, even peasant households were supposed to achieve self-sufficiency, relying on the market only in times of duress. Men were supposed to farm and women were supposed to spin and weave, both remaining in their home villages and producing only for their own consumption. Surpluses, a divine gift to the pious and industrious, were not to be sold but rather yielded up to the emperor at periodic intervals to express fealty and submission. Bureaucrats and scholars, who lived from these surpluses, kept track of them on paper.

Such was the ideal Neo-Confucian society. As we have seen, however, times of duress proved frequent in early modern China: droughts, floods, plagues, and even pirates took their toll. Peasants, as usual, suffered most, especially those driven to frontier lands by continued population growth. These stresses, along with increasing state demands for cash payment of taxes, compelled many individuals and families to migrate and sell their labor to whoever

Chinese Beggars

Although most early modern Chinese artists depicted idealized things of beauty, such as rugged landscapes and fanciful creatures in flight, some turned their attention to ordinary people. This c. 1500 Ming image depicts two wandering beggars, one apparently talking to himself as he walks and the other brandishing a serpent, presumably his helper at winning alms from curious or terrified passersby. The image offers a rare glimpse at an impoverished yet colorful Chinese subculture not often mentioned in historical documents. (The Granger Collection, New York.)

Silk Weavers in China

Chinese Silk Weaving
This rare detail from a Ming ceramic vase shows a group of Chinese women weaving silk on a complex loom. Chinese silk manufacture employed many thousands of women as well as men, doing everything from tending the mulberry bushes that produced the silkworms' food to finishing elaborate brocades and tapestries for export to the wider world, often in exchange for Spanish-American silver. Both highly technical and vast in scale, Chinese silk production was unmatched in early modern times. (Giraudon/ Bridgeman Art Library.)

Silk production, or sericulture, dates back several thousand years in China, but export volume grew most dramatically in early modern times, beginning with the late Ming. It was stimulated in particular by the massive influx of Spanish-American silver after China shifted to a silver-based economy in 1581. Most Chinese silk producers were concentrated in the southeast, especially along the lower Yangzi River (see again Map 21.2). Imperial factories were established under the Ming in Nanjing and Beijing, but most work was spread among peasants who worked at home at specific tasks assigned by private merchants. The merchants paid peasants for their mulberry leaves, cocoons, spun fiber, and finished fabrics.

Silk fiber is spun from the cocoons of the silkworm, produced by the worms' digestion of large quantities of

could pay. There is strong evidence that couples of even middling status practiced various forms of birth control to avoid the financial pressure of additional children.

The Newly Wealthy

Meanwhile, landlords and merchants accumulated increasing amounts of cash through market exchange. They were buying low and selling high, moving goods and getting rich. The social inequity resulting from this process was in part what bothered Chinese traditionalist intellectuals. What struck them as worse, however, since it had profound ethical and hence philosophical implications, was the market economy's tendency to reward non-productive and even outright dishonest behavior. It was the appearance of the uppity rich, not the miserably poor, that most bothered the educated old guard.

The Flourishing of Art and Culture

As in Golden Age Spain, the arts and literature thrived in China during an era of political decline. This seeming paradox was due in part to the patronage of merchants who had made fortunes in the economic upswing, but it was also a function of the surplus of unemployed, literate civil servants. More and more smart people, in short, were angling for work and recognition. The end of the Ming was an era of increased literacy and mass distribution of books as well, and ideas and scientific knowledge were disseminated more widely than ever before. Novels and plays were also hugely popular. The play *The Lute*, published in 1610, included woodblock prints of scenes, for readers not able to see a live performance. Some writers devoted themselves to adventure travel in the interior, describing rugged landscapes and wild rivers for curious urban readers.

mulberry leaves. The worms are fragile creatures susceptible to diseases and in need of constant supervision and feeding. Since they were tended in environments susceptible to drastic temperature changes, the worms' welfare was a constant source of worry. This codependent relationship between humans and insects was perhaps matched only by that of beekeeping for honey collection or cochineal dye production in Mexico (cochineal bugs thrive on prickly pear cacti).

Rather like the linen industry in early modern Holland and Ireland, silk production in Ming and Qing China was extremely labor-intensive and largely dependent on women. Care of silkworms added to a host of domestic and agricultural tasks, and spinning, which had to be finished rapidly before the cocoons rotted, often lasted late into the night. Many households stopped interacting with neighbors entirely until silk season had passed, so intense and delicate was the work. Silk for export had to be reeled twice to guarantee consistent fineness. Still, silk making was attractive to peasants since it allowed them to enter the market economy at greater advantage than with food products, which were heavy and susceptible to spoilage or consumption by rodents and other vermin. Because the industry itself was not taxed, many peasants planted mulberry bushes and tended cocoons to meet the emperor's silver cash tax demands.

Commercial producers eventually developed large reeling machines operated by men, but in early modern times most reeling was done by women on small hand-turned devices. Some peasants also wove textiles, but often not those who produced the raw fiber. With time, like European linen manufacture, Chinese silk production became a highly capitalized industry.

QUESTIONS TO CONSIDER

1. From its origins as an ancient Chinese art, how did silk manufacture change in early modern times?

2. Consider the Lives and Livelihoods essays in Chapters 17 and 18. How did silk weaving differ from sugar making in the Americas and gold mining in Africa?

For Further Information:
Shih, Min-hsiung. *The Silk Industry in Ch'ing China*. Translated by E-tu Zen Sun. 1976.
Vainker, S. J. *Chinese Silk: A Cultural History*. 2004.

In the years around 1600, foreign visitors, notably the Italian Jesuit Matteo Ricci in 1601, impressed the Chinese court with their knowledge of mathematics, alchemy, optics, and mechanics, though not with their religion. When he was not fixing European clocks brought as gifts for the emperor (see page 664), Ricci devoted his time to translating Confucius for a Western audience and composing religious tracts in court Chinese. As in Mughal India, Jesuit visitors at court had some influence on painting styles, particularly royal portraiture. Some artists also adopted European techniques of representing depth and perspective. The Jesuit presence at court and in the trading port of Macao remained important through the Qing era, even though the number of Chinese converts to Christianity remained very small in relation to China's population. They were never expelled from China, as happened in Japan.

Japan in Transition 1540–1750

Located in the temperate latitudes of the North Pacific Ocean, Japan was shut off from the rest of the world for most of the early modern period. A brief opening in the feuding sixteenth century allowed foreign ideas and technologies to flow in and permitted a large but ineffectual invasion of Korea. Soon after 1600, however, Japan's leaders enforced seclusion from the outside world and, like their neighbors in China, concentrated their efforts on consolidating power. Japan would not be reopened for over two centuries.

FOCUS
How did self-isolation affect Japan?

Most inhabitants of the three major islands, Honshu, Kyushu, and Shikoku, were peasants, nearly all of them subjects of regional lords, called **daimyo**. Above Japan's rice-farming peasant majority was a class of warriors called **samurai**, some of them mercenaries and others permanent employees of powerful daimyo. Above the daimyo a small group of generals, including the top-ranking **shogun**, jockeyed to become Japan's supreme ruler. By 1600 the royal family had been reduced to ceremonial figureheads. In the peace that came with closure, Japan's population expanded steadily and the arts flourished.

Tokugawa Japan

Rise of the Tokugawa Shogunate and the Unification of Japan

As we saw in Chapter 15, following what is often described in Japanese history as a golden age of imperial unity and courtly life in the eleventh and twelfth centuries there ensued a breakdown of central authority and a rise in competing military factions. This politically chaotic period, heyday of the samurai warriors, lasted several centuries. The daimyo sometimes succeeded in bringing a measure of order to their domains, but no one daimyo family could establish predominance over others.

At the end of the sixteenth century several generals sought to quell civil war and to unify Japan. One such general, Toyotomi Hideyoshi (1535–1598), not only conquered his rivals but, with the Kyoto emperor's permission, assumed the role of top shogun. After Hideyoshi died, Tokugawa Ieyasu (1542–1616), a powerful military leader, seized control. Assuming the title of shogun in 1603, he declared that thereafter rulership was hereditary. The Tokugawa (TOH-koo-GAH-wah) Shogunate would endure until 1867.

With the uncompromising Tokugawa shoguns in charge of Japan's core districts, regional lords and military men found themselves forced to accept allegiance to the emerging unified state or face its growing might. The vast majority chose submission, and a long period of peace ensued. Peasant rebellions occurred from time to time, sometimes led by disgruntled samurai, but the state's adoption of Neo-Confucian ideals similar to those embraced in contemporary China and Korea stressed duty and hierarchy over rights and individual freedom. No elaborate, Neo-Confucianist civil service exam system was developed to match those of the mainland, but most Japanese accepted the benefits of peace and worked within their assigned roles.

Containment of Foreigners   Hideyoshi's rule had been notable for tolerating Iberian Christian missionaries and launching two massive invasions of Korea in 1593 and 1597, part of a more ambitious project aimed at conquering China. Ieyasu reversed course, banning missionaries and making peace with Korea. Contact with foreigners, particularly Europeans—called *nanban*, or "southern barbarians," a reference to their arrival from southern seas—was restricted after 1614 to the tiny offshore island of Deshima near the city of Nagasaki, in westernmost Kyushu. Foreign families were not permitted to reside on Japanese soil, and by the 1630s all remaining Catholic priests and bachelor merchants had been expelled with the exception of one Dutch merchant. A representative of the Dutch East India Company, or VOC, he was strictly forbidden to discuss religion. The Dutch thus gained access, albeit limited, to the Japanese market, and the Tokugawa shoguns gained access to select information from the West, especially that regarding advances in science and technology. The much more numerous Chinese residents in Nagasaki, most of them silver-hungry merchants, were treated with similar suspicion. Scholars dispute the importance of Christianity in driving the early Tokugawa shoguns toward a policy of seclusion, but it clearly played a role. It was not the foreignness of the nanbans' religion that worried the shoguns, but rather its believers' insistence that it was the one true religion. Japan had long been a land of religious diversity, with a variety of foreign and local sects coexisting more or less peacefully. One

daimyo A regional lord in feudal and early modern Japan.

samurai The hereditary warriors who dominated Japanese society and culture from the twelfth to the nineteenth centuries.

shogun The supreme military commander in Japan, who also took political control.

nanban A Japanese term for "southern barbarians," or Europeans; also applies to hybrid European-Japanese artistic style.

could follow imported Confucian ethical principles, for example, as promoted by the Tokugawa state, yet also be a devout Buddhist. Taoist ideas and rituals were also embraced to a greater or lesser degree by most Japanese. Beyond this, one was expected to venerate nature spirits according to ancient Shinto traditions.

Suppression of Christianity

What was most unattractive about Christianity from the Tokugawa shogun's point of view was its intolerance of these or any other belief systems. Strictly monotheistic, focused on eternal salvation rather than everyday behavior, and fully understood only by foreign specialists, Christianity was branded subversive. Thus Roman Catholicism was harshly persecuted. The first executions of priests and followers began in 1597 and continued, with some breaks, to the end of the 1630s, when a major Christian-led rebellion was suppressed. Then, the shoguns ordered unrepentant priests and converts publicly beheaded, boiled, or crucified. The only remnants of Catholicism to survive this violent purge were scattered names of priests and saints, most of them venerated in older Japanese fashion by isolated peasants and fishing folk (see Reading the Past: Selections from the Hidden Christians' Sacred Book).

Harsh as it was, the shoguns considered their repression of Christianity a political rather than religious action. Stories of Spain's lightning-fast conquests in the distant Americas and nearby Philippines had long circulated in Japan, and Dutch and English contacts were quick to inform the Japanese of alleged Spanish cruelties. Portugal's similarly violent actions in India, Africa, and Southeast Asia were also well known, suggesting to Japan's new rulers that Catholic missionaries, particularly Iberians, were probably a spearhead for imperial designs. Several indiscreet Spanish visitors suggested as much in the 1590s, confirming Japanese fears.

Withdrawal from Global Connections

There was an economic basis for seclusion as well. Japanese exports of silver surged in about 1600 in response to China's shift to a silver cash economy, then declined precipitously. A mining crisis in southwest Honshu in the 1630s forced the shoguns to keep as much silver as possible within the country to avert a currency shortage. This further isolated Japan from outside contact. With silver in short supply, the Dutch exported Japan's other metals, gold and copper, but connections to China and other outsiders gradually diminished. Japan, in short, had little need for the outside world. Even matchlock handguns, which had been successfully copied from early European imports, were abandoned soon after 1600 in favor of more traditional swords. Gunpowder was relegated to fireworks.

Edo, the New Tokugawa Capital

Following Christian suppression in the 1630s, the shoguns established firm control of the interior by forcing subordinate lords to maintain households in the new capital of Edo (modern Tokyo). Wives and children lived in the city and its growing suburbs as virtual hostages, and the daimyo themselves had to rotate in and out of the capital at least every other year. A new version of court life was one result of this shifting center, and with it grew both a vibrant capital city and a complex road and inn system lacing the rugged topography of Japan together. With Edo's primacy firmly established, Osaka became a major marketplace, producing its own class of newly rich merchants, and Kyoto thrived as a major cultural center.

Conquest of the Ainu

Some Tokugawa subjects carried on trade with the Ryukyu Islands to the southwest, but only in the north was there anything like imperial expansion after the failed invasions of Korea in the 1590s. Japanese merchants had long traded rice for gold dust and rare seafoods with the Ainu of Hokkaido. The Ainu (EYE-new), who sported tattoos and whose men wore long beards, descended from Siberians from the north and probably also Austronesian islanders from the south. The Japanese considered them barbarians, and the Ainu considered the Japanese treacherous. By 1650 Japanese trading families had colonized portions of southernmost Hokkaido, but increasing pressures on the Ainu sparked rebellion. The Tokugawa state was reluctant to spend the necessary money to invade and fortify Hokkaido, but it did claim the island as Japanese territory. Only when the Russians threatened in the late eighteenth century to annex Ainu-inhabited islands farther north did the Japanese cement their claims and back them with force. Ainu culture was violently suppressed, but survives to the present day.

Selections from the Hidden Christians' Sacred Book

As seen in the last chapter with regard to Judaism and Islam in early modern Iberia, oppressed religions have survived in secret for centuries. Sometimes theologies endured with little change thanks to a preserved text or a sequence of tradition-keepers with good memories; in other cases only traces of old ritual behaviors persisted. In regions where a complex religious tradition had only recently been introduced before being harshly persecuted, considerable blending of local and imported ideas and forms was usually still in process. This yielded yet a third result, a kind of stunted blend. Thus Christianity's brief appearance in Japan produced an unusual underground religious tradition that was in general more Japanese than Christian. Compare the version of Genesis below to the standard Western text.

In the beginning Deusu [Dios] was worshiped as Lord of Heaven and Earth, and Parent of humankind and all creation. Deusu has two hundred ranks and forty-two forms, and divided the light that was originally one, and made the Sun Heaven, and twelve other heavens. The names of these heavens are Benbo or Hell, Manbo, Oribeten, Shidai, Godai, Pappa, Oroha, Konsutanchi, Hora, Koroteru, and a hundred thousand Paraiso [Paradise] and Gokuraku.

Deusu then created the sun, the moon, and the stars, and called into being tens of thousands of anjo [angels] just by thinking of them. One of them, Jusuheru [Lucifer], the head of seven anjo, has a hundred ranks and thirty-two forms. Deusu is the one who made all

things: earth, water, fire, wind, salt, oil, and put in his own flesh and bones. Without pause Deusu worked on the Shikuda, Terusha, Kuwaruta, Kinta, Sesuta, and Sabata [all days of the week, mostly from Portuguese]. Then on the seventh day Deusu blew breath into this being and named him Domeigosu-no-Adan [Adam], who possessed thirty-three forms. So this is the usual number of forms for a human being.

For this reason the seventh day of one cycle is observed as a feast day.

Deusu then made a woman and called her Domeigosu-no-Ewa [Eve], had the man and woman marry, and gave them the realm called Koroteru. There they bore a son and a daughter, Chikoro and Tanho, and went every day to Paraiso to worship Deusu.

Source: Christal Whelan, ed. and trans., *The Beginning of Heaven and Earth: The Sacred Book of Japan's Hidden Christians* (Honolulu: University of Hawai'i Press, 1996) (portions of an early nineteenth-century Tokugawa-era Kakure Kirishitan, or "Hidden Christian," manuscript).

EXAMINING THE EVIDENCE

1. What elements of Christian teachings survive in this origin tale of the world?

2. What elements of the story are distinctly Japanese?

Everyday Life and Culture in Tokugawa Japan

Agricultural Expansion

Japan's population grew from about 10 million in 1600 to nearly 30 million in 1700, when it stabilized. This rapid growth was made possible in part by relative peace, but expansion and integration of the rice economy contributed as well. Rice's high yields encouraged creation of even the smallest irrigated fields, and some daimyo proved to be skillful marketers of their tributaries' main product. Most rice was sold in cities and to elites, while peasants ate a healthier diet of mixed grains, vegetables, and soy products. Urban-rural reciprocity was key, and processed human excrement collected in cities and villages was the main fertilizer. As surprising as it may seem, Japan's complex system of waste collection and recycling was easily the most hygienic and efficient in the world. Whole guilds were dedicated to the collection and marketing of what in the West was regarded as dangerous filth. The water supply of Edo, with over half a million people by the eighteenth century, was cleaner and more reliable than that of London. Thus, this system improved the health of the Japanese population as it created connections between urban and rural Japanese.

New strains of rice introduced from Southeast Asia also allowed farmers to extend cultivation into previously unproductive areas. By contrast, American crops such as maize and peanuts were not embraced in Japan as they were in China. Only sweet potatoes were appreciated, and they saved millions of lives during times of famine. As in China, however, Japanese agricultural expansion and diversification had profound ecological consequences. Leaders immediately recognized that deforestation intensified floods, and they responded to this problem with striking efficiency, organizing armies of workers to replant many depleted woodlands by the eighteenth century.

Transportation infrastructure was everywhere improved, from roads and bridges to ports and canals. Shoguns kept daimyos in check after 1615 by permitting only one castle in each domain, and sharply limiting improvement or expansion, but peace encouraged other forms of private construction. Like agriculture, the construction boom soon took a toll on Japan's forests, as did increased shipbuilding and other transport-related industries. Vulnerability to earthquakes gave rise to building codes and design innovations. A German-born employee of the Dutch VOC, Engelbert Kaempfer, described this Edo scene in 1691: "Today, one hour before noon, in bright and calm weather, a terrible earthquake shook the house with a loud sound. . . . This earthquake taught me that the country's laws limiting the height of buildings are based on necessity. It is also necessary that buildings be constructed of light wood, partitions, boards, and wood chips and then, below the timbers, be topped with a heavy pole, which with its weight pushes together the whole construction so that it does not collapse during an earthquake."[2] Hence, in agriculture, infrastructure, and construction, the leaders of Tokugawa Japan demonstrated the power of centralized government, controlling Japan's growth and development and shaping the connections between their subjects.

Although the majority of Tokugawa subjects remained peasants, a genuine leisure class also emerged, mostly concentrated in Kyoto. Merchants imported raw silk from China, which Japanese artisans processed and wove. Other imports included sandalwood, sugar, and spices from Southeast Asia. Consumption of fine fabrics and other products by the wealthy greatly expanded the artisan sector, but did not spark industrialization. There was simply not a large enough wage-earning consumer class in Japan to sustain industrial production. Instead, the trend was toward increasingly high-quality "boutique" goods such as samurai swords and ceremonial kimonos, rather than mass-produced consumer goods.

The period did, however, see the emergence of a precursor to modern Japanese industrialization. Like elites, peasants had to be clothed, if less opulently. What they wore most were locally produced cotton garments. Both the demand and supply of these textiles were new developments historically. Most traditional peasant clothing prior to the sixteenth century had been made from hemp fiber, and only through trade with Korea and China had cotton come to figure in Japan's economy. Initially, cotton was in demand among sixteenth-century samurai warriors, who used it for clothing, lining for armor, and fuses for matchlock handguns. Fishing folk also consumed cotton sailcloth. Trade restrictions in the Tokugawa era stimulated internal production of cotton textiles to such a degree that it reached near-industrial levels by the eighteenth century.

Japanese commoners got by on a diet of just under two thousand calories a day according to population historians, mostly consisting of grain porridges. They consumed very little meat and no milk or cheese, and away from coastal areas where seafood and fish could be harvested, most protein came from beans and soy products such as tofu. A huge variety of fruits, vegetables, herbs, grasses, fungi, insects, and larvae were roasted or pickled for consumption in winter or in lean times. Tobacco, an American crop, grew increasingly popular under Tokugawa rule. It was smoked by men and women of all social classes in tiny clay pipes, serving a social function much like the sharing of tea. When tea was too expensive, as it often was, common folk drank boiled water, which was at least safe. In all, the peasant diet in Tokugawa Japan, though short of protein, was at least as nourishing as that of western Europe at the same time.

Both elite and ordinary Japanese folk lived according to a blend of agricultural and ritual calendars. In the simplest sense, time was measured according to lunar months and solar years, but there were numerous overlapping astrological and imperial cycles measured by Buddhist monks, who tolled bells to remind villagers and urbanites alike of ritual obligations. Western-style clocks, though known, were not adopted.

Improvements in Infrastructure

Rise of a Leisure Class and Expansion of the Artisan Sector

Growth of Cotton Textile Production

Commoners' Diet

The Japanese Calendar

Kyoto Festival

This c. 1750 painting of a festival in Kyoto, Japan, depicts not only the daimyo, or local lord, and his ox-drawn cart and procession of armed samurai, but also daily goings-on about town. Many people seem to be engaged in conversation indoors, although they are quite visible thanks to open screens, allowing them to view the procession. Near the top of the panel, women and children walk leisurely toward what appears to be a recitation, possibly given by a samurai, and accompanied by a drummer. The use of patterned gold clouds to fill in empty spaces was a standard convention of early modern Japanese art, and here it adds a foglike layer to the painting's depth. (The Granger Collection, New York.)

Women's Lives   Women of every class faced obstacles to freedom in Japan's male-dominated and often misogynist society. Most were expected to marry at an early age and spend the majority of their lives serving their husbands, children, and in-laws. Still, as in other traditional societies, there were significant openings for female self-expression and even access to power in Tokugawa Japan. At court, noblewomen exercised considerable influence over succession and the everyday maintenance of proper decorum, and in the peasant sphere women managed household affairs, particularly when men were away on military duty or business. Widows could become quite powerful, especially those managing the affairs of dead merchant husbands.

Emergence of a National Culture

With the growth of cities and rise of a leisure class, Japanese literature and painting flourished, along with flower arranging, stylized and puppet theater, board games, and music. The writer Ihara Saikaku (EH-hah-rah sigh-kah-KOO) grew immensely popular at the end of the seventeenth century with his tales contrasting elite and working-class life. Saikaku idealized homosexual relations between senior and junior samurai, and also those among actors and their patrons, mostly wealthy townsmen. In "The Great Mirror of Male Love," Saikaku described most of these relationships as temporary, consensual, and often purchased. More than a hint of misogyny pervades the writings of Saikaku, but that sentiment is less evident in his "Life of an Amorous Woman" and other stories relating the adventures of courtesans and female prostitutes. In short, homosexuality, bisexuality, and prostitution were not only accepted but institutionalized in Tokugawa society.

In Edo, Kyoto, and especially the rice-trading city of Osaka, entertainments were many and varied. Daimyo and samurai landlords came to Osaka to exchange their rice tributes for money, which they then spent locally or in Edo, where they had to pay obeisance to the emperor. The frequent visits by regional elites to these two cities helped make them economic and cultural crossroads for Japan as a whole. Many samurai moved to these cities permanently as their rural estates diminished in size across generations. Social tension arose as the old warrior class tried to adapt to the cooperative requirements of urban life, but fortunately, there was much to distract them. Some worked for little compensation as teachers or policemen, but the wealthier samurai found time for the theater, musical concerts, and poetry readings. **Sumo** wrestling matches were popular even among non-samurai urbanites, as were board games, the tea ceremony, calligraphy, bonsai cultivation, and garden landscaping. More costly pursuits such as gambling, drinking, and sexual diversions were restricted to the so-called Licensed Quarters of the major cities. In general these activities were not considered "vices" as long as they did not prevent individuals from performing their civil duties.

Early modern European visitors, especially Catholic priests, found the general Japanese tolerance of prostitution, female impersonation, and homosexuality shocking, but they made little effort to understand Japanese cultural attitudes about sex and shame. Prostitution often was degrading to women and in some places approached the level of sex slavery. Still, there were groups of female escorts such as the geisha whom outsiders mistook for prostitutes. The **geisha** were indentured servants who made their living as private entertainers to the wealthiest merchants and landowners visiting or inhabiting cities. Geisha dress, makeup, and general comportment were all highly ritualized and distinctive. Although the geisha had control over their adult sexual lives, their first coital experience, or "deflowering," was sold to the highest bidder. Many young male prostitutes also acted as female impersonators in kabuki theater.

Kabuki was a popular form of theater that first appeared in Kyoto in 1603 as a way to advertise a number of female prostitutes. Subsequent shows caused such violence among potential customers that the Tokugawa government allowed only men to perform. As these female impersonators became associated with male prostitution, the state established official theaters that punished actors and patrons who engaged in sexual relations. By the eighteenth century, kabuki performances had become so "sanitized" that they included moralizing Neo-Confucian speeches. Even so, playwrights such as Chikamatsu Monzaemon (1653–1724) managed to retain ribald humor amid lessons in correct behavior. At the other end of the spectrum was the somber and ancient tradition of Noh theater, associated with Buddhist tales and Shinto shrines.

Poetry flourished as never before during the era of seclusion, and poets such as the itinerant and prolific Matsuo Bashō (1644–1684) were widely read. Here is a sample of his work:

> On my way through Nagoya, where crazy Chikusai is said to have practiced quackery and poetry, I wrote:
>
> With a bit of madness in me,
> Which is poetry,
> I plod along like Chikusai
> Among the wails of the wind.

Urban Sophistication

sumo A Japanese professional wrestler known for his heft.

geisha A professional female entertainer in Tokugawa Japan.

kabuki A popular Japanese theater known for bawdy humor and female impersonation.

Kabuki Theater

Something of a counterpoint to Neo-Confucian ideals of self-control and social order was Tokugawa Japan's ribald kabuki theater tradition, which became wildly popular in major cities after 1600. Kabuki actors were initially prostitutes, first young women and then young men, but objections from the samurai led by 1670 to the creation of a class of older men licensed to act in drag. In this c. 1680 screen painting by Hishikawa Moronobu, actors, costume designers, makeup artists, washerwomen, and stagehands all appear to be absorbed in their own little worlds. The painting seems to confirm early modern Japan's inward gaze and seemingly total cultural and material self-sufficiency. (The Granger Collection, New York.)

Sleeping on a grass pillow
I hear now and then
The nocturnal bark of a dog
In the passing rain.[3]

Despite isolation, Japan was among the most literate societies in the world in early modern times. By 1700 there were some fifteen hundred publishers active between Edo, Kyoto, and Osaka, publishing at least 7300 titles. Books on everything from tobacco farming to how young brides could find marital bliss were sold or rented in both city and countryside. Early forms of comic books were circulating by the eighteenth century, with the greatest sellers resembling what today would be classed as pulp fiction. Most books continued to be published on woodblock presses despite the fact that movable type was known from both mainland Asian and European sources—another example of the fact that early modern Japan, like China, had little need of the West.

Korea, a Land in Between 1392–1750

The Korean peninsula falls between China and Japan, with the Yellow Sea to the west and the Sea of Japan to the east. In 1392 Korea came to be ruled by the Yi (or Choson) dynasty, which remained in power until 1910. Though unified since the late seventh century, the Korean peninsula developed its distinctive culture primarily during Yi times, partly in response to Chinese and Japanese invasions. Korea had long been influenced by China, and had likewise served as a conduit linking the Asian mainland to Japan. The guiding principles of the early Choson state were drawn from the work of Confucius, as in contemporary China and Japan, and grafted onto a society that mostly practiced Buddhism, yet another imported tradition. Still, Koreans regarded themselves as a distinct and autonomous people, unified by a language and culture.

FOCUS

How did life for common folk in early modern Korea differ from life in China or Japan?

Capital and Countryside

It was under the first Yi ruler that Seoul, then known as Hanyang, became Korea's undisputed capital. Following Chinese principles of geomancy, or auspicious site selection, the Choson capital, backed by mountains and spread along the Han River plains, was considered blessed. Successive rulers drafted nearby peasants to expand the city and add to its grandeur. By 1450 Hanyang was home not only to substantial royal palaces but also bureaucratic buildings, markets, and schools.

The Choson state was not secular, but its leaders did move quickly to reduce the political and economic power of Buddhist temples and monasteries. Temple lands were widely confiscated and distributed to loyal officials. A kind of Neo-Confucian constitution was drafted in the first years of Yi rule advocating more radical state takeover and redistribution of land to peasants, but nobles balked and for the most part tenant farming persisted. Early modern Korea's government mirrored neighboring China's in some ways, but a significant difference was the prominence of a noble class, the **yangban**. Ancient ruling clans dominated the highest ranks of the bureaucracy, which consisted of a broad range of councils and regional governorships. A uniquely Korean institution known as the Samsa, a kind of academic oversight committee, had power even over the king himself, acting as a type of moral police force. Official historians, also drawn from the educated noble class, were allowed to write what they observed, keeping their work secret from the king. The Korean state did follow the Chinese model of civil service examinations, however, and through the hardest of these a few rare individuals of medium rank gained access to positions of power. The pressure was so great that some enterprising students hid tightly rolled crib-notes in their nostrils. Military service proved unpopular, partly because it was associated with slavery, and enrollment in school won exemption.

Japanese invasions, 1592, 1597
Manchu invasions, 1627, 1637

Choson Korea

Korea still needed a defense apparatus, though, and the early Yi rulers responded directly. The nobles' private forces were consolidated into a national, standing army by the mid-fifteenth century, and a complex system of ranks and divisions was instituted. Professional military men took exams, and peasants soon faced periodic draft service in frontier outposts. The Jurchen and other horse warriors threatened Korea's northern provinces from time to time, but many chieftains were successfully co-opted by the Choson state in the fifteenth century. Another defense strategy was to settle the northern frontier with land-hungry peasants from the south.

Foreign Challenges

yangban The noble class in early modern Korea.

Social Order in Early Modern Korea

Korean life under the Yi dynasty was marked by sharp class divisions, with a large portion of the poorer country folk living as slaves. This eighteenth-century painting on silk shows a notable individual on promenade, elaborately dressed, shaded, and otherwise attended, as more humble figures kneel in submission in the foreground. The broad-brimmed black hats and flowing garments were typical of high-ranking Koreans. Although Korean artists also depicted humble workers with some dignity, the Neo-Confucian ideal of a rigid social order comes through most strongly here. (The Art Archive/Musée Guimet Paris/Gianni Dagli Orti.)

After these early initiatives, defense became less of a concern, and the general devaluing of military service, which some Neo-Confucian reformers tried to address through incentives and fund-raising schemes, left Korea vulnerable by the time the Japanese invaded the peninsula in 1593 and 1597. Despite their massive forces and lightning speed, the Japanese under Shogun Hideyoshi were soon driven out with aid from Ming China. The Manchus were not so easily subdued, however. They invaded Korea in 1627 and 1636, reducing it to tributary status by 1637. Still, Korea managed to retain considerable autonomy.

Korea exported ginseng, furs, and a few other items to China in exchange for silk and porcelain, but its overseas trade was generally small, and only a few Korean merchants ventured beyond Japan or the nearby Ryukyu Islands, especially Okinawa. Aside from a general lack of high-value exports, which also dampened European interest, Korean merchants in the south faced constant threats from mostly Japanese pirates, the same ones who menaced China and its merchants from the thirteenth to seventeenth centuries. The Choson government attempted to suppress the pirates through both force and diplomacy, but Japan's fractured political system and occasional sponsorship of the pirates had the same hindering effect on Korean overseas trade felt in coastal China.

Everyday Life in Choson Korea

Despite rugged terrain, most Koreans under Yi rule were rice farmers. Wet-field rice cultivation expanded dramatically in the south beginning in the fifteenth century thanks to government initiatives and adaptation of Chinese techniques. Southern populations grew accordingly. Population estimates are debated, but it appears that Korea grew from about 5 million inhabitants in 1450 to some 10 million by 1600. In colder and drier parts of the peninsula, especially in the far north, peasants relied on millet and barley. As in Japan, these healthy grains were widely disdained as hardship rations in early modern times. Soybeans were later planted, adding a new source of protein. Koreans also exploited seacoasts and rivers for mollusks and fish, and some raised pigs and other livestock. Vegetables such as cabbage were pickled for winter consumption, spiced by the eighteenth century with capsicum peppers introduced from the Americas.

Gender Roles and Religious Beliefs

Ordinary folk probably did not obsess over genealogies and proper marriage matches to the extent that the noble class, or yangban, did, but their mating customs could still be rigid. Some marriages were arranged, occasionally between young children. Women appear to have lost a great deal of their former autonomy thanks to the rise of Neo-Confucianism, and widows were even presented with a knife with which to kill themselves should they be sexually violated or otherwise dishonored. According to some sources,

Korean women more often used their suicide knives to kill attackers. Female entertainers, or **kisaeng**—like their Japanese counterparts, the geisha—were sometimes able to accumulate capital and achieve literary fame.

Teachers in Choson Korea took on the moral advisory role played by priests or imams in early modern Christian or Islamic societies, and in the seventeenth century Neo-Confucian scholars, following the lead of China's Wang Yangming, attempted to reform Korean society and government wholesale. Education in general was highly valued, and literacy widespread (see Reading the Past: Scenes from the Daily Life of a Korean Queen). It was in the Choson era that Korean students became outspoken critics of the state, launching a number of mass protests in the late seventeenth and early eighteenth centuries. Despite the ruling class's attachment to Neo-Confucian philosophy and suppression of Buddhist monasteries, popular religious ideas persisted, especially in the countryside. Alongside some rooted Buddhist beliefs, mountain deities and sacred stones or trees continued to be venerated on a regular basis, much as in western Africa and the Andes Mountains of South America, and shamanism was widely practiced for divination and healing. Many of the best-known healing shamans were women.

kisaeng A geisha-like female entertainer in early modern Korea.

READING THE PAST

Scenes from the Daily Life of a Korean Queen

The following selection is taken from the diary of Lady Hong (1735–1815), a queen during Korea's Yi dynasty. Unlike most male authors of the time, who wrote in Chinese (in part to show off their education, much as many European men at this time wrote in Latin rather than their own vernaculars), Lady Hong wrote in the Korean script. She also devoted great attention to the details of everyday life, including close observations of individual emotions. After stating that she began to write her memoirs at the urging of a nephew, Lady Hong describes her birth and early upbringing:

I was born during the reign of King Yongjo, at noon on 6 August 1735, at my mother's family's home in Kop'yong-dong, Pangsongbang. One night, before I was born, my father had dreamed of a black dragon coiled around the rafters of my mother's room, but the birth of a daughter did not seem to fit the portent of his dream. . . .

My paternal grandfather, Lord Chong-hon, came to look at me, and took an immediate fancy to me, declaring, "Although it is a girl, this is no ordinary child!" As I grew up, he became so fond of me that he was reluctant to let me leave his lap. He would say jokingly, "This girl is quite a little lady already, so she is sure to grow up quickly!". . .

The womenfolk of our family were all connected with the most respected clans of the day. My mother came from the Yi family—an upright clan. My father's eldest sister was married to a famous magistrate; while

his second sister was a daughter-in-law of Prince Ch'ong-nung; and his youngest sister was a daughter-in-law of the minister of the board of civil office. Despite these connections, they were not haughty or extravagant, as is so often the case. When the family gathered together on festival days, my mother always treated the elder members with respect, and greeted the younger ones with a kind smile and an affectionate word. Father's second brother's wife was likewise virtuous, and her esteem for my mother was exceeded only by that for her mother-in-law. She was an outstanding woman—noble-minded and well educated. She was very fond of me; taught me my Korean alphabet and instructed me in a wide range of subjects. I loved her like a mother and indeed my mother used to say I had grown too close to her.

Source: Lady Hong, *Memoirs of a Korean Queen,* ed. and trans. Choe-Wall Yangh-hi (London: KPI, 1985), 1–4, 49.

EXAMINING THE EVIDENCE

1. In what ways do these passages reveal Neo-Confucian values?

2. What do these passages tell us about gender roles in a Neo-Confucian court society?

Slavery   Choson Korea appears unique among early modern states in that it was both ethnically homogeneous and heavily reliant on slave labor. Korea's enslaved population, perhaps as much as 30 percent of the total by 1550, appears to have emerged as a result of several factors: debt peonage (self-sale due to famine or debt) and penal servitude (punishment for crimes, including rebellion). Debt peonage and penal servitude were not unusual in the early modern world, and both could be found in neighboring China. What made slavery different in Korea was that the legal status of the enslaved, once proclaimed, was likely to be inherited for many generations. Self-purchase was extremely difficult, and slave owners clung to their chattels tenaciously. Korea's rigid social structure, far more hierarchical than neighboring China's or Japan's, only reinforced the notion of perpetual bondage. Moralists criticized slavery as early as the seventeenth century, but it was not until forced contact with outsiders after 1876 that the institution died out. Korea's last slaves were freed only in 1894.

Consolidation in Mainland Southeast Asia 1500–1750

FOCUS

What trends did mainland Southeast Asia share with China, Korea, Japan, and Russia?

Mainland Southeast Asia, encompassing the modern nations of Burma (Myanmar), Thailand, Cambodia, Laos, and Vietnam, followed a path more like that of China than of the Southeast Asian islands discussed in Chapter 19. Overall trends on the mainland included political consolidation, mostly by Buddhist kings; growth of large, tribute-paying populations due to intensive wet rice cultivation; and a shift toward planting of cash crops such as sugar for export. Unlike the more politically fractured islands of Indonesia and the Philippines, which fell increasingly into the hands of European interlopers (see Counterpoint: "Spiritual Conquest" in the Philippines), mainland Southeast Asia in early modern times experienced gunpowder-fueled, dynastic state-building.

Political Consolidation

The mainland Southeast Asian kingdoms in place by 1700 formed the basis for the nation-states of today. As happened in Muscovite Russia, access to European guns enabled some emerging dynasties, such as those of southern Burma, to expand and even briefly conquer their neighbors in the sixteenth and seventeenth centuries. Another catalyst for change was the rapid growth of global maritime trade, evident since the early fifteenth century (see Map 21.3). Overseas commerce transformed not only traditional maritime hubs such as Melaka and Aceh, as seen in Chapter 19, but also Pegu in Burma, Ayudhya (or Ayutthaya) in Thailand, and Lovek (near modern Phnom Penh) in Cambodia. The Buddhist kings who dominated these cities used trade revenues to expand and enhance their realms by attracting scholars, building libraries and monasteries, and constructing temples and images of the Buddha. The most confident saw themselves as incarnations of the Buddhist ideal of the universal king. Funded in part by growing trade, a massive bronze Buddha and supporting temple complex were built in the city of Luang Prabang, in Laos, beginning in 1512. A solid gold Buddha was also commissioned. Religious monuments on this scale, as seen in Europe, the Middle East, and even Spanish America, are a lasting reminder of early modern devotion and wealth.

The Example of Burma   A notable example of mainland Southeast Asian state-building driven by commercial wealth and access to European gunpowder weapons arose in southern Burma beginning in the 1530s. Portuguese mercenaries aided a regional king's takeover of the commercial city of Pegu, and a new, Pegu-based Buddhist dynasty with imperial ambitions soon emerged. Under King Bayinnaung (r. 1551–1581) the Burmese expanded into neighboring Thailand and Laos, conquering the prosperous capital of Ayudhya in 1569 and Vientiane, on the

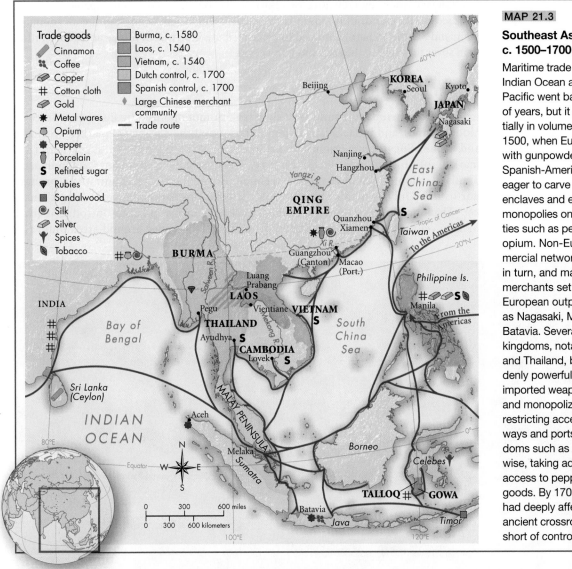

Trade goods

- Cinnamon
- Coffee
- Copper
- Cotton cloth
- Gold
- Metal wares
- Opium
- Pepper
- Porcelain
- **S** Refined sugar
- Rubies
- Sandalwood
- Silk
- Silver
- Spices
- Tobacco

Burma, c. 1580
Laos, c. 1540
Vietnam, c. 1540
Dutch control, c. 1700
Spanish control, c. 1700
Large Chinese merchant community
Trade route

MAP 21.3

Southeast Asian Trade, c. 1500–1700

Maritime trade between the Indian Ocean and the western Pacific went back thousands of years, but it grew exponentially in volume and value after 1500, when Europeans arrived with gunpowder weapons and Spanish-American silver, eager to carve out trading enclaves and establish monopolies on key commodities such as pepper and opium. Non-European commercial networks expanded in turn, and many Chinese merchants set up shop in European outposts such as Nagasaki, Manila, and Batavia. Several mainland kingdoms, notably Burma and Thailand, became suddenly powerful by adopting imported weapons technology and monopolizing exports or restricting access to waterways and ports. Island kingdoms such as Aceh did likewise, taking advantage of their access to pepper and other goods. By 1700, Europeans had deeply affected this ancient crossroads, yet fell far short of controlling it.

upper Mekong River, in 1574. After building numerous pagodas, or ceremonial towers, in his new conquests, admirers referred to Bayinnaung as the "Victor of Ten Directions." He preferred the title "King of Kings."

Vietnam followed a different path, largely as a result of Chinese influence. Even before Ming expansion southward in the fourteenth and early fifteenth centuries, Neo-Confucian principles of law and governance had been adopted by Vietnamese royalty under the Le dynasty (1428–1788). Yet like Korea, whose nobility had also embraced the kinds of reformist ideas promoted by Wang Yangming, the Chinese veneer in Vietnam barely masked a vibrant regional culture whose sense of distinct identity was never in question. China brokered power-sharing arrangements between the northern and southern halves of Vietnam in the 1520s, but new, competitive dynasties, led by the Trinh and Nguyen clans, were already in the making. Their battles for control lasted until the late seventeenth century and hindered Vietnamese consolidation despite the region's shared language and culture.

Mainland Southeast Asia resembled China more than neighboring islands in another sense: high overall population. This was largely the result of wet-rice agriculture and acquired immunity to a range of lowland tropical maladies. Massive water-control projects reminiscent of those in China and Japan allowed Vietnam's feuding clans to field tens of

Vietnam's Different Path

thousands of troops by 1700. Rice-rich Burma was even more populous, capable of fielding hundreds of thousands of troops as early as 1650. Unlike China, most of the kingdoms of mainland Southeast Asia continued to collect tribute in the form of rice and goods rather than silver throughout the early modern period.

Commercial Trends

Exports   Exports from mainland Southeast Asia were not monopolized by Europeans in early modern times, and in fact many commodities found their principal markets in China and Japan. Sugar cane originated in Southeast Asia, but refined sugar found no market until the late seventeenth century, when growers in Vietnam, Cambodia, and Thailand adopted Chinese milling technology and began to export their product northward. Only Taiwan competed with these regions for the Japanese "sweet" market. That most addictive of Columbian exchange crops, tobacco, introduced from Mexico via Manila, joined betel leaves (traditionally wrapped around areca nuts) as a

Buddha from Luang Prabang
This enormous gilt bronze Buddha was cast in the early sixteenth century in the former royal capital of Laos, Luang Prabang, where it is still at the center of an active temple. For several centuries the temple also housed a solid gold Buddha, which is now in the nearby palace museum. The remarkably well-preserved city and temples of Luang Prabang evoke the heyday of the Buddhist kings of mainland Southeast Asia, when new gunpowder weapons and access to more distant foreign markets stoked expansionist urges. (Yoshio Tomii Photo Studio/Aflo FotoAgency/Photolibrary.)

popular stimulant throughout the region by the seventeenth century. Other drugs had more profound consequences. The Dutch were the first to push the sale of opium from India in the 1680s (initially as a tobacco additive), and it soon created a class of addicts among Southeast Asia's many Chinese merchants and others willing to pay any amount of silver cash for it.

Imports to mainland Southeast Asia consisted primarily of cloth from India, an old "monsoon circuit" trade good that fostered resident communities of merchants, most of them Muslims, from as far away as Gujarat, in the Arabian Sea. Chinese merchants brought cloth from home, too, along with metal wares, porcelain, and a wide range of goods acquired through interregional trade. On the whole, the Chinese were by far more competitive and successful middlemen in mainland Southeast Asia than Europeans in early modern times, a fact that led to much resentment.

Imports

Interregional and interethnic commerce and urbanization enabled many Southeast Asian women to engage in trade as well, and whether they were Islamic, Buddhist, or otherwise observant, this pattern fit well with the general regional tendency toward female independence noted in Chapter 19. The wives and concubines of prominent long-distance merchants not only carried on important business transactions on land, they traveled with their husbands and lovers at sea. Some Southeast Asian women served as fully autonomous intermediaries for European merchants, most famously Soet Pegu, a Burmese woman who lived in the Thai capital of Ayudhya. She was the principal broker for the Dutch in Thailand (then known as Siam) for many years beginning in the 1640s.

Women's Commercial Pursuits

The global financial crisis of the seventeenth century, coupled with a number of regional wars, epidemics, and droughts, left mainland Southeast Asia in a weakened state. Burma contracted considerably, as did neighboring Siam. Laos survived as a separate kingdom only due to its isolation from these two neighbors, and it became even more inward-looking. Cambodia was similarly introverted under Khmer rule, and Vietnam suffered an even more severe decline. Mainland Southeast Asia submitted to paying tribute to China's Qing emperors in the course of the eighteenth century. In spite of the trend toward contraction, however, the region remained nearly impervious to European designs.

Economic Contraction

COUNTERPOINT
"Spiritual Conquest" in the Philippines

The Philippine Islands are a large volcanic chain in the warm tropical waters of the western Pacific (see Map 21.4). Like most Southeast Asian islands, the Philippines were settled by Austronesian mariners who left southern China and Taiwan some three thousand years ago. With the exception of a few small Islamic sultanates in the southern islands, the Philippines at the dawn of early modern times had no dynastic rulers or overarching religious or ethical traditions to unify its population. Over one hundred languages were spoken throughout the archipelago, and material culture differed radically from one river valley or island to the next.

> **FOCUS**
>
> In contrast to the general trend of political consolidation in early modern Asia, why did the Philippines fall to a European colonizing power?

Kin-based political units rarely exceeded two thousand members, and most were mutually hostile, sometimes murderously so. The islands' total population was relatively high, probably between 1 and 2 million in 1500, and acquired immunity to Old World diseases appears to have been relatively robust, certainly superior to that of Europeans who came later. As in most of Southeast Asia, women in the Philippines were relatively powerful and autonomous in politics, business, and domestic affairs. Both slavery and long-distance trade were established, though not deeply entrenched institutions, and a writing system using bamboo slats, now lost, was more or less common.

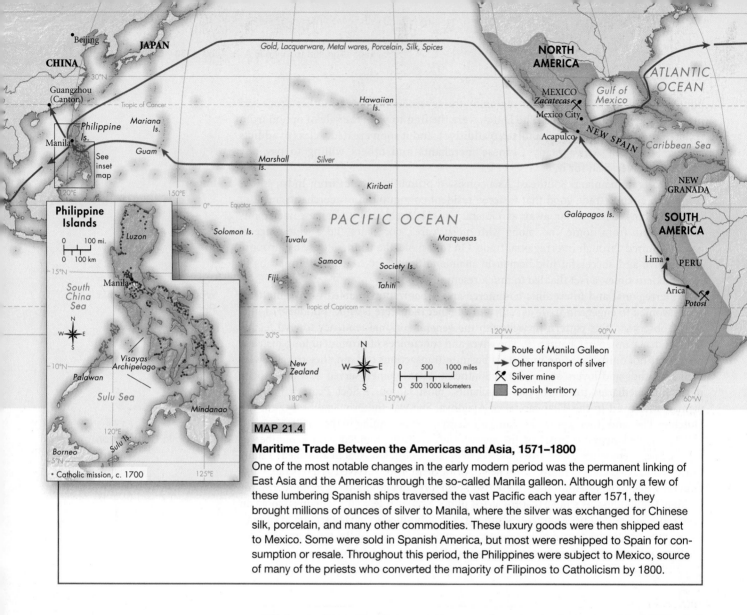

Maritime Trade Between the Americas and Asia, 1571–1800

One of the most notable changes in the early modern period was the permanent linking of East Asia and the Americas through the so-called Manila galleon. Although only a few of these lumbering Spanish ships traversed the vast Pacific each year after 1571, they brought millions of ounces of silver to Manila, where the silver was exchanged for Chinese silk, porcelain, and many other commodities. These luxury goods were then shipped east to Mexico. Some were sold in Spanish America, but most were reshipped to Spain for consumption or resale. Throughout this period, the Philippines were subject to Mexico, source of many of the priests who converted the majority of Filipinos to Catholicism by 1800.

Filipino traders sailing large outrigger vessels maintained contact with the East and Southeast Asian mainland, as well as with southern Japan, and Chinese merchants had long operated small trading posts in the Philippines, including one at Manila on the northern island of Luzon. Filipino exports included future plantation crops such as sugar and cotton, along with a bit of gold panned from mountain streams. Imports included metal goods, porcelain, spices, and a wide range of textiles. Most Filipinos mixed farming with fishing and the raising of small livestock, mostly pigs and chickens.

Arrival of the Spanish

Conquistadors

Filipino life was suddenly and forever altered when Spanish conquistadors arrived in 1565, following up on the claims of Ferdinand Magellan, who was killed on the islands in 1521. By 1571 the Spanish had made Manila their capital city: a base for trade with China and a springboard for regional conquest. Shipyards were established at nearby Cavite to outfit the great galleons sent annually to Mexico (see again Map 21.4). Conquest was not easy in such a divided region, but these same divisions prevented a unified effort to repulse the Spanish. European invaders managed to gradually dominate many regions of the Philippines by making alliances with local chieftains in exchange for gifts and favors. Where local headmen resisted, obedient substitutes were found and placed in power.

Early Spanish colonists feverishly searched for gold, pearls, and other exportable local commodities, but their hopes fizzled before the end of the sixteenth century. There was ultimately little to collect in the way of marketable tribute, and the small enclave around

An Elite Filipino Couple
When the Spanish established their Philippine capital at Manila in 1571, they began to deal regularly with local nobles as well as visiting Chinese merchants. This rare image from about 1600 shows a Filipino husband and wife with the local label of Tagalog. Although Filipinos spoke many languages and practiced many distinct religions, the Tagalog language was the one chosen by Spanish priests for evangelization. Alongside Spanish, it became the islands' official language. The couple shown here displays dress and grooming similar to those of Malay elites living throughout Southeast Asia. The man holds the hilt of a kris dagger, a key symbol of high status, while his demure wife stands draped in the finest Chinese silk.
(Courtesy, The Lilly Library, Indiana University, Bloomington, Indiana.)

Manila became, rather like a contemporary Portuguese outpost, the exclusive preserve of Spanish merchants, soldiers, and missionaries. A few bureaucrats eventually followed, linking Manila to its official capital in faraway Mexico City.

Outside Manila's Spanish core there grew a substantial Chinese merchant community, and many of its residents eventually converted to Catholicism and intermarried with local Filipino elites. In the end it was Catholic priests arriving on the annual ships from Mexico who proved responsible for what has come to be known as the "spiritual conquest" of the Philippines. As a result of lax crown oversight, the absence of precious minerals or other high-value exports, and general Filipino receptiveness to Roman Catholicism, before the end of early modern times a fairly small number of highly energetic priests managed to transform much of the archipelago into a veritable theocracy (a state ruled by religious authority), amassing huge amounts of territory and much political power in the process.

Missionaries

Missionaries from several Catholic orders learned to preach in Tagalog, the language of the greater Manila area, as well as a few other regional languages. Lack of standardized languages and writing systems complicated missionary efforts in some places, as did the racist refusal to train an indigenous clergy, yet the absence of a regionwide state religion or code of ethics similar to Buddhism or Confucianism probably eased acceptance of Catholicism's universalist claims. Indigenous deities and interpretations of Catholicism nevertheless persisted, usually manifested through the cult of the saints and in hybrid practices described by priests as witchcraft. In time, scores of Spanish and Mexican missionaries established hundreds of rural churches and frontier missions, most of them concentrated in the northern islands but some stretching south through the Visayas archipelago and into northern Mindanao.

The Limits of "Spiritual Conquest"

The Muslim South   Southern Mindanao and the Sulu Islands remained staunchly Muslim, however, and hence enemy territory in the Spanish view. Periodic battles pitted self-styled crusading Spaniards against the so-called Moors of this region, and some missionaries related harrowing stories of martyrdom and captivity among "pirate infidels" reminiscent of accounts from North Africa's Barbary Coast (discussed in Chapter 20). Indeed, hundreds of letters to Spain's kings and to the pope describe these mostly fruitless struggles.

Other threats to Christian hegemony came from bands of headhunters inhabiting the mountainous interior of Luzon and smaller islands. According to surviving documents, the ritual practice of headhunting, known in many parts of island Southeast Asia, was fairly widespread when the Spanish arrived, and it was periodically revived in some areas into modern times. Despite all these challenges to Spain's unarmed "Christian soldiers," the Philippines emerged from early modern times deeply transformed, in some ways more like Latin America than any other part of Asia. It would ironically be Filipino youths such as José Rizal, trained by the Jesuit and Franciscan successors of these early missionaries, who would lead the struggle to end Spanish colonialism at the last years of the nineteenth century.

Conclusion

China, Japan, Korea, and mainland Southeast Asia were home to a large portion of the world's peoples in early modern times. Russia was, by contrast, vast but thinly populated. In all cases, however, the most notable trend in northern and eastern Asia was toward internal political consolidation. The Philippines, though relatively populous, proved to be an exception, falling with relative ease into the hands of Spanish invaders. Outside Orthodox Russia and the Buddhist regions of Southeast Asia, Neo-Confucian principles of agrarian order and paternalistic harmony guided imperial consolidation. Despite some shocks in the seventeenth century, steady population growth and relative peace in China, Japan, and Korea only seemed to reinforce Confucius's ideal notions of educated self-sufficiency and limited need for foreign trade. Dynasty building and territorial expansion took on more charismatic and even prophetic religious tones in Orthodox Russia and Buddhist Southeast Asia.

Internal changes, however, particularly in China, did have profound effects on the rest of the world, and some regional political trends were accelerated by foreign imports such as gunpowder weapons. Wang Yangming, whose story began this chapter, was just one of many new imperial officials to use these deadly tools of power. Western weapons also aided Burmese and later Qing overland expansion in a way reminiscent of the Islamic "gunpowder empires" discussed in Chapters 19 and 20. Global trade also proved highly susceptible to East Asia's centralizing early modern policies. China's shift to a silver-based currency in the sixteenth century radically reordered world trade patterns. Suddenly, the Americas, Europe, and many Asian neighbors found themselves revolving in an increasingly tight, China-centered orbit. Virtually overnight, the village of Manila was transformed into one of the world's most vibrant trading crossroads. Manila was also an outlying colony, as will be seen in the next chapter, of an increasingly autonomous Spanish America. It was only in the nineteenth century that many parts of East and Southeast Asia began to experience the types of outside domination long experienced by these early established colonies.

NOTES

1. Peter the Great, quoted in Gérard Chaliand, ed., *The Art of War in World History from Antiquity to the Nuclear Age* (Berkeley: University of California Press, 1995), 578.
2. Engelbert Kaempfer, *Kaempfer's Japan: Tokugawa Culture Observed*, ed. and trans. Beatrice M. Bodart-Bailey (Honolulu: University of Hawai'i Press, 1999), 356.
3. Bashō, "The Records of a Weather-exposed Skeleton" (c. 1685), ed. and trans. Nobuyuki Yuasa, *The Narrow Road to the Deep North and Other Sketches* (London: Penguin, 1966).

RESOURCES FOR RESEARCH

General Works

Few works survey the many cultures treated as a cluster in this chapter, but some recent comparative studies have challenged established national categories of analysis. Liebermann and other contributors to the following volume try to relink Europe and Asia in early modern times.

Liebermann, Victor, ed. *Beyond Binary Histories: Re-imagining Eurasia to c. 1830*. 1999.

Straddling Eurasia: Rise of the Russian Empire, 1462–1725

The emphasis in early modern Russian history has largely moved away from court intrigues and suffering serfs toward broader processes of expansion into frontiers, environmental impacts, and cultural interaction. Other current scholarship focuses on the importance of the Orthodox Church. In economic history, classic works on the fur trade are still frequently cited.

For a broad-ranging Web site introduced by veteran Russian historian James H. Billington (author of *The Icon and the Axe: An Interpretive History of Russian Culture*, 1966), see http://www.pbs.org/weta/faceofrussia/intro.html.
Engel, Barbara A. *Women in Russia, 1700–2000*. 2004.
Kivelson, Valerie, and Robert H. Greene, eds. *Orthodox Russia: Belief and Practice Under the Tsars*. 2003.
LeDonne, John P. *The Grand Strategy of the Russian Empire, 1650–1831*. 2004.
Poe, Marshall T. *The Russian Moment in World History*. 2003.
Sunderland, Willard. *Taming the Wild Field: Colonization and Empire on the Russian Steppe*. 2004.

China from Ming to Qing Rule, 1500–1800

The literature on Ming and Qing China is vast. The following selections highlight both key internal developments and global interactions. Environmental history has experienced a recent boom.

Brook, Timothy. *The Confusions of Pleasure: Commerce and Culture in Ming China*. 1998.
Clunas, Craig. *Empire of Great Brightness: Visual and Material Cultures of Ming China, 1368–1644*. 2007.
Princeton University professor Benjamin Elman maintains a comprehensive Web site for Chinese history and culture: http://www.princeton.edu/~classbib.
Elvin, Mark. *The Retreat of the Elephants: An Environmental History of China*. 2004.
Mungello, D. E. *The Great Encounter of China and the West, 1500–1800*, 2d ed. 2005.
Struve, Lynn A., ed. *The Qing Formation in World-Historical Time*. 2004.
Von Glahn, Richard. *Fountain of Fortune: Money and Monetary Policy in China, 1000–1700*. 1996.

Japan in Transition, 1540–1750

The literature on Tokugawa Japan is extensive, and increasingly diverse. Some of the most exciting recent work treats cultural trends and environmental impacts.

Elison, George, and Bardwell L. Smith, eds. *Warlords, Artists, and Commoners: Japan in the Sixteenth Century*. 1981.
Fitzhugh, William W., and Chisato O. Dubreuil, eds. *Ainu: Spirit of a Northern People*. 1999.
Nakane, Chie, and Shinzaburō Ōishi, eds. *Tokugawa Japan: The Social and Economic Antecedents of Modern Japan*. Translated by Conrad Totman. 1990.
Perez, Louis G. *Daily Life in Early Modern Japan*. 2002.
The Public Broadcasting Service maintains a Web site with many Edo period images and links at http://www.pbs.org/empires/japan/.
Totman, Conrad. *The Lumber Industry in Early Modern Japan*. 1995.

Korea, a Land in Between, 1392–1750

Very few English-language histories of Korea give much attention to the early modern period. Seth is an exception.

Seth, Michael J. *A Concise History of Korea: From the Neolithic Period Through the Nineteenth Century.* 2006.

Consolidation in Mainland Southeast Asia, 1500–1750

Histories of mainland Southeast Asia are only beginning to break the old nationalist paradigm and take into account broad regional trends. Liebermann, a specialist on Burma, nicely complements Reid, whose work has mostly been on the islands.

Liebermann, Victor. *Strange Parallels: Southeast Asia in Global Context, c. 800–1830.* 2 vols. 2003–2004.

Northern Illinois University maintains a Southeast Asian digital library at http://sea.lib.niu.edu.

Reid, Anthony, ed. *Sojourners and Settlers: Histories of Southeast Asia and the Chinese.* 2001.

Tarling, Nicolas, ed. *The Cambridge History of Southeast Asia.* Vol. 1., *From Early Times to c. 1800.* 1992.

COUNTERPOINT: "Spiritual Conquest" in the Philippines

The colonial history of the Philippines still requires more scholarly examination, though many primary sources, such as that of Antonio de Morga, have been published in English translation. Phelan's account of early missionary endeavors remains a useful introduction.

Brewer, Carolyn. *Shamanism, Catholicism, and Gender Relations in the Colonial Philippines, 1521–1685.* 2004.

*de Morga, Antonio. *Sucesos de las Islas Filipinas.* Translated and edited by J. S. Cummins. 1971.

Majul, Cesar A. *Muslims in the Philippines.* 1973.

Phelan, John L. *The Hispanization of the Philippines: Spanish Aims and Filipino Responses, 1565–1700.* 1959.

Rafael, Vicente. *Contracting Colonialism: Translation and Christian Conversion in Tagalog Society Under Early Spanish Rule,* 2d ed. 1993.

*Primary source.

▶ **For additional primary sources from this period,** see *Sources of Crossroads and Cultures*.

▶ **For Web sites, images, and documents related to topics in this chapter,** see Make History at bedfordstmartins.com/smith.

The major global development in this chapter ▶ The general trend toward political and cultural consolidation in early modern Asia.

IMPORTANT EVENTS

1392–1910	Yi dynasty established in Korea
1542	Jesuits reach Japan
1555–1581	Expansion of Burma under King Bayinnaung
1565	Spanish conquest of Philippines begins
1571	Manila becomes Philippine capital and key Pacific trading post
1581	Chinese Ming emperor Wanli issues Single Whip Law
1584–1613	Time of Troubles in Russia
1597–1630s	Persecution of Japanese Christians
1601	Matteo Ricci demonstrates Western technology in Ming court
1602–1867	Tokugawa Shogunate in Japan
1614	Japanese contact with foreigners restricted
1627, 1636	Manchu invasions of Korea
1644	Manchu invasion of Beijing; Ming dynasty replaced by Qing
1661–1722	Qing expansion under Emperor Kangxi
1689–1725	Russian imperial expansion under Tsar Peter the Great
1751	Qing annexation of Tibet

KEY TERMS

daimyo (p. 698)   samurai (p. 698)
geisha (p. 703)   serf (p. 687)
kabuki (p. 703)   shogun (p. 698)
kisaeng (p. 707)   sumo (p. 703)
nanban (p. 698)   yangban (p. 705)
Neo-Confucianism
   (p. 683)

CHAPTER OVERVIEW QUESTIONS

1. What factors led to imperial consolidation in Russia and China? Who were the new rulers, and what were the sources of their legitimacy?

2. Why was isolation more common in these empires than overseas engagement, and what were some of the benefits and drawbacks of isolation?

3. In what ways did early modern Asians transform their environments, and why?

SECTION FOCUS QUESTIONS

1. What prompted Russian territorial expansion?

2. How did the shift to a silver cash economy transform Chinese government and society?

3. How did self-isolation affect Japan?

4. How did life for common folk in early modern Korea differ from life in China or Japan?

5. What trends did mainland Southeast Asia share with China, Korea, Japan, and Russia?

6. In contrast to the general trend of political consolidation in early modern Asia, why did the Philippines fall to a European colonizing power?

MAKING CONNECTIONS

1. How did imperial Russia's rise compare with that of the Ottomans or Habsburgs (see Chapter 20)?

2. How did China under the Ming and Qing compare with the other most populous early modern empire, Mughal India (see Chapter 19)?

3. How did Iberian missionaries' efforts in the Philippines compare with those in western Africa (see Chapter 18)?

AT A CROSSROADS ▲

Scenes of everyday life in eighteenth-century Brazil are extremely rare, but fortunately an Italian military engineer known in Portuguese as Carlos Julião chose to depict enslaved and free people of color in Salvador da Bahia, Rio de Janeiro, and the diamond diggings of northern Minas Gerais during several tours of duty. This image of a free woman of color in the diamond town of Tejuco, home of Chica da Silva (whose story opens this chapter), suggests that she is attracting the romantic attention of a bespectacled Portuguese immigrant. Both are clothed with a mix of fine Asian and European fabrics, testament to the wealth of the diamond diggings. Opulence, violence, and the constant mixing of peoples were core features of life on Brazil's colonial mining frontier. (Acervo da Fundação Biblioteca Nacional, Rio de Janeiro, Brazil.)

Transforming New Worlds: The American Colonies Mature

1600–1750

The World That Silver Made: Spanish America, 1570–1750

FOCUS How did mineral wealth steer the development of Spanish America?

Gold, Diamonds, and the Transformation of Brazil, 1695–1800

FOCUS How was Brazil transformed by the mining boom of the eighteenth century?

Bitter Sugar, Part Two: Slavery and Colonialism in the Caribbean, 1625–1750

FOCUS How did sugar production and slavery mold Caribbean societies?

Growth and Change in British and French North America, 1607–1750

FOCUS How did European relations with native peoples differ in the British and French colonies of North America?

COUNTERPOINT: The Maroons of Suriname

FOCUS How did the runaway slaves of Dutch Suriname create a lasting independent state of their own?

B orn of an enslaved African mother and a Portuguese father in a small diamond-mining camp deep in the highlands of Brazil, the legendary Chica da Silva, "the slave who became queen," has long fired the imagination. In 1753, when Chica was about twenty, she was purchased by João Fernandes de Oliveira, who had come from Portugal to oversee diamond mines granted by the Crown to his father. Before long, Chica became the overseer's mistress and the talk of Tejuco, capital of the diamond district. Freed on Christmas Day, 1753, less than a year after being purchased, Chica established a household of her own, in the most opulent style. In time, she would bear Fernandes de Oliveira thirteen children. Her lover lavished upon Chica and her children gifts, fine clothing, a large town-house, and country estates. Together, the couple owned hundreds of slaves. When Chica went down the street with her bright silk gowns and retinue of servants, people made way.

BACKSTORY

As we saw in Chapter 17, the Americas were transformed in early modern times, emerging as a global crossroads whose products, including silver, sugar, and tobacco, would change the world. The wealth of the Americas would be extracted at incalculable cost. By the early seventeenth century millions of native Americans had died from the effects of conquest, overwork, and epidemic disease. As a result, the Spanish and Portuguese enslaved West and West Central Africans and brought them to work the plantations and mines. Livestock imported from Europe roamed far and wide in the Americas, transforming the landscape and displacing native species.

Despite increasing challenges from northern Europeans, the Spanish remained dominant in the Americas through the early 1600s, and they retained control of all known sources of mineral wealth. Their colonies became increasingly mixed racially, and the people were ranked along a steep social hierarchy, but everyone was officially Catholic. In the early seventeenth century, Portuguese Brazil was a coast-hugging sugar colony dependent on the labor of enslaved Amerindians and Africans. Its European settler population was still a tiny minority, for whom most of Brazil was an unknown, untamed frontier. Although the great empires of the Aztecs and Incas had long since fallen, much of North and South America remained native territory.

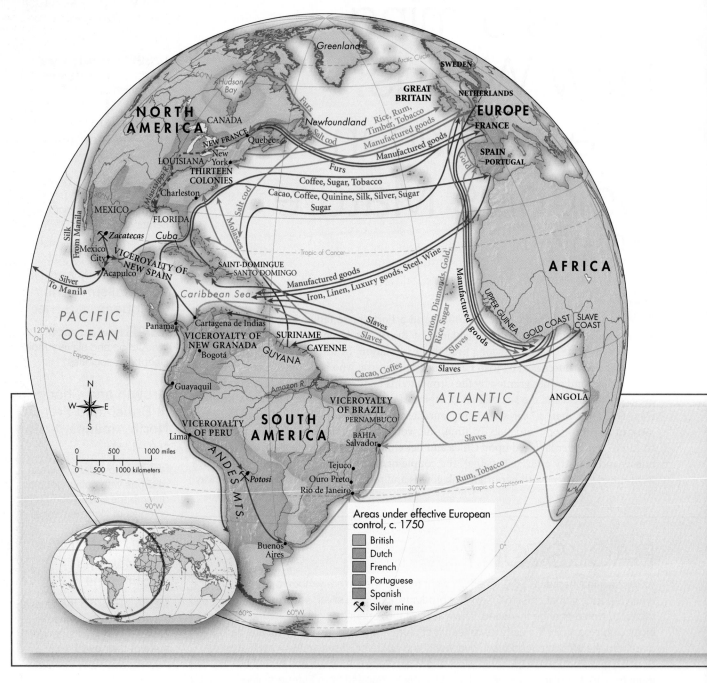

Areas under effective European control, c. 1750

British
Dutch
French
Portuguese
Spanish
✕ Silver mine

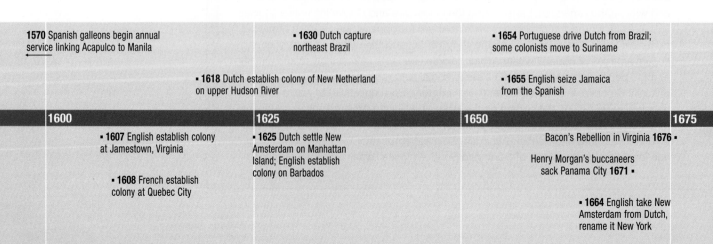

1570 Spanish galleons begin annual service linking Acapulco to Manila

- **1607** English establish colony at Jamestown, Virginia

- **1608** French establish colony at Quebec City

- **1618** Dutch establish colony of New Netherland on upper Hudson River

- **1630** Dutch capture northeast Brazil

- **1625** Dutch settle New Amsterdam on Manhattan Island; English establish colony on Barbados

- **1654** Portuguese drive Dutch from Brazil; some colonists move to Suriname

- **1655** English seize Jamaica from the Spanish

Bacon's Rebellion in Virginia **1676** -

Henry Morgan's buccaneers sack Panama City **1671** -

- **1664** English take New Amsterdam from Dutch, rename it New York

1600   1625   1650   1675

Visitors from Portugal were scandalized that an illegitimate "half-breed" woman could flaunt such extravagance. Indeed, numerous laws forbade such public display by persons of "free-colored" status. In Brazil's diamond and gold districts, however, such laws seemed made to be broken. After her death, storytellers surmised that Chica da Silva used cruelty and promiscuity to advance her wealth and status. According to the legends they constructed, Chica da Silva was a kind of Brazilian archetype: the sexually insatiable and power-hungry *mulata* (mulatto). In the popular imagination, the exceptional woman of color could make good only by seducing and manipulating her white oppressor.

However, the Brazilian historian Júnia Furtado has challenged this view of Chica. First, Furtado asks, how could a woman who bore thirteen children in fifteen years have been a seductress? Second, Chica was hardly unique: of 510 family residences in Tejuco, 197 were headed by free women of color, several of them recent slaves like Chica. Moreover, records show that Chica da Silva did attend to some matters of propriety: she did her best to educate her children and used much of her fortune to build churches, fund religious brotherhoods, organize church processions, and pay for baptisms, burials, and weddings, including those of her slaves. She was in these ways a typical elite "Portuguese" woman who happened to live in an atypical, racially mixed, mining frontier world.

The story of Chica da Silva highlights several features of colonial life in the Americas. First, these colonies were often born of the exploitation of slaves in the production of raw wealth for export. Second, the proximity of peoples of different colors, or "races," in these colonies led to racial mingling, a subject still marked by considerable taboo. For some, the

MAPPING THE WORLD

New World Colonies, c. 1750

Arguably the most profoundly transformed world region in the early modern period, the Americas soon came to be linked not only to western Europe, but also to Atlantic Africa and East Asia. Native American populations declined drastically due to disease and conquest. Their numbers began to rebound after 1650, however, and in Spanish America they served as the major producers of silver, dyes, hides, and other commodities exported to the rest of the world. Africa's role was also critical. The number of enslaved Africans forcibly brought to the Americas by 1750 far exceeded the number of Europeans who migrated voluntarily, and it was they and their descendants who produced the bulk of the world's sugar, cacao, tobacco, and eventually coffee. Colonial American life entailed more than forced labor and primary resource extraction, but both, like the Christianity introduced by missionaries and colonists, remained core features of the region long after colonialism ended.

ROUTES ▼

→ British trade route
→ Dutch trade route
→ French trade route
→ Portuguese trade route
→ Spanish trade route
-▶ Travels of Robert de la Salle, 1679–1682
→ Travels of Pehr Kalm, 1749

1695–1800 Discovery in Brazilian interior of gold and diamonds inaugurates Brazil's "gold rush"

▪ **1720** Brazil elevated to status of viceroyalty

1700   **1725**   **1750**

▪ **1694** Great Brazilian maroon community of Palmares destroyed

Rio de Janeiro elevated to status of capital of Brazil **1763** ▪

1701–1714 War of the Spanish Succession

emergence of new populations of mixed heritage upset notions of racial purity, ethnicity, hierarchy, and propriety. For others, breeding across color lines was a natural but not uncomplicated consequence of proximity. Although the abuses of colonialism can hardly be overstated, the life of Chica da Silva embodies the complexities and contradictions of colonial life in the Americas.

Beginning with the arrival of Columbus in the Caribbean in 1492 and Pedro Álvares Cabral on the coast of Brazil in 1500, waves of European conquerors, missionaries, and colonists, along with a host of alien plants, animals, and pathogens, swept across the Western Hemisphere. By 1750 few indigenous Americans remained unaffected. Even in the vast unconquered areas of the Amazon Basin and the Great Plains of North America, where native American refugee populations had been pushed by European encroachment, European-introduced diseases, animals, and trade goods steadily transformed everyday life. In some places native peoples were joined by runaway African slaves.

Despite its slower start, Portuguese Brazil came to resemble Spanish Mexico and Peru. Busy with their far-flung African and Asian colonies and trading posts, at first the Portuguese maintained only coastal plantations in Brazil. This situation began to change after 1695 when gold and diamonds were discovered in the interior. Along the northeast coast, the Portuguese created the first of several "neo-Africas" in the Americas, uprooting and enslaving hundreds of thousands of West and West Central Africans to plant, harvest, and refine sugar and other cash crops. The Atlantic slave trade and the plantation economy, both defining features of the Caribbean and of British North America after 1700, started in earnest in the Brazilian districts of Pernambuco and Bahia, where the Americas are nearest to Africa.

Desire for empire attracted the French, Dutch, and English to first prey on Spanish and Portuguese ships and ports, and then to establish American colonies of their own. They also searched desperately for a passage to China in hopes of outflanking the Spanish and Portuguese. Piracy and privateering, or state-sponsored piracy, proved to be serious problems for Iberian colonists and merchants until the end of early modern times, and both practices helped generate the initial capital and official interest needed to establish rival colonies. Despite some poor planning and occasional violent ejections, entrepreneurs and planters from northern European countries eventually developed thriving settlements. In time, Caribbean island and mainland colonies such as Barbados and Virginia came to compete with Spanish and Portuguese colonies in the export of sugar and tobacco.

Like the Spanish and the Portuguese, Dutch, French, and English planters in the Caribbean and eastern seaboard colonies of North America employed African slaves from an early date. Amerindian slavery was also practiced, despite proud claims by colonists that they treated native Americans more fairly than the Spanish and Portuguese had. Unlike their Iberian-American counterparts, however, northern European masters relied more heavily on indentured servants, poor women and men from their own countries who contracted terms of servitude in exchange for passage to the Americas, plus room and board. However, most terms of **indenture** were short, usually three years, and before long their masters reinvested the capital accumulated from their labors in African slavery.

In the far north, yet another model emerged. Here the French, Dutch, and English competed with a variety of indigenous groups for access to furs, timber, agricultural land, fish, and other natural resources. These European colonists, like their counterparts in the tropics, kept Amerindian and a few African slaves, but they did not rely wholly on them for subsistence or export products. Swedes, Germans, and Danes also entered into the competition for colonies in some regions, though less forcefully. To the chagrin of all northern Europeans, gold and silver were nowhere to be found in the regions not occupied by the Spanish and Portuguese. A water passage to China's fabled silk and porcelain was similarly elusive. The colonists would have to make do with less glamorous exports, such as salted cod and timber.

indenture A labor system in which Europeans contracted for several years of unpaid labor in exchange for free passage across the Atlantic and housing.

OVERVIEW
QUESTIONS

The major global development in this chapter: The profound social, cultural, and environmental changes in the Americas under colonial rule.

As you read, consider:

1. How did the production of silver, gold, and other commodities shape colonial American societies?

2. How and where did northern Europeans insert themselves into territories claimed by Spain and Portugal?

3. How did racial divisions and mixtures compare across the Americas by the mid-eighteenth century?

The World That Silver Made: Spanish America 1570–1750

FOCUS

How did mineral wealth steer the development of Spanish America?

As we saw in Chapter 17, following the discovery of precious metals in the early sixteenth century, the Spanish moved quickly to reconnoiter their claims while also building cities, widening roads, and fortifying ports. Their two great bases were Lima and Mexico City, each home to tens of thousands of Spaniards, Indians, Africans, mixed people of color, and even some Asians, mostly Filipinos, by the end of the sixteenth century. Although much territory remained in indigenous hands, the Spanish established themselves as far afield as northern New Mexico and southern Chile. A complex imperial bureaucracy functioned all over the colonies by 1570, and various arms of the Catholic Church were firmly in place, occupying stone buildings as imposing as many in Europe. Armed fleets hauled tons of gold and silver to Europe and Asia each year, returning with a wide array of luxury consumer goods, including Chinese silk and Dutch linen. The plundering of pirates could make only a small dent in this rich commerce in both Atlantic and Pacific waters (see Map 22.1).

Gold and silver also financed the purchase of slaves, and soon men, women, and children of African descent were found throughout Spanish America. Young Domingo Angola, whose story opened Chapter 18, was one of many such uprooted Africans. Captive Africans served on galleons in the Pacific, and some visited China, Japan, the Spice Islands, and the Philippines. Major port cities such as Lima and Cartagena de Indias counted black majorities soon after 1600, and highland mining boomtowns such as Zacatecas and Potosí had large African and African-descended populations throughout early modern times.

Perhaps the most significant trend in this long period, however, was the decline of the indigenous population. Ranking among the worst population collapses in world history, this decline was largely a result of sudden exposure to new diseases from Europe and Africa, against which native Americans had built up no natural immunities during thousands of years of isolation. From a total of some 40 million in 1500, the number of native Americans living within the sphere of Spanish dominance fell to less than 5 million by 1600. Labor conditions, displacement, and physical abuse greatly accelerated indigenous population decline in the early years. Although some recovery was evident by the mid-eighteenth century, native populations in the former Inca and Aztec realms never returned to precontact levels.

MAP 22.1

Spanish America, 1580–1750

In early modern times Spain was the most significant power in the Americas. Although Dutch, English, and French competitors gained ground in North America and the Caribbean after 1600, and the Portuguese finally moved to expand Brazil after 1700, during this period Spanish America, divided into three viceroyalties by 1750, remained the richest and most densely populated region in the Western Hemisphere by far. The mines of Potosí and Zacatecas alone supplied the bulk of the world's silver, and internal demand for cacao, sugar, and hides, among many other commodities, kept the colonies humming and interconnected. Meanwhile, the distant Philippines, governed from Mexico City, served as both a trade node with East Asia and a base for missionary expansion.

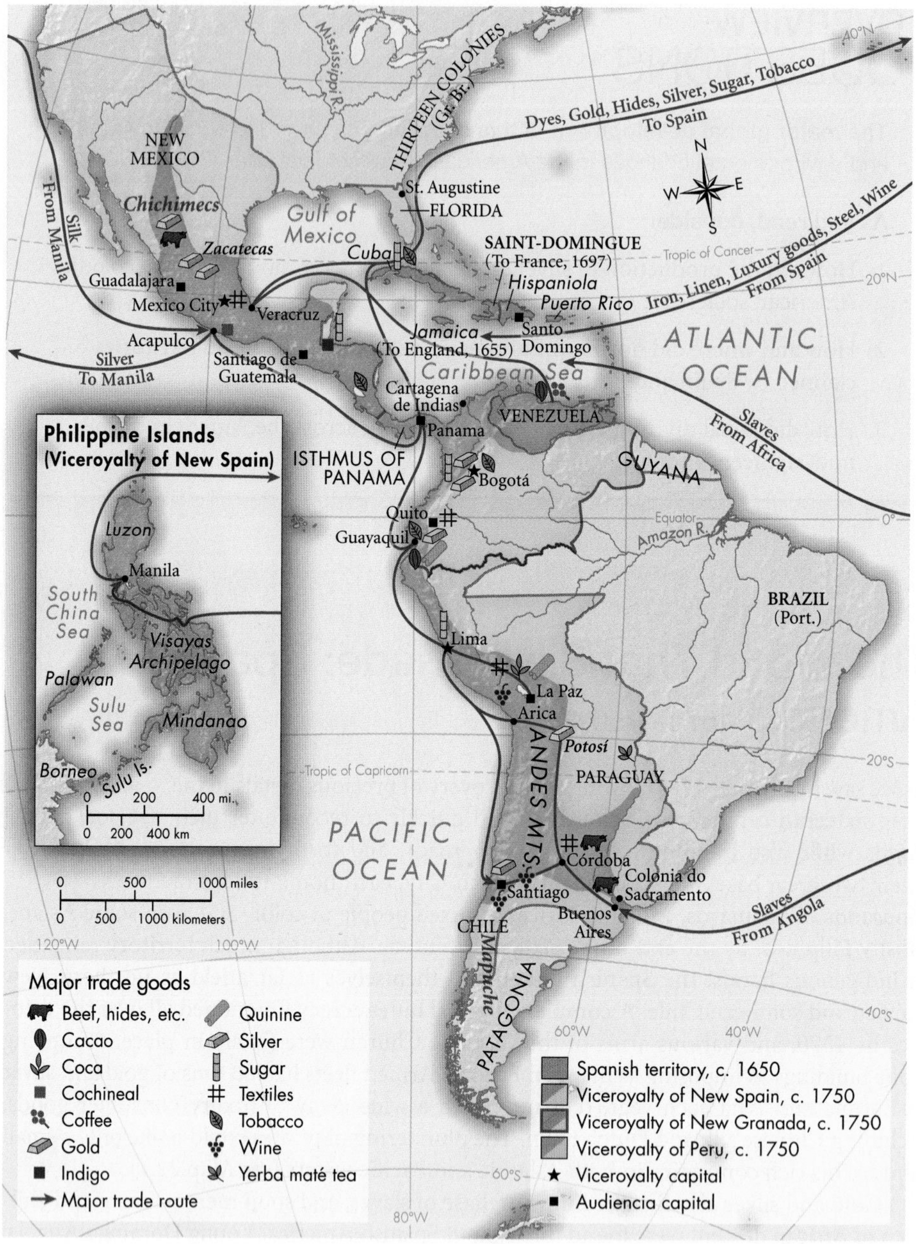

Governing and Profiting from the Colonies

Control Through Bureaucracy

To maintain control and authority over its ambitious settlers, the Spanish crown quickly spun a complex web of overlapping institutions for colonial governance. Some institutions, such as the high appeals court, or *audiencia*, were based on Spanish models; others were American innovations or hybrids. The process of bureaucratization was surprisingly rapid, in part thanks to Spain's growing ranks of university-trained lawyers. These lawyers often clashed with the conquistadors and their offspring, but by 1570 most government institutions were in place.

Spanish culture had long centered on towns and cities, and hundreds of new ones were founded throughout the Americas, some displacing pre-Columbian settlements. Santo Domingo, Mexico City, Lima, Bogotá, and Buenos Aires became capitals of vast districts,

audiencia The high appeals court in Spanish America.

Mexico City's Plaza Mayor

Mexico City's *plaza mayor*, or great square, painted here in 1695, served as the city's main marketplace, exposition grounds, and social crucible. In addition to ceremonial processions and religious devotions, the square was the site of public executions and *autos-da fé*, punishments of those convicted by the Inquisition. It was a place to see and be seen. In this anonymous painting one gets a sense of the size and grandeur of New Spain's capital at its height, although nature's wrath is on the horizon in the form of Popocatépetl, a huge, active volcano, spewing ash ominously into the darkened sky. (Corsham Court, Wiltshire/Bridgeman Art Library.)

but even small provincial towns exerted power over the surrounding countryside. As in Spain, town councils were the basic unit of governance throughout Spanish America.

Legally, the colonies were divided between a "republic of Indians," complete with separate legal codes, and a "republic of Spaniards." This divided system was created not out of fears of racial mixing, which occurred constantly regardless of the Crown's desires, but rather to shelter and thus more efficiently exploit Spanish America's indigenous population. In short, it was in the government's best interest to keep the number of officially registered "Indians" high, since only they were subject to tribute payment and labor drafts. Much like Russian peasants in the same period, native Americans under Spanish rule were legally bound to assigned villages. Officially recognized indigenous headmen were required to collect tributes from their subjects twice a year and to organize labor pools.

Spanish colonies were divided into provinces headed by crown-appointed governors or magistrates. Clusters of these provinces made up audiencia jurisdictions, or regions subject to the authority of a royal court of appeals. Audiencia judges were nearly all Spanish-born lawyers hoping to climb the ranks of colonial bureaucracy and one day return to Spain. Few subjects' legal appeals went beyond these courts, and indigenous groups quickly learned to use the audiencias to their advantage in disputes with Spanish landlords and mine owners.

Above the audiencias were two viceroyalties: New Spain and Peru. New Spain, with its capital at Mexico City, covered Spanish North America, Central America, the Caribbean islands, Venezuela, and the Philippine Islands across the Pacific. The Viceroyalty of Peru, which was subdivided in the eighteenth century, covered all of Spanish South America with the exception of Venezuela, but included the Isthmus of Panama (see again Map 22.1). Spain's king thus appointed only two viceroys for all of his overseas holdings. Both reported to the king and to a court council in Spain, the Council of the Indies. Consequently, at least in theory, all colonial officials were part of a political hierarchy headed by the Crown, the ultimate source of power and decision making.

Spain's transatlantic mail service was slow, and the transpacific one even slower, but both were surprisingly reliable once the annual fleet system was in place after the mid-sixteenth century. Word of trouble in the colonies—or new mineral finds—always reached the king, and his decrees and tax demands always made the return trip. Thanks to this complex bureaucracy and regular transportation system, Spain's many distant colonies felt connected to the motherland.

The first Spanish settlers in the Americas were few in number compared to the vast native populations. Still, these early settlers were an ambitious lot, and they quickly fanned out over an enormous area in search of gold, silver, and other commodities. Conquistadors gained land and encomiendas, or grants of the compelled labor and tribute of native Americans. Foreshadowing African slavery, the encomienda system allowed Spaniards to accumulate capital and gain access to credit without having to pay wages. The system persisted in frontier areas until the mid-eighteenth century, subsidizing development of cattle ranches, wheat farms, fruit orchards, and vineyards. The Spanish crown, meanwhile, also claimed its share of New World income.

Even without the encomienda, all men identified in census records as "Indian," with the exception of chiefs and nobles, were required to pay tribute to the Crown biannually as a reminder of their conquered status. By 1600, tribute had to be paid in cash, a requirement that forced native peoples to produce marketable goods or sell their labor. Tributes and taxes in raw commodities such as grains or textiles were no longer accepted; everyone had to participate in the market economy. Indigenous women and children were increasingly drawn into the workforce to help produce cash. In many cities, including Potosí, single indigenous women, exempt from tribute obligations and also exempt from the Spanish sales tax, became relatively

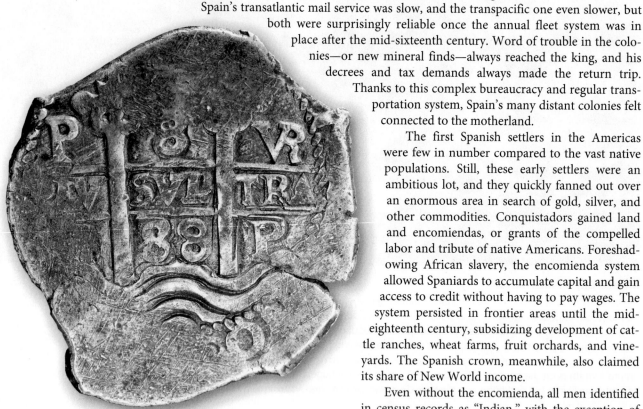

Spanish "Piece of Eight"

Most Spanish-American silver flowed out into the wider world in the form of large, brick-sized bars, but the Spanish also minted millions of coins throughout early modern times, both in the colonies and in Spain. This crudely struck *peso de a ocho*, or "piece of eight," was minted in the famous silver mining city of Potosí in 1688, during the reign of the last Habsburg king, Charles II. In addition to the coin maker's initials, "VR," the piece of eight bears symbols of Spain's overseas empire, including the Pillars of Hercules (the Strait of Gibraltar) and the great waves of the "Ocean Sea," or Atlantic. "Plus Ultra," or "Further Beyond," the motto of Spain's first Habsburg king and Holy Roman Emperor Charles V, became the motto of empire as well. The Spanish piece of eight served for several centuries as the standard world currency. (Hoberman Collection/Corbis.)

An Iraqi Traveler's Impressions of Potosí

The following selection was originally written in Arabic by an Iraqi Christian, Elias al-Musili, who traveled throughout Spanish America between 1675 and 1680 hoping to raise money for his church, which was located in Ottoman territory but sponsored by Rome. Al-Musili was among the very few foreigners permitted to visit Spain's colonies in the early modern era due to persistent crown fears of subversion and spying, and he was the only Middle Eastern Arabic speaker of whom we have record. He was given alms throughout the Andes, particularly by native Americans, for preaching in the ancient Aramaic language. He left Potosí with several mule-loads of silver.

A Visit to the Mint and Silver Mine

One day I went to the place where they minted dinars, piastres ["pieces of eight"], halves, and quarters. In this mint house there are forty black slaves and twelve Spaniards working. We saw the piles of coins, like hillocks on one side, the halves on another, and half-quarters still on another, heaped on the floor and being trampled underfoot like dirt that has no value.

On one side of this town is the mountain containing the mine[s]. It is known throughout the world on account of its excessive wealth; countless treasures have been extracted from all four sides of it for 140 years. They had fenced it off, dug it up, and reached the very bottom of it to extract the silver. They had prepared wooden props for it, to make sure the mountain did not cave in. From the outside it looks whole, but on the inside it is empty. Up to 700 Indians work inside to cut out stone for men who had already bought the rights from the king. Every miner has assigned a certain number of Indians to work his share of the mine. There is a royal decree ordering every village to offer a number of Indian men to mine. According to the law one out of five men is to be assigned to such a task.

Describing the Extraction of Silver

There are 37 mills used for grinding silver-bearing stones day and night, except for Sundays and holidays. After grinding it finely, they take it in quantities of fifty qintârs [about 5000 lbs.] and form separate piles with it. They add water to each . . . then add mercury to it according to need. They then stir it with shovels several times; and should it require more mercury, they add it up until perfected. If it is cold by nature, they add copper until it warms up. If it is warm by nature, they add lead until it cools. How can they tell whether it is warm or cool? They scoop up samples in a clay utensil and wash it with water until the dirt disappears and the mixture of silver and mercury remains. The sample is then smeared by finger on a piece of the aforementioned clay pot. If it crumbles, it is considered hot; if it sticks, it is considered cold. When perfect, or well tempered, it adheres to the clay and shines. Next they put it in a large basin with water flowing over it and stir it all the while with finesse. Silver and mercury settle on the bottom and dirt is carried off by the water. After thus completing the "washing" of this mixture, the overflow of water is cut off and the basin cleaned. The mixture of silver and mercury is taken out and put in gunnysacks hung from trees, under which are placed containers lined with cattle skin. Mercury flows out of the sacks into these containers underneath and only silver remains in them, like loaves of sugar.

Source: Cesar E. Farah, ed. and trans., *An Arab's Journey to Colonial Spanish America: The Travels of Elias al-Mûsili in the Seventeenth Century* (Syracuse, NY: Syracuse University Press, 2003).

EXAMINING THE EVIDENCE

1. What aspects of silver production seem to have most amazed al-Musili?

2. How does he portray workers in Potosí's mint, mines, and refineries?

wealthy, and soon ran afoul of town authorities for wearing silk garments and other adornments deemed inappropriate for their class.

Along with indigenous tributes, sales taxes, and customs duties, the Spanish crown and its many bureaucrats relied on mining taxes in the form of silver, the so-called *quinto real*, or "royal fifth," of the silver mined. The Crown also rented out the mercury monopoly, which was crucial in processing silver. However, by 1600 corruption was common, and crown control of mining and silver exports became weak. Mine owners and merchants found increasingly clever ways to avoid tax collectors. By the 1640s a vibrant contraband trade was flourishing, especially around Buenos Aires and along Caribbean shores, where newly arrived slaves and luxury merchandise were traded for silver ingots and "pieces of eight," all tax-free.

Despite a growing culture of corruption and tax evasion, some mine owners managed to follow the rules and still do very well for themselves. One who stood out was Antonio López de Quiroga, who used his profits from selling silver to the mint in Potosí to buy up abandoned mines, hire the most skilled workers available, and employ innovations such as black-powder blasting (see Reading the Past: An Iraqi Traveler's Impressions of Potosí). By the 1670s, López de Quiroga was the local equivalent of a billionaire, a major benefactor of churches, and even a sponsor of lowland conquest expeditions in the upper Amazon. Similar stories were repeated in the mining frontiers of northern Mexico.

Commodities Beyond Silver

Although the mining economy was most critical in stimulating the expansion of frontiers, much else was happening in Spanish America. Venezuela, for example, developed a vibrant economy based on the production of raw chocolate beans, or cacao. These were first destined for Mexico, a huge Spanish-American market, and subsequently for Europe, once the taste for chocolate developed there in the later seventeenth century. Partly due to Venezuela's location along the slave route to New Granada (present-day Colombia) and Mexico, in the cacao groves surrounding the regional capital of Caracas, African laborers soon displaced native Americans held in encomienda. Coffee was introduced from Arabia in the early eighteenth century and soon became another major export.

There were other ways to make money in Spanish America without entering the global export market. In Paraguay a tea called *yerba maté* was collected in the forest by native Guaraní speakers, many of whom lived on and around Jesuit missions. The tea was then carried by mule throughout the Andes, where it was consumed by all classes. This habit, unlike chocolate drinking, was not picked up in Europe. Huge cattle ranches developed in the hinterland of Buenos Aires and in north-central Mexico. Beef, tallow, and hides were consumed in great quantities in mining towns such as Potosí and Zacatecas. In seventeenth-century Mexico what historians call a "mining-ranching complex" developed, tying distant regions together across expanses of desert. Elites invested profits from mining in trade, and vice versa. By 1600, cheap cotton and woolen textiles were produced in quantity in both Mexico and the northern Andes, enough to nearly satisfy the substantial working-class market.

Spanish America's Unique Economy

Spanish America was unusual among early modern overseas colonies in that its economy was both export-oriented and self-sufficient from an early stage. Only luxury goods such as fine textiles and iron and steel items were not produced locally. Why a local iron industry did not develop might seem strange since iron deposits were available, but the short answer is silver. Spanish-American merchants simply had so much silver to export that they struggled to find enough imports to balance the trade. Spanish authorities later outlawed local iron production to protect merchant interests.

After textiles, which included vast quantities of Chinese silks and South Asian chintzes and calicoes along with a wide range of European cloths, common iron goods such as horseshoes were among the main items consumed. The Basques of northern Spain had long produced iron and steel products, and some artisan clans in cities such as Bilbao became wealthy by sending their wares to the colonies. Wine was another favorite import from Spain, mostly produced in the hinterland of Seville, but even this was being produced in large quantities on the coasts of Peru and Chile by the 1580s.

The net effect of silver exports on such a grand scale from both Mexico and the Andes was a colonial economy that was both internally interdependent in terms of food, common cloth, hides, and other basic items and dependent on the outside world for luxury products. As with iron, the Crown actively discouraged industrialization of the textile sector, but scientific innovations in mining and metallurgy—anything to increase the flow of silver—were rewarded with patents. Thus, the colonial system increased the density of economic connections within the Americas at the same time as it forged new connections between the Americas and the larger world.

As we saw in Chapter 20, Spain's Habsburg monarchs and ministers envisioned the colonial economy as a closed mercantile system, intended to benefit the mother country through taxation while enabling subjects of varying status to seek and consolidate wealth (although not to gain crown-challenging titles of nobility). No foreigners were supposed to trade with the American colonies except through approved monopoly holders based in Seville. These monopolists also controlled (theoretically) all trade through Acapulco to Manila and back. Although this closed-system ideal was realized to a surprising degree given the great distances, cultural divides, and other obstacles involved, it soon fell prey to individual wiles and corrupt cartels as Spain itself fell into decline under a succession of weak kings after Philip II (r. 1556–1598). Only after 1700, with the rise of the Bourbon dynasty, did the Crown manage to reassert itself forcefully in colonial economic affairs. As we will see in the next chapter, widespread rebellion would follow.

Spanish Mercantile Policy

Everyday Life in Spanish America

As the colonies matured, Spain's increasingly diverse American subjects found new possibilities for social and material improvement, but they also faced many bureaucratic and natural constraints. Life spans in colonial Spanish America were similar to those of contemporary Europe for elites, but as we have seen, they were considerably shorter for people of indigenous and African descent. Epidemics, particularly of smallpox, hit everyone from time to time. Slaves, draft workers, and mixed-race criminals sent to fight the Mapuche in Chile or the Chichimecs of northern Mexico were often described in identification documents as having smallpox scars on their faces. Infant mortality was very high at all levels of society.

Many of the regions settled by the Spanish were prone to earthquakes and volcanic eruptions, which led many to regard natural disasters as judgments of God. When in 1661 a volcano dumped several feet of ash on Quito, now the capital of Ecuador, Catholic priests ordered that an image of the Virgin Mary be paraded through the streets until the eruption ceased. Such religiosity was manifest in many aspects of colonial Spanish-American society, including art and literature, and it helped shape local norms of gender and race relations. In fact, Catholicism came to serve as a common cultural touchstone, connecting the members of an ethnically and culturally diverse society.

Unlike parts of English, French, and Dutch America, as we will see, Spanish America was never intended as a refuge for religious dissenters. From the beginning the region was a Roman Catholic domain. Even recent converts to Christianity were not allowed to emigrate for fear of allowing Judaism or Islam into the colonies. Spain's Romas, or gypsies, were likewise banned due to their alleged fondness for fortunetelling and witchcraft. Still, some recent converts and Romas, along with miscellaneous "unorthodox" foreigners from Portugal, France, Italy, Germany, the Low Countries, and even Greece, managed to sneak aboard Indies-bound ships leaving Seville. In the colonies, the beginning of the Inquisition after 1570, plus waves of anti-idolatry campaigns after 1560, soon led to widespread persecution of nonconformists.

Religious Conformity and Resistance

How did the mass of subject peoples, most of them indigenous peasants and enslaved Africans, respond to these demands for spiritual conformity? Faced with constant threats and punishments from priests and officials, along with the sometimes persuasive efforts of missionaries, the vast majority of native and African-descended subjects at least nominally accepted Catholicism. What soon emerged, however, was a complex fusion of Catholic practices with a more secretive, underground world of non-Christian cults, shamanistic healing practices, and witchcraft. Scholars have learned much about these alternative religious spheres in recent years from Inquisition and anti-idolatry records, and some have sought to trace their roots to parts of Africa and elsewhere.

According to Christian scripture, all human beings were redeemable in the creator's eyes, regardless of sex, age, status, color, or birthplace. Thus, many church leaders believed that non-Western habits such as nudity and even cannibalism could be reformed

Gentlemen of Esmeraldas

Andrés Sánchez Gallque, *Gentlemen of Esmeraldas* (The Art Archive/American Museum Madrid.)

In 1599 Andrés Sánchez Gallque, an indigenous artist from Quito, the former Inca capital located high in the Andes, painted a group portrait of three men who had climbed up from the Pacific coast province of Esmeraldas to sign a treaty with the colonial government. The three men, Don Francisco de Arobe and his two sons, Pedro and Domingo, were maroons, descendants of escaped slaves who swam ashore following a shipwreck in the 1540s. They were in Quito to sign a treaty agreeing not to ally with pirates. The Spanish honorific title "Don" was used for all three men since they were recognized as indigenous chiefs. As it happened, Don Francisco de Arobe was the son of an African man and a native woman from Nicaragua. Other Esmeraldas maroons had intermarried with local indigenous inhabitants.

In exchange for agreeing to defend the coast against intruders, the Arobes were sent to a professional tailor in Quito and given a wide variety of luxury textiles, including ponchos and capes made from Chinese silk brought to Acapulco by the Manila galleon, then south to Quito via Panama. The maroon leaders also received linen ruff collars from Holland and iron spearheads, probably from the Basque region of northern Spain. Their own adornments included shell necklaces and gold facial jewelry typical of South America's northwest Pacific coast. The painting was sent to Philip III in Madrid as a memento of peace. It is now housed in Spain's Museo de América.

Source: Kris Lane, *Quito 1599: City and Colony in Transition* (Albuquerque: University of New Mexico Press, 2002.)

EXAMINING THE EVIDENCE

1. **What might these men's wide array of adornments symbolize?**

2. **What image does Sánchez Gallque seem to wish to convey to the king of Spain?**

and did not justify permanent discrimination. It was on such grounds that Spanish priests such as Bartolomé de las Casas had argued so successfully against Amerindian slavery (see Chapter 17).

Condoning Slavery   By contrast, African slavery was hardly debated by Spanish priests and theologians. Some church leaders even sought to justify it. Settlers, particularly those in need of workers, were inclined to view both native Americans and Africans as inferior and uneducable; such racist views suited their interests. For its part, the Spanish crown sought protection of subject Amerindians not so much for reasons of faith, but because natives were a source of state revenue and paid their tributes in silver. Slaves, being outside the tributary economy, were left mostly to their own devices, although Spanish law contained some protections, certainly more than those developed by later colonists such as the Dutch, French, and English. It was assumed, often wrongly, that rational masters would be loath to harm their chattels.

By the seventeenth century, Spanish America was molded by a variety of religious, economic, and political forces. But it was only biology—some would say the law of human attraction—that could subvert the system. To start, a surplus of male European settlers, including farmers, artisans, and merchants, in the early years quickly led to *mestizaje* (mess-tee-ZAH-hey), Spanish for "mixture," and a significant mixed-heritage population. In some places it was indigenous women, ranging in status from servants such as Malintzin to Aztec and Inca princesses, who gave birth to a new generation of *mestizos*, as mixed-blood offspring were called. In other cases it was enslaved or free women of African descent who bore **mulatto** children to Spanish colonizers. There were many examples resembling Brazil's Chica da Silva throughout Spanish America, though none so rich or famous. Indigenous women also had children by African men, free and enslaved, and countless other "mixtures" occurred in the course of three centuries of colonial rule. The Mexican nation-state would later celebrate mestizaje as something dynamic and new, a "cosmic race."

To attribute all this to the power of physical attraction would be an oversimplification. Some relationships across color lines were forced and criminal, others merely fleeting, and still others were permanent and even church-sanctioned. Though some bureaucrats and bishops might have wished it so, neither state nor church outlawed interracial marriage in colonial Spanish America. Only marriage across huge status gaps, as, say, between a nobleman and a slave, was forbidden. By 1750 Spanish-American society was so "mixed" at virtually all social levels that the term *casta*, or "caste," formerly applied by the Portuguese in India, was adopted to categorize the bewildering range of soci02racial types. Hundreds of paintings depict the various unions and offspring comprising Spanish America's so-called *sistema de castas*, or "system of castes" (see Seeing the Past: *Gentlemen of Esmeraldas*).

The experiences of women in colonial Spanish America varied more by social class than color. In time, immigrants born in Spain looked down upon even the whitest **creole**, or locally born Spaniard. Under the influence of age-old superstitions about sub-Saharan Africa, Europeans believed that life in the tropics was inherently debilitating, even for aristocratic Christians from northern Spain. Still, most creole women in Spanish America brushed off such suggestions of inferiority and made the most of their situations.

Peruvian Blacksmiths

Although all iron and steel were imported by privileged wholesalers to the Spanish-American colonies, it was local blacksmiths who fashioned these raw materials into horseshoes, hinges, nails, tools, and many other items. In this mid-eighteenth-century watercolor from the Pacific-coast city of Trujillo, Peru, a man and woman work together to forge tools. By this time, nearly all artisans were of indigenous, African, or mixed background, since hand labor was generally disdained by those claiming to be of pure European stock. This pair appears to be of mestizo, or mixed Spanish and indigenous, heritage. (Iberfoto/The Image Works.)

Racial Mixing

mestizaje Spanish for "mixture," referring to racial blending of any type.

mestizo Spanish for "mixed," or offspring of Europeans and native Americans.

mulatto Offspring of Europeans and Africans.

creole A European born in the Americas and his or her descendants.

Late marriage by men left many Spanish-American women widowed at a relatively young age. This gave some women a boost in terms of economic security and independence. Despite a generally stifling patriarchal culture, Spanish inheritance law, similar to Islamic law from which it borrowed, was relatively generous to women. The wives of merchants, in particular, frequently found themselves in charge of substantial enterprises and estates, with much freedom to administer them. More significantly, widows wielded extraordinary influence over their children's marriage choices. When children married well, estates could be combined and expanded over time, cementing a family's fortunes in the face of uncertainties and disruption. Such was the story of the family of Simón Bolívar, whose story opens the next chapter. Among his ancestors, it was women who made many of the most important choices.

Although elite women were concerned with maintaining wealth and improving the status of their offspring, poor women had other worries. Virtually all poor women were engaged in market-oriented activity at some level, even if they lived in the countryside. Weaving, spinning, and pottery-making were often female tasks. Urban women of poor to middling status were usually either servants or vendors, with some working alongside artisan husbands as cobblers, tanners, tailors, cigar-rollers, and even blacksmiths. Along with their burdensome duties as wet nurses, cooks, and cleaners, female domestic servants and slaves were also hired out, handing over the wages to their masters. Despite harsh conditions, access to markets meant access to cash, and even some socially marginalized urban women accumulated small fortunes or purchased freedom for their children.

In a different category altogether were Catholic nuns. Most were of elite parentage, but some were of humble background, including women born out of wedlock. Every Spanish-American city of note had at least one convent, and often half a dozen or more. Inside lived not only the nuns themselves, but their female servants and slaves. Lima, for example, in 1630 counted over 1366 nuns served by 899 female African slaves out of a total city population of about forty thousand. Convents also served as shelters for widows and women facing hardships, and as reformatories for those accused of prostitution and minor crime. Though confining, Spanish-American nunneries occasionally nurtured female intellectuals and mystics of great renown, such as St. Rose of Lima (1586–1617) and Juana Inés de la Cruz (1651–1595). Famous for her biting wit, de la Cruz even took on the misogynist ways of Mexican society in verse:

> Who would have the greatest blame
> In an errant love affair,
> She who falls to him who begs
> Or he who plays the beggar?
>
> Or who should be more guilty
> Though each is evil-doing,
> She who sins for pay,
> Or he who pays for sinning?[1]

Gold, Diamonds, and the Transformation of Brazil 1695–1800

Beginning in around 1695, the coastal, sugar-based export economy of Portuguese Brazil began to change, sparked by the discovery of gold and diamonds in Brazil's south-central highlands. What followed was the greatest bonanza in world history prior to California's gold rush. The consequences were profound and lasting. First, over half a million Portuguese immigrants flowed into Brazil between 1700 and 1800. Second, the African slave trade was expanded,

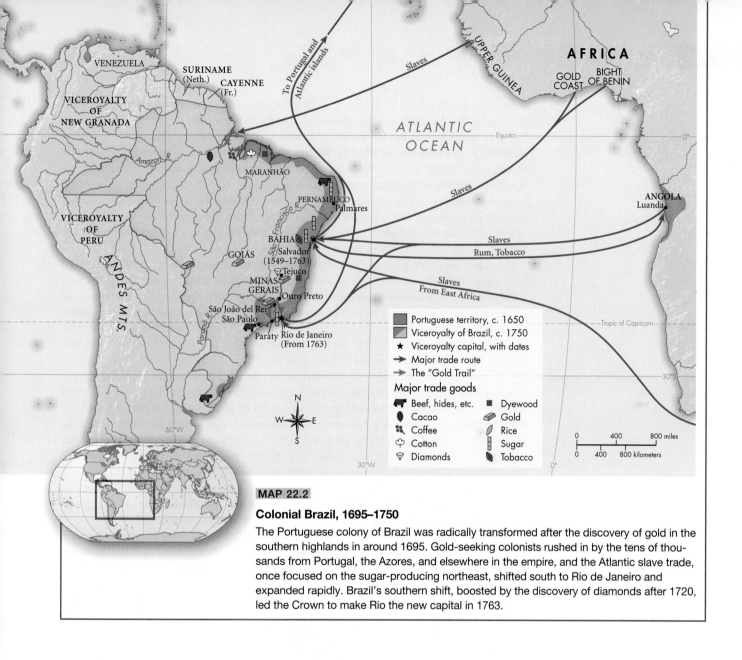

MAP 22.2

Colonial Brazil, 1695–1750

The Portuguese colony of Brazil was radically transformed after the discovery of gold in the southern highlands in around 1695. Gold-seeking colonists rushed in by the tens of thousands from Portugal, the Azores, and elsewhere in the empire, and the Atlantic slave trade, once focused on the sugar-producing northeast, shifted south to Rio de Janeiro and expanded rapidly. Brazil's southern shift, boosted by the discovery of diamonds after 1720, led the Crown to make Rio the new capital in 1763.

particularly in the hinterland of Angola. Third, the Portuguese crown elevated Brazil to the status of viceroyalty in 1720. Finally, Brazil's center of political and economic gravity shifted southward, away from the sugar zone of the northeast. Rio de Janeiro became Brazil's new capital in 1763 (see Map 22.2). On a global scale, Brazilian gold's importance briefly rivaled that of Spanish-American silver, flowing through Lisbon and into allied England, helping to finance the early stages of the Industrial Revolution.

Boom Times for Colonial Brazil

In the mid-1690s, while searching for indigenous slaves, a mulatto aide traveling with Brazilian backwoodsmen and slave hunters discovered gold in the rugged highlands northeast of São Paulo. By 1800 Brazil had exported between 2.5 and 4.5 million pounds of gold, and several million carats of raw diamonds. Up to this time diamonds had come almost entirely from India, and gold from West Africa and Spanish America. Soon after 1700, a district capital was set up in the town of Ouro Preto (OR-ooh PREH-too), or "Black Gold," and the region was dubbed Minas Gerais (MEAN-us jheh-HICE), or "General Mines." Prospectors and slaves flowed into Minas Gerais in droves, among them Chica da Silva's African mother and Portuguese father. Hordes of itinerant and wholesale merchants came close on their heels. As would happen in the later gold rush frontiers of

California, South Africa, and Australia, the greatest fortunes were made not by prospectors but by those selling clothing, shovels, and maps to the mines.

Mine Work

Due to the heavily eroded nature of its mountain ranges, Brazil's substantial gold and diamond mines were almost all of the surface, or "placer," variety. Wherever gold and diamonds were found, teams of enslaved workers, the vast majority of them young African-born men, excavated riverbanks while others panned or redirected streams to get at gravel beds and sandbars. Early commentators such as an Italian Jesuit using the pseudonym Antonil (since the Jesuits were officially forbidden from entering Minas Gerais, due to crown fears they would siphon away profits) described mining work as hellishly hard, and food shortages as common and severe.

Aside from chronic hunger and abuse, slaves in the mining country were endangered by a host of diseases, venomous snakes, and the constant threat of drowning in rain-swollen rivers. Murderous claim disputes and uprisings were common as well, especially in the early years, and many slaves ran away simply to avoid being caught in the crossfire. Slave mortality in the mines was much higher than in the sugar cane fields of the northeast. Some slave owners turned to the less risky activities of farming and livestock production, selling off only unruly slaves to the mines.

Environmental Impacts

Environmental historians estimate that in the course of the Brazilian gold rush tens of thousands of square miles of topsoil were overturned to a depth of at least one and a half feet. Resulting erosion led to widespread formation of gullies, deep ditches cut into the earth by running water after a downpour, and deforested regions were invaded by inedible grasses and weeds. Laws from as early as the 1720s called for preservation of forest and bush to control rainfall catchment and runoff, but these decrees were not observed. Uncontrolled digging and river diversion created vast badlands, areas of barren, arid land visible to the present day. Deforestation to support farming and the raising of livestock to feed the miners went even further, forever transforming the Brazilian highlands and greatly diminishing the Atlantic coast forest, only a tiny remnant of which remains.

Expansion of Portuguese Emigration and Atlantic Slave Trade

As happened in Spain soon after the discovery of Potosí and other major silver mines in Spanish America, a wave of emigration swept Portugal following the Brazilian bonanza of 1695. Never a very populous country, Portugal could ill afford the loss of tens of thousands of residents, especially when most of those leaving were young, able-bodied men. So many Portuguese men came to Minas Gerais in the first years after 1700 that a minor war broke out between them and the creole "Paulistas," or residents of São Paulo, who had discovered the mines. Crown authorities sided with the newcomers, and eventually sought to establish order in the backcountry by sending in troops.

The Atlantic slave trade expanded dramatically in response to the discovery of gold and diamonds in the Brazilian interior. Brazil's proximity to Africa and Portugal's long involvement in the slave trade led to a development quite distinct from the silver mines of Spanish America. In Mexico and Peru, most mine work was carried out by indigenous draft and later mestizo or mulatto wageworkers. By contrast, in the goldfields of Brazil, whose indigenous populations had been decimated by disease and slave raiding by 1700, African slavery quickly became the only form of labor employed. By 1800, there were nearly a million slaves in Minas Gerais. The few women to enter Minas Gerais in the early years of the rush were also primarily enslaved Africans, and they were in such high demand that most became the prized concubines of Portuguese men. Some were rented out as prostitutes in exchange for gold dust and diamonds. One such woman gave birth to Chica da Silva. Thus, the discovery of gold and diamonds in Brazil drew millions of migrants, some voluntary but many more forced, to the Americas. The cultural heritages these migrants brought with them have shaped Brazilian society to this day.

Royal Control and Its Limits

The Portuguese crown took an immediate interest in the Brazilian gold rush, establishing a taxation and monopoly trade system similar to that developed by the Spanish in Mexico and Peru. Gold taxes, the same "royal fifth" demanded by the Spanish crown, were collected at official sites in Ouro Preto and other towns, and all trade was directed along royal, stone-paved roads complete with official stations where mule-loads were inspected and taxed. The "gold trail" initially terminated in the tiny coastal town of Paraty, on Brazil's lush South Atlantic coast just beyond the Tropic of Capricorn, but soon it led to Rio de Janeiro, (see again Map 22.2). Rio became Brazil's largest city, and was elevated to the status of capital of the viceroyalty in 1763.

As in Spanish America, royal control over mining districts was more easily imagined than realized, and smuggling, particularly of diamonds, soon became a huge problem. Official control centered on the town of Tejuco (today's Diamantina) and was headed by royal contractors from Portugal, such as Chica da Silva's common-law husband, João Fernandes de Oliveira. Although the diamond mines were closely monitored and slaves were subjected to physical inspections, there were always ways of hiding and secretly trading stones. As an incentive to be honest and work hard, slaves were promised instant freedom if they found diamonds above a very large size, but few were so lucky.

Much more often, enslaved diamond miners set aside a few stones from time to time to trade to corrupt bureaucrats and merchants for cash. Slaves in the gold mines did the same. Wealth thus accumulated was then used to purchase the workers' freedom or the freedom of their children. One of the ironies of the Brazilian gold and diamond mines was that although the work itself was more dangerous than that of the cane fields and sugar mills of the northeast, the odds of obtaining freedom were considerably higher. Knowing that enslaved Africans outnumbered them by a huge margin here in the mountainous backlands, Portuguese masters and crown officials accepted a measure of secret trade and self-purchase.

Everyday Life in Golden-Age Brazil

With slavery such a central feature of Brazil's colonial economy, it is no surprise that this core institution deeply influenced society. Its influence would only increase over time. At first indigenous and then African cultural elements fused with Portuguese imports to create a new, hybrid culture. Only certain elites proved resistant to this hybridization, doing their best to mimic metropolitan styles and ideas. Some members of this elite class, such as the Portuguese diamond contractor João Fernandes de Oliveira, embraced "Afro-Brazil" in a more literal sense, by forming families of mixed ancestry. Other Brazilians practiced Catholicism while seeking the aid of numerous folk healers, clairvoyants, and other officially illegal religious figures, many of them of African ancestry.

As in Spanish America, a pressing matter for Portuguese authorities was the presence of Judaism and people of Jewish ancestry. In Brazil's early years some New Christians, or forced converts, had been allowed to immigrate. By the 1590s, some of these settlers were discovered to be secretly practicing Judaic rituals. Infrequent visits by the Inquisition, which never set up a permanent tribunal in Brazil, uncovered evidence of "heresy," or at least

Brazilian Diamond Diggers

Images of colonial mineworkers in the Americas are rare. Fortunately, the Italian military engineer Carlos Julião sought to depict the labors of Brazil's enslaved and mostly African-born diamond workers in Minas Gerais in the eighteenth century, precisely when Chica da Silva was the richest woman in the district and her common-law husband was possibly the wealthiest man in Portugal. The workers here are searching through diamond-bearing gravel under close surveillance (although the first overseer appears to be napping). When slaves found a diamond, they were to stand up and hold the stone above their heads before handing it to the overseer for safekeeping. Despite these and other controls, many slaves managed to hide diamonds in their mouths, ears, hair, and elsewhere, trading them later for food, clothing, alcohol, or cash. (The Art Archive/Biblioteca National do Rio de Janiero Brazil/Dagli Orti.)

unorthodox religious practices (such as kosher food preparation), but few were prosecuted. Brazil's Jewish community became more evident when several New Christians joined the Dutch during their occupation from 1630 to 1654 of Pernambuco in northeast Brazil. Under the Dutch, Brazil's Jews were allowed to build a synagogue and practice their religion openly. When the Portuguese regained control of the northeast in 1654, several New Christian planter families relocated to Dutch Suriname, where they set up slave-staffed plantations (see Counterpoint: The Maroons of Suriname). The Inquisition also persecuted secret Jews in Minas Gerais in the early eighteenth century, in part to confiscate their valuable estates and stocks of merchandise.

Afro-Brazilian Religion

The Portuguese Inquisition in Brazil also prosecuted Afro-Brazilian religious practitioners. None were burned, but many were publicly shamed, exiled, or sentenced to galley service. Usually denounced as "fetishists," devil-worshipers, and witches, these people maintained a wide variety of West and West Central African religious traditions, usually blended with some degree of Catholicism and native American shamanism. Often, Catholic saints were used to mask male and female West African deities, as later happened in Cuba and Saint-Domingue (Haiti). In other cases, religious brotherhoods combined West Central African spirit possession with Catholic Christianity. These brotherhoods, often devoted to black saints such as St. Benedict the Moor and St. Efigenia, were common throughout Brazil, but were especially powerful in Minas Gerais, where the missionary orders were banned for fiscal reasons. Orthodox black Catholics also enlivened their ceremonies, especially funerals and patron saints' days, with rhythmic music and dance.

Maroon Communities

Even before the discovery of gold, Brazil hosted the largest communities of **maroons** in the Western Hemisphere. By 1650 the maroon (from the Spanish term *cimarrón*, meaning "runaway") community of Palmares, really a confederation of a dozen fugitive villages, was home to some ten thousand or more ex-slaves and their descendants. Despite numerous military campaigns organized by planters in coordination with slave hunters, Palmares was only broken up in the 1690s and finally destroyed in 1694. With the development of Minas Gerais, dozens of new maroon villages popped up in the gold-rich backcountry. Several of their descendant communities have been formally recognized by the Brazilian government in recent years.

Artistic Legacies

As in Spanish America, it was in the cities most affected by the great mining boom—and later by sugar wealth—that Brazilian material culture grew most opulent. Churches modeled after European ones, such as those in Salvador in the northeast and Rio de Janeiro in the south, testify to the piety of both elites and poor religious brotherhoods. Even more stunning and original are the many churches and chapels of Minas Gerais, stretching from lonely Tejuco to São João del Rei (see again Map 22.2). A significant number of these extraordinary structures were designed, built, and decorated by slaves and their descendants. In Tejuco, several were commissioned by Chica da Silva, whose house still stands.

As the case of Chica da Silva illustrates, people of mixed heritage rose to prominent positions in Brazil, particularly in frontier districts. Arguably the colony's greatest artistic genius was the sculptor and architect Francisco Lisboa, like Chica the child of an enslaved African mother and free Portuguese father. Popularly known as Aleijadinho, or "Little Cripple" (due to leprosy), Lisboa was among the most original architects and sculptors of his era, carving fantastic soapstone façades with chisels strapped to the stumps of his hands.

Brazil's gold rush sputtered out around 1800, but by this time the northeastern sugar industry was undergoing a revival, along with tobacco, rice, cotton, and other cash crops. For the first time, Portuguese officials encouraged diversification and experimentation. The vast Amazon Basin was now being explored as a potential source of minerals, cacao, medicinal barks, and other export commodities. Coffee, which would later become Brazil's prime export, was also experimentally planted in various tropical climate zones, starting in the north. In export agriculture, Brazil's greatest competitors were in the Caribbean.

maroon In the seventeenth and eighteenth centuries, a runaway slave and his or her descendants.

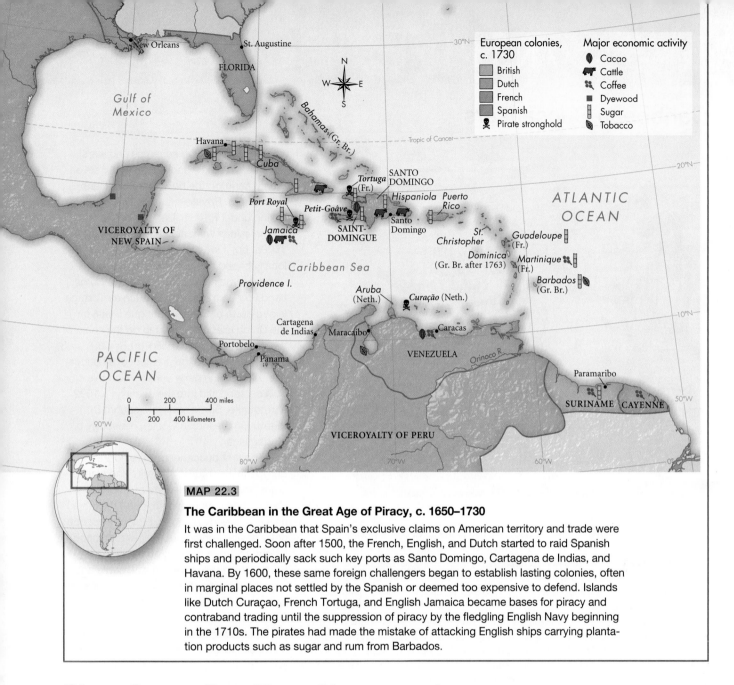

MAP 22.3

The Caribbean in the Great Age of Piracy, c. 1650–1730

It was in the Caribbean that Spain's exclusive claims on American territory and trade were first challenged. Soon after 1500, the French, English, and Dutch started to raid Spanish ships and periodically sack such key ports as Santo Domingo, Cartagena de Indias, and Havana. By 1600, these same foreign challengers began to establish lasting colonies, often in marginal places not settled by the Spanish or deemed too expensive to defend. Islands like Dutch Curaçao, French Tortuga, and English Jamaica became bases for piracy and contraband trading until the suppression of piracy by the fledgling English Navy beginning in the 1710s. The pirates had made the mistake of attacking English ships carrying plantation products such as sugar and rum from Barbados.

Bitter Sugar, Part Two: Slavery and Colonialism in the Caribbean 1625–1750

When the Dutch captured Pernambuco in 1630, they were most interested in sugar. How had the Portuguese managed to produce so much of it so cheaply? What the Dutch discovered was northeast Brazil's peculiar blend of loamy tropical soils, high-technology mills, and slave labor. By the time the Dutch abandoned Brazil in 1654, they had learned all they needed to know about the sugar business.

FOCUS

How did sugar production and slavery mold Caribbean societies?

English and French visitors had also taken careful notes as they displaced the Spanish in various parts of the Caribbean, such as Jamaica and western Hispaniola (later known as Saint-Domingue, then Haiti). These techniques of sugar manufacture were closely copied, and from the mid-seventeenth century onward the story of the Caribbean was but the story of sugar and slavery, continued. After Brazil, this diverse island region was the largest destination for enslaved Africans brought across the Atlantic—over one-third of the total (see Map 22.3).

Caribbean Buccaneers

Atlantic colonization schemes and wars gave rise to a new social type in the seventeenth century: the **buccaneer**, or Caribbean pirate. Privately financed sea raiders sailing under French, English, or Dutch commissions were active from the early 1500s, but it was only in the mid-1600s that locally based sea bandits acting on their own became an endemic problem. Some used French trading posts such as Tortuga Island north of Saint-Domingue (Haiti) or the Dutch island of Curaçao off the coast of Venezuela, but after 1655 Port Royal, Jamaica, became the greatest of all buccaneer bases. The party ended when this city built on sand slid into the ocean in a 1692 earthquake. Some survivors sought to regroup in the Indian Ocean, especially on Madagascar.

The first buccaneers were northern European indentured servants and war veterans, many of whom were sent to the Caribbean sugar islands to meet the labor needs of greedy planters. Either by escape or by having served out their terms, these indentures took to living off the land in Saint-Domingue, shooting wild cattle and roasting their meat on crude barbecues, or *boucans*. Known by 1650 as *boucaniers* in French, and buccaneers in English, the hunters began to organize raids on straggling merchant vessels in dugout canoes. Their guerrilla tactics and expert marksmanship

"Black Bart"

The great age of maritime commerce also gave rise to the great age of piracy, an activity that peaked between 1660 and 1730. Most pirates preyed on Spanish ships and towns, since these were imagined to be rich in silver and gold, but as Spain's competitors gained footholds in the Caribbean, coastal Africa, and parts of the American mainland after 1600, pirates expanded their reach and captured whatever they could, including slave ships belonging to their outraged countrymen. Among the most successful pirates was Bartholomew "Black Bart" Roberts, shown here near the African port of Whydah, where he captured and ransomed a number of English slave ships. Roberts was killed in 1722 in an engagement with the English Royal Navy near present-day Gabon. There followed a new and long-lasting era of policing the sea. (National Maritime Museum, London/The Image Works.)

Pirates and Planters

Development in the Caribbean was slow and not very methodical. Throughout the sixteenth century, French, English, and Dutch traders and raiders challenged Spanish monopolies, particularly on the mainland. Pirates and privateers preyed on slow-moving ships and lightly defended port towns. One of the most famous privateers was Sir Francis Drake, who in the late 1570s plundered one Spanish port after another. He also dabbled in the contraband slave trade, but the grateful English crown looked the other way to award him a knighthood. Only in around 1600 did these interlopers begin to establish permanent colonies. The Dutch focused on Guyana (later Suriname) and several small islands, such as Curaçao and St. Christopher. The English followed on Providence Island off the coast of modern Nicaragua. The French focused on western Hispaniola and Tortuga, a small island just offshore to the north. All these efforts combined experimental plantations, usually to grow tobacco or sugar, with contraband trade and piracy (see Lives and Livelihoods: Caribbean Buccaneers).

buccaneer A Caribbean-based pirate of the seventeenth century.

made them difficult to counter. Some, such as the Welshman Henry Morgan, made deals to share booty with colonial governors in exchange for legal protection, and later joined the colonial service. Others, such as François L'Ollonais, were unattached terrors of the Spanish Main. L'Ollonais was said to have carved the heart from a living victim and taken a bite. Piracy was about booty, not terror, however, and Spanish ships and towns, since they often contained silver and other portable treasures, were the main objects of buccaneer desire.

Once a raid was carried off, the pirates rendezvoused in the bars and brothels of Port Royal, whose markets thrived from the influx of stolen goods and money. When the buccaneers began to attack English, French, and Dutch ships with the same ferocity formerly reserved for Spanish ones in the late 1660s, the hunters became the hunted. Antipiracy laws from as early as the 1670s led to arrests and hangings, and by 1680 many buccaneers had fled to the Pacific and Indian oceans. A group of pirates who set out from the Virginia coast in the early 1680s returned to the Chesapeake with treasure stolen along the coast of Peru, only to land in jail and have their booty confiscated by royal officials. A portion of their loot was used to found the College of William and Mary in 1693.

At about the same time, a new pirate base was created on the island of Madagascar, which no Europeans had successfully colonized. From here buccaneers sailed north to stalk Muslim vessels traveling from India to the Arabian peninsula. The capture of several rich prizes by Henry Avery and other famous pirates in the 1690s led the English to send pirate hunters, among them the former buccaneer William Kidd. Kidd reverted to piratical activity off the coast of India; he was eventually arrested and jailed in New England before being sent to London for execution in 1701. After a break during the War of the Spanish Succession (1701–1714), which absorbed many buccaneers as privateers and even navy men, the war on Caribbean piracy returned in force, prosecuted mostly by the English Admiralty.

In the midst of England's war on piracy emerged some of the greatest figures of the era, among them Bartholomew Roberts. "Black Bart," as he was sometimes known, was one of the first pirates to prey on Portuguese ships carrying gold and diamonds to Europe from Brazil. When killed by English pirate hunters off the coast of Gabon in 1722, he was wearing a diamond-studded gold cross taken near Rio. By about 1725 the last wave of Anglo-American pirates, including the only known female pirate duo of Ann Bonny and Mary Read, was squelched.

QUESTIONS TO CONSIDER

1. What factors made buccaneer society possible in the seventeenth-century Caribbean?

2. What trends led to the sudden demise of the buccaneers' livelihood?

For Further Information:
Earle, Peter. *The Pirate Wars*. Boston: St. Martin's Griffin, 2006.

Spanish retaliation was fierce at first, but declined along with the empire's fortunes after 1648. The deepening seventeenth-century crisis rendered defense expenditures prohibitive. A massive English attack on Santo Domingo was successfully repulsed in 1655, but Jamaica was seized. Lacking minerals or a substantial native population, the Spanish had barely settled the island. Within a decade Port Royal, opposite Kingston Harbor on Jamaica's south coast, was a major base for contraband traders and buccaneers, among them Henry Morgan. Morgan and his followers sacked Panama City in 1671. The French followed a similar path on Martinique, Guadeloupe, and Saint-Domingue. Pirates of various nationalities meanwhile plagued the Spanish just as planters built a slave-staffed sugar economy farther inland. Some pirates, such as Henry Morgan, invested their plunder in their own Jamaican plantations, eventually gaining noble titles and general respectability.

Seizing Spanish Bases

The English colony of Barbados was a surprising success. A small and virtually uninhabited island at the easternmost edge of the Caribbean, Barbados had been of no interest

Developing Colonies

to the Spanish and Portuguese. The first English settlers came to plant tobacco in around 1625, and for a time the island's fortunes rested on production and export of this addictive drug. In time, capital accumulated from tobacco, along with advice and capital lent by Dutch refugees from Brazil, led the colony's planters to shift to sugar. Indentured servitude rapidly gave way to African slavery, and with slavery came rebellions. Even so, by the 1680s Barbados was a major world exporter of high-quality sugar, a position it held through the eighteenth century. Barbados showed that the Brazilian plantation model could transform even the smallest tropical island into a veritable gold mine.

With the expansion of slavery and sugar-growing on other Caribbean islands and parts of the mainland (especially Dutch Suriname), non-Iberian colonists began to surpass their predecessors in overall exports. In the course of the eighteenth century, the English, Dutch, and French embraced slavery on a scale and with an intensity not seen in Spanish America or Brazil. Slave codes grew increasingly harsh, and punishments cruel. There was virtually no interest expressed in protecting slaves' families or dignity, much less their souls. By 1750 the planters of Jamaica routinely tortured, raped, and otherwise terrorized enslaved Africans. They themselves admitted it, and wrote that such harsh measures were necessary to quell rebellion while maximizing production. Visitors to eighteenth-century Suriname described public executions as run-of-the-mill events, and those who visited Saint-Domingue wrote of sugar production on a vast, industrial scale. Slaves were consumed like so much timber.

The Rise of Caribbean Slave Societies

Whereas Brazilian planters used cheaper, enslaved native American workers as a bridge to mass African slavery, French, Dutch, and English planters in the Caribbean used indentured European servants. Throughout the seventeenth century thousands of poor servants and convicts staffed tobacco and sugar plantations alongside growing numbers of Africans and their descendants. If they survived the harsh conditions of the tropics, these servants could expect freedom within three to seven years. Many did not live to see that day, but the profits accumulated during these few years enabled plantation owners to purchase a permanently enslaved workforce. Scholars remain divided as to whether indentured Europeans were treated as badly as enslaved Africans.

Island Culture By the early eighteenth century, Caribbean plantation society had begun to achieve the opulent material culture and African-influenced diversity found in Brazil's mining districts. Great houses in the European style dotted many islands, and slave communities grew into neo-African villages. Churches in these often Protestant lands were far more modest than in Catholic Brazil, however, and of several denominations. African religious traditions flourished, often with little influence from the colonizers' faiths. In Jamaica and Saint-Domingue, the constant influx of African-born slaves, coupled with general disdain for slaves' spiritual lives among planters, priests, and missionaries, led to the formation of new, hybrid religious traditions, called Obeah and Vodoun (or Voodoo), respectively.

A great difference that did exist between Brazil and the Caribbean sugar colonies lay in the realms of racial mixture and shared religious traditions. European men routinely kept African and mulatto mistresses, as in Minas Gerais and other parts of Brazil, but they were usually loath to recognize their children, much less educate them in Europe and incorporate them into high society. Treated as a dirty secret and even a petty crime, racial mixture soon gave rise to sharply graded color categories quite distinct from Spanish America's fluid sistema de castas. As for religion, Europeans showed nothing but contempt for "Obeah men" and "Voodoo priestesses," treating them as frauds and quacks. Partly as a result, some of these new religious leaders, male and female, played key roles in slave uprisings.

Maroons and Slaves As in Brazil, *marronage* or slave flight was common throughout the Caribbean. Refuges for long-term runaways proved scarce on smaller, low-lying islands such as Barbados and Curaçao, but larger and more rugged islands such as Jamaica, Dominica, and Saint Domingue abounded with possibilities for safe haven. Here in rugged highlands such as Jamaica's Blue

Mountains, maroons were so successful they were able to negotiate treaties with planters and colonial officials by the early eighteenth century. Jamaican maroon leaders such as Nanny and Cudjoe were folk heroes to the enslaved and a constant thorn in the side of the British.

Sugar production as practiced by northern Europeans in the eighteenth century provided significant capital gains and, like Brazilian gold, probably helped to spark England's industrialization. Yet slavery of such horrific cruelty and scale also sowed the seeds of its own destruction. Slave traders responded to ratcheting Caribbean demand by packing their ships ever more tightly, turning slaving itself into an increasingly predatory exercise in more and more regions of West and West Central Africa. Some slaves were brought from as far away as the Indian Ocean island of Madagascar. By the late eighteenth century, white abolitionists at last began to join the long-ignored chorus of African and African-American voices against this enormous crime against humanity in the name of profit. For the first time, English tea drinkers thought twice before sweetening their brew.

Growth and Change in British and French North America 1607–1750

European colonization of the eastern seaboard of North America followed a different path than that of Spanish America or Brazil. There were, however, similarities: plantations developed, missionaries preached, people bred or married across color lines, and in places slave labor came to dominate. But overall, nontropical, Atlantic North America was characterized by a slow advance of European settler families practicing subsistence agriculture, livestock-raising, fishing, and commerce according to Old World norms. Eastern North America, both French and English, was to become, in the words of historian Alfred Crosby, a "neo-Europe" (see Map 22.4). Indigenous peoples, unlike in Spanish and Portuguese America where they had been absorbed and forcibly converted, were mostly driven from their lands or annihilated.

FOCUS

How did European relations with native peoples differ in the British and French colonies of North America?

Experiments in Commercial Colonialism

French, Dutch, and English colonization of eastern North America took root in the first decades of the seventeenth century. English Jamestown was founded on Virginia's Powhatan River (renamed "James" after the king) in 1607 and French Quebec, on Canada's St. Lawrence, in 1608. Henry Hudson, for a time an employee of the Dutch East India Company, began reconnoitering the river that took his name in 1609. Once it was clear that the Hudson River did not lead to the Pacific Ocean, a Dutch fur-trading post was established in 1618. As early as 1605 French Huguenots (or Protestant refugees) had also begun farming the coast of Maine and Nova Scotia, which they called Acadia.

Mariners such as Hudson continued searching in vain for a **northwest passage** to China. Others probed the soils of Newfoundland for signs of gold or silver. The survival of the earliest colonies in the tiny, fortified enclaves of "New France," "New Netherland," and "Virginia" depended on alliances with indigenous inhabitants. At the same time, all three European competitors were preoccupied with each other's designs on the region, a source of lasting conflict. Moreover, everyone worried about the Spanish, who had violently driven the French from Florida and the Dutch from Venezuela.

New France, first governed by Samuel de Champlain, marked France's renewed effort to colonize the Americas. Jacques Cartier and other mariners had explored the St. Lawrence Basin shortly after Columbus's time, and French colonists had planted forts in Florida and Brazil before being expelled by the Spanish and Portuguese in the 1560s. Only after France itself returned to calm, after the religious wars of 1562 to 1598 (discussed in Chapter 20), was a permanent colony deemed feasible. In North America, serious conflicts with the English

New France

northwest passage Searched-for sea route to Asia via North America.

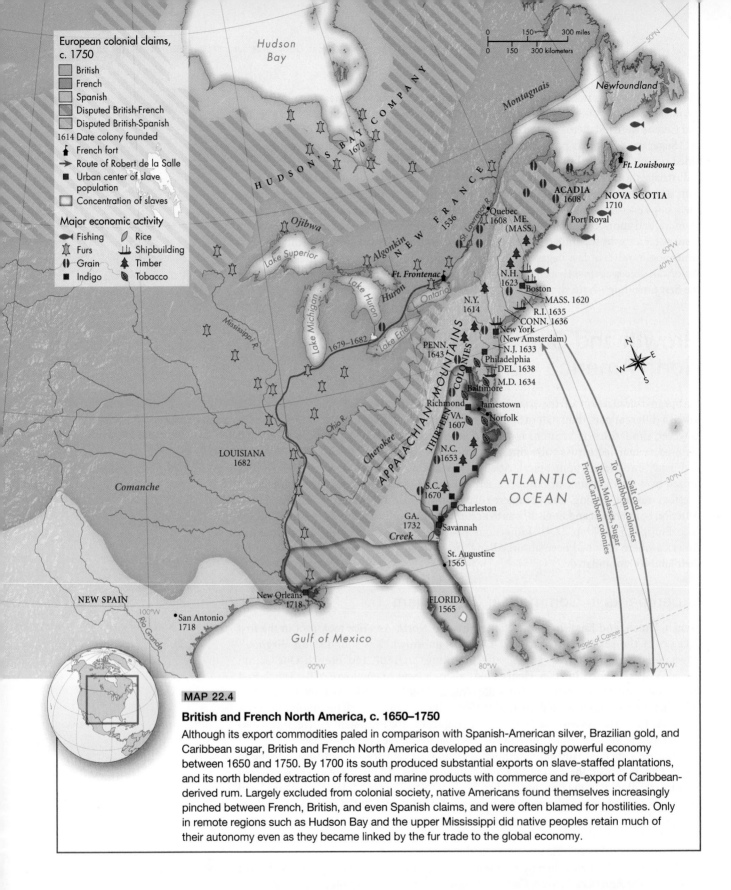

MAP 22.4

European colonial claims, c. 1750

- British
- French
- Spanish
- Disputed British-French
- Disputed British-Spanish

1614 Date colony founded

- French fort
- Route of Robert de la Salle
- Urban center of slave population
- Concentration of slaves

Major economic activity

- Fishing
- Furs
- Grain
- Indigo
- Rice
- Shipbuilding
- Timber
- Tobacco

British and French North America, c. 1650–1750

Although its export commodities paled in comparison with Spanish-American silver, Brazilian gold, and Caribbean sugar, British and French North America developed an increasingly powerful economy between 1650 and 1750. By 1700 its south produced substantial exports on slave-staffed plantations, and its north blended extraction of forest and marine products with commerce and re-export of Caribbean-derived rum. Largely excluded from colonial society, native Americans found themselves increasingly pinched between French, British, and even Spanish claims, and were often blamed for hostilities. Only in remote regions such as Hudson Bay and the upper Mississippi did native peoples retain much of their autonomy even as they became linked by the fur trade to the global economy.

broke out by the 1610s and 1620s; they were resolved by treaty in 1632. Quebec would subsequently survive for over a century as a fortified trading post funded by absentee investors. Military alliances with indigenous groups such as the Montagnais and Huron proved critical throughout New France's history.

Unlike the Spanish and Portuguese, French, English, and Dutch colonizers created **joint-stock companies** that attracted numerous investors in the mother country and took on a financial and even political life of their own. Amsterdam's stock market was by far Europe's most vibrant, and the Dutch VOC was considered the shining model of such enterprises, because it successfully combined commercial, military, and diplomatic functions to turn a private profit from colonialism.

New France managed to survive through many a long winter only by tapping into the long chain of indigenous and *métis*, or mixed-heritage, fur traders and trappers extending deep into the Great Lakes and beyond. The beaver pelts they brought from the interior were processed for the European hat market. Only these men in canoes, the famed *coureurs de bois* ("runners of the woods," as the independent fur traders were known), and a few Jesuits went much beyond the fort. Settlers concentrated mostly in the St. Lawrence Valley, eking out a living in subsistence agriculture supplemented by fishing and hunting.

The early government of Jamestown, Virginia, funded like New France by a group of absentee investors, blended business and military models. This proved to be a bad idea. Despite investment and high hopes, the Virginia Company experiment failed disastrously, and it was nearly abandoned after only a few years. Men such as John Smith, though in some ways capable leaders, could not keep restless fellow settlers from antagonizing local indigenous groups, many of which belonged to a confederacy headed by the chieftain Powhatan. The settler-soldiers refused to farm, and theft of indigenous food stores led to reprisals, spawning decades-long cycles of vengeance. Tsenacommocah (sen-uh-COMB-uh-cuh), as Powhatan's subjects called the Chesapeake Bay region, was not easily conquered, and indigenous attacks in the 1620s nearly wiped out the first English settlers' plantations.

Eventually, English settlers got the upper hand and began to make money from tobacco exports. Although enslaved Africans arrived as early as 1619, initially indentured English servants were the primary source of labor. Soil exhaustion was rapid, causing the tobacco frontier to sweep inland toward the Appalachian Mountains and southward into North Carolina. Soaring demand for land to cultivate tobacco prompted Indian attacks and culminated in a settler rebellion led by Nathaniel Bacon in 1676. Bacon and some five hundred followers ran Virginia's governor out of Jamestown for allegedly dealing too kindly with the Powhatan and other native groups. Although colonial authorities rejected Bacon's calls to uproot the Indians, English policy turned sharply toward "removal." As Indians were forced westward, indentured servitude and small plots gave way to African slavery and large plantations.

The stony region dubbed New England, initially settled by religious dissenters called "Puritans," followed a distinct trajectory. Soon after arriving more or less by accident in Plymouth, Massachusetts, in 1620 the first "pilgrims," as they called themselves, faced the problem of establishing a working relationship with indigenous peoples in a land of limited agricultural and commercial potential. The colony, farther north than initially planned, was sponsored by the Virginia Company, but in 1629 a new corporation, the Massachusetts Bay Company, was chartered by prominent Puritans in England. Elder churchmen latched onto the ample rights of self-governance entailed by this charter, and Boston emerged as capital of the deeply religious Massachusetts Bay colony. As in cold New France, survival was a challenge. Servants suffered most in the first hard years; indigenous peoples were largely ignored.

Religious and labor discipline led to some success for early New Englanders, but both also bred division. Dissenters fled southward to found Rhode Island and Connecticut; others were punished internally. Expansion of subsistence farms throughout the region yielded surplus wheat and other grains in time, and cod fishing in the Newfoundland Banks

Chesapeake Bay, c. 1650–1700

Areas settled and under tobacco cultivation
- By 1650
- By 1700

Jamestown

New England

joint-stock company A colonial commercial venture with a royal charter and private shareholders.

métis French for "mixed," or offspring of Europeans and native Americans.

Champlain Fires on the Iroquois

Violent European encounters with native Americans continued long after the arrival of Christopher Columbus in the Caribbean in 1492. Soon after Columbus, French navigators explored Canada's St. Lawrence estuary, partly in hopes of finding a northwest passage to the Pacific Ocean and to Asia. Yet it was only in the early seventeenth century that the French established a lasting colony based in Quebec City. This image shows French commander Samuel Champlain firing on Iroquois warriors in 1613 near what is today Fort Ticonderoga, New York. The engraving puts European technology in stark relief as Champlain (aided by two armed men in the trees above) confronts a mass of naked warriors flowing out of their stockade. Champlain's armor renders him immune to enemy arrows, which mostly sail overhead. According to an accompanying report of the engagement, a single shot by Champlain felled two of the most feared Iroquois warriors. (Bettmann/Corbis.)

grew ever more important, as did whaling. Colonial authorities signed treaties with compliant indigenous neighbors; those who resisted faced enslavement or death. The Puritans were not pacifists, and like Samuel de Champlain and John Smith, they knew how to use firearms to terrorizing effect. They also had no qualms about enslaving war captives. As in Virginia, missionary efforts were few, perhaps in part because of emerging English notions of individual religious freedom, but also because of racism. The general pattern of European-indigenous relations in New England, as it would eventually be throughout British North America, was total displacement.

New Commercial Ventures   Newfoundland and Nova Scotia were chartered for commercial reasons in the 1620s, the latter disputed with the French for over a century. Proprietary colonies soon followed to the south of New England. Court favorites were given vast tracts of American lands in exchange for promises to defend and develop them as havens for settlers and for the export of raw materials to benefit the mother country. These proprietary colonies later yielded states such as Pennsylvania, Delaware, and Maryland. In 1664, the English captured Dutch

Pilgrims Set Sail on the *Mayflower*

In this iconic seventeenth-century woodcut, a trio of English separatists leaves the temporary refuge of Leiden, a major Dutch university town, to sail to North America on the *Mayflower*. The Pilgrims, as they came to be known, hoped to found a colony in Virginia territory, but after landing by accident on the coast of Massachusetts in 1620, they chose to stay. (Private Collection/ Bridgeman Art Library.)

New Amsterdam, a fur-trading post established in 1625 and increasingly a site of contraband trade; they renamed it New York. By 1700, England dominated eastern North America from Newfoundland to the Carolinas. Religiously diverse, British North America lacked an overarching structure of governance. In this the English differed from the bureaucratic and centralizing Spanish.

Southeastern Plantations

By the early eighteenth century, Virginia, Maryland, the Carolinas, and England's other mid-Atlantic and southern colonies were home to huge, export-oriented plantations. Planters focused first on tobacco, then rice, indigo, and other cash crops. More like the Caribbean and parts of Iberian America than New France or New England, the mid-Atlantic and southeast colonies grew quickly into slave-based societies. The region's trade was dominated by port towns such as Norfolk, Baltimore, and Charleston, their vast hinterlands dotted with great plantation houses and substantial, almost townlike slave quarters. Pockets of indigenous resistance could still be found in the eighteenth century, but native groups wishing to remain independent were increasingly forced westward beyond the Appalachian Mountains.

Northeastern Commerce

The northeast seaboard colonies, including the thriving port of New York, followed a different, less export-oriented path, although mercantile connections to the Caribbean and other primary goods-producing regions were strong. Rum distilling and re-export became a major New England industry, alongside shipbuilding and fishing. All of these businesses connected northeastern British America to the Atlantic slave trade, and bulk items such as salt cod soon became central to the diet of enslaved Africans in Jamaica. Perhaps most significant compared with Spanish and Portuguese America was the great freedom to trade with foreigners that English colonists generally enjoyed. This was not legal, but as Chapter 23 will show, England failed to enforce its colonial trading policies until after 1750. When it finally did so, it provoked violent rebellion.

Everyday Life in the Northern Colonies

Given the long winters and relative isolation of the St. Lawrence River Basin, life for early French Canadians was both difficult and lonely. Food stores were a major concern, and settlers long relied on a blend of native generosity and annual supply ships from France. Thousands of colonists were sent to develop the land, along with soldiers to guard against English or Indian attacks. The result was the militarization of the backcountry, displacing and massacring native groups in a way reminiscent of England's uncompromising "removal" policy.

Jesuit Missionaries

Jesuit missionaries, meanwhile, set out to convert these embattled, indigenous inhabitants to Roman Catholicism. The priests, relatively few in number, concentrated on large semisedentary groups such as the Huron, Algonkin, and Ojibwa, among others. Sometimes the missionaries learned local languages, made friends with prominent chieftains or their sons, and found success. At other times, their failures ended in their deaths, memorialized by their brethren as religious martyrdom. French Jesuits did not give up on North American Indians, in any case, and eventually worked their way from the Great Lakes down the Mississippi Basin. Military explorers followed, including the nobleman Robert de la Salle, who in 1682 claimed the lower Mississippi, which he called Louisiana, for King Louis XIV (see again Map 22.4).

Frontier Society

Life in the American backcountry claimed by France was in many ways dominated by native peoples, a frontier arrangement historian Richard White has labeled "the middle ground." Here at the edge of imperial control indigenous Americans, métis fur traders, and European missionaries, soldiers, and homesteaders all found themselves interdependent, none claiming a monopoly. Not everyone found this arrangement to their liking, least of all crown representatives, but on the frontier the social divisions of race, religion, gender, and culture were blurred or overlooked (see Reading the Past: A Swedish Traveler's Description of Quebec). Put another way, "the middle ground" was the most egalitarian space in the early modern Americas. Like Chica da Silva's fluid world in backcountry Brazil, the possibilities could be astonishing, at least in the eyes of outsiders.

Limited Racial Relations

Unlike in Spanish or Portuguese America, sexual relations across color lines were relatively rare in British North America, except in frontier outposts. In part, this was a result of demography: European men and women migrated to the eastern seaboard in close to equal numbers over time, and indigenous peoples were relatively few and were rarely incorporated into settler society. When racial mixture occurred, it was most commonly the result of illicit relations between white men and enslaved women of African descent. Such relations, which according to surviving documents were more often forced than consensual or long-term, were most common in the plantation districts of the Chesapeake and Carolina Low Country. Still, some mixed-race children were born in northern cities such as New York and Boston, where considerable numbers of slaves and free people of color could be found in close proximity to whites. Throughout the British colonies, blatantly racist "antimiscegenation" laws dating to the seventeenth century also discouraged black-white unions, because these were thought to undermine the social hierarchy. Racial codes and covenants were most rigidly enforced in regions highly dependent on African slavery, namely the mid-Atlantic and southeast. Still, as Virginia planter and future U.S. president Thomas Jefferson's long-term, child-producing relationship with his slave, Sally Hemings, demonstrates, human urges and affinities could override even the strictest social taboos and legal codes.

Slave Culture and Resistance

Slavery existed in New France, but on a small scale. A few Africans could be found in growing towns such as Montreal, but most slaves were indigenous war captives used for household labor. In early New England, enslaved Africans and a few indigenous slaves served in similar roles, and also in artisan workshops and on board ships. Thousands of enslaved Africans lived and worked in the bustling shops and port facilities of New York City by the early eighteenth century, and many more lived and worked on farms in rural Pennsylvania. Slave rebellions were relatively rare in these regions, although the slaves of New York were highly outspoken and sometimes alarmed city authorities. Slave resistance mostly consisted of work stoppages, tool breaking, truancy, and other "passive" means. Faced with racist exclusion, small black religious communities, mostly of the Anglican, Methodist, and Baptist denominations, eventually formed.

Even more distinct slave cultures emerged in regions where Africans predominated, from Maryland to Georgia. Here plantation life took on some of the features of the English Caribbean, with large numbers of enslaved Africans and their descendants concentrated in prisonlike barracks within view of great plantation houses. As archaeologists

A Swedish Traveler's Description of Quebec

Pehr ("Peter") Kalm was a Swedish naturalist who visited Canada in around 1749. In the following passages, translated from the Swedish in the 1770s, Kalm describes the inhabitants of the Christian Huron village of Lorette, just outside the capital of French Canada, Quebec City.

August the 12. This afternoon I and my servant went out of town, to stay in the country for a couple of days that I might have more leisure to examine the plants that grow in the woods here, and the state of the country. In order to proceed the better, the governor-general had sent for an Indian from Lorette to show us the way, and teach us what use they make of the spontaneous plants hereabouts. This Indian was an Englishman by birth, taken by the Indians thirty years ago, when he was a boy, and adopted by them, according to their custom, instead of a relation of theirs killed by the enemy. Since that time he constantly stayed with them, became a Roman Catholic and married an Indian woman: he dresses like an Indian, speaks English and French, and many of the Indian languages. In the wars between the French and English, in this country [a reference to chronic conflicts preceding the Seven Years' War], the French Indians have made many prisoners of both sexes in the English plantations [i.e., farms], adopted them afterwards, and they married with people of the Indian nations. From hence the Indian blood in Canada is much mixed with European blood, and a great part of the Indians now living owe their origin to

Europe. It is likewise remarkable that a great part of the people they had taken during the war and incorporated with their nations, especially the young people, did not choose to return to their native country, though their parents and nearest relations came to them and endeavored to persuade them to it, and though it was in their power to do it. The licentious life led by the Indians pleased them better than that of their European relations; they dressed like the Indians and regulated all their affairs in their way. It is therefore difficult to distinguish them except by their color, which is somewhat whiter than that of the Indians. There are likewise examples of some Frenchmen going amongst the Indians and following their way of life. There is on the contrary scarce one instance of an Indian's adopting the European customs.

Source: Peter Kalm, *Travels into North America*, trans. John Reinold Forster (Barre, MA: Imprint Society, 1972) 3:184.

EXAMINING THE EVIDENCE

1. How does Kalm assess the "cultural divide" and racial mixture in French Canada?

2. What made Indian customs preferable to European ones in this region, according to Kalm?

and historians are increasingly discovering, enslaved Africans had a thriving religious and material world of their own, one that contrasted sharply to the tidy, well-heeled world of the English planter families who claimed lordship over them. African religious practices, while muted by comparison with those of the Caribbean or Brazil, were widely known and respected among the enslaved population. Secret shamanistic and medicinal practices were also common. Whites appear to have known virtually nothing about the slaves' hidden culture.

Violent rebellions and mass marronage along the Atlantic seaboard were rare in comparison with the Caribbean or even Brazil. There were simply far more whites who could be mustered to put down an uprising in Virginia or North Carolina than in Jamaica or Barbados, where slaves outnumbered white settlers by huge margins. Geography limited marronage as well. The mountains were distant and inhabited by Indians. During winter, maroons could be more easily tracked by hunters due to diminished forest cover, and they were hard-pressed to find food in the wild. Some slaves ran away to cities, and even to Spanish Florida, but it was nearly impossible to form lasting maroon communities. Unlike Spanish and Portuguese America, slaves' legal access to freedom through self-purchase or emancipation was severely limited, as was access to the religion of the planters. Only in places such as South Carolina were concentrations of recently arrived Africans great enough to create the kinds of "neo-Africas" found in much of Brazil and the Caribbean. Thus, while societies throughout the Americas included a mixture of Europeans, Africans, and indigenous Americans, the relationships among these groups and the hybrid cultures that emerged varied from region to region, depending on local conditions and the goals and beliefs of the colonizers in question.

COUNTERPOINT
The Maroons of Suriname

FOCUS

How did the runaway slaves of Dutch Suriname create a lasting independent state of their own?

In defiance of slavery on plantations and in mines, fugitive Africans and their descendants established free, or "maroon," communities throughout the Americas. Slaves ran away as soon as they could from brutal conditions in Hispaniola, Puerto Rico, Cuba, and Panama. Others fled into the hills east and southwest of Mexico City. Still others found refuge in backcountry Venezuela, Colombia, Ecuador, Peru, and Bolivia. Slaves in Portuguese Brazil did likewise, forming in the hills of Alagoas, a small province of northeastern Brazil, the largest maroon confederacy in history: the Quilombo (key-LOAM-boh) of Palmares. Similar maroon settlements emerged in English Jamaica, as well as French Saint-Domingue, Guadeloupe, and Martinique. But it was in the small colony of Dutch Suriname on South America's northern coast that African and African-American fugitives established the Americas' most resilient and distinctive maroon culture.

From Persecution to Freedom

Dutch and Portuguese Jewish planters ejected from Brazil after 1654 brought enslaved Africans to Suriname to grow and process sugar cane. By the 1660s, dozens of plantations dotted the banks of the Saramaka, Suriname, and Marowijne rivers. Faced not only with intensive, uncompensated labor in the hot sun but also with physical and psychological torture, many of the enslaved escaped upriver into dense forests once inhabited by Carib and Arawakan-speaking indigenous peoples. Sheltered by cataracts, rapids, and winding tributaries, dozens and then hundreds of runaways settled beyond the reach of planters and colonial authorities. If captured, the maroons, male and female, faced dismemberment and public execution, tactics of terror meant to dissuade those on the plantations from fleeing.

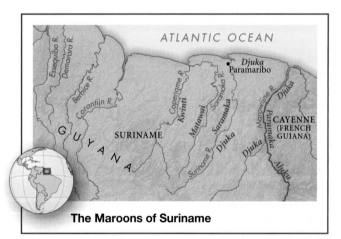

The Maroons of Suriname

By 1700 Suriname's maroons had formed several independent chiefdoms, each augmenting its numbers through periodic raids on the plantations downriver. Women were especially prized. Within a few decades the maroons numbered in the thousands. Taking advantage of the rugged geography of the Suriname interior and adapting to its challenging environment, the maroons carved out a "neo-Africa" in the backlands. After numerous failed expeditions to capture and re-enslave the maroons, plantation owners sought peace in the 1740s, only to return with even larger and better-armed expeditions after 1750. The maroons remained resolute and eventually won freedom from the Dutch government, which sent them arms and other trade goods to keep peace. As early as the late eighteenth century a few maroon groups allowed small numbers of Christian missionaries to visit them, but the missionaries won few converts and most of them soon died of malaria and other tropical diseases.

Suriname's Distinctive Maroon Culture

Six major maroon groups, the Saramaka, Djuka, Aluku, Paramaka, Matawai, and Kwinti, continue to live in Suriname and neighboring French Guiana, and many retain, thanks to vibrant oral traditions, substantial memories of the period of slavery and the punishing wars the planters prosecuted against them. Some maroon descendants began writing histories of these events as early as the 1880s. Others have moved in the decades following Suriname's independence from the Dutch in 1975 to the coastal capital of Paramaribo or even to Dutch cities such as Amsterdam and Leiden. Maroon culture nevertheless remains very much alive.

Maroon culture in Suriname, built around matrilineal villages, was so striking to early outside visitors that they assumed its rituals and complex artistic traditions to be direct transfers from some part of western Africa. The distinctive architecture, decorative patterns, textile traditions, and musical styles all hark back to Africa. Anthropologists looked for specific links in African art, language, and religion, but found no single traceable root—only broad associations and isolated words. Anthropologists Richard and Sally Price have argued that Suriname's distinctive maroon culture was something new, a product of resistance to colonialism. By combining archival and anthropological research they have shown how strands of western African thought and practice converged with the contingencies of fugitive life at the margins of a European-dominated plantation society. To survive, runaway Africans and their descendants learned to select the best local forest products such as wood for canoes and thatch for roofs, then planted known, imported crops such as bananas and plantains, as well as local ones like maize. Through raids and treaties they obtained cooking pots, textiles, and other manufactured goods, all of which they combined, then decorated, to create a new and distinctive material culture.

Descendants of the original maroon elders have preserved and passed along memories of the long-past horrors and escape from slavery, as in the following passage, recited by the Saramakan leader Lántifáya and recorded by Richard Price in 1978:

Maroon of Suriname

As slavery expanded throughout the Caribbean and many parts of the mainland Americas after 1650, so too did slave flight and the formation of "maroon," or runaway, communities. Although scattered throughout the tropics as well as the swamplands of the U.S. southeast, the largest and best-armed maroon communities in the Americas emerged in the backlands of Dutch Suriname, on the north coast of South America. Here escaped slaves armed themselves by raiding coastal plantations. Their raids sparked reprisals, which included full-blown wars by the later eighteenth century. A soldier in these wars, John Gabriel Stedman, wrote a sympathetic account of the struggles of slaves and maroons in Suriname that became evidence used by the emerging abolitionist cause in England. Engraver Francesco Bartolozzi followed Stedman's descriptions to depict this maroon warrior on the march, stolen gun in hand and death—or slain enemies—literally at his feet. (British Library/The Image Works.)

> In slavery, there was hardly anything to eat. It was at the place called Providence Plantation. They whipped you till your ass was burning. Then they would give you a bit of plain rice in a calabash [bowl made from the fruit of a tropical American tree]. (That's what we've heard.) And the gods told them that this is no way for human beings to live. They would help them. Let each person go where he could. So they ran.[2]

Conclusion

The colonial Americas underwent the deepest alterations of the world's regions in early modern times, environmentally and socially. Mining of precious metals for export to Europe and Asia drove the Spanish and Portuguese deep into the interior, transforming vast landscapes and giving rise to a wide range of new social and economic relations. Autonomous indigenous groups, followed later by enslaved Africans, were driven farther inland as they searched for refuge. Punishing forms of labor persisted at the old Aztec and Inca core through the eighteenth century, but indigenous populations began to recover from postconquest disease shocks. In the lawless mining frontier of Brazil, as in backcountry New France, racial mixing proved a pragmatic response to demographic realities, challenging notions of propriety and permissiveness.

More rigidly racist social orders developed in the French, Dutch, and English Caribbean and along the eastern seaboard of North America. That a successful and publicly recognized woman of color such as Chica da Silva could have emerged in such a place as Jamaica or Virginia is almost impossible to imagine. The intense religiosity of the seventeenth and early eighteenth centuries, manifested in both Spanish-American Catholicism and English Puritanism, faded only slowly and left a long-lasting legacy. American dependence on slavery and other forms of forced labor would also die a lingering death. In these and other key ways, the Americas and their European motherlands grew steadily and irreconcilably apart.

NOTES

1. Sor Juana Inés de la Cruz, quoted in Irving Leonard, *Baroque Times in Old Mexico: Seventeenth-century Persons, Places, and Practices* (Ann Arbor: University of Michigan Press, 1959), 189.
2. Saramakan elder Lántifáya, quoted in Richard Price, *First-Time: The Historical Vision of an Afro-American People* (Baltimore, MD: Johns Hopkins University Press, 1983), 71.

RESOURCES FOR RESEARCH

General Works

General surveys of the early modern Americas remain to be written, but the following are examples of border-crossing works. Benjamin and Egerton et al. are pioneering textbooks in Atlantic history, incorporating Africa and western Europe as well as the Americas.

Alchon, Suzanne Austin. *A Pest in the Land: New World Epidemics in a Global Perspective.* 2003.

Benjamin, Thomas. *The Atlantic World: Europeans, Africans, Indians, and Their Shared History, 1400–1900.* 2009.

Egerton, Douglas R., Alison Games, Jane Landers, Kris Lane, and Donald Wright. *The Atlantic World.* 2007.

Library of Congress: Hispanic Reading Room. This Web site features a wealth of materials on early Spanish and Portuguese America: http://www.loc.gov/rr/hispanic/onlinecol.html.

Socolow, Susan. *The Women of Colonial Latin America.* 2000.

University of Pennsylvania Library: Cultural Readings: Colonization and Print in the Americas. A useful mix of printed and pictorial sources on the early Americas: http://www.library.upenn.edu/exhibits/rbm/kislak/index/cultural.html.

The World That Silver Made: Spanish America, 1580–1750

Thanks to many researchers, Spanish America is at last beginning to come into focus as a global region. The following is a sampling of key studies and solid overviews. Bakewell is especially good on the mining economy, as are Guy and Sheridan on frontiers.

Andrien, Kenneth. *Andean Worlds: Indigenous History, Culture, and Consciousness Under Spanish Rule, 1532–1825.* 2001.

Bakewell, Peter. *A History of Latin America to 1825,* 3d ed. 2010.

Guy, Donna, and Thomas Sheridan, eds. *Contested Ground: Comparative Frontiers on the Northern and Southern Edges of the Spanish Empire.* 1998.

Hoberman, Louisa Schell, and Susan Socolow, eds. *Cities and Society in Colonial Latin America.* 1986.

Hoberman, Louisa Schell, and Susan Socolow, eds. *The Countryside in Colonial Latin America.* 1996.

Gold, Diamonds, and the Transformation of Brazil, 1695–1800

The story of Golden-Age Brazil is still being researched, but several classic and new works in English, including Charles Boxer's fine overview and Júnia Furtado's new biography of Chica da Silva, offer a solid start. Dean's is an excellent environmental study.

Boxer, Charles R. *The Golden Age of Brazil: Growing Pains of a Colonial Society.* 1964.

Dean, Warren. *With Broadax and Firebrand: The Destruction of Brazilian Atlantic Forest.* 1995.

Furtado, Júnia F. *Chica da Silva.* 2008.

Higgins, Kathleen. *"Licentious Liberty" in a Colonial Gold Mining Region: Sabará, Minas Gerais, in the Eighteenth Century.* 1999.

Schwartz, Stuart B. *Slaves, Peasants, and Rebels: Reconsidering Brazilian Slavery.* 1992.

Bitter Sugar, Part Two: Slavery and Colonialism in the Caribbean, 1625–1750

Caribbean history is a fast-growing field. This area is only starting to be treated as a region rather than as clusters of islands with a shared language, or "proto-nations." Dunn's work on the English Caribbean is classic, the Schwartz collection offers a sweeping update, and Moya Pons is a superb overview.

Burnard, Trevor. *Mastery, Tyranny, and Desire: Thomas Thistlewood and His Slaves in the Anglo-Jamaican World.* 2004.

Common-Place. A Web journal with research links sponsored by the American Antiquarian Society: http://www.common-place.org/.

Dunn, Richard S. *Sugar and Slaves: The Rise of the Planter Class in the English West Indies, 1624–1713,* 2d ed. 2000.

Moya Pons, Frank. *The Caribbean: A History.* 2007.

Schwartz, Stuart B., ed. *Tropical Babylons: Sugar and the Making of the Atlantic World, 1450–1680.* 2005.

Growth and Change in British and French North America, 1607–1750

The literature on British and French North America is vast. What follows is only a small sample of classic and recent contributions.

Gleach, Frederic W. *Powhatan's World and Colonial Virginia: A Conflict of Cultures.* 1997.

Hall, David D. *Worlds of Wonder, Days of Judgment: Popular Religious Belief in Early New England.* 1990.

Karlsen, Carol F. *The Devil in the Shape of a Woman: Witchcraft in Colonial New England.* 1987.

Morgan, Philip D. *Slave Counterpoint: Black Culture in the Eighteenth-Century Chesapeake and Lowcountry.* 1998.

Society of Early Americanists. Web site with links to teaching resources and documents: http://www.societyofearlyamericanists.org/.

White, Richard. *The Middle Ground: Indians, Empires, and Republics in the Great Lakes Region, 1650–1815.* 1991.

COUNTERPOINT: The Maroons of Suriname

Scholarship on maroon societies is growing, but few have written more on the maroons of Suriname than anthropologists Richard and Sally Price.

Price, Richard. *Alabi's World.* 1990.

———. *First-Time: The Historical Vision of an Afro-American People.* 1983.

———, ed. *Maroon Societies: Rebel Slave Communities in the Americas,* 3d ed. 1996.

Price, Richard, and Sally Price. *Maroon Arts.* 2000.

▶ **For additional primary sources from this period**, see *Sources of Crossroads and Cultures*.

▶ **For Web sites, images, and documents related to topics in this chapter**, see Make History at bedfordstmartins.com/smith.

The major global development in this chapter ▶ The profound social, cultural, and environmental changes in the Americas under colonial rule.

IMPORTANT
EVENTS

1570	Spanish galleons begin annual service linking Acapulco to Manila
1607	English establish colony at Jamestown, Virginia
1608	French establish colony at Quebec City
1618	Dutch establish colony of New Netherland on upper Hudson River
1625	Dutch settle New Amsterdam on Manhattan Island; English establish colony on Barbados
1630	Dutch capture northeast Brazil
1654	Portuguese drive Dutch from Brazil; some colonists move to Suriname
1655	English seize Jamaica from the Spanish
1664	English take New Amsterdam from Dutch, rename it New York
1671	Henry Morgan's buccaneers sack Panama City
1676	Bacon's Rebellion in Virginia
1694	Great Brazilian maroon community of Palmares destroyed
1695–1800	Discovery in Brazilian interior of gold and diamonds inaugurates Brazil's "gold rush"
1701–1714	War of the Spanish Succession
1720	Brazil elevated to status of viceroyalty
1763	Rio de Janeiro elevated to status of capital of Brazil

KEY
TERMS

audiencia (p. 724)   **mestizaje** (p. 731)
buccaneer (p. 738)   **mestizo** (p. 731)
creole (p. 731)   **métis** (p. 743)
indenture (p. 722)   **mulatto** (p. 731)
joint-stock company   **northwest passage**
  (p. 743)   (p. 741)
maroon (p. 736)

CHAPTER OVERVIEW
QUESTIONS

1. How did the production of silver, gold, and other commodities shape colonial American societies?

2. How and where did northern Europeans insert themselves into territories claimed by Spain and Portugal?

3. How did racial divisions and mixtures compare across the Americas by the mid-eighteenth century?

SECTION FOCUS
QUESTIONS

1. How did mineral wealth steer the development of Spanish America?

2. How was Brazil transformed by the mining boom of the eighteenth century?

3. How did sugar production and slavery mold Caribbean societies?

4. How did European relations with native peoples differ in the British and French colonies of North America?

5. How did the runaway slaves of Dutch Suriname create a lasting independent state of their own?

MAKING
CONNECTIONS

1. How did Spanish America's imperial bureaucracy compare with those of the Ottomans and other "gunpowder empires" discussed in Chapters 19 to 21?

2. How did the labor systems of the American colonies compare with those of western Eurasia (see Chapter 20)? With those of Russian and East Asia (see Chapter 21)?

3. What role did religious diversity play in colonial American life compared with contemporary South and Southeast Asia (see Chapter 19)?

4. In what ways did economic developments in colonial Brazil differ from developments in Spanish America?

PART 4

The World
from 1750 to the Present

MANY OF THE TRENDS of the early modern period continued after 1750. Global connections continued to intensify, and science and technology advanced at an ever-faster pace. As part of their growing competition for land, natural resources, and the control of populations, governments armed themselves with more destructive weaponry. As technology developed, the variety of livelihoods expanded across the globe, and many people enjoyed the opportunity to purchase an array of consumer products. The accelerating rate of change in technology, population growth, consumerism, and the introduction of new livelihoods and forms of government marks the shift from early modern times to what historians call the late modern era, the period from about 1750 to the present.

The great empires of the early modern period—the Qing, Mughal, Ottoman, and Spanish—faced challenges as the modern period opened. Many of these challenges arose from the inroads outsiders made on their rule, but these empires also faced problems within their borders, such as the enormous costs of military supremacy. Religious dissent, natural disasters, and the social changes that accompanied modernity also undermined their security. Newly wealthy or ambitious people and those wanting more modern forms of government contested the power of traditional rulers. The Qing, Mughal, Ottoman, and Spanish empires would all disappear in the late modern period.

Lives and livelihoods were transformed as mechanical power came to substitute for human power in the Industrial Revolution, which began in around 1750 in western Europe and spread throughout the globe. Newly created factory work moved production out of the home to mechanized workplaces, and a variety of other new occupations connected with the rise of industry developed, such as railroad builders, engineers, and conductors, and later, flight

754

CHAPTERS IN THIS PART ▼

23 Atlantic Revolutions and the World, 1750–1830

24 Industry and Everyday Life, 1750–1900

25 The Rise of Modern Nation-States, 1850–1900

26 Imperial Order and Disorder, 1850–1914

27 Wars, Revolutions, and the Birth of Mass Society, 1910–1929

28 Global Catastrophe: The Great Depression and World War II, 1929–1945

29 The Emergence of New Nations in a Cold War World, 1945–1970

30 Technological Transformation and the End of Cold War, 1960–1992

31 A New Global Age, 1989 to the Present

CH 26

attendants and workers in airplane plants. With the proliferation of science and technology, entirely new service work, in reproductive technology and systems analysis, for example, continued to transform work life. Nonetheless, agriculture remained a primary form of work for the vast majority of people until well into the twentieth century. That livelihood, too, was affected by farm machinery, the development of chemical fertilizers, and ultimately what was called in the late twentieth century a "green revolution" based on seeds and plants designed to flourish in particular parts of the world.

Modern industry did not displace older ways of doing things all at once. Slavery in fact gave a crucial boost to industrial growth by providing raw materials and food for industrial workers. Although a declining labor system, slavery has remained a livelihood down to the present. Women in the workforce often held the worst jobs and were paid less than men even for equivalent tasks.

Emboldened by new wealth and industrial technology, a cluster of European states, eventually joined by Japan and the United States, built cohesive, effective governments with modern military capabilities and mass armies. During this period, most of them developed constitutional governments based on the rule of law and the explicit elaboration of the rights of citizens. Constitutional government and legal rights were often gained through revolutions or other dramatic changes in rulership, but these states were backed by unified citizens. As dignified citizens, rather than servile subjects of kings, many felt empowered to join the commercial and industrial innovation that was going on around them. Historians characterize such states as "nation-states." As they became stronger because of their citizen support, the rising nation-states sought to extend their power through what is known as the "new imperialism." Unlike the expansionists of the early modern period, new imperialists had the "tools of empire" to take over the institutions

CH 27

CH 28

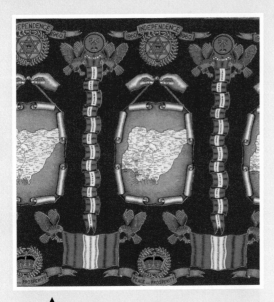

and economies of other parts of the world more completely. Late modernity saw the imperial nations try to dominate Africa, Asia, and other parts of the world both economically and politically in the nineteenth century.

Imperial countries justified their rule by celebrating the modern ideas and institutions they would bring to the world's "backward" peoples. Local peoples both resisted and cooperated with the imperialists; some grew incredibly wealthy from trade, manufacturing, and governmental work. However, imperialism also brought devastation and death because of exploitation and outright violence. Imperialism nonetheless developed global networks of unprecedented density, as steamships, telegraphs, and other forms of communications technology circled the earth at a faster pace than ever before.

Competition and conflict among these imperial nations intensified, as did organized resistance to their rule. In the twentieth century the imperial powers waged two horrific wars—World Wars I and II—in the course of which tens of millions of people died. Eventually, colonial people took advantage of the war-weakened imperialists, winning their freedom and setting up independent states after World War II ended in 1945. The rest of the twentieth century down to the present has been a story of these nation-states expanding their capacities and livelihoods and asserting their place in the modern world.

Our most recent modern history is filled with the struggles involved in asserting this independence, first under the conditions of the Cold War between the Soviet Union and United States that followed World War II, and then during the period of U.S. dominance after

CH 29

CH 30

	1750		1815	
Americas		1775–1781 North American Revolution U.S. Constitution formally adopted 1789 1791–1804 Haitian Revolution	1816–1825 Latin American revolutions of independence	U.S. Civil War 1861–1865 1846–1848 Mexican War
Europe	1750–1800 Spread of the Enlightenment beyond France 1750 Industrialization begins in Great Britain	1789–1799 French Revolution Napoleon comes to power 1799	1815 Napoleon defeated at Waterloo; Congress of Vienna	1853–1856 Crimean War Communist Manifesto 1848
Middle East		1798 Napoleon invades Egypt 1805 Muhammad Ali founds dynasty in Egypt		
Africa	Britain takes Cape Colony 1795 Sokoto caliphate founded 1809		1821 Republic of Liberia founded	
Asia and Oceania	1765 English East India Company rule of Bengal begins 1769–1778 Captain Cook's exploration of Australia, New Zealand		Taiping Rebellion 1840s 1839–1842 Opium War	

1989. Genocide, civil war, poverty, and an unprecedented migration of peoples globally have characterized human life in the past few decades. Terrorism, the pollution of the earth's atmosphere, and the spread of deadly diseases are also part of our most recent modernity.

Nonetheless, the world's peoples have simultaneously attempted to create new forms of world governance to eliminate the worst abuses of modern life. Writers and artists have innovatively explored modernity's difficulties. Historians and philosophers have also analyzed the consequences of growing military power on the one hand and life-enhancing developments such as medical breakthroughs and the communications revolution on the other. There is no alternative, many of these thinkers believe, to deliberate study of the past as the basis for informed decision-making in our world today.

CH 31

NORTH AMERICA

EUROPE

ASIA

MIDDLE EAST

ATLANTIC OCEAN

AFRICA

PACIFIC OCEAN

SOUTH AMERICA

INDIAN OCEAN

AUSTRALIA

1880

1945

2010

1880–1940 Immigration from Europe surges ▪ **1929** U.S. stock market crash sparks the Great Depression   NAFTA enacted ▪ **2001** Terrorists attack
 Spanish-American War   **1910–1920** Mexican Revolution   *The Feminine Mystique* **1963** ▪   ▪ **1969** U.S. astronauts **1994** ▪   the United States
      1898 ▪   ▪ **1917** United States enters World War I   **1945–1989** Cold War land on moon   **2007–2008** Global economic crisis unfolds

1861 Emancipation of the serfs in Russia **1914–1918** World War I   **1939–1945** World War II in Europe ▪ **1967** EEC established
1880–1900 Impressionism flourishes **1917–1918** Russian Revolution ▪ **1930s** Welfare state   ▪ **1960** Introduction of birth–control pill ▪ **1990s** New European nations
1891–1904 Construction of trans-Siberian railroad   begins in Sweden ▪ **1952** Discovery of structure of DNA   emerge in wake of Soviet collapse

1869   Young Turks' uprising   ▪ **1918** Breakup of Ottoman Empire ▪ **1948** Founding of Israel   **1980–1988** Iran-Iraq War ▪ **2003** United States
Suez Canal   **1908** ▪   Creation of OPEC **1960** ▪   Yom Kippur **1978–1979** Revolution in Iran invades Iraq
completed   **1922–1938** Mustafa Kemal modernizes Turkey   War **1973** ▪   Start of Arab Spring uprisings **2010** ▪

1867 End of Atlantic slave trade   Ghana gains independence **1959** ▪   Republic of South Sudan
1870–1914 New imperialism in Africa   ▪ **1962** Algeria wins independence   founded **2011** ▪
 1884–1885 Berlin Conference on Africa   **1948–1989** Apartheid in South Africa

1868 Meiji Restoration **1904–1905** Russo-Japanese War **1937–1945** World War II in the Pacific **1966–1976** Cultural Revolution ▪ **1992** Beginning of socialist
1870–1914 New imperialism in Asia   ▪ **1947** India and Pakistan win independence   market economy in China
1894–1895 Sino-Japanese War   Gandhi's Salt March **1930** ▪ **1950–1953** Korean War **1954–1975** Vietnam War

23

AT A CROSSROADS ▶

Simon Bolivar traveled the Atlantic world, gaining inspiration from the Enlightenment and revolutionary currents he felt firsthand in Spain, France, the United States, and the Caribbean. On his return to South America, he helped spearhead the movement for independence there. No democrat, Bolivar learned from hard experience that in an independent South America, the rich variety of slaves and other workers would need to be accommodated. (The Art Archive/Museo Historico Nacional Buenos Aires/Gianni Dagli Orti.)

Atlantic Revolutions and the World

1750–1830

Simon Bolivar (1783–1830) began life as the privileged son of a family that in the sixteenth century had settled in Caracas, a city in Spanish-controlled South America (now the capital of Venezuela). His early years were full of personal loss: his father died when he was three, his mother when he was five, and his grandfather, who cared for him after his mother's death, when he was six. Bolivar's extended family sent him to military school and then to Spain to study—typical training for prominent "creoles," as South Americans of European descent were called. Following the death of his young wife, he traveled to Paris to overcome his grief. There Bolivar's life changed: he saw the military hero Napoleon crown himself emperor in 1804 and witnessed crowds of patriotic French fill the streets of the capital with joy. "That moment, I tell you, made me think of the slavery of my country and of the glory that would come to the person who liberated it," he later wrote.[1] After a visit to the newly independent United States, Bolivar returned to his home in 1807, inspired by all he had seen, and determined to reform his homeland by freeing it from the oppressions of Spanish rule. He, too, took up arms, leading military campaigns, which along with popular uprisings eventually ousted Spain's government from much of Latin America. For his revolutionary leadership, contemporaries gave him the title "Liberator."

The creation of independent states in Latin America challenged centuries-old empires and was part of a powerful upheaval in the Atlantic world. North American colonists rebelled against Britain in 1776 and, with the help of the French and Spanish, successfully fought a war of independence, kindling other fires of liberty in the Atlantic world. The French rose up in 1789 against a monarchy that had bankrupted itself, ironically in part by giving military support to the American rebels. In 1791 a massive slave revolt erupted in the prosperous French sugar colony of Saint-Domingue, leading to the creation of the

The Promise of Enlightenment

FOCUS What were the major ideas of the Enlightenment and their impacts?

Revolution in North America

FOCUS What factors lay behind the war between North American colonists and Great Britain?

The French Revolution and the Napoleonic Empire

FOCUS What changes emerged from the French Revolution and Napoleon's reign?

Revolution Continued in the Western Hemisphere

FOCUS What were the motives and methods of revolutionaries in the Caribbean and Latin America?

COUNTERPOINT: Religious Revival in a Secular Age

FOCUS What trends in Enlightenment and revolutionary society did religious revival challenge?

BACKSTORY

Rising global trade and maturing slave systems brought wealth to merchants and landowners in many parts of the world during the seventeenth and eighteenth centuries. Emboldened by this newfound wealth, they joined bureaucrats and aristocrats in the struggle for more influence, not only in the great land-based empires such as the Qing, Mughal, and Ottoman states but also in some of the small states of Europe. These small European states had developed overseas empires, which after several centuries they hoped to exploit more efficiently. They had also built their military capability and gained administrative experience as they fought one another for greater global influence. Maintaining this influence was costly, however. Simultaneously the Scientific Revolution (see Chapter 20) and the beginnings of a movement to think more rationally about government were causing some critics in Europe to question the traditional political and social order.

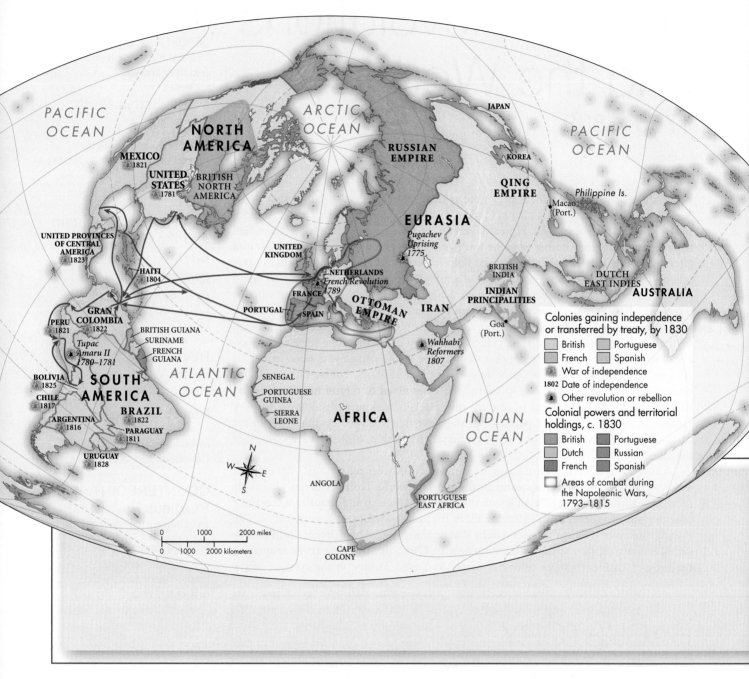

PACIFIC OCEAN

NORTH AMERICA

ARCTIC OCEAN

JAPAN

PACIFIC OCEAN

MEXICO
1821

UNITED STATES
1781

BRITISH NORTH AMERICA

RUSSIAN EMPIRE

KOREA

QING EMPIRE

Philippine Is.
Macao
(Port.)

UNITED PROVINCES OF CENTRAL AMERICA
1823

HAITI
1804

UNITED KINGDOM

NETHERLANDS
French Revolution
1789

FRANCE

PORTUGAL

SPAIN

EURASIA

Pugachev Uprising
1775

OTTOMAN EMPIRE

IRAN

BRITISH INDIA

INDIAN PRINCIPALITIES

Goa
(Port.)

DUTCH EAST INDIES

AUSTRALIA

GRAN COLOMBIA
1822

PERU
1821

Tupac Amaru II
1780–1781

BRITISH GUIANA

SURINAME

FRENCH GUIANA

ATLANTIC OCEAN

SENEGAL

PORTUGUESE GUINEA

SIERRA LEONE

Wahhabi Reformers
1807

INDIAN OCEAN

BOLIVIA
1825

CHILE
1817

SOUTH AMERICA

BRAZIL
1822

ARGENTINA
1816

PARAGUAY
1811

URUGUAY
1828

AFRICA

ANGOLA

PORTUGUESE EAST AFRICA

CAPE COLONY

N
W   E
S

0   1000   2000 miles
0   1000   2000 kilometers

Colonies gaining independence or transferred by treaty, by 1830
- British
- French
- Portuguese
- Spanish
- War of independence
- 1802 Date of independence
- Other revolution or rebellion

Colonial powers and territorial holdings, c. 1830
- British
- Dutch
- French
- Portuguese
- Russian
- Spanish
- Areas of combat during the Napoleonic Wars, 1793–1815

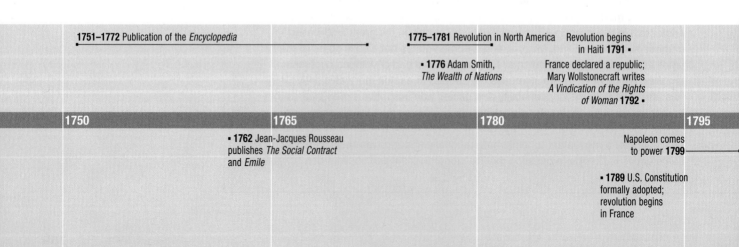

1751–1772 Publication of the *Encyclopedia*

1775–1781 Revolution in North America   Revolution begins in Haiti **1791** ▪

▪ **1776** Adam Smith, *The Wealth of Nations*

France declared a republic; Mary Wollstonecraft writes *A Vindication of the Rights of Woman* **1792** ▪

1750	1765	1780	1795

▪ **1762** Jean-Jacques Rousseau publishes *The Social Contract* and *Emile*

Napoleon comes to power **1799**

▪ **1789** U.S. Constitution formally adopted; revolution begins in France

independent state of Haiti. The independence of Latin American states took longer to achieve, but it was globally inspirational. The English poet Lord Byron named his yacht *Bolivar* and in the 1820s went off to liberate Greece from the Ottomans.

These upheavals were connected with a transformation of thought and everyday life in the West called "the Enlightenment." Traders in Asia, Africa, and the Americas had brought ideas and goods to Europe. The arrival of new products such as sugar, coffee, and cotton textiles had freed many Europeans' lives from their former limits, and this new-found abundance led them to readjust their thinking. Wanting even greater wealth, they became discontented with the old order's regulation of trade and livelihoods. Both ordinary people and the upper classes proposed changing society, adding to the calls from Enlightenment thinkers whom the Scientific Revolution, the English Revolution, and global contact influenced to demand more rational government. Such ideas affected North American politicians, Caribbean activists, and creole reformers like Simon Bolivar, transforming them into revolutionaries. Thus, global trading connections played a key role both in creating the conditions that prompted the development of new ideas and in providing pathways for the spread of those ideas.

Indeed, the impulse for change extended far beyond the Atlantic world. In Ottoman-controlled Egypt, French revolutionary forces under the command of Napoleon Bonaparte invaded, claiming to bring new political ideas of liberty. A determined leader, Muhammad Ali, helped drive out the French and then promoted reform himself. As ideas of freedom took hold and as the increasingly ambitious Bonaparte decided to push into Russia, the old powers united to fight him. Long-established empires faced new, often grave challenges in this age of revolution and political change.

By 1830 the map of the world had changed, but that change came at a great cost. Alongside the birth of new nations and a growing belief in political reform, there had been widespread hardship and destruction. Soldiers died by the hundreds of thousands;

MAPPING THE WORLD

Wars and Revolutions in the Atlantic World, 1750–1830

Between 1775 and 1830 transplanted Europeans, their descendants, and their slaves and servants overwhelmed the Spanish, British, and French empires in the Western Hemisphere and created many independent nations. Europe and the Mediterranean also experienced revolutionary change as the ideas of just government and citizens' rights traveled the crossroads of the world and caused both transformation and turmoil.

ROUTES ▼

→ Voyages of Simon Bolivar, 1799–1816

→ Independence campaigns of Simon Bolivar, 1817–1825

- **1804** Haiti becomes independent from France
- **1822** Brazil becomes independent from Portugal
- **1815** Napoleon defeated at Waterloo; Congress of Vienna resettles the boundaries of European states

1810	1825	1840

- **1811** Simon Bolivar first takes up arms against Spain
- **1825** Bolivia becomes independent from Spain
- **1816** Argentina becomes independent from Spain
- **1817** Chile becomes independent from Spain
- **1821** Mexico and Peru become independent from Spain

civilians also perished because political and social change set them against one another. The breakdown of established kingdoms was the work of the warriors, the masses, and determined leaders, but this age of revolution crushed many. Napoleon Bonaparte was condemned to exile, and even so privileged a revolutionary as Bolivar died of utter exhaustion in 1830 just as the new nations of Latin America began their independent existence.

OVERVIEW
QUESTIONS

The major global development in this chapter: The Atlantic revolutions and their short- and long-term significance.

As you read, consider:

1. What role did the Scientific Revolution and expanding global contacts play in the cultural and social movement known as the Enlightenment?

2. Why did prosperous and poor people alike join revolutions in the Americas and in France?

3. Why were the Atlantic revolutions so influential, even to the present day?

The Promise of Enlightenment

FOCUS

What were the major ideas of the Enlightenment and their impacts?

Intense rethinking of society, politics, and the workings of the economy was under way in Europe in the eighteenth century, spurred by the Scientific Revolution's call for observation and rational thinking. Travelers' and missionaries' reports from the rest of the world provided ideas about alternative forms of government and social organization. Those reports added to the questioning—already under way in Europe—of beliefs in a uniform, God-given order in all states of the world. New global products such as brightly printed cottons, lacquered furniture, and porcelain raised the issue of where the European artisans learning to produce all these goods fit in a supposedly unchanging social structure. How the social and political order should change inspired lively conversation in salons and cafés as well as profound philosophical reflection in books and essays. Even monarchs began rethinking how the state should be run and their own role in government reform.

A New World of Ideas

contract government A political theory that views government as stemming from the people, who agree to surrender a measure of personal freedom in return for a government that guarantees protection of citizens' rights and property.

Europeans in the eighteenth century had a great deal to think about. Science had challenged traditional views of nature and offered a new methodology for uncovering nature's laws. Changing techniques in agriculture and rising commerce led people to reflect on the meaning of greater abundance. Reports from around the world on foreign customs, ways of conducting government, and trade practices fueled intense discussion among Europeans. Moreover, participation in this intellectual ferment was not limited to the political and social elite. As literacy spread in Europe, ever more people were caught up in the debate over social, political, and economic change. These wide-ranging reconsiderations have come collectively to be called the Enlightenment.

Some Enlightenment writers hammered away at the abuses of monarchies and proposed representative rule based on the consent of the governed that later became the foundation of many states. The will of a monarch is not the best basis for government, the English philosopher John Locke wrote late in the seventeenth century. Rather, he maintained, governments should be established rationally, by mutual consent of the governed. The idea of compact or **contract government** grew from Locke's philosophy that people were born free, equal, and rational, and that natural rights, including personal freedoms, were basic to all humans. In Locke's view, governments were formed when people made the rational choice to give up a measure of freedom and create institutions that could express the people's will, guarantee natural rights, and protect everyone's property. If a government failed to fulfill these purposes, it ceased to be legitimate and the people had the right to replace it. Locke's ideas had centered on the situation in England, where citizens and the Parliament had, over the course of the seventeenth century, twice ousted their king.

John Locke

In contrast to Locke, French writers Voltaire and Baron Louis Montesquieu criticized their own society's religious and political abuses by referring to the political situation elsewhere—in China and outside Europe. They conspicuously set their widely read writings in faraway lands or used wise foreigners as foils to show Europe's backwardness. A wealthy trained jurist, Montesquieu in *The Persian Letters* (1721) featured a Persian ruler visiting Europe and writing back home of the strange goings-on. The continent was full of magicians, Montesquieu's hero reports, such as those who could turn wine and wafers into flesh—a mocking reference to the Christian sacrament of communion. Voltaire, a successful author thrown several times into jail for insulting the authorities, portrayed worthy young men cruelly treated by their supposed betters, such as priests and kings, in his rollicking novels *Zadig* (1747) and *Candide* (1759). From a prosperous family, Voltaire asked for a society based on merit, not on aristocracy of birth: "There is nothing in Asia that resembles the European nobility: nowhere in the Orient does one find an order of citizens distinct from all the rest by their hereditary titles or by exemptions and privileges given them solely by their birth."[2] Voltaire did not have the story quite right, but other Enlightenment thinkers joined his call for reason, hard work, and opportunity in both economic life and politics.

Voltaire and Montesquieu

Swiss-born Jean-Jacques Rousseau took up the theme of freedom and opportunity in his many influential writings. In *The Social Contract* (1762) he claimed that "man is born free," but because of despotic government "he is everywhere in chains." Moving beyond the form of government to the process of shaping the modern citizen, Rousseau's best-selling novel *Emile* (1762) describes the ways in which a young boy is educated to develop many practical skills. Instead of learning through rote memory, as was common, Emile learns such skills as carpentry and medicine by actually working at them, and he spends much time outdoors, getting in touch with nature by living a simple life away from corrupt civilization. Like China's Kangxi monarch, whom Enlightenment thinkers held up as a model, Emile becomes a polymath, that is, someone with a knowledge of many subjects and numerous skills—in this case, artisanal and agricultural techniques that could earn him a livelihood. At the end of his apprenticeship in nature, Emile has become the responsible citizen who can fend for himself and regulate his movements according to natural laws, not despotically imposed ones.

Jean-Jacques Rousseau

Enlightenment thinkers also redesigned ideas about the economy. In 1776, Scottish philosopher Adam Smith published one of the most influential Enlightenment documents, *On the Wealth of Nations*. Citing China as an important example of how specialization of trades leads to prosperity, Smith proposed to free the economy from government monopolies and regulations. Merchants from South America to the Caribbean and Europe embraced the idea of freedom from mercantilist regulations that forced them to send goods exclusively through their national ports before trading them in other markets. This idea of **laissez faire** (French for "let alone") became part of the theory called **liberalism**, which endorsed economic and personal freedom guaranteed by the rule of law. Smith saw trade itself as benefiting an individual's character because it required cooperation with others in the process of exchanging goods. The virtues created by trade were more desirable

Adam Smith

laissez faire An economic doctrine that advocates freeing economies from government intervention and control.

liberalism A political ideology that emphasizes free trade, individual rights, and the rule of law to protect rights as the best means for promoting social and economic improvement.

than the military swaggering and roughness of aristocratic lives, and he continually stressed that alongside individualism there needed to be concern for the well-being of the community as a whole. Slavery, he argued, was inefficient and ought to be done away with. Still other Enlightenment writers said that a middle-class way of life promoted sensibility, love of family, thrift, and hard work—again, in stark contrast to the unfeeling, promiscuous, and spendthrift habits these reformers saw in the behavior of the nobility.

Spread of Enlightenment Thought

As we have seen, Enlightenment thinkers explicitly drew on the knowledge of the world beyond Europe that global economic connections had allowed them to acquire. Such connections also made it possible for Enlightenment ideas to spread around the world. Some Japanese thinkers and officials were so interested in new ideas that they began "Dutch Studies," referring to the body of European information brought in by Dutch traders. They wanted to learn about recent breakthroughs in practical subjects as well as scientific practices based on rational observation and deduction. Chinese scholars, though not directly influenced by Enlightenment thought, were reflecting on issues of good government and the capacities of the individual within the imperial system. In contrast, future nation builders in the North American colonies—Benjamin Franklin, John Adams, and Thomas Jefferson—were steeped in both the practical and political sides of the Enlightenment, running businesses, designing buildings, conducting scientific experiments, and writing political documents.

The Public Sphere

Enlightenment thought had an impact on all of Western society—high and low, male and female. Population growth in cities such as Paris strained traditional work patterns and neighborhoods, causing old social structures to weaken and new ideas to flourish. Another cause of change was the initiative of women of the wealthier classes, who conducted salons—that is, meetings in their homes devoted to discussing the most recent issues and publicizing the newest books and findings. German Jewish women, often kept at a distance from Christian society, made a name for themselves by forming such groups. Along with coffeehouses in European and colonial cities, modeled on those in the Ottoman Empire, salons created a **public sphere** in which people could meet outside court circles to talk about current affairs. Together with the new public libraries, reading groups, and a host of scientific clubs that dotted the Atlantic world, they built new community bonds and laid the groundwork for responsible citizenship. Instead of a monarchical government single-handedly determining public policy, ordinary people in Europe and its colonies, relying on knowledge gained from public discussion, could express their opinions on the course of events and thereby undermine government attempts at censorship and traditional ideas about society.

The ideals of the Enlightenment were well represented in the *Encyclopedia* (1751–1772) of France's Denis Diderot. The celebrated work highlighted the contributions of ordinary working people, particularly artisans, to the overall improvement of the human condition; it contained dozens of technical drawings of practical machinery that could advance prosperity. The *Encyclopedia* described the freedoms and rights nature endowed on *all* people, not just aristocrats or religious authorities. Like Rousseau, Diderot maintained that in a natural state all people were born free and equal. French writer Olympe de Gouges further proposed that there was no difference among people of different skin colors. "How are the Whites different from [the Black] race? . . . Why do blonds not claim superiority over brunettes?" she asked in her "Reflections on Negroes" (1788). "Like all the different types of animals, plants, and minerals that nature has produced, people's color also varies."[3] Essayists in the *Encyclopedia* added that women too were born free and endowed with natural rights.

Many of the working people of Europe's growing towns and cities responded enthusiastically to the ideas set forth by the leading philosophers of the Enlightenment, such as Voltaire and Rousseau. The French glassworker Jacques Ménétra, for example, acquired and also distributed these new antireligious and egalitarian ideas as he moved from city to town and village, installing glass windows. With some religious schooling and then an apprenticeship in his trade, Ménétra, like his fellow journeymen artisans, led this

public sphere A cultural and political environment that emerged during the Enlightenment, where members of society gathered to discuss issues of the day.

Eighteenth-Century English Drawing Room

When drinking their tea imported from Asia, middle- and upper-class Europeans aimed for elegance, inspired by Asian tea rituals. They used porcelain, whose production European manufacturers had recently figured out, and an array of new furnishings such as the tea table on display here. These English tea-takers are wearing sparkling white muslin, probably imported from India, which produced high-quality cloth that Europeans valued above cotton from anywhere else, including, as we will see in the next chapter, the new European industrial mills. (Private Collection/Bridgeman Art Library.)

kind of mobile life as a young man before establishing his own shop in Paris. During the course of his travels, he provided news of the Parisian thinkers to artisans along his route. In his autobiography—one of the few written by an ordinary European worker—he referred to Jean-Jacques Rousseau and gossiped about aristocrats. Young journeymen like Ménétra helped spread news of politics and current ideas before the coming of mass media, making the Enlightenment an affair not only of the well-born in salons but also of many average people.

Enlightenment and the Old Order

Despite its critique of monarchs, church officials, and the aristocracy, "Enlightenment" was a watchword of some of Europe's most powerful rulers. "Enlightened" rulers came to sense that more rational government could actually strengthen their regimes, for example by increasing governmental efficiency and increasing tax revenues. Thus, instead of touting his divine legacy, Prussian king Frederick the Great (r. 1740–1786) called a ruler someone who would "work efficiently for the good of the state" rather than "live in lazy luxury, enriching himself by the labor of the people."[4] A musician and poet, Frederick studied several languages, collected Chinese porcelain, and wrote librettos for operas, some of them about toleration. For him, Enlightenment made monarchs stronger. Spreading to Russia, the Enlightenment moved Catherine the Great (r. 1762–1796) to sponsor the writing of a dictionary of the Russian language, to correspond with learned thinkers such as Diderot, and to work to improve the education of girls. Additionally, Catherine's goal was to put a stop to aristocrats' "idle time spent in luxury and other vices corrupting to the morals," as she put it, and instead transform the nobility into active and informed administrators of her far-flung empire and its diverse peoples[5] (see Seeing the Past: Portrait of Catherine the Great).

The Spanish monarchy in the eighteenth century likewise instituted a series of policy changes called the Bourbon Reforms, so named because many of them aimed to make the monarchy—headed by the Bourbon dynasty—financially sound by taxing the colonies

Enlightened Rulers

Portrait of Catherine the Great

Catherine the Great as the Roman Goddess Minerva
(Hillwood Estate, Museum & Gardens; Photo by Ed Owen.)

Catherine the Great was a monarch of towering ability and ambition. Although her regime was known for smashing peasant uprisings, it also promoted the arts and knowledge. Even as her armies conquered some two hundred thousand square miles of territory and added it to the Russian Empire, Catherine commissioned the first dictionary of the Russian language and communicated with the greatest thinkers of the Enlightenment. While sponsoring education, she tried to reform her government to increase its power. In this regard, Enlightenment was not just about the fine arts but also about generally raising the economic and political profile of the monarchy through rationally devised policies.

Although Enlightenment thinkers often referred to the excellent customs and the rational policies of non-Western monarchs of their day—especially those in China—they also prized classical Greece and Rome for their democratic and republican forms of government. In this spirit of classical enthusiasm, monarchs were sometimes depicted as mythical figures, despite the often dark side to their regimes. For this image, a skilled Parisian craftsperson of the 1760s chose Minerva—Roman goddess of both war and wisdom—as the figure closest to the celebrated Catherine. The luxurious detail on this round box assures us that it was destined for an aristocratic palace, perhaps that of the monarch herself.

EXAMINING THE EVIDENCE

1. What does this depiction of the empress as Minerva tell you about the society over which Catherine ruled?

2. How does this image of leadership compare with others you have seen, including those of U.S. presidents? How do you account for the differences? For the similarities?

---

more efficiently. Following Enlightenment calls for rational and secular policies, Spain's rulers also attempted to limit the church's independence. Often opposing slavery and promoting better treatment of native peoples, the Jesuit order, for instance, had many followers in Spain's "New World" empire. Thus, the order was an alternate source of allegiance, and the monarchy outlawed it.

Leaders of the Spanish colonies adopted many Enlightenment ideas, including scientific farming and improvements in mining—both of them subjects dear to forward-looking thinkers who read publications such as the *Encyclopedia*. In Mexico, reformers saw the education of each woman as central to building responsible government. As one local journalist put it, under a mother's care the young citizen "grows, is nourished, and acquires his first notions of Good and Evil. [Therefore] women have even more reason to be enlightened than men."[6] In this view, motherhood was not a simple biological act but a livelihood critical to maintaining a strong national life.

Justification of Slavery

European prosperity depended on the productivity of slaves in the colonies, and wealthy slave owners used the Enlightenment fascination with nature to devise scientific explanations justifying the oppressive system. Though many Enlightenment thinkers such as Olympe de Gouges wanted equality for "noble savages," in slave owners' minds Africans were less than human and thus rightly subject to exploitation. Scientists captured Africans for study and came up with a list of their biological differences from whites and their similarities to animals, contributing to a sense of racial inferiority as a "scientific fact." Others justified race-based slavery in terms of character: blacks were, one British observer explained, "conceited, proud, indolent and very artful"—a rationale for harsh plantation discipline.[7] Thus, some strands of Enlightenment thought helped buyers and sellers of Africans and native Americans argue that slavery was useful and rational, especially because slaves could produce wealth and help society as a whole make progress.

Popular Revolts in an Age of Enlightenment

Pugachev Rebellion

Enlightened officials hoped to improve government at a time of popular uprising in many parts of the world. In Russia, people throughout society came to protest serfdom's irrationality and unfairness. One aristocrat believed that such unfairness "spread a plague in the hearts of the common people."[8] In 1773 the discontent of many serfs crystallized around Emel'ian Ivanovich Pugachev, once an officer in the Russian army, who claimed to be Peter III, the dead husband of Catherine. Tens of thousands of peasants, joined by rebellious workers, serf soldiers in Catherine's overworked armies, and Muslim minorities rose up, calling for the restoration of Pugachev, alias Peter, to the throne. Pugachev promised them great riches for their support. Serfs responded by plundering noble estates and killing aristocrats. They justified revolt in slogans and songs: "O woe to us slaves living for the masters. . . . how shameful and insulting / That another who is not worthy to be equal with us / Has so many of us in his power."[9] The rebellion was put down only with difficulty. Once Catherine's forces captured Pugachev, they cut off his arms and legs, then his head, and finally hacked his body to pieces—just punishment, nobles believed, for the crimes of this "monster" against the monarchy and upper classes.

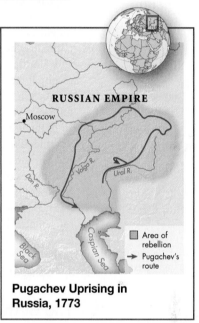

Pugachev Uprising in Russia, 1773

Uprisings among the urban poor, farmworkers, and slaves also occurred in the Caribbean and other parts of the Western Hemisphere. Over the course of the eighteenth century the Latin American population grew rapidly and cities expanded. Rebels protested harsh conditions, which included their enslavement and only grew worse with Spain's demand for more revenue. Some native peoples envisioned the complete expulsion of the Spaniards or the overthrow of the wealthy creoles, who owned estates and plantations. Between 1780 and 1783, several different groups in Peru attempted to restore Inca power and end the increased burden of taxation under the Bourbon Reforms. The charismatic trader and wealthy landowner Tupac Amaru II (TOO-pack a-MAH-roo), an indigenous leader who took his name from the Inca leader of the late sixteenth century, led tens of thousands in the region of Tinta against corrupt local leadership and then against the administration of the region as a whole. Eventually captured by the authorities, Tupac Amaru II had his tongue cut out, was drawn and quartered by four horses, and was finally beheaded—after first watching the execution of most of his family. Rebellions continued nonetheless.

Latin American Uprisings

Revolution in North America

The Atlantic world was part of a global trading network. Thus, Europeans in North America, participating in global livelihoods as merchants, fishermen, and sailors, were exposed to ideas and goods from around the world. A Boston newspaper in the 1720s advertised the sale of Moroccan leather, Indian chintz and muslin fabrics, South American mahogany, and Asian tea. Sending out lumber, dried fish, tobacco, and furs, the British colonies grew prosperous and cosmopolitan, interesting themselves in all facets of the Enlightenment and commercial growth.

> **FOCUS**
> What factors lay behind the war between North American colonists and Great Britain?

Many enlightened North American colonists came to resent Britain's attempts to tax and rule them more efficiently, and people from various walks of life soon rebelled against what they saw as government contempt for their own rights as English people. Amid growing wealth and intellectual ferment, North American colonists along the Atlantic seaboard came to forge an independent nation—the future United States of America.

The British Empire and the Colonial Crisis 1764–1775

In the eighteenth century European states continued to wage increasingly costly wars for global trade and influence. Where governments were poorly run and taxes did not cover the huge military debt, as in the case of France, financial disaster loomed. The expense of the Seven Years' War of 1756–1763 was enormous as, for the first time in history, Europeans fought to gain influence in South Asia, the Philippines, the Caribbean, and North America. Ultimately beating both the French and the Spanish, Britain received all of French Canada and Florida at the end of the war (see Map 23.1). It hoped to boost colonial taxation to recoup its expenses and pay the costs of administering its empire.

Taxation Without Representation

In 1764 the British Parliament raised taxes on molasses with the Sugar Act, and in the following year it passed the Stamp Act, which taxed printed material and legal documents—all of them important to colonists' everyday lives. The Townshend Acts of 1767 put duties on other useful commodities, such as paper, glass, and paint, resulting in increasingly radical protests. Driven by England's own history of revolution and by the new political theories, some colonial activists insisted that if they were going to be taxed, they needed direct representation in the English Parliament, which they currently lacked. This argument followed Locke's theory of the social contract: a government where citizens were not represented had no right to take their property in taxes. With a literacy rate of 70 percent among men and 40 percent among women in the North American colonies—among the highest rates anywhere—new ideas about government and reports of British misdeeds spread rapidly, especially among townspeople.

The Birth of the United States 1775–1789

When yet another tax was placed on prized imported tea, a group of Bostonians, disguised as native Americans, dumped a load of tea into the harbor in December 1773. The British government responded to the "Boston Tea Party" by closing the seaport's thriving harbor, while colonial representatives gathered for an all-colony Continental Congress that resulted in a coordinated boycott of British goods.

U.S. Declaration of Independence

Tensions escalated. In April 1775 artisans and farmers in Lexington and Concord fought British troops sent to confiscate a stockpile of ammunition from rebellious colonists. On July 4, 1776, the Continental Congress issued its "Declaration of Independence," a short, dramatic document written largely by Thomas Jefferson that aimed—like the Enlightenment itself—to convert its readers to the side of reason in matters of government. The Declaration argued that the monarchy was tyrannical and had forfeited its right to rule. It went on to articulate an Enlightenment doctrine of rights—the famous rights of "life, liberty, and the pursuit of happiness." Some of the rebel colonists likened themselves to "slaves" lacking individual freedom, drawing a parallel—even though Declaration author Thomas Jefferson was himself a slave owner—with slave rebels across the Western world.

The War of Independence

The British sent a powerful army and navy to defeat the colonists. British forces burned coastal towns and occupied New York, Philadelphia, and other crucial centers of commerce and government. George Washington of Virginia headed the Continental Army. His forces suffered from lack of clothing, food, pay, and efficient recruiting. Yet the British deployed their larger armies in battle formation, whereas colonists were effective at guerrilla warfare, sniping at the invaders from behind trees and using bows and arrows if they lacked guns. Others joined in: colonial women fed armies in their vicinity, knitted and sewed clothing, and cared for the wounded. Critical help arrived from countries interested in blocking

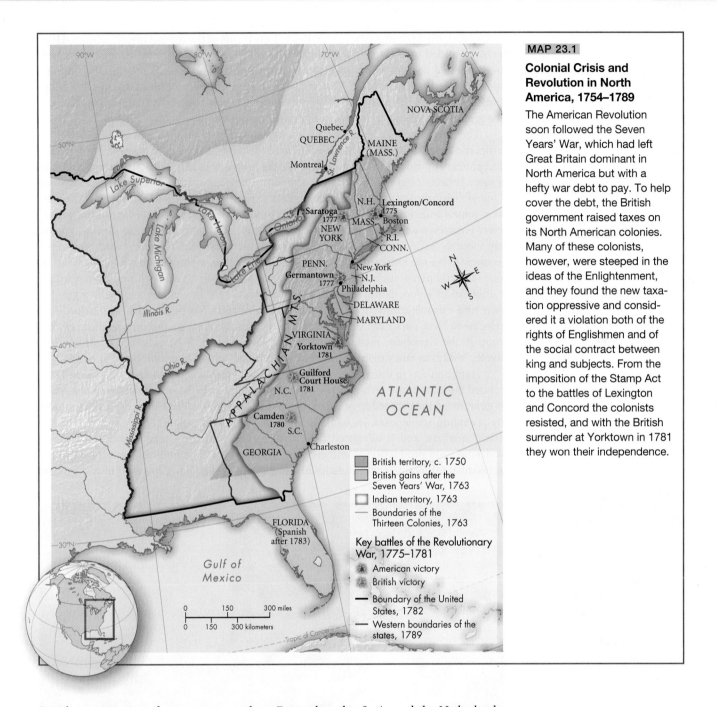

Colonial Crisis and Revolution in North America, 1754–1789

The American Revolution soon followed the Seven Years' War, which had left Great Britain dominant in North America but with a hefty war debt to pay. To help cover the debt, the British government raised taxes on its North American colonies. Many of these colonists, however, were steeped in the ideas of the Enlightenment, and they found the new taxation oppressive and considered it a violation both of the rights of Englishmen and of the social contract between king and subjects. From the imposition of the Stamp Act to the battles of Lexington and Concord the colonists resisted, and with the British surrender at Yorktown in 1781 they won their independence.

British expansionism, foremost among these France but also Spain and the Netherlands. Substantial assistance from the French under the Marquis de Lafayette ultimately brought the British down at Yorktown, where they surrendered their army in 1781 (see again Map 23.1).

Growing immigration had made the United States ethnically diverse well before its founding. Uprisings and disputes over trade and taxation followed the 1781 victory, showing that a strong **federation**, or union of states, was needed. The Articles of Confederation, drawn up in 1777 as a provisional constitution, however, proved weak because they gave the central government few powers. As the newly independent thirteen states pursued their own interests under the Articles of Confederation in the aftermath of the war, the "frail and tottering edifice [of the loosely aligned thirteen states] seems ready to fall upon our heads and crush us beneath its ruins," as Alexander Hamilton, Washington's trusted aide during the War of Independence, put it.[10] In 1787, a Constitutional Convention met

The U.S. Constitution

federation A union of equal and sovereign states rather than a thoroughly integrated nation.

in Philadelphia to draft a new constitution. Two-thirds of the delegates were educated lawyers, grounded intellectually in Enlightenment thought, but there were some of humble beginnings: a delegate from Connecticut had worked as a shoemaker before becoming a merchant, for example. Most, however, were men of property. Indeed, George Washington, who presided over the meeting, not only had a substantial plantation (like others in the group) but also was the owner of hundreds of slaves.

The Constitution reflected the broad understanding of just government shared by these propertied men. In it, the founders enshrined the contract theory of government from the Enlightenment with its opening words: "We the people of the United States in order to form a more perfect union." However, the document also reflected the authors' material interests. One of their primary motives in creating a strong government was to protect what they saw as a central individual right, the right to private property. The authors did not agree on every point, even when it came to private property. What, for example, should the Constitution say about slaves, individuals who were themselves property? Should slavery be acknowledged, as many of the representatives from the southern states wanted, or should it be abolished, as major participants such as Alexander Hamilton of New York believed? Born in the Caribbean of a poor family, Hamilton was a bookkeeper as a young teenager—a job that gave him valuable connections with merchant families in North America, who helped him relocate to New York City, where he attended Columbia College and then studied law. His roots in the Caribbean made him abhor the slave system. "The existence of slavery," he wrote, "makes us fancy many things that are founded neither in reason or experience."[11]

Hamilton was to lose this argument. The new Constitution, formally adopted in 1789, echoed the aims of the revolution and the rights of individuals—except slaves and women. It guaranteed the ownership of property and fostered commerce and the spirit of industry by providing stable laws. Its banking structure promised reliability in the international credit markets, and it advanced U.S. involvement with the global economy by lifting restrictions on production, commerce, and business life. The political rights given to the substantial minority—the enfranchised white men—by the U.S. Constitution and by state

Samuel Jennings, *Liberty Displaying the Arts and Sciences* (1792)

Enlightenment writers debated whether the ideals of liberty and equality should apply to everyone regardless of race, condition of servitude, and gender. This painting, commissioned early in U.S. history to urge the abolition of slavery, shows Liberty with the Cap of Liberty on a staff next to her; she is displaying Enlightenment accomplishments in the arts and sciences to freed slaves. Although in the United States and elsewhere Liberty was usually depicted as a woman, the principles of equal citizenship expressed in the Constitution and the Declaration of Independence did not apply to most women, African Americans, or native Americans. (The Library Company of Philadelphia.)

law inspired this burst of activity, innovation, and enterprise. To achieve the Constitution, the founders, as men of the Enlightenment, negotiated, made concessions, and came to hard-fought agreements. The U.S. Constitution thus became a monument to consensus politics and to the form of government called a **republic**. When the heated disputes were over and the Constitution finally framed, George Washington wrote to the Marquis de Lafayette in France that achieving the document was "little short of a miracle."

The French Revolution and the Napoleonic Empire

In 1780, on the eve of victory in its War of Independence, the fledgling United States had only about 2.7 million people, but its triumph had a powerful impact on the far larger population in Europe. "The [French] nation has been awakened by our revolution," Ambassador Thomas Jefferson wrote in 1788 to President George Washington, "they feel their strength, they are enlightened."[12] More directly, the cost of French participation in global warfare with Britain, including the North American War of Independence, hastened the collapse of the monarchy. France's taxation policy put the cost of warfare on the poor and exempted the wealthy from paying their share. In 1789, less than a decade after the victory at Yorktown, the French people took matters into their own hands, ultimately ousting the king and launching a republic. The French Revolution resonated far and wide, and under the French conqueror Napoleon Bonaparte, revolutionary principles advanced across Europe and beyond, even as Europe's monarchs struggled to halt the march of "liberty, equality, fraternity."

> **FOCUS**
> What changes emerged from the French Revolution and Napoleon's reign?

From Monarchy to Republic 1789–1792

Having borrowed recklessly (as had his predecessors) to pursue wars and princely living, the French monarch Louis XVI (r. 1774–1793) in 1787 met with a firm "no" when he asked for more loans from bankers and financial help from the aristocracy. The king was forced to summon the Estates General—a representative body that had not met since 1614—to the royal palace at Versailles to bail out the government. Members of the Estates General arrived at their meeting in May 1789, carrying lists of grievances from people of all occupations and walks of life, who had met in local gatherings across France to help representatives prepare for their momentous assembly.

There were several competing agendas at the meeting of the Estates General: those of the monarchy to repair its finances; those of the nobility to take power from the king; and those of the common people, who at the time were suffering from crop failures, heavy taxation, governmental restraints on trade, and a slowdown in business because of bad harvests. The meeting quickly broke down when representatives of the middle classes and common people left the general meeting. They were joined by sympathetic, reform-minded aristocrats and clergymen such as Abbé Sieyès, who asked what this mass of commoners meant to the kingdom. "Everything," he responded to his own question. "What has it been until now in the political order? Nothing."[13] These representatives declared themselves a National Assembly of "citizens" of France, not the lowly subjects of a king. The National Assembly included the lawyers and officials who had represented most of the people in 1789 as well as reform-minded deputies from the clergy and a substantial number of nobles.

Formation of the National Assembly

Soon much of France was overwhelmed by enthusiasm for this new government based on citizen consent. On July 14, 1789, crowds in Paris stormed the Bastille, a notorious prison where people could be incarcerated simply at the king's orders. The liberation of the Bastille by the people of Paris so symbolized the French Revolution that it became France's national holiday, just as the Declaration of Independence on July 4 eventually made that Independence Day in the United States.

Storming of the Bastille

republic A political system in which the interests of all citizens are represented in the government.

Declaration of the Rights of Man and of the Citizen

In its first years, the revolution was shaped by Enlightenment principles. Strong citizen protest also motivated the legislators of the National Assembly, who like U.S. revolutionary leaders were mostly from the propertied classes. With peasants rioting in the countryside against the unfair rule of aristocratic landowners, in August 1789 the nobility surrendered its privileges, such as its exemption from taxation. Later that month the National Assembly issued the "Declaration of the Rights of Man and of the Citizen," a stirring announcement of the basic rights possessed by each new citizen, including rights to free speech, to own property, and to be safe from arbitrary acts of the state. Soon, Olympe de Gouges would issue her own "Declaration of the Rights of Woman and the Female Citizen," declaring, "Woman is born free and lives equal to man in her rights."

Power to the People

In October 1789, the market women of Paris, protesting the soaring cost of food, marched to the palace of Versailles twelve miles away and captured the royal family, bringing it to live "with the people" in the city. In so doing, they showed that monarchs existed to serve the people—and that kings ignored this fact at their own peril. The government passed laws reducing the power of the clergy and abolishing the guild system and other institutions that would restrain trade. Suddenly people could pursue the jobs they wanted on their own terms outside guild restrictions. The liberal Enlightenment program of freedom for the person and for trade and property was now accomplished, pushed by enthusiastic demonstrations by newly empowered citizens.

These early acts of the French Revolution stirred the hearts and minds of many. Women petitioned for a range of rights, and for a time the power of the husband over his

Women's March to Versailles

Although the French Revolution began with the ceremonial meeting of the Estates General in May 1789, people from many walks of life soon became directly involved in the drive for fundamental change. That October, after the people of Paris had liberated the notorious Bastille prison, the market women of the city marched to the royal palace at Versailles. Joined by men who came from Paris to reinforce them, they captured the king and his family. This engraving shows the crowds escorting the monarch back to the city of Paris, where they could keep an eye on him. (The Art Archive/Marc Charmet.)

wife was eliminated. Across the English Channel, poet William Wordsworth captured the rush of youthful belief that through newly active citizens the world would be reborn: "Bliss was it in that dawn to be alive, / But to be young was very heaven!" The Declaration of the Rights of Man and of the Citizen inspired the addition of a Bill of Rights to the U.S. Constitution, which outlined the essential rights, such as freedom of speech, that the government could never overturn. English author Mary Wollstonecraft penned *A Vindication of the Rights of Man* (1790) in defense of the revolution.

Two years later Wollstonecraft wrote *A Vindication of the Rights of Woman*, a globally influential work that saw men's privileges over women as similar to the French aristocracy's privileges over the peasantry. Current laws in Britain made men into a privileged aristocracy that took women's property and wages on marriage, thus denying women their rights. Wollstonecraft knew all this from bitter experience. Born into a well-to-do family, her brother not only inherited most of the family estate but also confiscated his sisters' inheritances for himself. Destitute, they had to earn a living without having been trained to do so. Wollstonecraft first became a governess and then a journalist, whose classic works protested that the legal privileges of men allowed them to impoverish women.

Mary Wollstonecraft

War, Terror, and Resistance 1792–1799

As revolutionary fervor spread across national borders, the monarchs and nobility of Europe scrambled to survive. In the spring of 1792 the royal houses of Austria and Prussia declared war on France. Wartime brought to power the lawyer Maximilien Robespierre, leader in the popular Jacobin club, a political group that hoped to sweep away all institutions from the oppressive past. In the face of total defeat by Austria and Prussia and the counterrevolutionary efforts of Louis XVI, Robespierre and other politicians became convinced that it was time to do away with the monarchy, that the nation had to become a republic if the revolution were to survive. Patriotic holidays to replace religious ones, dishes with revolutionary slogans, an entirely new calendar, and new laws making the family more egalitarian turned the country upside down. Workshops were set up for the unemployed to earn a living by making war goods, and all citizens were urged to give their energy to help the war effort. In 1793 both King Louis XVI and Queen Marie Antoinette were executed by guillotine—an "enlightened" mode of execution because it killed swiftly and reduced suffering. France stood on the threshold of total transformation.

War Against France and Execution of the King

Claiming that there could be no rights in wartime, Robespierre and the newly created Committee of Public Safety stamped out free speech, squashed the various women's clubs that had sprung up to gain the rights of citizenship, and executed people such as Olympe de Gouges whom they judged to be traitors to the republic. This was the Terror, during which the government murdered people from all classes and livelihoods—from the highest to the lowest—because enemies of the republic, the government claimed, lurked on all rungs of the social ladder. To justify its actions, the Committee of Public Safety turned to Rousseau's idea of the **general will**. Rousseau's unique interpretation of the social contract maintained that once agreement among citizens had created a state, that state acted with a higher wisdom with which truly loyal citizens could not disagree, especially in wartime. The "general will" justified the Terror's mass executions and the suspension of individual rights and even free thought. The concept was one of the French Revolution's most powerful revolutionary legacies, enacted not only by totalitarian regimes in the twentieth century but even by democracies during times of stress.

The Terror

By 1794, largely because the war was turning in France's favor, moderate and propertied politicians were able to regain public support and overthrew Robespierre and the Committee of Public Safety. At the same time, France's revolutionary armies went on the offensive, taking the idea of rights, constitutions, and republicanism to countries such as Austria that had tried to stop the revolution. French pride, based on a belief in the superiority of a republican form of government and full, equal citizenship for men, blossomed,

general will The political concept that once agreement among citizens creates a state, that state is endowed with a higher wisdom about policies with which virtuous citizens could not disagree.

especially among citizen-soldiers who found upward mobility in the revolutionary army. No one took more advantage of this opportunity than a newly minted officer, the young Napoleon Bonaparte (1769–1821).

Napoleon's Reign 1799–1815

Napoleon's Rise to Power

Napoleon Bonaparte, born into a modest Corsican family, became commander in chief of the French revolutionary army in Italy at the age of twenty-seven. A student of Enlightenment thought and an avid reader of history throughout his life, Napoleon had the good fortune to enter the army just as its aristocratic officers were fleeing the revolution in France by moving to other countries. Rising to power through the ranks, he attempted the conquest of Egypt in 1798 but escaped the country as he began to lose the campaign. He returned to France months later, in 1799. There he used the uncertain political scene to establish himself first as co-consul and then, in 1804, as emperor. "As in Rome, it took a dictator to save the Republic,"[14] Napoleon said of the repression that followed his takeover. He reconciled France with the Catholic Church and even called back to his court some of the exiled aristocracy to help add grandeur to his regime.

The Napoleonic Code

Yet Napoleon solidified many revolutionary changes, notably those concerning citizenship and the right to private property, as outlined in the Code Napoleon (1803–1804), a new set of basic laws. The Code set rules for property, ending restrictions on sales of the nobility's land and establishing rules for assets such as bonds, stocks, and mortgages. The Code thus advanced prosperity by providing secure laws for commercial, industrial, and agricultural livelihoods; Napoleon's founding of national schools for teachers, engineers, and the military served this end too. In the realm of family law, however, the Code reversed gains made by women during the revolution by making the wages and other property of married women the legal property of their husbands, by forbidding them to appear as witnesses in court, and by not allowing them to be guardians of their own children. Financial impoverishment gave women no choices in life but to remain loyal wives—principles that Napoleon's triumphant armies spread through Europe and that encouraged imitators around the world. Instead of respecting the equality of women suggested by some Enlightenment thinkers, Napoleon enforced Rousseau's idea that women should raise the next generation of citizens but not be equal citizens themselves.

Napoleon's Military Campaigns

Maintaining his grip by keeping the nation at war and plundering other countries, Napoleon launched a series of successful wars against Spain, the German states, and Italy (see Map 23.2). Then, in 1812, he made a disastrous attempt to invade and conquer Russia. The Russian army, the Russian people, and deadly winter conditions combined to deal Napoleon a catastrophic defeat. After that, a coalition of German, Russian, Austrian, and British forces defeated Napoleon twice more, once in Paris in 1814 and then, in a victory that crushed Napoleon's forces, at Waterloo in 1815.

Congress of Vienna

At the Congress of Vienna (1814–1815), the coalition resettled the boundaries of European states. In doing so, many of Europe's rulers sought to overturn revolutionary and Napoleonic reforms to restore their old regimes. It was far too late to stamp out the principles of constitutional government and natural rights, however. Although monarchs (including France's) were restored to their thrones in 1815, there were now limitations on their powers. Moreover, Napoleon's military campaigns, which spread principles of rights and citizenship, ensured the continuation of these new values in people's minds and helped upset power arrangements around the world.

Muhammad Ali and the Revolutionary Spirit in Egypt

Despite Napoleon's ultimate defeat, the revolutionary legacy fomented reform activity for more rational government not only across Europe but also outside it. When the French revolutionary armies under Napoleon invaded Egypt in 1798, they faced the forces of the Ottoman Empire, whose administration, like that of other great land-based empires, was in decline. From time to time a modernizing sultan came to power hoping to enact reforms. The entrenched powers of the janissaries (elite troops) and ulamas (Muslim authorities), however, usually put a stop to such efforts. The similarly entrenched Mamluk (MAM-luke) military force that ran the Egyptian government increasingly alienated land-lords and other elites with its demands for more taxes.

Napoleon and Egypt

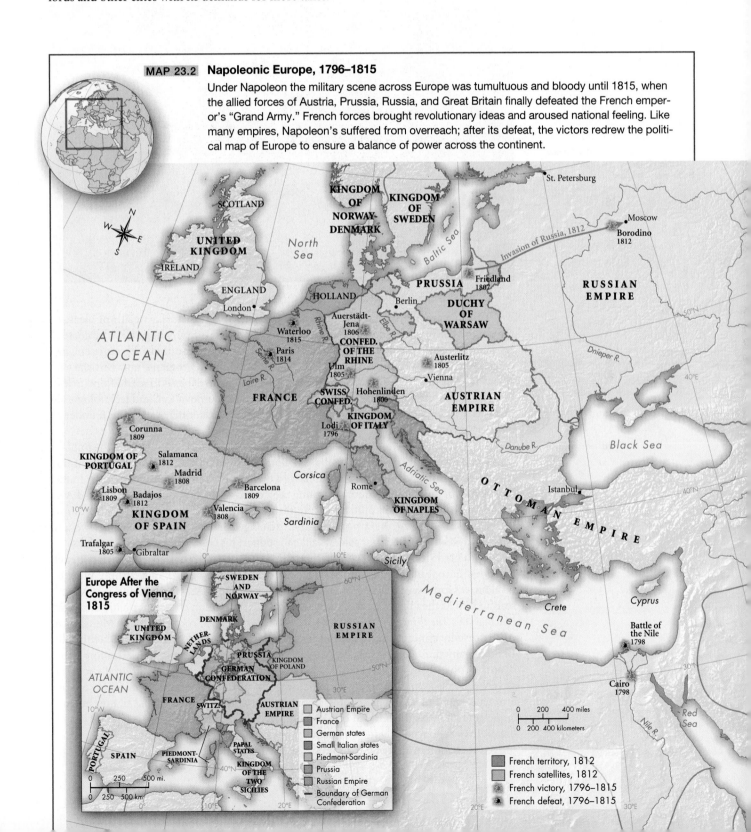

MAP 23.2 **Napoleonic Europe, 1796–1815**

Under Napoleon the military scene across Europe was tumultuous and bloody until 1815, when the allied forces of Austria, Prussia, Russia, and Great Britain finally defeated the French emperor's "Grand Army." French forces brought revolutionary ideas and aroused national feeling. Like many empires, Napoleon's suffered from overreach; after its defeat, the victors redrew the political map of Europe to ensure a balance of power across the continent.

Europe After the Congress of Vienna, 1815

- Austrian Empire
- France
- German states
- Small Italian states
- Piedmont-Sardinia
- Prussia
- Russian Empire
- — Boundary of German Confederation

- French territory, 1812
- French satellites, 1812
- ✳ French victory, 1796–1815
- ✴ French defeat, 1796–1815

Napoleon Celebrates the Birthday of Muhammad

Napoleon's invasion of Egypt simultaneously brutalized and tried to accommodate Egyptians. The French army ransacked homes and public buildings, but Napoleon himself made sympathetic gestures such as the celebration in 1799 of the birth of the Prophet Muhammad depicted here. Though they labeled the French as hypocrites, some Egyptians welcomed the books and scientific drawings Napoleon made available to them in the name of Enlightenment. (Private Collection/Roger-Viollet, Paris/ Bridgeman Art Library.)

To some among these elites, the Atlantic revolutions provided a wealth of ideas for reform. Napoleon entered the country not only accompanied by a huge team of doctors, artists, scientists, and other learned men, but also armed with proposals for more enlightened rule. Amid combined resistance from the Mamluks, Ottomans, and British, who aimed to stop the French, Napoleon and the French army departed Egypt. Nonetheless, they left behind rising interest in European ideas, political innovation, and technology. No one was a better student and imitator than Muhammad Ali, often called the founder of modern Egypt.

Muhammad Ali

An officer in the Ottoman forces, Muhammad Ali had worked his way up the military ranks during the anti-French campaign. Born in the Ottoman Balkans (present-day Albania), Muhammad Ali began his career as a merchant before the Ottoman army drafted him as part of the Albanian quota of young men owed to the Ottomans. Muhammad Ali's rise to power was based on military accomplishments, but also on the negotiating skills he learned as a merchant. As a politician he exchanged favors with ordinary people and persuaded wealthy traders and soldiers alike to support his ouster of the hated Mamluks.

Appointed viceroy in 1805, Muhammad Ali set out to modernize Egypt, hiring French and other European administrators, technicians, and military men to advise him. Illiterate until he was forty-seven, he had many works translated into Arabic, the translations being read to him as they progressed. One major work, a translation of Italian political theorist Machiavelli's *The Prince*, he cut short because the message was "commonplace," Muhammad Ali reportedly announced. "I see clearly that I have nothing to learn from Machiavelli. I know many more tricks than he knew."[15] He advanced economic specialization in the country, sponsoring the large-scale production of cotton by several hundred thousand slaves while discouraging agriculture that was not for the market. Centralization of government, founding of public schools, improvement of transportation, and tighter bureaucratic control of Islam rounded out Muhammad Ali's reforms. His death in 1849 left his dream to make Egypt fully independent of the Ottomans unfulfilled, but like Napoleon he proved successful in applying the rational programs of the age.

Revolution Continued in the Western Hemisphere

Such was the strength of late eighteenth-century global contacts that news of the French and American revolutions quickly spread to other parts of the Atlantic world. In the Western Hemisphere, revolutions broke out on the island of Hispaniola, motivating slave revolts elsewhere and arousing fear among whites. In Latin America, rebellion erupted not only among slaves and oppressed workers but also among middle- and upper-class creoles such as Simon Bolivar who wanted independence from Spain and Portugal. The Napoleonic Wars disturbed global trade, adding further to discontent and swelling the calls for political change. Soon concerted uprisings of peoples—rich, working-class, free peasants, and slaves—rose to fight for freedom in the Caribbean and across Latin America.

> **FOCUS**
>
> What were the motives and methods of revolutionaries in the Caribbean and Latin America?

Revolution in Haiti 1791–1804

News of the French Revolution spread to the Caribbean island of Hispaniola, where the sugar plantations and coffee farms enriched merchants, plantation owners, and sugar refiners—whites and free blacks alike. The western part of the island was the French colony of Saint-Domingue (san-doe-MANGH, modern Haiti). The eastern part of Hispaniola was Santo Domingo (modern Dominican Republic), a colony of Spain. Saint-Domingue was the wealthiest colony in the region, in part because the newly independent United States could now purchase sugar from French rather than British plantations, and it did so from Saint-Domingue. This thriving trade inspired investors and merchants in France to pour vast sums into expanding production there.

As we saw in Chapter 22, Caribbean slaves lived under inhumane conditions. The hot, humid climate made laborious work punishing and kept their life span short. Some committed suicide; women used plant medicines to induce abortions and prevent bearing children who would live in misery. Slaves also developed community bonds to sustain them. The spirit of community and resistance arose from the daily trade of vegetables grown by the slaves in their small garden plots, from the use of a common language made up of French and various African dialects, and from joint participation in Vodou—a religious tradition observed by slaves on the islands.

Solidarity and suffering made the Caribbean ripe for revolution. Slave uprisings took place regularly, and individual slaves escaped into the forests and hills to create new communities of independent people, as they did across the Hispanic world. Added to this, the Caribbean—like the entire Atlantic region—was a crossroads of ideas. Among those ideas were freedom and human rights, circulating not only among African and North American slaves but also among the several thousand free blacks and mulattos in Haiti, who constituted some 30 percent of the slave owners in the region. When their white counterparts passed legislation putting them at political and economic disadvantage despite their success as plantation owners and traders, these free blacks founded the Society for Friends of the Blacks in 1788 and used it to lobby enlightened politicians in Paris for equality. When the French Revolution broke out in 1789, their demands grew louder. "You must return to these oppressed citizens," a group of free blacks entreated the National Assembly in October 1789, "the rights that have been unjustly stripped from them." In the face of continuing white hostility, they became, as one free black put it in 1790, "more committed than ever to uphold [our rights] with the last drop of our blood."[16]

The slaves were roused by news of revolution too. Rumors that French revolutionaries had freed them spread among the slaves, and in 1791 an organized slave uprising erupted in Saint-Domingue (see Map 23.3). From a cluster of leaders, the free black Pierre-Dominique Toussaint Louverture (too-SAN loo-ver-CHURE) emerged as the most able military commander. The slave revolt moved from success to success, and an enthusiastic French official sent to calm the scene did quite the opposite of what the planters wanted: he issued

MAP 23.3   **Haitian Rebellion and Independence, 1791–1804**

The French colony of Saint-Domingue was a global crossroads for the sale of slaves and the sugar they produced. Commerce brought with it the flow of new ideas from around the world, whereas slavery produced not only grievances but solidarity. Even free blacks faced racism, and the Enlightenment ideas of human rights and dignity inspired them to protest. Soon after the French Revolution broke out in 1789, slaves in Saint-Domingue revolted and ultimately declared themselves the independent nation of Haiti.

a proclamation in 1793 granting slaves their freedom. In 1794, against the wishes of plantation owners and merchants—both black and white—the French revolutionary government formally declared that blacks had rights equal to those of whites. This news quickly passed across the Caribbean and Latin America, sparking further uprisings and rebellions against European rulers.

Conditions in Saint-Domingue evolved rapidly as Toussaint, himself a former slave and one grateful to France for its support of black equality, joined the French in driving back the British and Spanish, who hoped to conquer the French portion of the island for themselves. The black plantation owners refused to cooperate politically or economically with ex-slaves, and civil war broke out. In 1800 Toussaint defeated them too and issued a series of stiff reforms. Although slaves were free, they were to return to the sugar plantations, Toussaint legislated, and for their work they would receive a quarter of the profit from sugar production. The owners would receive another fourth, and the government would receive half.

By this time, however, Napoleon had come to power in France. Answering the appeal of Saint-Domingue plantation owners—who wanted far more profit than 25 percent—he determined to "pursue the rebels without mercy [and] flush them out," thereby regaining the upper hand in the colony.[17] The campaign led to the capture of Toussaint, who died in jail in 1803. With all blacks now uniting against any French takeover, however, the invading army suffered huge losses—some 50,000 of an army of 58,000—many of them from yellow fever. On January 1, 1804, the black generals who defeated the French proclaimed the independent republic of Haiti.

Revolutions in Latin America 1810–1830

The thirst for change gripped people in other empires. In Spain's Latin American empire discontent among artisans, agricultural workers, and slaves, along with rivalries among creoles and Spanish-born officials sent from the homeland, erupted under the pressures of the Napoleonic conquest of the Iberian peninsula in 1808. "It is now time to overthrow the [Spanish] yoke," a group of rebels in La Paz declared in 1809. "It is now time to declare the principle of liberty in these miserable colonies."[18] This spirit swept the Spanish lands, as the government back home in Europe crumbled.

Impact of the Napoleonic Wars

When Napoleon invaded Spain and Portugal in 1807, he sent the ruling dynasties packing to give his own family control. With British help, the Portuguese monarch fled to Brazil in hopes of ruling the empire from the colonies, while in Spain the monarch was replaced by Napoleon's brother Joseph. Guerrilla warfare erupted against the French while Spanish activists also organized **juntas** (HUN-tahs), or ruling councils, around the country despite French rule. In 1808, a national junta unveiled a broad program for reform. In the Spanish colonies, political confusion set in as news of the junta's plan for a constitution-based government spread. Some creole leaders welcomed the planned constitution, but other creoles in business and agriculture sensed an opportunity not simply for constitutional reform but for ousting officials from Spain altogether. Like imperial rulers elsewhere, the Spanish kings had come to treat their colonies as cash cows, milking them dry to pay for a lavish way of life in Europe. In the disorder brought on by the Napoleonic invasions and the appearance of reform-minded leaders in Spain, colonial leaders saw an opportunity to end these heavy burdens.

junta A ruling council.

The Napoleonic Wars opened up other avenues to economic and political change. Because Spain was allied with Britain in the wars against Napoleon, the people in the Spanish colonies had new contacts and new economic opportunities. Like Britain, Spain had formerly tried to prevent its colonies from manufacturing their own goods or trading directly with other countries. All goods were to be carried in Spanish vessels. Trade-minded local creoles resented these restrictions, as well as the privileged place of Spanish traders and the monopoly on good jobs enjoyed by Spanish aristocrats. The wars upset this state of affairs, throwing open ports to British vessels carrying both new ideas and exciting new products—both of them benefits of unrestricted trade. Mule drivers, parish priests, and market people also spread global news, alerting neighborhoods in distant towns to the possibility for change. Aspiring leaders saw a situation full of potential for new prosperity and freedom. Their struggles for independence would last until 1830 (see Map 23.4).

Reformers and rebels sprang into action throughout Latin America. In the lucrative colony of Mexico, Father Miguel Hidalgo, a Mexican priest trained in Enlightenment thought by the Jesuits and exiled by the Spanish to a rural parish because of his ideas, opened a campaign against colonial rule in 1810. His soldiers were his parishioners, most of them native Americans who worked as day laborers for the Spanish and creoles. The collapse of silver mining and the soaring prices of food made them desperate. Calling for the complete ouster of Spaniards, they wanted their jobs and their standard of living restored. Hidalgo's army swelled to some sixty thousand fighters, who hoped to get paid or fed as they fought. Drawn from the popular classes, the average fighter, in the opinion of the Mexican viceroy, was a "robber, assassin, and libertine."[19] Yet most of Hidalgo's followers were motivated by simple outrage at the poverty and oppression they faced—not by robbery or lust. They slaughtered entire contingents of Spaniards, creoles, and anyone else who stood in their path.

Father Hidalgo was captured and executed in 1811, but other armies appeared under the leadership of mulattos, mestizos (mixed-blood people of native American and European ancestry), and well-born creoles, who wanted the Spanish out and opportunity reborn. These armies—most notably that under the humbly born mestizo priest, Father José Maria Morelos—carried the uprising to the west of Mexico, using guerrilla tactics and living off the support of legions of women, who provisioned and tended the troops. The Spanish, however, were able to turn other native Americans, slaves, and mestizos against creole-led armies by pointing out that creoles owned the exploitative large farms. By 1815 the Spanish had put an end to this first stage of the Mexican drive for independence and had executed its leaders—adding to the hatred of colonialism that many felt.

Amid ongoing attacks from bandits and personal armies, new leadership emerged in Mexico, one that was more capable of victory. The key to its success lay in creoles' efforts to set aside their prejudices to unite with the native masses. Creoles adopted a nationalist sensibility, accepting the idea to distinguish *all* those inhabitants of Mexico born in the New World—the *Americanos*—from those born in Spain. Continued guerrilla fighting eroded the institutions of Spanish rule in Mexico, but the decisive move came when the creole leader Augustin de Iturbide (ee-tur-BEE-deh) allied his forces with Vicente Guerrero (goo-RER-eh), a leader of the popular armies, himself a mestizo and thus heir to the

Toussaint Louverture

In 1791, Toussaint Louverture, a freed slave and slave owner, joined a slave revolt that erupted in Saint-Domingue, the prosperous sugar colony of France in the Caribbean. Louverture, shown here in his general's uniform, possessed strong military skills and soon became the leader of the Haitian Revolution, writing the constitution of the fledgling nation and working to defeat the Spanish, British, and French, who in turn sought to take the former colony for themselves. Ironically, although he modeled his new nation on French ideals of freedom and citizenship, Louverture re-enslaved many Haitians. He died in a French prison in 1803. (Private Collection/ Bridgeman Art Library.)

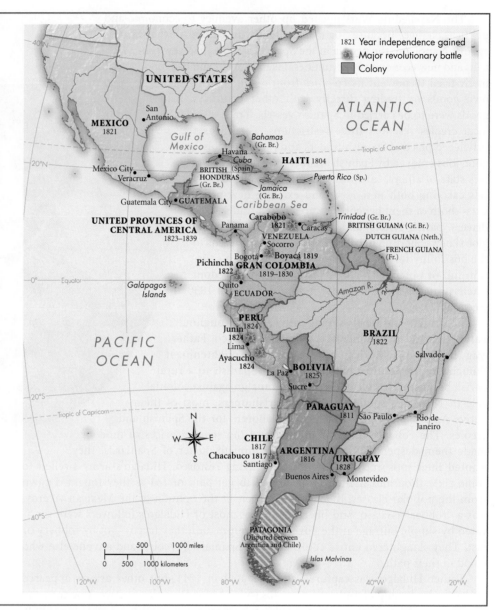

MAP 23.4

Revolutions in Latin America, 1810–1830

The Spanish government, influenced by Enlightenment ideas about rational government, attempted to streamline its rule and enhance colonial profitability. As revolution rolled across the Atlantic world, colonial subjects in Latin America were equally affected by Enlightenment ideas about liberty and the opportunities it would bring. Revolutions in Latin America were prolonged, however, and they were wide-ranging, bringing in people from many walks of life and ethnicities as well as soldiers from different parts of the world—all motivated by the potential for revolutionary transformation.

Independence for Mexico

Morelos legacy of native rights. Iturbide had once served the Spanish as an army officer, winning battles and collecting tribute for the government. As was so often the case, his creole birth blocked his advance in the Spanish colony, despite his record. Resentment of unearned Spanish privilege made him a natural ally of people who were also held back by what the Spanish saw as low birth—native American, black, mestizo, or mulatto. Iturbide's and Guerrero's forces reached an agreement for a constitutional monarchy independent of Spain. In 1821, the three hundredth anniversary of the Spanish conquest of Mexico, Iturbide entered Mexico City as Spanish rule disintegrated. Yet it was not this event but rather the start of Father Hidalgo's uprising of the common people on September 16, 1810 that came to mark Mexico's Day of Independence.

Across South America similar independent rebel armies sprang up, most of them controlled by a local strongman, or *caudillo* (kauh-DEE-yoh), who was able to raise armies from people of all classes and ethnicities. Such a caudillo was José Gervasio Artigas in Uruguay. Artigas was a rancher, cattle thief, and, by virtue of having his own army, a regional peacekeeper. While keeping peace locally, the *caudillos* had as many problems getting along with one another as they did enduring Spanish rule. One quality these creoles shared, however, was their contempt for native Americans, Africans, mulattos, and mestizos. Simon Bolivar mustered caudillo support to liberate Venezuela in 1811, but at the time he firmly believed that slavery could be maintained in the fight for national independence.

Independence for Peru

Nonetheless, with the Spanish monarch's return to power after the defeat of Napoleon in 1815, it became clear that creoles in Latin America needed to ally themselves with oppressed workers, agricultural laborers, and the *llaneros* (yah-NEH-rows), or local cowboys, of all races (see Lives and Livelihoods: The Cowboy Way of Life). Bolivar made himself one with the llaneros, demonstrating that his troops were militarily fit and daring riders; he called for the forging of a Gran Colombia—a united nation like the United States, composed of all the liberated lands. To create such a state, the foreign-born Spanish must be ousted for good. Increasing Spanish oppression and the appeal to all "Americans" did some good, enabling Bolivar, with the help of black troops, to take Bogotá, Caracas, and Quito by 1822. In the meantime Argentinean general José de San Martin was conquering Buenos Aires, western Argentina, and Chile, moving into Peru in 1818. His armies bogged down in Peru, however, leaving the final task of ousting the Spanish to Bolivar, whose armies finally took Lima in 1823 and upper Peru or Bolivia in 1825 (see again Map 23.4). Both San Martin and Bolivar had originally seen no conflict between their own freedom and the existence of slavery, but as the need for slave support became obvious, Bolivar declared it "madness that a revolution for liberty should try to maintain slavery."[20] To get the support of the vast number of slaves, many liberation leaders promised and awarded slave soldiers their emancipation, either immediately as a way of attracting fighters or after the wars as a reward for victory.

Independence for Brazil

Brazil gained its independence from Portugal more tranquilly than the Spanish colonies did from Spain, and with little change in the social situation: slavery and the bureaucracy alike were left intact. The ruling family, safe in Brazil, was summoned back to Portugal at the end of the Napoleonic Wars, but the king left his son Pedro behind in the capital of Rio de Janeiro. Pedro proceeded to cooperate with business and other leaders and in 1822 declared Brazil independent of Portugal and made himself king. With the masses set

Upper-Class Woman and Her Slaves in Eighteenth-Century Brazil
Many aristocrats and wealthy landowners in prerevolutionary South America followed European customs in such matters as display of class privileges. For instance, in Europe servants wore uniforms or livery, as do these slaves as they carry their upper-class mistress in a sedan chair and follow her on foot. Aristocratic status was often evident in the number of people accompanying a noble person, but these slaves also show the variety in slave livelihoods. (J. Bedmar/Iberfoto/The Image Works.)

The Cowboy Way of Life

Gauchos

Gauchos lived away from towns, cities, and settled ranches. Like cowboys, their North American counterparts, gauchos prided themselves on a range of skills with wild horses and other animals. In this nineteenth-century colored etching, a gaucho hurls a rope with a ball on its end to capture a rhea by entangling its legs in the rope. As South America developed commerce, manufacturing, and modern industry, the gaucho came to symbolize the independent spirit of the young nations. (akg-images.)

One of the most important livelihoods in the Western Hemisphere was that of cowboys or cattle hunters, who differed from the later settled ranchers for whom cowboys came to work. Called *gauchos* in Argentina, *llaneros* in Venezuela and Colombia, and *vaqueros* in Mexico, cowboys rode the prairies rounding up the wild horses and cattle that grazed there. They created their livelihood from scratch, for only after 1494 when Columbus first introduced cattle into the Caribbean did cattle spread across both North and South America. As the livestock multiplied, cowboys hunted down the wild animals and slaughtered them. Cowboys developed an entire range of skills, making lassos, for example, from horses' tails. But their most lucrative products were animal hides and byproducts such as leather and tallow for candle-making.

These herdsmen, similar to those on the Asian steppes, were usually nomadic, with their own customs and ways of life. Living as far as possible from cities and the centers of government, they aimed to keep their independence and to escape government regulation, which increased under the Bourbon Reforms. Cowboys in all areas usually refused to ride mares as an unmanly practice and generally prided themselves on maintaining the rough, masculine ways of frontiersmen. Enterprising landowners, however, set up vast ranches and challenged the claims of the gauchos, llaneros, and vaqueros, who saw wild horses as their own. Settled ranchers hired their own cattle tenders and then encouraged the government to see the independent cowboys as "cattle rustlers" and thieves.

Their independent way of life eventually led nation builders to mythologize gauchos, llaneros, and other cowboys as symbols of freedom for the nation as a whole. However, cowboys played a more direct role in both politics and nation building in the nineteenth century. Their experience with horses made them valuable fighters on both sides in the war for Latin American independence, and their survival skills helped them endure the rough conditions of battle.

QUESTIONS TO CONSIDER

1. For what reasons would some gauchos and llaneros ally themselves with upper-class creoles in the Latin American independence movements?

2. Why have cowboys become such icons in both North and South America?

For Further Information:
Loy, R. Philip. *Westerns and American Culture, 1930–1955*. 2001.
Oliven, Ruben George. *Tradition Matters: Modern Gaucho Identity in Brazil*. 1996.
Reding, Nick. *The Last Cowboys at the End of the World: The Last Gauchos of Patagonia*. 2001.
Slatta, Richard W. *Gauchos and the Vanishing Frontier*. 1983.

against Portuguese foreigners, there was widespread rejoicing at independence even with-out major social change. A frontier society like the United States, Brazil beckoned entre-preneurs, adventurers, and exiles from around the world as a land of opportunity.

For the most part, however, the new Latin American countries had been so devastated by years of exploitation, misrule, banditry, and armed uprising that except in Brazil, econ-omies lay in shambles. Instead of effecting social reform that would have encouraged eco-nomic initiative, most new governments worked to ensure creole dominance, often refus-ing the promised slave emancipation. In 1799 a Spanish bishop-elect had noted the "great conflict of interests and the hostility which invariably prevails between those who have nothing and those who have everything."[21] Independence did not transform this situation, and thus the popular forces that would have promoted innovation and increased activity at the grassroots did not materialize as effectively as in the newly independent United States.

New Ideologies and Revolutionary Legacies

The revolutions in the Americas and Europe achieved independence for some states but deliberately failed to bring full and free citizenship to slaves, women, and a range of inden-tured and oppressed peoples. Nonetheless, they left aspirations for the economic opportunity and personal freedom that define the term *liberalism*. Inspired by Enlightenment principles, revolutionaries sought to create centralized nation-states ruled under a constitution as opposed to monarchical governments given to arbitrary rulings by aristocrats and princes. In the early days of both the North American and French republics, this faith in a unified nation of like-minded peoples, which came to be known as **nationalism**, went hand in hand with liberalism. The idea was that the unified rule of law under a single nation, as embodied in the U.S. Constitution and the Declaration of the Rights of Man and of the Citizen, would guar-antee constitutional rights and economic growth through free trade. Latin American leaders such as Bolivar had much less faith in all the people of the nation being ready for participa-tion in government (see Reading the Past: Simon Bolivar on Latin American Independence).

The definition of nationalism became more complicated even as it was being born. For one thing, a host of opponents to the new governments of the United States and France believed that time-honored monarchical traditions were a better guarantee of a peaceful society than constitutions and republics. Such thought was called **conservatism**, and many prominent conservatives across Europe and the Americas argued the case for tradition, continuity, and gradual reform based on practical experience. Appalled by the violence and bloodshed of the French Revolution, Edmund Burke of England attacked Enlightenment ideas of a social contract, citizenship, and new fangled constitutions as destructive to the wisdom of the ages.

Like conservatism, **romanticism**—a philosophical and artistic movement that glori-fied nature, emotion, and the imagination—emerged partly in reaction to the Enlighten-ment's reliance on reason, especially after the violent excesses of the French Revolution. Closely related to early nationalism, romanticism was also a response to the political tur-moil of the Napoleonic Wars. There thus grew up a romantic nationalism, especially in territories such as the German states. Romantic nationalists revered language and tradi-tions as sources of a common feeling among peoples—for instance, among all the German peoples. "Perfect laws are the beautiful and free forms of the interior life of a nation," wrote one German jurist, criticizing reformers' desire to take the Napoleonic Code as a model for change. For him, the Napoleonic Code had not "come out of the life of the German nation."[22] Romantic nationalists took less pride in law codes, well-defined citi-zenship, and civic rights than in their ancient past and shared cultural experience.

To make the revolutionary legacy more complicated yet, Napoleon Bonaparte and Simon Bolivar ultimately became romantic heroes to rich and poor alike, even though they represented Enlightenment ideals of social mobility, consistent systems of laws, a rational approach to government, and economic modernizing. "My wife and I," said one distillery worker in southern France in 1822, "have the emperor in our guts."[23] The many poets,

nationalism A belief in the importance of one's nation, stemming from its unique laws, language, traditions, and history.

conservatism A political philosophy emphasizing the continuation of traditional institutions and opposition to sudden change in the estab-lished order.

romanticism A European philo-sophical and artistic movement of the late eighteenth and early nineteenth centuries that valued feeling over reason and glorified traditional customs, nature, and the imagination.

Simon Bolivar on Latin American Independence

Simon Bolivar was a heroic "Liberator" to some observers, an authoritarian creole to others. Some of these contradictory images come from Bolivar's own views of the situation in Latin America. This document is from Bolivar's "Letter from Jamaica," written in exile after his 1815 flight from Spanish forces. In it Bolivar expresses his thoughts about liberation from the Spanish and the possibilities for representative government thereafter.

The position of the inhabitants of the American hemisphere has for centuries been purely passive, its political role nonexistent. We are still at a level lower than slavery, and for that reason it is more difficult for us to raise ourselves to attain the enjoyment of freedom. . . . States are enslaved because of either the nature or the abuse of their constitutions; a people is therefore enslaved when the government by its essential nature or by its vices tramples on and usurps the rights of the citizens or subjects. . . .

As long as our countrymen do not acquire the political capacities and virtues that distinguish our brothers of the north, fully democratic systems, far from working to our advantage, will, I fear, bring about our downfall. Unfortunately, these traits, to the extent to which they are required, do not appear to be within our reach. On the contrary, we are dominated by the vices acquired during the rule of a nation like Spain, which

has only distinguished itself in brutality, ambition, vindictiveness, and greed. . . .

South Americans have tried to create liberal, even perfect, institutions, doubtless out of that instinct which all men have to attain the greatest happiness possible, which necessarily follows in civil societies founded on the principles of justice, liberty, and equality. But can we maintain in proper balance the difficult charge of a republic? Is it conceivable that a newly liberated people can soar to the height of freedom, . . . without falling into an abyss? Such a marvel is inconceivable and never before seen.

Source: Carta de Jamaica, September 6, 1815, in *Escritos políticos*. Selección e introd., de Graciela Soriano (Madrid: Alianza Editorial, 1969). Translated by Donald R. Kelley.

EXAMINING THE EVIDENCE

1. How does Bolivar characterize Spanish rule?

2. How does he think this rule has affected his contemporaries' capacity for self-government?

3. What seem to be the political options left to Latin Americans once they have obtained their independence?

---

musicians, and artists influenced by romanticism earned their livelihoods not only by glorifying feelings instead of reason but by spreading the myth of Napoleon and Simon Bolivar as superhuman rulers who overcame horrific obstacles to become conquerors. These powerful, if conflicting, ideas—liberalism, nationalism, conservatism, and romanticism—resonated down through the next centuries, shaping both local and global politics.

COUNTERPOINT
Religious Revival in a Secular Age

FOCUS

What trends in Enlightenment and revolutionary society did religious revival challenge?

As we have seen in this chapter, in the challenge to long-established empires, some peoples declared their sovereignty and set up states in opposition to centuries-old forms of rulership. In the influential cases of France and the United States, the principle of a secular state—one tied to no particular religion—flourished, supported by the Enlightenment idea that reason rather than faith should determine social, political, and economic regulations. The French under Robespierre devised national festivals to substitute for religious holidays and even, at the height of revolutionary fervor, converted churches into "temples of reason." But secularism did not prevail everywhere, and movements arose that countered the weakening of religious belief or its supposedly empty ritual. In Europe and North America, great surges of religious fervor took hold of people's daily lives, and in the Arabian peninsula reformers sought to restore Muslims to the fundamental teachings of Islam.

Christianity's Great Awakening

The spirit of Christian revival first took shape in Prussia, where Lutherans had called for a renewal of faith in the late seventeenth century. As Protestant revival spread across the European continent, people joined new evangelical churches, most of them focused on sharpening the inward experience of faith. In the middle of the eighteenth century, a wave of revivals that historians term the "Great Awakening" took place throughout Britain and the North American colonies. Emotional orators such as the English preachers John Wesley and George Whitefield appeared at large rallies, rousing the faithful to break off from the sterile ritual of established churches and to join new communities of faith such as Methodism, the evangelical Protestant church founded by Wesley and characterized by active concern with social welfare and public morals. Some observers were appalled by the sight of worshipers literally weeping at the perils of damnation; in the words of one, the Great Awakening was "horrible beyond expression."[24] Nonetheless, in the middle colonies of British North America alone, some 550 new Protestant congregations were organized between 1740 and 1770.

The Great Awakening

Beginning in around 1800, the United States experienced a Second Great Awakening, where thousands at a time flocked to revival meetings. Describing the scene, one commentator wrote that "some of the people were singing, others praying, some praying for mercy," as they testified to their faith in the face of the growth of science, rationalism, and emotional coldness in the old churches. At the same time, African American slaves were also fervent believers, finding in religion evidence of their humanity (see Reading the Past: Phillis Wheatley, "On Being Brought from Africa to America"). Religion later provided arguments for an end to slavery and were part of a rising democratic impulse among people who together addressed their comments directly and emotionally to God. Despite the surge in religious enthusiasm, governments such as that of the United States declined to proclaim an official faith because of their people's religious diversity and because of Enlightenment thinkers' suspicion of churches as institutions.

New Churches and the State

Government and Religion Allied

In some instances, ties between government and religion became stronger, not weaker. In the Arabian peninsula an eighteenth-century religious reformer, Muhammad ibn Abd al-Wahhabi developed a strong alliance with Muhammad ibn Sa'ud, the head of a small market town. Ibn Abd al-Wahhabi called on Muslims to return to the tenets of Islam, most importantly the worship of the single god, Allah. He felt that Islam had been betrayed by an overemphasis on the Prophet Muhammad and other human saints. At the time, in fact, people worshiped local fortunetell-

Mecca and Wahhabism
Wahhabis fought for a purified Islamic faith, one that eliminated the common practice in the Middle East and elsewhere in the Muslim world of worshiping at religious shrines and the tombs of saints. They destroyed the tombs of the Prophet Muhammad's family but were stopped from overturning the tomb of the Prophet himself. Because the pilgrimage to Mecca was one of the five "pillars" of the faith, Mecca itself, depicted here, remained a center of religious devotion that grew in importance as Islam spread around the world. (Popular Traditions Museum, Damascus/Giraudon/Bridgeman Art Library.)

READING THE PAST

Phillis Wheatley, "On Being Brought from Africa to America"

Born in Senegal in 1853, Phillis Wheatley was seven when she was sold into slavery to a Boston family, who educated her along with their children. Wheatley published celebrated poetry while a slave, becoming a sensation in New England and even traveling to England in 1773. A voyager to three continents, Wheatley was a true child of the Atlantic world. This celebrated poem, written while she was a teenager, contains a host of ideas and images about slavery and her own condition. As you read, consider why this short verse might pose problems for some modern readers.

'Twas mercy brought me from my Pagan land,
Taught my benighted soul to understand
That there's a God, that there's a Saviour too:
Once I redemption neither sought now knew,

Some view our sable race with scornful eye,
"Their colour is a diabolic die."
Remember, Christians, Negroes, black as Cain,
May be refin'd, and join th' angelic train.

EXAMINING THE EVIDENCE

1. In what ways does this poem reflect Enlightenment thought?

2. How does it relate to the Great Awakening?

3. Which ideas in the poem might present-day critics condemn? Which ideas might they praise?

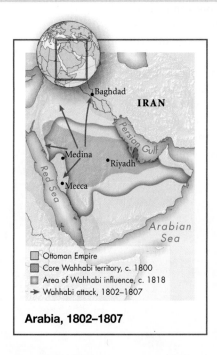

Arabia, 1802–1807

- Ottoman Empire
- Core Wahhabi territory, c. 1800
- Area of Wahhabi influence, c. 1818
- → Wahhabi attack, 1802–1807

Wahhabi-Sa'ud Alliance

ers and healers as well as graves, rocks, and trees. One traveler found Arabs "so negligent of religion" that they were "generally considered infidels." This was certainly the opinion of ibn Abd al-Wahhabi and his followers, who declared these departures from the tenets of Islam to be paganism itself. He got help in his quest to return Arabs to the basic principles of Islam not only from his large and active following but from the house of Sa'ud—the town's leading family. Unity of worship would come with political unity, led in ibn Abd al-Wahhabi's mind by the Sa'uds. They would unite the various tribes under a purified Islamic practice, realizing al-Wahhabi's belief that "Arab" meant Muslim.

Muslims, if they are physically able, are instructed to make a pilgrimage to Mecca during their lifetime as one of their basic obligations. The Wahhabis, as the reformer's followers came to be called (at first, by their enemies), were determined to take control of Mecca for the Sa'uds and for their cause of Islamic fundamentalism. In 1802, making their first attempt, they destroyed all mosques dedicated to the worship of Muhammad. Being connected with the Sa'uds put real muscle to the Wahhabis' religious fervor, and in 1807 they finally wrenched the religious sites of Mecca and Medina from Ottoman control. Although the Ottomans would regain possession in 1840, the alliance between the Sa'uds and the Wahhabis remained, to become ever more powerful in the twentieth century as the discovery of oil in the region fortified the Sa'uds and the Wahhabis along with them.[25]

Conclusion

This period saw widespread challenges to centuries-old empires in the Americas, Europe, the Caribbean, West Asia, and Egypt. The most direct of these challenges came from the popular uprisings known as the Atlantic revolutions. In these revolutions, state power and rigid social structures impinged on people's lives by promoting high taxes and controlling commerce. Deepening poverty and frustrated ambition afflicted ordinary folk, whether in

786

France or in Peru, causing both riots and political activism. These economic conditions awakened some revolutionaries. Others were inspired to push for political reform by Enlightenment ideas about government based on individual rights and the rational rule of law rather than on inherited privilege and notions of a divine order. Simon Bolivar was one such secular-minded revolutionary and state-builder. Other political actors, such as the Sa'ud family of the Arabian peninsula, drew on religious fervor in their state-building, forming a counterpoint to the general trend.

Independence in the Western Hemisphere affected the entire world. As frontier societies, North American and Latin American countries served as magnets for European investment and for people searching for better livelihoods. Still, countless people of all classes and ethnicities who participated in the uprisings in the Atlantic world benefited not at all or in the most limited way. Slavery remained entrenched in some countries; women, free blacks, and other people of color were usually disqualified from participating in politics. As representative government developed, it too was uneven, especially in Latin America, where a creole elite dominated the new nations.

These political revolutions nonetheless formed a platform for further social and economic change, and we remember them for their powerful and enduring influence. In the short term, the revolutions created conditions for heightened manufacturing and eventually the Industrial Revolution. In the long term, they gave citizens confidence to use their freedom. "It is harder to release a nation from servitude than to enslave a free nation," Bolivar had written, and in this respect the age of revolutions nurtured aspirations and opened up opportunities.

NOTES

1. Luis Peru de Lacroix, *Diario de Cucuramanga* (Caracas: Comité ejecutivo del Bicentenario de Simon Bolivar, 1982), 67, quoted in Charles Minguet, ed., *Simon Bolivar: Unité impossible* (Paris: La Découverte, 1983), 13.
2. Voltaire, *Essai sur les moeurs*, 3:179.
3. Quoted in Hilda L. Smith and Berenice A. Carroll, eds., *Women's Political and Social Thought* (Bloomington: Indiana University Press, 2000), 133.
4. "Political Testament," in George I. Mosse et al., eds., *Europe in Review* (Chicago: Rand McNally and Co., 1957), 111–112.
5. Quoted in Richard Wortman, *Scenarios of Power: Myth and Ceremony in Russian Monarchy, From Peter the Great to the Death of Nicholas I* (Princeton, NJ: Princeton University Press, 1995), 130.
6. *Seminario Económico de México*, 1811, quoted in Silvia Marina Arrom, *The Women of Mexico City, 1790–1857* (Palo Alto, CA: Stanford University Press, 1985), 18.
7. Edward Long, quoted in Barbara Bush, *Slave Women in the Caribbean, 1650–1838* (London: Heinemann, 1990), 15, 51.
8. Quoted in Paul Dukes, ed. and trans., *Russia Under Catherine the Great: Select Documents on Government and Society* (Newtonville, MA: Priental Research Partners, 1978), 112.
9. Dukes, *Russia Under Catherine the Great*, 112, 115.
10. Alexander Hamilton, *Federalist Papers*, Number 15.
11. Letter to John Jay, March 14, 1779, http://www.c250.columbia.edu/c250_celebrates/remarkable_columbians/alexander_hamilton.html.
12. Quoted in Ron Chernow, *Alexander Hamilton* (New York: Penguin, 2004), 316.
13. Quoted in Lynn Hunt, *The French Revolution and Human Rights: A Brief Documentary History* (Boston: Bedford/St. Martins, 1996), 65.
14. Quoted in Annie Jourdain, *Napoléon: Héros, Imperator, Mécène* (Paris: Aubier, 1998), 34.
15. Quoted in Albert Hourani, *Arabic Thought in the Liberal Age, 1798–1939* (London: Oxford University Press, 1962), "Address to the National Assembly, to Our Lords the Representatives of the Nation," quoted in Laurent Dubois and John D. Garrigus, eds., *Slave Revolution in the Caribbean, 1789–1804: A Brief History with Documents* (Boston: Bedford/St. Martins, 2005), 69.
16. Quoted Dubois and Garrigus, *Slave Revolution*, 77.
17. "Notes [from Napoleon Bonaparte] to Serve as Instructions to Give to the Captain General Leclerc," quoted in Dubois and Garrigus, *Slave Revolution*, 176.
18. "Proclamation of 1809," quoted in Peter Bakewell, *A History of Latin America: Empires and Sequels, 1450–1930* (Oxford, U.K.: Blackwell, 1997), 362.
19. Juan Ruiz de Apodaca, quoted in Richard Boyer and Geoffrey Spurling, eds., *Colonial Lives: Documents on Latin American History, 1550–1850* (New York: Oxford University Press, 2000), 305.
20. Quoted in George Reid Andrews, *Afro-Latin America, 1800–2000* (New York: Oxford University Press, 2004), 57.

21. Quoted in John Lynch, "The Origins of Spanish American Independence," in *The Cambridge History of Latin America* (Cambridge, U.K.: Cambridge University Press, 1985), 3:32.
22. Quoted in Martyn Lyons, *Napoleon Bonaparte and the Legacy of the French Revolution* (London: Macmillan, 1994), 232.
23. Quoted in Lyons, *Napoleon Bonaparte*, v.
24. William Briggs, quoted in Phyllis Mack, *Heart Religion in the British Enlightenment: Gender and Emotion in Early Methodism* (New York: Cambridge University Press, 2008), 2.
25. John Esposito, *Islam, the Straight Path* (New York: Oxford University Press, 1991).

RESOURCES FOR RESEARCH

The Promise of Enlightenment

The Enlightenment had a global reach, sparking interest in South America and Japan as well as in Europe. Scientific curiosity among a range of people, as featured in Schiffer's book, led to ongoing experimentation.

Dalton, Susan. *Engendering the Republic of Letters: Reconnecting Public and Private Spheres.* 2003.
Gorbatov, Inna. *Catherine the Great and the French Philosophers of the Enlightenment: Montesquieu, Voltaire, Rousseau, Diderot and Grimm.* 2005.
Rowe, William T. *Saving the World: Chen Hongmou and Elite Consciousness in Eighteenth Century China.* 2001.
Schiffer, Michael B. *Drawing the Lightning Down: Benjamin Franklin and Electrical Technology in the Age of Enlightenment.* 2003.
Stein, Stanley J., and Barbara H. Stein. *Apogee of Empire: Spain and New Spain in the Age of Charles III, 1759–1789.* 2003.

Revolution in North America

The revolution in North America engaged the European powers, not only Britain but also France and Spain, as Elliott's masterful work shows. Linda Kerber highlights the many aspects of North American women's involvement as participants as well as symbols of liberty and rights.

Appleby, Joyce. *Inheriting the Revolution: The First Generation of Americans.* 2004.
Elliott, John H. *Empires of the Atlantic World: Britain and Spain in America, 1492–1830.* 2006.
Kerber, Linda. *Women of the Republic: Intellect and Ideology in the American Revolution.* 1986.
Middlekauff, Robert. *The Glorious Cause: The American Revolution, 1763–1789.* 2005.
Wood, Gordon S. *Revolutionary Characters: What Made the Founders Different?* 2006.

The French Revolution and the Napoleonic Empire

More than the American Revolution, this was the uprising heard round the world, and it has given rise to exciting studies of many kinds. The Web site at George Mason University has one of the most comprehensive online presentations of documents, images, and songs from the French Revolution.

French Revolution: http://chnm.gmu.edu/revolution/.
Hunt, Lynn. *Inventing Human Rights: A History.* 2007.
Marsot, Afaf Lutfi Al-Sayyid. *Egypt in the Reign of Muhammad Ali.* 1984.
Napoleonic Empire: http://www.bbc.co.uk/history/historic_figures/bonaparte_napoleon.shtml.
Shovlin, John. *The Political Economy of Virtue: Luxury, Patriotism, and the Origins of the French Revolution.* 2006.
Todd, Janet. *Mary Wollstonecraft: A Life.* 2000.

Revolution Continued in the Western Hemisphere

As revolution continued in the Atlantic world, the Caribbean and Latin America saw a wave of uprisings. Dubois movingly describes the causes and conduct of revolution in Haiti; the State University of New York/Albany maintains an excellent Web site on it.

Dubois, Laurent. *Avengers of the New World: The Story of the Haitian Revolution.* 2004.
Haitian revolution: http://www.albany.edu/~js3980/haitian-revolution.html.
Masur, Gerard. *Simón Bolívar.* 2006.
Morgan, Jennifer. *Laboring Women: Reproduction and Gender in New World Slavery.* 2004.
Van Young, Eric. *The Other Rebellion: Popular Violence, Ideology, and the Mexican Struggle for Independence, 1810–1821.* 2001.

COUNTERPOINT: Religious Revival in a Secular Age

The religious fervor that accompanied the age of reason is well chronicled in the works below.

Mack, Phyllis. *Heart Religion in the British Enlightenment: Gender and Emotion in Early Methodism.* 2008.
May, Cedrick. *Evangelism and Resistance in the Black Atlantic, 1760–1835.* 2008.
Qadhi, Abu Ammar Yasir. *A Critical Study of Shirk: Being a Translation and Commentary of Muhammad b. Abd al-Wahhab's Kashf al-Shubuhat.* 2002.
Vassiliev, Alexei. *A History of Saudi Arabia.* 1998.

▶ **For additional primary sources from this period,** see *Sources of Crossroads and Cultures.*

▶ **For Web sites, images, and documents related to topics in this chapter,** see Make History at bedfordstmartins.com/smith.

Online Study Guide
bedfordstmartins.com/smith

The major global development in this chapter ▶ The Atlantic revolutions
and their short- and long-term significance.

IMPORTANT EVENTS

1751–1772	Publication of the *Encyclopedia*
1762	Jean-Jacques Rousseau publishes *The Social Contract* and *Emile*
1775–1781	Revolution in North America
1776	Adam Smith, *The Wealth of Nations*
1789	U.S. Constitution formally adopted; revolution begins in France
1791	Revolution begins in Haiti
1792	France declared a republic; Mary Wollstonecraft writes *A Vindication of the Rights of Woman*
1799	Napoleon comes to power
1804	Haiti becomes independent from France
1811	Simon Bolivar first takes up arms against Spain
1815	Napoleon defeated at Waterloo; Congress of Vienna resettles the boundaries of European states
1816	Argentina becomes independent from Spain
1817	Chile becomes independent from Spain
1821	Mexico and Peru become independent from Spain
1822	Brazil becomes independent from Portugal
1825	Bolivia becomes independent from Spain

CHAPTER OVERVIEW QUESTIONS

1. What role did the Scientific Revolution and expanding global contacts play in the cultural and social movement known as the Enlightenment?

2. Why did prosperous and poor people alike join revolutions in the Americas and in France?

3. Why were the Atlantic revolutions so influential, even to the present day?

SECTION FOCUS QUESTIONS

1. What were the major ideas of the Enlightenment and their impacts?

2. What factors lay behind the war between North American colonists and Great Britain?

3. What changes emerged from the French Revolution and Napoleon's reign?

4. What were the motives and methods of revolutionaries in the Caribbean and Latin America?

5. What trends in Enlightenment and revolutionary society did religious revival challenge?

MAKING CONNECTIONS

1. What was the relationship between the Enlightenment and the political revolutions of the late eighteenth and early nineteenth centuries?

2. What are the common challenges that centuries-old empires faced during this period?

3. What makes Napoleon a significant historical figure?

4. Why was there so much bloodshed in the various efforts to achieve political and social change?

KEY TERMS

conservatism (p. 783)
contract government (p. 762)
federation (p. 769)
general will (p. 773)
junta (p. 778)
laissez faire (p. 763)
liberalism (p. 763)
nationalism (p. 783)
public sphere (p. 764)
republic (p. 771)
romanticism (p. 783)

AT A CROSSROADS ▲

An artist from an elite samurai family, Kiyochika Kobayashi was so fascinated by technology and industry that in 1879 he placed a train front and center in this moonlit scene set in Takanawa Ushimachi, just outside of Tokyo. Earlier woodprints had portrayed the town as a slum called Oxtown with garbage strewn about its roads, but in this artist's eyes Takanawa Ushimachi became a prosperous, indeed alluring crossroads, thanks to the arrival of the railroad. Kiyochika changed the style of Japanese woodcuts by introducing into more traditional Japanese scenes such elements as clocks, cameras, electric lighting, and the massive cannons churned out by industry. (Santa Barbara Museum of Art, Gift of Dr. and Mrs. Roland A. Way.)

Industry and Everyday Life
1750–1900

As a seven-year-old in 1799, Robert Blincoe started working in a cotton mill outside the town of Nottingham, in central England. Robert was an orphan, and with others from his London orphanage he was sent to the mill. The idea was to have the orphans contribute to England's prosperity and learn the value of hard work, but it was not certain that Robert would even survive to adulthood. As his group of orphans reached the mill, he heard onlookers in the town mutter, "God help the poor wretches."[1] Robert soon found out why. He watched as his fellow child workers wasted away from the long hours and meager food, and he looked on in horror as the orphan Mary Richards was caught up in the machinery: he "heard the bones of her arms, legs, thighs, etc successively snap . . . her head appeared dashed to pieces, . . . her blood thrown about like water from a twirled mop."[2] Robert himself had to stand on a box to tend the machinery, but due to his small size he was less productive than the managers wanted, and he was constantly beaten. Robert's situation grew worse when his group was sent to another mill. The hours were even longer and the pace of work faster, and older workers tortured Robert, putting hot pitch into a blazing metal bowl and placing it on his head until his hair came off and his scalp was burned. Only when Robert reached age twenty-one, his entire body scarred for life from beatings, was he released from his grim "apprenticeship."

Robert Blincoe was a survivor of the Industrial Revolution—a change in the production of goods that substituted mechanical force for human energy. Beginning in Britain around 1750, European factories churned out machine-made products—first textiles and later manufactured items from sewing machines to automobiles—that came to replace

BACKSTORY

As we saw in Chapter 23, between 1750 and 1830 popular uprisings led to a revolutionary wave across the Atlantic world. Throwing off old political systems, revolutionaries also aimed to unchain their economies by eliminating stifling restrictions on manufacturing and commerce imposed by guilds and governments. Free global trade advanced further with the end of British control of the United States and Spanish control of much of Latin America. During the same period, slavery came under attack as an immoral institution that denied human beings equal rights and prevented a free labor force from developing. As Enlightenment ideas for good government flourished, reformers pushed to replace traditional aristocratic and monarchical privileges with rational codes of law. Free trade and free labor, promoted by enlightened laws and policies, helped bring dramatic changes to the global economy, most notably the unparalleled increase in productivity called the Industrial Revolution.

The Industrial Revolution Begins, 1750–1830

FOCUS What were the main causes of the Industrial Revolution?

Industrialization After 1830

FOCUS How did industrialization spread, and what steps did nations and manufacturers take to meet its challenges?

The Industrial Revolution and the World

FOCUS How did industrialization affect societies in China, South and West Asia, and Africa?

Industry and Society

FOCUS How did industrialization affect people's everyday lives and livelihoods?

The Culture of Industry

FOCUS How did writers and artists respond to the new industrial world?

COUNTERPOINT: African Women and Slave Agriculture

FOCUS What contributions did African women agricultural workers make to industrial development?

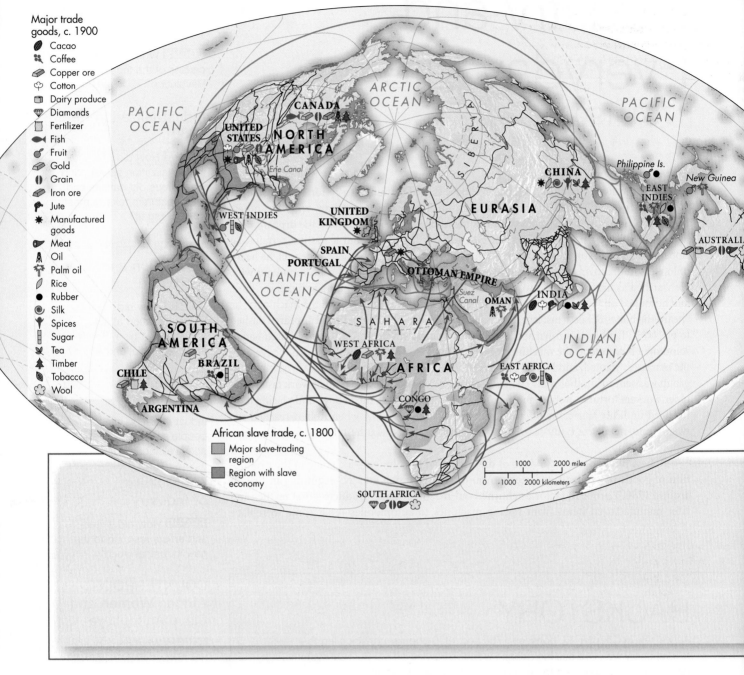

Major trade goods, c. 1900

- Cacao
- Coffee
- Copper ore
- Cotton
- Dairy produce
- Diamonds
- Fertilizer
- Fish
- Fruit
- Gold
- Grain
- Iron ore
- Jute
- Manufactured goods
- Meat
- Oil
- Palm oil
- Rice
- Rubber
- Silk
- Spices
- Sugar
- Tea
- Timber
- Tobacco
- Wool

African slave trade, c. 1800

- Major slave-trading region
- Region with slave economy

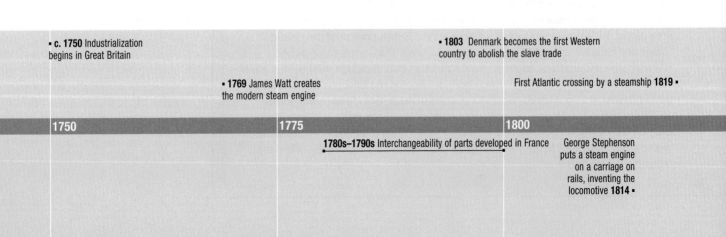

- **c. 1750** Industrialization begins in Great Britain
- **1803** Denmark becomes the first Western country to abolish the slave trade
- **1769** James Watt creates the modern steam engine
- First Atlantic crossing by a steamship **1819**
- **1780s–1790s** Interchangeability of parts developed in France
- George Stephenson puts a steam engine on a carriage on rails, inventing the locomotive **1814**

1750   1775   1800

higher-quality but more expensive artisanal goods. Agriculture continued to dominate the world economy, and farms such as those in Africa, worked largely by women, saw innovations in cultivation and irrigation techniques, as we will see in the Counterpoint to this chapter. In the twentieth century, industry would outstrip agriculture as the leading economic sector and the major source of employment in much of Europe and the United States, and eventually in other parts of the globe.

The Industrial Revolution transformed the livelihoods of tens of millions of people in the nineteenth century in a variety of ways. After his release, Robert Blincoe grabbed at opportunity, setting up a grocery store and even establishing a small factory of his own. The course of industrialization was thus ragged, offering both danger and advantage. Some were driven into factories where conditions were often dangerous and even criminal. Where countries industrialized, a working class arose to tend machines in the factories. These workers' lives were soon strikingly different from those of the artisans with whom they competed. The efficient new weaving machines gave jobs to some, but they impoverished artisans, such as the Indian and European handloom weavers who continued to follow traditional manufacturing methods. Industry also influenced agriculture around the world. Factories consumed more raw materials, and an increasing number of workers in cities no longer grew their own food, depending instead on distant farmers. With the global spread of industry, art, music, philosophy, and political thought echoed the transformation, as writers and painters described this new world in their art and theorists analyzed their new societies. Whether a region had comparatively few factories, as in India and South America, or a dense network of them, as in Britain, patterns of work and everyday life changed—and not always for the better, as Robert Blincoe's case shows.

MAPPING THE WORLD

The Spread of Industrialization

The world remained more agricultural than industrial in 1900. As the twentieth century opened, however, the Industrial Revolution that originated in eighteenth-century Britain was driving industry to ever higher peaks. Among its globally significant consequences was the decline of the slave trade and slavery itself, which had previously greatly increased the world's productivity.

ROUTES ▼

— Major sea trade route, c. 1775

→ African slave trade, to 1860

— Railroad, c. 1914

1839–1842 Opium War between China and Britain

1842 Treaty of Nanjing opens Chinese ports

1868 Meiji Restoration launches Japanese industrialization

1865 U.S. Civil War ends, rapid U.S. industrialization begins

1891–1904 Construction of trans-Siberian railroad

1825	1850	1875	1900

1840s–1864 Taiping Rebellion

1871 Germany gains resource-rich Alsace and Lorraine after defeating France

1848 *Communist Manifesto* published

1873–c. 1900 Deep global recession with uneven recovery

1853 U.S. ships enter Japanese ports

1890s Argentina's leading textile manufacturer produces 1.6 million yards of cloth annually

The Industrial Revolution Begins 1750–1830

FOCUS

What were the main causes of the Industrial Revolution?

The **Industrial Revolution** unfolded first in Britain and western Europe, eventually tipping the balance of global power to favor the West. The coming of mechanization expanded productivity as never before. Many historians believe the only transformation as important was the rise of settled agriculture thousands of years earlier. The Industrial Revolution had global roots, occurring in the context of worldwide trade, economic inventiveness, and agricultural improvement. Although Britain led in industry, the economies of Qing (ching) China and India were larger until almost 1900, when Britain surpassed them in overall productivity. A burning question for historians is how, in a climate of worldwide industriousness, Britain came to the forefront of the great industrial transformation.

The Global Roots of Industrialization

Industriousness and Population Growth

The Industrial Revolution took place amid a surge in productive activity. Industriousness rose, as people worked longer hours and tinkered to find new ways to make goods, developing thousands of new inventions in the process. In Qing China from the mid-1650s to 1800, productivity increased along with population, which soared from 160 million people in 1700 to 350 million in 1800. The dynamic economy improved many people's lifestyles and life expectancy, and encouraged people to work harder to acquire the new products constantly entering the market. Chinese life expectancy increased to the range of 34 to 39 years, longer than almost anywhere else in the world, including western Europe, where in 1800 it was 30 in France and 35 in Britain.

Global Trade

The new global connections created by European expansion into the Americas and Asia contributed to both economic dynamism and population growth. Crops from the Western Hemisphere helped raise the standard of living where they were imported and grown, and awareness of such popular Chinese products as cotton textiles, porcelain, and lacquer ware spread through international trade. Silver flowed into China as Europeans purchased its highly desirable goods. As the nineteenth century opened, Qing China was the most prosperous country on earth.

Europe, in contrast, produced little that was attractive to foreign buyers, and in the seventeenth century warfare, epidemics, and famine reduced its population from 85 million

Industrial Revolution A change in the production of goods that substituted mechanical power for human energy, beginning around 1750 in Britain and western Europe; it vastly increased the world's productivity.

MAP 24.1 **Industrialization in Europe, c. 1900**

Beginning in the workshops of England's tinkerers, industrialization spread across western Europe to Germany and then to Russia. The presence of raw materials such as coal and iron ore sparked industrial development, but so did curiosity and inventiveness. Sweden, for example, lacks mineral resources, so its people harnessed water power to develop electricity. Industrialization would remain uneven into the twenty-first century, however, and this imbalance often led to deadly political conflict.

to 80 million. After 1700, however, Europe's population surged, more than doubling by 1800, thanks to global trade that introduced nutritious foods and other useful goods. Population growth put pressure on British energy resources, especially fuel and food. With their populations rising rapidly, both Britain and China faced the limits of artisanal productivity and natural resources. The Industrial Revolution allowed the British to be the first to surpass those limits (see Map 24.1).

Great Britain: A Culture of Experimentation

Why did the Industrial Revolution happen when it did, and why did it happen in Britain first? After all, many regions have the coal, iron deposits, and other resources that allowed the British to make and power the first modern machines. Moreover, bursts of economic innovation have occurred at many times and in many places.

It was not just resources, however, that propelled Britain to the industrial forefront. As we saw in Chapter 20, the Scientific Revolution had fostered both new reliance on direct observation and deep curiosity about the world. Before the rise of industry, the British and other Europeans traveled the globe, which exposed them to technological developments from other societies. From China, for example, they learned about such implements as seed drills and winnowing machines to process grain. Publications like the *Encyclopedia*, composed in France during the Enlightenment and widely read in Europe (see Chapter 23), included mechanical designs from around the world, making them available to a public increasingly eager to tinker and experiment. Global trade and exchange, the Scientific Revolution, and the Enlightenment thus formed the backdrop for the Industrial Revolution. The massive expansion in productivity was initially not about theoretical science, however, but about trial and error—which especially flourished in Britain.

Artisans and Tinkerers

British artisans produced some of the early machinery of the Industrial Revolution. Britain had a particularly well-developed culture of experimentation and, as its population grew, the country's curious and industrious craftspeople worked to supply the surging population, to meet the shortage in energy due to declining wood supplies, and to devise products that the world might want to buy. "The age," wrote critic Samuel Johnson, "is running mad after innovation."[3] From aristocrats to artisans, the British latched onto news of successful experiments both at home and abroad. They tinkered with air pumps, clocks, and telescopes. European craftspeople worked hard to copy the new goods imported from China, India, and other countries. From the sixteenth century on, for example, European consumers bought hundreds of thousands of foreign porcelain pieces, leading would-be manufacturers in the Netherlands, France, and the German states to try to figure out the process of porcelain production. They finally succeeded early in the 1700s. Despite inventive activity across Europe, it was England that soon pulled ahead (see Reading the Past: Industry Comes to the British Countryside).

Wedgwood China

Josiah Wedgwood, the eighteenth-century English potter-turned-industrialist who founded a company still prosperous today, worked day and night to figure out the ingredients, formulas, and processes necessary to make "china"—that is, inexpensive, heat-resistant dishware patterned after China's renowned but costly and fragile porcelain. Wedgwood copied designs from around the world to brighten his dishware, but he is best known for his "Wedgwood blue" products, which were directly inspired by China's famed blue-and-white patterns. In this 1810 example, Wedgwood designers had fashioned a product that could compete with Chinese manufactures in the global marketplace. (Cotehele House, Cornwall, UK/Bridgeman Art Library.)

One English innovator who stands out is Josiah Wedgwood (1730–1795), founder of the Wedgwood dishware firm that still exists. Wedgwood developed a range of new processes, colors, and designs, expanding his business and making it a model for large-scale production. He grew up in a family that produced rough, traditional kinds of pottery on a very small scale. As a poor, younger son with an inquisitive mind, he used his bent for experimentation to devise many different types of ceramics. Helped by his wife and by the personal wealth she invested in the company, Wedgwood kept meticulous records of his five thousand experiments with "china" (so called because Chinese porcelain set the standard for ceramic production). He traveled widely in Britain, his agents searched the world for the right grade of clay to compete with Asian products, and he copied Asian designs unashamedly. Hence, in Wedgwood, the distinctive British culture of artisanal experimentation came together with the materials and inspiration provided by new global connections; the result was industrial innovation.

Life was not always easy for Wedgwood: an accident on a business trip eventually required that his leg be amputated. This setback only made him more determined to succeed. Born into poverty, he became the acclaimed manufacturer of fine dishes for British monarchs and for Catherine the Great of Russia, and he died one of the wealthiest men in his country. Wedgwood's fortune and spirit of experimentation passed down to his grandson Charles Darwin, who proposed the theory of evolution.

World Trade and the Rise of Industry

Global shipping, developed over three centuries, became ever more central to industrial progress in the eighteenth and nineteenth centuries. As population rose in Europe and as England, France, and other European countries

READING THE PAST

Industry Comes to the British Countryside

Industrialization transformed the human landscape and natural environment. In this passage from a promotional brochure, George Perry, co-owner of an ironworks in Coalbrookdale, England, describes how industrialization had changed the town by 1758. Dozens of travelers through the British countryside made similar observations as they noted the rise of industry in the eighteenth and nineteenth centuries and its complicated effects.

In the year One Thousand Seven Hundred, the whole Village consisted of only One furnace, Five Dwelling Houses, and a Forge or two. About Forty years ago the present Iron-foundry was establish'd, and since that time its Trade and Buildings are so far increas'd that it contains at least Four Hundred and Fifty inhabitants, and finds employment for more than Five Hundred People, including all the several Occupations that are connected with the Works. . . .

THIS place affords a number of delightful prospects. . . . Some of the Hills are cover'd with Verdure [greenery], others overgrown with Wood, and some again are naked and barren. These, with a View of a fine fertile Country, Water'd by the Severn [River], all contribute to form as agreeable a Variety to the Eye, as can well be conceiv'd. The Beauty of the scene is in the meantime greatly increas'd by a new view of the Dale itself. Pillars of Flame and smoke rising to vast height,

large Reservoirs of Water, and a number of Engines in motion, never fail to raise the admiration of strangers, tho' it must be confess'd these things join'd to the murmuring of the Waterfalls, the noise of the Machines, and the roaring of the Furnaces, are apt to occasion a kind of Horror in those who happen to arrive in a dark Night. UPON the whole, there are perhaps few Places where rural prospects, and Scenes of hurry and Business are so happily united as at COALBROOKDALE.

Source: Prospectus for "A View of the Upperworks of Coalbrook Dale" (1758) by George Perry. Quoted in Sally and David Dugan, *The Day the World Took Off: The Roots of the Industrial Revolution* (London: Macmillan, 2000), 44.

EXAMINING THE EVIDENCE

1. What is Perry's opinion of the industrial world in which he lives?
2. How might other people have viewed the industrial landscape differently?
3. Compare Perry's observations of Coalbrookdale with the story of Robert Blincoe that opens this chapter. Which do you think more accurately describes the effects of industrialization, and why?

fought wars worldwide over trade, they needed more resources to supply people at home and far-flung armies and navies. To supply industry and feed the growing number of urban workers, global shipping brought grain from North America, wood from Canada and Russia, cotton from Egypt and the United States, and eventually meat from Australia. Imports and Europe's own produce fed urban workers. Foreign commodities such as tea, coffee, chocolate, and opium derivatives, which the lower classes were just coming to use in the nineteenth century, helped them endure the rigors of industry. Thus, dense global trade networks and raw materials produced by workers from around the world were critical to the Industrial Revolution.

Slaves produced many elements crucial to industrial success. Eleven million Africans captured on the continent were sold into slavery in the Americas, raising capital to invest in commerce and industry. The slaves themselves produced low-cost agricultural products such as sugar and rice that enriched global traders and provided critical components in Atlantic trade networks (see Counterpoint: African Women and Slave Agriculture). Cheaper foodstuffs cut the expenses of factory owners, who justified low wages by pointing out that working families' costs had decreased. To clothe their slaves, wealthy African and American owners bought inexpensive factory-made textiles pumped out by British machines. In the northern United States, slave ironworkers were put to work building the metallurgical business, and in the Western Hemisphere generally slaves' skills played a crucial role in producing copper and tin for factory use. They also worked to produce raw materials such as cotton. Had free labor alone been used in these processes, some historians believe, the higher cost of raw materials and food would have slowed development of global trade and the pace of experiments with factories and machines.

Slavery and Industry

The Technology of Industry

Mechanizing Textile Production

New technology was a final ingredient in the effort to meet the needs of a growing and increasingly interconnected population. In the eighteenth century, clever British inventors devised tools such as the flying shuttle (1733) to speed the weaving of textiles by individuals working at home. This, in turn, led to improvements in spinning to meet the increased demand for thread created by more efficient weavers. The spinning jenny, invented in about 1765 by craftsman James Hargreaves and named, it is said, after his wife or daughter, allowed an individual worker, using just the power of her hand, to spin not one bobbin of thread, but up to 120 at once. At about the same time, Richard Arkwright and partners invented the water frame, another kind of spinning machine that used water power. When hand-driven spinning machines could be linked to a central power source such as water, many could be placed in a single building. Thus, the world's first factories arose from the pressure to increase production of English cloth for the growing global market.

The Steam Engine Breakthrough

Still another, even more important breakthrough arose when steam engines were harnessed to both spinning and weaving machines. Steam engines could power a vast number of machines, which drew more people out of home textile production and into factories. Almost two thousand people worked in the British factories of Richard Arkwright alone. Although born in poverty, by the time of his death in 1792, Arkwright was a wealthy man who owned mills across England and Scotland. Industrial spies infiltrated these factories and sent their mechanical and organizational secrets to businessmen in Belgium, northern France, the United States, and elsewhere. The most dramatic innovation in European textiles was thus the adaptation of mechanized spinning and weaving machines to the mass production of cheap cotton, which in turn clothed a swelling global workforce.

The steam engine proved to be a pivotal piece of technology not just for textiles, but for the Industrial Revolution as a whole. It was used first in the gold and silver mining industry, then in textile production, and finally in driving trains and steamboats. The steam engine had been invented earlier in China, and was used there and elsewhere to pump water from mines. It was improved throughout the eighteenth century in Britain. In 1765, James Watt, a Scottish craftsman, figured out how to make the steam engine more practical, fuel-efficient, and powerful—"Cheap as well as good" was how he put it.[4] A slew of ideas for using and improving the engine followed, and in 1814, British engineer George Stephenson placed the machine in a carriage on rails, inventing the locomotive. The first steam-powered ship crossed the Atlantic soon after, in 1819.

Interchangeability of Parts

The **interchangeability of parts** was a final critical aspect of the Industrial Revolution. The many wars Europeans fought over global trade and influence in the eighteenth and early nineteenth centuries produced incredible demand for less expensive weapons and more of them. By 1790 French gunsmith Honoré Blanc, experimenting with tools and gauges, had produced guns with fully interchangeable parts. This lowered the cost per weapon and made repair possible for merchants and soldiers based in any part of the world. The goal was to "assure uniformity [of output], acceleration of work, and economy of price," as a government official in charge of weaponry put it in 1781.[5] By the early nineteenth century Blanc was producing 10,000 muskets a year. The idea of interchangeability in weaponry and machinery was crucial to the unfolding Industrial Revolution.

Industrialization After 1830

FOCUS

How did industrialization spread, and what steps did nations and manufacturers take to meet its challenges?

One striking feature of industrialization is its spread within countries, across regions, and around the world. Although threatened workers and fearful rulers have from time to time resisted industrialization, it has proved impossible to stop. Industrialization brings ongoing efficiencies, which have proven important to meet the needs of a growing global population. From its birth in England and western Europe, entrepreneurs across the continent advanced the industrial system, as did innovators in the United States. Japan did not

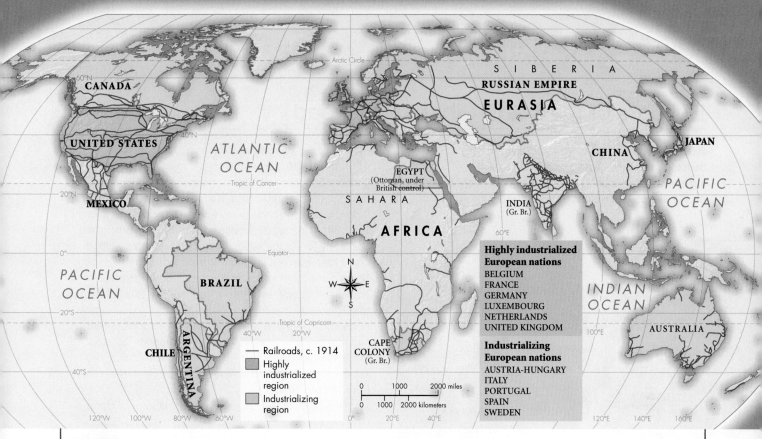

MAP 24.2

The Spread of Railroads, c. 1900

The spread of railroads throughout the world fostered industrialization because it required tracks, engines and railroad cars, and railway stations, which were increasingly made of iron, steel, and glass. Railroads generated economic growth beyond the building of trains and tracks, however. Entire cities grew up around railroad hubs, which attracted new migrants—not just hard-working builders but also professionals and service workers to fill the needs of the growing population. Railroads transported goods, turned handsome profits, promoted the fantasy world of tourism and travel, and almost immediately made warfare faster paced and more lethal.

industrialize until after 1870, but then it embraced technology enthusiastically. In many other countries, some enterprising individuals started factories, but full-scale industrialization across regions usually came later (see Map 24.2). Outside of Europe and the United States thorough industrialization generally did not develop until the twentieth century. Even though industry developed unevenly in different places, it affected the wider world by increasing demand for raw materials and creating new livelihoods.

Industrial Innovation Gathers Speed

By the end of the eighteenth century, entrepreneurs from the United States and across Europe joined British innovators, and the nineteenth century was one of widespread industrial, technological, and commercial innovation. Steam engines moved inexpensive manufactured goods on a growing network of railroads and shipping lanes, creating a host of new jobs outside of factory work (see Lives and Livelihoods: Builders of the Trans-Siberian Railroad). Around railroad hubs, for example, towns and cities filled with railroad and other workers who needed manufactured and agricultural goods. An increasing number of stores sold a soaring variety of products, ranging from the lowly cherry pitter to the reaping machine and bicycle, all of them proof of snowballing innovation in the nineteenth century.

Although independent craftsmen-tinkerers created the first machines, such as the spinning jenny and water frame, sophisticated engineers were more critical to later revolutionary technologies. In 1885 the German engineer Karl Benz devised a workable gasoline

interchangeability of parts
A late-eighteenth-century technological breakthrough in which machine and implement parts were standardized, allowing for mass production and easy repair.

Builders of the Trans-Siberian Railroad

Axes, saws, and wheelbarrows—these were the tools that built the greatest railway project ever undertaken. Stretching across Siberia from Moscow in the west to Vladivostok on the Sea of Japan (see again Map 24.2), the scale of the

Convict Railroad Workers in Siberia, 1895
The tsarist government of Russia mobilized hundreds of thousands of workers to build the trans-Siberian railroad, the main line of which took thirteen years (1891–1904) to complete. Convicts provided essential manpower, and this image shows their housing and conditions of life. The labor entailed moving mountains of soil and rock and bringing in lumber and iron track, all without benefit of machinery and in the harsh Siberian climate. (Corbis.)

trans-Siberian railroad was enormous by any measure: miles laid (5700), earth moved (100 million cubic yards), rail installed (more than 100 million tons), and bridges and tunnels constructed (60 miles). Because this remote wilderness lacked roads, the endeavor was difficult and expensive. Except for lumber, all supplies needed to be transported. Cut stone for bridge supports and gravel for the railbed came from quarries sometimes hundreds of miles away. Ships carried steel parts for bridges thousands of miles across the seas, from Odessa on the Black Sea to Vladivostok. They were then moved inland. In winter horse-drawn sleds and in summer horse-drawn wagons transported material to the work sites. Cut through forests, blasted through rock, raised over rivers and swampy lands, the project was completed in nine sections over thirteen years from 1891 to 1904.

Hundreds of thousands of manual laborers did the work. At the height of its construction, the trans-Siberian employed as many as ninety thousand workers on each of its original nine sections. Many were recruited by contractors who scoured Russian cities and villages for hefty men. Prisoners and soldiers were forced to work on the project. Around the large work sites, the army and police stood guard to prevent disruption as the grueling, dangerous labor progressed. The government set up state liquor stores near work camps to appease laborers in their off-hours.

Doing the job quickly and cheaply was the government's top priority. Worker safety was of little concern, and casualties were many among the unskilled workforce. Cutting through forests to lay rail and dynamiting through hills to construct tunnels took thousands of lives. The anonymous dead lived on only in poetry:

The New Inventors: Engineers

engine, and six years later France's Armand Peugeot constructed the first automobile. Benz produced his first car two years later in 1893. After 1880, electricity became more available, providing power to light everything from private homes to government office buildings. The Eiffel Tower in Paris, constructed for the International Exhibit of 1889 and for decades the tallest structure in the world, was a monument to the age's engineering wizardry; visitors rode to its summit in electric elevators. In 1900 the tower's system of electric lights dazzled nighttime strollers.

Innovations in Machinery and Chemicals

To fuel this explosive growth, the leading industrial nations mined and produced massive quantities of coal, iron, and steel during the second half of the century. Output by the major European iron producers increased from 11 million to 23 million tons in the 1870s and 1880s alone. Steel output grew just as impressively in the same decades, from half a million to 11 million tons. Manufacturers used the metal to build more than 100,000 locomotives that pulled trains, transporting 2 billion people annually.

Historians sometimes contrast two periods of the Industrial Revolution. In the first, in the eighteenth and early nineteenth centuries, innovations in textile machinery

The way is straight, the embankment narrow,

Telegraph poles, rails, bridges,

And everywhere on both sides are Russian bones—...

Brothers! You remember our reward!

Fated to be strewn in the earth.[1]

The only apparent safety precaution was forbidding prisoners to work with explosives.

Other kinds of livelihoods developed around the railroad: its planning and design preoccupied Russia's ablest engineers, and the skilled aspects of its construction attracted stonemasons and other master builders from foreign lands. Financiers from around the world and producers of raw materials from as far away as the United States participated as well. Construction began in May 1891 when Nicholas, heir to the Russian throne, drove the first golden spike into the ground at Vladivostok.

Minister of Finance Sergei Witte maintained that the railroad would make Russia the dominant global market in the world: "The silk, tea, and fur trade for Europe, and the manufacturing and other trade for the Far East, will likely be concentrated in Moscow, which will become the hub of the world's transit movement," he predicted.[2] Long after the line's completion the trans-Siberian railroad provided good jobs for railway workers in Siberia. In settlements along the rail line, business thrived, and cities such as Novisibersk opened scores of new opportunities for service workers supporting railroad personnel.

The trans-Siberian railroad did indeed transform the livelihoods of the empire as a whole. The government sent some 5 million peasants from western Russia to Siberia between 1890 and 1914. The massive migration was intended to extend Russian power across the empire's vast expanse. The government designated millions of acres of land—populated at the time by the nomadic Asian foragers and herders—for Russian, Ukrainian, and Belorussian settlers. Russian bureaucrats hoped that as the peasants intermingled with indigenous peoples, the non-Russian ethnic groups would become "Russianized." They thus justified occupation on grounds similar to those the U.S. government used to justify white settlers' migration westward and takeover of American Indian lands. The completion of the longest railroad line in the world meant that hundreds of nomadic tribes lost hunting lands and pasturage that were the basis of their livelihoods, and the population of Siberia soared with the influx of farmers. Russia would never be the same.

1. Nicholai Nekrasov, quoted in J. N. Westwood, *A History of the Russian Railways* (London: George Allen and Unwin, 1964), 33.
2. Quoted in Stephen G. Marks, *Road to Power: The Trans-Siberian Railroad and the Colonization of Asian Russia, 1850–1917* (London: I. B. Tauris, 1991), 117.

QUESTIONS TO CONSIDER

1. What jobs were needed to construct the trans-Siberian railroad, and how were workers treated?

2. How did the railroad affect livelihoods other than those directly connected with its construction?

3. How would you balance the human costs of building the railroad with the human opportunities it created?

4. What changes did the trans-Siberian railroad bring to Russia?

powered by steam energy predominated. The second, in the later nineteenth century, concentrated on heavy industrial products and electrical and oil power. This was indeed the pattern in Britain, but as other areas industrialized, textile factories and blast furnaces were built simultaneously. Moreover, the number of small workshops grew faster than the number of factories, though factories dominated production. Although industrialization reduced household production in traditional crafts such as weaving, livelihoods pursued at home—called **outwork**—persisted in garment making, metalwork, and such "finishing trades" as metal polishing. In fact, factory production fostered "industriousness" more than ever, and factory, small workshop, and home enterprise have coexisted down to the present.

Industrial innovations in machinery and chemicals also transformed agriculture. Chemical fertilizers boosted crop yields, and reapers and threshers mechanized harvesting. In the 1870s, Sweden produced a cream separator, a first step toward mechanizing dairy farming. Wire fencing and barbed wire replaced more labor-intensive wooden fencing and stone walls, allowing large-scale cattle-raising. Refrigerated railroad cars and

outwork A method of manufacturing in which raw or semifinished materials are distributed to households where they are further processed or completed.

steamships, developed between the 1840s and 1870 in several countries, allowed fruits, vegetables, dairy products, and meat to be transported without spoiling, increasing the size and diversity of the urban food supply.

Challenge to British Dominance

Although Great Britain maintained its high industrial output throughout the second half of the 1800s and profited from a multitude of worldwide investments, other countries began to narrow Britain's industrial advantage. The United States industrialized rapidly after its Civil War (discussed in Chapter 25) ended in 1865, and Japan joined in after 1870. Argentina, Brazil, Chile, and Mexico gained industries at varying rates between 1870 and 1914, producing textiles, beer, soap, cigarettes, and an array of other products. In Argentina, the introduction of cigarette-rolling machinery allowed the National Tobacco Company's twenty-eight hundred workers to turn out four hundred thousand cigarettes per day by the end of the 1890s. In the same decade, its leading textile company produced 1.6 million yards of cloth annually. Industry—if not full-scale industrialization—circled the globe.

Germany   Two countries in particular began to surpass Britain in research, technical education, innovation, and growth rates: Germany and the United States. Germany's burst of industrial energy occurred after its states unified as a result of the Franco-Prussian War of 1870–1871 (discussed in Chapter 25). At this time, Germany took the French territories of Alsace and Lorraine with their textile industries, mineral deposits, and metallurgical factories. Investing heavily in research, German businesses began to mass-produce goods such as railroad stock and weapons, which other countries had pioneered in manufacturing. Germany also spent as much money on education as on its military in the 1870s and 1880s, producing highly skilled engineers and technical workers who made Germany's electrical and chemical engineering capabilities soar.

The United States   After its Civil War, the United States began to exploit its vast natural resources intensively, including coal, ores, gold, and oil. The value of U.S. industrial goods vaulted from $5 billion in 1880 to $13 billion in 1900. Whereas German accomplishments relied heavily on state promotion of industrial efforts, U.S. growth depended on innovative individuals, such as Andrew Carnegie in iron and steel and John D. Rockefeller in oil. As the nineteenth century came to a close, then, Britain struggled to keep ahead of its industrial competitors.

Industrialization in Japan

Foundation of Industriousness   Between 1750 and 1850 merchants, peasant producers, artisans, and even samurai warriors laid the foundation for Japan's industrialization. They engaged in brisk commerce, especially with the East and Southeast Asian mainland. Japan exported its sophisticated pottery—some 2 million pieces to Southeast Asia alone in the first decade of the nineteenth century—and it imported books, clocks, and small precision implements, especially from China. Internal trade increased too. Businessmen and farmers produced sake, silk, paper, and other commodities required by Japan's vast network of regional lords, the daimyo, and their retainers, the samurai. By law, the daimyo traveled from their own lands to the court at Edo for long periods every year, and they spent lavishly to support the travels of their large entourages. Japan's roads were clogged with traffic in people and goods (see Seeing the Past: Japan's Industrious Society).

The samurai of this era were what we might describe today as underemployed. After two centuries of peace under the Tokugawa Shogunate (see Chapter 21), there were many more samurai than the country needed for administration and defense. To occupy their time, some samurai studied the new findings in the botany, chemistry, and engineering coming from China and Europe. They experimented with electricity, created important devices such as thermometers that helped improve silkworm breeding, and awaited Dutch ships in the port of Nagasaki with their information from around the world. Craft-based innovation produced new kinds of seeds, new varieties of silkworms, and improvements

Japan's Industrious Society

Hiroshige, *Nihon-bashi,* from the series, *Fifty-three Stations on the Tokaido* (Road to Tokyo) (Brooklyn Museum/Corbis.)

Famed Japanese artist Ando Hiroshige (1797–1858) is best known for his prints of nature and for his several series about work life in early-nineteenth-century Japan. In these works, Hiroshige combined his great print-making skills with knowledge of Dutch and other Western art. The exchange went both ways, as Western artists borrowed from Hiroshige in return. Impressionists were especially drawn to his focus on daily life and his vibrant use of color. Later, Hiroshige's serial method and drawing technique influenced the creators of comic strips.

Hiroshige depicted the many livelihoods of Japan in some of his works. In particular he showed commercial life on the road to Edo (now Tokyo), the capital of Japan, before it industrialized. The road is clogged with busy people loaded with goods and supplies. Collectively, Hiroshige's drawings show a remarkably active commercial and

productive life, demonstrating the prevailing view among historians today that many parts of the world enjoyed "industrious" economies in the seventeenth through the nineteenth centuries that laid the essential groundwork for full industrialization.

EXAMINING THE EVIDENCE

1. What attitude toward work comes through in this print?

2. How does it contrast with the attitude displayed in the document on pages 815 and 816 by Mexican women workers?

in their already highly technical looms. The inventive Japanese were more than ready to take advantage of Western machinery when the opportunity arose.

Merchants were also an economic force. As in Europe they supplied peasant families with looms and other machines for spinning and weaving at home. Under the Tokugawa regime, production was labor-intensive, and government encouraged these impressive levels of industriousness. Notable innovations took place in cotton and silk production and in manufacturing goods such as coins from precious metal, but output was limited. Japanese innovators aimed to replace this system with Western-style factory or mass production, beginning with textiles, guns, railroads, and steamships. It had become clear that, as one Japanese administrator wrote in 1868, "machinery is the basis of wealth."[6]

The final motive for change was concern about Western ships seeking access to Japanese ports and trade. Seeing outsiders as potential agents of social and political unrest, the Japanese had long restricted the flow of foreigners into the country. In the nineteenth century, however, they experienced for themselves the inroads they had seen Westerners make in China during the Opium War (discussed later in this chapter). In 1853 Commodore Matthew Perry steamed into Edo (now Tokyo) Bay and demanded diplomatic negotiations with the emperor. Some samurai urged resistance, but senior officials knew how defenseless the city would be against naval bombardment. The next year Perry signed an agreement on behalf of the United States under which Japan would open its ports on a regular basis.

Turn to Industry

Both individual Japanese and the government adjusted rapidly to the presence of these competitors. They were motivated in good part by the desire to learn the skills that would allow them to protect Japan through industrial prosperity and military strength. Inventors adapted European mechanical designs, using the country's wealth of skilled workers to make everything from steam engines to telegraph machines. The state sent delegations to Europe and the United States with the goal of "swiftly seizing upon the strengths of the Western industrial arts," as the minister of industry wrote in 1873.[7] By the early 1870s the reformed central government known as the Meiji Restoration (see Chapter 25) had overseen the laying of thousands of miles of railroad and telegraph lines, and by the early twentieth century the country had some 32,000 factories, many of them small; 5400 steam engines; and 2700 machines run by electricity. Although it is often said that Japan industrialized at state direction, a more accurate picture shows an effective mixture of state, local, and individual initiatives based on a foundation of industriousness. This combination eventually led to Japan's central role in the world economy.

Industrializing Japan, c. 1870–1900

Economic Crises and Solutions

Industry and the expansion of the global economy brought uneven prosperity to the world and seesawing booms and busts, especially in the second half of the nineteenth century. Because global trade bound industrialized western Europe to international markets, a recession—by today's definition, a period of negative economic growth lasting six months or longer—could simultaneously affect the economies of such diverse regions as Germany, Australia, South Africa, California, Argentina, Newfoundland, and the West Indies. At the time, economists, industrialists, and government officials did not clearly understand the workings of industrial and interconnected economies. When a stubborn recession struck in the 1870s and lasted in some places until the end of the century, they were stunned.

Late-Nineteenth-Century Recession

One reason for the recession of the 1870s was the skyrocketing start-up costs of new enterprises. Compared to steel and iron factories, the earliest textile mills had required little capital. After midcentury, industries became what modern economists call capital-intensive rather than labor-intensive: to grow, companies had to buy expensive machinery, not just hire more workers. This was especially true in developing countries such as those in Latin America, where the need to import machinery and hire foreign technicians added to costs.

Second, increased productivity in both agriculture and industry led to rapid price declines. Improved transportation allowed the expanding production of meat and grain in the United States, Australia, and Argentina to reach distant global markets rapidly, driving down prices. Wheat, for example, dropped to one-third its 1870 price by the 1890s. Consumers, however, did not always benefit from this persistent decrease in prices, or deflation, because employers slashed wages and unemployment rose during economic downturns. When this occurred, consumers just stopped purchasing manufactured goods.

Thus, a third major reason for the recession was underconsumption of manufactured products. Industrialists had made their fortunes by emphasizing production, not consumption. "Let the producers be many," went a Japanese saying, "and the consumers be few."[8] This attitude was disastrous because many goods were not sold, and the result was that prices for raw materials collapsed globally. People lost their land, jobs, and businesses, with consequences ranging from long stretches of unemployment to bankruptcy.

Governments and
Businesses Respond

In response to these conditions, governments around the world took action to boost consumption and control markets and prices. New laws protected innovation through more secure patents and spurred development of the limited-liability corporation, which protected investors from personal responsibility, or liability, for a firm's debt. **Limited liability** greatly increased investor confidence in financing business ventures. As prices fell in the 1870s and 1880s, governments broke any commitments they had made to free trade. They imposed tariffs (taxes) on imported agricultural and manufactured goods to boost sales of domestic products. Latin American countries levied tariffs that were some five times those in Europe. Without this protection from cheap European goods, a Mexican official predicted, new industries would "be annihilated by foreign competition."[9]

Business people also took steps to end the economic turmoil. They advanced the development of **stock markets**, which financed the growth of industry by selling shares or part ownership in companies to individual shareholders. In an international economy linked by telegraph, telephone, railways, and steamships, the London Stock Exchange was a center of this financial activity. In 1882 it traded industrial shares worth £54 million, a value that surged to £443 million by 1900, dramatically increasing the capital individuals made available to industry. At the same time, firms in single industries banded together in **cartels** to control prices and competition. One German coal cartel founded in 1893 dominated more than 95 percent of coal production in Germany. Thus, business owners deliberately blocked open competition to ensure profitability and economic stability.

Rise of Managers
and the "White-Collar"
Service Sector

Another way to address the economic crisis was to add managerial expertise. In the late 1800s, industrialists began to hire others to run their increasingly complex day-to-day operations, which was a revolutionary change in business practices. A generation and more earlier, factory owners such as Richard Arkwright had been directly involved in every aspect of the business and often ran their firms through trial and error. Now, separate managers specializing in sales and distribution, finance, and purchasing made decisions. The rise of the manager was part of the emergence of a "white-collar" service sector of office workers, with managers (generally male) at the high end of the pay scale and secretaries, file clerks, and typists (increasingly female) at the low end. These office workers were essential to guide the flow of business information that managers needed to make profits. Banks needed tellers and clerks, just as railroads, insurance companies, and government-run telegraph and telephone companies needed armies of white-collar employees.

The Department Store

A final solution to the economic crisis was the development of consumer capitalism, sparked by the recognition that underconsumption of manufactured goods had directly led to the late-nineteenth-century recession. The principal institution for boosting consumption was the department store, which daring entrepreneurs founded after midcentury to promote sales of manufactured products. Department stores gathered an impressive variety of goods in one place, in imitation of the Middle Eastern bazaar and the large Asian merchant houses, and they eventually replaced many of the single-item stores to which people were accustomed. Buenos Aires alone had seven major department stores, among them Gath y Chaves (GOT e shah-VEZ), which by 1900 had grown to occupy a multistoried building of 13,000-plus square feet, and which tripled its space five years later. From the Mitsui family in Tokyo to the Bloomingdales in New York, entrepreneurs set up institutions for mass consumerism, and some, such as Harrods of London, established branches around the world.

Just as factories led workers to greater productivity, these modern palaces aimed to stimulate more consumer purchases. Luxury items like plush rugs and ornate draperies spilled over railings in glamorous disarray. Shoppers no longer bargained over prices; instead they reacted to sales, a new marketing technique that could incite a buying frenzy. Department stores also launched their own industrial ventures to meet consumer needs: Gath y Chaves began a line of ready-to-wear clothing, recognizing that busy urban workers no longer had time to make their own. Women explained their often lengthy trips to these stores as necessary to a healthy home and family life. Stores hired attractive salesgirls, another variety of service worker, to lure customers to buy. Shopping was not only an urban phenomenon: glossy mail-order catalogs from the Bon Marché in Paris and Sears, Roebuck in the United States arrived regularly in rural areas to help farmers buy the products

limited liability Legal protection for investors from personal responsibility for a firm's finances.

stock market A site for buying and selling financial interests, or stock, in businesses; examples include the London and Hong Kong stock exchanges.

cartel A group of independent business organizations in a single industry formed to control production and prices.

Gath y Chaves Department Store

The first department stores, such as this one in Buenos Aires, Argentina, were built to resemble palaces and present the possibility of luxury to everyone. Shoppers could walk on lush carpets, climb stately marble staircases, and purchase or imagine buying the items displayed from around the world. By assembling an array of goods once sold in individual small stores, the department store was revolutionary because it focused on increasing consumption rather than driving production, as industry had done. The first department stores were the direct ancestors of today's megastores and Internet shopping.

of industry. Thus, department stores were both commercial crossroads where urban shoppers could purchase a wide variety of manufactured goods from around the world and a means of connecting otherwise isolated rural consumers to the industrial marketplace.

The Industrial Revolution and the World

FOCUS

How did industrialization affect societies in China, South and West Asia, and Africa?

The Industrial Revolution transformed life in many parts of the world, even those with few factories of their own. Increased industrial development caused hardships for economies outside the West, eventually tipping trade balances and ultimately political power. The once-dominant economies of China, India, and the Ottoman Empire declined due to the Industrial Revolution, despite the real wealth that some local merchants, landowners, and entrepreneurs created for themselves. The Industrial Revolution allowed Western nations to pull ahead of these former world leaders.

Western nations used their powerful and increasingly reliable weaponry to open trade. Like Japan, other nations in the early nineteenth century were often unwilling to trade with Europe, which was widely seen as both uncivilized and a source of inferior goods. Even an English man, commenting on the high quality of a shawl from India, agreed, "I have never seen a European shawl I would use, even if it were given to me as a present."[10] This attitude, common not just in England but around the world, led Europeans and Americans alike to use threats of violence to open markets. Europe's immense industrial productivity demanded outlets for manufactured goods, its factories needed raw materials, and its growing population of industrial workers depended on foreign food and stimulants.

Reaction abroad to these demands and needs was mixed. Some governments, merchants, and producers around the world saw that there was money to be made from trading in Western products, setting up their own factories, and adopting technology. Others saw only danger to local artisanal economies and to the political status quo. In the long run, the rise of industry changed lives and livelihoods everywhere, not only because of the interconnected economic consequences of rising productivity, but because the industrialized West was willing to use violence to gain access to raw materials and to open new markets for manufactured goods.

The Slow Disintegration of Qing China

At the beginning of the industrial era, Qing China was the wealthiest and most productive country in the world, its prosperity built on the silver that flooded China in exchange for its cottons, porcelains, and other coveted items (see Map 24.3). Yet the Qing Empire was facing difficult problems, and the Industrial Revolution only compounded them. Revolutionary upheavals in North and South America and the Napoleonic Wars in France suddenly stopped the flow of silver and curtailed trade, eating away at the source of China's wealth and strangling job opportunities. On world markets, cheap industrial European goods competed with Chinese products, and social unrest erupted among the affected workers. Commercial rivalry soon turned to war.

Europeans had grown dependent on a variety of products from India and China, especially tea. The five chests of tea Europeans had purchased annually in the 1680s had soared to more than 23 million pounds by 1800. At the time this meant a severe trade imbalance for Europe, whose cheap but inferior textiles did not appeal to the Indians and Chinese.

By the 1820s, however, the British had found something the Chinese would buy—opium. Grown legally in British-controlled India, opium was smuggled into China, where its import and sale were illegal. So great was the demand for opium in China that even after buying tea the British merchants and smugglers turned a handsome profit. China's big payout in silver caused a drain on its economy, and Chinese officials worried that opium use was out of control. A Chinese government official charged with ending the illegal trade commanded the British to turn over all the opium they possessed; he burned what they surrendered. Determined to force opium on the Chinese, the British sent a fleet to China to keep the opium market open.

In the Opium War (1839–1842) that followed, Western firepower won decisive victories, and with the 1842 Treaty of Nanjing, China agreed to pay the British an indemnity (or fine), allow British diplomats access to the country, open five ports to trade, and reduce tariffs (see again Map 24.3). The treaty shifted power to Europeans, forcing the Chinese to deal with them as full trading partners and respected diplomats. The opium trade was legalized, making fortunes for British merchants and paving the way for other goods to enter China.

The Opium War

The Opium War made life difficult for Chinese workers. During the conflict, many lost their jobs as dockworkers, tea exporters, and commercial agents. A severe depression followed the war's end, and floods and famines between 1846 and 1848 compounded the hardships. In the late 1840s peasant religious leader Hong Xiuquan (hung she-o-chew-on) built a following among the underemployed and unemployed. Hong had failed to get the career he desperately wanted—a place in the prestigious Chinese civil service. He first tried to pass the nationwide civil service exam in 1836, and like others flunked this initial try. As Hong failed successive attempts to pass the exam, he fell feverishly ill and had religious visions that convinced him he was the brother of Jesus.

By 1850, his charismatic preaching of his version of Christianity had attracted some 20,000 disciples. Hong's social message promised a better future: he promoted work for all, equality of the sexes, and communal living, which appealed to hard-pressed ordinary people. It emphasized industriousness: "The diligent husbandman will be rewarded and the idle husbandman punished."[11] Like some of the Christian missionaries infiltrating China, Hong asked his followers to give up alcohol and opium and reject oppressive customs such as foot binding as first steps toward a more prosperous future. Hong's movement envisioned a perfect society—the Heavenly Kingdom of Peace, or Taiping Tianguo—and it began to move in vast armies across the country, ultimately gathering millions of adherents.

MAP 24.3

Qing China, 1830–1911

Qing officials knew that opium was dragging China's people into addiction, but the resulting Opium War with Britain to restrict the supply only made matters worse. Led by the British, Europeans forced open Chinese ports, destroyed historic Chinese cities, and helped create uprisings such as the Taiping Rebellion. While its officials debated how to protect the Qing Empire's mighty legacy of conquest and productivity, China maintained its vigorous trade in porcelain and other manufactured goods.

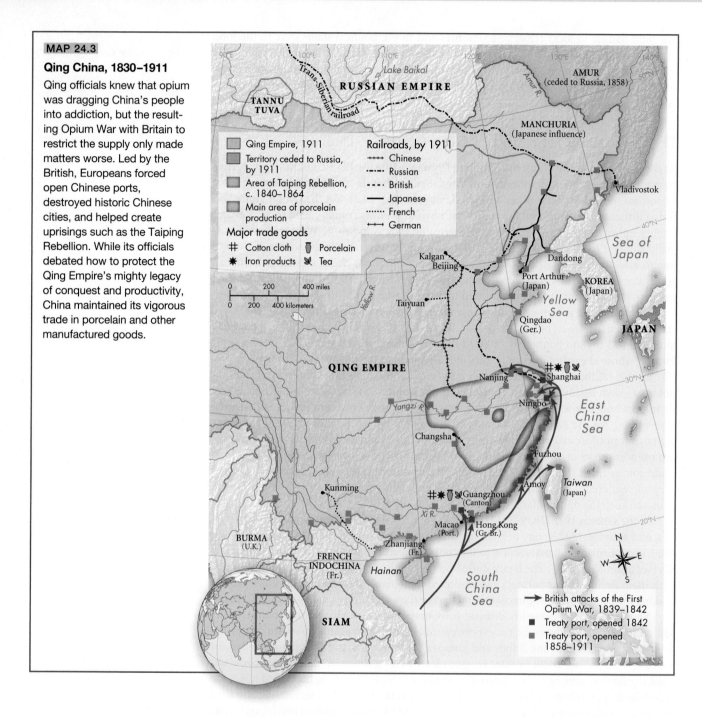

The Taiping Rebellion

To most Chinese, social discontent and economic distress were evidence that their rulers had lost "the Mandate of Heaven," their political legitimacy. The Taiping Rebellion accelerated the crisis of the Qing government, already weakened by the European economic and military assault. At this critical juncture, however, the movement's leaders began to quarrel among themselves and adopt a lavish lifestyle, which weakened the rebellion. The Hunan militia ultimately defeated the Taiping in 1864 under the leadership of the emperor's appointee, the scholar-official Zeng Guofan (zung gwoh-FAN). Hong himself died that year in the final siege of Nanjing.

The lesson learned by some intellectuals and officials—notably Zeng Guofan—was the value of Westernization, by which they meant modernizing the military, promoting technological education, and expanding industrialization. This led in the 1870s to the opening of mines and the development of textile industries, railroads, and the telegraph.

Weighing Opium in India

Opium grown in India went mostly to the Chinese market, though some found its way to Europe through Middle Eastern middlemen. Opium cured headaches, sleeplessness, and general aches and pains, but consumers in both Asia and Europe also welcomed the euphoric feeling of well-being the drug created. Many Chinese and European people became addicted, among them such famous Western artists as novelist Sir Walter Scott, poet Elizabeth Barrett Browning, and composer Hector Berlioz. British merchants and the British government, however, were concerned not with addiction but with sales, profits, and a favorable balance of payments. In the Opium Wars they crushed Chinese resistance with the help of their new steamships and industrially produced guns. (The Art Archive/ Victoria and Albert Museum London/Eileen Tweedy.)

However, the Dowager Empress Cixi, who had seized power during the uprising, focused more on maintaining imperial control of the government than on Western-style modernization. It was unclear which impulse would triumph.

Competition in West and South Asia

Since early modern times, the Ottoman Empire in West Asia had profited from its extensive system of textile manufacture—one so far-reaching that Europeans, Africans, and Asians had long coveted its silks, dyes, fine cottons, and woven rugs. As Western industrial powers sent inferior but less expensive thread, yarn, and woven cloth to markets around the world, it changed the balance of trade. As prices dropped, artisans spinning and weaving at home suffered, working longer hours just to earn a living wage. Textile manufacturing had traditionally been done in the home during winter to provide income during the agricultural off-season. These artisanal ways persisted, but in the last third of the nineteenth century some carpet factories were established across the Ottoman lands. Young unmarried girls, who were less expensive to hire than men and worked for just three or four years (that is, long enough to earn a dowry to attract a husband), replaced lifelong artisans. The Industrial Revolution altered centuries-old work patterns and left many Ottoman subjects, in the words of a British traveler, "ragged beyond belief."[12]

Although the Industrial Revolution hurt craftworkers globally, it boosted the fortunes of other workers. After 1815, the ruler of Egypt, Muhammad Ali, set his subjects to mastering the industry's "strange machinery," and he eventually exempted workers in silk factories from service in the army.[13] Ottoman merchants prospered, as did owners of large estates who could send cotton and other agricultural products to markets around the world on railroads and steamships. New jobs opened up: in 1911 there were thirteen thousand railroad workers in the empire, and thousands more had helped construct the lines. In the Ottoman Empire, regional rulers such as Muhammad Ali who recognized the need for modern skills founded engineering schools and expanded technical education. The Industrial Revolution opened opportunities for some even as it made life more difficult for others.

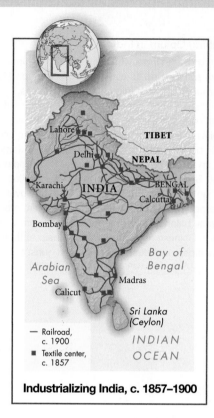

Industrializing India, c. 1857–1900

When Europe's cheap, lower-quality textiles flooded world markets, including those of the Indian subcontinent, the cut-rate competition hurt India's skilled spinners, weavers, and dyers. Furthermore, Britain taxed the textiles Indian craftsmen produced, tilting the economic playing field in favor of British goods. Even so, as in the Ottoman Empire, some in India's lively commercial economy adapted well. In Bengal between the 1830s and 1860s, entrepreneur Dwarkanath Tagore teamed up with British engineers and officials to found raw silk firms, coal mines, steamship companies, and an array of other businesses that made his family fabulously wealthy. The first textile factory started in Bombay in 1853, and by 1914 India had the fourth-largest textile industry and the fourth-longest railway system in the world. Some business people made fortunes. Yet the coming of industry hurt many of the region's independent artisans. The country did not industrialize enough to give them all factory jobs or business employment, and many returned to the countryside. As a result, India grew more rural as the West became more urban.

Besides textiles, India exported such manufactured goods as iron, steel, and jute, which contributed approximately 10 percent of the country's gross national product. Entrepreneurs such as Jamsetji Tata competed globally, founding a dynasty based first in textiles, then in iron and steel, and continuing in the twentieth century with airplanes and software. Yet the British presence was powerful. The East India Company and the British government filled their pockets by imposing high taxes and taking more than their share of the region's prosperity. Moreover, although the British improved the Indian infrastructure, building the rail system, for example, the benefits of such improvements were not spread evenly. By making it easier to extract and then sell agricultural goods on the world market, they favored large Indian landowners.

A New Course for Africa

Industrialization had long-term consequences for Africa as well. During the nineteenth century, the Atlantic slave trade declined quickly due to mounting protests against slavery and the growth of more profitable economic activities. As Denmark (1803) and Britain (1807) abolished the international slave trade, power in West Africa shifted away from the local rulers and traders who profited from it, and toward those who could provide raw materials to Western industry (see Map 24.4).

The Antislavery Movement   Since the Enlightenment, abolitionists had called for an end to the slave trade and to slavery itself. The antislavery message, often crafted by white religious leaders and blacks themselves, invoked Christian morality and the ideas of natural rights that had shaped the revolutions in the Atlantic world. In England, former slaves were eloquent participants in the antislavery movement, which expanded in the early nineteenth century to include international conferences. As the trade in humans was progressively outlawed, abolitionists worked to end slavery completely, a goal achieved in the Western Hemisphere in 1888 when Brazil became the last country in the Americas to outlaw it. Even after 1888, however, slavery continued in many parts of the world, including Africa and Asia.

The rationale for ending slavery also had an economic dimension, and many merchants, financiers, and workers supported the abolitionist movement. The price of slaves had risen during the eighteenth century, so the use of slaves became less profitable. Plantation owners, thinking that natural increase could supply them with slaves cheaply, tried to force slave women to have more children. Industrialists recognized that it was more profitable if Africans worked in Africa to produce raw materials such as palm oil and cotton. Factory workers supported abolition because they regarded slaves as cheap competition in the labor market. Free labor became a widely accepted ideology in industrial areas.

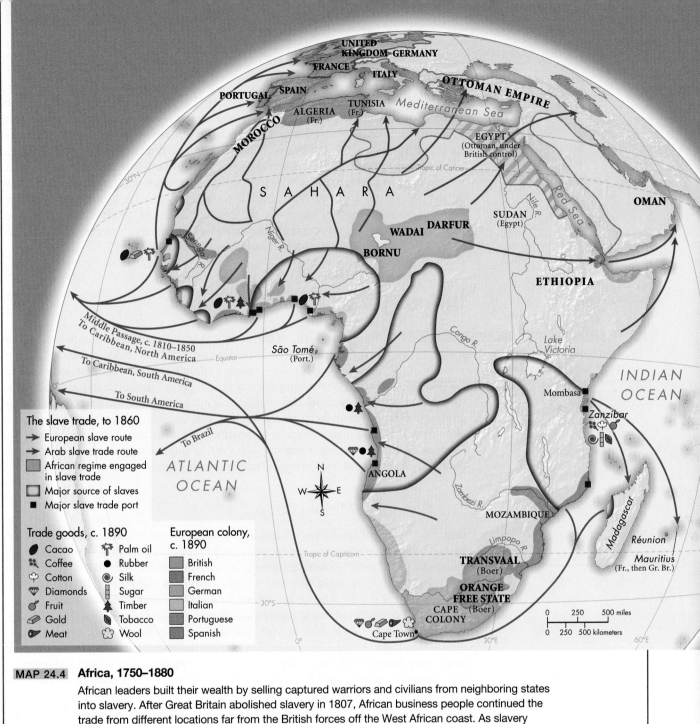

MAP 24.4 Africa, 1750–1880

African leaders built their wealth by selling captured warriors and civilians from neighboring states into slavery. After Great Britain abolished slavery in 1807, African business people continued the trade from different locations far from the British forces off the West African coast. As slavery further declined in the West, the Africans adapted once more, keeping their captives for themselves to provide raw materials for Western industrialists.

Expanding Slavery Within Africa

The decline of profits from the Atlantic slave trade threw some African elites into economic crisis. Many quickly adapted, simply moving the slave trade south to supply markets in Brazil and elsewhere. Slavers arriving in West African ports learned to load ships and depart in some 100 minutes to escape British surveillance. In the course of the nineteenth century, even as Europeans worked to abolish the trade, approximately 3.5 million slaves were taken from West Africa alone to sell in the Atlantic world. African rulers and business people used slaves to increase their efforts to provide raw materials for global manufacturing. They expanded slavery within Africa, waging war and kidnapping to capture slaves for their own use. For fear of enslavement, "One could not go to another town's sector of the market without being led by an armed elder," one Nigerian man recalled.[14]

Slaves in West Africa produced various materials for the textile industry: gum, redwood, and palm oil to lubricate machinery. The oil was also used to produce soap, which people in the West increasingly found essential to everyday life. Hundreds of thousands of slaves in Egypt worked the cotton fields. Other raw materials from Africa, such as gold, boosted the European economy; coffee, rubber, and diamonds followed. Many historians believe that the expansion of slavery to gain profits from these commodities condemned Africa to underdevelopment. West Africa, one British traveler noted in the 1830s, "is disorganized, and except in the immediate vicinity of the towns, the land lies waste and uncultivated, the wretched natives living under constant dread of being carried off into slavery."[15] In places both with and without factory labor, industrialization had far-reaching consequences.

Industry and Society

FOCUS

How did industrialization affect people's everyday lives and livelihoods?

The vast majority of the world's peoples remained rural until well into the twentieth century, but where industry did take hold, livelihoods changed and new social classes emerged. People were less and less self-sufficient. Factory owners and workers produced the manufactured goods that began to flood local, regional, national, and international markets. At first, these two growing social groups, workers and manufacturers, lived side by side because the first factory owners were often modest artisans themselves who personally put their inventions to work in their new factories. As industry advanced, this situation would change: both groups became important politically, but they were divided into increasingly distinct social classes.

The Changing Middle Class

Before the Industrial Revolution, traders around the world had formed a middle class, sandwiched between the aristocrats and the peasants and serfs. Now most factory owners joined this middle class, although some aristocrats invested in industry without losing their privileged class status. Early industrial innovators often led frugal lives full of hard work, and they tried to ensure that their children and others did too. The Tagore family in India thrived on hard work, leading Dwarkanath Tagore's son to refuse charity to a beggar-priest: "I shan't give you money. . . . you are able to work, and earn your bread."[16] While early businessmen directed the factories or went on distant sales trips, their wives often tended the accounts, dealt with subcontractors, supervised workers (especially if they were female), and organized shipments of finished goods. As factories grew and their owners became prosperous, they became society's leaders, rising far above the humble status of their workers. Leaders of industry built large houses and began to consume more goods, including luxuries. They removed their wives from factory supervision and from the working world, beginning what historians term a "cult of domesticity" for women that signaled a family's prosperity. These economic leaders have collectively been called the *bourgeoisie*, a French term for the middle-class groups at the center of the Industrial Revolution.

The Middle Class Promotes Progress

As we have seen, with the march of industry, scientists and engineers in research laboratories and universities replaced amateur tinkerers as industrial innovators. As part of the state's commitment to building national wealth, public monies often funded scientific research, which was increasingly expensive. The middle class grew to include those whose empirical and scientific knowledge benefited industrial society, and professionalization occurred in other fields as well. Doctors, lawyers, professors, and journalists—all of whom drew on the scientific method and objective analysis in their work—gained prestige as they served the wider population of industrial society.

Such prosperous men of the evolving middle class founded a range of societies and clubs to create solidarity and foster the exchange of knowledge. In Japan in 1876, the city fathers of Kanazawa opened an industrial museum to spread technical knowledge more widely among the public. Wealthy citizens around the world founded art, history, and science museums during these industrial years and worked to improve city life. "Reserve large areas for football, hockey, and parks," Indian industrialist Jamsetji Tata advised urban renovators. "Earmark areas for Hindu temples, Mohammedan mosques, and Christian churches."[17]

Well-to-do women banded together to provide baby clothes for newborn children and other goods to impoverished workers. Indian reformer Savithribai Phule, married at age nine, joined her husband in aiding the lowest-caste "Untouchables," despite mounting criticism and threats of violence against her. She founded schools for the girls of the Untouchable caste, claiming to feel "immeasurably happy" with her volunteer work. "Besides, it also demonstrates the horizons to which a human being can reach out," she wrote.[18] As industrialization and rapid urban growth disturbed centuries-old ways of life, these institutions, in the words of one English official, promoted "the protection of their [industrialists'] property" by reducing worker misery. Good works also helped to unite the middle classes in the face of challenges from those with "anti-social and revolutionary principles."[19]

The New Working Class

While the middle classes enjoyed increased comfort and prosperity, industrial workers led work lives governed by the machine, the factory whistle, and eventually the time clock of the office or department store. Initially, many industrial workers, whether in the United

An East Indian Middle-Class Family
Sometime in the late nineteenth century, this middle-class family donned their best clothes and sat for this formal portrait. The father may have worked for the British government or been an independent merchant or factory owner. Nevertheless, the British dominated the subcontinent politically, economically, and culturally. This family wore fashionable Western clothing, although some of the women adapted their outfits by adding elements of the traditional sari to their dress. (Dinodia Photos.)

States, Japan, Britain, or Argentina, were young, unmarried women whose families no longer needed them on farms, which now took fewer hands to run. Factories were magnets, offering steady wages and, often, supervised living quarters. Women and children were paid less than men, reducing labor costs, and this trend continued as industry spread. Despite the low pay, many women found factory work far preferable to domestic service as maids, where they were on call twenty-four hours a day. After her husband died in 1910, the Mexican widow Marcela Bernal del Viuda de Torres left her young sons to live with relatives and took her two daughters to Mexico City to find work for all three in its thriving factories. Marcela, like the underemployed around the world, sought opportunity. As she said when explaining the move to her daughters, "I'm sure not going to let you end up as maids."[20]

The worker's day was often long, grueling, and unsafe in the early days of industry, as Robert Blincoe witnessed firsthand. In 1844 England limited women's work to twelve hours per day, but in Japan men and women worked fourteen to seventeen hours a day even late in the century. They tended machines while they ate meals and usually had just half a day off per week. Machines lacked even minimal safety features, leading to amputated limbs, punctured eyes, torn-off scalps, and other crippling injuries. A Japanese observer described cotton workers in urban factories as "pale and exhausted with faces like invalids. . . . young girls with the lifeblood sucked out of them."[21]

Workers' health deteriorated in many cities, and critics said it was because the lower classes, as one British observer put it as early as 1795, lived "crowded in offensive, dark, damp and incommodious habitations, a too fertile source of disease."[22] The lure of industrial work swelled urban populations to the breaking point. There was not enough housing, and sanitary facilities were almost nonexistent. Europe's cities were usually surrounded by medieval walls, which limited their natural expansion, and humid factories nurtured disease. Wherever workers were crowded together, epidemics of deadly cholera

Working Conditions

might erupt, as happened, for example, in the camps housing thousands of Indian railroad builders. Deaths from tuberculosis and pneumonia soared. In its early days, industry's human costs were clear.

Fighting the Industrial Advance

Many people resisted the introduction of laborsaving machines into their towns and villages. Handloom weavers saw their livelihoods slipping away, and agricultural workers resented mechanization's threat to their livelihoods. Some handicraft workers—notably the Luddites (named after their leader, Ned Ludd), who attacked whole factories in northern England in 1812 and after—smashed the new machines, which they believed were putting them out of work. In the countryside, day laborers left menacing notes for those who introduced threshing machines, such as: "If providing you dont pull down your messhenes . . . we will burn down your barns and you in them this is the last notis."[23] The British government mobilized its armies to protect the new system from protesters. It executed and imprisoned many, and sent large numbers to populate Australia and New Zealand—which industrialized in turn.

Under the older values of city life, artisans mutually supported one another, but that system weakened. As rural folk migrated to cities in search of industrial jobs, workers were often strangers to one another. Between 1820 and 1840 the Russian government of Poland deemed that Lodz would become a textile center, for example, and thousands of migrant workers from the countryside and fledgling industrialists from several parts of Europe quickly moved there. Chinese migrated to the Caribbean to service the sugar industry, and South Asians took their commercial and other skills to East Africa. Single young people or widows migrating from the countryside lived beyond the reach of their families and old community networks. Prostitution soared, as did venereal disease and illegitimacy. Thus, as industrialization created dense networks of new economic connections throughout the world, it contributed to the breakdown of social connections in local communities.

Industrialization brought people's everyday lives into a mechanical orbit and changed the rhythms of earning a livelihood. No longer did sunrise and sunset determine the beginning and end of the workday. Now the clock, perfected in the early modern period to measure

Child Labor in Britain

Although the exploitation of children is still a feature of industrialization, the use of child labor by early industrialists was especially harsh, as the life of Robert Blincoe testifies and as this late-nineteenth-century illustration of children at work in the mines demonstrates. After these children were lowered side by side into claustrophobic conditions, they faced the rough job of physically hauling carts of coal out of the mines through narrow passageways. Like their adult counterparts, they suffered from coal dust and extremes of heat and cold. It is little wonder that even liberal British politicians of the time, who wanted no interference from government in business, agreed to governmental investigation and regulation of mining conditions. After parliamentary hearings on mine work, children's work and that of women who worked in and near the mines were regulated. (Photo: akg-images.)

even in seconds, set the hours for work of many kinds. Factory whistles signaled the start of the workday, while stopwatches timed the pace of work. The ongoing march of the machine, rather than the seasons, determined people's movements and organized their labor. Industrialists imposed heavy fines on anyone late by even a minute. With alcohol a prominent feature of life in a world where there was no safe water or milk supply, however, drunkenness sometimes undermined the strict discipline industrialists hoped to impose.

The Sexual Division of Labor

Factory Workers

The Industrial Revolution ushered in major changes in the sexual division of labor. Industrialists and manufacturers followed the tradition of dividing work along gender lines; now, however, the division was generally arbitrary. In some factory towns the weavers were all men, and women performed some processes in finishing the woven cloth. In other places, women tended the looms, and men only repaired and maintained the machines. Women's work in factories, even though it might be identical to men's, was said to require less skill; it always received lower pay. Men dreaded the introduction of women into a factory, which could signal that the owner intended to save on wages by cutting men's jobs. Sometimes the wife or daughter in an artisanal family went to work in a factory because the husband's work as a shoemaker or handloom weaver no longer paid enough to support the household. In such cases the husband's independent identity as handloom weaver or shoemaker may have been a proud one, providing freedom from the oversight of a foreman and an industrialist. His wife, however, may have surrendered her freedom to earn the extra income that permitted him to maintain his.

The vast majority of women, both unmarried and married, worked to support their families or themselves. Factory owners and supervisors often demanded sexual favors from women as the price of employment. The foreman supervising Adelheid Popp, a factory worker in late-nineteenth-century Germany, demanded kisses in exchange for higher wages. She quit the job, but others did not have such freedom. "Even the decent jobs, for example, those in banks," one Russian woman complained, "are rarely available unless one first grants favors to the director, the manager, or some other individual."[24] It was normal for supervisors to select one favorite woman, take her as a mistress, and then fire her once he tired of the relationship. Domestic service, which expanded with the rising prosperity of the middle class, was thought to be safer for young women, but many a housemaid fell victim to fathers and sons in middle-class families, who were regular harassers of working women. If these sexual relations became known, the women would be fired, and pregnant servants quickly lost their jobs. This is why Marcela de Torres feared for her daughters.

White-Collar Workers

The new white-collar sector advanced the sexual division of labor. Cost-conscious employers looking for workers with mathematical, reading, and writing skills gladly offered jobs to women. Since respectable lower-middle-class women had few other employment options, businesses in the service sector paid women much less than men for the same work, as in factories. As women increasingly filled lower-level white collar jobs, all sectors of the industrial economy perpetuated the idea that women were simply worth less than men and should receive lower wages (see Reading the Past: Mexican Women on Strike).

The Culture of Industry

Writers, artists, and ordinary people alike responded to the dramatic new sights and unexpected changes of industrialization. The railroad and expanded trade spread local customs, creating greater variety in everyday life and contributing to developing regional and national cultures. In Japan, for example, sashimi and sushi, once known in only a few fishing towns, became popular dishes across the nation. Better communication networks helped the spread of knowledge, and technological improvements helped knowledge flourish: gas lighting

FOCUS

How did writers and artists respond to the new industrial world?

Mexican Women on Strike

As industrialization progressed, factory workers increasingly responded to the harsh conditions of industrialization by organizing unions and banding together to strike. They directed their demands to factory owners and government officials, and they sought support from their fellow citizens. For instance, in 1881, women cigarette workers in Mexico City wrote a letter to a magazine for elite women in which they suggested that poverty might lead them to prostitution. At the same time, women cigar workers posted this placard around Mexico City to explain their strike against the factory owners.

Oppression by the Capitalist!

Until October 2, 1881, we used to make 2185 cigars for four reales [Mexican money], and now they have increased the number of cigars and lowered our salary. On October 3, 1881, through the mediation of El Congreso Obrero [The Congress of Workers], we agreed to make 2304 cigars for four reales. It is not possible for us to make more. We have to work from six in the morning until nine at night. . . . We don't have one hour left to take care of our domestic chores, and not a minute for education. The capitalists are suffocating us. In spite of such hard work, we still live in great poverty. What are our brother-workers going to do? What are the representatives of the Mexican press going to do? We need protection, protection for working women!

Source: Susie S. Porter, *Working Women in Mexico City: Public Discourses and Material Conditions, 1879–1931* (Tucson: University of Arizona Press, 2003), 80.

EXAMINING THE EVIDENCE

1. What major concerns do the women announce in this placard?

2. To what specific groups is the placard addressed? Why did the strikers single out these groups?

---

extended reading deep into the night, for example, and railroads exposed more travelers than ever to ideas far from home. The increased productivity associated with industrialization eventually led to more leisure time, and streams of workers entered cafés, dance halls, and parks to enjoy their new free time. Such changes in everyday life led to a torrent of artistic and literary reflections on the dramatic new industrial world.

Socialism and Marxism

In some, industry inspired optimism. For such thinkers, the rational calculation and technological progress that had produced industry raised the possibility that a perfect society could be created. A group of French and British thinkers, the "utopian socialists," spread this faith around the world. Their goal was to improve society as a whole, not just for the individual—hence the term **socialism**. They believed that rational planning would lead to social and political perfection—that is, to utopia—and to prove their point they often lived in communes where daily life could be as precisely organized as it was in the factory. The inefficient nuclear family became obsolete in their communes, where large numbers of people worked together to finish necessary tasks efficiently. At a time when many people still held monarchs and leisured aristocrats in the highest esteem, **utopian socialism** valued technicians and engineers as future rulers of nations.

socialism A social and political ideology dating from the early nineteenth century that stresses the need to maintain social harmony through communities based on cooperation rather than competition; in Marxist terms, a classless society of workers who collectively control the production of goods necessary for life.

Two middle-class German theorists—the lawyer and economist Karl Marx (1818–1883) and the wealthy industrialist Friedrich Engels (1820–1895)—had completely different ideas on how to best organize society. Although they shared the utopian socialists' appreciation of science, they saw the new industrial order as unjust and oppressive. In the 1840s they began to analyze the life of workers, publishing their results in Engels's *The Condition of the Working Class in England* (1844). In 1848 they published *The Communist Manifesto*, which became the bible of modern socialism. Marx elaborated on what he called "scientific socialism" in his most important work, *Das Kapital* (Capital), published between 1867 and 1894.

utopian socialism A goal of certain French and British thinkers early in the nineteenth century, who envisioned the creation of a perfect society through cooperation and social planning.

materialism In Marxist terms, the idea that the organization of society derives from the organization of production.

Marx held that the fundamental organization of any society derived from the relationships built into work, or what he called, simply, production. This idea, known as **materialism**, was that a society's structure was built on the class relationships that stemmed from production—such as those between serf and medieval lord, slave and master, or worker and factory owner. Marx referred to these systems—feudalism, slavery, and **capitalism**, respectively—as modes of production. In the industrial era, people were in one of two classes: the workers, or **proletariat**, and the owners, or capitalists (also the **bourgeoisie**, in Marxist terms), who owned the means of production—the land, machines, factories, and other forms of wealth. Rejecting the eighteenth-century liberal focus on individual rights, he held that the cause of the inequality between classes such as the proletariat and the capitalists was the owners' control of the means of production. When capitalist control disappeared, as Marx was certain it would, a classless society of workers would arise.

Economic liberals such as Adam Smith thought the free market would ultimately produce balance and a harmony of interests among people in all classes of society. Marx, however, believed that the workers' economic oppression by their bosses inevitably caused conflict. He predicted that as workers became aware of their oppression they would unite in revolt against their capitalist exploiters. Their revolt—not reform or legislation—would be the mechanism for worldwide historical change. The proletariat would overthrow capitalism, and socialism would reign. The moment for revolt, Marx thought, was near. "The proletarians have nothing to lose but their chains. They have a world to win. WORKING MEN OF ALL COUNTRIES, UNITE!" So ends *The Communist Manifesto*.

Marx never precisely described the classless society, but he believed it would involve workers' control of production in large factories. In a socialist society, private ownership of the means of production would end. This in turn would end the need for a state, whose only function, Marx claimed, was to protect the propertied classes. Like many male intellectuals in Europe, Marx devoted little analysis to inequalities based on race and gender. He did conclude, however, that women's lives would automatically improve under socialism. The possibility of achieving socialism inspired workers around the world. As we will see in later chapters, Marxist ideas shaped both the Russian Revolution of 1917 and the Chinese Revolution of 1949.

Industry and the Arts

The new industrial world inspired artists as well as intellectuals. Some celebrated industry, welcoming the artistic influences from far-off places that it made possible. Japanese woodblocks showed trains racing through a countryside of blossoming cherries. Hiroshige's prints depicting roads teeming with industrious people influenced Western artists to turn from mythical topics and great historic scenes to the subject matter of ordinary working lives (see again Seeing the Past: Japan's Industrious Society). Deeply influenced by the color, line, and delicacy of Japanese art as well as by its focus on scenes of ordinary daily life, French painters such as Claude Monet pioneered the artistic style known as "impressionism," so called for the artists' effort to capture a single moment by focusing on how the ever-changing light and color transformed everyday sights. Industry contributed to the new style as factories produced products that allowed Western painters to use a wider, more intense spectrum of colors.

Other Western artists interpreted the Industrial Revolution differently, focusing instead on the grim working conditions brought about by wrenching change. One was Germany's Käthe Kollwitz, whose woodcuts realistically depict starving artisans. British author Charles Dickens wrote of the dark side of industrialization in popular novels that even reached a Japanese audience. Among them was *Oliver Twist* (1837–1839), which many scholars speculate was based in part on the life of Robert Blincoe. *Uncle Tom's Cabin* (1852), U.S. writer Harriet Beecher Stowe's shocking tale of slave life in the American South, influenced some in the Russian nobility to lobby for freeing the serfs.

Even musical forms showed the impact of the Industrial Revolution. Utopian socialists composed music celebrating the railroad and the sounds of industry. Concert halls, like factories, became bigger to accommodate the increasing urban population, and orchestras grew larger and included more instruments to produce a massive sound. Military bands marched through the widening streets of capital cities. Their increasing precision and noise matched that of the new machines and the precise movements of the industrial workers tending them.

capitalism An economic system in which the means of production—machines, factories, land, and other forms of wealth—are privately owned.

proletariat Under capitalism, those who work without owning the means of production.

bourgeoisie Originally a term meaning the urban middle class; Marx defined it as the owners of the means of production under capitalism.

Workers Going Home at the Lehrter Railroad Station, 1897

German artist Käthe Kollwitz came from a family of socially active reformers and was married to the doctor Karl Kollwitz, who worked among the poor. "My real motive for choosing my subjects almost exclusively from the life of the workers was that only such subjects gave me in a simple and unqualified way what I felt to be beautiful," she wrote. Kollwitz spent her entire artistic career depicting the struggles of ordinary men and women, as in this image of workers going home exhausted after a day of hard labor. Many in the upper classes, including the German Kaiser, disapproved of such sordid subjects, but they are now considered to be among the most important art of modern times. (Käthe Kollwitz, *Workers on the Way Home at the Lehrter Station* (NT 146) 1897–1899 Brush and watercolor with accents in white Käthe Kollwitz Museum Köln © 2011 Artists Rights Society (ARS), New York/ VG Bild-Kunst, Bonn.)

COUNTERPOINT
African Women and Slave Agriculture

FOCUS

What contributions did African women agricultural workers make to industrial development?

The story of the Industrial Revolution often centers on individual inventors and the laborsaving machinery they pioneered. But entire groups, many of them anonymous and uncelebrated, piloted advances critical to industrialization. A good example comes from Africa, which nineteenth-century Europeans and Americans often regarded as a continent full of unskilled people; they used this perspective to justify both their enslavement and discrimination against all people of color. Africans, however, were foremost among the collective innovators of their day.

Women and Farming in Africa

Many of these unnamed inventors were women, who have dominated African farming both as cultivators of their own land or as slaves on African plantations. Armies of male slaves kidnapped individuals or captured entire communities of neighboring peoples for regional leaders to sell or enslave in turn. Male slaves also served in urban commerce, working as artisans, porters, and traders. Women slaves largely did agricultural work to feed the slave armies and other male slaves. Some slave men hunted such prized commodities as elephant tusks, which were fashioned into piano keys, gun handles, combs, and other objects characteristic of middle-class lives around the world. Women slaves also served as domestic servants and concubines for African elites.

Women's agricultural labor supported African life. When they married, women received land to provide for themselves and their children. Free and slave women alike could themselves own slaves to increase their agricultural productivity. As farm workers, women served as a counterpoint to independent and free male farmers, peasants and large landowners alike. In Africa it was women, either as independent farmers or more usually

Nayemwezi Women Pounding Sorghum, 1864

As industrialization advanced around the world, women in Africa were central to its agricultural foundation, as this drawing shows. They planted, weeded, and harvested major crops such as sorghum, a grass whose kernels were pounded into flour and whose stalks were pressed to produce a sweet syrup. Sorghum is native to Africa, and there is evidence that slave women brought it, along with rice and other crops, to the North American colonies, and that these crops fed both industrial workers and local slaves. (Photo: akg-images.)

as slave laborers, who introduced new varieties of seeds, new tools for farming, and more productive farming techniques. Today it is estimated that African women grow some 80 percent of all agricultural produce on the continent.

On the west coast of Africa, although men participated in some aspects of rice farming, rice cultivation was known as "women's sweat." Women developed complex systems for cultivating the important rice crop, especially a variety called "red" rice. To control water supplies, they installed canals, sluices, and embankments, depending on whether they were capturing water from rain, tides, or floods. They reaped bountiful harvests through this manipulation of the environment.[25]

Rice Cultivation

Women Slaves in the North American South

Many landowners in South Carolina and Georgia prized West African slave women, considering them "choice cargo" because of their knowledge of rice cultivation. In fact, it was slaves from West Africa who established the "red" rice variety as a preferred crop on American plantations and provided the initial technological systems for growing it. This rice was so important to the U.S. South's developing commercial economy that Thomas Jefferson, for one, sought more information about it. Its main advantage, he learned, was that if cultivated according to African techniques of water management, it could be grown outside of swamps. The more usual practice of cultivating rice in standing water "sweeps off numbers of the inhabitants with pestilential fevers,"[26] according to Jefferson, so a growing system that eliminated the threat of disease was advantageous.

Jefferson, like some other American planters, never succeeded in cultivating red rice. The first African rice to be widely grown in North America was fragile, demanding special skills that planters, such as Jefferson, usually lacked. In contrast, West African women possessed an extensive knowledge of this and other forms of agriculture and passed this knowledge down through their families.

Spread of Agricultural Technologies from Africa to the U.S. South

Slavers added these women to their cargo along with unhusked rice and many other plants and seeds. When they arrived in the United States, the technological knowledge to grow them moved from Africans to Europeans, not the other way around. In this regard West African women farmers form a counterpoint to the celebrated inventors of machines. Although they have been overlooked in history books, they created wealth for their owners, most of whom in the early days of rice cultivation were adventurers with little knowledge of how to grow these crops. Their story of the introduction of rice to North America, the perfection of seeds, and the complex technology of irrigation and processing that helped feed a growing workforce has seemed less heroic than that of an individual who invented one laborsaving machine.

Conclusion

The Industrial Revolution changed not only the world economy but the lives and livelihoods of tens of millions of people, from workers and manufacturers to the politicians trying to organize rapidly changing societies. By replacing simple machines operated by human energy with complex machines powered by steam engines, mechanization expanded productivity almost beyond measure. The results were both grim and liberating. Industrial laborers such as mill worker Robert Blincoe suffered abuse, and the flow of cheap goods from industrial countries drove down prices and threw artisans around the world into poverty. Slavery not only flourished but also allowed industry to advance. Unsung slave women spread rice cultivation to help feed the growing world population of workers. The new patterns of work in large factories transformed the rhythm of labor and the texture of urban life, and cities grew rapidly with the influx of migrants from the countryside and from other regions of the world. Political ideas and the arts also changed with the rise of industry and with the continuing global expansion of trade. Movements to end slavery and to create free workers succeeded in Europe and many parts of the Western Hemisphere.

Debate continues about whether industry was a force for good, but even opponents at the time saw that industrial life liberated people from the hardships and restrictions of rural life and gave them access to a wider array of inexpensive goods. Some theorists, such as Marx and Engels, believed that solidarity would grow among a global working class no longer isolated on individual farms, while artists depicted these new workers with paint and pen—occasionally romanticizing their productivity but more often presenting the poverty that accompanied industrialization. The middle and working classes that developed with industrialization led different lives even within the same industrial cities, but they often joined in a major global movement of the time—the development of the political form called the nation-state that increasingly shaped industrial society. As we will see in the next chapter, it was a form that spread around the world alongside industrialization and ushered in other conflicts and advances of the modern era.

NOTES

1. James R. Simmons Jr., ed., *Factory Lives: Four Nineteenth-Century Working-Class Autobiographies* (Peterborough, Ontario: Broadview, 2007), 110.
2. Ibid., 123.
3. Quoted in Brian Dolan, *Wedgwood: The First Tycoon* (New York: Viking, 2004), 54.
4. Quoted in Sally and David Dugan, *The Day the World Took Off: The Roots of the Industrial Revolution* (London: Macmillan, 2000), 54.
5. Quoted in Ken Alder, *Engineering the Revolution: Arms and Enlightenment in France, 1763–1815* (Princeton, NJ: Princeton University Press, 1997), 223.

6. Quoted in Tessa Morris-Suzuki, *The Technological Transformation of Japan from the Seventeenth to the Twenty-First Century* (Cambridge, U.K.: Cambridge University Press, 1994), 65.

7. Quoted in ibid., 73.

8. Quoted in T. R. Havens, "Early Modern Farm Ideology and Japanese Agriculture," in *Meiji Japan: Political, Economic and Social History*, ed. Peter Kornicki, 4 vols. (Routledge: New York, 1998), 1:235.

9. Quoted in Edward Beatty, *Institutions and Investment: The Political Basis of Industrialization in Mexico Before 1911* (Stanford: Stanford University Press, 2001), 59.

10. Thomas Munro, quoted in Romash Chunder Dutt, *The Economic History of India* (Delhi: Low Price, 1990 [orig. pub. 1902–1904]), 185–186.

11. "The Land System of the Heavenly Dynasty" (1853), quoted in *China: Readings in the History of China from the Opium War to the Present*, ed. J. Mason Gentzler (New York: Praeger, 1977), 56.

12. Quoted in Michael E. Meeker, *A Nation of Empire: The Ottoman Legacy of Turkish Modernity* (Berkeley: University of California Press, 2002), 103.

13. Afaf Lutfi Al-Sayyid Marsot, *Egypt in the Reign of Muhammad Ali* (Cambridge: Cambridge University Press, 1984), 169–171.

14. Quoted in Carolyn Brown, *"We Were All Slaves": African Miners, Culture, and Resistance at the Enugu Government Colliery* (Portsmouth, NH: Heinemann, 2003), 36.

15. Mr. Laird, quoted in Joseph Inicori, *Africans and the Industrial Revolution in England: A Study in International Trade and Economic Development* (New York: Cambridge University Press, 2002), 394.

16. Debendranath Tagore, quoted in Blair B. Kling, *Partner in Empire: Dwarkanath Tagore and the Age of Enterprise in Eastern India* (Berkeley: University of California Press, 1976), 184.

17. Quoted on the Tata Group Web site, http://www.tata.com/0_about_us/history/pioneers/quotable.htm.

18. Quoted in Susie Tharu and K. Lalita, eds., *Women Writing in India: 600 B.C. to the Early Twentieth Century*, 2 vols. (London: Pandora, 1991), 1:214.

19. Quoted in Caroline Arscott, "'Without Distinction of Party': The Polytechnic Exhibitions in Leeds, 1839–1945," in *The Culture of Capital: Art, Power, and the Nineteenth-Century Middle Class*, ed. Janet Wolff and John Seed (Manchester, U.K.: Manchester University Press, 1988), 145.

20. Quoted in Susie Porter, *Working Women in Mexico City: Public Discourse and Material Conditions, 1879–1931* (Tucson: University of Arizona Press, 2003), 3–4.

21. Quoted in E. Patricia Tsrumi, *Factory Girls: Women in the Thread Mills of Meiji Japan* (Princeton, NJ: Princeton University Press, 1990), 139.

22. Quoted in Ivy Pinchbeck, *Women Workers and the Industrial Revolution, 1750–1850* (London: Virago, 1981 [orig. pub. 1930]), 195.

23. Quoted in Eric Hobsbawm and George Rudé, *Captain Swing: A Social History of the Great English Agricultural Uprising of 1830* (New York: Norton, 1968), 208.

24. Quoted in Victoria E. Bonnell, *The Russian Worker: Life and Labor Under the Tsarist Regime* (Berkeley: University of California Press, 1983), 197.

25. Judith A. Carney, *Black Rice: The African Origins of Rice Cultivation in the Americas* (Cambridge, MA: Harvard University Press, 2001), 31.

26. Ibid., 147.

RESOURCES FOR RESEARCH

The Industrial Revolution Begins, 1750–1830

World history allows us to think differently about the Industrial Revolution, understanding it less as a radical departure and more as a burst of productivity and inventiveness taking place in many parts of the world. Bezis-Selfa's and Dolan's books depict the day-to-day toil of workers and manufacturers.

Bayly, C. A. *The Birth of the Modern World, 1780–1914: Global Connections and Comparisons.* 2004.

Bezis-Selfa, John. *Forging America: Ironworkers, Adventurers, and the Industrious Revolution.* 2004.

Clark, Gregory. *A Farewell to Alms: A Brief Economic History of the World.* 2007.

Dolan, Brian. *Wedgwood: The First Tycoon.* 2004.

Inikori, Joseph. *Africans and the Industrial Revolution in England: A Study in International Trade and Economic Development.* 2002.

Industrialization After 1830

Countries industrialized in different ways, though they often experienced similar problems. Morris-Suzuki and D'Costa show in exciting detail the road to industrialization in Japan and Argentina.

Beatty, Edward. *Institutions and Investment: The Political Basis of Industrialization in Mexico Before 1911.* 2001.

D'Costa, Anthony. *The Long March to Capitalism: Embourgeoisement, Internationalization, and Industrial Transformation in India.* 2005.

Morris-Suzuki, Tessa. *The Technological Transformation of Japan.* 1994.

Rappaport, Erica. *Shopping for Pleasure: Women in the Making of London's West End.* 2000.

Rocchi, Fernando. *Chimneys in the Desert: Industrialization in Argentina During the Export Boom Years.* 2006.

The Industrial Revolution and the World

Just as global innovation and trade provided much of the impetus for the Industrial Revolution, industrialists' efforts to sell their goods changed local and regional economies around the world. The books below describe the consequences for a variety of countries.

Bello, David Anthony. *Opium and the Limits of Empire: Drug Prohibition in the Chinese Interior, 1729–1850.* 2005.

Goswami, Manu. *Producing India: From Colonial Economy to National Space.* 2004.

Meeker, Michael E. *A Nation of Empire: The Ottoman Legacy of Turkish Modernity.* 2002.

Reilly, Thomas H. *The Taiping Heavenly Kingdom: Rebellion and the Blasphemy of Empire.* 2004.

Shepherd, Verene A. *A Maharani's Misery: Narratives of a Passage from India to the Caribbean.* 2002.

Industry and Society

The idea that a middle class arose during the Industrial Revolution is disputed, because world historians acknowledge that for centuries there had been merchants sandwiched between princes and peasants. At the same time, many believe that industrialist workers followed industrial rhythms and saw the world differently from their predecessors. For a real-life example of the opportunities seized by one striving industrialist, see the PBS Web site on Andrew Carnegie.

Banerjee, Swapna M. *Men, Women, and Domestics: Articulating Middle-Class Identity in Colonial Bengal.* 2004.

Igler, David. *Industrial Cowboys: Miller and Lux and the Transformation of the Far West, 1850–1920.* 2001.

Morgan, Kenneth. *The Birth of Industrial Britain: Social Change, 1750–1850.* 2004.

Porter, Susie. *Working Women in Mexico City: Public Discourses and Material Conditions, 1879–1931.* 2003.

Public Broadcasting Service. *American Experience*, "Andrew Carnegie." http://www.pbs.org/wgbh/amex/carnegie/.

The Culture of Industry

Those in the world of art and ideas responded to the sights and sounds of industry. The Metropolitan Museum of Art's Web site has many links to specific instances of cultural exchange during the nineteenth century, including the one listed on Japan's influence on the West during industrialization.

Callen, Anthea. *The Art of Impressionism: Painting Technique and the Making of Modernity.* 2000.

Izzard, Sebastian. *Hiroshige/Eisen: The Sixty-Nine Stations of the Kisokaido.* 2008.

Megill, Allan. *Karl Marx: The Burden of Reason.* 2002.

Metropolitan Museum of Art. *Timeline of Art History*, "Japonisme." http://www.metmuseum.org/toah/hd/jpon/hd_jpon.htm.

Peskin, Lawrence. *The Intellectual Origins of Early American Industry.* 2003.

COUNTERPOINT: African Women and Slave Agriculture

The unsung innovators of the past are in the process of being discovered. Carney looks at the West African women and men who brought rice cultivation, processing, and cooking to the U.S. South.

Carney, Judith A. *Black Rice: The African Origins of Rice Cultivation in the Americas.* 2001.

Carney, Judith A., and Richard N. Rosomoff. *In the Shadow of Slavery: Africa's Botanical Legacy in the Atlantic World.* 2009.

Hoerder, Dirk. *Cultures in Contact: World Migrations in the Second Millennium.* 2002.

▶ **For additional primary sources from this period,** see *Sources of Crossroads and Cultures.*

▶ **For Web sites, images, and documents related to topics in this chapter,** see Make History at bedfordstmartins.com/smith.

The major global development in this chapter ▶ The Industrial Revolution and its impact on societies and cultures throughout the world.

IMPORTANT EVENTS

c. 1750	Industrialization begins in Great Britain
1769	James Watt creates the modern steam engine
1780s–1790s	Interchangeability of parts developed in France
1803	Denmark becomes the first Western country to abolish the slave trade
1814	George Stephenson puts a steam engine on a carriage on rails, inventing the locomotive
1819	First Atlantic crossing by a steamship
1839–1842	Opium War between China and Britain
1842	Treaty of Nanjing opens Chinese ports
1848	*Communist Manifesto* published
1853	U.S. ships enter Japanese ports
1840s–1864	Taiping Rebellion
1865	U.S. Civil War ends, rapid U.S. industrialization begins
1868	Meiji Restoration launches Japanese industrialization
1871	Germany gains resource-rich Alsace and Lorraine after defeating France
1873–c. 1900	Deep global recession with uneven recovery
1890s	Argentina's leading textile manufacturer produces 1.6 million yards of cloth annually
1891–1904	Construction of trans-Siberian railroad

CHAPTER OVERVIEW QUESTIONS

1. In what ways did the Industrial Revolution change people's work lives and ideas?
2. How did the Industrial Revolution benefit people, and what problems did it create?
3. How and where did industrial production develop, and how did it affect society and politics?

SECTION FOCUS QUESTIONS

1. What were the main causes of the Industrial Revolution?
2. How did industrialization spread, and what steps did nations and manufacturers take to meet its challenges?
3. How did industrialization affect societies in China, South and West Asia, and Africa?
4. How did industrialization affect people's everyday lives and livelihoods?
5. How did writers and artists respond to the new industrial world?
6. What contributions did African women agricultural workers make to industrial development?

MAKING CONNECTIONS

1. How did the Scientific Revolution (see Chapter 20) and the Enlightenment (see Chapter 23) contribute to industrialization?
2. How did industrialization in the United States and in Japan differ, and why?
3. What was the role of slavery in industrial development?
4. In what ways was the Industrial Revolution a world event?

KEY TERMS

bourgeoisie (p. 817)
capitalism (p. 817)
cartel (p. 805)
Industrial Revolution (p. 794)
interchangeability of parts (p. 799)
limited liability (p. 805)
materialism (p. 816)
outwork (p. 801)
proletariat (p. 817)
socialism (p. 816)
stock market (p. 805)
utopian socialism (p. 816)

AT A CROSSROADS ▲

The Meiji Restoration of 1868 was the foundation of Japanese nation building and industrialization. Its Charter Oath, the founding document of Japan's new regime, is shown here being read in the presence of the emperor. The Charter Oath established the rule of law over "evil customs" of the past and opened the door to freedom in livelihoods. It also called on the Japanese to scour the world for new findings and advances, making Japan a crossroads of nation building and economic development. (Art Resource, NY.)

The Rise of Modern Nation-States

1850–1900

Modernizing Nations

FOCUS How did some states transform themselves into modern nations?

Emerging Powers: The United States and Japan

FOCUS How did the United States and Japan make their governments politically and economically powerful in the nineteenth century?

The Culture of Nations

FOCUS What part did culture play in forging a national identity?

COUNTERPOINT: Outsiders Inside the Nation-State

FOCUS Which groups were excluded from full participation in the nation-state, and why?

In 1862 Matsuo Taseko, a prosperous Japanese peasant, packed a few possessions and, leaving her family behind, made her way to the capital at Kyoto. The trip was an unusual one for a woman to make on her own, and even more so because of its goal: to overthrow the country's civilian leadership. Taseko belonged to a group of conservative activists eager to restore the power of the Japanese emperor, who for centuries had played second fiddle to the Tokugawa shogun, or first minister. So subordinate was the emperor that he received just 5 percent of the government's revenues while the shogun took 25 percent. To those in Taseko's group, the shogun's position was a reversal of the natural order. In a proper world, decision-making and revenue should have been the other way around. "Despicable charlatans," she called the shogun's administration. Even worse to Taseko was the presence of foreigners in the country's port cities, notably the Americans and British, who had demanded in the 1850s that Japan open its harbors to global trade. Taseko wrote this poem about them:

> The superficial
> foreign barbarians
> pile up mountains
> of silver,
> but even I, who am not
> a brave warrior
> from the land of the rising sun,
> I do not want their money,
> I would rather be poor.[1]

BACKSTORY

As we saw in Chapter 24, throughout the nineteenth century Europe and the United States industrialized rapidly, if unevenly, allowing the West to catch up economically with India and China. Industrialization offered a host of advantages to the West. Both Europe and the United States excelled in producing weaponry, which made them especially successful in opening trade and gaining diplomatic power. Industrializing nations engaged in increasingly global commerce, enjoyed greater productivity, and developed dense networks of swift transportation. As the West's newly industrialized states extended their power around the world, industrialization also produced internal transformations. It gave rise to new social classes and new occupations, swelling the middle and working classes and giving both a stake in the growing prosperity of their nations. These groups had the awareness, and some of them the wealth, to challenge the political and social values of kings and the aristocracy, sometimes overthrowing existing political institutions entirely and at other times working to modify them.

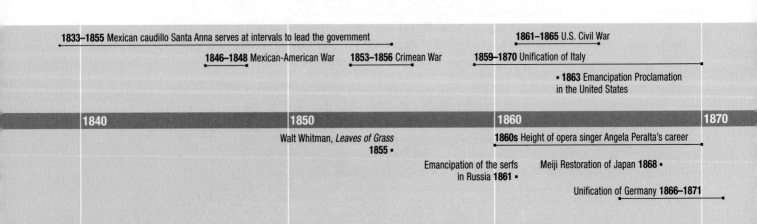

PACIFIC OCEAN

ARCTIC OCEAN

PACIFIC OCEAN

CANADA

JAPAN

UNITED STATES

SIBERIA

RUSSIAN EMPIRE

QING EMPIRE

MEXICO

GUATEMALA
EL SALVADOR
NICARAGUA
COSTA RICA
HONDURAS
HAITI
DOMINICAN REPUBLIC

UNITED KINGDOM

GERMANY

AUSTRALIA (Gr. Br.)

NEW ZEALAND (Gr. Br.)

ECUADOR
COLOMBIA
VENEZUELA

FRANCE
PORTUGAL   SPAIN   ITALY

OTTOMAN EMPIRE

PERU

ATLANTIC OCEAN

INDIAN OCEAN

BOLIVIA   BRAZIL
CHILE
ARGENTINA   PARAGUAY
URUGUAY

EGYPT

AFRICA

N
W   E
S

—— Boundaries, c. 1880

0   1000   2000 miles
0   1000   2000 kilometers

1833–1855 Mexican caudillo Santa Anna serves at intervals to lead the government

1861–1865 U.S. Civil War

1846–1848 Mexican-American War   **1853–1856** Crimean War   **1859–1870** Unification of Italy

▪ **1863** Emancipation Proclamation in the United States

1840   1850   1860   1870

Walt Whitman, *Leaves of Grass* **1855** ▪

1860s Height of opera singer Angela Peralta's career

Emancipation of the serfs in Russia **1861** ▪   Meiji Restoration of Japan **1868** ▪

Unification of Germany **1866–1871**

Beginning in 1862 members of Taseko's conservative group, aiming to free Japan from outside influences and to restore the emperor, took part in a virtual civil war with reformers who wanted trade, the latest technology, and a modern nation-state. Assassinations, riots, and street violence plagued the country, causing Taseko herself, who was sometimes seen as a spy by political opponents, to go into hiding in the spring of 1863 and eventually to return to her hometown. By 1868 the reformers had restored the emperor to his central position in a nation-building revolution that became known as the Meiji Restoration.

The Meiji Restoration was primarily the work of propertied individuals who wanted to update Japan's government and economy. It was part of a global nineteenth-century trend toward building strong states whose people felt bound together as part of a single political unity. In Latin America, leaders in Mexico, Argentina, and other states struggled to develop national institutions and to create connections between the central government and local elites. In Europe the nation-states of Germany and Italy unified amid economic ferment and calls for social and political reform. The United States fought a destructive civil war and killed and displaced native Americans to create a mighty nation-state stretching thousands of miles. Russia freed its serfs and reformed its legal and military systems—reforms designed to make it more competitive in a modernizing and global economic system.

Historians sometimes treat the rise of powerful nation-states and the sense of national identity among peoples as part of an inevitable process. However, it was not: as Italy and Germany were forming unified nations and Latin Americans were developing notions of modern citizenship, millions of individuals in the Austrian Empire, Africa, and Oceania, for example, held on to local identities based on village life or ethnic ties. Moreover, many

MAPPING THE WORLD

Nation-States, c. 1880

In many cases, but not all, industrial growth and revolutionary uprisings often led kingdoms to develop into nation-states. Around the world, nations reformed their administrative structures, created more effective armies, and encouraged national spirit. From Russia to Australia and across the Western Hemisphere, war and the seizure of native peoples' lands accompanied the rise of the nation-state.

ROUTES ▼

→ Forced migrations of Native Americans, 1832–1835

→ Travels of Florence Nightingale, 1820–1855

→ Travels of Camillo di Cavour, 1830–1838

→ Travels of Angela Peralta, 1862–1883

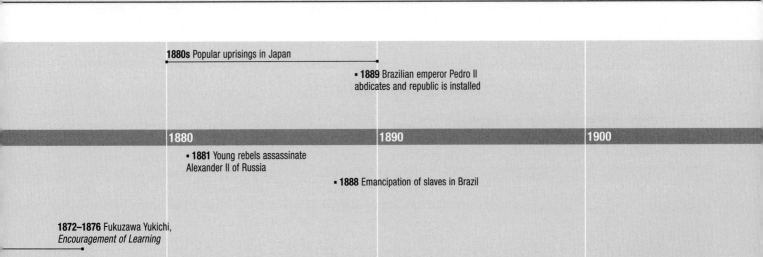

1880s Popular uprisings in Japan

▪ **1889** Brazilian emperor Pedro II abdicates and republic is installed

1880   **1890**   **1900**

▪ **1881** Young rebels assassinate Alexander II of Russia

▪ **1888** Emancipation of slaves in Brazil

1872–1876 Fukuzawa Yukichi, *Encouragement of Learning*

rulers had no interest in political and economic reforms, preferring to embrace tradition rather than change.

Other once-powerful states labored unsuccessfully to meet the challenges of global trade, rising population, and the growing industrial power of Europe. The Ottoman sultans found it difficult to modernize their administration of a complex empire; local governors such as the rulers of Egypt modernized cities, transportation, and other facilities on their own. China likewise failed to reform its governmental structures sufficiently to fight off the inroads made by the European powers, even though segments of its population were pushing for modern institutions and growing rich by dealing with the West.

Matsuo was a traditionalist—eager to restore the emperor to power and to rid Japan of outside influence. Although she was a peasant, she was well educated. Broader education also contributed to nation building as people circulated and debated political and philosophical writings, poetry, and other works. People came to be united not only by new institutions, but also by a common culture. However, modern nation-states also denied certain people within their borders full citizenship. Immigrants, women, and the conquered local peoples of Australia and the United States worked and paid taxes, for example, but they did not enjoy full equality and rights such as being able to vote. People hotly debated who did and did not belong to the nation, and Matsuo Taseko engaged in such debates, fighting for ideals that were centuries old. Even though she longed for an older way of doing things, she participated in the development of "the public"—that is, a wide arena of concerns and values that went beyond individual or family interests to create a shared national way of life. Thus, the era of nation building saw many forms of nation-states taking shape, all of them influenced by the public voices of many different people.

OVERVIEW
QUESTIONS

The major global development in this chapter: The causes and consequences of nation building in the nineteenth century.

As you read, consider:

1. Why did nation-states become so important to people in the nineteenth century?

2. What was the role of war in the rise of the nation-state?

3. What was the role of ordinary people in nation building?

4. Are nation-states still important today, and are there still outsiders inside nations?

Modernizing Nations

FOCUS
How did some states transform themselves into modern nations?

Politicians of this time and the citizens who backed them worked to bring varied peoples into cohesive nations and to develop more effective governments. This was an age of national growth and nation building when states industrialized and politicians changed the nature of government. To prosper in a more competitive and connected economic world, some even created entirely new entities, as occurred in Italy and Germany. Even where industry was slower to thrive, nation building occurred. People in the newly independent nations of Latin America began to develop a sense of themselves as citizens with common values. In Eurasia the mighty Russian Empire instituted dramatic reforms as part of a nationalizing effort after being decisively beaten in the Crimean War. What emerged from these efforts was a political and cultural form—the nation-state—that has shaped the course of modern world history, both for good and for ill.

"What Is a Nation?"

In an 1882 lecture, French writer Ernest Renan asked, "What is a nation?" The concept was a new one, and subject to debate. Nations came to be seen as political units in which citizens feel an allegiance to one another and are active in the government or state that represents them. Thus *nation-state* and *nation* are often treated as synonyms. A **nation** differs dramatically from a kingdom. A princely kingdom is the personal domain of a monarch, who sees people as subjects to be governed, not as active citizens with a political voice. Despite differences in their form, nations rely on the allegiance of a wide range of people within their geographic borders, who as citizens demand the rule of law and involvement in government. This active civic voice was essential to the rise of modern nations. Facing an enemy from without, people proudly protected the nation—that is, themselves and their community—as patriotic soldiers rather than military recruits forced to defend royal interests, as in a kingdom. Although women did not take up arms and lacked political rights, they too began to consider themselves active contributors to a nation's well-being, rearing young children to be virtuous citizens and volunteering their efforts in times of trouble.

In the nineteenth century and thereafter, politicians sought to mobilize whole populations to build powerful nation-states. Some waged external and civil wars in hopes of creating or maintaining national unity. The U.S. Civil War, for example, can be seen as a war for national unity waged by the North against the South. Other wars were fought to force outlying states to join a powerful military state permanently; this happened with Prussia, which formed the core of the new Germany. Historians have called the development of the nation-state a modernizing influence because the unity it created helped economic development spread over a wider territory. The nation-state also aided economic expansion by eliminating tariffs among cities and localities and by working to replace disruptive regional armies with a single fighting force operating to advance national, not local, power. Nation builders hoped to provide effective, centralized institutions—constitutions, bureaucracies, laws, and common military, education, and transportation systems. Theirs was a multifaceted undertaking in which centralizing authorities sought to challenge local identities and strengthen the connections and loyalties that bound populations together.

Latin American Nation Building

After the regions of South and Central America gained independence from Spain and Portugal early in the nineteenth century, they did not generally develop efficient or smoothly functioning democracies, but they did lay the groundwork for nation-states. Wars between states and civil wars between supporters of centralization and those wanting regional self-rule affected nation-building efforts. Although some people of individual nations were developing a sense of themselves as citizens, Latin American nation building was complex and often difficult (see Map 25.1).

Brazil's dominant ruler for more than five decades was the emperor Pedro II (r. 1831–1889)—a committed nation builder. "I have no rights; all I have is a power resulting from birth and chance," he claimed. "It is my duty to use it for the welfare, the progress, and the liberty of my people."[2] Pedro II tried to centralize government by gaining dominance over the wealthy landowning families and factions that controlled the countryside. As the capital of Rio de Janeiro prospered, Brazil fought a war against Paraguay

Brazil Takes the Lead

nation A sovereign political entity and defined territory of modern times representing a supposedly united people.

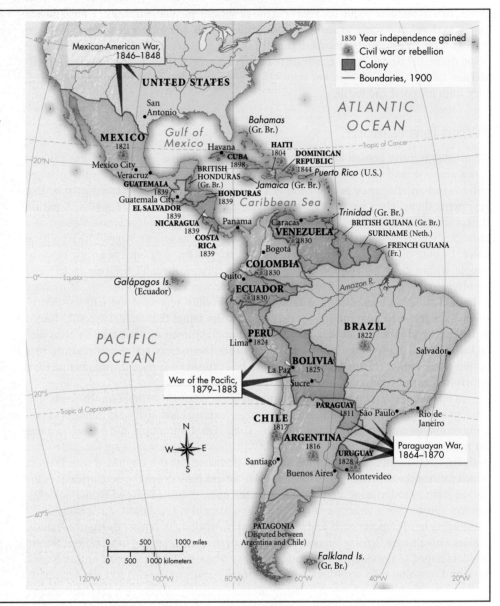

MAP 25.1

Latin America, c. 1900

The new nations of Latin America worked to create effective governments and engage citizens in the nation-building process. Like the new United States of America to the north, these nations often fought with their neighbors to expand boundaries and crushed native Americans to gain their lands. Simultaneously they created important institutions, such as systems of law, education, and culture, that would both enhance government power and advance citizens' capabilities.

Nation Versus Region

(1864–1870), which built allegiance to the central government. A firm believer that nation building depended on legal equality and opportunity, Pedro surrounded himself with people of all races. He ended the slave trade in 1850, partly in response to the growing voice of people of color expressed through their newspapers and clubs. Brazil ended slavery altogether in 1888, and it also tried to eliminate hierarchies based on skin color and racial ancestry. In its openness to change, Brazil seemed to be ahead of all its neighbors. It produced one of the greatest Latin American writers, Joachim Machado de Assis (ma-KA-do day ah-SEES). Of African descent, Machado de Assis's masterful novels do not portray a rosy society of the sort that Pedro hoped for. They are full of satire, as Machado explores the worlds of the old moneyed classes, the new bureaucracies of the rising nation-state, and the outsider status of women—all shaped by the legacy of slavery.

National cohesion quickly fell apart in Brazil. The emancipation of Brazil's slaves enraged plantation and mine owners in the countryside, who relied on cheap slave labor for their profits. Believers in small government, hierarchical social arrangements including slavery, and regional autonomy, they billed themselves as "federalists" and "liberals."

Brazilian Plantation Workers
Pedro II freed Brazil's slaves in 1888 as part of his nation-building efforts, believing that modern, unified nations needed to integrate all races into citizenship. Once regional leaders overthrew his monarchy, however, the weakened national authority could not protect newly freed workers from exploitation. The lack of protection for workers and the free hand given large landowners produced a huge disparity between the upper classes, who were virtually omnipotent, and impoverished ordinary people such as these workers on a manioc plantation in the 1890s. (The Art Archive/ Museu Nacional de Belas Artes Rio de Janeiro Brazil/Gianni Dagli Orti.)

In 1889 they overthrew Pedro's centralizing monarchy, returning power to provincial governments that they themselves controlled. Under the landlords' rule, movement toward a strong, tolerant nation-state seemed to go backward. As one newspaper complained in 1890 of the takeover, "In Brazil there are no more citizens; we are all slaves!"[3]

In fact, most of Latin America was shaped by the bold, powerful landowners in the countryside, who controlled the production of minerals, coffee, sugar, and other commodities sold on the global market. Such men believed that their wealth and power rested on the liberal, eighteenth-century belief in minimal government and the building of individual wealth. They felt that any policy or reform that challenged these principles should be resisted at all costs. In an age of nation building, their stance against strong centralized institutions went against the prevailing trend and kept individual states in turmoil. Almost every Latin American state experienced this contest between centralization and **federalism**.

Many wealthy landowners were themselves strongmen with their own armies, but there were also independent military leaders, *caudillos*, men at the head of unofficial bands of warriors who controlled the countryside by force. Caudillos ruled regions so far removed from the capital cities that they functioned as a law unto themselves. They gathered the support of peasants, workers, and the poor by offering protection in a turbulent countryside where the peasantry on large estates was intensely exploited.

Some caudillos stabilized the central government by acting as temporary dictators. General Antonio Lopez de Santa Anna was the quintessential caudillo. In Mexico, the period from the 1830s to 1855 is called the "Age of Santa Anna" because he wielded so much personal influence. In this period, conservatives favored the rule of large landowners, while the Catholic Church battled reformers who championed individual rights, foreign investment, and trade. During their disputes Santa Anna, who was called "Defender of the Homeland," was summoned some dozen times to head the government and stabilize the nation between 1833 and 1855. During this time of instability Mexico lost much of its territory to the United States in the Mexican-American War (1846–1848). Nonetheless, the

Caudillos

federalism A form of government in which power and administration are located in regions such as provinces and states rather than in a centralized administration.

caudillo remained an important figure in Latin American nation building, and at times even rescued nations from dissolution.

Although caudillos could mobilize masses of workers and peasants to political causes, gradually governments built state institutions such as national armies and military schools to train nationally oriented officers. Governments also took control of infrastructure such as railroads and ports along Latin America's extensive coastline. In the second half of the nineteenth century, state bureaucracies grew as the educated middle class came to fill government offices. Regional economic interests gave way to national economic interests; for instance, local tariffs exacted by the different regions of a nation gave way to tariffs collected at national borders.

A Sense of Citizenship   During the struggles to construct new, centralized governments, many people in individual Latin American countries developed a sense of belonging and citizenship that was crucial to nation building. José Gregorio Paz Soldán, a judge in Peru, had first supported slavery in the new republic but soon became an ardent supporter of liberty and equal treatment for all, commenting that "The Indians are no more savage or ferocious than other people who have been attracted to a social and civilized life."[4] Paz Soldán wanted solidarity among citizens of all classes. Employers, he urged, should give laborers "a salary and good treatment."[5] The Peruvian constitution of 1828 stated that "All citizens may be admitted to public employment, without any difference except that of their talents and virtues."[6] The qualifications for participating in the nation were in theory the same for everyone, uniting people of different ethnicities and classes instead of dividing them as the Spanish monarchy had done by giving preference to the Spanish-born.

Even in Cuba, where the Spanish crown still ruled, people came to believe in a common citizenship characteristic of an independent nation-state. Free blacks in Havana protested their exclusion from service in the militia because of their race, citing their commonality with other citizens. "Mulattoes and blacks, we are the ones who practice the mechanical arts to the highest degree of perfection, to the admiration and wonder of professors from other enlightened nations. We own property—houses that we live in with our families, workshops, and buildings to rent out to those who need them. We have farms and slaves in the same proportions as those other members of the people of Havana who possess such property."[7] The Spanish put down the protest, but they could not quell the sense of citizenship that gave rise to it.

After independence, cities in Latin American countries had thriving political clubs, mutual aid societies, newspapers and journals, and economic organizations that concerned themselves not only with the welfare of the community but with the nation as a whole. Although a nation might have a dictatorial ruler or a corrupt administration, commercial groups took part in public debate over building a strong national economy, and mutual aid societies focused on well-being in neighborhoods. "Clubs have enabled us to replace tyranny with liberty," was the opinion of one Mexican newspaper in 1855. "They have provided the government with a way to become acquainted with public opinion, and this is the reason we support them."[8] People became immersed in the public affairs of their nation as never before. Thus, the connections among citizens that were central to the nation-state were not solely the product of state policies imposed from the top down. They were also created from the bottom up by citizens themselves.

The Russian Empire's New Course

Other countries that seemed unlikely to embrace the institutions and values of modern nation-states were often transformed by events, such as peasant uprisings, inefficiencies, low productivity, and the revelation of internal problems from external defeat. The Russian Empire, for example, modernized its institutions when wartime defeat dramatically revealed the need for change. In the 1800s, Russia continued its centuries-old expansionism into Asia and the Middle East. Just as the British aimed for inroads in China, Tsar Nicholas I wanted to absorb much of the Ottoman Empire, which was fast becoming known as "the sick man of Europe" because of the disintegrating administration of its lands. As Russia grew more aggressive, war erupted in October 1853. The Crimean War (1853–1856) began as a conflict between the Russian and Ottoman empires but ended as a war with long-lasting consequences for Russia, much of Europe, and, indeed, for the world (see Map 25.2).

The war disrupted Europe's balance of power, as France and Great Britain, enemies for more than a century, united in declaring war on Russia to defend the Ottoman Empire's sovereignty. Their goal was to maintain power in the global economy by securing their full access to the eastern Mediterranean. British and French troops landed in the Crimea in September 1854 and waged a long siege of the Russian naval base at Sevastopol on the Black Sea. The war coincided with the continuing spread of the Industrial Revolution, which introduced powerful new technologies into warfare: the railroad, shell-firing cannon, breech-loading rifles, steam-powered ships, and the telegraph. With the telegraph and increased press coverage, the relationship of the home front to the battlefront changed. Home audiences received news from the Crimean front lines more rapidly and in more detail than ever before, intensifying national unity and thus nation building across Europe.

Despite the new weaponry, Sevastopol fell only after a year of savage and costly combat. Generals on both sides were incompetent, and governments failed to provide combatants with even minimal supplies, sanitation, and medical care. A million men died, more than two-thirds from disease and starvation. The casualties resulting from incompetence and poor sanitation showed that nations needed strong institutions. London reformer Florence Nightingale seized the moment to escape the confines of middle-class domesticity by organizing a battlefield nursing service to care for British troops. Through her tough-minded organization of nursing units, she pioneered nursing as a profession and also better sanitary conditions both in armies and in society in general. After the war, she contributed to nation building by publishing statistical studies showing that national effectiveness depended on public health and a scientifically prepared and centrally directed military.

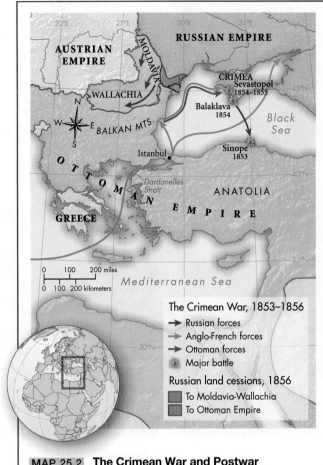

MAP 25.2   The Crimean War and Postwar Settlement, 1853–1856

The Crimean War has been called senseless, but it was rich in consequences. By splitting the conservative alliance between Austria and Russia that had effectively kept France and indeed all of Europe in check, it opened the way for ambitious politicians in Italy and Germany to unify their fragmented states into two strong nations. Additionally, its defeat caused Russia to free the serfs and institute significant reforms; the Ottoman Empire continued to attempt modern nation building as well.

The war exposed Russia's weakness and transformed the global balance of power. With casualties mounting, Tsar Alexander II (r. 1855–1881) asked for peace. As a result of the peace treaty of 1856, the Black Sea was declared neutral waters and Russia lost its claim to protect Christians in Ottoman lands. Austria's and Russia's grip on European affairs weakened, making way for the rise of new regional and global powers. The defeat forced the authoritarian Russian state to embark on a long-overdue renovation of the empire.

When Russia lost the Crimean War, the educated public, including some government officials, found the poor performance of serf-conscripted armies to be a disgrace. When a son was conscripted into the Russian army for the regular twenty-five-year term, parents held funerals because the army experience was so long and brutal and the chance of returning alive so slight. The system of serf labor was also seen as an intolerable liability for a country that needed economic and institutional modernization to be an effective nation-state on the world stage. The Russian economy had stagnated compared with western

Serfdom in Russia

Russian Peasants at a Soup Kitchen
Even after emancipation from serfdom in 1861 and other reforms that followed, Russian peasants were hard-pressed to earn a living. As a condition of emancipation, they were burdened with debt for farmland and could not migrate freely in search of greater opportunity. Tensions in the countryside grew, alleviated only by acts of charity and relief programs, such as the soup kitchen shown here. (©Sovfoto.)

Europe. Old-fashioned farming techniques led to worn-out soil and food shortages. For serfs, everyday life brought constant toil and obedience to flighty or cruel masters, who could marry them off at will or rent them out at great distances from home.

Challenges to serfdom had begun to grow during the decades before the Crimean War. Serf defiance ranged from malingering while at forced labor to small uprisings. Works of art such as novelist Ivan Turgenev's *A Hunter's Sketches* (1852) contributed to a spirit of reform with their sympathetic portrayals of serfs and frank depiction of brutal masters: "O Lord Jesus Christ!" one of his characters thunders. "Am I not free to use my slaves as I wish?"[9] But other inspiration came from serf artists and writers—the lucky ones among the serf population who were assigned artistic tasks such as piano tuning, fine cabinetry, or portrait painting on estates; some even became highly educated.

One of these was Alexander Nikitenko, born a serf in 1804. His father had been sent to sing in one of Russia's famous boys' choirs by his owner, a great landowner. Enraged at being returned to the estate still a serf, Nikitenko's father, who had learned to read while in the choir, made sure that his son received a good education. Alexander also fumed at the injustice of his serf condition, especially as he became known as one of the most learned young men in the land. In the late 1830s, a powerful Russian prince obtained Nikitenko's freedom, allowing him to become a high government official. Educated serfs such as Nikitenko were among the most bitter and vocal advocates of change (see Reading the Past: The Russian People Under Serfdom).

The Russian People Under Serfdom

Alexander Nikitenko gained his freedom from serfdom after proving himself a learned and conscientious teacher as well as an outstanding manager of households and general man of all work. Many serfs were accomplished; their achievements included painting and traveling in troupes of actors and singers, which brought Russians in contact with one another across vast spaces. Like Nikitenko, some of these serfs reached national eminence and came to be celebrated, but Nikitenko felt the degradation of serfdom long after he was free. These excerpts from his autobiography, first published in 1824, concern the early nineteenth century when he was between six and ten years old. They do not reflect the thinking of a child, however; Nikitenko observed serfdom for decades while honing this account of his life.

The peasants suffered beneath the yoke of serfdom. If a master was wealthy and owned several thousand serfs, they suffered less oppression because most of them were tenant farmers. . . . On the other hand, small [landowners] literally sucked out the strength of unfortunates in their power. Neither time nor land was at their disposal. . . . In addition, sometimes there was inhuman treatment, and often cruelty was accompanied by debauchery. . . .

People could be bought and sold wholesale or in small numbers, by families, or singly like bulls and sheep. . . . Tsar Alexander I, during the humanitarian phase of his reign, talked about improving the lot of his serf-subjects, but attempts to limit the [landowners'] power vanished without a trace. The nobility wanted to live in luxury befitting its station. . . .

[E]veryone bore the burdens generated by the People's War [Napoleon's 1812 invasion] without complaint.

They supplied and equipped recruits at great personal expense. Yet I did not detect in their conversations a sign of deep interest in the events of the time. Evidently everyone was interested solely in their own affairs. The mention of Napoleon's name evoked awe rather than hate. The nonchalant attitude of our community toward the disaster hanging over Russia was startling. This may have been due in part to the distance of the theater of war. . . .

But I think the main reason was apathy, characteristic of a people estranged from participation in society's affairs, as Russians were then. They were not accustomed to discussion [of] what went on around them and unconditionally obeyed the orders of the authorities.

Source: Alexander Nikitenko, *Up from Serfdom: My Childhood and Youth in Russia 1804–1824*, trans. Helen Saltz Jacobson (New Haven: Yale University Press, 2001), 54–56, 75.

EXAMINING THE EVIDENCE

1. How does Nikitenko characterize Russian serfs?

2. How did serfdom affect the Russian people and state more generally?

3. What was the mood of the Russian people as a nation facing the Napoleonic invasion of 1812? How might the emancipation of the serfs in 1861 have changed that mood?

Faced with Russia's dire situation, Alexander II proved more flexible than his predecessors in modernizing society. Better educated and more widely traveled, he ushered in what came to be known as the Great Reforms, granting Russians new rights from above as a way to ensure that violent action from below would not force change. The most dramatic reform was the emancipation of almost 50 million serfs beginning in 1861. Under the terms of emancipation, communities of former serfs, headed by male village elders, were given their personal freedom and grants of land. Each community, called a *mir* (mihr), was given full power to distribute this land among its members and to direct their own economic activity. Thus, although the serfs were free, the requirements of communal landowning and decision-making held back individuals with new ideas and those who wanted to find opportunity elsewhere. Nonetheless, millions surely received this news as former serf Alexander Nikitenko did: "with an inexpressible feeling of joy."[10] Ending serfdom and slavery was often the foundation for creating citizens and for nation building.

Emancipation of the Serfs

mir In Russia, the organization of land and former serfs following the emancipation of the serfs.

The state awarded peasant communities some 13 percent less land than they had tilled under serfdom, forced them to "redeem" or pay the government for this land in long-term loans, and in fact awarded the best land to the nobility. Although some landowners experimented with modern farming techniques, which made Russia the largest grain-exporting nation by 1900, the conditions of emancipation held Russian agriculture back. Nevertheless, idealistic reformers believed the emancipation of the serfs, whom the nobility once treated virtually as livestock, had produced miraculous results. As one writer put it, "The people are without any exaggeration transfigured from head to foot. . . . The look, the walk, the speech, everything is changed."

Other Nation-Building Reforms

The state also reformed local administration, the judiciary, and the military. The government set up *zemstvos* (ZEHMST-vohs), regional councils through which aristocrats could revive neglected public institutions for education, public health, and welfare. As aristocrats gained responsibility for local well-being, some became invested in Russia's health as a nation. Judicial reform in 1864 gave all Russians, even former serfs, access to modern civil courts, where ordinary people for the first time benefited from the principle of equality of all persons, regardless of social rank, under a unified set of laws. Military reform followed in 1874 when the government ended the twenty-five-year term of conscription, substituting a six-year term and devoting more attention to education, efficiency, and the humane treatment of recruits. These changes improved the fitness of Russian soldiers, helping them identify with the nation as a whole.

Limits of the Great Reforms

Alexander's reforms encouraged modernizers and gave many in the upper classes a more worldly outlook, but nation building also diminished the personal prerogatives of the nobility, leaving its authority generally weakened and sparking intergenerational rebellion. "An epidemic seemed to seize upon [noble] children . . . an epidemic of fleeing from the parental roof," one observer noted. Rejecting aristocratic values, youthful rebels from the upper class valued practical activity and sometimes identified with peasants and workers. Some formed communes, where they joined together in cooperative living to do humble manual labor. Others turned to higher education, especially the sciences, to gain modern knowledge. Rebellious daughters of the nobility flouted parental expectations by cropping their hair short, wearing black, and escaping from home through marriages in name only so they could study medicine and the sciences in European universities.

This repudiation of traditional society led Turgenev to label radical youth as *nihilists* (from the Latin for "nothing"), meaning people who lack belief in any values whatsoever. In fact, these individual rebellions showed a spirit of defiance percolating in Russian society that would soon fuel assassinations, including that of the reformer Alexander II in 1881, and ultimately produce the revolutions that would shape the world in the next century. For the time being, the tsarist regime only partially succeeded in developing the administrative, economic, and civic institutions that were strengthening nation-states elsewhere. The tsar and his inner circle held tightly to the reins of government, slowing the development of consensus politics and modern citizenship.

A Unified Italy and a United Germany

With the European powers divided over the Crimean War of 1853 to 1856, politicians in the German and Italian states took advantage of the opportunity to unify their respective countries. In 1848 workers, students, and professionals had revolted in many of the individual Italian and German states, hoping to reform and unify their countries. Despite their failure, the issue of unification simmered until two practical but visionary leaders took charge: Camillo di Cavour of the kingdom of Piedmont-Sardinia in the economically modernizing north of Italy, and Otto von Bismarck from the prosperous agrarian kingdom of Prussia. Both depended on modern railroads, strong armies, and power diplomacy to transform disunited states into coherent nations with a presence on the world stage.

Italy

The architect of the new Italy was Camillo di Cavour, prime minister of the kingdom of Piedmont-Sardinia from 1852 until his death in 1861. A rebel in his youth, the young

Cavour had conducted agricultural experiments on his aristocratic father's land. He organized steamship companies, played the stock market, and inhaled the fresh air of modernization during his travels to Paris and London. Cavour promoted economic development rather than democratic uprising as the means to achieve a united Italy. As prime minister, he helped develop a healthy Piedmontese economy, a modern army, and a liberal political climate to anchor Piedmont's drive to unite the Italian states.

Kingdom of Piedmont-Sardinia before 1859
To Kingdom of Piedmont-Sardinia, 1859
To Kingdom of Piedmont-Sardinia, 1860
To Kingdom of Italy, 1866, 1870
Boundary of Kingdom of Italy after 1870

Unification of Italy, 1859–1870

To achieve this goal, however, Piedmont would have to confront Austria, which governed the provinces of Lombardy and Venetia and had a strong influence on most of the peninsula. Realizing that Austria was too powerful for Piedmont to take on by itself, Cavour first got a promise of help from France and then provoked the Austrians to invade northern Italy in April 1859. Nationalists seeking unity and political liberals seeking constitutions and modern institutions in Tuscany and other central Italian states joined the Piedmontese cause. Using the newly built Piedmontese railroad to move troops, the French and Piedmontese armies achieved rapid victories in the north. In May 1860, Giuseppe Garibaldi, an inspired guerrilla fighter and veteran of the revolutions of 1848, set sail from Genoa to liberate Sicily with a thousand red-shirted volunteers, many of them teenage boys and half from the urban working class, "splendid in the dress and cap of the student, and in the more humble dress of the bricklayer, the carpenter, and the [blacksmith]," as Garibaldi himself put it.[11]

Across the Sicilian countryside peasant revolts against landlords and the corrupt government were under way in anticipation of ***Risorgimento***, the "rebirth" of a strong Italian state. Anger in the countryside was so violent against these oppressors that the farmers massacred opponents, leaving them to be "devoured by dogs . . . torn to pieces by their own brothers with a fury which would have horrified the hyenas."[12] Successfully mastering the scene in the south, Garibaldi threw his support to Piedmont-Sardinia's leadership. In 1861, the kingdom of Italy was proclaimed. Exhausted by a decade of overwork, Cavour soon died, but despite huge difficulties such as poverty in the south, many citizens of the new country took pride in the Italian nation and came to see themselves as one people.

A momentous act of nation building, for both Europe and the world, was the creation of a united Germany in 1871. The Prussian state brought an array of cities and kingdoms under its control within a single decade by using both the conservative military to wage war on behalf of unification and the liberal businessmen's enthusiasm for the profits to be gained from a single national market. The newly unified Germany prospered, continuing to consolidate its economic might as business people small and large enjoyed a bigger market to pursue profits. Its growing industrial and commercial wealth would make Germany the foremost power on the European continent by the end of the nineteenth century.

The architect of a unified Germany was Otto von Bismarck, the Prussian minister-president. Bismarck came from landed nobility on his father's side; his mother's family included high-ranking bureaucrats and middle-class intellectuals. As a university student, the young Bismarck had gambled and womanized; he was interested in only one course, on the economic foundations of politics. After failing in the civil service he worked to modernize operations on his family's estates while leading an otherwise rowdy life. His marriage to a pious Lutheran woman worked a transformation and gave him new purpose: to establish Prussia as a respected and dominant power.

In 1862, the king of Prussia appointed Bismarck prime minister in hopes that he would block the growing power of the liberals, who were the reformers and modernizers in the Prussian parliament, and instead build the army over their objections. Bismarck

Germany

zemstvo Regional council of the Russian nobility established after the emancipation of the serfs to deal with education and local welfare issues.

Risorgimento Italian for "rebirth," a nineteenth-century rallying cry for the unification of the Italian states.

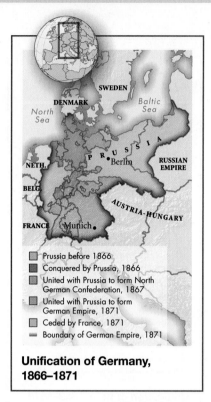

Unification of Germany, 1866–1871

Prussia before 1866

Conquered by Prussia, 1866

United with Prussia to form North German Confederation, 1867

United with Prussia to form German Empire, 1871

Ceded by France, 1871

Boundary of German Empire, 1871

indeed managed to ram through programs to build the army despite the opposition's belief in parliamentary control. His brand of nation building was based on *realpolitik*—a political strategy of hard-headed realism, armed might, and rapid industrial and commercial development. "Germany looks not to Prussia's liberalism, but to its power," he preached. "The great questions of the day will not be settled by speeches and majority decisions . . . but by iron and blood."

After his triumph over the parliament, Bismarck led Prussia into a series of victorious wars, against Denmark in 1864, against Austria in 1866, and, finally, against France in 1870. His victory over Austria-Hungary, which claimed to be the leader of the disunited German states, allowed Bismarck to create a North German Confederation led by Prussia. Prussia's swift victory over France persuaded all the German states to unify under Prussia's leadership. In January 1871, the king of Prussia was proclaimed the Kaiser, or emperor, of a new, imperial Germany.

Despite the growing wealth of liberal business people, the constitution of the newly unified empire ensured the continued political dominance of the aristocracy and monarchy. The Kaiser, who also remained Prussia's king, controlled the military and appointed Bismarck to the powerful position of chancellor for the Reich (empire). Bismarck balanced the right to vote, which the constitution granted to men, with an unequal electoral system in Prussia, which continued to be the dominant state within the German Empire. In the Prussian system, votes from the upper classes counted more than those from the lower. Bismarck's nation-building deals worked, allowing Germany, even more than Italy, to focus its national energy on industrial growth and power politics. Europe would never be the same.

Emerging Powers: The United States and Japan

FOCUS

How did the United States and Japan make their governments politically and economically powerful in the nineteenth century?

Two other newcomers, the United States and Japan, were also eager for global wealth and influence. These two states built national power in the nineteenth century and drastically reformed their societies and political structures to industrialize and to make their governments more focused and effective. By 1900 the United States and Japan were beginning to rival the great European powers as nation building promoted their economic strength and pumped ordinary people's ambitions.

Expansion and Consolidation of the United States

The United States went from a cluster of states hugging the eastern seaboard in the eighteenth century to a growing power in the nineteenth century. Like Germany and Italy, it did so through warfare. Confronted with the pressures of migration and the demands for raw materials, it fought Mexico and Indian peoples in order to seize their resources and land. It also engaged in a devastating civil war over issues arising from the brisk global trade in cotton, slaves, and—increasingly—industrial products. The series of wars the United States pursued in the nineteenth century expanded its territory and unified a rambunctious nation of adventurers, immigrants, farmers, ranchers, miners, entrepreneurs, and industrial innovators. Amid all this turmoil, the nation built up its common institutions, such as schools and transportation networks, and widened its global connections.

realpolitik A practical, tough-minded approach to politics, wielded most famously by Otto von Bismarck in Germany.

U.S. settlers continued to push westward in the nineteenth century, seeking more land to profit from the global trade in raw materials, particularly cotton. They drove into Mexican territory in the continent's southwest, where struggles for control of both trade and territory resulted in sporadic warfare. Between 1846 and 1848 the United States first provoked and then won a war with Mexico over land in Mexico's north, and as a result almost doubled its territory, annexing Texas as well as large portions of California and the Southwest (see Map 25.3). Simultaneously, immigrants from around the world flocked to California and later to other places where gold was discovered. Americans came to see this western expansion as part of the nation's **Manifest Destiny**—that is, the belief that white Americans had a God-given right to control the entire continent no matter how many native Americans were killed or displaced.

Westward Expansion and Manifest Destiny

Manifest Destiny The nineteenth-century doctrine that the United States had the right and duty to expand throughout the North American continent.

MAP 25.3 **U.S. Civil War and Westward Expansion**

U.S. nation building advanced through the war with Mexico, the Civil War, and ongoing battles to take the land of native Americans. Calls for unity during wartime and appeals asserting the superiority of white Americans welded the country together both politically and culturally. These shared values helped the United States forge ahead economically, with innovation coming to justify U.S. claims to being more advanced than those whose property the expanding nation took.

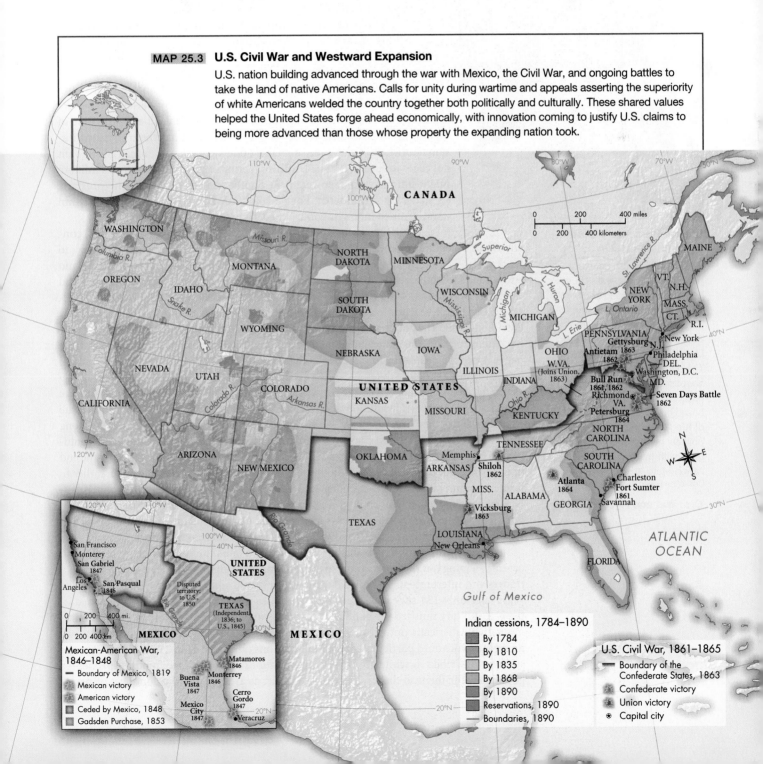

Mexican-American War, 1846–1848
- — Boundary of Mexico, 1819
- Mexican victory
- American victory
- Ceded by Mexico, 1848
- Gadsden Purchase, 1853

Indian cessions, 1784–1890
- By 1784
- By 1810
- By 1835
- By 1868
- By 1890
- Reservations, 1890
- — Boundaries, 1890

U.S. Civil War, 1861–1865
- — Boundary of the Confederate States, 1863
- Confederate victory
- Union victory
- Capital city

English Porcelain Statue of Abraham Lincoln

Although the British generally backed the Confederate cause because they needed southern cotton for its textile industry, the Staffordshire porcelain company issued this statue on Abraham Lincoln's inauguration in 1861. The oddly regal garment Lincoln is wearing and the highly decorated horse he is riding were based on an earlier representation of King George III. Portrayals of political heroes such as Lincoln grew with the spread of the nation-state. (The Art Archive/Private Collection/Eileen Tweedy.)

Civil War and Reconstruction

Politicians and citizens alike argued over the status of the new western lands. The greatest quarrels came over the expansion of slavery to the new territories, and the main issue was livelihoods. Should the West be settled by free white farmers, or could southern plantation owners bring in their slaves, against whose unpaid labor white farmers could not compete? Like some Latin American nation builders, many saw equal legal status of citizens as essential to a thriving nation, but others disagreed so strongly that the country became polarized. In the North, where abolitionists had a strong organization to fight against slavery, the new Republican Party called for "free soil, free labor, free men." However, few Republicans backed the abolitionists' demand for an immediate end to slavery in the South. In the months following Republican Abraham Lincoln's election to the presidency in 1860, most of the southern slaveholding states seceded to form the Confederate States of America.

Under Lincoln's leadership the North fought the South in a civil war from 1861 to 1865 to uphold the union. Lincoln did not initially aim to abolish slavery, but in January 1863 his Emancipation Proclamation came into force as a wartime measure officially freeing all slaves in the Confederate States and turning the war into a fight not only for union but for the end of slavery—thus creating a pool of workers who were entirely free *and* connecting nation building to the liberal program of rights and opportunity. While the war dragged on, northern industrialization flourished: "Believe me," remarked one Pennsylvania industrialist, "I am not eager for peace."[13] The North's superior industrial strength and military might ultimately overpowered the South, and in April 1865 the prostrate Confederacy surrendered. For Lincoln, the victory was short-lived. Within days a Confederate sympathizer had assassinated the president.

During the postwar period known as Reconstruction (1865–1877), constitutional amendments ended slavery and granted the rights of citizenship and voting to black males. For a time under Reconstruction, the newly liberated slaves received land and education, and some served in government or moved up in the world of business and work. The way was open for continent-wide industrial expansion and commercial agriculture, based on a free labor force, common rights for citizens, and migration from virtually every continent. The country would soon become a thriving nation-state.

A final piece of the nation-building effort in the United States was crushing the various native American peoples by forcibly taking their North American homelands or killing them to open up resources for whites. "Manifest Destiny" became a strong post–Civil War rallying cry. In the 1820s the state of Georgia simply took the land of the Cherokees, a group of native Americans who had a constitution and practiced settled farming, forcing them to migrate westward along the "Trail of Tears"—so named because of the number of deaths along the way. Pushed from the east coast westward by European settlers in the seventeenth century, tens of thousands of North American Indians had moved onto the Great Plains by the end of the eighteenth century. Numerous other native Americans had settled there far earlier in farming communities. Many were horse traders and herders of an estimated 40 million buffalo, exchanging goods with communities in New Mexico to the south and the British and French to the north. "There was always fat meat, glad singing, and much dancing in our villages," one Crow woman remembered of her people's mid-nineteenth-century prosperity.[14]

All that was before Europeans moved onto the Plains themselves in the nineteenth century, wiping out the buffalo and spreading European diseases widely, through Indian traders and interpreters. The Mandan tribes numbered some 15,000 in 1750; a hundred years later only 138 survived. Hundreds of thousands of native Americans perished as the U.S. military finished the conquest, carrying out government orders to drive remaining native Americans onto reservations in Oklahoma and other states, where they had no right to vote or to participate in U.S. institutions (see again Map 25.3). As one Apache survivor described it, whites considered reservations "a good place for the Apaches—a good place for them to die."[15] For white Americans at the time, the conquest of native

Americans across the continent helped industry thrive, helped immigrants find new livelihoods, and helped the nation to unify.

Dramatic Change in Japan

When the United States forced the opening of Japan to foreigners in the 1850s, it disturbed the country's peace and, as the activism of Matsuo Taseko shows, threw Japan into political turmoil. Strange, unruly white men walked the streets of port cities, and Western emissaries made demands on the government. All the same, even some of Japan's provincial rulers sensed the excitement and opportunity. There was money to be made, local notables suspected, and they resented the Tokugawa shogun's control of trade with the foreigners and thus his monopoly on profits. More conservative leaders found the break with the tradition of relative isolation an affront to Japan's greatness, and they were willing to use violence to suppress Japanese contact with the outside world. For example, conservatives assassinated an official who accepted trade treaties with foreigners and murdered a scholar who used a Western saddle on his horse. Such traditionalists shared Matsuo Taseko's desire to drive the "barbarians" from Japan and return the Japanese people to their traditions.

The furor over political and economic life led to a dramatic realignment of power in Japan. Many of the provincial rulers adopted the goal of restoring the emperor Komei to the full dignity of his office. The emperor was their "jewel," and Japanese of almost all political positions now unified around him. By late 1867, support for the shogun's long-standing power had dwindled to virtually nothing, and he was forced to resign.

Sioux Women Line Up for Rations

Nation building allowed many citizens to prosper because of the rule of law and new rights and opportunities. For many others, however, nation building was a disaster. Whereas once the Sioux had prospered, by the 1890s they were confined to small sections of the continent that was their homeland. Native Americans were the last group given the vote in the United States, although romanticized portrayals of native Americans who aided the European colonists as well as tales of native American "savagery" became staples of U.S. nation-building lore. (Denver Public Library. Western History Collection, photo by C.G. Morledge, Call number X-31445.)

Meiji Restoration   The restoration of power to the emperor did not, however, bring with it a straightforward return to Japanese isolation as conservatives such as Matsuo Taseko had hoped. Although a series of shoguns had recognized the importance of relationships with the West, Emperor Komei had been against it. Conveniently for the modernizers, he fell ill and died as the shogunate collapsed, leaving the throne to his fifteen-year-old son, Mutsuhito (r. 1868–1912). The resulting new government revived the imperial house and gave priority to Westernization and the shogun's more open, global policies—largely to protect Japan from further inroads by foreigners. Having fought to gain influence, the victorious, reform-minded elites crafted an assembly of high-ranking men such as themselves to determine the laws, making imperial rule much less than absolute. The government announced the "Meiji Restoration"—*Meiji* means "enlightened rule"—as a combination of "Western science and Eastern values" offering both innovation and restoration. Thus, the revival of imperial power partly masked the reality of revolutionary change. Japan would be transformed by its new relationship with the West, but its leaders hoped that by embracing aspects of Westernization they could control that transformation, ensuring that the process would serve Japan's interests, and not those of the West (see Map 25.4).

The Meiji government stabilized itself through a series of necessary changes. A pressing issue was overturning the older decentralization of power embodied in the system of local lords, the daimyo, and their loyal retainers, the samurai. The government successfully centralized power by forcing the daimyo to surrender their political and economic control of the countryside and giving them large payments or positions in the new government instead. The tens of thousands of samurai, who became unemployed once their local lords had no need for them, were potentially troublesome members of the new social order—a good many of them had no skills at all, except roughhousing. The government bought them off with pensions and later with government bonds. The samurai's status further declined as some of the most prominent politicians toured the world to gain ideas for modernization and concluded that a centralized conscript army would be far more reliable than Japan's traditional, samurai-based forces. Whereas the samurai mostly relied on a code of individual heroism, a national, conscript army was a disciplined fighting mass trained to cooperate in the use of modern weaponry. As a result of these findings, Japan instituted universal military conscription. It simultaneously created a hereditary nobility, as in Europe, and limited the powers of elected representatives who might come from the people. These last changes, enshrined in the constitution of 1889, showed that despite centralization, the government would not be fully based on republican institutions or popular rule.

The first two decades of the Meiji Restoration were tumultuous. Discontent and disorder persisted, as people from many walks of life remade the economy. The first to revolt were the displaced samurai, followed by farmers such as Matsuo Taseko, merchants, and countless others who had fought to bring back the emperor and face down the "barbarian" challenge. Now the same people struggled for the recognition of what were called "People's Rights" within

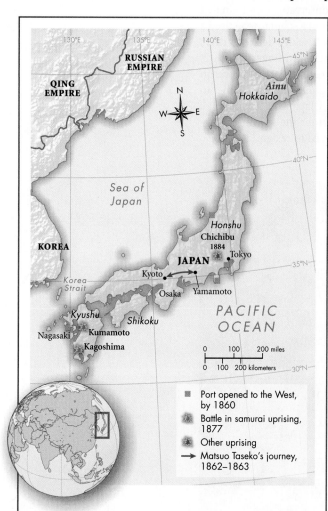

MAP 25.4   Japan, c. 1860–1889

Japan's rapid development of a more modern administration and economy cost many people their livelihoods, most notably the samurai. The changes the new government imposed during the Meiji Restoration of 1868 stirred uprisings and peasant revolts, particularly because Western nations appeared to be forcing Japan open with the goal of foreign domination.

the imperial system. They drafted constitutions of their own that laid out the fundamental powers of the people who, after all, were the building blocks of the nation. When their constitutions were ignored by the government during these first two decades of Meiji rule, they took up arms.

Throughout the early Meiji period, people of the rural lower classes launched a series of rebellions. They found themselves squeezed by high taxes, intended to finance Japan's modernization and industrialization, and by a drop in agricultural prices that resulted from increased global competition. The new officials of the Meiji government, instead of respecting those on the land, seemed to inflict them with hardship even as cities were thriving. In Chichibu outside Tokyo, one resident expressed his despair: "The wind blows, / The rain falls, / Young men die. The groans of poverty / Flutter like flags in the wind."[16] In 1884, an army of eight thousand peasants in Chichibu began fighting for the people's rights, fully believing that they could force the central government to negotiate. In the Chichibu uprising, the armed populace talked about "deposing evil rulers" and "changing the mandate" as part of the program of ousting corrupt officials. Government forces smashed the uprising, imprisoning and executing many participants. Meiji officials attributed the uprising to criminals, but in fact this revolt, like others occurring across Japan, showed that successful nation building required more attention to the needs of the Japanese population as a whole. In the decades to come, Japan would continue on the difficult path to the creation of a modern nation-state.

Social Unrest and Rebellion

The Culture of Nations

History, music, art, and other cultural works helped peoples forge national identities and built bonds across regions and localities. National cultures sometimes focused on reviving a country's literary past and celebrating long-dead authors' works. In other instances, people invented customs such as special dress or songs that over time came to be seen as "traditional." Still other peoples prized their nation's modernity, and citizens traveled miles to experience fast-paced new technology like the railroad or to see for themselves modern new structures such as the Eiffel Tower in Paris. Widely circulated books and newspapers for the masses also brought people together in national and even global unity. Cultural leaders such as composers, artists, editors, and even some university professors shaped the attitudes and experiences of a growing number of citizens, uniting them around shared knowledge and artistic achievement.

> **FOCUS**
> What part did culture play in forging a national identity?

The Culture of Tradition

In the early days of the Meiji Restoration, Matsuo Taseko was invited to the home of a prince, where she heard a Western organ played. Taseko was appalled at the declining appreciation for Japan's own instruments and sent a poem to the princess. "In Japan / the koto cannot be quick / but I ask you not to listen gladly / to this barbarian harp / no matter how clever it is."[17] Taseko's nationalism was built on imitating the past and indeed protecting it from outside influences and from cultural mixture such as the playing of a Western instrument. She herself wrote hundreds of poems modeled on those from earlier centuries. In the culture of tradition, one followed not only the form but even the exact words of earlier poetry. As public schools developed, children across the nation recited poetic masterpieces from the past as a way to create and to participate in a national culture.

Leaders of monarchies, republics, and empires became symbols of national unity. Taseko carefully guarded gifts from the emperor to show to her closest friends and to pass down to her children and grandchildren as emblems of patriotism. Monarchs' and presidents' portraits appeared on dishware and on household walls and adorned public

Forging National Unity

The Korean Flag

The Korean Flag
(Tetra Images/Corbis.)

like lions, eagles, stars, and the sun were selected to portray a nation's strength and magnificence.

In the 1880s, as China, Russia, and Japan greedily eyed Korea for conquest, the kings of Korea adopted the more impressive title of emperor, and they also designed a flag. Its central figure represents the balance of yin and yang in the cosmos, while the four corners indicate the elements—fire, water, earth, and air—and the four seasons. After Japan had defeated both China and Russia (discussed in Chapter 26), it established a protectorate over Korea in 1905 and then annexed it in 1910, replacing the Korean flag with its own. On the defeat of Japan in World War II, the nineteenth-century flag became the standard of South Korea.

Flags existed in ancient times to distinguish regiments of an army, as was the case with Egyptian standards. Over the centuries, most flags continued to be standards for armies, but they also became important symbols of the nation. Designing a single flag around which citizens of an entire country could rally became a crucial part of the process of nation building. Colors were carefully chosen to represent virtues such as courage and purity, and figures

EXAMINING THE EVIDENCE

1. What makes this flag or any flag distinctive to the nation?

2. Compare the Korean flag with the U.S. flag. What do the differences reveal about the political culture and national identity of each country?

spaces such as schools and office buildings, thus providing a unifying symbol. National flags were designed to serve a similar purpose (see Seeing the Past: The Korean Flag). Royal births were widely reported in the press, and in Britain, for example, officials carefully staged royal marriages, birthdays, and funerals as public ceremonies, which were not only viewed by the growing urban population but also commemorated with the new photographic technology. Nishimiya Hide, daughter of a samurai and lady-in-waiting to a member of the high Japanese nobility, found a way to use her knowledge of court traditions after the samurai and grand nobility had lost their leading role. She supported herself in part under the Meiji Restoration by teaching court ceremonies from an earlier time to members of the new elite.

Writing and teaching history became a popular way to legitimate nations (see Lives and Livelihoods: Historians of the Nation-State). The public latched onto the story of the rise of the nation-state from its origins as a princely kingdom to its current modern might. Historical pageantry was popular in the nineteenth century in the form of parades, theater, and the revival of rituals at shrines. Governments erected monuments in the capital and other cities to celebrate great moments in the nation's past; these suggested the nation's durability and antiquity, even though many nations were actually quite new. Official histories eventually integrated the story of native peoples to build pride in the nation's progress from barbarism to civilization. Governments built museums to house collections of national documents, coins, and other treasure, but also native artifacts such as baskets, arrowheads, and beadwork to illustrate the "primitive" condition before the nation took shape.

The reality of nation building was brutal, producing hundreds of thousands of casualties and entailing real suffering, but the stories of nation building told by artists and writers were often romantic and inspiring. From the late nineteenth century to the present, authors and artists have presented accounts of the birth of Latin American nations, the Meiji Restoration, and the U.S. Civil War as glamorous, heart-throbbing adventures. Towering heroes such as Simon Bolivar and their selfless officers and families were portrayed as sacrificing for a greater good—the nation. The idea of "founding fathers" erased the fact that people lived in the region before the nation-state appeared, and appeals to ancient gods and goddesses supported claims of a nation-state's eternal existence. Biographies of nation builders became popular reading from the nineteenth century on, which helped replace people's local identities with a shared national culture.

Romanticizing the Past

Westernization

The power of the nation-state fostered world trade, of both goods and ideas. Readers in East Asia and South America, for example, studied works by contemporary Western writers such as the Englishmen John Stuart Mill and Charles Darwin and the Russian novelist Fyodor Dostoevsky. The eighteenth-century French social and political theorist Jean-Jacques Rousseau was especially popular among reformers and modernizers for his ideas of the social contract and natural rights. Rapid steamships carried potential leaders from Asia, Africa, and South America to Europe for their education, and sometimes to the United States for firsthand observation of popular government and nation building. Japanese leaders were among those who identified military power as the foundation of Western success, and they visited Europe, especially Germany, and the United States to learn about new weaponry and modern military training techniques. Influences went in many directions: young Chinese people who wanted their nation to modernize studied in Japan, which was increasingly seen as strong and modern.

Back home, reformers popularized ideas from the West. Sometimes writers modified Western theories to suit the local situation. Japanese author and educator Fukuzawa Yukichi came from an impoverished samurai family but quickly achieved fame and fortune through his innovative reform message. Best-selling works such as *Encouragement of Learning* (1872–1876) made people aware of current thinking in the West. Fukuzawa maintained, like Rousseau, that the entire population created the state, agreeing to a social contract through a constitution, and that they entered this contract from a position of complete equality—a totally novel concept for the Japanese. Fukuzawa's theory differed from much of Western constitutional thought, however, when it maintained that once people had agreed to the formation of a state, they surrendered their right to criticize or protest. In this way, he recast Western liberal theory into a form that suited the Meiji Restoration, justifying reform but also fortifying an authoritarian, emperor-centered state.

Recasting Western Culture

Angela Peralta was a Mexican opera performer whose popularization of European operas helped build her country's national culture. Born in 1845, at a time when Mexicans were already wild about opera, she took audiences to new heights of rapture with her renditions of the most difficult European operas. Described as "angelic in voice and in name," Peralta sang across Europe and in Egypt. Her real triumphs, however, occurred in Mexico, where she traveled from city to city mobbed by fans—"an incomparable woman," they called her—and spreading her fame and the culture of opera. News of Peralta's comings and goings passed from city to village and back to other cities, uniting Mexicans culturally, as Santa Anna and other rulers were trying to do politically. By the time of her death from yellow fever at the age of thirty-seven, many a theater owner had become wealthy from her performances, and opera had received such a boost that Mexican composers began writing operas about Aztec princesses and other Mexican peoples, creating "national" traditions

Historians of the Nation-State

With the rise of the nation-state, the study of history became a profession in the nineteenth century. Historians—whether in Japan, Latin America, Europe, or North America—set out to collect the major documents that legitimated the rise of the unified nation-state. They concerned themselves above all with the story of institutional development, the formation of states and governments, and the expansion of imperial power. The tradition of official history writing went way back in China to the Han dynasty; in the eighteenth century, the Chinese emperors charged court historians with the job of celebrating their conquests to the west. Nineteenth-century nation builders appointed professional historians, trained in the study of the past, to posts in prestigious universities, where they were to research and write true, verifiable accounts of the national past.

The model of the new professional historian arose in Germany, and Leopold von Ranke and his followers became the most honored historians of their day, even in foreign lands. Merchants actually stood outside Ranke's classroom to sell his photograph to admiring students. Ranke was swept up by the enthusiasm for unity that gripped the German states. Nations drew individuals together, and he believed in a strong central government. He aimed in his investigation and verification of documents to provide an objective account of Germany's development over the centuries. Ranke had his disciples, such as Heinrich von Treitschke, who even as a supposedly dispassionate scholar lectured to his students about the genius of the German nation: "It is for us to stand together in manly discipline and self restraint, and to pass on the bulwark of our unity, the German kingdom, to our sons." These professional historians often advised rulers while they usually kept from their classrooms the same groups of people kept from citizenship—women and many people of color.

Source: Quoted in Andreas Dorpalen, *Heinrich von Treitschke* (New Haven, CT: Yale University Press, 1957), 156.

Leopold von Ranke

Historians wrote the story of a nation, giving it a solid foundation in facts and research. The most enduring figure in the professionalization of history is Leopold von Ranke, who took the writing of history out of the hands of amateurs and put it into those of university-trained scholars. Ranke wrote histories of Prussia and of Germany, basing his work on archival and documentary research and thus reinforcing the idea of the nation itself as true, reliable, and authoritative. (bpk, Berlin/ Nationalgalerie, Staatliche Museen, Berlin/Andres Kilger/Art Resource, NY.)

QUESTIONS TO CONSIDER

1. Why did nation-states promote history as a profession?

2. Compare this textbook with the description of Ranke's historical writing. What differences and similarities do you perceive, and what do these suggest about history as a field of study?

---

through a Western cultural form. Her tombstone reads: "She sang like no one has ever sung in this world."[18]

National Institutions

Institutional innovations helped consolidate and modernize the state. Citizens took pride in the modernization of their cities, especially capital cities such as Cairo, Tokyo, and Paris. Bureaucrats undertook efforts to improve sanitation, medicine, and other institutions to promote public health. Reformers recognized public education as a crucial ingredient of national development. A Japanese law of 1872, for example, mandated universal education so that in the modernized Meiji state there would be "no community with an illiterate family nor a family with an illiterate person."[19] Improved facilities, whether public transportation or cultural institutions such as opera houses, theaters, and museums, testified to a nation's power and greatness.

Ordinary persons in agrarian societies based on traditional rhythms of planting and harvest were often illiterate and untutored. The nation-state was based on citizen participation and required a more literate population with a common culture and common skills and ideals. China had long offered more widespread education than elsewhere because for centuries the positions of government officials had required literacy and extensive training. Nationally minded reformers sought not only to imitate the Chinese tradition of an educated officialdom but also to expand education more generally as the foundation of strong nations. Although he ruled an agrarian state, the emperor Pedro II of Brazil established a record number of schools as part of his commitment to nation building. When he came to power in 1831, the capital of Rio de Janeiro had 16 primary schools; when he abdicated in 1889, the number had climbed to 118. Schools built a sense of common purpose. "We must constantly strive to work diligently at our tasks," a third-grade Japanese textbook of 1892 instructed, "and, when an emergency arises, defend our nation."[20]

French emperor Napoleon I (r. 1803–1815) was among the first to see the importance of science, math, and engineering to national power, and he ordered the development of high-level technical schools to teach advanced skills such as engineering. Thereafter secondary and postsecondary education advanced across Europe and the United States. Universities added modern subjects such as science and math to the list of prestigious courses in the second half of the century, reshaping the curriculum to make it better serve the national interest in a competitive global environment.

Reformers bucked tradition when they opened public schools for girls and young women. Across the globe these activists touted the education of women as key to modernization, because ignorant or illiterate mothers would give children a poor start. By contrast, the educated mother, instructed in both national culture and practical skills, provided a living example of the cultured citizen and had the capacity to begin the educational process for preschool offspring (see Reading the Past: "Good Wives, Wise Mothers" Build Japan). Primary, secondary, and even university education for young women developed in the second half of the nineteenth century in most parts of the world. These changes were hotly contested, however; often, the education of women was seen as the final blow in the collapse of tradition.

Another tactic of nation building was to foster a uniform culture and uniform beliefs. The Russian Empire, comprising more than a hundred ethnicities, sought to reduce the threat of future rebellion by forcing all its ethnic groups, from Poles to Afghans, to adopt the Russian language and culture and to worship in the Russian Orthodox church. When resistance to this "Russification" mounted, the government showed some leniency to encourage continued acceptance of the nation-state. Across Latin America, plantation owners had tolerated the many different religious practices that African slaves had brought with them because the differences, it was thought, would keep slaves divided and less likely to rebel.

With independence, however, nation builders in some countries tried to impose greater control over religious life, seeking to replace loyalty to religion with loyalty to

Angela Peralta
Mexican singer Angela Peralta was famed in her time for her range as a soprano and for the delicate beauty of her voice—"like the trill of a goldfinch," one critic noted in his diary. Peralta sang before kings and emperors and performed in the major opera houses of Europe. She toured Mexico itself, becoming an icon as she helped build a shared culture for its people. (Library of Congress Prints and Photographs DivisionLC-USZ62-132102.)

Public Education

Cultural Unity

READING THE PAST

"Good Wives, Wise Mothers" Build Japan

In 1874 a group of reformers, many of them samurai, established a new Japanese journal, *Meiroku Zasshi*, to bring readers knowledge of Western philosophy, science, and customs—among them current attitudes toward women. Nakamura Masanao, of samurai background, brought to Japanese readers the new idea that mothers should actively raise their children as part of nation building. By 1900 the slogan "good wives, wise mothers" dominated the national ideology about women, making women's connection to children and love for their husbands part of patriotism.

> Thus we must invariably have fine mothers if we want effectively to advance the people to the area of enlightenment and to alter their customs and conditions for the good. If the mothers are superb, they can have superb children, and Japan can become a splendid country in later generations. We can then have people trained in religious and moral education as well as in the sciences and arts whose intellects are advanced, whose minds are elevated, and whose conduct is high. . . .
>
> Now to develop fine mothers, there is nothing better than to educate daughters. . . . It is then not excessive even to say that the foundations for [a man's] virtues of bravery, endurance, and perseverance of a later day were laid while he was still playing in his cradle and receiving his mother's milk. To fear harm from equal rights for men and women is no more than to fear that the uneducated woman will sit on her husband. This anxiety would not exist if women honored Divine Providence, respected noble sentiments, admired the arts, appreciated science, and helped their husbands, and if husbands and wives mutually loved and respected each other.
>
> Aside from the matter of equal rights, the training of men and women should be equal and not of two types. If we desire to preserve an extremely high and extremely pure level among human beings as a whole, we should accord both men and women the same type of upbringing and enable them to progress equally. . . . A wife possessed of a feeling of deep love will bring her husband ease and happiness and encourage him to exert himself in enterprises useful to the country.

Source: *Meiroku Zasshi: Journal of the Japanese Enlightenment*, trans. and ed. William Reynolds Braisted (Cambridge, MA: Harvard University Press, 1976), 401–403.

EXAMINING THE EVIDENCE

1. What are the groups of people that Nakamura identifies?

2. How are they supposed to support the nation?

3. How do men and women compare in their standing in the nation?

---

the nation-state. Latin American officials made Carnival celebrations less African and more uniformly Spanish. In Germany in the 1870s, Otto von Bismarck sought to build cultural unity by striking out against Catholicism; he expelled the Jesuits, increased the government's power over the clergy, and introduced obligatory civil marriage. His *Kulturkampf*, or culture war, aimed to weaken allegiance to religion and to redirect it to the German nation. German Catholics and other citizens rebelled at this attack on freedom of religion, but overall Bismarck's achievements fostered a strong sense of German identity, especially because an excellent public school system served the cause of cultural uniformity.

Support of Multiculturalism   Some nations built their common ideology around multiculturalism, which allowed citizens to take pride in their diversity or regional strengths. In the United States, for instance, the poet Walt Whitman's *Leaves of Grass* (1855) celebrated the many types of ordinary people working across the country. African Americans developed powerful musical forms such as blues and jazz from the African tradition of the *griot* (or oral poet) and the sounds, rhythms, and tonalities of African and local music. Many Americans increasingly saw this music as part of American rather than African heritage. In Japan, even as a Shinto religion was declared to be the "traditional" Japanese faith, religious pluralism existed, and cultural leaders announced that this pluralism was part of the nation's cultural evolution. Although multiple religious and cultural traditions were allowed, they argued, the Japanese should nonetheless choose the highest form of religion and culture—which was none other than Shintoism—and Japanese forms of poetry such as the brief verses called haiku. Controversies over culture persisted over the course of nation building down to the present, but these debates can also bring people together around the search for consensus.

COUNTERPOINT
Outsiders Inside the Nation-State

Defining who was a true Brazilian, Russian, Japanese, or other citizen was an essential part of the process of nation building. Nation-states saw no contradiction between the ideal of universal membership and the exclusion of certain people from political participation and thus full citizenship. Sometimes these people—native Americans, for example—were those who had resisted nation building, often because it threatened their livelihoods, took their land, and devalued their beliefs. Other outsiders, notably women, often had helped in nation building from the start but were still excluded. Nation building created a body of "we's," insiders who felt their citizenship most keenly when they discriminated against a set of "they's," the outsiders.

> **FOCUS**
>
> Which groups were excluded from full participation in the nation-state, and why?

People of Color

From Japan to South America, nation-building efforts had a devastating effect on indigenous peoples. Settlers in South America, Australia, New Zealand, and Siberia treated native peoples—who had lived in the territory for centuries and even for millennia—as remnants of barbarism. "In point of fact," the *New York World* told its readers in 1874, "the country never belonged to the Indians in any other sense than it belonged to the wolves and bears, which white settlers shoot without mercy."[21] Indigenous civilization was dismissed, even when settlement usually depended on learning the skills and receiving aid in food and medicine from local peoples. Native peoples generally lived within national borders but without the rights of citizens. In the United States they were excluded from voting and full protection of the law until 1924, and in Peru Indians paid an extra tax, which constituted almost half of Peru's national income. The Australian and Canadian governments took native children from their families, sending them to live in white homes or in boarding schools to be "civilized." Russian officials simply moved settlers into the far reaches of Siberia and displaced reindeer herders in the name of strengthening the nation. As an article in one U.S. newspaper argued, settlers "are the people who develop a country; who carry a civilization with them."[22]

 Ethnic and racial thinking justified exploitation in the name of civilized nation building, even though the people exploited were subject to the nation's laws and taxes. Japanese nation builders taught that the Ainu peoples on the country's outer islands were dirty and disheveled; their tattoos and physical features were judged as hideous. The caste systems of the Spanish Empire and of Brazil ranked people of pure European blood highest and those of native or African blood lowest; those of mixed blood fell in the middle. Whether it was the mother or father, a free or unfree parent, who had the darker skin could also alter one's status. In the long run, however, the hierarchy was simple: the darker the skin, the lower the person.

Native Peoples

Former U.S. Slaves

In the United States the withdrawal of Union troops from the South in 1877 marked the end of Reconstruction and the withdrawal of the rights to citizenship given to black men in the Fourteenth Amendment to the Constitution. Southerners passed "Jim Crow" laws segregating blacks from whites in public places and effectively disenfranchising them with a variety of regulations. The Ku Klux Klan, a paramilitary group of white Southerners, terrorized blacks and lynched and mutilated black men, whom they falsely accused of raping white women. Unprotected by U.S. laws, blacks fought back in ways both brave and subtle. One woman took as her goal in life keeping her daughter from the common livelihood for African American girls and women of domestic service in a white family, "for [Southern men] consider the colored girl their special prey."[23] The exclusion of blacks and native Americans from rights became a unifying ideal for many white Americans.

Women

From Italy and Germany to the United States, and in the case of Matsuo Taseko, Japan, women joined the effort to create and preserve strong nation-states. "I am a U.S. soldier," wrote Clara Barton, nurse on a U.S. Civil War battlefield.[24] Women such as Barton were subject to the laws and taxes of the nation-state, but they too were denied rights of citizenship, including the right to vote, to own property, and to participate in public life. In countries as distant from one another as Japan and France, the government made it a crime for women to participate in political meetings under pain of arrest and imprisonment. Rape, other forms of physical abuse, and inequality of wages (and sometimes no wages at all) were seen as normal treatment for women.

Nonetheless, women became central to national myths of origin. In almost every modernizing country, the self-sacrifice of women to their nation or family was held up as a common model for citizenship. Just as women put aside their self-interest when being "good wives, wise mothers," as the new, nationalist Japanese slogan went, so women sacrificed their personal interests to strengthen the nation, even if this meant accepting beatings and the taxation and confiscation of their property by men and governments. Countries such as the United States, France, and Germany took mythical women—in these examples, Columbia, Marianne, and Germania—as their symbols on coins and other official artifacts even as they denied women the rights of citizenship.

Frederick Douglass

Frederick Douglass was an escaped slave, journalist, and civil rights pioneer of the nineteenth century. His goal was freedom for slaves and civil rights for all, and as such he became a hero to all outsiders down to the present day. As outsiders have been integrated, national histories make heroes of them to build a portrait of the nation as all-encompassing and based on mass participation of its citizenry. (National Portrait Gallery, Smithsonian Institution/Art Resource, NY.)

Begum Rokeya Sakhawat Hossain

Begum Rokeya Sakhawat Hossain was an outsider to political life, as women generally lived in seclusion from society. In 1905 this Muslim woman, born in present-day Bangladesh, wrote an unusual short story that described what a nation—"Ladyland," she called it—would be like if women ruled with their brains instead of men ruling with their muscle. Ladyland ran smoothly because the women harnessed high-tech solar power; men remained safely tucked away in seclusion the way women had once been.

The Struggle for Citizens' Rights

Throughout the nineteenth century, reformers asserted the rights of native peoples, former slaves, and women. Juan Manuel de Rosas, the powerful caudillo of Buenos Aires, Argentina, and its countryside, combated prejudices against people of Indian and African ancestry by incorporating them into his armies, promoting them to high ranks in the military, and giving them farms for their service. He built a loyal following, not through discrimination, but through nondiscrimination. In the United States, Frederick Douglass had been an abolitionist before the Civil War; after it he worked for the rights of freed black men. Ida B. Wells, U.S. newspaper woman and daughter of a former slave, campaigned in the late nineteenth century to end segregation of public facilities and, more forcefully and dangerously, to stop the lynching of black men. "I felt I owed it to myself and to my race to tell the whole truth now," Wells explained in her autobiography.[25] She received death threats and was forced to go into hiding. Across Latin America and the United States reformers worked, often for free, with native peoples, freed slaves, and poverty-stricken urban dwellers to build solidarity, provide education, and teach new work skills—all in the name of improving the nation by improving conditions within it.

Simultaneously, however, minorities such as African Americans in the United States and former slaves in the Caribbean began to see the source of their common nationality not as the Western Hemisphere, which to them was a place of captivity, but as Africa. By the end of the century **pan-Africanism**, an ideology that stresses the common bonds of all people of African descent, had taken root. Similarly, Jews, who were discriminated against in many parts of the world, also fought back with thoughts of building a nation of their own where they would have full rights. "Why should we be any less worthy than any other . . . people?" one Jewish leader asked. "What about our nation, our language, our land?" Jewish intellectuals began drawing upon Jewish folklore, language, customs, and history to establish a national identity parallel to that of other Europeans. By the late nineteenth century, a nationalist movement called **Zionism**, led by Hungarian-born writer Theodor Herzl, advocated the migration of Jews to their ancestral homeland of Palestine and the creation there of a Jewish nation-state.

Because rising nation-states refused women a whole series of rights, activists began lobbying for women's full citizenship. As the Chinese moved toward a program of national strengthening, activists denounced foot-binding and the lack of education for women. Activists often blamed men directly—"the basest of roughs," one German doctor called

pan-Africanism Originating in the late nineteenth century, an ideology that stresses the bonds of all people of African descent, both on the African continent and beyond.

Zionism A movement that began in the late nineteenth century among European Jews to form a Jewish state.

them.[26] In the United States the leading activists among a wide variety of mostly white women's organizations were Susan B. Anthony and Elizabeth Cady Stanton; black feminists included Sojourner Truth and Maria Cooper, who worked for the more complicated ends of both racial and gender equality. In 1903 the most militant of suffrage movements arose in England; there Emmeline Pankhurst and her daughters founded the Women's Social and Political Union in the belief that women would accomplish nothing unless they threatened men's property. In 1907, WSPU members staged parades in English cities, and in 1909 they began a campaign of violence, blowing up railroad stations, slashing works of art, and chaining themselves to the gates of Parliament.

When nationalist movements became strong in India, Egypt, the Middle East, and China, activist women focused on gaining rights and equality within an independent nation. Although these groups often looked to Western **suffragists** for some of their ideas, European suffragists were themselves inspired by non-Western women's less restrictive clothing, ownership of property, and recognized political roles. Latin American activists were also vocal, concerning themselves with education, the status of children, and the legal rights of women. Feminism thus became a global movement as women's writings, fictional and nonfictional, were translated across national boundaries and women from around the world met at international suffrage meetings. By 1904 feminist organizations from countries on almost all continents joined to form the International Woman Suffrage Alliance. International connections among feminist, African, and African American groups showed the ways in which national movements for citizenship took shape within a global context. The goal of most, however, was no longer to be an outsider to the nation by gaining full insider rights.

Conclusion

Regions throughout the world witnessed revolutionary change in the second half of the nineteenth century as leaders joined with ordinary people to create strong, centralized nation-states. Sometimes these striving nations, such as many in Latin America, simultaneously felt the strong, divisive forces of regionalism. The United States experienced a devastating civil war over competing political and economic systems that threatened to divide the country in two. In Russia, fear of revolution made that government change policies, liberating the serfs as a way to strengthen the state. But Russia remained an autocracy that failed to listen to the voice of the people—even the wealthy ones. This meant that fundamental flaws, unrecognized at the time, were woven into its nation-building efforts, which around the world were promoting access to education; urban improvements in sanitation, transport, and communications; and the development of public institutions such as museums and libraries.

Though it became increasingly central to nation building in the nineteenth century, nationalism ultimately became a destructive force. Critics add that the widespread discrimination against "outsiders" such as women and people of other races and ethnicities is unfortunately a characteristic of how nation-states create unity among those privileged to be its citizens. Nation building did not happen everywhere, nor did it proceed evenly. It did not eliminate monarchies and empires, although, as Matsuo Taseko witnessed, it changed them. Nation builders around the world recognized that, given the global web of trade, communications, and industrialization, the nation-state was an effective means of focusing political, economic, and military power, even becoming a tool for moving beyond the nation-state to create far-flung empires. Those who lacked the concentrated force of the nation-state were ripe for colonization rather than independence and prosperity.

suffragist An activist on behalf of the vote for women.

NOTES

1. Anne Walthall, *The Weak Body of a Useless Woman: Matsuo Taseko and the Meiji Restoration* (Chicago: University of Chicago Press, 1998), 98, 107.
2. Quoted in John Armstrong Crow, *The Epic of Latin America*, 4th ed. (Berkeley: University of California Press, 1992), 542.
3. Quoted in George Reid Andrews, *Afro-Latin America, 1800–2000* (New York: Oxford University Press, 2004), 113.
4. Quoted in Sarah C. Chambers, *From Subjects to Citizens: Honor, Gender, and Politics in Arequipa, Peru, 1780–1854* (University Park: Pennsylvania State University Press, 1999), 234–235.
5. Ibid.
6. Quoted in ibid., 184.
7. Quoted in Andrews, *Afro-Latin America*, 107, 181.
8. *El Republicano*, October 29, 1855, quoted in Carlos Froment, *Democracy in Latin America, 1760–1900: Civic Selfhood and Public Life in Mexico and Peru* (Chicago: University of Chicago Press, 2003), 155.
9. Quoted in Richard Stites, *Serfdom, Society, and the Arts in Imperial Russia: The Pleasure and the Power* (New Haven, CT: Yale University Press, 2005), 38.
10. "Alexander Nikitenko Responds to the Emancipation of the Serfs, 1861," http://artsci.shu.edu/reesp/documents/nikitenko.htm.
11. Quoted in Jasper Ridley, *Garibaldi* (London: St. Martins, 2001), 443.
12. Ibid., 448.
13. Quoted in James L. Roark et al., *The American Promise: A History of the United States*, 4th ed. (Boston: Bedford/St. Martins, 2009), 537.
14. Quoted in Frank Linderman, *Pretty-shield, Medicine Woman of the Crows* (Lincoln: University of Nebraska Press, 1972), 83.
15. Daklugie quoted in Colin G. Calloway, *First Peoples: A Documentary Survey of American Indian History*, 3d ed. (Boston: Bedford/St. Martins, 2008), 312.
16. Quoted in Mikiso Hane, *Peasants, Rebels, and Outcastes: The Underside of Modern Japan* (New York: Pantheon, 1982), 24.
17. Walthall, *The Weak Body of a Useless Woman*, 269.
18. Quoted in Ronald H. Dolkart, "Angela Peralta: A Mexican Diva," in Judith Ewell and William H. Beezley, eds., *The Human Tradition in Latin America: The Nineteenth Century* (Wilmington, DE: Scholarly Resources, 1989), 165, 167, 173.
19. Quoted in Irokawa Daikichi, *The Culture of the Meiji Period*, ed. and trans. Marius B. Jansen (Princeton, NJ: Princeton University Press, 1985), 56.
20. Quoted in Mikiso Hane, *Peasants, Rebels, and Outcastes*, 58.
21. Quoted in Richard Slotkin, *The Fatal Environment: The Myth of the Frontier in an Age of Industrialization* (Norman: University of Oklahoma Press, 1985), 339.
22. Ibid., 347.
23. "The Race Problem: An Autobiography: A Southern Colored Woman," *The Independent* 56 (1904): 586–589.
24. Quoted in Stephen Oates, *A Woman of Valor: Clara Barton and the Civil War* (New York: Free Press, 1994), 157–158.
25. Ida B. Wells, *Crusade for Justice: The Autobiography of Ida B. Wells*, ed. Alfreda M. Duster (Chicago: University of Chicago Press, 1970), 49.
26. Grete Meisel-Hess, *The Sexual Crisis*, trans. Eden and Cedar Paul (New York: The Critic and Guide Company, 1917), 6.

RESOURCES FOR RESEARCH

Modernizing Nations

Nations modernized and built their strength in different ways, but one common trend involved upgrading the education and general welfare of a wider segment of the population. Froment's book describes popular movements and official policies that worked toward that change.

Blackbourn, David. *Fontana History of Germany, 1780–1918: The Long Nineteenth Century*. 1997.

Froment, Carlos. *Democracy in Latin America, 1760–1900: Civic Selfhood and Public Life in Mexico and Peru*. 2003.

Mexican-American War, 1846–1848. Kera. PBS Online. www.pbs.org/kera/usmexicanwar/.

Meyer, Michael C., and William H. Beezley. *Oxford History of Mexico*. 2000.

*Nikitenko, Alexander. *Up from Serfdom: My Childhood and Youth in Russia, 1804–1824*. Translated by Helen Saltz Jacobson. 2001.

Emerging Powers: The United States and Japan

Two surprising newcomers on the nineteenth-century international stage were the United States and Japan, whose rise to prominence was full of struggle and bloodshed, as described in these works.

Faust, Drew Gilpin. *This Republic of Suffering: Death and the American Civil War*. 2008.

Foner, Eric. *The Fiery Trial: Abraham Lincoln and American Slavery*. 2010.

Keene, Donald. *Emperor of Japan: Meiji and His World, 1852–1912*. 2002.

Love, Eric T. L. *Race over Empire: Racism and U.S. Imperialism, 1865–1900*. 2005.

Walthall, Anne. *The Weak Body of a Useless Woman: Matsuo Taseko and the Meiji Restoration*. 1998.

The Culture of Nations

Culture was an integral part of creating a national identity. Stites's book shows how serf artists shaped not only the culture of the Russian Empire but its national politics.

Andrews, George Reid. *Afro-Latin America, 1800–2000*. 2004.

Huffman, James L. *Creating a Public: People and Press in Meiji Japan*. 1997.

Marchand, Suzanne, and David Lindenfeld, eds. *Germany at the Fin de Siècle: Culture, Politics, and Ideas*. 2004.

Stites, Richard. *Serfdom, Society, and the Arts in Imperial Russia: The Pleasure and the Power*. 2005.

Walthall, Anne, ed. *The Human Tradition in Modern Japan*. 2004.

COUNTERPOINT: Outsiders Inside the Nation-State

In an age when nations were defining themselves, outsiders to the nation were those who lived within its boundaries but were kept from full citizenship. The battles for full rights continue to this day, especially as citizenship becomes global rather than national.

Bay, Mia. *To Tell the Truth Freely: The Life of Ida B. Wells*. 2009.

Calloway, Colin G. *First Peoples: A Documentary Survey of American Indian Peoples*. 2011.

*Douglass, Frederick. *Narrative of the Life of Frederick Douglass, an American Slave, Written by Himself*. 1993.

Lowy, Dina. *The Japanese "New Woman": Images of Gender and Modernity*. 2007.

Lynch, John. *Argentine Caudillo: Juan Manuel de Rosas*. 2001.

* Primary source.

▶ **For additional primary sources from this period,** see *Sources of Crossroads and Cultures*.

▶ **For Web sites, images, and documents related to topics in this chapter,** see Make History at bedfordstmartins.com/smith.

The major global development in this chapter ▶ The causes and consequences of nation building in the nineteenth century.

IMPORTANT EVENTS

1833–1855	Mexican caudillo Santa Anna serves at intervals to lead the government
1846–1848	Mexican-American War
1853–1856	Crimean War
1855	Walt Whitman, *Leaves of Grass*
1859–1870	Unification of Italy
1860s	Height of opera singer Angela Peralta's career
1861	Emancipation of the serfs in Russia
1861–1865	U.S. Civil War
1863	Emancipation Proclamation in the United States
1866–1871	Unification of Germany
1868	Meiji Restoration of Japan
1872–1876	Fukuzawa Yukichi, *Encouragement of Learning*
1880s	Popular uprisings in Japan
1881	Young rebels assassinate Alexander II of Russia
1888	Emancipation of slaves in Brazil
1889	Brazilian emperor Pedro II abdicates and republic is installed

KEY TERMS

federalism (p. 831)
Manifest Destiny (p. 839)
mir (p. 835)
nation (p. 829)
pan-Africanism (p. 851)

realpolitik (p. 838)
Risorgimento (p. 837)
suffragist (p. 852)
zemstvo (p. 837)
Zionism (p. 851)

CHAPTER OVERVIEW QUESTIONS

1. Why did nation-states become so important to people in the nineteenth century?
2. What was the role of war in the rise of the nation-state?
3. What was the role of ordinary people in nation building?
4. Are nation-states still important today, and are there still outsiders inside nations?

SECTION FOCUS QUESTIONS

1. How did some states transform themselves into modern nations?
2. How did the United States and Japan make their governments politically and economically powerful in the nineteenth century?
3. What part did culture play in forging a national identity?
4. What groups were excluded from full participation in the nation-state, and why?

MAKING CONNECTIONS

1. How did the spread of industrialization (see Chapter 24) affect the rise of modern nation-states?
2. What was the legacy of slavery in the new nations? Did it make a difference to nation building that some states—Germany and Italy, for example—did not have large numbers of slaves in their homelands?
3. Why did Russia fail to offer rights to citizens equal to those offered by Western nations?

26

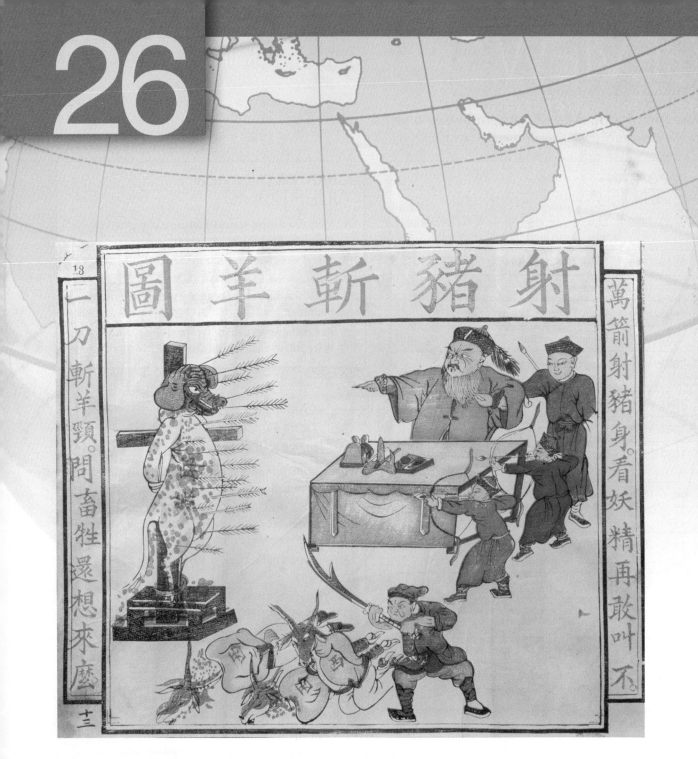

AT A CROSSROADS ▲

By 1900 China had become a crossroads of global ambitions. Japan, the United States, and the European powers had begun to exploit its markets and resources and in some cases to convert its population to Christianity. At the time, China was also a crossroads of famine and want, leading subjects of the Qing Empire to see their distress as the result of foreign inroads. The Chinese rebels known as the Boxers, illustrated here, were determined to "Kill the Pig"—that is, foreign missionaries, diplomats, and merchants. Armies from the foreign powers invaded China, suppressed the Boxers, rampaged across Chinese cities and farms, and further plundered the country's wealth. (Private Collection /Bridgeman Art Library.)

Imperial Order and Disorder

1850–1914

"Here come the foreign devils," a little boy shouted in 1900 in the northern Chinese city of Tianjin, "that's why we don't have any rain."[1] It was a time of intense drought in the region, and the Chinese were starving. Seedlings dried up in the fields, leaving peasants with time on their hands and with hunger killing both body and spirit. Many blamed the foreigners from Britain, Germany, Japan, and other parts of the world for these problems. On December 31, 1899, a British missionary, one of the many sent to convert the Chinese to Christianity, was assassinated in Shandong, an eastern province of China. By the summer of 1900, not only missionaries but also the German ambassador, European businessmen, and Chinese converts to Christianity by the thousands were being killed in antiforeign uprisings that came to be known as the Boxer Rebellion. The rebels believed that they were acting in self-defense, protecting their homeland from outsiders whose presence had brought the drought and the resulting hardship, devastation, and death.

Europeans had been fascinated by China for centuries. It had long been the most important power in the world with a tradition of excellence in philosophy, art, and literature; it was also the source of prized porcelain, silks, and cottons. In fact, it was the desire to gain a direct connection to the wealth and resources of Asia that had prompted early modern European expansion. The Japanese, too, had borrowed much from the Chinese, whose political and religious ideas played a key role in Japan's development. Nonetheless, in the nineteenth century the European powers, along with Japan and the expansionist United States, had come to see China—and most of the rest of the world—as areas to be dominated. Individual nation-states could increase their strength by gaining access to China's raw materials and cheap labor, and there was money to be made by seizing its taxes and financing development projects such as railroads. Britain, France, the Netherlands, Germany, Russia, Japan, and the United States all shared an impulse to control the wealth and, increasingly, even the governments of other regions of the world. In the second half

Building Empires

FOCUS What motivated the imperialists, and how did they impose their control over other nations?

Imperial Society

FOCUS How did imperialism change lives and livelihoods around the world?

Culture in an Imperial Age

FOCUS How did artists and writers respond to the age of empire?

Imperial Contests at the Dawn of the Twentieth Century

FOCUS What were the main issues in the contests over empire, and what were the results of these contests?

COUNTERPOINT: The West Copies from the World

FOCUS How did non-Western and colonized lands shape Western culture and society?

BACKSTORY

As we saw in Chapter 25, in the nineteenth century a number of states improved their governing institutions, expanded their bureaucracies, and attempted to build a shared sense of national identity in their often diverse populations. States also began to devote more attention to public education, seeing an educated population as a source of national strength. The drive to increase national power was a prime motive for commercial and military expansion, an outgrowth of state efforts to gain control of resources, markets, and strategic locations around the world. As states jostled with one another for power, their rivalries were increasingly played out in a competition for possessions outside of the nation-state's boundaries.

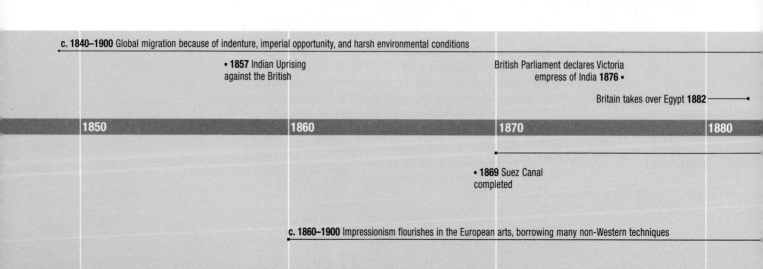

Hawaiian Is.
(U.S.)

PACIFIC
OCEAN

ARCTIC
OCEAN

CANADA

JAPAN

PACIFIC
OCEAN

Boxer Rebellion,
1899–1900

UNITED
STATES

MEXICO

RUSSIAN
EMPIRE

QING
EMPIRE

Fiji Is.
(Gr. Br.)

UNITED
KINGDOM

NETH.

TIBET

SIAM

BENGAL

ATLANTIC
OCEAN

BELG.

GERMANY

Young Turks'
uprising,
1908

INDIA

AUSTRALIA

NEW
ZEALAND

FRANCE

PORTUGAL

SPAIN

ITALY

OTTOMAN
EMPIRE

PERU

INDIAN
OCEAN

CHILE

BRAZIL

AFRICA

ARGENTINA

N
W   E
S

Imperial territories, 1914

Belgian	Japanese
British	Portuguese
Dutch	Russian
French	Spanish
German	U.S.
Italian	

0   1000   2000 miles
0   1000   2000 kilometers

c. 1840–1900 Global migration because of indenture, imperial opportunity, and harsh environmental conditions

▪ 1857 Indian Uprising
against the British

British Parliament declares Victoria
empress of India 1876 ▪

Britain takes over Egypt 1882

1850	1860	1870	1880

▪ 1869 Suez Canal
completed

c. 1860–1900 Impressionism flourishes in the European arts, borrowing many non-Western techniques

of the nineteenth century the word *imperialism* was used to describe this impulse toward global domination.

In the rush to dominate, these competing nations changed their tune, many claiming that they were bringing civilization and order to backward peoples of the world. Despite that promise, imperialism in China and elsewhere around the globe brought massive bloodshed and disorder, much of it inflicted by the imperialists themselves on those who would not bow to their rule. Empire builders in Asia, Africa, and the Mediterranean basin focused so exclusively on extracting wealth that they let the maintenance of traditional but crucial systems such as irrigation deteriorate because they did not yield immediate profit. The result was starvation and suffering. Imperialist inroads inspired heartfelt resistance, often increasing the bloodshed. Many in the colonies were inspired by some of the imperialists' accomplishments, including the creation of powerful nation-states and guarantees of liberal ideals such as self-determination and human rights. Even though such guarantees were hardly given to colonized peoples, the very existence of these ideals led many to fight for their freedom.

In the course of imperialism and the globalization of trade and finance that accompanied it, society and culture changed. Poets and artists reacted to the whirl of imperial activity around them, sometimes deploring the changes and at other times seizing on ideas from other cultures to spark their creativity. Tens of millions of people migrated either to find opportunity within empires or to escape the misery at home that imperialism brought. As they left their homes to take up livelihoods in other parts of the world, these migrants

MAPPING THE WORLD
The Spread of Imperialism, 1850–1914

The world's peoples interacted more in the late nineteenth century because of the spread of empire and increases in migration and travel. Behind this movement of peoples were the quest for opportunity and freedom, and also ambition and greed. Occasionally those driving imperialism had philanthropic and scientific motives, but imperialists often used naked violence to achieve their ends.

ROUTES ▼

Mass migrations, 1850–1910
- ⇢ African slaves, c. 1800–1860
- → Other European
- → African, c. 1840–1910
- → Indian
- → Chinese
- → Lebanese
- → European Jewish
- → Travels of Khaw Soo Cheang, c. 1820
- ⋯→ Travels of Nain Singh, 1873–1875

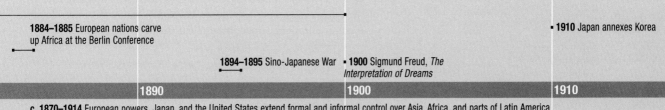

1884–1885 European nations carve up Africa at the Berlin Conference

1894–1895 Sino-Japanese War

1900 Sigmund Freud, *The Interpretation of Dreams*

1910 Japan annexes Korea

1890   **1900**   **1910**

c. 1870–1914 European powers, Japan, and the United States extend formal and informal control over Asia, Africa, and parts of Latin America

Spanish-American War 1898

1899–1902 South African War

1899–1900 Boxer Rebellion in China

1908 Young Turks' uprising against the Ottoman Empire

1904–1905 Russo-Japanese War

created new communities, such as the Chinese in Singapore and San Francisco and the Lebanese in Rio de Janeiro and Montreal. Thus, imperialism brought wrenching change as well as new opportunity for peoples throughout the world while pulling societies, willingly or not, into ever-closer contact. The Boxer Rebellion against the "foreign devils" was but one expression of the complex enterprise of imperialism.

OVERVIEW QUESTIONS

The major global development in this chapter: The accelerated competition among nineteenth-century nation-states for empire.

As you read, consider:

1. What are the arguments for and against imperialism?

2. How and why did some local peoples assist imperialists who took over their own countries?

3. Which were the major imperialist powers, and what made them so capable of conquest?

4. How did imperialism change the lives of people in the conquering countries and in the colonies?

Building Empires

FOCUS

What motivated the imperialists, and how did they impose their control over other nations?

The nineteenth century was an age of imperialism, a time when nations around the world built both formal and informal empires. The British government formally took over the governments of South Asian states, ending the East India Company's domination of the region through trade, taxation, and military might. It incorporated India into Britain politically and declared Queen Victoria empress. After midcentury, other nations instituted direct rule of areas once linked to them by trade alone. They sent soldiers and more settlers to distant lands and expanded their foreign office bureaucracies. Such takeovers—often called the "**new imperialism**" in contrast to the trader-based domination of preceding centuries—promoted both individual wealth and national power, albeit funded by ordinary taxpayers. The new imperialism was not, however, simply a story of violence inflicted by foreigners aiming for political and economic domination. Conquering nations provided social and cultural services such as schools to reflect the imperial power's values. In many instances local chieftains, merchants, and cultural leaders helped imperialists make their inroads abroad.

Imperialism: What Is It?

Imperialism is associated with the domination that European powers, Japan, and the United States began to exercise over much of the rest of the world in the second half of the nineteenth century. The term is used to describe the ambitions, conquests, and power exercised over the trade, taxation, and governments of other states and their peoples—somewhat similar to the way in which the word **globalization** is used today to describe a variety of

new imperialism The takeover in the second half of the nineteenth century of foreign lands by Western powers and Japan, which entailed political control as well as economic domination.

globalization A variety of behaviors and processes, such as trade, warfare, travel, and the spread of culture, that link the world's peoples.

behaviors and processes that link the world's peoples. There had been empires throughout history, but the new imperialism of the nineteenth and twentieth centuries was both more and less than empire. The word connotes not just formally claimed territory, indirectly ruled lands, and economic domination, but even the strong desire to possess territory. Although modern imperialism motivated both governmental and private actions right through World War II, it was never a coherent system or a consistent set of practices. It also describes a control that was never complete and that colonized peoples constantly contested.

One important feature of modern imperialism was colonization, that is, the creation of settlements in foreign territories intended to dominate the land and its native peoples and to take its wealth. Colonization shaped the Roman Empire and others, including the later Spanish and Portuguese empires of the sixteenth century, and it remained a prominent part of the new imperialism. Colonization, it was believed, could secure distant territories at less expense than armies would require; it could train a foreign population in the imperial power's culture; in some cases, it could alleviate crowding in the mother country. **Colonialism** is the term for the system that dominated people in these ways.

Colonization and Colonialism

A second feature of imperialism was the range of motivations behind it. Some national leaders saw more extensive landholdings in and of themselves as a major ingredient of national strength; others saw the wealth that could be siphoned off to strengthen nations. Business leaders aimed to make money in underdeveloped areas by building harbors, railroads, and roads, while merchants wanted to increase commerce and thus profits through imperial networks. "Business" or "informal" imperialism based on foreign investment, commerce, and manufacturing could also exist without political rule. Britain, and later the United States, exerted considerable power over Latin American states through investments in and control of key industries. **Business imperialism** included economic domination of sugar, coffee, and other plantation agriculture in many parts of the world. Finally, many envisioned imperialism as an almost saintly undertaking. As one French economist put it in 1891, taking over countries would bring civilization to "barbarous and savage tribes, some enduring wars without end and destructive ways of life, others knowing nothing of the arts and having so few habits of work and invention that they have no way of knowing how to get riches from the land."[2]

Imperial Motivations

For the Spanish and Portuguese, who saw firsthand the immense accomplishment and wealth of American peoples, their own superiority rested on their Catholic faith. Increasingly, Christianity blended with racism to justify domination. In the second half of the nineteenth century, new "scientific" theories of race reinforced this sense of cultural superiority. The ideas of European scientists and doctors—especially those of Charles Darwin, the English naturalist who developed the theory of evolution—appealed to imperialists. Darwin himself, along with people later called Social Darwinists, explicitly stated that nonwhites, women, and members of the working class were less highly evolved than white men and therefore in need of domination. This inferiority was affirmed by a number of bogus measurements in the nineteenth century, such as the size of the cranium. Scientific racism was not confined to whites: the Japanese considered themselves far in advance of native peoples such as the Ainu who lived far from the capital, and of foreigners such as the Koreans.

Confident of their superiority, imperialists proposed that they would uplift and liberate the people they conquered from their own backwardness. Paradoxically, cultural pride prompted some "civilizers" such as missionaries to support the most brutal military measures to accomplish their goals. Thus, the building of schools and churches occurred alongside massacres of local people who would not turn over their property, animals, or houses. Forcing others to accept cultural values such as Christian belief was also part of imperialism.

Takeover in Asia

Great Britain, the era's mightiest colonial power, made a dramatic change of course by instituting governmental control of India while the Russians and British were also in constant struggle to rule Central Asia and the French and Dutch struggled with local peoples

colonialism The establishment of settler communities in areas ruled by foreign powers.

business imperialism The domination of foreign economies without military or political rule.

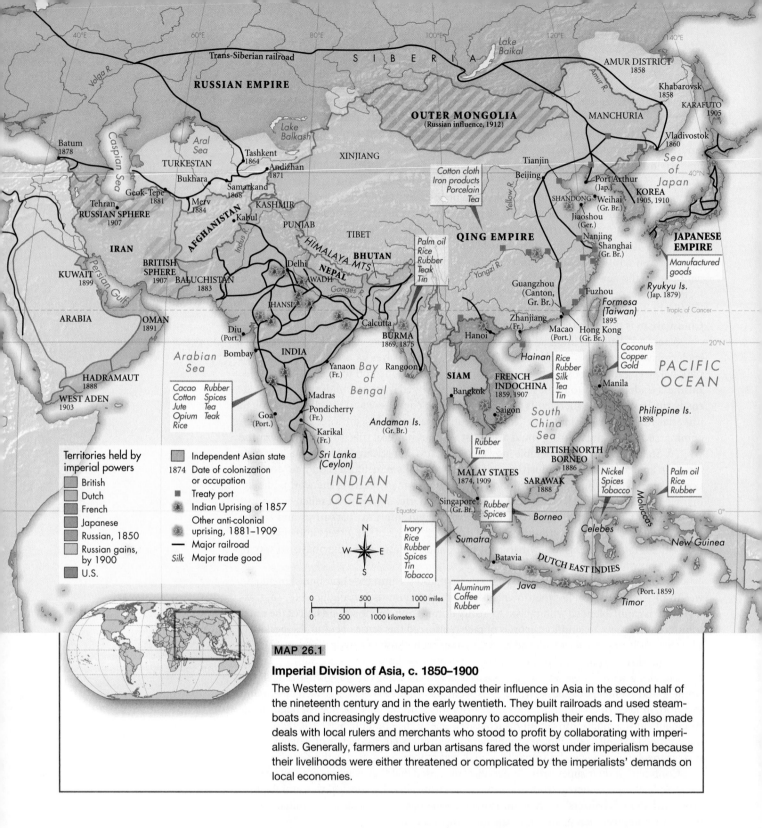

MAP 26.1

Imperial Division of Asia, c. 1850–1900

The Western powers and Japan expanded their influence in Asia in the second half of the nineteenth century and in the early twentieth. They built railroads and used steamboats and increasingly destructive weaponry to accomplish their ends. They also made deals with local rulers and merchants who stood to profit by collaborating with imperialists. Generally, farmers and urban artisans fared the worst under imperialism because their livelihoods were either threatened or complicated by the imperialists' demands on local economies.

for empire in Southeast Asia. The contest in Central Asia has been called the "Great Game," but that hardly conveys the destruction inflicted on local peoples and on the imperialists themselves—all in the name of advancing the nation by forging an empire (see Map 26.1).

The British in India   Since the eighteenth century and especially after the loss of Britain's thirteen North American colonies, the East India Company had expanded its reach to become the major tax collector for the Mughal emperor, princes, and other ruling officers on the subcontinent. The Company became the acting ruler of some of these Indian territories and later built railroads throughout the countryside to make commerce and revenue collecting more efficient. In 1856, wanting more revenue and control, the Company took over the wealthy northern kingdom of Awadh, contrary to formal treaties with the king about his sovereignty.

For Indians whose wealth and livelihoods derived from their connections with the Company, this event was of little importance. Outside of this small segment of the population, however, the takeover of Awadh fueled already rising anger over excessive taxation and the Company's increasingly high-handed ways. In 1857, Indian troops serving the Company, known as *sepoys*, heard rumors that the new Enfield rifles they were to use had cartridges greased with cow and pig fat, forbidden to Hindus (for whom cows are sacred) and Muslims (for whom pigs are unclean). The soldiers believed that they were deliberately being made impure and that the cartridges were part of a plot to convert them to Christianity. Spurred by the economic grievances of the peasant classes from which most of them sprang, the soldiers massacred their British officers and then conquered the Indian capital at Delhi, reinstating the emperor and declaring the independence of the Indian people.

Rebellions spread to the general populace, justified, so the emperor explained, by "the tyranny and oppression of the infidel and treacherous English." The Rani (Queen) Lakshmibai, widow of the ruler of the state of Jhansi in central India, led a separate military revolt when the East India Company tried to take over her lands, but she was only one among many to do so. The British had trouble motivating recruits to put down the uprisings. "All black men are one," said a newly recruited soldier, who vowed he would not fight the rebels.[3] Eventually British-led forces from other regions crushed the Indian Uprising of 1857, as this widespread revolt is now called. In the aftermath of the uprising, the British government substituted its control for that of the Company and in 1876 declared Queen Victoria the empress of India.

The British constructed India as a single colony formed from independent kingdoms and small princely territories, but in practice this apparent unity was partial at best. Many states remained semi-independent. Paradoxically, the British "unification" of India contributed to growing nationalist sentiment among Indian elites. It was in this context that, in 1885, wealthy and well-educated Indians created the Indian National Congress, an organization aiming to bring about reform, obtain rights and representation in the British government, and eventually gain independence.

British success in South Asia was part of a struggle for trade and empire that made entire continents a battlefield of competing interests and warring armies. In Central Asia, Russian and British armies blasted former centers of Silk Road trade into ruins and slaughtered Afghan resisters during decades of destructive conflict. After the fall of Kabul to British forces in 1842, a commander set his men loose on the city's population to avenge the killing of British soldiers and civilians by Afghani resisters. The Russian general who took the fortress of Geok-Tepe in modern Turkmenistan let his troops steal, rape, and butcher its inhabitants. He justified the sixteen thousand dead by saying, "The duration of peace is in direct proportion to the slaughter you inflict upon the enemy."[4] Publicly hanging only a few ringleaders of the rebellion, he explained, inspired further resistance to takeovers, whereas a reputation for massive killings would create fear—and thus obedience.

The British and Russians in Central Asia

Imperial moves inspired countermoves. The British added to their holdings in Asia partly to block Russian and French expansion. Russia absorbed the small Muslim states of West and Central Asia, including Turkestan; some provinces of Afghanistan; and extending into the Ottoman Empire, Persia, northern India, and China, often encountering British competition but mostly fighting local peoples. Russia built the trans-Siberian railroad to help integrate Siberia—once considered a distant colony—into an expanding Russian Empire. Once completed, the new rail line helped transport settlers and soldiers into the region (see again Map 26.1).

From India the British military pushed to the east, moving into Burma in 1869 and taking the Malay peninsula in 1874. The presence of British troops guaranteed the order necessary to expand railroads for greater access to interior markets and more efficient extraction of raw materials—tin, oil, rice, teak, and rubber. The environmental consequences were severe as the British built factories and leased forests in the north of Burma to private companies that stripped them bare, "denuding the country," as one official put it, "to its great and lasting loss."[5] Famine and drought followed this ecological nightmare, weakening the local population and making it easier to annex Burma in 1875.

The French in Southeast Asia

In the 1860s the French were establishing their own control in Cochin China (modern southern Vietnam). Missionaries in the area, ambitious French naval officers stationed in Asia, native officials looking for work, and even some local peoples making profits from European trade urged the French government on. After sending in troops, France used favorable treaties (backed by the threat of military action) to create the Union of Indochina from the ancient states of Cambodia, Tonkin, Annam, and Cochin China in 1887 (the latter three constitute the modern nation of Vietnam). Rubber plantations and other money-making projects followed. Laos was added to Indochina in 1893.

Like the British in India, the French brought some Western innovations to the societies they conquered. Modern agricultural projects spurred rapid growth in the food supply. The French also improved sanitation and public health in Indochina. Such changes proved a mixed blessing, however, because they led to population growth that strained resources. Furthermore, French landowners and traders siphoned off the profits from economic development. The French also transformed cities such as Saigon by constructing tree-lined boulevards inspired by those in Paris. French literature, theater, and art were popular with colonial officials and upper-class Indochinese alike. Nonetheless, in the countryside ordinary Vietnamese saw things differently. As one peasant protested to the governor general in 1907, "the French are treating us like animals, looking at us like wood and stone."[6] Such treatment, combined with the exposure of native elites to Western ideas of "the rights of man," helped produce an Indochinese nationalist movement.

Europeans Scramble for Africa

North Africa

Imperialism often involved seizures of people's lands and goods after their military defeat. In Africa, however, the cruelty was notorious, as Europeans trained their sights on the continent in the second half of the nineteenth century. European conquest of the continent began with North Africa, and then moved on to sub-Saharan Africa with its rich supplies of raw materials such as palm oil, cotton, diamonds, cacao, and rubber (see Map 26.2, page 866). With its empire in India, Britain additionally hoped to keep the southern and eastern coasts of Africa secure for stopover ports on the route to Asia. While North Africa had commercial value, the Mediterranean as a whole was most important for its strategic location.

French emperor Napoleon III, remembering his uncle's campaign in Egypt, helped sponsor the building of the Suez Canal, which would connect the Mediterranean with the Red Sea and the Indian Ocean and thus dramatically shorten the route from Europe to Asia. The canal was completed in 1869, and beginning with Muhammad Ali, Egypt's enterprising rulers made Cairo into a bustling city, boosting commerce and manufacturing and attracting European capital investment. In an effort to further enhance the connections between Egypt's economy and the rest of the world, Egyptian businessmen and government officials supported the construction of thousands of miles of railroad track, the improvement of harbors, and the installation of telegraph systems. Many of these ventures were paid for with money borrowed from European lenders at far higher rates of interest than Europeans paid. Nonetheless, many Egyptian elites believed that such modernization projects were essential to their country's future and, therefore, that an Egyptian-European financial alliance was necessary, whatever its cost.

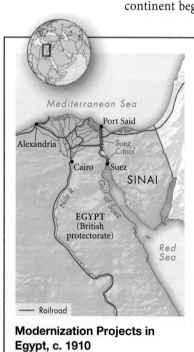

Modernization Projects in Egypt, c. 1910

Albert Rieger,
***Suez Canal* (1864)**

Workers from around the Mediterranean labored on the Suez Canal, which the French designed to connect the Mediterranean to the Red Sea and thus speed up commerce with Asia. The British saw the Suez Canal, completed in 1869, as important to protecting its Asian empire, and by 1882 they had taken over Egypt not only to control the canal but also to guarantee British financial investments in the canal and in other Egyptian modernization projects. The Suez Canal remains a major world crossroads to this day. (The Art Archive/Museo Civico Revoltella Trieste/Collection Dagli Orti.)

The alliance turned sour when Great Britain and France, eager to control business with Egypt, took over the Egyptian treasury with the excuse that they needed to guarantee loans that the Egyptian government found itself hard-pressed to repay. In 1882, after striking a deal with the French, the British invaded and essentially took control of the government, an act they claimed was necessary to put down those Egyptian nationalists who protested the seizure of the treasury. Soon Cairo had the air of "an English town," as one Egyptian local put it.[7] The English, in alliance with local entrepreneurs, shifted the Egyptian economy from a system based on multiple crops—a system that maintained the country's self-sufficiency—to one that emphasized the production of a few highly marketable crops, notably cotton and wheat, which were especially useful to the English. As the colonial powers and Egyptian elites grew rich, the bulk of the rural population, their livelihoods transformed, barely eked out an existence.

Meanwhile the French army, driving into the North African hinterland, occupied all of Algeria by 1870 and then neighboring Tunisia in 1881. As elsewhere, French rule in North Africa was aided by the attraction of local people to European trade and technology. Merchants and local leaders cooperated in building railroads, sought bank loans from the French, and sent their children to European-style schools. They became "evolved"—as the French called those who adopted European ways. Many local peoples, however, resisted French intrusions, attacking soldiers and settlers. Others died from European-spread diseases. By 1872, the native population in Algeria had declined by more than 20 percent from five years earlier.

In the 1880s, European governments raced to the African interior, both playing to local elites' self-interest and using military force to overwhelm resistance. The French, Belgians, Portuguese, Italians, and Germans jockeyed to dominate peoples, land, and resources—"the magnificent cake of Africa," as King Leopold II of Belgium (r. 1865–1909) put it. Driven by almost unparalleled greed, Leopold claimed the Congo region of central Africa, thereby initiating competition with France for that territory and inflicting on its peoples unspeakable acts of cruelty. German chancellor Otto von Bismarck established

Sub-Saharan Africa

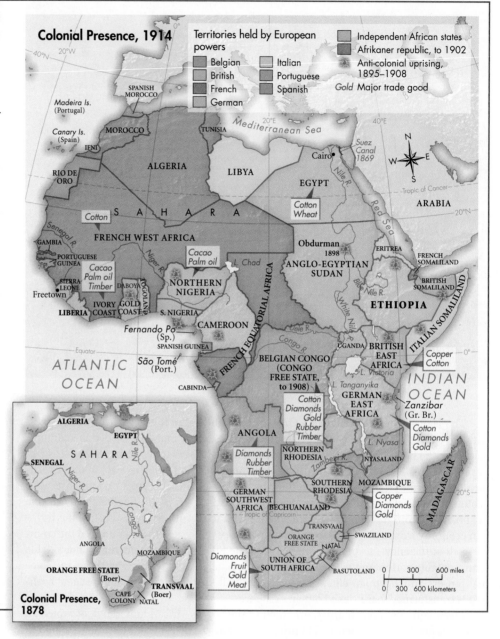

MAP 26.2

Imperial Division of Africa, c. 1880–1914

Though some Africans profited, most suffered from contacts with Europeans, which increased after the mid-nineteenth century, largely because the use of quinine cut down health risks for the invaders. Environmental factors also aided Europeans in their new pursuit of actual colonies on the continent. Where famine and drought failed to make Africans submit, the Europeans' outright brutality put down often stubborn resistance.

German control over Cameroon and a section of East Africa. Faced with stiff competition for African territory, the British spent millions of pounds attempting to take over the continent militarily "from Cairo to Cape Town," as the slogan went. The French cemented their hold on large portions of western Africa (see again Map 26.2).

Environmental disasters, regional tensions, and African rulers themselves scrambling for resources and territory helped the would-be conquerors. In 1882 the king of Daboya in northern Ghana explained his treaty with the British in these terms: "I want to keep off all my enemies and none to be able to stand before me."[8] The king expected guns and military backing from the British should it be necessary. The European powers put so much stake in the ability of local rulers to collect taxes and in the loyalty of African police and soldiers for maintaining order that during the 1890s, Germans in imperial Tanzania kept only one hundred military personnel to guard the entire territory.

Resistance in South Africa

The Zulu had maintained a powerful kingdom in southern Africa since early in the nineteenth century. Using excellent camouflage and stealthy movements, they consistently resisted the British, despite being outgunned. Finally, in the Anglo-Zulu War of 1879, they were defeated, and their king Cetshwayo was held and interrogated in an effort to prove he was a dictatorial savage and thus inferior to British rulers. Note that this painting makes it appear as if the British heroically fought dozens of Zulu individually. In fact, by the final battles the British were launching tens of thousands of African and European troops against the Zulu. (The Print Collector/HIP/The Image Works.)

South Africa

Violent struggle occurred for control of southern Africa, where farmers of European descent and immigrant prospectors, rather than military personnel, battled the Xhosa (KOH-suh), Zulu, and other African peoples for the frontier regions of Transvaal, Natal, the Orange Free State, Rhodesia, and the Cape Colony. Although the Dutch were the first Europeans to settle the area permanently, the British had gained control by 1815. Thereafter descendants of the Dutch, called *Boers* (Dutch for "farmers"), were joined by British immigrants in their fight to seize farmland and mineral resources from natives. British businessman and politician Cecil Rhodes, sent to South Africa for his health at age seventeen, just as diamonds were being discovered, cornered the diamond market and claimed a huge amount of African territory with the help of official charters from the British government, all before he turned forty. Pushing hundreds of miles into the interior of southern Africa (a region soon to be named Rhodesia after him), Rhodes moved into gold mining too. His ambition for Britain and for himself was boundless: "I contend that we are the finest race in the world," he explained, "and that the more of the world we inhabit the better it is."

The Berlin Conference

The scramble for Africa intensified tensions among the imperial powers, leading to a conference of European nations in 1884. Statesmen from the fourteen nations represented at the Berlin Conference echoed Rhodes's racial pride; as representatives of a "superior" civilization, they considered themselves fully entitled to determine the fate of the African continent. To resolve territorial disputes, they decided that any nation that controlled a settlement along the African coast was also guaranteed the rights to the corresponding interior territory. This agreement led to the linear dissection of the continent, a process that ignored the actual territorial borders of some 70 percent of Africa's ethnic groups. In theory the meeting was supposed to reduce bloodshed and temper ambitions in Africa, but European leaders remained more committed than ever to expanding their power. Newspaper reports of daring conquests only stirred up citizens to demand more imperialist excitement.

Japan's Imperial Agenda

Japan escaped the "new" European imperialism by rapidly transforming into a modern industrial nation with its own imperial agenda. The Japanese, unlike China, endorsed technology and the quest for colonies. In contrast to Europe where there was often heated debate about imperial conquest, the Meiji regime insisted on unity: "All classes high and low shall unite in vigorously promoting the economy and welfare of the nation," ran one of its statements. By 1894, Japan had become powerful enough to force traders to accept its terms for commerce and diplomatic relations. Then, it went further.

The Sino-Japanese War   To expand its influence and resource base, the Meiji government entered the imperial fray by invading the Chinese island of Formosa (present-day Taiwan) in 1874. In 1876, Japan forced unequal trading treaties on China-dominated Korea. Further Japanese encroachments in Korea led to the 1894 Sino-Japanese War. Modern military technology carried Japan to a swift victory that left the once powerful Qing China humiliated and Japan the colonial overlord of Taiwan and Korea. The European powers, alarmed at Japanese expansion, forced it to relinquish many gains, a move that outraged Japanese nationalists. Tensions between Japan and Russia continued to escalate over the course of the 1890s. The extension of the trans-Siberian railroad through Manchuria and the arrival of millions of Russian settlers accelerated Russian expansion into East and South Asia. Russia sponsored anti-Japanese groups in Korea, making the Korean peninsula appear, as a Japanese military leader put it, like "a dagger thrust at the heart of Japan." As we will see, war soon erupted between the Russians and Japanese, showing the deadly potential for conflict among imperial rivals.

The Sino-Japanese War, 1894

Technology, Environment, and the Imperial Advantage

Industrial Technology   Imperialists were helped immeasurably by both industrial technology and a series of ecological disasters that weakened Asian and African societies. Powerful guns, railroads, steamships, and medicines greatly accelerated imperial conquest. The gunboats that forced the Chinese to open their borders to opium played the same role in forcing African ethnic groups to give up their rights and independence. Improvements to the breech-loading rifle and the development of the machine gun, or "repeater," between 1862 and 1880 dramatically increased firepower. "The whites did not seize their enemy as we do by the body, but thundered from afar," claimed one resister at the 1898 Battle of Obdurman in Sudan, where the British, losing fifty men, mowed down some twenty-five thousand Africans with machine guns (see again Map 26.2). "Death raged everywhere—like the death vomited forth from the tempest," as one African put it. Railroads sped troops and weapons to wherever there was resistance and thus cemented imperial domination.

Environmental Disaster   The ecological balance of power changed too. Whereas once the tropical climate had given Africans an advantage, quinine extracted from cinchona bark from the Andes protected Europeans from the deadly tropical disease malaria, which had once made Africa the "White Man's Grave." Disastrously for Africans and Asians, El Niño weather currents of the last quarter of the nineteenth century brought drought that resulted in deadly famine across a wide swath of both continents. Mysore, India, one official wrote, contained "none but the dead and the dying."[9] Desperate for food, the population began resorting to theft, eating the dead, and, if they had the energy, rioting against big landowners and tax collectors. It was amid environmental catastrophe that Europeans seized land and cattle and generally expanded their holdings. "Europeans," one African man observed at the time, "track famine like a sky full of vultures."[10] The Chinese Boxers could not have said it better.

Imperial Society

Imperialism brought closer connections among peoples far distant from one another, through trade, migration, and warfare. These interactions reshaped societies around the world—both for good and for ill. In the colonies, violence and disorder increased because of the imperialists' heavy taxation, theft of property, and intrusion on everyday life. Migration and the rapid spread of disease added to the burdens of colonial societies. However, imperialists were only able to dominate distant colonies and informally held areas such as China with the help of local people, many of whom profited from the economic opportunities such as new jobs and new technologies that imperial globalization offered. Thus, imperialism was full of paradox and contradiction.

> **FOCUS**
> How did imperialism change lives and livelihoods around the world?

Changing Conditions of Everyday Life

Citizens paid heavy taxes to maintain empires, which usually cost the country as a whole more than it gained. In trade, manufacturing, and international banking, however, individual business people reaped profits. For certain businesses, colonies provided crucial protected markets: late in the century, for instance, French colonies bought 65 percent of France's exports of soap and 41 percent of its metallurgical exports. People in port cities around the world had better jobs because of imperialism. Other segments of the population, however, simply paid the taxes to cover the costs of imperialism, without reward. Many had to leave home and family behind to seek jobs—whether in mines, on newly opened farmland, or in the factories springing up around the world. Imperial interactions changed local life for native peoples, often making it unhealthy and oppressive for many and bringing stupendous wealth to the few.

Networks of guides and translators were among those who dealt successfully with imperialists from Europe, Japan, and the United States, just as their ancestors centuries earlier had dealt with Mongols or Mughals. Nain Singh was the principal of a village school in the Himalayas, but the expanding British Empire transformed his life. Talented and knowledgeable about the vast, uncharted region that included Tibet, Nain Singh took a job with the British colonial service. There he learned to take measured steps of thirty-three inches in order to map terrain, to take the temperature of water so as to chart altitudes, and to speak many languages. After several years of training, Nain Singh attached himself to caravans, posing as a Buddhist pilgrim or a merchant. In fact, he was a British spy against Russia in the contest for control of Central Asia. In that capacity, he charted the forbidden region of Tibet and even spent time in the forbidden Tibetan capital, Lhasa, where he met the Dalai Lama. At great personal risk and sacrifice, intrepid local travelers such as Nain Singh acquired the geographic knowledge on which imperialists depended.

Local elites served the imperialists as soldiers and administrators in both India and Africa, and others helped ward off foreign competition. Khaw Soo Cheang left his home in China for Thailand in the 1820s, beginning his career as a fruit vendor but ending it as a

Working with and for the Imperialists

Nain Singh

Indian explorer Nain Singh worked for the British as a spy and a guide in Central Asia. His livelihood shows how imperialism created complicated relationships between the colonizers and the colonized. Tens of thousands of local Asians and Africans served in European armies, civil service jobs, and commercial and industrial ventures. For most local people, however, the relationship was far from equal, and many such employees testified to being treated with contempt and even physical violence. (TopFoto/The Image Works.)

magnate in the shipping and mining business. He also became an official of the Thai government and handed down his position to his five sons, who efficiently managed the southern states, collected taxes, and made important improvements to roads, mines, and public buildings. As Khaw's family initiatives flourished, Khaw's sons and daughters married into the wealthy world of regional shippers and other businessmen; the sons partnered with Europeans and Australians in their ventures, making the area profitable under Khaw control. A British official complained of the lack of opportunity in a region where, as he described it, a Khaw "has his finger in every pie"; in so doing the family had effectively immunized the region from full-scale intervention by outsiders.[11] There were many ways to work with imperialism.

Under imperialism a system of indirect rule often emerged, one that used local officials, chiefs, and princes to enforce imperial laws and keep order. In India, the best-known example, a few thousand British officials supervised close to half a million local civilian and military employees, who were paid far less than British employees would have been. Other powers adopted similar systems. Indirect rule reduced the cost of empire and invested local officials in the imperial project. As elsewhere, British civil servants attacked Indian cultural practices, such as female infanticide, child marriage, and *sati*, a widow's self-immolation on her husband's funeral pyre. Some in the upper classes of colonized countries were attracted to Japanese reforms and Western ideals—"the lofty tree of liberty," as one high Tunisian official praised them—and to notions of a scientifically ordered society.[12]

The vast majority of colonized peoples, however, were exploited. For example, to prevent superior Indian textiles from competing with British cloth, the government worked to close down Indian manufacturing centers and force artisans to become day laborers producing raw materials such as wheat and cotton. On land seized from peasants, imperialists and local business people set up plantations and opened mines in Africa and Asia. Once self-sufficient farmers became landless workers, either on their former lands or wherever labor was needed, not only in their home region but around the world, as cash agriculture became an instrument of imperial rule. A British governor of the Gold Coast in Africa put the matter succinctly in 1886: the British would "rule the country as if there were no inhabitants," as if local traditions of political and economic life did not exist. By confiscating land for tea, cotton, or rubber plantations, Europeans forced native peoples to work for them to earn a living. The agents of Leopold II of Belgium chopped off hands or simply shot Africans who did not provide their quota of rubber. "All of us wanted only one thing," reported a foreign worker in a Belgian Congo mine, "to terminate our contract and return to our country—we were so frightened by the number of people who died each day"[13] (see Reading the Past: Rubber Workers in the Congo). Subsistence agriculture based on growing a variety of crops and raising animals that supported families declined around the world, and communities were undermined as men left their homes to work in mines or on plantations to earn cash to pay imperial taxes.

Social Disorder   Imperialists brought not just economic but social disorder, upsetting established patterns of life. Even though some local people profited from the presence of outsiders, whom they often viewed as barbarians, other locals were victims of theft or physical abuse. While earlier merchants, administrators, and sailors had arrived without families and mingled with the local population, in the late nineteenth century governments began sending wives and children to accompany colonial officials, often clearing local people out of desirable urban neighborhoods to make room for European families. Women from Europe and the United States appeared in public in Western garb, which was unwelcome in Muslim regions where segregation of the sexes was a strong social norm. As men left their families

Rubber Workers in the Congo

In 1896 American manager Edgar Canisius began working for the Belgians in the Congo Free State, where rubber was harvested by forced labor. Canisius was thus part of the global workforce at the turn of the century, as were the inhabitants of Congo, who labored for a distant king— Leopold II of Belgium. After describing the atrocities the Belgians inflicted on Congolese whose harvest fell the slightest bit short of the quota, he noted the punishing work process itself. Canisius's report on his time in the Congo was published early in the twentieth century.

    The Congo native, when about to gather rubber, generally goes with his fellow villagers far into the jungle. Then, having formed a rough, shelterless camp, he begins his search for the creepers [rubber vines that wind themselves around other trees]. Having found one of sufficient size, he cuts with his knife a number of incisions in the bark, and, hanging a small earthenware pot below the vine, allows the sap to slowly trickle into it. Should the creeper have been already tapped, the man must climb into the supporting tree at more or less personal risk and make an incision in the vine high above the ground where the sap has not been exhausted. . . . Not infrequently the natives slumber on their lofty perches, and, falling to the ground, become victims of the white man's greed. Few Africans will imperil their lives in rubber-gathering unless under compulsion. . . .

    Each tribe has only a limited extent of forest which it can call its exclusive domain, and it consequently very frequently happens, when their own "bush" is worked out, that natives from one village penetrate the territory of the other in defiance of tribal usage. Such an invasion is naturally resented by their neighbors, who, equally pressed no doubt by circumstances and the white man, are themselves experiencing difficulty in making up the quota of rubber definitely fixed for each village, and a deficient production of which may entail dire punishment and even death. In consequence, disputes arise between villages which heretofore, perhaps for quite a long period, have been at peace; and then come wars, involving more or less loss of life, destruction and cannibalism. Natives, I may add, have often come to me with bitter laments over the disappearance of their brothers after accidents when rubber-gathering, or the attacks of leopards or hostile tribesmen.

Source: Edgar Canisius, "A Campaign Amongst Cannibals," in Captain Guy Burrows, *The Curse of Central Africa* (London: R. A. Everett and Co., 1903), 74–80, quoted in Robert O. Collins, ed., *Central and South African History*, vol. 3, *African History: Text and Readings.* (New York: Markus Wiener, 1990), 111–112.

EXAMINING THE EVIDENCE

1. What were the conditions of life for those gathering rubber in the Congo?

2. What were rubber gatherers' attitudes in the face of their task?

3. What were the consequences of rubber gathering for the individual, the community, and the region at large?

---

to work in mines, on urban docks, or on plantations, imperialists recruited local women into prostitution around these new workplaces.

    Missionaries brought another kind of disorder, as the Boxer Rebellion demonstrated. European missionaries rushed to newly secured areas of Africa and Asia. A woman missionary working among the Tibetans reflected a common view when she remarked that the native peoples were "going down, down into hell, and there is no one but me . . . to witness for Jesus amongst them." In addition to their often unwanted arrival into native communities, missionaries fought among themselves, drawing locals into conflicts that sometimes led to military intervention and the expansion of imperial control. Women missionaries often found their new settings liberating as they left the domestic confines of their homelands for societies where they faced fewer restrictions. Their empowerment made some of them feel entitled to change local people's lives, and most earnestly hoped to improve daily life abroad. Christian missions attracted followers, upsetting local patterns of living.

    Imperialists also disordered the traditional landscape, not only with large plantations in rural areas but also with administrative buildings, theaters, and schools, designed in styles of the so-called mother country (see Seeing the Past: Imperial Architecture in Saigon). Wide

Imperial Architecture in Saigon

Not only did imperialism take the wealth of foreign regions and the labor of their inhabitants, but the imperial powers also attempted to impose their own culture and values on subjected lands. One way of doing this was building monuments to imperial rulers and transforming cities according to Western ideas of proper urban architecture. The French filled the Vietnamese city of Saigon, for example, with the same wide boulevards found in Paris and with buildings such as cafés, private dwellings, and government offices that resembled those in Paris as well.

An Imperial Cityscape: Saigon (ND/Roger-Viollet/The Image Works.)

EXAMINING THE EVIDENCE

1. What does this photograph reveal about changing livelihoods in imperial Saigon?

2. Why would local residents welcome this grand hotel in the French style? Why would they object to it?

---

boulevards allowed passage of fine carriages—and also military parades that demonstrated the empire's power.

Everyday Resistance and Accommodation

Those in contact with imperialists practiced everyday resistance such as slowdowns at work or petty theft. Indian merchants used traditional tactics to block tax increases: they closed up shop and left town by the thousands. African merchants protested conditions around ports that seemed to favor imperial traders. In Freetown, Sierra Leone, local merchants found that the pathway to the customs house was constructed to block their goods from entering while providing the European merchants direct access for their wares. Their protests forced European officials to negotiate and ultimately change the port's arrangements. There was also accommodation: the British employed Sikhs in the colonial army because of their warrior skills and bravery in battle. But they wanted the Sikhs to control their hair, which they kept long for religious reasons. Sikh soldiers complied to keep their good jobs by adopting a turban as part of their uniform, making it a proud symbol of their separate identity. Missionaries also had to adapt when, as the price for attending church, local people wanted lessons in the colonial culture, languages, and practical skills such as Western science and math.

Although resistance sometimes led to compromise, it often prompted violent repression. In early-twentieth-century German East Africa, local people refused to pay taxes. "We do not owe you anything. We have no debt to you. If you as a stranger want to stay in this country, you will have to ask us."[14] In this case resistance was met with force: in 1907, the Germans massacred these East Africans, seizing their food supplies and leaving survivors to die of starvation. Highly organized resistance usually met with brutal mass repression, making subtle opposition a better choice.

Medicine, Science, and Well-Being in the Colonies

Imperialism changed the life of local people in myriad ways. It crucially affected health and well-being, which declined on some fronts and improved on others. Trains efficiently transported food crops away from the colonies, and equally efficiently transmitted diseases from railroad hub to railroad hub, often leaving local people both hungry and sick. Simultaneously, colonial agents introduced modern health and hygiene programs; the contradictory agendas of imperialists affected local life in complex and profound ways.

Spread of Famine and Disease

Famine, made worse by the policies of imperial powers, helped empire builders expand their holdings. During the El Niño conditions of the late nineteenth century, when weather disturbances in the tropical Pacific dried up farming lands in Asia, Africa, and parts of Brazil, acreage that was once green and productive turned brown and hard. Rivers and shallow wells dried up, making safe water and fresh food unavailable. When such conditions had occurred before, traditional rulers in India, China, and the Ottoman Empire had sent aid and cut taxes. Instead of relenting on taxes during this disaster, the Europeans redoubled their efforts to collect them, sending in tax collectors "whip in hand." As British officials announced in India: "The revenue must at all costs be gathered in."[15] Those who could not pay lost their lands, which were then given to wealthy local peoples or Europeans; colonial agents then shipped these newly landless people to plantations and mines, saving them from starvation by forcing them to work in semislavery. The plantation owners' profits in the Caribbean and elsewhere soared with the arrival of this virtually cost-free labor.

Similarly, government policies going back centuries had ensured that reservoirs and irrigation systems collected scarce water to save for droughts. The British in India, however, had no interest in such projects. Maintaining irrigation systems cost money, and the British were in India to make money. In the Qing Empire as well, with foreign powers in control of revenue collection as a result of the Opium War, taxes were no longer used for upkeep of the reservoirs, irrigation systems, or even waterways that might have transported aid to stricken regions. Imperialist neglect further devastated both agriculture and the environment.

Industrialization worsened the situation. As people in drought-stricken areas lost their ability to buy goods, including food, imperialists made fortunes, using trains to carry grain out of poor regions and store it until shortages led to rising prices and bigger profits. As trains moved back and forth among regions, they helped spread diseases to weakened people. Mortality rates soared as smallpox, influenza, typhus, cholera, and other lethal diseases worked their way through China, India, and other areas. Influential Europeans believed that no relief should be provided because any relaxation of laissez-faire principles would simply spoil recipients of aid. Lord Lytton, viceroy of India during the 1870s, spent handsomely for grand ceremonials celebrating the ascension of Britain's Queen Victoria to the imperial throne of India, yet he refused to send food to the starving, calling the cost of such aid harmful to the economy as a whole. According to Lytton, people who wanted to restore the water storage infrastructure were "irrigation quacks," and those proposing to give food to the starving were "humanitarian hysterics." When some citizens in the imperial countries became so ashamed at the photos of skeletal Indians and Chinese that they set up relief funds, colonial governors—most of them strict believers in laissez faire—diverted these funds to colonial wars in Afghanistan, South Africa, and elsewhere to expand imperialism.

Science and Hygiene

At the same time, the imperial powers aimed to transform local life with new public health programs, in large part to protect their own soldiers and officials. Governments set up scientific stations to study and adapt local plant life to serve imperial interests. Simultaneously, foreign doctors ordered that entire villages be burned to the ground when contagious diseases were found in a single household. Europeans also worked to increase hospital births in the colonies as a way to build the colonial workforce. (By contrast, the vast majority of European women still gave birth at home.) Hospitalization of expectant mothers undermined local customs and sociability and ruined the livelihoods of midwives and other healers. Sometimes changes that were not directly related to public health were explained in hygienic terms: the wide boulevards that destroyed neighborhoods and changed the face of cities opened infested areas to sunlight and cleaner conditions, for example. Local people created their own stories to accompany medical explanations. In African lore, the vampire, with its bloodsucking habit, reflected the natives' concern about colonial doctors who took blood. In other countries, such as China, those interested in change translated books on Western hygienic methods.

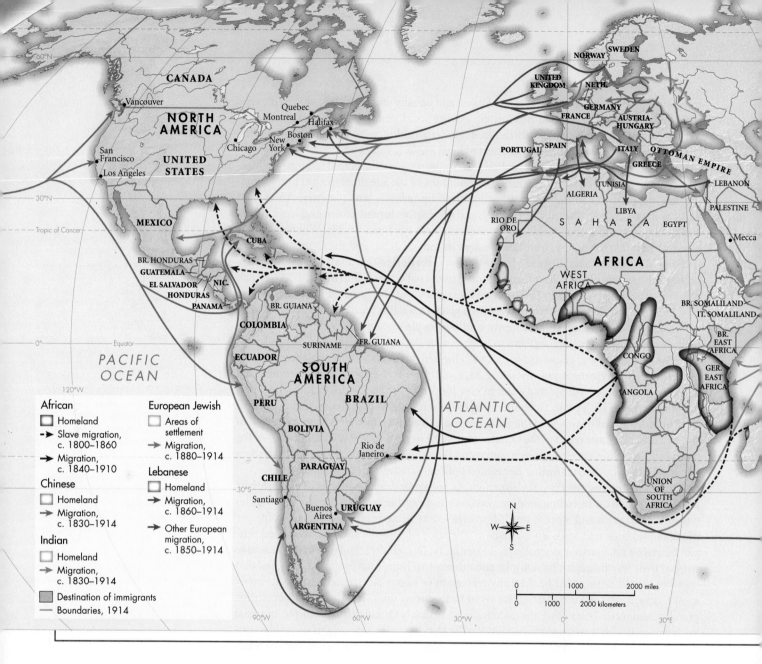

Migrants and Diasporas

The global expansion of industry and empire brought with it mass migration in the second half of the nineteenth century (see Map 26.3). In some cases, people moved because imperialists offered jobs outside their homelands. Others migrated simply because conditions at home were so bad: millions left the rural areas of Europe to escape persecution, crop failures, and eventually the hardship caused by global competition in agriculture. In Asia, Africa, and Latin America, people migrated regionally to cacao, rubber, coffee, and other plantations in response to the demands of imperialists that they pay new taxes and the lure of steady jobs.

Regional Migration   Both industrialization and imperialism affected the movement of people in search of livelihoods. Migrants left rural areas for industrialized cities, swelling their population to the bursting point. Migrants sometimes returned to the countryside at harvest time. Temporary migrants to the cities worked as masons, rickshaw drivers, or factory hands to supplement declining income from agriculture; in the winter, those remaining on the land turned to cottage industries producing a variety of goods, including bricks, pottery, lace, and locks. In Africa, dense networks of trade took Africans, Arabs, and Indians hundreds

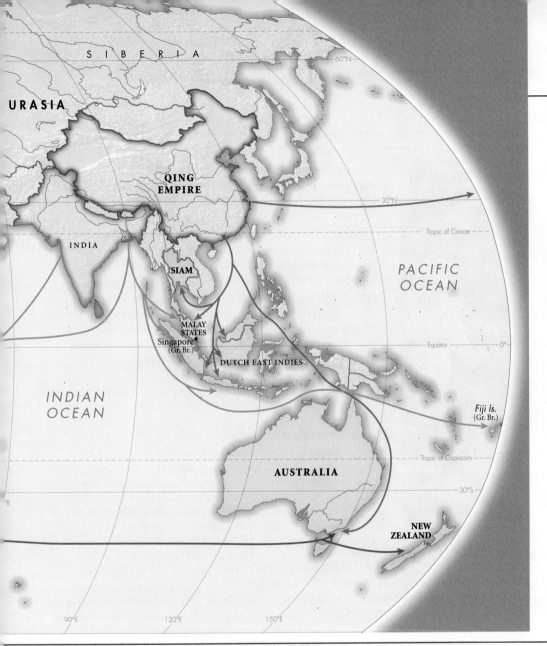

SIBERIA

URASIA

INDIA

QING EMPIRE

SIAM

MALAY STATES
Singapore (Gr. Br.)

DUTCH EAST INDIES

INDIAN OCEAN

PACIFIC OCEAN

Tropic of Cancer

Equator

Fiji Is. (Gr. Br.)

Tropic of Capricorn

AUSTRALIA

NEW ZEALAND

60°N

30°N

0°

30°S

90°E   120°E   150°E

MAP 26.3

Global Migration, c. 1800–1910

People were on the move during these decades for many different reasons. Most were concerned with finding better livelihoods, or finding any livelihood. The formal ending of the slave trade and then slavery itself led underemployed people from Asia and Africa to migrate as indentured servants, which many saw as a new type of slavery. Europeans migrated from rural areas because the global trade in grain drove down prices for produce; others, however, hoped to escape religious and personal persecution on the continent while simultaneously finding new means of support.

and even thousands of miles in caravans packed with goods. These temporary migrations were often interrupted to pay tribute to traditional rulers—not necessarily to imperialists. Yet in the colonies regional migration was also coercive and tested family ties.

Europeans, Asians, and Africans alike followed a pattern of global migration, moving well beyond their national borders to countries where land was being taken from native peoples to give to white settlers, or where imperialism created new job opportunities (see Lives and Livelihoods: Indentured Laborers). In parts of Europe, China, and India, for example, the land simply could not produce enough to support rapidly expanding populations, especially when drought, agricultural diseases, and famine struck. Millions of rural Jews, especially from eastern Europe, left their villages for economic reasons to populate many regions of the world, but Russian Jews also fled in the face of vicious anti-Semitic **pogroms**. In the course of such state-approved riots, Russian mobs brutally attacked Jewish communities, destroying homes and businesses and even murdering some Jews. "People who saw such things never smiled anymore, no matter how long they lived," recalled one Russian Jewish woman who migrated to the United States in the early 1890s.

News of commercial, agricultural, and industrial opportunity, often from recruiting agents working for governments or businesses, determined destinations. Railroads and steamships

Global Migration

pogrom A systematic attack on Jews, as carried out, for example, in the late-nineteenth-century Russian Empire.

Indentured Laborers

After slavery declined in many countries during the first half of the nineteenth century, owners of plantations, mines, and refineries complained that they needed more workers. Agents began to scour the countryside of colonized regions—especially where there was famine and other economic distress—to find workers to transport to other parts of the world. By the system of indenture, workers were cajoled or forced to sign contracts that obliged them to work for five to seven years in distant lands. Between 1830 and the outbreak of World War I in 1914, some 1.5 million Indians served as indentured laborers on European-owned plantations. Transported to Mauritania, British Guiana, Fiji, Trinidad, Guadeloupe, and Natal, to name a few destinations, their goal was to earn enough money to return home with some kind of savings.

An African Indentured Servant

The end of slavery left global business people searching for ways to secure cheap labor for plantations around the world. One source was indentured labor, a system in which agents scoured regions for underemployed workers who would serve an extended term of labor, usually in a far-off land. India, China, and West Africa thus provided workers for sugar and other plantations in the Pacific and Caribbean—to name a few destinations. This photograph shows an indentured servant planting coconut trees on Fiji, one of the Solomon Islands. Today, these regions have a rich heritage of multiculturalism in large part because of the traditions indentured laborers brought with them. (Art Media/Heritage/The Image Works.)

made journeys across and out of Asia and Europe more affordable and faster, even though most workers traveled in steerage. Once established in their new countries, migrants frequently sent money back home, and thus remained part of the family economy. They might use the funds they earned to educate a younger brother or set up a daughter or son in a small business, thus contributing to advancement. Nationalists in eastern and central Europe bemoaned the loss of ethnic vigor as the young and active departed, but peasants everywhere welcomed the arrival of "magic" income from their overseas kin. The connection between migrants and their homelands was not, therefore, completely severed by their departure. In fact, migration helped create new connections among distant parts of the world.

Migration to another part of the world did, however, often mean the end to the old way of life for the migrants themselves. Working men and women immediately had to learn new languages and civic practices and to compete for jobs in growing cities where they formed the cheapest pool of labor, often working in factories or sweatshops. Most of the first Chinese and Indian migrants were men, but when women migrants arrived with their husbands, they stayed at home and tended to associate with others like themselves, preserving traditional ways in dress and housekeeping. Their children and husbands,

"A new form of slavery," a British aristocrat and opponent called the system of indentured servitude that European powers developed after ending the slave trade. Indentured laborers endured horrendous conditions cutting sugarcane, growing other cash crops, or working in mines. "I haven't had food for three days, my body is weak, my throat is parched," reported one worker in Fiji. Another worker in the Fiji cane fields said, "We were whipped for small mistakes. If you woke up late, i.e. later than three A.M., you got whipped. No matter whether there was rain or thunder you had to work . . . otherwise we were abused and beaten up." Even those whose working conditions were somewhat better found themselves without any basic cultural institutions: "There are no temples, no festivals, no idols, . . . no schools for our children, who receive no education of any kind," an Indian indentured worker in Guadeloupe wrote in 1884. "It seems to us that animals are better treated than us in this colony."

Indentured workers kept in touch with their home culture through missionaries from India itself, adopting the ancient texts of the *Ramayana*—a tale of exile and deliverance—as their spiritual sustenance. Some African indentured laborers traveled back and forth between the Caribbean and the West African coast, even serving as recruiters after one term on the plantations.

Many indentured laborers never returned to their homeland, however, constituting extensive diasporas far from Africa and South Asia. Nonetheless, they maintained many traditions: performing scenes from the *Ramayana*, for example, remains a joyous public celebration in Trinidad today. Indentured workers also transported African religions and rituals, which are still influential in binding descendants of these workers to the African continent.

Source: Quoted in Marina Carter and Khal Torabully, *Coolitude: An Anthology of the Indian Labour Diaspora* (London: Anthem Press, 2002), 90–91, 110.

QUESTIONS TO CONSIDER

1. How does the system of indentured servitude compare to slavery?

2. How did Africans and others help in the system of indentured labor, and why might they have cooperated?

3. What is the cultural legacy of indentured servitude?

For Further Information:
Carter, Marina, and Khal Torabully. *Coolitude: An Anthology of the Indian Labour Diaspora.* 2002.
Kale, Madhavi. *Fragments of Empire: Capital, Slavery, and Indian Indentured Labor Migration in the British Caribbean.* 1998.

forced to remake their lives in the schools and factories of their adopted land, were more likely to embrace the new and search out opportunity.

As migrants from extended families or the same region settled near one another, they formed ethnic **diasporas**, clusters of people who shared an ethnic identity. Continuing enslavement of Africans, Russians, and others created the harshest diasporas, but imperialism also encouraged diasporas born of opportunity. For example, the British persuaded skilled Chinese traders to settle in Singapore, and thousands of them migrated—usually without establishing permanent attachments—to build this commercial city virtually from scratch (see again Map 26.3). Other Chinese settled around the world, depending for their success on global networks to supply goods and thereby maintaining close ties to their ancestral roots. The same was true of the Lebanese diaspora to France, the United States, Argentina, and Brazil. Many of these migrants were Christians who wanted to make money in trade without having to deal with Ottoman restrictions on non-Muslims. Thus they moved to areas of opportunity, expecting to prosper and eventually to return home. In fact, historians estimate that in the early twentieth century as many as 40 percent of these Lebanese migrants found their way back—mostly to the area around Beirut—for at least a period, if not permanently.

Global Diasporas

diaspora The dispersal of a population, often resulting in large settlements in different parts of the world.

Migrants even proved influential in politics back home. The "Song of Revolution" of the turn of the century called on members of the Chinese diaspora to help overthrow the Manchu dynasty and reform the Qing Empire: "What use is the cumulation of silver cash? / Why not use it to eject the Manchus? / Ten thousand each from you isn't much / To buy cannons and guns and ship them inland."[16]

Culture in an Imperial Age

FOCUS
How did artists and writers respond to the age of empire?

The imperial age led to new ways of thought and changing norms around the world. Exposure to new environments inspired scientists and led to fresh discoveries. Ordinary people adjusted their ideas and habits to suit new city neighborhoods. Books and art from around the world inspired artists and writers as they produced works that reflected on life in the imperial age. Global contacts sparked debates over gender roles and interest in alternative ways of life. Accelerating cultural change produced what is called "modernism" in the arts—a style based on sometimes disturbing transformations in artistic expression. In fact, we may interpret spreading modernity in the realm of behavior and culture as part of globalization.

The Culture of Everyday Life

Migration from countryside to city in an age of empire meant that people transplanted rural habits and cultural life to urban settings. Bengali women who migrated to Calcutta to work as potters, basketmakers, dyers, and occasionally as factory workers, for example, celebrated their holidays in traditional ways, singing and dancing to stories of the gods and goddesses. They amused city folk with their country poetry at weddings and births, poetry that often featured tales of seduction, jealousy, and betrayal. Drug-smoking husbands and lovers who stole women's possessions were a favorite topic:

> My tears dry up in my eyes,
> I go around making merry. I'm writing in pain,
> Yet I act coy
> Swinging my hips.[17]

Such popular amusement outraged Calcutta's elites, who now preferred British middle-class norms for "civilized" female behavior. In their view, women who performed in public, such as actresses or singers, were prostitutes. Certain middle-class attitudes became standard among many Bengalis and elites in other parts of the world. As a result, the number of women performers in Calcutta declined drastically, from over seventeen thousand in the 1870s to three thousand in 1890.

In other places, local leaders were able to maintain cultural values and patterns of life. In West Africa, the French allowed Islam to flourish and used religious leaders to maintain the peace even as the region lost its economic and political independence. In turn, religious leaders preached the doctrine of accommodation to French rule. "Support the French government totally," the Sufi leader Malik Sy urged in the early twentieth century. "God has given special victory, grace, and favor to the French. He has chosen them to protect our persons and property."[18] In West Africa, France financed pilgrimages to Mecca for Muslim leaders and local officials and supported the building of mosques and the observance of Islamic law.

Urbanization and globalization remained powerful forces, breaking down traditional customs. The development of the mass media—particularly the newspaper—made millions of readers aware of other ways of doing things. Photography displayed the triumphs of technology for viewers around the world, making railroads appear even more modern by juxtaposing their images with photos of "savages," whether from the U.S. West or Oceania.

Indian Woman Dancing with Musicians

Indian women traditionally danced on many occasions and in both public and private celebrations. One popular dance was the pot dance, which revolved around the imagery of a full container whose contents must be protected: any spillage would symbolize the emptying of one's own or one's family's being. Many in the growing Indian middle class came to see these dancers, whose entire bodies were in motion, as overly sexual and bordering on barbaric. (The British Library/HIP/The Image Works.)

To build circulation, Western journalists puffed up the triumphs of "explorers" and roused readers' emotions with lurid stories of the global trade in women and girls. In celebrations of such holidays as "Empire Day" in Britain and in imperial ceremonies in South Asia and Africa, people around the world participated in an invented global culture that seemed to endorse empire. Monuments and portraits of conquerors and rulers were aimed at reshaping local loyalties into imperial ones.

Clothing traveled the world too. When French painter Paul Gauguin arrived in Tahiti late in the nineteenth century, he noted that local women had already adopted Western-style dresses with long sleeves and high necks. Chinese women had their portraits painted wearing perky Western straw hats adorned with feathers. Traditional patterns of thought and behavior loosened their hold on everyday life, especially in the world's teeming cities.

Art and Empire

The arts felt influences from empire. Japanese, Indian, Chinese, and Latin American artists adapted Western techniques that they learned of through training in Western art schools and the increasing availability of photographs. Simultaneously, writers across the globe read one another's works. Global celebrities such as Rabindranath Tagore emerged. Tagore, who won the Nobel Prize for literature in 1913, was educated in Bengal and in London, but backed by the enormous wealth of his grandfather, a financier, he was able to travel the world at leisure while composing poems, songs, short stories, and other works of prose. In his works, Tagore commented on the difficult lives of Bengali peasants while emphasizing Indian nationalism and education in Western knowledge. This ability to consider and often integrate different cultural traditions is called **cosmopolitanism**.

Similarly aware of world developments and foreign educated, Soseki Natsumi, called the greatest writer of the Meiji period, wove insights on local Japanese life as it modernized into his novels and journalism. Soseki's *Botchan* (*Little Master*, 1906) focused on a cranky youth—a "misfit" in the Meiji world—who had been educated in math and science and sent to the provinces to teach. He insults his colleagues, no one more than an art teacher who wears a French-style smock and floppy bow tie around his neck, affecting the attitude

cosmopolitanism The merging or acceptance of a variety of national and ethnic values and traditions.

The Durbar for Edward VII in Delhi, India

Lavish celebrations and rituals were invented to cement imperial relationships between rulers and ruled. Held at the very end of 1902 and into 1903, this durbar—a formal state reception given by Indian princes for a British sovereign—marked the ascension of Edward VII to the imperial throne and thus to rule over India. Maharajahs and other local dignitaries attended, riding elephants and wearing luxurious clothing and jewels, appearing to accept this foreign ruler. Such ceremonies masked the violence with which the British and other imperial powers attempted to rule and the ever-present resistance to these foreign invaders. (Getty Images.)

of a Western artist. Soseki railed against consumers of Western-style journalism, especially readers who gobbled up news of fires, murders, and accidents with the idea that they were now in touch with a Western kind of reality. In Soseki's view, this foreign habit actually cut them off from a deeper reality. At the same time, he transformed Japanese literature by probing the psychology of his characters as writers in the West did. The leading writers of Asia were thus engaged with styles and worldviews brought from afar by imperialism and globalization.

Western literature traveled the world, arousing both acclaim and controversy. The Norwegian playwright Henrik Ibsen's *A Doll's House* (1879), a drama about a woman who leaves a loveless marriage, riveted global audiences. It influenced many to think that their countries' modernization required changes in the situation of women. Inspired by the play, Japanese women started a feminist movement; some Chinese women campaigned to eliminate foot-binding. Similarly, women in Ottoman countries abandoned their veils in the belief that it would help free their countries if they looked more Western. Under the influence of imperialism and globalization, literature influenced rebellion against the West even as it promoted the adoption of Western values and cultural patterns.

Imperial Contests at the Dawn of the Twentieth Century

FOCUS

What were the main issues in the contests over empire, and what were the results of these contests?

Although cultural influences were shaping city life and traveling around the world, imperialism was increasingly chaotic and deadly at the start of the twentieth century. Large-scale rebellions by ordinary people fighting against imperial domination, such as the Boxer Rebellion, became more common. Competition among the imperial powers themselves was also heating up as their ambitions swelled. The United States and Japan pursued global empire more vigorously in these years, fighting successful wars against older empires. International politics became menacing and imperial nerves were on edge, especially as military spending grew amid competition for power.

Clashes for Imperial Control

After centuries of global expansion, imperial adventure soured for empires both old and new. Some of this trouble arose from newcomers to imperial competition, such as Japan and the United States, both of which took territory and expanded their markets at the turn of the century, defeating older rivals. Empires faced constant challenges to their survival: as empires were competing among themselves for influence, the colonized and otherwise oppressed people were fighting back with increasing vigor.

The British experienced an unexpected setback to their imperial ambitions in 1896, when Cecil Rhodes, by then prime minister of the Cape Colony at Africa's southern tip, directed a raid on Johannesburg to stir up trouble between the Boers, descendants of early Dutch settlers, and the more recent immigrants from Britain who had come to southern Africa in search of gold. Rhodes hoped the raid would justify a British takeover of the Transvaal and the Orange Free State, which the Boers independently controlled. The Boers unexpectedly won, leading the British to wage the South African (or Boer) War directly against the Transvaal and the Orange Free State. As journalists reported on appalling bloodshed, rampant disease, and the unfit condition of the average British soldier, citizens back home were stunned. The British herded the Boers into a shocking and unfamiliar institution—the concentration camp, which became the graveyard of tens of thousands of women and children. Britain finally defeated the Boers in 1902 and annexed the area, but the cost of war in money, loss of life, and public morale was enormous.

Native Africans, who mostly had supported the British with the thought that they were more civilized and law-abiding than the Boers, were quickly disillusioned. Soon after the annexation, the government of South Africa passed a series of laws appropriating African-owned lands for whites, depriving Africans of free movement, and imposing an entire range of restrictions on their lives. It was the foundation for the policy of racial segregation and discrimination that would be called apartheid. "We expected deliverance," one local chieftain commented bitterly on postwar British policy, "whereas we have gone deeper into bond[age]."[19]

At about the time the British were fighting the Boer War, Spain lost Cuba, Puerto Rico, and the Philippines to the United States, which defeated it in the Spanish-American War of 1898. As Spanish imperial power declined, the Spanish government tried to support itself by raising taxes to exorbitant levels on its remaining colonies. Meanwhile, the United States, a newcomer to imperialism overseas, had been killing native Americans and driving them from their lands since the seventeenth century. In addition it had asserted its diplomatic influence in the Western Hemisphere in the Monroe Doctrine (1823), purchased Alaska in 1867, and annexed Hawaii in 1898 at the urgings of missionaries and businessmen, who had set up plantations on the islands (see Reading the Past: The United States Overthrows the Hawaiian Queen).

Before the Spanish-American War, both Cuba and the Philippines had vigorous independence movements backed by all classes of people. Expansionist-minded Theodore Roosevelt, then assistant secretary of the navy, and the inflammatory daily press goaded the U.S. government to help the independence movements with armed force. However, after its swift victory over Spain the United States annexed Puerto Rico and Guam and bought the Philippines from its former ruler. In theory, Cuba remained independent, but U.S. businesses virtually controlled its sugar-exporting economy—a clear example of business imperialism. The lesson for the imperial powers was the unpredictability of empire. After that, the triumphant United States, encouraged by British poet Rudyard Kipling to "take up the white man's burden" by bringing the benefits of Western civilization to the Philippines, waged a bloody war against the Filipinos, who wanted independence, not simply a different imperial ruler. Reports of American brutality in the Philippines, where some twenty

The South African War

The Spanish-American War

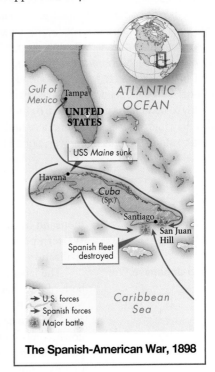

The Spanish-American War, 1898

The United States Overthrows the Hawaiian Queen

U.S. businessmen set themselves up in the Hawaiian Islands, establishing lucrative sugar plantations and other agricultural enterprises. With government support, they then worked to undermine the ruling monarchy, calling themselves the Committee of Safety. After imprisoning the Hawaiian queen under house arrest in 1893, they forced her to abdicate in a document that gave no indication of the trickery and violence behind their deeds. In this passage from her memoir of 1898, Queen Liliuokalani describes the threats that led to her abdication. The men she cites were members of the Committee.

For the first few days nothing occurred to disturb the quiet of my apartments save the tread of the sentry. On the fourth day I received a visit from Mr. Paul Neumann, who asked me if, in the event that it should be decided that all the principal parties to the revolt must pay for it with their lives, I was prepared to die? I replied to this in the affirmative, telling him I had no anxiety for myself, and felt no dread of death. He then told me that six others besides myself had been selected to be shot for treason, but that he would call again, and let me know further about our fate. . . .

About the 22d of January a paper was handed to me by Mr. Wilson, which, on examination, proved to be a purported act of abdication for me to sign. . . . For myself, I would have chosen death rather than to have signed it; but it was represented to me that by my signing this paper all the persons who had been arrested, all my people now in trouble by reason of their love and loyalty towards me, would be immediately released. Think of my position— sick, a lone woman in prison, scarcely knowing who was my friend, or who listened to my words only to betray me, without legal advice or friendly counsel, and the stream of blood ready to flow unless it was stayed by my pen.

My persecutors have stated, and at that time compelled me to state, that this paper was signed and acknowledged by me after consultation with my friends whose names appear at the foot of it as witnesses. Not the least opportunity was given to me to confer with anyone; but for the purpose of making it appear to the outside world that I was under the guidance of others, friends who had known me well in better days were brought into the place of my imprisonment, and stood around to see a signature affixed by me. . . . Then the following individuals witnessed my subscription of the signature which was demanded of me: William G. Irwin, H. A. Widemann, Samuel Parker, S. Kalua Kookano, Charles B. Wilson, and Paul Neumann. . . .

So far from the presence of these persons being evidence of a voluntary act on my part, was it not an assurance to me that they, too, knew that, unless I did the will of my jailers, what Mr. Neumann had threatened would be performed, and six prominent citizens immediately put to death. I so regarded it then, and I still believe that murder was the alternative. Be this as it may, it is certainly happier for me to reflect to-day that there is not a drop of the blood of my subjects, friends or foes, upon my soul.

Source: Liliuokalani, *Hawaii's Story by Hawaii's Queen* (Boston: Lothrop, Lee, and Shepard,1898), http://digital.library.upenn.edu/women/liliuokalani/hawaii/hawaii.html.

EXAMINING THE EVIDENCE

1. Why do you think that Queen Liliuokalani wrote this memoir?

2. What attitudes do you sense behind the actions of those who wanted to take over her lands and resources?

3. How does the queen portray herself in the face of these adversaries?

---

thousand freedom fighters and several hundred thousand civilians died, disillusioned the Western public, who liked to imagine native peoples joyously welcoming the bearers of civilization.

The Russo-Japanese War   The Japanese vigorously pursued empire, defeating China and then trouncing Russia— both of them Japan's rivals for influence in the Far East. Angered by Russian expansion in Manchuria, the Japanese attacked tsarist forces at Port Arthur in 1904 (see Map 26.4). Casualties were once again fearsome, as powerful new weaponry such as machine guns mowed down combatants on both sides. To the astonishment of the world, the Japanese completely destroyed the Russian fleet in the 1905 Battle of Tsushima Strait. The victory was the first by a non-European nation over a European great power in the modern age. As one

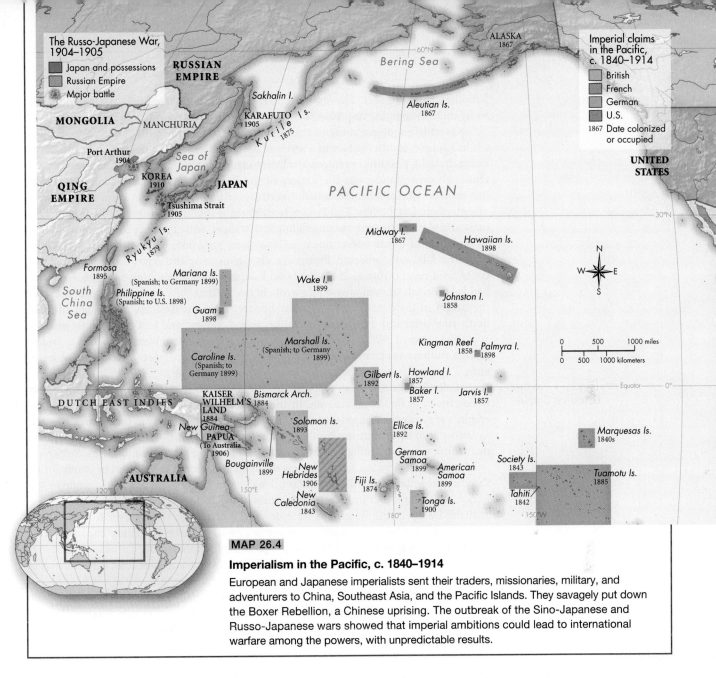

The Russo-Japanese War, 1904–1905
- Japan and possessions
- Russian Empire
- Major battle

Imperial claims in the Pacific, c. 1840–1914
- British
- French
- German
- U.S.
- 1867 Date colonized or occupied

RUSSIAN EMPIRE

Bering Sea

ALASKA 1867

60°N

MONGOLIA   MANCHURIA

Sakhalin I.

KARAFUTO Is. 1905

Kurile Is. 1875

Aleutian Is. 1867

Port Arthur 1904

Sea of Japan

QING EMPIRE

KOREA 1910

JAPAN

PACIFIC OCEAN

Tsushima Strait 1905

UNITED STATES

30°N

Ryukyu Is. 1879

Midway I. 1867

Hawaiian Is. 1898

Formosa 1895

Mariana Is. (Spanish; to Germany 1899)

Wake I. 1899

Johnston I. 1858

N W E S

South China Sea

Philippine Is. (Spanish; to U.S. 1898)

Guam 1898

Marshall Is. (Spanish; to Germany 1899)

Kingman Reef 1858   Palmyra I. 1898

0   500   1000 miles

0   500   1000 kilometers

Caroline Is. (Spanish; to Germany 1899)

Gilbert Is. 1892

Howland I. 1857

Baker I. 1857   Jarvis I. 1857

Equator   0°

DUTCH EAST INDIES

KAISER WILHELM'S LAND 1884

Bismarck Arch.

Solomon Is. 1893

Ellice Is. 1892

Marquesas Is. 1840s

New Guinea–PAPUA (To Australia 1906)

Bougainville 1899

New Hebrides 1906

Fiji Is. 1874

German Samoa 1899   American Samoa 1899

Society Is. 1843

Tuamotu Is. 1885

AUSTRALIA

150°E

New Caledonia 1843

180°

Tonga Is. 1900

Tahiti 1842

150°W

MAP 26.4

Imperialism in the Pacific, c. 1840–1914

European and Japanese imperialists sent their traders, missionaries, military, and adventurers to China, Southeast Asia, and the Pacific Islands. They savagely put down the Boxer Rebellion, a Chinese uprising. The outbreak of the Sino-Japanese and Russo-Japanese wars showed that imperial ambitions could lead to international warfare among the powers, with unpredictable results.

English general ominously observed of the Russian defeat, "I have today seen the most stupendous spectacle it is possible for the mortal brain to conceive—Asia advancing, Europe falling back." Japan went on to annex Korea in 1910 and to eye other areas for colonization. Russia itself erupted in the Revolution of 1905, forcing the tsar to institute a weak form of parliament, the Duma. The double blow of military defeat by Japan and social revolution exposed Russia's internal weaknesses, especially the widespread discontent of ordinary people.

Growing Resistance to Foreign Domination

The Japanese military victory over two important dynasties—the Qing in China and the Romanov in Russia—reverberated around the world. People under foreign domination responded to Japan's victory with enthusiasm and hope, believing that if a small non-Western nation such as Japan could defeat a Western power, they too could defeat outside forces.

In China, students, elites, and ordinary people felt humiliated by the 1895 defeat by Japan and the forced economic concessions to Western powers that followed. Students demanded reform, presenting a memorandum asking for modern institutions such as an efficient tax system and national railroad, postal, and banking networks. The memo insisted that the government sponsor technology and commerce, the latter through creating

Boxers in China

883

a modern shipping fleet. The Dowager Empress Cixi (kee-shee) (1835–1908), who effectively ruled the empire, responded by having the reformers rounded up and executed.

Nevertheless, defeat at the hands of Japan had rocked the faith of ordinary people in China's future, and in the face of a series of natural disasters, including floods and devastating drought, peasants organized locally into secret societies to restore Chinese integrity. One such organization was the Society of the Righteous and Harmonious Fists, or the Boxers, whose members maintained that ritual boxing would protect them from a variety of evils, including bullets. The Boxers reinvigorated themselves through the discipline of martial arts, often reciting charms, falling into trances, and appealing to the gods and spirits on behalf of China (see again At a Crossroads, page 856). Facing these young Boxers and their followers, however, Europeans also invoked spiritual powers: "We know God could send relief thru rain if He thot [*sic*] best, and we know all our interests are in His hands," a British woman missionary wrote in her journal.[20] By 1900 as the Boxers reached the height of their power, troops from Europe, the United States, and Japan invaded, destroying cities and the countryside alike, killing, raping, and looting to crush what the West had come to call "the yellow peril." The defeated Chinese were compelled to endure foreign military occupation and to pay a huge indemnity—more than twice the entire annual national income. The Qing dynasty faced its downfall.

Young Turks in the Ottoman Empire

Modern nationalism was sapping the Ottoman Empire, which for centuries had controlled much of the Mediterranean. In the nineteenth century, rebellions in several of the empire's provinces challenged Ottoman rule, and more erupted early in the twentieth century as resistance to the empire grew. Sultan Abdul Hamid II (r. 1876–1909) tried to revitalize the multiethnic empire by using Islam to counteract the rising nationalism of Serbs, Bulgarians, and Macedonians. Instead, he unwittingly strengthened Turkish nationalism in Istanbul itself. Rejecting the sultan's pan-Islamic solution, dissident Turks, the dominant ethnic group in Asia Minor, built their movement on the uniqueness of the Turkish culture, history, and language, as many European ethnic groups were doing. The Japanese victory over Russia in 1905 electrified Turkish nationalists with the vision of a modern Turkey becoming "the Japan of the Middle East," as they put it. In 1908, a group calling itself the Young Turks took control of the government in Istanbul, which had been fatally weakened by nationalist agitation and by the empire's economic dependence on Western financiers and businessmen.

The Young Turks' triumph motivated other groups in the Middle East and the Balkans to demand an end to Ottoman domination in their regions. These groups adopted Western values and platforms, and some, such as the Egyptians, had strong contingents of feminist

Young Turks

The Young Turks formed a group committed to the modernization of the Ottoman Empire—one of the longest imperial reigns in history. By the early twentieth century, the Young Turks had grown impatient with declining Ottoman power and, trained in western European military strategies and tactics, sought a complete overhaul of Ottoman institutions, economy, and culture. Complete success would not come, however, until after World War I, when officers in the defeated Ottoman army beat back Allied and Greek attempts to take over Turkey. (Mary Evans/Grenville Collins/The Image Works.)

nationalists who mobilized women to become modern and work for independence. But the Young Turks, now in control of the Ottoman government and often aided by European powers with financial and political interests in the region, brutally tried to repress movements in Egypt, Syria, and the Balkans modeled after their own nationalist success.

Further Blows Against Empire

Resistance to empire grew everywhere in the wake of the Japanese victory. In India, the fervently anti-British Hindu leader, B. G. Tilak, preached outright noncooperation. "We shall not give them assistance to collect revenue and keep peace. We shall not assist them in fighting beyond the frontiers or outside India with Indian blood and money." Tilak promoted Hindu customs, asserted the distinctiveness of Hindu values, and inspired violent rebellion in his followers. This brand of nationalism broke with that of the Indian National Congress, which was based on assimilating to British culture and promoting gradual change. Trying to repress Tilak, the British sponsored the Muslim League, a rival nationalist group, to divide Muslim nationalists from Hindus in the Congress.

Violence escalated, and inhabitants of the colonies—rulers and ruled alike—were often on edge. Imperial powers responded to growing resistance with harsh crackdowns. In German East Africa, colonial forces crushed native resistance in 1905 with a scorched-earth policy of destroying homes, livestock, and food, eventually killing more than one hundred thousand Africans there. Having set up police surveillance in colonies around the world, the French closed the University of Hanoi, executed Indochinese intellectuals, and deported thousands of suspected nationalists in an extreme attempt to maintain their grip on Indochina. A French general stationed there summed up the fears of many colonial rulers in the new century. "The gravest fact of our actual political situation in Indochina is not the recent trouble in Tonkin [or] the plots undertaken against us but in the muted but growing hatred that our subjects show toward us." Imperialists were right to worry.

COUNTERPOINT
The West Copies from the World

In the late nineteenth century, Western political thought, technology, and science were increasingly triumphant around the world. At the same time, however, interest in non-Western religion, art, and literature was growing in the West. Thus, alongside the political and military rule of the imperialist powers, cultural exchange flourished.

FOCUS

How did non-Western and colonized lands shape Western culture and society?

Changes in the Arts

Art from around the world resonated in the imaginations of Western artists. The most striking changes came in the work of impressionist painters such as Claude Monet and Vincent Van Gogh. As Japanese woodcuts came on the European market, Monet painted water lilies, Japanese bridges, and trailing wisteria vines, all of them gracefully depicted and seeming to shimmer in the light. The concept of the fleetingness of situations came from a centuries-old Japanese concept—*mono no aware*, serenity before and sensitivity to the fleetingness of life. The color, line, and delicacy of Japanese art, which many impressionists collected, is also evident in the work of the American expatriate Mary Cassatt. Cassatt was known for her paintings of women and children, which were strongly influenced by similar Japanese prints that she owned. Van Gogh filled the backgrounds of portraits with copies of intensely colored Japanese prints, even imitating classic Japanese woodcuts.

With increased global contact, poetry, music, dance, and literature changed in Europe and the United States, never to return to their preimperialism forms. The translation of haiku poetry influenced Western poets to give up formal meter, simplify their verse, and surrender lofty subjects in favor of the everyday topics of Japanese rhyme. William Butler Yeats, in his attempts to create an authentic Irish literature, copied themes and images from Japanese Noh and

Vincent Van Gogh, *Flowering Plum Tree* **(1887)**
Western culture soaked up influences from afar, whether in the fine arts or in practices of everyday life. By the late nineteenth century, ordinary people drank chocolate, tea, and coffee and filled their gardens with non-native plants that had become naturalized to the West. Western artists' indebtedness to non-Western styles is epitomized in this painting by Dutch painter Vincent Van Gogh, who modeled this work on a print by Hiroshige (see page 803). The brief flowering of trees so dear to the Japanese represented the fleetingness of life, and impressionists built their entire style on capturing the rapid changes in light. (akg-images.)

psychoanalysis A psychiatric therapy developed by Sigmund Freud; some elements, such as dream interpretation, were influenced by Freud's knowledge of African and Asian practices.

kabuki plays and, rejecting the ornate classical patterns of English poetry, stripped his verses of all embellishment. Yeats was but one of many who followed this path. Composers such as Claude Debussy largely abandoned centuries of Western musical patterns to create modern music based on sounds from around the world that Europeans encountered during their travels or at world fairs. In the same way, choreographers studied steps and movements practiced around the world to develop modern dance, a new way of performing that rejected the formality of classical Western ballet.

Expansion of Ideas

Outside the arts, Viennese physician Sigmund Freud, trained as a neurologist, led the West in the study of the human mind. Freud practiced telepathy (communication through means other than the senses), hypnosis, and dream therapies—all developed from ideas and therapies used in Africa and Asia. Dreams, he explained in *The Interpretation of Dreams* (1900), reveal an unseen, repressed part of the personality—the "unconscious," where all sorts of desires are more or less hidden. His new science for the treatment of mental disturbances, called **psychoanalysis**, centered on the "talking cure," that is, discussing one's dreams to uncover the reasons for mental problems. Freud read anthropological literature about the practices of witch doctors and shamans, coming up with ideas for his "talking cure" and for understanding fetishes such as fixations on shoes, gloves, or other ordinary objects.

Other Western intellectuals studied Hinduism, Buddhism, African religions, and many other bodies of thought and culture to develop new ideas. For example, at the beginning of the twentieth century, discussions of sexuality in the West expanded beyond biblically defined boundaries. South Asian ideas about reincarnation inspired the thought that the physical indications of a person's sex were merely temporary because an eternal self without sex was reborn across time in differently sexed bodies. So-called homosexuality and transgendering were explained by this process. People began discussing sexuality as variable, using ideas that came from beyond the West and that continue to be influential to this day.

Lifestyles Transformed

In Europe and the United States, people began to live in efficiently designed single-family homes styled after the Indian bungalow; they had porches and verandas, and they often decorated their homes with palms, bamboo furniture, and textiles of Asian or African designs. European cookbooks carried recipes for curry and cakes made from an array of global products, such as sugar, chocolate, vanilla, and coconut. Women joined men in wearing slimmer, more informal clothing, much of it modeled on non-Western styles. Late in the nineteenth century, women adopted looser "reform clothing"—kimono-like garments or those modeled after Middle Eastern caftans—and they began following Asian and African women in not wearing corsets.

To get and stay in shape, Westerners, who had generally not thought in such terms, began to exercise more. Men kept fit by practicing martial arts, all of which came from outside Europe and the United States. Even as national and international tensions were heating up and as the West thought itself superior in all things, Western military schools were using Sun Tzu's *The Art of War*, a Chinese classic from the sixth century B.C.E., in their courses on strategy. Despite the power of Western imperialism, ideas never followed a one-way street from West to East. Rather, imperialism was, among much else, a crossroads for ideas to travel in many directions.

Conclusion

The nineteenth century is called an age of imperialism because of the growing contest among Western nation-states to dominate the world's peoples politically and economically. New technology springing from ongoing industrialization helped people and ideas move more rapidly around the world, enabling the exercise of political and military power as well as cultural and economic exchange. Western technology gave its agents a real advantage in developing wealth globally and controlling the flow of resources. New forms of oppression such as indentured servitude developed; plantation agriculture increasingly replaced self-sufficient farming; and environmental catastrophes weakened societies and helped imperialism spread. Imperialism was complex. Some colonized peoples prospered by participating in the system and simultaneously developed goals such as national independence, based on the Western values of rights and freedom that were denied them.

Newly powerful countries vied with established ones for a share of world influence, fueling the "new" imperialism's explosive potential. Although global expansion led to increased wealth for some individuals and states, events such as China's Boxer Rebellion demonstrated that it brought violence and insecurity to most ordinary people and to governments. Imperial competition made the world more dangerous, as did the drive even within Europe to gain territory from the weakening Ottoman Empire. Thus, global and local battles raged during this period. Although it was meant to stabilize international politics, imperialism intensified distrust and insecurity among the powers. When global and local political ambitions met, as they did in the second decade of the twentieth century, catastrophic violence followed.

NOTES

1. Quoted in Paul A. Cohen, *History in Three Keys: The Boxers as Event, Experience, and Myth* (New York: Columbia University Press, 1997), 86–87.
2. Paul Leroy-Beaulieu, quoted in *Histoire de la colonisation française* (Paris: Fayard, 1991), 2:149.
3. Quoted in Rudrangshu Mukherjee, "The Sepoy Mutinies Revisited," in *War and Society in Colonial India, 1807–1945*, ed. Kaushik Roy (Delhi: Oxford University Press, 2006), 121.
4. General Skobelev, quoted in Peter Hopkirk, *The Great Game: The Struggle for Empire in Central Asia* (New York: Kodansha International, 1992), 407.
5. Quoted in Charles Lee Keeton, *King Thebaw and the Ecological Rape of Burma: The Political and Commercial Struggle Between British India and French Indo-China in Burma, 1878–1886* (Delhi, India: Manohar Book Service, 1974), 202.
6. Phan Chau Trinh, in Truong Buu Lam, *Colonialism Experienced: Vietnamese Writing on Colonialism, 1900–1931* (Ann Arbor: University of Michigan Press, 2000), 130.
7. William Morton Fullerton, *In Cairo*, quoted in Max Rodenbeck, *Cairo: The City Victorious* (New York: Knopf, 1999), 136.
8. Letter from the King of Daboya to Governor of the Gold Coast, 8 July 1892, quoted in A. Adu Boahen, *African Perspectives on Colonialism* (Baltimore, MD: Johns Hopkins University Press, 1987), 37.
9. Quoted in Mike Davis, *Late Victorian Holocausts: El Niño Famines and the Making of the Third World* (London: Verso, 2001), 46.
10. Davis, *Late Victorian Holocausts*, 139.
11. Quoted in Jennifer W. Cushman, *Family and State: The Formation of a Sino-Thai Tin-Mining Dynasty, 1797–1832* (Singapore: Oxford University Press, 1991), 62.
12. Khayr al-Din al-Tunisi, "The Surest Path to Knowledge Concerning the Condition of Countries," quoted in *Colonial Rule in Africa: Readings from Primary Sources*, ed. Bruce Fetter (Madison: University of Wisconsin Press, 1979), 57.
13. Quoted in Bruce Fetter, ed., *Colonial Rule in Africa*, 117.

14. Quoted in Robert O. Collins, ed., *Eastern African History*, vol. 2, *African History: Text and Readings* (New York: Markus Wiener Publishing, 1990), 124.

15. Quoted in Davis, *Late Victorian Holocausts*, 31, 57, 172.

16. "Song of Revolution," in Gungwu Wang, *Community and Nation: China, Southeast Asia and Australia* (St. Leonards, Australia: Allen and Unwin, 1992), 10.

17. Quoted in Sumanta Banerjee, "Women's Popular Culture in Nineteenth Century Bengal," in *Recasting Women: Essays in Indian Colonial History*, ed. Kumkum Sangari and Sudesh Vaid (New Brunswick, NJ: Rutgers University Press, 1990), 142.

18. Quoted in David Robinson, *Muslim Societies and French Colonial Authorities in Senegal and Mauritania, 1880–1920* (Athens: Ohio University Press, 2000), 204.

19. Chief Segale, quoted in Peter Warwick, *Black People and the South African War, 1899–1902* (Cambridge, U.K.: Cambridge University Press, 1983), 177.

20. Quoted in Cohen, *History in Three Keys*, 80.

RESOURCES FOR RESEARCH

Building Empires

There are many debates about the motivations for empire. Cain and Hopkins dispute the view that industrialists backed imperialism to provide them with markets, arguing instead that financial and other service providers were the major advocates of colonies. Steinmetz interestingly shows German imperialism as inconsistent, varying from one area to another, and he suggests that all colonies were similarly run, depending on the imperialists' evaluations of a particular region's culture.

Burbank, Jane, and Frederick Cooper. *Empires in World History: Power and the Politics of Difference.* 2010.

Cain, P. J., and A. G. Hopkins. *British Imperialism, 1688–2000.* 2002.

Feifer, George. *Breaking Open Japan: Commodore Perry, Lord Abe and the American Imperialism of 1853.* 2006.

Steinmetz, George. *The Devil's Handwriting: Precoloniality and the German Colonial State in Qingdao, Samoa, and Southwest Africa.* 2004.

Sunderland, Willard. *Taming the Wild Field: Colonization and Empire on the Russian Steppe.* 2004.

Imperial Society

Imperial powers showed their dominance through the exercise of military but also political and social power.

Armstrong, Charles K., et al., eds. *Korea at the Center: Dynamics of Regionalism in Northeast Asia.* 2006.

Carter, Marina, and Khal Torabully. *Coolitude: An Anthology of the Indian Labour Diaspora.* 2002.

Davis, Mike. *Late Victorian Holocausts: El Niño Famines and the Making of the Third World.* 2001.

Maugubane, Zine. *Bringing the Empire Home: Race, Class, and Gender in Britain and Colonial South Africa.* 2004.

Sahadeo, Jeff. *Russian Colonial Society in Tashkent, 1865–1923.* 2007.

Culture in an Imperial Age

The imperialists shaped colonial customs and attitudes, claiming to bring a superior civilization to their subjects.

Adas, Michael. *Dominance by Design: Technological Imperatives and America's Civilizing Mission.* 2006.

Berenson, Edward. *Heroes of Empire: Five Charismatic Men and the Conquest of Africa.* 2011.

Jansen, Marius B. *The Making of Modern Japan.* 2000.

Lowy, Dina. *The Japanese "New Woman": Images of Gender and Modernity.* 2007.

Robinson, David. *Muslim Societies and French Colonial Authorities in Senegal and Mauritania, 1880–1920.* 2000.

Imperial Contests at the Dawn of the Twentieth Century

The start of the twentieth century was a time of increasing global conflict. Several of the following authors describe the range of this conflict and the main issues in each example.

Cohen, Paul A. *History in Three Keys: The Boxers as Event, Experience, and Myth.* 1997.

Hobson, Rolf. *Imperialism at Sea: Naval Strategic Thought, the Ideology of Sea Power, and the Tirpitz Plan, 1875–1914.* 2002.

Parsons, Timothy. *The Rule of Empires: Those Who Built Them, Those Who Endured Them, and Why They Always Fall.* 2010.

Silbey, David J. *A War of Frontier and Empire: The Philippine-American War, 1899–1902.* 2007.

South African War. The Anglo-Boer War Museum maintains a helpful Web site. http://www.anglo-boer.co.za/.

Counterpoint: The West Copies from the World

As these works reveal, cultural exchange flourished alongside the rule of the imperialists.

Baas, Jacquelynn. *Smile of the Buddha: Eastern Philosophy and Western Art from Monet to Today.* 2005.

Brower, M. Brady. *Unruly Spirits: The Science of Psychic Phenomena in Modern France.* 2010.

Dixon, Joy. *Divine Feminine: Theosophy and Feminism in England.* 2001.

Treitel, Corinne. *A Science for the Soul: Occultism and the Genesis of the German Modern.* 2004.

▶ **For additional primary sources from this period,** see *Sources of Crossroads and Cultures.*

▶ **For Web sites, images, and documents related to topics in this chapter,** see Make History at bedfordstmartins.com/smith.

REVIEW

The major global development in this chapter ▶ The accelerated competition among nineteenth-century nation-states for empire.

IMPORTANT EVENTS

c. 1840–1910	Global migration because of indenture, imperial opportunity, and harsh environmental conditions
1857	Indian Uprising against the British
c. 1860–1900	Impressionism flourishes in the European arts, borrowing many non-Western techniques
1869	Suez Canal completed
c. 1870–1914	European powers, Japan, and the United States extend formal and informal control over Asia, Africa, and parts of Latin America
1876	British Parliament declares Victoria empress of India
1882	Britain takes over Egypt
1884–1885	European nations carve up Africa at the Berlin Conference
1894–1895	Sino-Japanese War
1898	Spanish-American War
1899–1900	Boxer Rebellion in China
1899–1902	South African War
1900	Sigmund Freud, *The Interpretation of Dreams*
1904–1905	Russo-Japanese War
1908	Young Turks' uprising against the Ottoman Empire
1910	Japan annexes Korea

KEY TERMS

business imperialism (p. 861)
colonialism (p. 861)
cosmopolitanism (p. 879)
diaspora (p. 877)
globalization (p. 860)
new imperialism (p. 860)
pogrom (p. 875)
psychoanalysis (p. 886)

CHAPTER OVERVIEW QUESTIONS

1. What are the arguments for and against imperialism?
2. How and why did some local peoples assist imperialists who took over their own countries?
3. Which were the major imperialist powers, and what made them so capable of conquest?
4. How did imperialism change the lives of people in the conquering countries and in the colonies?

SECTION FOCUS QUESTIONS

1. What motivated the imperialists, and how did they impose their control over other nations?
2. How did imperialism change lives and livelihoods around the world?
3. How did artists and writers respond to the age of empire?
4. What were the main issues in the contests over empire, and what were the results of these contests?
5. How did non-Western and colonized lands shape Western culture and society?

MAKING CONNECTIONS

1. How are the Industrial Revolution (see Chapter 24) and imperialism connected?
2. How are nation building (see Chapter 25) and imperialism connected?
3. In what ways might the globalization connected with imperialism undermine nation building?
4. Recall the empires discussed in Part 3. What were the key differences between empires in the early modern period and modern empires of the nineteenth century?

AT A CROSSROADS ▲

Diego Rivera spent most of the Mexican Revolution in Europe, where he learned a range of classical Western styles of painting. The bloodshed of the revolution and World War I and the coming of communism to Russia and elsewhere inspired him to become a communist and to take up the cause of oppressed native American peasants and workers on his return to Mexico. This mural, *Blood of the Revolutionary Martyrs Fertilizing the Earth* (1927), reflects the traditional Mexican idea that martyrdom makes the earth fertile. Rivera's strong belief in the value of workers and representations of this brutal era in human history make his art a crossroads of politics and cultural styles. The martyrs represented are peasant rebel leader Emiliano Zapata (right) and his follower Otilio Montano (left). (Schalkwijk/Art Resource, NY. /© 2011 Banco de México Diego Rivera Frida Kahlo Museums Trust, Mexico, D.F./ARS, NY.)

Wars, Revolutions, and the Birth of Mass Society

1910–1929

The rebel leader Emiliano Zapata was a dandy, wearing blinding white shirts and fitted black pants adorned with silver. Before 1910 he had worked the land of his part-Indian family in central Mexico, where small farmers such as Zapata struggled—usually unsuccessfully—to block the takeover of their traditional lands by big hacienda (plantation) owners producing sugar and other commodities for the global market. Zapata grew and sold watermelons, prospering by comparison with others in his village. A fighter against the takeover of local land, in 1910 he was galvanized by the call for revolution against the corrupt regime of Porfirio Diaz, a key ally of the big landowners. Gathering a peasant army, Zapata swept through central Mexico, motivating his followers with the slogan "It is better to die on your feet than live on your knees." During the long revolutionary struggle, Zapata became known as a shrewd, rational political leader, but he also provoked an emotional response: peasants who had never seen him boosted their spirits during the decade-long Mexican Revolution with cries of "Viva [Long Live] Zapata!"

By 1920, the Mexican Revolution had killed between 1 and 2 million people, some by rifles, machine guns, and bombs and others by disease, but it was just one of several lethal cataclysms in that decade. Between 1910 and 1920, tens of millions fought and died. In cities and villages, farms and battlefields around the world grew the grim sense that in this new century war would never end and that ordinary people would be endlessly called upon to support the slaughter. After Mexico, China erupted in revolution in 1911, throwing

Revolutions, Local Wars, and World War

FOCUS What factors contributed to the wars of the early twentieth century?

Revolution in Russia and the End of World War I

FOCUS Why did the Russian Revolution take place, and what changes did it produce in Russian politics and daily life?

Postwar Global Politics

FOCUS What were the major outcomes of the peacemaking process and postwar conditions?

An Age of the Masses

FOCUS How did the rise of mass society affect politics, culture, and everyday life around the world?

COUNTERPOINT: A Golden Age for Argentineans

FOCUS In what ways did Argentina's history differ from that of countries caught up in World War I?

BACKSTORY

The competition among Western powers heated up in the second half of the nineteenth century, fueled by the drive for overseas expansion known as imperialism (see Chapter 26). European nations used the economic and military advantages that resulted from industrialization to take direct and indirect control of territories in Asia, Africa, and Latin America. Newcomers Japan and the United States joined the race for empire, and many other states pursued policies intended to produce political centralization and national unification. Resistance to both new and old empires and to political elites mounted during these years, even as imperialism multiplied the connections among the world's peoples and intensified the pace of cultural and economic exchange. Both competition for power and resistance to existing power structures contributed to the violence that marked the early twentieth century. The application of industrial technology to warfare made conflicts between and within states more destructive than ever.

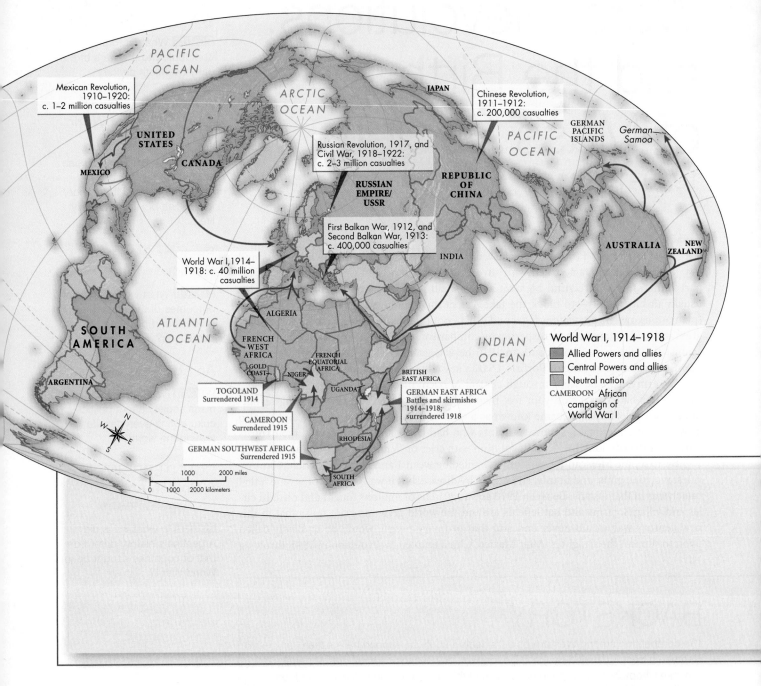

Mexican Revolution, 1910–1920: c. 1–2 million casualties

Chinese Revolution, 1911–1912: c. 200,000 casualties

Russian Revolution, 1917, and Civil War, 1918–1922: c. 2–3 million casualties

First Balkan War, 1912, and Second Balkan War, 1913: c. 400,000 casualties

World War I, 1914–1918: c. 40 million casualties

PACIFIC OCEAN

ARCTIC OCEAN

JAPAN

GERMAN PACIFIC ISLANDS

German Samoa

UNITED STATES

CANADA

MEXICO

PACIFIC OCEAN

RUSSIAN EMPIRE/ USSR

REPUBLIC OF CHINA

INDIA

AUSTRALIA

NEW ZEALAND

SOUTH AMERICA

ATLANTIC OCEAN

ALGERIA

FRENCH WEST AFRICA

GOLD COAST

NIGER

FRENCH EQUATORIAL AFRICA

UGANDA

BRITISH EAST AFRICA

INDIAN OCEAN

ARGENTINA

TOGOLAND
Surrendered 1914

CAMEROON
Surrendered 1915

GERMAN SOUTHWEST AFRICA
Surrendered 1915

GERMAN EAST AFRICA
Battles and skirmishes 1914–1918; surrendered 1918

RHODESIA

SOUTH AFRICA

N W E S

0   1000   2000 miles
0   1000   2000 kilometers

World War I, 1914–1918
- Allied Powers and allies
- Central Powers and allies
- Neutral nation

CAMEROON   African campaign of World War I

- **1910** Mexican Revolution begins

1911–1912 Revolutionaries overthrow Qing dynasty in China

- **1912** First Balkan War

Russian Revolution begins; United States enters World War I; Lenin returns to Russia **1917** ▪

- **1918** Bolsheviks take full control of Russian government; Treaty of Brest-Litovsk; armistice ends World War I

1910

1915

1920

- **1913** Second Balkan War

- **1914** World War I begins

Treaties comprising Peace of Paris signed, including the Treaty of Versailles with Germany **1919–1920**

Lenin introduces New Economic Policy in Russia **1921**

Germany forms Weimar Republic; May 4th movement in China **1919** ▪

off the Qing dynasty, and in 1912 and 1913 a host of Balkan peoples challenged the Ottoman and Austro-Hungarian empires. Their struggle led to World War I, which lasted from 1914 to 1918 and in turn spawned further wars and revolutions—most notably the Russian Revolution and the civil war that followed. The legacy of these conflicts shaped the rest of the century, and stories of soldiers' bravery—like that of Emiliano Zapata— filled the popular imagination through novels, films, and the new medium of radio.

These wars occurred on the crossroads of global trade and international politics. The Mexican Revolution, which was partly a struggle over U.S. control of the Mexican economy, led to American intervention, and even the peasant leader Emiliano Zapata corresponded with foreign leaders. The fall of the Qing left the future of a vast region in question and increased the interest of imperial powers in taking more of China's land and resources for themselves. World War I was a global war, fought not only on the European continent but in the Middle East, Africa, and the Pacific, as the powers pursued the goal of imperial expansion. All of these wars brought the masses into global politics, not only as soldiers but also as producers of the technology and supplies that soldiers needed. None of these wars, however, settled problems or restored social order as the combatants hoped. Instead, the Mexican Revolution destroyed the country's economy, while World War I produced political cataclysm, overturning the Russian, German, Ottoman, and Austro-Hungarian empires and changing the global balance of power. The Mexican Revolution, the fall of the Qing, World War I, and the Russian Revolution helped define early-twentieth-century history, and political uprisings continued into the 1920s, giving rise in turn to mass society.

Mass politics after the wars depended on mass culture, urbanization, and growing productivity, based on the postwar explosion of technology. Urban people from China to Argentina experienced the "Roaring Twenties," snapping up new consumer goods, drinking in the entertainment provided by films and radio, and relishing new personal freedoms. Modern communication technologies such as radio provided enjoyment, but they

MAPPING THE WORLD
Wars and Revolutions, 1910–1929

Wars and revolutions circled the globe in the early twentieth century. Areas where empire and imperial influence were at stake were especially hard hit, including a broad sweep of Eurasia. This era of local and global conflict brought dramatic political and other change, notably the fall of imperial dynasties, the exchange of colonial holdings and territory, and a stark toll in deaths from military campaigns, famine, and an influenza pandemic.

ROUTES ▼

→ Route of colonial and British Commonwealth troops in support of Allied Powers, 1914–1918

→ Route of U.S. forces during the Mexican Revolution, 1914–1916

→ Route of Pancho Villa, 1913–1916

- **1922** Civil war ends in Russia; Mussolini comes to power in Italy

1925   1930

- **1923** Founding of the independent republic of Turkey under Mustafa Kemal; formation of Union of Soviet Socialist Republics

1920s Mohandas Gandhi's nonviolent movement for India independence attracts millions; mass culture flourishes in film and publishing industries; growth of radio transmissions; technology increases global productivity

also spread political ideologies more widely than ever before. Some of these became the core of mass nationalist politics—some evil, like fascism, and some aimed at helping ordinary people, like the reform program of Emiliano Zapata.

OVERVIEW
QUESTIONS

The major global development in this chapter: The wars of the decade 1910 to 1920 and their role in the creation of mass culture and society.

As you read, consider:

1. Why did the Mexican Revolution, the Chinese Revolution, World War I, and the Russian Revolution cause so much change far from the battlefield?

2. How did these wars help produce mass culture and society?

3. What role did technology play in these developments?

Revolutions, Local Wars, and World War

FOCUS

What factors contributed to the wars of the early twentieth century?

The Mexican Revolution, the Chinese Revolution, and the Balkan wars opened one of the bloodiest decades in human history. The reasons for the violence were many and complex. Some fought to overthrow corrupt leaders, others to free their nations from outside threats, and still others to win the international competition for power and wealth. The conflicts of the early twentieth century did not always produce the social, economic, and political outcomes that had originally inspired individuals and nations to take up arms. Though some nations gained new territory, the fighting did not produce stability and order, but rather sowed the seeds for a new round of conflict and upheaval.

Revolutionaries and Warriors: Mexico, China, and the Balkans

The tensions created by imperialism and modern state-building were apparent in many parts of the world by 1910. In Mexico liberal reformers and peasant leaders, backed by local armies, attempted to reform a corrupt political order, while in China modernizers threw off the power of the Qing. In 1913 Balkan countries waged war against the weakening Ottoman Empire to claim more land and resources. When the victors fought against one another later that year, the chaos provoked further turmoil. In 1914, what some have called the Third Balkan War erupted, a regional conflict that sparked the global cataclysm of World War I.

The Mexican Revolution   In 1910, liberal Mexican reformers headed by the wealthy landowner Francisco Madero began a drive to force the dictator Porfirio Diaz from office. Diaz saw himself as a modernizer. During his forty years in power, Mexico had built some twelve thousand miles of railroads, and its mines yielded increasing amounts of lead, copper, and zinc. However, only a handful of wealthy families and foreign investors reaped the riches of Mexico's development. By encouraging the concentration of agricultural lands in the hands of a few, Diaz's policies had impoverished village people. By 1900, just 1 percent of the population held 85 percent of the land, much of it seized by the government for the wealthy. Compounding Mexican landlessness was the government's policy of granting huge tracts of this confiscated land for cattle-raising and mining to U.S. companies, which further hurt the prospects of ordinary citizens. Madero and his well-off friends were political reformers, seeking a more open political system and the rule of law, but peasants and workers, who were often paid in goods instead of cash, had survival on their minds.

Given this bleak situation, peasant armies arose to work for land reform—that is, for social, not just political, change—as conflict erupted on many fronts. Zapata described their situation and their goals: "Considering that for the great majority, villages and citizens of Mexico possess not even the land that they work and that they cannot ameliorate their condition in the slightest . . . because the land, the mountains, and the water are in the hands of a very small number, the following is decreed: one-third of all monopolies will be expropriated . . . and distributed to those villages and citizens who are now prevented from having their traditional rights to the land prevail."[1] In the north, butcher and landowner Pancho Villa headed another popular army that fought for the entire decade against U.S. citizens and others who were taking over local land and resources. Complicating the revolution was simple factional fighting for local and regional power.

The cause of the people was so strong, however, that in the end, long after the ouster of Diaz in 1911 and amid assassinations of leaders, including Zapata, the Mexican government announced land reform in its Constitution of 1917. The story of the hundreds of thousands of common warriors, many of them of Indian or mixed blood like Zapata, giving their lives for fundamental reform would inspire generations of Mexican writers and artists. The lasting cultural impact of this struggle is exemplified in the mural art of Diego Rivera, whose huge depictions of the Mexican Revolution were meant to show the masses their own past heroism and inspire them to remain committed to social justice.

As we saw in Chapter 26, the combination of Japan's lightning defeat of China in the Sino-Japanese War (1894) and the Boxer Rebellion (1899–1900) thoroughly discredited the Qing dynasty. These humiliating events ushered in a wave of reform, some of it sponsored by the Qing administration itself. Schools, urban planning, and women's rights all filled the agenda of reformers. Behind the flurry of change, modernizing businessmen, professionals, and intellectuals sensed that the Manchu dynasty was dangerously outdated and needed to be replaced by new rulers drawn from the Chinese people themselves. Influenced by Western ideas of evolution, reformers likened the Manchus, who descended from northern nomads, to undeveloped peoples of past times who "lived in dens and wore pelts."[2] In 1911 to 1912 a group of revolutionaries organized as the **Guomindang** (gwo-min-DAHNG), or Nationalist Party, overthrew the long-lived dynasty and declared China a republic. Their leader, the medical doctor Sun Yatsen (soon yot-SEN), who like many proponents of change had been educated outside of China, used a cluster of Western ideas in his slogan "nationalism, democracy, and socialism." However, he interpreted these ideas in the context of long-standing Chinese values. For example, whereas Marxist socialists called for an end to private property, Sun's socialism was based in such traditional charitable thinking as the view that all people should have enough food. Sun's Guomindang called for the revival of the Chinese belief in correct behavior between governors and the governed, economic and social reform in line with scientific theories, and the end of foreign domination over China.

Sun's stirring leadership helped set China on a modernizing course, but he was not a capable administrator and quickly resigned in favor of a powerful former Qing general, Yuan Shikai (yoo-ahn shee-KI). Yuan was no democrat, however, and in 1916 he broke with the Nationalists to declare the foundation of a new imperial dynasty. When regional generals rejected Yuan's imperial claims, formed their own armies, and began to act as warlords, the country descended into a decade of chaos.

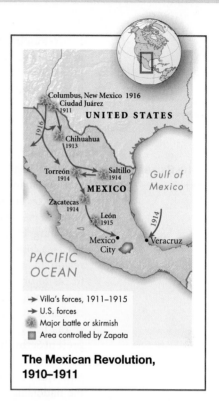

The Mexican Revolution, 1910–1911

→ Villa's forces, 1911–1915
→ U.S. forces
✳ Major battle or skirmish
▪ Area controlled by Zapata

The Chinese Revolution

Guomindang The Chinese nationalist party founded by Sun Yatsen that overthrew the Qing dynasty and fought to rule mainland China from 1911 to 1949.

Yet aspirations for a new way of life continued to grow, university life flourished, and literature became pointedly directed toward the need to modernize China. Reform-minded people were inspired by author Lu Xun, whose novella *The True Story of Ah Q* (1921–1922) presents what Lu called the typical Chinese, arrogant no matter how pathetic his station in life and full of useless maxims: "If a woman walks alone on the street, she must want to seduce bad men." Such backward thinking on Ah Q's part threatens his survival in modern times, just as China, in Lu's view, was held back by out-of-date ideas and the blindness of leaders who focused on China's glorious past and ignored the problems of its troubled present.

The Balkan Wars   In the Balkans politicians whipped up ethnic nationalism to challenge both Habsburg and Ottoman power. Greece, Serbia, Bulgaria, Romania, and Montenegro had recently emerged as autonomous states, almost all of them home to ethnically and religiously diverse populations. These small states sought strength as modern nations by taking Ottoman and Habsburg territory in which others from their own imagined majority ethnic group lived—a complicated desire, given the historic intermingling of ethnicities throughout the region. In the First Balkan War, in 1912, Serbia, Bulgaria, Greece, and Montenegro joined forces to break off Macedonia and Albania from the Ottomans. The victors divided up their booty, but they soon turned against one another. Serbia, Greece, and Montenegro contested Bulgarian gains in the Second Balkan War in 1913 and won a quick victory. In the peace treaty that followed the fighting, an alarmed Austria-Hungary managed to prevent Serbia from gaining parts of Albania, further inflaming Serb grievances toward the dual monarchy. Many Serbs dreamed of crushing Austria-Hungary with the help of their powerful Slavic ally Russia, a dream the Russian government did little to discourage. Thus, the nationalist aspirations of Slavic Serbs contributed to growing tensions between two great European powers, Austria-Hungary and Russia. Under these circumstances, events in the Balkans took on international importance.

Outbreak of World War I   The situation came to a head in June 1914 in the Habsburg-controlled Bosnian capital of Sarajevo when a Bosnian Serb, funded by the Serbian secret police, assassinated the heir to the Habsburg throne, Archduke Franz Ferdinand, and his wife Sophie. The young assassin hoped thereby to free his homeland from the Habsburgs and unite it with Serbia. According to its alliance with Germany, Austria-Hungary had the promise of full German support if it launched an offensive war to defeat the Serbians once and for all. So it issued a stern ultimatum: the Serbian government had just forty-eight hours in which to agree to demands that would amount to Austrian control of the Serbian state. When Serbia refused to meet one of these demands, Austria declared war on Serbia on July 28. Equipped with well-prepared war plans and armed to the teeth for war, the major European powers were eager to end the international tensions that existed among them over global, national, and even domestic issues. Thus, the origins of World War I lay in great-power interests in the Balkans, long-standing alliances and strategies for war among the powers, the buildup of military technologies, and a climate of rivalry for territory and influence. This so-called Third Balkan War proved to be more than any of the powers—or the world—bargained for.

Fighting World War I

World War I erupted in August 1914. On one side stood the Central Powers—Austria-Hungary and Germany—which had evolved from Bismarck's Triple Alliance of 1882 (see Chapter 25). On the other side were the Allies—France, Great Britain, and Russia—which had emerged as a bloc from an alliance between France and Great Britain that became the Triple Entente when Russia joined in 1907. In 1915, Italy, originally part of Bismarck's Triple Alliance, went over to the Entente (or Allies) in hopes of making postwar gains. As the fighting spread to the combatants' overseas colonies and non-European powers took sides, the war became a global conflict. Japan, eager to extend its empire into China, soon joined the Allies, while the Ottoman Empire united with the Central Powers against its traditional enemy, Russia (see Map 27.1, page 898). In time, the United States would enter the war as well, contributing to the Allied victory.

The antagonists hungered for the same power and prosperity that inspired imperialism. Germany hoped to acquire a far-flung empire by annexing Russian territory, parts of Belgium, France, and Luxembourg, and even Austria-Hungary. Austria-Hungary aimed to rebuild its power, which was under attack from the competing nationalist movements within its borders and by Serbs and other Slavs outside them. Russia wanted to reassert its great-power position as protector of the Slavs by adding all of Poland to the Russian Empire and by controlling other Slavic peoples. The French, too, craved territory, especially the return of Alsace and Lorraine, lost after the Franco-Prussian War of 1870 to 1871 (discussed in Chapter 25). The British sought to secure their world empire by defeating its competitors. The secret Treaty of London (1915) promised Italy territory in Africa, Anatolia (modern Turkey), and the Balkans in return for joining the Allies.

In August 1914, armies had at their disposal machine guns and rifles, airplanes, battleships, submarines, and cars, railroads, and other motorized transport. Newer technologies such as chlorine gas, tanks, and bombs would develop between 1914 and 1918. Nonetheless, officers on both sides held to a nineteenth-century strategy, the "cult of the offensive," in which continuous spirited attacks and flashing sabers and bayonets would be decisive. The colonies of the European powers were to provide massive assistance to wage such offensives. Some 1 million Africans, another 2 million Indians, and more than a million members of the British Commonwealth countries, notably Canada, Australia, and New Zealand, served on the battlefronts, while the imperial powers conscripted uncounted numbers of colonists as forced laborers. In the face of massive firepower, the outdated "cult of the offensive" would cost millions of these lives.

The first months of the war crushed hopes of quick victory. All the major armies mobilized rapidly. The Germans were guided by a strategy devised by Alfred von Schlieffen, a former chief of the general staff. The Schlieffen Plan outlined a way to avoid a two-front war by concentrating on one foe at a time. It called for a rapid and concentrated blow to the west against France, accompanied by a light holding action to the east against France's ally, Russia. According to the plan, France would be defeated in six weeks, and only then would German forces be concentrated against Russia, which, the Germans believed, would mobilize slowly. The attack on France began in the summer of 1914 and proceeded through Belgium, but there it met unexpected and spirited resistance, slowing the German advance and allowing British and French troops to reach the northern front. In massive battles neither side could defeat the other, and casualties were in the millions. The unprecedented firepower of modern weaponry turned what was supposed to be an offensive war of movement into a stationary, defensive stalemate along a line of trenches that stretched from the North Sea through Belgium and northern France to Switzerland. Deep within trenches dug along this front, millions of soldiers lived in nightmarish shelters.

Meanwhile, on the eastern front, the massive Russian army, some 12 million strong, mobilized more quickly than expected, driving into German territory by mid-August. The Russian generals believed that no matter how ill equipped their army was, no army could stand up to their massive numbers. Russian success was short-lived, however. The Germans crushed the tsar's army in East Prussia in the fall of 1914 and then turned south to Galicia. Victory against Russia emboldened the commanding generals to demand and get more troops for the eastern front. Nonetheless, by year's end Germany had failed to knock out the Russians and was bogged down in the very two-front war its military planners had taken such pains to avoid (see again Map 27.1).

War at sea proved equally indecisive. When the Allies blockaded ports to prevent supplies from reaching Germany and Austria-Hungary, the Germans responded with an intensive submarine, or U-boat ("underwater boat"), campaign against both Allied and neutral shipping. Despite U.S. deaths, President Woodrow Wilson maintained a policy of neutrality, and Germany, unwilling to provoke Wilson further, called off unrestricted submarine warfare—that is, attacks on neutral shipping. Throughout 1915 the British hoped to knock out the Ottomans and open ports to Russia by attacking at

The Blueprint for War

The Battlefronts, 1914–1916

Legend:

- Allied Powers and allies
- Central Powers and allies
- Greatest extent of territory gained by Central Powers
- German U-boat war zone
- Neutral nation
- → Major Allied Powers advance
- → Major Central Powers advance
- Farthest advance by Allied Powers on date marked
- Farthest advance by Central Powers on date marked
- British naval blockade
- Major battle

0   200   400 miles
0   200   400 kilometers

NORWAY

SWEDEN

• Petrograd (St. Petersburg)

North Sea

Jutland 1916

DENMARK

Baltic Sea

Farthest Russian advance, 1914

LITHUANIA

Masurian Lakes 1914

RUSSIA

• Moscow

Armistice line, December 1917

UNITED KINGDOM

Lusitania 1915

London •

NETHERLANDS

GERMANY

• Berlin

E. PRUSSIA

Tannenberg 1914

• Warsaw

Brest-Litovsk

Treaty of Brest-Litovsk, March 1918

BELGIUM

Somme 1916

Paris •

Marne 1914

Verdun 1916

LUXEMBOURG

Rhine R.

Elbe R.

Vistula R.

KINGDOM OF POLAND (Russia)

• Kiev

UKRAINE

Dnieper R.

Western front, 1914

ALSACE-LORRAINE

SWITZ.

Vienna •

AUSTRIA-HUNGARY

Budapest •

Eastern front, 1915

GALICIA

FRANCE

Caporetto 1917

Italian front, 1918

TRANSYLVANIA

CRIMEA

Farthest Ottoman advance, 1918

Caspian Sea

Adriatic Sea

BOSNIA

Sarajevo •

ROMANIA

Bucharest •

Black Sea

SPAIN

Corsica

ITALY

Rome •

MONTENEGRO

SERBIA

Danube R.

CAUCASUS

Balearic Is.

Sardinia

MACEDONIA

BULGARIA

Dardanelles Strait

• Istanbul

Middle Eastern front, 1918

IRAN

ALBANIA

See inset map

Gallipoli 1915

OTTOMAN EMPIRE

IRAQ

Al Kut 1915 1916 1917

Balkan front, 1916

GREECE

ANATOLIA

Baghdad 1917

Basra •

ALGERIA (Fr.)

Sicily

Tunis •

TUNISIA (Fr.)

Malta

Crete

Cyprus

SYRIA

LEBANON

• Damascus

PALESTINE

N
W   E
S

Mediterranean Sea

LIBYA (It.)

EGYPT (Gr. Br.)

Red Sea

Al Aqabah 1917

The Battle of Gallipoli, 1915

0   10   20 mi.
0   10   20 km

Aegean Sea

GALLIPOLI PENINSULA

Sea of Marmara

Hill 60 Aug. 21–29

Sari Bair Aug. 6–10

Dardanelles Strait

ANATOLIA

Krithia April 28

- → British forces
- → Australian and New Zealand forces
- — Ottoman mine belt
- ✷ Major battle

MAP 27.1

World War I in Europe and the Middle East, 1914–1918

World War I transformed many parts of Europe and the Middle East into wastelands because of the increasingly devastating weaponry. Farmlands were put out of commission for years, and livestock near battlefields was decimated. On the western front the damage was mostly confined to northern France, but on the eastern front the destructive power was mobile as armies crossed some areas several times. An effective blockade added to the hunger that central and eastern Europeans suffered as the war came to an end in 1918.

the Dardanelles Strait. At Gallipoli, casualty rates for both sides of 50 to 60 percent only yielded stalemate. "A miserable time," one Irish soldier called Gallipoli, as his comrades from New Zealand, Australia, and elsewhere in the empire had their heads blown off and their limbs smashed to pulp. Horrific suffering in this single battle

The Dead of World War I
Even as the death toll mounted during World War I, politicians and crowned heads of state across Europe refused to give up the idea of victory. For most soldiers, this political decision meant ongoing suffering in the trenches and, for millions, hysteria, crippling wounds, or death. The bones of the unburied were collected from the battlefield as shown here in Verdun, for placement in ossuaries, at the war's end. (Bettmann/Corbis.)

strengthened Australia's and New Zealand's will to break with British leadership, which had led them into the tragedy.

Both sides refused a negotiated peace: "No peace before England is defeated and destroyed," Kaiser William II railed against his cousin, Britain's King George V. "Only amidst the ruins of London will I forgive Georgy." French leaders called for a "war to the death." General staffs on both sides continued to prepare fierce attacks: after heavy artillery pounded enemy trenches and gun emplacements, troops obeyed the order to go "over the top" by scrambling out of their trenches and into battle, usually to be mowed down by machine-gun fire from the tens of thousands of defenders in their own trenches. On the western front, casualties of one hundred thousand and more for a single campaign became commonplace. In 1916, in an effort to break French morale, the Germans launched massive assaults on the fortress at Verdun, firing as many as a million shells in a single day during the attack. Combined French and German losses totaled close to a million men, whose anonymous bones today fill a vast shrine at the site.

The Soldiers' War

Had the military leaders thoroughly dominated the scene, historians judge, all armies would have been utterly demolished in nonstop offensives by the end of 1915. Yet ordinary soldiers in this war were not automatons, and in the face of what seemed to them suicidal orders, soldiers on both sides sometimes refused to engage in battle. Enemies facing each other across the trenches frequently ate their meals in peace, even though the trenches were within hand-grenade reach. Right up to the closing year of the war, soldiers fraternized with the "enemy," playing an occasional game of soccer, exchanging mementos, and entering into silent agreements not to fight. A British veteran of the trenches explained to a new recruit that the Germans "don't want to fight any more than we do, so there's a kind of understanding between us. Don't fire at us and we'll not fire at you." Male bonding aided survival: soldiers picked lice from one another's bodies and clothes and came to love one another, sometimes even passionately.

Troops from Asian and African colonies, taken like the European whites from their everyday lives, often had different experiences, especially because colonial soldiers were often put in the front ranks where the risks were greatest. Many suffered from the rigors of a totally unfamiliar climate and strange food, as well as from their encounter with Western war technology. Colonial troops' perspectives changed as they saw their "masters" completely undone and "uncivilized." For when fighting did break out, trenches became a veritable hell of shelling and sniping, flying body parts, rotting cadavers, and blinding gas. "I am greatly distressed in mind," one South Asian soldier wrote to his family, echoing the hopelessness that so many soldiers felt on seeing their comrades lose hands, feet, and entire limbs.[3] Colonizers and colonized could alike be reduced to hysteria through the sheer stress and violence of battle; others became cynical. "It might be me tomorrow," a young British soldier wrote his mother in 1916. "Who cares?"

Civilians at War: The Home Front

World War I quickly became a "**total war**," one in which all of the resources of each nation were harnessed to the war effort and lines between the home front and the battlefield were blurred. Civilians manufactured the machine guns, poisonous gases, bombs, airplanes, and eventually tanks that were the backbone of technological warfare. Increased and well-organized production of coffins, canes, wheelchairs, and artificial limbs was also a wartime necessity. Because their efforts were vital to military success, civilians were required to work overtime and sacrifice for victory. To supply the battlefront efficiently, governments took over the operation of the economy and suppressed dissent.

Politics Suspended   Initially, political parties in each combatant nation put aside their differences. For decades socialist parties had preached that "the worker has no country" and that nationalism was mere ideology meant to keep workers disunited and obedient to their employers. In August 1914, however, most socialists backed the war, trading worker solidarity for national unity in a time of crisis. Although many feminists were opposed to war, the British suffrage leader Emmeline Pankhurst was hardly alone in also becoming a militant nationalist. "What is the use of fighting for a vote if we have not got a country to vote in?" she asked. Others hoped that the spirit of nationalism could end prejudices. "In the German fatherland there are no longer any Christians and Jews, any believers and disbelievers, there are only Germans," one rabbi proudly announced. National leaders stressed ending political division in the name of victory: "I no longer recognize [political] parties," Kaiser William II declared on August 4, 1914. "I recognize only Germans." Governments mobilized the masses on the home front to endure long hours and food shortages with large doses of propaganda that promoted patriotism by demonizing the enemy (see Seeing the Past: Wartime Propaganda). New laws made it a crime to criticize official policies. For a time, it seemed as if old barriers would be broken down and new bonds formed among the citizens of each nation.

As the war dragged on, social and political tensions returned, and some individuals and groups began to lobby for peace. In 1915, activists in the international women's movement met in The Hague to call for an end to war. "We can no longer endure . . . brute force as the only solution of international disputes," declared Dutch physician Aletta Jacobs. Some socialists moved to neutral countries such as Switzerland to work for a negotiated peace settlement.

The Civilians' War   The requirements of total war upset the social and political order. In the early days of fighting many women lost their jobs when luxury shops, textile factories, and other non-military establishments closed. Wartime conditions, however, soon created new opportunities for women workers. As men left the workplace to join the fighting, women moved into a variety of high-paying jobs, including munitions production, metallurgy, and services like streetcar conducting and ambulance driving. Workingmen often protested that women, in the words of one metalworker, were "sending men to the slaughter" and robbing them of their role as breadwinner. Many people, including some women, objected to women's loss of femininity, as workers cut their hair short and wore utilitarian slacks and streamlined clothing. "The feminine in me decreased more and more, and I did not know

total war The vital involvement of civilians in the war industry, the blurring of home and battle fronts, and the use of industrial weaponry to destroy an enemy.

Wartime Propaganda

The French Are Using Monkeys: A German Magazine Cover
(Christel Gerstenberg/Corbis.)

Will Germany Take Over the World?: An Australian Poster
(K.J. Historical/Corbis.)

Propaganda agencies within governments on both sides in World War I touted the war as a patriotic mission to resist villainous enemies. They used both film and print to turn people who formerly saw themselves as neighbors into hate-filled enemies. British propagandists fabricated atrocities that the German "Huns" supposedly committed against Belgians, and German propaganda warned that French African troops would rape German women if Germany were defeated. Efforts were often clumsy: a British film, *The Battle of the Somme* (1916), so obviously sanitized the war's horrors that soldiers in the audience roared with laughter, though civilians found it riveting.

Brightly colored propaganda posters, representing the best lithographic technology, were pasted to walls and placed in windows. Government experts hired the best graphic artists to execute their carefully chosen themes. In the image on the left, German propagandists picked up on the widespread use of African soldiers in the French army to make their point, depicting the enemy in this magazine cover as monkeys. "The Ersatz Battalion—Senegal" speaks to the effectiveness of the

enemy. By contrast, an Australian artist drew the Allied poster on the right representing the German enemy with a frightening face and its hands dripping blood.

EXAMINING THE EVIDENCE

1. What accounts for these specific representations of the enemy?

2. How would the audience respond to each representation, and how would the images have aroused commitment to the war?

3. Alongside this type of caricature was sentimental wartime propaganda depicting brave soldiers, faithful wives, and children in need of their hardy fathers' and other male protection. Why was there such variety in propaganda, and which type of image would you judge to be most effective?

whether to be sad or glad about this," wrote one Russian nurse about putting on rough male clothing for the battlefield. Despite some alarm, a "new woman" with different clothing, a respectable job, and new responsibilities for supporting her family was emerging in great numbers from the war.

Rising social tensions revolved around issues of class as well as gender. Workers toiled longer hours eating less, while many in the upper classes bought abundant food and fashionable clothing on the black market (outside the official system of rationing). Governments allowed many businesses to keep raising prices and thus earn higher profits than ever, practices that caused the cost of living to surge and thus contributed to social strife. Shortages of staples such as bread, sugar, and meat caused hardships everywhere. A German roof-workers' association pleaded for relief: "We can no longer go on. Our children are starving." Civilians in occupied areas and in such colonies as German East Africa suffered oppressive conditions, facing harsh forced labor along with skyrocketing taxes and prices. Thus, even though political debate officially stopped during the war, the prolonged conflict created political grievances among people worldwide.

Revolution in Russia and the End of World War I

FOCUS

Why did the Russian Revolution take place, and what changes did it produce in Russian politics and daily life?

By 1917 the situation was becoming desperate for everyone—politicians, the military, and civilians. In February of that year, the German government, responding to public anger over mounting casualties, resumed unrestricted submarine warfare—a move that brought the United States into the war two months later, after German U-boats had sunk several American ships. Meanwhile, as prices soared, tenants across Europe conducted rent strikes, and factory hands and white-collar workers alike walked off the job. In the spring of 1917, French soldiers mutinied against further offensives, while in Russia, wartime protest turned into outright revolution.

Revolution in Russia

Of all the warring nations, Russia sustained the greatest number of casualties—7.5 million by 1917. Unlike other heads of state, Tsar Nicholas II failed to unify his government or his people. Nicholas was capable of making patriotic gestures, such as changing the German-sounding name of St. Petersburg to Petrograd, but he stubbornly insisted on conducting the war himself instead of using experienced and knowledgeable officials. "Is this stupidity or treason?" one member of the Russian Duma asked of the ineffective wartime effort. In March 1917, crowds of working women and civilians commemorating International Women's Day swarmed the streets of Petrograd and began looting shops for food. Other workers, furious at the government's inability to provide basic necessities, joined them. Many in the army defected, angered by the massive casualties caused by their substandard weapons. Nicholas abdicated that same month, bringing the three-hundred-year-old Romanov dynasty to an abrupt end.

The Provisional Government

Politicians from the old Duma formed a new ruling entity called the Provisional Government. At first hopes were high that under the Provisional Government, as one revolutionary poet put it, "our false, filthy, boring, hideous life should become a just, pure, merry, and beautiful life." However, the abdication of the tsar did not end internal conflict in Russia. Instead, the Russian Revolution unleashed social and political forces that had been building for decades. Spontaneously elected **soviets**—councils of workers and soldiers—campaigned to end favor of the wealthy and urged concern for workers and the poor. The peasantry, another force competing for power, began to seize aristocratic estates. Meanwhile, the Provisional Government seemed unwilling to end the war and unable to improve living conditions.

soviet A council of workers and soldiers elected to represent the people in the Russian revolutions of 1905 and 1917.

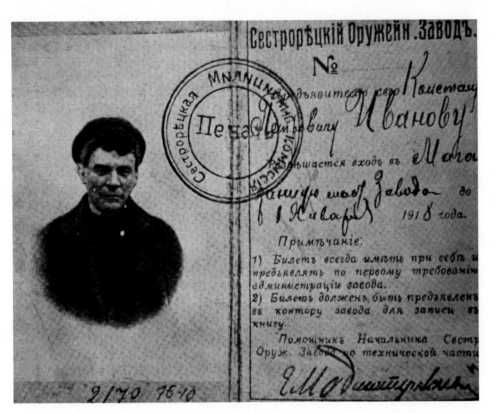

Lenin's False Identity Papers, 1917

Before the Russian Revolution began in 1917, Bolshevik leader V. I. Lenin had lived in forced exile, agitated among the Social Democrats in foreign lands, and preached loudly against World War I. During the Russian Revolution itself, he used many disguises and false identity papers such as the one shown here to escape notice by the Provisional Government, which he worked to bring down. By the autumn of 1917, the war was still going so badly for Russia and inflicted so much additional suffering that the Bolsheviks were able to take power. (Private Collection/The Stapleton Collection/Bridgeman Art Library.)

In April 1917, Vladimir Ilyich Lenin, leader of a faction of the Russian Socialist Party, returned from exile in Siberia, his safe rail transportation provided by the Germans, who hoped that Lenin might further weaken the Russian war effort. Son of a prominent provincial official, Lenin nonetheless lived his life as a revolutionary, beginning political activism while at university and then becoming a political organizer of Marxist and working-class groups across Europe. Among his principles was the belief that the Russian people needed to be led by an elite group of revolutionaries—not by the masses themselves. Those belonging to Lenin's faction were called **Bolsheviks**. On returning to Russia, Lenin quickly called on his countrymen to withdraw from World War 1, for the soviets to seize power on behalf of workers and poor peasants, and for all private land to be nationalized. The Bolsheviks challenged the Provisional Government with the slogans "All power to the soviets!" and "Peace, land, and bread!" In contrast, the Provisional Government—like governments across Europe—continued to seek popular support through battlefield victories, even as the Russian army continued to suffer staggering losses.

In November 1917, the Bolsheviks seized power in the name of the soviets. When in January 1918 elections for a constituent assembly failed to give the Bolsheviks a majority, the party took over the government by force. Observing Marxist doctrine, the Bolsheviks abolished private property, nationalizing factories in order to restore productivity. The new government asked Germany for peace and agreed to the Treaty of Brest-Litovsk (March 1918), which placed vast regions of the Russian Empire under German occupation (see again Map 27.1). Because the loss of millions of square miles put Petrograd at risk, the Bolsheviks relocated the capital to Moscow. To distinguish themselves from the socialists or Social Democrats who had voted for the disastrous war in 1914, the Bolsheviks formally adopted the name Communists, taken from Marx's writings. Lenin agreed to the huge loss of territory not only because he had promised to bring peace to Russia, but because he believed the rest of Europe would soon rebel and overthrow the capitalist order.

Opposition to Bolshevik policies swiftly formed and soon mushroomed into full-fledged civil war. The pro-Bolsheviks (or "Reds") faced an array of antirevolutionary forces

The Bolshevik Takeover

Bolshevik A faction of the Russian Socialist Party that advocated control of revolutionary activity by a disciplined group of the party elite instead of by the working class as a whole; renamed "Communist" by Lenin following the Russian Revolution.

Civil War

(the "Whites"). Among the Whites, the tsarist military leadership, composed of many aristocratic landlords, was joined by non-Russian-nationality groups eager to regain independence. Russia's former allies, notably the United States, Britain, France, and Japan, landed troops in the country, hoping to defeat the Bolsheviks. The Whites failed, however, because instead of conducting a united effort, the individual groups competed with one another: the pro-tsarist forces, for example, wanted a restored empire, whereas the nationality groups such as the Ukrainians and Lithuanians wanted freedom as individual nation-states.

In contrast, the Bolsheviks had a more unified leadership that essentially reshaped Marxism. Leon Trotsky, Bolshevik commissar of war, built a highly disciplined army by ending the democratic procedures, such as the election of officers, that had originally attracted soldiers to Bolshevism. The Cheka (secret police) set up detention camps for political opponents and often shot them without trial. The expansion of the Cheka, Red Army, and bureaucracy undermined the promise of Marxism that revolution would bring a "withering away" of the state.

Finally, the Bolsheviks organized revolutionary Marxism worldwide. In March 1919, they founded the **Comintern** (Communist International), a centrally run organization dedicated to preaching communism globally. By mid-1921, the Red Army had secured the Crimea, the Caucasus, and the Muslim borderlands in Central Asia, and in 1922 the Japanese withdrew from Siberia—the last of the foreign invaders to leave—ending the civil war. The Bolsheviks were now in charge of a state, the Union of Soviet Socialist Republics (USSR), as multiethnic as the former Russian Empire. In the meantime, civil war had brought Russia only unprecedented disease, hunger, and death. Nonetheless, people around the world saw in Soviet communism the promise of an improved life for the masses.

Ending the War: 1918

Although Russia was out of World War I by the spring of 1918, much of the rest of the world remained mired in the brutal conflict. Relying on Arab, African, and Indian troops, the British took Baghdad in 1917 as well as Palestine, Lebanon, and Syria from the Ottomans (see again Map 27.1). In sub-Saharan Africa, more than a million Kenyans and Tanzanians were conscripted by the Europeans to fight a vicious campaign for control of East Africa. African troops serving the imperial powers died by the thousands, as did the civilian population whose resources were confiscated and villages burned by competing powers. The Japanese seized German holdings in China to enlarge their influence on the mainland.

Allied Victory

In the spring of 1918 the Central Powers made one final attempt to smash through the Allied lines, but by then the British and French had started making limited but effective use of tanks that could withstand machine-gun fire. In the summer of 1918, the Allies, now fortified by U.S. troops, pushed back the Germans all along the western front and headed toward Germany. In an effort to shift the blame for defeat away from themselves, the German military leaders who had been running the country allowed a civilian government to form and ask for peace. After the war, the generals would claim that weak-willed civilians had dealt the military a "stab in the back," forcing Germany to surrender when victory was still possible. As the Central Powers collapsed on all fronts and mutinies and rebellions broke out across Germany, on November 11, 1918, delegates from the two sides signed an armistice ending the war.

In the course of four years, civilization had been sorely tested, if not shattered. Conservative figures put the battlefield toll at a minimum of 10 million dead and 30 million wounded, incapacitated, or eventually to die of their wounds. In every European combatant country, industrial and agricultural production had plummeted, and much of the reduced output had been put to military use. From 1918 to 1919, the weakened global population suffered an influenza epidemic that left as many as 100 million more dead. "They carried the dead people on mule-drawn carts without even being in boxes," one

Comintern An international organization of workers established by the Bolsheviks to spread communism worldwide.

Fourteen Points A proposal by U.S. president Woodrow Wilson for peace during World War I based on "settlement" rather than "victory" and on the self-determination of peoples.

fighter in Pancho Villa's army reported of the flu in Mexico. "Many poor people left their small children as orphans . . . without father, without mother, without anything."[4] The influenza pandemic only added to the horrifying fact that total war had drained society of resources and population and had sown the seeds of future catastrophes.

Postwar Global Politics

Across Europe, civilians and returning soldiers rose in protest after the war. Even as peace talks began in 1919, the red flag of socialist revolution flew from the city hall in Glasgow, Scotland, while in cities of the collapsing Austro-Hungarian Empire, workers set up soviet-like councils to reshape politics. The conduct of the war—including forced labor—damaged Western claims to be more advanced than other parts of the world, causing a surging resistance to colonialism even as the victorious Allies took steps to secure and expand their empires. Such was the highly charged backdrop for peacemaking.

FOCUS

What were the major outcomes of the peacemaking process and postwar conditions?

The Paris Peace Conference
1919–1920

The Paris Peace Conference opened in January 1919 with the leaders of the United States, Great Britain, and France dominating the proceedings. Western leaders worried about communism spreading far beyond Russia's borders and about pressure from their angry citizens, who demanded revenge. France, for example, had lost 1.3 million people—almost an entire generation of young men, more than a million buildings, and thousands of miles of railroad lines and roads had been destroyed while the war was fought on French soil. The British slogan "Hang the Kaiser!" captured the public mood. Italian officials arrived on the scene demanding the territory promised to them in the 1915 Treaty of London. Meanwhile U.S. president Woodrow Wilson, head of the growing world power that had contributed to the Allied victory, had his own agenda. His **Fourteen Points**, the peace proposal on which the truce had been based, were steeped in the language of freedom and called for open diplomacy, an "open-minded" settlement of colonial issues, and the self-determination of peoples—meaning the right of national groups to have autonomy if they wanted it. Amid disagreements over the need to punish the Central Powers or to prevent too harsh or humiliating a peace, representatives from Middle Eastern states, Japan, and other deeply interested parties lobbied for fair treatment from the victorious powers. World War I had drawn in non-European peoples from around the world, and now, having fought in the war, they wanted a say in the peace.

Paris Peace Conference, 1918

Allied heads of state, diplomats, military personnel, and policy experts dominated the peace conference that opened in Paris in 1918. Also attending were a variety of other participants in the war seeking a just peace, national independence, or special acknowledgment of their ethnic or other interest group. Among these were leaders from the Middle East, who had rallied their own armed forces to fight for the Allies on the promise of postwar independence. Their small presence in this picture symbolizes the utter disregard for those promises in the Peace of Paris settlement. (The Art Archive/Domenica del Corriere/Collection Dagli Orti.)

MAP 27.2

The Peace of Paris in Central and Eastern Europe, 1920

Where mighty empires had once reigned over central and eastern Europe, new states appeared and new forms of government replaced dynastic rule. These small states were generally fragile due to their very novelty, postwar economic difficulties, and the need to modernize agriculture and to develop industrial capacity. Their citizens faced more powerful neighbors—Germany and the Soviet Union—whose aspirations to expand would soon menace the region's security.

Map legend:
- Boundaries of German, Russian, and Austro-Hungarian empires in 1914
- New and reconstituted nations
- Demilitarized or Allied occupation zone
- Boundaries of 1920

The Peace of Paris Treaties

After six months, the Allies produced the Peace of Paris (1919–1920), composed of a cluster of individual treaties. The treaties separated Austria from Hungary, reduced Hungary by almost two-thirds of its inhabitants and three-quarters of its territory, and broke up the Ottoman Empire. The Habsburg Empire was replaced by a group of small, internally divided, and relatively weak states: Czechoslovakia, Poland, and the Kingdom of the Serbs, Croats, and Slovenes, soon renamed Yugoslavia. Austria and Hungary were both left reeling at their loss of territory and resources (see Map 27.2).

The settlement with Germany, the Treaty of Versailles (named after the palace where the treaty was signed), was the centerpiece of the Peace of Paris. France recovered Alsace and Lorraine, and Germany was ordered to pay substantial reparations for civilian damage during the war—terms that would cripple the German economy. It was also directed to give up its colonies, reduce its army, stop manufacturing offensive weapons, and deliver a large amount of free coal each year to Belgium and France. The average German saw in the terms of the Treaty of Versailles an unmerited humiliation of "war guilt" that was compounded by Article 231 of the treaty, which assigned "responsibility" for the war to "the aggression of Germany and her allies." Germany, a powerful nation, was branded an outcast in the global community.

Besides redrawing the map of Europe, the diplomats created the **League of Nations**, an organization whose members had a joint responsibility for maintaining peace through negotiation—a principle called **collective security**, which was to replace the divisive secrecy of prewar power politics. In Woodrow Wilson's vision, the League would peacefully guide the world toward disarmament, arbitrate its members' disputes, and monitor labor conditions around the world. However, the U.S. Senate, in an embarrassing defeat for the president, both failed to ratify the peace settlement and refused to join the League. Moreover, both Germany and Russia initially were excluded from the League and were thus blocked from participating in international consensus-building with the forty-two founding member nations. The absence of these three major powers weakened the League as a global peacekeeper from the outset.

The end to imperialism was at the top of many non-Western representatives' agenda, but they were to be denied. The covenant, or charter, of the League of Nations organized the new administration of the surrendered colonies and territories of Germany and the Ottoman Empire through a system of mandates (see Map 27.3). The European powers

League of Nations

League of Nations The international organization set up following World War I to maintain peace by arbitrating disputes and promoting collective security.

collective security The system of international diplomacy, especially involving the peaceful resolution of disputes, established by the League of Nations.

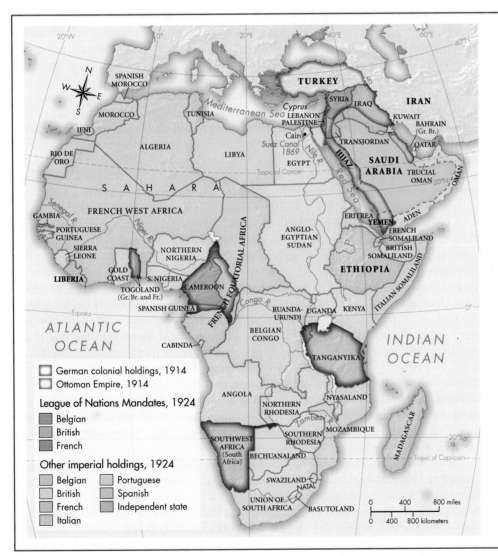

MAP 27.3

The Mandate System in Africa and the Middle East, 1924

Instead of granting Middle Eastern and African peoples the promised rights and independence that had brought them into the war, the Allies scooped up former territories controlled by the Germans and the Ottomans and converted them into "mandates"—in effect, colonies. The growing importance of oil and of other resources lay behind this seizure of control.

Mandate System

exercised political control over mandated territory, but some local leaders retained limited authority. The League covenant justified the **mandate system** as providing governance by "advanced nations" over territories "not yet able to stand by themselves under the strenuous conditions of the modern world."

Not surprisingly, the people of the new mandates were furious. Sharif Husayn ibn Ali had mobilized a substantial force to wage war against the Ottomans because of agreements with Britain for an independent Syria. His son Faisal was humiliated in Paris when it became clear that no such independence was forthcoming. On his return to the Middle East Faisal called on the crowds to "choose either to be slaves or masters of your own destiny."[5] Rebellions against France and Britain erupted in the Middle East, but they were put down. Outside of the Middle East, opponents of colonialism redoubled their organizational efforts in such movements as pan-Africanism, whose members now held regular international meetings with the goal of promoting solidarity among blacks everywhere and, eventually, a vast self-governing union of all African peoples. "Never again will the darker people of the world occupy just the place they had before," the African American leader W.E.B. Du Bois predicted in 1918. The postwar settlements, like the war itself, contributed to renewed activism among colonial peoples around the world.

Struggles for Reform and Independence

In the aftermath of war many of the world's peoples took advantage of Western weakness to seek independence from outside domination. These struggles occurred in remnants of the Ottoman Empire, China, India, and Africa. In the face of such determination, imperial powers from Japan to Britain not only resisted loosening their domination, but often resorted to violence to maintain and expand their empires.

Turkey Emerges from the Ottoman Empire

The Allied invasion of the Ottoman Empire caused chaos and suffering from Anatolia through Syria, Lebanon, and Egypt. Allied blockades during the war led to widespread starvation, and Allied agents provoked rebellion against the Ottoman grip to weaken the empire. From 1915 to 1916 the Ottoman leadership carried out the mass deportation of unknown numbers—estimates range from 300 thousand to 1.5 million—of Armenians in the empire, claiming that they were spying and plotting with the Russians to revolt in wartime. Armenians were rounded up and sent on marches into the desert to perish. Their considerable property was stolen, and their fellow villagers moved into abandoned Armenian homes. Witnesses based in the region sent horrifying reports around the world, but the Ottoman position was that "the Armenians have only themselves to blame." They were, in the words of one official, "a menace to the Turkish race."[6]

Once the war was over and the Ottoman Empire disbanded, determined Turkish military officers resisted the continuing presence of the Allies, who were inciting the Greeks to seize Ottoman lands. Led by General Mustafa Kemal, the remnants of the Ottoman army traveled the countryside calling for a democratically elected national assembly to represent the voice of the people. Kemal preached an anti-imperialist message in the face of the British occupation of Istanbul: "All we want is to save our country from sharing the fate of India and Egypt."[7] He and his followers also pushed for the primacy of ethnic Turks, despite the presence of many ethnic groups who had lived together for centuries. A war of independence broke out as the Allies tried to suppress the Turkish reformers and bring about a partition of Anatolia, but the spirit of nationalism proved too strong. Kemal, who later took the name Atatürk ("first among Turks"), led the Turks to found an independent republic in 1923 (see Map 27.4).

After victory in 1923, Kemal became head of the government. From the beginning he worked to bring the region into the orbit of Western modernity and to craft a capitalist economy. "A nation must be strong in spirit, knowledge, science and morals," he announced.[8] In an effort to Westernize Turkish culture and the new Turkish state, Kemal moved the capital from Istanbul to Ankara in 1923, officially changed the ancient Greek name *Constantinople* to the Turkish *Istanbul* in 1930, mandated Western dress for men

mandate system A system of regional control over former Ottoman lands awarded by the League of Nations' charter to the victors in World War I.

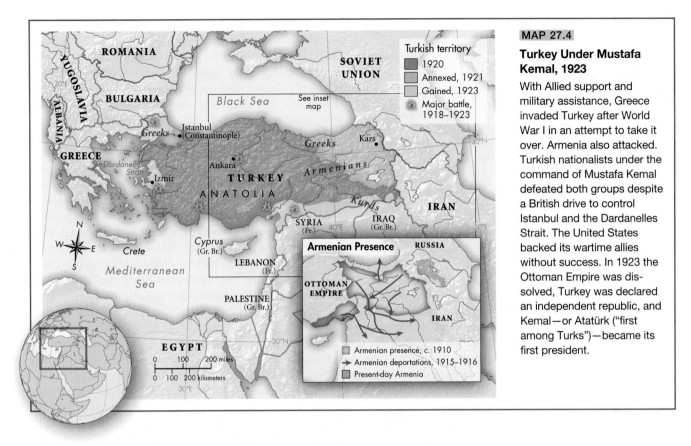

MAP 27.4

Turkey Under Mustafa Kemal, 1923

With Allied support and military assistance, Greece invaded Turkey after World War I in an attempt to take it over. Armenia also attacked. Turkish nationalists under the command of Mustafa Kemal defeated both groups despite a British drive to control Istanbul and the Dardanelles Strait. The United States backed its wartime allies without success. In 1923 the Ottoman Empire was dissolved, Turkey was declared an independent republic, and Kemal—or Atatürk ("first among Turks")—became its first president.

and women, introduced the Latin alphabet, and abolished polygamy. Ordinary people reacted to their world being turned topsy-turvy: "It's a Christian hat," a barber warned to a young soldier sporting a Western-style hat as part of his uniform. "If a Muslim puts such a shocking thing on his head the good God will surely punish him."[9] In 1936, women received the vote and were made eligible to serve in the parliament.

Reform in Turkey, 1923

Like many colonized countries and those seeking to free themselves from Western control, Turkey under Atatürk considered the condition of women an important element of modernization. Atatürk decreed that women and men alike should dress in Western clothes, receive a secular education, and switch from the Arabic to the Latin alphabet. There was much for the citizens of the new Turkey to learn and unlearn; women were at the center of this nation-building process, as we see in this image from a Turkish classroom. (Gamma-Keystone via Getty Images.)

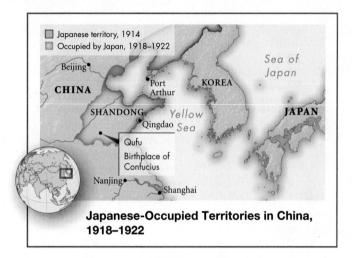

Japanese-Occupied Territories in China, 1918–1922

China Seeks a Modern Government

In China, the course of nation building stalled after the overthrow of the Qing dynasty in 1912, but the results of World War I gave it a new boost. People from many walks of life were outraged by Japan's 1915 takeover of Germany's sphere of influence in China, which included the birthplace of Confucius. The Allies' legal endorsement of that takeover, announced on May 4, 1919, galvanized student protest. Carrying signs that read, "China Belongs to the Chinese," they were joined by dockworkers, business people, and others from different walks of life. Among the middle and educated classes, the May 4th movement also targeted Chinese traditions—from Confucian values such as patriarchal control of women and the young to educational "backwardness"—as responsible for China's treatment on the world stage. Although they detested imperialism, some of these reformers came to see the value of Christian institutions that offered training in Western languages, modern science, and political theory. Like the leaders of the new Turkey and Meiji Japan, they had come to see selective Westernization as key to independence.

Many other Chinese, however, turned away from the West. Students and workers declared that Western leaders at the Paris conference were "still selfish and militaristic and that they were all great liars," as one student put it.[10] Some adopted an alternative—communism—just as the Soviet Union sent aid to the Chinese Communist Party with instructions that it should help Sun Yatsen's nationalist party, the Guomindang, to help organize and politicize the people (see Reading the Past: Communism Spreads in China). Politicization led to strikes, but also to tensions between Communists and the Guomindang, which had been taken over by the military leader Jiang Jieshi (Chiang Kai-Shek) after the death of Sun in 1925. Jiang led his troops to put down warlords to the north as the beginning of reunification. As he took the cities of Nanjing and Shanghai, his followers murdered the Communists in hopes of stopping their influence for good. Jiang then turned to mobilizing his countrymen for modernization.

Ireland Demands Independence

War and its aftermath inspired other attempts at liberation from combatant countries. In Ireland, pro-independence activists attacked government buildings in Dublin on Easter Monday 1916, in an effort to gain Irish freedom from Britain. Ill-prepared, their Easter rebellion was easily defeated and many of them were executed. Demands for home rule only intensified, and in January 1919, republican leaders proclaimed Ireland's independence from Britain. Instead of granting it, the British government sent in the "Black and Tans," a volunteer army of demobilized soldiers—so called for the color of their uniforms. Terror reigned in Ireland, as both the pro-independence forces and the Black and Tans waged guerrilla warfare, taking hostages, blowing up buildings, and even shooting into crowds at soccer matches. By 1921 public outrage at the violence forced the British to negotiate a treaty. The Irish Free State was declared a self-governing dominion owing allegiance to the British crown. Northern Ireland, a group of six northern counties containing many Protestants, gained a separate status as a self-governing British territory with representation in the British Parliament. Partial independence and the rights of religious minorities remained contentious issues, producing violence for decades thereafter.

Colonized peoples rose up after the war in virtually every empire. Those who had fought expected the rights that European politicians and military recruiters had solemnly promised in exchange for service. Instead, they met worsening conditions at home. "Is our reward to have our tax raised . . . and for our ownership of land to be called

Ireland, 1921

Communism Spreads in China

Communism was one alternative for middle- and upper-class Chinese reformers angry that the Western powers had given part of their country to Japan at the Peace of Paris. In this passage, P'eng P'ai, son of a prosperous landowning family, recounts the creation in the early 1920s of the Hai-Feng Peasant Union in the early 1920s based on Communist ideas. P'eng P'ai himself had much to learn about building a mass movement. At first he searched out peasant activists while wearing a fancy, Western-style white suit and a white hat; most of the peasants fled. After changing his clothing to simpler attire, P'eng had greater success. The Peasant Union grew to more than twenty thousand out of a population of one hundred thousand and undertook a range of activities to protect peasant livelihoods. Below are some of the Union's activities.

[W]e found that some peasants would try to get others' land to till, and landlords would increase rent and change tenants. So the Union drew up some regulations to prevent such incidents.

1. Unless permission is given by the member and by the Union, no one may encroach on a member's rented land.
2. Unless a member relinquishes his lease and the Union gives its permission, no one may rent the land already rented to a member of the Union. Violators are subject to severe punishment.
3. In case a landlord takes back his land from a member by means of increasing the rent, and as a result a member's livelihood is in danger, he may ask for help from the Union, which will either persuade nearby members to allow him to till part of their land, or will introduce him to another trade.

After the regulations were publicized, there was no longer any competition for land among our members, and the landlords also were afraid to raise the rent of members of the Union. . . .

Soon it was Chinese New Year of 1923. Dragon dancers and music troupes from all the villages came to celebrate, and the Union organized a New Year's Festival for all peasants in Hai-Feng. . . . More than six thousand members and three thousand non-members participated and the banners of each village's bands, dragon dancers, and music troupes danced in the open air. . . . The speakers . . . pointed out that before the proletarian revolution was realized, there could be no joyous New Year, for New Year's Day was a time for the exploiters to oppress us and to demand us to pay our debts. We were now united in our hardships, not in joy. However, this was an opportunity in which we might demonstrate our strength to our enemies and awaken the spirit of revolution in ourselves. We were prepared for a battle with our enemies. This was the reason why, on the one hand, we felt weighed down by our emotions, but on the other hand elated.

On that day, we issued two thousand new membership cards, and received over four hundred dollars in dues.

Patricia Buckley Ebrey. Adapted with permission of Free Press, a division of Simon & Schuster, Inc., from *Chinese Civilization and Society: A Sourcebook* by Patricia Buckley Ebrey. Copyright © 1981 by The Free Press. All rights reserved.

Source: Patricia B. Ebrey, ed., *Chinese Civilization and Society: A Sourcebook* (New York: Free Press, 1981), 273, 276.

EXAMINING THE EVIDENCE

1. What types of activities did the Hai-Feng Peasant Union sponsor, and why did these activities prove effective?

2. What would lead peasants to fear the Union, and what would make them want to join it?

3. What insight into mass movements does this document provide?

into question?" one group of East Africans asked in 1921 (see Reading the Past: Léopold Sédar Senghor, "To the Senegalese Soldiers Who Died for France").[11]

Rebellions mostly met a brutal response. Fearful of losing India, British forces shot into crowds of protesters at Amritsar in 1919 and put down revolts in Egypt and Iran in the early 1920s. The Dutch jailed political leaders in Indonesia; the French punished Indochinese nationalists; and in 1929 the British crushed Ibo women's tax protest. Maintaining empires abroad was crucial to covering debts incurred during World War I, spurring colonial rule to become more brutal in the face of protest.

Protesting Colonization

Léopold Sédar Senghor, "To the Senegalese Soldiers Who Died for France"

Among the colonial troops in World War I were the Senegalese Sharpshooters, who fought on the side of their French imperial masters. Though the Senegalese riflemen served on the front lines, they received little credit from the French and were even forced to march around, rather than through, villages so that white citizens would not have to set eyes on black soldiers. They were immortalized in a poem by Léopold Sédar Senghor, who himself fought in the French colonial forces and who became the first president of an independent Senegal in 1960. Among the thousands of poems memorializing World War I, the one from which this excerpt was taken also served as Senegal's national anthem after liberation.

> They put flowers on tombs and warm the Unknown
>   Soldier.
> But you, my dark brothers, no one calls your names.
> . . .
> Listen to me, Senegalese soldiers, in the solitude of the
>   black ground
> And of death, in your deaf and blind solitude,
> More than I in my dark skin in the depths of the Province,
> Without even the warmth of your comrades lying close
>   to you,
> As in the trenches back then or the village palavers
>   [conversations] long ago,
> . . .
> We bring you, listen to us, we who spelled your names
> In the months of your deaths, we bring you,
> In these fearful days without memory,

> The friendship of your age-mates.
> Ah! If I could one day sing in a voice glowing like embers,
> If I could praise the friendship of comrades as fervent
> And delicate as entrails, as strong as tendons.
> Listen to us, you Dead stretched out in water as far as
> The northern and eastern fields.
> Receive this red earth, under a summer sun this soil
> Reddened with the blood of white hosts
> Receive the salute of your black comrades,
> Senegalese soldiers
> WHO DIED FOR THE REPUBLIC!

Source: Léopold Sédar Senghor, *The Collected Poetry*, trans. Melvin Dixon (Charlottesville: University Press of Virginia, 1991), 46–47.

EXAMINING THE EVIDENCE

1. What emotions and values does Senghor express in this poem?

2. What views of World War I does the poem reveal?

3. Why do you think Senghor wrote this poem, and for whom?

4. Why would this poem about a specific group of people fighting on behalf of imperial powers become the national anthem of an independent country?

Postwar Imperial Expansion

Amid protest, imperialism reached its high tide in the 1920s and 1930s. Britain and France, enjoying control of Germany's African colonies and former Ottoman lands in the Middle East, were at the height of their global power. A new generation of adventurers headed for Middle Eastern and Indonesian oil fields, as the importance of oil increased along with the number of automobiles, airplanes, trucks, ships, and oil-heated homes. Investors from the United States and elsewhere grabbed land in the Caribbean and across Latin America, cornering markets in sugar, cocoa, and tropical fruit that were becoming a regular part of the Western diet. Competition for territory and business was alive and well.

The balance of power among the imperial nations was shifting, however. The most important change was Japan's growing competitiveness for markets, resources, and influence. During the war, Japanese output of industrial goods such as ships and metal grew some 40 percent because the Western powers outsourced their wartime needs for such products. As Japan took shipping, financial, and other business from Britain and France, its prosperity skyrocketed and officials touted its success as the key to an Asia free from Westerners. Ardently nationalist, the Japanese government was not yet strong enough to challenge Western powers militarily. Thus, although outraged at Wilson's abrupt rejection (with British backing) of a nondiscrimination clause in the charter of the League of Nations put forward by the Japanese, Japan cooperated in the Anglo-American-dominated peace, even agreeing both to restore Chinese possessions and to keep a ratio of English, American, and Japanese shipbuilding at 5:5:3 respectively. "Rolls Royce, Rolls Royce, Ford," a Japanese official commented bitterly.[12] This bitterness ultimately festered into war.

An Age of the Masses

War and revolutions demonstrated the centrality of the masses to modern life. With the collapse of autocratic governments from China to Germany, the sense of democratic potential based on mass participation grew. The condition of women came to symbolize the strength of the masses, which was reflected in the extension of the vote to many Western women during the 1920s. Modernizing the economy—a goal of many countries after the war—meant developing mass consumerism, while modern technology provided mass entertainment and news across the globe. By the end of the decade, a handful of political leaders were adopting new media to mobilize their citizenry.

> **FOCUS**
>
> How did the rise of mass society affect politics, culture, and everyday life around the world?

Mass Society

The development of mass society was a global phenomenon, fueled by the growing connections among economies. Urbanization surged in Asia, Latin America, Africa, and the United States as populations exploded and rural people migrated to cities in search of work. Global population, aided by the spread of medicine and improved sanitation, also soared. Tokyo had some 3.5 million inhabitants in 1920, New York 5.5 million, and Shanghai over 2 million. Calcutta's population quadrupled to 1.8 million from the late nineteenth century to 1920. City life was fast paced, brimming with trams, buses, and automobiles; in China rickshaws with cushioned wheels pulled by fast young men replaced the leisurely sedan chair as the conveyance of choice. Tall buildings lifted skylines, first in New York with its much-admired Chrysler and Empire State buildings, but soon in cities throughout the world. New urban cultural livelihoods arose, such as performing jazz and managing nightclubs. Across the globe class distinctions were blurred in the confusion of city life. Outside city centers, wealthy suburbs and exclusive beachside retreats flourished, such as that near the city of Bombay, India, started by the Tata family of industrialists (whom we met in Chapter 24). This mass society centered in cities depended on economic modernization—most notably, mass production and its byproduct, mass unionization.

Mass Production

Trade revived in the 1920s, and wartime innovations spurred new industries and created new jobs making cars, electrical products, and synthetic goods for peacetime use. The prewar pattern of mergers and cartels continued after 1918, giving rise to multinational food-processing firms such as Nestlé in Switzerland and global petroleum enterprises such as Royal Dutch Shell. Owners of these large manufacturing conglomerates wielded more financial and political power than entire small countries. By the late 1920s, many in Asia and Europe had survived the wild economic swings of the immediate postwar years to enjoy renewed economic growth.

Among economic leaders, the United States had become the trendsetter in modernization. Businessmen from around the world made pilgrimages to Henry Ford's Detroit assembly line, which by 1929 produced a Ford automobile every ten seconds. Ford claimed that this miracle of productivity resulted in a lower cost of living and increased purchasing power for workers, and indeed some 17 million cars were on U.S. streets by 1925. The new livelihood of scientific manager also played a part, as efficiency experts developed methods to streamline workers' tasks and motions for maximum productivity. Despite the rewards, many workers found the emphasis on efficiency inhumane, with restrictions on time and motion so severe that often they were allowed to use the bathroom only on a fixed schedule.

"When I left the factory, it followed me," wrote one French automobile worker. "In my dreams I was a machine."

Increased Unionization

As industry spread, the number of people in unions increased around the world, with both skilled and unskilled workers organizing to advance their collective interests. Sometimes the reasons for joining were basic: local workers on the French railroads in West Africa complained of "unsanitary food seasoned with dried fish and full of worms" and began unionizing.[13] White-collar workers and government clerks also had large, effective unions. Where male workers' jobs were threatened by laborsaving machinery, unions usually agreed with employers that women should receive lower wages, saving scarce high-paying jobs for men. Under these circumstances, women's participation in union activity was proportionally lower than men's.

Because they could mobilize masses of people, unions played a key role in politics, as they demonstrated when unionized workers in China struck against Britain's control of Hong Kong. "Down with imperialism!" was one of their cries, and they forced merchants to show that their goods did not originate in Britain.[14] India's ongoing industrialization during the war provided jobs, but in the postwar period some 125,000 Bombay textile workers were among those who struck to get their share of the profits. The British sent airplanes to attack strikers, first strafing civilians in 1920s India. As labor flexed its muscle around the world, union members blocked coups against Germany's newly elected democratic government, the Weimar Republic, and organized a general strike in Great Britain in the 1920s.

Changing Class Distinctions

Modernization and rising global productivity affected traditional social divisions. Advances in industrialization boosted the size of the modern middle class by expanding the need for managers and professionals and for skilled workers in new jobs. Often these opportunities reduced the influence of traditional elites and made society more complex in colonized areas such as India, where a modern working class and financial and industrialist classes grew alongside caste and religious divisions. Reformers such as those in China's May 4th movement pointed to the irrationality of traditional patterns of deference within families.

Class and racial prescriptions were also breaking down as a result of the war: men of all classes and ethnicities had served in distant trenches together and were even buried in common graves. As a result of the war, daughters around the world supported themselves in jobs, and their mothers did their own housework because people who once worked as servants could now earn more money in factories. A middle-class "look" became common around the world, promoted by global advertising that appealed to consumers with vivid images of sleek, modern styles.

The "New Woman"

One emblem of postwar modernity in most parts of the world was the "new woman," the "modern girl," or the "flapper," as she was called in the United States. In the 1920s many women around the world cut their hair, abandoned traditional clothes such as kimonos, smoked, had money of their own from working in the service sector, and went out unchaperoned, even dancing with men. Zhu Su'e, born in 1901 to a banking family in Changzhou, China, unbound her feet as a teenager and then left home in 1921 to study in Shanghai. She graduated from law school, married for love instead of having a traditional arranged marriage, and continued her career: "I understood that you must be able to earn money in order to be independent."[15] As an attorney, she often helped women in oppressive marriages, guiding them to become independent and educated. Attempts to impose "modern" standards were often rejected, however. When activists in the USSR urged Muslim women to remove their veils and change their way of life, fervent Muslims often attacked both the activists and the women who followed their advice.

Culture for the Masses

Wartime propaganda had aimed to unite classes, races, and countries against a common enemy. In the 1920s, phonographs, the radio, and film continued the development of mass or standardized culture. Print media, cheaper and more widely distributed to an increasingly literate global population, showed people what to buy and what to wear.

Mass media had the potential to create an informed citizenry, enhance democracy, and promote liberation in the colonies. Paradoxically, it also provided tools for dictatorship. Authoritarian rulers in the Soviet Union, Italy, Japan, and elsewhere were coming to see the advantage of mobilizing the masses through the control of information and culture.

By the 1920s, film flourished around the world, with Shanghai and Hong Kong joining the United States, Europe, and South Asia as important centers of production and regional distribution (see Lives and Livelihoods: The Film Industry). In India, where movie theaters had sprung up at the start of the century in Madras and Bombay, movies retelling the *Mahabharata* and history films on the story of the Taj Mahal developed Indians' sense of a common heritage. Bolshevik leaders underwrote the innovative work of director Sergei Eisenstein, whose films *Potemkin* (1925) and *Ten Days That Shook the World* (1927–1928) presented a Bolshevik view of history to Soviet and many international audiences, spreading standard Communist values. Films also showed the shared predicaments of ordinary people, helping to standardize behavior. Popular comedies of the 1920s and 1930s such as the Shanghai hits *Three Modern Women* (1933) and *New Woman* (1934) showed women viewers the ways of flappers.

Cinematic portrayals also played to postwar fantasies and fears, as threats to class and caste systems shaped movie plots from India to the United States. Impersonators, "gold diggers," and con artists abounded. The plight of gangsters appealed to veterans of revolutions and wars, who had seen that the modern world sometimes placed little value on life. English actor and producer Charlie Chaplin in *Little Tramp* (1914–1915) won international popularity as the defeated hero, the anonymous modern man, trying to keep his dignity in a mechanical world. Sporting events such as cricket, boxing, and martial arts were internationalized, and clips from matches were shown as newsreels before featured movies. As popular films and books crossed national borders, a cosmopolitan, global culture flourished.

Miss Brazil in Texas, 1929
Healthful sports and exercise, feats of daring, and a growing consumerism all signaled postwar revival in many parts of the world. In this photograph, Miss Brazil—an example of the new, modern woman with her trim clothing and cosmetically enhanced face—has traveled to the United States to participate in a beauty contest. International beauty contests introduced consumers around the world to global styles in fashion and self-presentation. (The Granger Collection, New York.)

Film and Radio

Radio was an even newer medium. Developed from the Italian inventor Guglielmo Marconi's wireless technology, radio broadcasts in the first half of the 1920s were heard by mass audiences in public halls (much like film theaters) and featured orchestras and song followed by audience discussion. The radio quickly became a relatively inexpensive consumer item, allowing public events to penetrate private homes. Specialized programming for men (such as sports reporting) and for women (such as advice on home management) soon followed. By the 1930s, politicians used radio to reach the masses wherever they might be—even alone at home.

Mass Marketing

The print media—newspapers and magazines—grew in popularity, and their advertising promoted mass consumption of modern conveniences such as electric clothes washers and irons. Mass marketing encouraged new personal habits, presenting mass-produced razors and deodorants as essential to modern hygiene. Politicians joined in as modernizers: Jiang Jieshi and Bolshevik leaders alike promoted toothpaste and toothbrushing as part of nationbuilding. "New woman" Rilda Marta of South Africa traveled to the United

The Film Industry

Butterfly Hu and Chinese Cinema

By the 1920s films were made and distributed throughout the world. *Twin Sisters* (1933), a product of Shanghai's bustling film industry, focused on the plight of twin sisters—raised apart with utterly different personalities—both played by the Chinese star Butterfly Hu. So easily could distant parts of the world now speak across cultural borders that the movie was a box office hit in China, Southeast Asia, Japan, and western Europe. (Still from "Zi Mei Hua" (Twin Sisters), directed by Zheng Zhengqiu.)

The development of the film industry worldwide from the late nineteenth century on led to the creation of dozens of new livelihoods. Although early films often were the work of a single author-director-cameraman, by the 1920s opportunities for new careers opened up as moviegoing became a mass phenomenon after World War I and as filmmaking itself came to involve many more jobs. Among the most notable new livelihoods were those of screenwriter, cameraman, art editor, and film financier, along with less-renowned jobs for stuntmen, animal trainers, baby actors, and in the United States especially, States to learn about African American cosmetics and on her return advocated the subtle use of lipstick and rouge: "The key to Happiness and Success is a good appearance," she proclaimed. "You are often judged by how you look."[16] A multibillion-dollar global cosmetics industry sprang up almost overnight, and women from Tokyo to Buenos Aires bought their products to imitate the appearance of film celebrities.

Mobilizing the Masses

The 1920s saw the rise of politicians mobilizing the masses for their political causes. When the Bolsheviks encountered opposition to their rule, for example, they began massive propaganda efforts to bring communism to villages and cities, peasants and workers, and Muslims, Christians, and Jews alike. So successful were these efforts that people around the world came to believe that the USSR was an ideal state, a utopia. In the colonies and mandates, leaders like Mohandas Gandhi in India and groups such as the Muslim Brotherhood in Egypt mobilized the masses around spiritual teachings. In Italy, where postwar resentment simmered, Benito Mussolini first staged a coup and then consolidated his rule with mass propaganda.

Gandhi's Movement in India   From the beginning of the twentieth century, Indian leaders objected to British rule of their country and urged boycotts of British products. Indian activist Mohandas Gandhi (1869–1948) transformed this cause into a nonviolent mass movement that appealed to

film censors. The Chinese focus on martial arts in film increased the number of jobs for and prominence of these experts. Before the "talkies," films with sound, were invented in the 1930s, silent movies featured pianists who provided mood-setting music and soloists who entertained the audience during intermission. In Japan the work of the *benshi* was to explain throughout the film the action on the screen, sometimes even singing and dancing as part of the job.

From Southeast Asia to Central America, lavish cinema houses attracted hundreds of millions of weekly viewers, the majority of them women. The importance of the cinema house itself gave jobs to architects, construction workers, and even the elegant usher, who in some countries accompanied viewers to their seats in exchange for a tip. With India producing some fifteen hundred films of its own between 1912 and 1927, the need for all the accoutrements of film viewing provided a rich array of livelihoods.

In the 1920s the "star" system developed, turning performers from humble backgrounds in burlesque or comedy into national, even global, celebrities. In Japan's thriving film industry, almost all stars were men, who played both male and female roles as they had done in kabuki and Noh theater (discussed in Chapter 21). By contrast, in China, the highest-paid star was the actress Butterfly Hu, who made her film debut in 1925 and starred in the first "talkie," *Sing Song Red Peony*, in 1930. Butterfly Hu also filled the pages of the print media as she became a style setter in terms of fashion and grooming. Hu, like other stars, was promoted by professional publicists and hired agents and managers, still other new livelihoods. Media entrepreneurs earned a handsome living founding magazines and engaging Hu and others to sell products. New lines of work opened for journalists to provide gossip about film celebrities, biographies of directors, and reviews of films. Celebrity for a few men and women in the film industry spawned hundreds of new livelihoods across mass culture.

QUESTIONS TO CONSIDER

1. What skills did those working in the film industry need, and to what extent were they new?

2. What accounts for the popularity of cinema in these decades?

3. In what ways was film important to global culture and the world economy?

For Further Information:
Grieveson, Lee, and Peter Krämer, eds. *The Silent Cinema Reader*. 2004.
Sklar, Robert. *A World History of Film*. 2002.
Wada-Marciano, Mitsuyo. *Nippon Modern: Japanese Cinema of the 1920s and 1930s*. 2008.
Zhang, Yingjin. *Cinema and Urban Culture in Shanghai, 1922–1943*. 1999.

millions. Born of middle-class parents in a village on the west coast of India, Gandhi studied law in England and then began practice in the Indian community in South Africa. The racism he experienced there made him determined to liberate the Indian masses from British imperialism. When he returned to India permanently in 1915, he began a full-time drive for Hind Swaraj (HIHND swah-RAJ), or Indian Home Rule, to escape the violent, even genocidal values of Westerners engaged in world war. Using the media and making speeches, he challenged the view that Britain was "civilized" and thus worthy of respect. To Gandhi's way of thinking his fellow citizens had the story backward. South Asia had a very long tradition of civilization, he pointed out, while Britain and other Western countries, above all the United States, valued only one thing: material wealth. "Many problems can be solved," Gandhi wrote early in his career, "by remembering that money is their God."[17]

Gandhi envisioned a nonviolent return to an India of small self-sufficient communities in which people grew their own food and spun the cloth for their own clothes. Rejecting the modernization brought by factories and railroads, he dressed in a simple loincloth and shawl made from cloth he had woven himself. For Gandhi, the root cause of India's subjection was that Indian merchants had handed the country over to "Satanic" Western values and turned away from the Indian goals of contemplation and humility. He opposed scientific developments such as birth control and rejected the modern sensibility that wanted to eliminate the caste system.

In rejecting the West, Gandhi's resembled another potent organization for the empowerment of ordinary people—the Muslim Brotherhood, founded in Egypt in 1928. This organization called for a return to Islam along with a rejection of the secular, "modern" mindset. "Islam is the solution" was the Brotherhood's watchword as it sought to end British influence in the country. Like Gandhi's movement, the Muslim Brotherhood would grow in mass appeal.

In contrast, communism promised a shining future and a modern, technological culture. The reality was that workers' living conditions declined while Communist Party supervisors enjoyed a privileged life. In the early 1920s, workers, sailors, and peasant bands alike revolted against harsh Bolshevik policies toward ordinary people. The government had many of the rebels shot, but as production dropped to 13 percent of its prewar output, Lenin changed course. His **New Economic Policy** compromised with capitalism by allowing peasants to sell their grain freely and entrepreneurs to engage in trade and keep the profits. More food soon became available, and some peasants and merchants did indeed prosper.

Nonetheless, grassroots opposition drove the Bolsheviks to make communism not just a political ideology but a cultural reality that would guide the masses' daily lives and reshape their thoughts. Party leaders invaded the countryside to set up classes on a variety of political subjects, and volunteers pushed the importance of literacy—on the eve of World War I, less than half the people in the USSR could read. As commissar for public welfare, Aleksandra Kollontai promoted birth-control education, classes in "domestic science," and the establishment of day care for children of working parents. To advance literacy, she wrote simply worded novels about love and work in the new socialist state. The government tried to develop a mass proletarian culture through workers' universities, a workers' theater, and workers' publishing. For many, it worked: as one teacher and worker on a veterinary farm wrote in her diary, "I have discovered a new world for me in Marxism. I read with deep interest."[18]

Authoritarian rule came as well to Italy, though of a different nature from communism. Benito Mussolini (1883–1945) came to power as a mass hero. Since the late nineteenth century, some Europeans had come to blame their parliaments for economic ills. Thus many Italians were enthusiastic when Mussolini, a socialist journalist who had turned to the radical right, built a personal army called the "Black Shirts" of veterans and the unemployed and used it to overturn parliamentary government. In 1922, his supporters, known as Fascists, started a march on Rome, leading to Mussolini's appointment as prime minister. Although in theory he ruled with the consent of the masses, Mussolini consolidated his power by making criticism of the state a criminal offense, violently attacking opposition, and beating up striking workers. Yet the sight of hundreds of Black Shirts marching through the streets like disciplined soldiers signaled to many Italians that their country was ordered and modern.

Besides violence, Mussolini used mass propaganda and the media to promote traditional values and prejudices, though **fascism**, unlike communism, was never an organized set of principles, except for the principle that the state had supremacy over the people. Peasant men huddled around radios to hear him call for a "battle of wheat" to enhance farm productivity on behalf of the state. Peasant women worshiped him for

Sheikh Hassan al-Banna, Founder of the Muslim Brotherhood

Sheikh Hassan al-Banna founded the Muslim Brotherhood in 1928 and worked to make it a mass movement that would revive the standing of Islam and Muslim culture in the world. Dismayed at the respect given Western culture and the power of the West's economy, al-Banna built his organization as a counterweight. His commitment to anti-colonialism and Islamic values made him an enemy of the West's allies in the Middle East; they had him assassinated in 1949. (AFP/Getty Images.)

New Economic Policy Lenin's compromise with capitalism that allowed peasants to sell their grain on the market and entrepreneurs to engage in trade and keep the profits.

fascism A political movement originating in postwar Italy under Mussolini that stressed the primacy of the state over the individual and the importance of violence and warfare in making nations strong.

appearing to value motherhood as a patriotic calling. In the cities the government built strikingly modern buildings and broad avenues for Fascist parades. Despite these signs of modernity, Mussolini introduced a "corporate" state that denied individual rights in favor of duty to the state, as in wartime. Decrees in 1926 outlawed independent labor unions, replacing them with state-controlled employer and worker groups, or corporations, that would settle grievances and determine conditions of work. Mussolini cut women's wages and banned women from the professions, confining them to menial and low-paying jobs. His popularity soared among war-torn men, making him a model for other militaristic leaders.

COUNTERPOINT
A Golden Age for Argentineans

World War I allowed some societies outside of Europe to flourish. Both Japan and Australia increased their trade during the war. Indian entrepreneurs, aided by nationalist boycotts of British goods early in the twentieth century, continued to build metallurgical and other factories, substituting their goods for those of the warring European powers. In the Western Hemisphere, as European, Mexican, and other leaders were marching their nations down the road to war, Argentineans were experiencing a "golden age" that offered a stark contrast to the suffering elsewhere.

FOCUS

In what ways did Argentina's history differ from that of countries caught up in World War I?

A Flourishing Economy and Society

Starting in the 1880s, immigrants flocked to Argentina. Between 1900 and the outbreak of World War I in 1914, hundreds of thousands of newcomers moved to the bustling commercial city of Buenos Aires and the surrounding area. Argentina offered a rich, exciting blend of livelihoods, as traders imported European goods and as ranchers supplied world markets with leather, meat, and agricultural products. Industry was also taking off in Argentina, adding a new, more prosperous type of worker to the laboring classes.

World War I broke Argentina's dependence on Britain's economy and turned its productivity inward, so that after the war the economy continued to grow even into the Great Depression of the 1930s (discussed in the next chapter). The landed elites controlled Argentina's politics for most of this time, although strikers and anarchists made vocal demands for change. Reform came in 1912 when President Roque Sáenz Peña, an outspoken advocate of honest government, ushered in universal and obligatory voting by secret ballot for all men. This led to the election in 1916 of Radical Civil Union leader Hipólito Yrigoyen, a candidate whose popularity with workers and the middle classes made for relatively stable politics. Instead of experiencing the surge of extremism seen in Russia and Italy, the Argentinean political scene remained relatively moderate during these years.

Argentina, c. 1920

But there was one glaring exception. In December of 1918, workers began a general strike, forcing the government to step in and negotiate in mid-January. Despite the successful end to the strike, the middle and upper classes, many of European heritage, began looking for scapegoats, encouraging vigilante groups to turn on Jews. From January 10 to 14, 1919, these groups attacked Jewish property and arrested Jews. This anti-Semitic frenzy, called the "tragic week," would repeat itself in the 1960s and 1970s in Argentina.

The Argentine Tango

The tango developed in the cafés frequented by the sailors, dockworkers, and sex workers of Argentina at the turn of the twentieth century. Starting in what was then considered low-life society, this creation of Argentina's golden age subsequently traveled to Europe, where it underwent some modification and then returned to the Americas as a newly respectable if somewhat daring dance. During the twentieth century many elements of popular culture, including films, jazz, and, more recently, video games and hip-hop music, followed complicated routes in their development, much like the tango. (Music Division, The New York Public Library for the Performing Arts, Astor, Lenox, and Tilden Foundations.)

Argentina's Cultural Riches

Argentina's overall climate of growth, prosperity, and immigration helped spark an outburst of cultural creativity. A rich working-class culture brought the world the tango, an erotic modern dance improvised from African, Spanish, and local music. Danced either by a man and woman or by two men together, the tango's sensuality shocked Argentina's polite society while it spread to dance halls and nightclubs around the world.

A participant in the 1920s cultural life of Buenos Aires was poet, essayist, and short story writer Jorge Luis Borges, one of the leading authors of the twentieth century. Determined to move beyond the fashionable literary modernism then shaping Latin America writing, Borges was fascinated both with questions of personal identity, including his own and his ancestors', and with the mysteries of learning, remembering, and forgetting. "Seek for the pleasure of seeking, not of finding," Borges wrote, and his whole life seemed more concerned with disorder than with order, as was suggested by his imagined "Chinese encyclopedia," which divided animals into categories from "belonging to the Emperor" to "that from a long way off look like flies." As he wrote,

> I think about things that might have been and never
>   were . . .
> The vast empire the Vikings declined to found.
> The globe without the wheel, or without the rose.
> John Donne's judgment of Shakespeare.
> The unicorn's other horn.
> The fabled Irish bird which alights in two places at
>   once.
> The child I never had.[19]

Borges's imagination laid the groundwork for "magical realism," the late-twentieth-century movement in Latin American fiction from Gabriel Garcia Marquez and Isabel Allende, among many others. Even as much of Latin America, including Argentina, came to feel economic stresses as the century advanced, the golden-age culture has remained powerful down to the present day.

Conclusion

Competition among nations and the clash of classes led to the loss of tens of millions of lives in the decade between 1910 and 1920. Major dynasties were destroyed and governments overthrown, the aristocratic classes collapsed, and millions more suffered starvation, disease, and permanent disability. The decade changed political institutions around the world, leading to demands for national liberation and for collective security such as that provided in the League of Nations. While dynasties fell, the centralization of power increased the scope of the nation-state. Internationally, the Peace of Paris that settled World War I rearranged the map of Europe and parts of the world beyond, dismantling the Habsburg and Ottoman empires into new, intentionally small states in eastern and central Europe—a settlement that, given the dense intermingling of ethnicities, religions, and languages in the area, failed to guarantee a peaceful future. Some political leaders, such as Emiliano Zapata in Mexico and Mustafa Kemal in Turkey, were inspired by Western ideals and models; others, such as Mohandas Gandhi in India, rejected them. In the midst of it all, the United States rose to the status of a world power.

Just as modern warfare had introduced mass armies, world war furthered the development of mass society and culture. It leveled social classes on the battlefield and in the graveyard and standardized beliefs and behaviors, first through wartime propaganda and then through postwar popular culture. Production techniques improved during wartime were turned in peacetime to churning out consumer goods and technological innovations such as air transport, cinema, and radio transmission for greater numbers of people. By the end of the 1920s, mass culture was a key ingredient in politicians' efforts to continue mobilizing the masses as they had in wartime. Among the leaders who saw cultural issues as central to reshaping society were Lenin, Gandhi, and Mussolini. The global economic collapse of 1929 would lead to further mobilization of the masses, this time to support cruel dictators and even genocide.

NOTES

1. Plan de Ayala, quoted in Manuel Plana, *Pancho Villa et la Révolution Mexicaine*, trans. Bruno Gaudenzi (Florence, Italy: Castermann, 1993), 28.
2. Wang Jingwei, quoted in Prasenjit Duara, *Rescuing History from the Nation: Questioning Narratives of Modern China* (Chicago: University of Chicago Press, 1995), 141.
3. Anonymous letter, 17 February 1915, in David Omissi, ed., *Indian Voices of the Great War: Soldiers' Letters, 1914–1918* (London: Macmillan, 1919), 38.
4. Quoted in Oscar J. Martinez, *Fragments of the Mexican Revolution: Personal Accounts from the Border* (Albuquerque: University of New Mexico Press, 1983), 52.
5. Quoted in Margaret Macmillan, *Paris 1919: Six Months That Changed the World* (New York: Random House, 2001), 403.
6. Quoted in Merrill Peterson, *"Starving Armenians": America and the Armenian Genocide, 1915–1930* (Charlottesville: University of Virginia Press, 2004), 48.
7. Quoted in Andrew Mango, *Atatürk: The Biography of the Founder of Modern Turkey* (Woodstock, NY: Overlook, 1999), 278.
8. Quoted in Mango, *Atatürk*, 219.
9. Irfan Organ, *Portrait of a Turkish Family* (London: Eland, 1993), 223.
10. Quoted in Macmillan, *Paris 1919*, 340.
11. Quoted in Geoffrey Hodges, "Military Labour in East Africa," in Melvin Eugene Page, ed., *Africa and the First World War* (New York: St. Martin's Press, 1987), 146.
12. Quoted in Sally Marks, *The Ebbing of European Ascendancy: An International History of the World, 1914–1945* (London: Arnold, 2002), 219.
13. Quoted in Babacar Fall, *Le travail force en Afrique occidentale française (1900–1946)* (Paris: Karthala, 1993), 181.
14. Quoted in Michael Tsin, *Nation, Governance, and Modernity in China: Canton, 1900–1927* (Palo Alto, CA: Stanford University Press, 1999), 151.
15. Quoted in Wang Zheng, *Women in the Chinese Enlightenment: Oral and Textual Histories* (Berkeley: University of California Press, 1999), 196.
16. Quoted in Lynn Thomas, "The Modern Girl and Racial Respectability in South Africa," *Journal of African History* 47 (2006): 3, 485.
17. Mohandas Gandhi, "Hind Swaraj," in *The Collected Works of Mahatma Gandhi* (Ahmedabad: Navjivan Trust, Government of India, Publications Division, 1963), 23.
18. Quoted in Jochen Hellbeck, *Revolution on My Mind: Writing a Diary Under Stalin* (Cambridge, MA: Harvard University Press, 2006), 146.
19. Jorge Luis Borges, "Things That Might Have Been," in *Selected Poems*, ed. Alexander Coleman (New York: Viking, 1999), 405.

RESOURCES FOR RESEARCH

Revolutions, Local Wars, and World War

The revolutionary and military enthusiasm of the second decade of the twentieth century was almost unprecedented in history, as nations and monarchies experienced bloodshed and political upheaval. The following selections provide either a broad picture of events or individual accounts of warfare.

Gordon, David B. *Sun Yatsen: Seeking a Newer China.* 2009.

Hart, Paul. *Bitter Harvest: The Social Transformation of Morelos, Mexico, and the Origins of the Zapatista Revolution, 1840–1910.* 2005.

Lear, John. *Workers, Neighbors, and Citizens: The Revolution in Mexico City.* 2001.

Morrow, John J. *The Great War: An Imperial History.* 2005.

Paice, Edward. *World War I: The African Front.* 2011.

Revolution in Russia and the End of World War I

The Russian Revolution was a cataclysmic event with worldwide repercussions throughout the twentieth century. Healy shows the suffering that occurred in Vienna, whereas Roshwald captures the ethnic chaos that existed in the wake of war and revolution.

Healy, Maureen. *Vienna and the Fall of the Habsburg Empire: Total War and Everyday Life in World War I.* 2004.

Holquist, Peter. *Making War, Forging Revolution: Russia's Continuum of Crisis, 1914–1921.* 2002.

Phillips, Howard, and David Killingray, eds. *The Spanish Influenza Epidemic of 1918–1919: New Perspectives.* 2003.

Reynolds, Michael A. *Shattering Empires: The Clash and Collapse of the Ottoman and Russian Empires, 1908–1918.* 2011.

Roshwald, Aviel. *Ethnic Nationalism and the Fall of Empires: Central Europe, Russia and the Middle East, 1914–1923.* 2001.

Postwar Global Politics

Politicians reworked the international order in the 1920s, with mixed results. One of the most striking leaders of this period is Mustafa Kemal (Atatürk), creator of modern Turkey. Mango's biography captures the difficulty of Atatürk's task, especially in the face of international opposition from the Western powers.

Callahan, Michael D. *A Sacred Trust: The League of Nations and Africa, 1929–1946.* 2005.

Macmillan, Margaret. *Paris 1919: Six Months That Changed the World.* 2001.

Manela, Erez. *The Wilsonian Moment: Self-Determination and the International Origins of Anti-Colonial Nationalism.* 2007.

Mango, Andrew. *Atatürk: The Biography of the Founder of Modern Turkey.* 1999.

Marks, Sally. *The Ebbing of European Ascendancy: An International History of the World, 1914–1945.* 2002.

An Age of the Masses

Radio, film, and print media expanded people's access to information and general culture during the 1920s and in so doing helped create mass society. Vaughan and Lewis's anthology shows the impact of the media on postrevolutionary Mexico.

Helstosky, Carol. *Garlic and Oil: The Politics of Food in Italy.* 2004.

Hu, Jubin. *Projecting a Nation: Chinese National Cinema Before 1949.* 2003.

Northrup, Douglas. *Veiled Empire: Gender and Power in Stalinist Central Asia.* 2004.

Vaughan, Mary Kay, and Stephen E. Lewis, eds. *The Eagle and the Virgin: Nation and Cultural Revolution in Mexico, 1920–1940.* 2006.

Weinbaum, Alys Eve, et al. *Modern Girl Around the World: Consumption, Modernity, and Globalization.* 2008.

COUNTERPOINT: A Golden Age for Argentineans

While much of the world suffered intense disruption during the early twentieth century, the period constituted a "golden age" in Argentina. The works below draw a picture of that multifaceted prosperity.

Rodriguez, Julia. *Civilizing Argentina: Science, Medicine, and the Modern State.* 2006.

Romero, Luis Alberto. *A History of Argentina in the Twentieth Century.* Translated by James P. Brennan. 2002.

Woodall, James. *Borges: A Life.* 1996.

▶ **For additional primary sources from this period,** see *Sources of Crossroads and Cultures.*

▶ **For Web sites, images, and documents related to topics in this chapter,** see Make History at bedfordstmartins.com/smith.

The major global development in this chapter ▶ The wars of the decade 1910 to 1920 and their role in the creation of mass culture and society.

IMPORTANT EVENTS

1910	Mexican Revolution begins
1911–1912	Revolutionaries overthrow Qing dynasty in China
1912	First Balkan War
1913	Second Balkan War
1914	World War I begins
1917	Russian Revolution begins; United States enters World War I; Lenin returns to Russia
1918	Bolsheviks take full control of Russian government; Treaty of Brest-Litovsk; armistice ends World War I
1919	Germany forms Weimar Republic; May 4th movement in China
1919–1920	Treaties comprising Peace of Paris signed, including the Treaty of Versailles with Germany
1920s	Mohandas Gandhi's nonviolent movement for India independence attracts millions; mass culture flourishes in film and publishing industries; growth of radio transmissions; technology increases global productivity
1921	Lenin introduces New Economic Policy in Russia
1922	Civil war ends in Russia; Mussolini comes to power in Italy
1923	Founding of the independent republic of Turkey under Mustafa Kemal; formation of Union of Soviet Socialist Republics

KEY TERMS

Bolshevik (p. 903)
collective security (p. 907)
Comintern (p. 904)
fascism (p. 918)
Fourteen Points (p. 904)
Guomindang (p. 895)

League of Nations (p. 907)
mandate system (p. 908)
New Economic Policy (p. 918)
soviet (p. 902)
total war (p. 900)

CHAPTER OVERVIEW QUESTIONS

1. Why did the Mexican Revolution, the Chinese Revolution, World War I, and the Russian Revolution cause so much change far from the battlefield?

2. How did these wars help produce mass culture and society?

3. What role did technology play in these developments?

SECTION FOCUS QUESTIONS

1. What factors contributed to the wars of the early twentieth century?

2. Why did the Russian Revolution take place, and what changes did it produce in Russian politics and daily life?

3. What were the major outcomes of the peacemaking process and postwar conditions?

4. How did the rise of mass society affect politics, culture, and everyday life around the world?

5. In what ways did Argentina's history differ from that of countries caught up in World War I?

MAKING CONNECTIONS

1. In what ways did conditions at the end of World War I differ from those expected at the outbreak of the war?

2. Consider the empires discussed in Chapter 26. How did they change in the 1920s, and why?

3. How did World War I affect work and livelihoods?

4. How did the mass political movements that emerged during and after the war differ from one another?

AT A CROSSROADS ▲

This photograph of a Nazi rally held in 1938 in Nuremberg reveals how young people, among others, admired Hitler and all that he stood for: quick fixes to a depressed economy and the promise of renewed global power. His rhetoric of hatred rallied Germans across the social order to envision a better future once their nation had been purified of enemies such as Jews, who were actually their neighbors and fellow Germans. Popular support for Hitler's violent bigotry has made historians aware that the history of Nazism is not just the story of one charismatic leader, but also of the masses whose devotion was the source of his power. (bpk, Berlin/Art Resource, NY.)

Global Catastrophe: The Great Depression and World War II

1929–1945

E va Kantorowsky worked as a secretary and teacher of English in Shanghai during World War II. A cosmopolitan city, Shanghai attracted refugees from war-torn Europe from the 1930s on, especially those fleeing Adolf Hitler's brutal Nazi regime in Germany. Eva Kantorowsky was one of these, helped by her uncle's successful acquisition of three exit visas so that she, her mother, and her father—a rabbi in Berlin—could make their way across two continents to China in 1940. They left only after Eva's father had been repeatedly beaten by the Nazis. Their reluctance to leave Germany had another cause: Eva's uncle had neglected to get an exit visa for her brother Hans, who, the uncle mistakenly thought, had already left the country. After World War II ended in 1945, Eva's family received the crushing news that Hans had died in Auschwitz, murdered along with millions of fellow Jews as well as Slavs, Roma ("gypsies"), and other persecuted groups, in the genocide the Nazis hoped would purify their empire.

Eva Kantorowsky escaped this genocide—the Holocaust—and survived the most destructive war in world history. World War II, with a death toll of some one hundred

1929: The Great Depression Begins

FOCUS What was the global impact of both the Great Depression and the attempts to overcome it?

Militarizing the Masses in the 1930s

FOCUS How did dictatorships and democracies attempt to mobilize the masses?

Global War, 1937–1945

FOCUS How did World War II progress on the battlefront and the home front?

From Allied Victory to the Cold War, 1943–1945

FOCUS How did the Allied victory unfold, and what were the causes of that victory?

COUNTERPOINT: Nonviolence and Pacifism in an Age of War

FOCUS In what ways did peace movements serve as a countertrend to events in the period from 1929 to 1945?

BACKSTORY

As we saw in Chapter 27, in 1918 World War I ended, and with it fell four major empires: the Ottoman, Russian, Austro-Hungarian, and German. The victorious Western powers took the colonies and other lands of the defeated German and Ottoman empires, expanding the "new imperialism" (see Chapter 26). Significant changes in the nature of government and in the relationship between governments and their peoples accompanied the new geopolitical order. In countries around the world, governments grew larger and more powerful, taking advantage of the new mass media to promote a uniform culture that stressed the central importance of patriotism and national identity. In the political and economic turmoil that followed the war, the same mass media contributed to the rise of stridently nationalist dictators. When a worldwide depression struck in the late 1920s, these dictators, backed by modern bureaucracies and military technology, grew more dangerous. Intent on expanding their nation's boundaries and empires, they posed a grave threat to world peace.

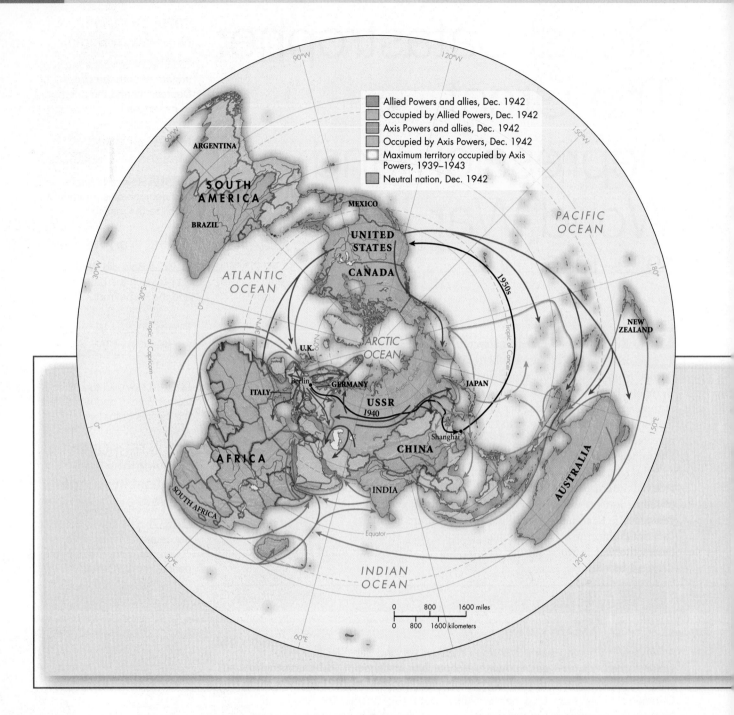

Allied Powers and allies, Dec. 1942
Occupied by Allied Powers, Dec. 1942
Axis Powers and allies, Dec. 1942
Occupied by Axis Powers, Dec. 1942
Maximum territory occupied by Axis Powers, 1939–1943
Neutral nation, Dec. 1942

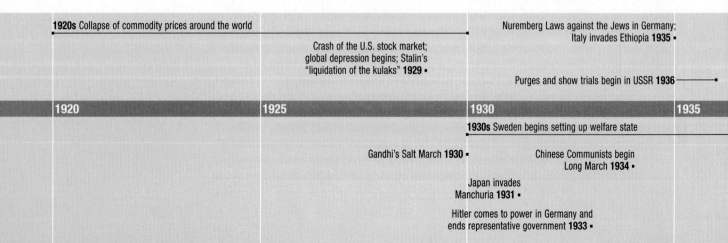

1920s Collapse of commodity prices around the world

Crash of the U.S. stock market; global depression begins; Stalin's "liquidation of the kulaks" **1929** ▪

Nuremberg Laws against the Jews in Germany; Italy invades Ethiopia **1935** ▪

Purges and show trials begin in USSR **1936** ▪

| 1920 | 1925 | 1930 | 1935 |

1930s Sweden begins setting up welfare state

Gandhi's Salt March **1930** ▪

Chinese Communists begin Long March **1934** ▪

Japan invades Manchuria **1931** ▪

Hitler comes to power in Germany and ends representative government **1933** ▪

million people, capped off a decade of suffering that began with the Great Depression of the 1930s, a global economic catastrophe that was sparked by the crash of the U.S. stock market in 1929. The crash opened a tragic era in world history, a time when people around the world were connected by their shared experience of economic hardship, war, and genocide. The Great Depression intensified social protest throughout the world. In Japan, China, Italy, Germany, and across Latin America, strongmen took power and militarized the masses, promising that disciplined obedience would end their troubles. Adolf Hitler roused the German masses to pursue national greatness by scorning democracy and scapegoating "inferior" and "menacing" Jews such as the Kantorowsky family. Joseph Stalin believed that the Soviet Union's rapid industrialization was worth the lives of the millions of citizens who died remaking their nation in the 1930s. For militaristic authoritarian regimes around the world, human rights and democratic institutions were nothing more than obstacles to national greatness.

Elected leaders in established democracies reacted ineffectively to the depression and the militarism it spawned. The League of Nations, formed after World War I to preserve world peace, ignored Japan's aggression in China, Italy's in Ethiopia, and Germany's in Europe. Whether in China or central Europe, aggression followed aggression until Hitler's invasion of Poland in 1939 and Japan's bombing of Pearl Harbor in 1941 finally pushed the democracies to declare war. By the end of 1941, Great Britain, France, the Soviet

MAPPING THE WORLD

World War II, 1937–1945

The Great Depression spread economic hardship, which was compounded by the advance of militarism and empire. Japan's drive to expand its empire early in the 1930s was followed by Italy's campaigns for empire in Africa and the German takeover of central and eastern Europe. These aspiring powers used increasingly formidable weaponry, lightning speed, and massive attacks on civilians. The culmination was World War II, which broke out in 1937 in East Asia and 1939 in Europe, ending only in 1945. The Great Depression and World War II stand out in human history as an era of unprecedented suffering.

ROUTES ▼

Troop movements during World War II

Axis offensive, 1939–1942

→ German

→ Japanese

Allied counteroffensive to front lines, 1942–1945

→ British

→ British colonial and Commonwealth

→ Soviet

→ U.S.

→ Probable travels of Eva Kantorowsky, 1940–1950s

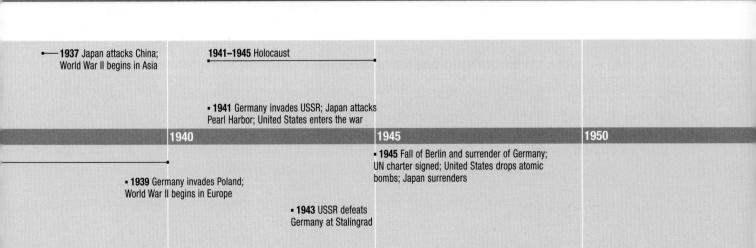

1937 Japan attacks China; World War II begins in Asia

1941–1945 Holocaust

• **1941** Germany invades USSR; Japan attacks Pearl Harbor; United States enters the war

1940   1945   1950

• **1945** Fall of Berlin and surrender of Germany; UN charter signed; United States drops atomic bombs; Japan surrenders

• **1939** Germany invades Poland; World War II begins in Europe

• **1943** USSR defeats Germany at Stalingrad

Union, and the United States were locked in combat with Germany, Italy, and Japan. The coalition that formed to stop Germany and its partners was an uneasy one, however, and by the end of the war the world's reigning military superpowers, the United States and the Soviet Union, regarded each other with deep distrust born of ideological differences. As hot war turned to cold war after 1945, tens of millions more became homeless refugees, among them Eva Kantorowsky. In this most destructive war in human history, however, she was among the lucky ones: global migration helped her survive. The dense network of economic and political connections that had made the Great Depression a global event and drawn the world into war also provided routes for some individuals to escape persecution and suffering in their home countries.

OVERVIEW
QUESTIONS

The major global development in this chapter: The causes and outcomes of the Great Depression and World War II.

As you read, consider:

1. How did ordinary people react to the Great Depression, and how did their reactions differ from country to country?

2. Why were dictators and antidemocratic leaders able to come to power in the 1930s, and how did all countries—autocratic and democratic alike—militarize the masses?

3. How are the Great Depression and World War II related historical events?

1929: The Great Depression Begins

FOCUS

What was the global impact of both the Great Depression and the attempts to overcome it?

A rapid decline in agricultural prices in the 1920s followed by the U.S. stock market crash of 1929 threw tens of millions out of work and wrecked the prospects of rural people worldwide. Economic depression spread from continent to continent as commerce and investment in industry declined, social life and gender roles were upset, and the birthrate plummeted. People everywhere, from farmers to industrial workers, saw their livelihoods destroyed. Despair turned to outrage, as many rose up in rebellion, embracing militaristic solutions to their nation's problems.

Economic Disaster Strikes

U.S. Stock Market Crash

In the 1920s, U.S. corporations and banks as well as millions of individual Americans invested their money (often borrowed) in the stock market, which seemed to churn out endless profits. Confident that stock prices would continue to rise, they used easy credit to buy shares in companies based on electric, automotive, and other new technologies. At the end of the decade, the Federal Reserve Bank—the nation's central bank, which controlled financial policy—tightened the availability of credit in an attempt to stabilize the market. To meet the new restrictions, brokers demanded that their clients immediately pay back the money they had borrowed to buy stock. As investors sold their stocks to raise cash and repay their loans, the wave of selling caused prices on the stock market to collapse. Between early October and mid-November 1929, the value of businesses listed on the U.S. stock market—and thus of people's investments through the stocks they owned in those businesses—dropped nearly two-thirds, from $87 billion to $30 billion. Individuals lost their money, and a breakdown of the economy as a whole followed.

The stock market crash helped spark the global economic collapse known as the **Great Depression**, because the United States, a leading international creditor, had financed the economic growth of the previous five years by lending money for business development around the world. Suddenly strapped themselves, U.S. financiers cut back drastically on loans and called in debts, weakening banks and industry at home and abroad. Creditors to newly created industries in India, for example, demanded repayment of loans and refused to finance further expansion. In Europe, the lack of credit and the decline in consumer buying caused businesses to close, workers to be laid off, and the European economy to slump. By 1933, almost 6 million German workers, or about one-third of the workforce, were unemployed, and many others were underemployed. The effects of the economic collapse were uneven, however: a few Latin American countries were able to expand domestic consumption enough at least partially to offset lost sales abroad.

In general, though, rural and urban folk alike suffered as tens of millions lost their livelihoods. For farmers, times had been tough for years. In the 1920s, technological innovation and a number of other factors combined to produce record crops and, consequently, falling farm prices. Canada, Australia, Argentina, and the United States had increased their production of wheat while World War I was raging in Europe; they did not cut back when the war ended and Europe became productive again. In the mid-1920s the price of wheat collapsed. Prices for other consumables, such as coffee and sugar, also tumbled, creating dire consequences in Africa, Asia, and some Latin American countries as large-scale farmers—either local magnates or white settlers—bought up the land of struggling small producers. Prices fell even for commodities such as rice, for which there was not a surplus, until by 1931 farmers were receiving 50 percent less for their crops than they had a few years earlier. As a result, rural consumption of manufactured goods dropped too. Thus, problems in agriculture were directly connected to industrial decline.

Government responses to the crisis made a bad situation worse. Great Britain went off the gold standard, which had the effect of depreciating its currency, thus making imports more expensive and cutting the sales of its trading partners. Other countries followed suit, blocking imports with high tariffs in hopes of sparking purchases of domestically produced goods. Measures such as cutting budgets were also part of accepted economic theory at the time, but reductions in spending only further undermined demand, leading to more business failures and higher unemployment. Governments in Latin America and eastern Europe often ignored the farmers' plight as they poured available funds into industrialization—a policy that increased tensions in rural society.

One solution for the imperial powers was to increase economic exploitation in the colonies. World War I and postwar investment had generated economic growth, a rising population, and explosive urbanization outside of Europe. Between 1920 and 1940, Calcutta ballooned from 1.8 million to 3.4 million residents and Saigon from 180,000 to 256,000, making them more attractive as markets and sources of tax revenue. Now the imperial powers demanded that colonial subjects pay higher taxes, no matter how desperate the local peoples' plight, to compensate for falling revenues back home. In the Belgian Congo, local farmers paid a per-person tax—called a poll or head tax—equivalent to one-sixth of their crops in the 1920s and one-fourth in the 1930s. Britain took its domestic economy off the gold standard, but it forced colonies such as India to pay taxes and other charges in gold. India's farmers stripped the subcontinent of its stores of gold to turn in every scrap of the precious metal, including women's jewelry, to meet British demands. During hard times, most imperial powers were able to shift at least some of their financial burden to their colonial subjects in Asia and Africa.

Global Economic Collapse

Government Response

Great Depression The economic crisis of the 1930s that began in agricultural regions through a severe drop in commodity prices in the 1920s and then, with the U.S. stock market crash of 1929, spread to industrial countries.

Promoting Business in the Great Depression

Winifred Tete-Ansa was an innovative businessman in Nigeria and the Gold Coast. He set up a cooperative so that Gold Coast cocoa growers could market their own products outside the imperial system. Then he established a bank to finance African-owned businesses such as trade in mahogany, palm oil, and other local commodities because European-owned banks would not. In 1930, at a time of economic depression and growing opposition to colonialism, Tete-Ansa explained to African Americans in this prospectus why he had started a bank to help finance African trade cooperatives. He urged these readers to contribute financially to his work.

Picture a land one-eighth as large as the United States and with a population one-fifth as great, where the people grow three-fifths of the world's cocoa supply. . . .

By the time this vast business has reached the ultimate consumer, over half a billion dollars have changed hands, and enormous profits have accrued to those of the white race who have furnished the necessary capital and directed the labor of thousands of the Negro race. A reasonable earning power on wealth of some five billion of dollars is thus developed, and the greater portion of these earnings go [*sic*] to the members of the white race. . . .

Realize, if you will, the cities to be built and rebuilt, harbors to be developed, rivers to be harnessed, power to be developed and transmitted, railroads to be built, trains to be run, the cities to be lighted, water to be piped, sanitary arrangements to be installed and metals to be found and processed, the engines, motors, shafting, buildings necessary to turn the potential of raw products into highly saleable commodities at a higher price. . . .

We of West Africa have taken the natural advantages of our country and have now fashioned them into a sphere of opportunity. On account of the vast area, the enormous number of our race habitant there and the sound foundation for progress that we have built, it now forms the most important sphere of opportunity for industrial success of the Negro and by the Negro; and a well-built, well-lubricated vehicle to carry on toward industrial emancipation.

This vehicle needs capital to furnish it power to propel itself, and passengers to occupy its seats. We have provided the driver to direct it and the roads for it to travel. It is to be hoped that you, Negroes of America, will help furnish this power and the passengers for this journey to the Industrial Precedence of the Race.

Source: Winifred Tete-Ansa, *Africa at Work* (n.p., 1930), 78, 86–87.

EXAMINING THE EVIDENCE

1. What kind of global vision does Tete-Ansa present?

2. How would you describe his approach to colonialism?

3. How does he address the problem of livelihoods in hard times for Africans?

Social Effects of the Great Depression

The Great Depression caused enormous hardship for many, but its social and economic effects were complex and not entirely negative. Despite the economic crisis, modernization proceeded, whether in the form of building new roads in Africa or bringing electricity to the Soviet Union (see Reading the Past: Promoting Business in the Great Depression). Wealthy individual Chinese living abroad poured money into modernizing their homeland, investing in profitable development projects. Bordering English slums, one British observer in the mid-1930s noticed, were "filling stations and factories that look like exhibition buildings, giant cinemas and dance halls and cafés, bungalows with tiny garages, cocktail bars, Woolworth's [and] swimming pools." Municipal and national governments modernized sanitation, and running water, electricity, and sewage pipes were installed in many homes throughout the world for the first time. New factories manufactured synthetic fabrics, new electrical products such as stoves, and improved automobiles.

The Fortunate   Despite oft-repeated stories of thousands of ruined stockbrokers committing suicide, many in the upper classes prospered during the Great Depression. In Kenya, southern

Indochina, and elsewhere, large landowners evicted tenants who were unable to pay their rents and replaced them with cheaper day laborers. Moneylenders in India and Burma loaned peasants money to pay their rising taxes—due before the harvest. When agricultural prices fell early in the 1930s, some could not repay these loans, and moneylenders and large landowners alike took over the peasants' lands. Moreover, whereas rising tariffs, the turn to self-sufficiency, and the loss of foreign markets such as Britain hurt many international traders, merchants engaged in domestic trade managed to survive. Colombia, Brazil, Chile, Mexico, and Argentina actually showed either rising production or increased exports by 1932–1933. Throughout the Great Depression arms manufacturers made huge profits as nations such as Germany militarized. The majority of Europeans and Americans had jobs throughout the 1930s, and those with steady employment benefited from the drastic drop in consumer prices.

Even employed people, however, saw the millions of others around them struggling for a bare existence. In Cuba, where sugar prices collapsed, workers who did not lose their jobs were no longer paid, but simply fed a meal of "black or *caritas* beans, with their accompanying scum of weevils and worms . . . garbage that had no market," as one sugar worker described the food.[1] Because of the slump in agricultural prices, Japanese farmers were often reduced to eating tree bark, grass, and acorns and even gave up working: "Better to remain idle and eat less than work hard and eat more than can be earned," was the motto of some.[2] In towns with heavy industry, sometimes more than half the population was out of work. In a 1932 school assignment, a German youth wrote: "My father has been out of work for two-and-a-half years. He thinks that I'll never find a job." Under these conditions, a storm cloud of fear, resentment, and hopelessness settled over many parts of the globe.

The Destitute

Economic catastrophe strained social stability and upset gender relations. The collapse of prices for rice and raw silk made some Japanese peasants so desperate that they sold their daughters into prostitution. As taxes increased in Africa, men migrated to regions hundreds of miles from their families in search of better jobs, weakening family ties. In urban areas of Europe and the United States unemployed men stayed home all day, increasing the tension in small, overcrowded apartments. Men who stayed at home sometimes took over housekeeping chores, but others found this "women's work" emasculating. Women around the world could often find low-paying jobs doing laundry and other domestic service; some brewed and marketed beer and prepared foods from their homes. As many women became breadwinners, albeit for low wages, men could be seen standing on street corners begging—a reversal of gender expectations that fueled discontent.

Gender Relations

Rural men also faced the erosion of patriarchal authority, which was once central to overseeing farm labor and allocating property among heirs. Some lost their land entirely, and others had fewer children because of the economic slump. Mandatory education—and thus more years of required schooling—reduced family income and increased expenses for parents. Working-class children no longer earned wages to contribute to household income and were no longer available to help the family in other ways; instead they cost money while they went to school. Family-planning centers opened to help working people reduce family size in hard times. In a wide variety of ways, hard times disrupted the most fundamental human connections–the relationships among family members.

Protesting Poverty

The Great Depression produced rising protest by the unemployed. Often led by activists trained in the USSR, Communist parties flourished in the Chinese countryside, Indochina, the United States, Latin America, and across Europe, because they helped organize strikes and promised to end joblessness and exploitation. Mexican artist Diego Rivera captured the experiences of ordinary working people and the appeal of communism to them in huge murals he painted for public buildings. These massive paintings featured workers in factories and on farms, with portraits of Marx, Lenin, and Trotsky prominently intermingled with those of ordinary laborers. Union members in cities as distant as Shanghai, Detroit,

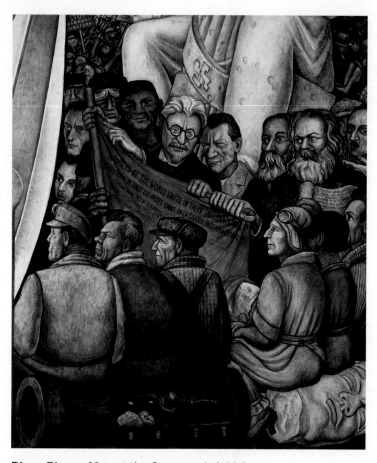

Diego Rivera, *Man at the Crossroads* (1934)
Communism and socialism appealed to workers both as ideologies and as political movements during the Great Depression, because they focused on ordinary people's needs. Mexican artist Diego Rivera had no love for the Soviet Union, yet he also considered communism to be an answer to the plight of native Americans and the oppressed around the world. In this mural, painted for Rockefeller Center in New York City but then torn down because of its image of Lenin, workers from many walks of life and ethnicities flock to the red flag and the message of Marx, Trotsky, and Lenin. (The Art Archive/Museo del Palacio de Bellas Artes Mexico/Dagli Orti.)

and Paris took to the streets to demand relief. In 1935, women textile workers in Medellin, Colombia, rose in angry protest about low wages and the insulting behavior of bosses. "Look, they'd go after the companies or whatever it was with rocks," said one woman of the strikers. "It was rough, it was bitter," she added.[3] Union leaders turned their wrath on big business. "Revolutions grow out of the depths of hunger," warned William Green, head of the American Federation of Labor, in 1931. For their part, governments and even factory owners responded with guns: police in Kobe, Japan, fought dockworkers, and government troops joined in crushing the demonstrators. U.S. automobile magnate Henry Ford turned his private police force on unemployed workers outside one of his plants, killing four of them and wounding far more. During the Great Depression, the masses had to defend their lives as well as their livelihoods.

Economic distress added to smoldering grievances in the colonies. As prices on commodities such as coffee, tin, and copper sank, colonial farmers withheld their produce from imperial wholesalers. Farmers in Ghana, for example, refused to sell cocoa in the 1930s. Discontent ran deep across the Middle East and Asia as well, fueled by the injustices of the World War I peace settlement, increasing colonial taxation, and hard economic times. General strikes rocked Palestine and India in 1936 and 1937, respectively. Their resolve fortified by bitter experiences, by the example of Japan's rising power, and by their own industrial development, colonial peoples roused themselves in an effort to overturn the imperial order.

Western-educated native leaders such as Ho Chi Minh, founder of the Indochinese Communist Party, led popular movements to contest their people's subjection. In 1930 the French government brutally crushed the peasant uprising Ho led. During the 1930s millions more working people came to follow Mohandas Gandhi, the charismatic leader of

Imperialist Response to Popular Uprisings

the Indian independence movement. The British jailed Gandhi repeatedly, stirred up Hindu-Muslim antagonism, and massacred protesters. Britain, France, and other European countries were quick to use their military might to put down colonial uprisings in an effort to preserve their empires. At the same time, however, they were slow to recognize a much greater threat to their well-being. As totalitarianism spread across Europe, the Western democracies responded with little more than words.

Militarizing the Masses in the 1930s

FOCUS

How did dictatorships and democracies attempt to mobilize the masses?

Representative government collapsed in many countries under the sheer weight of social and economic crisis. Japanese military men promoted overseas conquest as a solution to the depression, and even poor peasants donated funds to Japan's military cause. After 1929, Italy's Benito Mussolini, the Soviet Union's Joseph Stalin, and Germany's Adolf Hitler gained vast support for their regimes by mobilizing the masses in ways that had previously been attempted only in times of war. This common commitment to the use of political violence has led historians to apply the term **totalitarianism** to the Fascist, Communist, and Nazi regimes of the 1930s. The term refers to highly centralized systems of government that attempt to control society and ensure obedience through a single party and police terror. Many citizens admired Mussolini, Stalin, and Hitler for the discipline they brought to social and economic life, and overlooked the brutal side of totalitarian government. Unity and soldier-like obedience—not individual rights and open debate—were seen as keys to recovery.

To mobilize the masses, politicians also appealed to racist sentiment. "Superior" peoples were selfishly failing to flourish and breed, they charged, while growing numbers of "inferior" peoples were seeking to take their place. For the Japanese, the Chinese and Koreans were the "inferiors"; for Germans, Jews were the enemy and all others were inferiors. In the United States, some politicians built popular support by scapegoating Mexican Americans and other minorities. Targeting an enemy—whether fellow citizens of different faiths, colors, or ethnicities, or an entire country—enabled popular leaders to mobilize the masses to fight this internal or external enemy instead of building national unity around democratically solving economic problems.

The Rise of Stalinism

Joseph Stalin, who succeeded Lenin in 1929, led the astonishing transformation of the USSR in the 1930s from a predominantly agricultural society into a formidable industrial power. In 1929 Stalin ended Lenin's New Economic Policy, which (as we saw in Chapter 27) combined elements of Marxism and capitalism, and replaced it with the first of several **five-year plans** intended to mobilize Soviet citizens to industrialize the nation. Stalin's economic transformations reduced individual freedom and cost the lives of millions.

Transforming the Economy and Society

Stalin outlined a program for massive increases in the output of coal, iron ore, steel, and industrial goods over successive five-year periods. Without an end to economic backwardness, Stalin warned, "the advanced countries . . . will crush us." He thus established **central economic planning**, a policy of government direction of the economy, as used in World War I and increasingly favored by economists and industrialists around the world. Between 1929 and 1940, the number of Soviet workers in industry, construction, and transport grew from 4.6 million to 12.6 million, and production soared. Stalin's first five-year plan helped make the USSR a leading industrial nation, and one that was ultimately able to withstand the test of world war.

Central planning created a new elite class of bureaucrats and industrial officials, who dominated Soviet workers, forcing them to leave the countryside to work in state-run factories. While Communist officials enjoyed benefits such as country homes and luxurious vacations, untrained workers from the countryside were herded into barracklike dwellings or tents and endured dangerous factory conditions. Still, many believed in the promise of communism and took pride in learning new skills: "We mastered this profession—completely new to us—with great pleasure," a female lathe operator recalled. They tolerated intense suffering because, as one worker put it, "Man himself is being rebuilt." Nonetheless, new workers often lacked the technical education necessary to achieve the goals prescribed by the five-year plan, and official lying about productivity became a regular practice.

The Soviet government also drastically changed conditions on the land. Faced with peasants' refusal simply to turn over their grain to the government, Stalin called for the "liquidation of the kulaks" (koo-LAHKS). The word *kulak*, which literally means "fist," was first an insulting Soviet term for a prosperous peasant, but it came to apply to any independent farmer. One Russian remembered believing kulaks were "bloodsuckers, cattle, swine, loathsome, repulsive: they had no souls; they stank," and were "enemies of the state." Party workers robbed farmers of their possessions, left them to starve, or even murdered them outright. Confiscated kulak land formed the basis of the new collective farms,

totalitarianism A single-party form of government emerging after World War I in which the ruling political party seeks to control all parts of the social, cultural, economic, and political lives of the population, typically making use of mass communication and violence to instill its ideology and maintain power.

five-year plan One of the centralized programs for economic development instituted by Joseph Stalin in the USSR and copied by Adolf Hitler in Germany; these plans set production priorities and targets for individual industries and agriculture.

central economic planning A policy of government direction of the economy, established during World War I and increasingly used in peacetime.

Socialist Realist Art

The early days of the Bolshevik Revolution witnessed experimentation in social and sexual relationships and in the arts. Under Stalin the government sponsored the official artistic style called "socialist realism"; it featured smiling workers with glowing complexions who radiated a sense of supreme happiness. Often taken as hypocritical, given the actual living conditions in the Soviet Union, socialist realist art in fact looked to the future—what socialist society would be when it reached the state of perfection for which everyone should strive and sacrifice. (akg-images/Michael Teller.)

where the remaining peasants were forced to live and to share facilities and modern machinery. Traditional peasant life was brought to a violent end as the social and economic connections that bound rural residents to one another and to society at large were redrawn.

The result of the Communist experiment with collective farming was mass starvation, as Soviet grain harvests declined from 83 million tons in 1930 to 67 million in 1934. Economic failure became a political issue, and Stalin blamed the crisis not on inexperienced workers but on enemies of communism. He instituted **purges**—that is, state-approved violence that included widespread arrests, imprisonments in labor camps, and executions. Beginning in 1936, a series of "show trials" based on trumped-up charges and fabricated evidence resulted in the conviction and execution of former Bolshevik leaders and thousands of military officers for conspiring against the USSR. Simultaneously, the government expanded the system of lethal prison camps—called the *Gulag*, an acronym for the department that ran the camps—to stretch several thousand miles from Moscow to Siberia. Prisoners did every kind of work, from digging canals to building apartment complexes in Moscow. With 1 million dying annually from the harsh conditions, the casualties of the Soviet system far exceeded those in Nazi Germany in the 1930s.

Militarization in the 1930s curtailed personal freedom. As the population declined from famine, purges, and a rapid drop in the birthrate in the 1930s, the USSR ended the reproductive freedom of the early revolutionary years, restricting access to birth-control information and abortion and criminalizing homosexuality. Yet because of state programs, women across the Soviet Union made gains in literacy and received better health care. Positions in the lower ranks of the Communist Party opened to women as the purges continued, and women increasingly were accepted into the professions. Still, the burden on women was great. After working long hours in factories, they had to stand in line for scarce consumer goods and perform all household and child-care tasks.

Stalin used artists and writers—"engineers of the soul," he called them—to help mobilize the masses. In return for housing, office space, and secretarial help, the "comrade artist" adhered to the official style of "socialist realism," which depicted workers as full of rosy emotions—a rosiness reflecting less communist reality than its promises for future fulfillment. Some artists, such as the poet Anna Akhmatova (ahk-MAH-toh-vah), protested the harsh Soviet reality. "Stars of death stood above us, and Russia, / In her innocence, twisted in pain / Under blood-spattered boots," wrote Akhmatova of the 1930s, as she stood in line outside a Soviet prison, waiting for news of her son, who was being held there. Once a prosperous and celebrated writer, Akhmatova was reduced to living off the generosity of her friends as a result of her resistance.

purge In the USSR in the 1930s, one of a series of attacks on citizens accused of being enemies of the state.

Despite such notable exceptions, Stalin triumphantly militarized the masses in his warlike campaign to industrialize in the 1930s, becoming to them, as one worker put it, "a god on earth."[4] Admirers from around the world headed to the USSR to see the "workers' paradise" for themselves and to learn how to mobilize mass support in other countries.

Japanese Expansionism

The Great Depression struck Japan's economy as it was recovering from a catastrophic earthquake that had killed more than 140,000 people and laid waste to both the capital of Tokyo and the bustling port city of Yokohama. The earthquake sparked murders—led by the military—of Korean and Chinese workers in the area as somehow responsible for the devastation. In 1925, men over the age of twenty-five had received the vote and the young Hirohito (heer-oh-HEE-toh) had become emperor, but the economic downturn and social unrest made Japan unstable.

An ambitious military, impatient with Japan's weak democratic institutions, sought control of the government, as did politicians favoring improved representative government. A modernizing economy and growing world trade had unleashed social change, and reformers challenged traditional values such as women's obedience. Author Junichiro Tanizaki captured the clash of old and new worldviews in novels such as *Naomi* (1924–1925), in which an engineer is totally obsessed with an independent "new woman," and *The Makioka Sisters* (1943–1948), some of whose protagonists struggle to protect tradition amid relentless change.

The Japanese military won out over the liberal politicians. Military leaders offered their own solution to the depressed conditions of workers, peasants, and business people: conquer nearby regions to provide new farmlands and create markets. Japanese peasants, hampered in the pursuit of their livelihoods, would settle new areas such as Manchuria, while business people would benefit from a larger pool of consumers, workers, and raw materials in annexed lands. Viewing China and the Western powers as obstacles to Japan's prosperity, Japan's military leaders promoted the idea that the military was an institution unto itself, an "emperor's army" not subject to civilian control, and that it would bring about a new world order and the fulfillment of Japan's destiny. By the 1930s, Emperor Hirohito and his advisers had built public support for a militaristic imperial system. Renewed military vigor was seen as key to Japan's claims to racial superiority and its entitlement to the lands of people they considered "inferior"—such as the Chinese. Such claims linked Japan with Germany and Italy in the 1930s, setting the stage for a menacing global alliance.

The Japanese army took the lead in making these claims a reality: in September 1931 it blew up a Japanese-owned train in the Chinese province of Manchuria and made the incident look like an attack on Japan by placing corpses dressed in official Chinese uniforms alongside the tracks. The military then used the explosion as an excuse to invade the territory, set up a puppet government, and push farther into China (see Map 28.1). Journalists back in Japan rallied the public to condemn Chinese aggression and support expansion into China. China appealed to the League of Nations in protest. Although the League condemned the invasion, it imposed no penalties or economic sanctions against Japan. Meanwhile the Japanese army dealt with the democratic opposition by simply assassinating them.

The Chinese did not sit idly by in the face of Japan's invasion. In 1934 Jiang Jieshi (Chiang Kai-shek) introduced the "New Life" Movement, whose aim was "to militarize the

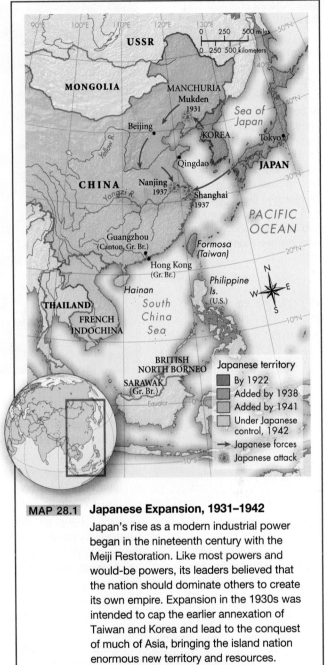

MAP 28.1 **Japanese Expansion, 1931–1942**

Japan's rise as a modern industrial power began in the nineteenth century with the Meiji Restoration. Like most powers and would-be powers, its leaders believed that the nation should dominate others to create its own empire. Expansion in the 1930s was intended to cap the earlier annexation of Taiwan and Korea and lead to the conquest of much of Asia, bringing the island nation enormous new territory and resources.

The Manchurian Incident

China's New Life Movement

Jiang Jieshi and Mai-ling Soong

Jiang Jieshi took control of the Nationalist government in China and campaigned to promote regular exercise and hygiene as part of his modernization efforts. At the time of this 1927 photograph, Mai-ling Soong, from one of China's wealthiest families and sister-in-law of Sun Yatsen, was Jiang's fiancée. Having crossed the globe, she represented the "new woman" with her U.S. college education, unbound feet, and Western clothing. (Bettmann/Corbis.)

life of the people" and to make them "willing to sacrifice for the nation at all times."[5] The New Life Movement was inspired by European fascist militarism, with its promise of national unity, but the program also promoted discipline in everyday life through cleanliness and exercise. Some nationalist reformers saw the position of women as key to modernizing and strengthening China. Traditions such as foot-binding were attacked as old-fashioned, and by the mid-1930s there were some six thousand institutions of higher education for women in China. To Jiang, national unity demanded mobilization on the political level against the Chinese Communist Party—not the Japanese. Ultimately, however, Jiang was forced to join the Communists in fighting the Japanese instead of fighting one another.

Mobilization of the Masses in Japan

Japanese army leaders, countering increasing Chinese unity and purpose, mobilized their own people, using the mass media to create a "people's patriotism" among poor farmers and factory workers. In 1933, the film *Japan in the National Emergency* depicted the utopian mission of Japan "to create an ideal land in East Asia" where under Japanese leadership the races would harmoniously join together. Decadent Western culture—notably its racism, the film claimed—showed that Japan as a whole needed to turn away from the West and return to protecting the "sacred spirit" of the nation.[6] Propagandists encouraged Japanese citizens to renounce individual rights: "even in our private lives we always remember to unite with the emperor and serve the state."[7] Labor unions supported militarization, pressing impoverished workers to contribute funds for the military. By 1937, Japan's government was spending 47 percent of its budget on weaponry, thanks to the successful mobilization of people from all classes.

Hitler's Rise to Power

Mass politics reached terrifying proportions in Germany when Adolf Hitler finally achieved his goal of overthrowing German democracy. In his book *Mein Kampf* ("My Struggle," 1925), he laid out his vision of "scientific" anti-Semitism and the rebirth of the German "race," a vision he attempted to implement through his leadership of the Nazi

Party (National Socialist German Workers' Party). When the Great Depression struck Germany, the Nazis began to outstrip their rivals in elections, thanks in part to support from some big businessmen and the press. Hitler's election as chancellor in 1933 launched twelve years of violent Nazi rule.

Foremost among the Nazis' supporters were idealistic youth, who believed that Germany could recapture its former glory only if Hitler took control, and also white-collar workers and the lower middle class, who were still hurting from the postwar inflation that had destroyed their savings. By targeting all their parliamentary opponents as a single, monolithic group of "Bolshevik" enemies, the Nazis won wide approval for confronting those they accused of causing the depression. Many thought it was time to replace democratic government with a bold new leader who would take on these enemies militarily, without concern for constitutions, laws, or individual rights.

Appeal of Nazism

Hitler devised modern propaganda techniques to build his appeal. Thousands of recordings of Hitler's speeches and other Nazi souvenir items circulated among the public, and Nazi rallies were masterpieces of mass spectacle. Hitler, however, viewed the masses with contempt: "The receptivity of the great masses is very limited, their intelligence is small. In consequence of these facts, all effective propaganda must be limited to a very few points and must harp on those in slogans." Germany's power brokers from the military, industry, and the state bureaucracy, fearing the Communists for their opposition to private property, saw to it that Hitler legally became chancellor in 1933. Millions celebrated. "My father went down to the cellar and brought up our best bottles of wine. . . . And my mother wept for joy," one German recalled. "Now everything will be all right," she said.

Hitler took command brutally and forcibly closed down representative government. Nazis suspended civil rights, imposed censorship of the press, and prohibited meetings of the political parties. Hitler made his aims clear: "I have set myself one task, namely to sweep those parties out of Germany." Storm troopers—the private Nazi army that existed in addition to Germany's regular forces—so harassed democratic politicians that at the end of March 1933 intimidated delegates let pass the Enabling Act, which suspended the constitution for four years and allowed Nazi laws to take effect without parliamentary approval. The elite SS (*Schutzstaffel*) was yet another military organization, and along with the Gestapo, or political police, it enforced complete obedience to Nazism. These organizations had vast powers to arrest Communists, Jews, homosexuals, and activists and either executed them or imprisoned them in concentration camps, the first of which opened at Dachau near Munich in March 1933.

Repression in the Nazi State

The Nazis knew that their power depended on improving economic conditions and, in that context, the government pursued pump priming, that is, stimulating the economy by investing in public works projects such as constructing tanks, airplanes, and highways. Unemployment declined from a peak of almost 6 million in 1932 to 1.6 million by 1936. The Nazi Party closed down labor unions, and government managers classified jobs and set pay levels, rating women's jobs lower than men's regardless of the level of expertise required. The belief grew that Hitler was working an economic miracle.

The Nazi government took control of all aspects of everyday life, including gender roles. A law encouraged Aryans (those people legally defined as racially German) to have children by providing loans to Aryan newlyweds, but only if the wife left the workforce. Nazi marriage programs enforced both racial and gender ideology; women were supposed to be subordinate so men would feel tough and industrious despite military defeat and economic depression. A woman "joyfully sacrifices and fulfills her fate," one Nazi leader explained. Censorship flourished. Radio broadcasts were clogged with propaganda; book-burnings destroyed works by Jews, socialists, homosexuals, and modernist writers. Hitler claimed to be rebuilding the harmonious community destroyed by modernity even as his government used very modern tools of surveillance and big government programs to enforce the Nazi program. For millions of Germans, however, Nazi rule brought anything but harmony and well-being.

The Nazis defined Jews as an inferior "race" dangerous to the superior Aryan "race" and as responsible for both Germany's defeat in World War I and the economic crisis that

Nazi Racism

followed. National Socialism, Hitler insisted in a 1938 speech, was not based on old fashioned anti-Semitism but on "the greatest of scientific knowledge." Jews were "vermin," "parasites," and "Bolsheviks," whom the Germans had to eliminate. In 1935, the Nuremberg Laws deprived Jews of citizenship and prohibited marriage between Jews and other Germans. Whereas women defined as Aryan had increasing difficulty obtaining abortions or birth-control information, these were readily available to Jews and other outcast groups. In the name of improving the Aryan race, doctors in the late 1930s helped organize the T4 project, which used carbon monoxide poisoning and other means to kill two hundred thousand "inferior" people—especially the handicapped.

Jews were forced into slave labor, evicted from their apartments, and prevented from buying most clothing and food. In 1938, a Jewish teenager, reacting to the harassment of his parents, killed a German official. In retaliation, Nazis attacked synagogues, smashed windows of Jewish-owned stores, and threw more than twenty thousand Jews—including Eva Kantorowski's father—into prisons and work camps. The night of November 9–10 became known as *Kristallnacht* (kris-TAHL-nahkt), or the Night of Broken Glass. Faced with this relentless persecution, by 1939 more than half of Germany's five hundred thousand Jews had emigrated. Hitler mobilized the masses by targeting an enemy—the Jews—not just in wartime but in peacetime, not outside the country but within it. Persecution of the Jews brought Germans new financial resources as they simply stole Jewish property and took Jewish jobs.

Democracies Mobilize

Facing the double-barreled assault of economic depression and totalitarian aggression, democracies rallied in support of freedom, individuals' rights, and citizens' well-being, though they often limited their efforts to whites. In the eyes of many, however, representative government appeared feeble compared with totalitarian leaders' military style of mobilizing the masses. Democracy was difficult to support in tough economic times, but as the depression wore on, some governments—notably the United States and Sweden—undertook bold experiments to solve social and economic crises while still maintaining democratic politics.

The United States   In the early days of the depression, U.S. lawmakers opposed giving direct aid to the unemployed and even used military force to put down a demonstration by jobless veterans in the nation's capital. Government policy changed, however, after Franklin Delano Roosevelt was elected president in 1932. Roosevelt pushed through a torrent of legislation: relief for businesses, price supports for struggling farmers, and public works programs for the unemployed. The Social Security Act of 1935 set up a fund to which employers and employees contributed to provide retirement and other benefits for citizens. Like other successful politicians of the 1930s and thereafter, Roosevelt used the new mass media expertly, especially in his radio series of "fireside chats" to the American people. In sharp contrast to Mussolini and Hitler, Roosevelt—with the able assistance of his wife Eleanor—aimed to build faith in democracy rather than denounce it: "We Americans of today . . . are characters in the living book of democracy," he told a group of teenagers in 1939. The president's bold programs and successful use of the media kept the masses, even those facing racial discrimination, mobilized to believe in a democratic future.

Sweden   Sweden's response to the crisis of the 1930s became a model for the postwar welfare state. The Swedish government turned its economy around by instituting social welfare programs and central planning of the economy. It devalued its currency to make Swedish exports more attractive. Pump-priming projects increased Swedish productivity by 20 percent between 1929 and 1935, a period when other democracies were floundering. Government programs also addressed the population problem, but without the racism and coercion of totalitarianism. One architect of the program to boost childbirth was the activist Alva Myrdal (MEER-dahl), a young sociologist and leading member of parliament. Myrdal's mother had been so against modern education that she forbade library books in the house, claiming that they promoted diseases. Myrdal made it to university, but after her topics for a doctoral dissertation were rejected, she turned to activism, promoting causes such as "voluntary parenthood" and improved work opportunities for women—even married ones. Following Myrdal's lead, the Swedish government started a loan program for married couples in 1937 and introduced prenatal care, free childbirth in a hospital, and subsidized housing for large families. Because all families—rural and urban, poor or prosperous—received these benefits, there was widespread support for this experiment with developing a welfare state alongside democracy. Alva Myrdal went on to become ambassador to India, a tireless worker for the United Nations and world peace, and a Nobel Prize recipient.

France

Like Germany, France faced economic and political turmoil and only narrowly avoided a fascist takeover. Deputies with opposing views frequently came to blows in the Chamber of Deputies, and right-wing paramilitary groups took to the streets, attracting the unemployed, students, and veterans to demonstrations against representative government. The growing attraction of fascism shocked French liberals, socialists, and Communists into an antifascist coalition known as the Popular Front. This alliance was made possible when Stalin allowed Communist parties, whose policies he determined, to join in the protection of democracy rather than work to destroy it. For just over a year in 1936–1937 and again very briefly in 1938, the French Popular Front, headed by socialist leader Léon Blum, led the government. Like American and Swedish reformers, the Popular Front enacted welfare benefits and mandatory two-week paid vacations for workers. Bankers and industrialists greeted Blum's costly programs by sending their savings out of the country, however, leaving France financially strapped and the government mortally wounded. "Better Hitler than Blum" was the slogan of the upper classes, and the Popular Front fell. The collapse of the antifascist Popular Front showed the difficulties of democratic societies facing economic crisis and the revival of militarism.

Cultural Mobilization in the West

Democratic cultural life also fought the lure of fascism. During its brief existence, the Popular Front encouraged the masses to celebrate democratic holidays such as Bastille Day with new enthusiasm. Artists made films, wrote novels, and produced art that celebrated ordinary people and captured their everyday struggles. In Charlie Chaplin's film *Modern Times* (1936), his famous character, the Little Tramp, was a worker in a modern factory molded by his monotonous job to believe that even his co-workers' bodies needed mechanical adjustment. Viewers laughed with him instead of growing resentful. Heroines in immensely popular musical comedies behaved bravely, pulling their men out of the depths of despair and thus away from fascist temptation. In the film *Keep Smiling* (1938), for example, British comedienne Gracie Fields portrayed a spunky working-class woman who remained cheerful despite the challenges of living in hard times.

Novelists affirmed human rights and the dignity of the poor in the face of dictatorial pomp and bombast. In a series of novels based on the biblical figure Joseph, German writer and Nobel Prize winner Thomas Mann conveyed the conflict between humane values and barbarism. The fourth volume, *Joseph the Provider* (1944), praised Joseph's welfare state, in which the granaries are full and the rich pay taxes so the poor might live decent lives. Chinese author Pa Chin used his widely influential novel *Family* (1931) to criticize the dictatorial powers of traditional patriarchy, which destroyed humane values and loving relationships. In one of her last works, *Three Guineas* (1938), English writer Virginia Woolf abandoned the experimental novel in favor of a direct attack on militarism, poverty, and the oppression of women, showing that these were interconnected parts of the single, dangerous worldview of the 1930s.

Global War 1937–1945

The depression intensified competition among nations as politicians sought to expand their country's access to land, markets, and resources. Mobilizing the masses around national and military might, Hitler, Mussolini, and Japan's military leaders marched the world toward another catastrophic war.

> **FOCUS**
>
> How did World War II progress on the battlefront and the home front?

Democratic statesmen hoped that sanctions imposed by the League of Nations would stop new aggression, but military assaults escalated with Japan's invasion of China and the outbreak of war in 1937. An era of destruction opened that at war's end left some 100 million of the world's peoples dead and tens of millions more starving and homeless.

Europe's Road to War

The surge in global imperialism that occurred during the 1930s has shaped international politics to the present day. Hitler's harsh anti-Jewish policies drove increasing numbers of European Jews to migrate to Palestine, bringing clashes between Palestinians and Jewish newcomers. Western imperialist powers, including Britain, France, the United States, and the Netherlands, increased their exploitation of resource-rich regions outside their borders amid mounting local resentment. The most severe challenge to the global order, however, came from Germany, Italy, and Japan, whose authoritarian regimes and drive for empire became ever bolder.

Uncontested Aggression

Like Japanese leaders, Hitler and Mussolini presented their countries as "have-nots" and demanded more power, resources, and land. Hitler's agenda included gaining more *Lebensraum* (LAY-buns-rowm), or living space, in which supposedly superior "Aryans" could thrive. This space would be taken from the "inferior" Slavic peoples, who would be moved to Siberia or would serve as slaves. In 1935 Hitler loudly rejected the Treaty of Versailles's limitations on German military strength and openly began rearming. In the same year, Mussolini invaded Ethiopia, one of the few African states not overwhelmed by European imperialism. "The Roman legionnaires are again on the march," one Italian soldier exulted at this colonial adventure. Despite the resistance of the poorly equipped Ethiopians, their capital, Addis Ababa, fell in the spring of 1936. The League of Nations voted to impose sanctions against Italy, but Britain and France opposed any embargo on oil, suggesting a lack of will to fight aggression.

Italian Invasion of Ethiopia, 1935–1936

Nazi territorial expansion began with the annexation of Austria in 1938 (see Map 28.2). Aiming to unite all German peoples, Hitler's troops entered Austria, and the enthusiasm of Nazi sympathizers there made Germany's actions appear to support Wilsonian "self-determination." Nazis generated support in Austria by building factories to solve the unemployment problem and by reawakening Austrians' sense that they belonged once more to a mighty empire. Hitler turned next to Czechoslovakia and its rich resources. Hitler gambled correctly that the other Western powers would not interfere with any takeover if he could

The Fall of Central Europe

convince them that this was his last territorial claim. In the fall of 1938, British Prime Minister Neville Chamberlain, French Premier Édouard Daladier, and Mussolini met with Hitler in Munich, Germany, and, despite strong Czech opposition, agreed to allow Germany's claim to the Sudetenland (sue-DAY-ten-lahnd)—the German-populated border region of Czechoslovakia. Their strategy was to make concessions for grievances (in this case, injustices to Germany in the Peace of Paris), a policy called **appeasement**. As Europe outside of Czechoslovakia rejoiced, Chamberlain announced that he had secured "peace in our time" for a continent fearing another devastating war. Appeasement proved a failure: in March 1939, Hitler invaded the rest of Czechoslovakia.

The Early Years of the War 1937–1943

While this expansion was unfolding, the first phase of World War II had begun in East Asia. In 1937, the Japanese military, after skirmishes around Beijing, attacked Shanghai, justifying its offensive as the first step in liberating the region from Western imperialism (see again Map 28.1). Moving to capture major cities along the coast, the Japanese army

appeasement The strategy of preventing a war by making concessions to aggressors.

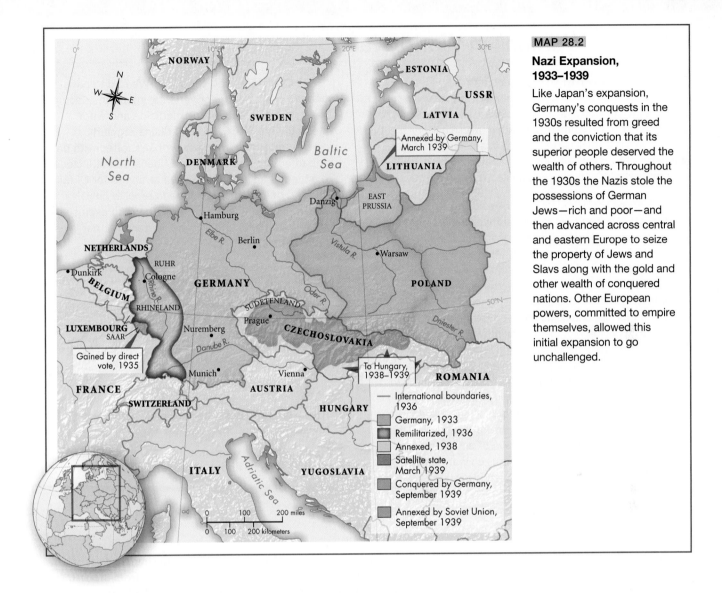

MAP 28.2

Nazi Expansion, 1933–1939

Like Japan's expansion, Germany's conquests in the 1930s resulted from greed and the conviction that its superior people deserved the wealth of others. Throughout the 1930s the Nazis stole the possessions of German Jews—rich and poor—and then advanced across central and eastern Europe to seize the property of Jews and Slavs along with the gold and other wealth of conquered nations. Other European powers, committed to empire themselves, allowed this initial expansion to go unchallenged.

took the Chinese capital of Nanjing, massacring hundreds of thousands of Chinese in the "Rape of Nanjing," an atrocity so named because of the special brutality toward girls and women before they were killed. Japan's invasion of China marked the Asian beginnings of World War II.

Despite the slaughter, many in the West continued to believe that the highly militarized and industrialized Japanese were more fit to rule China than the Chinese themselves. In 1938, the Japanese government described its expansionism as the foundation for a "New Order" in Asia, the **Greater East Asia Co-Prosperity Sphere** that Japan would use to help free Asians and indeed the world from the oppressive white race. In reality, however, the Japanese made enormous demands on Asians for resources while treating Chinese and Koreans with brutality (see Reading the Past: "Comfort Women" in World War II).

As the Japanese fought to conquer China, Hitler launched an all-out attack on Poland on September 1, 1939. The way was prepared a week earlier on August 23, 1939, when Germany and the USSR signed a nonaggression agreement—the Nazi-Soviet Pact—providing that if one country became embroiled in war, the other country would remain neutral. Feeling confident, German forces let loose an overpowering *Blitzkrieg* ("lightning war"), a stunning and concentrated onslaught of airplanes, tanks, and motorized infantry, to defeat the ill-equipped Polish defenders with overwhelming speed. Allowing the army

Greater East Asia Co-Prosperity Sphere A region of Asian states to be dominated by Japan, and in theory, to benefit from Japan's superior civilization.

"Comfort Women" in World War II

Oh Omok was sixteen when she left home in Chongup, Korea, in 1937 to take up a new livelihood: that, she was told, of a factory worker in Japan. Instead, like thousands of other young Korean women, she ended up in a military brothel. This is a small part of her story, among the mildest of those gathered in the 1990s from former "comfort women" and meticulously documented by researchers.

At first I delivered food for the soldiers and had to serve the rank and file, to have sex with them. . . . On receiving orders we were called to the appropriate unit and served five or six men a day. At times we would serve up to ten. We served the soldiers in very small rooms with floors covered with Japanese-style mats, *tatami.* . . . When the soldiers were away on an expedition it was nice and quiet, but once they returned we had to serve many of them. Then they would come to our rooms in a continuous stream. I wept a lot in the early days. Some soldiers tried to comfort me saying "*kawaisoni*" or "*naitara ikanyo*," which meant something like "you poor thing" and "don't cry." Some of the soldiers would hit me because I didn't understand their language. If we displeased them in the slightest way they shouted at us and beat us: "*bakayaro*" or "*kisamayaro*," "you idiot" and "you bastard." I realized that I must do whatever they wanted of me if I wished to survive.

The soldiers used condoms. We had to have a medical examination for venereal infections once a week. Those infected took medicine and were injected with "No. 606" [a medicine regularly injected into the forced sex workers, often with bad side effects]. Sometime later, I became quite close to a Lieutenant Morimoto, who arranged for Okhui [a friend of Oh Omok] and me to receive only high-ranking officers. Once we began to exclusively serve lieutenants and second lieutenants, our lives became much easier.

Source: Keith Howard, ed., *True Stories of the Korean Comfort Women: Testimonies Compiled by the Korean Council for Women Drafted for Military Sexual Slavery by Japan and the Research Association on the Women Drafted for Military Sexual Slavery by Japan*, trans. Young Joo Lee (London: Cassell, 1995), 66–67.

EXAMINING THE EVIDENCE

1. How would you describe Oh Omok's attitude toward her situation?

2. How might her experience as a "comfort woman" shape her ideas about gender and class relations?

The German Onslaught

to conserve supplies, the Blitzkrieg assured Germans at home that the human costs of conquest would be low. On September 17, 1939, the Soviets invaded Poland from the east, and the victors then divided the country according to secret provisions in the Nazi-Soviet Pact (see again Map 28.2). Within Germany, Hitler called for defense of the fatherland against the "warlike menace" of world Jewry.

In April 1940, the Blitzkrieg crushed Denmark and Norway; Belgium, the Netherlands, and France fell in May and June (see Map 28.3). Stalin meanwhile annexed the Baltic states of Estonia, Latvia, and Lithuania. As Winston Churchill, an early advocate of resistance, took over as prime minister, Hitler ordered the bombardment of Britain. Churchill, another savvy orator, rallied the British people by radio to protect the ideals of liberty with their "blood, toil, tears, and sweat." In the Battle of Britain, or the Blitz as the British called it, the Luftwaffe (German air force) bombed homes, public buildings, harbors, weapons depots, and factories. Britain poured resources into anti-aircraft weapons, its highly successful code-detecting group called Ultra, and further development of radar. By year's end, the British airplane industry was outproducing the Germans by 50 percent.

By the fall of 1940, German air losses had driven Hitler to abandon his planned conquest of Britain. Forcing Hungary, Romania, and Bulgaria to become its allies, Germany gained access to more food and oil. In violation of the Nazi-Soviet Pact, Hitler launched an all-out campaign in June 1941 against what he called the "center of judeobolshevism"—the Soviet Union. Deployed along a two-thousand-mile front, 3 million German and other Axis troops quickly penetrated Soviet lines and killed, captured, or wounded more than

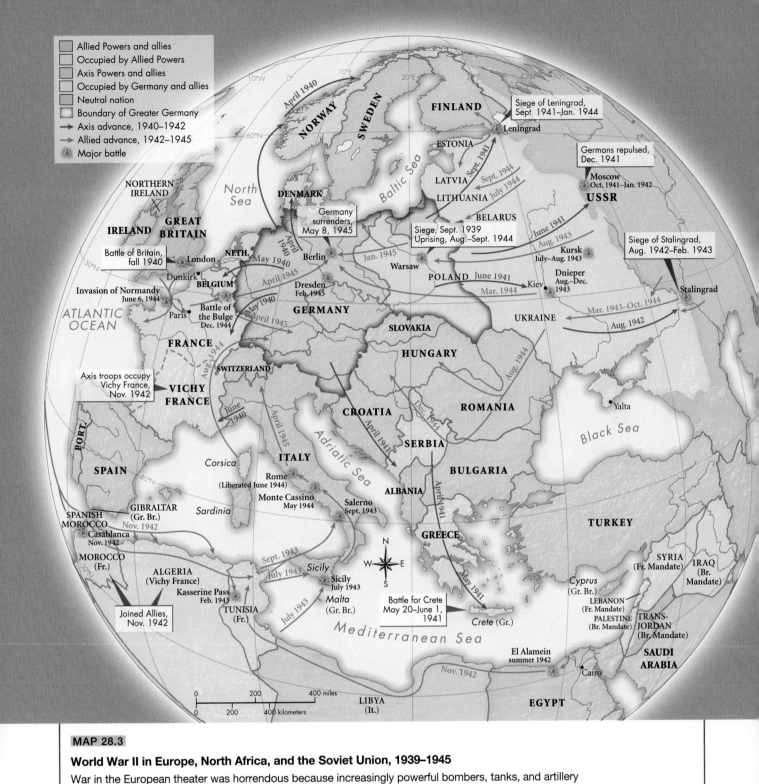

Legend
- Allied Powers and allies
- Occupied by Allied Powers
- Axis Powers and allies
- Occupied by Germany and allies
- Neutral nation
- Boundary of Greater Germany
- → Axis advance, 1940–1942
- → Allied advance, 1942–1945
- ✷ Major battle

Siege of Leningrad, Sept. 1941–Jan. 1944

Germans repulsed, Dec. 1941

Moscow Oct. 1941–Jan. 1942

Siege of Stalingrad, Aug. 1942–Feb. 1943

Germany surrenders, May 8, 1945

Siege, Sept. 1939 Uprising, Aug.–Sept. 1944

Kursk July–Aug. 1943

Dnieper Aug.–Dec. 1943

Battle of Britain, fall 1940

Invasion of Normandy June 6, 1944

Battle of the Bulge Dec. 1944

Dresden Feb. 1945

Axis troops occupy Vichy France, Nov. 1942

Rome (Liberated June 1944)

Monte Cassino May 1944

Salerno Sept. 1943

Casablanca Nov. 1942

Kasserine Pass Feb. 1943

Joined Allies, Nov. 1942

Sicily July 1943

Battle for Crete May 20–June 1, 1941

El Alamein summer 1942

MAP 28.3

World War II in Europe, North Africa, and the Soviet Union, 1939–1945

War in the European theater was horrendous because increasingly powerful bombers, tanks, and artillery were unleashed on soldiers and civilians alike. After its initial success in the spring of 1940, Germany was so ideologically driven that it pursued its military ambitions even after failing in the Battle of Britain and then in the war against the Soviet Union. Meanwhile, the Allies outproduced the Axis powers by a wide margin and lavishly used their own heavy weapons to achieve a final victory in May 1945. By then, much of the European continent and parts of the Middle East and North Africa had been reduced to rubble.

half of the 4.5 million Soviet soldiers defending the borders. As the campaign continued along the far-flung battlefront, the Soviet people fought back. Because Hitler feared that equipping his army for Russian conditions would suggest to civilians that a prolonged war lay in store, the Nazi soldiers were unprepared for the onset of winter. In this way, Hitler

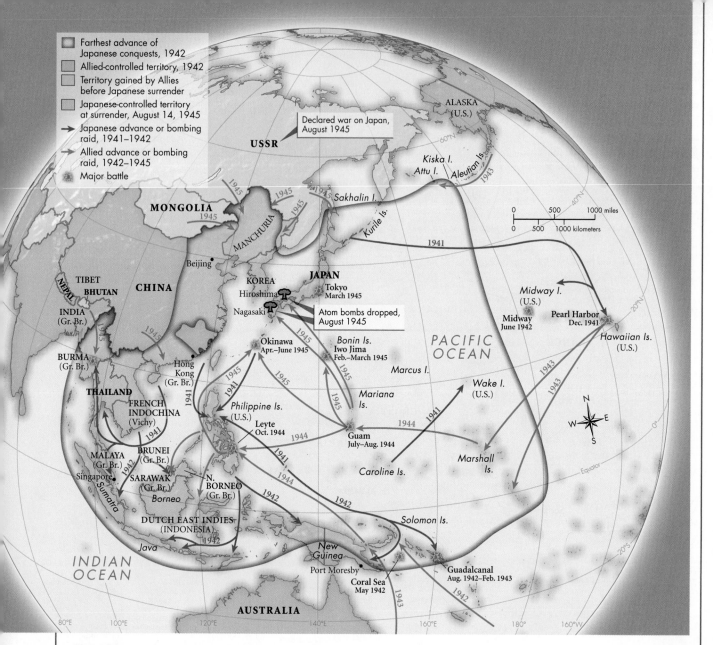

MAP 28.4

World War II in the Pacific, 1937–1945

The "Europe first" strategy of the Allies permitted Japan a comparatively free hand in the Pacific. Japan's victories were short-lived, however, despite the determined efforts of its civilians and military to sacrifice everything for victory. The many conquered peoples of the Pacific suffered mightily under Japanese rule, performing forced labor, serving as sex slaves, and bearing the brunt of the final Allied push to defeat the Axis in the Pacific.

preserved the average citizen's confidence in German might, but at the cost of undermining the actual effectiveness of his army.

As Japan swiftly captured British colonies in Asia and invaded French Indochina for its raw materials, the United States stopped supplying Japan with essential industrial goods. The Japanese government decided it should settle matters with the West, and in December 1941, its planes bombed American naval and air bases at Pearl Harbor in Hawaii and then destroyed a fleet of airplanes in the Philippines. President Roosevelt summoned the Congress to declare war on Japan. By spring 1942, the Japanese had conquered Guam, the Philippines, Malaya, Burma, Indonesia, Singapore, and much of the southwestern Pacific (see Map 28.4). As had happened with Germany's expansionist drive, the victories strengthened the appeal of the Japanese military's imperial ideology. "The era of democracy

War Intensifies in the Pacific

Allies The alliance of Great Britain, France, the Soviet Union, and the United States and their coalition partners in World War II.

Axis The alliance of Italy, Germany, and Japan and their client states in World War II.

is finished," the foreign minister announced confidently.[8] Japanese officials portrayed Emperor Hirohito as the pan-Asian monarch who would liberate Asians everywhere.

Germany and Italy quickly joined Japan and declared war on the United States—an appropriate enemy, Hitler proclaimed, as it was "half Judaized and the other half Negrified." The United States was ambivalent toward the Soviet Union despite Hitler's attack, and Stalin reciprocated the mistrust. Nonetheless, the Soviet Union joined with Great Britain, the Free French (an exile government based in London), and the United States to form the Grand Alliance. Twenty other countries joined this group of nations to form a coalition—known collectively as the **Allies**—who fought the **Axis** powers of Germany, Italy, and Japan. In the long run the Allies held distinct advantages in terms of manpower and access to resources, given the extensive terrain they controlled, but both sides faced the bloodiest fight in world history (see Lives and Livelihoods: Soldiers and Soldiering).

War and the World's Civilians

Victory in World War II depended on industrial productivity geared toward total war and mass killings. From the Rape of Nanjing to the horrors of the Holocaust, far more civilians than soldiers died in World War II. The Axis and the Allies alike bombed cities to destroy civilians' will to resist—a debatable tactic since it often inspired defiance rather than surrender. The Allied firebombing of Dresden and Tokyo alone killed tens of thousands of civilians, but Axis attacks caused far more civilian deaths. Chinese civilians, not Chinese soldiers, were the target of the Rape of Nanjing, and British people, not British soldiers, were the target of the Battle of Britain. Mass slaughter had a rationale behind it: in a total war, workers were as important as soldiers because they manufactured the tools of war. Neither Japan nor Germany took the resources and civilian morale of its enemies into full account, however.

The new "master races" believed it was their mission to rid the world of subhumans and then repopulate it themselves. As the German army swept through eastern Europe, it slaughtered Jews, Communists, Slavs, and others whom Nazi ideology deemed "racial inferiors" and enemies. The number of deliberately murdered civilian victims in China alone is estimated to be at least 2.5 million, with untold millions murdered elsewhere in the region. Some 3 million Japanese were then relocated as "civilizers" in conquered areas of East Asia, while "racially pure" Germans took over farms and homes in Poland and elsewhere. To lessen resistance, German occupiers tested the reading skills of those captured with the promise that they could avoid hard labor. Instead, those who could read were lined up and shot as potential rebel leaders.

The extermination of Jews became a special focus of the Nazis. Crowded into urban ghettos, stripped of their possessions, and living on minimal rations, countless eastern European Jews died of starvation and disease—the Nazis' initial plan for reducing the Jewish population. Soon the Nazis put into operation the "Final Solution," their bureaucratic plan for the extermination of all of Europe's Jews by rounding them up for transport to death camps. Soldiers, ordinary civilians, police, scientists, and doctors—all participated in the **Holocaust**. Extermination camps were developed specifically for the purposes of mass murder, though some, like Auschwitz-Birkenau in Poland, served as both death and labor camps. Captives, among them Hans Kantorowsky, were herded into gas chambers where they were killed by lethal gas, and then the corpses were burned in specially designed crematoria. As of 1943, Auschwitz had the capacity to burn 1.7 million bodies per year.

For all their anti-Semitic bluster, the Nazis took pains to hide the true purpose of the camps. Those not chosen for immediate murder in the camps had their heads shaved,

Major Concentration Camps and Extermination Sites in Europe

Holocaust The genocidal murder of some 6 million Jews by the Germans during World War II in an attempt to exterminate European Jewry.

Soldiers and Soldiering

African American Sailors in World War II

The U.S. military offered African Americans opportunity as well as danger in the struggle to defeat fascism. Even as they themselves faced discrimination in the armed forces, many saw the war as a campaign to promote universal rights and to defeat the forces of racism and ethnic supremacy. Having participated in the great moral victory of defeating violent bigotry abroad, they often joined the civil rights campaign after the war to defeat violent bigotry at home. (Bettmann/Corbis.)

Between 1930 and 1945 tens of millions of men and women worldwide became soldiers, joining both regular armies and paramilitary groups such as those run by the Chinese Communist Party and the German National Socialist (Nazi) Party. In 1927, for example, Mao Zedong, a young leader among Chinese Communists, helped decide that the groups should become a "Red Army" rather than organize into a traditional army. This paramilitary group marched northward through rural regions of China, adding recruits and ministering to the needs of peasants even as it indoctrinated them and took their resources. The German Nazi and Italian fascist paramilitary groups inflicted violence on strikers, on Communists,

and, in the case of the Nazis, on Jews. During tough economic times, when jobs in the civilian workforce were lacking, men found a livelihood in paramilitary armies.

Thus, well before World War II, there was active soldiering and warfare. Indeed, many people wondered if war ever really ended. In the deadly Chaco War (1932–1935) between Bolivia and Paraguay to increase territory, especially where oil exploration was taking place, teenage boys were drafted. One Bolivian survivor, drafted at age fifteen, recalled, "We had the luck to have bad commanders. They didn't lead us. . . . They sent all the soldiers to the front, and they stayed behind. They didn't give us a single thing to eat nor a single

The Holocaust were disinfected, and then given prison garments—many of them so thin and tattered that they offered no protection against winter cold and rain. So began life in "a living hell," as one survivor wrote of the starvation, overwork, and disease. In the name of advancing "racial science," doctors in German concentration camps performed unbelievably cruel medical experiments and operations with no anesthesia on pregnant women, twins, and other innocent people. But prisoners developed strategies for survival, forging friendships that sustained them. Thanks to the food and favors he received from fellow prisoners, wrote Auschwitz survivor Primo Levi, "I managed not to forget that I myself was a man." In the end, 6 million Jews, the vast majority from eastern Europe, along with a mosaic of

thing to drink. . . . For this simple reason [soldiers] collapsed . . . they died."[1]

The highest ranks of the military were generally staffed by social elites and treated well. In China, Jiang Jieshi, from a relatively prosperous family, attended Baoding Military Academy. He then trained in Japan, where high levels of literacy and knowledge of the classics were central, so officers usually came from homes that were cultured. In the United States, movie stars and children from the highest ranks of society, including the sons and daughters of senators and millionaires, volunteered for World War II and were often placed in less dangerous regions. Ordinary members of the infantry, however, were on the frontlines, where the most common activity was digging, especially the foxholes in which they lived and protected themselves.

For many, political belief was a major factor in warfare. "The only thing that keeps me always on my feet and always ready: faith in God and in the Duce," one Italian soldier wrote from the front. From their training, Japanese soldiers came to believe "we are all samurai now," and an Australian soldier observed that whatever the character of the individual Japanese soldier, "good or bad, kind or sadistic, they had one supreme virtue . . . a courage that I believe to be unequalled in our time."[2]

There were failures in instilling belief, however. After their increasing exploitation during the depression, Africans often hid from recruiters and village chiefs in charge of wartime forced labor. In Southern Rhodesia, they used colonial ideology to justify their draft-dodging: "We are women. The White people are our menfolk to whom we look for guidance and protection. We have never had the courage or the ability to fight in war."[3]

War was a grim experience for most—they might face starvation in prison camps, epidemic disease, horrific wounds, wrenching physical and mental torture, suicide, cannibalism, and death. Yet soldiers' lives also had a bright side based on the loyal comradeship that developed during combat. Many professed not to fight for a cause but for the well-being of those fighting alongside them, and others found love and support on ships, in hospitals, and on the battlefield. Some believed that the military offered opportunity, among them African Americans, even though many had grown cynical when their efforts in World War I brought no relief from lynching, job discrimination, and open racism more generally. Soldiers might gain new technological skills and even find wholly new livelihoods to pursue in the future.

---

1. Cristobal Arancibia, quoted in "Cristobal Arancibia: The Life of a Bolivian Peasant During the Chaco War, 1932–1935," ed. W. H. Beezley and J. Ewell, *Human Tradition in Latin America: The Twentieth Century* (Wilmington, DE: Scholarly Resources, 1987), 97.
2. Quoted in John Keegan, *Soldiers: A History of Men in Battle* (New York: Viking Penguin, 1986), 51.
3. Quoted in David Johnson, *World War II and the Scramble for Labour in Colonial Zimbabwe, 1939–1948* (Harare: University of Zimbabwe Press, 2000), 18.

QUESTIONS TO CONSIDER

1. What specific advantages did soldiers from many walks of life see in joining the military?

2. How would you describe soldiers' lives from 1930 to 1945, and how did they vary?

3. What were the class dimensions of the military?

For Further Information:

Cottam, Kazimiera Janina. *Soviet Airwomen in Combat in World War II*. 1983.
Johnson, David. *World War II and the Scramble for Labour in Colonial Zimbabwe, 1939–1948*. 2000.
Keegan, John. *Soldiers: A History of Men in Battle*. 1986.
Montgomerie, Deborah. *Love in a Time of War: Letter-Writing in the Second World War*. 2005.

millions of Roma, homosexuals, Slavs, and others, were murdered in the Nazis' organized, genocidal fury.

The Axis countries remained at a disadvantage throughout the war despite their early conquests. Although the war accelerated economic production some 300 percent between 1940 and 1944 in all belligerent countries, the Allies produced more than three times as much as the Axis in 1943 alone. Even while some of its lands were occupied and many of its cities besieged, the Soviet Union increased its production of weapons. Both Japan and Germany made the most of their lower capacity, with such tactics as Japan's suicide, or *kamikaze*, attacks in the last months of the war. Hitler had to prevent wartime shortages

Societies at War

The Warsaw Ghetto, 1943
From the 1930s on, the Nazis considered Jews and others to be both dangerous enemies and inferiors unworthy of living; they drove them into ghettos, confiscated their property, took away their livelihoods, and deprived them of food and fuel. Despite being confined to these ghettos, residents learned of the ongoing Holocaust, and in 1943 the people of the Warsaw ghetto staged an uprising. Those shown here were taken prisoner, and the uprising was brutally put down. (SZ Photo/ Bridgeman Art Library.)

because he had come to power promising to end economic suffering, not increase it. Japanese propaganda, however, persuaded civilians to endure extreme scarcity for the sake of the nation. The use of millions of forced laborers and resources from occupied areas reduced Axis deprivation.

Allied governments were overwhelmingly successful in generating civilian participation, especially among women. Soviet women constituted more than half the workforce by war's end. They dug massive antitank trenches around Moscow and other threatened cities, and eight hundred thousand volunteered for the military, even serving as pilots. As the Germans invaded, Soviet citizens moved entire factories eastward. In Germany and Italy, where government policy particularly exalted motherhood and kept women from the best-paying jobs, officials began to realize that women were desperately needed in offices and factories. Japanese women rushed to help, but even changing the propaganda to stress that they should take jobs did not convince German women to join the low-paid female workforce.

Even more than in World War I, propaganda saturated society in movie theaters and on the radio. People were glued to their radios for war news, but much of it was tightly controlled. Japan, like Germany, generally withheld news of defeats and large numbers of casualties to maintain civilian support. The antireligious Soviet government found radio programming from the Russian Orthodox clergy that boosted patriotism, and Japanese propagandists taught that both the war and the emperor were sacred. Filmmakers— subject to censorship unless their films conveyed the "right" message, including racial thinking—encouraged patriotism with stories of aviation heroes and faithful wives left behind. The German government continued to advertise ugly caricatures of Jews, Slavs, and Roma; Allied propaganda depicted Germans as gorillas and "Japs" as uncivilized, insectlike fanatics.

Such characterizations eased the way for the USSR to uproot Muslims and minority ethnic groups as potential Nazi collaborators and for the U.S. government to force citizens of Japanese origin into its own concentration camps. Fred Korematsu, born in Oakland,

California in 1919, was one U.S. citizen of Japanese descent who refused to leave his home on the grounds that only a handful of Americans of Italian and German descent were similarly interned. Korematsu was arrested and ultimately sent to a camp surrounded by barbed wire, machine guns, and watchtowers. Like that of many interned Japanese Americans, his family's property was taken and sold and he was left to find odd jobs, but he continued to fight his removal to a concentration camp and became a pioneer for civil rights.

Colonized peoples were drawn into the war through conscription into the armies and forced labor. Some 2 million Indian men served the Allied cause, as did several hundred thousand Africans, even as governments stripped their families of resources. To prevent Japanese confiscation of Indian resources, the British withdrew all shipping from Bengali ports, leaving the region with no food deliveries. "When I was nine years old we had the Bengal famine," one Indian remembered. "The victims suddenly emerged in millions—it seemed from absolutely nowhere, dying in incredible numbers."[9] Some 3 to 7 million Bengali civilians died of starvation—a British-inflicted Holocaust, as many have called it. Among the peoples of the great powers, Soviet children and old people were at the greatest risk of starvation; an adolescent alive during the siege of Leningrad would probably have been among the 1 million residents of the city who starved to death. Where there were resources, bureaucrats around the war-torn world regulated the production and distribution of food, clothing, and household products, all of which were of lower quality than before the war.

Collaboration with Axis conquerors was common among colonial people who had suffered the racist oppression of the Western powers. As the Japanese swept through the Pacific and parts of East Asia, they conscripted local men into their army; many volunteered willingly. Subhas Bose, educated

Forced Labor in Vietnam

Japan promised the colonized peoples of the world—especially those in Asia—that Japanese rule would bring liberation and real benefits to those who had been dominated by the Western powers. The reality was usually quite different. Korean, Chinese, and other women were made to serve as sex slaves to members of the Japanese military, and other civilians were forced to provide manual labor, such as these Vietnamese women digging what appears to be a trench to defend the military against tanks and other enemy vehicles. (bpk, Berlin/Art Resource, NY.)

in England and accepted into the Indian Civil Service, quit his post in 1921 and became a prominent member of the Indian Congress Party, spending time in British prisons for his activities. When World War II broke out and the British refused to grant India home rule, he went over to the Axis side and recruited an all-Indian army to fight the British in South Asia. "Gandhi wants to change human beings, and all I want to do is free India," Bose maintained, as he fought on Japan's side.[10] Throughout the Axis-occupied areas of Europe, collaborationist leaders such as Philippe Pétain in France and Vidkun Quisling in Norway provided workers and equipment for the Axis cause. Many an ordinary person moved up the economic ladder by spying for the Axis powers and working for the occupiers.

Collaboration

Resistance to the Axis also began early in the war. Escaping France in 1940, General Charles de Gaulle from his haven in London directed the Free French government, resisters on the continent, and Free French military—a mixed organization of troops of colonized Asians and Africans and soldiers and volunteers from France and other occupied

Resistance

Colonial Recruits in World War II

Colonial forces played as significant a role in World War II as they had in World War I. They participated by the millions in armies, and both the Axis and the Allies drove colonized people under their control into forced labor. Often colonized peoples used the war to work against their imperial masters. These North African soldiers, who were probably under the rule of the French before the war, appear to have joined forces with the Germans as they chat with an officer. (akg-images/ ullstein bild.)

countries. Other resisters, called partisans, planned assassinations of collaborators and enemy officers and bombed bridges and rail lines. Although the Catholic Church officially supported Mussolini, Catholic and Protestant clergy and their parishioners were among those who set up resistance networks, often hiding Jews and political suspects. Ordinary people also fought back through everyday activities. Homemakers circulated newsletters urging demonstrations at prisons where civilians were detained and in marketplaces where food was rationed. Jews rose up against their Nazi captors in Warsaw in 1943 but were mercilessly butchered. Resisters played on stereotypes: women often carried weapons to assassination sites and seduced and murdered enemy officers. "Naturally the Germans didn't think that a woman could have carried a bomb," explained one female Italian resister, "so this became the woman's task."[11]

From Allied Victory to the Cold War 1943–1945

FOCUS

How did the Allied victory unfold, and what were the causes of that victory?

Allied victory began to look certain by 1943, even though tough fighting still lay ahead. The Allies crashed through German lines in the east, south, and west of Europe, while war in the Pacific turned in the Allies' favor, despite the Japanese policy of resistance to the death. In a series of war-time meetings, Churchill, Stalin, and Roosevelt—nicknamed the Big Three—planned the peace that they expected to achieve, including the creation of a new organization called the United Nations to prevent another war. On the eve of victory, however, distrust among the Allies was about to provoke yet another struggle for supremacy—the Cold War between the United States and the Soviet Union.

The Axis Defeated

Germany and Italy Crushed

The Battle of Stalingrad in 1942–1943 marked a turning point in the war in Europe. In August 1942 the German army began a siege of this city, whose capture would give Germany access to Soviet oil. The fighting dragged on much longer than the Germans expected, and when winter arrived, the German army was ill-equipped to deal with harsh conditions. After months of ferocious fighting, in February 1943, the Soviet army captured the ninety thousand Germans who survived the freezing cold and near-constant combat. Meanwhile, the British army in North Africa faced off against German troops under General Erwin Rommel. Skilled in the new kind of mobile warfare, Rommel let his tanks move hundreds of miles from supply lines. He could not, however, overcome Allied access to secret German communication codes, and this access ultimately helped the Allies capture Morocco and Algeria in the fall of 1942. After driving Rommel out of Africa, the Allies landed in Sicily in July 1943. A slow, bitter fight for the Italian peninsula followed, lasting until April 1945, when Allied forces finally triumphed. After Italy's liberation, partisans shot Mussolini and his mistress and hung their dead bodies for public display.

The victory at Stalingrad marked the beginning of the Soviet drive westward, during which the Soviets still bore the brunt of the Nazi war machine. British and U.S. warplanes bombed German cities, and on June 6, 1944, known as D-Day, combined Allied forces attacked the heavily fortified French beaches of Normandy and then fought their way through the German-held territory of western France. Meanwhile the Soviets took Poland, Bulgaria, Romania, and finally Hungary during the winter of 1944–1945. As the military vice tightened, Hitler refused to spare the German people by surrendering. Instead, he committed suicide with his wife, Eva Braun, as the Soviet army took Berlin in April. Germany finally surrendered on May 8, 1945.

Turning the Tide in the Pacific

The Allies had followed a "Europe first" strategy for conducting the war, but had nonetheless steadily pursued the Japanese in the Pacific. In 1942, Allied forces destroyed some of Japan's formidable naval power in battles at Midway Island and Guadalcanal (see again Map 28.4). Japan lacked the capacity to recoup losses of ships or of manpower, while the Allies had not only their own productive power but access to materiel manufactured in Australia, India, and elsewhere around the world. The Allies stormed one Pacific island after another, gaining more bases from which to cut off Japanese supply lines and launch bombers toward Japan. In response to kamikaze attacks and the suicidal resistance of soldiers and civilians alike, the Allies stepped up their bombing of major cities, killing some 120,000 civilians in its spring 1945 firebombing of Tokyo.

The Atomic Bomb

Meanwhile a U.S.-based international team of more than one hundred thousand workers, including scientists, technicians, and other staff, had secretly developed the atomic bomb. The Japanese practice of fighting to the last man rather than surrendering persuaded Allied military leaders that the defeat of Japan might cost the lives of hundreds of thousands of Allied soldiers (and even more Japanese). On August 6, 1945, the U.S. government unleashed the new atomic weapon on Hiroshima. Three days later a second bomb was dropped on Nagasaki. The two bombings killed 140,000 people instantly; tens of thousands died later from burns, radiation poisoning, and other wounds. Hardliners in the Japanese military wanted to continue the war, but on August 15, 1945, Japan surrendered.

Postwar Plans and Uncertainties

Although the fighting had ended, conditions for lasting peace were poor at best. Japan, Europe, and large parts of East Asia and the Pacific lay in ruins. Governments and social order in many parts of the world were fragile if not totally broken. An estimated 100 million people had died in the war, and perhaps an equal number were homeless refugees, wandering the devastated land in search of food and shelter. Forced into armies or labor camps for war production, colonial peoples were in full rebellion or close to it. For a second time in three decades, they had seen their imperial masters killing one another, slaughtered by the very technology that was supposed to make Western civilization superior (see Seeing the Past: Technological Warfare: Civilization or Barbarism?). With their respect for empire undone, it was only a matter of time before colonized peoples would mount battles of their own for independence.

Technological Warfare: Civilization or Barbarism?

Hiroshima, September 2, 1945 (Bettmann/Corbis.)

This photograph of Hiroshima, Japan, shows the near-total destruction that resulted from the dropping of the first atomic bomb on August 6, 1945. The atomic bomb was the work of the world's top scientists during World War II, and its development resulted from the theories of brilliant people like Albert Einstein. So too, other increasingly sophisticated weaponry and methods for mass killing paralleled the great advances in a number of scientific fields. For some two centuries, the West characterized its scientific achievements as the hallmark of advanced civilization and viewed as backward those countries without them. It continued to make such claims as increasingly powerful nuclear weapons were tested in the Pacific and on the Asian continent, resulting in the annihilation of entire islands and the destruction of the environment. The visual and other evidence from Hiroshima can lead us to reflect to what degree the ability to destroy more lives than ever before and with less effort is a mark of high civilization or of barbarism.

EXAMINING THE EVIDENCE

1. **How is a moral argument for the atomic bomb possible?**

2. **How would you situate the atomic bomb and its use during World War II in the scientific and intellectual history of the West?**

The United Nations

Amid chaos, a wartime agreement led to the founding of the **United Nations** (UN). Franklin Roosevelt coined the term *United Nations* for the alliance of twenty-six countries formed on January 1, 1942, to fight the Axis. With the weakening of the League of Nations during the 1930s and its collapse after the outbreak of war, international institutions for collective security were absent, giving the formation of the United Nations a new urgency and the term a new meaning. In 1944, even as the war proceeded, delegates from the Big Three plus China met in Washington, D.C., to draw up plans for the UN. As a result of this often-ignored wartime conference, in June 1945, before the war was over, representatives from fifty countries signed the UN charter, setting the conditions for peaceful international cooperation. It remained to be seen whether this new organization would be more successful than its predecessor at maintaining world peace.

The Cold War

As the world sought to recover, a new struggle called the Cold War was taking root between the world's two military powers—the United States and the Soviet Union. At war's end, Stalin continued to see the world as hostile to his nation; the United States abruptly cut off many aid programs to the starving Soviet Union. In the face of this hostility, Stalin believed that Soviet security depended on not just a temporary military occupation of eastern Europe and Germany but a permanent "buffer zone" of European states loyal to the USSR as a safeguard against a revived Germany in particular and the anti-Soviet Western states more generally. Across the Atlantic, President Harry S. Truman, who had succeeded Roosevelt after his death in April 1945, saw the initial temporary occupation as the beginning of an era of permanent Communist expansion, especially since the Soviets were setting up friendly governments in the areas of eastern Europe they had liberated. By 1946, members of the U.S. State Department were describing Stalin as a "neurotic"

United Nations The international organization of nations established at the end of World War II to replace the League of Nations and to promote diplomacy and the peaceful settlement of disputes for countries worldwide.

Asian ruler prepared to continue the centuries-old Russian thirst for world domination. For his part, Stalin claimed that "it was the Soviet army that won" World War II and warned Anglo-American forces not to continue moving eastward. In a March 1946 speech, former British Prime Minister Churchill warned that an "iron curtain" had fallen across Europe, cutting off the East from the West and dividing the world into two hostile camps.

As the Cold War came to inflame global politics, it affected the world's peoples as World War II had done. Eva Kantorowsky was again ensnared as she and her family, like many of Shanghai's refugees, tried to emigrate to the United States. But many Americans, even though they had fought against Hitler, remained anti-Semitic, and the U.S. Congress passed legislation blocking the immigration of Jewish refugees after the war. Jews were Communists, members of Congress claimed, echoing Nazi ideology as they played the Cold War card. Eva eventually arrived in the United States despite the growing intensity of the Cold War.

COUNTERPOINT
Nonviolence and Pacifism in an Age of War

The wars of the twentieth century—hot and cold—focused the attention of peoples throughout the world on the exercise of military power. Leading nations from Germany and Japan to the Soviet Union and the United States saw military capacity as the measure of national greatness. Some activists and ordinary people, however, realized that nonviolent tactics could be powerful and effective tools to undermine colonialism and the doctrine of total war. Traditional modes of resistance shaped some efforts, while religious precepts underlay others.

> **FOCUS**
>
> In what ways did peace movements serve as a countertrend to events in the period from 1929 to 1945?

Traditional Tactics: The Example of Nigerian Women

In 1929, women in British-controlled Nigeria rebelled at the new tax the government tried to impose on them as part of its effort to resolve economic problems in England. They painted their bodies and sang and danced in the nude outside the homes of local tax collectors, who attacked and even burned some of the women's houses. Their method was called "sitting on a man," because it was generally used against rulings by men that the women considered unjust. British officials justified shooting the women, killing fifty-three of them, by calling the women's behavior irrational and dangerous. Throughout the 1930s and up into the 1980s, women in Nigeria used traditional nonviolent tactics, including removing all their clothing, to protest low prices for their palm products and the exploitative practices of oil companies in their region.

The women of Nigeria eventually became national heroes of the movement for independence, and other pacifist traditions were mobilized during the 1920s and 1930s as well. Jainism, an ancient South Asian religion, held to the belief in *ahimsa*—the idea of doing no harm—and other Asian religions adopted this belief, leading many to become pacifists.

Gandhi and Civil Disobedience

In the 1920s and 1930s, practitioners of peaceful protest adopted an approach that came to be variously called **civil disobedience** or nonviolent resistance. Mohandas Gandhi, for one, led his followers in 1930 on a twenty-three-day "Salt March" to break the law giving the British a monopoly on salt—a necessity of life that exists freely in nature. Professing to model his tactics on those of the British suffragists and the teachings of Jesus, Buddha, and other spiritual leaders, Gandhi's nonviolent protest highlighted India's difference

civil disobedience A political strategy of deliberately but peacefully breaking the law to protest oppression and obtain political change.

Mohandas Gandhi and Nonviolence

Indian leader Mohandas (Mahatma "great souled one") Gandhi led a mass movement, but his followers flocked to him because of a message entirely different from those of Mussolini and Hitler. Gandhi was neither bombastic nor wedded to material and militaristic display. Instead he denounced the violence and materialism of the West, preferring *Satyagraha*—soulforce—to physical conflict, and spinning by hand to parading tanks and rockets. (The Art Archive/Kharbine-Tapabor/ Collection NB.)

from militaristic, even genocidal Westerners, as he noted in more than one of his writings. He called his strategy *Satyagraha* (SAH-ty-ah-GRAH-hah)—truth and firmness—and rejected the view that his tactics were "passive." Rather, such acts as taking salt and then being beaten or arrested (as Gandhi was) demanded incredible discipline to remain opposed but at the same time nonviolent.

Pacifism, including the tactics of Gandhi, unfolded with real conviction both during the pre–World War I arms race and with even greater fervor in the aftermath of World War I. Feminists played key roles in the development of the Women's International League for Peace and Freedom after that war, and religious groups in many parts of the world contested what they saw as a new militarism developing in the interwar years. Many of these groups remained firmly pacifistic even with the rise of fascism, and were ridiculed either as deluded or as traitors. British novelist George Orwell called all pacifists in the 1930s "objectively fascist." After World War II, civil rights activists in the United States embraced nonviolence and civil disobedience. In the 1950s and early 1960s they "sat in" to desegregate lunch counters, buses, and public facilities that were closed to them, even as officials whipped, hosed, and murdered them. Many still see committed pacifists as deluded thinkers or as traitors to the nation-state, but none can deny that for some causes pacifists have been remarkably effective.

Conclusion

The Great Depression, which destroyed the lives and livelihoods of millions of people throughout the world, created conditions in which dictators and authoritarian rulers thrived because they promised to restore national greatness and prosperity. Mobilized by the mass media, people turned from the representative institutions that were accused of failing them and supported militaristic leaders who offered hope of a brighter future. Authoritarian leaders used aggression and violence to gain support, but others—both nonviolent resisters in the colonies and those with vivid memories of World War I—took up pacifism or a strategy of nonviolent civil disobedience to achieve their objectives, objectives that included the overthrow of authoritarian leaders.

Leaders of the Western democracies, hoping to avoid another war, permitted Hitler and Mussolini to menace Europe unimpeded throughout the 1930s. In Asia, the Japanese military convinced citizens that the nation deserved an extensive empire and that white domination must be ended. The coalition that formed to stop Germany, Italy, and Japan was an uneasy confederation among the Allied powers of France, Britain, the Soviet Union, and the United States. At the war's end, Europe's economies were shattered, its population reduced, its colonies on the verge of independence, its peoples starving and homeless. Occupied by the victorious U.S. Army, Japan was similarly devastated, as were large swaths of North Africa, Asia, and the Pacific Islands. People who had been dislocated by the war—such as Eva Kantorowsky and her family—were dislocated once again. The massive death and destruction of the war ended Europe's global dominance. Now the Soviet Union and the United States reigned as the world's superpowers, with the newly formed United Nations, a global organization, the only potential check on the two nations' unprecedented power.

In the decades following World War II, the United States and the Soviet Union competed for power and influence in every corner of the globe, seeing every local and regional development through the prism of the Cold War ideological split. Amid this growing divide, World War II brought another notable change: millions of people determined as a result of their experience of global war that colonialism, whether that of the French, British, or Japanese, would not long survive.

NOTES

1. Ana Núñez Machin, quoted in Angel Santana Suárez ,"Angel Santana Suárez: Cuban Sugar Worker," in *The Human Tradition in Latin America: The Twentieth Century*, ed. William H. Beezley and Judith Ewell (Wilmington, DE: Scholarly Resources, 1987), 85, 86.
2. Quoted in Piers Brendon, *The Dark Valley: A Panorama of the 1930s* (London: Jonathan Cape, 2000), 175.
3. Quoted in Ann Farnsworth-Alvear, *Dulcinea in the Factory: Myths, Morals, Men, and Women in Colombia's Industrial Experiment, 1905–1960* (Durham, NC: Duke University Press, 2000), 124, 125.
4. Edvard Radzinsky, *Stalin: The First In-Depth Biography Based on Explosive New Documents from Russia's Secret Archives*, trans. H. T. Willetts (New York: Doubleday, 1996), 363.
5. Jiang Jieshi, quoted in Patricia Buckley Ebrey, *Cambridge Illustrated History of China* (Cambridge, U.K.: Cambridge University Press, 1996), 277.
6. Herbert Bix, *Hirohito and the Making of Modern Japan* (New York: HarperCollins, 2000), 274–276.
7. Quoted in Bix, *Hirohito*, 315.
8. Matsuoka Yosuke, quoted in Bix, *Hirohito*, 374.
9. Amartya Sen, "Interview," *Journal of Economic Perspectives* (1994).
10. Quoted in *The Washington Post*, May 23, 2005.
11. Carla Capponi, interviewed in Shelley Saywell, *Women in War: From World War II to El Salvador* (New York: Penguin, 1986), 82.

RESOURCES FOR RESEARCH

1929: The Great Depression Begins

The Great Depression was a global event, affecting peasants and farmers, factory workers and shopkeepers, and the upper classes. Balderston and Rothermund provide excellent surveys of the worldwide impact.

Balderston, Theo. *The World Economy and National Economies in the Interwar Slump*. 2003.

Brendon, Piers. *The Dark Valley: A Panorama of the 1930s*. 2000.

Feinstein, Charles H., et al. *The World Economy Between the World Wars*. 2008.

Rothermund, Dietmar. *The Global Impact of the Great Depression, 1929–1939*. 1996.

Vernon, James. *Modernity's Hunger: How Imperial Britain Created and Failed to Solve the Problem of Hunger in the Modern World*. 2006.

Militarizing the Masses in the 1930s

Many postwar politicians promised relief of economic hardship through military conquest and discipline. Regimented parades and other displays of military power attracted mass audiences. Kushner's book captures the unfolding of those promises in the case of Japan in Manchuria.

Hammer, Joshua. *Yokohama Burning: The Deadly 1923 Earthquake and Fire That Helped Forge the Path to World War II.* 2006.

Kaplan, Marion. *Between Dignity and Despair: Jewish Life in Nazi Germany.* 1998.

Kushner, Barak. *The Thought War: Japanese Imperial Propaganda.* 2006.

Naimark, Norman. *Stalin's Genocides.* 2010.

* Pa, Chin. *Family.* 1931.

Wildt, Michael. *An Uncompromising Generation: The Nazi Leadership of the Reich Security Main Office.* 2009.

Global War, 1937–1945

The scholarship on World War II is extensive. These works cover facets of global warfare.

Browning, Christopher. *Remembering Survival: Inside a Nazi Slave Labor Camp.* 2010.

Fyne, Robert. *Long Ago and Far Away: Hollywood and the Second World War.* 2008.

Johnson, David. *World War II and the Scramble for Labour in Colonial Zimbabwe, 1939–1948.* 2000.

Peattie, Mark R. *Sunburst: The Rise of Japanese Naval Air Power, 1909–1940.* 2002.

St. Andrews University in Scotland provides a number of links to sources for the diplomatic history of the origins of World War II: http://www.st-andrews.ac.uk/~pv/courses/prewar/resources.html.

Weinberg, Gerhard L. *A World at Arms: A Global History of World War II.* 2005.

From Allied Victory to the Cold War, 1943–1945

Among the many fascinating books about the war is Spector's account of the conflict's end in Asia, where Japanese soldiers and conquered peoples did not believe the war had ended and where in many cases the Allies enlisted remnants of the Japanese army to crush independence movements.

Bucur, Maria. *Heroes and Victims: Remembering War in Twentieth-Century Romania.* 2009.

Krylova, Anna. *Soviet Women in Combat: A History of Violence on the Eastern Front.* 2010.

Miner, Steven Merritt. *Stalin's Holy War: Religion, Nationalism, and Alliance Politics, 1941–1945.* 2003.

Rhodes, Richard. *Arsenals of Folly: The Making of the Nuclear Arms Race.* 2007.

Spector, Ronald H. *In the Ruins of Empire: The Japanese Surrender and the Battle for Postwar Asia.* 2007.

COUNTERPOINT: Nonviolence and Pacifism in an Age of War

Pacifism and nonviolent resistance were global phenomena. The anthology of Brock and Socknat provides a look at worldwide pacifism in the interwar years.

Allman, Jean, Susan Geiger, and Nakanyike Musisi, eds. *Women in African Colonial Histories.* 2002.

Brock, Peter, and Thomas P. Socknat, eds. *Challenge to Mars: Essays on Pacifism from 1918 to 1945.* 1999.

Matera, Marc, Misty L. Bastian, and Susan Kingsley Kent. *The Women's War of 1929: Gender and Violence in Colonial Nigeria.* 2011.

Siegel, Mona. *The Moral Disarmament of France: Education, Pacifism, and Patriotism, 1914–1940.* 2004.

Tidrick, Kathryn. *Gandhi: A Political and Spiritual Life.* 2007.

* Primary source.

▶ **For additional primary sources from this period,** see *Sources of Crossroads and Cultures*.

▶ **For Web sites, images, and documents related to topics in this chapter,** see Make History at bedfordstmartins.com/smith.

The major global development in this chapter ▶ The causes and
outcomes of the Great Depression and World War II.

IMPORTANT EVENTS

1920s	Collapse of commodity prices around the world
1929	Crash of the U.S. stock market; global depression begins; Stalin's "liquidation of the kulaks"
1930	Gandhi's Salt March
1930s	Sweden begins setting up welfare state
1931	Japan invades Manchuria
1933	Hitler comes to power in Germany and ends representative government
1934	Chinese Communists begin Long March
1935	Nuremberg Laws against the Jews in Germany; Italy invades Ethiopia
1936	Purges and show trials begin in USSR
1937	Japan attacks China; World War II begins in Asia
1939	Germany invades Poland; World War II begins in Europe
1941	Germany invades USSR; Japan attacks Pearl Harbor; United States enters the war
1941–1945	Holocaust
1943	USSR defeats Germany at Stalingrad
1945	Fall of Berlin and surrender of Germany; UN charter signed; United States drops atomic bombs; Japan surrenders

CHAPTER OVERVIEW QUESTIONS

1. How did ordinary people react to the Great Depression, and how did their reactions differ from country to country?

2. Why were dictators and antidemocratic leaders able to come to power in the 1930s, and how did all countries—autocratic and democratic alike—militarize the masses?

3. How are the Great Depression and World War II related historical events?

SECTION FOCUS QUESTIONS

1. What was the global impact of both the Great Depression and the attempts to overcome it?

2. How did dictatorships and democracies attempt to mobilize the masses?

3. How did World War II progress on the battlefront and the home front?

4. How did the Allied victory unfold, and what were the causes of that victory?

5. In what ways did peace movements serve as a countertrend to events in the period from 1929 to 1945?

MAKING CONNECTIONS

1. What are the main differences between World War I (see Chapter 27) and World War II?

2. In what specific ways did World Wars I and II affect the African and Asian colonies of the imperial powers?

3. How do the strengths and weaknesses of the Allies and the Axis compare?

4. How would you describe the importance of World War II not only to the unfolding of history but also to present-day concerns?

KEY TERMS

Allies (p. 944)
appeasement (p. 940)
Axis (p. 944)
central economic planning (p. 933)
civil disobedience (p. 953)
five-year plan (p. 933)
Great Depression (p. 929)
Greater East Asia Co-Prosperity Sphere (p. 941)
Holocaust (p. 945)
purge (p. 934)
totalitarianism (p. 933)
United Nations (p. 952)

AT A CROSSROADS ▶

In 1957 Ghana became the first sub-Saharan nation to free itself from imperial rule. This woman celebrates not only Ghana's freedom but also its president, Kwame Nkrumah, who had led the campaign of civil disobedience against the British. Her clothing displays emblems of liberation, including Nkrumah's image—a preview of what would become the popular use of political heroes' faces on T-shirts and banners in the 1960s. At the time, Ghana marked a crossroads in global and African politics, as its leader and those who followed him advocated pan-Africanism and a political activism similar to that of Indian nationalist and spiritual leader Mohandas Gandhi. (Universal Images Group/SuperStock.)

The Emergence of New Nations in a Cold War World

1945–1970

During the early 1950s, on the first Thursday of the month, everyday life in Cairo and other major cities of the Arab world came to a standstill. Patrons of cafés huddled around the radio, and cabdrivers discharged their customers and dashed home to catch the broadcast. All were eager to tune in to a program featuring singer Umm Kulthum. Kulthum's repertoire included traditional desert songs, religious verses, and romantic ballads. Born at the beginning of the twentieth century, she began her career as a child disguised as a boy because girls were not supposed to perform in public. Singing verses from the Qur'an in her strong voice, she enraptured local audiences and her fame spread. By the 1950s she had become a national phenomenon, "the voice of Egypt" for the newly independent republic. In the words of one fan, her singing "shows our ordinary life." Even Egypt's leader Gamal Abdel Nasser, who in 1952 finally instituted a government totally free from British supervision, recognized the power of Umm Kulthum's popularity. He broadcast his speeches just before her program aired to link himself to her appeal. Traveling widely through the Middle East, Umm Kulthum used her vocal talent to encourage Arab-speaking people as a whole to celebrate their own culture as another way of shaking off the European powers.

The creation of a fully independent Egyptian republic was just one of the acts of liberation in the postwar world. From the Middle East through Africa and Asia, independence

World Politics and the Cold War

FOCUS Why was the Cold War waged, and how did it reshape world politics?

Decolonization and the Birth of Nations

FOCUS How did colonized peoples achieve their independence from the imperialist powers after World War II?

World Recovery in the 1950s and 1960s

FOCUS What were the major elements of recovery in different parts of the world in the decades following World War II?

Cultural Dynamism amid Cold War

FOCUS How did the experience of world war, decolonization, and Cold War affect cultural life and thought?

COUNTERPOINT: The Bandung Conference, 1955

FOCUS How did the Bandung Conference and its aims represent an alternative to the Cold War division of the globe?

BACKSTORY

As we saw in Chapter 28, imperial rivalries played a key role in the outbreak of World War II, the most destructive conflict in human history. By the time the war was over, as many as 100 million people had died, countries around the world lay in ruin, and the imperial system that had helped produce the war was in disarray. The chaos and confusion of the postwar world gave rise to a new set of global political trends. The formation of organizations such as the United Nations reflected new levels of cooperation among nations. At the same time, rising nationalism among colonized peoples sparked the process of decolonization. Finally, the Cold War between the United States and the Soviet Union shaped politics around the world and posed an unprecedented threat to world peace. These trends, along with the rising level of technological sophistication and the yearning of people around the world for peace and prosperity, would play major roles in defining the postwar world, a world that was more closely connected than ever before.

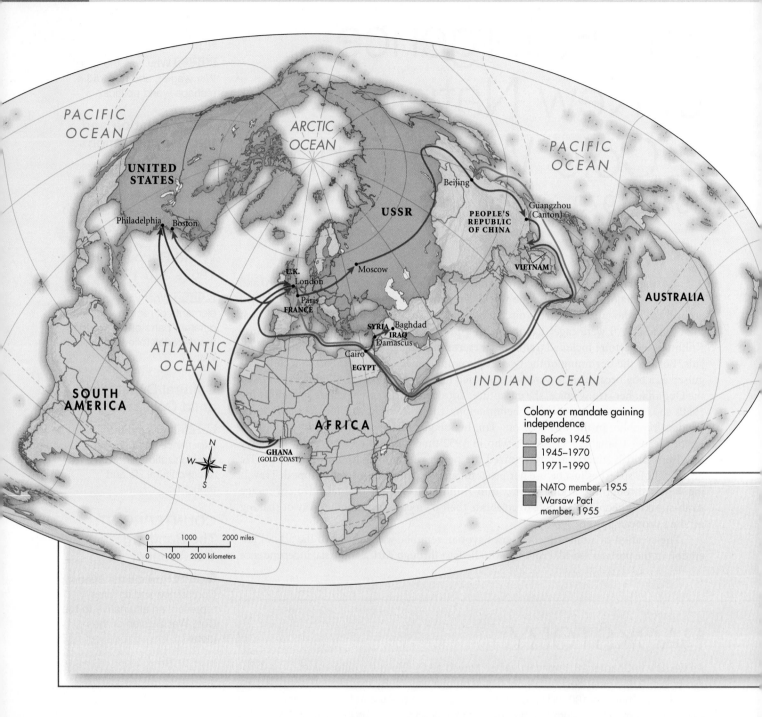

Colony or mandate gaining
independence
- Before 1945
- 1945–1970
- 1971–1990

- NATO member, 1955
- Warsaw Pact
  member, 1955

0 1000 2000 miles
0 1000 2000 kilometers

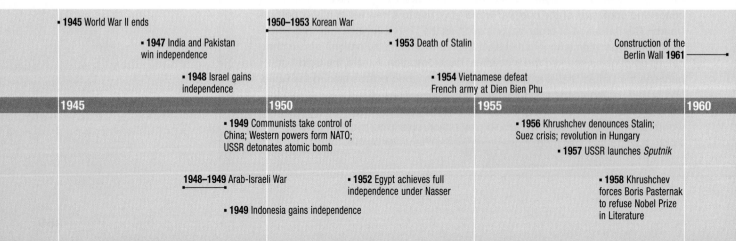

- **1945** World War II ends

- **1947** India and Pakistan
  win independence

- **1948** Israel gains
  independence

1950–1953 Korean War

- **1953** Death of Stalin

- **1954** Vietnamese defeat
  French army at Dien Bien Phu

Construction of the
Berlin Wall **1961**

1945　　　　**1950**　　　　**1955**　　　　**1960**

- **1949** Communists take control of
  China; Western powers form NATO;
  USSR detonates atomic bomb

- **1956** Khrushchev denounces Stalin;
  Suez crisis; revolution in Hungary

- **1957** USSR launches *Sputnik*

1948–1949 Arab-Israeli War

- **1952** Egypt achieves full
  independence under Nasser

- **1958** Khrushchev
  forces Boris Pasternak
  to refuse Nobel Prize
  in Literature

- **1949** Indonesia gains independence

movements toppled colonial governments that attempted to revive their control after World War II. Workers, professionals, veterans, and other activists took up arms to drive out British, French, Dutch, Belgian, and U.S. forces. **Decolonization** was followed by the difficult process of nation building. In addition to creating government structures, newly independent states had to rebuild roads destroyed in the war, erect public buildings, and create systems for educating citizens and maintaining their health. In sum, the destruction of the colonial system created the opportunity, and the necessity, for formerly colonized peoples to rebuild and redefine the connections among citizens and the relationship between newly independent nations and the rest of the world. Like Umm Kulthum, talented patriots throughout the Middle East, Asia, Africa, and Latin America devoted their livelihoods and capabilities to advancing this cause.

Postcolonial nation building took place in a vastly changed world. The old European-dominated international order was gone, replaced by the rivalry between the United States and the Soviet Union for control of a world in which many traditional political and economic systems had collapsed. The nuclear arsenals of these two "superpowers," a term coined in 1947, grew massively in the 1950s, but they were enemies who did not fight outright—at least not on their own soil. Instead, they preferred to confront each other in the developing world. The U.S.-USSR rivalry, known as the **Cold War**, set the so-called communist East against the democratic, capitalist West. When the United States discovered Soviet missile sites on the island of Cuba in 1962, the Cold War rivals took the world to the brink of nuclear disaster.

Yet there was a surge of optimistic activism after World War II. The birth of new nations and the defeat of authoritarian militarism inspired hope that life would become fairer and that people everywhere would gain the freedom to determine their own fate. Revolutionary-minded thinkers poured out new political theories, while novelists explored the often-harsh realities of independence. In rebuilding, some politicians championed the

decolonization The process of freeing regions from imperial control and creating independent nations.

Cold War The rivalry between the Soviet Union and the United States that followed World War II and shaped world politics between 1945 and 1989.

MAPPING THE WORLD

Independence Movements and New Nations

Earlier movements for freedom from colonialism were reinvigorated at the end of World War II; the Axis and Allied powers had been exhausted by this unprecedented conflict, and some were bankrupt. Independent nations emerged from the remnants of imperialism, some of them only after violent struggles with their rulers. These independent nations, however, faced a novel global situation—a bipolar world dominated by the Soviet Union and the United States and faced with a possible nuclear holocaust. This potentially disastrous confrontation was called the Cold War.

ROUTES ▼

→ Travels of Ho Chi Minh, c. 1912–1941

→ Travels of Kwame Nkrumah, c. 1930–1947

→ Travels of Umm Kulthum, c. 1932

→ Travels of Wu Guanzhong, c. 1947–1950

—**1962** Algeria wins independence; Cuban Missile Crisis

| 1965 | 1970 | 1975 |

c. 1966–1976 Mao Zedong's "Cultural Revolution"

well-being of their nation's citizens. Vast nation-building projects took shape; the welfare state expanded; and by the end of the 1950s economic rebirth, stimulated in part by the Cold War, had made many regions grow more rapidly than ever before. In many places, however, people caught up in events precipitated by Cold War rivalries faced a grim, and often deadly, reality. In the 1950s and 1960s, at the same time that Egyptian singer Umm Kulthum invigorated Arabs about the region's future, youthful followers of China's Mao Zedong banded together to bring about a "cultural revolution" that would transform society, killing and torturing millions of their fellow citizens in its name. The search for freedom thus differed drastically from place to place in this age of Cold War extremes.

OVERVIEW QUESTIONS

The major global development in this chapter: The political transformations of the postwar world and their social and cultural consequences.

As you read, consider:

1. How did the Cold War affect the superpowers and the world beyond them?

2. How did the Cold War shape everyday lives and goals?

3. Why did colonial nationalism revive in the postwar world, and how did decolonization affect society and culture?

4. Why did the model of a welfare state emerge after World War II, and how did this development affect ordinary people?

World Politics and the Cold War

FOCUS

Why was the Cold War waged, and how did it reshape world politics?

In 1945, Europe's world leadership ended and the reign of the United States and the Soviet Union as the world's new superpowers began. The United States, its territory virtually untouched in the war, had become the world's economic giant, and the Soviet Union, despite suffering immense destruction, had developed enormous military might. Occupying Europe as part of the victorious alliance against Nazism and fascism, the two superpowers came to use Germany—at the heart of the continent and its politics—to divide Europe in two. By the late 1940s, the USSR had imposed communist rule throughout most of eastern Europe, while the United States poured vast amounts of money, personnel, and military equipment into western Europe and parts of Asia, Africa, and Latin America to win the allegiance of new and old nations in those areas. Both superpowers maintained dense networks of spies and conducted plots, assassinations, and other undercover operations around the world. Unwilling to confront each other head-on, they fought **proxy wars** in smaller, contained areas such as Korea, while amassing huge stockpiles of weapons—including nuclear missiles and bombs—that could annihilate the world.

proxy war During the Cold War, a conflict in another part of the world backed by the USSR or the United States as part of their rivalry.

The New Superpowers

The situation of the two superpowers in 1945 could not have been more different. The United States was the richest country in the world. Its industrial output had increased a remarkable 15 percent annually between 1940 and 1944, a rate of growth that was reflected in workers' wages. By 1947, the United States controlled almost two-thirds of the world's gold bullion and more than half of its commercial shipping. Casting aside its post–World War I policy of nonintervention, the United States embraced its position as global leader and negotiated collective security agreements with many nations. Americans had learned about the world while tracking the progress of World War II; hundreds of thousands of American soldiers, government officials, and relief workers gained direct experience of Europe, Africa, and Asia. Although some Americans feared a postwar depression and nuclear annihilation, continued spending on industrial and military research, a baby boom, suburban housing development, and rising consumer purchases kept the economy buoyant, and most Americans were optimistic about their futures.

The Soviets emerged from the war with a well-justified sense of accomplishment. Withstanding horrendous losses, they had successfully resisted the most massive onslaught ever launched against a modern nation. Soviet citizens believed that a victory that had cost the USSR tens of millions of lives would improve everyday conditions and continue the war's relatively relaxed politics. "Life will become pleasant," one writer prophesied at war's end. "There will be much coming and going, and a lot of contacts with the West." In the 1930s, the Soviets had industrialized their nation, and in the 1940s they had defeated Nazism. With these achievements behind them, many expected an end to decades of hardship and looked forward to building a new, more open Soviet society.

Taking a very different view of the situation, Stalin moved ruthlessly to reassert control. In 1946, his new five-year plan increased production goals and mandated more stringent collectivization of agriculture. Stalin cut back the army by two-thirds to beef up the labor force, and also turned his attention to the low birthrate brought about by wartime conditions. He introduced an intense propaganda campaign emphasizing that working women should hold down jobs and also fulfill their "true nature" by producing many children.

The Cold War Unfolds 1945–1962

The Cold War, the political, economic, and ideological competition between the United States and the Soviet Union, would afflict the world for more than four decades, with lingering effects even today. Its origins remain a matter of debate. Some historians point to consistent U.S., British, and French hostility that began with the Bolshevik Revolution in 1917 and continued through World War II. Others stress Stalin's aggressive policies, notably the Nazi-Soviet alliance in 1939 and his quick claims on the Baltic states and Polish territory when World War II broke out. Even during that war, suspicions among the Allies ran deep. Stalin felt that Churchill and Roosevelt, as part of their anticommunist policy, were deliberately letting the USSR bear the brunt of Hitler's onslaught on Europe. Some Americans believed that dropping the atomic bomb on Japan would also frighten the Soviets away from seizing more land. As early as 1946, the U.S. State Department described Stalin as continuing the centuries-old Russian thirst for "world domination." In late August 1949, the USSR tested its own atom bomb, and from then on the superpowers built and stockpiled ever-more-sophisticated nuclear weapons, including hydrogen and neutron bombs. From this point on, the conflict between the superpowers carried with it the threat of global annihilation.

The United States acknowledged Soviet influence in areas the USSR occupied, but worried that the Soviets were intent on spreading communism around the world. The difficulties of postwar life in western and southern Europe made communist programs promising better conditions attractive to workers, and communist leadership in the resistance movements of World War II gave the party a powerful appeal. When in 1947 communist insurgents threatened to overrun the right-wing monarchy the British had installed in Greece, U.S. President Harry S. Truman announced what quickly became known as the Truman Doctrine, the countering of political crises that might lead to communist rule with economic and military aid. Fearing that Americans would balk at backing an antidemocratic Greece, the U.S. Congress

American Aid to Tokyo's Orphans

In addition to the homelessness, disease, and starvation caused by the war, many of Japan's citizens lost their families in the atomic- and fire-bombings. As part of the Cold War effort to win allies, the United States hurried to make things better for those most in need—including defeated enemies such as Japan and Germany—by giving them aid. These orphans in Tokyo are photographed gratefully receiving this aid. What in this image suggests both a humanitarian and a propaganda purpose to such aid programs? (Bettmann/Corbis.)

agreed to the program only if Truman would "scare the hell out of the country," as one member of Congress put it. Truman thus promoted a massive aid program as necessary to prevent global Soviet conquest, warning that "the seeds of totalitarian regimes are nurtured by misery and want."[1] As the Communists backed off in Greece, the Truman Doctrine began the U.S. Cold War policy of **containment**—the attempt to keep communism from spreading.

The Truman Doctrine was quickly followed by enactment of the European Recovery Program, popularly called the Marshall Plan, a program of massive U.S. economic aid to Europe. Announced by Secretary of State George C. Marshall in 1947, the Marshall Plan claimed to be directed not "against any country or doctrine but against hunger, poverty, desperation, and chaos." Stalin, however, saw it as a U.S. political trick that caught him without resources to offer similar economic aid to the Soviet satellite countries and thus designed to open avenues to American influence in eastern Europe. By the early 1950s, the United States had sent western Europe more than $12 billion in food, equipment, and services, and it sent the same amount to Japan alone, helping even former enemies to rebuild and thus stay in the U.S. orbit.

Taking advantage of its military occupation of the region, the Soviet Union turned its military occupation of eastern Europe into a buffer zone of satellite states directed by "people's governments." In such Soviet-allied states as Poland, Czechoslovakia, and Hungary, Stalin enforced collectivized agriculture, centralized industrialization, and the nationalization of private property. In Hungary, for example, communists seized and reapportioned all estates over twelve hundred acres. Land redistribution won the support of the poorer peasants, but enforced collectivization of farming was a brutal process for many. Others felt that ultimately their lives and their children's lives had improved. "Before we peasants were dirty and poor, we worked like dogs. . . . Was that a good life? No sir, it wasn't. . . . I was a miserable sharecropper and my son is an engineer," said one Romanian peasant.

Modernization of production in the Soviet bloc opened new technical and bureaucratic careers, but economic development in the satellite states remained slow because the USSR bought goods from these satellite states at bargain prices and sold to them at exorbitant ones. Despite this inequity, people's livelihoods changed dramatically, as they moved to cities to receive better education, health care, and jobs, albeit at the price of severe political repression. They also experienced intense immersion in Russian rather than their own national cultures.

Germany Divided

Cold War competition led to the division of Germany. The terms of Allied agreements reached at Yalta in 1945 provided for the division of Germany and its capital city, Berlin, into four zones, each of which was occupied by one of the four principal victors in World War II—the United States, the Soviet Union, Britain, and France (see Map 29.1). The agreements provided for economic coordination among the zones, with agricultural surplus from Soviet-occupied areas feeding urban populations in the Western-controlled zones; in turn, industrial goods would be sent to the USSR. The Soviets upset this plan and instead sent equipment and dismantled industries from its zone to the Soviet Union. They transported skilled workers, engineers, and scientists to the USSR to work as virtual slave laborers. In response, France, Britain, and the United States agreed to merge their zones

containment The U.S. policy developed during the Cold War to prevent the spread of communism.

into a West German state that would serve as a buffer against the Soviets. The Soviets then created an East German state to act as a buffer against the West German state.

On June 24, 1948, Soviet troops blockaded Germany's capital, Berlin, located more than one hundred miles deep in the Soviet zone. The Soviets declared all of Berlin part of their zone of occupation and, expecting to starve the city into submission, refused to allow highway, railroad, and barge traffic into West Berlin. Instead of handing over Berlin, the United States flew in millions of tons of provisions to the city that just three years earlier had been the capital of the Nazi state. During the winter of 1948–1949, the Berlin airlift—"Operation Vittles," U.S. pilots called it—even funneled coal to the city to warm some 2 million isolated Berliners. The blockade was lifted in May 1949 and West Berlin remained tied to the West—a symbol of freedom to many. More than a decade later, in the summer of 1961, the East German government began construction of the Berlin Wall. The divided city had served, embarrassingly to the Soviets, as an escape route by which some 3 million people had fled to the freer, more prosperous West.

The People's Republic of China 1949

At the same time that the conflict between the superpowers in Europe was heating up, the Cold War entered a new phase with the triumph of Chinese Communist forces over the Nationalists in 1949. Before, during, and after World War II, the Nationalist government led by Jiang Jieshi (Chiang Kai-shek) and his unpopular armies had fought to eliminate rival communist forces to consolidate the Nationalist regime. With varying degrees of success, the United States and its allies did much both to prop up Jiang and to force these two Chinese enemy factions to concentrate on defeating Japan during World War II instead of annihilating one another. Once the war was over, however, the Nationalists and Communists went at each other once more.

In 1949, Mao Zedong (MOW zuh-DOONG) and his army of Communists won. From a prosperous peasant family, Mao had little in common with the farmers whom he targeted for support. He never worked as an agricultural laborer but rather spent his entire life as a politician, taking advantage of the opportunities for advancement created by the fluid conditions of modern nation building in China. At the outset he gravitated toward communism with USSR financial support. Once in power, Mao announced that Chinese communism in the new People's Republic of China would focus above all on the welfare of the peasantry rather than the industrial proletariat. Mao's government instituted social reforms such as civil equality for women and at the same time copied Soviet collectivization, rapid industrialization, and brutal repression of the privileged classes. Jiang and many of his Nationalist forces were forced to the island of Taiwan, where they refused to accept the legitimacy of Mao's communist government. With Jiang supported by the United States, Cold War fires spread to East Asia.

Proxy Wars and Cold War Alliances

The Chinese Communists' victory over the Nationalists in 1949 spurred both superpowers not only to increase their involvement in Asian politics but to form alliances with nations around the world, pulling much of the globe into the Cold War. Africa and Latin America

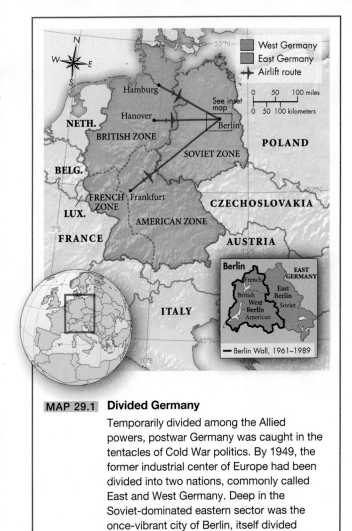

MAP 29.1   Divided Germany
Temporarily divided among the Allied powers, postwar Germany was caught in the tentacles of Cold War politics. By 1949, the former industrial center of Europe had been divided into two nations, commonly called East and West Germany. Deep in the Soviet-dominated eastern sector was the once-vibrant city of Berlin, itself divided east and west.

Mao Zedong and the Communist Victory

Cosmonauts and Astronauts

Soviet Leaders Honor Yuri Gagarin and Valentina Tereshkova

Soviet cosmonauts, like U.S. astronauts, were heroes not only in their own countries but in their Cold War blocs. The Soviets made these two cosmonauts special heroes: Gagarin (second from the left) because he was the first man in space, and Tereshkova because she was the first woman in space and represented the equality for women said to exist only in the Soviet bloc. Even today, one can find mementos of these heroes on T-shirts and caps across the former Soviet Union, reminders of the Cold War. (akg-images/RIA Nowosti.)

The space race gave rise to many new livelihoods, but none more celebrated than that of cosmonaut and astronaut, as space travelers were called in the USSR and United States, respectively. As an occupation, it attracted people of both genders and all ethnicities and classes. The parents of cosmonaut Yuri Gagarin, the first person in space, worked on a communist collective farm, and Gagarin himself labored in a foundry before the Soviet government selected him for technical education and

eventual training as a pilot. His small stature, 5 feet 2 inches, helped him fit into the small cockpit of the first manned spacecraft—*Vostok I*. Television programs and films celebrate pioneers of space travel, both real and imaginary, and even today in small villages in eastern Europe one can buy T-shirts with pictures of Gagarin and other space heroes. The enduring human fascination with voyages and the longing to travel beyond the earth was on its way to being satisfied during these years.

felt the Cold War's impact as guerrilla fighters, spies, and activists for both sides blanketed their regions. The Cold War even reached into space: in 1957, the Soviets successfully launched the first artificial earth satellite, *Sputnik*, and in 1961 they put the first cosmonaut, Yuri Gagarin, in orbit around the earth. The Soviets' edge in space technology shocked the Western bloc as the superpowers continued their rivalries on the ground with more traditional weapons (see Lives and Livelihoods: Cosmonauts and Astronauts).

The Korean War　　The two superpowers faced off indirectly in Korea, which after World War II had been divided into two nations, North and South Korea. After border skirmishes by both sides, in 1950 the North Koreans, supported by the Soviet Union, invaded the U.S.-backed South. The United States maneuvered the UN Security Council into approving a "police action" against the North, and UN forces quickly drove well into North Korean territory, where they were met by the Chinese army supported by Soviet planes. Fighting continued for another two and a half years, with 3 million civilian deaths, but the war remained a stalemate. The opposing sides finally agreed to a settlement in 1953 that changed nothing: Korea would remain divided as before. The United States increased its military spending from

After the successful 1957 launch of *Sputnik*, the Soviets' edge in space so shocked the Western bloc that it motivated the creation in 1958 of the U.S. National Aeronautics and Space Administration (NASA). U.S. astronauts followed Gagarin, and like him became heroes: astronaut John Glenn, for example, served as a U.S. senator. Despite the dominance of the superpowers in space, citizens of some thirty-five countries, including Afghanistan, Belgium, Brazil, China, Cuba, Malaysia, Mexico, and Saudi Arabia, contributed their citizens to the world's various space programs. In addition, individual countries such as China, Brazil, and Iran recognized that capabilities in space were needed to participate in satellite technology and to create an independent military capability. Brazil, with the most developed space program in Latin America, began its work with sounding rockets in 1964. As countries beyond the superpowers initiated their own programs and cooperated with multinational ventures, livelihoods in space multiplied, including monitoring and spying on other nations' space capabilities.

Trained space travelers are generally drawn from the ranks of jet pilots (like Gagarin) and space engineers, with mathematicians and scientists added to oversee the execution of experiments in space. Recently, teachers and space tourists have joined the ranks of those more explicitly trained for space, to give these costly and time-consuming programs more widespread appeal. Whatever their backgrounds and missions on the spacecraft, however, candidates for space travel undergo rigorous instruction in experiencing weightlessness, enduring space environments, and other space techniques. Participants in multinational space ventures also need to speak other languages well to communicate, and thus they undergo extensive language training.

Space travel is one of the more dangerous livelihoods created since the end of World War II. Not only have dozens of trained astronauts and cosmonauts died, but so have ground workers involved in space programs. In 2003, twenty-one workers and scientists died in a rocket explosion at Brazil's space site, and the next year six people in India's space program were killed when a rocket motor burst into flames. Yuri Gagarin himself died in 1968 during a jet training flight.

QUESTIONS TO CONSIDER

1. What roles did astronauts and cosmonauts play in the Cold War?

2. Why did so many countries besides the superpowers begin their own space programs?

3. What livelihoods are comparable to those of astronaut and cosmonaut?

For Further Information:

Brzezinski, Matthew. *Red Moon Rising: Sputnik and the Hidden Rivalries that Ignited the Space Age*. 2007.
De Groot, Gerard. *Dark Side of the Moon: The Magnificent Madness of the American Lunar Quest*. 2006.
Dickson, Paul. *Sputnik: The Shock of the Century*. 2001.
Wolfe, Tom. *The Right Stuff*. 1979.

$10.9 billion in 1948 to almost $60 billion in 1953 to "contain" the global threat of communist expansion. The fear that communist regimes would be established in decolonizing areas led U.S. President Dwight Eisenhower to characterize Asian countries as a row of dominoes: "You knock over the first one and what will happen is that it will go over [to communism] very quickly."[2] Thus, the Cold War mentality helped create a perception of connections between global developments, even in cases where those connections did not really exist.

Viewing the Cold War as a global conflict, the USSR and the United States formed competing military alliances that split most of the world into two opposing camps. In 1949 the United States, Canada, and their European allies formed the **North Atlantic Treaty Organization** (NATO). NATO provided a unified military force for its member countries. In 1955, after the United States forced France and Britain to invite West Germany to join NATO, the Soviet Union retaliated by establishing its own military organization, commonly called the **Warsaw Pact**, which included Albania, Bulgaria, Czechoslovakia, East Germany, Hungary, Poland, and Romania. These two massive regional alliances formed the military muscle for Cold War politics in Europe and replaced the individual might of the European powers (see Map 29.2).

North Atlantic Treaty Organization A Cold War alliance formed in 1949 among the United States, its western European allies, and Canada.

Warsaw Pact A Cold War alliance formed in 1955 among the Soviet Union and its eastern European satellite states.

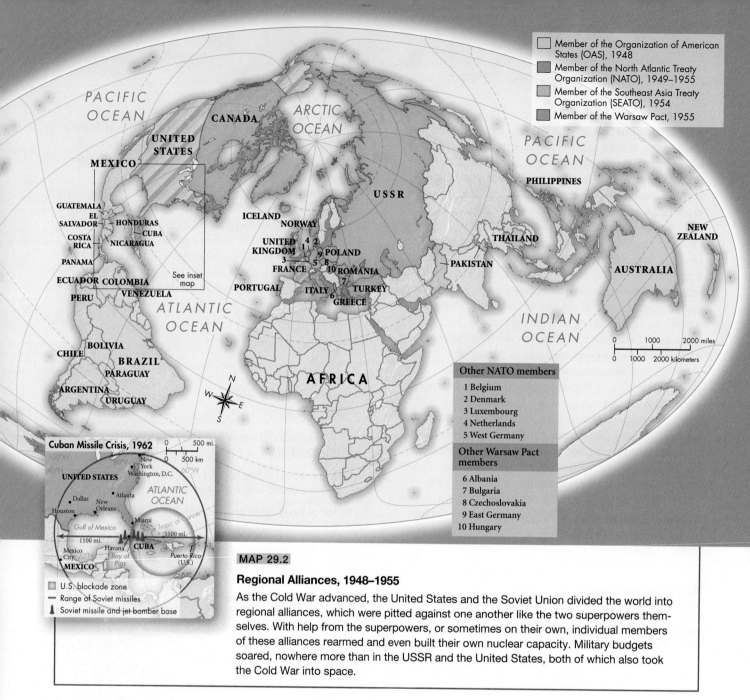

Member of the Organization of American States (OAS), 1948

Member of the North Atlantic Treaty Organization (NATO), 1949–1955

Member of the Southeast Asia Treaty Organization (SEATO), 1954

Member of the Warsaw Pact, 1955

Other NATO members

1 Belgium
2 Denmark
3 Luxembourg
4 Netherlands
5 West Germany

Other Warsaw Pact members

6 Albania
7 Bulgaria
8 Czechoslovakia
9 East Germany
10 Hungary

Cuban Missile Crisis, 1962

U.S. blockade zone

Range of Soviet missiles

Soviet missile and jet bomber base

MAP 29.2

Regional Alliances, 1948–1955

As the Cold War advanced, the United States and the Soviet Union divided the world into regional alliances, which were pitted against one another like the two superpowers themselves. With help from the superpowers, or sometimes on their own, individual members of these alliances rearmed and even built their own nuclear capacity. Military budgets soared, nowhere more than in the USSR and the United States, both of which also took the Cold War into space.

Regional Alliances

Even though the most heated Cold War activity seemed to center on Europe, the largest and earliest regional alliance was far away. In 1948, some twenty-one nations from the Western Hemisphere banded together to form the **Organization of American States** (OAS). To strengthen the alliance as a Cold War vehicle, the United States gave individual Latin American countries of the OAS greater economic assistance as well as military aid and training for officers. U.S. aid guaranteed Latin American military regimes' increased prestige and power over civilians and prevented movements for democracy from succeeding. The expansion of the Cold War to Asia prompted the creation of an Asian counterpart to NATO. Established in 1954, the **Southeast Asia Treaty Organization** (SEATO) included Pakistan, Thailand, the Philippines, Britain, Australia, New Zealand, France, and the United States. Collectively, the new organizations reflected the determination of the United States to pull as much of the world as possible into its orbit.

One Latin American nation, however, refused to align with the United States. In 1959 a revolution in Cuba brought to power the young Fidel Castro. Born in 1926 to the owner of a large plantation and his housekeeper, Castro as a child played with others far less privileged than he, and he saw up close the ways of the local poor. Soon, however, the boy was separated from his poorer friends and given an elite education, leading eventually to

Organization of American States An alliance formed in 1948 among nations in the Western Hemisphere.

Southeast Asia Treaty Organization A Cold War coalition of U.S. Asian allies formed in 1954.

968

law school. At the university, Castro was a political leader, and eventually he became a major opposition figure in Cuban politics. In 1959 Castro's forces overthrew the island's corrupt regime, which was controlled in large part by U.S. sugar interests and the mob. Peasants and well-educated guerrilla fighters like Castro banded together to end the economic plunder not only of the Cuban island but of individual workers. After being rebuffed by the United States, Castro, initially opposed to communist organizations, turned to the Soviet Union for aid to rebuild the country.

Cuba's connection to the Soviet Union frightened American decision makers, including John F. Kennedy. Elected U.S. president in 1960, Kennedy intensified the arms race and escalated the Cold War to a frightening pitch. In 1961 he authorized an invasion of Cuba by CIA-trained Cuban exiles at the Bay of Pigs to overthrow Castro. The CIA had backed similar coups in Iran, where it overthrew a populist nationalist regime to install the Shah, and in Guatemala, where it devised an invasion by so-called exile forces who imposed a president friendly to U.S. interests. The Bay of Pigs invasion, however, failed miserably and humiliated the United States, as Castro's tiny air force sank U.S. ships and captured more than a thousand invaders.

Revolution in Cuba

Another incident involving Cuba brought the world even closer to the brink of nuclear war. In October 1962, the CIA reported the installation of launching pads for Soviet medium-range nuclear missiles in Cuba (see again Map 29.2). In response, Kennedy called for a blockade of Soviet ships headed for Cuba and threatened nuclear war if the installations were not removed. For several days, superpower leaders were acutely aware that the world hovered on the brink of nuclear disaster. A high Soviet official called his wife telling her to leave Moscow immediately; men in Kennedy's cabinet reported looking at the sunset, believing it to be the last they would see. Then, between October 25 and 27, Nikita Khrushchev, Stalin's successor, and Kennedy negotiated an end to the crisis. The two leaders, who had looked deeply into the nuclear future, clearly feared what they saw.

Cuban Missile Crisis

Decolonization and the Birth of Nations

In World War II colonized peoples had been on the frontlines defending the West. They had witnessed the full barbarism of the imperial powers' warfare—and also the West's weaknesses. "We felt that the British were not supermen as we used to think," one Singapore worker put it. Another was enraged at seeing "the same old arrogance that you saw before the war."[3] Excluded from victory parades and other ceremonies so the Allies could maintain the illusion of white supremacy, veterans from the colonies were determined to be free. Workers and farmers in Asia, Africa, and the Middle East felt that they too had borne the brunt of the war effort. People from many walks of life, often led by individuals experienced in warfare and steeped in Western nationalism, fought for liberation as the postwar period opened.

> **FOCUS**
>
> How did colonized peoples achieve their independence from the imperialist powers after World War II?

The path to independence was paved with difficulties. In Africa, a continent whose peoples spoke several thousand languages, the European conquerors' creation of administrative units such as "Nigeria" and "Rhodesia" had obliterated divisions based on ethnic ties and local cultures. Religion also played a complicated role in independence movements. In the Middle East and North Africa, pan-Arab and pan-Islamic movements might seem to have been unifying forces. Yet many Muslims were not Arab, not all Arabs were Muslim, and Islam itself encompassed many competing beliefs and sects. In India, Hindus, Sikhs, and Muslims battled one another, though they shared the goal of eliminating British rule. Differences in religious beliefs, ethnic groups, and cultural practices—many of them invented or promoted by the colonizers to divide and rule—overlapped and undermined political unity. Despite these complications, in the three decades after World War II colonized peoples succeeded in throwing off the imperial yoke, often to become entangled in the battle between the United States and the USSR for world supremacy.

The End of Empire in Asia

At the end of World War II, Asians demonstrated against the inflation, unemployment, and other harsh conditions the war had imposed on them, while politicians continued to mobilize this mass discontent against the colonial powers. White colonizers often fought back, but able leaders and ordinary people worked together to drive out foreign rulers. Slipping as the major imperial power, Britain in 1947 finally parted with India, the "jewel in its crown." As some half a billion Asians gained their independence, Britain's sole notable remaining colony was Hong Kong.

India   During World War II, soldiers, workers, and farm tenants actively protested conditions under colonialism, sometimes using Gandhi's tactic of civil disobedience and at other times attacking the workplaces of moneylenders and landlords. Britain had promised in the 1930s to grant India its independence, but postponed the plan when war broke out. Two million Indian veterans, who had participated in the war in the Middle East and Asia, joined forces with powerful Indian Congress politicians, many of whom had helped finance the British war effort by buying out British entrepreneurs short of cash. India was now one of Britain's major creditors, and Britain had to face the inevitable by granting the colony its independence.

Independent countries emerged along the lines of religious rivalries that Britain had fomented under colonialism as a strategy to divide and conquer. In 1947, political leaders agreed to partition British India into an independent India for Hindus and the new state of Pakistan for Muslims; both were artificial divisions, because there were people from many religions living together across the subcontinent. The new state of India, in fact, had the second largest Muslim population in the world after Indonesia. Ordinary people had violent reactions as **Partition** unfolded (see Map 29.3). A powerful religious minority—the Sikhs—bitterly resented receiving nothing. Because independence as determined by the British occurred along religious rather than secular lines, tensions exploded among opposing religious groups, who used partition to struggle for resources and power. Hundreds of thousands were massacred in the great shift of populations between India and Pakistan—"appalling sights," a journalist reported, as trains reached their destination filled with nothing but corpses and hospitals treated the wounded whose hands had been cut off.[4] Indian and Pakistani soldiers began fighting for control of Kashmir along the border between the two countries. In the midst of this tragic bloodshed, in 1948 a radical Hindu assassinated Gandhi, who had loudly championed religious reconciliation and a secular Indian democracy. Delayed by bitter feelings, a Constitution emerged for India that forced wealthy, autonomous Indian states into the union.

In Indonesia in the closing days of World War II, the Japanese, eager to foil the Dutch, allowed a group of nationalist leaders, headed by the Western-educated Achmed Sukarno, to declare Indonesia an independent state. Sukarno's distinctive nationalist vision brought all the islands of the archipelago into a unified nation. His task was complicated by three factors. First, Indonesia had a tradition of local princely rule, even under Dutch control. Second, from the beginning of the twentieth century Indonesians had built an array of organizations, including a variety of Islamic ones, that pushed for freedom from Dutch exploitation. Third, Allied military forces had helped the Dutch to reclaim their empire, and after the defeat of Japan they even enlisted the occupying Japanese troops to put down all movements for independence.

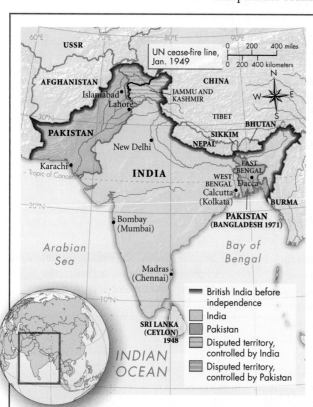

MAP 29.3   Partition of India, 1947

The British had whipped up religious antagonisms as part of their strategy of divide and conquer in India, and they used the same strategy in planning for decolonization. Thus, despite the commitment of Gandhi and other leaders to unity and religious toleration, Britain, along with some Indian leaders, arranged for a partition into a Muslim-dominated Pakistan and a Hindu-dominated India. Given the many religions in the region, the partition was a recipe for independence plagued by violence.

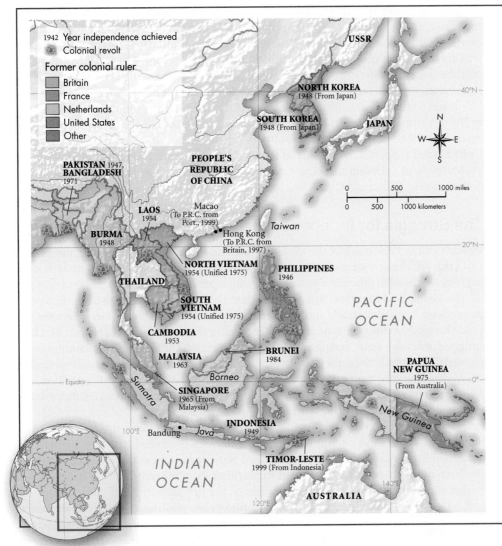

MAP 29.4

New States of Southeast Asia, 1945–1999

The French were determined to keep their empire in Southeast Asia, but their forces were handily defeated by the Vietnamese in 1954. Even as the Bandung Conference was held in Indonesia, the emerging nations of Southeast Asia became pivotal to the Cold War, as communist leader Ho Chi Minh stood steadfast in his vision for the region. One of the longest and most lethal proxy wars of the Cold War was fought in Vietnam, where genocide in neighboring Cambodia erupted adjacent to the war for liberation.

Indonesia

The popular forces of independence used **guerrilla warfare** that was unstoppable. In 1949 the Dutch conceded Indonesian independence, and in 1957 Sukarno, as head of the new state, legislated that all Dutch leave the country. Sukarno's policies entailed economic modernization and a cultural unity based on the belief in one God, whether Islamic, Christian, or other. Although the new Ministry of Religion fostered unity through Islamic institutions, sponsoring the building of mosques and institutions for Islamic welfare programs, ethnic, religious, and economic interests diverged and kept the archipelago involved in constant governmental struggle against dissenters. For a time, Sukarno himself was the mainstay of unity, becoming a charismatic leader by championing the power of newly independent countries (see Map 29.4).

Indochina

In Indochina nationalists struggled to prevent the postwar revival of French imperialism. From the 1930s on, their leader, Ho Chi Minh (hoe chee min), built a powerful organization, the Communist Viet Minh, to fight colonial rule. He began his career, however, by working aboard a French ocean liner, then taking jobs in London and Paris at the time of World War I, experiences that brought him in direct contact with white racism. Ho became interested in Marxism, which led him to Moscow and training as a political operative; he was first assigned to organizing strikers in China in the 1920s. Once head of the Viet Minh, he advocated the redistribution of land held by big landowners, especially in the rich agricultural area in southern Indochina where some six thousand owners held more than 60 percent of the land.

Partition The division of the Indian subcontinent into different states in 1947 and the violence accompanying it.

guerrilla warfare Unconventional combat, often undertaken by those who are not members of official armies.

During World War II, Ho worked to overthrow the Japanese, who had taken over Indochina, and at the end of the war, he declared Vietnam independent. The French, however, reasserted their control. Viet Minh peasant guerrillas ultimately forced the French to withdraw from the country after the bloody battle of Dien Bien Phu in 1954. Later that year the Geneva Conference—a meeting held in Switzerland to settle the war between the Indochinese and the French—carved out an independent Laos and divided Vietnam into North and South, each free from French control. Ho established a communist government in North Vietnam, and a noncommunist government was installed in South Vietnam (see again Map 29.4). Fearing that Ho would further the spread of communism in Asia, the United States supported the regime in South Vietnam, even its cancelling of elections in 1956 to prevent a communist victory. Ho and North Vietnam, in turn, received aid from both the Soviet Union and China.

The Struggle for Independence in the Middle East

By war's end in 1945, much of the world had become almost fully dependent on the Middle East's rich petroleum resources to fuel cars and airplanes, heat homes, and create products such as plastics. "The oil in this region is the greatest single prize in all history," as one geologist put it.[5] The Middle Eastern nations that emerged from their political domination by the European powers were thus economically and strategically important enough to maneuver between the Cold War rivals. At the same time, newly independent nations such as Syria, Lebanon, and Iraq struggled to develop a sure footing and autonomous identity. The legacy of the Holocaust complicated the political scene as the Western powers' commitment to secure a Jewish homeland in the Middle East stirred up Arab determination to hold onto their lands. From 1945 on, the Middle East was the scene of coups, power struggles, and ethnic and religious conflict, even as new nations were being born and older ones were strengthened by oil.

Israel   When World War II broke out, six hundred thousand Jewish settlers and twice as many Arabs lived, amid intermittent conflict, in British-controlled Palestine. In 1947, an exhausted Britain ceded the area to the United Nations to work out a settlement between the Jews and the Arabs. The UN voted to partition Palestine into an Arab region and a Jewish one, and in May 1948 Israelis proclaimed the new state of Israel. "The dream had come true," Golda Meir, future prime minister of Israel, remembered, but "too late to save those who had perished in the Holocaust."[6] Arguing that the UN had no right to award land to the Jewish minority in Palestine, five neighboring Arab states attacked Israel and were beaten. A UN-negotiated truce in 1949 to the Arab-Israeli War gave Israel even more territory than had been granted earlier. The result was that some two-thirds of Palestinian Arabs became stateless refugees and the war itself became but one more confrontation in a longer Arab-Israeli conflict over territory, rising Jewish immigration, and Palestinian rights to a homeland that continues to the present day.

Israel's neighbor, Egypt, had been a center of Allied efforts in North Africa and the Middle East during the war and demanded complete independence from British domination at the war's end. Britain, however, was determined to keep its control of Middle Eastern oil and Asian shipping through the Suez Canal, which was owned by a British-run company. Early in the 1950s the people of Cairo took to the streets, destroying flags of the puppet monarchy and other symbols of British rule. In 1952, army officer Gamal Abdel Nasser took part in the military ouster of the Egyptian king, a puppet of Britain's behind-the-scenes rule. The son of a postal inspector, Nasser rose quickly to become president of Egypt in 1956. As president, Nasser worked to improve the economic well-being of the peasants by redistributing land from the very wealthiest estates. Most notably, he faced down the European powers

UN partition of Palestine, 1947

▪ Proposed Jewish state
▫ Proposed Arab state
— Boundary of Israel after UN truce, 1949

The Arab-Israeli War of 1948–1949

that wanted to keep control of Egyptian resources. A prime goal was reclaiming the Suez Canal, "where 120,000 of our sons had lost their lives in digging it [by force]," Nasser stated. In July 1956, after being denied a loan from the United States to build the projected Aswan Dam, he nationalized the Suez Canal so that Egypt would receive the income from tolls paid by those who used the canal. Nationalization of the Suez Canal sent Nasser's reputation soaring, making him the most popular and respected leader in the Arab world.

Nasser's nationalization sent an angry tremor through the imperial powers, however. The Egyptians, Britain claimed, were hardly advanced enough as a people to run as complex an operation as the Suez Canal. Britain, with assistance from Israel and France, then invaded Egypt, bringing the Suez crisis to a head. American opposition made the British back down. Nasser's triumph in gaining the canal inspired confidence that the Middle East could confront the West and win.

> **Egypt**

New Nations in Africa

Displaced from their traditional agricultural livelihood during the war, many Africans flocked to cities such as Lagos and Nairobi, where they lived in shantytowns and survived by scavenging and doing menial labor for whites. After the war, struggling urban workers, including civil servants, professionals, and ordinary laborers, formed the core of the nationalist movement. High taxes imposed by white settlers gave added impetus to the decolonization movement. Another element in the drive toward independence was the transnational vision of Africans involved in trade and intellectual contact with the wider world. Leaders who had studied abroad were determined to have Western-style freedom.

In sub-Saharan Africa, these nationalists led increasingly discontented peoples to challenge the European imperialists. In the British-controlled Gold Coast of West Africa, Kwame Nkrumah (KWAH-may ehn-KROO-mah), formerly a poor school teacher, led the region's diverse inhabitants in Gandhian-style civil disobedience. A student in the United States in 1936, Nkrumah had been radicalized by Italy's invasion and defeat of Ethiopia. After the war, he joined a group of fellow West Africans in London, forging with them plans for liberation. Nkrumah returned to the Gold Coast, where he led protests that, despite determined British opposition, resulted in the formation of the independent country of Ghana in 1957 (see Seeing the Past: African Liberation on Cloth, page 975).

> **Sub-Saharan Africa**

Nkrumah lobbied for the unity of all African states: "How except by our united efforts will the richest and still enslaved part of our continent be freed from colonial occupation . . . ?" he asked the heads of African governments in 1963 before all of Africa had been liberated.[7] But individual nation building was the order of the day. In the most populous African colony, Nigeria, workers and veterans recognized how important they were to Britain's postwar recovery and struck for higher wages, better working conditions, and greater respect. Respect did not come quickly: during a miners' strike in 1949 the British police commissioner ordered his troops to shoot because, he said, the miners were "dancing around and around" and chanting "We are all one."[8] Nonetheless, Nigeria gained its freedom in 1960 after the leaders of its many regional groups, unions, and political organizations reached agreement on a federal-style government. In these and other African states where the population was mostly black, independence came less violently than in mixed-race territory (see Map 29.5, page 974).

The numerous European settlers along Africa's eastern coast and in the southern and central areas of the continent violently resisted independence movements. In British East Africa, where white settlers ruled in splendor, the increasing mechanization of agriculture during the war drove blacks off the land. Displaced people filled cities like Nairobi or tried to eke out a living on infertile land. From the middle of World War II on, some of these displaced persons, including returning veterans, began forming secret political groups to oppose British rule. Violence erupted in the 1950s, when these rebels—including women who served as provisioners, messengers, and weapons stealers—tried to recover land from the whites. The rebels, who were mostly from the Kikuyu (kih-KOO-you) ethnic group, called themselves the Land and Freedom Army, but the whites referred to them as "Mau

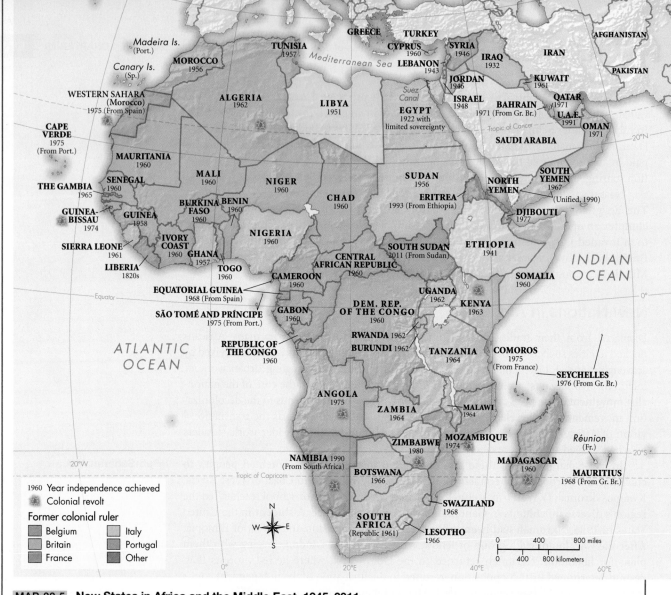

Madeira Is. (Port.)
Canary Is. (Sp.)
GREECE
TURKEY
CYPRUS 1960
SYRIA 1946
IRAQ 1932
IRAN
AFGHANISTAN
PAKISTAN
TUNISIA 1957
LEBANON 1943
JORDAN 1946
KUWAIT 1961
QATAR 1971
MOROCCO 1956
Mediterranean Sea
Suez Canal
ISRAEL 1948
BAHRAIN 1971 (From Gr. Br.)
U.A.E. 1991
OMAN 1971
WESTERN SAHARA (Morocco) 1975 (From Spain)
ALGERIA 1962
LIBYA 1951
EGYPT 1922 with limited sovereignty
Tropic of Cancer
SAUDI ARABIA
20°N
CAPE VERDE 1975 (From Port.)
MAURITANIA 1960
MALI 1960
NIGER 1960
SUDAN 1956
NORTH YEMEN
SOUTH YEMEN 1967 (Unified, 1990)
THE GAMBIA 1965
SENEGAL 1960
CHAD 1960
ERITREA 1993 (From Ethiopia)
DJIBOUTI 1977
GUINEA-BISSAU 1974
GUINEA 1958
BURKINA FASO 1960
BENIN 1960
SIERRA LEONE 1961
IVORY COAST 1960
NIGERIA 1960
SOUTH SUDAN 2011 (From Sudan)
ETHIOPIA 1941
LIBERIA 1820s
GHANA 1957
TOGO 1960
CENTRAL AFRICAN REPUBLIC 1960
SOMALIA 1960
INDIAN OCEAN
Equator
CAMEROON 1960
EQUATORIAL GUINEA 1968 (From Spain)
SÃO TOMÉ AND PRÍNCIPE 1975 (From Port.)
GABON 1960
UGANDA 1962
KENYA 1963
0°
DEM. REP. OF THE CONGO 1960
RWANDA 1962
BURUNDI 1962
ATLANTIC OCEAN
REPUBLIC OF THE CONGO 1960
TANZANIA 1964
COMOROS 1975 (From France)
SEYCHELLES 1976 (From Gr. Br.)
ANGOLA 1975
ZAMBIA 1964
MALAWI 1964
ZIMBABWE 1980
MOZAMBIQUE 1974
Réunion (Fr.)
20°S
NAMIBIA 1990 (From South Africa)
BOTSWANA 1966
MADAGASCAR 1960
MAURITIUS 1968 (From Gr. Br.)
Tropic of Capricorn
SWAZILAND 1968
SOUTH AFRICA (Republic 1961)
LESOTHO 1966

1960 Year independence achieved
Colonial revolt
Former colonial ruler
Belgium
Britain
France
Italy
Portugal
Other

N W E S

0 400 800 miles
0 400 800 kilometers

20°W 0° 20°E 40°E 60°E

MAP 29.5 New States in Africa and the Middle East, 1945–2011

To maintain their empires, the British, French, and Belgians fought lethal wars in Kenya, Algeria, and Congo, which featured brutal attacks against the local populations and killed tens of thousands. Inspired by their leaders, other African countries became independent relatively peacefully, although the costs of nation building were crushing in areas that had been so overexploited. The Middle East, in contrast, had enormous assets that drew the superpowers and other nations to compete fiercely for oil and control of the region's other assets, such as the Suez Canal.

Mau." The British responded by rounding up Kikuyus by the hundreds of thousands and placing them in secret concentration camps where conditions were so grim and mortality so high that the British deny their existence to this day. Nonetheless, despite the coordinated slaughter of an estimated 150,000 to 320,000 Kikuyus, the Land and Freedom Army finally wore the British down in costly military actions. Kenya gained formal independence in 1963.

North Africa   As the tide of liberation spread, colonial leaders in Tunisia, Morocco, and French West Africa successfully convinced France to leave peaceably, in large part because European settlers were few and there was little military involvement running these areas. Having earlier been declared an integral part of France, Algeria was another story altogether. In 1954 the newly formed Front for National Liberation (FLN) rose up, attacking French government buildings, radio stations, and utility plants. A radio station in Cairo announced the FLN's goal: the "restoration of the Algerian state, sovereign, democratic, and social, within the framework of the principles of Islam." The French sent in more than four hundred thousand troops to crush the uprising, determined to keep Algeria French and to guard the well-being of over 1 million European settlers.

African Liberation on Cloth

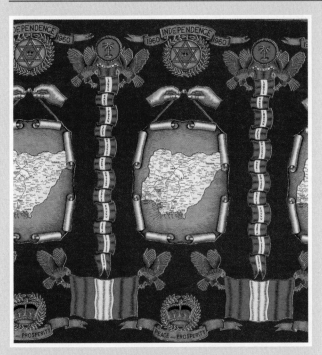

Nigerian Commemorative Textile (Textile Museum of Canada.)

Many African societies used commemorative textiles such as this vividly colored one from Nigeria to mark special occasions. Nations gaining their independence from the European powers issued such textiles in the 1960s and 1970s as they threw off imperial rule. This cloth clearly proclaims "Independence," but others presented the portraits of liberation heroes as they announced their freedom to the world. The textiles were immensely popular, hanging in homes and public buildings or serving as clothing (see At a Crossroads, page 958). Paradoxically, the independence textiles symbolized unity in the face of divisions among regions and ethnic groups within a country that had been artificially created by imperialist designs. In so doing, commemorative textiles, sometimes fashioned by women artisans, stood at the crossroads of pre-war and postwar world history.

EXAMINING THE EVIDENCE

1. What was the purpose of these commemorative textiles?

2. What accounts for their popularity, given the many divisions among the peoples of new nations?

3. Why would some commemorative textiles feature brutal dictators?

Neither side fought according to the rules of warfare: the French tortured native people, mutilating and then beheading them. The FLN fought a guerrilla war, fading into the mountains and countryside, while Algerian women, defying gender stereotypes, planted bombs in European cafés and carried weapons to assassination sites. Although France won the war with Algeria in military terms, the Algerian nationalists knew how to win the war of world opinion. Using modern public relations methods, they turned the United States and other influential nations against the French, convincing them that France stood in the way of Algerian economic development and the fight against communism. In 1962 Charles de Gaulle, leader of the Free French during World War II and new president of France, negotiated a settlement that resulted in independence for Algeria. Fearing retribution, hundreds of thousands of Europeans in Algeria as well as their Arab supporters fled to France. Having won its independence, Algeria, like the other newly independent states, now faced the challenge of establishing an effective, unified nation.

World Recovery in the 1950s and 1960s

The struggles against colonialism and the ideological clash between the United States and the Soviet Union took place alongside remarkable economic growth and social change. Some parts of the world had prospered during the war. Latin America, for example, benefited from the wartime demand for raw materials and manufactured goods. Cuba's exports of

FOCUS

What were the major elements of recovery in different parts of the world in the decades following World War II?

sugar grew almost 300 percent between 1938 and the end of the war. The population of Latin America steadily grew. Other peoples, within a few decades after suffering the deprivation and devastation of total war, came to live longer lives and to enjoy a higher standard of living than ever before in history. In Europe this newfound prosperity was celebrated as an "economic miracle." As governments took increasing responsibility for the health and well-being of citizens, the menacing Cold War was also the backdrop for rapid development of the welfare state pioneered by Sweden (see Chapter 28).

Political changes fostered some of the movement toward economic growth. New nations faced the enormous task of building effective government. India, for example, had experienced the horrors of Partition and was additionally composed of more than five hundred small and several quite large states that had enjoyed local rule under the British. "We have to make [people] feel they are parts of India, not only politically but emotionally and otherwise, and that their future is tied up with India," the first prime minister, Jawaharlal Nehru (JAH-wa-HAR-lahl NAY-roo), wrote in 1955.[9] To build loyalty to new nations and the superpowers alike, governments often turned to expensive projects such as building dams, extending railroads, and electrifying rural areas—all of which contributed to the postwar pattern of economic growth.

Expanding Economic Prosperity

In the immediate aftermath of the war, governments in new and old nations alike diverted labor and capital into rebuilding infrastructure—transportation, communications, and industrial capacity. The scarcity of consumer goods sparked unrest in many parts of the world, but the influx of U.S. funds into nations worldwide as part of its Cold War mission fueled economic recovery. Food and consumer goods became more plentiful, and demand for them increased. The growth in production alleviated unemployment among those whose livelihoods the war had destroyed. Oil-rich countries imported people from many parts of Asia and Africa to perform menial labor: women from the Philippines, Indonesia, and the Caribbean were among those who migrated as nurses, nannies, and household help. Northern Europe, short of labor, arranged for "guest" workers to arrive from Sicily, Turkey, and North and sub-Saharan Africa to help rebuild cities. The outbreak of war in Korea in 1950 encouraged economic recovery in Japan and elsewhere. Korea itself, however, was devastated. The Cold War thus spurred economic advance in some parts of the world while labor shortages led to ongoing migration and further interconnectedness of peoples and livelihoods.

During the postwar recovery, wartime technology was adapted to civilian use, and military spending continued. Civilian travel expanded globally as nations organized their own air systems based on improved airplane technology. Developed to relieve wartime shortages, synthetic goods such as nylon now became part of peacetime civilian life. Factories churned out a vast assortment of electronics, and plastic products ranging from pipes to household goods and rainwear. In the climate of Cold War, governments ordered bombs, fighter planes, tanks, and missiles, and they continued to conduct military research. Governments in decolonized countries courted the superpowers to provide up-to-date weaponry to secure their rule against internal and external foes. The number of radios in homes grew steadily around the world, and by the 1960s television had become a widely popular consumer item and the source for a host of new occupations.

The Common Market   International cooperation and economic growth led to the creation in 1957 of the **European Economic Community** (EEC), known popularly as the Common Market, the foundation of the European Union of the 1990s. In 1957, Belgium, the Netherlands, Luxembourg, France, West Germany, and Italy established the EEC, which reduced tariffs among the six partners and worked to develop common trade policies. According to its founders, the EEC aimed to "prevent the race of nationalism, which is the true curse of the modern world." Increased cooperation produced great economic rewards for the six members, and it reduced the threat of war: the Italian economy, which had lagged behind that of France and Germany, boomed, and as additional countries joined from the 1970s on, many of them flourished too.

European Economic Community A consortium of European countries established in 1957 to promote free trade and economic cooperation among its members.

Even as new nations came into being, the trend in postwar and postcolonial government was to intervene in people's everyday lives to improve social conditions and to prevent the political extremism and discontent of the 1930s. This policy of intervention became known as the **welfare state**, a term suggesting that, in addition to building their military power, states would guarantee a minimum level of well-being for their citizens. Postwar governments promoted both the advance of industry and the welfare of the general population with various forms of financial assistance. Imitating the sweeping Swedish programs of the 1930s, nations expanded or created family allowances, health-care and medical benefits, and programs for pregnant women. The combination of better material conditions and state provision of health care dramatically extended life expectancy. Contributing to the overall progress, the number of medical doctors and dentists soared between 1920 and 1950, and vaccines greatly reduced the global death toll from such diseases as tuberculosis, diphtheria, measles, and polio.

State initiatives in other areas also helped raise the standard of living. Government-built atomic power plants brought electrification to many more rural areas. States legislated for better conditions and more leisure time for workers and sponsored construction to alleviate housing shortages resulting from three decades of economic depression and war. Such efforts often drained the economies of newly independent countries. Moreover, despite the new construction, housing shortages persisted, and growing cities like Rio de Janeiro were surrounded by shantytowns. Nonetheless, the modernized appearance of many of the world's largest cities suggested that the century's two cataclysmic wars had swept away much that was old and traditional.

The welfare state became the backbone of politics in many regions. Juan Perón, a colonel in the Argentine army, became president in 1946 on a platform of welfare for workers and independence from the financial domination of Britain and the United States. During the war, as manufacturing jobs multiplied and migration to cities in search of industrial jobs swelled, Perón had forced American meatpacking plants around Buenos Aires to raise wages. Hundreds of thousands of workers backed Perón's array of economic benefits for "the shirtless ones," and his dramatic use of surplus government funds to buy out British-owned telephone companies and railroad lines was said to free Argentina from Western business imperialism domination. While Perón added to workers' wallets with rising social security and wages, his wife Eva, who was from the lower class, won their hearts. During the depression,

The Welfare State

Welfare for Workers in Argentina

welfare state The postwar system of government-sponsored programs designed to provide citizens with basic standards of health care, housing, and income.

The Great Leap Forward in China

In 1949, life in China changed for most people because of the communist revolution that brought Mao Zedong to power. Kang Zhengguo was a student in the 1950s as the full weight of change began. His grandfather owned land and was a Buddhist leader; his father was a highly trained engineer. In this early passage from Zhengguo's memoir, he describes one of Mao's earliest programs, "The Great Leap Forward," when China was supposed to industrialize rapidly as the Soviets had done. Later parts of his memoir present bloody and terrifying incidents, including those that he himself endured.

In 1958, the year of the Great Leap Forward, the nation became caught up in a frenzy of smelting "backyard steel." It was our "glorious mission" to donate scrap iron to this cause, so our school playground, like most other work units, was heaped with it, along with piles of burned charcoal. Some enthusiasts had tossed in their pots and pans or drawer handles for good measure, even if they were made of copper or tin. The student cafeteria had been temporarily converted into a foundry, equipped with a mighty blower that shook the classrooms with its roar and filled the air with a sooty purplish haze. Nobody seemed to have time for mundane pursuits like eating and sleeping. The upperclassmen manned the furnaces around the clock with holiday spirit, belting out all of their new songs and

cheering for the molten "steel" as it poured out of the furnaces. Once it congealed into hard black slag, we deemed it a success and swathed it in bright red silk. Then, banging on drums and gongs and carrying big red paper placards that read "SURPASS ENGLAND AND CATCH UP TO AMERICA," we marched it triumphantly over to the district party committee.

Classes were canceled more often than not, and even we younger students had to help out at the foundry.

Source: Kang Zhengguo, *Confessions: An Innocent Life in Communist China,* trans. Susan Wilf (New York: W. W. Norton, 2007), 14–15.

EXAMINING THE EVIDENCE

1. What impression does this passage give you of the Great Leap Forward?

2. What is the place of politics in education, as suggested by this excerpt?

3. How would you describe the industrialization taking place during the Great Leap Forward?

4. How would you describe the student life?

---

at the age of fifteen, she had migrated from the countryside to Buenos Aires, quickly leaving her poverty behind when she succeeded in radio and film. As Perón's wife, "Evita" joined him in providing the poor with housing, unemployment funds, and personal charity, which she virtually extorted from businesses. In exchange, the masses loyally supported the Peróns, even as the upper and middle classes stewed in silent protest. Eva Perón died from cancer at the age of thirty-two, leaving the Argentine masses heartbroken and the government strapped for funds to continue its welfare policies. In 1955, the military drove Perón out, reducing both the welfare state and the anti-American rhetoric.

Building and Rebuilding Communism

Two countries in particular bore the brunt of World War II in terms of population loss and outright destruction. The Soviet Union lost between 42 and 47 million people, new estimates suggest, while the Japanese invasion and more than a decade of civil war killed some 30 million people in China. Both Stalin and Mao Zedong were committed to rebuilding and modernizing their countries, and both revived the crushing methods that had served before to modernize and industrialize traditional peasant economies. An admirer of American industrial know-how, Stalin prodded all Soviet-bloc nations to match U.S. productivity. In China Mao had similar goals, and reaching them produced losses in both lives and jobs.

The Soviet Union   Stalin's death in 1953 created an opportunity to create a less repressive society in the USSR. Political prisoners in the labor camps pressed for reform, leading to the release of millions. Cold War competition and growing protests over shortages of food and other consumer items led the government to increase production of consumer goods. Nikita Khrushchev, an illiterate coal miner before the Bolshevik Revolution, outmaneuvered other rivals to become in 1955 the undisputed leader of the Soviet Union, but he did so without the usual executions. At a party congress in 1956, Khrushchev attacked the "cult of personality" Stalin had built about himself and announced that Stalinism did not equal socialism. The so-called Secret Speech—it was not published in the USSR but became widely known—sent tremors through hard-line Communist parties around the world.

In 1956, discontented Polish railroad workers successfully struck for better wages. Inspired by the Polish example, Hungarians rebelled later that year against forced collectivization and wage cutbacks, but the protest soon targeted the entire communist system. Tens of thousands of protesters filled the streets of Budapest, urged on both publicly and privately by the United States and its allies. When Hungary announced that it might leave the Warsaw Pact, Soviet troops moved in, killing tens of thousands and causing hundreds of thousands more to flee to the West. The U.S. refusal to act showed that, despite its rhetoric of "liberation," it would not risk World War III by military intervention in the Soviet sphere of influence.

In the People's Republic of China, Mao Zedong faced the problem of rebuilding a war-torn peasant society. Like Stalin, Mao saw modernization as the answer, but to keep Chinese communism and himself in power, Mao tacked back and forth, uncertain of what to do. In 1959 he initiated the **Great Leap Forward**, an economic plan intended to increase industrial production. The plan ordered country people to stop tending their farms and instead produce steel from their shovels, pots, and pans in their own small backyard furnaces (see Reading the Past: The Great Leap Forward in China). This decentralized plan of industrial production proved to be a disaster, as much of the do-it-yourself iron and steel was worthless. Meanwhile, the halting of agriculture resulted in massive famine. An estimated 30 million people died, and millions more went hungry. "Communism is not a dinner party," Mao remarked with grim irony, and his government touted the virtues of being thin. During this and other projects, livelihoods deteriorated and education was devalued in the name of participating in different communist schemes.

In the early 1960s, Mao's slipping popularity and rising threats from outside the country led to the brutal development known as the **Cultural Revolution**. To break the opposition that had emerged during the Great Leap Forward, Mao turned against his associates in the Communist Party, appealing to China's youth to reinvigorate the revolution. Brought up to revere Mao, young people responded to his call to rid society of the "four olds"—old customs, old habits, old culture, and old ideas. In Mao's name they destroyed artistic treasures and crushed individual lives, striking yet another blow at ordinary people's ability to pursue productive lives.

During the Cultural Revolution, any kind of skilled person was branded uncommunist and thus criminal, as seen in the experience of painter Wu Guanzhong. Wu went to Paris in 1947 on a government scholarship to learn the techniques of Western masters, but after three years Mao's administration summoned him back to teach in Beijing. By the mid-1950s, the Chinese leadership had come to see Wu's work, which mixed Chinese and Western

Wu Guanzhong, *Willows on a Hillside*

Wu Guanzhong's studies in Europe influenced his art after his return to China to teach in Beijing in the 1950s. Forbidden to paint during the Cultural Revolution of the 1960s, Wu returned to his hybrid style, which mixed abstract representations from the West with Chinese styles that he modernized in his work. For many critics, Wu's work reflects both his own artistry and the influence of other contemporary artists, such as Jackson Pollock (see page 983). (Christie's Images/Corbis.)

China

Great Leap Forward The Chinese communist program of the mid-1950s designed to push the country ahead of all others in industrial and other production.

Cultural Revolution The Chinese communist program of the 1960s and early 1970s carried out by Mao Zedong's youthful followers to remake Chinese thought, behavior, and everyday life.

styles, as a "poisonous weed." In their view, the only acceptable approach to art was Soviet-style socialist realism. Wu was removed from his prestigious teaching post and sent to farm in the countryside, where he was forbidden to paint or to talk to his wife, who accompanied him. In 1972 Wu was allowed to resume his artwork "for relaxation" one day a week, but he had trouble finding materials and came ultimately to describe himself as a "cow-dung painter." After Mao's death in 1976 the brutality of the Cultural Revolution eased. Wu Guanzhong's reputation as one of the world's outstanding artists was restored, and the skills of the Chinese people in artistic, agricultural, industrial, and other pursuits were once again valued.

Cultural Dynamism amid Cold War

FOCUS

How did the experience of world war, decolonization, and Cold War affect cultural life and thought?

As the Cold War unfolded, people around the world vigorously discussed the devastating World War II experience, the rationale for decolonization, and the dangers of the Cold War itself. Writers tried to understand the meaning of war and genocide. Literature exploring concepts of freedom and liberation poured out of Africa, Latin America, and Asia and reached the West, where oppressed minorities were likewise demanding better treatment. Thus, the postwar period was one of intense cultural ferment and unprecedented levels of cultural exchange within each Cold War bloc.

Confronting the Heritage of World War

In 1944, during the last months of the war, University of Tokyo professor Tanabe Hajime began a soul-searching book, turning to Buddhism for enlightenment. In *Philosophy as Matonetics* (the title refers to an act of repentant confession), Tanabe urged the Japanese to enter higher realms of wisdom as they faced defeat. His program for a return to Buddhist values allowed the Japanese to see in their defeat a lofty purpose, elevating them above the brute power politics of the Western victors. Such programs for exalting the wartime losers took place alongside intense indoctrination in democratic values and the dramatic trials of Axis leaders conducted at Nuremberg, Germany, in 1945 and in Tokyo, Japan, in 1946. Both sets of trials revealed a horrifying panorama of crimes and led to death sentences or long imprisonment for most of the defendants. These trials introduced the concept of "crimes against humanity" and an international politics based on demands for human rights.

Nonetheless, as civilians in the defeated Axis nations struggled with starvation, rape, and other postwar hardships, many Japanese and Germans came to believe that they were the main victims of the war. The Cold War helped reinforce that view. American officials themselves, eager to fight the communists, began to rely on the expertise of high-ranking Japanese militarists, fascists, and Nazis, overlooking war crimes as trivial when compared to the evil menace of the USSR. The work of Tanabe and others justified the speedy rehabilitation of the Axis powers, as the war temporarily came to be explained as one of idealism on both sides.

Memoirs of the death camps and tales of the resistance evoked a starkly different side of the events of the 1930s and 1940s. Anne Frank's *Diary of a Young Girl* (1947) was the poignant record of a German Jewish teenager hidden with her family for two years in the back of an Amsterdam warehouse before they were discovered and sent to concentration camps, where all died except Anne's father. Confronted with the small miseries of daily life and the grand evils of Nazism, Frank wrote that she never stopped believing that "people are really good at heart." Histories of the resistance addressed the public's need for inspiration after the savagery of World War II. After years of censorship and privation, Japanese publishers tapped a market thirsty for books by putting out moving collections of letters from soldiers that quickly became best sellers. Only phrase books teaching the language of the conquerors outsold the books of soldiers' letters. Filmmakers from around the world also depicted war, as memories and nightmares of World War II haunted the screen into the twenty-first century.

By the end of the 1940s, **existentialism** had become popular among the cultural elites and students in universities around the world. This philosophy explored the meaning of human

existentialism A philosophy prominent after World War II, developed primarily by French thinkers, that stresses the importance of active engagement with the world in the creation of an authentic existence.

existence in a world where evil flourished. The principal theorists of existentialism, Frenchmen Jean-Paul Sartre and Albert Camus, wrote plays and essays in which they asked what "being" meant, given what they saw as the absence of God and the breakdown of morality under Nazism. Their answer was that "being," or existing, was not the automatic process either of God's creation or of birth into the natural world. Instead, through action and choice, the individual created an "authentic" or meaningful and valuable existence. As existentialists, Sartre and Camus emphasized political activism and resistance to totalitarianism.

In 1949, Simone de Beauvoir, Sartre's lifetime companion, published *The Second Sex*, the twentieth century's most influential work on the condition of women. Examining women's status as mothers, wives, and daughters, de Beauvoir concluded that most women had failed to take the kind of action necessary to lead authentic lives. Instead of acting based on their individual reasoning, they devoted themselves to reproduction and motherhood because it was a social expectation. Failing to create an authentic self through considered action, they had become its opposite—an object, or "Other," who followed cultural norms set by men. Translated into many languages, de Beauvoir's book asked women to change by creating their own freedom.

Liberation Culture

In decolonizing areas, thinkers mapped out new visions of how to construct the future. In the 1950s and 1960s Frantz Fanon, a black psychiatrist from the French Caribbean colony of Martinique, wrote that the mind of the colonized person had been

Frantz Fanon

Frantz Fanon was one of the most influential thinkers during anti-imperial liberation struggles of the 1950s. He justified the use of violence against colonizers by arguing that brute force was all the imperialists understood, and indeed it was what colonized peoples themselves understood best because of the violence regularly inflicted on them. He also raised the question of how one "decolonized" one's mind of such propagandistic notions as the superiority of whites and the inferiority of blacks. (© Abdelhamid Kahia/Kaha Studio.)

traumatized by the brutal imposition of an alien culture. Ruled by guns, the colonized person knew only violence and would thus naturally decolonize by means of violence. Translated into many languages, Fanon's *Black Skin, White Masks* (1952) and *The Wretched of the Earth* (1961) posed the question of how to "decolonize" one's mind. South African writer Bessie Head, the daughter of a white mother and an African father, developed Fanon's themes in her novels. Her characters danced on the edge of madness because of their complicated identities springing from colonialism, clashing ethnicities, and education. A teacher in Head's novel *Maru* (1971) has an English education but is despised and disdained by other Africans because she belongs to the darkest-skinned group of Bushmen. Liberation culture characterized independence as something emotionally confusing for individuals, with the meaning of freedom remaining to be puzzled out.

Ideas about the meaning of liberation circled the world. Mao Zedong's "Little Red Book" contained brief maxims intended to guide hundreds of millions of postcolonial citizens. Fanon's ideas also circulated among Africans, North Americans, and Latin Americans. They intersected with those of Jamaica-born Marcus Garvey, who in the interwar years had promoted a "back to Africa" movement as the way for African Americans to escape racial discrimination in the United States. In the 1960s the physician and upper-class guerrilla warrior Che Guevara, though a Marxist, wrote of avoiding the centralized and dictatorial Marxism of both the USSR and China. His popular works advocated a compassionate Marxism based on an appreciation of the oppressed rather than on a determination to direct them.

The Spread of Ideas

Inspired not only by their own situation in the United States but by decolonization movements throughout the world, African Americans intensified their agitation for civil rights in the 1950s. In principle, African American troops had fought to defeat the Nazi idea of white racial supremacy; now African Americans hoped to end ideas of white racial superiority in the United States. In 1954, the U.S. Supreme Court declared segregated education unconstitutional

The U.S. Civil Rights Movement

The "New Look" for Women After World War II
Designers and marketers aimed to return women in the West to a state of hyperfemininity in the postwar world, even though women in war-torn areas often lacked the bare necessities. In some places, clothing and food were rationed into the early 1950s, making the attire shown here more a fantasy than a reality. (Bibliotheque des Arts Decoratifs, Paris/Archives Charmet/Bridgeman Art Library.)

in *Brown v. Board of Education*, a case initiated by the National Association for the Advancement of Colored People (NAACP). Over the course of the 1950s, many talented individuals emerged to lead the civil rights movement, foremost among them Martin Luther King, Jr., a minister from Georgia whose powerful oratory galvanized African Americans to peaceful resistance in the face of brutal white retaliation. By the 1960s, other activists came to follow thinkers such as Fanon, proclaiming "black power" to achieve rights through violence if necessary.

The Culture of Cold War

In the effort to win the Cold War, both sides poured vast sums of money into high and popular culture. The United States secretly channeled government money into foundations to promote favorable journalism around the world and to sponsor specific artists. In the USSR, official writers churned out spy stories, and espionage novels topped best seller lists as well in the West. *Casino Royale* (1953), by the British author Ian Fleming, introduced James Bond, British intelligence agent 007, who survived tests of wit and physical prowess at the hands of communist and other political villains. Soviet pilots would not take off for flights when the work of Yulian Simyonov, the Russian counterpart of Ian Fleming, was playing on radio or television. Daily reports of Soviets and Americans—fictional or real—facing one another down fed many of the world's fantasies and nightmares.

In postwar Europe and the United States, everyday life also revolved around the growing availability of material goods and household conveniences. A rising birthrate and a bustling youth culture encouraged spending on newly available goods. The advertising business boomed, confronting the thriftiness of the Great Depression and wartime with messages that described new products and encouraged the desire to

Consumerism in the West

buy them. These were the years when American-style consumerism came to stand for freedom and plenty versus the scarcity in the communist world. Women's magazines in the West publicized a "new look" that encouraged women to be sexy and feminine—unlike women in communist countries—and urged them to return to the "normal" life of domesticity and shopping. European communists debated the "Americanization" they saw taking place. Many wanted American products; nonetheless, Communist parties worked to get American products banned. The Communist Party in France, for example, led a successful campaign to ban Coca-Cola for a time in the 1950s, and the Soviets tried unsuccessfully to match the West's production of consumer goods.

Spreading Cold War Culture

Radio was key to spreading Cold War culture and values; both the United States and the USSR used the medium to broadcast news and propaganda. During the late 1940s and early 1950s, the Voice of America, broadcasting in thirty-eight languages from one hundred transmitters, provided an alternative source of news for people around the world. The Soviet counterpart broadcast in Russian around the clock but initially spent much of its wattage jamming U.S. programming. Russian programs stressed a uniform communist culture and values. The United States, by contrast, emphasized diverse programming and promoted debate about current affairs—even while a U.S. senator, Joseph McCarthy, began a witch hunt for communists to win an election in 1950. Radio and television helped the events and developments of the Cold War acquire a far-reaching emotional impact: both the United States and USSR whipped up fear of enemies within, persecuting millions of citizens for allegedly favoring the opposing side. People heard reports of nuclear build-ups; in school, children rehearsed what to do in case of nuclear war; and families built bomb shelters in their backyards.

As leadership of the art world passed from Europe to the United States, art became part of the Cold War, along with consumer goods and books. **Abstract expressionism**, developed primarily by American artists, encompassed many diverse styles but often featured large canvases depicting nonrepresentational forms in bold colors. Abstract expressionists spoke of the importance of the artist's self-discovery, spiritual growth, and sensations in the process of painting. American artist Jackson Pollock produced abstract works by dripping, spattering, and pouring paint. Dutch-born artist Willem de Kooning commented on his relationship with his canvas, "If I stretch my arms next to the rest of myself and wonder where my fingers are, that is all the space I need as a painter." Said to exemplify Western freedom, such painters were awarded commissions at the secret direction of the U.S. Central Intelligence Agency. Pro-Soviet critics in western Europe condemned abstract art as "an infantile sickness" and favored socialist realist art with "human content," showing the condition of the workers and the oppressed races in the United States. When a show of abstract art opened in the Soviet Union, Khrushchev yelled that it was "dog shit."

Abstract Expressionism

The USSR promoted an official communist culture based on the socialist realist style highlighting the heroism of the working classes. The government sponsored classical training in ballet and music and harassed innovators in the arts. Communist culture emphasized Soviet successes, celebrating Soviet wartime victories and the USSR's progress toward Stalin's goal of economic modernization. Dissenters in the USSR were both feared and bullied. For example, Khrushchev forced Boris Pasternak to refuse the 1958 Nobel Prize in Literature because Pasternak's novel *Doctor Zhivago* (1957) cast doubt on the glory of the Bolshevik Revolution and affirmed the value of the individual. Yet Khrushchev himself made several trips to the West and was a more cosmopolitan, public figure than Stalin had been. With growing confidence and affluence, the Soviets concentrated their efforts on spreading official socialist culture and influence in Asia, Africa, and Latin America.

Official Communist Culture

COUNTERPOINT
The Bandung Conference 1955

In April 1955, Achmed Sukarno, who led the struggle for Indonesian independence from the Dutch, hosted a conference in Bandung, Indonesia, of emerging nations. The Bandung Conference, also known as the Asian-African Conference, was meant to ensure the independence of the emerging Asian and African nations despite the temptations of loans and military aid from the superpowers. The conference was thus a counterpoint to the seemingly global grip of the Cold War and the superpowers' hold on international politics.

> **FOCUS**
> How did the Bandung Conference and its aims represent an alternative to the Cold War division of the globe?

Cosponsored by Egypt, Indonesia, Burma, Sri Lanka, India, and Pakistan, the conference was attended by representatives from twenty-nine countries, most of them newly independent. They constituted a who's who of anticolonialism: Kwame Nkrumah of Ghana, Gamal Abdel Nasser of Egypt, Zhou Enlai of China, and Ho Chi Minh of Vietnam attended alongside Sukarno and Jawaharlal Nehru, prime minister of India. Activists throughout the world were inspired

abstract expressionism A postwar artistic style characterized by nonrepresentational forms and bold colors; often associated with the freedom of the Western world.

The Bandung Conference

In 1955, leaders from Asia and Africa met in newly independent Indonesia at the Bandung Conference, with the goal of building unity among emerging nations. Participants listened to inspiring and hard-hitting speeches as they began a policy of "nonalignment" in the Cold War. This policy was a refusal to become pawns of the superpowers, but it was hard for many to maintain because the need for support was so great in regions devastated by imperial greed and total war. (AP Photo/Asia-Africa Museum, HO.)

by the independent, even defiant stand against the superpowers taken by the leaders gathered at Bandung. African American author Richard Wright, who attended the conference, was riveted by the meaning of such an assembly: "The despised, the insulted, the hurt, the dispossessed—in short, the underdogs of the human race were meeting. Here were class and racial and religious consciousness on a global scale. Who had thought of organizing such a meeting? And what had these nations in common? Nothing, it seemed to me, but what their past relationship to the Western world had made them feel. This meeting of the rejected was in itself a kind of judgment upon the Western world!"[10] Leaders at the conference, speakers noted, represented more than half the world's population.

Shared Goals

Issues discussed at the Bandung Conference included economic development outside the structures of colonialism, and the achievement of political well-being without following the dictates of either the Soviet Union or the United States. Nehru argued strongly for nonalignment, maintaining that nations affiliating with one side or another would lose their identity. Moreover, Nehru claimed, the superpowers had come to equate a nation's worth with its military power. To his mind this was evidence that "greatness sometimes brings quite false values, false standards. When they begin to think in terms of military strength—whether it be the United Kingdom, the Soviet Union, or the U.S.A.—then they are going away from the right track and the result of that will be that the overwhelming might of one country will conquer the world."[11] In India, Nehru tried to follow a middle course between the superpowers in his own economic policies, even though he simultaneously offered support to communist China.

Nehru had high hopes for Bandung, but he also had concerns that proper conditions such as first-rate accommodations and sanitary facilities be provided for delegates of the emerging nations to the conference. They needed to be recognized as valuable through their treatment, as they were at the meetings of the United Nations in New York. Nehru admired the more lofty goals of the UN, including the charter outlining a collective global authority that would adjudicate conflicts and provide military protection to any member threatened by aggression. Meetings of both the UN and emerging nations began shifting global issues away from superpower priorities. Human rights and economic inequities among developing countries and the West nudged their way into public consciousness.

Divisive Issues

Yet for all the desire to be an influential third force between the superpowers, serious issues divided participants at the Bandung Conference. For one, the legacy of mistrust between India and Pakistan grew increasingly bitter and violent over their rival claims to the state of Kashmir. The leaders at Bandung argued both in favor of nationalism and in support of movements that transcended nationalism, such as pan-Islam and pan-Africanism. Although the Bandung Conference did not yield an enduring world power bloc, it did articulate a position that after the end of the Cold War would evolve into the idea of a North-South divide. Those living in the northern half of the globe were wealthy compared with those in the south, impoverished because imperialism's legacy had relegated them to poorly remunerated production of commodities. In the 1950s and 1960s, however, the notable achievement of the Bandung Conference was that it strengthened the commitment of new nations to remain independent in the face of the superpowers' military and economic might.

Conclusion

The Cold War began the atomic age and transformed international power politics. The two new superpowers, the Soviet Union and the United States, each built massive atomic arsenals, replacing the former European leadership and facing off in a Cold War that menaced the entire world. The Cold War saturated everyday life, producing a culture of bomb shelters, spies, and witch-hunts. Yet within this atmosphere of division and nuclear rivalry an astonishing worldwide recovery occurred. New housing, transport, and industrial rebuilding—often sponsored by a burgeoning welfare state and using wartime technology—made many people healthier and more prosperous.

World War II promoted further discontent and activism—like that of Umm Kulthum—among the colonized peoples of the world and simultaneously loosened the grip of the colonial powers. From India to Ghana and Nigeria, colonial peoples, often led by Western-educated and nationalist politicians, won their independence and turned to nation building. Many, as in the case of Algeria and Kenya, had to take up arms against the brutality of the imperialists to become free. Nation building in newly independent states, however, turned out to be slow and halting, even though many of these nations also enjoyed a burst of postwar prosperity.

As the world grew overall in prosperity, its cultural life focused on eradicating the evils inflicted by the Axis and on surviving the atomic rivalry of the superpowers. Frantz Fanon and other thinkers developed theories to explain the struggles of decolonized peoples for their full independence. In the midst of postwar intellectual introspection and heated Cold War rhetoric, many came to wonder whether Cold War was really worth the threat of nuclear annihilation and whether there might be an alternative way of living as individuals and as a world community. Leaders of newly independent nations, through such activities as the Bandung Conference, promoted the idea of nonalignment with either superpower, but they often had difficulty overcoming their own differences, rivalries, and internal corruption. These hopes matured into a burst of technological creativity and further activism to improve the world—including putting an end to the Cold War.

NOTES

1. Harry S. Truman, "Truman Doctrine Speech," March 12, 1947.
2. Dwight D. Eisenhower, press conference, April 7, 1954.
3. Quoted in Ronald J. Spector, *In the Ruins of Empire: The Japanese Surrender and the Battle for Postwar Asia* (New York: Random House, 2007), 78.
4. Quoted in Alex von Tunzelmann, *Indian Summer: The Secret History of the End of an Empire* (New York: Henry Holt, 2007), 225.

5. Everette Lee DeGoyler, quoted in Daniel Yergin, *The Prize: The Epic Quest for Oil, Money, and Power* (New York: Simon and Schuster, 1991), 393.
6. Golda Meir, *My Life* (New York: Putnam, 1975).
7. "Africa Must Unite" (1963), quoted in Michael Hunt, *The World Transformed, 1945 to the Present* (Boston: Bedford/St. Martin's, 2004), 144.
8. Superintendent of Police Philip, quoted in Carolyn A. Brown, *"We Were All Slaves": African Miners, Culture, and Resistance at the Enugu Government Colliery* (Portsmouth, NH: Heinemann, 2003), 310.
9. Quoted in Judith M. Brown, *Nehru: A Political Life* (New Haven, CT: Yale University Press, 2003), 229.
10. Richard Wright, *The Color Curtain: A Report on the Bandung Conference* (Jackson, MS: Banner, 1995).
11. *Selected Works of Jawaharlal Nehru: 1 February–31 May 1955*. vol. 28.

RESOURCES FOR RESEARCH

World Politics and the Cold War

The Cold War replaced the great-power politics of the previous hundred years, making the world increasingly dangerous. Spector's history of the immediate postwar years in Asia shows the chaos and violence that provided the setting for the Cold War division of the world and the transformation of world politics.

Cumings, Bruce. *Korea's Place in the Sun: A Modern History*. 2005.
The Korean War Educator. http://www.koreanwar-educator.org.
Meisner, Maurice. *Mao Zedong: A Political and Intellectual Portrait*. 2007.
Skierka, Volker. *Fidel Castro: A Biography*. 2007.
Spector, Ronald H. *In the Ruins of Empire: The Japanese Surrender and the Battle for Postwar Asia*. 2007.
Statler, Kathryn, and Andrew Johns, eds. *The Eisenhower Administration, the Third World, and the Globalization of the Cold War*. 2006.

Decolonization and the Birth of Nations

New nations emerged in a variety of ways, with differing levels of violence and styles of leadership. Elkins's book starkly details the British torture and slaughter of Kenyans who wanted freedom.

Connelley, Matthew. *A Diplomatic Revolution: Algeria's Fight for Independence and the Origins of the Post–Cold War Era*. 2002.
Danielson, Virginia. *Umm Kulthum, Arabic Song, and Egyptian Society in the Twentieth Century*. 1998.
Duara, Prasenjit, ed. *Decolonization: Perspectives from Then and Now*. 2004.
Elkins, Caroline. *Imperial Reckoning: The Untold Story of Britain's Gulag in Kenya*. 2005.
Guha, Ramachandra. *India After Gandhi: The History of the World's Largest Democracy*. 2008.
Hyam, Ronald. *Britain's Declining Empire: The Road to Decolonisation, 1918–1968*. 2007.

World Recovery in the 1950s and 1960s

Recovering from the devastation of World War II and the trials of nation building was no easy task. Notable leaders of new nations worked to overcome poverty, illiteracy, and lingering factionalism. Brown's biography of Nehru provides a good example.

Allen, Larry. *The Global Economic System Since 1945*. 2005.
Brown, Judith M. *Nehru: A Political Life*. 2003.
Estévez-Abe, Margarita. *Welfare and Capitalism in Postwar Japan*. 2008.
Rhodes, Richard. *Arsenals of Folly: The Nuclear Arms Race*. 2007.
Sturgeon, Janet C. *Border Landscapes: The Politics of Akha Land Use in China and Thailand*. 2005.
Tignor, Robert. *W. Arthur Lewis and the Birth of Development Economics*. 2006.

Culture Dynamism amid Cold War

An array of thinkers and artists considered the birth of new nations amid immense postwar suffering. Frantz Fanon was one of the most influential theorists of decolonization of his time, but Cold War rivalries also led to cultural competition, as seen in Von Eschen's work.

Fanon, Frantz. *The Wretched of the Earth*. 1963 [orig. pub. 1961].
Hoerder, Dirk. *Cultures in Contact: World Migrations in the Second Millennium*. 2002.
Igarashi, Yoshikuni. *Bodies of Memory: Narratives of War in Postwar Japanese Culture, 1945–1970*. 2000.
Von Eschen, Penny. *Satchmo Blows Up the World: Jazz Ambassadors Play the Cold War*. 2005.
Wright, Michelle M. *Becoming Black: Creating Identity in the African Diaspora*. 2004.

COUNTERPOINT: The Bandung Conference, 1955

Taylor's people-oriented book provides the Indonesian background to Bandung and shows the stresses and strains of nation building amid postwar turbulence.

Jankowitz, Odile, and Karl Sauvant, eds. *The Third World Without Superpowers: Collected Documents of Non-Aligned Countries*. 1973–1993.
Legge, John David. *Sukarno: A Political Biography*. 2003.
Taylor, Jean Gelman. *Indonesia: Peoples and History*. 2003.
Wright, Richard. *The Color Curtain: A Report on the Bandung Conference*. 1995.

▶ **For additional primary sources from this period**, see *Sources of Crossroads and Cultures*.

▶ **For Web sites, images, and documents related to topics in this chapter**, see Make History at bedfordstmartins.com/smith.

The major global development in this chapter ▶ The political transformations of the postwar world and their social and cultural consequences.

IMPORTANT EVENTS

1945	World War II ends
1947	India and Pakistan win independence
1948	Israel gains independence
1948–1949	Arab-Israeli War
1949	Communists take control of China; Western powers form NATO; USSR detonates atomic bomb
1949	Indonesia gains independence
1950–1953	Korean War
1952	Egypt achieves full independence under Nasser
1953	Death of Stalin
1954	Vietnamese defeat French army at Dien Bien Phu
1956	Khrushchev denounces Stalin; Suez crisis; revolution in Hungary
1957	USSR launches *Sputnik*
1958	Khrushchev forces Boris Pasternak to refuse Nobel Prize in Literature
1961	Construction of the Berlin Wall
1962	Algeria wins independence; Cuban Missile Crisis
c. 1966–1976	Mao Zedong's "Cultural Revolution"

CHAPTER OVERVIEW QUESTIONS

1. How did the Cold War affect the superpowers and the world beyond them?

2. How did the Cold War shape everyday lives and goals?

3. Why did colonial nationalism revive in the postwar world, and how did decolonization affect society and culture?

4. Why did the model of a welfare state emerge after World War II, and how did this development affect ordinary people?

SECTION FOCUS QUESTIONS

1. Why was the Cold War waged, and how did it reshape world politics?

2. How did colonized peoples achieve their independence from the imperialist powers after World War II?

3. What were the major elements of recovery in different parts of the world in the decades following World War II?

4. How did the experience of world war, decolonization, and Cold War affect cultural life and thought?

5. How did the Bandung Conference and its aims represent an alternative to the Cold War division of the globe?

KEY TERMS

abstract expressionism (p. 983)
Cold War (p. 961)
containment (p. 964)
Cultural Revolution (p. 979)
decolonization (p. 961)
European Economic Community (p. 976)
existentialism (p. 980)
Great Leap Forward (p. 979)

guerrilla warfare (p. 971)
North Atlantic Treaty Organization (p. 967)
Organization of American States (p. 968)
Partition (p. 971)
proxy war (p. 962)
Southeast Asia Treaty Organization (p. 968)
Warsaw Pact (p. 967)
welfare state (p. 977)

MAKING CONNECTIONS

1. Recall Chapters 27 and 28. Why did economic well-being seem so much stronger a decade and longer after World War II than it had been after World War I?

2. Why did proxy wars play such a constant role in the Cold War? Some historians see these wars as part of a new imperialism. Do you agree?

3. What was the role of culture in shaping the Cold War?

4. What remnants of decolonization and the Cold War still affect life today?

30

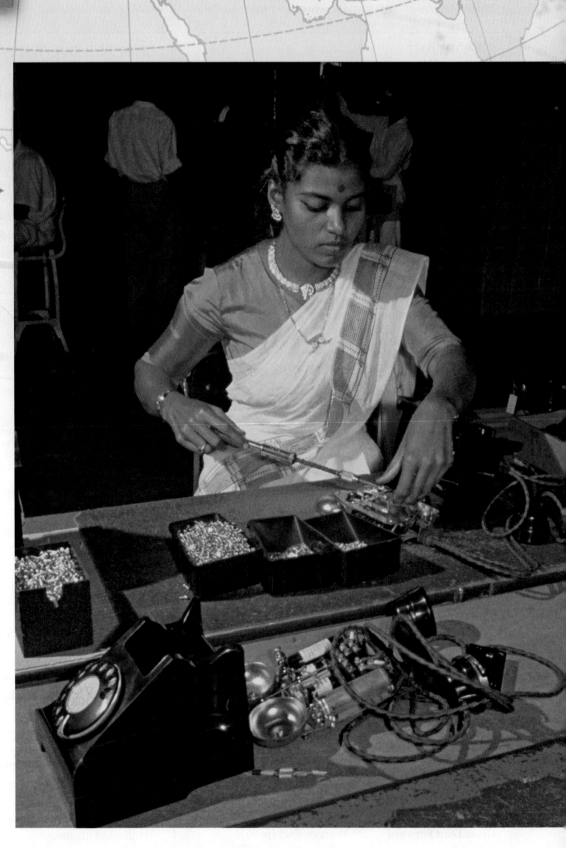

AT A CROSSROADS ▶

This technician, working in 1962 in a telephone plant in Bangalore, India, stands at a crossroads of global technological innovation. Not only would satellites come to connect a range of communication devices such as telephones throughout the world, but telephones would evolve into such instruments as the iPhone, which would incorporate almost all other means of communication. By the twenty-first century, Bangalore itself would become a leader in global service work because of these and other innovations. (National Geographic/Getty Images.)

Technological Transformation and the End of Cold War

1960–1992

I n 1973 the film *Bobby* opened to packed houses in cities across India. The film tells the story of Raj and Bobby, teenagers who fall in love after Raj returns to Bombay from boarding school. Infatuated with each other and the world, Bobby wears long chiffon scarves floating from her ponytail and Raj races around on his motorbike, both of them setting consumer trends among young Indians tired of postindependence seriousness. As Raj's wealthy industrialist father works to stop his son from marrying someone of a lower class, moviegoers cheered the young couple's determination to stay together, even as thugs kidnap them to obtain ransom money from the father. Rebellious young love, new fashions, and lots of song and dance filled *Bobby* and other hit Indian films, which helped "Bollywood," as the film industry centered in Bombay (Mumbai) came to be called, outpace Hollywood in ticket sales and popularity in the 1970s. Thanks to new video-recording technology, developed by the Japanese as a mass market item late in the 1970s, *Bobby* came to circulate worldwide, especially among South Asian fans who had migrated to Western countries.

Hundreds of Bollywood writers, composers, actors, designers, cameramen, editors, agents, and the other service workers who constituted an ever-growing segment of the global workforce contributed to the making of *Bobby*. Bollywood films represented the

Advances in Technology and Science

FOCUS What were the major postwar advances in technology and science, and why were they important?

Changes in the World Economy

FOCUS How did changes in the global economy affect livelihoods and family life?

Politics and Protest in an Age of Cold War

FOCUS What developments challenged the superpowers' dominance of world politics, and how did the superpowers attempt to address those challenges?

The End of the Cold War Order

FOCUS Why did the Cold War order come to an end?

COUNTERPOINT: Agrarian Peoples in a Technological Age

FOCUS How did some agrarian peoples resist the scientific and technological developments that threatened their ways of life?

BACKSTORY

As we saw in Chapter 29, by 1960 the two superpowers had pulled much of the world into the Cold War, using their considerable military and economic power to attract allies and counter each other's efforts. Their ability to extend their influence into developing countries rested on their successful adoption and application of the technological and industrial developments of the past two centuries. Since 1750 the Industrial Revolution (discussed in Chapter 24) had substituted mechanical energy for human power and then proceeded to develop electrical, chemical, and nuclear capacity. By the postwar period all of these technologies were being enhanced and democratized, widely improving civilian life. Those societies that could innovate, adapt, and then efficiently coordinate the use of these technologies moved ahead, as Japan and Western countries understood early on.

Exxon
IBM
Ford
General Electric
Mobil
Grace
McDonald's
Coca Cola

Toyota
Honda
Sony
Toshiba

Royal Dutch Shell
(U.K.)
Nestlé (SWITZ.)
Philips (NETH.)
Asea Brown Boveri
(SWE./SWITZ.)

Daewoo

Tata Steel

- OPEC member
- Other major oil-producing country
- International borders, 1975
- Pacific tiger, c. 1990
Sony Major multinational corporation, 1990s; listed by size

PACIFIC OCEAN

ATLANTIC OCEAN

INDIAN OCEAN

SOUTH AMERICA

AFRICA

BELIZE   MEXICO
ECUADOR
JAMAICA   CUBA
HAITI
VENEZUELA
DOM. REP.
UNITED STATES
CANADA
NORWAY
U.K.
FRANCE
Frankfurt
Moscow
USSR
JAPAN
S. KOREA
Taiwan
Hong Kong
P.R. CHINA
VIETNAM
BANG.
AUSTRALIA
INDONESIA
SINGAPORE
MALAYSIA
ALGERIA
LIBYA
EGYPT
KUWAIT
SAUDI ARABIA
IRAQ   IRAN
QATAR
U.A.E.
OMAN
PAK.   INDIA
NIGERIA
GABON

0   1000   2000 miles
0   1000   2000 kilometers

Arab-Israeli Six-Day War **1967** ▪

Vietnam War ends;
Vietnam reunited **1975**

▪ **1957** USSR launches *Sputnik*

"Prague Spring" in
Czechoslovakia **1968** ▪

▪ **1969** U.S. astronauts
land on moon

1950

1960

1970

Betty Friedan, *The Feminine
Mystique* **1963** ▪

U.S. president Richard Nixon visits China;
SALT I agreement **1972** ▪

1973–1976 Aleksandr Solzhenitsyn, *Gulag Archipelago*

Arab-Israeli Yom Kippur War; OPEC raises oil
prices and imposes embargo **1973** ▪

fantasies of an increasingly service-oriented population and those aspiring to join it. Across the world, sophisticated technology devised by highly educated service workers transmitted productions via satellite and circulated them on DVDs. In **postindustrial**, service-driven economies, institutions of higher education sprang up at a dizzying rate, drawing more students away from traditional families than ever before—among them bright-eyed young people like Raj and Bobby. The high-tech youthfulness and rebellion represented by *Bobby* and Bollywood were one aspect of the unsettled, dynamic social and economic environment of the late twentieth century.

Although Bollywood presented social and economic change in lighthearted fantasies, people were also making serious efforts to tackle the most pressing problems of modern society. The same young people targeted by the makers of Bollywood films joined a wide variety of activists to strike out against the effects of technology, as well as against war and the Cold War, social inequality and repression, and prevailing attitudes of racism and sexism. Many of these activists participated in grassroots protests against national dictatorships—in Latin America, for example—and against the way high-tech nations in general and the superpowers in particular were directing society. Between 1945 and 1990, more than one hundred major rebellions and civil wars erupted around the world as countries in both the Soviet and U.S. blocs headed toward political revolution. Whole nations—often with the young on the frontlines—challenged the superpowers' monopoly of international power. Agonizing wars in Vietnam and Afghanistan sapped the resources of the United States and the Soviet Union, respectively. Other states emerged to exercise surprising economic and military power as they grasped the reins of technology. The oil-producing states of the Middle East combined their efforts and reduced the export of oil to the leading industrial nations in the 1970s while also raising prices.

As the USSR failed to keep pace with high-tech innovation or to heed youthful calls for change, an invisible erosion of Soviet legitimacy took place, and soon a reform-minded leader—Mikhail Gorbachev—set the country on a new course. It was too late: in 1989, the

postindustrial An economy or society in which service work rather than manufacturing or agriculture predominates.

MAPPING THE WORLD
OPEC, Pacific Tigers, and World Migration

In the decades from 1960 to 1990, the world seemed bogged down in the Cold War order, but it was actually in tremendous flux. Technological change was transforming society and would continue to do so through the twenty-first century. Economic power was beginning to shift away from the West, and this shift would accelerate over the coming decades. Finally, under the influence of technology and global economic change, livelihoods became postindustrial in some areas and more attuned to manufacturing in formerly agricultural regions.

ROUTES ▼

→ Major oil trade routes, c. 1975

⇢ South Asian migrations, 1970–present

→ Southeast Asian migrations, 1975–present

→ Routes of Aleksandr Solzhenitsyn, 1945–1974

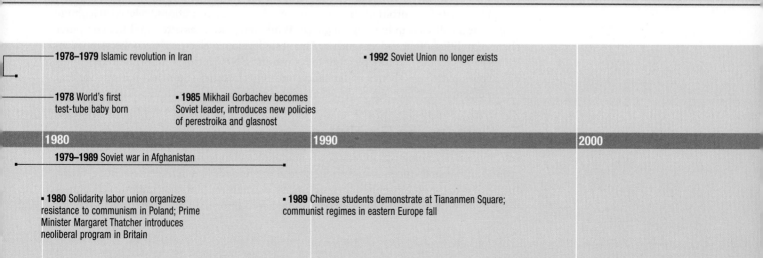

1978–1979 Islamic revolution in Iran

▪ **1992** Soviet Union no longer exists

1978 World's first test-tube baby born

▪ **1985** Mikhail Gorbachev becomes Soviet leader, introduces new policies of perestroika and glasnost

1980   1990   2000

1979–1989 Soviet war in Afghanistan

▪ **1980** Solidarity labor union organizes resistance to communism in Poland; Prime Minister Margaret Thatcher introduces neoliberal program in Britain

▪ **1989** Chinese students demonstrate at Tiananmen Square; communist regimes in eastern Europe fall

Soviet bloc collapsed, and by 1992 the USSR itself had dissolved. The dissolution of the Soviet bloc occurred in part as a result of the transformations in the rest of the world. Among these transformations were the growth of rapid global communications, revolutionary developments in technology, and the raised voices of educated young people like Raj and Bobby.

OVERVIEW QUESTIONS

The major global development in this chapter: The technological revolution of the late twentieth century and its impact on societies and political developments around the world.

As you read, consider:

1. How did the technological developments of these decades transform social and economic conditions?

2. What were the attitudes of young people toward technology and social change during these years, and how did they reflect the Cold War climate in which these changes occurred?

3. How did the technological developments influence the fall of communist regimes in Europe and the dissolution of the Soviet Union?

4. How did the scientific and technological developments of the second half of the twentieth century affect the waging—and the end—of the Cold War?

Advances in Technology and Science

FOCUS

What were the major postwar advances in technology and science, and why were they important?

Revolutionary developments in technology and science reshaped global society after World War II, if unevenly. Wartime technology adapted for civilian use—such as the massive development of nuclear power—continued to improve daily life and boost prosperity. The spread of technology allowed billions of people access to instantaneous radio and television news, to new forms of contraceptives to control reproduction, and to the advantages of computers. Satellites orbiting the earth reported weather conditions, relayed telephone signals, and collected military intelligence. While television, cassettes, and the computer changed politics, other gadgets such as Japanese-developed electric rice cookers and electronic games made life more pleasant for consumers. New forms of information technology allowed citizens to better understand conditions in other countries—knowledge that inspired people around the world to demand more from employers and politicians alike.

The Information Revolution

Information technology catalyzed social and political change in these postwar decades just as innovations in textile making and the spread of railroads had in the nineteenth century. In the first half of the twentieth century, mass journalism, film, and radio had begun to forge a more homogeneous society based on shared information and images; in the last third of the century, television, computers, and telecommunications made information even more accessible and linked once-remote towns to urban capitals on the other side of the globe. In effect, the new information technology acted as a new kind of crossroads, giving individuals access to the ideas, beliefs, and products of societies around the world.

Americans embraced television in the 1950s; following the postwar recovery television became a major entertainment and communications medium in countries around the world. In many places the audience for newspapers and theater declined. "We devote more . . . hours per year to television than [to] any other single artifact," a French sociologist commented in 1969.[1] As with radio, many governments funded television broadcasting with tax dollars and initially controlled TV programming to tap its potential for sending political messages and to avoid what they perceived as the substandard fare offered by American commercial TV. The Indian official in charge of early television programming forbade pop music, for example, and some European countries broadcast mostly classical drama and news. Thus, states assumed a new obligation to organize their citizens' leisure time, thereby gaining more influence over daily life.

Television

With the emergence of communications satellites and video recorders in the 1960s, state-sponsored television encountered competition. Satellite technology transmitted sports broadcasts and other programming to a worldwide audience. In 1969 the Sony Corporation of Japan introduced the first color videocassette recorder to the consumer market; it was widely purchased late in the 1970s. What statesmen and intellectuals considered the junk programming of the United States—soap operas, game shows, sitcoms—arrived dubbed in the native language. More interesting to Brazilians, however, were their own soap operas and those imported from Mexico. Although under the Brazilian dictatorship news was censored from the 1960s into the 1980s, soap operas seemed to show real life, and Mexican programming added to their pool of information. By the 1980s people migrating from one continent to another could keep in touch with their home culture by watching sporting events broadcast via satellite or viewing films such as *Bobby* on videocassettes.

East and west, television exercised a powerful political and cultural influence. Educational programming united the far-flung population of the USSR by broadcasting shows featuring Soviet specialties such as ballet. At the same time, with travel forbidden or too expensive for many people globally, shows about foreign lands were often the most popular. By late in the century even some of the poorest houses in remote African oases sported satellite dishes. Heads of state such as Fidel Castro in Cuba used the medium to maintain national leadership, often preempting regular programming to address fellow citizens. Because electoral success increasingly depended on a successful media image, politicians came to rely on media experts—a new service job—as much as they did policy experts.

Just as revolutionary as television, the computer reshaped work in science, defense, and industry and eventually came to affect everyday life. As large as a gymnasium in the 1940s, computing machines shrank to the size of an attaché case in the mid-1980s and became far less expensive and fantastically more powerful, thanks to the development of sophisticated digital electronic circuitry implanted on tiny silicon chips, which replaced the clumsy radio tubes used in 1940s and 1950s computers. Within a few decades, the computer could perform hundreds of millions of operations per second and the price of the integrated circuit at the heart of computer technology would fall to less than a dollar, allowing businesses and individuals access to computing power at a reasonable cost.

Computers

Computers changed the pace and patterns of work by speeding up tasks and making them easier. By performing many operations that skilled workers had once done themselves, they rendered many livelihoods obsolete. In garment making, for example, experienced workers no longer painstakingly figured out how to arrange patterns on cloth for maximum efficiency and economy. Instead, a computer gave instructions for the best positioning of pattern pieces, and workers, usually women, simply followed the machine's directions. In 1981 the French phone company launched a public Internet server, the Minitel—a forerunner of the World Wide Web—through which French users made dinner reservations, performed stock transactions, and gained information. As in earlier

Computer Programmers in the 1940s

Early computers were massive, and programming required plugging and unplugging multiple cables, as this photograph shows. Many women, such as these U.S. workers, were among the first programmers, perhaps because the process resembled large telephone operations. Technological advances brought increasing miniaturization of ever more powerful computers—a true knowledge revolution that advanced the development of postindustrial society and globalization. (Corbis.)

times, people could work in their homes, but technology now allowed them to be connected to a central mainframe.

Failure to profit from high-tech efficiencies could have dire political consequences, as we shall see. But debate raged over the social effects of computers. Whereas in the Industrial Revolution, machine capabilities had replaced human power, in the information revolution computer technology augmented brainpower. Many believed that computers would further expand mental life, providing, in the words of one scientist, "boundless opportunities . . . to resolve the puzzles of cosmology, of life, and of the society of man."[2] Others maintained that computers programmed people, reducing human capacity for inventiveness and problem solving. Widespread access to the Internet and World Wide Web in the 1990s provoked debates over privacy, property rights, and the transmission of pornography, debates that continue to the present day.

The Space Age

The Space Race

New information and computer technology both contributed to and grew out of another mid-twentieth century development—the space race. After the Soviets' launch of the satellite *Sputnik* in 1957, the space race took off. The competition produced increasingly complex space flights that tested humans' ability to survive space exploration and its effects. Astronauts walked in space, endured weeks (and later, months) in orbit, docked with other craft, fixed satellites, and carried out experiments for the military and private industry. Meanwhile, a series of unmanned rockets filled the earth's gravitational sphere with weather, television, intelligence, and other communications satellites. In July 1969, U.S. astronauts Neil Armstrong and Edwin "Buzz" Aldrin walked on the moon's surface—a climactic moment in the space race.

Global Communication

Although the space race grew out of Cold War rivalry, the space age also offered the possibility of global political cooperation and communication. The exploration of space by a single country came to involve the participation of other countries. In 1965, an international consortium headed by the United States launched the first commercial communications satellite, *Intelsat I*, and by 1969, with the launch of *Intelsat III* covering the Indian Ocean region, the entire world was linked via satellite. Although some 50 percent of satellites were for military and espionage purposes, the rest promoted international communication and were sustained by transnational collaboration: by the 1970s some 150 countries collaborated to maintain the global satellite system. Satellite transmission allowed 500 million people to watch live reporting from the moon in 1969, and in 1978 one billion fans—or one quarter of the world's population at the time—tuned in to the World Cup soccer game. Global linkages only grew in magnitude and importance over the next decades.

Lunar landings and experiments in space brought advances in pure science. For example, astronomers used mineral samples from the moon to calculate the age of the solar system with unprecedented precision. Unmanned spacecraft provided data on cosmic radiation, magnetic fields, and infrared sources. Utilizing a range of technology, including the radiotelescope, which depicted space by receiving, measuring, and calculating nonvisible rays, these findings reinforced the so-called big bang theory of the origins of the universe and brought other new information, such as data on the composition of other planets, to scientists around the world. Long before politicians resolved Cold War differences, scientists were sharing their knowledge of the universe.

Scientific Advances

A New Scientific Revolution

Sophisticated technologies extended to the life sciences, bringing dramatic health benefits and ultimately changing reproduction itself. In 1952, English molecular biologist Francis Crick and American biologist James Watson discovered the configuration of DNA, the material in a cell's chromosomes that carries hereditary information. Simultaneously, other scientists were working on "the pill"—an oral contraceptive for women that tapped more than a century of scientific work in the field of birth control. More breakthroughs lay ahead—ones that would revolutionize conception and make scientific duplication of species possible.

Crick and Watson, young men working as a team from laboratories in Cambridge, England, solved the mystery of the gene and thus of biological inheritance when they demonstrated the structure of DNA. They showed how the double helix of the DNA molecule splits in cellular reproduction to form the basis of each new cell. This genetic material, biologists concluded, provides the chemical pattern for an individual organism's life. Beginning in the 1960s, genetics and the new field of molecular biology progressed rapidly. Growing understanding of nucleic acids and proteins advanced knowledge of viruses and bacteria, leading to effective worldwide campaigns against polio, tetanus, syphilis, tuberculosis, and such dangerous childhood diseases as mumps and measles—boosting the world's population.

Understanding DNA

Understanding how DNA works allowed scientists both to alter the makeup of plants and to bypass natural animal reproduction in a process called cloning—obtaining the cells of an organism and dividing or reproducing them (in an exact copy) in a laboratory. The possibility of genetically altering species and even creating new variations (for instance, to control agricultural pests) led to concern about how such actions would affect the balance of nature. Adding to medical breakthroughs, in 1967 Dr. Christiaan Barnard of South Africa performed the first successful heart transplant, and U.S. doctors later developed an artificial heart. By the end of the twentieth century, transplant technology circled the globe. Critics questioned whether the enormous cost of new medical technology to save a few people might be better spent on improving basic medical and health care for the many.

Technology also influenced the most intimate areas of human relations—sexuality and procreation. In traditional societies, community and family norms dictated marital arrangements and sexual practices, in large part because too many or too few children threatened the crucial balance between population size and agricultural productivity. As societies industrialized and urbanized, however, not only did these considerations become less important, but the growing availability of reliable birth-control devices permitted young people to begin sexual relations earlier, with less risk of pregnancy. These trends accelerated in the 1960s when the birth-control pill, developed in a Mexican research

Transforming Reproduction

institute and later mass-produced in the United States and tested on women in Puerto Rico and other developing areas, came on the Western market. By 1970, its use was spreading around the world. Millions also sought out voluntary surgical sterilization through tubal ligations and vasectomies. New techniques brought abortion, traditionally performed by amateurs, into the hands of medical professionals, making the procedure safe, though still controversial.

Childbirth and conception itself were similarly transformed. Whereas only a small minority of Western births took place in hospitals in 1920, more than 90 percent did by 1970 and this trend spread worldwide. Obstetricians performed much of the work midwives had once done. As pregnancy and birth became a medical process, innovative procedures and equipment made it possible to monitor women and fetuses throughout pregnancy, labor, and delivery. In 1978, the first "test-tube baby," Louise Brown, was born to an English couple. She had been conceived when her mother's eggs were fertilized with her father's sperm in a laboratory dish and then implanted in her mother's uterus—a complex process called *in vitro fertilization*. If a woman could not carry a child to term, the laboratory-fertilized embryo could be implanted in the uterus of a surrogate, or substitute, mother.

The Green Revolution

Science also helped boost grain harvests around the world. In Mexico City in the 1940s, a team of scientists led by Norman Borlaug experimented with blending Japanese strains of wheat with Mexican ones, devising hardier seeds that raised yields by some 70 percent. Borlaug became part of "an army of hunger fighters," as he called those who next worked to devise rice that would thrive in India, the Philippines, and other countries.[3]

Those most able to profit from the breakthrough, however, were large landowners who could afford the irrigation, fertilizers, and the new seeds themselves. High costs led many small farmers to fail. As a result of the **Green Revolution**, however, rural poverty nonetheless declined in countries such as India, where it fell from close to 50 percent of the population in the 1960s to 30 percent in the 1990s. Although technological innovation did not affect all societies to the same degree or in the same ways, the rate of scientific discovery and its overall impact on life around the world increased steadily in the late twentieth century. Moreover, as the century came to a close, Western nations lost their monopoly on scientific and industrial power.

Changes in the World Economy

FOCUS
How did changes in the global economy affect livelihoods and family life?

Beginning in the 1960s industrial and agrarian entrepreneurship and the development of technology rose dramatically outside the West, especially in Asia and the Middle East. Profits from both manufacturing and the sale of commodities soared during these years. In contrast, reshaped by the spread of technology, the economies of Western countries took what has been labeled a postindustrial course. Instead of being centered on industry and agriculture, the postindustrial economy emphasized intellectual work and the distribution of services such as health care and education. As Asia and Latin America in particular developed their manufacturing and service sectors in the last third of the century, the share in the world economy of the traditional industrial powers declined.

The Rising Pacific Economy

Green Revolution The application of DNA and other scientific knowledge to the production of seeds and fertilizers to raise agricultural productivity in developing parts of the world.

From Japan to Singapore, explosive productivity began to spread economic power through the Pacific region. Japan's government determined to oversee the nation's economic rebirth, with the Ministry of Trade and Industry announcing in 1959 a goal of "income doubling" within ten years. In an effort to strengthen its Cold War allies, the United States pumped some $12 billion into East Asian allies such as South Korea, contributing to its

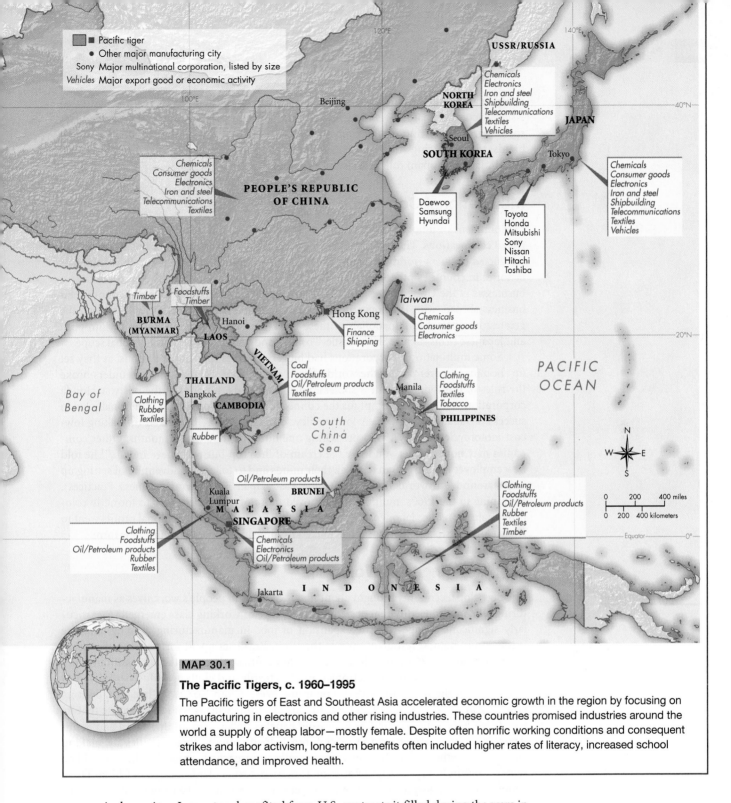

Legend:
- Pacific tiger
- Other major manufacturing city
- Sony Major multinational corporation, listed by size
- *Vehicles* Major export good or economic activity

USSR/RUSSIA

NORTH KOREA
- Chemicals
- Electronics
- Iron and steel
- Shipbuilding
- Telecommunications
- Textiles
- Vehicles

JAPAN

Seoul
SOUTH KOREA

Tokyo

PEOPLE'S REPUBLIC OF CHINA
- Chemicals
- Consumer goods
- Electronics
- Iron and steel
- Telecommunications
- Textiles

Beijing

Daewoo
Samsung
Hyundai

- Chemicals
- Consumer goods
- Electronics
- Iron and steel
- Shipbuilding
- Telecommunications
- Textiles
- Vehicles

Toyota
Honda
Mitsubishi
Sony
Nissan
Hitachi
Toshiba

Taiwan
- Chemicals
- Consumer goods
- Electronics

Timber

Foodstuffs
Timber

BURMA (MYANMAR)

Hanoi

LAOS

VIETNAM

Hong Kong
- Finance
- Shipping

- Coal
- Foodstuffs
- Oil/Petroleum products
- Textiles

THAILAND

Bangkok

CAMBODIA

- Clothing
- Rubber
- Textiles

Rubber

Bay of Bengal

South China Sea

Manila

- Clothing
- Foodstuffs
- Textiles
- Tobacco

PHILIPPINES

PACIFIC OCEAN

- Oil/Petroleum products

BRUNEI

Kuala Lumpur

MALAYSIA

SINGAPORE

- Chemicals
- Electronics
- Oil/Petroleum products

- Clothing
- Foodstuffs
- Oil/Petroleum products
- Rubber
- Textiles
- Timber

- Clothing
- Foodstuffs
- Oil/Petroleum products
- Rubber
- Textiles

INDONESIA

Jakarta

Equator

0   200   400 miles
0   200   400 kilometers

MAP 30.1

The Pacific Tigers, c. 1960–1995

The Pacific tigers of East and Southeast Asia accelerated economic growth in the region by focusing on manufacturing in electronics and other rising industries. These countries promised industries around the world a supply of cheap labor—mostly female. Despite often horrific working conditions and consequent strikes and labor activism, long-term benefits often included higher rates of literacy, increased school attendance, and improved health.

economic dynamism. Japan, too, benefited from U.S. contracts it filled during the wars in Korea and Vietnam. By 1982, Asian Pacific nations accounted for 16.4 percent of global production, a figure that had doubled since the 1960s. China abandoned Mao's disastrous economic experiments in 1978, achieving economic growth rates of 8 percent by the mid-1990s. Japan and China joined the United States and Germany as the world's top trading nations, while South Korea, Taiwan, Singapore, and Hong Kong came to be called **Pacific tigers** for the ferocity of their growth in the 1980s and 1990s (see Map 30.1).

Japan led the way in developing innovative high-tech industries. In 1982, Japan had more than four times as many industrial robots in operation as the United States. Constant government spending on technological innovation paid off as buyers around the

Pacific tiger One of the East Asian economies with ferocious rates of growth in the 1980s and 1990s.

world snapped up automobiles, videocassettes, and computers from Japanese and other Asian Pacific companies. As the United States poured vast sums into Cold War military spending, the resulting profits from the Pacific Rim went to purchase U.S. government bonds, thus financing America's national debt. Forty years after its total defeat in World War II, Japan was bankrolling its former conqueror.

Multinational Corporations

One of the major innovations of the postindustrial era was the growing number of **multinational corporations**. These companies produced goods and services for a global market and conducted business worldwide, but unlike older international firms, they established major factories in countries other than their home base. For example, of the five hundred largest businesses in the United States in 1970, more than one hundred did over a quarter of their business abroad, with IBM operating in more than one hundred countries. Although the greatest number of multinationals in these years were U.S.-based corporations, European and Japanese firms such as Shell, Nestlé, Toshiba, and Sony also had a broad global scope.

Some multinational corporations had bigger revenues than entire nations, as they set up shop in whatever part of the world offered cheap labor. Many of their founders broke the rules of traditional business success. Soichiro Honda, founder of the postwar Honda corporation, had only contempt for the connections and diplomas that traditionally led to success in Japanese business. A former bicycle repairman, he pioneered in making low-cost motorcycles that by 1961 were selling one hundred thousand a month. "Other companies may not consider you to be the cream of the crop but we believe in you,"[4] he told new employees, urging them to speak their minds and to follow his adventure of setting up firms around the world (see Reading the Past: Japan Transforms Business Practices). Beginning in the 1960s, multinationals moved more of their operations to formerly colonized states to reduce labor costs, taxes, and regulations. Most multinational profits went to enrich foreign stockholders and thus looked to some like imperialism in a new form.

Global Changes in Work

New Manufacturing Areas   The new global economy brought about major changes in people's work lives as manufacturing jobs moved to different areas and a new type of working class emerged. A particularly significant change was the expansion of jobs in manufacturing, mining, and the extraction of natural resources outside the West. Brazil set up all sorts of manufacturing enterprises in the 1960s, including what would eventually become the successful production of automobiles. Jobs in electronics and the textile and clothing industries moved to other parts of the world while declining in the West. South Korea, for instance, built its economy in the 1960s and 1970s by attracting electronics firms with the promise that its female workers would accept low wages and benefits. In sweatshops in Central and South America, young women and even children helped support their families by making sneakers and other goods. In China, rural families chose which single daughters would be sent to work in European toy factories or Taiwanese textile plants located in China. These young women performed repetitive work, yet still learned to move from plant to plant to gain small advantages either in pay or conditions in the few years during which their families allowed them to leave the village. People learned new skills: "The first time I saw those English letters I was scared to death. I couldn't recognize them, so I copied them down and recited them at night," one young Chinese worker recalled of learning English.[5] With the influx of manufacturing jobs, educational standards rose, along with access to birth control and other medical care that improved health.

Change also occurred in the West, where the number of manufacturing workers who had once labored to exhaustion declined, a trend that slowly spread to the rest of the world. Resource depletion in coal mines, the substitution of foreign oil for coal and of plastics for steel, the growth of offshore manufacturing, and automation in industrial

multinational corporation A company that produces goods and services for a global market and that operates businesses worldwide.

Japan Transforms Business Practices

Alongside technological innovation from the 1960s on came a fundamental change in the way many multinational companies were run. Japan led the way, as it did in much innovation in these years, and its businessmen introduced new responsibilities for workers—a real break from the relationships between bosses and workers in the first two hundred years of the Industrial Revolution. Akio Morita was a cofounder of Sony, the Japanese electronics pioneer that quickly became a global corporation. Its founders ushered in the cutting-edge practice of spreading responsibility for innovation and productivity across the firm instead of confining it to the managerial ranks as had been the previous practice. Morita explained the concept in his autobiography *Made in Japan* (1986).

A company will get nowhere if all of the thinking is left to management. Everybody in the company must contribute, and for the lower-level employees their contribution must be more than just manual labor. We insist that all of our employees contribute their minds. Today we get an average of eight suggestions a year from each of our employees, and most of the suggestions have to do with making their own jobs easier or their work more reliable or a process more efficient. Some people in the West scoff at the suggestion process, saying that it forces people to repeat the obvious, or that it indicates a lack of leadership by management. This attitude shows a lack of understanding. We don't force suggestions, and we take them seriously and implement the best ones. . . . After all, who could tell us better how to structure the work than the people who are doing it? . . .

I always tell employees that they should not worry too much about what their superiors tell them. I say,

"Go ahead without waiting for instructions." To the managers I say this is an important element in bringing out the ability and creativity of those below them. Young people have flexible and creative minds, so a manager should not try to cram preconceived ideas into them, because it may smother their originality before it gets a chance to bloom.

In Japan, workers who spend a lot of time together develop an atmosphere of self-motivation, and it is the young employees who give the real impetus to this. Management officers, knowing that the company's ordinary business is being done by energetic and enthusiastic younger employees, can devote their time and effort to planning the future of the company. With this in mind, we think it is unwise and unnecessary to define individual responsibility too clearly.

Source: Akio Morita with Edwin M. Reingold and Mitsuko Shimomura, *Made in Japan: Akio Morita and Sony* (New York: E. P. Dutton, 1986), 149.

EXAMINING THE EVIDENCE

1. What is Akio Morita's attitude toward employees in this statement?

2. What are the innovative aspects of his policies?

3. What role does Akio Morita see for young people in businesses?

4. How have industrial attitudes, as described in this excerpt, changed from those discussed in Chapter 24?

processes reduced the blue-collar workforce. Remaining blue-collar workers enjoyed improved conditions as work in manufacturing became cleaner and more mechanized than ever before. Huge new agribusinesses forced many struggling farmers to take different jobs. Governments, cooperatives, and planning agencies set production quotas and handled an array of marketing transactions for the modern farmer-entrepreneur.

Meanwhile, the ranks of service workers swelled with researchers, health-care and medical workers, technicians, planners, and government functionaries. Jobs in banks, insurance companies, and other financial institutions also surged because of the vast sums needed to finance technology and research. Entire categories of employees such as flight attendants found that much of their work focused on the psychological well-being of customers. Already by 1969, the percentage of service-sector employees had passed that of manufacturing workers in several industrialized countries: 61.1 percent versus 33.7 percent in the United States alone (see Lives and Livelihoods: Global Tourism).

Changes in the Workforce in the West

Global Tourism

International Tourism Workers in Japan

These guides at the Imperial Palace in Japan are part of the vast global pool of service workers, whose fields range from medicine and health care to teaching, law, and personal service such as beautification and domestic help. Tourism workers number in the millions and are found in thousands of capital cities, historic locations, and sites of natural beauty. (Robert Holmes/Corbis.)

Mr. Ibrahim stands outside the hotel gates near the Great Pyramids of Giza looking for customers who might want a guide around the nearby city of Cairo. Friendly, speaking several languages, he asks passersby if they need directions or a ride into town in his car. Like him, women in Guatemala wait by bus and train stations with ponchos and other craft items they have made themselves in hopes that a tourist will buy something. Native Americans ring the main square of Santa Fe, New Mexico, with lavish displays of leatherwork, jewelry, and paintings. In Bamako, capital of Mali, Muhammad waits to do such services for visitors as finding a telephone, delivering a message, or guiding them around the museums. All of these workers make their living through the growing presence of tourists eager to visit every part of a shrinking world, and to make purchases when they get there. They are the uncounted laborers in one of the fastest-growing global livelihoods—tourism.

In 1841 Thomas Cook, a Baptist evangelist in Britain, arranged for a special train to take some six hundred people to a temperance rally. His belief was that going to a rally and then seeing the local sights was a far better way to spend time than frequenting cafés and taverns. Cook's enterprise was so financially successful that he made deals with trains and found lodging for ever-larger groups of travelers.

The Knowledge Economy

Research and education were the means by which nations now advanced their economic and military might. Common sense, hard work, and creative intuition had launched the earliest successes of the Industrial Revolution. By the late twentieth century, success in business or government demanded humanistic or technological expertise and ever-growing staffs of researchers. As one French official put it, "the accumulation of knowledge, not of wealth, . . . makes the difference" in the quest for power. Thus governments around the world expanded the welfare state's mandate for intensive development of educational and research facilities.

Research and Applied Science

Investment in research fueled economic leadership. The United States funneled more than 20 percent of its gross national product into research in the 1960s, in the process enticing many of the world's leading intellectuals and technicians to work in America—

In 1851 he provided package tours for people wanting to attend the Crystal Palace Exhibition in London—over one hundred thousand travelers from Yorkshire alone. Cook's Tours, the company he eventually founded, became so skilled in arranging long-distance travel that the government even hired it to move troops in such distant regions as Africa. With Cook's Tours, some say, tourism became an official line of work—and that was a century before the postwar boom in transportation and communication.

There have been travelers, pilgrims, and even tourists for thousands of years, using guides and drivers, porters, cooks, laundresses, and innkeepers to smooth the way. None of these could avail themselves of transport by air, of course, but in the twentieth century, flight went from being primarily a military phenomenon to one that involved tens of millions of consumers around the world after World War II. At that point the tourist industry grew to comprise employees of large multinational corporations such as airlines and banks. Transcontinental hotel chains employed so many different types of workers that postsecondary schools came to offer programs in hotel and restaurant management. These service workers made up the booming postindustrial economy of the late twentieth and early twenty-first centuries. The United Kingdom estimates tourism currently as one of its largest industries, generating approximately £74 billion annually and employing 2.1 million people in a variety of livelihoods, including those in hotels, restaurants, and tour companies. Still growing in the decolonized areas where women and children struggle to earn a living is sex tourism from wealthy societies such as western Europe and Japan.

Besides small-scale workers in tourism and large and vigorous multinational companies dealing with hundreds of thousands of people, tourism has generated livelihoods for bureaucrats, statisticians, and, increasingly, public relations experts, translators, and Web site designers. Every country and most cities had Web sites for tourists by the twenty-first century. The World Tourism Organization (WTO), which took shape in 1925 and became an agency of the UN in 1974, provided work for people who monitored, counted, and encouraged travel. Employees of the WTO, for example, have recently worked to boost tourism in eastern European countries and sub-Saharan Africa—all of these livelihoods developing the service sector still further.

QUESTIONS TO CONSIDER

1. What is the range of service occupations you can connect to tourism?

2. What skills are necessary in the tourism industry, and how do these fit the knowledge-based, technological society of the postwar world?

3. Why do you think tourism has grown so dramatically since the time of Thomas Cook?

For Further Information:

Baud, Michiel, and Annelou Ypeij, eds. *Cultural Tourism in Latin America: The Politics of Space and Imagery.* 2009.

Dallen, J. Timothy, and Gyan P. Nyaupane, eds. *Cultural Heritage and Tourism in the Developing World: A Regional Perspective.* 2009.

Segreto, Luciano, et al., eds. *Europe at the Seaside: The Economic History of Mass Tourism in the Mediterranean.* 2009.

the so-called brain drain. Soon, however, Japan was outpacing Western countries in research and new product development. Complex systems—for example, nuclear power generation with its many components, from scientific conceptualization to plant construction to the supervised disposal of radioactive waste—required intricate coordination and oversight. In the realm of space programs, weapons development, and economic policy, scientists and bureaucrats frequently made more crucial decisions than did elected politicians. Developing and developed nations alike set up special cities and research hubs where scientists lived and worked, but Soviet-bloc nations proved less successful at linking their considerable achievements in science and technology to actual applications because of bureaucratic red tape. In the 1960s, an astounding 40 percent of Soviet-bloc scientific findings became obsolete before the government approved them. Falsification of information in the Soviet system also hampered efforts to make technology work to the nation's benefit.

Growth in Higher Education

The new criteria for success fostered unprecedented global growth in education, especially in the size and number of universities and scientific institutes. The number of university students in South Korea soared from 11,358 in 1950 to 3.4 million by 2000. Countries set up networks of universities specifically to encourage the technical research that traditional elite universities often scorned and established schools to train high-level experts in administration. Meanwhile, institutions of higher learning added courses in business and management, information technology, and systems analysis. Students enrolled in schools outside their home nations as education became internationalized. In principle, education equalized avenues to success by basing them on talent instead of wealth, but in fact, broad societal leveling did not occur in many universities. So long as socioeconomic background remained a key factor in determining university attendance, universities would reinforce inequality, not reduce it.

Postindustrial Family Life

Just as education changed dramatically to meet the needs of postindustrial society, in urban areas family structure and parent-child relationships shifted significantly from what they had been a century earlier. A steady flow of migrants produced enormous variety in urban households. These varied from patriarchal households consisting of several generations to those headed by a single female parent, unmarried couples cohabitating, or traditionally married couples who had few or no children. Daily life within the urban family became increasingly mechanized. The wages that young Chinese workers earned enabled them to buy more consumer items, even in villages distant from cities, and radio and television often formed the basis of the household's common social life, yielding conversations from Australia to Chile about the plots of soap operas and the outcomes of sporting matches. By the end of the century, appliances became increasingly affordable and more households were able to own them. The increase of appliances within the home reduced the time women devoted to household work, but did not eliminate it, as the standards of cleanliness also increased. Still, the mechanization of domestic chores freed more women to work outside the home. Young women's wages went to finance the education of brothers, and working mothers supported the prolonged economic dependence of their children, who spent more years in school. Working mothers still, however, did the housework and provided child care almost entirely themselves.

Whereas early modern families organized labor, taught craft skills, and monitored reproductive behavior, the primary focus of the modern urban family was most often on psychological and financial assistance. Many children in industrialized regions did not enter the labor force until their twenties but instead attended school, thus requiring their parents' backing. Japanese parents doled out the most resources: they financed their children's after-school education beginning as early as the primary grades to give the children a competitive edge

***Bobby* and the Youth Revolution**

In the late 1960s and 1970s, young people around the globe asserted their rights to sexual freedom and independent private lives. The 1973 hit film *Bobby*, in which the main character rebelled by choosing a partner from a different social class, featured the youth culture of these years. Made at the height of postwar prosperity, just before the first oil embargo, the film also reflected youthful consumerism, as young people bought such items as motorcycles and up-to-date fashions. (RK FILMS LTD/Ronald Grant Archive/Mary Evans/The Image Works Editorial.)

in exams, and ambitious parents never let their children do housework or hold part-time jobs. Parents could also rely on an array of psychologists and other service workers to counsel them.

Most notably, modern society transformed teenagers' lives; they gained new roles as the most up-to-date consumers. Advertisers and industrialists saw youth as a multibillion-dollar market and wooed them with consumer items such as rock music recordings, electronic games, and eventually computers and iPods. Rock music celebrated youthful rebellion against adult culture in biting and often sexually explicit lyrics. This youth music, in the words of one 1960s Latin American commentator, was "a threat to the family."[6] Sex roles for the young did not change, however. Despite the popularity of a few individual women rockers, promoters focused on men, setting them up as idols surrounded by worshiping female groupies. Advanced technology and savvy marketing for global mass consumption contributed to a worldwide youth culture and a growing generation gap—phenomena depicted in the film *Bobby*.

The global media helped spread knowledge of birth-control procedures and allowed for public discussion of sexual matters in many parts of the world. Although highly sexualized film, music, and journalism permeated the world, widespread use of birth control (by some 80 percent of the world's people at the end of the twentieth century) meant there was no corresponding rise in the birthrate—evidence of the increasing separation of sexuality from reproduction. Statistical surveys showed that regular sexual activity began at an ever-younger age, and people talked more openly about sex—another component of cultural change. Critics as early as the mid-1950s worried about the level of sexuality in media: "Reduce the sex appeal in [motion] pictures," one Indian official urged. "How can we progress in other matters if every young man is thinking of this [sex] stuff all the time?"[7] Finally, in a climate of increased publicity about sexuality, homosexual behavior became more open and accepted. Some media announced the arrival of a "sexual revolution," but many political voices denounced it as a particularly dangerous form of Westernization.

Politics and Protest in an Age of Cold War

Scientific sophistication and high-tech military elevated the United States and the Soviet Union to the peak of their power in the 1960s. Simultaneously, however, other nations' aspirations for freedom and their own growing access to technology began to limit the superpowers' ability to shape world politics. Expanding European Common Market and Pacific Rim economies were innovative and had muscle of their own. People in eastern Europe had greater contact with the West via satellite and other technology and contested Soviet leadership. Elsewhere, people refused to endure superpower-backed dictatorships. At the same time, both superpowers discovered that there were limits to their ability to dictate the outcomes of foreign struggles, notably in Vietnam and Afghanistan. Thus, popular struggles around democratization, technology, and economic well-being strained the international political order of the Cold War.

> **FOCUS**
>
> What developments challenged the superpowers' dominance of world politics, and how did the superpowers attempt to address those challenges?

Democracy and Dictatorship in Latin America

World War II and the early Cold War had boosted prosperity in many countries of Latin America, but a hefty percentage of profits went to multinational corporations that had taken control of resources and often shaped the economy around one or two crops such as coffee or bananas or raw materials such as copper. When prices for commodities dropped after the war, workers in undiversified economies suffered and activism grew. By providing aid to Cuba, the Soviet Union came to dominate the Cuban government, while the United States sent money and personnel to overthrow democratic leaders in Guatemala,

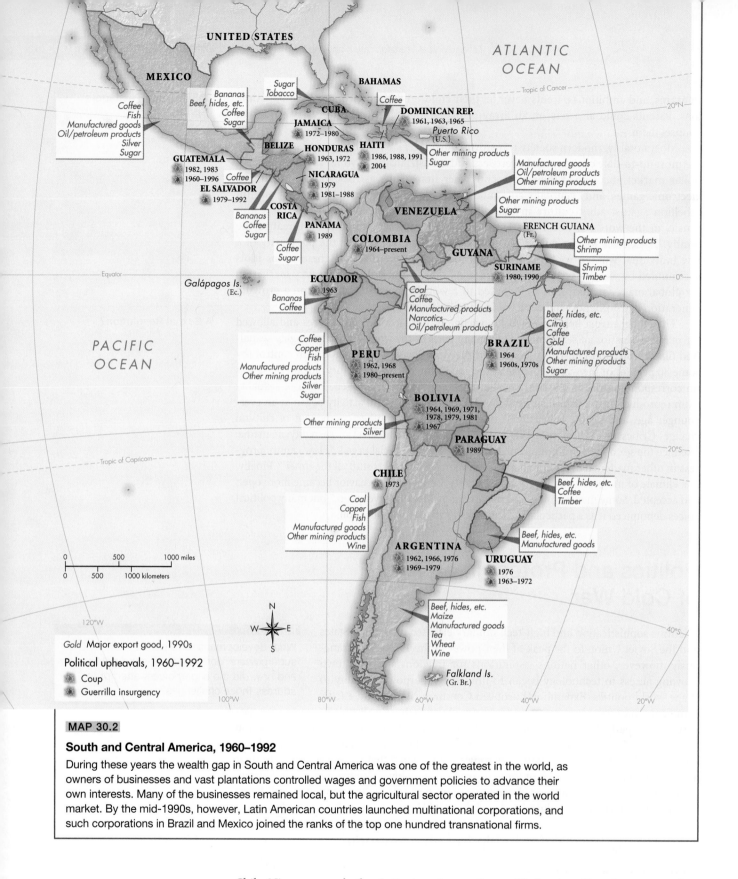

MAP 30.2

South and Central America, 1960–1992

During these years the wealth gap in South and Central America was one of the greatest in the world, as owners of businesses and vast plantations controlled wages and government policies to advance their own interests. Many of the businesses remained local, but the agricultural sector operated in the world market. By the mid-1990s, however, Latin American countries launched multinational corporations, and such corporations in Brazil and Mexico joined the ranks of the top one hundred transnational firms.

Map labels:

UNITED STATES

ATLANTIC OCEAN

MEXICO
Coffee
Fish
Manufactured goods
Oil/petroleum products
Silver
Sugar

Bananas
Beef, hides, etc.
Coffee
Sugar

Sugar
Tobacco

BAHAMAS

Coffee

CUBA

JAMAICA
1972–1980

DOMINICAN REP.
1961, 1963, 1965

Puerto Rico
(U.S.)

BELIZE

HONDURAS
1963, 1972

HAITI
1986, 1988, 1991
2004

Other mining products
Sugar

GUATEMALA
1982, 1983
1960–1996

Coffee

NICARAGUA
1979
1981–1988

Manufactured goods
Oil/petroleum products
Other mining products

EL SALVADOR
1979–1992

COSTA RICA

Bananas
Coffee
Sugar

PANAMA
1989

Coffee
Sugar

VENEZUELA

Other mining products
Sugar

FRENCH GUIANA
(Fr.)

COLOMBIA
1964–present

GUYANA

Other mining products
Shrimp

Equator

Galápagos Is.
(Ec.)

ECUADOR
1963

Bananas
Coffee

Coal
Coffee
Manufactured products
Narcotics
Oil/petroleum products

SURINAME
1980, 1990

Shrimp
Timber

PACIFIC OCEAN

Coffee
Copper
Fish
Manufactured products
Other mining products
Silver
Sugar

PERU
1962, 1968
1980–present

BRAZIL
1964
1960s, 1970s

Beef, hides, etc.
Citrus
Coffee
Gold
Manufactured products
Other mining products
Sugar

Other mining products
Silver

BOLIVIA
1964, 1969, 1971,
1978, 1979, 1981
1967

PARAGUAY
1989

Tropic of Capricorn

CHILE
1973

Beef, hides, etc.
Coffee
Timber

Coal
Copper
Fish
Manufactured goods
Other mining products
Wine

ARGENTINA
1962, 1966, 1976
1969–1979

URUGUAY
1976
1963–1972

Beef, hides, etc.
Manufactured goods

Beef, hides, etc.
Maize
Manufactured goods
Tea
Wheat
Wine

Falkland Is.
(Gr. Br.)

Gold Major export good, 1990s

Political upheavals, 1960–1992
Coup
Guerrilla insurgency

Chile, Nicaragua, and other Latin American nations with the aim of keeping communism at bay. Generous financing by the superpowers gave rise to repressive dictatorships allied to one side or the other in the Cold War. In many Latin American countries citizen activists protested against both economic difficulties in an increasingly technological world and foreign-backed political oppression (see Map 30.2).

Argentina

Dictatorships grew up across Latin America to crush democratic movements for change and to provide the kind of bureaucratic planning for a technology-driven economy that was helping Common Market countries advance. Argentineans, burdened by rising prices and wage freezes along with dictatorship, took their protests to the streets in the 1960s and early 1970s. In response, the Argentinean military, having taken over from Perón in 1955, launched what came to be known as "the dirty war," silencing critics through kidnapping, torture, and murder. Mothers of the Plaza de Mayo became celebrated for opposing the "dirty war." Beginning in April 1977, a group of women, whose relatives were among the "disappeared" ones, began meeting at three-thirty in the afternoon in the plaza that fronted important government buildings. Walking in silent protest around the bustling center where Argentineans gathered to chat or conduct business, the "Mothers"—women from all livelihoods and conditions—wordlessly demanded an account of their missing brothers, husbands, and children. Hebe de Bonafini, whose two sons had "disappeared," explained the change in her everyday existence: "My life had been the life of a housewife—washing, ironing, cooking, and bringing up my children, just like you're always taught to do, believing that everything else was nothing. . . . Then I realized that that wasn't everything, that I had another world too. You realize that you're in a world where you have to do a lot of things."[8] She became an activist, helping bring the human rights abuses of the Argentinean government to the attention of a global audience (see Reading the Past: Terror and Resistance in El Salvador).

The many protests against the Argentinean government, combined with a disastrous economic situation, led to the election of civilian Raúl Alfonsin to the presidency in 1983. Alfonsin tried to deal with the nation's economic troubles brought on by a lack of investment in industry, large public expenditures, and an unequal balance of payments, but his failure to solve these problems quickly and his decision to freeze wages led to the return of a military-backed candidate in 1989. But one thing had changed: the military's policy of torture and murder was ended—a crucial victory. "There's no more official torture here; there are no more 'disappeared,'" one reporter exclaimed of the more open political climate. "Whatever else may be happening, this is terribly terribly important."[9]

Chile

Brazil also took the Argentine route of dictatorship in the name of orderly technological development, but until the mid-1970s Chile remained democratic even as it experienced the chaotic postwar rush to the cities. In country and city alike, however, poverty remained pervasive. In 1970 Chileans elected socialist candidate Salvador Allende (ah-YEHN-day), whose platform for improving the economy included taking over the country's copper resources from foreign investors, notably many Americans. The U.S. fought back against both Allende's socialism and his potential to reduce U.S. economic interests, pouring vast sums into political opposition and sending CIA operatives to murder Allende's supporters in the military. Allende hoped to improve Chile's economic position, but the measures he used failed miserably. He mandated a wage increase, but he also imposed price controls that discouraged domestic manufacturers. Inexperienced bureaucrats could not make newly nationalized industries function either well enough or fast enough. As inflation soared, opposition to Allende mounted, much of it sponsored by the CIA. In 1973 Allende was murdered in a military coup.

Chile's multiple political parties depended on the support of people from different classes. Allende's had come from the working classes, whereas professionals and small shopkeepers backed more centrist parties. General Augusto Pinochet (pin-oh-CHET), who emerged to rule after the coup, ended this tradition of political participation, closing down the elected Congress and suspending the constitution. While working to stabilize the economy, Pinochet's government kidnapped and killed dissidents. Determined opponents, braving torture and facing murder, slowly gained a foothold and finally became strong enough to defeat Pinochet. Mothers for Life, one of the opposition groups, launched a series of demonstrations, sending letters to foreign embassies and the press: "We are Chilean women from a variety of fields: workers, professionals, students, peasants, artists, and housewives, women of all ages who have survived more than a decade of a system of

Terror and Resistance in El Salvador

In a number of Latin American countries, dictators came to power in the second half of the twentieth century, using the military and private armed forces to "disappear" those who opposed them. Teenage critics, protesters, relatives of protesters, and sympathetic Catholic clergy were kidnapped, tortured, raped, and most often killed, frequently with the assistance of the superpowers. In El Salvador, the disappearance of family members beginning in 1975 sparked the development of the CoMadres ("co-mothers"), a group of mostly peasant women who—like women in other Latin American nations—gave up their normal livelihoods to protest these conditions. In the face of the increasing number of disappeared and even the torture and rape of virtually all the "mothers" themselves, the group regularly marched in protest and collected information about the capture of family members—their own and others'. Here, one of the founders explains the protest movement to an American anthropologist.

> In the beginning of our struggle, it was an individual problem. But one began to discover that there were others in the same situation, and we realized we couldn't be isolated, that our struggle had to be collective. It had to be a group of people who participated in the same fight, in the same search, trying to discover the truth. . . .
>
> We borrowed from a march of mothers dressed in black during a march in 1922 to protest a massacre of male and female teachers. They went out into the street to protest the killing of their children. We borrowed our black dress from them. . . . Black signified the condolences and affliction we carry for each person killed. And the white headscarf represents the peace we are seeking—but it must be a peace with justice, not a peace with impunity! We also carry a red and white carnation: the red for the spilled blood, the white for the detained—disappeared and the green leaves, the hope for life. That is our complete dress. . . .
>
> Most of us at this time were from Christian-based communities. . . . Mons[eigneur] Romero would read our public letters out loud in his Sunday homily in the Cathedral so that the CoMadres became known nationally. One month before he was assassinated, I remember that Mons[eigneur] Romero gave us his blessing by telling us, "Ah, women, you are the Marys of today. . . . All of you are suffering the same loss, the same pain."

Source: Interviews conducted by Jennifer Schirmer, "The Seeking of Truth and the Gendering of Consciousness: The CoMadres of El Salvador and the CONAVIGUA Widows of Guatemala," in *"VIVA": Women and Popular Protest in Latin America*, ed. Sarah A. Radcliffe and Sallie Westwood (London: Routledge, 1993), 32–33, 36.

EXAMINING THE EVIDENCE

1. What caused these women to leave their ordinary livelihoods to protest on a regular basis?

2. To what extent would you say that protest and the search for their children became a new livelihood for them?

3. Why did the CoMadres and similar groups of Latin American women activists become such a powerful symbol around the world?

death. . . . We accuse the military regime of throwing our nation into the greatest crisis of history. . . . It is a crisis of the future, a crisis of life."[10] The Mothers for Life were hardly alone, and by 1988 a broad coalition of the Chilean people had swept Pinochet from office, bringing in a representative government and leaving him to face international tribunals for crimes against humanity. Thus, while global developments contributed to the rise of dictatorships in Latin America, some of the same developments made it possible for ordinary individuals to forge connections with sympathetic people around the world and to serve as models for others who wanted change.

Domestic Revolution and a Changing International Order

Political change surged around the world, undermining allies of both superpowers, upsetting the Cold War order, and generally highlighting the need to advance technologically, economically, and politically. In Spain, the death of dictator Francisco Franco in 1975

The Rule of Idi Amin in Uganda

New nations emerging from colonial rule were often plagued by dictatorships headed by the military leaders who fought the imperialists. Idi Amin took power in Uganda in 1971, and during his eight-year reign his forces murdered some five hundred thousand Ugandans, forcing many thousands more to flee the country to safe havens around the world. In this image of a public execution in 1973, a supposed guerrilla fighter becomes one of Amin's victims. (Mohamed Amin/Africa Media Online/The Image Works.)

ended more than three decades of authoritarian rule. Franco's handpicked successor, King Juan Carlos, surprisingly steered his nation to Western-style constitutional monarchy that ushered in Spain's economic modernization and membership in the Common Market. In Africa, brutal killers such as Idi Amin of Uganda were overthrown, and other dictators fell, making Cold War stability uncertain.

South Korea

In 1960 some thirty thousand South Korean university and high school students mounted a peaceful demonstration in Seoul to call for clean elections in their country. They stood before the presidential residence, where Syngman Rhee (SING-man REE), a U.S.-educated and U.S.-supported dictator, had ruled since before the Korean War. Playing the Cold War card, Rhee labeled any critic or democratic politician a communist and had that person arrested or assassinated. Rhee employed his usual tactics in response to the student protesters' call for honest democracy: the police fired into the crowd and killed and wounded hundreds. Citizen outrage caused the government to collapse and free elections brought to power leaders oriented toward openness and constitutional government.

In May 1961, however, Park Chung Hee, a major general in the military, overthrew the new democratic government and instituted a dictatorship, which the U.S. praised as "Korean-style democracy." Instead of democracy, however, Park opted to give Koreans economic growth, using repressive measures such as torture and imprisonment of critics as the government lured hi-tech multinationals to its shores. Student protests continued through the late 1960s and 1970s, and workers denounced the influence of General Motors and other foreign corporations even as the police beat them up. Working people fought the regime: textile worker Chon T'ae-il immolated himself in 1970, shouting as he died "Don't mistreat young girls," a reference to the fifteen-hour days with one day off per month worked by teenagers in unheated textile factories to meet the government's goals for economic development.[11] In 1979, Park ordered more severe police retaliation against demonstrators; opposing the directive, the head of the Korean CIA shot Park. A military junta took over, again with U.S. backing to keep South Korea loyal, and ruled until 1987, when a newly elected president, backed by the military, instituted reforms, including guarantees of civil rights and democratic procedures. It appeared that popular activism had finally brought greater democracy while technological advances made South Korea a looming economic power.

Vietnam

The Cold War remained a potent force in world politics as the United States became increasingly embroiled in Vietnam. After the Geneva settlement in 1954 formally ended French domination of the region, the United States escalated its commitment to the corrupt and incompetent leadership of noncommunist South Vietnam. North Vietnam, China, and the Soviet Union backed the rebel Vietcong, or South Vietnamese communists. The strength of the Vietcong seemed to grow daily, and by 1968, the United States had more than half a million soldiers in South Vietnam. Before the war ended in 1975, the United States would in its effort to defeat communism drop more bombs on North Vietnam than the Allies had launched on Germany and Japan combined during World War II.

U.S. president Richard Nixon promised to bring peace to Southeast Asia. In 1970, however, he ordered U.S. troops also to invade Cambodia, the site of North Vietnamese bases. Americans erupted in protest, and political turmoil followed in Cambodia. The communist Khmer Rouge, led by Pol Pot, a zealot intent on returning the country to preindustrial conditions, took control in 1975 and launched genocidal murders of minority Vietnamese, Chinese, and political opponents that ultimately killed 21 percent of the population. As this brutal situation unfolded, the United States and North Vietnam agreed to peace in January 1973, but the fighting continued. In 1975, South Vietnam collapsed under a determined North Vietnamese offensive and Vietnam was forcibly reunited. The United States reeled from the defeat, having suffered the loss of some fifty-eight thousand young lives and countless billions of dollars, along with a serious blow to its international prestige. Vietnam had demonstrated that the awesome technological might of the United States did not always ensure an easy victory, or even any victory at all.

Lessons from the U.S. defeat in Vietnam did not stop the Soviet Union from becoming entangled with Islamic forces in Afghanistan when it unleashed its own high-tech military to support a communist coup against Afghanistan's government in 1979. Afghanis who saw their traditional way of life being threatened by communism's modernizing goals put up stiff resistance. By 1980, tens of thousands of Soviet troops were fighting in Afghanistan, using the USSR's most advanced missiles and artillery in an ultimately unsuccessful effort to overcome Muslim leaders. The United States, China, Saudi Arabia, and Pakistan provided aid to a group of Muslim resisters, some of whom later coalesced into the Taliban. After the Soviets pulled out of their own "Vietnam" in 1989, the fundamentalist Taliban movement took over in the 1990s, imposing strict rules said to represent true Islamic teachings and causing millions of political and religious refugees to flee the country. Involvement in the wars in Vietnam and Afghanistan undermined both superpowers, sapping them of resources despite their technological advantages over their enemies.

Afghanistan

Revolution in Iran

In Iran, religiously inspired protests by students, clerics, shopkeepers, and unemployed men in 1978 and 1979 brought to power the Islamic religious leader Ayatollah Ruhollah Khomeini (a-yat-ol-LAH ROOH-ol-LAH ko-MAY-nee). The uprising was directed against Shah Mohammed Reza Pahlavi (REH-zah PAH-lah-vee), whose repressive regime the United States supported to protect its oil interests. Employing audiocassettes to spread his message, Khomeini called for a transformation of the country into a truly Islamic society, proclaiming "Neither East, nor West, only the Islamic Republic." Overturning the Westernization policy of the deposed shah, Khomeini's regime required women to cover their bodies almost totally in special clothing, restricted their access to divorce, and eliminated a range of other rights. Islamic revolutionaries believed these restrictions would restore the pride and Islamic identity that imperialism had stripped

The United States and the Vietnam War, c. 1968–1975

from Middle Eastern men. Khomeini won widespread support among Shi'ite Muslims, who constituted the majority but had long been subordinate to Sunni Muslims.

In the autumn of 1979, supporters of Khomeini seized hostages at the American embassy in Tehran, keeping them captive until Ronald Reagan's inauguration in January 1981. U.S. paralysis in the face of Islamic militancy, following on the heels of defeat in Vietnam, showed the possibility of superpower decline (see Seeing the Past: The Iranian Revolution as Visual News).

Activists Challenge the Superpowers

The Cold War, technological transformation, and bloody conflict gave rise to social activism that challenged the superpowers. Prosperity and the benefits of a high-tech, service-oriented economy made people eager for peace instead of the violence of war, just as those living in Latin American and South Korean dictatorships wanted to "take back the streets." Activists sought a fair chance to get education, jobs, and political influence. Students, blacks and other minorities, Soviet-bloc citizens, women, environmentalists, and homosexuals joined in what became increasingly fiery protests in the 1960s and 1970s. They protested the Cold War order that they believed denied an equal share of well-being and democracy for all.

The Soviet War in Afghanistan, 1979–1989

African Americans in the United States led the way in demanding equal rights early in the 1960s, even as white segregationists murdered and maimed those attempting to integrate lunch counters, register black voters, or simply march on behalf of freedom. This violent racism was the weak link in the American claim to moral superiority in the Cold War, prompting President John F. Kennedy to introduce civil rights legislation, which, following Kennedy's assassination, was pushed through Congress in 1964 by his successor, Lyndon B. Johnson. This legislation forbade segregation in public facilities and created the Equal Employment Opportunity Commission to fight job discrimination based on "race, color, national origin, religion, and sex."

Activism in the U.S. Bloc

Despite the civil rights legislation, change came too slowly for some minority activists. Among those were César Chavez and Dolores Huerta, who in the 1960s led oppressed Mexican American migrant workers in the California grape agribusiness to nonviolent resistance in their struggle for their right to collective bargaining and for an end to discrimination. Chavez knew their plight firsthand—he had lived in miserable conditions as a son of migrant workers. A teacher had put a sign around his neck reading "I am a clown. I speak Spanish." Huerta, his co-organizer, had led a somewhat different life but was equally committed to the cause—"a firebrand," she was called. She had attended community college but faced racial discrimination as a Chicano despite her education.

Some African American activists, frustrated by the lack of any real change in their condition, turned militant, and urban riots erupted across the United States in 1965 and subsequent years. In 1968, civil rights leader Martin Luther King, Jr., was assassinated by a white racist. More than a hundred cities in the United States erupted in violence as African Americans vented their anguish and rage. Many felt they had more in common with decolonizing people than with Americans. They aimed for "black power," and some took up arms in the belief that, like decolonizing people elsewhere, they needed to protect themselves against the violent whites around them.

Young people, who had been critical of racism, the war in Vietnam, and the militaristic and environmentally harmful effects of technology, closed down classes in campuses around the world. In western Europe, students went on strike, invading administration offices to protest their inferior education and status. They called themselves a proletariat—an exploited working class in the new high-tech, service society—and, rejecting the Soviets, considered

The Iranian Revolution as Visual News

U.S. Hostages During the Iranian Revolution (Bettmann/Corbis.)

Supporters of the Ayatollah Khomeini
(Abbas/Magnum Photos.)

The Iranian Revolution was a shock to the West and the world because it overthrew the ruler of a major Middle Eastern client state of the United States. Moreover, the Ayatollah Khomeini refused to ally the country with either of the superpowers because he saw them both as corrupt. In 1979, militant Iranian students stormed the U.S. Embassy in Tehran and took those in it hostage. With the development of satellite communications, images of current events circled the globe almost immediately, and newspapers and television repeatedly broadcast the two photographs shown here. The first photograph features the blindfolded hostages the day after their capture. In the second, women supporters of the hostage-taking hold their own demonstration before the U.S. Embassy to chastise the United States for backing the authoritarian rule of the Shah for so many years. The global news regularly portrayed women in Iran in this way.

EXAMINING THE EVIDENCE

1. What responses might each of these two photographs individually have provoked in viewers? What responses might they have provoked when seen together?

2. What is the historic value of these photographs? What propagandistic goal might they have served?

themselves part of a New Left. After French police beat up students, some 9 million French workers went on strike, calling not only for higher wages but also for participation in everyday decision making both in politics and in work life. With their long hair, communal living, and scorn for sexual chastity, students proclaimed their rejection of middle-class values.

Women around the world turned to feminist activism, calling for equal rights and an end to gender discrimination. Middle-class women eagerly responded to the international best seller *The Feminine Mystique* (1963) by American journalist Betty Friedan. Pointing to the stagnating talents of many housewives, Friedan helped organize the National Organization for Women in 1966 to lobby for equal pay and legal reforms. Women demonstrated on behalf of such issues as abortion rights, and they were soon joined by gays demanding the decriminalization of their sexuality. Many flouted social conventions in their attire and attitudes, speaking openly about taboo subjects such as their sexual feelings. African American women pointed to the "double jeopardy" of being "black and female." Women engaged in the civil rights and student movements soon realized that many of those protest organizations devalued women just as society at large did. As African American activist Angela Davis complained, women aiming for equality supposedly "wanted to rob [male protesters] of their manhood."[12]

Women's activism engendered some concrete changes. Just after the war, women in Chile and other Latin American countries had lobbied successfully for the vote. In Catholic Italy, feminists won the rights to divorce, to gain access to birth-control information, and to obtain legal abortions. The demand for protection from rape, incest, and battering became the focus of thousands of women's groups from the 1970s to the present, as they combated a long-held value in virtually every society—the inferiority of women.

Protests erupted in the Soviet bloc too, with students at a Czech May Day rally in 1967 publicly chanting, "The only good communist is a dead one." In 1967 the Czechoslovak Communist Party took up the cause of reform when Alexander Dubçek (DOOB-chehk), head of the Slovak branch of the party, called for more social and political openness, striking a chord among frustrated party officials, technocrats, and intellectuals. Arguing that socialism should have "a human face," Dubçek was made head of the entire party and quickly changed the communist style of government, ending censorship, instituting the secret ballot for party elections, and allowing competing political groups to form. The Prague Spring had begun—"an orgy of free expression," one Czech journalist called the almost nonstop political debate that followed.[15]

Dubçek was unsuccessful in devising policies acceptable to both the USSR and reform-minded Czechs, and in August 1968, Soviet tanks rolled into Prague in a massive show of antirevolutionary force. Citizens turned to sabotage to defend their new rights: they painted graffiti on the tanks and removed street signs to confuse invading troops. Illegal radio stations broadcast testimonials of resistance, and merchants refused to sell food or anything else to Soviet troops. These responses could not stop the determined Soviet leadership, and the moment of reform-minded change passed even as some students, like those in Korea, immolated themselves in protest.

Activists' protests challenged superpower dominance, but little turned out the way reformers had hoped. Governments in both the Soviet and U.S. blocs turned to conservative solutions: the Soviets announced the Brezhnev Doctrine, which stated that reform movements, as a "common problem" of all socialist countries, would face swift repression and that those countries in any case had only limited independence. In 1974, Brezhnev

Mexico City Protest, 1968

Following World War II, a rising standard of living encouraged young people around the world to enter universities in greater numbers than ever before, which helped them see social and political ills more clearly. In Mexico City, which in the spring of 1968 was about to host the summer Olympics, university students protested police violence and government repression after the slaying of several high school students. They too were mowed down by the police. During the late 1960s and 1970s, reactions to student demonstrations varied worldwide. Notice in this photograph a common denominator of student protest across the world: emblems of rebellion such as the banner featuring the revolutionary Che Guevara. (Bettmann/Corbis.)

Activism in the Soviet Bloc

The Superpowers Restore Order

expelled author Aleksandr Solzhenitsyn from the USSR after the first volume of Solzhenitsyn's *Gulag Archipelago* (1973–1976) was published in the U.S.-led bloc. Solzhenitsyn's story of the Gulag (the Soviet system of internment and forced-labor camps) documented the brutal conditions Soviet prisoners endured under Stalin and his successors. More than any other single work, the *Gulag Archipelago* disillusioned loyal communists around the world. Brezhnev also expelled feminists who dared speak about communist sexism, Jews who became scapegoats for the failures of the Soviet system, and other dissenters. The brain drain from the Soviet bloc was severe, enriching the rest of the world.

In the U.S. bloc the reaction against activists was different, though order was restored there too. A current of public opinion turned against young people with the idea that somehow they—not the defeat in Vietnam or government corruption—had brought the United States down. Protesters had opened all leadership to question, helping conservatives gain power in the name of bringing back traditional values. As order returned, some young reformers turned to open terrorism in the West. In this atmosphere of reform, reaction, and radicalization, the future of prosperity became uncertain.

The End of the Cold War Order

FOCUS

Why did the Cold War order come to an end?

During the 1970s the superpowers faced internal corruption, competition from oil-producing states and rising Asian economies, and the increasing costs of attempting to control the world beyond their borders. Oil-producing nations brought a crashing halt to postindustrial prosperity in the West even as innovation continued. In response, reformers Margaret Thatcher in Great Britain and Mikhail Gorbachev in the USSR began implementing strikingly new policies in the 1980s to get their economies moving, just as Latin American countries were turning away from dictatorship. In the Soviet bloc, however, restoring prosperity was virtually impossible because a corrupt and inefficient system failed to take full advantage of technology and an unpopular war drained scarce resources. Suddenly, in 1989, the Soviet Empire collapsed and the Cold War came to an abrupt end. The USSR itself slowly dissolved, finally disappearing by January 1, 1992.

A Shifting Balance of Global Power

The United States seemed to overcome all obstacles when in 1972 it achieved a foreign policy triumph over the USSR by opening diplomatic relations with the other communist giant—China. Almost immediately a Middle Eastern oil embargo hit the United States hard, and the relationship between the United States and the Middle East began to overtake the Cold War as a major issue in global politics. In this arena, technology and Cold War muscle gave no advantage.

The United States Reaches Out to China

In the midst of turmoil at home and the draining war in Vietnam, Henry Kissinger, Nixon's national security adviser, decided to take advantage of growing tensions between China and the Soviet Union. Kissinger's efforts to forge closer ties with this other communist power led Nixon to visit China in 1972, opening up the possibility of contact and exchange between the two very different great nations. Nixon's visit served the domestic interests of both the Nixon administration and the Chinese leadership. For Nixon, the visit represented a high-profile diplomatic victory at a time when his conduct of the war in Vietnam was increasingly unpopular. Within China, the meeting helped stop the brutality of Mao's Cultural Revolution while advancing the careers of Chinese pragmatists interested in technology and economic growth.

U.S.-Soviet Rapprochement

The diplomatic success also advanced U.S.-Soviet relations. Fearful of the Chinese diplomatic advantage and similarly confronted by popular protest, the Soviets made their own overtures to the U.S.-led bloc. In 1972, the superpowers signed the first Strategic Arms Limitation Treaty (SALT I), which set a cap on the number of antimissile defenses each country could have. In 1975, in the Helsinki accords on human rights, the Western bloc officially acknowledged Soviet territorial gains in World War II in exchange for the Soviets' guarantee of basic human rights.

The Middle East's oil-producing nations dealt Western dominance and prosperity a major blow by withholding exports of oil. Tension between Israel and the Arab world provided the catalyst. On June 5, 1967, Israeli forces, responding to the buildup of Syrian, Egyptian, and other Arab armies on its border, seized Gaza and the Sinai peninsula from Egypt, the Golan Heights from Syria, and the West Bank from Jordan (see Map 30.3). Israel's stunning victory, which came to be called the Six-Day War, so humiliated the Arab states that it led them to forge common political and economic strategies. In 1973, Egypt and Syria attacked Israel on Yom Kippur, the most holy day in the Jewish calendar. Israel, with assistance from the United States, stopped the assault.

Having failed militarily, the Arab nations took economic action, striking at the West's weakest point—its enormous dependence on Middle Eastern oil. Arab member nations of **OPEC** (Organization of Petroleum Exporting Countries) quadrupled the price of its oil and imposed an embargo, cutting off all exports of oil to the United States in retaliation for U.S. support of Israel. For the first time since imperialism's heyday, the producers of raw materials—not the industrial powers—controlled the flow of commodities and set the prices. The West and many parts of the world now faced an oil crisis.

Throughout the 1970s, oil-dependent Westerners watched in astonishment as OPEC upset the balance of economic power, bringing about a recession in the West. The oil embargo and price hike caused a significant rise in unemployment in Europe and the United States,

The Politics of Oil

OPEC A consortium of oil-producing countries in the Middle East established to control the production and distribution of oil.

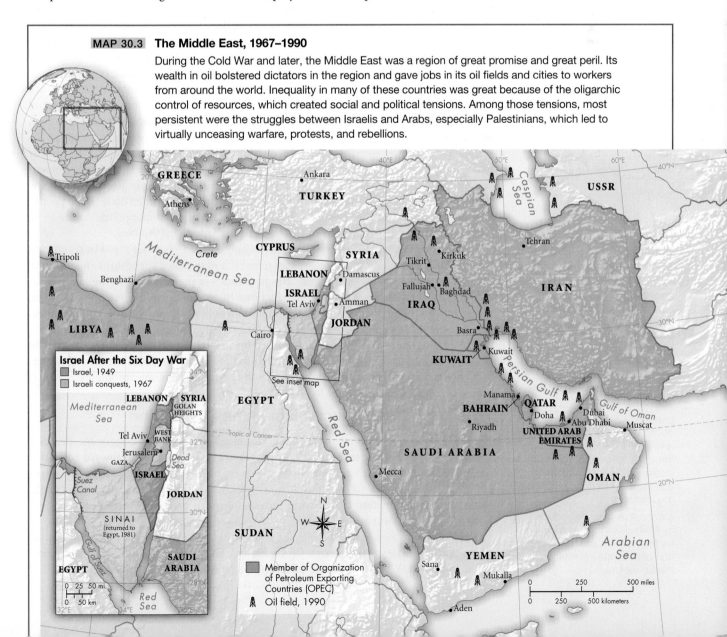

MAP 30.3 **The Middle East, 1967–1990**

During the Cold War and later, the Middle East was a region of great promise and great peril. Its wealth in oil bolstered dictators in the region and gave jobs in its oil fields and cities to workers from around the world. Inequality in many of these countries was great because of the oligarchic control of resources, which created social and political tensions. Among those tensions, most persistent were the struggles between Israelis and Arabs, especially Palestinians, which led to virtually unceasing warfare, protests, and rebellions.

Israel After the Six Day War
- Israel, 1949
- Israeli conquests, 1967

Member of Organization of Petroleum Exporting Countries (OPEC)

Oil field, 1990

and by the mid-1970s inflation soared around the world. Skyrocketing interest rates discouraged both industrial investment and consumer buying. With prices, unemployment, and interest rates surging—an unusual combination of economic conditions dubbed **stagflation**—some came to realize that both energy resources and economic growth had limits. Western Europe and Japan drastically cut back on their oil dependence by undertaking conservation measures, improving public transportation, and raising the price of gasoline to encourage the development of fuel-efficient cars. But more was clearly needed.

A Change of Course in the West

At the beginning of the 1980s, stagflation and the realignment of global economic power forced noncommunist governments in the West to put their economic houses in order. Conservative politicians, who blamed welfare state programs for the West's economic problems, were handily elected in a number of countries. Tough times also intensified feelings that the unemployed and new immigrants from around the world were responsible for the economic downturn. An emphasis on competitiveness, individualism, and privilege replaced the twentieth-century trend of promoting economic democracy—a dramatic change of political course.

Thatcherism and Reaganomics

More than anyone else, Margaret Thatcher, the outspoken leader of Britain's Conservative Party and prime minister from 1979 to 1990, reshaped the West's political and economic ideas to meet the crisis. She called herself "a nineteenth-century liberal" in reference to the economic individualism that she wanted to restore. Believing that only more private enterprise could revive the sluggish British economy, the combative prime minister rejected the politics of consensus building, targeting unions and welfare recipients as enemies of British well-being.

The policies of Thatcherism were based on monetarist, or supply-side, economic theories, which state that inflation results when government pumps money into the economy at a rate higher than a nation's economic growth rate. Supply-siders thus advocate tight control of the money supply to keep prices from rising rapidly. They maintain that the economy as a whole flourishes when businesses grow and their prosperity "trickles down" throughout the society. To implement such theories, the British government cut income taxes on the wealthy to encourage new investment and increased sales taxes on everyday purchases to compensate for the lost revenue. The result was fairly successful, but economic growth came at the price of cuts to education and health programs and an increased burden on working people, who bore the brunt of the sales tax. Thatcher's package of economic policies came to be known as **neoliberalism**, and it immediately came to shape global thinking.

In the United States, President Ronald Reagan followed Thatcher's lead in combating the economic crisis. Blaming both "welfare queens" and so-called spendthrift and immoral liberals for stagflation, he introduced "Reaganomics"—a program of income tax cuts for the wealthy combined with massive reductions in federal spending for student loans, school lunch programs, and mass transit. In foreign policy, Reagan warned of the communist threat and demanded huge military spending to fight the "evil empire." The combination of tax cuts and military expansion pushed the federal budget deficit to $200 billion by 1986. Other western European leaders limited welfare-state benefits in the face of stagflation, though without blaming poor people for their nation's economic problems.

The Collapse of Communism in the Soviet Bloc

The Soviet Union faced far more difficult challenges than the West. Since the death of Stalin in 1953, Soviet leaders had periodically taken small, halting steps toward economic and political reform. Such reforms were, however, halfhearted and often quickly abandoned. In 1985 a new Soviet leader, Mikhail Gorbachev, introduced much more thoroughgoing reforms, but instead of fortifying the economy, his programs stirred up rebellion. The corrupt system was beyond cure.

Mikhail Gorbachev, who became leader of the Soviet Union in 1985, unexpectedly opened an era of change. The son of peasants, Gorbachev had firsthand experience of the costs of economic stagnation. Years of weak and then negative growth led to a deteriorating standard of

stagflation A surge in prices and interest rates combined with high unemployment and a slowdown in economic growth.

neoliberalism A theory first promoted by British prime minister Margaret Thatcher, calling for a return to nineteenth-century liberal principles, including the reduction of welfare-state programs and tax cuts for the wealthy to promote economic growth.

perestroika A policy introduced by Mikhail Gorbachev to restructure the Soviet economy through improved productivity, increased capital investment, and the introduction of market mechanisms.

glasnost A policy introduced by Mikhail Gorbachev allowing for free speech and the circulation of accurate information in the Soviet Union.

living. After working a full day, Soviet homemakers stood in long lines to obtain basic commodities. Alcoholism reached crisis levels, diminishing productivity and straining the nation's morale. Despite its tremendous agricultural potential, the USSR imported massive amounts of grain because 20 to 30 percent of homegrown grain rotted before it could be harvested or shipped to market, so great was the mismanagement of the state-directed economy. A massive and privileged party bureaucracy stifled effective use of technology, while Soviet military spending of 15 to 20 percent of the gross national product (more than double the U.S. proportion) further lowered living standards. A new generation came of age lacking the fear instilled by World War II or Stalin's purges. "They believe in nothing," a mother said of Soviet youth in 1984.

Gorbachev Attempts Reform

Gorbachev knew from experience and travels to western Europe that the Soviet system was not keeping up, and he quickly proposed several new programs. A crucial economic reform, *perestroika* ("restructuring"), aimed to reinvigorate the Soviet economy by encouraging more up-to-date technology and introducing such market features as prices and profits. Alongside economic change was the policy of *glasnost* (translated as "openness"), which called for disseminating "wide, prompt, and frank information" and for allowing Soviet citizens freer speech.

Glasnost stirred debate across the USSR and affected superpower relations as well. Television reporting adopted the outspoken methods of American investigative journalism, and newspapers, instead of publishing made-up letters praising the Soviet state, printed real ones complaining of shortages and abuse. One outraged "mother of two" protested that the cost-cutting policy of reusing syringes in hospitals was a source of AIDS. "Why should little kids have to pay for the criminal actions of our Ministry of Health?" she asked. "We saw television programs about U.S. racism," one young man reported, "but blacks there had cars, housing, and other goods that we didn't."[14] Gorbachev cut missile production, defusing the Cold War, and in early 1989 withdrew Soviet forces from the disastrous war in Afghanistan. By the end of the year the United States started to reduce its own vast military buildup.

Solidarity Protests in Poland, 1981–1983

Even before Gorbachev's reforms of the mid-1980s unleashed free speech in the USSR, dissent had risen across the Soviet bloc. In the summer of 1980, Poles had reacted to rising food prices by going on strike and forming an independent labor movement called **Solidarity** under the leadership of electrician Lech Walesa and crane operator Anna Walentynowicz. The organization attracted much of the adult population, including a million members of the Communist Party. Waving Polish flags and parading giant portraits of the Virgin Mary and Pope John Paul II—a Polish native—Solidarity workers occupied factories in protest against inflation, the scarcity of food, and the deteriorating conditions of everyday life. The scarcity of food likewise drove tens of thousands of women, who were both workers and the caretakers of home life, into the streets crying, "We're hungry!" With Soviet support, the Communist Party imposed a military government and in the winter of 1981 outlawed Solidarity. Dissidents, using global communications, kept Solidarity alive as a force both inside and outside of Poland. Workers kept meeting and a new culture emerged, with poets reading verse to overflow crowds and university professors lecturing on such forbidden topics as Polish resistance in World War II. The stage was set for communism's downfall.

Rebellion in Poland

The disintegration of communist power in Europe was also inspired by Gorbachev's visit to China's capital, Beijing, in the spring of 1989. There, hundreds of thousands of students massed in the city's Tiananmen Square to demand democracy and greet Gorbachev as democracy's hero. They used telex machines and satellite television to rush their message of reform to the international community. China's communist leaders, while pushing economic modernization, refused to introduce democracy. Workers joined the mass of prodemocracy students: "They say and they do what I have only dared to think," one man commented after giving money to the cause.[15] As numbers swelled and the international press broadcast the events, government forces crushed the movement, killing untold numbers and later executing as many as a thousand rebels.

Revolutions of 1989

Solidarity An independent Polish trade union that confronted the communist government in the 1980s and eventually succeeded in ousting the party from the Polish government.

The televised protests in Tiananmen Square offered an inspirational model to opponents of communism in Europe. In June 1989, the Polish government, lacking Soviet support for further repression, held free parliamentary elections. Solidarity candidates overwhelmingly defeated the communists, and in early 1990, Walesa became president of Poland. In Hungary, where citizens had boycotted communist holidays and lobbied against ecologically unsound projects such as the construction of new dams, popular demand led the Parliament in the fall of 1989 to dismiss the Communist Party as the official ruling institution. Meanwhile, Gorbachev reversed the Brezhnev Doctrine, refusing to interfere in the politics of satellite nations.

East Germans had likewise long protested communism, holding peace vigils throughout the 1980s and ceaselessly attempting to cross the Berlin Wall. Satellite television brought them visions of postindustrial prosperity and of open public debate in West Germany. In the summer of 1989, crowds of East Germans flooded the borders of the crumbling Soviet bloc, and hundreds of thousands of protesters rallied against the regime throughout the fall. On November 9, East Berliners crossed the wall unopposed and protest turned to festive holiday. Soon thereafter, citizens—East and West—released years of frustration by assaulting the Berlin Wall with sledgehammers and then celebrated the reunification of the two Germanys in 1990.

Protesters in Tiananmen Square, 1989
Student activists for democracy mounted a massive and prolonged demonstration for democracy in the spring of 1989. The protests in Tiananmen Square, where Mao Zedong had often addressed mass rallies, captured the imagination of the world and showed the protesters' own global imagination. Students displayed images of the Statue of Liberty and carried signs in English, playing to a worldwide audience. As workers joined the movement, Chinese authorities struck back, dispersing the crowds and executing many participants. (Jacques Langevin/Sygma/Corbis.)

The fall of communism in Czechoslovakia and Romania formed two extremes. In November 1989 Alexander Dubček, leader of the Prague Spring of 1968, addressed the crowds in Prague's Wenceslas Square after police had beaten students who had called for the ouster of Stalinists from the government. Almost immediately, the communist leadership resigned, in a bloodless or "velvet" revolution. By contrast, Romanian president Nicolae Ceauşescu (nee-koh-LIE chow-SHES-koo), who had ruled as the harshest dictator in communist Europe since Stalin, met a far different end. Workers and much of the army rose up and crushed the forces loyal to Ceauşescu. On Christmas Day 1989, viewers watched on television as the dictator and his wife were executed. For many, the death of Ceauşescu meant that the very worst of communism was over.

The revolutions of 1989 accelerated the breakup of Yugoslavia into multiple states (see Map 30.4). Yugoslavia had the most ethnically diverse population in eastern Europe, and when Serbian president Slobodan Milosevic attempted in 1991 to seize territory and unite all Serbs (and in effect much of the former Yugoslavia) into a "greater Serbia," a tragic civil war broke out. Throughout the 1990s, the peoples of the former Yugoslavia fought one another, murdering neighbors of different ethnicities.

Meanwhile, amid deteriorating conditions and the threat of violence, the Soviet Union itself collapsed. Perestroika had failed to revitalize the Soviet economy, and by 1990 people faced unemployment and an even greater scarcity of goods than before. In 1991 a group of eight antireform top officials, including the powerful head of the Soviet secret police (the KGB), attempted a coup,

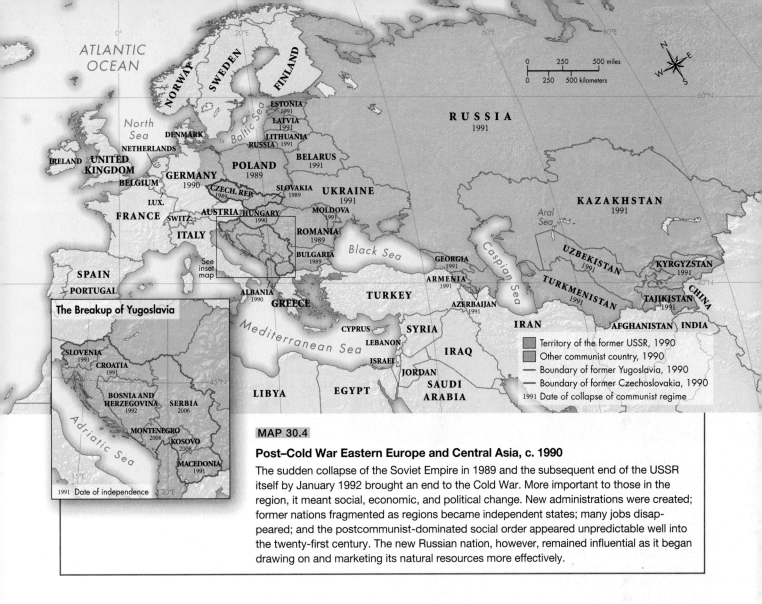

MAP 30.4

Post–Cold War Eastern Europe and Central Asia, c. 1990

The sudden collapse of the Soviet Empire in 1989 and the subsequent end of the USSR itself by January 1992 brought an end to the Cold War. More important to those in the region, it meant social, economic, and political change. New administrations were created; former nations fragmented as regions became independent states; many jobs disappeared; and the postcommunist-dominated social order appeared unpredictable well into the twenty-first century. The new Russian nation, however, remained influential as it began drawing on and marketing its natural resources more effectively.

holding Gorbachev under house arrest. Hundreds of thousands of residents of Moscow and Leningrad filled the streets, and units of the army defected to protect the headquarters of Boris Yeltsin, the reform-minded president of the Russian Parliament. People used fax machines and computers to coordinate internal resistance and send messages to the rest of the world. As the coup failed, the Soviet Union disintegrated and officially dissolved by January 1, 1992.

The USSR Dissolves

COUNTERPOINT
Agrarian Peoples in a Technological Age

As high-tech society expanded, millions of people in the world's rural areas felt themselves more hurt than helped. Even as breakthroughs in science and technology led to improved health and a higher standard of living for the majority, there were many others whom scientific advances harmed. Some farmers found that the application of scientific techniques damaged both their livelihoods and the environment. They objected especially to the genetic modification of plants and animals made possible by the discovery of DNA.

FOCUS

How did some agrarian peoples resist the scientific and technological developments that threatened their ways of life?

Contesting the Results of Technological Advance
As societies around the world developed technologically and economically, some of the results were shocking. Cubotão, a city in southeastern Brazil, is home to some two dozen steel, petrochemical, and other industries, which daily send about 875 tons of toxic gasses, 473 tons of carbon monoxide, and 182 tons of sulfuric oxide into the atmosphere. Residents call the area the "Valley of Death" because of the extreme air and water pollution and have lobbied successfully to curtail the most damaging dumping of toxic waste. This photograph shows a cement-producing section of the complex. (Miguel Rio Branco/Magnum Photos.)

Local Farmers Against Multinational Corporations

Farmers were especially angry about the ways in which companies took seeds from them and then patented them so that those same farmers could be sued for harvesting and using their own seeds. They also objected to the multinationals' practice of sterilizing seeds so that the resulting plants would not produce sowable seeds that farmers could harvest and plant the next year. In Africa, Asia, and Latin America, grassroots movements developed to stop the use of chemical fertilizers, the patenting of medicinal plants and seeds by multinational chemical companies, and the genetic modification of seeds, insects, fish, and other living organisms.

The immediate, practical problem of the failure of seeds to germinate and the erosion of soil caused by large-scale planting of a single crop led to the creation in the 1980s of the Institute for Production and Research in Tropical Agriculture in Venezuela. Officials from the Institute argued that the directives imposed by specialists and chemical companies from the North harmed Latin American farmers engaged in tropical agriculture. Whereas the many microclimates and diverse conditions found in Latin America should have led to the cultivation of many different crops, the Green Revolution of the 1950s and 1960s began directing farmers toward growing one crop and insisting that they use chemical pesticides. Top-down direction had depleted the soil and brought increasing poverty to many farmers. To correct this situation, the Institute collected the know-how of small and medium-sized rural producers. "We get knowledge from farmers," one worker for the Institute claimed. "We evaluate knowledge from farmers."[16]

Grassroots activists in other areas—India, for example—worked to protect local agricultural knowledge from being abused by the new postindustrial economy. Activists labeled the phenomenon of patenting plants and then suing farmers who continued to grow crops like rice in their own way as "biopiracy." "Patents are a replay of colonization as it took place five hundred years ago in a number of ways," farmers' rights activist Vandana Shiva maintained.[17] "The Basmati seed, the aromatic rice from India, which we have grown for centuries, right in my valley is being claimed as a novel invention by Rice-Tec." Biopiracy by the multinational corporations, activists charged, contributed to the impoverishment of Third World peoples: "Neem, which we have used for millennia for pest control, for medicine, . . . which my grandmother and mother have used for everyday functions in the home, for protecting grain, for protecting silks and woolens, for pest control, is treated as an invention held by Grace, the chemical company."[18] Entrepreneurs, while harming farmers, were seizing control of and profiting from their knowledge.

Government Measures to Protect Farmers

Moved by citizens' activism, governments in developing economies began taking steps to stop the piracy by multinational businesses. India, for example, began creating a database of its medicinal plants, teas, and yoga positions. The idea was to patent these as Indian property so that enterprises in other countries could not simply steal and market them as their own. The Indian government claimed to be doing just what industrialized nations had been doing for years: France, for example, sued any foreign firm that used the name *champagne* for sparkling wine. "Champagne" had been registered as a trademark branding wines from the Champagne region of France, one protected by law just as Toyota and Heinz were trademarks with full legal protection from theft by another company. These actions provided a strong counterpoint to postindustrial society's drift toward multinational markets seizing knowledge-based products and using them against the traditional livelihoods of tens of millions of agricultural workers around the world.

Conclusion

The last half of the twentieth century witnessed a surge in technological and scientific discovery with vast potential for improving people's lives and connecting them to one another. Asian Pacific nations advanced by adopting new technology and transforming their economies. Work changed, as societies across the globe expanded the service sector of their economies and entered a new, postindustrial stage. New patterns of family life, new relationships among the generations, and revised standards for sexual behavior also characterized these years. Youth culture spread globally, touching teens around the world like Raj and Bobby in India. A high-tech society demanded levels of innovation, efficiency, and coordination that spread unevenly and was especially lacking in the Soviet bloc. Despite improved postindustrial conditions, brutal coercion continued to plague workers in rapidly industrializing economies such as that of South Korea.

Inequalities in the distribution of goods and the persistent support of military dictators by the superpowers frustrated citizens worldwide, and especially pushed youths like Raj and Bobby to rebellion. From the 1960s, youth joined ethnic and racial minorities and women in condemning existing conditions, including the threat posed by the Cold War. By the early 1980s, wars in Vietnam and Afghanistan, protests against privations in the Soviet bloc, the power of oil-producing states, and the growing political force of Islam had weakened superpower pre-eminence. In the Soviet Union Mikhail Gorbachev attempted to bring about technological efficiencies and cultural reform, but he released dissent and exposed the flaws of communism. By 1992, the failure of the brutal experiment with communism had brought about both the dissolution of the Soviet Union and the end of the Cold War order. Although the former Soviet Empire faced painful adjustments, this development opened the world as a whole to the further spread of technology and the complex processes of globalization.

NOTES

1. Quoted in Ray Brown, "Children and Television," *Social Science* (1978): 7.
2. W. O. Baker, "Computers as Information-Processing Machines in Modern Science," *Daedalus* 99, no. 4 (Fall 1970).
3. Norman Borlaug, Nobel Prize Acceptance Speech, 1970, http://www.nobel.se.
4. Quoted in Sam Fiorani, "Soichiro Honda," *Automotive History Online,* http://www.autohistory.org/feature_7.html.
5. Quoted in Pun Ngai, *Made in China: Women Factory Workers in a Global Workplace* (Durham, NC: Duke University Press, 2005), 83.
6. Quoted in Peter Winn, *Americas: The Changing Face of Latin America and the Caribbean* (Berkeley: University of California Press, 2006), 447.
7. Ramachandra Guha, *India After Gandhi: The History of the World's Largest Democracy* (New York: HarperCollins, 2008), 710.
8. Quoted in Temma Kaplan, *Taking Back the Streets: Women, Youth, and Direct Democracy* (Berkeley: University of California Press, 2004), 113.
9. Quoted in Thomas E. Skidmore and Peter H. Smith, *Modern Latin America,* 3d ed. (New York: Oxford University Press, 2002), 111.
10. Quoted in Kaplan, *Taking Back the Streets,* 38.

11. Quoted in *Korea Observer* 32 (2001): 264.
12. Quoted in Paula Giddings, *Where and When I Enter: The Impact of Black Women on Race and Sex in America* (New York: William Morrow, 1984), 316.
13. Quoted in David Caute, *Sixty-Eight: Year of the Barricades* (London: Hamish Hamilton, 1988), 165.
14. Russian citizen's interview with author, July 1994.
15. Quoted in Orville Schell, "China's Spring," in *The China Reader: The Reform Era*, ed. Orville Schell and David Shambaugh (New York: Vintage, 1999), 194.
16. Quoted in *In-Motion Magazine*, http://www.inmotionmagazine.com/global/man_int.html#AnchorKnowledge-49575.
17. Quoted in *In-Motion Magazine*, 2003, http://www.inmotionmagazine.com/shiva.html.
18. Ibid.

RESOURCES FOR RESEARCH

Advances in Technology and Science

Although the powers that waged World War II led the way in converting wartime technology to peacetime uses, the impact of scientific advances was felt around the world. Marks's book on reproductive technology provides a look at science's global reach.

Borlaug, Norman. "The Green Revolution, Peace, and Humanity," Nobel Lecture, 1970. http://www.nobel.se.

Dickson, Paul. *Sputnik: The Shock of the Century*. 2001.

Marks, Lara V. *Sexual Chemistry: A History of the Contraceptive Pill*. 2004.

O'Mara, Margaret Pugh. *Cities of Knowledge: Cold War Science and the Search for the Next Silicon Valley*. 2005.

Schefter, James L. *The Race: The Uncensored Story of How America Beat Russia to the Moon*. 1999.

Changes in the World Economy

As technology swept the globe, manufacturing power began to move from the West to the rest of the world. Chu et al., Kynge, and Mazlish describe these developments.

Chu, Yun-Peng, and Hal Hill, eds. *The East Asian High-Tech Drive*. 2006.

Davis, Deborah, ed. *The Consumer Revolution in Urban China*. 2000.

Kynge, James. *China Shakes the World: A Titan's Rise and Troubled Future and the Challenge for America*. 2006.

Mazlish, Bruce. *Leviathans: Multinational Corporations and the New Global History*. 2005.

Sony history. http://www.sony.net/SonyInfo/CorporateInfo/History/SonyHistory/.

Politics and Protest in an Age of Cold War

As the Cold War advanced, citizens rose to fight off dictators and to protest superpower dominance. Suri's book shows the worldwide maneuverings that accompanied domestic instability, while Kaplan's work gives accounts of resistance to Latin American dictators.

Kaplan, Temma. *Taking Back the Streets: Women, Youth, and Direct Democracy*. 2004.

Lam, Andrew. *Perfume Dreams: Reflections on the Vietnamese Diaspora*. 2005.

Lesch, David. *1979: The Year That Shaped the Modern Middle East*. 2001.

Ngai, Pun. *Made in China: Women Factory Workers in a Global Workplace*. 2005.

Suri, Jeremy. *Power and Protest: Global Revolution and the Rise of Détente*. 2003.

The End of the Cold War Order

The year 1989 saw a series of threats to communist nations. These works describe the events in both Europe and China from a variety of perspectives.

Human Rights in China, ed. *Children of the Dragon: The Story of Tiananmen Square*. 1990.

Kenney, Padraic. *Carnival of Revolution: Central Europe, 1989*. 2002.

Kotkin, Stephen. *Escaping Armageddon: The Soviet Collapse, 1970–2000*. 2001.

Ost, David. *The Defeat of Solidarity: Anger and Politics in Postcommunist Europe*. 2005.

Thomas, Daniel C. *The Helsinki Effect: International Norms, Human Rights, and the Demise of Communism*. 2001.

Tolstoya, Tatyana. *Pushkin's Children: Writings on Russia and Russians*. 2003.

COUNTERPOINT: Agrarian Peoples in a Technological Age

The Green Revolution in agriculture provoked opposition, sometimes passionate, from many ranks of global society, as these books reveal.

Rosegrant, M., and P. Hazell. *Transforming the Rural Asian Economy: The Unfinished Revolution*. 2000.

Shiva, Vandana. *Biopiracy: The Plunder of Nature and Knowledge*. 1997.

▶ **For additional primary sources from this period**, see *Sources of Crossroads and Cultures.*

▶ **For Web sites, images, and documents related to topics in this chapter**, see Make History at bedfordstmartins.com/smith.

REVIEW

The major global development in this chapter ▶ The technological revolution of the late twentieth century and its impact on societies and political developments around the world.

IMPORTANT EVENTS

1957	USSR launches *Sputnik*
1963	Betty Friedan, *The Feminine Mystique*
1967	Arab-Israeli Six-Day War
1968	"Prague Spring" in Czechoslovakia
1969	U.S. astronauts land on moon
1972	U.S. president Richard Nixon visits China; SALT I agreement
1973	Arab-Israeli Yom Kippur War; OPEC raises oil prices and imposes embargo
1973–1976	Aleksandr Solzhenitsyn, *Gulag Archipelago*
1975	Vietnam War ends; Vietnam reunited
1978	World's first test-tube baby born
1978–1979	Islamic revolution in Iran
1979–1989	Soviet War in Afghanistan
1980	Solidarity labor union organizes resistance to communism in Poland; Prime Minister Margaret Thatcher introduces neoliberal program in Britain
1985	Mikhail Gorbachev becomes Soviet leader, introduces new policies of perestroika and glasnost
1989	Chinese students demonstrate at Tiananmen Square; communist regimes in eastern Europe fall
1992	Soviet Union no longer exists

KEY TERMS

glasnost (p. 1014)
Green Revolution (p. 996)
multinational corporation (p. 998)
neoliberalism (p. 1014)

OPEC (p. 1013)
Pacific tiger (p. 997)
perestroika (p. 1014)
postindustrial (p. 991)
Solidarity (p. 1015)
stagflation (p. 1014)

CHAPTER OVERVIEW QUESTIONS

1. How did the technological developments of these decades transform social and economic conditions?
2. What were the attitudes of young people toward technology and social change during these years, and how did they reflect the Cold War climate in which these changes occurred?
3. How did the technological developments influence the fall of communist regimes in Europe and the dissolution of the Soviet Union?
4. How did the scientific and technological developments of the second half of the twentieth century affect the waging—and the end—of the Cold War?

SECTION FOCUS QUESTIONS

1. What were the major postwar advances in technology and science, and why were they important?
2. How did changes in the global economy affect livelihoods and family life?
3. What developments challenged the superpowers' dominance of world politics, and how did the superpowers attempt to address those challenges?
4. Why did the Cold War order come to an end?
5. How did some agrarian peoples resist the scientific and technological developments that threatened their ways of life?

MAKING CONNECTIONS

1. Why is late-twentieth-century society in many parts of the world described as postindustrial?
2. How did technological development and the social changes it produced affect national and world politics?
3. Why did the economic, scientific, and political developments of the late twentieth century spark so many grassroots protests, and what did those protests achieve?

AT A CROSSROADS ▶

The Burj al Arab (Tower of the Arabs) makes a statement about its home—Dubai, the United Arab Emirates—as a global crossroads. Its name signals a regional pride, while the tower itself is a hotel that welcomes visitors from around the world. With vast international experience, Tom Wright from England and Kunan Chew from Singapore designed the exterior and the interior, respectively. Like the designers and visitors, many of the men and women who built the tower come from beyond Dubai's borders. (akg-images/Bildarchiv Monheim.)

A New Global Age

1989 to the Present

O n February 11, 1990, South Africans celebrated the news that Nelson Mandela, deputy head of the African National Congress (ANC), had been freed after three decades in prison. Later that day Mandela stood before some fifty thousand cheering supporters in Cape Town, announcing his determination to end apartheid, the brutal South African system of racial discrimination. "Our path to freedom is irreversible," he stated. "Now is the time to intensify the struggle on all fronts." These were brave words in a society where the minority white population controlled the military and for decades had not hesitated to murder anyone who criticized white racist rule. But by 1990 black youth had taken up arms, protesting repression and unemployment. Their elders backed them with protests of their own, as the crowded South African ghettos became more miserable and more dangerous. Many whites hoped that Mandela's release would appease the protesters, but it became clear that white rule would not hold, and in April 1994 nearly 90 percent of South Africans went to the polls, many of them standing for hours in mile-long lines to vote in a free and fair election. One voter summed up his feelings at participating in democracy: "Now I am a human being." The ANC won 62 percent of the vote, and on May 10 that same year Nelson Mandela became president of South Africa.

Nelson Mandela's release from prison was noted not only by South Africans but by people around the world. Multinational companies had come to insist on racial equality in hiring at their South African plants, but as the apartheid government continued to torture and kill blacks, Coca-Cola, IBM, and others closed down their factories. The U.S. Congress

The Impact of Global Events on Regions and Nations

FOCUS How has globalization affected the distribution of power and wealth throughout the world in the early twenty-first century?

Global Livelihoods and Institutions

FOCUS How has globalization reshaped national economies and political institutions?

The Promises and Perils of Globalization

FOCUS What major benefits and dangers has globalization brought to the world's peoples?

Cultures Without Borders

FOCUS What trends suggest that globalization has led to a new mixing of cultures?

COUNTERPOINT: Who Am I? Local Identity in a Globalizing World

FOCUS How have peoples sought to establish and maintain distinctive local personal identities in today's global age?

BACKSTORY

As we saw in Chapter 30, a burst of technological innovation from the 1960s on changed the way many people lived and worked. In much of the West, the service sector surpassed industry and manufacturing as the most important components of the economy, with knowledge-based jobs leading the way. At the same time, industrial jobs were shipped overseas, and countries such as Korea and China joined the United States and Germany as centers of global manufacturing. As the economic balance of power began to shift, the United States and the Soviet Union found it more and more difficult to shape and control events around the world. In 1989, internal tensions led to the collapse of the Soviet Union, bringing the Cold War to a close and opening the way for still more dramatic change in the global economic and political order. With the Cold War over, technology flowed more freely across borders, and the increased pace of globalization created new connections among the peoples of the world. International tensions remained, however, and the new global landscape raised hopes around the world even as dangers persisted.

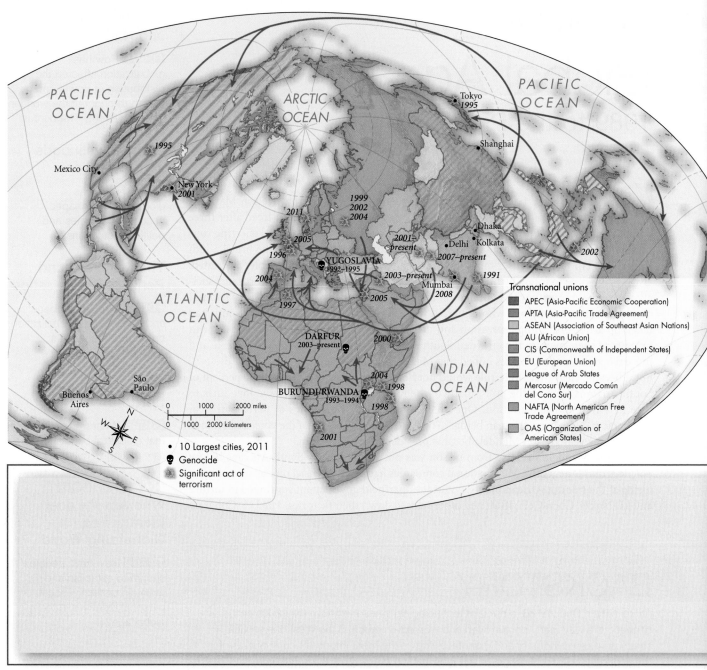

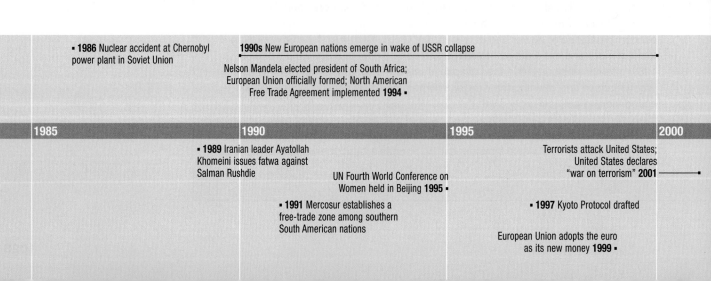

Timeline content:

■ **1986** Nuclear accident at Chernobyl power plant in Soviet Union

1990s New European nations emerge in wake of USSR collapse

Nelson Mandela elected president of South Africa; European Union officially formed; North American Free Trade Agreement implemented **1994** ■

1985 **1990** **1995** **2000**

■ **1989** Iranian leader Ayatollah Khomeini issues fatwa against Salman Rushdie

UN Fourth World Conference on Women held in Beijing **1995** ■

■ **1991** Mercosur establishes a free-trade zone among southern South American nations

Terrorists attack United States; United States declares "war on terrorism" **2001**

■ **1997** Kyoto Protocol drafted

European Union adopts the euro as its new money **1999** ■

banned the sale of South African gold coins, or Krugerrands, and legislated a boycott of South African products. Other countries took similar measures. The collective effect was devastating to the South African economy, whose leaders came to understand, as so many did from the 1970s on, that they were living in a world far more tightly connected than ever before. As satellite television and human rights groups brought the brutality of apartheid to the attention of the world, freedom in South Africa—like many other issues—became a concern of people everywhere. Nelson Mandela's release from prison and his election as president of South Africa symbolized a new and more intensely global stage in human history.

The end of the Cold War accelerated the continuing process of **globalization**—that is, the economic, political, social, and cultural interconnectedness of the world's regions. Now, instead of being forced to choose between two powerful and dangerous adversaries, people around the world could envision working and living together as global citizens and enjoying all aspects of one another's culture, including food, music, films, and books. Global organizations, regional trade alliances, and international businesses multiplied and drew more people into their tightening networks. Migration increased, with many migrants moving in search of opportunity. Others, however, sought to escape the dangers that cropped up after the Cold War as bitter conflicts among competing political and ethnic groups in Africa, the former Soviet Empire, India, and elsewhere brought horrific suffering. Radicals around the world publicized their aims with acts of terrorism. While improvements in medicine benefited much of the world, globalization facilitated the spread of infectious diseases, threatening people everywhere. Many soon realized that the same interconnectedness that fueled the economic boom of the late twentieth century also increased the potential for worldwide economic and environmental disasters.

Although the process of globalization drew people ever closer together, it also produced a backlash. Rejecting anything beyond the local community where they conducted their livelihoods, groups and individuals sought to retain their distinctive personal identities built on family ties and local traditions. In some cases, resistance to globalization took

globalization The economic, cultural, political, and social interactions and integration of the world's peoples.

MAPPING THE WORLD

A New Global Age

By the start of the twenty-first century, the world's peoples were bound together more significantly than ever. Migration brought unprecedented ethnic and cultural diversity to entire regions. At the same time, large regional alliances brought military, economic, and even political unity—at least superficially. No less real in their impact on everyday life were the mixing of cultures and the shared experience of terrorism and disease. Finally, the earth, humanity's common habitat, felt the effects of technological change, advancing industry, and growing population.

ROUTES ▼

→ Global migration, 1970s to present

2002 Luiz Inácio Lula da Silva elected Brazilian president

2003 United States invades Iraq

2007–2008 Global economic crisis begins to unfold

2005

2010

2015

2004 Manmohan Singh becomes prime minister of India

2005 Kyoto Protocol goes into effect

violent forms, including terrorist attacks on those seen as responsible for the erosion of traditional values and beliefs. Despite these efforts, the interdependence of the world's peoples, the connectedness of nations, and the sharing of culture that globalization had brought were nearly inescapable. In 1994 the European Economic Community (or Common Market) transformed itself from a mainly economic alliance into the European Union, which looked as if it might become a United States of Europe. When Barack Obama was elected the first African American president of the United States in 2008, it was a moment shared by the world, just as the release of Nelson Mandela had been less than two decades earlier.

As historians, the authors of this book have no firm idea how these recent events will appear a century from now, but in this chapter we follow trends that have evolved over decades and even centuries. In choosing events to recount in this analysis of the very near past we have also used generally accepted criteria for spotting historical significance. We hope—and you can be the judge several decades from now—that this account of our own global age stands the test of time and of history.

OVERVIEW
QUESTIONS

The major global development in this chapter: The causes and consequences of intensified globalization.

As you read, consider:

1. What were the elements of globalization at the beginning of the twenty-first century?

2. How did globalization affect lives and livelihoods throughout the world?

3. How did globalization affect local cultures?

4. What people do you know whose roots and livelihoods are global?

The Impact of Global Events on Regions and Nations

FOCUS

How has globalization affected the distribution of power and wealth throughout the world in the early twenty-first century?

The end of the Cold War brought many advantages in terms of free speech, human rights, and economic opportunity. Peoples around the world no longer had to toe the line set by the superpowers, and some nations began to flourish as never before, often thanks to adopting new technology. Yet the aftermath was not all positive—the weapons and other military goods given as aid by the superpowers promoted dictatorships and civil wars. Vast differences appeared between many regions emerging from colonialism and those that had long enjoyed freedom and prosperity.

North Versus South

During the 1980s and 1990s, world leaders tried to address the growing economic schism between the earth's northern and southern regions. Other than Australians and New Zealanders, southern peoples (those from Africa, South Asia, Southeast Asia, and Latin

America) generally had lower standards of living than northerners. Long ruled as colonies or exploited economically by northerners, citizens in the southern regions could not yet count on their new governments to provide welfare services or education. International organizations such as the World Bank and the International Monetary Fund provided loans for economic development, but the conditions tied to them, such as cutting government spending for social programs, led to criticism that there was no real benefit if education and health care were sacrificed in the name of balancing national budgets. Disease soared and the pace of literacy and capacity-building slowed.

Although the Southern Hemisphere had highly productive agriculture and abundant natural resources, southern peoples often found it difficult to export their products to developed countries. Both the United States and the European Union advocated free trade but nevertheless imposed tariffs on imported agricultural products and subsidized their own farmers, raising prices for imported products and lowering them for domestic ones in the process. As Amadou Toumani Touré, president of Mali, complained in 2002, "the North cannot massively subsidize its farm exports and at the same time try and give lessons in competitiveness to the South."[1] Tariffs and financial aid to wealthy farmers in the north diverted an estimated $100 billion worth of business away from poorer nations. "We cannot compete against this monster, the United States," one Mexican farmer claimed in 2008. "It's not worth the trouble to plant. We don't have the subsidies."[2] Understanding the situation but unwilling to challenge domestic agribusinesses, leaders from wealthy nations met in 2004 to draft plans to alleviate the debt of southern countries and to sponsor health-care and education initiatives as an alternative to lifting subsidies. It remained to be seen whether these programs would materialize and whether poverty, disease and death would decline as a result.

Southern regions experienced a number of internal barriers to peaceful development. Latin American nations grappled with government corruption, multibillion-dollar debt owed to international banks, widespread crime, and grinding poverty. The situation was not, however, universally grim. Some countries—Mexico and Brazil, for example—began to strengthen their economies by marketing their oil and other natural resources effectively on the global market.

Sub-Saharan Africa suffered from drought, famine, and civil war. In the African nations of Rwanda, Burundi, and Sudan, a lethal mixture of military rule, ideological factionalism, and the ethnic antagonism that had been encouraged under imperialism resulted in conflict and genocide in the 1990s. Millions perished; others were left starving and homeless while leaders drained national resources to build up their militaries and enrich themselves. Arms dealers and aid workers poured into these regions, both groups bringing resources that governments often used against their own people. In Sudan, children were among the first victims of starvation, disease, and outright murder in the half-century-long civil war between the north and south of the country. Those in southern Sudan opposed the north's creation of an Islamic republic and its control of the country's oil and agricultural wealth. As the dispute intensified and spread to central and western Sudan (Darfur) between 1985 and 2005, an estimated 2 million people were killed and some 4 million left homeless. Common to Africa and other embattled regions was the recruitment of children into armies, a practice that contributed to the long-term militarization of affected societies. Although negotiators achieved truces, political uncertainty and the lack of stable economic institutions continued to plague many southern regions.

Obstacles to Development

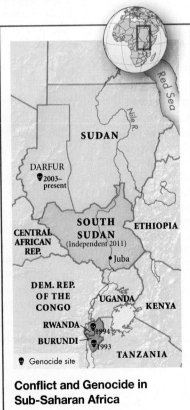

Conflict and Genocide in Sub-Saharan Africa

Advancing Nations in the Global Age

Despite the challenges, the developing world was also the site of dramatic successes. After decades of strife and economic underperformance, officials, business people, farmers, and artisans rebuilt prosperity in India, Brazil, South Africa, and China as they took advantage of global technology and markets. The same groups also helped democracy materialize in Brazil and South Africa and mature in India. Politicians worked to accommodate opposition parties instead of stifling their critics, and they pulled supporters and rivals alike into the common cause of advancing representative government.

India

By the twenty-first century, democratic India had become an economic powerhouse, possessing robust industrial and service sectors connected to markets around the world. India's path to prosperity was hardly smooth, however. Its leaders had to overcome ethnic, religious, class, and caste conflict as they tried to integrate India's diverse peoples. The Congress Party, founded in 1885 to combat British domination, remained powerful, but Nehru's daughter and grandson, who followed him as prime ministers, were assassinated by offended members of religious and ethnic minorities, leaving Gandhi's and Nehru's goals of integration unfulfilled. Nonetheless, India remained the world's largest democracy.

For a brief period the Bharatiya Janata Party (BJP), which advocated a Hindu nationalist program aimed in part at halting the technological development behind India's growing wealth and secularization, attracted voters struggling with rapid economic change. In 2004, however, Indian voters soundly defeated the BJP, rejecting Hindu nationalism in favor of the economic fairness promised by an alliance of the Congress Party and smaller parties, including the communists. New prime minister and the first Sikh to hold that position, Manmohan Singh, was an economist with international experience, having served as a director of the International Monetary Fund and other global organizations. Known as "the cleanest politician in India,"[3] Singh supported a mixed economy—that is, one with both privately and publicly owned enterprises. Even as its economy soared under Singh, however, India continued to face problems that were part of the legacy of colonialism: lack of modern infrastructure and education for all, the poverty of several hundred million citizens, and persistent ethnic and religious terrorism. Amid both turmoil and prosperity, India's cities grew and its middle class expanded, in large part thanks to the global economic activities of its innovative business people. India's internal integration and development were also importantly linked to its continued connections with peoples and markets around the world.

Globalized Agriculture in India

This up-to-date Indian farmer harvests a bumper crop of wheat using machinery from the U.S.-based John Deere corporation. Not only did this harvester have parts made in other countries, but the seeds he used were probably developed in Mexico-based scientific laboratories. These laboratories produced seeds suitable for different agricultural conditions, such as varying climate and soil composition. The result was the "Green Revolution" that began in the 1960s. (akg-images/Yvan Travert.)

Like other Latin Americans in the 1960s and 1970s, Brazilians had endured military dictatorship, soaring inflation, rising poverty, and a grossly inadequate system of education and social services. In 1985 Brazilian voters, tired of government brutality and human rights abuses, ousted the military dictatorship and installed an elected government. Civilian rule brought with it an emphasis on human rights and economic expansion, especially in the 1990s and thereafter. By the 1990s, government leaders had adopted a tight monetary policy and a commitment to pay down debts. In 2004 Brazil's economy expanded at a rate of 5.2 percent, despite the persistence of serious social problems, including crime and poverty.

There were several forces behind these developments. In the slums or *favelas* of the country's major cities, Rio de Janeiro and São Paulo, where the dictatorship provided no sanitary, educational, or other services, poverty-stricken residents organized themselves in the spirit of change, holding self-education meetings, teaching one another to read, and taking turns collecting and disposing of garbage. "I go to meetings every week now," one woman reported of her growing activism. "I think we women should participate in political parties."[4] Unions also played an important role. Luiz Inácio Lula da Silva, born in poverty in the countryside, had become a metalworker and then boosted his leftist union's membership to more than one hundred thousand. In the 1980s he brought together a broad coalition to found the Workers Party. On his fourth try for office in 2002, Lula da Silva was elected president—an incredible journey for a poor child who only learned to read when he was ten.

Global journalists described Lula da Silva as another Stalin or Mao. Yet Lula da Silva adopted an effective, pragmatic style: as president he promised that increased tax revenues on the wealthy would be used to pay off the dictatorship's foreign loans and thus free Brazil from indebtedness to the West. Alongside indebtedness, the populace was outraged at the brutal murders of reformers who wanted to stop the destruction of Brazil's rain forests by both global and local developers. The issue was one not only of murder, but of whether local peoples could keep their land in the forests or whether the government would let loggers strip the forests and murder opponents in the name of economic development. Although Lula negotiated a path between antiglobalizers and globalizers, some of the worst poverty was alleviated and the Brazilian economy surged, becoming a rising economic star in the Southern Hemisphere and indeed in the world as a whole.

As president of South Africa, Nelson Mandela faced numerous pressing issues. Foremost among them were calming interethnic tensions, ending political violence, and unifying the nation around consensus-building rather than violence. Violence against blacks and white critics had been the main political strategy of the **apartheid** government; it included taking blacks' homes and land and herding them by force into small "townships." In 1976 government troops killed and wounded some three thousand youth and children at Soweto as they protested the lack of educational opportunities. "We want equal education, not slave education," they had chanted while being mowed down. The white apartheid government also pursued a divide-and-conquer strategy, doing what it could to encourage conflict between the Zulu Inkatha Freedom Party and Mandela's African National Congress. In the 1980s, violence from many sides kept the country in turmoil. After Mandela took control, the government set up in 1995 a Truth and Reconciliation Commission to hear testimony about the violence. The Commission allowed those whom the apartheid government had persecuted to talk about their experiences in public; then it allowed those who had participated in the persecutions to confess to what they had done and request amnesty. The aim was to provide some relief to victims and to construct a new model for nation building (see Reading the Past: Testimony to South Africa's Truth and Reconciliation Commission).

While the Commission did its work, Mandela's presidency opened world markets to South African products, increased the flow of technology to the country, and created policies based on fairness to all social groups. For example, South African women had played a leadership role in opposing apartheid, and they received a quota of seats in the new government. Health care was declared a constitutional right of all citizens. The government's

apartheid The South African system of laws and behaviors that enforced segregation of the black from the white population, with the intention of creating a society dominated by whites; apartheid laws were repealed in 1991.

Testimony to South Africa's Truth and Reconciliation Commission

In 1995 the South African government established the Truth and Reconciliation Commission to hear testimony from accusers and perpetrators alike about violence and human rights abuses during the apartheid regime. Usually the commission imposed fines, but in the aftermath of the hearings victims were often angrier than before. They saw the punishment as inadequate and complained that the fines were ridiculously low or never paid. Despite the drawbacks and objections, many around the world hailed the Truth and Reconciliation model as one with great potential.

Accounts by perpetrators of the violence make for especially horrific reading. In this excerpt, researchers followed up with one member of the government security forces to hear in more depth how he pursued his grim job in the 1970s and 1980s, getting paid by the head for black resisters captured and for black resisters killed.

We would volunteer for a three-month stint on the border for the Security Branch up there. . . . It sounded like a bit of an adventure and [a] nice getting away kind of ploy, because my girlfriend and I were having hassles, probably because we were staying at my parents' place. I'd always been interested in doing something unconventional anyway, and I thought, well, this is it. This is my chance. . . .

The amount of adrenaline that we were producing on a daily level, constantly aware that we could die or be wounded at any moment. . . . Having that adrenaline pumping, we became adrenaline junkies. . . . It became like a drug to me, to go out there and follow up on those tracks. . . . [It is] almost a sexual kind of stimulation. Not physical sexual, but mental sexual. . . .

[On one particular captive] I knew that he was a veteran and that he would have been an excellent source of info. Sean, the Army medic, started patching him up while I was busy interrogating him. . . . Even at that stage he was denying everything and I just started to go into this uncontrollable [expletive deleted] rage and I remember thinking, "How dare you?" And then—this is what I was told afterwards—I started ripping. I ripped all the bandages, the drip that Sean had put into this guy . . . pulled out my 9 mm, put the barrel between his eyes and . . . I executed him.

Source: Don Foster et al., *The Theatre of Violence: Narratives of Protagonists in the South African Conflict* (Oxford, U.K.: James Currey, 2005), 130, 137, 140.

EXAMINING THE EVIDENCE

1. What values appear to have motivated this member of the security forces as he pursued his livelihood?

2. Do you detect a change over time in his conduct, and if so, how do you explain it?

3. Why do you think the Truth and Reconciliation Commission came to be viewed as a powerful model in nation building?

---

approach to land reform reflected its commitment to national integration and consensus-building. Instead of simply seizing land held by whites and giving it to blacks, the government set up a process by which the claims of dispossessed whites and blacks alike could be resolved. Nonetheless, South African blacks still remained an underclass, and migrants from neighboring Zimbabwe, Mozambique, and other hard-pressed African regions competed with them for jobs (see Map 31.1). Business people and farmers often fired their former employees and hired the migrants at rock-bottom wages.

At the same time, the rapid spread of HIV/AIDS (discussed later in the chapter) engulfed the nation in a horrific health crisis. South Africans themselves contracted the disease, and because of South Africa's growing prosperity, tens of thousands of other afflicted Africans came there to receive treatment. Twenty-four percent of all inhabitants of South Africa were HIV-positive in 2007. This trend, combined with ethnic tensions, economic inequalities, and the rise of new political factions, challenged the gains made after South Africa's hard-won victory over apartheid.

China   Of all the developing nations, China's was the most striking success story. Deng Xiaoping came out on top in the power struggle that followed Mao's death in 1976. Under his leadership, China began its drive to become an economic titan, at once producing an array of inexpensive products for the global marketplace and providing its citizens with jobs that raised their standard of living. As people from the countryside flocked to cities to find jobs in China's global workplace, skyscrapers sprouted like mushrooms, transforming China's urban landscape. One- and two-story buildings were demolished in a flash: "Buildings are being knocked down at such a rate that one doesn't even have time to film them anymore," said one Beijing resident.[5] With rising prosperity, consumers sought out luxury goods that would have been unimaginable just two decades earlier. Even relatively poor workers could afford pirated DVDs, and thousands supported themselves by counterfeiting imported goods in much the same way that U.S. hustlers more than a century earlier had helped build American prosperity through counterfeiting products.

Economic development was not, however, accompanied by democratization. The Communist Party kept its grip on government, clamping down hard on free speech, even on the Internet, and meting out harsh punishments to political and religious dissidents. While maintaining control at home, China sought business partners around the world, making deals for raw materials and even for used factories, which it dismantled piece by piece and then reconstructed in new Chinese industrial parks. It also used its trade surpluses to buy vast quantities of debt, especially from the United States, making this communist country the bankroller of capitalist economies and thus an increasingly powerful player on the global stage. The flow of wealth and productive energy appeared to have changed direction away from the Atlantic and toward the Pacific.

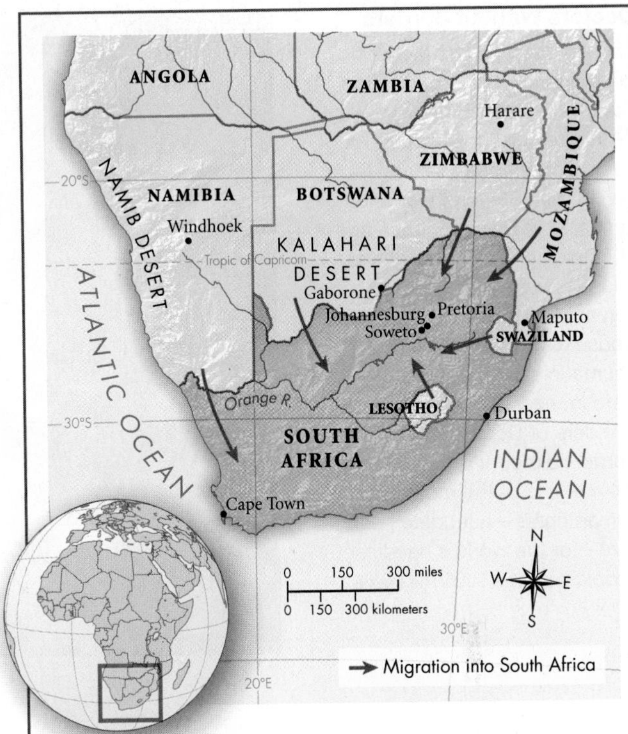

MAP 31.1   South Africa After Apartheid

Before the end of apartheid, legal migration into South Africa was restricted to whites and to African contract laborers who worked in the mines. After 1994, refugees seeking opportunity from the region around South Africa entered the country. The new South Africa also deported many illegal immigrants, and South Africans themselves migrated, creating a "brain drain" from the country, including people in the professions and those with technical skills.

Global Livelihoods and Institutions

The same forces that created a global market for products and services created a global market for labor. Increasingly, companies took their operations to wherever labor was cheapest. As a result, workers around the world found themselves in competition for employment. At the

FOCUS

How has globalization reshaped national economies and political institutions?

same time, workers found it easier to move to where the jobs were. Better transportation and communication led people to travel thousands of miles to work: Indonesian village women, for instance, left their families to work as domestic servants in the Middle East; nurses from the Philippines went to Japan and other countries as health-care providers in a better-paying environment. Migration, innovations in communication technology, and the globalization of business combined to create global cities. London, Tokyo, and New York became crossroads for global finance, engineering, and legal decision-making. Finally, global financial, political, and activist institutions such as the World Trade Organization, the United Nations, and Doctors Without Borders operated worldwide, transcending the borders of the nation-state and even throwing the nation-state itself into question.

Doctors Without Borders
This doctor from the global nongovernmental organization Doctors Without Borders distributes plastic sheeting to construct refugee shelters during the 1994 civil war and genocide in Rwanda. In an age of ethnic conflict and civil war, refugees were an all-too-common type of global citizen, whose displacement was traumatic and whose needs were immense. The French founders of Doctors Without Borders aimed for this NGO to provide one of the most basic human rights—adequate health care—for the world's neediest peoples. (Louise Gubb/The Image Works.)

Global Networks and Changing Jobs

The Internet and Service Work

The Internet in particular advanced the globalization that multinational corporations and satellite communications had fostered in the first decades after World War II. By the early twenty-first century, as skills spread around the world, the Internet brought service jobs to a number of previously impoverished countries. One of the first to recognize the possibilities of computing and call desk services was Ireland, which attracted global business by stressing computer literacy. From the 1990s on, the people of this traditionally poor country began to prosper as the Internet allowed them to perform service jobs for clients throughout the world. The trend reached other nations as well. Moroccans could do help-desk work for French or Spanish speakers, and Nigerians could tend to U.S. telephone and credit card bills. India and China, both of which had good if unequally distributed systems of education, and eastern Europe with its well-educated workforce profited from the Internet revolution. Three percent of Indian domestic product came from the outsourcing work it did in payroll and other services for Europe, the United States, and Austronesia, but jobs flowed in multiple directions: jobs outsourced to the United States rose from 4.9 million in 1991 to 6.4 million in 2001 and continued to grow.

Global Consumerism

Those who worked in outsourced jobs were more likely to participate in the global consumer economy. Thus, consumption soared in India, China, Brazil, and other emerging markets. Service workers in these areas received intense language training to sound like American, Spanish, or British consumers, and global advertising introduced them to products from around the world. A twenty-one-year-old Indian woman, working for a service provider in Bangalore under the English name "Sharon," was able to buy a cellphone from the Finnish company Nokia with her salary. "As a teenager I wished for so many things," she said. "Now I'm my own Santa Claus."[6] North Africans, Indians, Chinese, and eastern Europeans had access to automobiles, CD players, and personal computers that would have been far beyond their means before the 1990s. Critics called the phenomenon "Consumania."[7]

Consumerism developed unevenly, however: 30 to 40 percent of the people in eastern Europe and even larger percentages in China and Indonesia could not participate fully in the consumer economy because they lacked the means for even basic purchases. The lion's share of global consumer benefits went to urban rather than rural workers. Urban workers in the global service economy also used their rising incomes to educate their families and themselves, hoping to advance even further.

Globalization produced acute competition among lower-level workers in industrial countries for good jobs. "How can I prepare my children for a knowledge-based society when I can't even put food on the table," one French mother complained.[8] Minimum-wage workers in the urbanized countries of the north competed for jobs with people around the world. Much as rural people in the late nineteenth and early twentieth century had faced a drop in prices for their produce and a deterioration in their way of life with the development of global markets in grain and other agricultural products, now lower-level industrial and service workers faced lower wages because they competed with workers worldwide. In contrast, those with advanced managerial, technological, and other skills derived from university education fared better, showing the increasing importance of education to prosperity.

Neoliberalism and the Global Economy

In the 1990s neoliberalism as pioneered by Margaret Thatcher and Ronald Reagan (see Chapter 30) became a central economic model for promoting growth. Reducing social programs such as health care and education for ordinary people would lower costs to employers and boost profits and investment. Neoliberal policy encouraged business mergers, the elimination of rules for the industries and banks, and the free flow of capital across national borders. German companies, like U.S. firms, increased investments abroad in the early 1990s and thereafter; Germans set up companies in the United States where benefits to the workforce were low, and U.S. firms headed to places where benefits and taxes were even lower. An important tenet of neoliberalism was that profit and investment increase through downsizing—that is, reducing the number of jobs and enhancing the productivity of any individual worker. The resulting growth would eventually produce more jobs, thus creating new opportunities for those who were put out of work.

The neoliberal model continued to challenge that of the postwar welfare state in which the government tried to create a minimum level of well-being for society as a whole. Although Europeans still believed government should provide social services and education for all, the tightening of budgetary rules in the European Union meant that these services had to constitute a smaller part of the budget. Some labor unions protested that neoliberals wanted to keep workers at bare subsistence levels. The Swedish government drastically cut pensions, leading one union member to complain: "It means that we have to work our entire life."[9] Because employers (like workers) paid taxes for social service programs, any reduction in benefits or education costs meant smaller employer contributions. Reductions in employer contributions freed up money for investment, thus advancing neoliberalism. Despite neoliberal convictions, some nations believed that certain services were too important to be left to those whose main concern was profit rather than the public good; for that reason these governments continued to run high-quality transportation systems and pave roads, for example.

Beyond the Nation-State

Supranational organizations fostered globalization by creating worldwide networks to improve and regulate societies, economies, and politics. In the 1990s Europeans made immense strides in moving their governmental institutions beyond those of the traditional nation-state, while countries of the "southern cone" of South America joined the effort to speed up economic and social progress. People from around the world packed into cities such as Tokyo, New York, and London, bringing new ideas and new customs.

Supranational Organizations

The International Monetary Fund (IMF) and the World Bank had been in existence for decades, but with globalization these supranational organizations gained in power and importance. Raising money from individual governments, the IMF made loans to developing countries to support modernizing projects or to pay off debts. Such assistance, however, came on the condition that the recipient countries restructure their economies according to neoliberal principles. Other supranational organizations not connected to governments and therefore called **nongovernmental organizations** (NGOs) were charitable or policy-oriented foundations. Because they controlled so much money, these NGOs often shaped national policies. After the fall of the Soviet bloc, NGOs used their resources to bring about political reform. Some NGOs, such as the France-based Doctors Without Borders, used global contributions to provide medical aid in such places as the former Yugoslavia, where people at war lacked any medical help except what outsiders could provide.

Activists Against Globalization

Globalization entailed the rise of global activism, even against globalization itself. For example, the Association for Taxation of Financial Transactions (known as ATTAC), founded in 1998, had adherents in forty countries who opposed the control of globalization by the forces of high finance. ATTAC's major policy goal was to tax financial transactions (just as purchases of household necessities were taxed) and use the money raised to create a fund for people in underdeveloped countries. By 2011, the European Union indeed proposed such a tax, although it was to support poorer countries in the EU itself. ATTAC held a conference at Porto Alegre, Brazil, in 2002 to develop policy alternatives that would protect ordinary people from the worst effects of globalization; political leaders flocked to "alternative" Porto Alegre just as they attended the more traditionally global Davos forum held annually in Switzerland for the world's leading executives.[10]

Women Activists and Globalization

Women activists also held global meetings. Feminists gathered in Beijing, China, in 1995 to discuss common issues and agree on a common platform that could serve as the basis for political action in individual countries. The event was eye-opening for many participants, especially those from industrialized countries who had thought themselves more advanced and active than women from Africa and South America. The reverse proved to be true. Sharp differences in agendas and priorities emerged, as well as dissent in shaping the final report, especially on matters of birth control and abortion. In the end, the activists created a declaration of principles and a set of specific actions designed, in the words of the Declaration, "to advance the goals of equality, development, and peace for all women everywhere in the interest of all humanity"[11] (see Reading the Past: Assessing Livelihoods for Women in a Global Economy). In the early twenty-first century, women became heads of state in Germany, Liberia, Chile, Argentina, and Brazil, a sign of women's increasing influence in politics and business.

The European Union

In 1992, the twelve countries of the European Economic Community (or Common Market) ended national distinctions in the spheres of business activity, border controls, and transportation. Citizens of member countries carried a common burgundy-colored passport, and governments, whether municipal or national, had to treat all member nations' firms the same. In 1994 by the terms of the Maastricht Treaty, the European Economic Community became the **European Union** (EU) (see again Mapping the World, page 1025), and in 1999 a common currency, the European Currency Unit—the ECU, or euro—was established. Common policies governed everything from the number of American soap operas aired on television to pollution controls on automobiles to standardized health warnings on cigarette packages. The EU parliament convened regularly in Strasbourg, France, and with the adoption of a common currency by most members, the EU's central bank gained more control over regionwide economic policy.

Between 2004 and 2007 the EU admitted ten new members, mostly from central and eastern Europe: Estonia, Latvia, Lithuania, Poland, the Czech Republic, Slovakia, Hungary, Malta, Cyprus, Slovenia, Bulgaria, and Romania. All new members hoped to

nongovernmental organization A group devoted to activism outside the normal channels of government, such as Doctors Without Borders.

European Union An expanded version of the European Economic Community, established in 1994 to increase political and economic cooperation among European nations.

Assessing Livelihoods for Women in a Global Economy

In 1995 delegates from around the world met in Beijing, China, for the Fourth World Conference on Women sponsored by the United Nations. The delegates listened, debated, and negotiated to come up with a platform for action addressing women's health, education, role in politics, safety, and—in this excerpt—their situation in the increasingly globalized economy of the 1990s.

Although some new employment opportunities have been created for women as a result of the globalization of the economy, there are also trends that have exacerbated inequalities between women and men. . . .

These trends have been characterized by low wages, little or no labor standards protection, poor working conditions, particularly with regard to women's occupational health and safety, low skill levels, and a lack of job security and social security, in both the formal and informal sectors. Women's unemployment is a serious and increasing problem in many countries and sectors. Young workers in the informal and rural sectors and migrant female workers remain the least protected by labor and immigration laws. Women, particularly those who are heads of households with young children, are limited in their employment opportunities for reasons that include inflexible working conditions and inadequate sharing, by men and by society, of family responsibilities.

In countries that are undergoing fundamental political, economic, and social transformation, the skills of women, if better utilized, could constitute a major contribution to the economic life of their respective countries. Their input should continue to be developed and supported and their potential further realized.

For those women in paid work, many experience obstacles that prevent them from achieving their potential. While some are increasingly found in lower levels of management, attitudinal discrimination often prevents them from being promoted further. The experience of sexual harassment is an affront to a worker's dignity and prevents women from making a contribution commensurate with their abilities. The lack of a family-friendly work environment, including a lack of appropriate and affordable child care, and inflexible working hours, further prevents women from achieving their full potential.

In the private sector, including transnational and national enterprises, women are largely absent from management and policy levels, denoting discriminatory hiring and promotion policies and practices. The unfavorable work environment as well as the limited number of employment opportunities available have led many women to seek alternatives. Women have increasingly become self-employed and owners and managers of micro, small, and medium-scale enterprises.

Source: The United Nations Fourth World Conference on Women, "Action for Equality, Development and Peace," Beijing, China, September 1995, http://www.un.org/womenwatch/daw/beijing/platform/.

EXAMINING THE EVIDENCE

1. According to this statement, what are the effects of globalization on women's place in the economy?

2. What other issues besides economic ones affect women's ability to pursue productive and fulfilling livelihoods?

3. Judging from this statement, what relationship do you see between women's economic participation and the well-being of nations?

emulate the case of Greece, which had long been considered the poor relative of other EU countries. Greece had joined the European Common Market in 1981; in 1990 its per capita gross income was 58.5 percent of the European average. By the early twenty-first century, thanks to advice from the EU and an infusion of funds, the country reached 80 percent of the EU per capita gross domestic product. Candidates in 2010 for membership included Turkey, Croatia, and Macedonia.

The economic and political successes of the EU prompted the creation of other cooperative zones that imitated the early Common Market (see again Mapping the World,

Other Transnational Unions

Mercosur, 2011

page 1024). In 1967 five countries—Indonesia, Malaysia, the Philippines, Singapore, and Thailand—formed the **Association of Southeast Asian Nations** (ASEAN), later expanded to include Brunei Darussalam (1984), Vietnam (1995), Laos and Myanmar (1997), and Cambodia (1999). ASEAN members engaged in a range of cooperative ventures, but they particularly set their sights on rapid economic cooperation and expansion. The **North American Free Trade Agreement** (NAFTA), implemented in 1994, eliminated nearly all tariffs on goods traded between Canada, the United States, and Mexico. **Mercosur**, formed in 1991, established a free trade zone among South America's "southern cone" countries: Argentina, Brazil, Uruguay, and Paraguay, all of which were full members, and Chile and Bolivia as associates. These transnational organizations hardly matched the integration of the EU, and NAFTA explicitly rejected the kind of borderless opportunities for workers that the EU allowed. Workers in the United States watched in dismay as many jobs moved to Mexico, but as trade blossomed among the partners, the country's industrialists, financiers, and traders came to regard NAFTA and Mercosur as successes.

Global Cities

The changing function of cities in a global world reshaped livelihoods and identities. Cities had always served as regional crossroads, acting as centers of economic, political, and cultural activity. Now, as the twentieth century came to a close, some old urban areas, including Hong Kong, Paris, Tokyo, London, and New York, became global crossroads. Taking advantage of innovations in transportation and communication, they claimed critical roles in the global economy and became magnets for migrants from all over the world. Residents of other cities who took pride in maintaining their distinctive national culture or local way of life denounced global cities, often portraying them as corrupt and cold. Global cities, many of which were in the north, also drew criticism for their concentrated wealth, as their rise to global power and influence was seen by some to come at the expense of poorer people in rural areas or southern nations.

Life in Global Cities

A global city's institutions—its stock markets, legal firms, insurance companies, and financial service organizations—operated across national borders and were linked to similar enterprises in other global cities. Within these cities, high-level decision-makers interacted with one another to set global economic policy and to transact business worldwide. Their high pay drove up living costs and sent middle managers and engineers to live in lower-priced suburbs that nonetheless provided good schools and other amenities for these well-educated white-collar workers. Living in squalid conditions in the run-down neighborhoods of global cities were the lowest of service providers—the maintenance, domestic, and other workers who needed to be at the beck and call of global enterprise. According to one commentator, those at the top envisioned these people—many of them immigrants—as "lumpentrash." Thus, suburbanization and ghettoization alike flourished as part of globalization.

Association of Southeast Asian Nations A transnational organization formed in 1967 to facilitate economic cooperation among Southeast Asian countries.

North American Free Trade Agreement An agreement among Canada, Mexico, and the United States established in 1994 that eliminated most tariffs on goods traded among the signatories.

Mercosur The establishment in 1991 of a free trade zone among nations of South America's "southern cone."

Huge numbers of willing migrants flocked to leading global cities. In the mid-1990s, for example, an estimated ninety thousand Japanese lived in England staffing Japan's global enterprises located there. Sometimes said to be "invisible migrants," they did not aim to become citizens, nor did they make any economic or political claims on the adopted country. The presence of massive numbers of like-minded wanderers and a rich array of cultures and peoples in their communities often kept these global citizens from suffering the trauma of exile from their native country. Global cities were sometimes criticized for producing a "de-territorialization of identities"—meaning that residents of these areas lacked both a national and a local sense of themselves, so much so that they were at home anywhere in the world (see Seeing the Past: The Globalization of Urban Space).

The Globalization of Urban Space

The New Louvre, Paris, France (The Art Archive/Richard Nowitz/NGS Image Collection.)

One everyday sign of globalization is the homogenization of urban architecture. Travelers to urban capitals may see carefully preserved and distinctive buildings from centuries past that differ from one continent to another. Alongside these ancient buildings are recent ones, similar in style whether they are in Dubai, Malaysia, Japan, Brazil, or the United States. The similarity arises not only from the globalization of style but from the globalization of architects themselves, who bid on and construct buildings far beyond their home countries, often in collaboration with architects from other parts of the world.

The Louvre was once a royal palace. It evolved from a twelfth-century fortified residence of kings to a museum not only for the French but for millions of tourists from around the world. In the 1980s the French government undertook a major renovation of the central entrance to the Louvre, which was no longer adequate to deal with the throngs of visitors. The architect I. M. Pei, who designed buildings around the world, produced this entryway through a glass pyramid.

EXAMINING THE EVIDENCE

1. Why might so ancient a structure as a pyramid have been chosen to be placed in front of the Louvre?

2. Why might glass have been used instead of the stone from which the Egyptian pyramids were constructed?

3. What message does this update of the entrance to the Louvre convey?

The Promises and Perils of Globalization

Despite growing prosperity for many, the global age was filled with challenges. First, the health of the world's peoples and their environments came under a multipronged attack from industrial disasters, acid rain, epidemics, and global warming. Second, a surging population, especially

FOCUS

What major benefits and dangers has globalization brought to the world's peoples?

in southern regions, although fueling economic growth in many places, increased demands on resources and often fed strife. Migration from imperiled areas mushroomed, and transnational religious and ethnic movements also competed for power around the world, sometimes through the use of terrorism. Growing prosperity in regions outside the West boosted confidence that the time had come for the redistribution of global power, especially as the West was hit with a devastating economic crisis.

Environmental Challenges

In the late twentieth century people became concerned that technological development threatened the environment and human well-being on a disastrous scale. In 1984 poisonous gas leaking from a Union Carbide plant in Bhopal, India, killed an estimated ten to fifteen thousand people, with many tens of thousands more permanently harmed and the region completely contaminated by chemicals. This was followed by the 1986 explosion at the Chernobyl nuclear power plant in present-day Ukraine, which killed thirty people instantly and left many more dying slowly from the effects of radiation. Levels of radioactivity rose for hundreds of miles in all directions, and by the 1990s cancer rates in the region were soaring, particularly among children. Fossil-fuel pollutants such as those from natural gas, coal, and oil mixed with atmospheric moisture to produce acid rain, a poisonous brew that destroyed forests and inflicted ailments such as chronic bronchial disease on children. In less populated areas, clearing the world's rain forests depleted the global oxygen supply and threatened the biological diversity of the entire planet.

Climate Change   By the late 1980s, scientists determined that the use of chlorofluorocarbons (CFCs), chemicals found in aerosol and refrigeration products, had blown a hole in the earth's ozone layer, the part of the blanket of atmospheric gases that prevents harmful ultraviolet rays from reaching the planet. Simultaneously, automobile and industrial emissions, especially of carbon dioxide produced by the burning of fossil fuels, were adding to that thermal blanket. The buildup of CFCs, carbon dioxide, and other atmospheric pollutants produced a "greenhouse effect" that resulted in **global warming**, an increase in the temperature of the earth's lower atmosphere. Changes in temperature and dramatic weather cycles of drought or drenching rain indicated that a greenhouse effect might be permanently warming the earth and thus causing climate change. Already in the 1990s, the Arctic ice pack was breaking up, and scientists predicted dire consequences: the rate of global ice melting, which had more than doubled since 1988, would raise sea levels 27 centimeters by 2100, flooding coastal areas, disturbing fragile ecosystems, and harming the fresh water supply (see Map 31.2).

Environmental Activism   Activism against unbridled industrial growth took decades to develop as an effective political force. American biologist and author Rachel Carson wrote a powerful critique, *Silent Spring* (1962), which advocated the immediate rescue of rivers, forests, and the soil from the ravages of factories and chemical farming. In 1979, the Green Party was founded in West Germany, and across Europe Green Party candidates came to force other politicians to voice their concern for the environment.

Competing voices and the demands of nation building, however, led politicians to push massive and questionable projects such as superhighways and dams. Egypt's Aswan Dam, built in the 1960s, and China's Three Gorges Dam, on which construction began in the 1990s, destroyed miles of villages and farmland and cost thousands of lives even as they produced much-needed hydroelectric power. Chinese Nobel Laureate Gao Xingjian explored questions of ecological disaster, as he described peasant reactions to the destruction and invoked the responsibilities of the human community for the earth's well-being in his novel *Soul Mountain* (2000). Gao had been punished more than once during times of political extremism in China, the final time leading to his self-imposed exile, during which he gathered thoughts, stories, and impressions for his novel. Modernizers around the world denounced Gao's work and that of other environmental critics, and there were many attempts to silence protesting voices. In 2007, former U.S. vice president Al Gore

global warming An increase in the temperature of the earth's lower atmosphere, resulting in dramatic weather cycles and melting of glaciers.

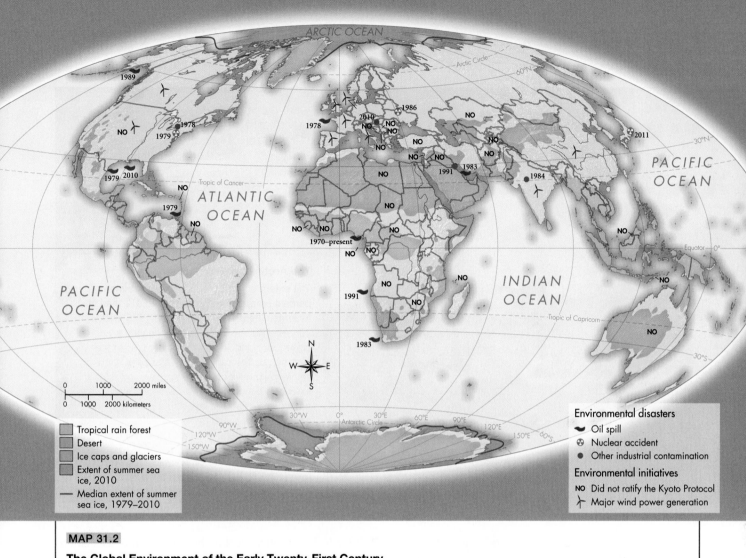

MAP 31.2

The Global Environment of the Early Twenty-First Century

As industry advanced and population grew, the earth itself came under assault. Degradation of the environment— including desertification (the transformation of formerly agrarian land into desert), depletion of rain forests, climate extremes, industrial catastrophes, and other changes caused by humans—threatened the sustainability of life.

won the Nobel Peace Prize for his fight to relieve the environmental crisis—"a moral and spiritual challenge to all of humanity," he called it.

People attacked environmental problems on both the local and global levels. Beginning in 1977, Wangari Maathai (wan-GAH-ree mah-DHEYE) enlisted women to plant trees to create green belts around Kenya's capital city of Nairobi. Born in Kenya, Maathai had studied botany in the United States and then returned to Africa to receive her doctorate in veterinary medicine. Local deforestation led her to take action and create a citizens' movement. "It's important for people to see that they are part of the environment and that they take responsibility for it," she explained. Maathai's project went against the wishes of powerful politicians and business people, who had her beaten up and run out of the country. Maathai returned, more powerful than ever, and in 2004 won the Nobel Peace Prize for her efforts to improve the environment and livelihoods of Africans.[12]

Frankfurt, Germany, and other European cities developed car-free zones. In Paris, when pollution reached dangerous levels, cars were banned. The Smart, a very small car using reduced amounts of fuel, became a popular way for Europeans to cut their use of fossil fuels. Cities also developed bicycle lanes on major city streets. Germany, Spain, the

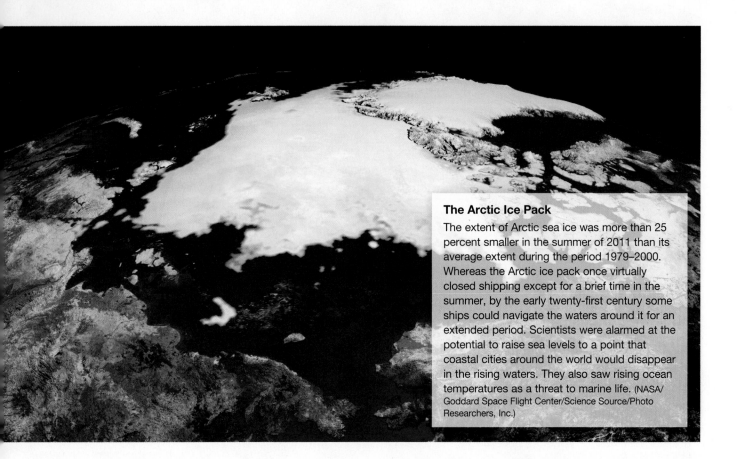

The Arctic Ice Pack

The extent of Arctic sea ice was more than 25 percent smaller in the summer of 2011 than its average extent during the period 1979–2000. Whereas the Arctic ice pack once virtually closed shipping except for a brief time in the summer, by the early twenty-first century some ships could navigate the waters around it for an extended period. Scientists were alarmed at the potential to raise sea levels to a point that coastal cities around the world would disappear in the rising waters. They also saw rising ocean temperatures as a threat to marine life. (NASA/ Goddard Space Flight Center/Science Source/Photo Researchers, Inc.)

United States, Denmark, and China had some 80 percent of the world's wind installations to generate electricity in 2005, and in 2007 China and the United States led in the creation of new capacity. By 2007 some one hundred ninety countries had signed and ratified the **Kyoto Protocol**, an international treaty fashioned in 1997 to reduce the level of emissions of greenhouse gases and other pollutants around the world. Even though the United States refused to ratify the agreement, much of the rest of the world began working to preserve the environment (see again Map 31.2).

Population Pressures and Public Health

Nations with less-developed economies struggled with the pressing problem of rapidly rising population. The causes of the population surge were complex. By 1995 Europe was actually experiencing negative growth (that is, more deaths than births), but less industrially developed countries accounted for 98 percent of worldwide population growth, in part because the spread of medicine enabled people there to live much longer than before. By late 2011, the earth's population had reached 7 billion and by 2050 was projected to reach 8 to 10 billion (see Map 31.3).

Life Expectancy and Birthrates

Life expectancy globally rose by an average of sixteen years between 1950 and 1980. The world's sole remaining superpower did not fare particularly well by this measure of social health: by 2009, the United States had fallen to fiftieth place in average life expectancy, below Albania and Puerto Rico. However, life expectancy in Russia and its former satellites was catastrophic, falling from a peak of seventy years for Russian men in the mid-1970s to fifty-three in 1995 and to fifty-one at the beginning of the twenty-first century. Although birthrates in nonindustrial countries were much higher than in industrialized ones, overall birthrates were rapidly declining, leading to great uncertainty in forecasting population growth. These rates had been dropping in the West for decades, and by 1995

Kyoto Protocol An international treaty fashioned in 1997 to reduce emissions of pollutants around the world.

they had also begun to fall in the less economically developed world, where an estimated 58 percent of couples used birth control.

Non-Western governments were alarmed at their nation's rising population and took action. In 1979 Deng introduced the idea of a one-child policy for urban Chinese families, with a considerable number of exceptions. Chinese families had their own methods of population control, mostly focused on female infanticide. Finding that its population was growing rapidly, the Iranian government under Ayatollah Khomeini at first welcomed robust growth as strengthening Islam, but by the 1990s the government was urging families to space their children: the birthrate fell from 6.5 live births per Iranian woman in the 1970s to below 2 in 2010. For a time in the 1970s, the Indian government used a policy of forced sterilization; its recent stress on voluntary family planning has kept population growth at a high level. Yet family planning appeared in unexpected places: mullahs in Afghanistan studied the problems of population. "If you have too many children and you can't control them," one reported after a class on birth control, "that's bad for Islam."[13]

Vaccines and drugs for diseases such as malaria and smallpox helped improve health in developing nations. However, half of all Africans lacked access to basic public health facilities such as safe drinking water. Drought and poverty, along with political machinations in some cases, spread famine in Sudan, Somalia, Ethiopia, and elsewhere. In the West, specialists performed heart bypass surgery, transplanted organs, and treated cancer with radiation and chemotherapy, while preventive care for the masses received less attention. Wealthy people traveled the globe to find the best medical treatment, but although the poor and unemployed suffered more chronic illnesses than those who were better off, they received less care. The distribution of health services was a hotly debated issue.

In the early 1980s, technological expertise was challenged by the spread of a global epidemic disease: acquired immunodeficiency syndrome (AIDS), caused by human immune deficiency virus (HIV). A deadly disease that shuts down the body's entire immune system, AIDS is transmitted through contact with bodily fluid (blood or semen) of an infected person. The disease initially afflicted heterosexuals in central Africa; later it turned up in Haitian immigrants to the United States and in homosexual men worldwide. The disease spread quickly among the heterosexual populations of Africa and Asia. Action against AIDS was often sporadic, targeting the wrong audiences, and in some cases the disease was even dismissed as nonexistent. The government of Vietnam launched a dramatic campaign, with

Population Control

Medical Treatment

HIV/AIDS

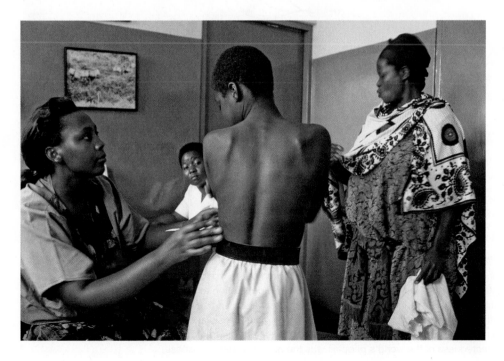

Treatment of AIDS in Uganda

Even as many Africans gained professional and technological expertise and as the continent's nations participated in the global economy, health remained a burning issue in the twenty-first century. Many diseases that had been eradicated elsewhere in the world still threatened the continent's population. Alongside the ravages of civil wars and genocide and the migration that followed, Africans also attempted to address the AIDS pandemic, often through the mobilization of local unions, doctors and nurses, and activists. (Véronique Burger/Photo Researchers, Inc.)

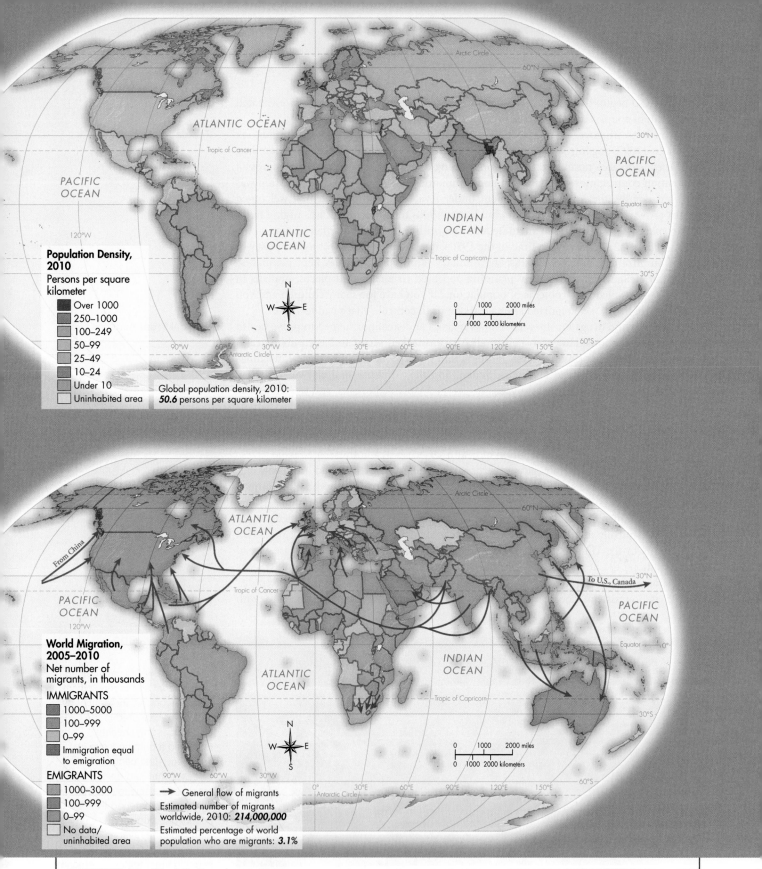

Population Density, 2010

Persons per square kilometer

- Over 1000
- 250–1000
- 100–249
- 50–99
- 25–49
- 10–24
- Under 10
- Uninhabited area

Global population density, 2010: **50.6** persons per square kilometer

World Migration, 2005–2010

Net number of migrants, in thousands

IMMIGRANTS
- 1000–5000
- 100–999
- 0–99
- Immigration equal to emigration

EMIGRANTS
- 1000–3000
- 100–999
- 0–99
- No data/ uninhabited area

→ General flow of migrants

Estimated number of migrants worldwide, 2010: **214,000,000**

Estimated percentage of world population who are migrants: **3.1%**

From China

To U.S., Canada

MAP 31.3 **The World's Peoples, c. 2010**

Migration, disease, and global religions contributed to the integration of the world's peoples in the early twenty-first century. Rising life expectancy caused the world's population to surge to 7 billion in late 2011, which led many people to migrate in search of opportunity and living space. Most of these migrants brought with them their ideas and traditions, including religious beliefs and practices, making their new homelands more culturally rich and diverse. A frightening and often tragic result of globalization and the interconnectedness of the world's peoples was the global spread of disease.

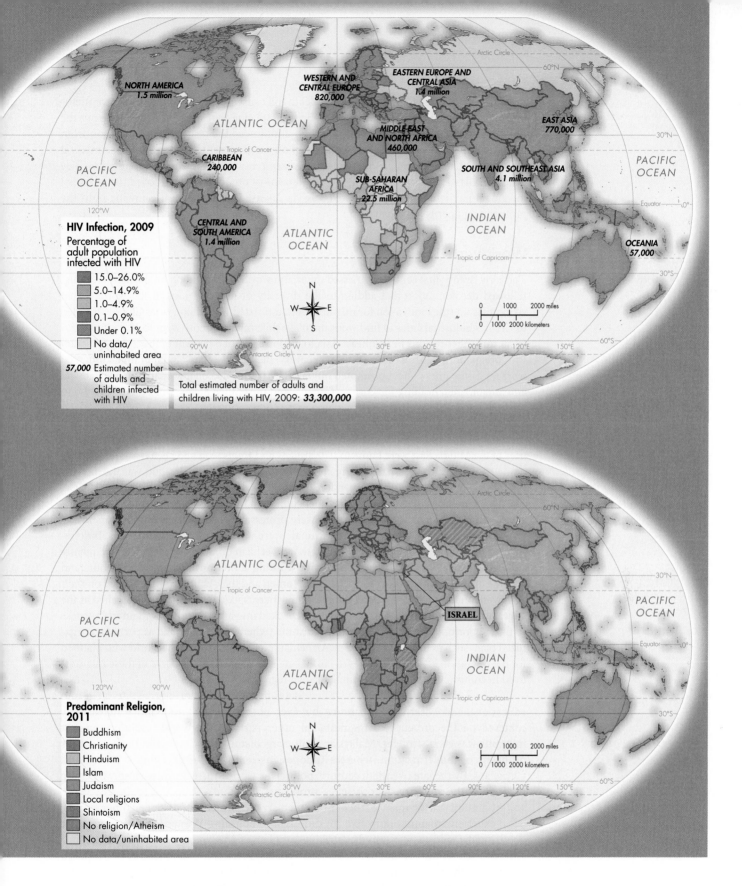

HIV Infection, 2009

NORTH AMERICA
1.5 million

WESTERN AND
CENTRAL EUROPE
820,000

EASTERN EUROPE AND
CENTRAL ASIA
1.4 million

EAST ASIA
770,000

MIDDLE EAST
AND NORTH AFRICA
460,000

CARIBBEAN
240,000

SUB-SAHARAN
AFRICA
22.5 million

SOUTH AND SOUTHEAST ASIA
4.1 million

CENTRAL AND
SOUTH AMERICA
1.4 million

OCEANIA
57,000

Percentage of
adult population
infected with HIV

- 15.0–26.0%
- 5.0–14.9%
- 1.0–4.9%
- 0.1–0.9%
- Under 0.1%
- No data/
  uninhabited area

57,000 Estimated number
of adults and
children infected
with HIV

Total estimated number of adults and
children living with HIV, 2009: **33,300,000**

**Predominant Religion,
2011**

- Buddhism
- Christianity
- Hinduism
- Islam
- Judaism
- Local religions
- Shintoism
- No religion/Atheism
- No data/uninhabited area

ISRAEL

posters blanketing public space that blared "Do not use or accept harmful cultural products. Do not become addicted to smoking or injecting drugs." In fact, the major culprits for the spread of AIDS in Vietnam were privileged and sexually adventurous public officials.

By 2010, no cure had yet been discovered, though strong drugs that alleviated the symptoms had been developed (see again Map 31.3). Activists in Africa and Asia raised their voices louder still, protesting that these costly drugs existed but only the lives of white victims were being saved. The mounting death toll caused some to call AIDS the twentieth-century version of the Black Death, the bubonic plague that ravaged Eurasia during the fourteenth century. In 2005 Nelson Mandela announced the death of his grown son from AIDS in hope that such publicity would help advance prevention and encourage medical attention. AIDS was not the only epidemic disease ravaging the world's population. The deadly Ebola virus, bird flu, swine flu, and dozens of other viruses harbored the potential for global pandemics. Interconnectedness via disease was all too real, showing both the promises and perils of globalization.

Worldwide Migration

Motives for Migration

The early twenty-first century witnessed migration worldwide, building on the migration that followed decolonization and adding to the diversity of many regions of the world. Often economics was the motivation for migration. An estimated 190 million rural Chinese traveled to China's industrial cities to find work in 2004, while millions more went to Malaysia, Indonesia, and other regions in Southeast Asia to get jobs. About 5 percent of the U.S. population was foreign born in the early twenty-first century, including some 11 million undocumented workers. Sometimes danger prompted migration. Africans fled civil wars in Rwanda, Congo, and Sudan, often heading for Europe, Canada, and the United States, while an easier path to safety led people in the more southerly regions of the continent to migrate to South Africa. Civil wars and ethnic oppression drove civilians from states of the former Soviet Union and its satellites to Germany, Scandinavia, Austria, France, and England. Jordan and other countries of the Middle East were home to Palestinians and Iraqis who had been driven from their homelands by violence. A particularly abhorrent form of coerced migration was the increasing trafficking in children and women for sexual and other kinds of forced labor.

Conditions of Migration

The conditions of migration varied depending on one's class, gender, and regional origin. Among the most fortunate migrants were professionals and talented innovators in science and technology. Among the less fortunate were women from the Philippines, Indonesia, and other southern regions who migrated to perform domestic service. They frequently suffered rape by their employers, oppressive working conditions including long hours and no time off, and confiscation of their wages. Women and their children who escaped on their own were often unprotected from exploitation, whereas men and women alike waited at the edges of deserts such as the Sahara or traveled packed into airless storage containers in trucks to find opportunity or to escape political turmoil. Other people migrated as part of an organized plan, such as those of Chinese or Armenian merchants around the world who planned for the migration of young relatives to participate in trade or services. Most of these migrants lived in communities of people from their own region or ethnicity.

The diverse population of the United States made it easier for migrants to meld into educational and workforce institutions, but even in the United States politics increasingly centered on the presence of migrants. In other parts of the world, prejudice against migrants was even stronger. Malaysian politicians blamed the Chinese in their midst for problems of modernization, whereas Indonesians rampaged against both Chinese and Christians. By the late twentieth century, politicians worldwide won votes simply by citing migrants as the source of their societies' problems.

The Literature of Migration

Migration stories, many of them best sellers, related dreams of magnetic other worlds, often experienced amid oppressive conditions. The appeal of Western culture, consumer goods, and democracy inspired a striking number of these. Expatriate Russian author Andrei Makine, who emigrated to France, produced lyrical accounts of Soviet people in Siberia and their powerful imaginings of a better world. *Once Upon the River Love* (1998) recounts the fantasies of a group of Siberian teens who see a French adventure film and begin to dream of Western women and life in western Europe. In this tale, the teenagers' later lives outside of the USSR are bleak and even bitterly disillusioning. *Reading Lolita in Tehran* (2003), a memoir by Iranian author Azar Nafisi, who published her book after emigrating to the United States, and *Balzac and the Little Chinese Seamstress* (2003) by Dai

Sijie, a Chinese refugee in Europe, detail the powerful influence of Western literature under conditions of oppression. Nafisi, who left her post at a Tehran university during the Iranian theocracy, writes of bringing a group of young women to her home to read forbidden literature. As they read, both teacher and students discover that forbidden works contain beauty, values, and examples of personal courage. The two young men in Sijie's novel are banished to the countryside during China's Cultural Revolution and discover there a supply of nineteenth-century Western classics.

Terrorism Confronts the World

Even as insightful literature served as a force for global understanding, the world's people also experienced their interconnectedness in terrifying ways as radicals began to use violence rather than peaceful protests or regular politics to accomplish their goals. Many such radicals came from countries with dictatorships or dysfunctional democracies, but others simply saw violent tactics as a more effective means to publicize their cause. In the 1970s, terrorist bands in Europe, such as Italy's Red Brigades, responded to the restoration of political order after 1968 with kidnappings, bank robberies, bombings, and assassinations. In 1972, Palestinian terrorists kidnapped and murdered eleven Israeli athletes at the Olympic Games in Munich. The terrorists demanded the release of Palestinian prisoners held in Israeli jails. After Bloody Sunday (January 30, 1972) in Northern Ireland, when British troops fired on unarmed civil rights demonstrators, a cycle of violence ensued that left thousands dead. Protestants, fearful of losing their dominant position, battled a reinvigorated Irish Republican Army, which carried out bombings and assassinations to end the oppression of the Catholic minority in Northern Ireland and reunite Northern Ireland with the Republic of Ireland.

Terrorists aimed at the highest levels of government and at ordinary people alike. Prime Minister Indira Gandhi was assassinated by her Sikh security guards in 1984 after the Indian government attacked a Sikh temple; Tamil separatists from Sri Lanka assassinated Indira Gandhi's son Rajiv for his lack of support for their independence in 1991; antigovernment U.S. terrorists blew up a government building in Oklahoma City in 1995; in the same year Japanese religious radicals released deadly poisonous gas in the Tokyo subway system to promote their beliefs; in 2011 a Norwegian fundamentalist Christian and anti-Muslim extremist massacred close to eighty young political activists and wounded hundreds more.

Terrorism began to play an ever-larger role in world politics. Although it appeared that growing belief in religion, nationalism, and the power of oil would naturally make the Middle East a leader in the preservation of international order, the charismatic leaders of the 1980s and 1990s—Iran's Ayatollah Ruhollah Khomeini, Libya's Muammar Qaddafi, Iraq's Saddam Hussein, and Osama bin Laden, leader of the Al Qaeda transnational terrorist organization—all used violence to gain leverage. Throughout the 1980s and 1990s, terrorists from the Middle East and North Africa planted bombs in many European cities, blew up European airplanes, and bombed the Paris subway system—among other acts. Some attacks were said to be punishment for the West's support for both Israel and repressive regimes in the Middle East. **Terrorism and the Middle East**

On September 11, 2001, Middle Eastern militants hijacked four planes in the United States and flew two of them into the World Trade Center in New York and one into the Pentagon in Virginia. The fourth plane crashed in Pennsylvania. The hijackers, most of whom were from Saudi Arabia, were inspired by Osama bin Laden, who was supported by the United States during the Cold War but now wanted U.S. military forces removed from Saudi Arabia. The loss of some three thousand lives led the United States to declare a "war against terrorism." **September 11, 2001**

Global cooperation followed the September 11 attacks and the continuing lethal bombings around the world. European countries rounded up terrorists and conducted the first successful trials of them in the spring of 2003. Ultimately, Western cooperation fragmented when the United States invaded Iraq in March 2003, claiming falsely that Iraq's Saddam Hussein had weapons of mass destruction and suggesting ties between Saddam Hussein and Al Qaeda, bin Laden's terrorist group (see Map 31.4). Great Britain, Spain, and Poland were among those who joined the U.S. invasion, but Germany, Russia, and **U.S. Invasion of Iraq**

MAP 31.4

Wars in Afghanistan and Iraq, 2001–2011

In the aftermath of the terrorist attack on the United States on September 11, 2001, the U.S. government, with the help of Western allies and the Northern Alliance of Afghani groups, launched an attack on the Taliban. This group had taken control of Afghanistan in the wake of the Soviet withdrawal and supported the Al Qaeda terrorist group behind "9/11." In 2003, the United States and its allies invaded Iraq on the grounds that it had weapons of mass destruction—which was not true. Both wars caused tens of thousands of deaths and produced millions of refugees.

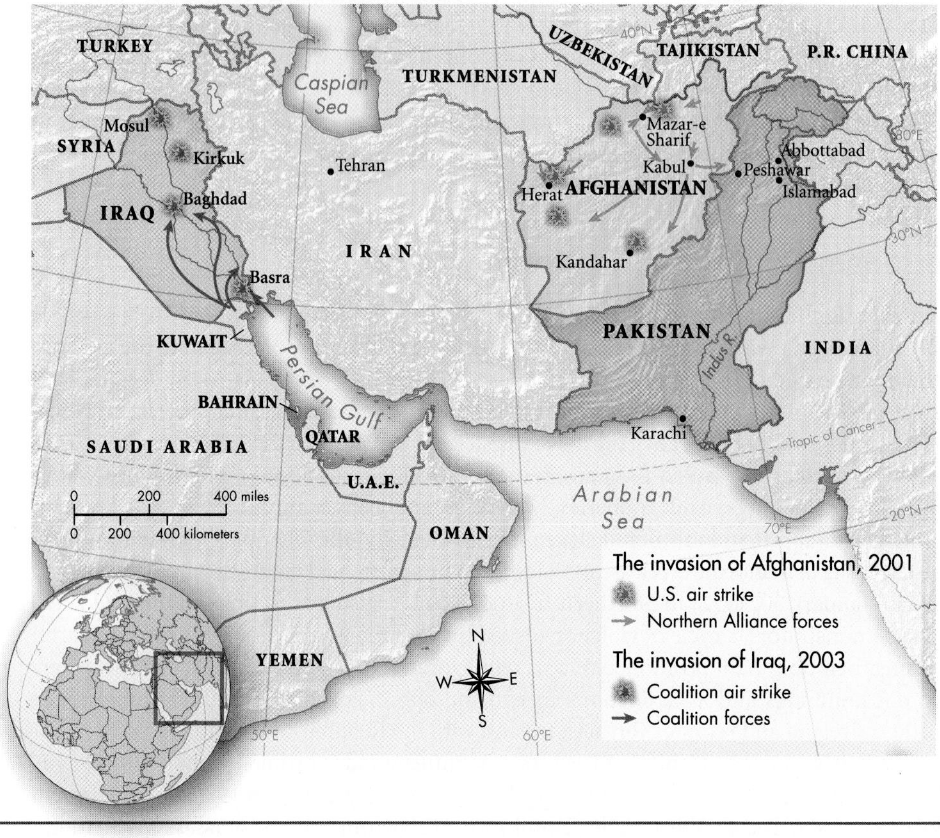

France refused. The public in much of the world accused the United States of becoming a world military dictatorship to preserve its only value—wasteful consumerism. Supporters of the invasion countercharged that Europeans were too selfish in their enjoyment of democracy and creature comforts to protect freedom under attack. The Spanish withdrew from the U.S. occupation of Iraq after Al Qaeda–linked terrorists bombed four commuter trains in Spain on March 11, 2004. The British reeled too, when terrorists left bombs in three subway cars and a bus in July 2005. In 2011 American forces scored a symbolic victory in the "war against terror" through the capture and execution of Osama bin Laden. Nonetheless, as the wars in Iraq and Afghanistan continued into the second decade of the twenty-first century, terrorism became an additional ingredient in the globalization of warfare.

Terrorism in the twenty-first century knew no bounds. Chechens protested the Russian destruction of their country by bombing Moscow apartment buildings, blowing up packed buses and airplanes, and taking hundreds of hostages, including schoolchildren. In Bali, terrorists blew up nightclubs and resorts, while in Jordan Al Qaeda suicide bombers slaughtered wedding guests. Alongside the many promises of globalization—including the rich mixture of peoples and cultures and the victory for democracy wrought by people like Nelson Mandela—was the incredible toll in lives taken by terrorism, civil wars and genocide, disease, and other instruments of death around the globe.

The Promise of Arab Spring

Even as terrorism continued, a new manifestation of antigovernment sentiment appeared that brought hope and promise throughout the Middle East. In late 2010, an "Arab Spring" began in a series of popular uprisings, some of which forced dictators in North Africa and the Middle East to step down in favor of democracies and representative government. Uprisings in Tunisia, Egypt, and Libya succeeded, even in the face of brutal repression. In Egypt, long-time dictator Hosni Mubarak was forced from power and put on trial for the murder of many protesters. Hard on the heels of the Egyptian success, protest mounted against dictators in Libya and Syria, with NATO planes helping the Libyan rebels defeat Muammar Qaddafi.

Hopes for a speedy transition to a full-blown democracy in liberated countries were not high. Working against representative institutions and civil rights were two facts: dictators had prevented the institutions of civil society, including open debate, from developing; in their place tribal organizations often controlled decision-making. However, others who saw a more hopeful future in the near-term pointed to the sophisticated means by which protesters had mobilized: they used features of the World Wide Web such as e-mail and social networking to create meeting points and devise strategies. The protesters were relatively peaceful, unless governments fought back, forcing protesters to defend themselves. Even as the situation often appeared chaotic and uncontrolled in the face of government repression, in fact, the promise of the Arab Spring was not just in its accomplishments but in the "virtual" societies young and older citizens had constructed through technology. The Arab Spring may have looked rough and ragged, but it showed the ever-changing capacities that can be brought to bear on human problems.

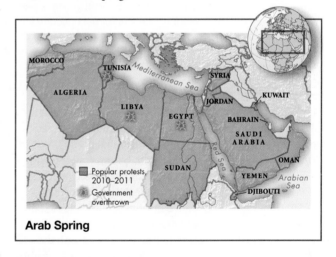

Arab Spring

Global Economic Crisis

Globalization meant tighter financial connections and a faster pace of doing business. As the twenty-first century opened, the global economy suffered a series of shocks, followed by the bursting in 2008 of a real estate bubble in the United States. Housing prices had escalated because of mortgage financing available on easy or even dishonest terms. Then, financiers distributed this often fraudulent debt around the world to those who hoped to make handsome profits because adjustable mortgage rates were set to rise dramatically. When people became unable to repay their rising debt, including credit card debt, credit became unavailable both to ordinary people and to banks and industry. A credit collapse followed, just as it had in the stock market collapse of 1929 (see Chapter 28). Banks and industries became insolvent, and governments around the world tried to prop them up with the infusion of billions of dollars. Unemployment rose as businesses and consumers alike stopped purchasing goods. Although by late 2009 Pacific economies had returned to growth, in 2011 European governments including Greece, Italy, and Spain faced possible bankruptcy. The globalization of economic crises remained yet another peril faced by the world's population.

Readers of the Qur'an

Readers of the Qur'an in Kazan, Russia

Despite the Soviet Union's official policy of atheism, Kazan has remained a center of Islamic culture and practice. It is the site of magnificent mosques and hosts expert readings of the Qur'an. In this 2008 photograph, a reader participates in a Qur'an reading contest, in which young experts from across Russia vie with one another for the best and truest performance. Although this contest is a national one, echoing secular contests in music, beauty, and even game shows, Islam remains a powerful global religion with a rising number of believers. (RIA Novosti/The Image Works.)

Among the most popular and prestigious stars in the global media are those who chant the Qur'an on cassettes, CDs, and radio. Specially trained and tested Qur'an reciters—literally thousands of them—make their recordings in dozens of cities in the Islamic world, but only after being certified to do so by official examining boards. The apprenticeship is arduous, for readers must know the Qur'an to perfection, because errors such as stopping in the middle of a word would mar recipients' understanding of the holy words of Allah as handed down through the Prophet Muhammad. Cassettes allow the Qur'an to inspire Muslims at home or work; for example, a carpenter in Cairo keeps his tape playing during the day. "I have two ears," the carpenter reports, "one for work, and one for listening to the Qur'an." Readings of the Qur'an can make up a third of sales by record companies, and cell phones now deliver Qur'an readings.

Although most reciters of the Qur'an are men, one of the best known is Maria Ulfah, a reciter from Indonesia.

Taught as a child that men and women are equal, she has traveled to many parts of the world to read. Like Ulfah, well-loved readers of the Qur'an become celebrities. In Egypt Sheik Mohammed Gebriel is the most appreciated; listeners immediately recognize his voice. He is known to bring in crowds of over half a million when reading in public. "When I hear Sheik Gebriel, I feel that the angels are reading with him," a retired army officer said.

Despite the standardization involved in procedures for certification, the reading of the Qur'an and the issuing of calls to prayer five times a day have their variations according to region and language. Muslims in Kenya, for example, prefer the sounds of the call to prayer by their country's readers to those recorded in Egypt. Saudis object to musical recitations of the Qur'an, preferring those that are direct and plain-spoken. Recordings by the thousands of reciters show, in fact, differences and nuances by region that are welcome to local worshipers, again proving that even in the face of standardization and globalization at the highest levels of religion and faith, local identities remain both powerful and important to carrying out one's daily life. "You can get bored by a song in a few days," a record store owner said in analyzing the popularity of cassettes of the Qur'an, "but no one gets bored listening to the Qur'an."

QUESTIONS TO CONSIDER

1. In the case of the Qur'an in people's lives, what has been the effect of modern communications technology?

2. How would you describe the role of the reciter of the Qur'an in modern society? Is he or she a religious leader, service worker, or media personality?

3. Over time, what has been the effect of books, television, CDs, and other media on religion generally?

For Further Information:
Douglas Jehl, "Above the City's Din, Always the Voice of Allah," *New York Times International*, March 6, 1996.
    Ali Asani lecture, November 2005.
Qur'an Explorer (recordings of recitations of the Qur'an in several languages, including Arabic, Urdu, and
    English). http://www.quranexplorer.com/.
Qur'an Reciters, including images of especially important reciters of the past. http://www.quranreciters.com/wp/.

Cultures Without Borders

In the global age, positive cultural values such as the quest for human rights began to mature. Communication and more extensive contact allowed widespread sharing and enjoyment of the world's cultural accomplishments in literature, art, and music. The global age, for all its deadly flaws, was rich in possibilities for improving human life and connecting people around the world.

> **FOCUS**
> What trends suggest that globalization has led to a new mixing of cultures?

The Quest for Human Rights

At the end of the twentieth century, human rights constituted a newly invigorated global value supported by people from many countries and traditions. Notions of human rights as transnational guarantees of just treatment for all people had grown up gradually over the course of the twentieth century. The idea of human rights as transcending any individual government's policies—that is, as being universal and not limited to citizens of a particular nation-state—emerged powerfully with the creation of supranational bodies such as the United Nations. In 1948 the General Assembly of the United Nations adopted a Declaration of Human Rights, which proclaimed the inalienable rights and fundamental freedoms of all people, including the rights to life, liberty, security, and equal protection of the law. In 1975 the Helsinki Accords, part of a series of agreements between the two sides in the Cold War, acknowledged Soviet gains in World War II in exchange for Soviet endorsement of human rights. This commitment to human rights, at first a pro forma statement, became central to dissidents within the Soviet bloc, and with globalization, it became a lynchpin of international activism. Some critics denounced the accords as simply another ploy for powers in the north to interfere in the political affairs of people from the south—a powerful critique once the United States began using torture during its war on terrorism.

Human Rights as a Global Value

Human rights activists found much to correct in the world around them, and after the 1970s they were better organized globally to take action. Human rights activists spoke out against the genocide in Rwanda and the former Yugoslavia in the 1990s, and the international community joined them in backing prosecution for these crimes in the International Tribunal at The Hague. Human rights activists investigated other abuses, such as violations of political freedoms, immunity from violence and torture, and the guarantee of food, clothing, and shelter. Activists protested the torture of prisoners in Turkey and the trial of Turkish novelist Orhan Pamuk for asserting Turkey's role in the Armenian genocide of 1915–1917. Latin American governments and China also wracked up long lists of abuses, which human rights activists publicized, often at their own peril. They targeted powerful leaders such as Russian president Vladimir Putin, who closed down independent television stations and imprisoned critics. Human rights activists were suppressed and sometimes murdered for speaking out. Shirin Ebadi, an Iranian lawyer who won the Nobel Peace Prize in 2005 for her human rights activism, was constantly attacked by the government; her offices were raided in December 2008 for tax fraud, even though she did not charge those she defended. Political opponents of Belarus's president Aleksandr Lukashenko, including young demonstrators on behalf of human rights, were murdered or beaten.

Targeting Human Rights Abuses

Religion Worldwide

Many religions surrendered any national identity and sought out the faithful globally. Roman Catholicism had more adherents in Latin America and Africa than in its western European heartland, where many had embraced secularism. Beginning in the 1970s, Roman Catholic popes—most notably John Paul II—traveled widely to almost every corner of the world. Although some believers found the church's message against homosexuals, birth control, and abortion distasteful, Catholic clergy, such as the nuns assassinated in Brazil or Rwanda, gained a strong record as advocates for the poor around the world. They were said to practice "liberation theology," which stressed bringing Christian compassion

Growth of World Religions

to those suffering—wherever they lived. The Buddhist sect Soka Gakkai, once identified with its Japanese origins, also had a far-flung global membership, with more than a million adherents each in Brazil and South Korea and major followings in New York, Los Angeles, Sydney, and many other parts of the world. Soka Gakkai precepts include chanting for specific goals, most important among them world peace, compassion for others, and respect for all human life. The sect sponsored cultural events, hosted conferences for women, and supported environmental protection movements, thereby, like the Catholic Church, promoting transnational values and good works.

Spread of Islam

Islam also expanded worldwide, becoming the world's second-largest faith after Christianity (see again Map 31.3). Although Muslims held Mecca and Medina in Saudi Arabia in special regard as the birthplace of their faith, the population center of Islam by the late twentieth century lay in a more easterly direction, falling on a line from eastern Pakistan through western India. As many Muslims lived east of that line, in centers such as Jakarta and Kuala Lumpur, as lived west of it in Cairo and Istanbul. While practicing the Five Pillars of their faith, including charitable giving, Muslims embraced a wide variety of interpretations of Islam. In the 1990s, young Turkish people, raised with the nation's republican and secular beliefs, began to follow "green pop" stars and to read "green romances"—green being the color of paradise in the Muslim faith. While enjoying gossip, jokes, and the company of their best friends, young women decided to wear headscarves and follow the call to prayer, maintaining "we pray like you have fun."[14] Islam spread to the New World, and places where it had mostly been rejected, such as Europe, included centers of Islamic faith. Muslims also recruited members globally, often using sophisticated techniques based on marketing and demographic knowledge (see Lives and Livelihoods: Readers of the Qur'an).

Global Literature and Music

The Boom in Latin American Literature

A crucial ingredient of globalization was the deepening relationship among cultures as books and music from many different national traditions gained a worldwide audience. Latin American authors, for example, developed a style known as magical realism, which melded everyday events with elements of Latin American history, myth, magic, and religion. The novels of Colombian-born Nobel Prize winner Gabriel García Márquez were translated into dozens of languages. His lush fantasies, including *One Hundred Years of Solitude* (1967), *Love in the Time of Cholera* (1988), and many later works, portray people of titanic ambitions and passions who endure war and all manner of personal trials. García Márquez described the tradition of dictators in Latin America, but he also emphasized the legacy of business imperialism. *One Hundred Years of Solitude*, for example, closes with the machine-gunning in 1928 of thousands of workers at the request of the U.S. United Fruit firm because they asked for a single day off per week and breaks to use the toilet. Five years of rain flood the region, erasing all trace of the slaughter, even from local memory. Wherever they lived, readers snapped up the book, which sold 30 million copies worldwide. A host of other outstanding novels in the magical realism tradition followed, including Laura Esquivel's *Like Water for Chocolate* (1989). In the 1990s the work was translated into two dozen languages and became a hit film. Set in a Mexican kitchen during the revolution of 1910, it intertwines such themes as cooking, sexuality, and brutality.

The Latin American "boom," as it was called, continued into the early twenty-first century, with innumerable authors writing in the style of Márquez and his predecessor, Jorge Luis Borges (see Chapter 29). While acknowledging these geniuses, younger novelists such as Chilean-born Roberto Bolaño questioned the right of literary-minded people to focus on aesthetics amid the brutal dictatorships, torture, and poverty that were so powerful a part of Latin American reality.

Cultural Challenges to Traditional Values

In a global age, the power of literature seemed magnified because it challenged deeply held local beliefs and widespread values. Some writers faced real danger for producing controversial works: García Márquez went into hiding from time to time and rode in a bullet- and bomb-proof car. Feminist authors were menaced and even exiled from Pakistan and other countries that felt threatened by works describing women's oppression and calling for women's equality. Egyptian feminist, medical doctor, and writer Nawal El Saadawi was criticized for producing accounts of women's plight in the region. Her opponents charged her with trying to appeal to Westerners with chilling stories of abuse and backwards customs. Indian-born Salman Rushdie, who had settled in Great Britain, produced *Midnight's Children* (1981), a novel whose fantastic characters formed part of Rushdie's fictional depiction of India's history and whose style was influenced by the magical realism of Latin American authors. Rushdie's novel *The Satanic Verses* (1988) ignited outrage among Muslims around the world because it appeared to blaspheme the Prophet Muhammad. Banned in South Africa and India, the book led to riots worldwide. In 1989 Iran's Ayatollah Khomeini issued a fatwa, or edict, promising both a monetary reward and salvation in the afterlife to anyone who would assassinate the writer. In the 1990s Rushdie went into hiding, but assassins succeeded in murdering his Japanese and Italian translators. The conflict over *The Satanic Verses* reflected a "clash of civilizations," pitting the right to free speech against the right not to have one's religion slandered.

Popular music also flourished in the global marketplace. Pop musicians mixed styles from all over the world, and people brought their music with them as they migrated. Hip-hop, rap, and salsa music, for example, combined African, Latin American, and African American traditions into new musical genres. African hip-hop artists claimed hip-hop and rap as part of an African heritage based on the poet singers, or griots, who for centuries had lyrically recited history and legends. In 1988 the South African group Black Noise produced the region's modern version of rap, and they participated in the antiapartheid movement. Other groups from East Africa rapped about the problems of HIV/AIDS and the urban crime that ruined many of their neighbors' lives. Hip-hop and rap music circled the world, soaking up influences from various cultures. Salsa music did likewise, flourishing not just in Latin America and the Caribbean, but also in the United States as more Hispanics migrated there. African influences shaped salsa too via the slave heritage of the Western Hemisphere. Countries made their own adaptations of musical styles, but the mixing of global styles remained constant, especially as promoters sought new products and novel sounds to sell globally.

Contemporary popular music was the music of diasporas as the world's peoples migrated and interacted with others. Raï, the popular music of North African cities, echoed in the Algerian suburbs of Paris, and performances by raï stars attracted tens of thousands of fans. Dangdut, a form of popular music in Indonesia, used tunes from Bollywood film while its lyrics expressed Islamic values—the combination appealing to diasporas in the world's largest Islamic state. "Chutney" generally described the fusion music of the Caribbean, but particularly the influence of the many South Asian indentured workers who settled there in the nineteenth and early twentieth centuries. As with political and economic institutions, the globalization of people's lives made literary and musical culture a dense crossroad of influences.

Global Pop Culture

Inul Daratista, a sensation in Indonesia and beyond for her singing and dancing performances, blends Indian, Middle Eastern, Malay, and Portuguese styles into unique rock routines. Inul's body moves sensuously and rapidly, and Muslim clergy object to her lack of modesty. The controversy is reminiscent of Elvis Presley's notoriety back in the 1950s in the West, but some see her moves as looking simply like sped-up aerobics, albeit with many Indian and Indonesian gestures. Although Inul Daratista's "dangdut" music originates in folk performances, she has made it not just a local but a global phenomenon. (BAZUKI MUHAMMAD/Reuters/Corbis.)

COUNTERPOINT
Who Am I? Local Identity in a Globalizing World

FOCUS

How have peoples sought to establish and maintain distinctive local personal identities in today's global age?

As globalization linked the world's people in multiple ways, individuals also claimed local, personal identities as a counterpoint to the globalizing trend. Traditionally, individuals took their identities from families, villages, and eventually nation-states. The advance of globalization produced both a sense of loss and a feeling that something other than global forces and even nation-states was needed to provide values. People sought various ways to proclaim their personal identities: through local religious customs or by emphasizing age-old local traditions of dress, food, and celebration. Personal identity also developed through showing loyalty to local sports teams, despite the fact that many such teams were allied with global business, including television networks and marketers of consumer goods.

Ethnic Strife and New Nations

One countermovement to globalization aimed at empowering smaller units of political alliance. Such groups as the Tamils in Sri Lanka and Sikhs in India struggled for autonomy for their people, threatening nation-states with fragmentation. These groups did not achieve their aims. However, by 2000 there were more nations than there were at the end of World War II in 1945. This was not only because of decolonization but because the rising tide of ethnic distinctiveness divided some countries. Since 1990, twenty-nine new nations have been born, including South Sudan in 2011. Yugoslavia splintered into several states in bloody civil wars among ethnic groups, including Serbs, Bosnians, Croatians, and Slovenians. New Asian states such as Kazakhstan and Uzbekistan came into being when they separated from Russia.

Activists also worked to assert regional autonomy, fostering movements for the independence of Quebec from Canada. Basques assassinated tourists, police, and other public servants in their quest for independence from Spain. Many a politician found campaigning for ethnic secession to be the path to public office.

Movements to Protect Tradition

The desire to maintain a local identity also encompassed the movement to preserve local customs and practices, including some of the world's thousands of languages, which were under threat of being swallowed up by Chinese, Hindi, Spanish, and English. In January 2005 Guatemalan forces killed a Maya-Kakchiquel man who sought to block a global mining firm's inroads into his community. At issue in hundreds of other similar protests across Central America was the preservation of local customs and traditional rights, including age-old rights to specific plots of land and sources of water. In late 1993 a group of activists in the Chiapas state of Mexico declared themselves a local liberation army devoted to stanching the "bleeding" of their locality by stopping the flow of oil, coffee, bananas, and other resources out of the area, leaving the local people destitute. These activists, known as the Zapatistas (recalling the name of the hero of the 1910 revolution), also decried the decline in the use of their language and the national and international ridicule heaped on their way of life. Many of these Mexicans still worshiped at ancient Maya shrines, just as locally oriented people around the world focused on their own ancient altars. In seeking to preserve their local identity, the activists were similar to the pilgrims in Vietnam, who brought fruit to special shrines around Hanoi so that it could be blessed by local gods. Native Americans in the United States worked to preserve their ancestral burial sites against industrial and agricultural development. The rap group

Local Customs in a Global Age: Mexico
This image from 2004 shows a Mexican father carrying a bouquet to the Holy Death temple in Mexico City as he presents his infant to Mictlantecuhtli and Mictecacihuatl, the "Señor and the Señora" of Mictlan—that is, the region of the dead people. In so doing, he keeps alive an Aztec custom from the fifteenth century, some six hundred years later in a much changed, cosmopolitan world. (AFP/Getty Images.)

Xplastaz in Tanzania promoted the wearing of traditional garb to fight the globalization of clothing that threatened to erase their local culture.

Although the global media have worked to make family life more standardized, individuals continued to take their identities from their families and to promote distinctiveness. They spent more effort to trace their genealogies. Despite high divorce rates, in fact there are more marriages in the twenty-first century than ever before in human history. National politicians often invoke "family values" to get people to vote for them, and in fact daily family life remains for many a shelter for individual identity, just as local activism is a bulwark against global national forces.

Conclusion

"Sometimes I tell myself, I may only be planting a tree here, but just imagine what's happening if there are billions of people out there doing something. Just imagine the power of what we can do." Wangari Maathai's motivation reflected a belief that billions of citizens, acting as individuals, can effect change on a global scale. Innovations in global communications, transportation, migration, and the development of strong transnational organizations have accelerated the pace of globalization in the past four decades. Globalization is evident everywhere: in the worldwide spread of disease and the worldwide consequences of industrialization. It is seen in the spread of campaigns like Nelson Mandela's on behalf of human rights and in dastardly acts of global terrorism.

As the world's peoples come to work on common projects and share elements of one another's cultures, their mental outlook has become more global, more cosmopolitan. The Chinese painter Wu Guanzhong, even after years of repression for his cosmopolitan style, combined elements from around the world in his work. "In my art," Wu said, "I really belonged to a hybridized breed."[15] Many rightly protest that much of value can be lost at the hands of global forces at work in the world today; others foresee some great irreconcilable clash among civilizations. The question remains whether, given the meeting of humans on the world's crossroads, we are not all hybrids—that is, mixtures of one another's thoughts, traditions, cultures, and livelihoods. Isn't this mixture of peoples and cultures what has given texture to the recent history of the world?

NOTES

1. Quoted in *Guardian Weekly*, September 19–25, 2002.
2. Quoted in James C. McKinley, Jr., "Mexican Farmers Protest End of Corn-Import Taxes," *New York Times*, February 1, 2008.
3. Soutik Biswas, "India's Architect of Reforms," *BBC News*, May 22, 2004.
4. Quoted in Yvonne Corcoran-Nantes, "Female Consciousness or Feminist Consciousness: Women's Consciousness-Raising in Community-Based Struggles in Brazil," in *Global Feminisms Since 1945*, ed. Bonnie G. Smith (London: Routledge, 2000), 89.
5. Quoted in Michael Dutton, et al., *Beijing Time* (Cambridge, MA: Harvard University Press, 2008), 10.
6. Saranya Sukumaran, quoted in Saritha Rai, "India Is Regaining Contracts with the U.S.," *New York Times*, December 25, 2002, W7.
7. Georges Quioc, "La 'consomania' de l'Europe de l'Est électrise les distributeurs de l'Ouest," *Le Figaro économie*, January 13, 2003.
8. Quoted in *Le Monde*, June 2, 2002.
9. Quoted in *Le Monde*, January 17, 2003.
10. Quoted in *Libération*, January 20 and 21, 2002.
11. Fourth World Conference on Women Beijing Declaration, 1995. http://www.un.org/womenwatch/daw/beijing/platform/declar.htm.
12. Quoted in "Nobel Peace Prize for Woman of 30m Trees," *The Guardian*, October 9, 2004.
13. Quoted in "At Birth Control Class, Mullahs Face New Reality," *International Herald Tribune*, November 12, 2009.
14. Quoted in Ayse Saktanber, "'We Pray Like You Have Fun': New Islamic Youth in Turkey Between Intellectualism and Popular Culture," in *Fragments of Culture: The Everyday of Modern Turkey* (London: I. B. Tauber, 2006), 254.
15. Wu Guanzhong, "Preface by the Artist," in Anne Farrer, *Wu Guanzhong: A Twentieth-Century Chinese Painter* (London: British Museum, 1991), 9.

RESOURCES FOR RESEARCH

The Impact of Global Events on Regions and Nations

The decades around the turn of the twenty-first century were full of events that shifted balances of economic and political power. The South African Web site provides a look at the innovative postapartheid constitution, which ensures an array of human rights.

Bayly, Susan. *Asian Voices in a Post-Colonial Age: Vietnam, India and Beyond*. 2007.
Kynge, James. *China Shakes the World: A Titan's Rise and Troubled Future and the Challenge for America*. 2006.
Prunier, Gérard. *Darfur: The Ambiguous Genocide*. 2005.
Rosefielde, Steven. *Russia in the 21st Century: The Prodigal Superpower*. 2006.
South Africa. http://www.info.gov.za/documents/constitution/1996/96cons2.htm.
Taylor, Lance, ed. *External Liberalization in Asia, Post-Socialist Europe, and Brazil*. 2006.
van Kessel, Ineke. *Beyond Our Wildest Dreams: The United Democratic Front and the Transformation of South Africa*. 2000.

Global Livelihoods and Institutions

The spread of global communication brought on by the Internet dramatically affected livelihoods and institutions. Greenspan and Rowen chart developments in information technology.

Greenspan, Anna. *India and the IT Revolution: Networks of Global Culture.* 2004.

Rowen, Henry S., Marguerite Gong Hancock, and William F. Miller. *Making IT: The Rise of Asia in High Tech.* 2007.

Sassen, Saskia. *Cities in a World Economy.* 2006

United Nations. http://www.un.org/womenwatch/. Provides ample information on women around the world and also on the UN's programs for women.

Wasserstrom, Jeffrey N. *China's Brave New World—and Other Tales for Global Times.* 2007.

The Promises and Perils of Globalization

Globalization is hotly debated, and this selection of works shows why. AIDS, terrorism, and environmental decline increased as the world's peoples became more tightly linked. Louie and Smith and Siplon, however, discuss activism and spirited movements for change.

Baldwin, Peter. *Disease and Democracy: The Industrialized World Faces AIDS.* 2005.

Hefner, Robert W. *Civil Islam: Muslims and Democratization in Indonesia.* 2000.

Khalid, Adeeb. *Islam After Communism: Religion and Politics in Central Asia.* 2007.

Louie, Miriam Ching Yoon. *Sweatshop Warriors: Immigrant Women Workers Take on the Global Factory.* 2001.

McNeill, J. R. *Something New Under the Sun: An Environmental History of the Twentieth Century.* 2000.

Smith, Raymond A., and Patricia Siplon. *Drugs into Bodies: Global AIDS Treatment Activism.* 2006.

Cultures Without Borders

As the media became a global force, culture knew even fewer boundaries than it had in the past. These works chart a variety of trends and global mixing of cultures.

Allison, Anne. *Millennial Monsters: Japanese Toys and the Global Imagination.* 2002.

Iwabuchi, Koichi. *Recentering Globalization: Popular Culture and Japanese Transnationalism.* 2002.

Kato, M. T. *From Kung Fu to Hip Hop: Globalization, Revolution, and Popular Culture.* 2007.

Lopez, A. M. *To Be Continued . . . Soap Operas Around the World.* 1995.

Osumare, Halifu. *The Africanist Aesthetic in Global Hip-Hop: Power Moves.* 2007.

Seager, Richard. *Encountering the Dharma.* 2006.

COUNTERPOINT: Who Am I? Local Identity in a Globalizing World

Whether praying or shopping, people around the world maintain local customs and practices. Even a global chain such as McDonald's needs to adjust to local preferences, as Watson's work shows.

Benjamin, Thomas. "A Time of Reconquest: History, the Maya Revival, and the Zapatista Rebellion." *The American Historical Review.* 2000.

Malarney, Shaun Kingsley. *Culture, Ritual and Revolution in Vietnam.* 2002.

Parkin, David, and Stephen C. Headley, eds. *Islam: Prayer Across the Indian Ocean and Outside the Mosque.* 2000.

Saxenian, Anna Lee. *The New Argonauts: Regional Advantage in a Global Economy.* 2006.

Watson, James L., ed. *Golden Arches East: McDonald's in East Asia,* 2d ed. 2006.

▶ **For additional primary sources from this period**, see *Sources of Crossroads and Cultures.*

▶ **For Web sites, images, and documents related to topics in this chapter**, see Make History at bedfordstmartins.com/smith.

The major global development in this chapter ▶ The causes and
consequences of intensified globalization.

IMPORTANT EVENTS

1986	Nuclear accident at Chernobyl power plant in Soviet Union
1989	Iranian leader Ayatollah Khomeini issues fatwa against Salman Rushdie
1990s	New European nations emerge in wake of USSR collapse
1991	Mercosur establishes a free-trade zone among southern South American nations
1994	Nelson Mandela elected president of South Africa; European Union officially formed; North American Free Trade Agreement implemented
1995	United Nations Fourth World Conference on Women held in Beijing
1997	Kyoto Protocol drafted
1999	European Union adopts the euro as its new money
2001	Terrorists attack United States; United States declares "war on terrorism"
2002	Luiz Inácio Lula da Silva elected Brazilian president
2003	United States invades Iraq
2004	Manmohan Singh becomes prime minister of India
2005	Kyoto Protocol goes into effect
2007–2008	Global economic crisis begins to unfold

KEY TERMS

apartheid (p. 1029)

Association of Southeast
  Asian Nations
  (p. 1036)

European Union (p. 1034)

globalization (p. 1025)

global warming (p. 1038)

Kyoto Protocol (p. 1040)

Mercosur (p. 1036)

nongovernmental
  organization (p. 1034)

North American Free
  Trade Agreement
  (p. 1036)

CHAPTER OVERVIEW QUESTIONS

1. What were the elements of globalization at the beginning of the twenty-first century?

2. How did globalization affect lives and livelihoods throughout the world?

3. How did globalization affect local cultures?

4. What people do you know whose roots and livelihoods are global?

SECTION FOCUS QUESTIONS

1. How has globalization affected the distribution of power and wealth throughout the world in the early twenty-first century?

2. How has globalization reshaped national economies and political institutions?

3. What major benefits and dangers has globalization brought to the world's peoples?

4. What trends suggest that globalization has led to a new mixing of cultures?

5. How have peoples sought to establish and maintain distinctive local identities in today's global age?

MAKING CONNECTIONS

1. What have been the most important features of globalization—good and bad—in the past thirty years, and why are they so significant?

2. Consider Chapter 24. How have livelihoods changed since the era of industrialization, and what factors have caused these changes?

3. Do you consider local or global issues more important to people's lives? Explain your choice.

4. How do you describe your identity—as global, national, local, familial, religious—and why?

ADDITIONAL CREDITS

Text Credits

Chapter 15

Richard A. Newhall. *The Chronicle of Jean de Venette*, edited by Richard A. Newhall, Columbia University Press, 1953. Used by permission of Columbia University Press.

Chapter 16

Miguel Leon-Portilla. *Pre-Columbian Literatures of Mexico*, by Miguel Leon-Portilla, translated from the Spanish by Grace Lobanov. Copyright © 1969 by The University of Oklahoma Press. Used by permission of the publisher.

Matthew Restall, Lisa Sousa, and Kevin Terraciano, editors. *Mesoamerican Voices: Native-Language Writings from Colonial Mexico, Oaxaca, Yucatan, and Guatemala*. Copyright © 2005 Matthew Restall, Lisa Sousa, and Kevin Terraciano. Reprinted with the permission of Cambridge University Press.

Frank Salomon and George L. Urioste. From *The Huarochirí Manuscript: A Testament of Ancient and Colonial Andean Religion*, translated and edited by Frank Salomon and George L. Urioste, Copyright © 1991. By permission of the University of Texas Press.

Chapter 17

William Brooks Greenlee. *The Voyage of Pedro Alvares Cabral to Brazil and India*, translated by William Brooks Greenlee, Hakluyt Society, 1938; as it appears in Kraus Reprint Limited, Nendeln/Liechtenstein, 1967. Used by permission of the Hakluyt Society.

Chapter 18

Kate Ferguson Masters. "Travels in the Interior of Africa," in *Travels in the Interior Districts of Africa* by Mungo Park, edited by Kate Ferguson Masters, pp. 264–267. Copyright 2000, Duke University Press. All rights reserved. Reprinted by permission of the publisher.

John O. Hunwick. *Timbukto and the Songhay Empire: Al-Sadi's Tarikj al-sudan down to 1613 and Other Contemporary Documents,* edited and translated by John O. Hunwick, Brill 1999. Used by permission of Koninklijke BRILL NV.

Nicole Von Germeten. *Treatise on Slavery,* by Alonso de Sandoval, edited and translated by Nicole Von Germeten. Hackett Publishers, 2008. Used by permission of the publisher.

Chapter 19

Anthony Reid. *Southeast Asia in the Age of Commerce,* Volume 2. Yale University Press, 1993. Copyright © Yale University Press, 1993. Used by permission of the publisher.

Chapter 20

Abraham of Erevan, *History of the Wars* (1721–1738), edited and translated by George A. Bournoutian (Costa Mesa, CA: Mazda Publishers, 1999), 77–78. Used by permission of Mazda Publishers.

Chapter 21

C. Whelan. From "An early 19th-century Tokugawa-era Kakure Kirishitan, or 'Hidden Christian,'" manuscript, edited and translated by C. Whelan. © 1966 University of Hawaii Press. Reprinted with permission.

Nobuyuki Yuasa. "The Records of a Weather-exposed Skeleton," by Matsuo Basho, c. 1685, in *The Narrow Road to the Deep North and Other Sketches*, edited and translated by Nobuyuki Yuasa, Penguin, 1966. Reproduced by permission of Penguin Books Ltd.

Map 21.4: Maritime Trade Between the Americas and Asia, 1571–1800. From John Leddy Phelan, *The Hispanization of the Philippines: Spanish Aims and Filipino Responses, 1565–1700.* © 1959 by the Board of Regents of the University of Wisconsin System. Reprinted by permission of The University of Wisconsin Press.

Choe-Wall Yangh-hi. Lady Hong, *Memoirs of a Korean Queen,* edited and translated by Choe-Wall Yangh-hi (London: KPI, 1985), pp. 1–4, 49. Used by permission of Taylor & Francis Books.

Chapter 22

Cesar E. Farah. *An Arab's Journey to Colonial Spanish America: The Travels of Elias al-Musili in the Seventeenth Century,* edited and translated by Cesar E. Farah, Syracuse University Press, 2003. Used by permission of Syracuse University Press.

Richard Price. *First-Time: The Historical Vision of an Afro-American People* (Baltimore: Johns Hopkins University Press, 1983), p. 71. Used by permission of the author.

Chapter 23

Paul Dukes. *Russia Under Catherine the Great: Select Documents on Government and Society,* edited and translated by Paul Dukes, Oriental Research Partners, 1978. Reprinted by permission of the publisher.

Chapter 24

J. N. Westwood. *A History of the Russian Railways*, George Allen and Unwin, 1964. Used by permission of the author.

Chapter 25

Alexander Nikitenko. *Up from Serfdom: My Childhood and Youth in Russia 1804–1824,* translated by Helen Saltz Jacobson. Copyright © 2001 Yale University Press. Used by permission of Yale University Press.

Anne Walthall. *The Weak Body of a Useless Woman: Matsuo Taseko and the Meiji Restoration.* © 1998 by The University of Chicago. Used by permission of the University of Chicago Press.

William R. Braisted. From *Meiroku Zasshi: Journal of the Japanese Enlightenment* by William R. Braisted, pp. 401–403, Cambridge, Mass.: Harvard University Press, Copyright © 1976 by the University of Tokyo Press.

Chapter 26

Wang Gungwu. *Community and Nation* by Wang Gungwu (2000), published by Allen & Unwin, Sydney (www.allenandunwin.com).

Chapter 27

Patricia Buckley Ebrey. Adapted with permission of Free Press, a division of Simon & Schuster, Inc., from *Chinese Civilization and Society: A Sourcebook* by Patricia Buckley Ebrey. Copyright © 1981 by The Free Press. All rights reserved.

Léopold Sédar Senghor. *The Collected Poetry*, pp. 47–48. Translated by Melvin Dixon. © 1991 by the Rector and Visitors of the University of Virginia. Reprinted by permission of the University of Virginia Press.

Chapter 28

Keith Howard. "Comfort Women" from *True Stories of the Korean Comfort Women*, edited by Keith Howard. Continuum Books, 1995. By the kind permission of Continuum International Publishing Group.

Chapter 29

Isidore Ndaywel è Nziem. *Histoire générale du Congo: De l'héritage ancien à la République Démocratique,* De Boeck & Larcier, 1998. Used by permission of Edition le Cri. [English translation by Bonnie G. Smith.]

Khang Zhengguo. From *Confessions: An Innocent Life in Communist China* by Khang Zhengguo, translated by Susan Wilf. Copyright © 2005, 2004 by

Chapter 30

Art Credits

Opener to Part 3

Opener to Part 4

INDEX

A note about the index:

Letters in parentheses following pages refer to:
- (*b*) boxed features
- (*i*) illustrations, including photographs and artifacts
- (*m*) maps

Abd al-Wahhabi, Muhammad ibn (Islamic reformer), 785, 786
Abdul Hamid II (Ottoman sultan), 884
Abolition and abolitionism, 606
    in Denmark, 810
    in England, 601, 810
    religion and, 785
    white, 741
Abortion and abortion rights, 934, 938, 996, 1011
Abraham of Erevan, on Ottomans vs. Safavids in Baghdad, 655(*b*)
Absolutism, 650, 673–675
    in Asia, 686
    in France, 673–674
Abstract expressionism, 983
Acadia, 741
Accommodation, of imperialism, 872
Aceh, Indonesia, 616, 640–642, 640(*m*), 708
    Dutch merchants in, 641(*b*)
Acid rain, 1038
Aclla girls (Peru), 513
Activism
    Bandung Conference and, 983–984
    by farmers, 1018–1019
    feminist, 1009–1010
    global, 1034
    for human rights, 1049
    protests by, 1009–1012
    in Soviet bloc, 1011–1012
    in United States, 1012
    of women, 851–852
    after World War II, 961–962
    youth, 1009
Adams, John, Enlightenment and, 764
Addis Ababa, 940
Administration. *See* Government
Advancement of Learning, The (Francis Bacon), 671
Advertising, middle-class "look" promoted by, 914
Afghanistan
    British in, 863
    population growth in, 1041
    Soviet Union and, 1008, 1015
    wars in (2001–2011), 1046, 1046(*m*)
Afghan warlords, 625
Afonso I (Nzinga Mbemba, Kongo), 599
Afrasian Sea, 616. *See also* Indian Ocean region
Africa. *See also* Afro-Eurasia; North Africa; specific locations
    Asia and, 617
    Christianity in, 598–599
    East African links with interior, 620
    Europeans in, 593, 864–868
    exploration and, 554(*m*)
    famine in, 868

    c. 1450–1800, 582(*m*)
    during Great Depression, 931
    HIV/AIDS in, 1030
    indentured servants in, 876(*i*)
    industrialization and, 810–812
    mandate system in, 907(*m*)
    migration from, 1044
    migration in, 858(*m*), 874–875
    missionaries in, 871
    modernity in, 509
    new nations in, 973–975, 974(*m*)
    paramount chiefs in, 586–587
    Portugal and, 555, 581, 598
    religion in, 598
    resistance to imperialism in, 872
    1750–1880, 811(*m*)
    slave trade and, 597(*m*), 598, 606–607
    textiles and independence in, 975(*b*), 975(*i*)
    troops in World War I, 904
    underdevelopment of, 812
    women farmers in, 818–820, 819(*i*)
    World War I soldiers from, 897
African Americans, 840, 850
    in armed forces, 947(*b*)
    civil rights and, 851, 981–982, 1009
    music of, 848
    sailors in World War II, 946(*i*)
    as U.S. president, 1026
African diaspora, 584
African National Congress (ANC), 1023, 1029
African people
    African enslavement of, 595
    in Americas, 722
    as New World sugar workers, 572–573(*b*)
    in Spanish America, 723
Afro-Brazilians, 735
    Inquisition in Brazil and, 736
Afro-Eurasia, 475–478
    in early 15th century, 476(*m*)
Agra, 631
    Taj Mahal in, 615
Agrarianism
    agricultural productivity and, 672
    literacy and, 847
    in technological age, 1017–1019
Agriculture. *See also* Farms and farming
    in Africa, 581, 870
    African women in, 594
    after Black Death, 482–483
    cinnamon harvest in Ceylon and, 636–637(*b*), 636(*i*)
    in eastern Europe, 964
    in Great Depression, 929
    Inca, 530
    in India, 1028(*i*)
    in Japan, 503, 701

    in Korea, 706
    in Little Ice Age, 479
    Mamluk Sultanate and, 480, 481
    in Mughal Empire, 631
    Ottoman, 491
    productivity in, 672
    scientific help for, 996
    seed sterilization and, 1018
    slave workers in, 797
    in Southeast Asia, 709–710
    women and slave agriculture, 818–820, 819(*i*)
Aguilar, Jerónimo de (interpreter for Cortés), 549
AIDS. *See also* HIV
    epidemic of, 1041–1044
    in South Africa, 1030
    treatment in Uganda, 1041(*i*)
Ainu people (Japan), 699, 849
Airplanes, in World War II, 942
Akan peoples, 592–593
Akbarnama (Mughal court history), 612(*i*)
Akbar the Great (Mughal Empire), 612(*i*), 624, 626–627
Akhmatova, Anna, 934
Alagoas, Brazil, 748
Alam II (Shah, Mughal Empire), 628
Alaska, U.S. purchase of, 881
Albania
    First Balkan War and, 896
    Ottoman Balkans as, 776
Alberti, Leon Battista (Italian architect), 500, 501
Alchemy, 587
Alcohol, in industrial society, 815
Aldrin, Edwin ("Buzz") (U.S. astronaut), 994
Aleppo
    commerce in, 650, 656, 657
    Timur and, 488
Alexander II (Russia), 833, 835, 836
Alexandria, Egypt, plague in, 480
Algeria
    France and, 865, 974–975
    independence for, 975
    World War II in, 951
Ali, Muhammad (Egypt), 761, 776, 809, 864
Ali, Sharif Husayn ibn (Syria), 908
Allende, Isabel, 920
Allende, Salvador, 1005
Alliances. *See also* specific alliances
    in Cold War, 966–969
    Egyptian-European, 864–865
    French-Indian, 742
    Mughal, 628
    in North America, 539–540
    regional, 968–969, 968(*m*)
    in West Africa, 590
    before World War I, 896
    in World War I, 896

Allies (World War I), 896
    in Ottoman Empire, 908
    at Paris Peace Conference, 905
    Russian civil war and, 904
    treaties of, 906–907
    victory of, 904
Allies (World War II), 943(m), 944(m), 945,
        948, 951
    division of Germany and Berlin by, 964
Alpaca, 537
    Inca, 536
Al Qaeda, 1045, 1046(m)
Alsace, 897
    after World War I, 906
Aluku maroons, 749
Amazon River region, 514(m)
    European claims in, 568(m)
    Inca in, 532
America(s). See also Latin America; Native
        Americans; Spanish America; specific
        locations
    Africans and, 722
    Columbian Exchange and, 561–562
    crops in Europe from, 672
    cultures of, 516–517
    empires and kingdoms of, 513, 567–573
    encomienda system and, 559–560
    environment of, 516
    European claims in (c. 1600), 568(m)
    Europe and, 659–660
    European diseases in, 562
    exploration of, 510–511, 546(i), 547–550,
        551–562
    foods from, 562
    Iberians and, 550
    maritime trade with Asia, 712(m)
    migration to, 511
    native peoples of, 547
    population density in, 516
    racism in, 602–604
    settlement of, 517(m)
    silver shipments from, 691
    slavery in, 575, 598, 600
    Spanish, 723–732
    transformation of, 719
    West Central African crops from, 593
American Federation of Labor (AFL), 932
American Revolution (1775–1789), 768–771,
        769(m)
Amerindians, as slaves, 722
Amin, Idi, 1007, 1007(i)
Amritsar, protests at, 911
Amur River region, China and, 693
Anatolia (Turkey). See also Turkey
    Christianity in, 491
    Ottomans in, 475, 491, 908
Ancestors
    Huron, 542
    in Inca society, 532
Andean region
    creation story in, 533(b)
    Inca and, 529, 532
    Inca vertical archipelago in, 530, 530(m)
    Pizarro in, 565
    potatoes from, 537

Anglican Church (England), 662, 676
Anglo-Zulu War (1879), 867
Angola
    Christianity in, 599
    Ndongo kingdom in, 594
    Portugal and, 599–600
    slaves from, 583, 600, 601
Angola, Domingo (slave), 583–584, 723
Animals
    in Columbian Exchange, 561
    genetic modification of, 1017, 1018
    spirits in Americas, 518–519
    for sugar industry, 574(b)
    in western Africa, 585
Ankara, as Turkish capital, 908
Ann, Queen Nzinga as, 599
Anne of Austria (queen), 674
Annexation, of South Africa, 881
Anthony, Susan B., 852
Anticolonialism, 918(i)
    Bandung Conference and, 983
Anticommunism, after World War II, 963
Antiforeign uprisings, in China, 857, 860
Anti-Semitism. See also Jews and Judaism
    in Argentina, 919
    of Hitler, 936–937
    migration due to, 875
    in Nazi Germany, 937–938
    in United States, 953
Apache Indians, 840–841
Apartheid
    in South Africa, 1023–1024, 1029
    South Africa after, 1031(m)
Appeasement, of Hitler, 940
Appliances, family life and, 1002
Arabia, in 1802–1807, 786(m)
Arabian peninsula, al-Wahhabi and, 785, 786
Arabs and Arab world. See also Middle East
    decolonization and, 969
    Israeli wars with, 1013
    as Muslims, 786
    Palestinians and, 972
    tensions in (1967–1990), 1013(m)
Arab Spring (independence movements),
        1046–1047, 1047(m), 1047(i)
Aragon, 665
Araucanians. See Mapuche people
Archaeology. See Culture(s)
Archangel, 690
Architecture. See also Housing
    in China, 1031
    of cities, 913
    globalization of, 1037
    Inca, 532–533
    in India, 615, 625
    Taj Mahal and, 615, 626(i)
Arctic pack ice, melting of, 1038, 1040(i)
Argentina, 919(m)
    culture of, 920
    "dirty war" in, 1005
    economy of, 919
    golden age of, 919–920
    human rights in, 1005
    Inca in, 532
    industrialization in, 802

    in Mercosur, 1036
    Perón in, 977–978
    San Martín in, 781
    society in, 919
Aristocracy. See also Nobility
    in Japan, 504
Aristotle, geocentrism and, 671
Arkwright, Richard (English inventor), 798, 805
Armada. See Spanish Armada
Armed forces. See also Military; specific battles
        and wars
    of Bolsheviks in civil war, 904
    French in North Africa, 865
    in Japan, 842
Armenia
    attack on Turkey, 909(m)
    genocide in (1915–1917), 1049
Armenians, Ottoman deportations of, 908
Armistice, ending World War I, 904
Arms manufacturers, militarization during
        Great Depression and, 931
Arms race, Kennedy, John F., and, 969
Armstrong, Neil (U.S. astronaut), 994
Art(s). See also specific arts and artists
    Aztec, 526
    in Brazil, 736
    in China, 696–697
    imperialism and, 879–880
    in industrial society, 815–816, 817
    in Italian Renaissance, 501
    in Japan, 702, 790(i), 803(b), 803(i)
    modernism in, 878
    non-Western impact on Western, 885–886
    of slave trade, 592(b), 592(i)
    socialist realism in, 934, 934(i)
    after World War II, 983
Articles of Confederation (U.S.), 769–770
Artigas, José Gervasio, 780–781
Artisans
    Inca, 535
    in industrial age, 814
    in Industrial Revolution, 796
    in Mughal Empire, 631
Art of Metals, The (Barba), 672
Art of War, The (Sun Tzu), 887
Aryans, in Nazi Germany, 937
ASEAN. See Association of Southeast Asian
        Nations
Ashikaga Shogunate (Japan), 503–504
Asia. See also Afro-Eurasia; Eurasia; specific
        locations
    Black Death in, 478
    in Cold War, 966–967
    economy in, 494–498, 913, 997
    end of empires in, 970–972
    famine in, 868
    1450–1750, 683–686
    imperialism in, 861–864, 862(m)
    maritime trade with Americas, 712(m)
    missionaries in, 871
    Russia and, 690, 868
    sea routes to, 547
    trade in, 494–498, 547
    World War II in, 940–941, 944–945, 944(m)
Asia Minor. See Anatolia (Turkey)

Asian-African Conference. *See* Bandung Conference
Askeri (Ottoman military class), 655–656
Askiya (hereditary lord), 590
Assassinations, of Mexican leaders, 895
Association for Taxation of Financial Transactions (ATTAC), 1034
Association of Southeast Asian Nations (ASEAN), 1036
Astrolabe, 553
Astronomy
  big bang theory of universe and, 995
  Copernicus and, 671, 671(*i*)
Aswan Dam, 973, 1038
Atatürk. *See* Kemal, Mustafa
Atawallpa (Atahualpa, Inca ruler), 538, 566
  Pizarro and, 565, 565(*i*)
Atlantic creoles, intermediaries of exchange as, 597
Atlantic Ocean region. *See also* Exploration
  East Atlantic region (c. 1500), 554(*m*)
  c. 1450–1800, 582(*m*)
  Portugal and, 633
  revolutions in, 759–762
  slave trade in, 597(*m*), 600–607, 602(*m*), 722
  sugar in, 572–573, 574–575(*b*), 574(*i*)
  trading network in, 767–768
  wars and revolutions in (1750–1830), 760(*m*)
Atomic bomb
  Soviet, 963
  in World War II, 951, 952(*b*), 952(*i*)
Atomic power, after World War II, 977
ATTAC. *See* Association for Taxation of Financial Transactions
Atzcapotzalco, Aztecs and, 523
Audiencia (Spanish-American high appeals court), 724, 726
Aurangzeb (Mughal Empire), 627
Auschwitz-Birkenau, 925, 945
Australia
  native children in, 849
  World War I and, 897, 898–899
Austria
  French Revolution and, 773
  German war with, 838
  Italy and, 837
  Nazi annexation of, 940
  Peace of Paris treaties and, 906
  Piedmont and, 837
  war against France and, 773
Austro-Hungarian Empire. *See also* World War I
  Balkans and, 893, 896
  in Triple Alliance, 896
  World War I and, 896, 897
Austronesia, Indian outsourcing for, 1032
Authoritarianism, control of information and culture in, 915
Autocracy. *See also* Dictators and dictatorships
  collapse of, 913
  Russia as, 852
Automation, industrial, 998–999
Automobiles and automobile industry, 799–800, 913
Autosacrifice, 525–526
Awadh, India, 863

Axis powers (World War II), 943(*m*), 944(*m*), 945, 947–948
  postwar trials of leaders, 980
Ayudhya (Ayutthaya), Thailand, 496, 708
Azores, 554(*m*)
Aztec Empire (1325–1521), 516, 519–529, 520(*m*)
  core features of, 524–526
  Cortés in, 562–564, 563(*m*)
  culture of, 518
  daily life in, 526–529
  Florentine Codex in, 528(*b*)
  midwives in, 528(*b*), 528(*i*)
  peoples of, 547
  sacrifices in, 524–526, 525(*i*), 529
  Spanish and, 529, 562–566, 564(*b*)
  Spanish horses, technology, and, 566
  warfare in, 526
  women in, 527
Aztlán, 519

Babur (Timurid Muslims), 623, 625
Baburnama (Babur's memoir), 625
"Back to Africa" movement (Garvey), 981
Bacon, Francis (English writer and statesman), 671
Bacon, Nathaniel (American colonial rebel leader), 743
Baghdad
  Ottomans and, 654
  Ottomans vs. Safavids in, 655(*b*)
  in World War I, 904
Bahamas, Columbus in, 555–556
Bahia, Brazil, 722
Bahrain, 1046
Baka Pygmies, 608(*i*)
Balance of power
  Crimean War and, 833
  economic, 1023
  military revolution and, 477
  after Napoleonic Wars, 774
  shifts in, 912–913, 1012–1017
Balance of trade. *See* Trade
Bali, Hinduism in, 493
Balkan region
  Ottomans and, 489, 491, 894
  wars in, 892(*m*), 893, 894, 896
Baltic region
  Russia and, 688
  Soviet Union and, 963
  World War II in, 942
Balzac and the Little Chinese Seamstress (Sijie), 1044–1045
Bandung Conference (Indonesia, 1955), 971(*m*), 983–985, 984(*i*)
Bangalore, India, global service work in, 988(*i*)
Bangladesh, women in, 851(*i*)
Banking, in Gold Coast, 930(*b*)
al-Banna, Sheikh Hassan (founder of Muslim Brotherhood), 918(*i*)
Bantu peoples
  in East Africa, 617
  Pygmies and, 608–609
Baptism
  of native Americans, 570
  of Nzinga, 601(*i*)

Barba, Alvaro Alonso, 672
Barbados, 722, 738, 739–740
Barbarossa brothers, Oruç and Hayreddin (Algiers), 653
Barbary pirates, 677–679, 677(*m*), 678(*i*)
Barbary Wars, 678–679
Barbed wire, 801
Barnard, Christiaan, 995
Barriers to development, in global South, 1027
Barton, Clara, 850
Basho, Matsuo (Japan), 703–704
Basmati seed, 1018
Basques, independence and, 1052
Bastille (Paris), storming of, 771
Battle of Britain, 942, 943(*m*), 945
Battle of the Somme, The (film), 901(*b*)
Battles. *See* Wars and warfare; specific battles and wars
Batwa culture and people (Pygmies), 586(*m*), 607
Bayinnaung (Burma), 708–709
Bay of Pigs, invasion of, 969
Beauvoir, Simone de, 981
Beg, Sayyid (Persian ambassador), 612(*i*)
Beggars, in China, 695(*i*)
Begum, Arjumand Banu (Mumtaz Mahal, Mughal empress), 613–615, 626(*i*)
Beijing, China, 487. *See also* Dadu (Beijing)
  feminist gathering in, 1034
  Gorbachev in, 1015
  Tiananmen Square riots in (1989), 1015–1016, 1016(*i*)
Belarus, human rights and, 1049
Belgian Congo, 870
  poll (head) tax in, 929
Belgium
  Africa and, 865
  World War I and, 897
  World War II and, 942
Belgrade
  diversity in, 657
  Ottomans in, 653
Belief systems. *See also* Christianity; Hindus and Hinduism; Ideologies; Islam; Jews and Judaism; Muslims; Philosophy; Religion(s)
  in China, 895
  in Enlightenment, 762–765
  in Mexico, 890(*i*)
  non-Western impact on Western, 885–887, 886(*i*)
  in Spanish America, 570
  uniformity of, 847–848
  in warfare, 947(*b*)
Benares, India, pilgrimages to, 615
Bengal, 625
  Dutch VOC headquarters in, 639(*i*)
  famine in, 949
Benguela (port), 600
Benin, 581(*i*), 590–592
  art of slave trade from, 592(*b*), 592(*i*)
  Portugal and, 555
  sculpture from, 592, 592(*b*)
  statue of Portuguese soldier from, 598(*i*)
Benz, Karl (German car designer), 799

Berlin, postwar zones in, 964–965, 965(*m*)
Berlin airlift, 965
Berlin Conference, 867
Berlin Wall, 965
    fall of, 1016
Betel leaves, 710–711
Bhakti (Hindu devotional worship), 497(*b*)
Bharatiya Janata Party (BJP, India), 1028
Bhopal, India, Union Carbide gas leak in, 1038
Bicycles, in cities, 1039
Big bang theory, of universe, 995
Big business, labor unions and, 932
Bight of Benin, 602(*m*)
Bight of Biafra, 602(*m*)
Big Three (Roosevelt, Churchill, Stalin), 952
Bill of Rights (U.S.), 773
Bin Laden, Osama, 1045, 1046
Biological exchange. *See* Columbian Exchange
Biology, molecular, 995
Biopiracy, 1018
Bird flu, 1044
Birth control, 995
    in China, 696
    Gandhi and, 917
    in Nazi Germany, 938
    population and, 1041
    in Soviet Union, 918, 934
Birthrate
    in Iran, 1041
    in Soviet Union (1930s), 934
    in Sweden, 939
Bismarck, Otto von (Prussia), 836, 837–838
    Cameroon and, 866
    Triple Alliance of, 896
"Black Bart." *See* Roberts, Bartholomew
Black Death (1347–1350), 477, 478–482
    causes of, 479
    European population and, 479
    French theologian on, 482(*b*)
    in Italy, 499–500
    Muslims on, 482
    spread of (1347–1451), 480(*m*)
Black market, in World War I, 902
Black Noise (musical group), 1051
Black power, 982, 1009
Blacks, 581. *See also* African Americans
    racism toward, 603
    slavery and, 595
    in Spanish America, 723
    whites compared with, 766–767
Blacks and Tans, in Ireland, 910
Black Sea region, 687(*m*)
Black Shirts (Italy), 918
Black Skin, White Masks (Fanon), 981
Blacksmiths, in West Central Africa, 593–595, 594(*i*)
Blanc, Honoré (French inventor), 798
Blincoe, Robert (English author and former child laborer), 791–793, 813, 817
Blitz (Battle of Britain), 942, 943(*m*), 945
Blitzkrieg (lightning war), 941–942
Blockades, in World War I, 897, 908
Blood offerings, Aztec, 525–526
Blood of the Revolutionary Martyrs Fertilizing the Earth (Rivera mural), 890(*i*)

Bloody Sunday (January 30, 1972), in Northern Ireland, 1045
Blue-collar workers, decline in, 999
Blues music, 848
Blum, Léon (French Socialist Party leader), 939
Bobby (film), 989, 991, 1002(*i*), 1003
Boccaccio, Giovanni, on Black Death, 479
Boers, 867, 881
Boer War, 881
Bogotá, 781
Bohemia, in Thirty Years' War, 668
Bolaño, Roberto (Chilean writer and poet), 1050
Bolivar, Simon, 732, 758(*i*), 759, 781, 783
Bolivia, 946(*b*). *See also* Potosí
    Bolivar in, 781
    in Mercosur, 1036
Bollywood, 989–991
Bolshevik Revolution (1917), 963
Bolsheviks
    civil war and, 903–904
    as Communists, 903
    takeover by, 903
Bombards (cannons), 474(*i*), 477
Bombs and bombings. *See also* Nuclear weapons
    in England (2005), 1046
    in World War II, 945, 951
Bonafini, Hebe de (Argentinean activist), 1005
Bonaparte family. *See* Napoleon I
Bond, James (book and film character), 982
Book-burnings, in Nazi Germany, 937
Books. *See also* Literature
    Catholic bans on, 665
Borges, Jorge Luis (Argentinean writer and poet), 920, 1050
Boriquen. *See* Puerto Rico
Borlaug, Norman (U.S. founder of Green Revolution), 996
Bose, Subhas (member of Indian Congress Party), 949
Boston Tea Party (1773), 768
Botchan (Soseki), 879–880
Bourbon dynasty, 676(*m*)
    in Spain, 729
Bourbon Reforms, 767
    in Spain, 765–766
Bourgeoisie, 812
    growth of, 672
    Marx on, 817
Boxer Rebellion (China, 1899–1900), 857, 860, 884, 895
Brahe, Tycho, 671
Brahman (priestly) caste (India), 622
Brain drain, 1001
    from South Africa, 1031(*m*)
Brass, from Benin, 592
Braun, Eva, 951
Brazil, 1029
    Cabral's report on, 571(*b*)
    colonization of, 732(*m*)
    dictatorship in, 1005
    economy in, 736, 998, 1029
    in 18th century, 718(*i*)
    environment in, 734
    ethnic and racial exploitation in, 849
    France and, 572

    gold and diamonds in, 732–733
    independence of, 781–783
    industrialization in, 802
    lifestyle in, 735–736
    in Mercosur, 1036
    mining in, 734
    modernization of, 829–831
    multinational corporations in, 1004(*m*)
    plantations in, 575
    plantation workers in, 831(*i*)
    pollution of Cubotão in, 1018(*i*)
    Portugal and, 555, 559, 568(*m*), 570–573, 719
    Rio de Janeiro and, 977(*i*)
    slavery and, 596, 598, 601, 606, 748, 830
    space program in, 967(*i*)
    sugar in, 572
    television in, 993
    trade in, 571–572
    women in, 781(*i*)
Brazilwood, 571
Brest-Litovsk, Treaty of (1918), 903
Brezhnev, Leonid, 1011–1012
Brezhnev Doctrine, 1011–1012, 1016
Britain. *See also* England (Britain)
    Battle of, 942, 943(*m*), 945
British Commonwealth, World War I and, 897
British Empire. *See also* England (Britain)
    colonial crisis in (1764–1775), 768
    independence in, 970
British North America
    slavery in, 746
    slave trade and plantation economy in, 722
Bronze
    from Benin, 592(*b*), 592(*i*)
    in Inca Empire, 536
Bronze Age, Inca and, 535–536
Brotherhood(s)
    ikki (Japan), 503
    Muslim, 916, 917
    Sufi, 489
Brown, Louise (first person successfully conceived by in vitro fertilization), 996
Brown v. Board of Education (1954), 981–982
Brunei Darussalam, in ASEAN, 1036
Bubonic plague. *See* Black Death
Buccaneers, in Caribbean region, 738–739(*b*), 738(*i*)
Buddha and Buddhism
    in Burma, 708
    in Japan, 699, 980
    in Korea, 707
    from Luang Prabang, 710(*i*)
    Soka Gakkai, 1050
    in Southeast Asia, 683
    Western study of, 886
    Zhu Xi on, 486
Budget(s)
    deficit in United States, 1014
    reduction in government, during Great Depression, 929
Buenos Aires, 781, 919
    department stores in, 805
    exploration and, 560
    slave trade in, 597(*m*)
Buffer zone, Stalin and, 952

Bulgaria
   as autonomous state, 896, 898(*m*)
   in World War II, 942, 951
Bulgarians, nationalism of, 884
Bullion, in trade with India, 629
Bureaucracy. *See also* Civil service examinations
   in China, 691
   Inca, 534
   in Korea, 705
   Ottoman, 489–490
   in Spanish America, 723
   in Vietnam, 487
Burial(s)
   ancestral native American, 1052
   Inca, 513–515
Burj al Arab (Dubai tower), 1022(*i*)
Burke, Edmund, 783
Burma (Myanmar), 944
   British in, 863
   China and, 693
   development of, 708
   ecological destruction in, 864
Bushidō (way of the warrior), 501
Business. *See also* Commerce; Corporations;
      Merchant classes
   Chinese, 1031
   in Egypt, 865
   in Great Depression, 930(*b*)
   in Japan, 999(*b*)
   mergers of, 1033
   worldwide transactions of, 1036
Business imperialism, defined, 861. *See also*
      Imperialism
Byron, Lord, 761
Byzantine Empire. *See also* Constantinople
   end of (1453), 474(*i*), 477
   Ottoman expansion and, 489

Cabral, Pedro Alvares, 570–571, 571(*b*)
Caffa, Crimean peninsula, 479, 480
Cahokia, 513
Cairo, Egypt
   commerce and, 650
   Kulthum, Umm, in, 959
   modernization of, 864
   trade in, 656
Cajamarca (Inca sacred city), 565
Calcutta, 638, 929
Calendar
   Aztec, 524–525
   in France, 773
   in Japan, 701
Calicut, 494
Caliphs and caliphates, use of term, 590
Call desk services, in Ireland, 1032
Calvin, John, 662
Cambay, India, exchanger of, 619(*i*)
Cambodia, 1008
   China and, 693
   development of, 708
   genocide in, 971(*m*)
   Khmer in, 711
   U.S. invasion of, 1008
Cameroon
   Baka Pygmies of, 608(*i*)

Germany and, 866
Caminha, Pero Vaz de (Portuguese explorer), 571
Camões, Luiz Vaz de (Portuguese writer and
      poet), 635
Camus, Albert (French writer and philosopher),
      981
Canada, 514(*m*), 741
   British in, 768
   in NAFTA, 1036
   native children in, 849
   World War I and, 897
Canals, in Tenochtitlán, 523
Canary Islands, 554
   Columbus in, 556
   slaves to, 606
   sugar and, 575
Candide (Voltaire), 763
Canisius, Edgar, in Congo Free State, 871(*b*)
Cannibalism, 559(*i*)
   Caribs and, 558–559
   Inca and, 532
   rumors about, 583–584
   Vespucci on, 560
Cannons, 474(*i*), 477, 484(*i*)
   in Mughal India, 625, 627
   at siege of Constantinople, 474(*i*)
Canton, China. *See* Guangzhou
Capacocha sacrifice, by Inca, 513, 515, 534(*i*),
      537
Cape Colony, 867
   South African War and, 881
Cape of Good Hope, Dias' voyage around, 555
Cape Verdes, 554(*m*)
Capital (financial). *See also* Capitalism
   international flows of, 1033
Capitalism
   consumer, 805
   emergence of, 672–673
   English East India Company and, 672
   Marx on, 817
Captives. *See also* Slaves and slavery; Wars and
      warfare
   from Gambia River region, 595
   Mande and Mane invasions and, 596
   as slaves, 590
Caracas, 781
   Bolivar in, 759
Caravans, 494
   in Central Asia, 475
Caravanserais (travelers' lodges), 656
Caravels, 553
Carbon dioxide, from fossil fuels, 1038
Car-free zones, 1039
Caribbean region, 514(*m*), 912. *See also* specific
      locations
   buccaneers in, 738–739(*b*), 738(*i*)
   colonialism in, 737–741
   Columbus in, 556–560
   exports from, 722
   migrants to, 814
   origins of name, 558
   piracy in (c. 1650–1730), 737(*m*)
   plantations in, 575, 722
   revolts in 18th century, 767
   slavery in, 737–741, 777–778

slave trade in, 598
Spanish in, 561, 563
Carib people, 558–559, 560
Carnegie, Andrew, 802
Carolinas, 745
Carracks (ships), 553(*i*)
Carreira da India (voyage to India), by Portugal,
      614(*m*), 634
Carson, Rachel, 1038
Cartagena, Inquisition in, 570
Cartagena de Indias, 723
Cartels, 805
Cash crops
   in Asia, 616
   Dutch and, 635
Cash economy, in China, 690
Casino Royale (Fleming), 982
Caspian Sea region, 687(*m*)
Cassatt, Mary, 885
Cassava, in central Africa, 593
Castes and caste system. *See also* Class(es)
   cinematic portrayals and, 915
   Gandhi and, 917
   in India, 496(*b*), 622, 631, 813
   of Spanish Empire and Brazil, 849
Castile, 665
Castro, Fidel, 968–969, 993
Catherine the Great (Russia), 765, 766–767(*b*)
Catholic Church. *See* Roman Catholic Church
Catholic Reformation, 661–665, 663(*m*)
Cattle, raising of, 801
Caucasus region, Ottomans and, 654
Caudillos (strongmen), in South America,
      780–781, 831–832
Cavour, Camillo di (Italy), 827(*m*), 836–837
Ceauşescu, Nicolae (Romania), 1016
Censorship
   of films, 917(*b*)
   in Nazi Germany, 937
Central Africa, Baka Pygmies of, 593, 607–609,
      607(*m*), 608(*i*)
Central America. *See also* Latin America; specific
      locations
   Aztecs in, 516
   1960–1992, 1004(*m*)
   protests for traditional rights, 1052
Central Asia
   British in, 863
   after Cold War (c. 1990), 1017(*m*)
   imperialism in, 861–862
   Islam in, 488–489
   Russia in, 863
Central economic planning, in Soviet Union,
      933
Central Europe, Peace of Paris in (1920), 906(*m*)
Central Intelligence Agency. *See* CIA (U.S.)
Centralization, political, 891
Central Powers (World War I), 896, 904
Ceramics
   from China, 494–495
   English, 796
Cerro Rico (Potosí, Bolivia), 569(*i*)
Cervantes Saavedra, Miguel de, 647, 653, 678,
      679
   voyages of, 648(*m*)

Ceuta (Islamic port city), 554
Ceylon. *See* Sri Lanka
Chaco War (1932–1935), 946(*b*)
Chamberlain, Neville, 940
Chamber of Deputies (France), 939
Champlain, Samuel de, 741
  Iroquois and, 744(*i*)
Chaplin, Charlie, 915, 939
Charity, in India, 631
Charles I (England), 675–676
Charles II (Habsburg Empire), 726(*i*)
Charles V (Spain, Holy Roman Empire), 563,
  564, 572, 665, 668
Charles XII (Sweden), 688(*i*)
Charqui (jerky), as Inca food, 537
Charter Oath (Japan), 824(*i*)
Charters, constitutions as, 675
Charts, portolan, 546(*i*)
Chattel slavery. *See also* Slaves and slavery
  Aztec, 527
  China and, 693
  Inca, 535
  Korea and, 693, 708
Chavez, César, 1009
Chechens, terrorism by, 1046
Cheka (secret police), in Russia, 904
Chemicals
  fertilizers and, 1018
  industrial, 801
  as pesticides, 1018
Chernobyl nuclear power plant, explosion at,
  1038
Cherokee Indians, 840
Chettis (traders), 494
Chew, Kunan (designer), 1022
Chiapas, Mexico, local liberation army in, 1052
Chica da Silva (Brazilian celebrity), 719–722, 736
Chicimec people (Mexico), 729
Chiefs, in Africa, 586–587
Childbirth
  Aztec, 528(*b*), 528(*i*)
  in Europe, 661
  Inca, 536
  scientific transformation of, 996
Child care, in Sweden, 939
Child labor, 813
  in England, 814(*i*)
Children
  in African mining, 595
  Aztec, 527
  in Eastern Woodlands society, 541
  during Great Depression, 931
  Inca, 536–537
  Inca sacrifice of, 513–515
  in postindustrial families, 1002–1003
  in Sudan, 1027
  trafficking in, 1044
Chile
  democracy in, 1005
  Inca in, 532
  industrialization in, 802
  Mapuche people of, 573–576, 573(*m*),
    576(*i*)
  in Mercosur, 1036
  San Martin in, 781

  U.S. and, 1003–1004
  women in, 1011
Chimú people, 531
China
  arts in, 696–697
  ceramics from, 494–495
  Communists in, 910, 911(*b*), 936, 965–966,
    1031
  conditions in (1900), 856(*i*)
  consumerism in, 1032
  Cultural Revolution in, 962, 979–980, 1002
  culture in, 696–697
  disintegration of Qing, 807–809
  drought in, 670
  East Africa and, 619
  economy in, 690–691, 690–693, 794, 997,
    1030–1031
  Enlightenment and, 764
  exports from, 496–498
  famine in, 857
  film industry in, 916(*i*), 917(*b*)
  foreign trade in, 807
  gifts for emperor, 664(*b*), 664(*i*)
  Great Leap Forward in, 978(*b*), 979
  gunpowder in, 552
  Guomindang in, 895
  imperial conditions in (1850–1914), 857–860
  Japan and, 487, 504, 691, 868, 868(*m*),
    910(*m*), 940–941
  Korea and, 487
  Manchurian Incident and, 935
  maritime trade of, 494, 498–499
  Marx and, 817
  May 4th Movement in, 910
  merchants in Philippines, 713
  as middlemen in Southeast Asia trade, 711
  migration and, 814, 858(*m*), 877, 1044
  Ming dynasty in, 477, 485–487
  from Ming to Qing rule in (1500–1800),
    690–697
  modernity and, 510
  Nationalists in, 910
  New Life Movement in, 935–936
  opium and, 807
  People's Republic of (1949), 965
  plague in, 479
  population of, 691, 1041
  porcelain from, 494–495, 692, 692(*b*), 692(*i*)
  Qing dynasty in, 693–697, 694(*m*)
  republic in, 895
  resistance to imperialism in, 883–884
  revolution in (1911–1912), 891–893, 895–896
  route to, 722
  Russia and, 683, 693, 863
  sense of superiority in, 486–487
  silk in, 696–697(*b*), 696(*i*)
  silver in, 691–692, 794
  strikes in, 914
  tea from, 807
  textiles in, 692–693
  Three Gorges Dam in, 1038
  Tiananmen Square riots in (1989),
    1015–1016, 1016(*i*)
  trade in, 692–693, 694(*m*)
  U.S. and, 1002

  Vietnam and, 487, 499, 709
  wealth in, 696
  women in, 487, 851, 914, 965
Chinampas, 523
Chinaware
  Chinese porcelain as, 494–495, 692
  Wedgwood pottery as, 796, 796(*i*)
Chinese Communist Party, 910, 1031
Chintz, 494
Chitor, India, 627
Chlorofluorocarbons (CFCs), 1038
Chon T'ae-il, 1008
Chontal Maya language, 547–549
Choson Korea. *See* Yi (Choson) dynasty
Christendom. *See also* Latin Christendom
  Islam and, 485(*m*)
Christianity. *See also* Crusades; Latin
    Christendom; Orthodox Christianity
  in Africa, 598–599
  in Anatolia, 491
  in China, 697
  in East Africa, 621
  European expansion and, 650
  explorers and, 550
  Hong Xiuquan and, 807
  intolerance of diversity by, 647
  Japanese Hidden Christians and, 700(*b*)
  Japanese persecution of, 698–699
  missionaries and, 554
  Muslims and, 475
  Ottomans and, 490–491, 651, 657
  plague as divine punishment and, 481, 482
  ransoming Christians from pirates and, 678(*i*)
  in Thirty Years' War, 668
  Tokugawa Japan and, 698
  as world's largest faith, 1050
Church(es), in French Revolution, 784–785
Churchill, Winston, 942, 953
Church of England. *See* Anglican Church
"Chutney" music, 1051
CIA (U.S.)
  Allende (Chile) and, 1005
  Castro and, 969
Cinema houses, 917(*b*)
Cinnamon
  in Ceylon, 636–637(*b*)
  harvesting, 636(*i*)
Ciompi uprising (Florence), 483
Cities and towns. *See also* Urban areas
  in Africa, 973
  bombings of (World War II), 945, 951
  car-free and bicycle zones in, 1039
  East African trade and, 617–618
  European, 660–661
  global, 1031, 1036–1037
  growth of, 913
  in India, 1028
  in Italy, 919
  in Japan, 503, 703
  modernization of, 846
  railroads in, 799
  in Spanish America, 724–725
  in West Africa, 590
Citizens and citizenship
  equality for women and, 770(*i*)

literacy and, 847
struggles for rights of, 851–852
women and, 850
City-states
in Italy, 500
of Maya, 517
in West Africa, 592–593
Civil disobedience, 953–954
by Gandhi, 954–955
Civilians
in World War I, 900–902
in World War II, 945–950
Civil justice system, Aztec, 526
Civil rights. *See also* Rights
for African Americans, 981–982
in Nazi Germany, 937
in United States, 849–852, 850(*i*)
Civil rights movement (U.S.), 954, 1009
Civil service examinations
in China, 486
in Korea, 705
Civil war(s)
in England (1642–1646), 676
in former Yugoslavia, 1016
in Russia, 903–904
in Sudan, 1027
in United States, 839(*m*), 840
Cixi (Chinese empress), 884
Clans, matrilineal, 540
Class(es). *See also* Castes and caste system;
specific groups
in Aztec society, 526–529
bourgeoisie as, 672
cinematic portrayals and, 915
in cities, 913
Inca, 534–535
industrialization and, 914
in Japan, 504, 701
in Korea, 705, 708
Marx on, 816–817
in Ottoman Empire, 655–656
after World War I, 914
Class conflict, in World War I, 902
Clergy. *See also* Religious orders
in Africa, 598
in Mali, 492
Climate. *See also* Ice age
greenhouse effect and, 1038
Little Ice Age and, 479, 667, 669
in North America, 539
Clive, Robert (British imperial officer), 632
Clocks, gifted to China, 664(*b*), 664(*i*), 697
Cloning, 995
Cloth and clothing. *See also* Textiles and textile
industry
in Japan, 701
migration of, 879
non-Western impact on Western, 886
in slave trade, 604
South Asian, 619
in Southeast Asian trade, 711
Western dress in Turkey, 908–909
Clubs, political, 832
Coal and coal industry
cartel in Germany, 805

coke (refined coal), 832
decline of, 998–999
Coalitions
Napoleonic Wars and, 774
in World War II, 928
Coatepec, in Tenochtitlán, 522
Coca, 513–515
Cochin China. *See also* Vietnam
France in, 864
Cocoa growers cooperative, 930(*b*)
Code Napoleon, 774, 783
Codes of law. *See also* Law(s)
of Napoleon, 774, 783
Codex Mendoza, 521(*i*)
Codices, Aztec, 520–521
Coerced labor
of colonized peoples in World War II, 949,
949(*i*)
Jews in, 938
of Nazis, 945–946
World War I and, 905
Coerced migration, trafficking in children and
women as, 1044
Coffee, Dutch and, 635
Coffeehouses, Ottoman, 658–659(*b*), 658(*i*)
Coins and coinage. *See also* Money
Spanish, 726(*b*), 726(*i*)
Colbert, Jean-Baptiste (French finance minister),
674
Cold War (1945–1989), 928, 959, 961, 963–965
alliances in, 965–969
beginning of, 952–953
culture of, 982–983
eastern Europe and central Asia after
(c. 1990), 1017(*m*)
end of, 989–991, 1012–1017, 1023
nonalignment in, 984(*i*)
protests against, 1009
Southeast Asian nations and, 971(*m*)
Soviet Union and, 978–979
Vietnam War and, 1008
weapons production in, 976
world politics and, 962–969
Colhuacan, Aztecs and, 521(*b*)
Colhua people, Aztecs and, 522, 523
Collaboration
on communications satellites, 994–995
in World War II, 949
Collective farms, in Soviet Union, 933–934
Collective security, 907
Collectivization
in China, 965
in eastern Europe, 964
Collectivized agriculture, in Soviet Union, 964
Colombia, Inca and, 532
Colonialism. *See* Colonies and colonization
Colonies and colonization
American, 719–722, 720(*m*)
American Revolution and, 768–771, 769(*m*)
in Brazil, 572, 732(*m*)
British India as, 863
in Caribbean region, 737–741
collaboration with Axis conquerors in, 949
criminal settlement in, 571–572
decolonization and, 969–975

Dutch in Southeast Asia, 638(*m*)
end of system, 961
English in Southeast Asia, 638(*m*)
Enlightenment and U.S. government, 764
European, 511
exploitation in, 870
Great Depression in, 929
imperial culture and values in, 872(*b*), 872(*i*)
imperialism and, 861
independence revolts in, 910–911
Japanese, 883
lifestyle in northern North American,
745–748
mandate system and, 907–908, 907(*m*)
as markets, 869
medicine in, 872–873
in North America (1754–1789), 769(*m*)
plantation, 617
Portuguese, 554(*m*)
protests during Depression in, 932
Spanish-American, 559
textiles sold to, 673
after World War I, 925
World War I and, 896, 897, 899–900, 904,
912(*b*)
World War II and, 944–945, 949, 949(*i*),
950(*i*)
Columbian Exchange, 550, 561–562
epidemic diseases, population, and, 562, 563
Mughal Empire and, 631
Southeast Asian markets and, 710–711
Columbus, Christopher, 551–552
native Americans and, 556–559, 558(*i*)
portolan charts and, 546(*i*)
sea route to Indies and, 555
voyages of, 484, 548(*m*), 557(*m*)
CoMadres (El Salvador), 1006
Comintern (Communist International), 904
Commerce, 477. *See also* Business; Trade
in Atlantic region, 767–768
Aztec, 523
Chinese, 690–691, 692–693
exploration for, 551–552
in India, 629
in Islamic West Africa, 491–493
Istanbul and, 650
Italian, 477, 500
in Japan, 802
monopolies in, 481
Mughal, 623–624
in Newfoundland and Nova Scotia, 744
in Ottoman Empire, 657
Portugal and, 553–555
Portuguese African, 596–598
in Renaissance, 499–500
in Southeast Asia, 708, 710–711
Commercial colonialism, in British and French
North America, 741–745
Commercial farming, in Europe, 660
Committee of Public Safety (France), 773
Common Market. *See* European Economic
Community; European Union
Communication(s)
in Crimean War, 833
devices for, 988(*i*)

Communication(s) (*continued*)
  in industrial society, 815–816
  technologies for, 893–894
Communications satellites, 993, 994–995
Communism. *See also* Communists
  in China, 910, 911(*b*)
  in eastern Europe, 962, 964
  fall in eastern Europe, 1014–1017
  fears of spread, 963–964
  in Nazi Germany, 937
  in Soviet Union, 978–979
Communist Manifesto, The (Marx and Engels),
    816, 817
Communist parties
  in China, 910, 1031
  during Great Depression, 931
  Indochinese, 932
Communists. *See also* Communism
  Bolsheviks as, 903
  in China, 965
  McCarthy witch-hunt for, 983
  Rivera, Diego, as, 890(*i*)
  in Vietnam, 1008
Compass, 553
Competition
  for empire, 891
  of global workers, 1033
  of imperial powers, 880, 881–882
  in Japan, 804
Computers, 993
  Irish economy and, 1032
  programmers for (1940s), 994(*i*)
Concentration camps
  for Japanese Americans, 948–949
  Nazi, 937, 945(*m*)
Conception, scientific transformation of, 996
Concord, Battle of, American Revolution and,
    768, 769
Condition of the Working Class in England, The
    (Engels), 817
Confederacies, in North America, 539–540
Confederate States of America, 840
Conflict. *See also* Revolts and rebellions;
    Violence; Wars and warfare
  over African independence, 973–975
  class, 902
  English-French in North America, 741–742
  between English king and Parliament,
    675–677
  French, 675
  global, 1025
  in South Africa, 1029
  in sub-Saharan Africa, 1027, 1027(*m*)
  in western Africa, 587
Confucianism, in Japan, 699
Conglomerates, 913
Congo
  Belgium and, 865–866, 870
  lifestyle in rain forest of, 607–608
  rubber workers in, 871(*b*)
Congo River region, 586(*m*), 593, 594, 607
  peoples of middle region, 594
Congress of Vienna (1814–1815), 774
Congress Party (India). *See* Indian Congress
    Party

Conquistadors, 562–566
  in Chile, 573–574
  myths and realities about, 565–566
  Portuguese in India, 632–635
  Spanish, 548(*m*)
Conscription. *See* Draft (military)
Consensus politics, in U.S. Constitution, 771
Conservatism, 783
  of Catholic Church, 665
  in Japan, 826, 827
Consolidation, in mainland Southeast Asia,
    708–711
Constantinople. *See also* Istanbul
  fall of (1453), 474(*i*), 477, 485(*m*), 491
  as Istanbul, 491, 651–652, 908
  Ottomans in, 650
Constitution, 675
  Mexican (1917), 895
  U.S., 770, 773
Constitutional Convention (U.S., 1787),
    769–770
Constitutionalism, 650, 673, 675–677
Constitutional monarchy, in Spain, 1007
Consumer capitalism, 805
Consumer prices, during Great Depression, 931
Consumers and consumerism, 915(*i*)
  bourgeoisie and, 672
  in China, 1031
  global jobs and, 1032–1033
  in Japan, 701
  in United States, 982
Containment policy, 964, 967
Continental Congress, 768
Contraband, in Spanish America, 727–728
Contraceptives, oral, 995
Contract government, 763
Conversion (religious)
  in American colonies, 569–570, 572
  forced, 735
  to Islam, 657
  in Kongo, 599
  of Muslims to Christianity in Spain, 669(*b*)
Cook, Thomas (English entrepeneur),
    1000–1001, 1001(*b*)
Cook's Tours, 1001(*b*)
Cooper, Maria (U.S. feminist activist), 852
Cooperative zones, 1035–1036
Copernicus, Nicolaus, 671, 671(*i*)
Copper
  in Africa, 587, 594
  in Inca Empire, 536
Corn (maize), 537, 563
  Aztec, 529
  in central Africa, 593
Corporations
  conglomerates, 913
  limited-liability, 805
  multinational, 913, 998
Corruption, in Spanish America, 727–728
Cortés, Hernando, 549–550, 562–564, 563(*m*),
    566(*b*), 566(*i*)
Cosa, Juan de la (Spanish explorer), 546(*i*)
Cosmetics industry, 915–916
Cosmonauts, 966–967(*b*), 966(*i*)
Cosmopolitanism, 879–880

Cotton and cotton industry
  in China, 487
  Inca, 536
  in India, 494, 616
  in Japan, 701
Councils (Christian), of Trent (1545–1563), 665
Countryside. *See* Rural areas
Coups, in Soviet Union, 1016–1017
Coureurs de bois (fur traders), 743
Court (royal)
  in China, 693
  in France, 674
  in Japan, 699
  Mughal, 625, 627, 628(*i*)
Courtier class, in Japan, 504
Covenant, of League of Nations, 907
Cowboys
  gauchos as, 782(*b*), 782(*i*)
  llaneros as, 781, 782(*b*)
  vaqueros as, 782(*b*)
Cowry shells, 594
Crafts, in Africa, 587
Craftworkers, Industrial Revolution and, 809
Credit, collapse of, 1047
Creoles
  Atlantic, 597
  independence for, 779
  in Latin America, 767, 780–781
  in Spanish America, 731
Crick, Francis, 995
Crimean War (1853–1856), 833, 833(*m*)
Crimes against humanity, 980
Criminals, as settlers in Brazil, 571–572
Croatia, as EU membership candidate, 1035
Cromwell, Oliver, 676
Crops. *See also* Agriculture; Foods
  in Egypt, 865
  globalization of, 794
  in Japan, 700–701
  in Korea, 706
  in Mughal Empire, 631
  from New World, 659–660, 672
  in West Central Africa, 593
Crosby, Alfred, 741
Cross-cultural exchange. *See also* Exchange;
    Trade
  in Mediterranean region, 475
Crusades (1095–1291), as religious wars, 475
Crystal Palace Exhibition (London, 1851),
    1001(*b*)
Cuba, 968–969
  Columbus in, 557
  Cortés in, 562
  during Great Depression, 931
  nation building in, 832
  Soviet aid to, 1003
  Spanish-American War and, 881
  sugar exports from, 975–976
  television and, 993
Cuban missile crisis (1962), 961, 969
Cult(s), Inca, 533
Cult of domesticity, 812
"Cult of personality," in Soviet Union, 979
"Cult of the offensive," 897
Cultural Revolution (China), 962, 979–980, 1002

Culture(s)
of Aceh, 640–641
Afro-Eurasian trade patterns and, 478
Ainu, 699
in Americas, 514(*m*), 516–517
of Argentina, 920, 920(*i*)
of Aztecs and Incas, 518
in Caribbean slave societies, 740–741
Chinese, 696–697
during Chinese Revolution (1911–1912), 896
in Cold War, 980–983
communist, 918, 983
cosmopolitan, global, 915
democratic, 939
global, 879
in imperial age, 878–880
imperial impact on, 872(*b*), 872(*i*)
in India, 620–632
of industry, 815–817
Japanese, 702–704, 935, 936
of liberation, 981–982
maroon, 749
mass, 893–894, 914–916
mass proletarian, 918
Mexican Revolution's impact on, 895
national, 843–849
and political styles, 890(*i*)
and race in British North America, 746
in Renaissance, 499–500
of slaves, in British and French North America, 746–748
in Spanish America, 724–725
uniformity of, 847–848
urban, 913
in West Africa, 492
in West Central Africa, 593–595
Westernization of Turkish, 908–909
Curaçao, 738
Currency. *See also* Coins; Money
manillas as, 587
Cuzco, Peru, 513
in c. 1500, 530(*m*)
Incas and, 530–531
Cyprus, Ottomans and, 653
Czechoslovakia
fall of communism in, 1016
Nazi invasion of, 940
Prague Spring in, 1011
Soviet Union and, 964
after World War I, 906, 906(*m*)

Daboya (king of Ghana), England and, 866
Dachau concentration camp, 937
Dadu (Beijing), 485, 487
Da Gama, Vasco, 553(*i*)
on Roman Catholicism in East Asia, 633
voyages of, 555, 557(*m*), 633
Daimyo (local lord, Japan), 698, 702(*i*), 802
Dairy farming, 801
Daladier, Édouard (French premier), 940
Damascus
Timur and, 488
trade in, 656
Dams, environment and, 1038

Dance
Indian woman and, 879(*i*)
non-Western impact on Western, 886
tango, 920, 920(*i*)
Dance of death, 481(*i*)
Dangdut (Indonesian music), 1051, 1051(*i*)
Daratista, Inul (dangdut performer), 1051(*i*)
Dardanelles Strait, World War I and, 898
Darfur, 1027
Darwin, Charles, 845, 861
Das Kapital (Marx), 816
Davis, Angela, 1011
Davos forum, 1034
D-Day invasion, 951
Death. *See also* Burial(s); Mortality
Black Death images of, 481, 481(*i*)
in Eastern Woodlands groups, 541–542
Inca belief in, 515
Death camps. *See also* Concentration camps
memoirs of, 980
Debt
in Brazil, 1029
fraudulent, 1047
Debt peonage, in Korea, 708
Debussy, Claude, 886
Declaration of Human Rights (UN), 1049
Declaration of Independence (U.S.), 768
"Declaration of the Rights of Man and Citizen" (France), 772, 773
"Declaration of the Rights of Woman and the Female Citizen," 772
Decolonization, 958(*i*), 959–961, 969–975
Decorative objects. *See* Art(s)
Deductive reasoning, 670–671
Deforestation, 660
in Brazil, 734
in Japan, 701
De Gaulle, Charles, Free French and, 949–950, 975
De Kooning, Willem, 983
De la Cruz, Juana Inés (Spanish-American intellectual and mystic), 732
Delaware (U.S.), 744
Delhi
British in, 863
Persian sack of (1739), 625
Safavids and, 628
Democracy
during Great Depression, 927–928
in India, 1028
in Latin America, 1003–1006
in Middle East, 1047
Demography. *See also* Population
Black Death and, 477, 479
in British North America, 746
Columbian Exchange and, 562
of England, 479
population and, 1040–1041
Demonstrations. *See also* Protest(s); Resistance; Revolts and rebellions
in Egypt, 972
in South Korea, 1007
Deng Xiaoping (China), 1030, 1041
Denmark
German war with, 838

slave trade and, 600, 810
in Thirty Years' War, 668
World War II in, 942
Department stores, 805–806, 806(*i*)
Depressions (economic). *See also* Great Depression
in China, 807
silver and, 668
Description of Africa (al-Wazzan), 492
Deshima, Japan, 698
Detention camps, of Cheka, 904
Developed nations, research in, 1001
Developing nations
economic inequities in, 984–985
research in, 1001
Devshirme conscription system (Ottoman), 490, 651
Dhows (ships), 552, 619
Diamonds, in Brazil, 718(*i*), 719, 722, 732–733, 735(*i*)
Diary of a Young Girl (Frank), 980
Dias, Bartolomeu, 555
Diaspora, 877
African, 584
contemporary popular music and, 1051
migration and, 874–878
of Muslims and Jews from Europe, 647
Nigerian, 598
of trade, 492–493
Diaz, Porfirio, 891, 894, 895
Dickens, Charles, 817
Dictators and dictatorships
in Brazil, 1029
in Korea, 1007
in Latin America, 1003–1006
in Uganda, 1007, 1007(*i*)
Diderot, Denis, 764
Dien Bien Phu, Battle of (1954), 972
Diet (food). *See also* Foods
Aztec, 529
in Europe, 659
Inca, 537
in Japan, 700, 701
Diplomacy
by Hongwu, 487
U.S.-China, 1002
Dirschau, Battle of, 668(*i*)
Disabled people, in Nazi Germany, 938
Discovery. *See also* Exploration
European voyages of, 555–561, 557(*m*)
Discrimination
racial, in U.S., 938
in South Africa, 1023
Diseases, 1027. *See also* AIDS; specific diseases
Black Death and, 477
in colonies, 873
Columbian Exchange and, 562
from Europe in Americas, 723
global spread of, 1042(*m*)
influenza epidemic (1918–1919), 904–905
in Mexico, 563
research after World War II, 995
in Spanish America, 729
vaccines and drugs for, 1041
of workers, 813–814

Dissent. *See also* Protest(s); Revolts
　　and rebellions
　　in New England, 743–744
　　in Soviet Union, 983
Diversity. *See also* Ethnic groups
　　of Americas, 516–517
　　in Balkan region, 896
　　global migration and, 1024(*m*)
　　in Mediterranean region, 649–650
　　in Ottoman Empire, 657
Divinity, of Hindu kings, 622
Division of labor, sexual, 815
Divorce, in Ottoman Empire, 656, 657
Djuka, maroons, 749
DNA, 995
Doctors Without Borders, 1031, 1032(*i*), 1034
Doctor Zhivago (Pasternak), 983
Doll's House, A (Ibsen), 880
Domesticity, after World War II, 982(*i*)
Dominican Republic, 777
Domino effect, in Asia, 967–968
Don Quixote (Cervantes), 649, 678, 679
Dostoevsky, Fyodor, 845
Douglass, Frederick, 850(*i*), 851
Draft (military)
　　of colonized peoples, 949
　　devshirme system and, 490
　　in Japan, 842
Draft-dodging, 947(*b*)
Drake, Francis, 600, 666, 738
　　voyages of, 557(*m*)
Drama
　　in China, 696
　　Japanese theater and, 504
　　kabuki and, 703
　　non-Western impact on Western, 885–886
　　Spanish, 647
Dresden, firebombing of, 945
Drought, 1041
　　in China, 693
　　in colonies, 873
　　1641–1644, 670
Drugs
　　in Europe, 660
　　in Southeast Asia, 710–711
Dual monarchy, in Austria-Hungary, 896
Dubai, Burj al Arab in, 1022(*i*)
Dubček, Alexander (Czechoslovakia), 1011, 1016
Du Bois, W. E. B., 908
Duma (Russian parliament), 883, 902
Dutch. *See also* Boers; Netherlands
　　in Aceh, 640, 641–642, 641(*b*)
　　Caribbean colonialism and, 737
　　colonial protests and, 911
　　Indonesian independence and, 971
　　Japan and, 691, 802
　　land reclamation by, 660
　　Portugal and, 635
　　slave trade and, 598, 600, 603
　　South American silver and, 638
　　Southeast Asian colonies of, 638(*m*)
　　sugar plantations and, 574
　　in Thirty Years' War, 668
　　trade route of, 614(*m*)
　　wealth in, 668–669

Dutch East India Company (VOC), 635–638, 666
　　Bengal headquarters of, 639(*i*)
　　capitalism and, 672
　　cinnamon and, 636(*i*), 637(*b*)
　　Dutch economy and, 669
　　Japan and, 698
　　North America and, 741
　　in Southeast Asia, 638(*m*)
Dutch Republic, Spain and, 666
Dutch Revolt (1566–1648), 665
"Dutch Studies," in Japan, 764
Dutch Suriname
　　Jews in, 736
　　maroons of, 748–749, 749(*i*)
Dutch West India Company, 666
　　slaves and, 603
Duties. *See* Taxation

Earthquakes, in Japan, 935
East Africa. *See also* Africa
　　African interior and, 620
　　China and, 619
　　Germany and, 866, 885
　　port cities in, 617(*m*)
　　resistance to imperialism in, 872
　　Roman Catholicism in, 633
　　trading cities and inland networks in,
　　　617–618
　　violence in, 973
　　World War I in, 902, 904
East Asia. *See also* Asia
　　modernity in, 510
East Atlantic region (c. 1500), 554(*m*)
East Berlin, Berlin Wall and, 1016
Eastern Europe. *See also* specific locations
　　after Cold War (c. 1990), 1017(*m*)
　　consumerism in, 1032
　　fall of communism in, 1014–1017
　　Peace of Paris in (1920), 906(*m*)
　　as Soviet buffer zone, 964
Eastern front, in World War I, 897
Eastern Woodlands peoples (North America)
　　1450–1530, 538–542
　　organization of, 540
　　sacrifice by, 541
　　society of, 540–542
Easter rebellion (Ireland, 1916), 910
East Germany, 964(*m*), 965
　　Berlin Wall and, 1016
East India, Portuguese spice trade and, 635
East Prussia, World War I in, 897
Ebadi, Shirin (Iran), 1049
Ebola virus, 1044
Ecology. *See also* Environment
　　of Africa, 868–869
　　of Americas, 516–517
　　Aztec, 529
　　changes in human community and, 1038
　　of Japan, 701
Economic classes. *See* Class(es)
Economic depressions. *See* Depressions; Great
　　Depression
Economy and economic systems. *See also*
　　Finances; Great Depression; Industrial
　　Revolution; Industry; Livelihood(s); Trade

abolition of slavery and, 810
　　in Americas, 722
　　in Argentina, 919
　　balance of power in, 1023
　　Black Death impact on, 477
　　in Brazil, 736, 1029
　　capitalism and, 672–673
　　in China, 690–693, 794, 997, 1030–1031
　　consumer, 1032–1033
　　crises and solutions in 19th century, 804–806
　　in developing countries, 984
　　Dutch, 668–669
　　in Egypt, 864, 865
　　in Europe (c. 1600), 668
　　expansion of prosperity, 976–978
　　global, 493–498, 996–1003, 1027, 1047
　　global North vs. South and, 1026–1027
　　growth after World War II, 975–978
　　in India, 631–632, 794, 976, 1028
　　in Industrial Revolution, 794
　　in Ireland, 1032
　　in Italy, 499–500
　　in Japan, 503, 935, 996–997
　　in Korea, 1007
　　in Mamluk Egypt, 480, 481
　　and maritime trade in Asia (1350–1450),
　　　494–498
　　Marxian socialism and, 816–817
　　mercantilism and, 673
　　in Mexico, 893
　　modernization of, 913
　　as motive for migration, 1044
　　in Nazi Germany, 937
　　neoliberalism and, 1033
　　in 1970s, 1014
　　in North Africa, 865
　　plantation, 722
　　postindustrial, 991
　　in Russia, 834
　　Smith, Adam, on, 763–764
　　in South Asia, 624–625
　　in South Korea, 996–997
　　Soviet, 918, 933–934, 963
　　in Spanish America, 728
　　in Sweden, 938
　　in United States, 963
　　in the West, 1014
Ecosystems. *See also* Environment
　　global warming and, 1038
　　Russian fur trade and, 690
Ecuador, Inca battles and, 532
Edict of Nantes (France, 1598), 665, 674
Edo, Benin, 590
Edo (Tokyo), Japan, 699
　　water supply of, 700
Education
　　family life and, 1002–1003
　　reforms of, 846–847
　　of Russian serfs, 834
Edward VII (England), celebration for, 880(*i*)
EEC. *See* European Economic Community
Egypt. *See also* Cairo
　　Ali, Muhammad, in, 761, 776, 809
　　Arab spring in, 1047(*i*)
　　Aswan Dam in, 1038

economy in, 864, 865
modernization of, 864, 864(*m*)
Muslim Brotherhood in, 916, 917
Napoleon and, 760, 774, 776, 776(*i*)
Nasser and, 972–973
nationalism in, 959
revolt in, 911
in Six-Day War, 1013
Suez Canal and, 864
uprising in, 1046
in Yom Kippur War, 1013
Eiffel Tower, 800
Einstein, Albert, 952(*b*)
Eisenhower, Dwight, 967
Electricity, 800, 815–816
Electronic circuits, 993
Electronic networks, for protests, 1047
Elephants, ivory trade and, 620
"El Inca" Garcilaso de la Vega, 647–649
Elites. *See also* Class(es)
    in Africa, 810
    in Argentina, 919
    Aztec, 527
    after Black Death, 483
    in Egypt, 775–776
    Filipino, 713(*i*)
    imperialism and, 869–870
    in military, 947(*b*)
    in Soviet Union, 933
Elizabeth I (England), 666
    Aceh and, 642
El Niño
    famine from, 869
    taxation during, 873
El Saadawi, Nawal (Egyptian feminist and
        writer), 1051
El Salvador, terror and resistance in, 1006b(*b*)
Emancipation, of Russian serfs, 834–836, 834(*i*)
Emigration. *See also* Immigrants and immigra-
        tion; Migration
    to Brazil, 734
    of Jews from Nazi Germany, 938
Emile (Rousseau), 763
Emissions, environmental damage from, 1038
Emperors. *See also* Empires; specific rulers
    in Japan, 825, 841–842
Empires. *See also* Imperialism; specific locations
    in Africa, 589–590
    in Americas, 513, 514(*m*), 722
    arts and, 879–880
    in Asia, 970–972
    Aztec, 519–529
    German, 838
    Inca, 529
    in Indian Ocean, 613–616, 614(*m*), 635
    of Ming China, 485–487
    race for, 891
    Russian, 687, 687(*m*), 689–690
    in South Asia, 613–616, 620–625
    Spanish, 665–666
    of Timur, 488
    World War I and, 893
Empire State Building, 913
Employment. *See also* Livelihood(s); Work
    in global manufacturing, 1023

global networks and, 1032–1033
during Great Depression, 931
in India, 631–632
as managers, 805
of samurai, 802–803
of women, 815
Enabling Act (1933), 937
Enclosure, of land, 672
Encomenderos, 560
Encomienda system, 559–560, 651, 726
Encouragement of Learning (Fukuzawa Yukichi),
        845
Encyclopedia (Diderot), 764
Energy crisis, oil embargo and, 1013–1014
Enfield rifles, 863
Engels, Friedrich, 817
Engineering
    German, 802
    Inca, 535
    industrial, 799–800
England (Britain). *See also* Britain; World War I;
        World War II
    abolition of slave trade in, 810
    Aceh and, 642
    Africa and, 866
    American Revolution and, 768–769
    in Barbados, 739–740
    at Battle of Omdurman, 868
    Bengali famine and, 949
    Black Death and population of, 479
    Blitz in, 942, 943(*m*), 945
    Caribbean colonialism and, 737
    child labor in, 814(*i*)
    colonial protests and, 911
    colonial taxation by, 768
    constitutionalism in, 675–676
    contract government in, 763
    Egypt and, 865
    18th century drawing room in, 765(*i*)
    enclosure in, 672
    expansion of, 863–864
    Germany after World War II and, 964–965,
        965(*m*)
    Glorious Revolution in (1688), 676–677
    Great Awakening in, 785
    during Great Depression, 929
    Hundred Years' War and, 484
    imperialism by, 912
    India and, 813(*i*), 916–917, 929, 932
    Industrial Revolution in, 794, 795–796
    industry in, 797(*b*)
    innovation in, 796
    Ireland and, 910
    labor unions and, 914
    Luddites in, 814
    Napoleon and, 776
    Navigation Acts and, 745
    in North America, 741–745, 742(*m*)
    opium trade and, 807
    Palestine and, 972
    at Paris Peace Conference, 905
    Protestantism in, 662
    revolt by Nigerian women against, 953
    as secular state, 784–785
    after Seven Years' War, 768

slave trade and, 598, 600, 601, 603
South Africa and, 867–868, 867(*i*)
South African War and, 881
Southeast Asian colonies of, 638(*m*)
Spanish Armada and, 666, 666(*m*)
Suez crisis and, 973
taxation in, 483
Thatcher in, 1014
in Thirty Years' War, 668
tourism in, 1001
in Triple Entente, 896
women in, 773
World War I and, 897
English Civil War (1642–1646), 676
English East India Company (EIC), 637,
        638–639, 810, 862–863
    capitalism and, 672
    Mughal Empire and, 625
    in Southeast Asia, 638(*m*)
English West Indies, slaves to, 606
Enlightenment, 510, 761, 762–771
    in American colonies, 769
    French Revolution and, 772
    ideas in, 762–765
    Old Order and, 765–767
    revolts in, 767
    spread of, 764
Entertainment
    in Japan, 703
    after World War II, 993
Entrepreneurs, industrial, 798–799
Entrepreneurship, 483
Environment. *See also* Ecosystems
    of Africa, 866
    of Americas, 516
    Brazil gold rush and, 734
    of China, 694–695
    Columbian Exchange and, 561–562
    consequences of British in Burma, 864
    of English North American colonies,
        743
    of Europe, 660
    global, 1039(*m*)
    as global issue, 1038–1040
    imperialism and, 868–869, 871–872
    Inca, 530
    of India, 622–623
    of Japan, 701
    mining in Spanish America and, 567
    of 17th-century China, 693
    of western Africa, 585
Epidemic disease. *See also* Diseases
    Columbian Exchange and, 562
    influenza as, 904–905
    in Spanish America, 729
Equal Employment Opportunity Commission
        (U.S.), 1009
Equality
    for African Americans, 1009
    racial and gender, 852
    for women, 1010
Equiano, Olaudah, 606, 606(*i*)
    voyage of, 582(*m*)
Escorial (Spanish palace), 674
Española. *See* Hispaniola

Espionage. *See* Spies and spying

Esquivel, Laura, 1050

Estates General (France), 771

Estonia, 942

Ethiopia, 617
famine in, 1041
Mussolini's invasion of, 940, 940(*m*)

Ethnic groups and ethnicity. *See also* specific groups
in Africa, 868
in Balkans, 896
diasporas of, 877
as global issue, 1038
in North America, 539
as outsiders, 849
strife among, 1052
in Yugoslavia, 1016

Eunuchs, in China, 693

Eurafrican communities, in West Africa, 597

Eurasia. *See also* Afro-Eurasia; Asia; Europe and Europeans
in 14th century, 478–487
gunpowder empire in, 616
modernity in, 509

Euro (European Currency Unit), 1034

Europe and Europeans. *See also* Afro-Eurasia; Eurasia; specific locations
in Africa, 593, 865–868
American claims by (c. 1600), 568(*m*)
Black Death and, 478, 479
bourgeoisie and, 672
China and, 857
diaspora of Muslims and Jews from, 647
divisions in (1500–1650), 658–670
economy and, 477, 913
empires in Americas, 722
end of Ottoman threat to, 654
Enlightenment and, 762–767
expansion into Indian Ocean, 616
exploration by (c. 1450–1600), 548(*m*), 551–576
India and, 632–639
Indian outsourcing for, 1032
industrialization in (c. 1900), 795–796
Japanese expansion and, 868
Napoleonic (1796–1815), 775(*m*)
nation-states and, 686
in North America, 538–539
Ottomans and, 489, 652–653
political power in (1453), 485(*m*)
population increase and, 659
postwar prosperity and, 976
production and, 794–795
Protestant and Catholic Reformations in, 661–665, 663(*m*)
Renaissance and, 478, 499–501
Scientific Revolution and, 670–672
17th-century crisis and, 667–670
in c. 1600, 648(*m*)
slaves and, 606
societies after Black Death, 482–484
in Southeast Asia, 708
U.S. Great Plains and, 840–841
U.S. aid to, 964
voyages of discovery by, 555–561, 557(*m*)

West and West Central African slave trade and, 598
Western Hemisphere and, 722
witchcraft trials and, 670

European Economic Community (Common Market), 976, 1026, 1034

European Recovery Program. *See* Marshall Plan

European Union (EU), 1026, 1034
membership of (to 2010), 1034–1035

Europe first strategy (World War II), 944(*m*), 951

Evangelicalism, in Great Awakening, 785

Evil empire, communist world as, 1014

Ewuare (Benin), 590–592

Examination system. *See also* Civil service examinations
Neo-Confucianism and, 486

Exchange. *See also* Cross-cultural exchange; Trade
expansion and, 891
Inca, 530

Exercise, non-Western impact on Western, 886

Existentialism, 980–981

Expansion. *See also* Imperialism
Aztec, 522, 523–524
European, 650
by Germany, 926(*m*)
Inca, 529, 530–532, 537–538
by Italy, 926(*m*)
by Japan, 926(*m*), 935–936, 935(*m*)
migration and, 874–875
Mughal, 627
Nazi, 940, 941(*m*)
in 19th century, 857
Ottoman, 489–491, 490(*m*), 651–655
overseas, by Western powers, 891
postwar imperial, 912–913
Russian, 683, 684(*m*), 686–690, 832–833
by Songhai, 590
of United States, 838–841

Exploration. *See also* Conquistadors; Settlement; Space exploration
European (c. 1450–1600), 547–576, 548(*m*)
Iberian, 508
motives for, 551–552
by Portugal, 548(*m*), 553–555, 570–571
by Spain, 484, 548(*m*), 555–560
technologies for, 552–553

Exports
from China, 496–498, 693
of Russian grain, 836
from Southeast Asia, 496, 710–711

Extermination camps, 945, 945(*m*)

Factories. *See also* Industrialization; Industry
in India, 810
in Japan, 803
Luddites and, 814

Faisal (Syria), 908

Families
in China, 1041
female support of, 815
during Great Depression, 931
Ottoman, 491
postindustrial, 1002–1003
samurai, 503

standardization of, 1053
in Sweden, 939

Family (Pa Chin), 939

Family planning, 1041
centers for, 931

Famine, 1041. *See also* Starvation
in Africa, 868
in Asia, 868
in China, 857
in colonies, 873
in India, 949
in Valley of Mexico, 529

Fanon, Frantz, 981, 981(*i*), 982

Farms and farming. *See also* Agriculture; Crops
in Americas, 519
collective farms, 933–934
dairy farming, 801
government protection of, 1018–1019
during Great Depression, 929, 931
in Mexico, 891
in Mughal Empire, 631
multinational corporations and, 1018
Ottoman, 656
scientific techniques for, 1017
in Spanish colonies, 560
tax farming, 491
in West Central Africa, 593–594
women in Africa and, 818–819

Farrukhsiyar (Shah, India), 632

Fascism. *See also* Italy; Nazi Germany; Spain
in France, 939
of Mussolini, 918–919

Fatwa (decree), 642

Federalism, in Latin America, 831

Federation, in United States, 769

Feitorías (fortified trading posts), 554, 595, 620, 633

Female impersonators, in Japan, 703

Female infanticide, in China, 1041

Females. *See* Women

Feminine Mystique, The (Friedan), 1010

Femininity, during World War I, 900–902

Feminists
activism by, 1009–1010
as authors, 1050–1051
Brezhnev and, 1012
global meetings by, 1034
nationalism and, 884–885
pacifism and, 954
World War I and, 900

Ferdinand (Holy Roman Empire), 665

Ferdinand II (Holy Roman Empire), 668

Ferdinand of Aragon, 484. *See also* Isabella and Ferdinand (Spain)

Fernandes de Oliveira, João (Brazilian mine owner and companion of Chica da Silva), 719, 735

Fertility, Inca, 536

Fertilizers, 801
chemicals and, 1018

Fetishism, 598

Fiji, 877

Filipino people
elite, 713(*i*)
U.S. and, 881–882

Films, 893, 914
    in Bollywood, 989
    star system in, 917(*b*)
    about warfare, 980
    after World War I, 915, 916–917(*b*)
    World War I propaganda in, 901(*b*)
    in World War II, 948
"Final Solution," Holocaust as, 945
Finances
    of European monarchs, 484
    Italy and, 500
Firearms. *See* Weapons
First Balkan War (1912), 892(*m*), 896
First World War. *See* World War I
Fishing, in Newfoundland, 743–744
Fitness, non-Western impact on Western, 886
Five Pillars of Islam, 1050
Five-year plans (Soviet Union), 933
Flagellants, 481
Flags, as national symbols, 844(*b*), 844(*i*)
Flappers, 914, 915
Fleming, Ian, 982
FLN. *See* Front for National Liberation
Flooding, in Bible, 533(*b*)
Florence
    Medici family in, 483
    revolt in (1378), 483
Florentine Codex (Aztecs), 528(*b*), 566(*b*), 566(*i*)
Florida
    British in, 768
    French in, 741
Flowering Plum Tree (Van Gogh), 886(*i*)
Flying shuttle, 798
Foods. *See also* Agriculture; Farms and farming
    American, 519, 562, 659–660
    Aztec, 529, 563
    Inca, 537
    in Mughal Empire, 631
Foot-binding, in China, 487, 851
Ford, Henry, violence against unemployed
    workers and, 932
Foreign aid
    to defeated enemies, 964(*i*)
    to Europe, 963–964
    to Japan, 964, 964(*i*)
    to Latin America, 1003–1004
Foreign-born population, of United States, 1044
Foreigners
    in Japan, 803–804, 825
    in Ming China, 487
Forests
    environmental changes and, 660
    in Japan, 701
    in West Central Africa, 593
Formosa, Japanese invasion of, 868
Forts, slaving, 603
Fossil fuels, gases from burning, 1038
Fourteen Points, 905
France. *See also* French Revolution; World War I
    absolutism in, 673–674
    Algeria and, 974–975
    Alsace and Lorraine and, 802
    Brazil and, 572
    Caribbean region and, 737, 739
    colonial uprisings and, 911, 932

colonies of, 869
education in, 847
Egypt and, 864, 865
expansion of, 863, 864
Germany after World War II and, 964–965,
    965(*m*)
Haiti and, 777–778
Huguenots in, 665
Hundred Years' War and, 484
imperialism by, 912
independence of African nations and, 974
Indochina and, 864, 885
Italian unification and, 837
July 14 as national holiday, 771
monarchy in, 483–484
in North Africa, 679, 865
North America and, 741–745, 742(*m*)
at Paris Peace Conference, 905
Popular Front in, 939
republicanism in, 773–774
response to Great Depression, 939
royal court in, 674
Saint-Domingue and, 777
St. Lawrence region and, 744
as secular state, 784–785
slave trade and, 600, 603
in Southeast Asia, 864
strike in, 1010
Suez crisis and, 973
in Thirty Years' War, 668
in Triple Entente, 896
U.S. consumerism and, 982
women in, 773, 774
World War I and, 897, 905
World War II in, 942
Francis Xavier (Jesuit missionary), 633
Franco, Francisco, Spain after, 1006–1007
Franco-Prussian War (1870–1871), 838, 897
Frank, Anne, 980
Franklin, Benjamin, Enlightenment and, 764
Franz Ferdinand (Austria-Hungary), 896
Frederick the Great (Prussia), 765
Free blacks, in Haiti, 777
Freedom(s). *See also* Rights
    economic, 763–764
Free France, 949–950
    de Gaulle and, 975
Free labor. *See also* Labor; Slaves and slavery
    costs of production and, 797
Free soil, in United States, 840
Freetown, Sierra Leone, 872
Free trade, 1027
    zones, 1034–1036
French Indochina. *See also* Indochina
    World War II in, 944
French Revolution (1789–1799), 771–774
    European war against, 773
    Napoleon and, 774
French West Africa, independence in, 974
French West Indies, slaves to, 606
Freud, Sigmund, 886
Friedan, Betty, 1010
Fronde (French resistance), 674
Front for National Liberation (FLN, Algeria),
    974, 975

Frontiers
    Chinese, 693
    Ottoman, 657
Fundamentalist Muslims, Taliban as, 1008
Furtado, Júnia (historian), 721
Fur trade, 743
    Dutch, 741
    route of, 684(*m*)
    Russia and, 690

Gagarin, Yuri (Soviet cosmonaut), 966,
    966–967(*b*), 966(*i*)
Galicia, World War I in, 897
Galilei, Galileo, 671, 672
Gallipoli, Battle of, 898–899
Gambia River region, Portugal and, 595
Gandhi, Indira, assassination of, 1045
Gandhi, Mohandas (Mahatma), 958(*i*)
    activism by, 916–917
    assassination of, 970
    civil disobedience by, 954–955
    jailing of, 932
    Satyagraha strategy of, 954, 954(*i*)
Gandhi, Rajiv, assassination of, 1045
Gao, 590
Gao Xingjian (China), 1038
García de Loyola, Martín, 574–575
García Márquez, Gabriel, 920, 1050
Garcilaso de la Vega ("El Inca"), 647–648
Garibaldi, Giuseppe (Italy), 837
Garvey, Marcus, 981
Gasoline engine, 799–800
Gatherer-hunters
    in Americas, 514(*m*), 516, 519, 540
    Pygmies (Batwa) as, 607
Gath y Chaves (department store), 805, 806(*i*)
Gays. *See also* Homosexuality
    equal rights for, 1011
Gaza, 1013
Gebriel, Mohammed (Sheik), 1048
Geisha, in Japan, 703
Gender and gender issues
    cultural change and, 878
    during Great Depression, 931
    Inca, 536
    in Korea, 706
    in Nazi Germany, 937
    World War I and, 900–902
    youth culture and, 1003
"General Points Relating to Slavery" (Sandoval),
    596(*b*)
General will, in France, 773
Genetics, 995
    modification of plants and animals, 1017,
    1018
Geneva Conference (1954), 972
Génies (sacred places), in western Africa, 585
Genoa
    Black Death and, 479, 480(*m*)
    declining power of, 651
Genocide
    in Armenia (1915–1917), 1049
    in Cambodia, 971(*m*)
    Holocaust as, 925
    in Rwanda, 1049

Gentlemen of Esmeraldas (Sanchez Galque), 730(*b*), 730(*i*)

Geocentrism, 671, 671(*i*)

George V (England), 899

German East Africa, 866, 872, 885

German Empire, 838

Germany. *See also* Nazi Germany; World War I; World War II

    Africa and, 865

    Alsace and Lorraine and, 802

    coal cartel in, 805

    East Africa and, 866

    historiography in, 846(*b*), 846(*i*)

    industrialization of, 802

    international capital flows and, 1033

    League of Nations and, 907

    mutinies and rebellions in, 904

    Napoleon and, 774

    nation building in, 837–838

    postwar division of, 964–965, 965(*m*)

    Protestantism in, 662

    reparations and, 906

    reunification of (1990), 1016

    Schlieffen Plan of, 897

    in Thirty Years' War, 668

    Treaty of Versailles and, 906–907

    in Triple Alliance, 896

    unification of (1871), 837–838, 838(*m*)

    Venezuela grants to, 572

    war guilt and, 907

    World War I and, 896, 897

    World War I homefront in, 900

Germ warfare, by Mongols, 479

Gestapo, 937

Ghana, 592–593

    cocoa protest in, 932

    England and, 866

    feitoria in, 595–596

    gold in, 588(*i*)

    independence of, 958(*i*), 973

Ghazi (holy warrior) bands, 489–490

Gibraltar, 676(*m*)

Gift exchange, in Peru, 513

Glasnost (openness), 1015

Glenn, John, 967(*b*)

Global cooling, in Little Ice Age, 669

Global economy, 996–1003. *See also* Economy and economic systems

    neoliberalism and, 1033

    networks and job changes in, 1032–1033

    trade in, 794–795

    United States in, 770–771

Global issues, 1037–1047

    economic crisis as, 1047

    migration as, 1044–1045

    terrorism as, 1045–1047

Globalization, 860–861, 1024(*m*), 1025. *See also* Global issues

    of cities, 1036–1037

    of communications linkages, 995

    culture and, 878–879

    early, 508

    environment and, 1039(*m*)

    ethnic strife and, 1052

    global activism and, 1034

    impact of events on regions and nations, 1026–1031

    of literature and music, 1050–1051

    livelihood and, 1031–1037

    migration and, 1024(*m*)

    protecting tradition and, 1052–1053, 1052(*i*)

    resistance to, 1025–1026

    of technology, 988(*i*)

    of trade and finance, 859–860

    worker competition and, 1033

Global networks, 1032–1033

Global politics, terrorism in, 1045

Global recovery, in 1950s and 1960s, 975–980

Global structures and organizations. *See also* Globalization

    capitalism and, 672–673

    Cold War alliances and, 967–969

    early, 508

    economic development and, 1027

    supranational, 1033–1036

Global trade, 796–798

    crop movements and, 593–594

Global war, World War I as, 893, 896

Global warming, 1038

Glorious Revolution (England, 1688), 676–677

Goa

    Christians in, 633

    Portugal and, 622, 633

Gobind Singh (guru), 632

Golconda, diamonds of, 616

Gold

    in Africa, 547, 586, 587, 587–588(*b*), 587(*i*)

    in Brazil, 722, 732–733

    in Chile, 573–574

    exploration for, 551–552

    Inca, 536, 565

    silver vs., 691

Gold Coast, 595–596

    British in, 870

    cocoa growers cooperative in, 930(*b*)

    Nkrumah in, 973

Golden age

    in Brazil, 735–736

    in Spain, 647–648

Golden Horde (Mongols), Russia and, 689

Gold rush, in Brazil, 733–735, 736

Gold standard, England and, 929

Gonzalez de Clavijo, Ruy (Spanish traveler and ambassador), 490(*b*)

"Good wives, wise mothers," in Japan, 848(*b*)

Gorbachev, Mikhail (Soviet Union), 991–992, 1002

    KGB coup against, 1016–1017

    reforms of, 1014–1015

Gouges, Olympe de, 764, 766, 772, 773

Governance. *See* Government

Government

    absolutism as, 650, 673–675

    in Asia, 686

    Aztec, 523–524

    after Black Death, 483–484

    of Brazil, 1029

    changes in nature of, 925

    of China, 486, 693

    constitutionalism as, 673, 675–677

    contract, 763

    of East African coastal cities, 620–621

    of Eastern Woodlands peoples, 540

    economies and, 805

    of Egypt, 775

    of English North American colonies, 743

    farm protection by, 1018–1019

    imperial, 870

    intellectual thought on, 763, 764

    in Latin America, 1003–1006

    of Meiji Japan, 842

    of Mughal Empire, 629

    Nazi, 937

    Ottoman, 656

    religion and, 785

    responses to Great Depression, 929, 932

    of South Africa, 1029–1030

    of Spanish America, 724–729

    standard of living and, 977

    of Timur's empire, 488–489

    TV programming and, 993

    of United States, 769–771

    of Vijayanagara, 622

    in West Africa, 590

    during World War I, 900, 901(*b*)

Grain

    Russian exports of, 836

    science and, 996

Gran Colombia, 781

Grand Alliance (World War II), 945

Grand Army (France), 775(*m*)

Grand Vizier (Ottoman Empire), 651

Grassroots activism, in farming, 1018

Great Awakening, 785

Great Britain. *See* England (Britain)

Great Depression (1929–1941), 919, 926(*m*), 927

    business in, 930(*b*)

    commodity prices in, 929

    communism and socialism ideologies during, 932(*i*)

    democracies' responses to, 938–939

    gender relations during, 931

    government response to, 929

    protests during, 931–932

    social effects of, 930–931

    U.S. stock market crash and, 927, 928–929

Greater East Asia Co-Prosperity Sphere, 941

"Greater Serbia," 1016

Great Famine (1315–1317), 479

Great Flood (Bible), 533

Great Game, imperialism in Asia as, 862

Great Lakes region, French Jesuits in, 746

Great Leap Forward (China), 978(*b*), 979

"Great Mirror of Male Love, The" (Saikaku), 703

"Great mortality." *See* Black Death

Great Plains (North America), 538

    native Americans in, 840

Great Wall (China), 499

Great Zimbabwe, 620

Greece

    as autonomous state, 896, 898(*m*)

    communists in, 963

    EU and, 1035

    invasion of Turkey, 909(*m*)

    U.S. aid to, 964

Greek church. *See* Greek Orthodox Church; Orthodox Christianity
Greek Orthodox Church. *See also* Orthodox Christianity
    Ottomans and, 491
Green, William (head of American Federation of Labor), 932
Greenhouse effect, 1038
Green movement. *See* Green Party; Green Revolution
Green Party, 1038
Green Revolution, 996
    in India, 1028(*i*)
Griot (oral poet), 848
Guadalcanal, Battle of, 944(*m*), 951
Guadeloupe, 739
Guam, 944
    Magellan in, 561
    U.S. annexation of, 881
Guanabara Bay, Brazil, French colony in, 572
Guanahani (Bahama Islands), 556
Guanajuato, silver in, 567
Guanches (native Canary Islanders), 554
Guangzhou (Canton), China, 497–498, 691
Guaraní speakers, 728
Guatemala
    Maya in, 519
    Spanish and, 562
    tradition in, 1052
    U.S. and, 1003–1004
Guerrero, Vicente, 779–780
Guerrilla warfare, in Indonesia, 971
Guest workers, 976
Guevara, Che, 981, 1011(*i*)
Guilds, in India, 496(*b*)
Guillotine, in France, 773
Guinea, invasions of, 596
Gujarat
    kingdom of, 625
    merchants from, 494, 623
    Muslims in, 497–498
Gulag Archipelago (Solzhenitsyn), 1012
Gulags, in Soviet Union, 934
Gulf of Guinea, Portugal and, 555
Gunpowder and gunpowder weapons, 478, 483–484, 552, 625–626
    in China, 693
    in India, 627
    in Southeast Asia, 710(*i*)
Gunpowder empires
    in Eurasia, 616
    Ottoman Empire as, 650
    Russia as, 690
Guomindang (China), 895, 910, 935–936
Gustav II (Sweden), 668(*i*)
Guyana (Suriname), 738

Habsburg dynasty, 676(*m*)
    Balkan wars and, 896
    Ottomans and, 653–654
    Peace of Paris treaties and, 906
    in Spain, 654
Hague, The
    International Tribunal on human rights abuses and, 1049

peace meeting in, 900
Hai-Feng Peasant Union, 911(*b*)
Haiku poetry, 885
Haiti
    Columbus in, 557
    revolution in, 777–778, 778(*m*), 779(*i*)
Al-Hajari, Ahmad Ibn Qasim, 669(*b*)
Hallucinogenic drugs, in Americas, 518
Hamilton, Alexander, 769, 770
Hampi, Vijayanagara, 621(*i*), 623
Hanyang, Korea. *See* Seoul
Hargreaves, James, 798
Hawaii
    U.S. annexation of, 881
    U.S. overthrow of queen in, 882(*b*)
Head, Bessie (South African writer), 981
Headmen, Inca, 532, 534–535
Health. *See also* Diseases; Medicine
    in colonies, 872–873
    of Eastern Woodlands peoples, 541
    as global issue, 1037, 1041–1044
    HIV/AIDS crisis and, 1030
    of Japanese people, 700
    Spanish-American mining and, 567, 568–569
    vaccines and, 1041
    of workers, 813–814
    after World War II, 977
Health care. *See also* Health; Medicine
    in South Africa, 1029
Heart transplant, 995
Heiji Revolt (Japan, 1159), 504(*i*)
Heliocentrism, 671
Helsinki Accords (1975), 1049
Hemings, Sally (slave), 746
Henry III (Castile), embassy in Samarkand of, 490(*b*)
Henry IV (France), 665, 674
Henry VIII (England), 662
Henry "the Navigator" (Portugal), 554, 555
Herat, as Mongol capital, 489
Heresy. *See* Christianity; Reformation
Herzl, Theodor (founder of Zionism), 851
Hidalgo, Miguel (Mexican rebel leader), 779, 780
Hidden Christians (Japan), 700(*b*)
Hideyoshi, Toyotomi (Japanese shogun), 698, 706
Hierarchies. *See also* Society
    in Aztec society, 526–529
    in Inca society, 536
Higher education, for postindustrial economy, 991
High-tech industries, 993–994, 997–998
High-tech society, agrarian peoples and, 1017–1019, 1018(*i*)
Highway. *See* Roads and highways
Hijackings, on September 11, 2001, 1045
Hind Swaraj (Indian Home Rule), 917
Hindus and Hinduism
    in India, 613
    in Majapahit kingdom, 493
    nationalism of, 885
    Partition of India and, 970
    Shivaji (Maratha), 627
    in Vijayanagara, 621, 623
    Western study of, 886

Hip-hop music, 1051
Hirohito (Japan), 935, 945
Hiroshige, Ando, 803(*i*), 817
Hiroshima, atomic bombing of, 951, 952(*b*), 952(*i*)
Hispaniola, 738, 777
    Columbus in, 557
History and historiography
    on Aztecs, 520, 521–522
    on Black Death, 479
    on China's environment, 694–695
    Chinese silver revenues and, 691–692
    nationalism and, 844–845
    on nation-states, 829, 846(*b*)
    of Pygmies (Batwa), 608
    Al-Sa'di on Jenne, 591(*b*)
    on Spanish-American conquests, 566
Hitler, Adolf, 927, 933, 945. *See also* Nazi Germany
    expansionism of, 940
    Lebensraum and, 940
    masses and, 924(*i*)
    propaganda use by, 937
    rise to power of, 936–938
    suicide of, 951
    World War II and, 947–948
    young people and, 924(*i*), 937
HIV. *See also* AIDS
    in 2009, 1042(*m*)
Ho Chi Minh (Vietnam), 932, 960(*m*), 971, 971(*m*), 983
Hodgson, Marshall, 616
Hokkaido, Ainu people of, 699
Holidays, in France, 773
Holland. *See also* Dutch; Netherlands
    land reclaimed in, 660
Holocaust, 925, 945–947, 945(*m*)
    Israel and, 972
Holy Roman Empire
    Ottomans and, 653–654
    in Thirty Years' War, 668
Home front, in World War I, 900–902
Home rule, for India, 917
Homosexuality
    criminalization in Soviet Union, 934
    gay rights and, 1011
    in Japan, 702–703
    Nazis and, 947
Honda, Soichiro, 998
Hong (Lady) (Korea), 707(*b*)
Hong Kong, 970, 997, 1036
    British in, 914, 970
Hongwu (Zhu Yuanzhang), 486
Hong Xiuquan (China), 807
Honshu, 698
Horses
    Latin American cowboys and, 782(*b*), 782(*i*)
    Mapuche people and, 576, 576(*i*)
    Spanish, 566
Horticulture. *See* Ecosystems
Hostage crisis, in Iran (1979), 1009, 1010(*b*), 1010(*i*)
Hotel industry, 1001(*b*)
Housing
    of Eastern Woodlands peoples, 540
    non-Western impact on Western, 886

Hu, Butterfly (Chinese film star), 916(*i*), 917(*b*)
Huancavelica
    labor in mines, 568–569
    mercury mines of, 567
Huarochirí, Peru, 533(*b*)
Huascar (Inca ruler), 538
Hudson, Henry, 741
Huerta, Dolores (U.S. civil rights activist), 1009
Huguenots (French Protestants), 674
    Catholic persecution of, 665
    in North America, 741
Huitzilopochtli (god), 522, 526
Humanism, 498, 499
Human rights
    activism for, 1049
    Bandung Conference and, 984
    as global value, 1049
    in Soviet Union, 1012
Human sacrifice. *See also* Sacrifice
    Aztec, 524–526, 525(*i*)
    Inca, 513–515, 534(*i*)
Human traffickers, slave trade and, 604
Humayun, Muhammad (Mughal Empire),
    625–626
Hundred Years' War (1337–1453), 484
Hungary
    Ottomans and, 654
    Peace of Paris treaties and, 906
    rebellion in (1956), 979
    Soviet Union and, 964
    in World War II, 942, 951
Hunger, scientific advances against, 996
Hunter's Sketches, A (Turgenev), 834
Hunting. *See also* Gatherer-hunters
    in Americas, 519
Huron Indians, 540, 540(*i*), 542, 742
Husbandry, animal, 585
Hydroelectric power, from dams, 1038
Hydrogen bomb, 963
Hygiene
    in Japan, 700
    promotion of, 915–916

Iberians. *See also* Portugal; Spain
    exploration by, 508, 550
IBM, 998
Ibn al-Wardi (Muslim cleric), 482
Ibn Battuta (Moroccan Muslim scholar), 492
Ibn Majid (Arab shipmaster), 493
Ibo women's tax protest, 911
Ibsen, Henrik, 880
Ice, global melting of, 1038, 1040(*i*)
Ice Age, Little Ice Age, 479
Ideas
    in Enlightenment, 762–765
    non-Western impact on Western, 886
Identity
    in globalizing world, 1052–1053, 1053(*i*)
    local, 827
    national, 649, 827–828
    resistance to globalization and, 1025–1026
Ideologies
    communication technology and political,
        893–894
    communism in Depression and, 932(*i*)

conservatism as, 783
Japanese military, 944–945
liberalism as, 763, 783
nationalism as, 783
revolutionary Marxism as, 903, 904
romanticism as, 783
socialism in Depression and, 932(*i*)
Idolatry. *See* Fetishism
Ieyasu Tokugawa (Japan), 698
Ife people, 592
Ignatius of Loyola, 574, 662
Ijaw peoples, slave trade and, 598
Imams (Muslim religious scholars), coffee and,
    658–659(*b*)
Imbangala people (Angola), 599, 600
Immigrants and immigration. *See also* Migration
    to Argentina, 919
    in global cities, 1036
    to United States, 769
Imperialism. *See also* Empires
    arts and, 879–880
    business, 861, 998
    competition among powers and, 881–882
    contests over, 880–885
    culture and, 878–880
    decolonization and, 969
    defined, 860–861
    1850–1914, 858(*m*)
    environment and, 868–869, 871–872
    European cooperation with, 869–870
    global (1930s), 940
    governments under, 870
    in India, 632
    by Japan, 868
    migration and, 874–875
    motivations for, 861
    nationalism and, 959
    new, 925
    post–World War I expansion, 912–913
    resistance to, 883–885
    scramble for Africa and, 867–868
    social disorder under, 870–871
    society under, 869–878, 872(*b*), 872(*i*)
    technology and, 868–869
    tensions from, 894
    by United States, 881–882
    World War I and, 893, 897
Imports
    into Japan, 701
    to Southeast Asia, 711
Impressionism, 817
Inca Empire (1430–1532), 529–538
    culture of, 518
    expansion of, 530–532
    human sacrifice in, 534(*i*)
    land in, 537
    lifestyle in, 534–537
    Machu Picchu and, 512(*i*)
    mummies in, 532, 534(*i*), 538
    origins of, 530
    peoples of, 547
    religion in, 532
    roads in, 514(*m*), 535(*i*)
    Spanish conquest of, 564–565, 564(*m*)
    1325–1521, 531(*m*)

Inca people
    Garcilaso de la Vega on, 649
    revolt in 18th century by, 767
Income tax, cuts for wealthy, 1014
Indenture and indentured labor, 722,
    876–877(*b*), 876(*i*)
    African slaves and, 602–603
Independence
    in Africa, 975
    African textile for, 975(*b*), 975(*i*)
    for Algeria, 975
    decolonization and, 969–975
    in Haiti, 778, 778(*m*)
    in Latin America, 759–761, 778–783, 832
    in Middle East, 972–973
    movements for, 932, 960(*m*)
    nation builders after, 847–848
    in sub-Saharan Africa, 958(*i*)
    after World War I, 908–911
India. *See also* Pakistan
    in Afrasian Sea trade, 616
    Amritsar massacre in, 911
    anti-British nonviolent mass movement in,
        916–917
    Awadh takeover and, 863
    Basmati rice from, 1018
    Britain and, 813(*i*), 861, 862–863
    castes in, 914
    celebration for Edward VII in, 880(*i*)
    classes, castes, and religious divisions in, 914
    consumerism in, 1032
    da Gama voyage to, 555
    Dutch in, 635
    economy in, 631–632, 794, 976, 1028
    environment in, 622–623
    Europeans in, 632–639
    Gandhi, Indira, and, 1045
    Gandhi, Mohandas, in, 916–917
    general strike in, 932
    gunpowder weapons in, 627
    imperial government in, 870
    imperialism in, 632
    indentured workers in, 877
    independence for, 970
    industrialization in, 810, 810(*m*)
    literature in, 879
    middle-class family in, 813(*i*)
    movies in, 915
    Mughal dynasty in, 616
    nationalism in, 885, 958(*i*)
    opium in, 809(*i*)
    outsourcing in, 1032
    partition of (1947), 970(*m*)
    population control in, 1041
    Portugal and, 614(*m*), 616, 632–635
    protection of farmers in, 1018–1019
    railroads in, 810
    resistance to imperialism in, 872
    Russia and, 863
    sati in, 630–631
    sepoys in, 863
    Southeast Asia trade with, 711
    strikes in, 914
    taxation of, 929
    tea from, 807

textiles from, 810
trade and, 494
Untouchables in, 813
urban weavers in, 496–497(b)
Vijayanagara kingdom in, 621–623, 621(i)
women in, 630–631
World War I soldiers from, 897
World War II in, 949
Indian Congress Party, 949, 1028
"Indianization," of Mughal emperors, 626–627
Indian National Congress, 863, 885
Indian Ocean region. See also specific locations
China and, 487
Dutch Empire in, 635
East Africa trade and, 619–620
Europeans in, 616
in c. 1450, 495
modernity in, 509
Ottomans and, 652
Portuguese in, 633
rulers of, 615
trade in, 587, 613–616, 614(m), 618(m)
Zheng He in, 498–499
Indians. See also Native Americans
Columbus on, 556–557
in Spanish America, 726
Indian Uprising (1857), 863
India voyage, of Portugal (Carreira da India), 634
Indies, sea route to, 555
Indigenous peoples. See also Native Americans
in Atlantic region, 554
decline in Columbian Exchange, 562
as outsiders, 849–850
in South America, 726
in Spanish-American mines, 734
in Spanish–native American encounters, 566
Indochina
France and, 864, 885
nationalists in, 911, 971
Indochinese Communist Party, 932
Indonesia, 616, 911, 944
in ASEAN, 1036
Dutch in, 635
Europeans in, 708
exploration of, 560
independence for, 970
Inductive reasoning, 670
Indulgences, Luther on, 662
Industrialization. See also Industrial Revolution; Industry
in Africa, 810–812
in China, 978(b)
in colonies, 873
costs of, 804
after 1830, 798–806
in Europe (c. 1900), 795–796
European expansion and, 891
global roots of, 794–795
in India, 810, 810(m)
innovation and, 796, 799–802
interchangeability of parts and, 798
in Japan, 701, 802–804, 804(m), 935(m)
middle class and, 812–813
migration and, 874–875

non-European, 802–804
railroads and, 790(i)
in Soviet Union, 933, 963
spread of, 792(m)
in United States, 802
workers and, 791–793, 813–815
Industrial Revolution, 791–793
Crimean War and, 833
in England, 794, 795–796
middle class and, 812–813
periods of, 800–801
in western Europe, 794
world and, 806–812
Industry
arts and, 817
culture of, 815–817
in Depression, 929
domestic, 484
environmental damage from, 1038
everyday life and (1750–1900), 791–793
globalization of, 794
resources for, 797
in rural England, 797(b)
slavery and, 797
society and, 812–815
technology of, 798
women and children in, 813
after World War I, 913
Infant mortality
in Europe, 661
in Spanish America, 729
Inflation. See also Economy and economic systems
in Ottoman Empire, 654
Influenza, 563
epidemic of (1918–1919), 904–905
Information evolution, 993–994
Infrastructure
colonial taxation and, 873
Inca, 535
in Japan, 701
in Latin America, 832
Ottoman, 656
Inheritance
in Aceh, 640–641
Inca, 534
in Ming China, 487
Innovation. See also Inventions; Technology
industrial, 796, 799–802
in Japan, 802–803
Inquisition
in Americas, 570
in Brazil, 735–736
prosecutions by, 670
in Spanish America, 729
Institute for Production and Research in Tropical Agriculture (Venezuela), 1018
Institutions
global, 1031–1037
national, 846–849
Intellectual thought. See also Learning
in China, 696–697
in Enlightenment, 510, 763–765
industrial knowledge and, 812–813
non-Western impact on Western, 886

in Renaissance, 498, 501
Scientific Revolution and, 670–672
in Timbuktu, 492(i)
after World War II, 980–981
Intelsat I and III, 994
Intendants (French officials), 674
Interchangeability of parts, 798
Interest rates, in mid-1970s, 1014
Intergroup conflict, in western Africa, 587
International Exhibit (Paris, 1889), 800
International Monetary Fund, 1027
International order, changes in, 1006–1009
International organizations
Cold War alliances and, 967
economic development and, 1027
International trade. See Trade
International Tribunal (The Hague), human rights abuses and, 1049
International Women's Day, in Russia, 902
International women's movement, 900
Internet, global employment and, 1032
Interpretation of Dreams, The (Freud), 886
Interstate relations. See Commerce; Diplomacy; Wars and warfare
Intervention, in society, 977
Intolerance, of diversity by Christianity, 647
Invasions. See also specific invasions
of Iraq by U.S., 1045–1046
of Korea, 698
Inventions. See also Innovation
in Japan, 804
navigational, 553
In vitro fertilization, 996
iPhone, 988(i)
Iran. See also Persia
hostage crisis in (1979), 1009, 1010(b), 1010(i)
population growth in, 1041
religious uprising in, 1008–1009
revolt in, 911
Iraq
independence for, 973
U.S. invasion of (2003), 1045
wars in (2001–2011), 1046(m)
Ireland. See also Northern Ireland
Cromwell and, 676
Easter rebellion in, 910
economy of, 1032
in 1921, 910(m)
Irish Free State, 910
Irish Republican Army, 1045
Iron and iron industry
in Africa, 586–587
in Spanish America, 728
Iron curtain, 953
Iroquois Five Nations, 539
Iroquois Indians, 744(i)
Irrigation
in colonies, 873
Inca, 535
Isabella and Ferdinand (Spain), Columbus and, 556, 559
Isabella of Castile, 484, 556. See also Isabella and Ferdinand (Spain)
Isabella of Portugal, 666

Iskandar Muda Shah (Aceh sultan), 642
Islam. *See also* Muslims
    African trade and, 581
    Black Death and, 480
    in Central Asia, 488–489
    Christendom and, 475, 485(*m*)
    expansion of, 1050
    in Kazan, 1048
    in Mughal Empire, 616
    Muslim Brotherhood and, 918
    nationalism in Ottoman Empire and, 884
    Ottomans and, 651
    sciences in, 670
    in Southeast Asia, 492–493
    in Sudan, 1027
    Wahhabism in, 785–786, 785(*i*)
    in West Africa, 491–493, 585, 588–589
    in West Central Africa, 593
Islamic law. *See* Shari'a (Islamic law)
Islamic world
    Black Death and, 477
    Chinese porcelains in, 495–496
    land empires of, 616
Isolation, of Japan, 501, 697
Israel. *See also* Jews and Judaism
    Arab wars with, 1013
    Palestine and (1949), 972(*m*)
    in Six-Day War, 1013
    Suez crisis and, 973
Istanbul, 656(*i*). *See also* Constantinople
    British in, 908
    commerce and, 650
    Constantinople as, 491
    population of, 651–652
    skyline of, 653(*i*)
Isthmus of Panama, 726
Italy
    in Africa, 865
    Cavour and, 836
    commercial opportunities for, 477
    Ethiopia and, 940, 940(*m*)
    expansion by, 926(*m*)
    fascism in, 918–919
    financing of exploration and, 550
    Mussolini in, 916, 918–919
    Napoleon and, 774
    paramilitary groups in, 946(*b*)
    Red Brigades in, 1045
    Renaissance in, 499–500
    revolt in Florence (1378), 483
    Treaty of London and, 897
    in Triple Alliance and Entente, 896
    unification of, 836–837, 837(*m*)
    World War II in, 951
Iturbide, Augustin de, 779–780
Ivan III (Russia), 688–689
Ivan IV ("the Terrible," Russia), 689
Ivory, trade in, 620
Ivory Coast, invasions of, 596

Jacobin club, 773
Jahangir (Mughal Empire), 613, 626, 627, 628(*i*)
Jahangirnama (Jahangir memoir), 627, 628(*i*)
Jainism
    in East Africa, 621

    nonviolence and, 953
Jamaica, 739
James II (England), 676–677
Jamestown, 741, 743
Janissaries (Ottoman Empire), 489–490, 651,
    652, 775
Japan
    agrarian economy in, 503
    Ainu in, 849
    Asian imperialism by, 862(*m*)
    atomic bombing of, 963
    business practices in, 999(*b*)
    China and, 478, 487, 504, 694(*m*), 868,
        868(*m*), 884, 904, 910, 910(*m*), 935–936
    colonization by, 883
    diet in, 701
    earthquake in, 935
    economy in, 976, 996–997
    c. 1860–1889, 842
    1185–1392, 503(*m*)
    Enlightenment and, 764
    expansion by, 926(*m*), 935–936, 935(*m*),
        940–941
    in 15th century, 683
    films in, 917(*b*)
    foreigners in, 803–804
    Great Depression in, 931, 935
    Greater East Asia Co-Prosperity Sphere of,
        941
    high-tech industries in, 997–998
    imperialism by, 868
    Indonesian independence and, 970
    industrialization in, 802–804, 803(*i*), 804(*m*)
    industrial museum in, 812–813
    Korea and, 698, 706, 868, 883
    lifestyle in, 700–702
    literature in, 879
    Meiji Restoration in, 824(*i*)
    merchants in, 803
    militaristic imperial system in, 935
    militarization in, 932
    modernity and, 510
    modernization of, 841–843
    national culture in, 702–704
    at Paris Peace Conference, 905
    population of, 700
    research and development in, 1001(*b*)
    Russia and, 868
    Russo-Japanese War and, 882–883
    samurai in, 501–503
    shogun in, 503
    Siberia and, 904
    silver from, 691, 699
    tourism workers in, 1000–1001(*b*), 1000(*i*)
    trade and, 798, 803–804
    transition in (1540–1750), 697–704
    U.S. aid to, 964, 964(*i*)
    Western arts and, 885
    Westernization of, 845
    women in, 504, 702, 848(*b*)
    woodblocks in, 817
    workday in, 813
    after World War I, 912–913
    in World War I, 896
    in World War II, 940–941

Japanese Americans, relocation of, 948–949
Japan in the National Emergency (film), 936
Jati class (occupational caste, India), 496
Java
    Dutch in, 635
    Islam in, 493
Jazz, 848
Jefferson, Thomas
    Barbary Wars and, 679
    Continental Congress and, 768
    Enlightenment and, 764
    and Hemings, Sally, 746
Jenne
    Al-Sa'di on, 591(*b*)
    trade in, 492
Jennings, Samuel (U.S. painter), 770(*i*)
Jerusalem, Ottoman control of, 650
Jesuits, 581–582, 662
    in China, 664(*b*), 697
    in New France, 743
    in North American colonies, 746
    in Spanish America, 766
Jewelry, in Africa, 587
Jews and Judaism
    in Argentina, 919
    Black Death blamed on, 480(*m*), 481
    in Brazil, 735–736
    in East Africa, 621
    Holocaust against, 925, 945–947, 945(*m*)
    homeland for, 972
    migrations in 19th century, 858(*m*)
    in Nazi Germany, 937, 938
    in Ottoman Empire, 657
    pogroms against, 875
    in Spain, 484
    U.S. anti-Semitism and, 953
    in Warsaw Ghetto (1943), 948(*i*)
    Zionism and, 851
Jiang Jieshi (Chiang Kai-Shek, China), 910,
    935–936, 936(*i*), 947(*b*), 965
Jiangxi, China, 683
Jim Crow, in United States, 850
Jingdezhen, China, porcelains in, 495
Job discrimination, outlawing of, 1009
Jobs. *See also* Employment; Livelihood(s); Work
    global networks and, 1032–1033
Johannesburg, 881
John Paul II (pope), 1015, 1049
Johnson, Lyndon B., civil rights legislation and,
    1009
Johnson, Samuel, 796
Joint-stock companies, 743
Jordan
    Al Qaeda suicide bombers in, 1046
    independence for, 973
    in Six-Day War, 1013
Joseph the Provider (Mann), 939
Juan Carlos (Spain), 1007
Judaism. *See* Jews and Judaism
Julião, Carlos (Italian artist), 718(*i*)
Junichiro Tanizaki (Japanese author), 935
Junks (Chinese ships), 494
Juntas, 778
    in South Korea, 1007
Jurchen Jin, in Korea, 705

Kabir (bhakti preacher), 497(b)
Kabuki theater (Japan), 703, 704(i)
Kabul, British in, 863
Kaiser (Germany), 838
Kalahari Desert, Pygmies (Batwa) of, 607
Kalm, Pehr, 720(m)
Kamakura Shogunate (Japan, 1185–1333), 503
Kamalat Shah (Aceh sultana), 642
Kamikaze attacks, 947, 951
Kandy kingdom, Ceylon, 637
Kangxi (Qing dynasty, China), 693
Kang Zhengguo (China), on Great Leap
    Forward, 978
Kantorowsky, Eva (Holocaust survivor), 925,
    928, 953
Kantorowsky, Hans (brother of Eva), 925, 945
Kasanje kingdom, 600
Kashmir, 970
Kazan, Russia, Qur'an in, 1048(b)
Keep Smiling (film), 939
Kemal, Mustafa, Turkey under, 908–909, 909(m)
Kennedy, John F.
    civil rights movement and, 1009
    Cuba and, 969
Kenya, 633
    independence of, 974
Kepler, Johannes, 671
KGB (Soviet secret police), 1016–1017
Khaw Soo Cheang, 869–870
    travels of, 858(m)
Khipus (Inca record-keeping method), 530, 536,
    537
Khmer Rouge (Cambodia), 1008
Khmer rule, 711
Khoikhoi people, 586(m), 607
Khomeini, Ayatollah Ruhollah, 1008–1009,
    1010(b), 1010(i), 1041, 1045
Khrushchev, Nikita (Soviet Union), 979
    Cuban missile crisis and, 969
    Soviet culture and, 983
Kidd, William, 639
Kikongo language, 600
Kikuyu people, 973–974
Kilwa, 618
Kimbundo language, 600
King, Martin Luther, Jr., 982, 1009
Kingdom of the Serbs, Croats, and Slovenes.
    See Yugoslavia
Kings and kingdoms. See also State (nation);
    specific rulers and locations
    in Americas, 513
    Aztec, 523–524
    Hindu, 613, 621–623
    Kongo, 598–599
    nation-states and, 826(m)
    in Southeast Asia, 493, 708
    in West Africa, 580(i), 581, 590
    in West Central Africa, 593–595
Kin relationships, in Inca society, 536
Kip, Johannes, 603(i)
Kipling, Rudyard, 881
Kisaeng (female entertainers, Korea), 707
Kissinger, Henry, 1002
Kitomi (deities), 599
Kiyochika Kobayashi, 790(i)

Knowledge-based society, 1033
Kobe, Japan, workers' demonstration in, 932
Kollwitz, Käthe (German artist), 817, 818(i)
Komei (Japan), 837, 841, 842
Kongo
    Christianity in, 599
    kingdom of, 598–599
    slaves from, 600
Kongo territory, 594
    c. 1550, 594(m)
Korea, 935(m)
    chattel slavery in, 693
    China and, 478
    "comfort women" and, 942(b)
    defensive measures in, 705–706
    in 15th century, 683
    flag of, 844(b), 844(i)
    gender issues in, 706
    Japan and, 698, 706, 868, 883
    lifestyle in, 706(i)
    population of, 706
    slave labor in, 708
    1392–1750, 705–708
    trade in, 706
Korean language, 707(b)
Korean War (1950–1953), 967
    economy after, 976
Korematsu, Fred (Japanese American civil rights
    activist), 948–949
Krishna Deva Raya (Vijayanagara king), 622, 623
Kristallnacht (Night of Broken Glass), 938
Kshatriya (warrior) caste (India), 622
Kubilai (Qubilai) Khan (Mongols), 479, 485
Ku Klux Klan, 850
Kulaks, 933
Kulthum, Umm (Arab singer), 959, 961, 961(m),
    962
Kulturkampf (Bismarck), 848
Kwakiutl culture, 519
    area of (c. 1500), 519(i)
Kwinto maroons, 749
Kyoto, Japan, 503
    festival in, 702(i)
Kyoto Protocol, 1040
Kyushu, 698

Labor. See also Serfs and serfdom; Slaves and
    slavery; Workers; Working class
    abolition of slavery and, 810
    after Black Death, 480
    for Ceylon's cinnamon crops, 637(b)
    child, 813
    in Chile, 573–574
    in China, 692–693, 695–696
    in colonies, 873
    encomienda system and, 559–560
    free vs. slave, 797
    global market and, 1031–1032
    in imperial societies, 872
    indentured, 876–877(b), 876(i)
    in Korea, 708
    migrations of, 976
    sexual division of, 815
    in society after Black Death, 482–483
    for Spanish-American mines, 567–568

    for sugar plantations, 572–573
    women's agricultural, 818–820
Laborsaving machines, 814
Labor unions. See also Strikes
    in Brazil, 1029
    in Great Depression, 931–932
    growth of, 914
    in Italy, 919
    Japanese, 936
    Nazis and, 937
    neoliberalism and, 1033
Lady Hong (Korea), 707(b)
Lafayette, Marquis de, American Revolution
    and, 769
Lagos, 973
Laissez faire, 763–764
Lake Texcoco, 519, 520, 521(b), 522(m), 523
Lakshmibai (Jhansi, India, queen), 863
Land
    after Black Death, 483
    in Brazil, 1029
    in colonies, 870
    confiscation in Soviet Union, 933–934
    Dutch reclamation of, 660
    in eastern Europe, 964
    enclosure of, 672
    to former Russian serfs, 835–836
    Inca, 530, 531, 534–535, 537
    in Mexico, 891, 894–895
    in Ottoman Empire, 491
    in South Africa, 1030
    in Tenochtitlán, 523
    in western Africa, 585
Land and Freedom Army, of Kikuyu, 973, 974
Landlords, in West Africa, 588
Landowners
    eviction of tenants in Depression, 931
    in Mexico, 894–895
Language(s). See also Writing
    Chontal Maya, 547–549
    disappearance of, 1052
    Guaraní, 728
    Inca, 531
    Kimbundu and Kikongo as, 600
    Korean, 707(b)
    Nahuatl, 520, 523, 528(b), 549, 564(b)
    in Philippines, 713(i)
    Quechua, 531, 533, 564
    Tagalog, 713(i)
    Tupi-speaking peoples and, 571(b)
Lántifáya (Saramakan leader), 749
Laos
    in ASEAN, 1036
    Burma and, 708
    development of, 708
La Paz, rebels in, 778
La Salle, Robert de, 720(m), 746
Las Casas, Bartolomé de, 560, 730
Lateen sails, 552
Latin alphabet, in Turkey, 909
Latin America, 912. See also Spanish America;
    specific locations
    Carnival in, 848
    democracy in, 1003–1006
    dictatorships in, 1005–1006

Latin America (*continued*)
  economy in, 975–976
  federalism in, 831
  feminist activists in, 852
  during Great Depression, 929
  independent states in, 759–761
  literature in, 1050–1051
  nationalism and, 783
  nation building in, 829–832
  in c. 1900, 830
  Organization of American States and, 968
  population growth in, 976
  problems in, 1027
  rebellions in 18th century, 767
  revolutions in (1810–1830), 778–784,
    780(*m*)
  tariffs in, 805
  women's rights in, 1011
Latin Christendom. *See also* Roman Catholic
    Church
  Black Death and, 481
Latvia, 942
Law(s). *See also* Codes of law; specific laws
  nationalism and, 783
  reforms in, 791
Law codes. *See* Codes of law
Laws (scientific), of motion, 671–672
League of Nations
  covenant (charter) of, 907, 908
  creation of, 907
  Japan and, 913, 935
  mandate system of, 907–908, 907(*m*)
Leagues, in North America, 539
Learning. *See also* Education; Intellectual
    thought
  classical, 499
Leaves of Grass (Whitman), 848
Lebanon
  diaspora from, 877
  migrations in 19th century, 858(*m*)
Lebensraum (living space), 940
Le dynasty (Vietnam), 487, 709
Legal systems. *See also* Law(s)
  Inca, 534
Legislation. *See also* Law(s); specific laws
  U.S. segregation forbidden by, 1009
Leisure class, in Japan, 701
Lenin, V. I., 903(*i*)
  New Economic Policy of, 918, 933
  Russian Revolution and, 903
Leningrad, starvation in, 949
Leonardo da Vinci (Italian artist), 501, 502(*b*),
    502(*i*)
Leopold II (Belgium), Africa and, 865–868, 870,
    871(*b*)
Lepanto, Battle of (1571), 647, 653, 665
Léry, Jean de, 665
Lesbians. *See* Gays
Less developed economies, population control
    and, 1040–1041
Levi, Primo, 946
Lexington, Battle of, American Revolution and,
    768, 769(*m*)
Liberalism, 783
  economic, 763

Liberation, culture of, 981–982
Liberation army, in Chiapas, Mexico, 1052
Liberation theology, of Catholic Church,
    1049–1050
Liberia, invasions of, 586
Liberty Displaying the Arts and Sciences
    (Jennings), 770(*i*)
Libraries, in West Africa, 492
Libya
  in 2011, 1047(*i*)
  uprising in, 1047
Life expectancy
  in Europe, 661
  increasing, 1040
  in Spanish America, 729
  world population and, 1042
"Life of an Amorous Woman" (Saikaku), 703
Lifespan, of Eastern Woodlands peoples, 541
Lifestyle. *See also* Livelihood(s); Standard of
    living
  of African American slaves, 747
  American silver and, 569
  Aztec, 526–529
  in Brazil, 718(*i*), 735–736
  in Cold War, 982–983
  in colonies, 873
  in Congo rain forest, 607–608
  in early modern Europe, 659–661
  of Eastern Woodlands groups, 540–541
  in 18th-century England, 765(*i*)
  of gatherer-hunters, 519
  imperialism and, 869–872
  Inca, 534–537
  industrial, 791–793
  in Japan, 699, 700–702
  in Korea, 706(*i*)
  of migrants, 876–877
  in Ming and Qing China, 695–696
  in Mughal Empire, 630–632
  non-Western impact on Western, 886–887
  in Ottoman Empire, 655–657
  of postindustrial families, 1002–1003
  of Pygmies, 608
  of soldiers, 947(*b*)
  in Soviet Union, 1014–1015
  in Spanish America, 729–732
  in Vijayanagara, 622
  in West Africa, 590
Like Water for Chocolate (Esquivel), 1050
Liliuokalani (Hawaiian queen), 882(*b*)
Lima, Peru, 533, 723
  Bolivar in, 781
  Inquisition in, 570
Limited liability, 805
Lincoln, Abraham, 840(*i*)
  Civil War and, 840
Linen industry, expansion of, 673
Lisboa, Francisco, 736
Literacy, 1027
  in agrarian societies, 847
  in Europe, 658, 762
  in Japan, 704
  in North American colonies, 768
  in Soviet Union, 918
  after World War I, 914–915

Literature. *See also* Poets and poetry; specific
    works and authors
  in Argentina, 920
  in Brazil, 830
  in China, 696, 896
  global, 1050–1051
  in Japan, 704, 935
  Lusíads, The (Portuguese epic), 635
  Mexican Revolution and, 895
  in 1930s, 939
  non-Western impact on Western, 885
  Western, 880
Lithuania, 942. *See also* Poland-Lithuania
Little Ice Age (1550–1700), 479, 667, 669–670
"Little Philip" (Andean interpreter), 565(*i*)
"Little Red Book" (Mao Zedong), 981
Little Tramp (film), 915
Livelihood(s). *See also* Economy and economic
    systems; Employment; Labor; Work
  American silver bonanza and, 569
  global, 1031–1037
  in India, 631–632
  industrialization and, 814–815
  migrations for improved, 859–860
  silver and, 569–570
  in Soviet Union, 964
  in West Central Africa, 593–595
Li Zicheng (Manchu emperor), 693
Llamas, 537
Llaneros (cowboys), 781, 782(*b*)
Locke, John, contract government and, 763
Locomotives, 798
Lodz, 814
Lombardy, 837
London, England, 1031, 1036
  Treaty of (1915), 897, 905
Longhouses, of Eastern Woodlands peoples, 540
López de Quiroga, Antonio (Latin American
    silver producer), 726
Lords. *See also* Nobility
  in Japan, 503, 802
Lorraine, 897
  after World War I, 906
Louis XIV (France), 673–675, 675(*i*)
Louis XVI (France), French Revolution and,
    771, 773
Louisiana, 746
Louvre (Paris), 1037(*b*), 1037(*i*)
Love in the Time of Cholera (García Márquez),
    1050
Lovek, Cambodia, 708
Loyola, Ignatius, 574, 662
Luanda, Angola, 581, 599, 603
  Benguela and, 600
Luang Prabang, Buddha from, 710(*i*)
Ludd, Ned, 814
Luddites, 814
Lukashenko, Aleksandr (president of Belarus),
    1049
Lula da Silva, Luiz Inácio (president of Brazil),
    1029
Lumber, from Swahili Coast, 620
Lunar landings, 995, 996
Lusíads, The (Portuguese epic), 635
Lute, The (China), 696

Luther, Martin, 661–662
Lutheran church, 662
Luxembourg, 897
Lu Xun (China), 896
Luxury goods, 805
    consumption of, 672
    Italian, 500
    Spanish America and, 728
Luzon, Philippines, 714
Lytton, Lord (viceroy of India), 873

Maastricht Treaty (1994), 1034
Maathi, Wangari, 1039, 1053
Macao, 633, 691
Macedonia
    as EU membership candidate, 1035
    First Balkan War and, 896
Macedonians, nationalism of, 884
Machado de Assis, Joachim, 830
Machiavelli, 776
Machine guns, 868
    in World War I, 904
Machinery. *See also* Industrialization
    laborsaving, 814
Machu Picchu (Peru), 512(*i*)
Madagascar, 601, 617, 741
Made in Japan (Morita), 999(*b*)
Madeiras, 554(*m*)
    sugar and, 575
Madero, Francisco (president of Mexico), 894, 895
Madras, India, 638
    English East India Company in, 639
Madrid, 665
Magazines, 915
Magellan, Ferdinand, voyages of, 557(*m*), 560–561
Magical realism, in Latin American literature, 1050
Magnetic compass, 553
Mahabharata epic, movies retelling, 915
Mail, Spanish transatlantic, 726
Mai-ling Soong, 936(*i*)
Maine, 741
Maiolica (ceramic ware), 500
Maize. *See* Corn (maize)
Majapahit kingdom (Southeast Asia, 1292–1528), 493, 496
Makioka Sisters, The (Junichiro Tanizaki), 935
Malabar, India, 616, 623
Malaria, 562, 585, 868, 1041
    in Africa, 598
Malaya, 944
    in ASEAN, 1036
    people of, 493
Malay peninsula, British in, 863
Mali, 1027
    Islam in, 491
    kingdom of, 589, 590
    Portugal and, 595
    trade and, 492
    women in, 593
Malik Ibrahim (Islamic preacher), 493
Malindi, 618

Malintzin (Malinche, Aztec woman), 547–549, 562, 566, 566(*b*), 566(*i*)
Malta, Ottomans and, 651, 653
Maluku. *See* Molucca Islands
Mamluk Sultanate (Egypt), 475, 775, 776
    decline of, 480–482
    economy of, 480
Management, 805
Man at the Crossroads (Rivera mural), 932(*i*)
Manchuria
    Russia and, 868
    Russo-Japanese War and, 882–883
Manchurian Incident (1931), 935
Manchus (China), 895
    as Qing dynasty, 693
Mandate system (League of Nations), 907–908, 907(*m*)
Mandatory education, Great Depression and, 931
Mandela, Nelson, 1023–1024
    on AIDS, 1044
    as South African president, 1029–1030
Mande peoples, 588–589(*b*)
    invasions by, 596
Mane peoples, invasions by, 596
Manifest Destiny, in United States, 839
Manikongos (blacksmith king of Kongo), Kongo and, 594
Manila, Philippines
    commerce in, 691
    Spanish in, 712
Manillas (currency), 587
Mann, Thomas, 939
Manoel (Portugal), 571(*b*), 572
Mansas (Mali), 589, 590
Manufacturing
    in China, 495
    in Europe, 673
    of firearms, 552
    global, 1023
    Italy and, 500
    underconsumption of, 804
Mao Zedong (China), 946(*b*), 962, 966–967
    Cultural Revolution and, 1002
    Great Leap Forward and, 978(*b*)
    "Little Red Book" of, 981
    modernization by, 978, 979–980
Maps
    Aztec, 521(*b*), 521(*i*)
    portolan charts as, 546(*i*)
Mapuche people (Chile), 550, 573–576, 573(*m*), 576(*i*), 729
al-Maqrizi (Egyptian historian), 480
Maracaña (Rio de Janeiro), 977(*i*)
Marathas (India), 627
Marconi, Guglielmo, 915
Mariana Islands, Magellan in, 561
Marie Antoinette (France), 773
Maritime empires, of Portugal (c. 1600), 634(*m*)
Maritime exploration, European, 548(*m*)
Maritime trade, 478
    in Americas, 517
    between Americas and Asia, 712(*m*)
    in Asia (1350–1450), 494–498
    Muslim Arabs in, 492–493

Market(s)
    Aztec, 523
    capitalistic, 672
    colonies as, 869
    laissez faire and liberalism on, 763–764
    slave, 596
    South African, 1029
    in South Asia, 624–625
    youth, 1003
Marketing, mass, 915–916
Maroons, 736
    in North America, 747–748
    in Palmares, Brazil, 736
    slaves and, 740–741
    of Suriname, 748–749, 748(*m*), 749(*i*)
Marriage
    Aztec, 527
    Aztec-Colhua, 522
    in Eastern Woodlands society, 541
    in Europe, 661
    in Korea, 706
    in Nazi Germany, 937
    in Spanish America, 732
Marronage (slave flight), 740–741
Marshall, George C., 964
Marshall Plan (1947), 964
Marta, Rilda, 915–916
Martinique, 739
Martyrdom, Mexican belief about, 890(*i*)
Maru (Head), 981
Marx, Karl, 816–817
Marxian socialism, vs. Sun Yatsen's socialism, 895
Marxism, 816–817
    revolutionary, in Russia, 903, 904
    worldwide revolutionary, 904
Mary (England), 677
Maryland, 744, 745
Masculinity. *See also* Gender and gender issues; Men
    cowboy way of life and, 782(*b*)
Massachusetts Bay colony, 743
Mass culture, 893–894
Masses
    age of, 913–919
    culture for, 914–916
    Hitler and, 924(*i*), 937
    militarization of, 934
    mobilization of, 916–919, 932–939
Mass marketing, 915–916
Mass media
    development of, 878–879
    dictators and, 915, 925
    in Japan, 936
    Roosevelt, Franklin D., use of, 938
    uniform culture and, 925
    after World War I, 914–915
Mass politics, 893–894
Mass production, 913
    in Germany, 802
    industrial, 802
Mass proletarian culture, 918
Mass society, 893, 913–914
Mass unionization, 913
Master race, 945

Matamba kingdom, 594
Matawai maroons, 749
Materialism, Marx on, 816–817
Mathematics
    Galileo on, 671
    science and, 670
Matrilineal clans, of Eastern Woodlands peoples, 540
Matrilineal societies, in West Africa, 593
Mau Mau, 973–974
Maximilian I (Holy Roman Empire), 484(*i*)
May 4th movement (China), 910, 914
Maya Empire, 517. *See also* Teotihuacán
    in Guatemala, 519
Maya-Kakchiquel people, 1052
May Day rally (Czechoslovakia,1967), 1011
Mayflower (ship), Pilgrims on, 745(*i*)
Mazarin (Cardinal), 674
Mbanza, Kongo, 599
Mbuti people, 608
McCarthy, Joseph, witch-hunt for communists by, 983
McNeill, William, on Black Death, 479
Measles, 562
Mecca
    Ottomans in, 650, 652
    pilgrimages to, 615, 785
    Sa'uds in, 786
    Wahhabism in, 785(*i*)
Mechanization
    agrarian productivity and, 672
    of textile industry, 798
Medellín, Colombia, protest by women textile workers in, 932
Media. *See also* Mass media
    Gandhi's use of, 917
    sexuality in, 1003
Media experts, 993
Medici family (Florence), 483
Medicine. *See also* Health; Health care
    in colonies, 872–873
    growth of, 977
    population growth and, 1040
    after World War II, 995
Medina, 786
    Ottomans in, 652
Medina, Bartolomé de, 567
Mediterranean region. *See also* specific locations
    Barbary pirates and, 677–679
    Black Death in, 480, 480(*m*)
    Mamluks in, 475
    Ottomans in, 475, 651–652, 652(*m*)
    piracy in, 653
    political power in (1453), 485(*m*)
    17th-century crisis in, 667–670
    in c. 1600, 648(*m*)
Mehmed II ("the Conqueror," Ottoman Empire), 474(*i*), 477, 491, 651
Mehmed IV (Ottoman Empire), 654
Meiji Restoration (Japan), 804, 824(*i*), 842, 935(*m*)
Mein Kampf (Hitler), 936
Melaka, Malaysia, 640–642, 708
    Muslims of, 493
    Portugal and, 633

Men. *See also* Gender; Women
    Aztec, 527
    in Eastern Woodlands Indians, 540
    during Great Depression, 931
    imperialism and, 870–871
    as Inca weavers, 536
    Mapuche, 576(*i*)
    sexual division of labor and, 815
Mendes family (Ottoman Jews), 657
Ménétra, Jacques, 764–765
Mercantilism, 673, 763
    in Spanish America, 729
Merchant classes, 477
Merchants
    Aztec, 523, 527
    Dutch, in Aceh, 641(*b*)
    exploration and, 550
    in Japan, 803
    migration by, 1044
    in Ming China, 487
    Ottoman, 656
    in Russia, 690
    in West Africa, 590
    women as, 711
Mercosur, 1036
Mercury, mining of, 567
Mergers, business, 1033
Meritocracy, Ottoman, 656
Mesoamerica. *See also* Central America
    Aztec Empire in, 519–529
    Spanish in, 562–566
Mesopotamia
    Ottomans in, 654
    in World War I, 904
Mestizaje (mixture), 731
Mestizo (mixed offspring), 570, 731
Metals and metalwork. *See also* Bronze; Gold; Iron; Silver
    in Africa, 586
    Barba on, 672
    Inca, 535–536
    industrial, 800
    refining in Americas, 567
    in Spanish America, 723
    in West Central Africa, 594–595, 594(*i*)
Methodism, 785
Métis (mixed-heritage fur traders), 743
Mexican Americans, protests by, 1009
Mexican-American War (1846–1848), 831–832, 839
Mexican Revolution (1910–1920), 891, 892(*m*), 894–895, 895(*m*)
    factions in, 895
    Rivera mural of, 890(*i*)
Mexica people, 519, 562. *See also* Aztec Empire
Mexico, 562. *See also* Teotihuacán
    Aztecs in, 516, 519–529
    economy and, 1027
    European claims in, 568(*m*)
    European diseases in, 563
    fall of Aztecs in, 562–566
    gold from, 549
    Hidalgo in, 779
    Independence Day in, 780
    industrialization in, 802
    influenza epidemic in, 904–905

    Inquisition in, 570
    land grants to U.S. companies in, 895
    land reform in, 895
    mining in, 734
    multinational corporations in, 1004(*m*)
    in NAFTA, 1036
    as New Spain, 564(*b*)
    revolt in, 779–780
    Santa Anna in, 831–832
    silver in, 567
    television and, 993
    U.S. war with, 839
    U.S. intervention in, 893
Mexico City, 520(*m*), 550, 1011(*i*)
    plaza mayor in, 725(*i*)
Michael Romanov (Russia), 689
Middle class
    growth of, 914
    in India, 813(*i*), 1028
    Industrial Revolution and, 812–813
Middle East. *See also* Arabs and Arab world; specific locations
    independence struggle in, 972–973
    mandate system in, 907(*m*)
    1967–1990, 1013(*m*)
    oil in, 972, 1013
    at Paris Peace Conference, 905, 905(*i*)
    rebellions in, after World War I, 908
    Six-Day War in (1967), 1013
    terrorism and, 1045
    World War I in, 898(*m*)
"Middle ground," in North American colonies, 746
Middle Passage, 583, 605–606
Midnight's Children (Rushdie), 1051
Midway Island, Battle of, 944(*m*), 951
Midwife, Aztec, 528(*b*), 528(*i*)
Migrant workers, industrialization and, 814
Migration, 1042–1043(*m*)
    in Africa, 973
    to American colonies, 511
    to Brazil, 734
    in China, 695–696
    culture and, 878
    diasporas and, 874–878
    1850–1910, 858(*m*)
    family life and, 1002
    global, 875(*m*), 928, 990(*m*), 1024(*m*), 1042–1043(*m*), 1044–1045
    to global cities, 1036
    as global issue, 1038
    of labor, 976, 1031
    of Lebanese, 877
    lifestyle and, 876–877
    in 19th century, 859
    on Trail of Tears, 840
    from Valley of Mexico (1450s), 529
Mihr un-nisa. *See* Nur Jahan (Mughal Empire)
Milan, Leonardo's *Virgin of the Rocks* in, 502(*b*), 502(*i*)
Militarism
    Great Depression and, 927
    revival of, 939
Militaristic authoritarian regimes, Great Depression and, 927

Militarization
    during Great Depression, 931, 932–933
    in Japan, 935, 936
    in 1930s, 934
Military. *See also* Armed forces; specific battles
        and wars
    in Argentina, 978
    balance of power and, 477
    elites in, 947(*b*)
    in France, 674
    German, 802
    in India, 632
    in Korea, 705
    Ottoman, 651, 655–656
    in South Korea, 1007
Military occupation, by Soviets of eastern
        Europe, 964
Military spending
    in Cold War, 968(*m*), 976
    Soviet, 1015
Mill, John Stuart, 845
Mills. *See also* Textiles and textile industry
    in England, 798
    workers in, 791–793
Milosevic, Slobodan (Serbia), 1016
Mina, São Jorge da, 596
Minas Gerais, Brazil, 733, 734, 736
Mindanao, Philippines, Muslims in, 714
Minerals. *See also* Mines and mining
    industry and, 802
    from Mexico, 894
Mines and mining
    in Brazil, 718(*i*), 734, 735(*i*)
    of gold (West Africa), 588–589
    in Honshu, 699
    for industry, 800
    labor draft for, 568–569
    in Mexico, 894
    of silver, 567
    in Spanish America, 567, 727–728
    in West Africa, 586–587
    West Africans in Spanish colonies and, 595
    in West Central Africa, 595
Ming dynasty (China), 477, 478, 485–487,
        690–693
    empire of, 486(*m*), 683
    environment in, 693
    fall of, 670
    lifestyle in, 695–696
    Mongols and, 499
    Southeast Asian maritime trade and, 498
    trade in late period, 691–693
Miniatures, Mughal, 630(*i*)
Minimum wage, workers and, 1033
Ministry of Trade and Industry (Japan), 996
Minorca, 676(*m*)
Minorities. *See also* specific groups
    activism by, 1009
    in East Africa, 621
    rights of, 851
Mir (peasant communities), 835–836
Miscegenation, laws against, 746
Missiles, in Cuba, 969
Missions and missionaries
    in Africa, 598

    in Americas, 569–570
    in China, 857
    in imperial Africa and Asia, 871
    in Japan, 698–699
    in New Spain, 564(*b*)
    in Philippines, 714
    Spanish, 554
Mississippi River region
    Cahokia in, 513
    French exploration of, 746
Mita (labor draft), 568, 573
Mixed economy, in India, 1028
Mixed races
    in Americas, 719–722
    in Spanish America, 731–732
Mobility. *See* Migration
Mobilization
    of democracies, 938–939
    of masses in Japan, 936
    for World War I, 897
Moctezuma II (Aztecs), 529, 562–563, 566(*b*),
        566(*i*)
Modernism, cultural change and, 878
Modernity, early period of (1450–1750),
        508–511, 647
Modernization
    of Brazil, 829–831
    of China, 895, 896, 979–980
    of cities, 846
    ecological destruction and, 1038
    of Egypt, 776, 864, 864(*m*)
    during Great Depression, 930
    of Japan, 841–843
    national, 828–838
    of Russia, 834–836
    in Soviet bloc, 964
    of Soviet Union, 978–979
    in Turkey, 908–909, 909(*i*)
    women and, 847
Modernizers, in Mexico, 894
Modern Times (film), 939
Mogadishu, 618
Mohacs, Battle of (1526), 646(*i*)
Molecular biology, 995
Molucca Islands, voyages to, 560
Mombasa, 618, 633
Monarchs and monarchies. *See also* Palaces; spe-
        cific rulers and locations
    absolutism and, 673–674
    in France, 483–484
    taxation by, 484
Monet, Claude, 817
Monetarism, 1014
Money. *See also* Coins
    in India, 629
    Italian attitudes toward, 500
Moneylenders, in Depression, 931
Mongol Empire. *See also* Mongols
    Timur in, 488–489
Mongols. *See also* Mongol Empire
    China and, 485, 693
    germ warfare by, 479
    last empire of, 477–478
    Ming dynasty and, 499
    as Mughals, 623

    Timur and, 488–489
    Yongle and, 487
Mono no aware concept (serenity), 885
Monopolies
    in Indian Ocean trade, 620
    in Spanish-American trade, 729
    in trade, 481
    trading companies as, 601–604
Monroe Doctrine (1823), 881
Monsoons, 614(*m*), 615
    in China, 694
Montagnais people, 742
Montano, Otilio, 890(*i*)
Montenegro, as autonomous state, 896, 898(*m*)
Montesquieu, Louis (Baron), 763
Monuments
    national, 844–845
    in Southeast Asia, 708
Monzaemon, Chikamatsu, 703
Moon landing, 994
More, Thomas, 662
Morelos, José Maria, 779
Morgan, Henry, 739
Moriscos (Spanish Muslims), 669(*b*)
    in West Africa, 590
Morita, Akio, 999(*b*)
Morocco
    Barbary pirates and, 677, 678
    Ceuta in, 554
    France and, 974
    help desk services in, 1032
    Songhai and, 590
    World War II in, 951
Moronobu, Hishikawa, 704(*i*)
Mortality
    of Black Death, 479
    in colonies, 873
    in Europe, 661
    in Middle Passage, 605
    in West, 1040–1041
Mortgages, economic crisis and, 1047
Moscow, 687
    Chechen bombings in, 1046
    Tatars in, 689
Mothers, in El Salvador, 1006
Mothers for Life (Chile), 1005–1006
Motion, laws of, 671–672
Mountains, spiritual significance of, 515
Mount Ampato (Peru), 513
Movable type, 552
Movement of peoples. *See* Immigrants and
        immigration; Migration
Movies. *See* Films
Mozambique, 601, 617, 1030
Mubarak, Hosni (Egypt), 1046, 1047(*i*)
Mughal Empire (India), 616, 623–625
    Akbar in, 612(*i*)
    economy in, 631–632
    English East India Company and, 862–863
    lifestyle in, 630–632
    miniature from, 630(*i*)
    Nur Jahan in, 613–615
    in c. 1700, 625(*m*)
Muhammad Shah (Mughal Empire), 627–628
Mulata (mulatto), Chica da Silva as, 721

Mulatto, 731
  communities in West Africa, 597
Multiethnic empires
  Ottoman Empire as, 884
  regional societies evolving into, 508
Multinational corporations, 913, 998
  farmer protests against, 1018
  in Latin America, 1004(*m*)
  South African apartheid and, 1023–1024
Mummies
  Inca, 532, 534(*i*), 538
  in Peru, 513
Mumps, 562
Mumtaz Mahal, 614–615, 626(*i*)
Munich, terrorism at Olympic Games in (1972), 1045
Murad III (Ottoman Empire), 654
Murad IV (Ottoman Empire), 654
Murals, by Rivera, Diego, 890(*i*), 895, 931, 932(*i*)
Murasaki Shikibu (Lady), 504
Murra, John, 530
Musa, Mansa (Mali), 589
Muscovy, 687–688
  Romanovs and, 689–690
Music. *See also* Dance
  culture and, 848
  global, 1051
  Industrial Revolution and, 817
  national Mexican, 845–846
  non-Western impact on Western, 886
  youth, 1003
Muslim Brotherhood, 916, 917
Muslim League, 885
Muslims. *See also* Arabs and Arab world; Islam
  Black Death and, 482
  Christianity and, 475
  in East Africa, 617
  in Europe and Mediterranean region, 649
  Gujarati merchants as, 623
  identities in Indian Ocean region, 616
  in India, 627
  Moriscos as, 590
  Ottomans as, 657, 775
  Partition of India and, 970
  in Philippines region, 561
  piracy by, 653
  Portugal and, 598
  range of interpretations of, 1050
  in Southeast Asia, 714
  in Spain, 484
  Spanish refugee in Netherlands, 669(*b*)
  Taliban and, 1008
  Timurid, 623, 627
  USSR and, 948
  as West African rulers, 589
  women and, 914
Mussolini, Benito, 916, 918–919, 932, 933, 940
Mutapa kingdom, 620
Myanmar, in ASEAN, 1036
Myrdal, Alva, 938–939
Mythology, Andean creation, 533(*b*)

NAACP. *See* National Association for the Advancement of Colored People
Nadir Shah (Iran), 628, 655(*b*)

Nafisi, Azar, 1044, 1045
NAFTA. *See* North American Free Trade Agreement
Nagasaki, Japan, 698
  atomic bombing of, 951
  port of, 802
  trade in, 691
Nahuatl language, 520, 523, 528(*b*), 549, 564(*b*)
Nain Singh (Indian explorer), 858(*m*), 869, 870(*i*)
Nairobi, 973
Nanban (Europeans), 698
Nanjing, China
  as Chinese capital, 486–487
  Japanese massacre in, 941
  Nationalists in, 910
  Treaty of (China, 1842), 807
Naomi (Junichiro Tanizaki), 935
Napoleon I (Bonaparte, France), 761, 774
  education and, 847
  Egypt and, 776(*i*)
  French Revolution and, 771
  Muhammad's birthday and, 776(*i*)
Napoleonic Code. *See* Code Napoleon
Napoleonic Europe (1796–1815), 775(*m*)
Napoleonic Wars, 774–775, 779
Napoleon III (France), 864
NASA (National Aeronautics and Space Administration), 967(*b*)
Nasser, Gamal Abdel (Egypt), 972–973, 983
Natal, 867
Nation(s). *See also* National states; Nation building; Nation-state; State (nation)
  in Africa, 973–975, 974(*m*)
  in Brazil, 829–831
  creation of, 969–975
  culture of, 843–849
  defined, 829
  in global age, 1027–1031
  independent, 960(*m*)
  institutions in, 846–849
  modernization of, 828–838
National Assembly (France), 771, 772, 783
National Association for the Advancement of Colored People (NAACP), 981–982
National identities, 649
Nationalism, 783
  in Balkans, 896
  at Bandung Conference, 985
  decolonization and, 959
  in Egypt, 959
  feminists and, 884–885
  Hindu, 1028
  history writing and teaching and, 844–845
  in India, 885
  in Indochina, 971
  in Italy, 837
  in Japan, 843, 912
  migration and, 876
  nation-states and, 827–828
  in Ottoman Empire, 884–885
  romantic, 783
  of Slavic Serbs, 896
  in World War I, 900
Nationalist China, 965

Nationalist Party (China). *See* Guomindang (China)
Nationalization, of Suez Canal, 973
National Organization for Women (NOW), 1010–1011
National states
  in East Asia (1368–1500), 485–487
  rise of, 483–484
National Tobacco Company, 802
Nation building, 828, 829. *See also* State-building
  in Brazil, 830–832, 831(*i*)
  ethnic and racial thinking in, 849
  in Germany, 837–838
  after imperialism, 961
  in Italy, 836–837
  in Latin America, 829–832
  national culture and, 843–849
  native Americans and, 840–841, 841(*i*)
  in Russia, 832–836
  in United States, 838–841
  Westernization and, 845–846
  after World War II, 962
Nation-state
  citizens' rights in, 851–852
  c. 1850, 826(*m*)
  in Europe, 686
  historians of, 846(*b*), 846(*i*)
  literacy in, 847
  nation and, 829
  outsiders in, 849–852
  rise of, 827–828
  supranational organizations and, 1033–1036
Native Americans, 719
  ancestral burial sites of, 1052
  Aztec and Inca, 516
  as Brazilian sugar workers, 572
  Columbus and, 556–559, 558(*i*)
  decline of, 723
  enslavement of, 559–560
  c. 1500, 539(*m*)
  forced migrations of, 827(*m*)
  Manifest Destiny and, 840
  Mapuche people of Chile, 573–576, 573(*m*)
  in Mexico, 890(*i*)
  Portugal and, 570–572
  "removal" policy toward, 743
  as slaves, 722
  in Spanish America, 725
Native peoples. *See also* Native Americans
  in Algeria, 865
  lands seized from, 827(*m*)
  missionaries and, 871
  of North America (c. 1500), 539(*m*)
  as outsiders, 849–850
NATO (North Atlantic Treaty Organization), 967
Natural resources
  decline in, 998
  industrialization and, 795–796, 797
  in United States, 802
Navigation
  in Americas, 517
  exploration and, 550, 552–553
Navy
  in France, 674
  Ottoman, 653

in World War I, 897–898
in World War II, 951
Nayaks (Vijayanagara administrators), 622
Nayemwezi women, sorghum and, 819(*i*)
Nazi Germany. *See also* Germany
    annexation of Austria, 940
    civilians in conquered regions and, 945
    expansion by, 926(*m*)
    Frank, Anne, and, 980
    Holocaust of, 945–947, 945(*m*)
    Jews in, 937–938
    Nuremberg rally in, 924(*i*)
    paramilitary groups in, 946(*b*)
    propaganda in, 937
    racism of, 937–938
    repression in, 937
    women in, 937, 938
Nazi Party (National Socialist German Workers'
    Party), 936–937
Nazi-Soviet Pact (1939), 941, 942, 963
Ndongo kingdom, 594, 599, 600
Nehru, Jawaharlal, 976, 983, 984, 1028
Neo-Africas, in American colonies, 748–749
Neo-Confucianism
    in China, 486, 487, 695
    in Japan, 684(*m*)
    in Korea, 706, 707
    spread of, 684(*m*)
    in Vietnam, 487, 683
Neoliberalism, 1014, 1033
Nepal, China and, 693
Nestlé, 913
Netherlands
    European Muslims in, 669(*b*)
    revolt against Spain, 665
    World War II in, 942
Networks, global, 1032–1033
Neutrality, U.S., in World War I, 897
Neutron bomb, 963
New Amsterdam, 745
New Christians, in Brazil, 735
New Economic Policy, 918, 933
New England, 743
Newfoundland, 743–744
    commerce in, 744–745
New France, 741, 743. *See also* Canada
    slavery in, 746
New imperialism, 860. *See also* Imperialism
    expansion of, 925
New Left, 1010
New Life Movement (China), 935–936
"New look," for women after World War II,
    982(*i*)
Newly independent countries, Bandung
    Conference and, 983–984
New Netherland, 741
New Order, in Asia, 941
New Spain, 550, 564, 564(*b*), 567–570
    slave trade in, 598
    as viceroyalty, 726
Newspapers, 878, 915
Newton, Isaac, 671
New Woman (film), 915
New woman, World War I and, 902, 914
New World. *See also* America(s)

American colonial development and, 719–722
    cannibals and, 559(*i*)
    crops from, 672
    division of, 559
New York, 1031, 1036
    colonial, 745
New Zealand, World War I and, 897, 898–899
NGOs. *See* Nongovernmental organizations
Nguyen clan (Vietnam), 709
Nicaragua, U.S. and, 1003–1004
Nicholas I (Russia), 832–833
Nicholas II (Russia), 902
Nigeria
    help desk services in, 1032
    independence in, 975
    revolt by women in, 953
"Nigerian diaspora," 598
Niger River region, 586(*m*), 588(*b*), 589, 593
    Ijaw peoples in, 598
Nightingale, Florence
    in Crimean War, 833
    travels of, 826(*m*)
Nihilists, in Russia, 836
Nihon-bashi (*Fifty-three Stations on the Tokaido*)
    (Hiroshige), 803(*i*)
Nikitenko, Alexander (Russia), 834, 835(*b*)
Ninety-five Theses (Luther), 662
Nixon, Richard
    in China, 1002
    Vietnam and, 1008
Nkrumah, Kwame, 958(*i*), 961(*m*), 973, 983
Noah (Bible), 533
Nobility. *See also* Lords
    Inca, 534
    in Korea, 705
    peasant revolts and, 483
    in Russia, 836
    in society after Black Death, 482–483
Noble savages, slaves and, 766
Noh theater (Japan), 504, 703, 885–886
Nomads
    end of, 477–478
    Ottomans on, 491
Nonalignment, in Cold War, 984(*i*)
Nondiscrimination clause, League of Nations
    charter and, 913
Nongovernmental organizations (NGOs),
    1032(*i*), 1034
Nonindustrial nations. *See also* Industrialization;
    Industrial Revolution
    economic inequities in, 984–985
    research in, 1001
    underdevelopment of Africa and, 812
Nonviolent resistance
    Gandhi and, 916, 917, 954(*i*)
    by Mexican Americans, 1009
    by Nigerian women, 953
    in 20th century, 953–954
Normandy, D-Day invasion in, 951
North (U.S.), 840
    colonial lifestyle in, 745–748
North (global), vs. South (global), 985,
    1026–1027
North Africa
    Barbary pirates and, 677–678, 677(*m*)

consumerism in, 1032
    Europeans in, 865
    France in, 679, 865
    World War II in, 943(*m*), 951
North America
    colonial crisis and revolution in, 769(*m*)
    commercial colonialism in, 741–745
    Eastern Woodlands people in (1450–1530),
        538–542
    England and France in (c. 1650–1750), 742(*m*)
    European claims in, 568(*m*)
    lifestyle in northern colonies, 745–748
    plantations in, 722
    revolution in, 767–771
North American Free Trade Agreement
    (NAFTA), 1036
Northeast, in United States, 745
Northern Europe, Atlantic slave trade and
    (1600–1800), 600–607
Northern Ireland, 910
    Bloody Sunday in (January 30, 1972), 1045
North German Confederation, 838
North Korea, 967
North-South divide (global), Bandung
    Conference and, 985
North Vietnam, 972, 1008. *See also* Vietnam War
Northwest passage, in North America, 741
Norway
    massacre of political activists in (2011), 1045
    World War II in, 942
Nova Scotia, 741
    commerce in, 744–745
Novels, 893. *See also* Literature
    in 1930s, 939
Nuclear war, Cuban missile crisis and, 969
Nuclear weapons, 963
Nuns, in Spanish America, 732
Nuremberg, Germany
    Nazi rally in, 924(*i*)
    trials in, 980
Nuremberg Laws (1935), 938
Nur Jahan (Mughal Empire), 613–615, 627
Nursing
    in Crimean War, 833
    women in, 900–902
Nzinga (Ndongo queen), 599–600, 601(*i*)

Oba (king of Benin), 580(*i*)
Obama, Barack, 1026
Obas (Yoruba political leaders), 592
Occupation (military). *See* Military occupation
Occupations (labor). *See* Livelihood(s)
Offshore manufacturing, 998
Oh Omok, as comfort woman, 942(*b*)
Oil and oil industry
    imperialism and, 912
    in mandates, 907(*m*)
    in Middle East, 972
    trade routes in (c. 1975), 990(*m*)
    uses of, 998
Oil embargo, 1013–1014
Okinawa, 706
Oklahoma, native Americans in, 840
Oklahoma City government building,
    destruction of (1995), 1045

Old Ghana, 590
Old Order, Enlightenment and, 765–767
Oligarchy, in Venice, 483
Oliver Twist (Dickens), 817
Olympic Games
    in Mexico City (1968), 1011(*i*)
    terrorism at Munich games (1972), 1045
Omdurman, Battle of (Sudan), 868
Once Upon the River Love, 1044
One-child policy (China), 1041
One Hundred Years of Solitude (García Márquez),
        1050
On Restoring Ethiopian Salvation (Sandoval), 596
On the Revolutions of the Heavenly Spheres
        (Copernicus), 671
On the Wealth of Nations (Smith), 763–764
OPEC (Organization of Petroleum Exporting
        Countries), 990(*m*), 1013
Opera, in Mexico, 845
"Operation Vittles," 965
Opium, 660, 807
    China and, 807
    Dutch and, 711
    India and, 809(*i*)
Opium War (1839–1842), 807
    taxation and, 873
Oprichnina (Russian land system), 689
Orange Free State, 867, 881
Organization of American States (OAS), 968
Organization of Petroleum Exporting Countries.
        See OPEC
Organizations. *See* Global structures and
        organizations
Original sin, Black Death as divine punishment
        and, 482
Orphans, as industrial labor, 791
Orthodox Christianity. *See also* Greek Orthodox
        Church
    in Russia, 687
Orwell, George, on pacifists, 954
Osman (Ottomans), 489–490
Osman dynasty (Ottoman Empire), 655–656
Otomí people, Aztecs and, 526
Otranto, Battle of, 651
Ottoman Balkans (Albania), 776
Ottoman Empire (1453–1750), 475, 650–657,
        652(*m*)
    Armenian deportations by, 908
    Balkans and, 893, 894, 896
    Battle of Lepanto and, 653, 665
    Battle of Mohacs and, 646(*i*)
    Christianity and, 490–491
    coffeehouses in, 658–659(*b*), 658(*i*)
    consolidation of, 651–655
    Crimean War and, 833, 833(*m*)
    dissolution of, 909(*m*)
    East African trade and, 617
    expansion of, 489–491, 490(*m*), 651–655
    Habsburgs and, 653–654
    industrialization and, 809
    as Islamic power, 651
    lifestyle in, 655–657
    Mamluks conquered by, 481
    Mecca, Medina, and, 786
    Napoleon and, 775, 776
        nationalism in, 884–885
        Nicholas I and, 832–833
        Peace of Paris treaties and, 906
        Persia and, 654
        rise of, 650
        Russia and, 863
        Sultanate of the Women and, 654–655
        Timur and, 488
        World War I and, 896, 898(*m*), 904, 908
        Young Turks and, 884–885, 884(*i*)
Ottoman Turks
    Christianity and, 490–491
    East African trade and, 617
    expansion of (1354–1453), 489–491
    fall of Constantinople to (1453), 474(*i*)
    vs. Safavids in Baghdad, 655(*b*)
    Timur and, 488
Ouro Preto, Brazil, 733, 734
Outsiders, in nation-states, 849–852
Outsourcing, to India, 1032
Outwork, 801
Overland trade. *See also* Silk Road
    in Americas, 517–518
    Black Death carried by, 479
    on Silk Road, 494
Oxygen, depletion of, 1038
Ozone layer, hole in, 1038

Pachacuti Inca Yupanki (emperor), 531–532
Pa Chin, 939
Pacific Northwest, Kwakiutl people of, 519,
        519(*m*)
Pacific Ocean region
    economies in, 1047
    endemic disease, population decline, and, 562
    wealth and production in, 1031
    World War II in, 944–945, 944(*m*), 951
Pacific tigers, 990(*m*), 997(*m*)
Pacifism
    Asian religions and, 953
    in 20th century, 953–954
    after World War I and World War II, 954
Paes, Domingos, on Vijayanagara festival, 624(*b*)
Pagodas, in Southeast Asia, 709
Pahlavi, Mohammed Reza (Shah of Iran), 1008
Painting
    impressionism in, 817
    in Renaissance Italy, 501, 502(*b*), 502(*i*)
    after World War II, 983
Pakistan, 970, 985. *See also* India
    in SEATO, 968
Palaces
    Red Fort complex, 675(*i*)
    Topkapi, 675(*i*)
    Versailles, 674, 675(*i*)
Palestine and Palestinians, 1013(*m*)
    Israel and (1949), 972(*m*)
    Jewish homeland and, 972
    migration of Jews to, 940
    strike in, 932
    terrorists at Munich Olympic Games, 1045
    in World War I, 904
Palmares, Brazil, 736
    maroon confederacy in, 748
Pampas (plains), 573
        Pamuk, Orhan, 1049
Pan-Africanism, 851, 908, 958(*i*)
Pandemics. *See also* Disease
    AIDS, 1041(*i*)
    Black Death as, 478
    in New World, 562
Panipat, Battle of, 625
Pankhurst, Emmeline, 900
Papacy. *See* Popes; Roman Catholic Church;
        specific popes
Papermaking, 552
Paraguay, 946(*b*)
    in Mercosur, 1036
Paramaka maroons, 749
Paramilitary groups, 946(*b*)
Paramount chiefs, in Africa, 586–587
Paraty, Brazil, 735
Parganas (zones), 629, 651
Paris, 1036
    battle in (1814), 774
Paris Peace Conference (1919–1920), 905–908,
        905(*i*)
Park, Mungo (Scottish traveler), 588–589(*b*)
Park Chung Hee, 1007
Parliament (England), Charles I and, 675–676
Parliaments
    constitutionalist, 675
    in Russia (1905), 883
Parsees (Zoroastrians)
    in East Africa, 621
    in India, 627
Partisans, in World War II, 950
Partition, of India, 970, 970(*m*)
Pasternak, Boris, 983
Patagonia, 561
Patel, Pierre, 675(*i*)
Patents, 805
    agricultural, 1018–1019
    as colonization, 1018
Patriarchal authority, Great Depression and, 931
Patriarchy
    in China, 487
    Ottoman, 491
Patrilineal societies, in West Africa, 593
Patriotism, in World War I, 900
Paz Soldán, José Gregorio, 832
Peace movements, during World War I, 900
Peace of Paris treaties, 906–907
Peanuts, in central Africa, 593
Pearl Harbor, Japanese bombing of, 927, 944
Peasant Revolt (England, 1381), 483
Peasants
    Aztec, 526–527
    after Black Death, 482
    in China, 694–695, 911(*b*), 965
    displacement of, 660
    in eastern Europe, 964
    in Europe, 658
    in French Revolution, 772
    Inca, 531
    in Italy, 918–919
    in Japan, 698
    Mexican Revolution and, 895
    Ottoman, 491, 656
    in Russia, 834(*i*), 835–836, 902

Peça (accounting unit), 595
Pedro I (Brazil), in Rio de Janeiro, 781
Pedro II (Brazil), 829–831, 830(*i*), 847
Pegu, Burma, 608
Pegu, Soet (Burma), 711
Pei, I. M., 1037
P'eng P'ai, 911(*b*)
Pennsylvania, 744
　September 11, 2001, terrorist attack and, 1045
Pensions, cuts in, 1033
Pentagon, terrorist attack on, 1045
People of color, as outsiders, 849–850
People's patriotism (Japan), 936
People's Republic of China, 965. *See also* China
"People's Rights," in Japan, 842–843
Pepper trade. *See also* Spices and spice trade
　Aceh and, 642
Peralta, Angela (Mexican opera singer), 845–846, 847
　travels of, 827(*m*)
Perestrelo, Felipa de (Columbus' wife), 555
Perestroika (restructuring), 1015
Pernambuco, Brazil, 722
　sugar in, 572, 574(*i*)
Perón, Eva, 977
Perón, Juan, 977–978, 1005
Perry, George, English industrialization and, 797(*b*)
Persia. *See also* Iran
　Mughal India and, 625
　Ottomans and, 654
　Russia and, 863
　Safavid Empire in, 612(*i*), 628, 652, 654
Persian Gulf region, Portugal and, 633
Persian Letters, The (Montesquieu), 763
Peru. *See also* Inca Empire
　European claims in, 568(*m*)
　Indians taxed in, 849
　Machu Picchu in, 512(*i*)
　mummies in, 513
　nation building in, 832
　revolt in, 767
　San Martin in, 781
　slave trade in, 598
　Spanish, 564–565, 564(*m*), 567–570
　as viceroyalty, 726
Pesticides
　chemical, 1018
　after World War II, 562
Pétain, Philippe, 949
Peter III (Russia), Pugachev as, 767
Peter the Great (Russia), 688(*i*), 689
　Russian Empire under, 687, 689–690
Petrograd, St. Petersburg as, 902
Peugeot, Armand, 800
Philip II (Spain), 665, 673
　and Ottomans at Lepanto, 653
　Portugal and, 635
Philip III (Spain), 669(*b*)
Philip V (Spain), 676
Philippines, 711–712, 944
　in ASEAN, 1036
　Europeans in, 708
　in 15th century, 683

languages in, 713(*i*)
Magellan and, 557(*m*), 561
naming of, 665
"spiritual conquest" by Catholic Church, 713–714
trade in, 712
U.S. control of, 881–882
Philosophy as Matonetics (Tanabe), 980
Phonographs, 914
Photography, 878–879
Pieces of eight, Spanish, 726(*b*), 726(*i*)
Piedmont, 837
Piedmont-Sardinia, 836
Pigafetta, Antonio de, 560
Pilgrimages, 614(*m*), 615
Pilgrims, 743, 745(*i*)
"Pill, the" (oral contraceptive), 995
Pinochet, Augusto, 1005–1006
Pirates and piracy, 649, 678(*i*), 722. *See also* Buccaneers; Privateers
　Barbary, 677–679
　bio-, 1018
　in Caribbean region, 737(*m*)
　Dutch, 669
　English, 639
　in Indian Ocean region, 619
　Muslim, 653
　by Portugal, 632
Pires, Tomé (Portuguese traveler), 496(*b*)
Pizarro, Francisco, 562, 564–565
　Atawallpa and, 565(*i*)
　Inca Empire conquered by, 562, 564–565, 564(*m*)
Plague. *See* Black Death
Planetary motion, 671
Plantation colonies, 617
Plantation economy, in Americas, 722
Plantations
　in Atlantic Ocean region, 555
　in Brazil, 722, 831(*i*)
　in Caribbean and North America, 722
　Dutch and, 635
　in Haiti, 777–778
　slaves for, 555
　in southern North America, 745, 746–747
　for sugar industry, 572–573, 574(*b*), 574(*i*)
Plants
　in Columbian Exchange, 561–562, 561(*i*)
　genetic modification of, 1017, 1018
Plaza mayor (Mexico City), 725(*i*)
Pluralism, in national tradition, 849
Plymouth, Massachusetts, 743
Pneumonia, 814
Pochteca (merchants), 523, 527
Poets and poetry
　in Japan, 703–704
　non-Western impact on Western, 885
Pogroms, anti-Semitic, 875
Poland
　industry in, 814
　rebellion (1956), 979
　Russia and, 897
　Solidarity movement in, 1015
　Soviet Union and, 963, 964
　in Thirty Years' War, 668, 668(*i*)

after World War I, 906, 906(*m*)
World War II in, 927, 941–942, 951
Poland-Lithuania, in Thirty Years' War, 668(*i*)
Political clubs, in Latin America, 832
Political diversity, in Americas, 517–518
Political heroes, in United States, 840(*i*)
Political parties
　in Chile, 1005
　Green Party and, 1038
　World War I and, 900
Political power
　in Africa, 810
　in Europe and Mediterranean region (1453), 485(*m*)
　of European royalty, 483
　as global issue, 1038
　in Japan, 841–843
　of monarchs, 484
　in West Central Africa, 594
Political structures. *See also* Economy and economic systems; Political power
　absolutism as, 650, 673–675
　capitalism and, 673
　constitutionalism as, 650, 673, 675–677
　mercantilism and, 673
　in West Africa, 590
Political styles, culture and, 890(*i*)
Political systems, consolidation in mainland Southeast Asia, 708–711
Political thought, socialism, Marxism, and, 816–817
Politics. *See also* Political power
　Cold War and, 962–969, 1003–1012
　global, 893
　in Holy Roman Empire, 668
　labor unions in, 914
　mass, 893–894
　mobilization of masses and, 916–919
　post–World War I, 905–913
　radio use and, 915
　rights in United States, 770–771
　television and, 993
　World War I and, 900
Pollock, Jackson, 983
Poll (head) tax, 929
Pollution
　global warming from, 1038
　mercury, 567
　technology and, 1018(*i*)
Polo, Marco
　Columbus and, 555
　travel by ship, 494
Pol Pot (Cambodia), 1008
Poltava, Battle of, 688(*i*)
Polygamy
　abolished in Turkey, 909
　in India, 631
Pombeiros (Kongo traders), 599
Poor people, uprisings by, 767
Popes. *See also* Christianity; specific popes
　Portuguese slave trade and, 597(*m*)
　Treaty of Tordesillas and, 559
Popocatepetl (volcano), 725
Popp, Adelheid (Austrian feminist), 815
Popular Front (France), 939

Population
    agriculture and, 481
    of Algeria, 865
    Aztec, 563
    Black Death and, 478, 479
    characteristics of worldwide, 1042–1043(m)
    of China, 479, 691
    China's environment and, 694–695
    in colonial cities, 929
    density in Americas, 516
    of East African trading ports, 618
    of England, 479
    of Europe, 659
    of European cities, 660–661
    European diseases in Americas and, 562
    global (1920), 913
    as global issue, 1037–1038, 1040–1041
    indigenous in Spanish America, 723
    in Iran, 1041
    of Islam, 480
    of Istanbul, 651–652
    of Japan, 700
    of Korea, 706
    of Latin America, 976
    migrants in U.S. and, 1044
    of Russia, 689
    of Tenochtitlán, 522
    of West and West Central Africa, 585
Porcelain
    Chinese, 494–495, 692, 692(b), 692(i)
    efforts to copy Chinese, 796
    Wedgwood pottery as, 796
Pornography, transmission of, 994
Port Arthur, 882
Port cities, in East Africa, 617, 617(m)
Porto Alegre, Brazil, 1034
Portolan ("port finder") charts, 546(i)
Port Royal, 739
Portugal
    Africa and, 555, 581, 865
    Angola and, 599–600
    Benin trade and, 592
    Brazil and, 568(m), 570–573, 719, 722,
        781–783
    cinnamon trade and, 636(i)
    East African trade and, 617, 620
    emigration to Brazil from, 734
    exploration by, 547, 548(m), 553–555
    imperialism of, 861
    India and, 614(m), 616, 632–635
    Ndongo and, 600
    seaborne empire of (c. 1600), 634(m)
    ships of, 553(i)
    slave trade and, 596–598, 601
    soldier from, 598(i)
    sugar and, 572
    trade and, 634–635
    Treaty of Tordesillas and, 559, 571
    Vijayanagara and, 622
    in West Central Africa, 594
    western Africa and, 595–600
Posters, propaganda, 901(b), 901(i)
Postindustrial course, 996
Postindustrial economies, 991
    family life in, 1002–1003

Postsecondary education, in France, 847
Potatoes, 672
    in Inca diet, 537
Potemkin (film), 915
Potosí, 723
    decline of silver in, 666
    silver in, 567, 569(i), 726(i)
    slave trade in, 597(m)
Poverty, 1041
    in Brazil, 1029
    in China, 695(i)
    rural, 996
Power (political). See Political power
Power (energy), steam engine and, 798
Powhatan, 743
Powhatan Confederacy, 539
Powhatan (James) River, 741
Prague Spring, 1011
Price, Richard and Sally (anthropologists), 749
Prices
    of commodities, 929
    declines in, 804
Priest(s), in Africa, 598
Primogeniture, Inca, 534
Prince, The (Machiavelli), 776
Príncipe, 555
Principia Mathematica (Newton), 671–672
Printing
    in Japan, 704
    movable type and, 552
Print making. See also Woodblock printing
    in Japan, 803(b)
Print media
    advertising in, 915
    newspapers as, 878, 915
    after World War I, 914–915
Prison camps, Gulags in Soviet Union, 934
Prisoners, Chinese work by, 693
Privacy rights, 994
Privateers, 722
    Drake as, 738
    Kidd, William, as, 639
Private property, 483
Production
    European, 794–795
    industrial, 794–795
    mass, 913
    in Soviet Union, 964
Productivity
    growth in, 893
    price declines and, 804
Proletariat, Marx on, 817
Propaganda
    Bolshevik, 916
    Hitler's use of, 937
    Japanese, 936
    in World War I, 900, 901(b), 901(i)
    in World War II, 948
Property, in Aceh, 640–641
Property rights, 994
Proprietary colonies
    in Brazil, 572
    in North America, 744–745
Prosperity
    expansion of, 976–978

    in middle class, 812–813
    in 19th century, 804
    after World War II, 975–976
Prostitution
    during Great Depression, 931
    industrialization and, 814
    in Japan, 703
Protest(s). See also Revolts and rebellions
    against globalization, 1052–1053
    during Great Depression, 931–932
    against Japan in China, 910
    in Latin America, 1005
    in Middle East, 1046–1047
    by young people, 1009–1010
Protestant Reformation, 509–510, 661–665,
        663(m)
Protestants and Protestantism
    in Brazil, 572
    in England, 676
    freedoms in France, 665
    Great Awakening and, 785
    in Northern Ireland, 1045
    Scientific Revolution and, 670
    in Thirty Years' War, 668
    in World War II, 950
Providence Island, 738
Provisional Government (Russia), 902, 903
Proxy war, 962
Prussia
    Bismarck and, 836
    Danish war with, 838
    Enlightenment and, 765
    king as German Kaiser, 838
    war against France and, 773
Psychoanalysis, 886
Public, the, 828
Public affairs, in Latin America, 832
Public health, in colonies, 873
Public sphere, 764–765
Public works, in Mughal Empire, 631
Publishing, in Japan, 980
Puerto Rico, 558
    U.S. annexation of, 881
Pump priming
    by Nazis, 937
    in Sweden, 938
Punjab, Sikhs in, 632
Purges, by Stalin, 934
Puritans
    in England, 676
    in New England, 743, 744
Putin, Vladimir, 1049
Pygmies
    Bantu peoples and, 608–609
    of central Africa, 593, 607–609, 607(m)
Pyramids, in Tenochtitlán, 525

Qaddafi, Muammar, 1045, 1047, 1047(i)
Qadis (judges), 657
    in Mongol Empire, 489
Qianlong (China), 682(i), 693–694(m)
Qing (Manchu) Empire (China), 808(m), 893,
        894, 910
    disintegration of, 807–809
    downfall of, 884

gifts to, 664(*b*), 664(*i*), 684(*m*)
infrastructure in, 873
lifestyle in, 695–696
reform and, 895
in 1644–1799, 694(*m*)
Southeast Asia and, 711
Quanzhou, China, 498
Quebec, 741, 742
independence and, 1052
Quechua language, of Inca, 531, 533, 564
Queens. *See* specific rulers
Quelimane, 618
Quilombo maroon confederacy, Palmares, 748
Quilon, 494
Quinine, 660
malaria and, 868
Quinto real ("royal fifth"), taxation as, 727–728
Quipus. *See* Khipus
Quisling, Vidkun (president of Norway), 949
Quito, Ecuador, 583, 781
Qur'an
in Kazan, Russia, 1048(*b*)
readers of, 1048(*b*), 1048(*i*)

Race and racism
African Americans and, 981–982
American, 602–604
in Brazil, 719–722
in British North America, 746
as cause of slavery, 603
in English North American colonies, 744
Enlightenment thinkers on, 764
of Hitler, 936–937
inferiority of blacks as, 767
Japanese militarism and, 935
mixed races in American colonies and, 722
mobilization of masses and, 933
outsiders and, 849
scientific, 861
slavery and, 595, 603
in South Africa, 1023
in Spanish America, 725, 730–732
in United States, 850, 1009
youth protests against, 1009
Radar, 942
Radical Civil Union (Argentina), 919
Radicals and radicalism, terrorism and, 1025
Radio, 893, 914, 915
Cold War culture and, 982–983
Nazi use of, 937
politicians use of, 915
in World War II, 948
Radiotelescope, 995
Raffia palm fiber, 593
Railroads, 790(*i*), 798, 816, 818(*i*)
in Africa, 868
in Egypt, 864
in India, 810, 863
in Italy, 837
in Mexico, 894
in c. 1914, 792(*m*)
in North Africa, 865
refrigerated cars for, 801–802
spread of (c. 1900), 799(*m*)
trans-Siberian, 799–802, 800(*b*), 800(*i*)

Rain forests
in Brazil, 1029
clearing of, 1038
in Congo, 607–608
Rajas (subject princes), in Vijayanagara, 622
Ramaraja (Vinjayanagara), 623
Ramayana, 877
Ranches, in Spanish America, 728
Ranke, Leopold von (German historian), 846(*i*)
Rape of Nanjing, 941, 945
Rap music, 1051
Rationing, in World War I, 902
Raw materials. *See* Natural resources
Reading Lolita in Teheran (Nafisi), 1044
Reagan, Ronald, 1033
economy and, 1014
Iran hostage crisis and, 1009
Reaganomics, 1014
Realpolitik, in Germany, 838
Reasoning
deductive, 670–671
inductive, 670
Reaya (flock, Ottoman Empire), 656
Rebellions. *See* Revolts and rebellions
Recessions, in 19th century, 804
Reciprocity, Inca, 536
Reconquista (Reconquest of Spain), 484, 550
Reconstruction (U.S.), 840
Red Army (China), 904, 946(*b*)
Red Brigades (Italy), 1045
Red Fort (Mughal palace complex), 631, 675
Reds, in Russian civil war, 903–904
Red Sea region, Portugal and, 633
Refining, in Americas, 567, 568–569
Reform(s), 846–849. *See also* Reformation
in China, 895
in Czechoslovakia, 1011
of education, 846–847
in Egypt, 776
emancipation of Russian serfs and, 834–836
in Latin America, 778
legal, 791
Meiji Restoration as, 826–827
in Mexico, 894, 895
after Napoleonic Wars, 774–775
NGOs and, 1034
political, in Mexico, 894, 895
Soviet Union and, 1011–1012
Western ideas and, 845
after World War I, 908–911
Reformation. *See also* Protestant Reformation
Protestant and Catholic, 661–665, 663(*m*)
Refrigerated railroad cars, 801–802
Refugees
blocking of Jewish, 953
in World War II, 925, 928
Regional alliances, 968–969, 968(*m*)
Regionalism, migration and, 874–875
Regional societies, as multiethnic empires, 508
Reich (empire), in Germany, 838
Reincarnation, South Asian ideas of, 886
Reinhard, Johan (anthropologist), 513
Religion(s). *See also* Buddha and Buddhism;
Christianity; Hindus and Hinduism;

Inquisition; Islam; Jews and Judaism;
specific groups
of African Americans, 747
of Akbar, 627
Aztec, 522
in Brazil, 735
conformity of, 484
in East Africa, 621
of Eastern Woodlands peoples, 541
in England, 676
in France, 674
in Germany, 848
as global issue, 1038
government and, 785
Inca, 532, 534
in Indonesia, 971
in Japan, 698–699
in Korea, 707
mountains and, 515
Mughal expansion and, 627
in New England, 743–744
New World exploration and, 559
in Ottoman Empire, 657
Portugal and, 633–634
Portuguese in Africa, 598
revival in secular age, 784–787
in Russia, 687, 689
shamanism and, 518
skepticism in, 650
in Spanish America, 729
in Spanish and Portuguese colonies, 861
in western Africa, 585
Western study of non-Western, 886
worldwide, 1043(*m*), 1049–1050
Religious orders, Jesuits as, 662
Religious revivalism, 785–787
Religious toleration
Mughal, 624, 628
in Ottoman Empire, 657
in Vijayanagara, 723
Religious wars, Crusades as, 475
"Removal" policy, toward native Americans,
743, 745
Renaissance (Europe), 478, 498
Renan, Ernest (French philosopher and writer), 829
Reparations, German (World War I), 906
Repartimiento (labor system), 568
Republic, in United States, 771
Republicanism, in France, 773–774
Research and development
military, 976
in science and technology, 1001
Reservations, for native Americans, 840
Resistance. *See also* Revolts and rebellions
by Aceh, 640
in El Salvador, 1006(*b*)
to foreign domination, 883–885
to globalization, 1025–1026
to imperialism, 872, 891
by Mapuche people, 573–576
by slaves, 746–747
in Soviet Union, 934
by Suriname maroons, 749
in World War II, 949–950

Resources. *See* Natural resources
Restaurants, 1001(*b*)
Retailing, 805
Reunification, of Germany (1990), 1016
Réunion, 617
Revivals and revivalism, Great Awakening as, 785
Revolts and rebellions
   Boxer Rebellion (China), 857
   in China, 693
   in colonies, 880
   English Peasant Revolt (1381), 483
   in Enlightenment, 767
   Florentine wool workers (1378), 483
   Heiji (Japan, 1159), 504(*i*)
   in Hungary, 979
   in India (1857), 863
   in Iran, 1008
   in Mexico (1810), 779
   between 1945 and 1990, 991
   in North American colonies, 746
   in Poland, 979
   by proletariat, 817
   by Sikhs (1710–1715), 632, 632(*i*)
   by slaves, 747–748
   in Soviet Union (1920s), 918
   against Spanish in Chile, 574–575
   Taiping (China), 808–809
   after World War I, 910–911
Revolution(s). *See also* Scientific revolution
   in Atlantic Ocean region, 760(*m*)
   in Balkan region, 893
   in China (1911–1912), 891–893, 895–896
   domestic, 1006–1009
   economic constraints and, 791
   Enlightenment and, 761
   in Haiti, 777–778, 779(*i*)
   in Latin America (1810–1830), 778–784,
     780(*m*)
   in Mexico, 890(*i*), 891
   from 1910–1929, 892(*m*)
   of 1989, 1016–1017
   in North America, 767–771
   in Poland, 1015
   in Russia (1905), 883
   in Russia (1917), 893
Rhee, Syngman, 1007
Rhodes, Cecil, 867, 881
Rhodes, Ottomans in, 653
Rhodesia, 867
Ricci, Matteo (Jesuit priest), 664, 672, 697
   travels of, 684(*m*)
Rice and rice industry
   in Japan, 503, 700
   in Korea, 706
   in Southeast Asia, 709
   in Vijayanagara, 623
Richard II (England), 483
Rieger, Albert (Austrian painter), 865(*i*)
Rights
   of citizens, 851–852
   in Declaration of Independence, 768
   exclusion of Americans from, 850
   in French Revolution, 772–773
   in United States, 840
   of women, 656, 850

Rio de Janeiro, 733(*m*), 781, 1029
   schools in, 847
   after World War II, 977(*i*)
Río de la Plata region, European claims in,
   568(*m*)
Risorgimento (rebirth, Italy), 847
Rivera, Diego, 890(*i*), 895, 931, 932(*i*)
Rizal, José (Philippines), 714
Roads and highways, Inca, 535, 535(*i*)
"Roaring Twenties," 893
Roberts, Bartholomew ("Black Bart"), 738
Robespierre, Maximilien, 773
Rockefeller, John D., 802
Rockefeller Center, 932(*i*)
Roma (gypsies), Nazis and, 925, 947
Roman Catholic Church, 1049–1050. *See also*
     Christendom; Christianity; Crusades;
     Popes
   American silver funding for, 569–570
   in Brazil, 572
   in Ireland, 1045
   Japanese persecution of, 698–699
   Jesuits and, 581–582
   Kongo aristocracy and, 599
   Napoleon and, 774
   New World exploration and, 559
   in North American colonies, 746
   in Philippines, 712(*m*), 713–714
   Portuguese exploration and, 633–634
   Reformation in, 661–665, 663(*m*)
   Scientific Revolution and, 670
   in Spanish and Portuguese colonization, 861
   in World War II, 950
Romania
   as autonomous state, 896, 898(*m*)
   fall of communism in, 1016
   in World War II, 942, 951
Romanov dynasty (Russia), 684(*m*), 689
   end of, 902
Romanticism, 783
Rommel, Erwin, 951
Roosevelt, Eleanor, 938
Roosevelt, Franklin Delano, 944, 952
   fireside chats of, 938
   response to Great Depression, 938
Roosevelt, Theodore, Spanish-American War
     and, 881–882
Rosas, Juan Manuel (Argentinean dictator), 851
Rose of Lima (Saint), 732
Rousseau, Jean-Jacques, 763, 765, 773
Royal African Company, 603
Royal Commentaries of the Incas (Garcilaso de la
     Vega), 649
Royal court. *See* Court (royal)
Royal Dutch Shell, 913
Royalty. *See also* Kings and kingdoms; Monarchs
     and monarchies; Palaces
   power of, 483
Rubber industry, in Congo, 871(*b*)
Rucellai, Giovanni (Florentine merchant), 500
Rulers. *See* Kings and kingdoms; Monarchs and
     monarchies; specific rulers
Rum, in slave trade, 605
Runasimi language (Quechua), of Inca, 531
Runaways

in Caribbean region, 740–741
   in Suriname, 748
Rural areas
   British industry in, 797(*b*)
   Great Depression and, 931
   Green Revolution and, 996
Rushdie, Salman, 1051
Russia, 684(*m*). *See also* Russian Revolution;
     Soviet Union; World War I
   Bolshevik takeover in, 903
   Catherine the Great in, 765, 766–767(*b*)
   Chechnya and, 1046
   China and, 693
   civil war in, 903–904
   Crimean War and, 833, 833(*m*)
   emancipation of serfs in, 834–836, 834(*i*)
   Enlightenment in, 765
   expansion by, 683, 686–687
   Japan and, 868
   League of Nations and, 907
   life expectancy in, 1040
   Napoleon and, 761, 774
   peasants in, 834(*i*)
   peoples moved within, 850
   pogroms in, 875
   Poland and, 814
   Provisional Government in, 902
   Pugachev's revolt in, 767, 767(*m*)
   rise of (1462–1725), 687(*m*)
   serfdom in, 834, 835(*b*)
   trade in, 690
   trans-Siberian railroad in, 800(*b*), 800(*i*)
   in Triple Entente, 896
   women in, 836
   World War I and, 897, 903
Russian Empire, 687, 687(*m*)
   German occupation of, 903
   nation building and, 832–836
Russian Orthodox Church, 687
Russian Revolution
   of 1905, 883
   of 1917, 817, 893, 902–904, 963
Russification, 847
Russo-Japanese War (1904–1905), 882–883
Rwanda, 1027
   Doctors Without Borders and, 1032(*i*)
   genocide in, 1049
Ryukyu Islands, 706

Sacrifice. *See also* Human sacrifice
   Aztec, 524–526, 529
   by Eastern Woodlands peoples, 541
   Inca, 513–515, 534
   in Peru, 513
Saddam Hussein, 1045
Al-Sa'di (historian), 591(*b*)
Sa'di people, 591(*b*)
Sáenz Peña, Roque (president of Argentina), 919
Safavid Empire (Persia), 489, 612(*i*), 654
   Mughals and, 628
   Ottomans and, 652
Safi al-Din (Safavid founder), 489
Safiyat al-din Shah, sultana Taj al-Alam (ruler of
     Aceh), 642
Sahel, in Africa, 585

Saigon, 929
　colonialism in, 872(*b*)
　France and, 864
Saikaku, Ihara (Japanese poet), 702–703
Sailors, African American in World War II, 946(*i*)
St. Christopher, 738
Saint-Domingue, 739, 777. *See also* Haiti
　revolt in, 759–760
St. Gabriel (ship), 553(*i*)
St. Lawrence River region, 741
St. Petersburg, 689, 689(*m*)
Salé (city), 677
Salsa music, 1051
Salt, trade in, 593
SALT I. *See* Strategic Arms Limitation Treaty (SALT I)
Salvador, Brazil, 572
Samarkand
　as Mongol capital, 489
　Spanish ambassador on, 490(*b*)
Samurai (Japanese warriors), 501–503, 698, 842
　Japanese industrialization and, 802–803
Sanchez Galque, Adrian (Spanish artist), 730(*b*), 730(*i*)
Sandoval, Alonso de, 596(*b*)
Sanitation, in Crimean War, 833
San Martin, José de (Argentinean independence fighter), 781
Santa Anna, Antonio Lopez de, 831–832
Santo Domingo, 739
São Jorge da Mina, 603
São Paulo, 733, 1029
São Salvador, Kongo, 599
São Tomé, 554(*m*), 555, 575, 606
Sapa Inca (Inca emperor), 531, 532, 534, 565
Sarajevo, Franz Ferdinand assassinated in, 896
Saramaka maroons, 749
Sari, in India, 813(*i*)
Sartre, Jean-Paul, 981
Satanic Verses, The (Rushdie), 1051
Satellites (artificial)
　communications, 988(*i*), 993, 994–995
　Sputnik as, 966
　technology for, 994
Sati (widow suicide, India), 630–631, 870
Satyagraha strategy (Gandhi), 954, 954(*i*)
Sa'ud, house of, 786
Sa'ud, Muhammad ibn, 785
Savannas, 491
　in Africa, 585
Scholar-official class, in China, 486
Scholars, Muslim, in West Africa, 492
Scholarship. *See* Intellectual thought; Learning
School and schooling. *See* Education
Science
　astronomy and, 995
　revolution in, 510
Scientific management, 913
Scientific racism, 861
Scientific revolution, 650
　in Europe, 670–672
　after World War II, 995–996
Scientific socialism, 816
Scotland, Cromwell and, 676

Scripture, religious, 729–730
Sculpture, from Benin, 592, 592(*b*)
Seaborne trade, in East Africa, 618
Sea routes, to Asia, 547
SEATO. *See* Southeast Asia Treaty Organization
Sebastian (Portugal), 666
Sebu, Philippines, 561
Secondary education, in Europe, 847
Second Balkan War (1913), 892(*m*), 896
Second Great Awakening, 785
Second Sex, The (Beauvoir), 981
Second World War. *See* World War II
Secret Speech (Soviet Union), 979
Secularism, religion and, 784–787, 1049–1050
Security, collective, 907
Security Council (UN), Korean War and, 967
Segregationism, in U.S., 1009
Self-determination, 905
Selim I ("the Grim," Ottoman Empire), 652
Selim II (Ottoman Empire), 653
Seminaries, in Africa, 598
Senate (U.S.)
　League of Nations and, 907
　World War I peace settlement and, 907
Senegalese soldiers, 912(*b*)
Senegal River region, 588(*b*)
Senghor, Léopold Sédar, 912(*b*)
Seoul, 705
　as Hanyang, 705
Separatists, English, 745(*i*)
Sephardim, Ottoman Jews as, 657
Sepoys, 863
September 11, 2001, terrorism, 1045
Serambi Mekkah, Aceh as, 640
Serbia
　as autonomous state, 896, 898(*m*)
　World War I and, 896
Serbs
　Balkan wars and, 896
　Milosevic and, 1016
　nationalism of, 884
Serfs and serfdom
　demise of, 477
　protests against, 767
　in Russia, 690, 833–834, 834(*i*), 835(*b*)
Servants. *See also* Slaves and slavery
　indentured, 722, 876–877(*b*), 876(*i*)
Services, social, 1033
Service sector, 805, 1023
　global, 991
　growth of, 999
　technological, 988(*i*)
Settlement(s)
　of Americas, 517(*m*)
　Spanish-American conquests and (1519–1600), 562–566
Sevastopol, 833
"17th-century crisis," 650
Seven Years' War, 768
Sex and sexuality
　birth control and, 995–996
　comfort women, 942(*b*)
　in Japan, 703
　South Asian ideas and, 886
　youth culture and, 1003

Sex slaves, in World War II, 942(*b*), 949(*i*)
Sex tourism, 1001(*b*)
Sexual division of labor, 815
Shah Jahan (Mughal Empire), 614–615, 626(*i*), 627
Shamans and shamanism, 518–519
　in Eastern Woodlands groups, 540
　in Korea, 707
　women as, 518, 527
Shanghai, China
　film industry in, 916(*b*)
　Nationalists in, 910
　refugees in, 925
Sharafs, 494
Shari'a (Islamic law), women under, 656
Shayks (elders), in Mongol Empire, 489
Shi'a Islam (Shi'ism)
　Ottomans and, 654
　Sufism and, 489
Shikoku, 698
Ships and shipping
　Chinese junks as, 494
　exploration and, 552–553
　global, 796–797
　in Indian Ocean, 619
　in Japan, 803–804, 913
　Portuguese, 553–554, 553(*i*)
　slave trade and, 603(*i*), 605–606, 607
　in World War I, 897–898
Shivaji (Hindu Marathas, India), 627
Shoguns and shogunate (Japan), 503, 698, 825
　Tokugawa, 698–699
Shona speakers, 620
Show trials, Soviet, 934
Siam. *See* Thailand
Siberia
　fur trade and ecosystem of, 690
　Japanese withdrawal from, 904
　in Russian Empire, 863
Sicán kingdom (Peru), 513
Sicily, Garibaldi in, 837
"Sick man of Europe," Ottoman Empire as, 832–833
Siderus Nuncius (The Starry Messenger, Galileo), 672
Sierra Leone, invasions of, 586
Sieyès, Abbé, 771
Sigoli, Simone, 500
Sijie, Dai (Chinese writer), 1044–1045
Sikhs, 497(*b*), 632, 1052
　in India, 1028, 1045
　rebellion by (1710–1715), 632, 632(*i*)
Silent Spring (Carson), 1038
Silicon chips, 993
Silk and silk industry
　in China, 487, 494, 692–693, 696–697(*b*), 696(*i*)
　in Japan, 802
Silk Road, 476(*m*), 494
　caravanserai along, 656
　Russia and British destruction of, 863
Silver
　in China, 691, 794
　decline of Spanish, 666
　depression in 1600s and, 668

Silver (*continued*)
Dutch East India Company and, 638
Japanese exports of, 699
Spanish-American, 567, 629, 654, 728
transpacific shipping from Americas, 691
world livelihoods and, 569–570
Simyonov, Yulian (Russian novelist), 982
Sinai peninsula, 1013
Singapore, 944
in ASEAN, 1036
Chinese traders in, 877
Singh, Manmohan (prime minister of India), 1028
"Single Whip Law" (China, 1581), 691
Sino-Japanese War (1894), 868, 868(*m*), 895
Sioux Indians, 841(*i*)
Sistema de castas, 731
Six-Day War (1967), 1013
Skin color, Enlightenment thinkers on, 764
Slave Coast, 598, 602(*m*)
Slave labor, Jews as, 938
Slaves and slavery, 583–584. *See also* Chattel slavery
abolition and, 810
in Africa, 590
African enslavement of Africans and, 595
Amerindian, 722
Aztec, 526–527
in Brazil, 734, 830
captives and, 590
in Caribbean region, 737–741, 777–778
Dutch and, 635
Enlightenment ideas and, 766–767
European claims in Americas and, 568(*m*)
Inca, 535
indentured servitude as, 877
Indians and, 556–557
industry and, 797
in Korea, 708
Mamluks and, 490
markets for, 596
Middle Passage and, 583, 605–606
native American, 559–560
number from West Central Africa, 600
racism and, 603
in Saint-Domingue, 759–761
slave ships and, 603(*i*)
Smith, Adam, on, 764
in South America, 583
in Spanish America, 567–568, 730–731
for sugar industry, 572–573, 575
for tobacco industry, 601–602
Uncle Tom's Cabin and, 817
U.S. Constitution and, 770
in United States, 840
West African trading posts and, 596
Wheatley as, 786(*b*)
women and agriculture in, 818–820
Slave trade
abolition of, 810
African, 581, 596–599
African rumors about, 583–584
in Angola, 599
Atlantic, 597(*m*), 602(*m*), 722
Benin art of, 592(*b*), 592(*i*)

to 1860, 792(*m*)
exploration and, 552
functioning of, 604–605
in Indian Ocean region, 613
in Kongo, 599
monopoly trading companies and, 601–604
northern Europeans in, 600–607
ports for, 600
Portuguese, 596–598
Spanish, 676(*m*)
volume of, 606–607
Slaving forts, 603
Slavs, Nazis and, 925, 947
Smallpox, 562, 563, 729, 1041
Smith, Adam, 763–764
Smith, John, 743, 744
Smyrna, trade in, 656
Soccer, in Rio de Janeiro, 977(*i*)
Social classes. *See* Class(es); Hierarchies
Social Contract, The (Rousseau), 763
Social Darwinism, 861
Social health, in United States, 1040
Socialism, 816–817
in Czechoslovakia, 1011
of Sun Yatsen, 895
World War I and, 900
Socialist realism, in Soviet art, 934, 934(*i*)
Social order
after Black Death, 483
in Italy, 483
Social Security Act (U.S., 1935), 938
Social services, taxes for, 1033
Society
African, 587
in Argentina, 919, 977–978
Aztec, 522
Black Death and, 478–482
in Brazil, 1029
Caribbean slave, 740–741
in China, 965
complexity of, 914
disorder under imperialism, 870–872
of Eastern Woodlands group, 540–541
Enlightenment thinkers on, 763
Great Depression and, 930–931
imperial, 869–878
Inca, 532–533
industry and, 812–815
in Italy, 499–500
in Japan, 501–505, 842
mass, 893, 913–914
in Nazi Germany, 937–938
Ottoman, 491
public sphere and, 764–765
in Russia, 836
in Siberia, 690
Soviet, 978
West Central Africa, 594–595
western European after Black Death, 482–484
in World War II, 947–948
Society for Friends of the Blacks (1788), 777
Society of Jesus. *See* Jesuits
Society of the Righteous and Harmonious Fists (Boxers, China), 884
Sofala, 618

Soil
in Brazil, 734
depletion of, 1018
in English North American colonies, 743
Soka Gakkai (Buddhist sect), 1050
Soldiers. *See also* Armed forces; Military; specific battles and wars
colonial, in World War I, 897, 898, 899–900, 899(*i*), 904, 912(*b*)
in France, 674
Portuguese, 598(*i*)
in Vietnam, 1008
in World War II, 946–947(*b*), 949, 950(*i*)
Solidarity movement (Poland), 1015, 1016
Solís, Juan de, 560
Solzhenitsyn, Aleksandr, 990(*m*), 1012
Somalia, famine in, 1041
Songhai Empire, 586(*m*), 589, 590
women in, 593
"Song of Revolution" (Chinese diaspora), 878
Sony, 999(*b*)
Sophie (Austria-Hungary), 896
Soseki Natsumi (Meiji writer), 879–880
Soul Mountain (Gao Xingjian), 1038
South (U.S.)
Civil War and, 840
slave culture in, 746–747
women farmers in, 819–820
South (global), vs. North (global), 985, 1026–1027
South Africa, 1029–1030. *See also* Africa
after apartheid, 1031(*m*)
Boers in, 881
British annexation of, 881
HIV/AIDS in, 1030
Mandela and, 1023–1024
resistance to Britain in, 867–868, 867(*i*)
South African (Boer) War, 881
South America. *See also* specific locations
Bolivar and, 758(*i*)
caudillos in, 780–781
Dutch silver from, 638
economic and social progress in, 1033
European claims in, 568(*m*)
Inca in, 513–516
Magellan and, 560–561
Mercosur free trade zone in, 1036
1960–1992, 1004(*m*)
slaves in, 583
South Asia. *See also* India
migrations in, 990(*m*)
Mughal Empire in, 623–625
trade and empire in, 613–616, 614(*m*), 620–625
Western ideas and, 886
South China Sea, Portugal and, 633
Southeast Asia. *See also* specific locations
Aceh in, 640–642
China and, 693, 694(*m*)
commerce in, 710–711
Dutch and, 669
Dutch and English colonies in (to 1750), 638(*m*)
in c. 1450, 495
France in, 864

imperialism in, 862
Islam in, 492–493
mainland consolidation in, 708–711
migrations in, 990(m), 1044
Muslims in, 714
new states of (1945–1999), 971(m)
17th-century financial crisis in, 711
spices from, 496
trade in, 709(m)
Vietnam War and, 1008
Southeast Asia Treaty Organization (SEATO), 968
Southern cone (South America), 1033, 1036
Southern Hemisphere, trade and, 1027
South Korea, 967
    demonstrations in, 1007
    economy in, 996–997, 998
South Vietnam, 972, 1008. See also Vietnam War
Southwest (U.S.), European claims in, 568(m)
Soviet bloc, 964–965
    activism in, 1009
    collapse of, 991–992, 1014–1017
    protests in 1967, 1011
    science and technology applications in, 1001
Soviets, 903
    defined, 902
Soviet Union, 904. See also Cold War; Russia;
        Soviet bloc; World War II
    Afghanistan and, 1008
    communism and, 963–964, 978–979
    cosmonauts in, 966–967(b), 966(i)
    Cuba and, 969
    dissolution of (1992), 1017
    eastern Europe and, 964
    economy in, 963
    end of, 991–992, 1012, 1014–1017
    film industry in, 915
    five-year plans in, 933
    Germany after World War II and, 964–965, 965(m)
    in Grand Alliance, 945
    human rights and, 1049
    modernization of, 978–979
    Nazi invasion of, 942–943
    New Economic Policy in, 918, 933
    nonaggression pact with Nazis, 941
    postwar radio in, 982
    Prague Spring and, 1011
    propaganda by, 916
    secret police (KGB) in, 1017
    socialist realism in, 934, 934(i)
    space exploration by, 966–967(b), 966(i)
    as superpower, 962
    Warsaw Pact and, 967
    after World War II, 962–970
    in World War II, 942, 943(m), 948, 950–951
Soviet Union (former), migration from, 1044
Space Age, 994–995
Space exploration, 994–995
    countries with programs, 967(b)
    Soviet and U.S., 966–967(b), 966(i)
Space race, 966–967(b), 966(i)
    Cold War and, 994
Spain. See also Latin America; New Spain; Peru;
        Spanish Empire

in Americas, 567–570, 719
Armada of, 666, 666(m)
Aztec Empire and, 529
Bourbon dynasty in, 729
Chile and, 573–574
conquistadors and, 562–566
conversion of Muslims to Christianity in, 669(b)
Dutch Revolt against, 665
Enlightenment and, 765–766
exploration by, 547, 548(m), 555–560
after Franco, 1006–1007
"Golden Century" in, 647–649
Habsburg dynasty in, 654
imperialism of, 861
Inca Empire conquered by, 564–565
Latin American rebellions against, 778–781
missionaries from, 554
Moriscos (Muslims) in, 590
Napoleon and, 774
national monarchy in (1469), 484
Philippine conquest by, 712–713
Portugal and, 635
Reconquista in, 484
religious conformity in, 484
revolutions in Latin American empire of, 778–784
Spanish-American War and, 881–882
in Thirty Years' War, 668
Treaty of Tordesillas and, 559
Spanish America, 723–732. See also Latin America
    1580–1750, 724(m)
    government in, 724–729
    Jesuits in, 766
    lifestyle in, 729–732
    mining economy in, 728
    mixed races in, 731–732
    silver in, 567, 691
    slavery and, 596, 603–604, 606
    women in, 726–727, 732
Spanish-American War (1898), 881–882, 881(m)
Spanish Armada (1588), 666, 666(m)
    defeat of, 667(i)
    route of, 648(m)
Spanish Empire, 665–666
    Battle of Lepanto and, 665
    coin from, 726(b)
    ethnic and racial exploitation in, 849
Spanish language, in Philippines, 713(i)
Spheres of influence, in China, 910
Spices and spice trade
    cinnamon and, 636–637(b), 636(i)
    Dutch and, 635, 669
    European diet and, 660
    exploration and, 552
    in Indian Ocean and Arabian Sea, 614(m)
    Portuguese, 635
    from Southeast Asia, 496
Spies and spying
    satellites for, 995
    in World War II, 949
Spinning jenny, 799
Spinning machines, 798
"Spiritual conquest," of Philippines, 713–714

Sputnik, 966, 994
Sri Lanka (Ceylon), 616
    cinnamon harvest in, 636–637(b), 636(i)
    Dutch and, 635
    Tamil separatists in, 1045
SS (Schutzstaffel), 937
Stagflation, 1014
Stalin, Joseph
    central economic planning and, 933
    death of (1953), 978
    industrialization and, 927
    kulaks and, 933–934
    modernization and, 978
    purges by, 934
    Soviet security and, 952
    after World War II, 963
Stalingrad, Battle of, 950–951
Stalinism, 933–934
Stamp Act (1765), 768, 769(m)
Standard of living. See also Lifestyle
    in global North and South, 1027
    in Soviet Union, 1014–1015
    after World War II, 977
Stanton, Elizabeth Cady, 852
Starvation. See also Famine
    in Soviet Union, 934
    World War I blockades and, 908
    in World War II, 949
State (nation). See also City-states; National
        states; Nation-state
    in East Asia, 485
    in West Africa, 588–593
State-building. See also Nation building; Nation-
        state; State (nation)
    in central and eastern Europe (1920), 906(m)
    in China, 910
    in 1910, 894
    Peace of Paris treaties and, 906
    in Southeast Asia, 708–711
    in Turkey, 908–909, 909(i)
State Department (U.S.), 952
States (U.S.), 769
Status (social). See Class(es)
Steam engine, 798
Stedman, John Gabriel (soldier and author), 749(i)
Stephenson, George (inventor), 798
Sterilization
    forced, in India, 1041
    voluntary, 996
Stock market, 805
    crash of (1929), 927, 928–929
Storm troopers (Nazi Germany), 937
Stowe, Harriet Beecher, 817
Strasbourg, Jews of, 481
Strategic Arms Limitation Treaty (SALT I), 1012
Strikes (labor)
    in Argentina, 919
    in China, 910
    in colonies, 932
    in France, 1010
    in postwar period (World War I), 914
    during World War I, 902
Submarines, in World War I, 897, 902

Sub-Saharan Africa
   animals of, 585
   conflict in, 1027, 1027(*m*)
   Islam in, 491
   peoples of, 584
   problems in, 1027
   in World War I, 904
Subsistence agriculture, in Africa, 589, 870
Succession
   Inca, 534, 538
   in Russia, 689
Sudan, 1027
   Battle of Omdurman in, 868
   famine in, 1041
Sudetenland, Hitler and, 940
Suez Canal, 864, 972–973
   England and, 972
   nationalization of, 973
Suez Canal (Rieger), 865(*i*)
Suffragists, 852
Sufism, 658(*b*)
   in Central Asia, 488–489
   Indian castes and, 497(*b*)
   in Southeast Asia, 493
Sugar Act (England 1764), 768
Sugar and sugar industry
   in Atlantic world, 572–573, 574–575(*b*),
      574(*i*)
   in Caribbean region, 737, 740, 741
   Cuban exports and, 975–976
   exploration and, 552
   in São Tomé, 555
   slaves for, 601
   sources of, 574(*b*)
   in Southeast Asia, 710
Sukarno, Achmed (Indonesia), 970, 971
   Bandung Conference and, 983
Suleiman ("the Magnificent," Ottoman Empire),
      646(*i*), 653–654
Sultans. *See also* Mamluk Sultanate
   of Aceh, 642
   Ottoman women and, 654–655
Sulu Islands, Muslims in, 714
Sumatra
   Dutch and, 635
   Islam in, 493
Sumo wrestling, in Japan, 703
Sun, Inca and, 531, 533, 534
Sunni Ali (Songhai Empire), 590
Sunni Islam, Ottomans and, 654
Sun Tzu (Chinese military strategist), 887
Sun Yatsen (China), 895, 910
Superpowers
   activist challenges to, 1009–1012
   Cold War alliances and, 966–969
   end of, 989
   after World War II, 928, 962–963
Supply-side economics, 1014
Supporter of Religion Against the Infidels, The
      (Al-Hajari), 669(*b*)
Supranational organizations, 1033–1036
   NGOs as, 1034
Supreme Court (U.S.), *Brown v. Board of
   Education* (1954) and, 981–982
Surat, 638

Suriname
   Dutch and, 738, 740
   Jews in, 736
   maroons of, 748–749, 748(*m*), 749(*i*)
Swahili Coast, 617
   lumber exports from, 620
Swahili peoples, 620
Sweden
   cream separator in, 801
   pension cuts in, 1033
   response to Great Depression, 938–939
Swine flu, 1044
Synthetic goods, 976
Syria, 908
   Mamluk Sultanate in, 480
   Timur in, 488
   uprising in, 1047
   in World War I, 904

Tabasco, Malintzin in, 547–549
Tagalog language, 713(*i*)
Tagore, Dwarkanath (India), 810, 812
Tagore, Rabindranath, 879
Taino people, 556, 557–559, 560
Taiping Rebellion (China), 808–809
Taiping Tianguo, 807–809
Taiwan, 935(*m*), 997
   China and, 694(*m*)
Taj Mahal, 615, 626(*i*), 631
Tale of Genji, The (Murasaki Shikibu), 504
Taliban, 1008, 1046(*m*)
"Talkies," 917(*b*)
Tamerlane. *See* Timur
Tamil people, 1052
   as separatists, 1045
Tanabe Hajime (Japanese philosopher), 980
Tango, 920, 920(*i*)
Tanks
   in World War I, 904
   in World War II, 951
Tanzania, Germany and, 866
Taoism, in Japan, 699
Tarascan people, 520(*m*)
   Aztecs and, 526, 529
Tariffs
   in Depression, 931
   in EEC, 976
   free trade and, 1027
   in Latin America, 805
Taseko, Matsuo (Japanese activist), 825, 826, 828,
      841, 842, 843–844
Tata family (India), 913
   Jamsetji, 810, 813
Tatars, Moscow and, 689
Tawantinsuyu (Inca Empire), 564–565
Taxation
   of American colonies, 768, 769
   ATTAC and, 1034
   in China, 691
   of colonies, 929
   in England, 483
   by English East India Company, 625
   in France, 674
   imperialism and, 869
   in India, 810, 872

   by monarchs, 484
   in Mughal Empire, 629, 631
   revolts against, 483
   for Seven Years' War, 768
   in Spanish America, 726
   in Spanish Bourbon Reforms, 765–766
Tax farming, 491
Tea
   in England, 765(*i*)
   trade in, 807
Teachers. *See also* Education
   in Korea, 707
Technology, 992. *See also* Industrialization;
      Printing; Writing
   agrarian peoples in age of, 1017–1019
   AIDS and, 1041–1042
   in Crimean War, 833
   environmental damage from, 1038
   for exploration, 552–553
   global, 988(*i*)
   imperialism and, 868–869
   industry and, 798, 799–802
   information revolution and, 992–994
   navigational, 552–553
   pollution from, 1018(*i*)
   postwar, 893
   Scientific Revolution and, 670
   service sector and, 1023
   sexuality, procreation, and, 995–996
   in South Asia, 616
   in Spanish-American metal refining, 567
   in Spanish–native American encounters, 566
   transformation of, 989–992
   warfare and, 891, 952(*b*)
   World War I weapons, 897
Tehran, Iran, hostage crisis in (1979), 1009
Tejuco, Brazil, 719–721
Telescope, of Galileo, 671
Television, 993
   in 1960s, 976
   state-sponsored, 993
Temples
   Aztec, 522
   in Luang Prabang, Laos, 708, 710(*i*)
   in Tenochtitlán, 525
   in Tiwanaku, Bolivia, 532
Tenant farmers, after Black Death, 483
Tenayuca, Aztecs and, 521(*b*)
Ten Days That Shook the World (film), 915
Tenochtitlán, 520(*m*), 522
   Aztec map of, 521(*b*), 521(*i*)
   c. 1500, 522
   land in, 523
   Spanish in, 562–563, 564(*b*)
Tenochtli (Aztec emperor), 521(*b*)
Teotihuacán, Mexico, 519
Tereshkova, Valentina (Soviet cosmonaut),
      966(*i*)
Terror, the (France), 773
Terrorism
   by Aztecs, 526
   in El Salvador, 1006(*i*)
   in England, 1046
   global, 1025, 1038, 1045–1047
   in India, 1028

in Ireland, 910
on September 11, 2001, 1045
"Test-tube babies," 996
Tete-Ansa, Winifred (African businessman), 930(b)
Texcoco. See Lake Texcoco
Textiles and textile industry. See also Cloth and clothing
 African liberation and, 975(b), 975(i)
 in China, 692–693
 expansion of, 673
 Inca, 536
 in India, 496–497(b), 496(i), 810
 industrial, 793
 in Japan, 701
 mechanization of, 798
 slaves and, 812
 in Spanish America, 728
 workers in, 813
T4 project, 938
Thailand
 in ASEAN, 1036
 Burma and, 708–709
 China and, 693
 development of, 708
 trade in, 496
Thatcher, Margaret (England), 1012, 1014, 1033
Theater. See Drama
Theocracy, Safavid, 489
Thevet, André (French priest), 521(b)
Third Balkan War, 894, 896. See also World War I
"Third Rome," Moscow as, 687
Third World, biopiracy in, 1018
Thirty Years' War (1618–1648), 667–668, 668(i)
Three Gorges Dam (China), 1038
Three Guineas (Woolf), 939
Three Modern Women (film), 915
Tiananmen Square, Beijing, riots in (1989), 1015–1016, 1016(i)
Tibet, 869
 China and, 693
Ticonderoga, Fort, 744
Tierra del Fuego, Magellan and, 560–561
Tigers. See Pacific tigers
Tilak, B. G. (Indian Hindu leader), 885
Timar (Ottoman land grant) system, 629, 651
Timber, Russian, 690
Timbuktu, 589, 590
 manuscript from, 492(i)
 trade in, 492
Time of Troubles (Russia, 1584–1613), 689
Timur (Tamerlane, Mongols), 477–478, 488–489
Timurid Muslims, 623, 627
Tiwanaku, Bolivia, 532
Tlacopan, Aztecs and, 523
Tlaloc (god), 522, 523
Tlatelolco (Aztec city), 523
 fall to Spanish, 563, 564(b)
Tlatoque (Aztec male rulers), 523
Tlaxcalan people, 520(m), 526, 529, 563
Tobacco
 in Caribbean region, 740
 industrialization of, 802
 in Japan, 701
 slaves for, 601–602

in slave trade, 605
in Southeast Asia, 710–711
Tokugawa Shogunate (Japan, 1603–1868), 503, 698–699, 841
Tokyo, Japan, 1031, 1036. See also Edo
 attack on subway system, 1045
 earthquake in, 935
 firebombing of, 945, 951
 postwar trials in, 980
 U.S. aid to, 964(i)
Toleration. See Religious toleration
Toltecs, 519, 523, 539
Tools, Inca, 535
Topkapi (Ottoman palace), 675(i)
Tordesillas, Treaty of (1494), 559, 571
Torres, Marcela de, 815
Tortuga, 738
Torture, human rights and, 1049
Totalitarianism, 932, 933
Total war
 World War I as, 900
 World War II as, 945
"To the Senegalese Soldiers Who Died for France" (Senghor), 912(b)
Touré, Amadou Toumani (Mali), 1027
Touré, Muhammad (Songhai), 590
Tourism
 Cook, Thomas, and, 1000–1001(b)
 in Japan, 1000–1001(b), 1000(i)
Toussaint Louverture, Pierre-Dominique, 777–778, 779(i)
Towns. See Cities and towns
Townshend Acts (1767), 768
Toxic wastes, 1018(i)
Trade, 1027. See also Commerce
 African gains and losses from slave trade, 604–605
 in African gold, 586
 Afro-Eurasian, 475, 476(m), 478
 in Atlantic region, 767–768
 Aztec, 523
 Black Death carried by, 479
 in Brazil, 734–735
 capitalism and, 672
 of China, 494, 692–693, 694(m)
 China's environment and, 694–695
 Chinese–East African, 619–620
 commercial power and, 477
 competition for, 547
 domestic, in Great Depression, 931
 Dutch and, 635–638
 in East Africa, 617–618
 English in India, 638–639
 global, 794–795, 796–798
 Inca, 530
 India and, 494, 629
 Indian maritime, 631–632
 in Indian Ocean, 587, 613–616, 614(m), 615, 618(m)
 Italian, 500
 Japanese, 698, 802
 Korean, 706
 laissez faire and, 764
 of land in India, 632

in late Ming China, 691–693
in Manila, 691
maritime, 494–498, 712(m)
in Ming China, 487
monopolies in, 481, 601–604
Muslim, 492–493
opium, 807
Ottoman, 654, 656
in Philippines, 712
Portuguese, 633, 634–635
in Portuguese Africa, 596–598
in Portuguese Brazil, 571
Russian, 690
in South Asia, 613–616, 614(m), 620–625
in Southeast Asia (c. 1500–1700), 709(m)
in Spanish America, 724(m), 728
tea, 807
in Vijayanagara, 623
in West Africa, 492
in West Central Africa, 593–594
women in, 711
world economy and, 997
worldwide, 661(m), 806–807
Trade diaspora, 492–493, 497–498
Trademark branding, 1018–1019
Trade routes
 in Africa, 581
 in Afro-Eurasia (15th century), 477(m)
 Dutch, 614(m)
 Portuguese to India, 614(m)
 by sea (c. 1775), 792(m)
 in Western Hemisphere, 514(m)
Trading companies, Dutch and English (1600–1750), 635–639
Trading posts
 Dutch takeover of Spanish-Portuguese, 666
 slave, 596
Tradition
 culture of, 843–845
 protecting, 1052–1053, 1053(i)
Trail of Tears, Cherokee Indians and, 840
Transplants, 995
Transportation. See also Automobiles; Railroads
 in Americas, 517
 in cities, 913
 in Japan, 701
Transregional structures. See also Global structures and organizations; United Nations
 Mercosur as, 1036
 NAFTA as, 1036
 NATO as, 968
 SEATO as, 968
Trans-Saharan trade, in West Africa, 492
Trans-Siberian railroad, 800(b), 800(i), 863, 868
Transvaal, 867, 881
Treaties. See also specific treaties
 Chinese ports and, 807
 ending World War I, 906–907
 after Second Balkan War, 896
Trench warfare, in World War I, 897, 899
Trent, Council of (1545–1563), 665
Tribute
 Aztec, 523, 526
 Inca, 532

Tribute (*continued*)
  in Southeast Asia, 710
  in Spanish America, 726
Trickle-down economy, 1014
Trinh clan (Vietnam), 709
Triple Alliance, 896
Triple Entente, 896
Tropical areas, diseases in, 562
Trotsky, Leon, 904
True Story of Ah Q, The (Lu Xun), 896
Truman, Harry, 963–964
Truman Doctrine (1947), 963–964
Truth, Sojourner, 852
Truth and Reconciliation Commission (South
    Africa), 1029, 1030(*b*)
Tsenacommocah (Chesapeake Bay), 743
Tsetse flies, in West Central Africa, 593
Tsimshian inhabitants, 518(*i*)
Tsushima Strait, Battle of (1905), 882
Tuberculosis, 814
Tunis, Ottomans and, 653
Tunisia
    France and, 865, 974
    protests in (2010), 1047(*i*)
    uprising in, 1046
Tupac Amaru II (Inca), 767
Tupi-speaking peoples, in Brazil, 571(*b*), 572
Turgenev, Ivan, 834
Turhan (mother of Mehmed IV), 654
Turkestan, Russia and, 863
Turkey. *See also* Anatolia; Ottoman Empire
    as EU membership candidate, 1035
    under Kemal, Mustafa, 908–909, 909(*m*)
    Young Turks and, 884–885
Turks. *See* Ottoman Empire; Ottoman Turks
Tuscany, 837
Twin Sisters (film), 916(*i*)

U-boats. *See* Submarines
Udai Singh (Rajput Hindu prince), 627
Uganda, 1027
    AIDS in, 1041(*i*)
    dictatorship in, 1007(*i*)
Ukraine, Chernobyl power plant in, 1038
Ulama (Islamic learned persons), 488, 656
    in Egypt, 775
Ulfah, Maria, 1048
Ultra (code-detecting group), 942
Uncle Tom's Cabin (Stowe), 817
Underconsumption, of manufactured goods, 804
Undocumented workers, 1044
Unemployment
    from Arab oil embargo, 1013
    during Great Depression, 929
Unification
    of Germany, 837–838, 838(*m*)
    of Italy, 836–837, 837(*m*)
    of Spain (1469), 484
Union Carbide, gas leak from, 1038
Union of Soviet Socialist Republics (USSR). *See*
    Soviet Union
United Nations (UN), 1031
    Declaration of Human Rights, 1049
    founding of, 952
    Israeli independence and, 972

Korean War and, 967
Nehru and, 984
United States. *See also* Cold War
    African Americans in, 850
    Barbary Wars and, 678–679
    civil rights movement in, 954
    as economic leader, 913
    economy in, 963
    expansion and consolidation of, 838–841
    foreign policy in, 1002
    Germany after World War II and, 964–965,
        965(*m*)
    government of, 769–771
    in Grand Alliance, 945
    Great Awakening in, 785
    Great Depression and, 931, 938
    immigration to, 769
    imperialism by, 881–882
    Indian outsourcing for, 1032
    industrialization in, 799, 802
    international capital flows and, 1033
    League of Nations and, 907
    life expectancy in, 1040
    Mexican-American War and, 831–832
    migrants in, 1044
    music in, 848
    in NAFTA, 1036
    nationalism and, 783
    neutrality policy of, 897
    outsourcing of jobs and, 1032
    overthrow of Hawaiian queen by, 882(*b*)
    at Paris Peace Conference, 905
    Pearl Harbor bombing and, 927, 944
    relocation of Japanese Americans by, 948–949
    South Korea and, 1007
    space exploration by, 966–967(*b*)
    Spanish-American War and, 881–882
    stock market crash in (1929), 927, 928–929
    Suez Canal and, 973
    as superpower, 962
    television in, 993
    Versailles Treaty and, 907
    Vietnam War and, 1008(*m*)
    in World War I, 896, 902
    after World War II, 962–970
    in World War II, 944, 945
Universal empire, Mongol model of, 478
Universe. *See also* Astronomy
    big bang theory of, 995
Universities and colleges. *See* Higher education
Unrestricted submarine warfare, 897
Untouchables, in India, 631, 813
Upper classes. *See also* Elites; Nobility
    in France, 939
    during Great Depression, 930–931
Urban areas. *See also* Cities and towns
    family life in, 1002
    Indian weaving in, 496–497(*b*)
    Renaissance in, 500
    in West Africa, 590, 592–593
Urbanization, 893
    culture and, 878–879
    after World War I, 913
Uruguay
    in Mercosur, 1036

revolt in, 780–781
USSR (Union of Soviet Socialist Republics).
    See Soviet Union
Utopia (More), 662
Utopian socialism, 816
Utrecht, Treaty of (1713–1714), 676(*m*)

Vaccines, 977, 1041
Valdivia, Pedro de (Spanish conquistador),
    573
Valley of Mexico, 520(*m*). *See also* Mexico
    Aztecs in, 519, 522
Valverde, Vicente de (Spanish bishop), 565(*i*)
Van Gogh, Vincent, 885, 886(*i*)
Vaqueros (cowboys), 782(*b*)
"Velvet" revolution (Czechoslovakia), 1016
Venereal disease, 814
Venetia, 837
Venette, Jean de (French theologian), on Black
    Death, 482(*b*)
Venezuela, 726
    agricultural modifications in, 1018
    grants to Germans, 572
    independence fight in, 781
Venice
    declining power of, 651
    oligarchy in, 483
    trade in, 477
Veracruz, 562
Verdun, battle at, 899
Versailles, Treaty of, 906–907
    Hitler and, 940
Versailles palace, 674, 675
    women's march to (1789), 772, 772(*i*)
Vertical archipelago, Inca land use as, 530,
    530(*m*)
Vespucci, Amerigo, 560
Viceroyalties, in Spanish America, 726
Victoria (England), 860
Vicuña, fiber from, 536
Video recorders, 993
Vienna, Ottoman siege of, 654
Vientiane, 708
Vietcong, 1008
Viet Minh, 971, 972
Vietnam, 684(*m*)
    AIDS in, 1041–1042
    in ASEAN, 1036
    bureaucracy in, 487
    China and, 478, 487, 499, 693
    development of, 708, 709
    division of, 972
    forced labor in, 949(*i*)
    France and, 864, 872(*b*), 872(*i*)
    Ho Chi Minh in, 971(*m*)
    Neo-Confucianism in, 487, 683
    pilgrims in, 1052
Vietnam War (1968–1975), 1008, 1008(*m*)
    protests against, 1009–1010
Vijayanagara, kingdom of
    Portuguese report on festival in, 624(*b*)
    rise and fall of (1336–1565), 621–623
Villa, Pancho (Mexico), 905
Villages. *See also* Cities and towns
    in West Central Africa, 593

Vindication of the Rights of Man, A
  (Wollstonecraft), 773
Vindication of the Rights of Woman, A
  (Wollstonecraft), 773
Violence. *See also* Conflict; Wars and warfare
  civil rights, 1009
  in colonies, 885
  in East Africa, 973
  European–native American, 557–558
  in Middle East, 1045
  political, 933
  in South Africa, 1029
  by Spanish against Aztecs, 563
Virginia, 722, 741, 743, 745
Virginia Company, 743
Virgin of the Rocks (Leonardo), 502(*b*), 502(*i*)
Virupaksha (god), 622
Viruses, 1044
Vision quest, in Americas, 518
VOC. *See* Dutch East India Company
Voice of America, 982–983
Voltaire (French writer), 763
Volta River region, 586(*m*), 588(*b*)
Voodoo, 740
Vostok I (spacecraft), 966(*b*)
Voting and voting rights
  in Argentina, 919
  in Japan, 935
  in United States, 770–771
  for women, 852, 1011
Voyages. *See also* Exploration
  of Columbus, 484
  European, of discovery, 555–561, 557(*m*)
  by Portugal, 570–571
  slave, 582(*m*)
  by Vespucci, 560
  of Zheng He, 476(*m*), 487, 498–499
Vroom, Hendrik Cornelisz (Dutch painter),
  667(*i*)

Wages
  after Black Death, 483
  for women, 914
  workers and, 1033
Wahhabism, 785(*i*), 786
Wakas (Inca sacred places), 532
Walentynowicz, Anna (Polish activist), 1015
Walesa, Lech (Polish activist), 1015, 1016
Wampum, 540, 540(*i*)
Wang Yangming (China), 683
Wanli (Ming emperor, China), 664, 691
War against terrorism, 1045
War club, Canadian, 518(*i*)
War crimes. *See also* Human rights
  in World War II, 980
War guilt, Germany and, 907
War of the Spanish Succession (1701–1714),
  676(*m*)
Warriors
  in Japan, 501–505
  sacrifice by Aztecs, 525
Wars and warfare. *See also* specific battles and
    wars
  in Africa, 587
  African agriculture and, 589

in Atlantic Ocean region, 760(*m*)
Aztec, 526, 529
Barbary, 678–679
in Crimean War, 833
in early modern period, 649
against France, 773
guerrilla warfare, 971
industrial technology applied to, 891
of Louis XIV (France), 675
Mapuche, 573–574
Napoleonic, 774–775, 779
from 1910–1929, 892(*m*)
political beliefs in, 947(*b*)
submarine, 897
technological, 952(*b*)
trench, 897
by United States, 838
Warsaw Ghetto (1943), 948(*i*)
Warsaw Pact, 967
Washington, George, 768, 769
  on Constitution (U.S.), 771
Waste collection, in Japan, 700
Water, for drinking, 1041
Water frame, 798, 799
Waterloo, battle at (1815), 774
Water power
  for sugar industry, 574–575(*b*)
  in textile industry, 798
Watson, James, 995
Watt, James, 798
al-Wazzan, Hasan (Muslim diplomat), 492
Wealth. *See also* Gold; Silver
  in China, 696
  decline in silver and, 668
  in Italian Renaissance, 500
  in Mexico, 894
  in new imperialism, 860
  Spanish, 665, 666
  in suburbs, 913
  tax cuts and, 1014
  in World War I, 902
Weapons. *See also* Cannons; Missiles
  atomic, 951, 952(*b*)
  Cold War production of, 976
  in Crimean War, 833
  exploration and, 552
  firearm manufacturing and, 552
  gunpowder, 478, 483–484, 552, 625–626, 627
  in gunpowder empires, 616
  in Hundred Years' War, 484(*i*)
  imperialism and, 868
  in India, 627, 863
  interchangeability of parts and, 798
  nuclear, 963
  Ottoman, 654
  Russia and, 688
  in World War I, 897, 904
  in World War II, 942
Weapons of mass destruction, 1045
  Ottomans vs. Safavids in Baghdad, 655(*b*)
Weather. *See also* Climate
  global warming and, 1038
  greenhouse effect and, 1038
Weaving, 793. *See also* Textiles and textile
    industry

improvements in, 798
  by Inca, 536
  in India, 496–497(*b*)
  industrialization and, 798
Wedgwood, Josiah, 796, 796(*i*)
Weimar Republic (Germany), labor unions and,
  914
Welfare benefits, in United States, 1014
Welfare state, 977
  in Sweden, 938–939
Wells, Ida B., 851
Wesley, John, 785
West, in United States, 839–841, 839(*m*)
West Africa
  empires and trade in, 589–590
  in c. 1500, 586(*m*)
  Gold Coast in, 595–596
  gold in, 588–589(*b*), 588(*i*)
  Islam in, 491–493, 588–589
  kingdoms of, 581
  lifestyle in, 590
  nations in, 973
  peoples of, 588–593
  political structure in, 590
  Portugal and, 595–600
  power in, 810
  religions in, 585
  slave trade and, 582–584, 606–607, 812
  urban life in, 592–593
  women in, 587(*i*), 593
West Asia, Russia and, 863
West Central Africa, 586(*m*). *See also* West Africa
  Angola and, 599–600
  blacksmith kings in, 593–595
  c. 1500–1635, 600(*m*)
  kingdom of Kongo and, 598–599
  Portugal in, 594
  slaves from, 600
  women in, 594–595
Western Africa. *See* West Africa; West Central
    Africa
Western Europe. *See also* specific locations
  Industrial Revolution in, 794
  societies after Black Death (1350–1492),
    482–484
Western front, in World War I, 897
Western Hemisphere
  Europeans and, 722
  Haitian revolution in (1791–1804), 777–778
  trade routes in, 514(*m*)
  U.S. influence in, 881
Westernization, 845–846
  of China, 808–809, 910
  in French Indochina, 864
  of Turkey, 908–909
Western powers
  competition between, 891
  after World War I, 925
Western world
  economic change in, 998–999
  economics in, 1014
  global commerce and, 825
  imperialism in Asia by, 862(*m*)
  Japan and, 842
  literature from, 880

Western world (*continued*)
  medicine in, 1041
  non-Western industrialization and, 806–812
  non-Western religion, art, literature, and, 885–887
West Germany, 965, 965(*m*)
  Berlin Wall and, 1016
  Green Party in, 1038
West Indies, 561
  slavery and, 598, 606
Westward expansion, of United States, 839–841, 839(*m*)
Wet-field rice cultivation
  in Korea, 706
  in Southeast Asia, 709
Wheat, production of, 929
Wheatley, Phillis, 786(*b*)
White-collar service sector, 805
White-collar workers, 815, 914
Whitefield, George, 785
"White man's burden" (Kipling), 881
Whites
  as abolitionists, 741
  African slaves compared with, 766–767
  Darwinism and, 861
  native Americans and, 840–841
  racism and, 603
  in South Africa, 1023, 1029
Whites, in Russian civil war, 904
White supremacy, decolonization and, 969
Whitman, Walt, 848
Widows
  in Japan, 702
  in Korea, 706
  sati (India) and, 630–631
  in Spanish America, 732
William II (Germany), 900
  World War I and, 899
William of Orange (England), 677
Wilson, Woodrow
  Fourteen Points of, 905
  League of Nations and, 907
Wind power, 1040
Wiracocha (god), 536
Wiracocha Inca (emperor), 531
Wire fencing, 801
Witchcraft
  of Eastern Woodlands peoples, 541
  trials in Europe, 670
Witch-doctors, in Americas, 518
Witch-hunt, by McCarthy, 983
Wollstonecraft, Mary, 773
Women. *See also* Feminists; Gender and gender issues; Men
  in Aceh, 640–641
  as African farm labor, 818–820, 819(*i*)
  in American Revolution, 769
  Aztec, 527
  Beauvoir on, 981
  in Brazil, 781(*i*)
  in Chile, 1005–1006
  in China, 965
  as citizens, 829
  "comfort women," 942(*b*)
  cult of domesticity and, 812

  in England, 773
  environment and, 1039
  family life and, 1002
  feminist activism by, 1009–1010
  films for, 915
  in France, 773, 774
  as global activists, 1034
  during Great Depression, 931, 932
  imperialism and, 870
  Inca, 534, 536
  in India, 630–631
  in Italy, 918–919
  in Japan, 504, 702
  labor unions and, 914
  Latin American dictatorships and, 1005
  Mapuche, 576(*i*)
  march to Versailles by (1789), 772, 772(*i*)
  in Minas Gerais, 734
  in Ming China, 487
  modernization and, 847
  native American, 570
  in Nazi Germany, 937, 938
  "new look" after World War II, 982(*i*)
  new woman and, 902, 914, 915(*i*)
  Ottoman, 491, 654–655, 656
  rights and status of, 850–852
  in Russia, 836
  sexual division of labor and, 815
  as shamans, 518, 527
  in South Africa, 1029
  in South Asia, 613–615
  in Southeast Asia, 711
  in Soviet Union, 963
  in Spanish America, 726–727, 731
  as sugar workers, 575
  as sultans of Aceh, 642
  trafficking in, 1044
  in Turkey, 909, 909(*i*)
  in United States, 770(*i*)
  voting rights for, 1011
  wages for, 914
  in West Africa, 593
  in West Central Africa, 594–595
  in western Africa, 587(*i*)
  witchcraft trials and, 670
  in working class, 813
  during World War I, 900–902
  in World War II, 946(*b*), 948, 949(*i*)
Women's International League for Peace and Freedom, 954
Women's Social and Political Union, 852
Wood, 660. *See also* Forests
  Russian, 690
Woodblock printing, Japanese, 790(*i*), 817
Wool and woolen industry, expansion of, 673
Woolf, Virginia, 939
Wordsworth, William, 773
Work. *See also* Labor; Livelihood(s); Workers
  computers and, 993–994
  global changes in, 998–999
  outwork as, 801
  sexual division of labor and, 815
Workday, 813, 814–815
Workers. *See also* Labor
  in Brazil, 831(*i*)

  in China, 807
  competition for jobs among, 1033
  efficiency and, 913
  industrial, 793
  Industrial Revolution and, 809
  Marx on, 816–817
  in Mexico, 890(*i*)
  Ottoman, 809
  in Soviet German zone, 965
  in Soviet Union, 918, 933
  on trans-Siberian railroad, 800(*b*), 800(*i*)
  undocumented, 1044
Workers Going Home at the Lebrter Railroad Station, 1897 (Kollwitz), 818(*i*)
Workers Party (Brazil), 1029
Workforce, women and, 900
Working class
  in Argentina, 920
  industrial, 813–815
Workplace, global, 998
World Bank, 1027
World Tourism Organization (UN), 1001(*b*)
World Trade Center, September 11, 2001, terrorist attack on, 1045
World Trade Organization, 1031
World War I (1914–1918)
  casualties in, 898, 899, 899(*i*), 904
  eastern front in, 897
  end of, 904–905
  in Europe and Middle East (1914–1918), 898(*m*)
  events leading to, 893
  as global war, 893, 896
  home front during, 900–902
  imperialism and, 897
  outbreak of, 896
  Paris Peace Conference after, 905–908
  Russian withdrawal from, 903
  soldiers in, 898, 899–900, 899(*i*)
  strategies, 897, 899
  as total war, 900
  United States in, 896, 902
  war at sea, 897–898, 902
  weapons in, 897
  western front in, 897, 899
  women during, 900–902
World War II (1937–1945), 926(*m*)
  atomic bombings in, 951, 952(*b*), 952(*i*)
  Axis and Allies advantages/disadvantages in, 947–948
  Axis defeat in, 950–951
  casualties in, 925–927, 945, 951
  civilians in, 945–950
  collaboration in, 949
  "comfort women" in, 942(*b*)
  economic growth after, 975–978
  in Europe, 941–944, 943(*m*)
  events leading to, 939–940
  Germany divided after, 964
  Holocaust in, 925, 945–947, 945(*m*)
  India and, 970
  Japanese invasion of China, 940–941
  Jewish homeland after, 972
  from 1937–1943, 940–945
  in North Africa, 943(*m*), 951

in Pacific, 944–945, 944(*m*), 951
Pearl Harbor bombing and, 927
programs exalting losers of, 980
resistance in, 949–950
soldiers in, 946–947(*b*)
in Soviet Union, 942–943, 943(*m*)
weapons in, 942
women in, 948
Wretched of the Earth, The (Fanon), 981
Wright, Richard, 984
Wright, Tom (architect), 1022(*i*)
Writing, in New Spain, 564(*b*)
Written records, Aztec, 520–521
Wu Guanzhong (China), 960(*m*), 979–980, 1054

Xhosa people, 867
Xolo dogs, 529
Xplastaz rap group (Tanzania), 1053

Yale, Elihu, 632
    English East India Company and, 638–639
Yalta Conference (1945), 964
Yangban (Korean noble class), 705
Yeats, William Butler, 885–886
Yellow fever, 562
"Yellow peril," China and, 884

Yeltsin, Boris, 1017
Yerba maté (tea), 728
Yi (Choson) dynasty (Korea), 683, 705–708
Yokohama, earthquake in, 935
Yom Kippur War (1973), 1013
Yongle (China), 487, 498, 499
Yorktown, Battle of, 769
Yoruba people, city-states of, 592
Young people. *See also* Youth culture
    in Nazi Germany, 924(*i*), 937
    protests by, 1009–1010
Young Turks, 884–885, 884(*i*)
Youth culture, 1002(*i*), 1003
Yrigoyen, Hipólito (president of Argentina), 919
Yuan Empire (China), 485
Yuan Shikai (Chinese leader), 895
Yucatan peninsula, Cortés in, 562
Yugoslavia
    breakup of, 1016
    former, 1049
    after World War I, 906, 906(*m*)
Yukichi, Fukuzawa (Japanese author and
    educator), 848

Zacatecas, Mexico, 724(*m*)
    silver in, 567

Zadig (Voltaire), 763
Zaire. *See* Congo
Zambezi River region, 619, 620
Zamindars (administrators), 629
Zapata, Emiliano, 890(*i*), 891, 893, 894, 895
Zapatistas, 1052
Zemstvos (regional councils), 836
Zeng Guofan (Chinese official), 808
Zheng He (Chinese admiral), voyages of,
    476(*m*), 487, 498–499, 619
Zhou Enlai (Chinese leader), 983
Zhu Chen-hao (Chinese prince), 683
Zhu Su'e (New Woman, China), 914
Zhu Xi (Neo-Confucian scholar), 486
Zhu Yuanzhang (Chinese emperor), as Hongwu,
    486
Zimbabwe, 1030
Zionism, 851
Zones, in Berlin and Germany, 964–965, 965(*m*)
Zoroastrianism, in East Africa, 621
Zulu Inkatha Freedom Party, 1029
Zulu people, Anglo war with, 867(*i*)
Zwingli, Ulrich, 662

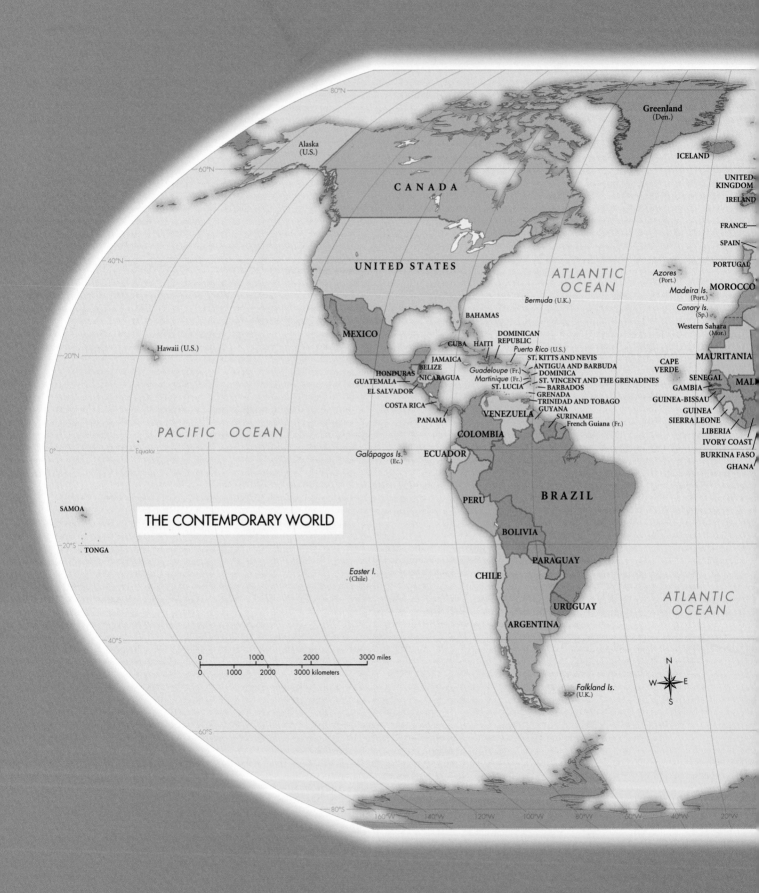

THE CONTEMPORARY WORLD

Greenland
(Den.)

ICELAND

Alaska
(U.S.)

UNITED
KINGDOM

IRELAND

FRANCE

SPAIN

CANADA

PORTUGAL

Azores
(Port.)

MOROCCO

UNITED STATES

ATLANTIC
OCEAN

Madeira Is.
(Port.)

Canary Is.
(Sp.)

Western Sahara
(Mor.)

Bermuda (U.K.)

BAHAMAS

Hawaii (U.S.)

MEXICO

DOMINICAN
REPUBLIC

CUBA   HAITI

Puerto Rico (U.S.)

ST. KITTS AND NEVIS

MAURITANIA

JAMAICA

ANTIGUA AND BARBUDA

CAPE
VERDE

BELIZE

Guadeloupe (Fr.)

DOMINICA

HONDURAS

NICARAGUA

Martinique (Fr.)

ST. VINCENT AND THE GRENADINES

SENEGAL

MALI

GUATEMALA

ST. LUCIA

BARBADOS

GAMBIA

EL SALVADOR

GRENADA

GUINEA-BISSAU

COSTA RICA

TRINIDAD AND TOBAGO

GUYANA

GUINEA

PANAMA

VENEZUELA

SURINAME

SIERRA LEONE

French Guiana (Fr.)

LIBERIA

COLOMBIA

IVORY COAST

PACIFIC OCEAN

Galápagos Is.
(Ec.)

ECUADOR

BURKINA FASO

GHANA

Equator

BRAZIL

SAMOA

PERU

THE CONTEMPORARY WORLD

TONGA

BOLIVIA

Easter I.
(Chile)

PARAGUAY

CHILE

ATLANTIC
OCEAN

URUGUAY

0   1000   2000   3000 miles

ARGENTINA

0   1000   2000   3000 kilometers

Falkland Is.
(U.K.)

N

W   E

S

80°N

60°N

40°N

20°N

0°

20°S

40°S

60°S

80°S

160°W   140°W   120°W   100°W   80°W   60°W   40°W   20°W

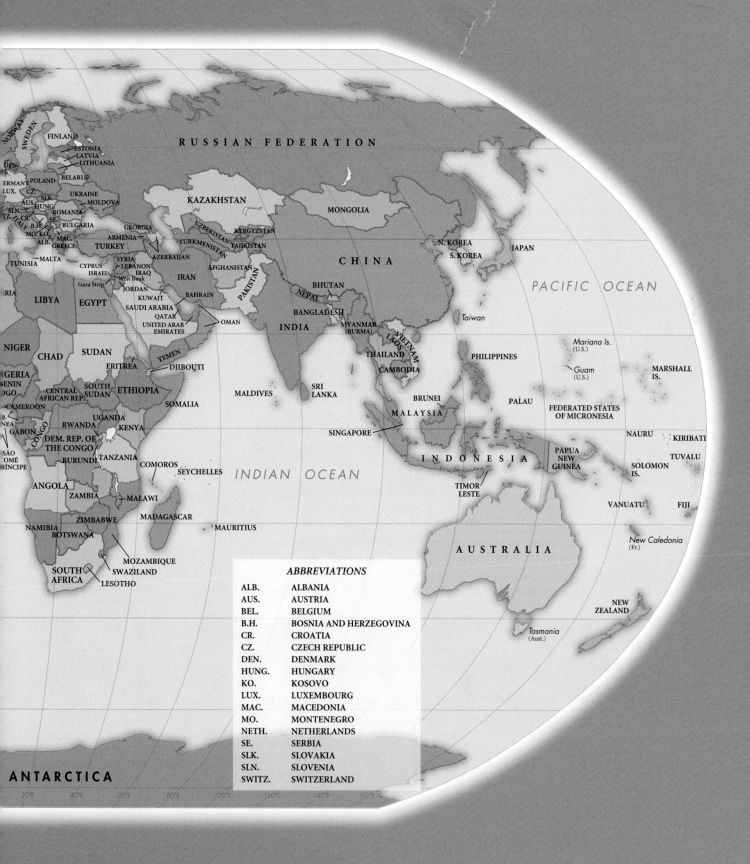

RUSSIAN FEDERATION

NORWAY
SWEDEN
FINLAND
ESTONIA
LATVIA
LITHUANIA
DEN.
GERMANY
LUX.
POLAND
BELARUS
CZ.
SLK.
UKRAINE
AUS.
HUNG.
MOLDOVA
SLN.
TZ.
ITALY
CR.
ROMANIA
MO.
KO.
SE.
BULGARIA
ALB.
MAC.
GREECE
TURKEY
TUNISIA
MALTA
CYPRUS
ISRAEL
Gaza Strip
West Bank
JORDAN

KAZAKHSTAN

MONGOLIA

GEORGIA
ARMENIA
AZERBAIJAN
UZBEKISTAN
KYRGYZSTAN
TURKMENISTAN
TAJIKISTAN

SYRIA
LEBANON
IRAQ
IRAN
AFGHANISTAN
PAKISTAN

CHINA

N. KOREA
S. KOREA
JAPAN

PACIFIC OCEAN

LIBYA
EGYPT
KUWAIT
SAUDI ARABIA
QATAR
UNITED ARAB
EMIRATES
BAHRAIN
OMAN
INDIA
NEPAL
BHUTAN
BANGLADESH
MYANMAR
(BURMA)
VIETNAM
LAOS
THAILAND
CAMBODIA
PHILIPPINES
Taiwan

Mariana Is.
(U.S.)
Guam
(U.S.)
MARSHALL
IS.

NIGER
CHAD
SUDAN
YEMEN
ERITREA
DJIBOUTI

GERIA
BENIN
OGO
CAMEROON
NEA
GABON
SÃO
TOMÉ
RÍNCIPE

CENTRAL
AFRICAN REP.
SOUTH
SUDAN
ETHIOPIA
SOMALIA
MALDIVES
SRI
LANKA
BRUNEI
MALAYSIA
SINGAPORE
PALAU
FEDERATED STATES
OF MICRONESIA
NAURU
KIRIBATI
TUVALU

CONGO
UGANDA
RWANDA
KENYA
DEM. REP. OF
THE CONGO
BURUNDI
TANZANIA
COMOROS
SEYCHELLES

INDONESIA
PAPUA
NEW
GUINEA
SOLOMON
IS.

ANGOLA
ZAMBIA
MALAWI
INDIAN OCEAN
TIMOR
LESTE

NAMIBIA
ZIMBABWE
BOTSWANA
MADAGASCAR
MAURITIUS
AUSTRALIA
VANUATU
FIJI
New Caledonia
(Fr.)

SOUTH
AFRICA
MOZAMBIQUE
SWAZILAND
LESOTHO
NEW
ZEALAND
Tasmania
(Aust.)

ABBREVIATIONS	
ALB.	ALBANIA
AUS.	AUSTRIA
BEL.	BELGIUM
B.H.	BOSNIA AND HERZEGOVINA
CR.	CROATIA
CZ.	CZECH REPUBLIC
DEN.	DENMARK
HUNG.	HUNGARY
KO.	KOSOVO
LUX.	LUXEMBOURG
MAC.	MACEDONIA
MO.	MONTENEGRO
NETH.	NETHERLANDS
SE.	SERBIA
SLK.	SLOVAKIA
SLN.	SLOVENIA
SWITZ.	SWITZERLAND

ANTARCTICA

20°E   40°E   60°E   80°E   100°E   120°E   140°E   160°E

About the authors

BONNIE G. SMITH (Ph.D., University of Rochester) is Board of Governors Professor of History at Rutgers University. She has written numerous works in European and global history, including *Ladies of the Leisure Class*; *Changing Lives: Women in European History since 1700*; and *Imperialism*. She is editor of *Global Feminisms since 1945* and *Women's History in Global Perspective*; coeditor of the New Oxford World History series; and general editor of *The Oxford Encyclopedia of Women in World History*. Currently she is studying the globalization of European culture and society since the seventeenth century. **Bonnie treats the period 1750 to the present (Part 4) in *Crossroads and Cultures*.**

MARC VAN DE MIEROOP (Ph.D., Yale University) is Professor of History at Columbia University. His research focuses on the ancient history of the Near East from a long-term perspective and extends across traditionally established disciplinary boundaries. Among his many works are *The Ancient Mesopotamian City*; *Cuneiform Texts and the Writing of History*; *A History of the Ancient Near East*; *The Eastern Mediterranean in the Age of Ramesses II*; and *A History of Ancient Egypt*. **Marc covers the period from human origins to 500 C.E. (Part 1) in *Crossroads and Cultures*.**

RICHARD VON GLAHN (Ph.D., Yale University) is Professor of History at the University of California, Los Angeles. A specialist in Chinese economic history, Richard is the author of *The Country of Streams and Grottoes: Expansion, Settlement, and the Civilizing of the Sichuan Frontier in Song Times*; *Fountain of Fortune: Money and Monetary Policy in China, 1000–1700*; and *The Sinister Way: The Divine and the Demonic in Chinese Religious Culture*. He is also coeditor of *The Song-Yuan-Ming Transition in Chinese History* and *Global Connections and Monetary History, 1470–1800*. His current research focuses on monetary history on a global scale, from ancient times to the recent past. **Richard treats the period 500 to 1450 (Part 2) in *Crossroads and Cultures*.**

KRIS LANE (Ph.D., University of Minnesota) is the France V. Scholes Chair in Colonial Latin American History at Tulane University. Kris specializes in colonial Latin American history and the Atlantic world, and his great hope is to globalize the teaching and study of the early Americas. His publications include *Pillaging the Empire: Piracy in the Americas, 1500–1750*; *Quito 1599: City and Colony in Transition*; and *Colour of Paradise: The Emerald in the Age of Gunpowder Empires*. He also edited Bernardo de Vargas Machuca's *The Indian Militia and Description of the Indies* and *Defense and Discourse of the Western Conquest*. **Kris treats the period 1450 to 1750 (Part 3) in *Crossroads and Cultures*.**

About the cover image

Samarkand, Uzbekistan

Timur, the last of the great Mongol conquerors, rebuilt the ancient trading city of Samarkand as a capital dedicated to Islamic culture and learning. Timur's successors constructed the three majestic *madrasas* (Islamic schools) that surround Registan Square at the heart of the city. Looming over the madrasas is Timur's domed mausoleum, which inspired great architectural monuments of the later Mughals such as the Taj Mahal.